D0984383

ORIGINS TO CONSTANTINE

The first of the nine-volume *Cambridge History of Christianity* series, *Origins to Constantine* provides a comprehensive overview of the essential events, persons, places and issues involved in the emergence of the Christian religion in the Mediterranean world in the first three centuries. Over thirty essays written by scholarly experts trace this dynamic history from the time of Jesus through to the rise of imperial Christianity in the fourth century. The volume provides thoughtful and well-documented analyses of the diverse forms of Christian community, identity and practice that arose within decades of Jesus' death, and which through missionary efforts were soon implanted throughout the Roman empire. *Origins to Constantine* examines the distinctive characteristics of Christian groups in each geographical region up to the end of the third century, while also exploring the development of the institutional forms, intellectual practices and theological formulations that would mark Christian history in subsequent centuries.

MARGARET M. MITCHELL is Professor of New Testament and Early Christian Literature at the University of Chicago. She is the author of *Paul and the rhetoric of reconciliation: an exegetical investigation of the language and composition of 1 Corinthians* and *The heavenly trumpet: John Chrysostom and the art of Pauline interpretation*, and is co-executive editor of Novum Testamentum Supplements monograph series.

FRANCES M. YOUNG is a Fellow of the British Academy and received an OBE for services to Theology in 1998. She became Professor and Head of the Department of Theology, University of Birmingham, in 1986, Dean of the Faculty of Arts in 1995, served as Pro-Vice Chancellor from 1997–2002 and is now Emerita Professor of Theology. Her many publications include *From Nicaea to Chalcedon* and *Biblical exegesis and the formation of Christian culture*, as well as more popular works such as *The making of the creeds, Can these dry bones live?* and *Face to face*.

THE CAMBRIDGE HISTORY OF

CHRISTIANITY

The *Cambridge History of Christianity* offers a comprehensive
chronological account of the development of Christianity in all its
aspects – theological, intellectual, social, political, regional, global –
from its beginnings to the present day. Each volume makes a substantial contribution in its own right to the scholarship of its period
and the complete *History* constitutes a major work of academic
reference. Far from being merely a history of western European
Christianity and its offshoots, the *History* aims to provide a global
perspective. Eastern and Coptic Christianity are given full consideration from the early period onwards, and later, African, Far Eastern,
New World, South Asian and other non-European developments
in Christianity receive proper coverage. The volumes cover popular piety and non-formal expressions of Christian faith and treat
the sociology of Christian formation, worship and devotion in a
broad cultural context. The question of relations between Christianity and other major faiths is also kept in sight throughout. The
History will provide an invaluable resource for scholars and students alike.

List of volumes:

Origins to Constantine
EDITED BY MARGARET M. MITCHELL AND FRANCES M. YOUNG

Constantine to c. 600
EDITED BY WINRICH LÖHR, FRED NORRIS AND AUGUSTINE CASIDAY

Early Medieval Christianity c. 600–c. 1100
EDITED BY THOMAS NOBLE AND JULIA SMITH

Christianity in Western Europe c. 1100–c. 1500
EDITED BY MIRI RUBIN AND WALTER SIMON

Eastern Christianity
EDITED BY MICHAEL ANGOLD

Reform and Expansion 1500– 1660
EDITED BY RONNIE PO-CHIA HSIA

Enlightenment, Reawakening and Revolution 1660–1815
EDITED BY STEWART J. BROWN AND TIMOTHY TACKETT

World Christianities c. 1815–c. 1914
EDITED BY BRIAN STANLEY AND SHERIDAN GILLEY

World Christianities c. 1914–c. 2000
EDITED BY HUGH MCLEOD

THE CAMBRIDGE
HISTORY OF
CHRISTIANITY

★

VOLUME 1

Origins to Constantine

★

Edited by

MARGARET M. MITCHELL

and

FRANCES M. YOUNG

Assistant editor

K. Scott Bowie

CAMBRIDGE
UNIVERSITY PRESS

CAMBRIDGE UNIVERSITY PRESS
Cambridge, New York, Melbourne, Madrid, Cape Town, Singapore, São Paulo

Cambridge University Press
The Edinburgh Building, Cambridge CB2 2RU, UK

Published in the United States of America by Cambridge University Press, New York

www.cambridge.org
Information on this title: www.cambridge.org/9780521812399

First published 2006

Printed in the United Kingdom at the University Press, Cambridge

A catalogue record for this book is available from the British Library

Library of Congress Cataloguing in Publication data
Origins to Constantine / edited by Frances M. Young, Margaret M. Mitchell ; assistant editor,
K. Scott Bowie.
p.   cm. – (The Cambridge history of Christianity; v. 1)
Includes bibliographical references and index.
ISBN 0 521-81239-9 (hardback)
1. Church history – Primitive and early church, ca. 30–600.
1. Young, Frances M. (Frances Margaret)   II. Mitchell, Margaret Mary, 1956–
III. Bowie, Kenneth Scott.   IV. Title.   V. Series.
BR165.066   2006   270.1 – dc22   2005012926

ISBN-13 978-0-521-81239-9 hardback
ISBN-10 0-521-81239-9 hardback

Contents

Contents

PART V

THE SHAPING OF CHRISTIAN THEOLOGY

Contents

PART VI

'ALIENS' BECOME CITIZENS: TOWARDS
IMPERIAL PATRONAGE

Illustrations

Maps

Contributors

HAROLD W. ATTRIDGE, Yale Divinity School

JOHN BEHR, St Vladimir's Orthodox Theological Seminary

DAVID BRAKKE, Indiana University

AVERIL CAMERON, Keble College, Oxford

A. J. DROGE, University of California, San Diego

MARK EDWARDS, Christ Church, Oxford

†W. H. C. FREND, emeritus, University of Glasgow, Bye-Fellow of Gonville and Caius College, Cambridge

SEAN FREYNE, Trinity College, Dublin

HARRY Y. GAMBLE, University of Virginia

STUART GEORGE HALL, emeritus, King's College London, University of St Andrews, Scotland

SUSAN ASHBROOK HARVEY, Brown University

ROBIN M. JENSEN, Vanderbilt Divinity School

HANS-JOSEF KLAUCK, University of Chicago

JUDITH LIEU, King's College London

JOEL MARCUS, Duke Divinity School

GERHARD MAY, emeritus, Johannes Gutenberg-Universität, Mainz

DENIS MINNS, Blackfriars, Oxford

WAYNE A. MEEKS, emeritus, Yale University

MARGARET M. MITCHELL, University of Chicago

CAROLYN OSIEK, Brite Divinity School

BIRGER A. PEARSON, emeritus, University of California, Santa Barbara

TESSA RAJAK, University of Reading

ADOLF MARTIN RITTER, Ruprecht-Karls-Universität, Heidelberg

MAUREEN A. TILLEY, University of Dayton

CHRISTINE TREVETT, University of Cardiff

FRANK TROMBLEY, University of Cardiff

MARKUS VINZENT, University of Birmingham

FRANCES M. YOUNG, emerita, University of Birmingham

Preface

Once upon a time, historians of the early church wrote a simple story of a pristine faith received from Jesus Christ and communicated to his disciples. With an agreed gospel summed up in the Apostles' Creed, they dispersed to spread the word in all directions. In time, however, this unified message was frustrated by distortions called heresies, which produced their own offspring, multiplying and diversifying, by contrast with the one truth entrusted to the apostles. Despite heresy and persecution, however, Christianity triumphed with the conversion of Constantine.

Doubtless that is an over-simplification of an over-simplification, yet it is towards the goal of emancipation from such a schematised view of earliest Christianity (a perspective inherited from the ancient sources themselves) that much modern critical scholarship has been directed. The recognition of diversity within Christianity from the very beginning has transformed study of its origins. Simple models of development, or single theory explanations, whether they be applied to organisational, liturgical, doctrinal or other aspects of early church history, are recognisably inadequate. We have endeavoured to capture the complexity of early Christianity and its socio-cultural setting, whilst also indicating some of the elements that make it possible to trace a certain coherence, a recognisable identity, maintained over time and defended resolutely despite cultural pressure that could have produced something other.

It is thanks to interdisciplinary scholarship, together with the variety of new evidence provided by archaeological activities and by chance finds such as the Dead Sea scrolls and the Nag Hammadi library, that this project is possible. Inevitably, the essays assembled here are brief overviews of what have become vast areas of research, but we hope that their virtue is the fact that, both severally and together, they provide balance and perspective, coherence and diversity, as well as the means to explore further the complex topics with which they engage.

Perhaps the greatest conundrum for the historian of Christian origins is how to deal with the figure of Jesus. Most movements are generated by a founder whose biography would seem to be the natural starting-point. But in the case of Jesus, it is not so simple. In a significant sense, Christian faith is founded upon the person of Jesus Christ himself. The Prelude to the volume, 'Jesus Christ, foundation of Christianity', engages the consequent problems: is it possible to write the kind of historical biography of Jesus that we expect in the case of other significant figures, and, even if it were, would it do justice to what he has actually represented for Christian believers?

In part I, 'The political, social and religious setting', we present three essays which sketch the three major formative contexts within which early Christianity developed. The first outlines the local setting of the life of Jesus and his earliest Jewish followers in Galilee and Judea. The second moves onto a wider stage, as it considers the presence of Jews outside that immediate locality, in the 'diaspora', and their response to the broader context of Graeco-Roman culture. It was both within and alongside the Greek-speaking Jewish communities outside Palestine that Christianity first spread, and it owed a considerable debt to Jewish precursors in developing an apologetic stance towards 'pagan' society. The third sketches the political and social realities of the Roman empire which both facilitated and thwarted the growth of Christian communities, as subsequent chapters demonstrate. The story of the first three centuries of Christianity may be depicted, broadly speaking, as a process whereby a counter-cultural movement is increasingly enculturated, and the task of writing that story may be undertaken through an analysis of the ways in which the movement both fitted within and challenged the various cultural environments in which it found itself.

The essays in part II, 'The Jesus movements', explore the forms of Christianity that can be traced behind the New Testament documents, the final essay considering the nature of early Christian communities as social entities in the world of the late first century. It is clear that Jesus was a Jew, and his immediate followers were likewise Jews. The continuing existence of Jewish Christianity has become a subject of significant historical research, though bedevilled by questions of definition. It is also clear that our earliest Christian documents, namely the Pauline epistles, bear witness to the rapid incorporation of non-Jews into the community of believers in Jesus Christ, as well as to controversy about the terms on which that incorporation should take place. The first two essays therefore seek to trace the lineaments of Jewish and Gentile Christianity respectively. Their ultimate separation obscures the difficulties of differentiation in some New Testament texts, not least the gospel of John, where hostility to 'the Jews' may betray disputes within a Jewish community about where true Jewishness is to be found, rather than the more obvious possibility of a community defining itself over against Judaism. Be that as it may, the Johannine literature merits special attention, seeming as it does to represent Christian communities with a distinctive interpretation of the Jesus tradition, despite its ultimate acceptance within the common canon of New Testament writings. Yet these differing Christian groups have a family likeness, and their characteristic community ethos, organisational patterns and ritual forms are considered as a climax to the section.

The following section, part III, 'Community traditions and self-definition', considers various ways in which Christian identity was formed in the next generation or two. The first essay examines the emergence of the written record, and the way in which the Christian movement early on developed a literary culture that was crucial to its sense of self and its propagation. The second is devoted to the complex figure of Marcion, whose legacy for the history of the Christian canon as well as its theological foundations is inestimable. What Marcion and his opponents had in common was the same process of identity formation through differentiation from others. In each such case, both among those who called themselves Christians, and between Christians and 'others' (Jews and 'pagans'), this was a complex interactive process as the significant others were themselves undergoing identity transformations even as they were being configured as the opponent in Christian consciousness or apologetic. Attempts to capture such a process may take several forms: one might paint on a broad canvas, endeavouring to collect the broadest possible base of information and produce a carefully nuanced position; or one might present a more detailed analysis of a particular dialectical interchange. The essay on 'Self-definition vis-à-vis the Jewish matrix' appropriately adopts the first approach, given the intense debates about the parting of the ways between Judaism and Christianity which have characterised scholarship in the late twentieth century. The other tactic is evident in the following essay on 'Self-definition vis-à-vis the Graeco-Roman world', which offers insight into the complexity of defining exactly what distinguished the Christian discourse from that of others through a case study of Justin Martyr and Celsus, the opponent of Christianity. When over-arching models have essential similarities, the question of differentiation becomes the more urgent: Jews, philosophers and Christians had subtly different versions of a hierarchically ordered universe with a single divine Being at its apex but argued profoundly over what or who should be worshipped and how.

A defining discourse was necessitated also by groups (often uncritically lumped together as 'Gnostic') experienced by Christians as too close for comfort and, therefore, doubly threatening. Their teachings were eventually rejected by the 'great church' because they were perceived to subvert sharply the core legacy from Judaism, characterised as insistence on the one true God who created the universe, declared it good, and through the prophets revealed the divine providential plan to be realised at the climax of history. Both sides of that dialogue are presented and considered in this section. By the end of the second century, a sense of what constituted the true tradition of Christian teaching was being articulated and claimed as universal, notably in the work of Irenaeus, who may be regarded as the first great systematiser of Christian theology. The final essay moves the issues of Christian self-definition into a broader social framework, turning from questions of doctrine, discourse and world-view to matters of family life and social practice, highlighting the ambivalent status of Christians in Graeco-Roman society. This reflects a notable shift in scholarship at the turn of the twenty-first century towards social history, in response to what some have perceived as an over-emphasis on intellectual history. Broadly speaking, section III brings us to the end of the second century.

Part IV, 'Regional varieties of Christianity in the first three centuries', focuses on the spread of Christianity 'from Jerusalem . . . to the ends of the earth' (as Luke terms it, in Acts 1:8) within the first three centuries. An essay on 'the geographical spread of Christianity' first engages the evidentiary and methodological issues involved in making demographic estimates of 'Christianisation' in the empire. Subsequent chapters are devoted to each of the major regions where Christian populations were found in the period up until Constantine: Asia Minor (and Achaea), Egypt, Syria and Mesopotomia, Gaul, North Africa and Rome. The chapters in this section reflect a notable historiographic shift in the study of earliest Christianity. Since the work of Walter Bauer,[1] which suggested that in some regions the earliest form of Christianity was heretical rather than orthodox, there has been radical reappraisal of the history of the early period: maybe diversity rather than uniformity characterised Christianity from the beginning; maybe what was heretical was only discerned by hindsight; maybe uniformity was imposed by the dominance of an emerging authority such as the Roman church. The last was Bauer's thesis, a view that has been demolished in subsequent discussion. Nevertheless much else has directed scholars to regional variations, not least because different parts of the Roman empire had different roots and differing responses to

1 *Orthodoxy and heresy.*

Romanitas, especially the ruler cult, so that the religio-political context of Christian communities was not uniform, and this produced some variety in cultural and confessional ethos. In addition, research has turned up local varieties of liturgical practice and organisational structure in the churches. Scholars increasingly recognise the need for in-depth studies of the evidence for the presence of Christian communities, and an analysis of their particular character, in different localities.[2] Each of the essays in this section gathers the key pieces of literary, documentary and archaeological evidence and sketches the outlines of the principal events, controversies and personalities for that particular region, while also highlighting the essential fact that no area stood in complete isolation. Indeed, letters and travellers brought influences from one end of the Roman empire to another, and interaction was a significant reality.

Part v, 'The shaping of Christian theology', mediates between these regional varieties and the ideologies of institutional unity that made the church appear to Constantine as a useful vehicle for his programme of uniting the empire. Here we trace the creation of a Christian world-view which instantiated itself in institutional structures which were pan-Mediterranean as well as local. Classic debates about doctrine we have set in a broader context than earlier church histories would have placed them, and we have avoided notions of development which imply a necessary outcome. Struggles over monotheism and the doctrine of creation set up the context for arguments about the nature of Jesus Christ and his relationship with the one God, while particular local controversies with more universal implications provide material for the discussion of Christology and ecclesiology. The section concludes by drawing attention to the fact that the larger context for doctrinal affirmations was the school-like character of early Christian discourse and the self-conscious development of a Christian intellectual culture to rival the *paideia* of the Graeco-Roman world. In the late fourth century and beyond, the traditional pagan educational programme, so far from being replaced, was gradually Christianised, but this process owed much to the earlier adaptation to study of the Bible of the curriculum and techniques traditionally taught in Graeco-Roman schools of rhetoric and philosophy.

Part vi, '"Aliens" become citizens: towards imperial patronage', traces the way in which Christians became increasingly at home in the world, despite their initial tendency to adopt the biblical motif of the resident alien or sojourner,[3]

---

2 Two notable examples are Lampe, *Paul to Valentinus* (on Rome) and Pearson, *Gnosticism and Christianity in Roman and Coptic Egypt*.

3 Phil 3:20; 1 Pet 1:17; 2:11; *Ep. Diognet.* 5.5.

claiming that their citizenship was in heaven. From the time of Paul, individual Christians may have held Roman citizenship, yet there was an ambivalence in their civic attitude as the diaspora mentality was, in a way, carried over to Gentile converts, and loyalty to Christ displaced loyalty to Caesar. Experience of persecution reinforced this, though it is important to grasp that, as the first essay shows, persecution was largely local and sporadic, and official empire-wide procedures directed against Christians mostly appear late in our period. The Roman perception that in some sense Christians did not belong is reflected in Christian views of the Roman empire, and the second essay provides a nuanced view of shifting attitudes to the question that is later phrased as the relation between 'church and state'. The chapter on Constantine reflects on the crucial impact of this first 'Christian emperor', while also warning against oversimplified accounts of the socio-political and religious shifts that came with his reign. The essay on the Council of Nicaea provides a sense of the interplay of doctrinal and political factors as the search for unity was driven by the one who claimed to be 'the bishop for those outside', namely the emperor Constantine. The climax to the section is provided by a review of art and architecture spanning the whole story of this counter-cultural movement to its incorporation into the socio-cultural patterns of the Roman world and eventual articulation of a distinctive material culture. The section as a whole traces the changing parameters within which the question about the place of Christians in the world was considered in the pivotal period of the early fourth century. We conclude with a few remarks about how ancient Christianity is, in some complex configurations, foundational for the long and varied history to come.

This conspectus is intended to show that, so far from being a 'hotch-potch' of unrelated essays, this collection as a whole has a sequence which hangs together, despite the various perspectives represented. The volume may be read as a consecutive history of the period, which the essays address from a multiplicity of angles. Readers are encouraged to follow up the subjects and questions raised in each essay by drawing on the chapter bibliographies each author has provided, and consulting the full details for primary and secondary literature cited across the essays, which can be found in the general bibliography.

The editors would like to acknowledge with gratitude the efforts of all the authors, with thanks for their gracious response to feedback so that the volume as a whole could come together as effectively as it has. They have particularly appreciated the invaluable assistance provided by K. Scott Bowie, who, amongst other things, compiled the unified bibliography from the many provided by the authors, sorted out standard abbreviations, and produced the final copy in both hard and electronic form. They thank the University of Chicago Divinity School for generous institutional and financial support of this project. They would also like to express their gratitude to Cambridge University Press for the support of this project from inception through production. Finally they would like to dedicate this volume to Robert M. Grant, by whom both were taught and inspired.

FMY & MMM
December 2004

Acknowledgements

The editors acknowledge with gratitude permission to reprint maps from the *Cambridge Ancient History* and *Cambridge History of Judaism*, and *Der Neue Pauly*/*Brill's New Pauly* (vol. III, pp. 262–3, our map 4), published by Metzler Verlag and E. J. Brill.

We are grateful also to the University of Michigan, Yale University Art Gallery, and the International Catacomb Society for granting us permission to reprint images from their photo archives. All the photographs by individual photographers are reprinted here with their written permission and our thanks. We would particularly like to express gratitude to Professor Robin M. Jensen for valuable assistance in procuring the images.

Chart: Roman emperors and bishops of Rome and Alexandria

Roman emperors		Bishops of Rome		Bishops of Alexandria	
27, BCE–14, CE	Augustus				
14–37	Tiberius				
37–41	Gaius (Caligula)				
41–54	Claudius			42–62	St Mark
54–68	Nero		St Peter (mart. c. 64)	62–84	Annianus
		67–76	Linus		
68–9	Galba				
69	Otho				
69	Vitellius				
69–79	Vespasian	76–88	Anacletus		
79–81	Titus				
81–96	Domitian	88–97	Clement	84–98	Abilius
96–98	Nerva	97–105	Evaristus		
98–117	Trajan	105–15	Alexander	98–109	Cerdo
		115–25	Xystus I	109–19	Primus
117–38	Hadrian	125–38	Telesphorus	119–31	Justus
				131–44	Eumenes
138–61	Antoninus Pius	138–41	Higinus	144–54	Marcus
		141–55	Pius	154–67	Celadion
		155–66	Anicetus		
161–80	Marcus Aurelius	166–75	Soter	167–79	Agrippinus
161–69	Lucius Verus coregent				
		175–89	Eleutherus		
180–92	Commodus	189–99	Victor	179–89	Julian
				189–232	Demetrius I
193	Pertinax				
	Julianus				
193–211	Septimius Severus	199–217	Zephyrinus		
211–17	Caracalla	217–22	Callistus		
217–18	Macrinus				
218–22	Elagabalus				

Roman emperors				Bishops of Rome		Bishops of Alexandria	
222–35	Alexander Severus			222–30	Urban	232–47	Heraclas
				230–5	Pontianus		
235–8	Maximinus Thrax			235–6	Anteros		
				236–50	Fabian		
238	Gordiani						
	Pupienus						
238–44	Gordian III						
244–9	Philip the Arabian					247–64	Dionysius
249–51	Decius						
251–3	Decius's sons and others			251–3	Cornelius		
253–60	Valerian			253–4	Lucius		
				254–7	Stephen		
				257–8	Xystus II		
				259–68	Dionysius		
260–8	Gallienus			269–74	Felix	265–82	Maximus
268–70	Claudius Gothicus			275–83	Eutychianus		
270–5	Aurelian						
275–6	Tacitus						
	Florianus						
276–82	Probus						
282–3	Carus					282–300	Theonas
	WEST		EAST				
283–4	Carinus	283–4	Numerian	283–96	Gaius		
284–6	Diocletian	284–305	Diocletian				
286–305	Maximian			296–304	Marcellinus	300–11	Peter I
305–6	Constantius	305–11	Galerius	308–9	Marcellus		
	Chlorus	310–12	Maximinus				
306–	Constantine	308–	Constantine	309–10	Eusebius	311–12	Achillas
		308–24	Licinius	311–14	Miltiades	313–26	Alexander I
				314–35	Silvester		
324–37		Constantine alone		336	Marcus	326–73	Athanasius I

Sources: for Roman emperors and bishops, Robert M. Grant, *Augustus to Constantine*, 313–14; for Alexandrine bishops, Birger A. Pearson (produced for this volume, as adapted from the traditional list).

Abbreviations

General

ET	English translation
LXX	The Septuagint
NRSV	The Bible, New Revised Standard Version, ed. Bruce M. Metzger *et al.* (New York: Oxford University Press, 1990)
NTApoc	*New Testament Apocrypha*, 2 vols., W. Schneemelcher and R. McL. Wilson (eds.), rev. ed. (Cambridge: James Clarke & Co. Ltd.; Louisville, KY: Westminster John Knox Press, 1991–2)
NHL	*Nag Hammadi Library in English*, J. M. Robinson (ed.), 4th rev. ed. (Leiden: Brill, 1996).

Primary sources

Books of the Bible

Old Testament

Gen	Genesis	Prov	Proverbs
Exod	Exodus	Eccl	Ecclesiastes
Lev	Leviticus	Song	Song of Songs
Num	Numbers	Isa	Isaiah
Deut	Deuteronomy	Zeph	Zephaniah
Josh	Joshua	Hag	Haggai
Judg	Judges	Jer	Jeremiah
Ruth		Lam	Lamentations
1–2 Sam	1–2 Samuel	Ezek	Ezekiel
1–2 Kgs	1–2 Kings	Dan	Daniel
Nah	Nahum	Hos	Hosea
Hab	Habakkuk	Joel	
1–2 Chr	1–2 Chronicles	Amos	
Ezra		Obad	Obadiah
Neh	Nehemiah	Jon	Jonah
Esth	Esther	Mic	Micah
Job		Zech	Zechariah
Ps	Psalms	Mal	Malachi

LXX/Deuterocanonical books cited

1–4 Macc	1–4 Maccabees
Sir	Sirach
Wis	Wisdom of Solomon

New Testament

Matt	Matthew	1–2 Thess	1–2 Thessalonians
Mark		1–2 Tim	1–2 Timothy
Luke		Tit	Titus
John		Phlm	Philemon
Acts		Heb	Hebrews
Rom	Romans	Jas	James
1–2 Cor	1–2 Corinthians	1–2 Pet	1–2 Peter
Gal	Galatians	1–3 John	
Eph	Ephesians	Jude	
Phil	Philippians	Rev	Revelation
Col	Colossians		

Ambrose

Exp. Ps. 118	*Explanatio psalmi* CXVIII
Ob. Theo.	*De obitu Theodosii*

Apocryphal Acts of the Apostles

Acts Joh.	*Acts of John*
Acts Pet.	*Acts of Peter*
Acts Thom.	*Acts of Thomas*

Apostolic fathers

1–2 Clem.	*1–2 Clement*
Did.	*Didache*
Ep. Barn.	*Epistle of Barnabas*
Ep. Diognet.	*Epistle to Diognetus*
Herm. *Mand.*	Shepherd of Hermas, *Mandates*
Herm. *Sim.*	Shepherd of Hermas, *Similitudes*
Herm. *Vis.*	Shepherd of Hermas, *Visions*
Ign. *Eph.*	Ignatius, *To the Ephesians*
Ign. *Magn.*	Ignatius, *To the Magnesians*
Ign. *Phild.*	Ignatius, *To the Philadelphians*
Ign. *Pol.*	Ignatius, *To Polycarp*
Ign. *Rom.*	Ignatius, *To the Romans*
Ign. *Smyr.*	Ignatius, *To the Smyrneans*
Ign. *Trall.*	Ignatius, *To the Trallians*
Poly. *Phil.*	Polycarp, *To the Philippians*

Apuleius (Apul.)

Fl.	*Florida*
Met.	*Metamorphoses*
Pl.	*De Platone*

[Aristeas]

Ep. Arist.	*Epistle of Aristeas*

Aristides

Apol.	*Apologia*

Aristotle (Arist.)

Pol.	*Politica*

Arnobius

Adv. nat.	*Adversus nationes*

Athanasius (Ath.)

Apol. sec.	*Apologia (secunda) contra Arianos*
Decr.	*De decretis Nicaenae synodi*
Dion.	*De sententia Dionysii*
Ep.	*Epistulae*
Ep. Jov.	*Epistula ad Jovianum*
H. Ar.	*Historia Arianorum ad monachos*
Syn.	*De synodis*
Tom.	*Tomus ad Antiochenos*

Athenagoras

Leg.	*Legatio pro Christianis*
Res.	*De resurrectione mortuorum*

Augustine (August.)

Cresc.	*Contra Cresconium Donatistam*
De civ. D.	*De civitate Dei*
Doctr. Chr.	*De doctrina Christiana*
Retract.	*Retractationes*
Trin.	*De Trinitate*

Aurelius Victor (Aurel. Vict.)

Caes.	*Liber de Caesaribus*

Basil (Bas.)

Ep.	*Epistulae*

Julius Caesar (Caes.)

B. Gall.   *Bellum Gallicum*

Cassius Dio (Cass. Dio)

Chrysostom, John (Chrys.)

Adv. Jud.   *Adversus Judaeos*
Hom. 1–88 in Jo.   *Homiliae 1–88 in Johannem*

Cicero (Cic.)

Acad.   *Academicae quaestiones*
Clu.   *Pro Cluentio*
Fin.   *De finibus*
Har. resp.   *De haruspicum responso*
N.D.   *De natura deorum*
Rep.   *De republica*

Clement of Alexandria (Clem. Al.)

Paed.   *Paedagogus*
Protr.   *Protrepticus*
q.d.s.   *Quis dives salvetur*
Str.   *Stromateis*

Clementina ([Clem.])

Asc. Jas.   *Ascents of James*
Ep. Petr.   *Epistula Petri ad Jacobum*
Hom.   *Homiliae*
Keryg. Pet.   *Kērygmata Petrou*
Recogn.   *Recognitiones*

Constantine (Const.)

Or. s.c.   *Oratio ad sanctorum coetum*

Cyprian (Cypr.)

Ep.   *Epistulae*
Hab. virg.   *De habitu virginum*
Laps.   *De lapsis*
Unit. eccl.   *De catholicae ecclesiae unitate*

Cyril of Jerusalem (Cyr. H.)

Catech. 1–18   *Catecheses illuminandorum*
Catech. 19–23   *Catecheses mystagogicae*
Ep. Const.   *Epistula ad Constantium de visione crucis*

Dead Sea scrolls and related texts

1QH*ᵃ*	*Hodayot*ᵃ *or Thanksgiving hymns*ᵃ
1QS	*Rule of the community*
1Qsa	*Rule of the congregation* (appendix a to 1QS)
1QM	*War scroll*
CD	Cairo Geniza copy of the *Damascus document*
4QShirShab*ᵃ*	*Songs of the sabbath sacrifice*ᵃ
4QDibHam*ᵃ*	*Dibre hame'orot*ᵃ *or Words of the luminaries*ᵃ
11QPs*ᵃ*	*Psalm scroll*ᵃ

Diodorus Siculus (Diod. Sic.)

Diogenes Laertius (Diog. Laert.)

Epiphanius (Epiph.)

Mens.	*De mensuris et ponderibus*
Pan.	*Panarion seu Adversus lxxx haereses*

Eusebius (Euseb.)

Chron.	*Chronicon*
D.E.	*Demonstratio evangelica*
E.Th.	*De ecclesiastica theologia*
Ep. Caes.	*Epistula ad Caesarienses*
HE	*Historia ecclesiastica*
L.C.	*Laus Constantini*
Marcell.	*Contra Marcellum*
Mart. Pal.	*De martyribus Palestinae*
Onomast.	*Onomasticon*
P.E.	*Praeparatio evangelica*
V.C.	*De vita Constantini*

Gelasius of Cyzicus (Gel.)

HE	*Historia ecclesiastica*

Gregory of Nazianzus (Gr. Naz.)

Or.	*Orationes*

Gregory of Nyssa (Gr. Nyss.)

V. Gr. Thaum.	*De vita Gregorii Thaumaturgi*

Gregory Thaumaturgus (Gr. Thaum.)

Ep. can.	*Epistula canonica*

Herodotus (Hdt.)

Hist.	*Historiae*

Hilary of Poitiers (Hil. Poit.)

Ad. Val. et Ur.	*adversus Valentem et Ursacium*

Hippolytus (Hipp.)

Antichr.	*Demonstratio de Christo et antichristo*
Ben. Is. Iac.	*De benedictionibus Isaaci et Jacobi*
Dan.	*Commentarium in Danielem*
Fr. 1–81 in Gen.	*Fragmenta in Genesim*
Haer.	*Refutatio omnium haeresium*
Noët.	*Contra Noëtum*
Trad. ap.	*Traditio apostolica*

Irenaeus (Iren.)

Epid.	*Epideixis tou apostolikou kērygmatos*
Frag. Syr.	*Fragments in Syriac*
Haer.	*Adversus haereses*

Jerome

Comm. Am.	*Commentariorum in Amos*
Comm. Ezech.	*Commentariorum in Ezechielem*
Comm. Gal.	*Commentariorum in Epistulam ad Galatas*
Comm. Habac.	*Commentariorum in Habacuc*
Comm. Isa.	*Commentariorum in Isaiam*
Comm. Jer.	*Commentariorum in Jeremiam*
Comm. Mt.	*Commentariorum in Matthaeum*
Ep.	*Epistulae*
Onom.	*Onomasticon*
Vir. ill.	*De viris illustribus*

Josephus

AJ	*Antiquitates Judaicae*
Ap.	*Contra Apionem*
BJ	*Bellum Judaicum*
Vit.	*Vita*

Justin

1 Apol.	1 Apologia
2 Apol.	2 Apologia
Dial.	Dialogus cum Tryphone Judaeo

Juvenal (Juv.)

Sat.	Satires

Lactantius (Lactant.)

Div. inst.	Divinae institutiones
Mort.	De morte persecutorum

Lucian (Luc.)

Alex.	Alexander (Pseudomantis)
De mort. Peregr.	De morte Peregrini
Men.	Menippus (Necyomantia)

Martyrologies

Musurillo	H. Musurillo (ed. and trans.), *Acts of the Christian martyrs*, OECT (1972)
M. Crisp.	Martyrium Crispinae
M. Cypr.	Martyrium Cypriani
M. Iust.	Martyrium Iustini et septem sodalium
M. Mar.	Martyrium Mariani et Iacobi
M. Mont.	Martyrium Montani et Lucii
M. Perp.	Martyrium Perpetuae et Felicitatis
M. Pion.	Martyrium Pionii
M. Polyc.	Martyrium Polycarpi
M. Saturn.	Martyrium Saturnini, Dativi et aliorum plurimorum
M. Scil.	Martyrum Scillitanorum acta

Maximus of Tyre (Max. Tyr.)

Melito of Sardis (Mel.)

Fr.	Fragmenta
Pass.	Homilia in passionem Christi (= Peri pascha)

Methodius of Olympus (Meth.)

Res.	De resurrectione mortuorum
Symp.	Symposium

Minucius Felix (Min. Fel.)

Oct.	*Octavius*

Nag Hammadi Codices

The Nag Hammadi codices (NHC) are identified by the codex number (I) followed by treatise number (1).

NHC	Nag Hammadi Codices
NHL	*Nag Hammadi library in English*, J. M. Robinson (ed.), 4th rev. ed. (Leiden: Brill, 1996)
BG	Berlin Codex
CG	Cairensis Gnosticus
Pr. Paul	I, 1 *Prayer of the apostle Paul*
Treat. res.	I, 4 *Treatise on the resurrection*
Tri. trac.	I, 5 *Tripartite tractate*
Ap. John	II, 1 *Apocryphon of John*
Gos. Thom.	II, 2 *Gospel of Thomas*
Gos. Phil.	II, 3 *Gospel of Philip*
Hyp. Arch.	II, 4 *Hypostasis of the Archons*
Thom. cont.	II, 7 *Book of Thomas the contender*
Eugnostos	III, 3 *Eugnostos the blessed*
Dial. sav.	III, 5 *Dialogue of the saviour*
Gos. Eg.	IV, 2 *Gospel of the Egyptians*
Eugnostos	V, 1 *Eugnostos the blessed*
1 Apoc. Jas.	V, 3 *(First) Apocalypse of James*
2 Apoc. Jas.	V, 4 *(Second) Apocalypse of James*
Apoc. Adam	V, 5 *The Apocalypse of Adam*
Acts Pet. 12 apos.	VI, 1 *Acts of Peter and the twelve apostles*
Thund.	VI, 2 *Thunder: perfect mind*
Disc. 8–9	VI, 6 *Discourse on the eighth and ninth*
Pr. thanks.	VI, 7 *Prayer of thanksgiving*
Asclepius	VI, 8 *Asclepius 21–29*
Paraph. Shem	VII, 1 *Paraphrase of Shem*
Steles Seth	VII, 5 *Three steles of Seth*
Zost.	VIII, 1 *Zostrianos*
Ep. Pet. Phil.	VIII, 2 *Letter of Peter to Philip*
Melch.	IX, 1 *Melchizedek*
Norea	IX, 2 *Thought of Norea*
Marsanes	X, 1 *Marsanes*
Interp. know.	XI, 1 *Interpretation of knowledge*
Val. exp.	XI, 2 *A Valentinian exposition*
Allogenes	XI, 3 *Allogenes (foreigner)*
Hypsiph.	XI, 4 *Hypsiphrone*
Trim. Prot.	XII, 1 *Trimorphic protennoia*
Act Pet.	BG, 4 *Act of Peter*

New Testament Apocrypha and Pseudepigrapha

NTApoc	*New Testament Apocrypha*, 2 vols., W. Schneemelcher and R. McL. Wilson (eds.), rev. ed. (Cambridge: James Clarke & Co. Ltd.; Louisville, KY: Westminster John Knox Press, 1991–2).
Gos. Eb.	*Gospel of the Ebionites*
Gos. Heb.	*Gospel of the Hebrews*
Gos. Naass.	*Gospel of the Naassenes*
Gos. Naz.	*Gospel of the Nazareans*

Novatian

Trin.	*De Trinitate*

Old Testament Pseudepigrapha

APOT	*The Apocrypha and pseudepigrapha of the Old Testament*, 2 vols., R. H. Charles (ed.) (Oxford: Clarendon Press, 1913)
OTP	*The Old Testament pseudepigrapha*, 2 vols., J. H. Charlesworth (ed.) (Garden City, NY: Doubleday, 1983–5).
1–4 Bar.	*1–4 Baruch*
Odes Sol.	*Odes of Solomon*

Optatus of Milevis (Opt.)

Donat.	*De schismate Donatistarum*

Oracula Sibyllina (Orac. Sib.)

Origen (Or.)

C. Cels.	*Contra Celsum*
Comm. Heb.	*Commentarii in epistulam ad Hebraeos*
Comm. Jo.	*Commentarii in evangelium Joannis*
Comm. Matt.	*In Matthaeum commentariorum series*
Dial.	*Dialogus cum Heraclide*
Hom. Ezech.	*Homiliae in Ezechielem*
Hom. Gen.	*Homiliae in Genesim*
Hom. Jer.	*Homiliae in Jeremiam*
Hom. Luc.	*Homiliae in Lucam*
Hom. Num.	*Homiliae in Numeros*
Or.	*De oratione*
Princ.	*De principiis*
Sel. Lev.	*Selecta in Leviticum*

Orosius (Oros.)

Hist.	*Historiae adversum paganos*

Ovid (Ov.)

Am.	*Amores*

Palladius (Pall.)

H. Laus.	*Historia Lausiaca*

Pamphilus (Pamph.)

Ap. Or.	*Apologia pro Origene*

Panegyrici Latini (Pan. Lat.)

Papyri

P. Amh.	Amherst papyri
P. Köln	Kölner papyri
P. Oxy.	Oxyrhynchus papyri
P. Ryl.	John Rylands papyri

Pausanias (Paus.)

Philo

Contempl.	*De vita contemplativa*
Decal.	*De decalogo*
Flacc.	*In Flaccum*
Legat.	*Legatio ad Gaium*
Migr.	*De migratione Abrahami*
Opif.	*De opificio mundi*
Prov.	*De providentia*
Quaest. Ex.	*Quaestiones et solutiones in Exodum*
Spec.	*De specialibus legibus*
Virt.	*De virtutibus*

Philostorgius (Philost.)

HE	*Historia ecclesiastica*

Philostratus (Philostr.)

VA	*Vita Apollonii*

Plato (Pl.)

Epin.	*Epinomis*
Lg.	*Leges*
Prt.	*Protagoras*
Res.	*Respublica*
Ti.	*Timaeus*

Pliny (the Elder) (Plin.)

HN	*Naturalis historia*

Pliny (the Younger) (Plin.)

Ep.	*Epistulae*
Pan.	*Panegyricus*

Plotinus (Plot.)

Enn.	*Enneades*

Plutarch (Plut.)

Adol. poet. aud.	*Quomodo adolescens poetas audire debeat*
Cam.	*Camillus*
Def. orac.	*De defectu oraculorum*
De Is. et Os.	*De Iside et Osiride*
Lib. ed.	*De liberis educandis*
Princ. inerud.	*Ad principem ineruditum*
Quaest. conv.	*Quaestiones convivales*
Superst.	*De superstitione*

Polybius (Polyb.)

Hist.	*Historiae*

Porphyry (Porph.)

Christ.	*Contra Christianos*
De antr. nymph.	*De antro nympharum*
Vit. Plot.	*Vita Plotini*

Ptolemaeus

Flor.	*Epistula ad Floram*

Rabbinic Works

A prefixed '*y.*' before a Tractate name denotes the Jerusalem Talmud (Yerushalmi), and a prefixed '*b.*' the Babylonian (Bavli). Additionally, a prefixed '*t.*' indicates the *Tosefta* and an '*m.*' the *Mishnah*. A prefixed '*bar.*' indicates a *baraita*.

'Abod. Zar.	*Avodah Zarah*
'Abot	*Avot*
Ber.	*Berakhot*
Git.	*Gittin*
Ḥul.	*Hullin*
Sanh.	*Sanhedrin*

Sukk.	*Sukkah*
Ta'an.	*Ta'anit*
Yad.	*Yadayim*
Midr. Teh.	*Midrash Tehillim*
Pesiq. Rab.	*Pesiqta Rabbati*

Rufinus (Ruf.)

HE	*Historia ecclesiastica*

Seneca

Ep.	*Epistulae morales*

Socrates Scholasticus (Socr.)

HE	*Historia ecclesiastica*

Sozomen (Soz.)

HE	*Historia ecclesiastica*

Spartian

Sept. Sever.	*Vita Septimii Severi*

Strabo

Geog.	*Geographica*

Suetonius (Suet.)

Claud.	*Divus Claudius*
Dom.	*Domitianus*
Jul.	*Divus Julius*
Nero	*Nero*
Tit.	*Divus Titus*

Tacitus (Tac.)

Agr.	*Agricola*
Ann.	*Annales*
Hist.	*Historiae*

Tatian (Tat.)

Orat.	*Oratio ad Graecos*

Tertullian (Tert.)

Ad ux.	*Ad uxorem*

Adv. Jud.	*Adversus Judaeos*
An.	*De anima*
Apol.	*Apologeticus*
Bapt.	*De baptismo*
Carn. Chr.	*De carne Christi*
Cor.	*De corona militis*
Cult. fem.	*De cultu feminarum*
Exh. cast.	*De exhortatione castitatis*
Herm.	*Adversus Hermogenem*
Idol.	*De idololatria*
Marc.	*Adversus Marcionem*
Mart.	*Ad martyras*
Mon.	*De monogamia*
Nat.	*Ad nationes*
Or.	*De oratione*
Paen.	*De paenitentia*
Praescr.	*De praescriptione haereticorum*
Prax.	*Adversus Praxean*
Pud.	*De pudicitia*
Res.	*De resurrectione carnis*
Scap.	*Ad Scapulam*
Scorp.	*Scorpiace*
Spect.	*De spectaculis*
Val.	*Adversus Valentinianos*
Virg.	*De virginibus velandis*

Theodoret (Thdt.)

HE	*Historia ecclesiastica*

Theophilus of Antioch (Thph. Ant.)

Autol.	*Ad Autolycum*

Valentinus (Val.)

Gos. truth	*The gospel of truth*

Vergil (Verg.)

Aen.	*Aeneid*

Xenophon (Xen.)

Mem.	*Memorabilia*

Zosimus (Zos.)

Hist.	*Historia nova*

Secondary Sources

Reference works and series

AAR Academy series	American Academy of Religion Academy series (New York: Oxford University Press)
AB	Anchor Bible (Garden City, NY: Doubleday)
ABD	*Anchor Bible dictionary*, 6 vols., D. N. Freedman (ed.) (New York: Doubleday, 1992)
ACW	Ancient Christian writers (New York: Newman Press)
AGJU	Arbeiten zur Geschichte des antiken Judentums und des Urchristentums (Leiden: Brill)
AKG	Arbeiten zur Kirchengeschichte (Berlin: De Gruyter)
AnBib	Analecta Biblica (Rome: Pontifical Biblical Institute)
ANF	*Ante-Nicene Fathers* (Grand Rapids, MI: Eerdmans)
Ant.	Antiquitas (Bonn: R. Habelt)
ANRW	*Aufstieg und Niedergang der römischen Welt* (Berlin: De Gruyter)
ANTF	Arbeiten zur neutestamentlichen Textforschung (Berlin: De Gruyter)
ATD	Acta theologica Danica (Copenhagen: Munksgaard; Leiden: Brill)
AzBiG	Arbeiten zur Bibel und ihrer Geschichte (Leipzig: Evangelische Verlagsanstalt)
BAC	Biblioteca de autores cristianos (Madrid: Biblioteca de autores cristianos)
BBET	Beiträge zur biblischen Exegese und Theologie (Bern: Peter Lang)
BCTH	*Bulletin archéologique du Comité des travaux historiques et scientifiques* (Paris: Editions du CTHS)
BDR	Blass, F., A. Debrunner and F. Rehkopf, *Grammatik des neutestamentlichen Griechisch*, 14th ed. (Göttingen: Vandenhoeck & Ruprecht, 1976)
BETL	Bibliotheca ephemeridum theologicarum lovaniensium (Leuven: Peeters)
BFCT	Beiträge zur Förderung christlicher Theologie (Gütersloh: Bertelsmann)
BHT	Beiträge zur historischen Theologie (Tübingen: Mohr Siebeck)
BibS(F)	Biblische Studien (Freiburg: Herder, 1895–)
BibS(N)	Biblische Studien (Neukirchen-Vluyn: Neukirchener Verlag, 1951–)
BIS	Biblical interpretation series (Leiden: Brill)
BJS	Brown Judaic studies (Providence, RI: Brown University)
BSRel	Biblioteca di scienze religiose (Rome: LAS)

BZNW	Beihefte zur Zeitschrift für die neutestamentliche Wissenschaft und die Kunde der älteren Kirche (Berlin: De Gruyter)
*CAH*¹	*Cambridge Ancient History*, 12 vols. (Cambridge: Cambridge University Press, 1923–39)
*CAH*²	*Cambridge Ancient History*, 2nd ed., 14 vols. (Cambridge: Cambridge University Press, 1970–2001)
CBET	Contributions to Biblical exegesis and theology (Leuven: Peeters)
CBQMS	Catholic Biblical quarterly monograph series (Washington, DC: The Catholic Biblical Association of America)
CCSA	Corpus Christianorum: series Apocryphorum (Turnhout: Brepols, 1983–)
CCSG	Corpus Christianorum: series Graeca (Turnhout: Brepols, 1977–)
CCSL	Corpus Christianorum: series Latina (Turnhout: Brepols, 1953–)
CII	*Corpus inscriptionum Iudaicarum*, 2 vols., J. B. Frey (ed.) (Rome: Pontificio istituto di archeologia cristiana, 1936–52).
CIL	*Corpus inscriptionum Latinarum* (Berlin: Akademie der Wissenschaften, 1862–).
CJA	Christianity and Judaism in antiquity (Notre Dame, IN: University of Notre Dame Press)
ConBNT	Coniectanea Biblica: New Testament series (Stockholm: Almqvist & Wiksell International)
ConBOT	Coniectanea Biblica: Old Testament series (Stockholm: Almqvist & Wiksell International)
CPJ	*Corpus papyrorum Judaicarum*, 3 vols., V. Tcherikover and A. Fuks (eds.) (Cambridge, MA: Harvard University Press, 1957–64).
*CPL*³	*Clavis patrum Latinorum*, 3rd ed., E. Dekkers and E. Gaar (eds.), CCSL (1995)
CRINT	Compendia rerum Iudaicarum ad Novum Testamentum (Assen: van Gorcum and Minneapolis: Fortress Press)
CSCT	Columbia studies in the Classical tradition (Leiden: Brill)
CSCO	Corpus scriptorum Christianorum orientalium (Louvain: Peeters)
CSEL	Corpus scriptorum ecclesiasticorum Latinorum (Vienna: Hoelder-Pichler-Tempsky)
DACL	*Dictionnaire d'archéologie chrétienne et de liturgie*, 15 vols., F. Cabrol (ed.) (Paris: Letouzey et Ané, 1907–53)
DJD	Discoveries in the Judean desert (Oxford: Clarendon Press)
DMAHA	Dutch monographs on ancient history and archaeology (Amsterdam: J. C. Gieben)
EBib	Études bibliques (Paris: J. Gabalda)
EECh	*Encyclopedia of the early church*, 2 vols., A. di Berardino (ed.), A. Walford (trans.) (New York: Oxford University Press, 1992)
EKKNT	Evangelisch-katholischer Kommentar zum Neuen Testament (Düsseldorf: Benziger Verlag; Neukirchen-Vluyn: Neukirchener Verlag)

EPRO	Études préliminaires aux religions orientales dans l'empire romain (Leiden: Brill)
ER	*The encyclopedia of religion*, 16 vols., M. Eliade (ed.) (New York: Macmillan, 1987)
FC	Fathers of the church (Washington, DC: Catholic University of America Press)
FGrH	*Die Fragmente der griechischen Historiker*, 3 vols., F. Jacoby (ed.) (Leiden: Brill, 1954–64)
FKDG	Forschungen zur Kirchen- und Dogmengeschichte (Göttingen: Vandenhoeck & Ruprecht)
Foerster, *Gnosis*	*Gnosis: a selection of Gnostic texts*, 2 vols., W. Foerster (ed.), R. McL. Wilson (trans.) (Oxford: Clarendon Press, 1972–4).
FRLANT	Forschungen zur Religion und Literatur des Alten und Neuen Testaments (Göttingen: Vandenhoeck & Ruprecht)
GCS	Die griechische christliche Schriftsteller der ersten drei Jahrhunderte (Berlin: Akademie Verlag)
GNS	Good news studies (Collegeville, MN: Liturgical Press)
Goodspeed, *Die ältesten Apologeten*	*Die ältesten Apologeten: Texte mit kurzen Einleitungen*, E. J. Goodspeed (ed.) (Göttingen: Vandenhoeck & Ruprecht, 1984, original 1914)
GTA	Göttinger theologische Arbeiten (Göttingen: Vandenhoeck & Ruprecht)
HBS	Herders biblische Studien (Freiburg: Herder)
HDR	Harvard dissertations in religion (Minneapolis: Fortress Press)
HNTC	Harper's New Testament commentaries (San Francisco: Harper & Row)
HO	Handbuch der Orientalistik (Leiden: Brill)
HTS	Harvard theological studies (Cambridge, MA: Harvard University Press)
HUT	Hermeneutische Untersuchungen zur Theologie (Tübingen: Mohr Siebeck)
ICC	International critical commentary on the holy scriptures of the Old and New Testaments (Edinburgh: T. & T. Clark)
IG	*Inscriptiones Graecae*, 14 vols. (Berlin: de Gruyter, 1913–)
IGUR	*Inscriptiones Graecae urbis Romae*, L. Moretti (ed.), Studi pubblicati dall' istituto italiano per la storia antica 17 (Rome, 1968–)
ILCV	*Inscriptiones Latinae Christianae veteres*, 3 vols. E. Diehl, J. Moreau and H. I. Marrou (eds.), 4th ed. (Berlin: Weidemann, 1925–85)

ILS	*Inscriptiones Latinae selectae*, Hermann Dessau (ed.), 3rd ed., 3 vols. (Berlin: Weidmann, 1962)
JDS	Judean Desert studies (Jerusalem: Israel Exploration Society)
JRASup	Journal of Roman archaeology, supplementary series (Portsmouth, RI: Journal of Roman Archaeology)
JRSM	Journal of Roman studies monographs (London: Society for the Promotion of Roman Studies)
JSNTSup	Journal for the study of the New Testament: supplement series (Sheffield: Sheffield Academic Press)
JSOTSup	Journal for the study of the Old Testament: supplement series (Sheffield: Sheffield Academic Press)
JSPSup	Journal for the study of the Pseudepigrapha: supplement series (Sheffield: Sheffield Academic Press)
JSS Sup	Journal of Semitic studies supplement (Oxford: Oxford University Press)
KAV	Kommentar zu den apostolischen Vätern (Göttingen: Vandenhoeck & Ruprecht)
KEK	Ergänzungsreihe zum kritisch-exegetischen Kommentar über das Neue Testament (Göttingen: Vandenhoeck & Ruprecht)
Der kleine Pauly	*Der kleine Pauly: Lexikon der Antike*, 5 vols., H. Gärtner, W. Sontheimer, K. Ziegler and A. F. von Pauly (eds.) (Munich: Druckenmüller, 1964–75)
LCC	Library of Christian Classics (Grand Rapids, MI: Christian classics Ethereal Library)
LCL	Loeb Classical library (Cambridge, MA: Harvard University Press)
LEC	Library of early Christianity (Philadelphia: Westminster)
MAMA	*Monumenta Asiae Minoris antiqua*, 10 vols., C. W. M. Cox, A. Cameron, J. Cullen and B. Levick (eds.), JRMS (1928–1993).
MBPF	Münchener Beiträge zur Papyrusforschung und antiken Rechtsgeschichte (Munich: C.H. Beck)
MBT	Münsterische Beiträge zur Theologie (Münster: Aschendorff)
MDOP	Monograph, Dakhleh Oasis project (Oxford: Oxbow Books)
Mnemos. Sup.	Mnemosyne, bibliotheca classica Batava, Supplementum: history and archaeology of Classical antiquity (Leiden: Brill)
Musurillo	Musurillo, Herbert (ed.), *Acts of the Christian martyrs: introduction, texts, and translations*, OECT (1972)
Nestle-Aland NTG²⁷	*Novum Testamentum Graecae*, 27th rev. ed., E. E. Nestle, B. Aland and K. Aland (eds.) (Stuttgart: Deutsche Bibelstiftung, 1993, 1979)
Der neue Pauly	*Der neue Pauly: Enzyklopädie der Antike*, 15 vols., H. Cancik, H. Schneider and A. F. von Pauly (eds.) (Stuttgart: Metzler, 1996–)

NewDocs	*New documents illustrating early Christianity*, 9 vols., G. H. R. Horsley and S. Llewelyn (eds.) (North Ryde, NSW: Ancient History Documentary Research Centre, Macquarie University, 1981)
NHMS	Nag Hammadi and Manichaean studies (Leiden: Brill)
NHS	Nag Hammadi studies (Leiden: Brill)
NICNT	New international commentary on the New Testament (Grand Rapids, MI: Eerdmans)
NovTSup	Novum Testamentum supplements (Leiden: Brill)
NPNF¹	*Nicene and post-Nicene fathers*, series 1 (Grand Rapids, MI: Eerdmans)
NPNF²	*Nicene and post-Nicene fathers*, series 2 (Peabody, MA: Hendrickson)
NTAbh	Neutestamentliche Abhandlungen (Münster: Aschendorff)
NTOA	Novum Testamentum et orbis antiquus (Freiburg, Switzerland: Universitätsverlag)
OCD³	*The Oxford Classical dictionary*, 3rd ed., S. Hornblower and A. Spawforth (eds.) (Oxford: Oxford University Press, 1996)
OCT	Oxford Classical texts (Oxford: Oxford University Press)
OECS	Oxford early Christian studies (Oxford: Oxford University Press)
OECT	Oxford early Christian texts (Oxford: Oxford University Press)
OGIS	*Orientis Graeci inscriptiones selectae*, 2 vols., W. Dittenberger (ed.) (repr. Hildesheim: Olms, 1970)
OrChrAn	Orientalia Christiana analecta (Rome: Pontificio Istituto Orientale)
OTM	Oxford theological monographs (Oxford: Oxford University Press)
PatrMS	Patristic monograph series (Macon, GA: Mercer University Press)
P. Coll. Youtie	*Collectanea papyrologica: texts published in honor of H. C. Youtie*, 2 vols., A. E. Hanson (ed.) (Bonn: Habelt, 1976)
PG	*Patrologia Graeca*, 162 vols. [= *Patrologiae cursus completus: series Graeca*], J.-P. Migne (ed.) (Paris, 1844–64)
PHC	Pelican history of the church (New York: Penguin Books)
PL	*Patrologia Latina*, 221 vols. [= *Patrologiae cursus completus: series Latina*], J.-P. Migne (ed.) (Paris, 1857–66)
PO	*Patrologia orientalis* (Turnhout: Brepols)
PTS	Patristische Texte und Studien (Berlin: De Gruyter)
PW	*Paulys Realencyclopädie der classischen Altertumswissenschaft*, 70 vols., A. F. Pauly, G. Wissowa and G. Krolls (eds.) (Stuttgart: Metzler, 1894–1972)
RA	Revealing antiquity (Cambridge, MA: Harvard University Press)
RAC	*Reallexikon für Antike und Christentum: Sachwörterbuch zur Auseinandersetzung des Christentums mit der antiken Welt* (Stuttgart: Hiersemann, 1950–)
RFCC	Religion in the first Christian centuries (London: Routledge)
RGG³	*Religion in Geschichte und Gegenwart*, 3rd ed., K. Galling (ed.) (Tübingen: Mohr Siebeck, 1957–65)
RGG⁴	*Religion in Geschichte und Gegenwart*, 4th ed., H. D. Betz, *et al.* (eds.) (Tübingen: Mohr Siebeck, 1998–)
RGRW	Religions in the Graeco-Roman world (Leiden: Brill)

RVV	Religionsgeschichtliche Versuche und Vorarbeiten (Berlin: De Gruyter)
SAC	Studies in antiquity and Christianity (Philadelphia, PA: Fortress; Harrisburg, PA: Trinity Press International)
SBB	Stuttgarter biblische Beiträge (Stuttgart: Katholisches Bibelwerk)
SBLDS	Society of Biblical Literature dissertation series (Atlanta: Society of Biblical Literature)
SBLMS	Society of Biblical Literature monograph series (Atlanta: Society of Biblical Literature)
SBLRBS	Society of Biblical Literature resources for Biblical study (Atlanta: Scholars Press)
SBLSBS	Society of Biblical Literature sources for Biblical study (Atlanta: Scholars Press)
SBLSymS	Society of Biblical Literature symposium series (Atlanta: Scholars Press)
SBLTT	Society of Biblical Literature texts and translations (Atlanta: Scholars Press)
SBS	Stuttgarter Bibelstudien (Stuttgart: Katholisches Bibelwerk)
SC	Sources chrétiennes (Paris: Éditions du Cerf)
SCH	Studies in church history (Woodbridge, Suffolk: Ecclesiastical History Society / Boydell Press)
SD	Studies and documents (London: Christophers)
SEAug	Studia ephemeridis Augustinianum (Rome: Institutum Patristicum Augustinianum)
SEG	*Supplementum epigraphicum Graecum*, J. Hondius, H. W. Pleket, R. S. Stroud, *et al.* (eds.) (Amsterdam: J. C. Gieben, 1923–)
SHR	Studies in the history of religions (Leiden: Brill)
SIG	*Sylloge inscriptionum Graecarum*, 4 vols., 3rd ed., W. Dittenberger (ed.) (repr. Hildesheim: Olms, 1960).
SJLA	Studies in Judaism in late antiquity (Leiden: Brill)
SNTSMS	Society for New Testament Studies monograph series (Cambridge: Cambridge University Press)
SSEJC	Studies in early Judaism and Christianity (Sheffield: Sheffield Academic Press)
StEv	*Studia evangelica* (Berlin: De Gruyter)
StPB	Studia post-Biblica (Jerusalem: Magnes Press)
SVF	*Stoicorum veterum fragmenta*, 4 vols., H. von Arnim (ed.) (Leipzig: Teubner, 1903–24)
TANZ	Texte und Arbeiten zum neutestamentlichen Zeitalter (Tübingen: Francke)
TBA	Tübinger Beiträge zur Altertumswissenschaft (Stuttgart: Kohlhammer)
TCH	Transformation of the Classical heritage (Berkeley: University of California Press)
TCL	Translations of Christian literature (London: SPCK; Atlanta: Scholars Press)
Teubner	Bibliotheca scriptorum Graecorum et Romanorum Teubneriana (Leipzig: Teubner)

ThH	Théologie historique (Paris: Beauchesne)
TNTC	Tyndale New Testament commentaries (Leicester: Inter-Varsity Press)
TRE	*Theologische Realenzyklopädie*, G. Krause and G. Müller (eds.) (Berlin: De Gruyter, 1976–)
TS	Texts and studies (Cambridge: Cambridge University Press)
TSAJ	Texte und Studien zum antiken Judentum (Tübingen: Mohr Siebeck)
TTH	Translated texts for historians (Liverpool: Liverpool University Press)
TU	Texte und Untersuchungen zur Geschichte der altchristlichen Literatur (Berlin: De Gruyter)
VCSup	Supplements to *Vigiliae Christianae* (Leiden: Brill)
WBC	Word Biblical commentary (Nashville: Nelson)
WMANT	Wissenschaftliche Monographien zum Alten und Neuen Testament (Neukirchen-Vluyn: Neukirchener Verlag)
WUNT	Wissenschaftliche Untersuchungen zum Neuen Testament (Tübingen: Mohr Siebeck)

Periodicals

ABR	*Australian biblical review*
AJA	*American journal of archaeology*
AJAH	*American journal of ancient history*
AJT	*American journal of theology*
AmAnth	*American anthropologist*
AnBoll	*Analecta bollandiana*
AnSt	*Anatolian studies*
AThR	*Anglican theological review*
BA	*Biblical archaeologist*
BASOR	*Bulletin of the American Schools of Oriental Research*
Bib	*Biblica*
BibInt	*Biblical interpretation*
BTB	*Biblical theology bulletin*
BZ	*Biblische Zeitschrift*
CBQ	*Catholic biblical quarterly*
CH	*Church history*
CTJ	*Calvin theological journal*
ExpT	*Expository times*
GRBS	*Greek, Roman and Byzantine studies*
HeyJ	*Heythrop journal*
Historia	*Historia: Zeitschrift für alte Geschichte/Revue d'histoire ancienne/Rivista di storia antica/Revista de historia antigua/Ancient history bulletin*
HTR	*Harvard theological review*
HUCA	*Hebrew Union College annual*
IEJ	*Israel exploration journal*
INJ	*Israel numismatic journal*
JAAR	*Journal of the American Academy of Religion*
JAC	*Jahrbuch für Antike und Christentum*

JBL	*Journal of biblical literature*
JEA	*Journal of Egyptian archaeology*
JECS	*Journal of early Christian studies*
JEH	*Journal of ecclesiastical history*
JJS	*Journal of Jewish studies*
JQR	*Jewish quarterly review*
JR	*Journal of religion*
JRA	*Journal of Roman archaeology*
JRS	*Journal of Roman studies*
JSJ	*Journal for the study of Judaism in the Persian, Hellenistic and Roman periods*
JSNT	*Journal for the Study of the New Testament*
JTS	*Journal of theological studies*
KD	*Kerygma und Dogma*
MTZ	*Münchener theologische Zeitschrift*
NKZ	*Neue kirchliche Zeitschrift*
Nouv. Clio	*La nouvelle Clio: revue mensuelle de la découverte historique*
NovT	*Novum Testamentum*
NTS	*New Testament studies*
OrChr	*Oriens christianus*
OrChrAn	*Orientalia christiana analecta*
RB	*Revue biblique*
RSR	*Recherches de science religieuse*
SCI	*Scripta classica Israelica*
SCO	*Studi classici e orientali*
SecCent	*Second century*
SJT	*Scottish journal of theology*
SPhilo	*Studia philonica*
ST	*Studia theologica*
StPatr	*Studia patristica*
SVTQ	*St Vladimir's theological quarterly*
ThLZ	*Theologische Literaturzeitung*
ThSt	*Theologische Studien*
TS	*Theological Studies*
VC	*Vigiliae Christianae*
VF	*Verkündigung und Forschung*
VL	*Vetus Latina: die Reste der altlateinischen Bibel*, 26 vols., E. Beuron, B. Fischer, H. J. Frede, P. Sabatier, W. Thiele *et al.* (eds.) (Freiburg: Herder, 1949–).
VT	*Vetus Testamentum*
ZAC / JAC	*Zeitschrift für antikes Christentum / Journal of ancient Christianity*
ZKG	*Zeitschrift für Kirchengeschichte*
ZTK	*Zeitschrift für Theologie*
ZNW	*Zeitschrift für die neutestamentliche Wissenschaft und die Kunde der älteren Kirche*

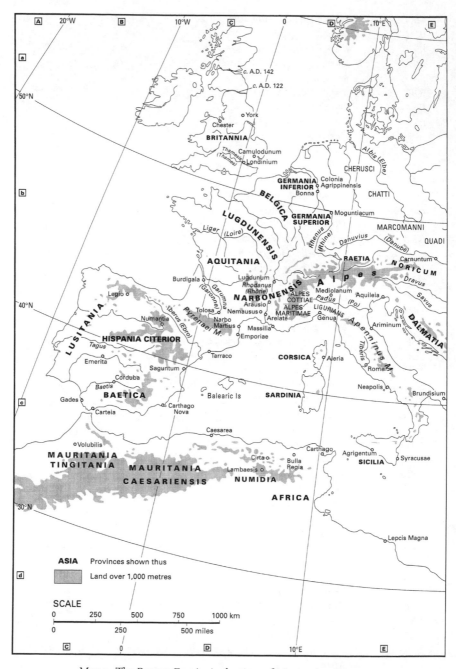

Map 1. The Roman Empire in the time of Marcus Aurelius

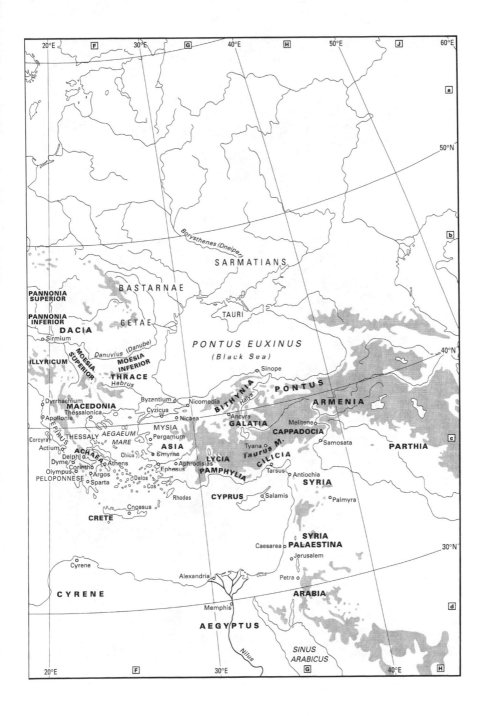

Figure 1. *Titulus* in reliquary, Santa Croce in Gerusalemme (Rome)

Prelude: Jesus Christ, foundation of Christianity

FRANCES M. YOUNG

The Jesus of early imperial Christianity

The death of Jesus by crucifixion, together with his resurrection from the dead, lies at the heart of Christianity. In about 326 CE, at the end of the period covered by this volume, Helena, mother of emperor Constantine, made a legendary pilgrimage to the Holy Land and is purported to have found the true cross, as well as the tomb in which Christ's body had been laid. By exploring this story at the very beginning of this history of Christianity, we shall both open up the particular tensions surrounding the figure of Jesus, who may be regarded as at once the historical instigator and the foundation of Christianity – tensions often captured in the distinction between the 'Jesus of history' and the 'Christ of faith' – and also illustrate with an instructive parallel the problems of reconstructing the life and teaching of a historical figure around whom apparently legendary features have clustered.

To this day, visitors to Rome may make their way to the basilica of Santa Croce in Gerusalemme, just inside the remains of the Aurelian walls of the ancient city, and there find relics of the crucifixion of Jesus and associations with Helena's pilgrimage. Entering a doorway to the left of the altar, the eye is first caught by the supposed crossbeam of the righteous robber (crucified with Jesus, according to Luke 23:39–43). Pilgrims may then follow the traditional Stations of the Cross before turning to the right and entering a twentieth-century chapel. There, standing on the altar are various elaborate reliquaries, and just visible within are what purport to be minute fragments of the true cross, a thorn from the crown of thorns, and part of the board (generally known as the *titulus*) on which Pilate had inscribed in various characters that the one there crucified was Jesus of Nazareth, king of the Jews. Given the measures taken to keep people at a secure distance, the marks scratched on this fragment of wood are barely visible, let alone legible. Yet the story of this unprepossessing piece of board is intriguing.

In 1492 repairs were being made to a mosaic in a niche above the triumphal arch inside this church,[1] and here this fragment was found, sealed behind a brick inscribed with the words *TITULUS CRUCIS*. The mosaic behind which this unexpected discovery was made (now long since gone, though a fifteenth-century copy of it can be found in the chapel of St Helena) went back to the fourth century, the same sort of date as the historians who first recorded the tale of Helena's discoveries. The church is in fact built on the site of a Roman imperial palace, which originated in the early third century, as is evident from certain inscriptions and the fact that the Aurelian walls of 276 CE cut across it, but later was owned by Constantine's mother, the empress Helena. One of the palace halls was adapted into the original fourth-century church, and externally its masonry is partially visible despite the elaborations that have taken place over the centuries. In a crypt chapel, which was once part of the palace, Helena is supposed to have prayed on earth which she brought back from the Holy Land. There too the relics were once housed. The rough writing on the fragment of the *titulus* is curious, for the characters all run from right to left: Hebrew, Greek and Latin. They look hastily inscribed by someone who was familiar with the Hebrew or Aramaic convention while apparently regardless of the fact that Greek and Latin run from left to right. So, could these treasured fragments actually have some connection with events that took place nearly 2,000 years ago, despite the gaps in the evidence and the hidden 300 years between the time of Christ and the purported discoveries of Helena?[2]

Needless to say, scepticism has reigned since the time of Gibbon's *Decline and fall of the Roman empire* (1776–88). He noted the absolute silence of Eusebius of Caesarea with respect to the discovery of the true cross. Now Eusebius was a Palestinian bishop, and a contemporary of Helena who rhetorically celebrated both her pilgrimage and the founding of the Church of the Holy Sepulchre, so naturally his silence has convinced most scholars that the story is a legend – indeed, legendary elements, such as miracles and visions, have clearly entered the story in the 100 years between the event and our first written accounts. Scepticism has seemed the appropriate stance for the post-Reformation, post-Enlightenment historian, especially given the trade in largely spurious relics that seduced Christendom in the medieval period.

---

1 For details about this building, see Webb, *Churches and catacombs*, 52–5.
2 The case has been made by Thiede and d'Ancona, *Quest of the true cross*, though against the general trend of scholarship. The most important study is Drijvers, *Helena Augusta*.

The full story is told by four church historians who, in one way or another, produced continuations of the first ecclesiastical history to be compiled – the work of the same Eusebius of Caesarea, which covered the period from church origins to his own day.[3] Rufinus translated Eusebius' work into Latin and continued the story through the fourth century, writing about 402 CE. Some thirty or forty years later, Socrates Scholasticus, Sozomen and Theodoret continued Eusebius' work in Greek. According to Rufinus[4] and Socrates,[5] Helena went to Jerusalem in response to divinely directed dreams in order to find the sepulchre of Christ. She discovered that a mound had been piled up to cover it, and on the mound a temple to Venus had been erected, a fact attributed to hostility to Christians venerating the tomb. She had the statue thrown down, the earth removed, and the ground entirely cleared, and there she found three crosses in the sepulchre, together with the *titulus*. By a miracle of healing, it was determined which was the cross of Christ. A portion of the true cross was left in the church she built over the site; another part was sent to Constantine who enclosed it in a statue of himself that was erected in Constantinople. The nails she found were used to make a helmet and bridle bits for the emperor.

Sozomen,[6] writing perhaps a little later than Socrates, provides a largely corroborative account, though differing in some details. He indicates that some attributed the discovery to information from a Hebrew who had inherited some relevant documents, though Sozomen himself preferred divine communication through signs and dreams to human information! He also distinguishes between the discovery of the cave where the body was buried and the place where the crosses were found,[7] and notes that the *titulus* had been wrenched from the cross so that it provided no clue as to which was the cross of Christ – hence the need for a miracle. Theodoret[8] attributes to Helena the making of a helmet and bridle bits from the nails to protect her son. In other words, although the story is essentially the same, there are variations and additions.

It was long supposed that the earliest witness to the story is Ambrose of Milan, who tells it as a generally known fact in 395 in *De obitu Theodosii*,

---

3 Thus Eusebius' history, still a vital resource, covered the same ground as this volume.
4 *HE* 10.7–8.
5 *HE* 1.17.
6 *HE* 2.1.
7 Sozomen's version corresponds better with what one is shown today on a visit to the Church of the Holy Sepulchre in Jerusalem.
8 *HE* 1.18.

his funeral oration for the emperor Theodosius.[9] Unlike the other sources, Ambrose attributes the identification of the true cross to the *titulus*, which was placed there by providence for this purpose. Does he perhaps know of the fragment of the *titulus* brought back to Italy by Helena? A comment by John Chrysostom,[10] again dating from the 390s, also appears to link the *titulus* with the identification of the true cross, though he does not attribute the discovery to Helena. So how far back can we trace Helena's connection with the discovery? It is now generally agreed that the lost history of Gelasius, bishop of Caesarea from 357 CE, was the source for all the other historians, and what Rufinus added to Eusebius was, at least in books 10 and 11, largely a translation of Gelasius.[11] Prior to Gelasius, however, there is nothing to link the discovery of the true cross with Helena's well-attested pilgrimage in 326–7, a gap of some thirty years. Eusebius makes much of her involvement with the building of churches in Bethlehem and on the Mount of Olives, but does not in any way connect her with the discovery of the Holy Sepulchre or the building of the church in Jerusalem. Besides, his silence about the discovery of the true cross is absolute. It is time to consider his evidence.

The important work is his *De vita Constantini* ('Life of Constantine'). Written soon after the death of the Emperor, it celebrates Constantine's deeds and his character, and focuses among other things on his church building programme in the Holy Land. Eusebius[12] confirms the discovery of the sepulchre under a pagan temple at the heart of the Roman colony of Aelia Capitolina, and quotes the letter from Constantine to bishop Macarius of Jerusalem, instructing him to build a church there. It has been pointed out,[13] however, that, while Eusebius emphasises 'the memorial of the Resurrection', Constantine wrote of a 'token of that holiest Passion', and that Constantine focuses on the basilica (or Martyrion) associated with Christ's death, while Eusebius is largely interested in the resplendent courtyard constructed around the tomb (the Anastasis). Eusebius, then, may appear to suppress the story of the finding of the cross, while betraying himself, both by recording this letter and also in hints elsewhere – speaking before the emperor[14] he states that the basilica was constructed to honour the 'saving sign', which naturally means the cross.

---

9 *Ob. Theo.* 43–8.
10 *Hom.* 85 *in Jo.*
11 For a discussion of the reconstruction of Gelasius' history, and Rufinus' debt to it, see Drijvers, *Helena Augusta*, 96–101.
12 *V.C.* 3.25–47.
13 Drake, 'Eusebius on the true cross'.
14 *L.C.* 9.16; this text is Eusebius' address on the thirtieth anniversary of Constantine's reign, appended to the *V.C.*

Political and theological reasons have been proposed to explain Eusebius' silence[15] – there is plenty of evidence that elsewhere he suppressed material that did not suit his purpose. Alternatively, it is not impossible that he doubted the authenticity of the find – his predecessor, Origen, was quite prepared to use the ancient critical techniques of *kataskeuē* and *anaskeuē* to consider the historicity of stories in the gospels.[16]

Nevertheless, by 348 CE, Cyril, the bishop of Jerusalem, was telling his cate-chumens that 'the holy wood of the cross, shown among us today . . . has already filled the entire world by means of those who in faith have been taking bits from it',[17] and in a letter to the emperor Constantius II he referred to the discovery of the saving wood of the cross in the time of Constantine.[18] Inscriptions and casual references in other fourth-century literature confirm that relics of the cross spread rapidly, and were even worn as jewellery.[19] Despite protests from preachers, in the popular mind fragments of the cross had become amulets, capable of protecting the wearer from harm. Turning the nails into a bridle and a diadem for Constantine reflects the same kind of belief in the potency of the cross, as does the story of the healing miracle. Yet, there is little trace of the cross as a symbol in pre-Constantinian art[20] – something has changed! For Constantine,[21] the standard of the cross was like a trophy ensuring victory – purportedly a cross of light above the noonday sun had been revealed to him on the eve of his battle for the empire. It was claimed that with this sign he had conquered.[22] Through the cross the supreme God had shown himself Constantine's patron, while Christ, his Son, had been Constantine's preserver and aid in battle against the forces of evil, polytheism, and idolatry. So it is not entirely inconceivable that Helena had motives for seeking the true cross, or that Constantine should have taken a personal interest in the building of a basilica over the place where the wood was found.

Historically speaking, of course, the plausibility of the full story depends on such inferences, not on solid data. Furthermore, there are bound to be questions about the identification of the site and the authenticity of the cross

---

15 Discussed by Drake, 'Eusebius on the true cross'; cf. also Hunt, *Holy Land pilgrimage*; and Drijvers, *Helena Augusta*.
16 Grant, *Earliest lives of Jesus*; see pt V, ch. 27, below.
17 *Catech.* 10.19.
18 *Ep. Const.* 3.
19 Drijvers, *Helena Augusta*, 89–93; also Gibson and Taylor, *Beneath the Church of the Holy Sepulchre*, 83–5.
20 Snyder, *Ante pacem*; but, cf. Hurtado, 'Earliest evidence'.
21 See pt VI, ch. 30, below; the history surrounding Constantine's vision and conversion is likewise contested, of course.
22 Euseb. *V.C.* 1.28–31.

and tomb which were uncovered. Recent discussion has tended to be more sympathetic to the idea that a continuous tradition identified Golgotha and the site of the tomb beneath the pagan temple erected when Hadrian founded the Roman colony of Aelia Capitolina.[23] Be that as it may, it would seem that Helena could have had political reasons for specifically searching out the cross. But what else did she know of the historical Jesus? What picture of Jesus Christ shaped her Holy Land pilgrimage?

That question is not easy to answer directly, but we can make some inferences. If Helena was a convert, as seems likely,[24] she would have recited a creed at her baptism. The statement about Christ would have gone something like this:

> [I believe] in Christ Jesus, [God's] only Son, our Lord, who was born by the Holy Spirit from the Virgin Mary, crucified under Pontius Pilate and buried, on the third day he rose again from the dead, he ascended to heaven, he sits at the Father's right hand, thence he will come to judge the living and the dead.

What is immediately noticeable is the absence of any information about the historical life and teaching of Jesus, apart from the fact that he was born of Mary and crucified under Pontius Pilate. Helena is associated in the sources with the founding of churches in Bethlehem and on the Mount of Olives to mark the sacred locations of the birth and ascension of Jesus, both important events in the creedal summary of who he was.[25] Nevertheless, Helena must have been familiar with the gospels, though the stories would have been heard episodically in the liturgy; it is worth asking how they were understood and what kind of perceptions of Jesus she had gleaned from them.

Constantine's *Oratio ad sanctorum coetum* ('Oration to the assembly of the Saints'), a text appended to Eusebius' *De vita Constantini*,[26] might provide clues. From this text we may deduce that Helena, like her son, was aware of Jesus' baptism in the river Jordan where, 'from infancy possessing the wisdom of God', he was gifted with 'the spirit of universal intelligence, with knowledge and power to perform miracles'. She would have admired his teaching, instilled

---

23 Hunt, *Holy Land pilgrimage*; Drijvers, *Helena Augusta*; Gibson and Taylor, *Beneath the Church of the Holy Sepulchre*; Taylor, 'Golgotha: a reconsideration'; and Biddle, *Tomb of Christ*, 54–70.
24 According to Eusebius she was converted by her son, Constantine. Discussion in Drijvers, *Helena Augusta*.
25 E.g. Euseb. *V.C.* 3.41–3.
26 Appended in Greek, it was delivered in Latin on a Good Friday between 321 and 324 at Serdica or Thessalonica, and probably distributed as propaganda. Discussion in Barnes, *Constantine and Eusebius*, 73–6.

with prudence and wisdom, as well as the benefits he bestowed – 'for blindness, the gift of sight; for helpless weakness, the vigour of health; in place of death, restoration to life again . . .'. She would know also of incidents such as 'the abundant provision in the wilderness, whereby a scanty measure of food became a complete and enduring supply for the wants of a mighty multitude', and the stilling of a raging storm at sea; but like her son she might also have regarded his loving kindness to be the chief thing to be noted. She would have remembered that he told his followers to endure injury with dignity and patience, that he came to associate with the lowly, and prepared people for contempt of danger, teaching them genuine confidence in himself, and that he restrained one of his followers, telling him to return his sword to the sheath.[27] She would have taken it for granted that he provided a model for people to follow. It is noticeable how little the language actually reflects that of the gospels themselves!

Her over-riding sense of Jesus Christ, however, would not belong simply to the past. For her, he would be the King of kings, the regent providentially governing the whole universe on behalf of the transcendent supreme God. She would probably be aware of the flattery that turned her son into the earthly imitation of that heavenly ruler. She would certainly have accepted that the ascended Lord Jesus Christ shared God's sovereignty and divine majesty.[28] Almost certainly she would have believed that his divine life was communicated to her when she partook of his body and blood in the sacrament. Christian belief in Helena's time meant receiving immortality through physical contact with the material realities that had been transformed and sanctified by the presence of the divine. Even the cross had its talismanic power because it was a sign of immortality, a trophy of the victory over death gained in time past when the Son of the one and only God had sojourned on earth.[29] Eusebius tells us she wanted to pray in the places where Christ's feet had touched the ground[30] – indeed, as noted before, she is reputed to have prayed in Rome on earth she had brought back from the Holy Land. She needed to be in touch with the Jesus of history because he was more than a merely historical figure. He represented not just the historical origins of Christianity but was the foundation of her faith. Helena's faith in Jesus, on the one hand, moves him beyond the reality of a first-century Jew condemned to death as 'king of

---

27 Abstracted from Const. *Or. s.c.* 11, 12, 15.
28 The classic example of how the Hellenistic 'king ideology' was Christianised is found in Euseb. *L.C.*, from which these sentiments are drawn, along with Const. *Or. s.c.*
29 Euseb. *V.C.* 1.32.
30 *V.C.* 3.42–7. For discussion of the importance of touch, see Wilken, *Land called holy*, 114ff.

the Jews' (this much, at any rate, can be inferred from the *titulus*), and, on the other hand, stimulates an interest in being in touch with that very concrete reality. Even if legendary, her story is a kind of quest for the Jesus of history.

The purpose in telling Helena's story has been twofold – to illustrate what people knew and thought about Jesus at the end of the period covered by this volume, and to provide a parallel to the historical problems associated with Jesus himself. If we review the preceding paragraphs we observe the following difficulties in reconstructing what really happened:

- Post-Enlightenment questions about the perspectives and beliefs of those who told the story, not least the belief in miracles and supernatural power
- The nature of the sources and the question of their mutual compatibility
- Considerable time-spans between the events and the accounts
- Questions about the validity of oral traditions
- Gaps in the evidence
- Issues about the authenticity of material remains
- Post-Reformation rejection of relics and their veneration.

Such factors likewise affect the quest of the historical Jesus. Since the nine-teenth century,[31] there have been repeated attempts to reconstruct the facts behind the gospels, to distinguish the 'Jesus of history' from the 'Christ of faith'. Thus, the case of Helena exemplifies the dilemma for anyone approaching the subject of Jesus at the start of a history of Christianity. It may be customary to open the history of a movement with a biography of its founder, but is Jesus the founder and can we write his biography? Even if we could, would that explain the rise of Christianity?

Lord Jesus Christ, Son of God, Saviour

It is said that the early Christians used the symbol of the fish because in Greek the word for fish (*ichthus*) is an acronym of 'Jesus Christ, Son of God, Saviour';[32] so here was a handy secret sign of the full significance of Jesus. The aura accorded to Jesus through devotion and doctrine parallels the blend of history and fantasy that made up the legend of Helena. In Helena's time the fiercest battles over the nature of God's Son and the manner of his incarnation in Jesus still lay in the future, though the turmoil of the Arian controversy[33] was their

---

31 Historical scepticism prior to this was largely identified with the opponents of Christianity such as Celsus and Porphyry; Origen's critique of gospel stories (n. 16, above) served his spiritualising agenda, and its motivations were quite different from those of the modern quest for the historical Jesus, for which see further below.
32 Snyder, *Ante pacem* finds little evidence to confirm this.
33 See further pt vi, ch. 31, below.

harbinger. The resulting dogma became problematic for post-Enlightenment historians: as in the case of Helena, they wished to remove the veil of legend, or in this case, doctrine, so as to find the facts about Jesus. Yet it is precisely Christology, the dogmas concerning the divinity and humanity of Christ, which have made Christianity what it is. The clarification of these doctrines, against all the variant forms of Christianity around in the earliest period, was impelled by the 'cult' of Jesus, and by the fact that his story was quickly incorporated into an over-arching cosmic narrative. Both of these features belong to the period of this volume.

The overarching story is best presented in the *Epideixis tou apostolikou kērygmatos* ('Demonstration of the apostolic preaching'), a work of Irenaeus, bishop of Lyons at the end of the second century.[34] It begins with creation and culminates in the call of the Gentiles to faith in resurrection and eternal life. It tells how Adam and Eve were innocent, like children, how they failed to keep God's commandment, were misled by a fallen angel (known as Satan, or the devil), and so were excluded from paradise. A summary of biblical stories reinforces the sense of humanity's fall, and God's repeated attempts to put things right: Cain and Abel; Noah and his sons; the tower of Babel; Abraham, Isaac and Jacob; Moses and the giving of the Law; the promised land and the temple; the prophets. The most important function of the prophets, however, was to be 'heralds of the revelation of our Lord Jesus Christ, the Son of God, announcing that . . . he would be, according to the flesh, son of David, . . . while according to the Spirit, Son of God'. So the story turns to 'the Word made flesh'. We have already been told that the Word and Wisdom of God were God's 'two hands', the instruments of creation, and that the Son of God and the Spirit were to be identified as God's very own Word and Wisdom. Now we read that 'He united man with God and wrought a communion of God and man'. He 'recapitulated all things' in himself: he was obedient where Adam was disobedient, and 'the transgression which occurred through the tree was undone by the obedience of the tree', for 'the Son of Man, obeying God, was nailed to the tree' (= the cross). 'In this way, He gloriously accomplished our salvation and fulfilled the promise made to the patriarchs', namely, that

> to those who believed and loved the Lord, and <who lived> in holiness, righteousness and in patience, the God of all would offer eternal life by means of the resurrection from the dead, through him who died and rose, Jesus Christ, <to whom> He has entrusted the kingship over all things, the authority over the living and the dead, and the judgement.

34 See further pt III, ch. 13, below; ET quoted here, Behr, *On the apostolic preaching.*

With this narrative in mind, the gospels have been read within the Christian tradition, not as biographical accounts of a Jew named Jesus, but as epiphanies.[35] The divine has shone through the earthly story, because it is about the Son of God, who pre-existed creation, yet, for love of the human race, emptied himself of divinity, became human by being born of the Virgin Mary and the Holy Spirit, lived a human life marked by miracles and healings, gave his disciples the supreme ethical teaching, towards which seers and philosophers had aspired but never reached, and above all, took upon himself the sins and sufferings of the human race and overcame them by dying and rising again. In Christ human nature is united with the divine: the image and likeness of God, once granted to Adam, is restored to humanity, and the gift of immortality made available. Thus the time-scale of this story is not simply the span of Jesus' human life, but the whole providence of God from the beginning to the end. Believers are taken up into this narrative, which gives meaning to their lives. Everything about Jesus is seen through these cosmic perspectives.

Early Christian texts reveal writers[36] revelling in the rhetorical paradoxes of the invisible God becoming visible in Jesus Christ, the intangible being touched, the incomprehensible made comprehensible, the impassible suffering, the immortal dying – patterns of liturgical and homiletic rhetoric that would live on in Christian discourse over the centuries. This presupposes the whole cosmic story into which the story of Jesus was taken up. Melito concludes his *Homilia in passionem Christi* ('Homily on the passion of Christ'; perhaps the Haggadah for a Quartodeciman Passover)[37] as follows:

> This is he who made the heavens and the earth, and formed humanity in the beginning, who is announced by the Law and the prophets, who was enfleshed in a virgin, who was hanged on the tree, who was buried in the earth, who was raised from the dead and went up to the heights of heaven, who is sitting on the right hand of the Father, who has authority to judge and save all things, through whom the Father made the things which exist, from the beginning to all the ages. This one is 'the Alpha and the Omega', this one is 'the beginning and the end' – the beginning which cannot be explained and the end which cannot be grasped. This one is the Christ. This one is the king. This one is Jesus. This one is the leader. This one is the Lord. This one is he who has risen from the dead. This one is he who sits on the right hand of the Father. He bears the Father and is borne by the Father. 'To him be the glory and the power to the ends of the ages. Amen.'

---

35 See pt III, ch. 8, below.
36 E.g. Ign. *Eph.* 7.2, *Pol.* 3.2; Mel. *Pass.* 2 and *Fr.* 13; Iren. *Haer.* 3.16.6.
37 Stewart-Sykes, *Lamb's high feast*; for the Quartodecimans see pt IV, chs. 17 and 22, below.

Dogma was the outcome of struggles to devise a conceptual discourse adequate to this overarching story. Origen, the great Christian intellectual and biblical scholar of the third century,[38] expresses the difficulty of this:

> Of all the marvellous and splendid things about him there is one that utterly transcends the limits of human wonder and is beyond the capacity of our weak mortal intelligence to think of or understand, namely how this mighty power of the divine majesty, the very Word of the Father, and the very Wisdom of God in which were created all things visible and invisible, can be believed to have existed within the compass of that man who appeared in Judaea.[39]

He wonders how on earth God's Wisdom could have entered into a woman's womb, been born as a baby and made noises like crying children. He can hardly credit the story of how he was troubled and said, 'My soul is very sorrowful, even unto death.' He is amazed that 'at the last he was led to that death which is considered by man to be the most shameful of all, even though on the third day he rose again'. The difficulty lies in the fact that 'we see in him some things so human that they appear in no way to differ from the common frailty of mortals and some things so divine that they are appropriate to nothing else but the primal and ineffable nature of deity'. 'The human understanding . . . is baffled,' he says; 'struck with amazement at so mighty a wonder', it does not know where to turn.

The wonder of God's self-emptying would remain at the heart of Christian understanding. It was assumed to be scriptural, and based on Philippians 2:5–11, where Christ Jesus is described as being 'in the form of God'; but he

> did not regard equality with God as something to be exploited, but emptied himself, taking the form of a slave being born in human likeness. And being found in human form, he humbled himself and became obedient to the point of death – even death on a cross. Therefore God also highly exalted him and gave him the name that is above every name, so that at the name of Jesus every knee should bend in heaven and on earth and under the earth, and every tongue confess that Jesus Christ is Lord, to the glory of God the Father.

This perspective on the story of Jesus was rooted, not just in the overall cosmic story which shaped the reading of scripture, but also in its celebration in worship, as is confirmed by the following prayer, which probably goes back to the third century and is found incorporated into the liturgy of Addai and Mari:

38 See pt IV, ch. 18, and pt V, ch. 27, below.
39 *Princ.* 2.6.

And with these heavenly powers we give Thee thanks, O my Lord, we also, Thy unworthy, frail and miserable servants, because Thou hast dealt graciously with us in a way that cannot be repaid, in that Thou didst assume our humanity that Thou mightest restore us to life by Thy divinity. And didst exalt our low estate, and raise up our fallen state, and resurrect our mortality, forgive our sins, and acquit our sinfulness, and enlighten our understanding, and, our Lord and God, overcome our adversaries, and give victory to the unworthiness of our frail nature in the overflowing mercies of Thy grace.[40]

This prayer is addressed to the Lord and God who put on humanity. At the heart of the Christian cult lay worship of the Son of God, who pre-existed with God, was incarnate in Jesus, is risen from the dead, and now lives and reigns with the Father in glory.

'It was their habit on a fixed day to assemble before daylight and *sing a hymn to Christ as to a god*'; so Pliny, the Roman governor of Bithynia, reported to the emperor Trajan round about 112 CE.[41] There is good reason to believe that already in the third century the *Phōs hilaron* was sung at vespers as lamps were lit. This hymn has been continuously used in the eastern Orthodox churches ever since, and from the seventeenth century entered western church traditions, where it is best known in Keble's translation:

> Hail, gladdening Light of his pure glory poured,
> Who is the immortal Father, heavenly blest;
> Holiest of holies, Jesus Christ our Lord!
> Now we are come to the sun's hour of rest;
> the lights of evening round us shine,
> we hymn the Father, Son and Holy Spirit divine.
> Worthiest art thou at all times to be sung
> With undefiled tongue, Son of our God, giver of life alone;
> Therefore in all the world thy glories, Lord, they own.[42]

The image of light reflects biblical language of God, as well as the idea in John's gospel that Christ is the light of the world; but the word *hilaron* ('joyous') is not scriptural and was widely used in the mysteries of Isis and Cybele.[43] In Christian art before Constantine, we find adapted to Christ the figure of Apollo,

---

40 ET Gelston, *Eucharistic prayer of Addai and Mari*, 51. Gelston argues that this is probably the earliest extant anaphora with a relatively fixed form, and could go back to the second or early third century, though a definite date cannot be proved.

41 *Ep.* 10.96.

42 ET John Keble (1792–1866).

43 R. Garland Young in Kiley, *Prayer from Alexander to Constantine*, 316.

the sun god, as charioteer.[44] That Christians prayed to Christ as to a god is clear, and also undeniable is assimilation to the cultic language and imagery of the religious world around them.

A hymn composed by Clement of Alexandria, and so dating from the turn of the second and third centuries, piles up celebratory epithets in a poem which echoes Greek forms and vocabulary:

> King of saints,
> all-taming word
> of the most high Father,
> ruler of wisdom.
> ever joyful support
> for the mortal race
> in toil and pain.
> Saviour Jesus,
> shepherd, ploughman,
> helm, bridle,
> heavenly wing,
> of the most holy flock,
> fisher of men,
> of those saved
> from the sea of evil,
> luring with sweet life
> the chaste fish
> from the hostile tide.
> Holy shepherd
> of sheep of the *logos* . . .
> Let us sing together
> to Christ, the king,
> artless praise
> and truthful songs,
> holy wages
> for the teaching of life.[45]

This may never have been used in liturgy, but it represents the composition of prayers to Christ that incorporated the language and patterns of pagan prayer.

---

44 See pt VI, ch. 32, below, and fig. 9.
45 Selections from *Paed.* 3.12.101, ET by van den Hoek in Kiley, *Prayer from Alexander to Constantine.*

Already analogies between Christ and the deity of a mystery cult are implicit in 1 Corinthians 10:19–21 and in Justin's assertion that the devil imitated the eucharist of Christians in the mysteries of Mithras: both rites involved participation in bread and drink, but for Christians this represented the flesh and blood of 'Jesus Christ our Saviour'.[46] The gospels, or 'memoirs of the apostles', are quoted: 'Jesus took bread, and when he had given thanks, said, "Do this in remembrance of me, this is my body"'; and 'having taken the cup and given thanks, he said, "This is my blood", and gave it to them.' Justin adds that at the weekly gatherings on Sunday, the 'memoirs of the apostles' were read for as long as time permitted. The earthly life of Jesus was recalled in the context of cultic rites that assumed his divinity. Eventually, though probably beyond our period, the gospel books would be processed with incense in the same kind of way as a pagan idol, and with a similar cultic function, namely, to make the divine present to the worshipper. Already in 1 Corinthians (11:23–6), Paul had recalled what happened at the Last Supper as if the story were an aetiological cult-myth, and had insisted that there could be no communion between the 'table of the Lord' and the 'table of the daemons'. Papyri found at Oxyrhynchus reveal invitations to 'sup at the table of the lord Sarapis'.[47] The analogies ran deep.

The earliest and most insistent analogy between the way Christ was celebrated and pagan cultic activity is to be found in the use of language from the ruler-cult tradition,[48] by then associated with the divinisation of the Roman emperor, particularly but not solely in Asia Minor. An inscription from Ephesus speaks of Julius Caesar as 'the god made manifest, offspring of Ares and Aphrodite and common saviour of human life'. For Christians, Jesus was God manifest, God's offspring and the Saviour of all. In Pergamum an inscription reads: 'Caesar, absolute ruler (*autokrator*), son of god, the god Augustus, overseer of every land and sea'. For Christians, God was the *autokrator* who oversees everything, seeing even into the hearts of human beings, ultimately their judge, and Jesus was the one who exercised these powers on God's behalf. Inscriptions accord to the emperors titles such as 'lord' and 'god', 'king of kings', 'saviour', and 'high priest' (*pontifex maximus*), all of which Christians ascribed to Christ. Martyrologies show how Christians refused to call Caesar 'lord' in

---

46 1 *Apol.* 66–7.
47 *P. Oxy.* 110 and 523.
48 To show the depth of this observation in scholarship, my examples are deliberately drawn from the classic presentation of the evidence, that of Deissmann, *Light from the ancient East*. The point has been strongly reinforced by the subsequent publication of many more inscriptions and papyri. The argument is taken further by Brent, *Imperial cult*.

competition with their 'Lord Jesus Christ': asked to 'swear by the genius of our lord the emperor', Speratus of Scilli answered, 'I know no *imperium* of this world . . . I know my Lord, the King of kings, and emperor of all nations.'[49] And it is not just titles that provide parallels: the birthday of the emperor Augustus was 'good news' (evangel or gospel); the 'presence' (*parousia* or *advent*) of the sovereign was a matter of hope and expectation for a city. For Christians hope and expectation were focused on the return of Christ, and they knew it as his *parousia*. Given all this evidence, it is hardly surprising that many scholars, especially since Bousset,[50] come to the conclusion that it was only in the context of Hellenistic syncretism that the cult of Jesus could have developed. Here apotheosis was accepted for kings, heroes and philosophers – indeed, the Euhemeran theory of religions was that the gods were all divinised men. Here mystery cults provided models of initiation into secret rituals whereby divine life might be assimilated. None of this was acceptable within the monotheistic framework of Judaism. So it came to be widely accepted that only the spread of Christianity to the Gentiles could have enabled a Jewish rabbi to become the Lord Jesus Christ, Son of God, the Saviour, whose life was but the brief and visible expression of his eternal invisible being.

If the earliest Christian writings (namely, the epistles of that great missionary to the Gentiles, the apostle Paul) are already coloured by such beliefs, how much more the gospels! The quest of the historical Jesus had long since sought to probe behind the gospels to rediscover the facts and tear away this veil of doctrine and devotion.

The Jesus of the quest

Helena's quest for Jesus was apparently motivated by the need to be in touch with the one who could impart to her eternal life. By contrast, the modern quest had its roots in the Enlightenment need to be emancipated from the chains of church dogma, and the story is usually begun with Reimarus (1694–1768). A well-respected scholar during his lifetime, it was only after his death that his controversial views were published. He found 'cause to separate completely what the apostles say in their own writings from that which Jesus himself actually said and taught'.[51] Basing his claims on careful study of the gospel sources, Reimarus showed that classic Christian doctrines, such as the Atonement and the Trinity, were not revealed by Jesus, and that Jesus was a Jew

---

49 M. *Scil.* 6.
50 *Kyrios Christos.*
51 *Reimarus: Fragments*, 64.

who upheld the Law, did not preach to the Gentiles, and did not institute baptism or eucharist, but rather simply called the Jews to repentance and promised the arrival of the expected Messiah who would restore the kingdom of God in Jerusalem. Reimarus rejected miracles and the fulfilment of prophecy as proofs of Christianity, regarding the Christian religion as based on a fraud. The natural explanation for the resurrection claims was that the disciples stole the body, and, out of disappointment at the failure of Jesus' mission, altered the entire doctrine. Attempts to reply, and in the process renew Christianity in the post-Enlightenment world, produced historical reconstructions which explained away the miraculous elements in the gospels. True, many of those involved sought to be in touch with a Jesus that was credible in these circumstances, but this was hardly the physical or sacramental contact sought by Helena and believers like her.

The legacy of these Enlightenment roots is a persistent sense that there is a tension between history and faith.[52] Nineteenth-century scholarship only reinforced this. One of the many controversial acts of the woman novelist who wrote under the name of George Eliot was to translate into English the work of David Friedrich Strauss, *The life of Jesus critically examined*. The work was published in England in 1846. It is clear that Strauss himself did not view his work as destructive of the heart of Christianity, but his claim that the whole story of Jesus is intertwined with myth was perceived to be profoundly disturbing to faith.

In his book, Strauss works through the whole story, from the birth narratives, through the public life, claims, teaching and miracles of Jesus, to his suffering and death, resurrection and ascension, demonstrating the all-pervasive mythologising of the Jesus tradition as it appears in the gospels. He develops this against previous approaches, noting the attempt by Heinrich Paulus[53] to distinguish fact and interpretation: naturalistic accounts of the miracles had been used to explain away all supernatural intervention, so that 'the historical truth of the Gospel narratives' could be maintained as they were woven 'into one consecutive chronologically-arranged detail of facts'.[54] Strauss accepts criteria for distinguishing the unhistorical in the gospel narrative: the first is when the narration is irreconcilable with the known and universal laws which govern the course of events; the second rests on inconsistency within and contradiction between narratives; the third is when the characteristics of legend

---

52 A useful survey of the quest, which brings out this tension, is to be found in Dunn, *Jesus remembered*.
53 His two-volume work, *Das Leben Jesu*, had been published in 1828.
54 Strauss, *Life of Jesus*, 49.

or fiction are evidently present. But in his view the real difficulty is that facts and mythical features are intertwined – history is entirely overlaid with myth. Between the various editions of this work some of Strauss' views shifted: as he came to recognise more value in the gospel of John, his early emphasis on Jesus' apocalyptic fanaticism and messianic delusions gave way to an emphasis on his God-consciousness. So, in the end, Strauss concluded that all this need not affect the heart of Christianity. The antithesis of the human and divine was dissolved in the self-consciousness of Jesus; in this Jesus was unique and, for Strauss, the paradigm of the truly religious person – for he defined religion as the 'awakening in the human spirit of the relationship between God and man'. It would seem that he ended up wanting to be in touch with a credible Jesus, though his critics hardly saw it that way.

The nineteenth-century response to Strauss was the production of many so-called 'liberal lives of Jesus' in which scholars, such as Renan, Holtzmann and Harnack, tried to present a personality capable of inspiring the legendary gospel material. Strauss had concentrated more on narratives than teaching; the liberal lives concentrated on the teaching and saw the message of Jesus as the fatherhood of God and the brotherhood of Man. They tried to characterise his ethics and his God-consciousness, believing that this made him universally relevant. Jesus became the supreme religious genius, a great personality who founded a new religion at a turning-point in history. But this was a Jesus abstracted from first-century Jewish society, a Jesus made acceptable to the nineteenth-century European mind, a fact exposed in the classic phrase of Albert Schweitzer suggesting that what these authors saw was a reflection of their own faces at the bottom of a deep well. In his notorious work of 1906, known in English as *The quest of the historical Jesus*, Schweitzer reviewed the whole story of the quest, concluding that the results were a series of modern projections onto the past. He depicted Jesus as a stranger to the modern world, a prophet of the end-time whose predictions were not fulfilled, who died disillusioned. 'He comes to us as one unknown,' he famously wrote. So, by the early twentieth century, the modern liberal quest for Jesus had apparently collapsed.

Schweitzer's challenge, however, shifted the way in which historians approached early Christianity.[55] Enlightenment rationalism, together with historico-critical study of the prophets in the Old Testament, had under-mined confidence in the notion that specific prophecies were fulfilled in Jesus – here were not mysterious oracles or precise predictions, but messages for the

---

55 Allison, *Jesus of Nazareth*.

prophet's contemporaries. Now, however, it was recognised that historically the roots of early Christian belief were to be found in the expectation that apocalyptic prophecies would be fulfilled, and as the twentieth century progressed, study of the numerous apocalypses produced in the inter-testamental and early Christian periods, not to mention the discovery of new material, such as the Dead Sea scrolls, reinforced the importance of eschatology for understanding Jesus and his followers. The genre of apocalyptic literature[56] emerged from a complex of precedents and took various forms; key characteristics included the use of symbolic language and numerology to sketch world history and to demonstrate God's providential purposes from the beginning to the end, in order to justify God's ways and give comfort to God's oppressed people. A cosmic struggle between good and evil was mirrored on earth, but, in the end, God would overcome the powers of evil, everyone would be raised up and judged, and God's people would be redeemed. After Schweitzer most scholars felt they had to attend to the fact that the earliest Christians expected the imminent end of the world, and looked forward to the second coming of Jesus Christ to bring justice and peace. The question was whether Jesus himself had promulgated such ideas. Certainly the majority came to agree that his message had been about the kingdom of God and its imminent arrival, though the gospel reports also contained material suggesting its hidden presence.[57] Modern Christians might have to find ways of 'demythologising' the message for it to be credible;[58] but historians after Schweitzer could ignore neither the emphasis on fulfilment of prophecy in the time of Jesus, nor the importance of apocalyptic expectation for early Christianity.

Meanwhile movement on another trajectory had impinged on the questions. This was the development of source-criticism of the gospels. If the quest had highlighted the mythical world-views that coloured the sources, rationalist analysis of them had exposed their lack of independence. Clearly the authors of the first three gospels had plagiarised one another. The question was who had copied whom. Then there was the issue raised by the very different fourth gospel: did the author know and use the others or not? To get to the sources behind the sources became an obsession. The results have largely held the field for about a hundred years, though from time to time contested. Mark is regarded as the earliest gospel; a reconstructed source known as Q (from the German *Quelle*, 'source') is deduced from the material common to Matthew

---

56 For study of apocalyptic, Rowland, *The open heaven*.
57 Long discussion was provoked by Dodd, who (*Parables of the kingdom*) suggested that in Jesus eschatology was 'realised'.
58 Bultmann in particular espoused such a programme.

and Luke; *M* is the source of Matthew's unique material and *L* of Luke's. As for John, that gospel is later, whether dependent or not, so, the natural assumption being that the best picture of the historical Jesus lay in the earliest sources, it could be largely disregarded. Conveniently, given the scepticism of the questers about myth, Mark and *Q* have no birth narratives or post-resurrection appearances, and *M* and *L* are different at these points; so source-criticism appeared to facilitate attempts to go back to Jesus' teaching and the events of his public ministry. In the 'liberal lives', Mark's outline was taken as the basis for writing a chronological account of the public ministry. Yet, at the point where Schweitzer demolished the liberal accounts of Jesus as projections, Wrede[59] showed that Mark was itself the product of post-resurrection faith. The gospel presented the message of the church about Christ the Saviour, and this was quite different from the message of Jesus about God and his kingdom. The Markan device of the 'messianic secret' was deployed to conceal this.

Besides, there was still a gap between the sources and the life of Jesus. So there arose form-criticism: the attempt to analyse the oral traditions behind the discrete units in the written sources. Notoriously this led one of its greatest practitioners, Rudolf Bultmann, to declare, 'I do indeed think that we can now know almost nothing concerning the life and personality of Jesus.'[60] Everything in the gospels was remembered and shaped to serve community needs. So interest shifted to plotting the way in which the gospel writers crafted their accounts, whether out of previous written sources or disparate oral units (redaction criticism). Jesus was elusive, since all that was available were the portraits painted by his faithful followers or their followers, coloured by the emerging beliefs of the early church. The stages in the development of christological doctrine constituted the new history to be written. A sharp break was drawn between the Jewish context of Jesus' life and ministry and the Greek environment of the spreading Gentile church, and this drew upon the theories of the History of Religions school[61] to attribute to Hellenistic culture the development of Christianity as a religion focused on Jesus Christ as Lord, a cult regarded as inconceivable within the context of Jewish monotheism. Paul became the 'founder of Christianity', and both he and the author of the gospel of John were regarded as influenced by Gnosticism. Importantly, espousing

---

59 Wrede, *The messianic secret*.
60 *Jesus and the Word*, 8. The classic form-critical analysis of the gospel material is Bultmann's *History of the synoptic tradition*. Despite his much-quoted remark, Bultmann did sketch a picture of Jesus both here and in his *Theology of the New Testament*.
61 See Neill and Wright, *Interpretation of the New Testament*; Bousset (see above) is a representative of this school.

this kind of theory enabled some Jewish scholars, such as Klausner,[62] to reclaim Jesus as a prophet and teacher within their own tradition, while discounting the development of Christian doctrine.

Some still hoped to reconstruct the facts behind the dogma. Scholars such as T. W. Manson, F. C. Grant, Joachim Jeremias and C. H. Dodd[63] felt that to be in touch with the historical Jesus was vital for a historical religion like Christianity, and developed arguments that purported to get back to the characteristic voice of Jesus, to his sayings and parables, even to an outline of his career. However, the survey of the quest so far has clearly shown how the difficulties in reconstructing what really happened paralleled those found in Helena's case:

- Post-Enlightenment questions about the perspectives and beliefs of those who told Jesus' story, not least the belief in miracles and supernatural power
- Critical enquiry into the nature of the sources and their mutual compatibility
- Recognition of the considerable time-span between the events and the accounts
- Debate about the validity of oral traditions
- Gaps in the evidence.

In addition, in the case of Jesus, there was

- Scepticism about prophecy and its fulfilment, and so challenges to the over-arching story which has traditionally given Christian meaning to the life of Jesus.

Modernity thus eschewed the credulity of those who simply accepted Helena as the saint who found the true cross, and Jesus as the divine Saviour and Lord whose life and teaching is to be found in the gospel records. Instead, critical analysis sought to reconstruct the facts behind the stories, or came to the conclusion that such results were unattainable.

So, through the first half of the twentieth century, it seemed to many that the quest had run into the sand. Then in the post-war period, some of Bultmann's pupils, notably G. Bornkamm and E. Käsemann, initiated a New Quest. This built on Bultmann's analyses and led to the articulation of a series of criteria for establishing what was and was not authentic. Seeming as they did to facilitate the process of sifting the material, these criteria have had a continuing influence

---

62 Klausner, *Jesus of Nazareth*.
63 See Neill and Wright, *Interpretation of the New Testament*.

on scholarship as the world approached the third Christian millennium and a surge of questing activity emerged, particularly in the United States, now often referred to as the Third Quest.[64]

The criterion of multiple attestation holds that something that appears in more than one independent source is more likely to be authentic than something that appears in only one. This is comparable to the need for several independent witnesses in a court of law. Collusion in itself does little to substantiate the evidence. The dependence of the gospels on one another means they are not independent witnesses. The sources behind the gospels, however, could well be independent. Suppose something appears in Mark and Q, or even L and John, assuming John's independence – then, the argument goes, there is a good chance of some basis in the facts behind the streams of oral tradition that fed these sources. The earliest Christian writings are the epistles of Paul, which could provide another source, except that most questers find his interest in Jesus' life and teaching surprisingly limited. The Third Quest has taken seriously the need to add to the canonical gospels a number of newly discovered texts, such as the gospels of Thomas and Peter, an argument having been made that such material is not only independent of the canonical gospels but also has an early pedigree. Building on this, John Dominic Crossan argued for careful stratification of the various sources, assigning the materials to specific decades of the first century. The problem is that not all scholars are agreed about the value of some of the sources, let alone their date, and the use of hypothetical documents like Q means that hypothesis is built on hypothesis. Nevertheless this criterion continues to command respect – it is its application which is problematical.

The criterion of double dissimilarity seeks to differentiate what is unique to Jesus (a) from parallels in the Jewish background and (b) from developments in Christian belief. It is a summation of the key aims of the early quest: to identify Jesus' originality while distinguishing the historical Jesus from church dogma. The criterion of coherence means that once a kernel of original Jesus material has been identified, then other material consistent with this can be accepted. The problem, however, is that (a) focuses methodologically on what makes Jesus different and so abstracts him from his immediate social environment – an approach which is both historically unrealistic and seems tainted by anti-Jewish bias, while (b) deprives Jesus of any explanatory power in relation to the

---

64 For a summary account of this Third Quest see Powell, *The Jesus debate*. Major contributors include the members of the Jesus Seminar, led by Funk, who succeeded in generating wide public interest in the USA, Crossan, Sanders, Meier and Wright.

rise of Christianity. One radical attempt to cut through these difficulties was Sanders' proposal to focus on the deeds rather than the words of Jesus, and to interpret them within the political and religious context of first-century Judaism.[65] Coupled with regard for features retained in the Gospels which would be embarrassing for subsequent Christian belief (a refinement of the dissimilarity criterion),[66] this seemed to create a picture of Jesus less easily dismissible as the product of the investigator's interests.

From this critique came the proposal to replace the criterion of double dissimilarity with a criterion of historical plausibility: 'each individual historical phenomenon is to be considered authentic that plausibly can be understood in its Jewish context and that also facilitates a plausible explanation for its later effects in Christian history.'[67] Of course what is plausible to one investigator will not necessarily be plausible to another. The nineteenth century did not find miracles plausible. The late twentieth century, exploiting the approach of social anthropology, is more prepared to acknowledge that, in pre-modern cultures, the way the world works is differently conceived and that there are many parallels in ancient literature to the kind of charismatic healer we find in the gospels, and so judge the plausibility issues rather differently. Indeed, one proposal characterises Jesus as a magician like the well-attested magicians known from other ancient sources.[68] So, this criterion means setting the figure of Jesus within the social, cultural and religious environment of the time, and accepting what fits.

The application of these criteria has produced a huge amount of detailed analysis of sources, non-Christian and Christian, canonical and non-canonical. Enthusiasm has been further fired by the publication of discoveries such as the Dead Sea scrolls, a collection of material that turned up in caves at Qumran in 1947. Deposited by members of a Jewish community, possibly Essene in character, they offer a number of parallels with the roughly contemporary Jesus movement. More recently archaeology has contributed greater knowledge of the social and material realities of life in first-century Galilee.[69] Such comparative material adds much to the interest of the quest, and despite encouraging some far-fetched leaps of imagination, has become more and more significant in the reconstructions of scholars. So the quest at the turn of the millennium

---

65 Sanders, *Jesus and Judaism*.
66 A criterion of embarrassment is explicitly promulgated by Meier, *A marginal Jew*.
67 Theissen and Winter, *Quest for the plausible Jesus*; quotation from preface.
68 Smith, *Jesus the magician*; Davies, *Jesus the healer*.
69 See, for example, Reed, *Archaeology and the Galilaean Jesus*; Crossan and Reed, *Excavating Jesus*.

is characterised by the production of different 'types' of figure which more or less plausibly capture the Jesus of history: the Jewish 'holy man',[70] the rabbi,[71] the Pharisee,[72] the Galilean peasant,[73] the Cynic philosopher,[74] the social revolutionary,[75] the sage, the seer,[76] the prophet of the end-time,[77] the true Messiah.[78]

To review the many contributions is outside the scope of this chapter. Perhaps the most important feature of the late-twentieth-century quest is the insistence that Jesus was a Jew, and the contribution of Jewish scholars to the field.[79] But interest in Jesus the Jew itself raises questions about what kind of Jew and what the Judaism of Galilee was like. It is now generally recognised that there were diverse, and competing, ways of being Jewish at the time when Jesus lived, and indeed many would now argue that multiple forms of Christianity emerged more or less independently. But these recognitions could be a retrojection into the first century of post-modern acceptance of pluralism. For, indeed, the Third Quest hardly escapes being shaped by concurrent interests just like the Old Quest, marked as it is by the use of social scientific models, and coloured by ideological analysis of sources (e.g. liberationist, feminist and others). There is also some reaction against the positivist and rationalist assumptions of earlier investigations, as well as a post-Holocaust sensitivity to tendentious interpretation and to the historically deleterious effects of influential texts.

The major gain, then, is the recovery of Jesus the first-century Jew, a Jesus open to investigation by all whose interest he captures, and no longer constrained by the boundaries set up by Christian dogma. The Jesus recovered by the quest, however, is hardly Helena's Jesus; so the question remains: was Helena in some ways more in touch with the Jesus who gave rise to Christian faith? Before considering that, however, we must acknowledge that the milieu of the quest demands some attempt at a historically plausible sketch of Jesus of Nazareth.

---

70 Vermes, *Jesus the Jew* and *The religion of Jesus the Jew*.
71 Chilton, *Rabbi Jesus*.
72 Maccoby, *Jesus the Pharisee*.
73 The Jesus Seminar and Crossan, *The historical Jesus*.
74 Crossan; and Downing, *Christ and the Cynics*.
75 Horsley, *Bandits, Prophets and Messiahs* and *Jesus and the spiral of violence*.
76 Witherington, *Jesus the sage* and *Jesus the seer*.
77 Sanders, *Jesus and Judaism* and *The historical figure*; Allison, *Jesus of Nazareth*; Ehrman, *Jesus*.
78 Wright, *Jesus and the victory of God*.
79 E.g. Vermes, Maccoby and Fredriksen.

Jesus the Jew: towards a plausible portrait

It is worth stating at the outset that there can be no definitive account in historical research, and we should not confuse reconstructions of any significant figure of history with the real person. Despite the claims of some investigators, it is always only possible to assess probabilities, and the more significant the statement the more contentious it is likely to be – different perspectives and endless revisions are inevitable, for any given portrait tends to highlight a few specifics and cannot do justice to the complexities. The Jesus of history remains elusive, tantalising, intriguing – still he comes to us as one unknown – and the gospels themselves indicate a certain enigma about the person whose story they tell.

Nevertheless, curiosity still drives the questions: what really happened? What was Jesus really like? What was his mission all about? Can we be in touch with the Jesus who once lived and died a Jew in first-century Palestine? Perhaps a few plausible inferences are possible. Clearly Jesus and his activities must be set as far as possible within the social context of the Galilee and Judaea of his time. Also some explanation must be offered for his crucifixion by the Romans, for his handing over by the Jewish authorities (probably), and for the response of his followers – for it is likely that an account of his words, deeds and personality which makes plausible this threefold reaction will have some truth in it. It is inevitable that the brief account here offered implicitly mirrors or rejects the work of the many scholars who have attended to these questions in the past 200 years.[80]

The crucifixion is the best-attested fact concerning Jesus. The display of the *titulus* on the cross accords with known practice: the intention in thus advertising the charge was to make a public example of someone condemned. The gospels report that it read, 'The king of the Jews'. The stories of the soldiers' horseplay revolve around that royal claim. At the heart of the trial scenes lies the same accusation. The memory of Jesus in the gospels is of someone who provoked speculation that he might be the 'Messiah' (or 'anointed one'), the 'son of David', in other words the hoped-for king who was to restore Israel. Scholarship has revealed a wide range of hopes for the future in the literature of Second Temple Judaism, of which one was the return of a Davidic kingdom. It is said (John 6:15) that the crowds tried to make him king after the miraculous feeding; whatever happened on that occasion, the story enshrines expectation

---

80 To justify every point made in the following is impossible; footnotes only make specific acknowledgements. See further pt II, chs. 4 and 7, below.

of a replay of the Exodus and of God's direct intervention to restore his people's freedom. There seems little doubt that Jesus was handed over to the occupying Romans as a messianic pretender. Josephus, the Jewish historian, provides examples of such figures, and it is reported that 'after the capture of Jerusalem Vespasian issued an order that, to ensure no member of the royal house should be left among the Jews, all descendants of David should be ferreted out'.[81] A generation earlier Pilate presumably acted to get rid of such a claimant when he sent Jesus to be crucified. It seems clear why the Romans put him to death.

The question is to what extent this was a trumped-up charge. Jesus quietly withdrew when the crowds wanted to make him king. He is usually depicted in the gospels as trying to silence those suggesting he was God's Messiah (though there have been various assessments of Mark's 'messianic secret' since Wrede). The earliest Christian preaching undoubtedly laid claim to Jesus' messiahship – that he becomes known as 'Jesus Christ' is evidence in itself, since 'Christ' is the Greek for 'anointed one'. Jesus is depicted as acknowledging that he was the Christ at Caesarea Philippi (Mark 8:27ff), though his words there suggest both acceptance and ambivalence – did his kingly role lie in the future rather than now? The staged incident known as the 'triumphal entry' (Mark 11:1–10 / Matt 21:1–11 / Luke 19:29–40 / John 12:12–19) contrives the fulfilment of a kingly prophecy while challenging the picture of a king riding to his capital on a war-horse – Jesus rode a donkey. His followers remembered him as saying, 'Love your enemies.' Repeatedly scholars have observed that the message of Jesus seems to have focused on the coming kingdom of God, rather than on his own position, so the question about his claim remains a teasing one. Besides, would the messianic claim have been sufficient to account for the move against him by the Jewish authorities? Some have suggested it would not.

There was no monolithic 'Judaism' in this period. The Pharisees sought the purity of Israel by scrupulous practice of the Torah, but debated among themselves as to what that meant. The priestly caste tried to protect the temple and the people from contamination by judicious negotiation with their Roman overlords. The members of the community we now know from the Dead Sea scrolls sought the restoration of Israel and the purity of the temple, having separated themselves from what they regarded as a corrupt situation. Each group claimed to represent the true tradition, tended to exclude those who did not belong to their own community and used vituperative language of the

---

81 Hegesippus, as reported by Euseb. *HE* 3.12. According to 3.19–20, Domitian ordered the execution of all who were of David's line, and the descendents of Jude, Jesus' brother, were caught up in this investigation. See further Bauckham, *Jude and the relatives of Jesus*.

others.[82] But they did not, generally speaking, take legal proceedings against one another for some kind of 'heresy'. Jesus may well have challenged the general tendency to draw boundaries – he is, after all, accused of eating with sinners and tax gatherers, of breaking the sabbath and of disregarding purity rules, and stories are told of his inappropriate attitudes to women and children, Samaritans and Gentiles. Yet contemporary inner-Jewish debates are reflected in the controversies reported in the gospels, especially those between Jesus and the Pharisees; in fact, Jesus appears very like a Pharisee. At first sight it is by no means clear why the Jerusalem authorities collaborated with Pilate against Jesus.

The gospel accounts present us with procedural problems as far as the trial scenes are concerned, and the passion narratives display a tendency to decrease Roman responsibility and increase the blame resting on the Jews. Certainly crucifixion was a Roman punishment, so the Romans not the Jews should be regarded as responsible for what happened. Yet conflict between Jesus and Jewish leaders is a persistent feature of the gospels. It seems quite plausible that the act of riding into Jerusalem hailed by crowds or, perhaps even more likely, the incident in the temple provoked the authorities to move against Jesus. In the presence of the high priest, so-called false witnesses attributed to Jesus a saying against the temple (Mark 13:2 / Matt 24:2 / Luke 21:6); but other evidence (Matt 23:38 / Luke 13:35; John 2:19 and *Gos. Thom.* 71) suggests it was not false – he did say something about destroying and rebuilding the temple.[83] The demonstration in the temple, then, might well have led the Jewish authorities to feel it was wise to proceed against this trouble-maker before the Romans acted to quell popular disturbances.[84] The Roman occupation was both the context and reason for taking action.

The best explanation of Roman action, Jewish collaboration and later Christian claims is that Jesus' message and activity centred upon the immediacy of God's kingdom, and the crucial importance of responding to the crisis of his own coming. The imminent realisation of God's kingdom was anticipated in his prophetic act of 'cleansing' the temple, as it probably had been in other staged acts – the triumphal entry, the re-enactment of the giving of manna in the desert, the miracles of healing and exorcism. Jesus announced the consummation of God's sovereignty on earth as something to be shortly

---

82 See Dunn, *Jesus remembered*, 260–92, on the factionalism and unity of Judaism; also pt I, ch. 1 and pt III, ch. 10, below.
83 Young, 'Temple, cult and law'.
84 Both Josephus and the gospels bear witness to the Romans taking violent and, to the Jews, blasphemous action when disturbances arose in the temple.

manifest – the church would surely not invent embarrassing unfulfilled predictions such as Mark 9:1: 'Truly I tell you, there are some standing here
who will not taste death until they see the kingdom of God has come
with power.' That the church struggled with the consequences of unfulfilled expectations is clear from the earliest Christian writings, the epistles of
Paul. The hopes of early Christianity surely had their roots in the teaching of
Jesus.

So was he just a failed apocalyptic prophet? This solution has seemed plausible since Albert Schweitzer. Yet throughout the New Testament we find
what might be called 'eschatological tension', a sense of 'now' and 'not yet'. It
appears in the epistles of Paul and the gospel of John,[85] as well as in the reports
of Jesus' teaching about the kingdom of God in the other gospels – so there
is a kind of multiple attestation. We might argue, then, that the characteristic
thing about Jesus' teaching is found in his declarations that God's sovereignty
is already being anticipated, indeed is present, if people can only recognise
the signs. The immediate presence of God is demonstrated in the exorcism of
unclean spirits, a manifestation on earth of God's victorious progress against
the cosmic powers of evil. Jesus' opponents accuse him of acting through the
power of Beelzebul (Mark 3:22), in other words practising black magic, yet he
offers no proofs or signs against that view. He expects people to open their
eyes and see that it must be God's Spirit which is effecting the healing and
forgiveness which attends his presence with people. There are prophetic pronouncements of judgement on those who do not respond. Yet his teaching
has an enigmatic quality: whoever has ears to hear, let them hear. His parables
and similitudes seem to point to the idea that the ways of God are discernible,
one way or another, in everyday things, in God's creatures and their activities –
trees and their fruit, sheep and sparrows, salt and light, builders and sowers,
masters and servants, wedding feasts. His sayings suggest an upside-down
world in which the poor, those who are humble – even humiliated, and those
who mourn, are blessed. Thus he challenged people to live 'in the light of the
coming Kingdom',[86] and that meant living with radical trust in God's mercy
and goodness:

> Look at the birds of the air; they neither sow nor reap nor gather into barns,
> yet your heavenly Father feeds them . . . Consider the lilies of the field, how
> they grow; they neither toil nor spin, yet I tell you, even Solomon in all his

---

85 Rom 5:9 and John 11:25, together with their contexts, provide examples of ambiguities
about present and future which pervade their writings.
86 Dunn, *Jesus remembered*, 610.

glory was not clothed like one of these. But if God so clothes the grass of the field, which is alive today and tomorrow thrown into the oven, will he not much more clothe you – you of little faith? (Matt 6:25–34)

He spoke of God as Father and encouraged the kind of trust a child has in its parents.

It seems that Jesus shared his contemporaries' views on the importance of temple and Torah, while offering a critique of the way in which both were honoured in current practice. Like other rabbis, Jesus summed up the Torah in two commandments: to love God and to love the neighbour. He implied that God's kingdom, shortly to be consummated on earth, was already present when his people were properly obedient; and this obedience meant a deepening of the Torah, a focus on interiority rather than on externals.[87] In calling Israel back to obedience, Jesus resembled the prophets, appealing for justice, mercy and love, and perhaps implying the 'new covenant' predicted by Jeremiah when the Law would be written on the heart. Indeed there are many ways in which Jesus is like the prophets of the Jewish scriptures, calling the people to a restoration of Israel as it was meant to be. The visionary and eschatological character of that restoration is betrayed by the symbolic choice of twelve disciples, representatives of the original twelve tribes, regardless of the fact that ten had been lost many centuries before. The New Testament repeatedly reflects on the fact that prophets are unwelcome among their own people. Jesus certainly provoked opposition.

John the Baptist marks the genesis of Jesus' activity. Both appear to have heralded the imminent arrival of God's final dénouement, thus presupposing the kind of cosmic panorama delineated in apocalyptic literature. Both called for repentance and renewal, though the Baptist's message of judgement would seem the harsher. Despite overlap, some contrast developed between the two, John living as an ascetic, Jesus accused of being 'a glutton and a drunkard, a friend of tax gatherers and sinners!' (Matt 11:18–19). John met with a violent end at the hands of Herod Antipas. Maybe this explains why the gospels are silent about Jesus visiting Herod's cities, Sepphoris and Tiberias – they were deliberately avoided.[88] This precedent also makes it not entirely implausible that Jesus predicted his own suffering and death, as the gospels indeed report. If so, the question arises whether he attempted to provide any explanation for his disciples. He may have seen himself in a line of prophets who, like Jeremiah, had suffered rejection (Matt 23:29–39 / Luke 13:33–5; cf. 1 Thess 2:15); and maybe

---

87 Vermes, *The religion of Jesus the Jew*.
88 Reed, *Archaeology and the Galilean Jesus*.

early Christian interest in the suffering servant of Isaiah (e.g. Acts 8:32–5) can be traced back to Jesus himself.[89] Possibly the symbolic actions and words of the Last Supper (1 Cor 11:23–6; Matt 26:26–9 / Mark 14:22–5 / Luke 22:14–20) reflect his way of indicating what meaning might be put upon the crisis about to face them. In roughly contemporary texts, the Maccabaean martyrs were being depicted as offering a redemptive sacrifice for their people (4 Macc 6:28–9 and 17:20–2; cf. Mark 10:45). Whatever the answer to that specific question, the fulfilment of prophecy seems deeply embedded in the gospel traditions, not to mention traditions embedded in the Pauline epistles (e.g. 1 Cor 15:3–4).

Jesus was a complex figure, appearing now like a sage and holy man, now like a prophet, now like a seer or visionary – in many and various ways he fits such analogies from his first-century Jewish world. He had a charisma that divided people for and against him. But he probably died quite specifically as a messianic pretender. Subsequently, his followers asserted the truth that he had fulfilled the prophecies, while many of his own people rejected their claims and treated them as blasphemers[90] because they by now regarded him as worthy of receiving the honour and worship due to God alone. The gospels reflect the viewpoint of those who believed in him. But the crucial question is: how did they sustain such claims in the light of his apparent failure to achieve anything – indeed, his despicable death on the cross?

The answer must lie in the resurrection. Few would begin an investigation into the historical Jesus with the resurrection – it is not easy to assess either the evidence or the validity of a claim to a unique event. Yet given the multiple attestation provided not merely by the gospel traditions but by all the other documents that now make up the New Testament, it would be hard to dispute the fact that, whatever actually happened, his followers believed that he had been raised from the dead, that his tomb was empty and that some had seen – even touched – him. It might be possible in principle to establish that the tomb was empty, a matter accepted as fact by the Jewish scholar Geza Vermes[91] – for a natural explanation can always be surmised. It might in principle be possible to establish that Jesus was resuscitated, but that would imply further life and subsequent death for which we would require evidence, and there is none, despite some novelistic speculations. The New Testament belief in resurrection is not in any case simply about resuscitation. What it was about could well provide further clues to Jesus' message and activity; for the claim that Jesus

89 Though Hooker, *Jesus and the servant*, offered a critique of that view.
90 Note the implications of e.g. Matt 9:3; 26:65; Mark 14:64; Luke 5:21; John 10:33, etc. Also Justin, *Dial* 17.
91 Vermes, *Jesus the Jew*.

had risen from the dead is even more extraordinary than might be supposed. The idea of resurrection was associated with the final dénouement when God would appear to judge the living and the dead, and the dead would rise to face that judgement. No prophecies pointed to the raising of an individual in advance of those eschatological events, not even the Messiah – he was not after all expected to die! So the resurrection of Jesus was, as it were, 'out of time', an anticipation of events still to come – it meant that the end-time had begun.

If the disciples responded to the charisma of Jesus during his life, they responded with awe after his death and resurrection. The problem of the historical Jesus to a large extent lies in the fact that all the material is coloured by the resurrection belief. Yet the resurrection claim is itself a confirmation of the eschatological 'reading' of Jesus' career. Readings which make him simply a prophet, a sage, a holy man or a philosopher cannot account for his politically motivated condemnation to death, nor the subsequent effects of his life and death. The remarkable thing is that the memories which the gospels record – in Greek for urban, Gentile believers – retain so much that fits into what we can discern of rural Jewish Galilee and Jerusalem under Pilate.

The risen Jesus: towards Christian faith

The resurrection meant that Jesus became the Christ, and the risen Christ became the focus of the message of the church rather than the kingdom of God. The earliest Christians looked for the return of Jesus in glory, as Christ and king. They thought they now knew the identity of the one who would come to be judge at the end and establish God's kingdom on earth. After the events in Jerusalem, they searched the scriptures for prophecies of the Christ's death and subsequent vindication, because what had happened shifted the generally expected pattern of eschatological events. These features of the earliest Christian belief are confirmation of the fact that Jesus proclaimed the fulfilment of God's promises and the coming kingdom of God, provoking messianic speculations. They also indicate why the life of Jesus was subsumed into the over-arching cosmic story outlined earlier, why fulfilment of prophecy was so fundamental to early Christianity, why belief in his pre-existence began to complement his post-existence (for the pre-existence in heaven of what was later to be revealed was commonly presumed in apocalyptic literature),[92] and why the earliest Christians came to venerate him without imagining any

---

92 Lincoln, *Paradise now and not yet.*

threat to the priority of the one true God in whose providence the Christ was pre-ordained to act as agent in bringing his purposes to fruition.

Jesus did not teach Christianity, because Christianity is about Jesus. The earliest writings in the New Testament are the epistles of Paul. Their difference from the gospels, particularly the apparent lack of interest in the life and teaching of Jesus, is one of the great conundrums of early Christianity. Yet there are some elements that provide a remarkable confirmation of the tenor of Jesus' teaching. For example, Paul tells his readers to 'have this mind in you which was in Christ Jesus', who emptied himself of 'equality with God', 'took the form of a slave' and 'became obedient to the point of death – even death on a cross' (Phil 2:5–11). The message of self-denial and radical trust in God, which Jesus taught and exemplified, becomes the basis of Christian behaviour. The ideal of radical love is portrayed in 1 Corinthians 13 and would seem to confirm the memory found in the gospels that Jesus saw love as the fulfilling of the law. Again, it is likely that the term 'Son of God' was originally a messianic designation; but the disciples remembered Jesus speaking of God as his Father and teaching them too to pray to, and trust in, God as Father. In Paul's epistles we find the idea that through Jesus Christ, the Son of God, believers may become adopted sons of God (e.g. Rom 8:14–17). Such developments, though apparently assuming already a transcendent origin for the Christ, seem best explained by some continuity of tradition.

Jesus himself and his teaching must have contributed to the generation of the ideas about him and about his significance that are traceable in early Christianity. The quest has too easily assumed that getting back to the earliest sources guarantees greater reliability – is it not true that the significance of a historical event is better understood by hindsight? The post-resurrection tendency to venerate Jesus both defines the majority of emerging Jesus movements and differentiates them from the Jewish matrix within which they were formed. (The exception proves the rule: we hear of some known as 'Ebionites' – appropriately named, Eusebius suggested,[93] 'in view of the poor and mean opinions they held about Christ. They regarded him as plain and ordinary, a man esteemed as righteous through growth of character and nothing more, the child of a normal union between a man and Mary.' He adds that they felt every detail of the Law should be observed, and salvation could not be attained by faith alone. Most scholars have deduced that he was describing Jewish Christians.)[94] It has been argued that it is precisely the 'cult' of Jesus

93 *HE* 3.27.
94 See pt II, ch. 4, below.

within the exclusive monotheistic framework of Judaism which gave emerging Christianity its distinctiveness,[95] as well as guaranteeing the profound and bitter doctrinal debates of succeeding centuries. Devotion to the risen Jesus can be documented extremely early, within predominantly Jewish groups of Christians and not least in the writings of the ex-Pharisee, Paul of Tarsus. If by the third century prayers can be cited that suggest pagan influence (see above), even more evident is the Jewishness of most early Christian liturgical expression. The 'Lord's Prayer', which Jesus taught his disciples, is made up of phrases to which parallels can be found in Jewish liturgy. The doxologies incorporated into the New Testament writings provided precedent for adapting Jewish forms of prayer, which would in any case come naturally to Jesus' first Jewish followers. The long prayer at the end of 1 *Clement* betrays both the debt and the adaptation: the creator of the universe is asked to 'open the eyes of our heart to know you, that you alone are the highest in the highest and remain holy among the holy'. God is addressed as 'merciful and compassionate' and characterised as 'faithful in all generations, righteous in judgement, wonderful in strength and majesty, wise in your creation . . . gracious among those that trust in you'. The content lies firmly in the Jewish biblical tradition, yet it ends:

> We praise you through Jesus Christ, the high priest and guardian of our souls, through whom be glory and majesty to you, both now and for all generations and for ever and ever. Amen.

Such devotional responses to the Lord Jesus both predated and impelled the defining of dogmatic discourse, as people tried to make sense of a mythopoeic rhetoric which pushed at the boundaries of what was acceptable within a religious tradition focused exclusively on the one God of the scriptures.[96] The history of early Christianity is usually presented as doctrinal development. But this common approach would seem to reflect the assumptions of modern evolutionary ideas. Rather what happened was that people searched for adequate ways of expressing what had so unexpectedly occurred, finding it in one cultural context after another.[97] Doctrine belongs to a time when logic and philosophy began to shape the discourse. It sought to articulate in a new way and with increasing precision and sophistication what was assumed to have been implicit in the beginning.

95 Hurtado, *Lord Jesus Christ*.
96 See further pt v, ch. 25, below.
97 See Young's essays in Hick, *Myth of God incarnate*.

One of the most obvious features of the second century is that what became mainstream Christianity had to struggle against a possibly more dominant movement which would have lost touch with the earthly Jesus. Indeed, it is entirely possible that, during the second century, developing Christianity could have lost its moorings in the Jesus of history, as over the centuries it did lose its anchorage in Judaism. There were apparently two ways in which the significance of the fleshly historical person of Jesus was downplayed. The first involved separating the heavenly being from the earthly body. For Cerinthus, who is purported to have been challenged by the apostle John in the baths at Ephesus,[98] the Christ was a spiritual being which descended on Jesus at the baptism and departed before the crucifixion. Only the human Jesus suffered while the spiritual Christ remained impassible.[99] The second involved, in some ways, a more radical denial, and was hardly possible for any who had walked and talked with Jesus in his lifetime – for the Docetists seem to have regarded the whole human presence of Jesus as a kind of mirage, like an angel in disguise, such as we find the book of Tobit. The alienation from the material and fleshly which apparently characterised Gnosticism[100] would seem to have reinforced this view. Whichever position he had in mind, Ignatius, bishop of Antioch in the early second century, spelt out the danger:

> Be deaf when anyone speaks to you apart from Jesus Christ, who was of the stock of David, who was from Mary, who was truly born, ate and drank, was truly persecuted under Pontius Pilate, was truly crucified, and died in the sight of beings heavenly, earthly and under the earth, who was truly also raised from the dead, His Father raising him.[101]

This debate points to the widespread acceptance of the Christ's heavenly origin, and at the same time to determination to hold onto the reality of his earthly life, suffering and death.

What was recognised by hindsight as the 'true tradition' among the plurality of early Christian movements needed to be in touch with the Jesus of history. For an apologist like Justin Martyr, it was vital that Jesus Christ really had lived a life that fulfilled the prophecies, really had taught people how to live so as to satisfy the demands of the one true God who created all things, and really had been crucified 'under Pontius Pilate, procurator of Judaea in the time of Tiberius Caesar'.[102] He tried to confirm it, appealing to other evidence,

98 Euseb. *HE* 3.28.
99 Iren. *Haer* 1.26.
100 See further pt III, ch. 12, below.
101 *Trall.* 9.
102 1 *Apol.* 13.

claiming that the birth of Jesus was recorded in the tax declarations submitted under the procurator Quirinius and available in Rome for inspection, and that the *Acts of Pilate* confirm the miracles, as well as details of the crucifixion.[103] The gospels were transmitted through a period in which Jesus might have been dissolved into a spiritual visitant, or remained just a good man adopted by God – the gospel texts themselves show traces of the impact of these controversies.[104] But despite this they tell a story that fulfils divine providential intentions that go back behind the immediate narrative, retaining a cosmic perspective derived from apocalyptic, and they invite the reader to be in touch with a genuinely human life, which was nevertheless epiphanic.

It is this dual perspective on Jesus Christ that lies at the heart of Christianity as a religion. He was, for believers, the 'wholly human and visible icon of the wholly transcendent and invisible God'[105] – and the wholly material or bodily being of the one wholly immaterial or incorporeal God. Through what became known as the 'incarnation' or 'enfleshment' of God's Word or Wisdom, the life of God was communicated to his creatures, so they could be 'in touch' with that life. We began by showing how fundamental this was for Helena. Even if the Christian religion had by then baptised into itself some of the superstition of the ancient world (discerned, for example, in her treatment of the cross as a magic talisman), this fundamental instinct is true to the incarnational thrust of Christianity. The physical is sanctified as the vehicle of the divine presence, whether it be the actual living and dying of saints and martyrs, who themselves become 'types' of Christ, or the concrete reality of the eucharistic bread and wine received in communion. Being 'in touch' with the one who was God incarnate meant the assimilation of divine life, and the articulation of Christian doctrine, in the period of this volume and beyond, was shaped by the need to guarantee this reality. The incarnation is what turns Jesus into the foundation of Christianity.

103 1 *Apol.* 34, 35 and 48.
104 Ehrmann, *Orthodox corruption*.
105 Bockmuehl, *Cambridge companion to Jesus*, 1.

PART I

*

THE POLITICAL, SOCIAL AND RELIGIOUS SETTING

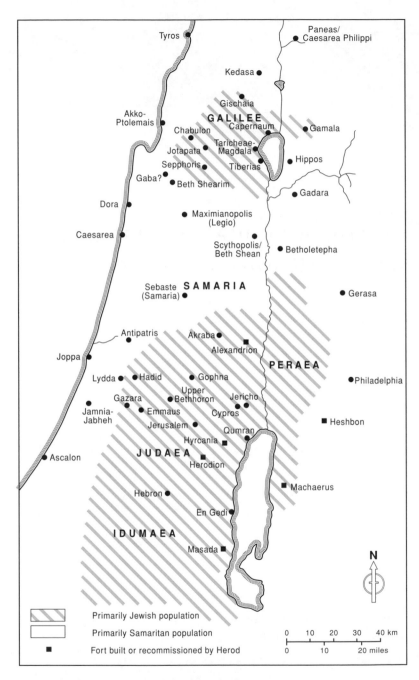

Map 2. Palestine in the first century CE

Galilee and Judaea in the first century

SEAN FREYNE

The gospels provide contrasting theatres for the public ministry of Jesus. Whereas the Synoptics have a shared focus on Galilee, with one final journey to Jerusalem, the fourth gospel views Galilee virtually as a place of refuge from a ministry conducted for the most part in Judaea and Jerusalem. In the most recent wave of historical Jesus research, there has been a marked preference for Galilee, due to a variety of factors, not the least of which are current trends among scholars interested more in the social than the theological significance of Jesus' life. Historians are missing an important clue to his career, however, if they ignore the fact that it was in Jerusalem rather than in Galilee that he eventually met his fate.[1]

Geographical factors

As one moves from west to east, both Galilee and Judaea follow a similar pattern in geomorphic terms – coastal plain, central hill country, rift valley and the uplands of Transjordan. On a north–south axis, however, real differences emerge due to the variety of climatic conditions. The marked decrease in annual rainfall from north to south is quite obvious in the landscape. Whereas the central Galilean hill country, with its rich alluvial soil and many springs, has a number of wide valleys running in an east/west direction, the Judaean hill country has much less soil covering and tapers off quickly into the dry, arid desert region of the Dead Sea valley. These variations, which were recognised by such ancient writers as Strabo (*Geog.* 16.2.16), Josephus (*BJ* 3.41–3; 3.506–21) and Pliny the Elder (*HN* 5.66–73), also point to diversity in lifestyles and settlement patterns in both regions. The threefold division of upper and lower Galilee and the valley reflects a recognition that, even in Galilee itself, there

---

1 Crossan, *Birth of Christianity*, 407–17; Freyne, 'Geography of restoration'.

are several micro-regions from an ecological perspective (*m. Shevi'it* 9.2; cf. *BJ* 2.573; 3.41–3; 3.506–21).

Historical outline

Early history

These differences should not be neglected when the historical factors having to do with the ministry of Jesus are investigated.[2] The name Galilee, meaning 'the circle', is derived in all probability from the experience of the early Israelites inhabiting the interior highlands and surrounded by Canaanite city-states. Judaea, on the other hand, is a tribal name which came to particular prominence in the period of the Davidic monarchy, inasmuch as David himself was from the tribe of Judah. The Galilean tribes were Zebulon, Naphtali and Asher, with the tribe of Dan migrating north later. The accounts of tribal characteristics and behavioural patterns, found especially in the Blessings of Jacob (Gen 49) and Moses (Deut 33), as well as in the Song of Deborah (Judg 5), suggest that the northern tribes were exposed to greater cultural diversity over the centuries. Certainly the region bore the brunt of the Assyrian onslaught in the eighth century BCE, with Tiglathpilesar III's invasion resulting in the destruction, and possible depopulation, of many centres in upper and lower Galilee (2 Kgs 15:29; Isa 8:23, LXX). Judah succumbed to the Babylonians a century and a half later with the destruction of the temple and the deportation to Babylon of the king and the leading members of the aristocracy in 587 BCE. Unlike the north, however, restoration in Judaea occurred quickly under the Persians, with the edict of Cyrus in 515 BCE allowing the Jews to return and rebuild the temple. Josephus acknowledges the significance of these events for later Judaean history, linking the return from Babylon to the etymology of the name *Ioudaioi*/Judaeans (*AJ* 11.173).

A firm grasp of the history of both regions during the intervening centuries before the Common Era is vital to an understanding of the religious, cultural, and political context of Galilee and Judaea in the first century CE.[3] The Persian province of *Yehud*, as it was officially named, remained a fairly insignificant temple territory for several centuries, despite the hopes of restoration expressed by various prophets. All that was to change after the conquest of Alexander the Great and the advent of the Hellenistic kingdoms. In the second century BCE, the Seleucid empire in Syria began to collapse and various ethnic

---

2 Freyne, *Galilee from Alexander*, 3–21; Frankel, 'Galilee'.
3 For a detailed account of this history, cf. Schürer, *History of the Jewish People*, esp. vol. I.

groups, including Judaeans, were able to establish themselves within national territories. Once the threat from Antiochus Epiphanes (175–164 BCE) of forced assimilation of the Judaean temple cult of Yahweh to that of Zeus had been averted under the leadership of the Maccabees, the desecrated temple was rededicated in 164, and the foundation of an autonomous Jewish state soon followed in its wake. Thereafter the second generation of the Maccabees, the Hasmoneans (135–67 BCE), initiated campaigns of expansion, which eventually led to the establishment of a kingdom that was as extensive territorially as that of David and Solomon in the tenth to the ninth centuries (1 Macc 15:33).

For the first time in almost a millennium, therefore, Galilee and Judaea were under the same native rulership, and significantly in the literature of the period the name *Ioudaios*/Judaean begins to be used, not just for the inhabitants of Judaea in the strict sense, but for all who embraced the Jewish temple ideology by worshipping in Jerusalem.[4] By the mid-first century BCE, Rome was emerging as master of the eastern Mediterranean, and the Hasmoneans had been replaced by the Herodians, an Idumean dynasty entrusted by Rome with maintaining its interests in the region as client kings. Galilee, with Sepphoris – only approximately six kilometres from Nazareth – as its administrative centre, was recognised as a Jewish territory, together with Judaea in the south and Perea across the Jordan. These sub-regions were soon incorporated into the kingdom of Herod the Great, and were expected to make their contribution to the honouring of his Roman patron, Augustus.

The Herodian period

The long reign of Herod (37–4 BCE) made a deep impact on both Galilean and Judaean society, so much so in fact that on his death an embassy was sent to Rome requesting that none of his sons should replace him. Augustus responded by dividing the kingdom between Herod's three sons, assigning Antipas to rule over Galilee and Peraea, Archelaus over Judaea and Philip over Batanaea, Trachonitis and Auranitis in northern Transjordan. Galilee was once again, therefore, administratively separate from Judaea, as reflected in the gospel of Matthew's explanation of how Jesus, though born in Judaea, came to live in Galilee (Matt 2:23). Josephus gives a broader background to the political situation. Archelaus had so outraged his subjects that he was deposed by Rome in 6 CE; and thereafter Judaea proper was administered by a procurator who resided in Caesarea Maritima, thus reducing Jerusalem to the role of a temple city controlled by a priestly aristocracy.

4 Freyne, 'Behind the names'.

Antipas, called simply 'Herod' in the New Testament (cf. e.g. Matt chs. 2 and 14; Mark chs. 6 and 8; and Luke chs. 1, 3, 9, 13 and 23), aspired to, but was never given, the title 'king'. He ruled in Galilee and Perea until 37 CE, when he too was deposed and his territory was handed over to his nephew Agrippa I. Despite his lesser status as 'tetrarch', Antipas continued with the style and policy of his father in ensuring that Roman concerns be addressed in his territories. John the Baptist suffered at his hands, probably for the reasons given by Josephus rather than those of the gospels, namely, that John's popularity and espousal of justice for the poor was cause for concern that an uprising might occur (AJ 18.116–19; Mark 6:14–29; Matt 14:1–12; Luke 9:7–9). This would have been deemed a serious failure in imperial eyes, since client rulers were tolerated only if they could ensure stability and loyalty to Rome and its values.

Apart from a major renovation of the Jerusalem temple, Herod the Great had for the most part confined his building projects to the periphery of the Jewish territories: Samaria was renamed Sebaste (in Latin, 'Augustus'), with a temple to Roma and Augustus constructed there, as also at Caesarea Maritima on the coast where he developed a magnificent harbour. In the north, Herod constructed a temple to Augustus at Paneas, which his son, Philip, later renamed Caesarea (Philippi). Antipas continued this tradition of honouring the Roman overlords through monumental buildings in Galilee. Sepphoris was made 'the ornament of all Galilee' and named *autokrator*, probably honouring the sole rule of Augustus (AJ 18.27). Tiberias on the sea of Galilee was a new foundation, in 19 CE, honouring the new emperor who had succeeded Augustus, and Bethsaida got the additional name Julias, in honour Augustus' wife, Livia/Julia.

Social and economic conditions in Galilee

In the past twenty-five years, no region of ancient Palestine has received more attention than Galilee, because of Jewish and Christian interest in the career of Jesus and the emergence of rabbinic Judaism there after the revolt of Bar Kochba (132–5 CE).[5] In addition to the study of the literary evidence – mainly Josephus' works, the gospels, and the rabbinic writings – the focus has been on archaeology, both at key sites like Sepphoris and in surveys of various sub-regions. These studies give varied, sometimes even contradictory, accounts, as

---

5 Two international conferences and a number of important collections of essays have appeared: Levine, *The Galilee in late antiquity*; Edwards and McCollough, *Archaeology and the Galilee*; Meyers and Martin-Nagy, *Sepphoris in Galilee*; Meyers, *Galilee through the centuries*; Arav and Freund, *Bethsaida*, vols. I and II. Cf. also Stemberger, *Jews and Christians*.

scholars from various disciplines attempt a complete description of the region in Hellenistic and Roman times. Nowhere is this tendency more in evidence than when historical Jesus studies and Galilean studies become intertwined. Ever since Albert Schweitzer exposed the anachronistic concerns of many of the nineteenth-century liberal lives of Jesus,[6] it has become increasingly evident that objectivity is often asserted but rarely fully achieved, as various proposals for the ministry of Jesus are advanced.[7]

Gerhard Lenski's description of advanced agrarian empires from a social scientific perspective has been highly influential in many recent studies, providing, as it does, a model for understanding social stratification in advanced agrarian empires such as that of Rome. In such societies agriculture is the main industrial occupation and the management of labour is directed towards achieving a surplus rather than mere subsistence.[8] This exercise of modelling through an ideal type must, however, always take account of local factors. In first-century Palestine the evidence of two major revolts, both of which had a social as well as a religious component, has convinced many scholars of the need to supplement the Lenski model with another approach which highlights the causes of social conflict and the strategies adopted by elites for its management.[9]

Cultural identity

Discussion of the ethnicity of the Galilean population during the first century CE is concerned with the identity of the *dominant* strand in the ethnic mix of the region by examining traces of cultural and religious affiliations, comprising Israelite, Judaean, Iturean and even Babylonian elements. Certain claims can be ruled out as highly unlikely on the basis of our present knowledge of the situation. Thus, the argument for a pagan Galilee is poorly supported by the literary evidence and receives no confirmation from the archaeological explorations.[10] Nor is there any real evidence of a lasting Iturean presence in the region, even though they may have infiltrated upper Galilee briefly before the arrival of the Hasmoneans. There are several problems with the idea of Galilean Israelites also. It is difficult to imagine a largely peasant population having maintained a separate Yahwistic/Israelite identity over the centuries

6 Schweitzer, *Quest of the historical Jesus*.
7 Cf. Freyne, 'Archaeology and the historical Jesus' and 'Galilean questions'.
8 Lenski, *Power and privilege*.
9 Horsley, *Sociology and the Jesus movement*, is critical of Theissen's use of a functionalist approach in his application of sociological models to the study of early Christianity. Cf. Theissen, *Sociology of early Palestinian Christianity*, as well as his *Social reality*.
10 Betz, 'Jesus and the Cynics', 453–75; Freyne, *Galilee from Alexander*, 101–45.

in the absence of a communal cultic centre. Mount Gerazim, the sacred site of the Samaritans, who styled themselves 'Israelites who worshipped on holy Argarizin', might have been expected to play such a role.[11] Yet all indications are that the Samaritans were as hostile to Galileans as they were to Judaeans, especially when they went on pilgrimage to Jerusalem (Luke 9:52; Josephus *AJ* 20.118–36).[12] Thus, the theory of the Judaisation of Galilee in the sense that adherents to the Jerusalem temple in Judaea were settled there, would appear to be the most likely hypothesis, in our present state of knowledge. Archaeological surveys have shown a marked increase in new foundations from the Hasmonean period onwards, and at the same time the destruction of older sites, like Har Mispe Yamim (between upper and lower Galilee) which had a pagan cult centre.[13] Excavations at various sites have uncovered such instruments of the distinctive Jewish way of life as ritual baths (*miqvaot*), stone jars and natively produced ceramic household ware. These finds indicate a concern with ritual purity emanating from Jerusalem and its temple as well as an avoidance of the cultural ethos of the encircling pagan cities.[14]

Social stratification

Lenski's model envisages a pyramid view of society in which most of the power, prestige and privilege resides at the top among the narrow band of ruling elite and native aristocracy (if and when these are to be distinguished). Beneath these are the retainer classes, who help to maintain the status quo on behalf of the elites, thereby gaining for themselves some measure of relative prestige. On a rung further down the ladder, as the base broadens, are the peasants, the free landowners who are the mainstay of the society, but cannot themselves aspire to a higher position on the social scale. Instead, they are in constant danger of falling among the landless poor, due either to increased taxation, a bad harvest or simple annexation of property by the ruling elites. Lenski's model indeed corresponds generally with what we know of Roman Galilee, once certain adjustments are made to this ideal picture to account for local circumstances.

While Antipas never seems to have been given the title king, despite the attribution by Mark (6:14), there is no doubt that within Galilee itself he and his court represented the ruling elite. In one sense they could be considered

---

11 Kraabel, 'New evidence'.
12 Freyne, 'Behind the names', 116–19; Kraabel, 'New evidence'.
13 Frankel, 'Har Mispe Yamim'; Frankel and Ventura, 'Mispe Yamim bronzes'.
14 Chancey, *The Myth of a Gentile Galilee*, is the most detailed and up-to-date report of the evidence. Cf. also Reed, *Archaeology and the Galilean Jesus*, 23–62.

retainers on behalf of the emperor, since Antipas was prepared to accept the role that Roman imperial policies in the east had dictated for him. Josephus informs us that he 'loved his tranquillity' (*AJ* 18.245), a characterisation that fits well with the gospel portraits, despite his attempts to upstage the governor of Syria at Rome on one occasion (*AJ* 18.101–4). Augustus had decreed that he could have a personal income of 200 talents from the territories of Galilee and Perea, and presumably he could also introduce special levies for building and other projects, especially when these were intended to honour the imperial household (*AJ* 17.318). Not only Antipas and his immediate family benefited from these concessions, but a new class seems to have emerged around Antipas, whom the gospels refer to as the Herodians (cf. e.g. Mark 3:6; 12:13). While the identity of this group is unclear, a discussion of various other groups mentioned in the gospels may shed some light on their social role.[15]

One passage that opens up an interesting perspective on Galilean society is Mark's account of Herod's birthday celebration, where three different groups are distinguished among the attendees: *megistanes, chiliarchoi* and *protoi tēs Galilaias* (Mark 6:21). The first term ('great men') is known both in the LXX (Dan 5:23) and Josephus (*Vit.* 112; 143), where it refers to courtiers of king Agrippa II, and so should probably be understood in the same way here. Their special relationship to Antipas is underlined by the use of the possessive pronoun *autou*/'his' with reference to this group only of the three mentioned. The presence of military personnel (*chiliarchoi*) suggests that the tetrarch had some form of permanent army, as distinct from a militia which he might call up for a particular engagement (*AJ* 18.251–2). 'The leading men of Galilee' (*hoi protoi*) are also known from Josephus' writings, as he uses the expression some seventy times in all. In two separate incidents, the *protoi* are influential Jews, at least ostensibly concerned about religious values, but they are also interested in the maintenance of law and order and the payment of the tribute to Rome (*AJ* 18.122, 261–309). They represent, therefore, an aristocracy of birth, similar to the senatorial class at Rome. At the time of the first revolt (*c*.66 CE), two people bearing the name Herod were numbered among the ruling class of Tiberias, each of whom, as landowners across the Jordan, recommended loyalty to Rome (*Vit.* 33). The Herodians in Galilee could best be described, therefore, as a wealthy aristocracy, stoutly loyal to the Herodian house and its policies, presumably because they were its beneficiaries and possibly also involved in administrative duties.

15 Hoehner, *Herod Antipas*, 331–42.

From our knowledge of village administration in other parts of the Roman east, we can presume a whole network of lesser officials within the highly bureaucratic structures that had been put in place in the early Hellenistic period by the Ptolemies, who ruled Palestine from Egypt in the third century CE. These officials would have included market managers (*agoranomoi*), tax collectors (*telōnai*), estate mangers (*oikonomoi*), judges (*kritai*) and prison officers (*hypēretai/ praktores*), all of whom are alluded to in the gospels. The tax collectors appear to be ubiquitous, an indication of the high levels of taxation – religious as well as secular – that obtained. The *tributum soli* (land tax) was probably paid in kind, as we hear of imperial and royal granaries in both upper and lower Galilee at the outbreak of the first revolt (*Vit.* 71.119). Tolls were another important source of revenue for local rulers and landowners; in all probability the tax collectors of the gospels, with whom Jesus seems to have had friendly relations, belong to this category.[16] Like some other professions, theirs was suspected of dishonesty by the more religious circles, but Jesus does not exclude them from his retinue, even when this meant a certain opprobrium for fraternising with 'sinners' (Matt 11:19; Luke 7:34; Mark 2:16).

Landowning patterns in Galilee, as elsewhere in the ancient world, are difficult to determine with any degree of precision.[17] Large estates farmed by lease-paying tenants rather than freeholding peasants were already present in Persian times (Neh 5:1–11). Under Ptolemaic rule this trend continued, as we learn from the account of the Egyptian businessman Zenon's inspection tour of royal estates – including some in Galilee – in the mid-third century BCE.[18] The gospel parables also reflect this pattern (Mark 12:1–9; Luke 16:1–9). On the basis of scattered pieces of information from Josephus, as well as from archaeological surveys, the trend was towards larger estates, and thus a move away from mere subsistence farming of the traditional Jewish peasant class. Pressure could fall on small landowners as the ruling aristocracy's needs had to be met. In a pre-industrial context, land was the primary source of wealth, but it was in short supply in a Galilee that was densely populated by the standards of the time (*BJ* 3.41–3). Increased taxation to meet the demands of an elite lifestyle meant that many were reduced to penury. These landless poor and urban destitute correspond to the lowest level on Lenski's pyramid (*Vit.* 66f). The slide from peasant owner to tenant farmer, to day labourer – all recognisable characters from the gospel parables – was inexorable for many

---

16 Herrenbrück, *Jesus und die Zöllne*; Oakman and Hanson, *Palestine in the time of Jesus*.
17 Fiensy, *Social history of Palestine*.
18 Tcherikover, 'Palestine under the Ptolemies'.

and, thus, gave rise to social resentment, debt, banditry and, in the case of women, prostitution.

Economic realities: roots of conflict

Relatively speaking, Galilee was well endowed with natural resources. The melting winter snows from Mt Hermon and seasonal rains ensured good yields and allowed for the production of a variety of crops. Josephus speaks lyrically about the climatic conditions of the plain of Gennesareth in the region of Capernaum, with its luxuriant range of fruits (*BJ* 3.506–21). But, according to both Josephus and rabbinic sources (*BJ* 3.42–3), the valleys of lower Galilee also yielded a variety of grains and flax.[19] The slopes of upper Galilee were suitable for the cultivation of the vine and the olive tree, supporting the abundant production of wine and oil, so graphically illustrated in the entrepreneurial activity of John of Gischala, as reported by Josephus (*Vit.* 74f; *BJ* 2.259f).[20] In addition to this agricultural activity, the lake of Gennesareth supported a thriving fish industry. The names of Bethsaida and Magdala suggest a connection with fish, and Jesus' first followers were actively engaged in this industry (Mark 1:16f). The Greek name of Magdala, Tarichaeae, refers to the practice of salting fish for export, and this industry must have necessitated such specialised services as potters making vessels for export of liquid products, as well as boat, sail and net makers.[21]

The most pressing question about the Galilean economy is the extent to which the benefits of these products accrued to the peasants themselves.[22] Was the Galilean economy a politically controlled entity in which the peasants were mere serfs? In whose interest were the primary resources utilised? If, as we have suggested, the Galilean landownership pattern represented a combination of large estates and family-run holdings, then some degree of commercial independence would have been granted to the Galilean peasants. However, the refurbishment of Sepphoris and the building of Tiberias must have marked a turning-point in the Galilean economy, one which coincided with Jesus' public ministry. This provides the most immediate backdrop to his particular emphasis on the blessedness of the destitute and his call for trust in God's providential care for all.[23] The new Herodian class required

---

19 Cf. Safrai, *Economy of Palestine*.
20 Frankel, 'Some oil-presses'.
21 Hanson, 'The Galilean fishing economy'.
22 Horsley, *Galilee*, 202–22.
23 Freyne, 'Geography, politics and economics'.

adequate allotments in order to maintain a luxurious lifestyle (cf. Matt 11:19), and, inevitably, this brought further pressure on the native peasants.[24]

Yet this picture has to be balanced by evidence from later sources which shows that a Jewish peasant class did survive the crisis of two revolts. The rabbinic sources are replete with references to markets, village traders and laws having to do with buying and selling.[25] This cannot be dismissed as the mere idealisation of later generations, but is rather a continuation of patterns already discerned in such first-century sources as the gospels and Josephus' writings. The dividing line, however, between subsistence and penury was always a thin one, as the threatened strike by the Galilean peasants in the reign of the emperor Gaius (Caligula) demonstrates (39/40 CE). In protest at the proposed erection of the emperor's statue in the Jerusalem temple, they decided not to till the land. Significantly, some members of the Herodian family were dismayed, fearing that there would not be sufficient resources to pay the annual tribute, which would lead to social anarchy (AJ 18.273–4). Julius Caesar had recognised the problem caused for Jewish peasants by his restoration in 47 BCE of their rights to support their temple, and, consequently, he reduced the annual tribute due to Rome (AJ 14.190–216). The 200 talents (the equivalent of 600,000 Tyrian silver shekels) from Galilee and Peraea to which Antipas was annually entitled as a personal income made a considerable demand on the populace. A direct tribute to Rome was presumably still applicable on top of this, even though this is not mentioned explicitly.[26]

A monetary system is essential for any developing economy, since as stored value it allows for a wider and more complex network of trading than the barter of goods, which can only occur at a local level. Tyrian coinage seems to dominate the numismatic finds at locations not just in upper Galilee, such as Meiron, Gischala and Khirbet Shema, but even at Gamala and Jotapata as well, both lower Galilean strongholds of Jewish nationalism in the first revolt.[27] This suggests trading links with the important Phoenician port, despite the cultural differences between the city and its Jewish hinterland, which could often boil over into open hostility (BJ 4.105). Most surprising is the fact that despite its pagan imagery, the Tyrian half-shekel was deemed to be 'the coin of the sanctuary' which all male Jews were obliged to pay for the upkeep of the Jerusalem temple. The usual reason given is that the Tyrian money retained

24 Horsley and Hanson, Bandits, prophets, and Messiahs.
25 Safrai, Economy of Palestine, 224–72; Oakman, Jesus and the economic questions.
26 Hoehner, Herod Antipas, 298–301.
27 Hanson, Tyrian influence; Raynor and Meshorer, Coins of ancient Meiron; Barag, 'Tyrian currency'; Ben-David, Jerusalem und Tyros; Syon, 'Coins from Gamala'.

a constant value in terms of its silver content for over a century and a half (126 BCE–56 CE).

In order to maintain their elite lifestyle, the Herodians siphoned off the wealth of the land for their own benefit, without giving anything back in return. The Jewish ideal on the other hand affirmed an inclusive community in which all shared in the blessings of the land and its fruits. During the long reign of Antipas, the upkeep of Sepphoris and Tiberias drained the countryside of its resources, natural and human, causing resentment and opposition.[28] The conflict comes into clear light during the first revolt, when both cities were attacked by Galileans venting their resentment of the aristocratic inhabitants and their opulent lifestyles (*Vit.* 66.301, 373–80). This feeling of distance, even antipathy, however, can be detected some forty years earlier during the ministry of Jesus to the villages of Galilee. Neither Herodian centre is mentioned in the gospels, and the lifestyle of those dwelling 'in the houses of kings' is viewed critically when contrasted with the values advocated by both Jesus himself and his mentor, John the Baptist (Matt 11:8).[29]

Much of Jesus' public ministry, as portrayed in the gospels, was conducted against the backdrop of an unjust economic system. The gospels, even when they are presenting Jesus' ministry in a post-resurrection situation, provide us with a window on the economic conditions in Galilee as these can be discerned from other sources also. In order to understand the full impact of statements such as 'Blessed are the poor,' or 'Forgive us our debts as we also forgive our debtors', they need to be heard in the context of attitudes and values surrounding wealth and possessions within both Graeco-Roman society and standard Jewish covenantal thinking. To be poor was to be lacking in honour, the most prized possession of all in Mediterranean society, and cursed by God according to the Deuteronomic principle that the good will prosper and the wicked will perish (Deut 30:15–20).

Yet Jesus was no starry-eyed romantic. Wealthy people who can lend money and then exact it back with interest are part of the landscape of his ministry, and thieves are a constant threat for those who seek to hoard their money (cf. e.g. Matt 6:19; 18:23–35; 19:16–22; 25:14–30). The poor or the destitute are never far away, and they are frequent characters in his parables (Mark 12:41–4; Luke 16:19–31). On the other hand, it is important to recognise that this picture may be somewhat distorted because of the particular emphasis of Jesus' ministry. Certainly, not everybody who was attracted to him was poor. The

28 Freyne, 'Herodian economics in Galilee'.
29 Theissen, *Gospels in context*; Freyne, 'Jesus and the urban culture of Galilee'.

inhabitants of such places as Capernaum, Corazin and Bethsaida, all large villages situated in the fertile plain of Gennesareth, do not seem to have accepted his radical message (cf. Matt 11:19–21). This points to the fact that the more affluent Galileans were not prepared to abandon possessions and family, even when they may have been happy to accept Jesus because of his healing powers.

Judaea and Jerusalem

While still in Galilee, Jesus was for the most part active among *Ioudaioi*, that is, adherents of the Jerusalem temple and its laws. Yet the social ethos he would have encountered in Jerusalem would have been considerably different from that of Galilee. Because of the particular character of Jerusalem as the holy city of Jews, everywhere the tensions went deeper than those generally operative between provincials and residents of the national capital. The pre-eminence of Jerusalem was recognised even by pagan writers, and, as previously mentioned, Herod the Great had sought to enhance this by his building projects (*AJ* 15.267–91).[30] However, its political status was diminished through the development as an alternative capital of Caesarea Maritima in 10 BCE, with its altar dedicated to Roma and Augustus and its impressive harbour. Thus, after the deposition of Herod's son, Archelaus, the Roman procurator had a suitable location in which to establish the trappings of Roman administration, leaving Jerusalem to the Jews as the religious, but no longer the administrative, capital of the province.[31]

This separation of the religious and administrative centres points to a deep cleavage in first-century Judaean society between the ruling elite and the native aristocracy, something that did not occur to the same extent in Galilee. As Herod the Great enhanced the physical splendour of Jerusalem, he moved to take control of the most important institution of the temple state, that of the high priesthood. Early in his reign, he had appointed Aristobulus III as high priest, only to realise quickly that this was a major political mistake because of popular support for a young Hasmonean. Aristobulus was removed, and thereafter Herod appointed various diaspora Jews to the office, first a Babylonian, and then an Alexandrine, thus introducing into Judaean society a new dynasty, the Boethusians, whom he could control at will (*AJ* 15.22, 15.39–41 and 15.320–2). As a consequence, Herod's control of the high priesthood

---

30 Netzer, 'Herod's building projects'; Richardson, *Herod*, 174–215.
31 Mendels, *Rise and fall of Jewish nationalism*, 277–331.

eroded the effectiveness of the office for inner-Judaean life. Similarly, Herod replaced the Hasmonean lay nobility with Hellenised Idumeans loyal to him, apportioning to them some of the best lands in the district described as *har hamelek*, 'the king's mountain' (probably in north-west Judaea) which he had inherited from previous rulers.[32]

Thus, when the Romans sought to introduce direct rule, they discovered a native aristocracy, clerical and lay, who lacked credibility with the Judaean populace and were therefore devoid of the authority to play effectively the role that Rome expected from their ilk, namely, to render the population of a region amenable to its rule. The failure of the Judaean aristocracy in this regard is most clearly evident in the fact that, in a last desperate effort to cling to power, they were forced unwillingly into a revolt against Rome, simply to retain some credibility with the people as a whole. This situation of a disaffected peasantry and an ineffectual native aristocracy had, as Goodman persuasively argues, deep roots in the social realities of Judaean life.[33] None of the usual status criteria of Graeco-Roman society, such as wealth or claims to noble lineage, could cloak historical realities. In Galilee, it was the Herodian ruling class emanating from Sepphoris and Tiberias that was resented, but in Judaea, the aristocracy was supposed to share a common symbolic system with all the people, one which in theory meant that all shared in the fruits of Yahweh's land. Ostentatious wealth was, therefore, unacceptable; yet, as recent excavations in the Jewish quarter of the city clearly demonstrate, the Jerusalem priestly aristocracy lived a life of luxury, even when this required violent action in the villages in order to ensure that the offerings were paid to them rather than to the country priests (*AJ* 20.180–1, 20.206–7). The imbalance, then, between rich and poor that characterised all ancient economies was greatly exacerbated in this instance because in Judaea and Jerusalem it was directly at odds with the shared religious ethos emanating from the national saga, the Torah of Moses.

As a temple city, Jerusalem generated considerable revenue, both from gifts intended for the sanctuary and from services rendered to the many pilgrims (including non-Jews) who visited annually. Herod's refurbishment was a major boost, not just for the citizens of Jerusalem itself, but for Jews in the diaspora as well (*AJ* 16.62–5). Indications are that the number of pilgrims increased greatly in the first century (cf. Acts 2:9–13). The rebuilding project begun by Herod continued throughout the first century, and provided work for an estimated 20,000 men. In addition to the various ranks of cultic ministers

---

32 Fiensy, *Social history of Palestine*, 49–55.
33 Goodman, *Ruling class of Judaea*.

residing in or near Jerusalem, there were many different 'lay' functionaries
associated with the temple and its daily rituals, requiring thereby a variety
of specialisations: woodcutters, incense makers, market inspectors, money
changers, water carriers, providers of doves and other sacrificial animals and
the like. Many of these professions were looked down upon by the elites, due to
suspicion with regard to the observance of purity regulations, several featuring
in various lists of trades viewed as despicable in rabbinic literature.[34] This form
of social segregation meant that Jerusalem had more than the usual share of
urban poor. Thus, despite all its obvious advantages, the economy of Jerusalem
was out of balance. The wealth of the temple itself was non-productive, and
its benefits did not flow back into the country. Those who stood to gain most
from the temple system, the aristocratic priestly families, were its immediate
guardians who jealously sought to protect their privileged status (AJ 15.247–8).
In contravention of the biblical ideal that the tribe of Levi should have no share
in the land, the best plots in the Judaean countryside were in the hands of the
priests or their wealthy (Sadducean) supporters (BJ 6.115).[35] Yet, an attempt
was made to conceal this anomalous situation by claims of religious loyalty,
as is evident from Josephus' own posturing in Galilee, while freely admitting
that he owned lands adjacent to Jerusalem (Vit. 63.80, 63.348, 63.442).

It is not surprising, then, that the first century saw an increase in social
turmoil in the Judaean countryside: banditry, prophetic movements of protest
and various religious ideologies which can be directly related to prevailing
conditions. Thus the Essenes' practice of a common life in the Judaean desert
away from the city, as well as the Pharisees' espousal of a modest lifestyle (AJ
18.12 and 18.18) represent classic counter-cultural responses to the prevailing
aristocratic ethos, treating poverty as an ideal rather than shameful. A similar
stance seems to have been adopted by the Jesus movement both in its Galilean
and later, Jerusalem, forms, as we can infer from the earliest strata of the gospels
as well as from Acts of the Apostles (Acts 2:44–7, 4:32–5). However, it is in the
various revolutionary groups and their strategies that one can best judge the
resentment felt towards the native aristocracy. The refusal to pay the tribute,
the cessation of 'the loyal sacrifice' on behalf of Rome, the burning of the debt
records and the election by lot of a 'rude peasant' to replace the aristocratic
Ananus as high priest (BJ 2.404, 2.409, 2.427, 4.151) were all acts prompted
as much by resentment of the native aristocracy as by hatred of the Roman
presence.[36] The comment of Josephus on these events – himself a member

---

34 Jeremias, *Jerusalem*, 303–17.
35 Stern, 'Aspects of Jewish society'.
36 Goodman, *Ruling class of Judaea*, 152–97.

of this class – is revealing in terms of how his ilk viewed the developments: 'I should not be wrong in saying that the capture of the city began with the death of Ananus; and that the overthrow of the walls and the downfall of the Jewish state dated from the day on which the Jews beheld their high priest, the captain of their salvation, butchered in the heart of Jerusalem' (*BJ* 4.318).

Even when full account is taken of the rapid changes occurring in Judaean society throughout the first century, it still seems clear that the systemic causes of the breakdown, so graphically illustrated during the revolt, were already operative in the first procuratorial period (6–41 CE). To some extent these factors were the legacy of Herod the Great's domination of the religious institutions of Judaism for his own political ends. While he was able to contain any show of dissent by his strong-arm tactics, the reaction among the Jewish people upon his death and the subsequent failure of Archelaus to maintain order are clear indicators that Judaean society was already in turmoil in a way that Galilee was not.

This was the world in which Jesus grew up and which shaped his distinctive understanding of Israel's destiny and his own role in it. Within the broad contours of the gospels' portrayals and allowing for their later kerygmatic concerns, it is possible to discern two different though related strategies operating in the career of Jesus. In Galilee, he sought to address the social needs of the village culture, whose lifestyle and values were being eroded by the new level of Herodian involvement in the region as a result of Antipas' presence.[37] As a *Jewish* prophet, however, he had also to address the centre of his own religious tradition in Jerusalem, like other country prophets before and after him (Amos, Jeremiah and Jesus the son of Ananus, for example), whose unenviable task it was to proclaim judgement on the temple and the city.[38] Thus, in their separate ways, both the Synoptics and John have retained different, but plausible, aspects of a single career that spanned both Galilee and Jerusalem.

37 Freyne, 'Urban–rural relations in first-century Galilee'.
38 Freyne, *Galilee, Jesus and the gospels*, 224–39.

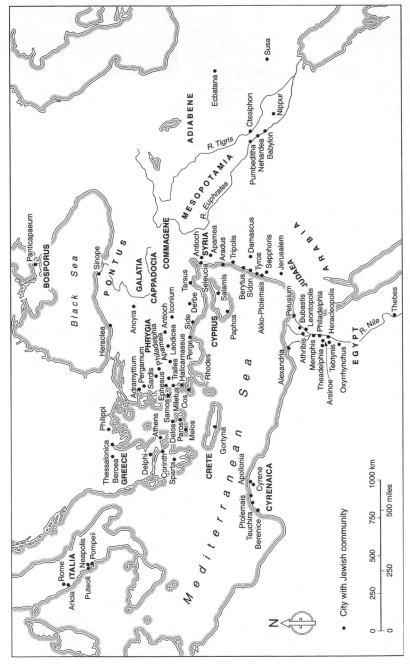

Map 3. Centres of Jewish population in the Herodian period

• City with Jewish community

N

0   250   500   750   1000 km
0   250   500   miles

2

The Jewish diaspora

TESSA RAJAK

Development and legacy

The era of the Second Temple in Jewish history, from the return from the Babylonian captivity in 538 BCE to the Roman sacking of Jerusalem in 70 CE, has aptly been described as the period of 'formative Judaism'. Many of the features and institutions of Judaism as we understand it took shape during this period. Among these developments, there can be no disputing the overwhelming historical importance of the diaspora, or dispersion – in other words, the adjustment to a division of the people between the homeland and communities elsewhere. After the disaster of 70, and even more after the Jewish exclusion from Jerusalem following the defeat of Bar Kochba's rebellion of 135 CE, the diaspora grew in significance. None the less, the rabbinic movement had its first major flowering in Judaea and the Galilee; thus the split existence continued.

The history of the diaspora is usually taken to begin in 587/6 BCE, when Nebuchadnezzar took the inhabitants of Jerusalem into captivity. When permitted to return by Cyrus the Persian king, many remained voluntarily in Babylonia. There, communities existed for centuries, saw periods of flowering, and produced, in late antiquity, the Babylonian Talmud, rabbinic learning's most important monument. That vast compendium is the repository also of much tradition from the land of Israel, but it was the product of diaspora-based academies. The spread of Jews in significant numbers around the Mediterranean, on the other hand, had followed Alexander the Great's conquest of the east, and was consolidated under Greek and then Roman sovereignty (see Map 3). The major literary products of Hellenistic Judaism – the Greek translation of the Hebrew Bible (the 'Septuagint' (LXX)) and the works of Philo and Josephus – have been largely embedded, until the modern period, in Christian culture, and they have survived through Christian transmission. Archaeology has yielded a sufficient number of tangible remains from this Mediterranean Jewish diaspora after the literary record comes to an end.

Ideology

Reflection upon the condition of exile evolved at the same time as the circumstances of life away from the homeland. The term 'diaspora' itself is a coinage of the Alexandrian Greek Torah translation, appearing first in Deuteronomy (28:25; 30:4–5). A derivation of the Greek root meaning 'to scatter', this rendering collects together a number of different Hebrew words, among them *galut*, 'exile', thereby creating a more coherent construction than had existed before. Dispersion, as in the Hebrew Bible, is a temporary condition of dislocation, to be surely followed by an ingathering (e.g. Ps 146; Isa 49:6; Esdras 11:9 = Neh 1:9; and especially the prayer in 2 Macc 1:27). At times, especially in the prophetic books, this is taken as a state of disgrace and interpreted as national punishment (e.g. Jer 41:12–22; Dan 12:2). But a more positive representation of the dispersal gains ground in Greek Jewish writing through the Hellenistic-Roman periods, expressed not only by the Alexandrian Philo but also by Josephus, a priest from Judaea, albeit writing in the diaspora after the fall of Jerusalem (*AJ* 4.115, 14.110).[1] The noun 'diaspora' in its specialised sense is absent from their vocabulary, though Josephus has the verbal form from the same root; these authors do not, in fact, make a sharp conceptual divide between Jews in the land of Israel and those everywhere else.[2] On the other hand, they contain ample reference to an existing or longed-for homeland, and Philo, though not Josephus, speaks of an eventual ingathering. This attachment was implicit in the standard appellation for a Jew, *ioudaios/a*, a person from Judaea.[3] It is summed up by Philo's much-quoted statement where, drawing on the Greek vocabulary of colony and mother-city, he asserts that the inherited place of residence was a Jew's *patris*, but Jerusalem their *metropolis* (*Flacc.* 46).[4]

Diaspora locations and populations

While Jewish communities were responsive to local circumstances, the interests and concerns of Palestine and the diaspora came together in various spheres of thought and action: the gap in outlook was essentially a matter of emphasis and balance. Moreover, in geographical terms, the boundaries between Judaea and Galilee on the one hand, and the diaspora on the other,

---

1 These constructions, with their rabbinic continuation, are discussed in Gafni, *Land, center and diaspora*, 19–78.
2 See Rajak, 'Josephus in the diaspora', 81–3.
3 See ch. 1, above.
4 Nuances explored by S. Pearce, 'Jerusalem as "mother-city" in the writings of Philo of Alexandria', in Barclay, *Negotiating diaspora*, 19–37.

were neither clearly defined nor fully definable. Graeco-Syrian cities in which Jews co-existed with pagans (and later with Christians) ringed the small Jewish territory, both on the coast and in the Decapolis, across the Jordan. Notable among them was Caesarea, the capital of the Roman province. Outside the major centres, rural Galilee too, as distinct from Judaea, was a mixed area. An expert on this region can thus quite reasonably ask whether living in Galilee was 'a form of Diaspora existence for a Jew'.[5] The question has, of course, no single or simple answer.

Major Jewish settlements were located in the cities of the Roman provinces of Asia (both coastal and inland Asia Minor), in Greece and in Egypt. There, the pre-Hellenistic Jewish military colonists on the island of Elephantine (at Aswan), established perhaps as early as the seventh century BCE, were joined by new military and civilian settlers in both towns and villages. A window onto the life of these communities is provided by a range of private and public documents preserved on papyrus.[6] The Alexandrian community was the most important in the Graeco-Roman diaspora. In spite of harassment and persecution, it maintained a vigorous life until damaged by the Jewish uprising in the reign of Trajan. This community stood out because of its numbers; its strong hinterland of smaller Jewish communities;[7] its visibility in the city (where there were two Jewish quarters out of the five divisions and Jews resided in other areas too); the size and splendour of its synagogue, which was still mentioned with awe in Talmudic literature (*t. Sukk.* 4.6; *y. Sukk.* 5.1.55a–b; *b. Sukk.* 51b); the high status of some members of its elite in both Hellenistic and Roman periods; and its creative Jewish Greek culture, which sprang from and built upon the Septuagint. We are fortunate in the survival of most of the output of its principal luminary, Philo, the first century CE exegete, philosopher and communal spokesman.[8]

In Rome, a Jewish community established before the mid-second century BCE was increased to number several thousands, not only by general immigration, but by subsequent waves of enslaved Jewish individuals.[9] Many of these were captured after the various wars in Palestine and were able to achieve citizenship within two generations through manumission in accordance with Roman law. Prosperity and elevated social status were undoubtedly harder to

5 See S. Freyne, 'Introduction: studying the Jewish diaspora in antiquity', in Bartlett, *Jews in the Hellenistic and Roman cities*, 1–5; see also ch. 1, above.
6 See Mélèze-Modrzejewski, *Jews of Egypt*. For the documents, see *CPJ*.
7 Detailed account in Kasher, *Jews in Hellenistic and Roman Egypt*.
8 For an introduction to Philo's copious and complex writings, see Schürer, *History*, vol. III. 2, 809–89.
9 See Leon and Osiek, *Jews of ancient Rome*; Rutgers, *Jews in late ancient Rome*.

achieve in the capital than in the provincial cities. The surviving epitaphs from the Roman Jewish catacombs, dating mainly from the third to fourth centuries CE, seem to suggest that the deceased and their relatives were for the most part people of quite modest means, who remained, with some exceptions, speakers of Greek rather than of Latin, in common with a large part of the Roman plebs. We find mention of eleven or twelve separate synagogues, and it is conceivable that there was an over-arching community structure.[10]

The extent of the Jewish diaspora in the Roman empire can be roughly but not precisely mapped, and there undoubtedly existed communities which have left no trace.[11] But Philo, in words attributed to a letter from the Herodian Agrippa I to the emperor Gaius (Caligula), gives a useful conspectus, which we may take to be as complete as the author could make it, since its purpose was to emphasise the extent of Jewish settlement:

> Egypt, Phoenicia, Coele-Syria and the rest of Syria too, through to the further inhabited lands – Pamphylia, Cilicia, most of Asia up to Bithynia and the corners of Pontus [the Black Sea area] – and likewise into Europe – Thessaly, Boeotia, Macedonia, Aetolia, Attica, Argos, Corinth and most of the finest parts of the Peloponnese . . . but also the best-regarded of the islands, Euboea, Cyprus, Crete. I say nothing of the countries beyond the Euphrates. (*Legat.* 281–4).

Philo omitted Italy, Rome (the setting for his text), as well as Cyrenaica and Carthage in North Africa. The area which was to become the Roman province of Arabia also contained Jews. Communities in Spain, Gaul and Germany are scarcely attested prior to late antiquity, although a few artefacts of earlier date associated with Judaism have been found here and there.

For snapshots of life in the Jewish diaspora, we draw upon individual episodes in Josephus' *Antiquitates judaicae* ('Jewish antiquities'), and the contro- versial accounts of Paul's dealings with successive synagogues and their leaders in the later chapters of Luke-Acts. The locations on which momentary light is shed by these two very different sources overlap surprisingly little. Thus, Jose- phus tells us nothing of the Jews of mainland Greece: had we depended entirely on his writing we would not have known of the existence of communities in Beroea or Philippi. On the other hand, an important centre and apparently a collecting point for the decrees on Jewish privileges cited by Josephus was Pergamum, well known both as a provincial capital and as one of the seven

---

10 Williams, 'Structure of the Jewish Community'.
11 Magisterial survey in Schürer, *History*, vol. III. 1, 1–86.

cities of Revelation (cf. Rev 2:12–17), yet not a place which fell within Paul's sphere.

When it comes to estimates of Jewish population sizes, the deficiencies in our evidence are even greater, and indeed an ancient historian who has recently addressed the problem argues persuasively that the attempt should simply be abandoned.[12] Philo's figure of one million for the Jews in Egypt may well be no more than a rhetorical flourish, and the startlingly high estimate of eight million Jews for the entire population of the Roman empire espoused by a few scholars[13] rests on dubious medieval evidence.

Jewish identity and religious practice in the diaspora

Jewish identities in the ancient Mediterranean varied widely, as might be expected. But it is possible still to speak of common features. The understanding of what was meant by a 'Jew' comprised, as in later ages, both ethnic and religious elements.

In the absence of a central authority, and across a long stretch of time and a wide range of localities subject to diverse regional influences, it might seem rash even to attempt a generalization about diaspora religious practice.[14] Nevertheless, we can cautiously address the question in terms of a customary minimum requirement for being a Jew. We can derive a modicum of information as to external appearances from the mocking observations of Greek and Roman writers on Jewish practices and conduct. Albeit dependent upon stereotype and hostile caricature, they do serve as some kind of report upon those practices that caught the attention of outsiders.[15] It is reasonable to suppose that, as a rule, diaspora Jews saw fit to aspire to the central practices prescribed by the Torah and carried out by the individual within the context of home and family. Male circumcision was the mark of the biblical covenant, and the chief defining mark of Jews to outsiders.[16] Sabbath observance was particularly puzzling to pagans, appearing as idleness and folly. Nonetheless, some Jews might seek and receive exemption from the military so as to avoid the need to fight on the sabbath, and Augustus excused them from court

12 B. McGing, 'Population and proselytism: how many Jews were there in the ancient world?', in Bartlett, *Jews in the Hellenistic and Roman cities*, 88–106.
13 E.g. Feldman, *Jew and Gentile*.
14 As argued by T. Kraabel, 'The Roman diaspora: six questionable assumptions' and 'Unity and diversity among diaspora synagogues', in Overman and MacLennan, *Diaspora Jews and Judaism*, 1–33.
15 Texts collected in Stern, *Greek and Latin authors*.
16 Cohen, *Beginnings of Jewishness*, 39–49; Isaac, *Invention of racism*, 472–4.

appearances on that day (Philo, *Legat.* 23; 158; Josephus, *AJ* 16.27); rearrangement of the grain distributions was another Jewish request. The almost certainly erroneous but quite common supposition among pagan writers that the sabbath was a fast day reveals at least that certain fasts, either fixed or supernumerary, were a part of Jewish observance. The three agricultural and pilgrim festivals (Passover, Sukkoth – Tabernacles, and Shavuot – the Feast of Weeks) expressed the connection of diaspora Jews with the land and asserted the significance of the temple. The Levitical dietary laws figure frequently in diaspora narratives, whose authors, no doubt in part with an exhortatory purpose, have the participants avoid prohibited foods or those prepared by Gentiles. In the Pauline literature, we are made aware of the aversion to sacrificial meat (1 Cor 8 and 10; cf. Acts 15:29; Rev 2:14). Purity through ablution was associated with prayer and, interestingly, in contrast with Palestine, handwashing is better attested than immersion in pools for effecting purification.[17] Intermarriages with unconverted Gentiles were not approved but no doubt occurred.[18]

Legal rulings made in Jerusalem may indeed sometimes have been sent abroad, but we may concur with the assumption that 'diaspora Jews were capable of interpreting the Bible, and that they did not sit, patiently waiting for the Houses of Hillel and Shammai to send them their disagreements'.[19] Even in the post-destruction era, the claims to authority of the developing rabbinic movement, with the code for living embodied, around 200 CE, in the Mishnah of Rabbi Judah Hanasi, are likely to have made few inroads in regions far from their Galilean seats, despite the impression given by all the stories that have come down to us of travelling rabbis.[20] Diaspora inscriptions do not mention rabbis before the fourth century CE.[21]

Erwin Goodenough, in a monumental study, sought to construct diaspora Judaism as an independent and highly distinctive religious system, highlighting Philonic allegory, the repertoire of characteristic visual symbols and their possible meanings and the thoroughgoing syncretism of the many magical papyri which have prominent Jewish elements. But the first of these components could hardly form the basis of belief for the ordinary person; the second was much over-interpreted by Goodenough; and the third represents a world of

---

17 Sanders, *Jewish law*, 260–72.
18 Goodman, 'Jewish proselytizing', 63–6; Barclay, *Negotiating diaspora*, 410–12.
19 Sanders, *Jewish law*, 256.
20 Main sources in Williams, *Jews among Greeks and Romans*, 81.
21 Cohen, 'Epigraphic rabbis'.

activity shared by Jews, pagans and Christians alike. Rather, 'common Judaism', as defined by E. P. Sanders, bound Palestine and diaspora together.[22] Until 70 CE, the expected allegiance to the temple and to Jerusalem was signalled by the two-drachma (half-shekel) temple tax, whose collection and shipment was permitted by the Romans, and also through pilgrimage, an act of piety which we happen to know Philo performed once in his life (*Prov.* fr. 2.64). The temple founded by the dissident Oniad high priests at Leontopolis in lower Egypt during the second century BCE had only a local importance, and it was presumably by way of intimidation and to eliminate any possible focus for the remnants of resistance that Vespasian had it closed in 73 CE, after the complete defeat of the revolt in Judaea (Josephus, *BJ* 7.433–5).

There are weak reflections in the diaspora of the striking religious diversity found in Second Temple Palestine. Philo talks in *De vita contemplativa* of the *therapeutai* of Lake Mareotis who led an ascetic communitarian existence comparable to that of the Essenes. The diaspora Jewish family of Saul of Tarsus might be taken as Pharisaic on the basis of the studies with Gamaliel ascribed to him (Acts 22:3). And the invective against the Pharisees in Matt 23:15 has been interpreted by Goodman[23] as referring to a specifically Pharisaic mission to the diaspora. The destruction of the Jerusalem temple probably led to the dispersal of surviving elements of the Sadducaean high priesthood. And, if the rebels of 66–73 can be regarded, following Josephus, as embodying a separate strand or 'philosophy' within Judaism, then we should mention here the information given by the historian concerning the transference of the activity of *sicarii* ('assassins') to Cyrenaica after the failure of the revolt (*BJ* 7.437–41). Another divergent tendency is represented by those allegorical interpreters of the Law who incurred Philo's strictures (*Migr.* 89) for proceeding then to disregard it.

The destruction of the temple undoubtedly lent momentum to the development of the synagogue as a source of local self-sufficiency, though it is hard to judge the pace of change. The Greek word itself means simply 'assembly' or 'association'. The synagogue came to be almost exclusively associated with the practice of Judaism, whether referring to the religious community or to its communal building. Apart from Torah reading, study, recitation and prayer, this became a key physical venue for charitable, social and political activity. Archaeologically, the fifteen or so excavated diaspora synagogues have been

---

22 Sanders, *Judaism: practice and belief*, 47–303; cf. Rutgers, *Jews in late ancient Rome*, 201–9.
23 Goodman, 'Jewish proselytizing', 61–2.

identifiable less by their design and layout, in which there was no uniformity, but rather by the presence of a small repertoire of specific symbols appearing as decorative features carved, incised or embedded in mosaic. Alongside the menorah, the most widespread and secure identifying marks of Judaism were symbols associated with the temple cult (shofar, incense shovel, ewer) and with the festival of Tabernacles (palm branches, citrons). A Torah shrine, or occasionally two shrines, can often be located. At Dura Europos, the rich sequence of third-century CE biblical illustrations leaves one in no doubt of the identity of the building's users, even in the absence of surviving parallels.[24] By contrast, the Stobi inscription sets out in detail the arrangements for turning over part of the private dwelling of Polycharmus to communal use. Assembly in private houses will have been far from unique.[25]

The Jewish community

Commitments from the ruling power to Jewish communities were by nature impermanent and subject to local pressures. Swings of the pendulum, following the typology of the new Pharaoh of Exodus and of the reversals of the Esther plot, are a favourite topic of diaspora writing.[26] But in the best circumstances, stability and the continuity of rooted communities could be achieved in the diaspora.

The Alexandrian community achieved a degree of legal autonomy in the age of Augustus, as noted even by an outsider, the Greek writer Strabo: 'an ethnarch stands over them, who administers the community and judges lawsuits and takes care of contracts, just as if he were the ruler of an independent polity' (quoted in Josephus, *AJ* 14.117). Occasionally, in relation to Egypt and also to the city of Berenice in Cyrenaica, the term *politeuma*, in the sense of a self-governing unit, makes an appearance.[27] Elsewhere, Jewish groups simply availed themselves of the administrative and social space within the city offered to associations, guilds and cultic societies of various kinds.[28] *Synagōgē* was

---

24 For all this material, see Hachlili, *Ancient Jewish art*.

25 For the evidence and interpretive issues involved in the history of synagogues, see Levine, *The ancient synagogue*; Fine, *Jews, Christians and polytheists*; Runesson, *Origins of the synagogue*; Olsson and Zetterholm, *The ancient synagogue*; Rajak, 'The ancient synagogue'.

26 Gruen, *Heritage and Hellenism*, analyses various such tales. For Josephus, see Rajak, 'Josephus and diaspora', 92–7.

27 Data from Egypt: Kasher, *Jews in Hellenistic and Roman Egypt*, 29–38, 208–11. Text from Berenice, Cyrenaica: Applebaum, *Jews and Greeks*, 167. On the recent reconstruction of a papyrological dossier from an Egyptian Jewish *politeuma*, see Honigman, 'The Jewish *politeuma* at Heracleopolis'. Smallwood, *Jews under Roman rule*, understood the term *politeuma* as a legal definition of status for diaspora Jewish communities.

28 Harland, *Associations, synagogues and congregations*.

but one term for such a collectivity. A marked fluidity in the terminology continued in Jewish circles, however, varying, as far as our evidence allows us to see, from place to place and group to group. Terms such as *synodos*, *syllogos*, *laos* (people) and the Latin *universitas* also occur, and some Jewish groups describe themselves in inscriptions simply as *hoi ioudaioi*, 'the Jews'. *Proseuchē*, 'prayer house' (literally 'prayer'), a term apparently coined in Ptolemaic Egypt and appearing in texts from as early as the third century BCE, is still found occasionally in the Roman period.[29]

The honorific titles for the leaders and post-holders of Jewish associations were also variable. Echoing the term by which the wider city described its magistrates, a Jewish community often had its own *archontes*. The synagogue head, *archisynagōgos*, continued through the period as a figure of great importance: the honorific and public role of this dignitary emerges from the inscriptions, where liturgical functions and associations are notably absent.[30] The striking presence of some women post-holders in synagogues again has a counterpart in the wider society, in the unusual prominence of independent women in the cities of Roman Asia Minor.[31]

Social and cultural identities: interaction with non-Jews

The continuity of Jewish communal existence in the diaspora was secured, as we have seen, by pragmatic stances, and, beyond this, by a sophisticated appreciation of the complexities of plural identities and of the possibilities and the limits of interaction. Accommodation to the environment and a level of integration into the wider society are observable as a general pattern.[32] Assimilation to the point where some Jewish individuals and groups merged into their environment and disappeared must have taken place on a considerable scale, but remains in the nature of things undocumented.

A fundamental determinant of cultural identity was the primary use of the Mediterranean lingua franca, Greek, as spoken and written language, not only in everyday usage, but also for religious purposes. The latter was made possible by the momentous decision, made probably as early as the mid-third century BCE, and quite probably – as the Letter of Aristeas would have it – under the auspices of an inquiring and cultured Ptolemy, to translate the 'Jewish Law'

---

29 For the variety, see Rajak, 'Synagogue and community'.
30 T. Rajak and D. Noy, in Rajak, *The Jewish dialogue*, 393–430.
31 Brooten, *Women leaders*, was a landmark study.
32 These phenomena are skilfully distinguished in Barclay, *Negotiating diaspora*.

into Greek. The foundation legend ascribes the work to scholars from Judaea. This was followed by the production of Greek versions of the other books of the Hebrew Bible, using variants of the same carefully forged and highly individual 'translation language' and spreading over several centuries and probably to locations outside Alexandria. Translation was an important branch of literary activity, as emerges from the preface to the Greek Ben Sira, where the author's grandson explains how and why, on arrival in Egypt, he laboured to translate his learned grandfather's book of wisdom and instruction. This demonstrates that esteem for Hebrew as holy tongue and national language persisted, and it presupposes a functioning bilingualism at least within a scholarly element of the diaspora population.

Yet this activity also demonstrates a high level of acculturation. The surviving evidence offers the rarest of glimpses as to how this expressed itself in terms of Jewish participation in the educational and cultural institutions of the *polis*. But from the literary legacy it emerges that Philo's immersion in Greek philosophy and literature had its counterpart among writers of lesser stature, such as the (anonymous) authors of the third and fourth books of Maccabees and of the Wisdom of Solomon (included within the Apocrypha), or the lost source summarised in 2 Maccabees and named there as Jason of Cyrene, or again, the pseudepigraphic writer known as pseudo-Hecataeus. Also revealing are the genres and style adopted by writers such as Demetrius the Chronographer, Aristobulus the philosopher (known as 'the peripatetic'), Philo the epic poet and Ezekiel the author of an Aeschylean tragedy on the Exodus. These are preserved in fragmentary form by Clement and Eusebius.[33]

Eschewing a picture of two world-views in opposition, expressed by those time-honoured abstractions, 'Hellenism' and 'Judaism', we do better to conceive of the culture of this diaspora as a complex interweaving of traditions, to produce, in the distinctive culture of Greek-speaking Judaism, a fabric in which the threads are no longer separable. At the same time, it is now widely accepted that a process of Hellenisation was integral to the development of Judaean society too, even if the extent, depth and significance of its impact continue to be contested.[34]

In the sphere of material culture, burial practices and funerary epigraphy shed light upon on the Jews' adaptation to their varied diaspora environments.

---

33 For this literature, see Schürer, *History*, vol. III. 2, 470–704; Collins, *Between Athens and Jerusalem*; Holladay, *Fragments*, vols. I–IV; Doran, 'Jewish Hellenistic historians'; Bar-Kochva, *Pseudo-Hecataeus*.

34 Hengel's *Judaism and Hellenism* continues to be debated; see, e.g. Collins and Sterling, *Hellenism in the land of Israel*.

Jews normally adopted the burial patterns and epitaph types used in the wider society.[35] The common artistic styles of tomb decoration were often adopted. Among the more remarkable of the Jewish tombs found in common burial grounds are those of the vast surviving necropolis of Hierapolis in Phrygia, which is still yielding new treasures. Within this general conformity, Jewish group identity was maintained by a range of subtle cultural markers. In a period where incineration was giving way to inhumation among pagans, Jews practised only inhumation. At Rome, this might be coupled with the distinctive practice of secondary burial of the bones in ossuaries, apparently following the practice prevalent in Jerusalem and its environs. The distinctive Jewish catacombs of Rome (such as the Vigna Randinini catacomb, or those under the Villa Torlonia) foreshadow the extensive Christian underground burial systems.[36] Here at least, the strictures against elaborate tombs advertised by Josephus (*Ap.* 2.205) appear to have been consciously regarded.

Epigraphy supplies evidence on participation in city life. The two thousand or so surviving Jewish inscriptions include short honorific texts in which, also, the Jews perhaps show a distinctive restraint.[37] From the first century CE, a text from Cyrenaica attests Jewish ephebes associated with the gymnasium. By the third century, Jewish town councillors (*bouleutai*) appear in Asia Minor. In assessing their significance, however, we should remember that they appear in a period when civic office was becoming burdensome to the old elites. Our finest evidence for this development is the famous inscription from Aphrodisias in Caria which, on one side of the pillar, lists the members of an association of Jews and proselytes, and, on the other, a group of God-fearers, including a number of town councillors; the dating of this text now seems, however, to be later than was first thought.[38] We can be sure that the holding of municipal office involved at least passive participation in pagan cultic practices, for these were inseparable from city ceremonial life and part of every civic activity.

Some non-Jews expressed support for the Jewish community by becoming benefactors. Julia Severa, builder of the 'house' where a synagogue was

---

35 van der Horst, *Ancient Jewish epitaphs*; Rutgers, *Jews in late ancient Rome*, 100–38.
36 Rajak, 'Reading the Jewish catacombs of Rome'; Rutgers, *Jews in late ancient Rome*, 50–67; see also pt IV, ch. 16 and pt VI, ch. 32, below.
37 The older work *CII* (ed.) Frey is still necessary. More recently, see Horbury and Noy, *Jewish inscriptions of Graeco-Roman Egypt*; Noy, *Jewish inscriptions of Western Europe*, vols. I and II; introduction in Williams, *Jews among the Greeks and Romans*; studies in van Henten and van der Horst, *Studies in early Jewish epigraphy*.
38 Reynolds and Tannenbaum, *Jews and God-fearers*; Chaniotis, 'The Jews of Aphrodisias'. Recent approaches to God-fearers are to be found in Levinskaya, *Book of Acts*, 51–82 and 117–26; and Lieu, 'Race of the Godfearers'.

established at Acmonia in Phrygia, was no less than a priestess of the imperial cult under Nero. The building was refurbished by three men bearing the
Roman *tria nomina*. Since such philanthropy was a two-way process, we may
conclude that some Jewish communities were groups to be reckoned with in
the civic context. The diaspora synagogue here emerges as an outward-looking
institution serving to foster engagement with the world outside.[39]

That there was a more permanent route by which outsiders could mark an
affiliation to the Jewish group which fell short of full membership is suggested
by the widespread use of the description 'God-fearer', found in variant forms,
either as *theosebeis* (literally 'godly pious' found in some inscriptions) or as
phoboumenoi or *sebomenoi ton theon* (literally 'fearers' or 'fearers of God', the
latter in the book of Acts[40] and other epigraphy), but surely referring, in both
cases, to sympathisers who had not undergone conversion. The interest of
such persons in Judaism may, again, have been determined as much by social
factors as by religious or spiritual inclination. Whether or not this appellation
declares that its holder belongs to a formal and universally recognised category
of affiliates to Jewish communities is a puzzle around which inconclusive
debate continues. It is at all events clear that Judaising was a highly visible
phenomenon, and one in which Josephus takes pride and pleasure. He claims
that every city in Syria had both its Jews and its Judaisers (*BJ* 2.462–3), and also
that a large number of the citizens of Antioch in Syria were attracted by Jewish
practices and incorporated 'in a way' into the body of the Jews (*BJ* 7.45). In
Damascus, men were concerned by the effect on their wives (*BJ* 2.560). Certain
regional groups of inscriptions, notably Lycian curse texts, show elements of
Judaism (or Christianity) so thoroughly mixed with the local pagan formulae
that it is not easy to say whether we should speak of conscious Judaising by those
who wrote them, of traces of Jewish influence or perhaps simply of a religious
mix whose exponents were not even aware of the Judaic elements in their
traditions. Worshippers of 'the Most High God', a designation used both for
the God of the Hebrews and for Zeus, include the authors of the manumission
inscriptions from the Crimean Bosphorus, where the manumitted slaves retain
residual obligations 'to the synagogue'.[41]

It would be simplistic to assume that the designations 'God-fearer' and
'Judaiser' always served to identify individuals travelling part of a difficult
road towards conversion but stopping short at a particular point. Rather, such

---

39 Rajak, in *Jewish dialogue*, 463–78.
40 E.g. Acts 13:43, 16:14, 17:4, 17:17, 18:7.
41 Mitchell, 'The cult of Theos Hypsistos'; Gibson, *Jewish manumission inscriptions*, 96–123;
   Levinskaya, *Book of Acts*, 83–116.

descriptions reflected the range and complexity of options and the multiplicity of overlapping identities in the religious 'market place' of the Roman city.[42] The word *prosēlytos*, another Septuagint coinage, is less ambiguous. Becoming a full Jew stood as a real option and, although converts seem rarely if ever during this period to have been actively sought by Jewish authorities, they were evidently not uncommon and often not unwelcome.[43] The royal dynasty of Adiabene, converted as the result of the activities of a trader-missionary, went on to associate itself with important donations to the temple and assistance to Jerusalem, as well as to support the revolutionaries of 66–73 CE. But for the most part, personal contact or the local visibility of the synagogue brought people to Judaism. Philo praises the courage of proselytes who abandoned everything to journey to 'a better home'.[44] Josephus writes that, of the many who joined, some 'lacked the necessary endurance and fell away again' (*Ap.* 2.123). It was not an easy route to take. But, whatever the numbers, this was a mainstream phenomenon. There is perhaps a paradox in the cultivation of such open boundaries by a group whose historic self-understanding fostered separation by choice.

Conflict with neighbours and with the ruling power

In spite of – or because of – Jewish acculturation, friction between Jews and their neighbours was not uncommon. Anti-Judaism in Hellenistic Alexandria took both literary and popular forms.[45] But it was the Roman annexation of Egypt that created serious antagonism between Jews and Greeks, undermining the status of both. Violence erupted in 38 CE, during the very short but provocative reign of Caligula: synagogues were burnt, shops looted, and the Jews herded into a ghetto and assaulted, with many killed. His successor, the emperor Claudius, investigated and issued a firm edict which restored the balance between the warring parties, but which still did not shrink from speaking of the Jews in Alexandria as inhabiting 'a city which was not their own', and of the trouble allegedly caused by Jewry as a 'general . . . disease'.[46] In 66 CE, the tensions in Palestine provoked Greek–Jewish violence in a number of Syrian cities. Roman handling of an ethno-religious dispute over the use of space in Caesarea was a trigger for the first Jewish revolt. The failure of this revolt led to

---

42 Cohen, *The beginnings of Jewishness*, 140–97.
43 As argued in Goodman, *Mission and conversion*.
44 Philo, *Spec.* 1.52; *Virt.* 102–8. Cohen, *The beginnings of Jewishness*, 157.
45 Schäfer, *Judaeophobia*.
46 *CPJ*, vol. II, 153.

further city conflict and more attacks on Jewish minorities in the cities around Palestine.

The Jews showed a lively awareness of the determining role of the ruling power on their fortunes and an appreciation of the vital importance of governmental support (whatever the kind of government). This is epitomized in the widely told story of how the Septuagint was translated at the enthusiastic command of king Ptolemy II Philadephus. A precedent was set by the decree of the Seleucid conqueror Antiochus III to protect the purity and sacred rights of the Jerusalem temple, with obvious significance for *ioudaioi*, wherever they were. Diplomacy, in which the members of the Herodian dynasty played a leading role, gained for Jewish communities in the Roman provinces the patronage successively of Julius Caesar, of Marcus Antonius and of Augustus. Synagogues were exempted by Julius Caesar from his ban on *collegia* ('associations'). In their disputes with their neighbours, communities were assisted by Roman pronouncements which upheld their right to observe their customary practices (*nomoi*) and required regular reiteration. Josephus' *Antiquitates judaicae* bears witness to the resolute and vigilant manner by which the edicts and decrees of senate, magistrates or governors of the Roman republican, triumviral and early imperial period supporting Jews in Greek cities were sought, generated, guarded and archived.[47] They were a source of pride as well as of practical assistance throughout the period. Christian authors were later to perceive Judaism as having legitimate status as, in Tertullian's words, a *religio licita* ('lawful religion') in the Roman empire, by contrast with the church (*Apol.* 21.1).

Yet, in reality, the history of the Jews under Rome was often deeply troubled. Three temporary expulsions of Jews from the city of Rome are recorded: the first as early as 139 BCE and the others under the emperors Tiberius and Claudius. These measures were consistently ascribed to Jewish proselytising activity and this, at least as a perception, exacerbated the general religious and social anxiety which induced sporadic Roman actions against eastern cults and against philosophers.[48] Only in the reign of Septimius Severus was conversion to Judaism officially forbidden.

The crushing of the revolt in 70–3 CE, celebrated by Rome's issue of the famous 'Judaea capta' coins, resulted in a degradation of the standing of Jews everywhere. Rebuilding of the temple was not permitted. The consequent diversion of the former temple tax to a new Roman *fiscus iudaicus* used to

---

47 Rajak in *The Jewish dialogue*, 301–34; Pucci Ben Zeev, *Jewish rights*; Gruen, *Diaspora*.
48 Isaac, 'Roman religious policy'.

rebuild the temple of Jupiter on the Capitoline in Rome, its extension to women and children, and its harsh exactions by the emperor Domitian in the early years, was a collective punishment. Domitian's successor, Nerva, announced in 97 CE some alleviation of the abuses, but the exaction continued into late antiquity.

In 115/16 CE, the Jews of the diaspora revolted in waves, against both their pagan neighbours and the Roman authorities, in Cyrenaica, in Egypt and in Cyprus (Cass. Dio 68.32; Euseb. *HE* 4.2.4; Oros. *Hist.* 7.12.6–7). The background was the aftermath of the revolt in Palestine, and there were perhaps messianic overtones. A little earlier than the main revolt (it seems), the Jews of Babylonia had become involved in the successful rebellion of Trajan's newly conquered Mesopotamian province. The Jewish uprisings were suppressed by Roman forces only with considerable effort. The Alexandrian community took many years to recover and some rural communities disappeared altogether. These uprisings were followed, very soon after Trajan's death, by a dramatic uprising in Palestine against his successor, Hadrian, under the leadership of Bar Kochba, 'prince of Israel', apparently supported by some rabbinic leaders. The historical record is poor, but if the emperor's prohibition on circumcision (whatever its purpose) was indeed the trigger for this last major outburst of resistance, as alleged by the *Historia Augusta* (Hadrian 14.2), then diaspora Jews will have been hit just as hard as the Jews of Palestine.[49] The ban was allegedly revoked by Antoninus Pius.[50] The diaspora will surely also have experienced the full misery of the aftermath, when the Roman colony of Aelia Capitolina rose on the ruins of Jerusalem and the cult of Jupiter Capitolinus was established on the temple site itself. Babatha, whose papers have been found in the Dead Sea cave where she presumably took refuge from the revolt and perished, was a diaspora Jewish woman who had been living among the Nabateans and owning land (and litigating) in the Roman province of Arabia.[51]

It was only after a century which must be rated as one of its low points that Jewish history perhaps entered, in the second half of the second century, a less turbulent era. To this era belong most of the excavated remains of diaspora synagogues and the inscriptions. In Sardis, a large-scale synagogue adjoining the city's main baths–gymnasium complex was probably a former civic build-ing, somehow acquired in the second or third century CE, and elaborately

---

49 The historicity of this ban is rejected by Oppenheimer, 'Ban on circumcision' and Abusch, 'Negotiating difference'; see ch. 3, below.
50 Linder, *Jews in Roman imperial legislation*, 99–102.
51 Texts in Lewis *et al.*, *Documents from the Bar Kochba period*; discussion in Kraemer, 'Typical and atypical family dynamics'.

refurbished more than once, right down to the sixth century. It has come, in modern interpretation, to stand as a symbol of Jewish integration into the life of a city which was a prominent centre of late paganism.[52] This may be allowed, provided we are aware of the ambiguity which symbols are capable of carrying. The physical record may give us a reassuring sense of harmonious integration and of the power of a community. At the same time the essence of diaspora circumstances lies in powerlessness more than in power and might always turn to acrimony. This was surely the lesson learnt by Mediterranean Jewry through the half millennium which we have surveyed of their existence in dispersion. The early Christian communities shared many of the same experiences; they brought to bear on them both old techniques and new.

52 General assessment in Rajak, *The Jewish dialogue*, 447–62.

3

The Roman empire

HANS-JOSEF KLAUCK

The *imperium romanum* and its subjects

The local and global impact of Roman power

The Roman empire forms the broader political, social and religious context for the emergence of early Christianity. Two developments are especially important for the situation we find in the first century CE. The first one, beginning perhaps in 229–228 BCE with the first Illyrian war, is the successive conquest of the eastern part of the Mediterranean world by the Romans, who were able to capitalise on the spread of Hellenism to all of Asia Minor, Persia and Egypt in the wake of Alexander and his successors, the *Diadochoi*. Then, in the second half of the first century BCE, the Roman republic was transformed into something new, retaining the name republic, but in fact now an autocracy of one man, who later took the eponymous title *Caesar* (*Kaisar* in Greek).

The beginnings: Caesar and Augustus. The path leading to Rome's imperial history was set by Gaius Julius Caesar, who was assassinated in 44 BCE by senators fearing that he was trying to become a new Roman king. His grand-nephew and adoptive son Octavian won the struggle for power with his decisive victory over Mark Antony at the battle of Actium in 31 BCE. Warned by Caesar's fate, Octavian avoided claiming for himself the title of king, but, owing largely to the military strengths of his legions which were strictly loyal to him, he now was without doubt Rome's most powerful individual. Through his discretion, political skill and long reign, he succeeded in establishing the principate as the new form of Roman government.

In 27 BCE, when he had formally declared Rome a republic again, the senate bestowed on him the title *Augustus*,[1] which means the 'venerated' or the 'revered one', with religious connotations. Religion played an important role in

---

1 Cf. his testamentary *Res gestae* 34.

the conceptualisation of the emperor's role (see below). The famous calendar decree of 9 BCE from Asia Minor calls the birthday of the divine emperor the beginning of 'the good news' (*euangelia*).[2]

The great achievement of Augustus in the eyes of his contemporaries that earned him these honours was the establishing of the *pax Augusta* (or *Romana*), an unprecedented time of peace, which meant primarily an end of the cruel civil wars and their repercussions throughout the whole empire. This peace had its price: wars were still fought to protect the frontiers; Roman legions, commanded by legates, were kept standing in the imperial provinces like Egypt and Syria (as opposed to the senatorial provinces where the senate nominated the proconsul); and, so, taxes had to be paid. Greek philosophers like Plutarch and Dio Chrysostom accepted the Roman domination, but at the same time also levelled veiled criticism against it.[3] But all this should not be used to deny the fact that the Roman peace was seen as a real improvement by many.[4]

The feeling that the task of ruling the Mediterranean world had fallen to the Romans is encapsulated in a 'prophecy' in Vergil's *Aeneid* (written at the time of Augustus). The ghost of his dead father Anchises tells Aeneas: 'Roman, remember: your arts will be to reign the nations with your power, to establish peace by law, to spare the conquered, but to battle to the end against the rebellious' (*Aen.* 6.851–3).

The next hundred years. Of the following hundred years, which were formative for the process which is called 'Romanisation' in modern scholarship,[5] we shall highlight only those events that are of structural importance or involve the earliest Christian groups. Since Augustus did not really create the formal position of an emperor (theoretically Rome remained a republic with the senate as governing body and two consuls as its spokesmen), the succession of a new *princeps* always proved to be a major weakness of the new system. Individual solutions had to be found in nearly every instance, beginning with Tiberius and Caligula.

Of special interest for us is Claudius, a nephew of Tiberius and Caligula's uncle. In religious matters, he favoured a conservative approach that stressed

2 *OGIS* 458.40–1; with an improved text, U. Laffi, 'Le iscrizioni'; see, too, Sherk, *Roman documents*, 328–37.
3 See Swain, *Hellenism and empire*, 135–241; see, too, Tac. *Ann.* 1.10.4: 'peace without doubt – but a cruel one'.
4 This has to be stressed against the overly critical perspective in Wengst, *Pax romana*, 7–54.
5 See Woolf, 'Romanisierung', 124.

the old Roman traditions, but he only intervened against other religious groups when he felt that they were disturbing the public order.[6] In his famous letter to Alexandria,[7] he did not grant citizenship to the Alexandrine Jews, but he gave them other privileges and protected them against insults and persecution by the Greek population. In Rome, on the other hand, where the Jews had become very numerous, he had already prohibited their gatherings in 41 CE (Cass. Dio 60.6.6), and in 49 CE he expelled from Rome a group of unruly Jewish subjects, perhaps community leaders and Jewish Christian missionaries, whose clash had created some disturbances.[8]

Under Nero in 64 CE, a devastating fire burned down several quarters of the city of Rome. Since Nero himself was thought to have ordered this act of arson (Suet. *Nero* 38.1–3),[9] he looked for another scapegoat and found the Roman Christians (see their unfavourable description in Tac. *Ann.* 15.44.2–4). This led to the first official persecution of Christians, which still was confined to Rome. There was no organised worldwide persecution of Christians under Domitian, despite what Eusebius says (*HE* 3.17). What we hear of in our sources (e.g. the death of the 'true witness' Antipas in Rev 2:13) are isolated actions of local authorities, especially in Asia Minor. Domitian's image, which was denigrated by senatorial historiography and early Christian polemic, has undergone a recent change.[10]

Around 111 CE, when Trajan reigned as emperor, Pliny the Younger was responsible for the provinces of Bithynia and Pontus in northern Asia Minor, and there he was confronted with accusations against Christians, too. Since no fixed procedure for handling their case seems to have been instituted yet, he wrote to Trajan to ask for advice. This letter and the emperor's reply 'are perhaps the most important non-Christian texts on Christianity during its first two centuries'.[11] Trajan's approach is a pragmatic one: Pliny doesn't have to search for Christians, and he shouldn't accept anonymous accusations. But if Christians, nevertheless, have been identified as such, they have to offer incense and libations to the Roman gods, or they must die. This is not completely

---

6 Cf. Alvarez Cineira, *Religionspolitik*, esp. 22–159.

7 *PLondon* 1912; *CPJ*, vol. II, 153.

8 Cf. Suet. *Claud.* 25.4: *Iudaeos impulsore Chresto assidue tumultuantis Roma expulit*. For a critical discussion of these two incidents, which are identified by several authors, see Alvarez Cineira, *Religionspolitik*, 194–210.

9 But Suetonius doesn't make the link to Nero's persecution of the Christians which he had mentioned already in *Nero* 16.2.

10 Cf. Urner, *Kaiser Domitian*, 321.

11 Novak, *Christianity and the Roman empire*, 47. An extended analysis of these letters may be found in Freudenberger, *Das Verhalten der römischen Behörden*.

logical, as Tertullian, a lawyer himself, clearly saw: *o sententiam necessitate confusam!* (*Apol.* 2.8). But by this procedure some moderation is shown by the Roman authorities.

Further perspectives. A frame had now been created, which, crises of all kinds and intensities not withstanding, proved elastic and firm enough to stabilise (see below) the Roman empire for the next two centuries. Struggle for leadership, often rather fierce, was finally decided by emperors coming exclusively from military ranks and by sharing power with co-regents. There were organised persecutions of Christians on a larger scale later on, under Decius (249–51), Valerian (253–60) and especially Diocletian (303–5),[12] but then Constantine (306–37) came and made Christianity his favourite form of religion (if for better or for worse, no one really knows).[13] During the whole of that period, Roman power and presence were felt throughout the Mediterranean world, east and west, though with regional varieties (we shall come back to the special example of Judaea below) and in different ways on different social levels. In the following sections, we shall discuss several religious, social, military and cultural aspects of this complex phenomenon.

The emperor cult. The predecessor of the Roman emperor cult[14] is the ruler cult in the Hellenistic empires of the *Diadochoi* which honoured the reigning king with forms of veneration formerly used only for the Olympian gods. In Rome the emperor was declared a god of the state by the senate only after his death, but that did not hinder people in the provinces, first in the east, but then gradually in the west, too, from presenting divine honours and titles to the living emperor. In Rome Augustus found the elegant solution that sacrifices and libations might not be brought to him, but to his *genius*, seen as the divine force inspiring and guarding his personality (which also shows a Roman penchant for making abstract ideas into gods (such as the goddesses Roma and Pax)). But there always remained a difference between what was allowed and accepted in the provinces (and here again with a slightly different emphasis in the east with its long tradition of ruler cult compared to the west) and what went on in Rome itself. Exceptions like Caligula, who tried to take over the role of the Olympian gods in the city itself, and – perhaps – Domitian (though the relevance of his title *dominus ac deus* is disputed)[15] prove the rule.

---

12 See pt VI, ch. 28, below.
13 See pt VI, ch. 30, below.
14 Of the abundant literature, cf. esp. Price, *Rituals and power*, and Clauss, *Kaiser und Gott*.
15 See now Boyle, 'Introduction', 17, and Newlands, 'The emperor's *saturnalia*', 515–16.

The emperor cult was not seen as an alternative to the inherited religions, but as a kind of superstructure which could be added onto the local cults. It functioned as a kind of institutional metonymy: it evoked the fact of Roman rule, gave an ideological foundation for it and furthered its social acceptability, at least for members of the leading classes to whom new and honourable careers as provincial priests of the emperor cult were offered.

Stabilising elements

Political and military structures. It is a surprising fact that the Romans were able to rule their huge empire with a rather small number of officials, drawn from the leading families. This was only possible because they left existing local structures basically intact and depended heavily on them. In the Greek cities, for example, the city council and the assembly still existed and had a say, and most judicial cases were decided by local courts. The institution of client kingship belongs to this policy, too.

Another stabilising factor was the Roman army.[16] The Romans had twenty to thirty legions under arms. Each legion, led by a legate of senatorial rank, ideally consisted of 5,000 to 5,500 men (the real numbers often were smaller), drawn from the free population of Italy (later from the provinces, too), organised in six cohorts led by tribunes, each cohort itself subdivided into ten groups of eighty to one hundred soldiers called a century and led by a centurion. The centurion of the first century of the first cohort was called *primipilus* – the highest rank that could be reached by a simple soldier. The legionaries were heavy infantry. They were supplemented by auxiliary forces taken from the local population and used as cavalry, light infantry and archers. Legionaries could expect to receive a grant of money and of land at their retirement. They sometimes settled in newly created 'colonies', like Philippi in Macedonia or Corinth in Greece.

Members of auxiliary forces could expect to receive Roman citizenship after twenty-five years of service. Roman citizenship, initially granted only to inhabitants of the city of Rome and later of all Italy, was more widely diffused under the emperors of the first and second centuries CE, conferring such privileges as the right to appeal to the emperor in criminal cases.

Transportation and communication. Legions had to be moved as quickly as possible to zones of conflict; the officials had to travel to their assigned posts

---

16 On the Roman army, see e.g. Campbell, *The Roman army*, or Roth, *The logistics of the Roman army*; a description of the legions at work may be found in Josephus, *BJ* 3.59–109, 5.39–70.

and, once in place, keep up contact with Rome. Hence, transportation and communication were of vital importance to the maintenance of the empire.[17] Consequently, the Romans developed their excellent road system and *cursus publicus*, a postal and courier system. Though designed for military and official purposes, the roads nevertheless facilitated travel and communication on a more general scale.

The main language spoken in the whole of the empire still was Greek, used even in Rome and Italy by some writers. Latin was the next most important language, used especially in imperial administration. But local languages, e.g. Aramaic in Judaea, Punic at Carthage and Lycian in Asia minor (cf. Acts 14.11), were still very much alive.

Graeco-Roman culture to a great extent still remained an oral one (or a semi-oral one, since orality already interacted smoothly with the written record). Reading was often (not always) done aloud and in a communal setting, and writing meant dictating to a scribe (cf. Rom 16:22). It is very difficult to estimate the level of literacy at this time, but one proposal which has found some following estimates it at ten per cent of the population, with up to thirty or even forty per cent (but only of the freeborn men) in a few cities and only five per cent in the Latin west.[18]

The social pyramid. The emperor was situated at the very top of the Roman social pyramid, the pinnacle of which was quite small indeed.[19] The ruling class consisted of approximately 600 families, the heads of which were members of the senate. Such families must have a net worth of one million sesterces. The equestrians, who had to possess 400,000 sesterces or more, followed. The members of the local aristocracy, each with property valued over 100,000 sesterces, were called *decuriones*. They held the municipal offices in the provinces. These groups, the so-called *honestiores*, 'noble ones', did not form much more than one per cent of the whole population of the Roman empire, which may have numbered some fifty or sixty million.[20] Whether or not there was a middle class to speak of, consisting, e.g. of artisans, salesmen, house owners and farmers, is disputed.[21] Most of the population had to work hard for a modest

---

17 Cf., Casson, *Travel in the ancient world*, esp. 163–96, and still Riepl, *Das Nachrichtenwesen des Altertums*.
18 This is the conclusion of Harris, *Ancient literacy*, 328–30.
19 Cf. Garnsey and Saller, *The Roman empire*; Alföldi, *Social history*, 94–156, esp. fig. 1 on p. 146. Rich source material is found in Shelton, *As the Romans did*.
20 Heichelheim, 'Bevölkerungswesen', 879.
21 Alföldy, *Social History*, 147: 'the prerequisites for an independent middle order did not exist'.

living or, especially in the city of Rome, were poor and dependent on public food distribution.

The bottom of the pyramid was formed by the slaves. In most modern estimates they made up one-third of the total population, at least in the cities.[22] Their conditions of living depended very much on the attitude of their owners. That led to a kind of 'slave pyramid', too, with slaves from Caesar's household at the top and industrial labourers and mine workers at the bottom. In the first century CE many slaves (though probably not most, as is sometimes said)[23] could expect that they would be freed at some time during their life, often when their owner died. The new supply of slaves constantly required came from children born to slave parents, infant exposure, conviction of criminals, victims of piracy, people selling themselves into debt slavery and, especially, prisoners of war.

Social relations. Cultural differences notwithstanding, the family and household, composed of husband, wife, children and slaves, remained a basic component of the fabric of social life in Roman times, too.[24] Roman law granted special privileges to the male head of the household (*pater familias*).[25] Family and house were major themes of social theory and admonition (see the household codes in the New Testament) and the basis for the creation of fictive kinship terminology (e.g. the emperor being called *pater patriae*).

A typical component of Roman social structure was the patronage system. This involved a personal, asymmetrical and continuous relationship between persons of unequal social standing, i.e. patron and client, with a reciprocal exchange of goods, material and immaterial (like *fides*, 'loyalty' or 'devotion', etc.).[26] There is no exact Greek equivalent to Roman patronage, but the Greek world knew a phenomenon that is now called 'euergetism' (from *euergetēs*, 'benefactor'), which was based on such exchanges as public honours for contributions to the public good (e.g. by inscriptions, by a crown, by a tomb and even by funeral games).[27]

Friendship is another important category, working both on political, private and metaphorical levels (see John 15:15, 19:12).[28] For the Greeks and even

---

22 See Harrill, *Manumission*, esp. 11–67; Bradley, *Slavery*; see also pt III, ch. 14, below.
23 Harrill, 'Slavery', 1126, calls this 'A common misunderstanding among some NT scholars'.
24 Cf. Rawson, *The family in ancient Rome*, esp. 1–57.
25 See pt III, ch. 14, below.
26 Saller, *Personal patronage*, 1.
27 See Veyne, *Le pain et le cirque*, and Danker, *Benefactor*.
28 Cf. Fitzgerald, *Greco-Roman perspectives*.

more for the Romans, friendship is not opposed to (reciprocal) utility, but includes it.

Voluntary associations, which began in Hellenistic times and still flourished in the *imperium romanum*, were an additional type of social grouping.[29] Associations formed around common trade, common nationality, a specific household or the cult of a deity. Typical features were the drawing up of statutes, often recorded on inscriptions, the paying of fees, the offering of sacrifices and the celebration of common meals. The provision for a proper burial was added later as a secondary function, but it shows that most of the associations consisted of members of the lower stratum of society. Therefore Roman authorities always regarded associations with some scepticism and tried to control them by strict regulations and prohibitions, as in Trajan's rejection of Pliny's quite sensible proposal to form a company (*collegium*) of firemen at Nicomedia.[30]

A special case: Judaea. How stabilising and disruptive elements, produced by the display of Roman presence and power, could go hand in hand, may be seen in the example of Judaea. Conquered by Pompey in 63 BCE, it was partly ruled by a series of client kings, from Herod the Great (37–4 BCE) through Herod Antipas (4 BCE–39 CE) and the other tetrarchs to (Herod) Agrippa I (37–44 CE) and Agrippa II (50[?]–92/93 CE).[31]

Though often called a 'province', Judaea was in fact in the first century CE neither a senatorial nor an imperial one, but belonged technically to the province of Syria, where a legate was stationed with two legions. But the unruly small country had its own Roman governors, usually of equestrian rank, who made Caesarea Maritima their headquarters and tried to keep peace and order with a small contingent of auxiliary troops. Their title first was *prefectus*, as in the case of the best known of them, Pontius Pilate,[32] and later, under Claudius, *procurator*, which is used anachronistically for Pilate too by Tacitus, when he speaks of those called *Chrestiani*: 'The founder of this name, Christ, had been put to death by sentence of the governor (*per procuratorem*) Pontius Pilate, when Tiberius reigned' (*Ann.* 15.44.3).

The very death of Jesus by crucifixion, a Roman capital punishment for slaves and non-Roman insurgents, demonstrates that the first century CE in Judaea was a time of unrest and conflict, too. One early crisis should be

29 Cf. e.g. van Nijf, *Civic world of professional associations*. See pt II, ch. 7 below.
30 Pliny *Ep.* 10.34. See now Harland, *Associations*.
31 See Braund, *Rome*, on the Herods, esp. 75–85, 108–12, 139–43; Millar, *The Roman near east*, 27–79.
32 The inscription of Caesarea Maritima, found in 1961, gives this correct title; cf. Lémonon, *Pilate*, 23–32 (a plausible new reconstruction is now proposed by Alföldy, 'Pontius Pilatus').

mentioned, namely Caligula's order to set up a huge golden statue of himself in the inner part of the temple at Jerusalem (Philo, *Legat.* 203), which might even have left traces in the Synoptic tradition (cf. Mark 13:14). The legate of Syria, P. Petronius, delayed the execution of his task. The Jewish king (Herod) Agrippa I, who lived at the Roman court for some time, tried to intervene.[33] But the nightmare only ended when officers of his guard finally assassinated Caligula in January 41.

These conflicts resulted in the Jewish war of 66–73 CE, which had deep repercussions also for Roman history. When, after Nero's death, Vespasian successfully competed for the position of the emperor, he commanded the Roman legions in Judaea and was just laying siege to Jerusalem. Titus, his oldest son and future successor, took over the command and conquered the city of Jerusalem, which was completely destroyed, the temple included.

Some decades later, Hadrian again had to fight an unusually fierce war in 132–5 CE against Simeon ben Kosiba (Bar Kochba), the leader of a Jewish rebellion in Judaea, which perhaps broke out because Hadrian re-founded Jerusalem as a pagan city named Aelia Capitolina and interdicted circumcision (which he contemptuously termed 'castration').[34] This war finally put an end to two centuries of rather convoluted interactions between Roman military power and Jewish striving for religious and political survival.

Roman culture and religion

In his aforementioned 'prophecy' on the worldwide reign of Rome, Anchises had also conceded: 'Others, I believe, will form the living bronze with softer lines, will create features of life from marble, will plead more forcefully their causes (in court), will describe the heaven's path with the rod and tell of the rising stars' (Verg. *Aen.* 6.847–50). Vergil, perhaps Rome's greatest poet, thereby admits that in art, science, rhetoric and, we may add, in philosophy and literature, the Greeks remained the leaders, and what Romans created in these fields usually started with imitation of some Greek paradigm.

Philosophy

This holds especially true for philosophy. Greek philosophy of the Hellenistic age,[35] which was divided into several currents (e.g. Platonic, Peripatetic, Stoic,

---

33 Cf. Schwartz, *Agrippa* I, 18–23, 77–89.
34 The main source is Cass. Dio 69.21.1–14.3; see Schürer, *History*, vol. I, 542–52; Millar, *The Roman near east*, 106–8, 372–4; cf. ch 2, above.
35 On philosophy in the imperial age in general cf. Reale, *Schools*.

Epicurean, Sceptic, Pythagorean), was appropriated by Roman thinkers and gradually introduced into Latin language and thought. This process found an early culmination in Cicero's extensive philosophical writings. Cicero himself preferred a sceptical academic position, but in his treatises, which often take the form of a dialogue, he has some of the speakers also quote Stoic and Epicurean teachings extensively.

Another channel for transmitting Greek philosophy and literature to the Romans was the presence of Greek teachers in Italy. A fine example is the Epicurean philosopher and poet Philodemus of Gadara (110–40 BCE), who lived in Piso's villa at Herculaneum, where papyrus remains of his library were found in the eighteenth century.[36] An Epicurean approach was also emphatically chosen by Lucretius (c.96/4–55 BCE) in his great poem *De rerum natura* ('On the nature of things').

But on the whole, Stoicism proved more congenial to the Romans, especially when concentrating on ethics.[37] In the first century CE, Seneca favoured an eclectic Stoicism in his collection of essays on several topics and his influential *Epistulae morales* ('Moral epistles') addressed to Lucilius.

Another Stoic philosopher who lived first as a slave at Rome is Epictetus (50–125 CE), a former student of the Roman Stoic Musonius Rufus, who wrote in Greek. Epictetus taught in Greek, too, and a selection of his lectures (*Dissertationes*) is preserved by his sometime pupil Arrian. In the second century CE, the Roman emperor and Stoic thinker Marcus Aurelius also preferred Greek for his personal notes called *Meditations* (*ta eis heauton* in Greek). But Stoicism also could become a last resort against political oppression and misuse of imperial power. This is evident in the Stoic opposition first to Nero (by Thrasea Paetus and Seneca) and then to Domitian, with the resultant banishment of philosophers (including Epictetus and Dio Chrysostom) from Rome in 89 or 92/3 CE.

Therefore, the old philosophical schools were still very much alive in the first to second centuries CE, though some had undergone considerable transformation. Because of their relevance for everyday life, Stoicism and Epicureanism seem to have been the more popular ones (cf. Acts 17:18). But the existence of Middle Platonism, which in the second and third century CE developed into the all-embracing synthesis of Neoplatonism, is testified to by the voluminous writings of Plutarch of Chaeronea (about 40–120 CE) and, not to be forgotten, by Philo of Alexandria. The rediscovery of the esoteric works of Aristotle in

---

36 For one of his works, see Philodemus, *On piety.*
37 See Colish, *Stoic tradition.*

the first century BCE gave a new impetus to the Peripatetics, too. Some philosophical orientations were more or less reinvented in the early imperial age, among them Cynicism and Pythagoreanism.[38]

The importance of Graeco-Roman philosophy for early Christianity can be seen especially in two areas: the question of god(s), later called 'theology', was treated only by philosophers, and philosophers felt responsible for 'pastoral care',[39] since *eudaimonia*, the well-being of the human person, was their declared aim. Philosophical theology included such diverse topics as cosmology, metaphysics, anthropology and ethics. Textual traditions (e.g. the Homeric epics) served as a main source for the philosopher's knowledge of the divine, and allegorical interpretation was the most important tool in deciphering these texts.[40]

Religion

Roman religion and syncretism. In Cicero's *De natura deorum* ('On the nature of the gods'), Cotta, himself *pontifex maximus* but at the same time the defender of a sceptical academic position in religious matters, utters the conviction that 'the Roman state would never have been able to rise to such height, if the immortal gods would not have been placated in the fullest measure' (*N.D.* 3.5). Placating the gods by carefully observing their rites and searching their will through signs, especially by *auspicium* (watching the flight and behaviour of birds), was the pillar of the Roman state religion, which was felt to be a central element of Roman identity. Its priestly offices, therefore, were entrusted only to state officials.[41]

For a rather long period, Rome proved more or less resistant to the importation of Greek and oriental forms of religion. Though the cults of the Great Mother (from Asia Minor), of Asclepius and of Isis were admitted to Rome in times of crisis, their temples remained exotic enclaves compared, for example, to the eighty-two temples of Roman divinities Augustus claims to have restored in Rome (*Res gestae* 20).

Distinctions were blurred mainly on the conceptual level by the *interpretatio graeca* of Roman religion, when the gods and goddesses of the Roman pantheon were equated with the Greek Olympian gods (Jupiter is Zeus, Juno is Hera, and so on) and overruled by them. This *interpretatio graeca*, which also

---

38 Cf. Reale, *Schools*, 145–63, 237–62.
39 See Malherbe, *Paul*; Glad, *Paul and Philodemus*.
40 See pt v, ch. 27, below.
41 On Roman religion, see the two volumes by Beard *et al.*, *Religions of Rome* (with extensive bibliographies).

involved other local religions like Egyptian (Isis is Athena, Osiris is Dionysos, etc.)[42] or Jewish (YHWH is Dionysos) cults,[43] is foundational for the so-called 'syncretism', that is, the mixture of originally different forms of religion in imperial times that resulted from a bi-directional reinterpretation of the traditional pantheons throughout the empire.

Options. In this context, religious options are best seen not as alternate but as embedded phenomena, which means that they could co-exist peacefully and might simply be added to form individual profiles of religious commitment. The main framework was still formed by the public and civic religion of city and state with its feasts, processions, sacrifices, meals and games (for the imperial cult, see above). Embedded in it was, for example, the domestic cult which reproduced some features of the public cult in the context of house and family and, in the case of the Romans, put an emphasis on the memory of the ancestors (*penates*). Also included were perhaps oracles and other forms of divination (by signs, portents and dreams), but later on astrology, too, which came more and more to the foreground. Another personal option was the mystery cults,[44] based on individual initiation. Their older types (e.g. Eleusis) were enriched now by the mysteries of Isis and Osiris[45] and, since the end of the first century CE, by the mysteries of the Persian god Mithras, which proved especially popular with the Roman army.

A peculiar personal option was magic, which can be understood as religion gone underground and ostracised socially, at least in the eyes of some.[46] There were Roman laws against the practice of magic, and these were enacted from time to time against magicians (as well as astrologers and soothsayers). But there was a secure market for magic, too, and some of the collections of texts used for professional purposes have even survived (as the *Greek magical papyri*).[47] Especially here the impact of the east is felt, since the best magicians were thought to come from oriental countries like Egypt and Babylonia (even if this reputation is partly based on a misunderstanding of indigenous oriental religions which simply seemed enigmatic to Greek and Roman visitors).

---

42 See Plut. *De Is. et Os.* 354C, 362B, etc.; a long list of these equations is given in Griffiths (ed.), *De Iside et Osiride*, 572–8.
43 See Plut. *Quaest. conv.* 4.6.1–2.
44 See Burkert, *Cults*, 4: 'They appear as varying forms, trends, or options within the one disparate yet continuous conglomerate of ancient religion.'
45 See Apul. *Met.* 11.
46 The task of defining magic presents nearly insurmountable difficulties, but a good description is given by Graf, *Magic*.
47 Easy access to them is given by Betz, *Greek magical papyri*. For another kind of magical texts, indigenous to the western part of the empire, too, see Gager, *Curse tablets*.

Literature

'Literature' is a very broad category.[48] Taken to the extreme, it includes all written material except documentary inscriptions and papyri. There exists, for example, a considerable body of scholarly, scientific and professional literature, e.g. on medicine and pharmacology (see Dioscurides, *De materia medica*, 'Concerning medicinal materials'), on law, on grammar, lexicography and literary criticism (see Pseudo-Longinus, *De sublimitate*, 'On the sublime'), on astronomy or astrology (Manilius), on architecture (Vitruvius) and geography (Strabo), but also on farming (Columella) and cooking (Apicius). The letter form, which had been brought to unusual heights already by Cicero, developed into its own literary genre with Ovid's *Heroides* and with the pseudonymous letter collections.[49] Aesop's fables were put into Latin verse by Phaedrus, a freedman of Augustus.

If we stick instead to the more classical concept of literature, i.e. epic, poetry and drama, we have to note immediately that the Augustan period was the golden age of Latin literature. Vergil with his *Aeneid* created the national epic of the Romans; Horace excelled in the genre of satire; Ovid wrote his *Metamorphoses*, to name only a few of their works, and on the field of elegy they were joined by Tibullus and Propertius. Compared to that, the time from Tiberius to Hadrian is often seen as the silver age of Latin literature. Of these authors, we mention only Lucan, Seneca's nephew, with his epic *Pharsalia* on the civic war, the new masters of satire, Persius and Juvenal, and Martial, who excelled in the miniature genre of the epigram.

The first century CE also saw the emergence of a new genre of which contemporary literary criticism took no note at all: the Graeco-Roman novel.[50] A surprisingly original and early example of the novelistic genre was produced in Latin by Petronius, who died in 66 CE. Unfortunately only fragments of his *Satyrica* have survived.

Education and rhetoric

The Greek educational curriculum (*paideia*) included a long tradition of instruction in the arts of rhetoric (i.e. modes of oral communication, especially in law courts, assemblies and festival crowds) at least since Plato, Aristotle and

---

48 On the Greek and Latin literature of this time, see Dihle, *Greek and Latin literature*, 62–212; on Latin literature, Albrecht, *History*, 639–1277.
49 Cf. Rosenmeyer, *Ancient epistolary fictions*, 193–233.
50 See the collection by Reardon, *Collected ancient Greek novels*.

the sophists.[51] A representative of this important branch of Greek knowledge in the first century CE is Dio Chrysostom (i.e. the 'golden mouth'), whose eighty speeches, mostly deliberative (counsel to assemblies), but partly also epideictic (festive praise) and apologetic (defence in court), give a vivid picture of civic life in the eastern part of the empire.

The Romans developed a natural affinity with the Hellenistic rhetorical tradition. The anonymous *Rhetorica ad Herennium*, written in Latin in the first century BCE, clearly enumerates the five tasks of the orator: invention, arrangement, style, memory and delivery. Cicero, himself the greatest orator of all speakers of Latin, composed seven treatises on rhetorical matters. Tacitus, perhaps the most reliable of the Roman historians, also wrote an insightful and perceptive *Dialogus de oratoribus* ('Dialogue on oratory'). It is therefore not by chance that it was a Latin writer, Quintilian (*c.*35–95/6 CE), who by his voluminous compendium with the title *Institutio oratoria* ('Education of the orator') created the canonical handbook of rhetoric for centuries to come.

Art and architecture

The first and second century CE also saw the acme of Roman art and architecture[52] which had developed through a blending of Etruscan and Italian with Greek and Hellenistic elements and which then was diffused from the capital through the cities of the empire where it interacted with local traditions. The Julio-Claudian age specifically is characterised by a new classicism,[53] i.e. an emphasis on the great Greek models.

In sculpture, the Romans showed a specific interest in the portraiture of living personalities, creating canonical models from which copies were to be made, as, e.g. for the representation of the reigning emperor.[54] The magnificence of Roman painting is revealed by extant murals in Nero's *domus aurea* ('golden house') in Rome, in the Villa of the Mysteries on the outskirts of Pompeii, and that at Boscoreale next to Pompeii. Often mosaics on floors and walls recreate paintings that are otherwise lost, but also present on their own an art form brought to perfection. This also holds true for the emblematic reliefs on sarcophagi with scenes from mythology, agriculture and the life of the dead.

At Rome, Augustus began a widespread building programme which was continued by his successors. One of his most inspired creations is the *ara pacis*

---

51 For Hellenistic and Roman times, see the selection of articles in Porter, *Handbook of Classical rhetoric.*

52 See Pollitt in Boardman, *Oxford history of classical art*, 217–95.

53 Torelli, 'Roman art', 930–1.

54 See Zanker, *Power of images*, 79–100.

('altar of peace'),[55] completed in 9 BCE. The Flavians built the huge amphitheatre called the Colosseum.[56] Trajan's building activity is best known from the forum bearing his name. There the column of Trajan also found its place; on a spiral-like frieze of 200 m length, it describes the emperor's Dacian wars.[57] On the site of Agrippa's Pantheon, destroyed by fire, Hadrian had constructed a new Pantheon, a temple with an unusual circular form for the main hall and a dome with a central opening designed to bring heaven down to the temple. Similar building projects were executed not only at Rome, but on an empire-wide scale. They helped to promote Roman imperial ideology throughout the Mediterranean world.

We can mention only in passing smaller forms like pottery, jewellery, glass and metal ware, coins and other objects of everyday use.[58] In literature, works of art were represented by the technique of *ekphrasis*, 'description' (see the opening scenes of the novels of Achilles Tatius and Longus). By art and archi-tecture, i.e. by visual communication, a kind of omnipresence of religious and political themes was produced in the public space that contributed to the establishment of a 'force field' of the Roman empire, both in Rome and in the provinces, i.e. the milieu inhabited by the earliest Christians.[59]

55 Torelli, 'Roman art', 943.
56 Cf. Colledge, 'Art and architecture', 968.
57 Coarelli, *Column of Trajan*; on the importance of these wars, see Strobel, *Untersuchungen zu den Dakerkriegen Trajans*.
58 See pt VI, ch. 32, below; for the whole subject, cf. Elsner, *Art and The Roman viewer*, and his *Imperial Rome*.
59 See Friesen, *Twice Neokoros* and Radt, *Pergamon*, esp. 209–54.

PART II

*

THE JESUS MOVEMENTS

Figure 2. Santa Pudenziana (Rome) altar mosaic, Church of Gentiles, Church of Circumcision (photo: Margaret M. Mitchell)

4

Jewish Christianity

JOEL MARCUS

Jesus and the earliest church

To some readers, the title of this chapter may seem like a contradiction in terms, since 'Judaism' and 'Christianity' are generally perceived to be opposites. But 'from the beginning it was not so' (Matt 19:8); Jesus and his first disciples were Jews, and for several centuries after his death Christians of Jewish origin were a significant presence both inside and outside of the land of his birth.

His own legacy, to be sure, was ambiguous; he was remembered, for example, as having claimed that it was not what entered people's mouths that defiled them but what came out of their mouths (Mark 7:15; Matt 15:11; Gos. Thom. 14). If taken literally, this principle would suggest that foods have no power to defile, a conclusion flatly contradicting the Old Testament kosher regulations (Lev 11). It has been argued, however, that Jesus' saying employs a Semitic idiom in which 'not this but that' actually means 'not so much this as that'.[1] Although Mark 7:19 interprets the saying as an assertion that all foods may be consumed, that is Mark's exegesis not Jesus', and it is omitted in the Matthean parallel (Matt 15:17).[2] If Jesus had made an unambiguous statement abrogating the Old Testament kosher laws, these scholars say, those within the later church who claimed that Christians were free to eat anything probably would have invoked it to end discussion – but they did not. Similarly, the early church struggled over the question of whether or not male converts from Gentile backgrounds needed to be circumcised, as the Jewish Law, the Torah, required of Israelite males (Gen 17:9–14; Lev 12:3). But in the records of these debates within the New Testament, no one ever invokes a saying of Jesus on this disputed subject – presumably because he never made one. The issue had not come up because Jesus' followers were Jews, his mission was to Israel, and he simply took circumcision for granted.

---

1 Westerholm, *Jesus and scribal authority*, 83.
2 On the ambiguity of Mark 7:15, see Dunn, 'Jesus and ritual purity'.

After his death and resurrection, however, things began to change. The book of Acts, to be sure, is no doubt historical in portraying the earliest Christians as addressing only their fellow Jews and experiencing the extension of the mission to Gentiles as a divine surprise (cf. the stories of the Ethiopian eunuch and of Cornelius in Acts 8 and 10). But as these fellow Jews came, for the most part, to reject the Christian message, while Gentiles proved astonishingly receptive to it, a problem surfaced that had not arisen before – did Gentile believers in Jesus need to convert to Judaism? Different Christians developed different answers to this question, and various factions emerged, distinguished above all by their attitudes towards the Law, as encapsulated in the title of Raymond Brown's article: 'Not Jewish Christianity and Gentile Christianity, but types of Jewish/Gentile Christianity'.[3] Some Jews who had embraced Jesus insisted on full observance of the Mosaic Law by those who claimed to be followers of the Jewish Messiah, Jesus. Gentiles who converted under their influence took 'the yoke of the Torah' upon themselves and thus for all practical purposes became Jewish. Other Jews who believed in Jesus, such as Paul, thought that the Mosaic Law as commandment essentially belonged to the old regime that had now been swept aside by Jesus' death and resurrection (Gal 3:13, 23–5; Rom 10:4). Gentiles who converted under *their* influence were not required to make any gesture towards Old Testament requirements such as food laws, circumcision and sabbath observance. In between were leaders and Gentile converts with intermediate stances, such as that *some* of the Law, but not all of it, was binding on Christians (cf. Acts 15:19–21; contrast Gal 5:3; Jas 2:10–11).

Definition

But which of these groups should be termed 'Jewish Christian'? Study of ancient Jewish Christianity is, indeed, bedevilled by the problem of definition, especially of the adjective 'Jewish'.[4] In modern discourse, Jewishness has both an ethnic and a religious component, and the exact weight to be accorded to each in the definition of the term is a matter of dispute – as witness contemporary intra-Jewish debates on the 'who is a Jew' question.[5] Both a one-sidedly ethnic approach and a one-sidedly religious approach raise questions. If 'Jew' is defined ethnically, is the idea of conversion to Judaism – which most Jews through the centuries have accepted – excluded from the outset? If, on the

---

3 Brown, 'Types of Jewish/Gentile Christianity'.
4 On the definition of Jewish Christianity, see especially Carleton Paget, 'Jewish Christianity', as well as his 'Definition of the term "Jewish Christian/Jewish Christianity"'.
5 See Casey, *From Jewish prophet to Gentile God*, 11–22.

other hand, a 'religious' approach is taken, what exactly are the religious tests for Jewishness? With regard to the present subject, the picture is further complicated in that the terms 'Jewish Christian' and 'Jewish Christianity' are modern coinages, not appearing in ancient texts at all,[6] and that, in some ancient writings, 'Jews' are simply inhabitants of Judaea, irrespective of their religious commitments or ethnic origins.[7]

In the scholarship of the past three centuries or so, however, the terms 'Jewish Christian' and 'Jewish Christianity' have usually been reserved for the subset of ancient Christians who manifested a commitment to Jewish religious institutions, especially the Torah, and saw themselves as bound to fulfil its commandments literally. Some scholars even prefer to speak of such believers as 'Christian Jews' in order to underline the stress these believers in Jesus placed on the defining religious characteristic of Jews, observance of the Torah.[8] Under this definition, Paul and other Christians of Jewish ethnic origin who felt themselves to be released from ordinances such as circumcision, sabbath observance and kosher food laws would not be considered 'Jewish Christians'. This Torah- and praxis-centred definition of Jewish Christianity, which will be adopted in the present chapter, has the advantage of relative clarity and of accordance with the way in which most outsiders perceived Jews in antiquity – i.e. as people who *did* certain things.[9] It also corresponds to the persistent and usually negative attention given by the church fathers to groups of Christians who stubbornly insisted on observing the Jewish Law. This emphasis on Torah sometimes went along with a de-emphasis on the importance of Christology, but not always; as we shall see, Torah-observant Jewish Christians held a variety of christological positions.

To be sure, this Torah-centred definition has its problems, the greatest one being the question, as M. Simon put it, of the 'dose' of Torah observance required for a person to be deemed a *Jewish* Christian.[10] For example, what if a male Christian who was born a Gentile went to synagogue, celebrated some but not all Jewish holidays, observed some but not all Mosaic food regulations – but did not get circumcised? Did such 'God-fearers' qualify as

---

6 The closest approach is from Jerome, who speaks about people who want to be both Jews and Christians but end up as neither (*Ep.* 112.13). Significantly, modern scholarship disagrees, as attested by the fact that there is an article about Jewish Christianity both in the *Cambridge history of Judaism* (Carleton Paget, 'Jewish Christianity') and, here, in the *Cambridge history of Christianity*!

7 On the problems of defining Jewishness in antiquity, see Cohen, *Beginnings of Jewishness*.

8 See e.g. Sim, *Gospel of Matthew and Christian Judaism*, 24–7.

9 See Carleton Paget, 'Jewish Christianity', 734; his assertion can be confirmed by study of the sources in Stern, *Greek and Latin authors on Jews and Judaism*.

10 M. Simon, 'Réflexions sur le judéo-christianisme', 56–7.

Jewish Christians?[11] Despite such grey areas, the Torah-centred approach seems superior to that championed by J. Daniélou, who considers *all* early Christianity to be 'Jewish Christianity', because the first few generations of Christians were so heavily influenced by the thought-patterns of Judaism.[12] At the same time, however, the sort of data Daniélou cites for the pervasiveness of Jewish Christian patterns of thought may actually be an indirect testimony to the influence of Jewish Christianity more narrowly conceived.

Our search for ancient Jewish Christianity must often proceed by such indirect routes because the direct evidence for the phenomenon is neither plentiful nor easy to interpret. This is largely because Torah-observant Jewish Christianity was eventually squeezed out between the ascendant Gentile church and developing rabbinic Judaism, both of which opposed it. More often than not, therefore, our scanty knowledge of it depends on the witness of its enemies (e.g. Paul, the church fathers, rabbinic traditions), a fact that makes deliberate or unintentional distortion inevitable.[13] Moreover, though we can sometimes be reasonably sure that an ancient author is describing or attacking a form of Jewish Christianity, in other instances it is uncertain whether the foil is a Jewish Christian or a non-Christian Jew (e.g. Eph 2:11–22; Col 2:8–23;1 Tim 1:6–11). In the rare cases where we have connected Jewish Christian sources, they have generally been incorporated into contexts that move their interpretation away from the Jewish particularism in which they arose;[14] nor is it always possible to be sure where a Jewish Christian source leaves off and a Gentile Christian redactor's work begins.

---

11 On the God-fearers, see Lieu, *Neither Jew nor Greek?*, 31–68, and pt III, ch. 10, below.

12 See Daniélou, *Theology of Jewish Christianity*.

13 Important sources for Jewish Christianity include (1) *texts arguably written by Jewish Christians*, such as Matt, John, Jas, Jude, Rev, *Did.* 1–6 or the whole, the putative sources within the Pseudo-Clementines (*Ep. Petr., Keryg. Pet., Asc. Jas.*), fragments of Jewish Christian gospels (*Gos. Naz., Gos. Naass., Gos. Eb., Gos. Heb.*); (2) *'historiographic accounts'* (e.g. Acts chs. 6–7; 15; 21:17–26; Josephus, *AJ* 18.63; 20.197–203; Euseb. *HE* 1.7.14; 2.23; 3.27.1–6; 5.8.10 5.17, etc.); (3) *theological description and response from opponents, both Christian* (e.g. Gal; Rom, esp. 14:1–15:13; Phil 3:2–7; Justin *Dial.* 16, 46–7, 110; 1 *Apol.* 31; Iren. *Haer.* 1.26.2; 3.11.7; 3.21.1; 5.1.3; Tert. *Carn. Chr.* 14, 18; *Praescr.* 32.3–5; 33.11; *Virg.* 6.1; Hipp. *Haer.* prol. 7.8; 7.34.1–2; 9.13.1–17.2; 10.22.1, 29.1–3; Or. *Hom. Luc.* 17; *Hom. Gen.* 3.5; *Comm. Mt.*, sermon 79; *C. Cels.* 2.1, 3; 5.61, 66; Euseb. *D.E.* 3.5; 7.1; Epiph. *Pan.* esp. bks 19, 28–31, 51; Jerome, *Ep.* 112.13, 16; 125.12.1; *Comm. Gal.* on 1.11–12; 3.13–14; 5.3; *Onom.* 112; *Comm. Habac.* on 3.10–13; *Comm. Mt.* on 12.2; *Comm. Am.* on 1.11–12; *Comm. Isa.* on 1.12; 5.18–19; 8.11–15, 19–22; 9.1; 31.6–9; 49.7; 52.4–6; *Comm. Ezech.* on 44.6–8; *Comm. Jer.* on 3.14–16; *Didasc. apost.* and *Apost. const.* passim), *and rabbinic* (e.g. *m. Sanh.* 4.5; *t. 'Avot* 13(14).5; *t. Hul.* 2.20–1; *t. Yad.* 2.13; *b. 'Abod. Zar.* 16b–17a, 26ab; 27b–28a; *b. Ber.* 28b–29a; *t. Avot.* 116ab; *b. Sanh.* 38b, 107ab; *b. Sukk.* 48b; *b. Git.* 45b; *b. Ta'an.* 27b; *Siphre Numbers* 143; *Genesis Rabbah* 8.9; 25.1; *Exodus Rabbah* 19.4).

14 The epistle of James, for example, becomes a less nomistic document by its inclusion in the same canon as Paul's letter to the Galatians, and the *Kerygmata Petrou* has been absorbed into the Pseudo-Clementines, which endorse the views of Gentile Christianity (see Jones, 'Pseudo-Clementines').

James and Peter

Despite such difficulties, something like a sketch of the history of Jewish Christianity in the first few Christian centuries may be attempted; and this attempt should begin with Jesus' brother James, the leader of the Torah-observant faction in the Jerusalem 'mother church' – the predominant faction in that church until its dispersal in the Jewish revolt of 66–73 CE, and perhaps even afterwards.[15] Sometimes called 'James the Just' because of his reputation for piety, this man, who was martyred in 62 CE, was remembered as a strict observer of the Torah who encouraged others to follow suit. His reputation for Torah observance and the memory of his martyrdom are linked in Josephus' report that the high priest Ananus executed him as a transgressor of the Law, but 'those of the inhabitants of the city who were considered the most fair-minded and were strict in observance of the Law were offended at this' (AJ 20.201). His enthusiasm for the Torah is also remembered in the New Testament (see e.g. Acts 21:20–1). Although Acts 15:13–21 and Gal 2:1–10 portray James as acquiescing to the decision of the 'Jerusalem council' that full observance of the Law should not be imposed on Gentile converts to Christianity, Galatians 2:11–14 suggests that he still regarded the Law as binding at least on Jewish Christians, since it portrays 'people from James' influencing the Jewish believers in Syrian Antioch to withdraw from table fellowship with Gentiles.

This image of James as an advocate of Christian Torah observance is reinforced in later canonical and non-canonical Christian works. The probably pseudonymous epistle of James, which is addressed to 'the twelve tribes in the diaspora' (1:1), has only positive things to say about the Torah, which is described in classically Jewish fashion as 'the perfect law of liberty' (Jas 1:25; cf. m. 'Abot 6.2). Indeed, so lofty are the epistle's claims for the saving function of the Law (cf. 1.21: 'the implanted word that is able to save your souls') that little room is left for the saving function of Jesus, who is mentioned only twice, and in an incidental way (1:1, 2:1).[16] James continues to be a model of Torah piety in the second–third century Jewish Christian sources embedded in the fourth-century Pseudo-Clementine literature. Not coincidentally, these same sources also highlight the position of Peter, so that two of the three 'pillars' of the

---

15 On James, see Painter, *Just James* and Bernheim, *James, brother of Jesus*. For the fragmentary evidence of the continued influence of the family of Jesus in the Jerusalem church and elsewhere in Palestine between the first revolt and the Bar Kochba revolt in 132–5, see Bauckham, *Jude and the relatives of Jesus*.

16 On James as a Jewish Christian document, see Marcus, 'James' and Allison, 'Fiction of James'. In the two references to Jesus, James calls him 'the Lord' and 'the Lord of glory' (1:1; 2:1), but this nomenclature does not necessarily imply divinity; see Laws, *Commentary on James*, 46–7.

earliest church (Gal 2:9) are depicted as strong advocates of Torah observance, whereas Paul is vilified.

This depiction of Peter probably to some degree reflects historical reality, since Paul in Galatians 2:11–14 describes him as following the lead of 'certain people from James' and withdrawing from table fellowship with Gentile Christians because of scruples related to the Law.[17] On the other hand, there may have been a certain ambiguity in Peter's position, since both the book of Acts (chs. 10–11 and 15:7–11) and the probably pseudonymous 1 Peter cast him in a Pauline light.[18] Paul's description of Petrine vacillation in Gal 2:11–14 suggests that both aspects of this depiction have some basis in reality, but we may suspect that he fell more towards the James side of the spectrum than the Pauline one.[19]

Jewish Christians encountered by Paul in his mission

James and Peter were important figureheads, but they themselves were only the tip of a huge Jewish Christian iceberg that is mostly invisible to us because of the eventual triumph of Gentile Christianity. Paul himself, in his battle against it, provides compelling evidence of its power, for example in his letter to the Galatian Christians. The latter had come under the influence of a group of Law-observant Christian missionaries who insisted that not only Jewish but also Gentile males must be circumcised and observe the Torah in order to become members in good standing of 'the Israel of God' (cf. Gal 6:16). These missionaries, whom Paul calls 'agitators' (Gal 1:7, 5:10), were probably part of a broadly based Law-observant Christian mission to Gentiles, against which Paul also battles in his letter to the Christians in Philippi, where he warns against 'dogs' who insist on 'mutilating the flesh', i.e. circumcision (Phil 3:2–3). He also attacks Christian missionaries of Jewish descent in

17 Exactly what those scruples were is not clear, since there is nothing in the Torah itself proscribing Jews from table fellowship with Gentiles. Common guesses include fear of contracting ritual impurity through casual contact with unclean Gentiles, apprehension that the food served might not be kosher, and anxiety that it might not have been properly tithed (see Sanders, 'Jewish association').

18 On Pauline theological elements in 1 Pet, see Achtemeier, *1 Peter*, 15–19.

19 One of the weaknesses of the great work of F. C. Baur, who first brought the term 'Jewish Christianity' to prominence, is that he does not recognize this Petrine ambiguity, but identifies Peter totally with the anti-Pauline, Torah-observant party in the 'battle royal between Jewish Christianity and Gentile Christianity' (Carleton Paget, 'Jewish Christianity,' 751) that for him constitutes the first two centuries of Christian history. For a review of Baur's major contribution to the study of Jewish Christianity, see Luedemann, *Opposition to Paul*, 1–7.

2 Corinthians, where he denounces 'superapostles' who boast in their status as 'Hebrews', 'Israelites' and 'seed of Abraham' (2 Cor 11:5, 22–3), though it is unclear whether or not these 'superapostles' insisted on circumcision and robust observance of the Torah and thus were 'Jewish Christians' according to our definition.[20]

Paul's attitude toward Jewish Christians, however, was not always so negative. Turning from Galatians to Romans, one is struck by the way in which sharp polemic against such people evaporates. In this letter Paul shows himself to be aware of the existence and influence of a faction within the Roman church that abstains from meat and observes certain holidays (Rom 14:1–15:13); many scholars think that this party, whom Paul calls the 'weak', are Jewish Christians who have become vegetarians because they can no longer obtain kosher meat.[21] But, in contrast to the fierce polemic of Galatians, Paul calls on the opposing party, 'the strong', who believe that they are free to eat anything, to put up with the 'weakness' of the 'weak', and elsewhere in the letter he shows himself extraordinarily sympathetic to Jewish concerns – even circumcision (3:1–2)! The different attitude here probably has something to do with the non-aggressive nature of the Jewish Christian community in Rome; they made up a minority of the Roman house churches, and they were not trying to impose their view of the Torah on the 'strong' – merely to be faithful to it themselves.

Frequently throughout his ministry, then, Paul encountered Law-observant Jewish Christians, sometimes of a zealous and proselytising sort, and much of his surviving correspondence is an attempt to refute their insistence that Christians need to observe the Law.

Later first-century evidence

James, Peter and Paul all died in the early sixties CE, and shortly thereafter, in 66, the Jews of Palestine began the revolt against the Romans that climaxed in disaster in 70 when the Romans burned the temple, destroyed Jerusalem, and effectively terminated Jewish sovereignty in the Holy Land until the twentieth

---

20 See the opposing positions of Georgi, *Opponents of Paul* and Barrett, *Essays on Paul*, 1–107.
21 See the contributions by Donfried and Watson in Donfried, *The Romans debate*; also Marcus, 'The circumcision and the uncircumcision in Rome'. Suetonius' statement (*Claud.* 25) that the Jews were expelled from Rome under Claudius (49 CE) because of disturbances over 'Chrestus' is often interpreted as a reference to tension between Jewish Christians and non-Christian Jews in Rome. After the Jews, including Jewish Christians, were allowed to return, the latter may no longer have had access to kosher butchers because of their estrangement from the rest of the Jewish community.

century. These dramatic changes produced a need, evident in the Christian literature written between the seventies and approximately the end of the century, to affirm theological continuity in the face of the death of the apostles, the changed political situation of the Jews and hardening Jewish attitudes toward Christianity. One of the primary responses of the Jewish Christians to this need was a redoubled emphasis on the Law. We have already noted, for example, the way in which the epistle of James, which was probably penned in this period, exalts the importance of the Torah even at the expense of Christology.

Not all Jewish Christians, however, thought that one had to choose between a high evaluation of the Torah and a high view of Jesus. The author of Matthew, for example, seems to combine a belief in Jesus' functional divinity (see e.g. 1:23, 28:16–20) with a typically Jewish veneration for the Law (Matt 5:17–20). We have observed, moreover, that Matthew omits the Markan note about Jesus declaring all foods pure. Other Matthean reinterpretations of Markan passages seem to move in a similar Torah-upholding direction; the sayings in 12:8 and 24:20, for example, are more sabbath-affirming than their Markan counterparts (Mark 2:27–8, 13:8). This tendency to tone down Jesus' clashes with the Law goes along with other indications that Matthew, most probably a Jew by birth, takes his heritage seriously; his genealogy of Jesus, for example, traces him back to Abraham, the first Jew (1:2), and the famous 'fulfilment citations' explicitly link events in Jesus' life with Old Testament scriptures (1:22–3, 2:15, 2:17–18, etc.). These Jewish elements, however, co-exist with sharp denunciations of the Pharisees, the party whose spiritual offspring became the leaders of post-70 CE Judaism, and even with a passage in which the author speaks of 'the Jews' as a foreign body hostile to Jesus (28:15). These seeming contradictions probably reflect the tension-filled existence of a Jewish Christian church that identified itself as the true Israel (cf. 21:43) while experiencing rejection and persecution from the leaders of the larger Jewish community in its locality.[22]

In addition to these relatively clear reflections of first-century Jewish Christianity in the Pauline correspondence, James and Matthew, New Testament exegetes have discerned other possible traces of the phenomenon. Regarding the Pauline sphere of influence, for example, the present author has argued both that Mark is a Pauline writing and that 7:18, 'Are you also without understanding?', suggests that some within his community are resisting the message of freedom from kosher regulations.[23] Jervell, similarly, contends that

---

22 See Overman, *Matthew's gospel*; Stanton, *Gospel for a new people*; Saldarini, *Matthew's Christian-Jewish community*; Sim, *Gospel of Matthew*, 24–7.
23 See Marcus, 'Mark – interpreter of Paul'; and Marcus, *Mark 1–8*, 458.

Luke-Acts, though written by a Gentile Christian, responds to the concerns of the 'mighty minority' of Jewish Christians within the first-century church, for example in the lengthy Lukan justification of the circumcision-free Gentile mission.[24] The long passage in the probably deutero-Pauline Ephesians 2:11–21, moreover, may be directed not only against non-Christian Jews who regard Gentiles as 'strangers to the covenants of promise', but also against Jewish Christians who hold similar opinions.[25] Jewish Christian opponents may also be reflected in another deutero-Pauline passage, Colossians 2:8–23, which emphasises that Christians are the true 'circumcision', and defends them against people who censure them on matters of food and drink, festivals, new moons and sabbaths.[26] The Pastoral Epistles certainly reflect some sort of tension with Jewish Christianity in their polemic against Christians who desire to be teachers of the Law (1 Tim 1:8–11; cf. Tit 3:9) and who, being 'of the circumcision', encourage attention to 'Jewish myths' (Tit 1:10, 14). As for Hebrews, its title suggests Christian addressees of Jewish background, and many exegetes think that this (later) title is in fact accurate and that the epistle is addressed to Jewish Christians tempted to 'fall back' into a theology whose starting-point is the Levitical Law rather than the Christ event (see 9:10; 13:9).[27]

Jewish Christianity was also a factor to be reckoned with outside the Pauline sphere of influence. Martyn, for example, has described 'the history of the Johannine community from its origin through the period of its life in which the Fourth Gospel was composed' as 'a chapter in the history of Jewish Christianity'.[28] In favour of this opinion, there is in the gospel no attack on ordinances such as the Levitical food laws and circumcision, and 7:22–3 seems to assume observance of the latter, using its acknowledged importance as the point of departure for Jesus' own practice of healing on the sabbath. On the other hand, the evangelist concludes an earlier sabbath controversy with the frank admission that Jesus 'broke the sabbath' (5:18) – an acknowledgement that creates some difficulties for the idea that his community was sabbath observant. It may be that the Johannine community, after an initial Torah-observant phase (reflected in 7:22–3), ended up being non-observant (as reflected in 5:18).[29]

24 See Jervell, *Luke and the people of God*; and Jervell, *Theology of Acts*.
25 See Käsemann, 'Epheserbrief', 517; and Marcus, 'The circumcision and the uncircumcision in Rome', 77–81.
26 See Shepherd, 'Gospel of John', 708.
27 See Lane, *Hebrews*, cxxv–cxxxv and index s.v. 'Paul'.
28 See Martyn, *Gospel of John*, 121. On Martyn's linkage of the Johannine situation with the *birkat hamminim* of the rabbis, see below, n. 55.
29 For attempts to reconstruct the history of the Johannine community, including changing attitudes towards the Torah, see Martyn, *Gospel of John*, as well as his *History and theology*; Brown, *Community of the beloved disciple*; de Boer, *Johannine perspectives*, 43–82.

Other exegetes have demonstrated points of contact between the eschatolog-
ically oriented New Testament works of Jude and Revelation on the one hand
and Jewish apocalypticism on the other, and some have taken these agree-
ments as evidence for a Jewish Christian provenance for these New Testament
works.[30] Revelation in particular, which attacks people who 'say that they are
Jews and are not' (2:9, 3:9), may do so in the name of the 'true Jews', i.e. the
Jewish Christians.[31]

Even if some of these suggestions of Jewish Christian provenance are not
totally secure, their cumulative effect is impressive: the vast majority of New
Testament writers feel the necessity of engaging the issues of Torah observance
and/or Jewish identity, and this compulsion probably reflects, among other
factors, the strong influence of Jewish Christianity in the New Testament era.

The continuing influence of Jewish Christianity

This influence continued as the first century gave way to the second, and
remained an important factor for some time thereafter. In Rome, *1 Clement*
and *The Shepherd of Hermas*, which are dated respectively to the end of the first
century and the beginning or middle of the second, both have markedly Jewish
traits, which are probably in part attributable to the continuing impact of Jewish
Christianity in the capital city.[32] Jewish Christianity continued to be influential
in Rome in the late second and early third century, as is demonstrated by
the works of Hippolytus and Novatian and the controversy about the date of
Easter.[33] Things were similar in the eastern part of the empire; the *Didache*, a late
first- or early second-century text that comes from Syria-Palestine or Egypt, is
probably either in part or in full the product of a Jewish Christian community.[34]
The continued vitality of Jewish Christianity across a wide geographical area
in the early to middle second century is also attested by the existence of three
Jewish Christian gospels, The *gospel of the twelve*, The *gospel of the Nazaraeans*,
and The *gospel of the Hebrews*, which probably originated during this period in
Transjordan, Syria and Egypt respectively.[35] Although the works themselves
have not survived, they are occasionally quoted by the church fathers, usually

---

30 On Jude, see Wolthuis, 'Jude and Jewish traditions'.
31 Cf. Shepherd, 'Gospel of John', 708 and Frankfurter, 'Jews or not?
32 See Brown and Meier, *Antioch and Rome*, 158–83, 211–16 and Lampe, *From Paul to Valentinus*,
75–6.
33 See Frend, *Rise of Christianity*, 340–3.
34 See Niederwimmer, *The Didache*, 1–54 and Draper, 'Torah and troublesome apostles'.
35 See Klijn, *Jewish-Christian gospel tradition*, 27–43.

in order to refute them; paradoxically, these refutations now provide our sole knowledge of the otherwise vanished documents.[36]

Other texts that criticise Jewish Christianity provide evidence for its continued importance. In Syria, for example, the early second-century *Gospel of Thomas* opposes the Jewish practices of prayer, fasting, almsgiving, dietary rules, circumcision and sabbath observance (sayings 6, 27, 14, 27, 53, 89, 104), apparently because some of *Thomas'* addressees remain bound to their Jewish past.[37] In Asia Minor, similarly, Ignatius of Antioch's early second-century letter to the Christians in Philadelphia grapples with the issue posed by Torah-observant Jewish Christianity, attacking people, apparently Christians, who 'propound Judaism' (6.1) and declare that they will accept no doctrine unless they find it clearly enunciated in the Old Testament 'charters' (8.1). Against these people, who are perhaps Gentile 'fellow travellers' with Jewish Christiantiy, Ignatius declares that he would rather hear Christianity from the circumcised than Judaism from the uncircumcised, and resoundingly affirms that for him the only 'charter' is Christ's cross, death and resurrection (8.2). Ignatius' statements reveal the fluidity of the boundary between Gentile and Jewish Christianity in the early second century,[38] and his denigration of Torah-centred Christians provides a glimpse into an influential Gentile bishop's uneasiness with a form of the faith too heavily indebted to Judaism and too little influenced by Christology.[39]

This late first- and early to middle second-century evidence for the vitality of Torah-observant Jewish Christianity coheres with the thesis of Walter Bauer's classic work, *Orthodoxy and heresy in earliest Christianity*, that in the early church the predominant form of Christianity was often one that would later be termed heretical.[40] Hence the picture in Acts and Eusebius' *Historia ecclesiastica* of an originally unitary Christian community later invaded by heresy is tendentious; 'heretical' views were widespread from the beginning, and in some areas predominated until the Roman emperor Constantine, following his conversion in 312 CE, began to give 'orthodox' bishops the authority to root out heresy. Bauer does not treat Jewish Christianity extensively, but in an appendix to a

---

36 As Carleton Paget, 'Jewish Christianity', 761 points out, however, Jerome, in his commentary on Isaiah, frequently cites the exegesis of the Nazareans as an authority, not just as an example of mistaken exegesis; cf. the translation and analysis in Pritz, *Nazarene Jewish Christianity*, 57–70.
37 See Marjanen, '*Thomas* and Jewish religious practices', esp. 180–2.
38 Cf. Strecker, 'On the problem of Jewish Christianity', 243.
39 See also the polemic against 'living according to Judaism' in Ign. *Magn.* 8.1, against 'talking of Jesus Christ and practising Judaism' in 10.3, and against observing the sabbath rather than the Lord's Day in 9.1.
40 Bauer, *Orthodoxy and heresy*.

later edition of his monograph Strecker fills this lacuna, focusing in particular on the *Kerygmata Petrou* ('Teachings of Peter') document, which comes from late second- or early third-century Greek-speaking Syria and is preserved in the Pseudo-Clementine *Homilies* and *Recognitions*. Strecker concludes that 'in the world from which the *Kerygmata* derives, Jewish Christianity was the sole representative of Christianity and the problem of its relationship to the 'Great Church' had not yet arisen'.[41]

Strecker's conclusion that Jewish Christianity dominated in the Syrian area that produced the Pseudo-Clementine sources is strengthened by the facts that Tatian's *Diatessaron*, a harmony of the gospels compiled in Syria (*c.*170 CE), appears to reflect the influence of the Jewish Christian gospels,[42] and that Syriac translations of Old Testament, apocryphal and pseudepigraphal books, as well as the biblical exegesis of the fourth-century Syriac writers Aphrahat and Ephrem, incorporate targumic and midrashic Jewish traditions.[43] Ter Haar Romeny, moreover, argues that only *Jewish* Christians would have had the linguistic expertise required to translate the Hebrew Old Testament into the Syriac of the Peshitta.[44] Rouwhorst, similarly, contends that the liturgical practices of the Syrian church in the first four or five centuries were heavily indebted to Judaism and that the conduit for this influence was Jewish Christianity.[45]

Jewish Christianity, however, was not limited to Syria. Justin Martyr, who was born in Samaria, sojourned in Ephesus in Asia Minor and eventually settled in Rome, describes different groups of Torah-observant Jewish Christians in his *Dialogus cum Tryphone Judaeo* (46–7), which was written in Rome about mid-second century and may reflect contacts with Jewish Christians in all three localities.[46] The continuing influence of Jewish Christianity in Asia Minor throughout the second century is attested by the Asian Christians' stubborn insistence on reckoning the date of Easter by Passover and perhaps by Montanism, a late second-century apocalyptic movement that may have originated as a Jewish Christian heresy.[47] As for Palestine, the homeland of Christianity, most of the Christians encountered in early rabbinic literature

41 Strecker, 'On the problem of Jewish Christianity', 271.
42 See Petersen, 'The Diatessaron of Tatian'. Epiphanius (*Pan.* 30.13.7) says that 'the Hebrew gospel' mentioned light at Jesus' baptism, a feature also found in the Diatessaron.
43 See Brock, 'Jewish traditions'.
44 Ter Haar Romeny, 'Hypotheses on the development of Judaism'.
45 Rouwhorst, 'Jewish liturgical traditions'.
46 See Pritz, *Nazarene Jewish Christianity*, 19–21 and Wilson, *Related strangers*, 258–84.
47 On the Quartodeciman controversy (so named from the Jewish celebration of Passover on the 14th of Nisan), see Wilson, *Related strangers*, 235–41. On Montanism, see Ford, 'Was Montanism a Jewish-Christian heresy?'.

appear to be Jewish, and they are important enough to be refuted in numerous passages.[48]

Bauer's general point about the diversity of pre-Constantinian Christianity, however, also applies to pre-Constantinian *Jewish* Christianity. We have already seen NT evidence that Christians of Jewish extraction differed from each other on the issue of the Law, and this debate continued into the second century, as is shown by Justin's *Dialogus cum Tryphone* (ch. 47). Pritz has argued that second- and third-century Torah-observant Jewish Christians also differed over Christology.[49] Some of them, who came to be known as 'Nazarenes', combined Torah observance with a high Christology, viewing Jesus as the Son of God who was born of a virgin. Others, who came to be known as 'Ebionites', combined Torah observance with a view of Jesus as a mere man born of Mary and Joseph. This distinction corresponds to the variation already observed in New Testament Jewish Christian thought – Matthew's Christology, for example, is high and pervasive, whereas James' is incidental.

The demise of Jewish Christianity

Despite the widespread presence of Torah-observant Jewish Christianity in the first several centuries of the Christian era, however, it was not to be the wave of the future, and it was weakened by several historical developments in the Jewish and Christian world. Of primary importance were the two Jewish insurrections against the Romans in Palestine (the great revolt of 66–73 CE and the Bar Kochba rebellion of 132–5) and the one in the diaspora (the revolt of 115–17, about which little is known). The first of these wars not only destroyed the temple, a unifying force for all Jews, including Jewish Christians, but it also devastated Jerusalem, the birthplace of Torah-observant Jewish Christianity.[50] The Jewish Christian 'mother church' seems to have removed from Jerusalem to Pella in the the Transjordan region before or near the beginning of this war, and this desertion of the spiritual centre of Judaism probably weakened the cause of the movement and was viewed by other Jews as traitorous.[51] It is also probable, as Alexander has argued, that the relatively greater success of the

---

48 For the sources, see Herford, *Christianity in Talmud and Midrash*; for analysis, see Alexander, 'The parting of the ways'.
49 Pritz, *Nazarene Jewish Christianity*.
50 See Bauckham, 'The parting of the ways'.
51 On the historicity of the tradition about the flight to Pella, see Koester, 'Origin and significance', and Carleton Paget, 'Jewish Christianity', 746–8; on the Jewish Christians' difficulties in coping with Jewish nationalism, see Alexander, 'The parting of the ways', 22–3.

church's mission to Gentiles made it 'increasingly difficult to establish itself in the eyes of Jews as a *Jewish* movement'.[52] The first revolt, moreover, may have been led by one or more Jewish messianic pretenders, as the second revolt certainly was (by Bar Kochba himself), and these messianic claims presented the Jewish Christians in Israel with a painful conflict of loyalties between identification with their native people and faithfulness to their Lord.[53]

In the aftermath of the first revolt, moreover, Jewish leadership in Palestine fell more and more into the hands of the rabbis, the successors to the Pharisees, a religious party with which Jesus had clashed in his lifetime.[54] Partly as a way of consolidating their power and pulling the shattered people together after the devastation of the war, the rabbis sought to define the parameters of acceptable Jewish thought and practice and even to codify their understanding in a portion of the standard daily prayer, the Eighteen Benedictions, that cursed the 'heretics' (*minim*). One version of this *birkat hamminim* = 'cursing (lit. "blessing") of the heretics' damns not only heretics in general but Christians in particular, and it is probable that, even if they were not specifically mentioned in its earliest form, they were its primary target (cf. Justin, *Dial.* 16 and 110, which speaks of Jews cursing Christians in the synagogues).[55] It is probable that one reason for this condemnation was the rabbinic perception that at least some of the Jewish Christians venerated Jesus as God and thus impugned monotheism – an issue that already arises in the disputes between the Johannine Jesus and 'the Jews' in John 5:18 and 8:57–9 (cf. later rabbinic disputes with 'two powers in heaven' heretics).[56]

For all these reasons, the outreach of Christian Jews to their co-religionists became less and less effective over time. They fared no better with Gentiles, for

---

52 Alexander, 'The parting of the ways', 23.
53 See Pritz, *Nazarene Jewish Christianity*, 109, and Marcus, 'The Jewish war'.
54 The extent of their control in the early centuries of the Christian era, however, is a matter of intense debate. If, as many recent scholars have emphasised (e.g. Schwartz, *Imperialism and Jewish society*), their hegemony was very limited until the Middle Ages, the effect of enactments such as the *birkat hamminim* (see below) may have been restricted; see Alexander, '"The parting of the ways"'.
55 See also Epiph. *Pan.* 29.9.1 and Jerome, *Comm. Am.* (on 1:11–12); *Comm. Isa.* (on 5:19 and 52:4–6). On the echoes of the *birkat hamminim*, or measures related to it, in John 9:22; 12:42; 16:2, and perhaps Luke 6:22, see Martyn, *History and theology*, 37–62. Some scholars have questioned that the *birkat hamminim* was directed against Christians; see e.g. Kimelman, '*Birkat hamminim* and the lack of evidence for an anti-Christian Jewish prayer in late antiquity'. Despite his title, however, Kimelman does acknowledge that the *birkat hamminim* 'was aimed at Jewish sectarians among whom Jewish Christians figured prominently' (232). For a cautious sifting of the issues with regard to the Johannine passages, which concludes that there is some relation to the *birkat hamminim*, see Smith, 'Contribution of J. Louis Martyn'. See also ch. 6 and pt III, ch. 10, below.
56 See Segal, *Two powers in heaven;* and Brown, *Community of the beloved disciple.*

they simply could not compete with the popular message of Christian thinkers such as Paul, Justin, Irenaeus (e.g. *Haer.* 4.1–34) and Tertullian (e.g. *Adv. Jud.*) that Gentile converts could enjoy all the benefits of membership in Israel without suffering the inconveniences associated with strict observance of the Law. As a result, the church became more and more Gentile in complexion, and the question arose as to how to deal with the increasingly marginalised Jewish Christian minority – the mirror image of the earliest church's dilemma about coping with the influx of Gentiles. Justin Martyr, for example, describes various kinds of Jewish Christian groups that continue to observe the regulations of the Torah, specifically circumcision, the sabbath, months and purifications (*Dial.* 46–7). Some, like Paul's Galatian opponents, try to persuade other Christians to observe the Law. Others, however, while personally observant, do not object to their fellow Christians remaining unobservant. Justin is prepared to put up with the latter group but not the former; he adds, however, that not all Gentile Christians are so tolerant.

A comparison of these passages from Justin with the evidence examined earlier from Acts and Paul's letters brings to light a striking change in tone. In Acts and some of the Pauline correspondence, readers encounter an aggressive Jewish Christianity centred in Jerusalem and influential throughout the Christian world, a self-confident movement against which Gentile Christianity has to defend its legitimacy. In Justin, on the other hand, they meet a self-assured Gentile Christianity dictating the terms under which Jewish Christianity may still be countenanced. Although Justin's presentation may reflect his desires as well as the reality in which he lives, and although, as noted above, Jewish Christianity was still dominant in his time in some parts of the Christian world, a shift in the balance of power had nevertheless occurred. It is not accidental that neither Irenaeus, the great refuter of heretics in the second century, nor Epiphanius, his counterpart in the fourth, devotes to Jewish Christians a fraction of the attention that he pays to Gnostics. Already by Justin's time the battle for the legitimacy of the Torah-free mission, while not over, was at least in the process of being won in most portions of the Christian world, and the question on the agenda would increasingly be whether any place might still be found for Torah-observant followers of Jesus. And the writing was already on the wall: the Great Church's answer would be 'no'.

What was lost through this 'no' to Jewish Christianity, which eventually turned 'Jew' and 'Christian' into antonyms in most people's minds? As Paul said in a related context, 'Much in every way' (Rom 3:2). The Gentile church forfeited its sense of a living connection with 'Israel according to the flesh' (1 Cor 10:18; cf. Rom 9:3–4) and began to think of Jews as 'those people' rather than 'us'. This way of thinking turned out to be a tragedy for the Jews; the question has even been raised whether the bloody history of ecclesiastical anti-Semitism, culminating in the Holocaust, would have been possible if there had continued to be a middle group that was recognisably Christian and recognisably Jewish at the same time.[57] But it was also a misfortune for the Gentile church, which lost Paul's appreciation for the way in which God's continuing faithfulness to the original chosen people – as evidenced, among other ways, by the existence of a substantial Jewish Christian 'remnant' – proves his unswerving commitment to humanity in general and bears witness to his redemptive purpose for the world.

57 Martyn, in private conversation; cf. Wyschogrod, 'Letter to a friend', 171.

5

Gentile Christianity

MARGARET M. MITCHELL

Definitions and designations

In the years after his death, the adherents of Jesus of Nazareth – a Galilean, Aramaic-speaking Jew – multiplied, but there was as yet no word 'Christianity'.[1] The telltale term in our sources refers not to the believers, but to their defining message: *to euangelion*, 'the good news'. In a letter written to 'the assemblies of Galatia', a figure of unmatched importance for what was to become 'Gentile Christianity' – a Jew named Paul – recounted a meeting in Jerusalem in the 40s between himself and other Christ-believing preachers to discuss the nature and provenance of their respective efforts. Paul reports that Peter and James and John (the 'so-called pillars' of the Jerusalem church), on the one hand, and himself and Barnabas and Titus, on the other, executed a formal agreement, sealed by handshake, that called for two distinct but equally divinely mandated and empowered missions. In calling them 'the gospel of the uncircumcision' and 'the gospel of the circumcision' (Gal 2:7–8), these early Christian missionaries appear to be plotting the new term *euangelion*, 'good news', onto a fixed dichotomy between Jews and Gentiles. But it was not so simple.

There were different sociological maps at work in the world of the first century, but all present themselves as an absolute polarity of 'us' versus 'them'. The Jewish world-view – which was the template for all early Christians – uses such biblical distinctions as 'Jews' versus 'the nations' (*ta ethnē* = 'Gentiles'), and 'circumcised' versus 'uncircumcised'.[2] The former is political terminology ('Jew' as 'Judaean,' a resident of Judaea),[3] which corresponds with the ancient assumption that one worships the gods in one's own location. For Jews it was

---

1 *Christianismos* is first found in Ignatius (*Rom.* 3.3; *Magn.* 10.1–3; *Phild.* 6.1). The adjective *Christianos* ('Christian') appears only in late New Testament documents, such as Acts 11:26; 26:28, and 1 Pet 4:16.
2 E.g. Lev 18:24; Deut 28:10; 29:23; Jud 14:3; Isa 52:1.
3 Cohen, *Beginnings*, 69–106.

also based in a theology of election, on the self-understanding that they are the nation – both people and land – God has chosen from among all the others (Deut 14:2; cf. Acts 15:14). Circumcision is a cultic marker of difference, rooted in God's covenant with the ancestor Abraham (Gen 17).[4] The covenant also prescribed a broad terrain of laws or norms for everyday life, such that 'living like a Jew' (*ioudaikōs zēn*) stands apart from 'living like a Gentile' (*ethnikōs zēn*) (Gal 2:14). The contrast between 'Jew' and 'Greek' can also denote the linguistic divide between the Hebrew and Greek tongues,[5] with 'Greek' also serving as a metonymy for the entire cultural and cultic difference between those who worship 'the God of Israel' and those whose world-view is circumscribed by the polytheistic pantheon of Greek religion and literature. From a Jewish monotheistic point of view, such 'idolatry' was traditionally associated with immorality,[6] thus setting up a rhetorically powerful moral boundary between the two groups.[7]

While these dichotomies seem firmly defined and absolutely opposed, life on the ground was messier. Not all 'Jews' were 'Judaeans,' but many lived in the diaspora, among non-Jews, and spoke Greek as their native language.[8] While circumcision would seem to be a non-negotiable distinction, it was not restricted to those born to Jewish parents and circumcised on the eighth day (adult proselytism was practised), nor was it irreversible, and, even more importantly, its significance in relation to these other identifying markers was a matter of dispute.[9] Further complicating that picture were individuals and whole groups who shared some, but not all, of these features, such as Samaritans (who worshipped the same one God, called themselves 'Hebrews', some in Palestine, but others in synagogues in places like Thessalonica), and 'God-fearers' (who were probably not a clearly defined group, but one term for a boundary status of Gentiles who participated in Jewish life in certain ways but not others, such as circumcision). Moreover, what it meant to 'live like a Jew' or live 'under the Law'[10] was the essential religious question – not just of

4 Abrahamic ancestry implies also 'race' through his 'seed'. The categories of race and ethnicity were as much matters of construction and debate in antiquity as today (see Buell and Hodge, 'Politics of interpretation').

5 Bilingualism in 'Hellenistic Judaism' obviously confounds this map. In Acts 6:1 Luke refers to 'Hellenists' and 'Hebrews' in the Jerusalem church. Estimates of the historicity of this account of the origins of the Gentile mission vary greatly (contrast e.g. Hengel, *Between Jesus and Paul*, 1–29, and Hill, *Hellenists and Hebrews*).

6 Num 25 (1 Cor 10:1–11); Hos 3–4; Wis 12–14; Rom 1:18–3.

7 On the Gentiles as 'sinners' see e.g. Isa 14:5; 1 Macc 1:34; Gal 2:15; cf. 1 Cor 6:9–11.

8 See pt I, ch. 2, above.

9 Fuller discussion in Hall, 'Circumcision', and Cohen, *Beginnings*.

10 Gal 2:14; 1 Cor 9:20.

Gentiles seeking admission on some terms – but of Jews themselves and their teachers who sought to comprehend, live and pass on the Law.[11]

Non-Jews did not think of themselves as 'Gentiles'. The standard classical mindset, which had been taken over by the Romans from the Greeks, plotted 'Greeks' (or 'Romans') against 'barbarians'. Such a polarity was itself territorial (the barbarians lived on the 'frontiers'), linguistic (the term barbarian is apparently onomatopoetic for the way foreign tongues sounded) and cultural, in that barbarians were seen as beyond the pale of 'civilisation', as defined by the *imperium Romanum*. From the Roman point of view Jews were barbarians from the east.[12] But a Jew like Paul could be culturally ambidextrous enough to think in such terms himself, and regard people living beyond Rome, such as in Spain, as barbarians (Rom 1:14). And even 'barbarian' was not a unified category, as the addition of the infamously uncivilised 'Scythians' alongside 'barbarians' in Col 3:11 shows (cf. Gal 3:28; 1 Cor 12:13).[13]

This complex cartography of self- and other-definition provides the backdrop and the vocabulary for the debates among earliest Christians about who could be included in the community, and on what terms. The Pauline 'apostolate to the Gentiles' had as its most fundamental task the reappraisal and renegotiation of these criteria of difference in order to substantiate its mandate to bring the gospel of Jesus to non-Jews who were (if we may combine these indices into a general composite overview) uncircumcised, spoke Greek, worshipped 'idols',[14] and lived outside the land of Judaea. In so doing Paul opened up a third category (if not yet the 'third race' of later patristic authors)[15] at the intersection of the bipolar map: 'Jews ask for signs, and Greeks seek wisdom, but we preach Christ crucified, a scandal to Jews and foolishness to Gentiles, but to *the very ones who are called, both Jews and Greeks*, Christ is the power of God and the wisdom of God' (1 Cor 1:22–4; cf. 10:22). The success of the mission to these 'called ones' among the Gentiles, which could hardly have been predicted during the life of Paul (let alone Jesus), by all indications was so great as to eclipse and far outrun the mission to Jews.[16]

---

11 Sanders, *Paul and Palestinian Judaism* and *Paul, the Law and the Jewish people* are the classic treatments.

12 Tacitly accepted by Justin, Tatian and others (see Lightfoot, *Colossians and Philemon*, 216–19).

13 Lightfoot, *Colossians and Philemon*, 218–19. Epiphanius in the fourth century will speak of five original pre-Christian nations (from whom all the heresies spring): barbarians, Scythians, Hellenes, Jews and Samaritans (*Pan.* 1.157).

14 I.e. gods other than 'the Lord,' the God of Israel, called 'the Father'.

15 Tert. *Nat.* 1.8, responded to Christians being designated *tertium genus*, by saying, 'what about the Phrygians, the Greeks or the Egyptians?'

16 *Pace* Stark, *Rise of Christianity*, 49–72.

Sources for Gentile Christianity

We do not possess a single Christian source from the first generations in Aramaic or Hebrew. All extant Christian documents from the first and early second centuries are written in Greek.[17] Although Aramaic or Hebrew idioms and loan words, such as *abba, maranatha* or *amen* are found within early Christian literature, on the whole it is a Greek literary culture that emerged, one based upon the Septuagint as its Bible. By far the majority of the earliest Christian literary sources reflect Gentile Christianity, which may simply be due to the fact that their perspective ultimately won out. But it may equally attest to the very agent of success of that movement. Gentile Christianity from very early on was engaged in writing texts, and those writings, in the most widely spoken language of the Mediterranean world, became a crucial factor in community organisation, self-understanding, worship and propagandisation among others.[18]

The earliest and most important sources for Gentile Christianity are the seven authentic letters written by Paul *c.*50–60 to assemblies of Christians: Romans, 1 and 2 Corinthians, Galatians, Philippians, 1 Thessalonians and Philemon. The next two generations of Gentile mission foundations can be traced through an epistolary tradition that takes Paul as its foundation:[19] letters written by his admirers in the 70s–90s (2 Thessalonians, Colossians, Ephesians, 1 Clement, Hebrews), and still others from the first decades of the second century (the Pastoral Epistles, letters of Ignatius of Antioch, of Polycarp, Barnabas). The earliest extant Christian narratives – the Synoptic Gospels (Mark, Matthew and Luke), which were probably written between *c.*70 and 100 CE – all three presume a Gentile mission and Jesus' conformity with it, although in different ways they reflect the tensions between the Jewish roots of the founder and early movement, and its now predominantly Gentile face.[20]

The Acts of the Apostles, Luke's second volume, is a later and in many ways legendary account which seeks to present a harmonious and unified picture of the earliest church.[21] The work represents an advanced stage of

17 Papias' tradition that Matthew was written in Hebrew (fr. 2.16 (Funk-Bihlmeyer, 136) = Euseb. *HE* 3.39.16) is overturned by critical scholarship which recognizes its use of Mark, a Greek source.
18 See pt III, ch. 8, below.
19 Tellingly, even the letters attributed to Peter and James, with whom the church of the circumcision is identified, actually bear very much the imprint of Paul, the apostle to the Gentiles, as literary author and epistolary theologian.
20 See Fredriksen, *From Jesus to Christ*.
21 Haenchen, *Acts*, 99–103, etc.

Paulinism[22] that adopts the form of apologetic historiography[23] to demonstrate both that the gospel is a legitimate and non-threatening religious movement within the Roman *imperium*, and that, while it has venerable roots in Judaism, the Christian faith has found a new present among the Gentiles.[24] Scholarly assessment of the historicity of individual narratives and speeches in this great work varies greatly; many who recognise the constructive rhetorical role and purpose of any author in a hellenistic historiographical writing[25] still seek by detailed redaction-critical work to uncover reliable source material that is pre-Lukan and secure, a quest that remains always uncertain. It is precisely on the topic of this chapter – the origin and progression of the Gentile mission[26] – that Luke's account differs in significant respects from the evidence given in Paul's letters. All scholarly work on 'Gentile Christianity' must proceed from some assumptions about the relative weight of these sources; the present essay gives priority to the Pauline letters as the earliest primary source material, drawing on Acts when it corroborates or at least does not overtly contradict the seven undisputed letters.[27]

None of these literary sources is a neutral witness to 'Gentile Christianity'. In fact, they tumble over one another in their efforts to attribute its inauguration to different figures. Paul insisted that it was due to divine not human initiative. He claims a plan for it was in place before his own birth (*à la* Jer 1), and was communicated to him in the call experience[28] he refers to as an *apokalypsis*, 'revelation' (Gal 1:15–16; cf. 1:12) when God made known his son to Paul 'so that I might evangelise him among the Gentiles/nations' (*ta ethnē*). Indeed, Paul dubs himself *ethnōn apostolos*, 'the Gentiles' apostle' in Rom 11:13 (cf. Rom 1:5: 'an apostolate . . . among all the nations').[29] For Mark already Jesus carried out his ministry on the Jewish and Gentile sides of the sea of Galilee (but cf. 7:24–30!). Further, Mark signals by the events that immediately follow Jesus' crucifixion – the rending of the temple curtain, and the Roman centurion's confession (15:38–9) – God's own openness to Gentiles. Luke also gives pride of place to

---

22 Mount, *Pauline Christianity*; Haenchen, *Acts*, 112–16.
23 Sterling, *Historiography*.
24 See esp. the powerful penultimate line in 28:28.
25 Aune, *Westminster dictionary*, 215–18, with further literature.
26 Johnson, 'Luke-Acts', 408, says trenchantly that Acts 'has become the etiological myth of Gentile Christianity'.
27 With Knox, *Chapters*.
28 See Stendahl, *Paul among Jews and Gentiles*, 7–22 ('call' rather than 'conversion' of Paul); contrast Segal, *Paul the convert*.
29 There were other *apostoloi* in his day, but we have no evidence that any laid claim to 'the Gentiles' as their special province.

the conversion of a centurion: Cornelius is the test case which convinces Peter (not Paul!) that 'God does not show partiality' (Acts 10:34f.), a decision which is endorsed and legislated by the apostles and elders in Jerusalem in formal session (Acts 15). Luke had already usurped even the new role he had given to Peter as the 'apostle to the Gentiles' (Acts 15:7), by Philip's earlier conversion of Samaritans (Acts 8:4–14), and then the Ethiopian eunuch (Acts 8:26–40), a man who clearly represents Gentiles and outcasts, those at 'the ends of the earth' (cf. Acts 1:8, which presents the spread of the mission to the Gentiles in geographical terms). But for Luke these three different inaugural missions to the Gentiles – Philip's, Peter's, Paul's – do not really conflict, for in his theological and literary design the true agent of the Gentile mission is the Holy Spirit, whose transnational, cross-cultural and multilingual proclivities had already been so powerfully prefigured in the Pentecost event (Acts 2:5–13). Even Matthew's gospel, the one that appears most rooted in the people and traditions of Israel (esp. 5:17–20), nonetheless points to the ultimate success of the Gentile mission and relative failure of that to the Jews.[30] The written record of the Christian movement as it has come down to us shows all clambering on board the Gentile mission.

The Pauline mission in the Roman world

There may have been individual Gentile converts before Paul, but scattered Gentile Jesus-believers do not make a movement. It is Pauline *ekklēsiai*, 'assemblies' or 'churches', that first do this. Paul was the most influential preacher to the Gentiles,[31] and, even more, its theological architect and chief exponent. 'Gentile Christianity' refers not just to a missionary target, but to a theological orientation that regards the conversion of the Gentiles as an apocalyptic sign of the culmination of God's decisive plan for human history and salvation for the whole world.[32]

In recounting the geographical spread of the Pauline mission to the Gentiles,[33] we shall follow the terms of Roman provincial organisation and urban place names (see Map 1, pp. xlv–xlvi above) which Paul himself chose to

---

30 See esp. Matt 21:43 and 28:19. On John's gospel, see ch. 6, below.
31 However, Paul was not a loner, but a member of a missionary team (see Ollrog, *Paulus und seine Mitarbeiter*).
32 Rom 11:25, and the full argument of chs. 9–11 with its succession of scriptural proofs from prophetic literature; Frederiksen, 'Judaism, the circumcision of Gentiles, and apocalyptic hope'; Munck, *Paul and the salvation of mankind*.
33 On the chronology of Paul's life compare Knox, *Chapters*, and Becker, *Paul*, 17–32.

employ in his letters.[34] This was an important means by which Paul created a self-consciousness among his converts of being part of an empire-wide movement with local outposts called *ekklēsiai*.[35]

Arabia, Syria and Cilicia

We have no details about Paul's first missionary years in Arabia (Gal 1:17). Likely he forged here his strategy of seeking out Gentiles in Hellenised urban centres (such as Bostra and Petra). Afterwards he proclaimed the gospel in Syria and Cilicia in Asia Minor, in cities like Damascus and Antioch (Gal 1:17–2:2). He did not engage in missionary work in Judaea (1:22), but journeyed to Jerusalem just twice for brief consultations with the 'pillars', with whom he entered into the parallel gospels concordat authorising him to go to Gentiles (Gal 2:9; 1:17; 2:7). A territorial understanding of this agreement could not, by definition, account for mixed churches. Hence Paul was furious when representatives of James[36] came to Antioch (Gentile territory) and treated it as an extension of *their* apostolate, 'compelling Gentiles to *ioudaizein*' ('live like Jews', Gal 2:14). He publicly accused Cephas (Peter) of hypocrisy for vacillating in Law observance there (Gal 2:11–14).[37]

Galatia and Asia Proconsularis

Probably because he failed in the showdown with Cephas at Antioch, and lost Barnabas as his partner, Paul struck out on his own into the territories of Asia Minor, travelling long distances despite physical infirmity and hardships (Gal 4:13–14; cf. 2 Cor 1:8; 11:26). The '*ekklēsiai* of Galatia' (1:2; cf. 3:1) he founded were probably in the Roman province by that name formed by Augustus in 25 BCE.[38] Paul did not stop in every small village along the way in this vast province, but likely walked or rode on the major Roman road, the Via Sebaste, concentrating his attention on Hellenised, urban centres, such as Perge, the Roman veteran colony of Pisidian Antioch, Iconium and Lystra, maybe reaching as far north as

---

34 With Riesner, *Paul's early period*, 289. Even if Paul has some concept of the Table of Nations of Genesis 10 (so Scott, *Paul and the Nations*), tellingly he does not invoke it.

35 Whether Paul saw his mission as a deliberate challenge or alternative to the Roman *imperium* is currently a matter of intense interest (see e.g. Horsley, *Paul and empire*; Elliott, *Liberating Paul*).

36 This picture of James' viewpoint is at odds with Acts 15:13–21, a later attempt to reconcile him to Pauline teaching (Haenchen, *Acts*, 447–64).

37 Betz, *Galatians*, 105–112; further essays in Nannos, *Galatians Debate*.

38 On the 'north Galatian' or 'south Galatian' hypothesis see Lightfoot, *Galatians*, 18–21; Betz, *Galatians*, 1–5; Martyn, *Galatians*, 15–17. Decisive for me is the fact that Paul in general does overwhelmingly use Roman provincial terminology in his letters (Asia, Macedonia, Achaea, Judaea, Syria, Spania/Hispania, Illyricum).

Pontus.[39] Although he spent a good amount of time in the capital of the Roman province of Asia Proconsularis, Ephesus (1 Cor 16:8; 15:32), and other coastal regions in Asia,[40] no genuine letters from Paul to those cities are extant.[41]

The Asian church letter which we do have, Galatians, recounts what was in Paul's eyes an initially triumphal success (4:12–14; cf. 1:7; 5:7a). At the 'telling of the gospel' (4:14) about 'the son of God who loved [us] and gave himself on [our] behalf' (2:20), an untold number of non-Jews throughout the province came 'to know God, and even more be known by God' (4:9). In addition to moving these Gentiles from idolatry to adherence to 'God the Father', Paul instructed them in some essential ethical guidelines (5:21) that he apparently thought necessary to complete their conversion to the God of Israel. But his proselytising message included more than Israelite monotheism (though that was an important precondition for the 'gospel message'). He taught his Galatian hearers that, if they had 'faith in Jesus Christ'[42] and were baptised, they would put on the prophetically promised Christ – that one God's son – and would become one in Christ (3:26–8), receiving his spirit into themselves (an experience Paul later recounts as a recognised fact (3:2–5)).[43]

Paul's 'gospel' proclamation to the Galatian Gentiles (as we glimpse it behind the argument of the later letter) was a narrative of divine activity[44] highlighting the death of Jesus on the cross out of love for his followers (Gal 1:4; 2:20), his vindicating resurrection by God, and his imminent return to rescue those who believe in him from the present evil age (1:4), and ensure them a promised place in the 'kingdom of God' (5:21), 'justification' and 'eternal life' (2:16–21; 5:4–5; 6:8). The God whose will animates these events is the God of Israel, the God of Abraham, Isaac and Jacob, the God known in the Law (the Torah) as having laid down sacred promises for the children, the heirs, of Abraham. The media of Paul's proclamation of this crucified Son of God included Paul's own bodily weakness and disabilities, which he interpreted as the 'marks of Jesus' he bore in his own flesh (Gal 4:13–14; 6:17b).[45] Paul's bold claim to be Christ's epiphanic

---

39 A convergence here of Pauline terminological preference with Acts (chs. 13–14).
40 The Troad in particular (2 Cor 2:12; cf. Ign. *Phild.* 11.2; *Smyr.* 12.1; *Pol.* 8.1).
41 Ephesians is a pseudepigraphic letter which originally did not contain the phrase 'in Ephesus' (see Metzger, *Textual commentary*, 601); but Paul is connected with Ephesus elsewhere (Ign. *Eph.* 1.12 ('co-initiates of Paul'); 1 Tim 1:3; cf. Acts 19). If Colossians is authentically Pauline, however, one gains two Pauline letters to specific Asian cities, for it appears to mention a letter to Laodicea (4:16).
42 Some scholars have recently argued that this crucial phrase should be translated instead 'the faith(fulness) of Jesus Christ' (see Hays, *Faith of Jesus Christ*, with bibliography).
43 Betz, *Galatians*, 128–36.
44 Hays, *Faith of Jesus Christ*; Mitchell, 'Rhetorical shorthand'.
45 Güttgemanns, *Der leidende Apostel*.

envoy[46] meant he and his gospel were an indivisible entity. To accept Paul was to accept Christ Jesus (4:14), and to reject his gospel was to reject him and the one who called him (1:6). This crucial identification between the apostle (i.e. 'sent one') and the Lord who sent him was both the strength and the Achilles heel of the Pauline mission, for Paul's 'apostolate', for which he vigorously claimed solely divine authorisation, could easily be called into question, as it was soon to be.

Paul's apocalyptic urgency to spread the gospel through the whole world meant that he moved on after founding these local *ekklēsiai*. Sometime after departure he learned that the situation had shifted significantly. Other missionaries had traced his footsteps, proclaiming 'another gospel' (Gal 1:6–9). The main feature of their gospel (as best we can reconstruct it from Paul's outraged rebuttal) was that these Gentile Jesus believers were *compelled*[47] to become circumcised (6:12; cf. 5:3). It is less clear why they taught this. Paul maintains it is so they can 'boast in the flesh' of these converts (6:13), perhaps to avoid persecution by non-Jesus-believing Jews through a token gesture towards the Law. Yet Galatians 4:10 suggests the Galatians were also practising sabbath and festival observance.[48] For Paul, nothing less than the Galatians' very salvation was at stake. He argued that if one is 'justified' (that is, proleptically found innocent of blame at the coming eschatological judgement) by faith in Jesus Christ, then 'works of the Law' (of which circumcision is the crucial test) cannot bring justification, and therefore cannot be required (so the thesis of the letter (2:16)). Indeed, Paul takes it one step further: for his Gentile converts to undergo circumcision would be to accept an entirely different economy of divine salvation, a mistake which could nullify their faith in Jesus Christ (5:3–4) and would, ironically, be a return to a form of slavery as sure as their earlier enslavement to idols (4:8–11).[49] He caricatured circumcision as bondage in the flesh that contradicts the freedom in the spirit his gospel brought them (3:3; 5:13).

Paul's audacious argument in this letter was to become the Magna Carta of the Gentile Christian movement: an ingenious case that 'those who are from faith' (Gal 3:7) are the true 'children of Abraham'. They receive all the

46 Mitchell, 'Epiphanic evolutions'.
47 Gal 6:12; cf. 2:3, 14.
48 The 'Jerusalem Council' Luke depicts did not impose these requirements on Gentiles, but the so-called 'Noachide commandments' of abstinence from meat sacrificed to idols, with blood in it or from strangled beasts, and from sexual immorality (Acts 15:28–9; cf. 15:20). Paul gives no hint in his letters of knowing such stipulations.
49 It is important to note here that Paul's argument really does not address the issue of Jewish Christians' obligation or lack of obligation to keep the commandments of the Torah.

promises and blessings of the chosen people, but through a new route ('faith'), that circumvents the obligations of the Mosaic covenant. Ironically the letter to the Galatians may not have won the battle,[50] though it certainly did win the war, as the letter itself – even if not persuasive to its original addressees – paved the way for the 'Law-free' Gentile Christianity that was to predominate throughout Christian history. Amazingly, within just a generation of this bitter struggle one of Paul's followers would write a letter in his name to proclaim to a new generation of believers[51] the completion of the Pauline mission to the Gentiles as the fulfilment of the very purpose of the gospel:

> remember that you once were the Gentiles in the flesh, those who are called 'the uncircumcision' by the so-called 'circumcision' which is done by hand in the flesh. Because you were at that time apart from Christ, separated from the commonwealth of Israel and estranged from the covenants of the promise, having no hope, the godless in the world. But you, the very ones who then were far away, have now become near in Christ Jesus by the blood of Christ. For he himself is our peace, the one who made the two into one, by destroying the dividing wall of partition . . . for the sake of this I, Paul, am the prisoner of Christ Jesus on behalf of the Gentiles. (Eph 2:11–13)

Macedonia

By the early 50s Paul moved beyond the continent of Asia towards Europe. Probably landing at the seaport of Neapolis (Acts 16:11; cf. 2 Cor 11:25–6), Paul set out on the Via Egnatia, a major Roman road, to Philippi, a Roman veteran colony. From there, after a period of preaching amidst resistance and persecution (1 Thess 2:1–2), he took the same road to the lively port city of Thessalonica, capital of the Roman province of Macedonia. Acts describes Paul seeking out 'God-fearing' Gentiles associated with the Jewish community in Macedonia by finding the local place of prayer (Philippi) or synagogue (Thessalonica) and having more success with them – particularly with upper-class women – than with Jews (Acts 16:13–15; 17:4). Paul's own letters address the Thessalonian converts as Gentiles; he recounts with pride how they 'turned to God from the idols to serve a living and true God' (1 Thess 1:9–10).

Although his missionary presence and activity in Philippi and Thessalonica followed closely upon each other, the letters we have from Paul to those churches may have been written as much as a decade apart. First Thessalonians,

---

50 Despite 1 Cor 16:1, the Galatians appear not to have joined Paul's collection effort (Rom 15:26).
51 The pseudepigraphy assumes these converts are used to experiencing Paul's presence among them in letters (such as Galatians!).

likely Paul's earliest extant letter, was written relatively soon after his departure from there, probably from Athens (3:1). The letter reports how Paul had sent his fellow missionary Timothy back to Thessalonica in his absence to shore up their flagging faith in a time of stress and doubt. As in Galatia, the indivisibility of Paul and his gospel message meant that the doubts the Thessalonians had about his gospel's truthfulness – especially since some of their company had died before Jesus' promised return, in apparent disconfirmation of the gospel message – extended to him (see 1:5–2:13). He writes them a letter that is meant to bolster the quality of his *logos* ('speech'), both past and present, and to update his original apocalyptic scenario to ensure that they have complete hope in the coming resurrection of the dead at the *parousia*, the second coming, of Christ (4:13–18).[52] In 1 Thessalonians we see the importance of the pithy teaching triad 'faith, hope and love' in the Pauline mission,[53] and especially the key role that hope for a future divine rescue, including resurrection of the dead, played in his 'good news' (4:13–18). Paul does not here treat circumcision as the defining issue for Gentile converts, but divine election, its expected consequences – persecution (1:5–6; 2:14–16; 3:4) – and the requisite demand for sanctification it entails (3:13; 4:3–8; 5:23). On these terms Paul can even warn his Thessalonian converts away from sexual sins characteristic of 'the Gentiles who do not know God' (4:5; cf. 1 Cor 5:1). We also glimpse here Paul setting up local leaders and presiders to carry on after he and the team had moved on to the next site (5:12–13), and making strategic use of envoys and letters to provide ongoing instruction, calm fears and disconfirm doubts from a distance.[54]

Philippians was written at some remove from these events, later recalled as 'the beginning of the gospel' (4:15). Paul writes in the recognition that the Philippians have heard that he is in prison (in an undisclosed location, likely either Ephesus or Rome), and are expressing concern about him, and about the fate of one of their own, Epaphroditus, who is with Paul (1:12f; 2:25–30). Paul sent this letter to thank them for their financial partnership with him, an arrangement of 'accounts payable and receivable' which he describes in customary business language (Phil 4:10–20; cf. 2 Cor 11:9).[55] Philippians also reveals the presence of *episkopoi* and *diakonoi* (Phil 1:2), which may already be formal offices ('bishops and deacons') or perhaps more likely descriptive titles of local leaders in the house churches ('overseers and ministers').[56] Paul wrote also

52 Mitchell, '1 and 2 Thessalonians', 51–8.
53 1:2–3; 5:8; cf. 3:6; but see Gal 5:5–6; also 1 Cor 13:13.
54 Mitchell, 'New Testament envoys'.
55 Sampley, *Pauline partnership*.
56 See ch. 7, below.

to address divisions within the Philippian *ecclēsna*, which he views as rooted especially in conflicts between two prominent women, Euodia and Syntyche, whom he urges to reconcile (4:2). The consistent theme of this letter is a call to unity through humility and subservience for the greater good, as exemplifed by Christ (2:5–10), Paul's co-worker Timothy (2:19–24) and Paul himself (3:17f.). The cultural hybrid that was Paul's gospel is nicely illustrated by his reminder to the Christ-believers to orient their life around the solemn apocalyptic promise that 'we have a *politeuma* ('commonwealth') in the heavens, from which we eagerly await the Lord Jesus Christ as saviour' (3:20), which is followed quickly by a set of ethical exhortations entirely consonant with Stoic popular ethics (4:8), but now rooted in Paul's own life and example (4:9). Because of the potential threat of Jewish Christian missionaries (disparaged as 'dogs'), Paul addressed the distinguishing mark of circumcision, this time with a simpler construal than in Galatians: his Gentile converts do not need to be circumcised because they *already are* – in the spirit (Phil 3:3).[57]

The continuity of Paul's Gentile mission in Macedonia into the next generations is confirmed by a later letter of Polycarp to the Philippians (*c.* 117):

> the firm root of your faith, proclaimed from ancient times until now remains and bears fruit for our Lord Jesus Christ. (1.2)

> Neither I nor anyone else like me is able to follow upon the wisdom of the blessed and glorious Paul, who when he was with you, face to face before those who were alive then, taught with precision and solidity the word of truth. And when absent he wrote you letters which, if you peer closely into them, will give you the power to be built up into the faith which was given to you. (3.2)

Achaea

From Macedonia Paul and co-workers Timothy and Silvanus moved into mainland Greece. Details of his time in Athens (1 Thess 3:1) remain largely unknown to us. Luke paints an epic encounter between the apostle and Greek philosophy (Acts 17), which, although probably not a true account of any single day, surely captures some of the intellectual quandaries Paul's gospel would have raised in the Graeco-Roman world. Some time later he moved south-west to

---

57 Paul's sarcastic play in 3:2 between circumcision and mutilation (a pun that works only in Greek) is not paralleled in biblical or Second Temple Jewish texts, but the idea of spiritual circumcision – of hearts, ears, etc. – is (e.g. Deut 10:16; Jer 4:4; 9:25; 1QH*ᵃ* 19.5; Philo, *Quaest. Ex.* 2.2).

the major city of Corinth. Like Philippi it was a Romanised city and colony, the provincial capital of Achaea, a major commercial and trading centre with dual ports allowing transport from the Aegean to the Ionian and beyond.[58] Paul later reports how he 'planted' the gospel there, in the process apparently forming a number of house churches,[59] such as that hosted by Gaius (Rom 16:23), which would also periodically come together 'in one place' for the Lord's Supper and worship (1 Cor 14:23; cf. 11:20). The earliest Corinthian converts were predominantly Gentiles (1 Cor 12:2; Acts 18:7: God-fearers), and also some Jewish believers, for after Paul's departure there were serious disputes over issues such as meat sacrificed to idols (see 1 Cor 8 and 10). Gentiles would have eaten this food all their lives (when they could afford it),[60] but for those born Jews its consumption involved idolatry. Rather than debating points of *halachah* (legal interpretation), or training his full attention on the philosophical defence of monotheism (but see 1 Cor 8:4–7; cf. 10:20), Paul seeks a practical solution vis-à-vis the consumption of this food that urges compromise for the sake of the church's unity.[61] In Corinth Paul's Gentile mission again comes into direct conflict with other missionaries: Cephas (Peter) and Apollos (1 Cor 1:12; 3:5, 22), and unnamed figures who bring 'another Jesus' (2 Cor 11:4) from outside, as well as local antagonists from within the *ekklēsia* itself (such as the unnamed figure in 2 Cor 10:10; cf. 2:5–8; 7:12).

Paul's extant correspondence with the Corinthian church comprises as many as six letters revealing a dramatic history of conflict and, ultimately, reconciliation – among the Corinthians themselves, and between them and the apostle.[62] Because he sees the Corinthians as crucial allies (see 1 Cor 9:2), these controversies were particularly intense.[63] The initial conflict arose out of success: as the number of Christian converts expanded, divisions and sub-groups formed which (from Paul's point of view) threatened the unity in Christ which he proclaimed. Paul responded to that situation (from Ephesus) with 1 Corinthians, a carefully composed argument in which he addresses the series of issues dividing them (marriage and sexual practices, eating of idol meat, behaviour in worship, the resurrection of believers) by urging concord

---

58 Grant, *Paul in the Roman world*, 13–20.
59 Klauck, *Hausgemeinde*; Balch and Osiek, *Families*.
60 Theissen, *Social setting*, 69–119, 145–74.
61 Note that Paul terms it a matter of 'custom' (*synētheia*) rather than commandment (8:7; but see 10:14: 'Flee from idolatry!').
62 See Mitchell, 'Paul's letters to Corinth', and 'The Corinthian correspondence and the birth of Pauline hermeneutics'. Differently Young and Ford, *Meaning and truth*.
63 Strangely, Luke has not a word to say of them!

in terms which strongly evoke Graeco-Roman cultural values. Paul adapts conventional political appeals in service of his call for unity, giving them a unique Christian cast, such as the stock appeal to the harmonic balance of the mixed body politic which becomes an appeal to 'the body of Christ' (1 Cor 12:12–31).[64] Before closing, Paul adds instructions for the Corinthians to participate actively in a major monetary campaign in his absence (16:1–4).

The letters which follow 1 Corinthians (now redacted into the canonical 2 Corinthians) allow us to trace the bitter conflicts that ensued, involving accusations that Paul was not an apostle (3:1–6; 11:5f.; 12:11–13), but an imposter engaging in a fraudulent long-distance fund-raising campaign (2 Cor 2:17; 4:4:1–4; 11:7–9; 12:14–18). Paul deepened his theology in relation to these challenges. When under fire Paul amplified his apostolic self-understanding as the *apostolos*, 'envoy', of Christ, by turning around the criteria by which his opponents sought to discredit him, especially his bodily weakness which they interpreted as a sign of divine punishment and condemnation. Paul argued that the 'signs of an apostle' (2 Cor 12:12) were more than miracles and powerful acts, but also, paradoxically and profoundly, weakness which embodied the very 'dying of Jesus' which bears in itself the promise of resurrection (2 Cor 4:10–12; 13:4). The logic of Paul's gospel as expressed in these letters is emphatically centered in the cross,[65] the dying of Jesus which implies also his resurrection.[66] Powerful letters (cf. 2 Cor 10:10) and the ambassadorial labours of Titus[67] eventually succeeded in qualming the Corinthians' fears that Paul was an illegitimate preacher and charlatan seeking to take their money (2 Cor 12:14). In the end, they agreed to join the Macedonians in his collection for the saints in Jerusalem (2 Cor 9; Rom 15:26), an undertaking that was to satisfy real hungers among the poor in Judaea while also symbolising the alliance of these transformed Gentiles with the church in Jerusalem (2 Cor 8:13–15; 9:11–15). Like Jews in the diaspora paying their temple tax, Paul wished his Gentile churches' wealth to 'stream to Jerusalem'[68] in a spiritual bond that would also fulfil his part of the original 'two missions agreement', that he should 'be mindful of the poor' (Gal 2:10).[69]

---

64 Mitchell, *Paul*.
65 1 Cor 1:18: 'the word of the cross'; 2:1–5.
66 See esp. 1 Cor 15; 2 Cor 4:7–12; 13:3–4.
67 Mitchell, 'New Testament envoys.'
68 Mic 4:1–2; Isa 2:2–3; 60:5–7.
69 Betz, *2 Corinthians 8 and 9*; Georgi, *Remembering the Poor*.

As was the case for Asia and Macedonia, the descendants of Paul's first Corinthian Christians were to be the recipients of a letter from another *ekklēsia* (Rome), calling upon it, in the epistolary medium Paul had made so popular among Christians, to heed the voice of the now-dead apostle (*1 Clem.* 5.7) and cease from the fresh contentions that have arisen among them. Once again we can see how remarkably quickly the Pauline mission had created a sense of its own history as the sure foundation for its future:

> Take up the letter of the blessed apostle Paul. What first did he write to you in the beginning of the gospel . . . because even then you had made divisions for yourself. . . . It is shameful, beloved, both terribly shameful and unworthy of conduct in Christ for it to be heard that the most firmly rooted and ancient assembly of the Corinthians is factionalised. (*1 Clem.* 47.1–7)

Rome, Italy and west

From Corinth Paul wrote ahead to Christians at Rome, the capital of the *imperium Romanum*, to set the stage for further missionary work (Rom 15:23; cf. 1:13). His famous letter to 'all the beloved of God who are in Rome, called saints' demonstrates that Christianity had arrived in Rome before Paul.[70] Paul regards these believers as 'among the Gentiles' (Rom 1:5–7, 13), and therefore within his missionary responsibility.[71] Despite his acknowledgement that he had never been there (Rom 1:10–13; cf. 28:20–1), at least some of the house churches in Rome were apparently (assuming Romans 16 is original to the letter) hosted by missionaries in league with Paul, such as Prisca and Aquila,[72] or Epainetus.[73] Both had apparently moved there from Asia, bringing their evangelising efforts into a context that may already have included some groups of Jewish Christians.[74] These Jewish Christians may have been exiled under Claudius' edict in 49 CE,[75] but returned after his death in 54 CE, a scenario that may account for the rise in Gentile Christianity there during the interval.

---

70 The letter says nothing of other Christian communities on the Italian penninsula, but see Acts 28:14 (Puteoli); cf. Heb 13:24.

71 See Klein, 'Paul's purpose in writing to the Romans' (they are lacking an apostolic foundation).

72 His 'co-workers in Christ Jesus' who have an *ekklēsia* in their house (Rom 16:3–4; cf. 1 Cor 16:19; Acts 18:1–3, 26).

73 Rom 16:5. Yet an early history of the gospel among Roman Jews, thoroughly independent of Paul, is also possible (Lampe, *From Paul to Valentinus*, 11–16).

74 Such as Paul's *syngeneis*, 'relatives,' Andronicus and Junia, and Herodion (Rom 16:7, 11).

75 Fitzmyer, *Romans*, 31–4.

Paul had several reasons for writing his now famous letter to the Romans,[76] all of which unite in this letter of introduction for his gospel of salvation,[77] and appeal for Roman material support for the mission bearing it beyond them to the west. As in 1 Corinthians (but not Galatians), the argument of Romans emphasises the theological unity that prevails among all believers in the gospel, over and against the old maps of Jew and Gentile division. The thesis of 1:16–17 emphasises that 'the gospel is the power of God for salvation for everyone who believes' even as all – Jew and Greek – stand united (paradoxically) in being helpless to the power of sin without it. Although he begins on moral grounds, with excoriation of Gentiles for idolatry and the litany of sins it spawns (1:18–32), Paul turns the same harsh critique onto Jews, who do the same things (2:1) and hence are without defence before the divine wrath (2:5, 8; cf. 1:18). Divine impartiality is declared over and above the election of Israel (2:11; cf. 9–11), and some bold reversals of expected identities are invoked: Gentiles who do not have the Law but do its requirements by nature (2:14–15; 9:30); Jews who become uncircumcised by transgressions of the Law (2:25); Gentiles who are 'secret Jews' with spiritually circumcised hearts (2:29). The dense argument of this missive serves to justify Paul's Gentile mission, but without repudiating Jewish Christians, and even non-Christian Jews, for whom the gospel still holds out hope of salvation (ch. 11, esp. 11:1–2, 23–31).[78] But Paul, 'apostle of the Gentiles' (11:13; 15:16), asks from the Roman Christians assistance so that he might be sent forth to proclaim this saving gospel beyond them (10:11–15), in Spain (15:24). However, he wishes first to finish one more piece of business in the east: bringing the collection for the saints from the provinces of Macedonia and Achaea to Jerusalem (15:25–8). He sends the deacon Phoebe of Cenchreae likely as the advance team for the expedition to Spain (Rom 16:1–2).

Paul's own letters do not tell us if these plans were carried out. But within a few decades, traditions of his death at Rome and his journeys west were jointly celebrated:

> having been a herald in the east and in the west, Paul received the noble credit for his faith; after teaching justification extending throughout the whole world, and having come to the far borders of the west, and testified before rulers, he was thus departed from the world and taken up into a holy place. (1 Clem. 5.6–7)

---

76 See Donfried, Romans debate.
77 Paul had learned from his conflicts with the Corinthians the dangers of appearing to write a letter of introduction for himself (2 Cor 3:1–3; 5:12; 10:12–18; 12:11).
78 With Becker, Paul, 457–72; Gager, Reinventing Paul, among others.

Reasons for success

Why would Gentiles have been persuaded to respond with 'faith' and leave their traditional religious practices and orientations to turn to Paul's 'gospel'? While caution is necessary about personal motives in any case, or uniformity among individuals or different locations in the empire, we can identify some contributing factors.

There is probably historical truth behind Luke's picture of Paul finding adherents to his gospel among the 'God-fearers' or 'devout,'[79] Gentiles who were already in some way associated with Jews, attending synagogue, learning Jewish sacred texts and lore or serving as benefactors, but not undergoing circumcision to become full converts.[80] That Paul's missionary activity intersected with the orbit of the synagogue seems confirmed by his having received the punishment of thirty-nine lashes (2 Cor 11:24), and by the urban centres he chose.[81] This can also explain how a message that relies so much on scriptural interpretation for its cogency and credibility[82] could have been intelligible to Gentiles who would otherwise have been befuddled by claims about 'the anointed one', 'the fulfilment of scripture', and the necessity for deliverance from divine wrath. But we need not imagine that Paul's message was attractive simply because it gave these God-fearers an easy ride into Judaism (bypassing circumcision, food laws and other restrictions), nor that it was for them simply another Hellenistic mystery cult of a dying and rising god symbolising the fertility cycles of the earth and offering an entryway to immortality (as the 'history of religions school' is taken to have argued).[83] Paul's was a different pattern of religion akin to both but also unique – a self-proclaimed *sui generis* message fundamentally about soteriology (a means of salvation) but plotted onto the Jewish grand narrative of divine intent and election as made known in history, propelled by apocalyptic logic and, above all, centred in the utterly new figure, Jesus Christ. In exploring the meaning of this Christ being 'Lord',

79 See Acts 13:16, 26, 43; 14:1; 16:14; 17:4; 18:7.
80 Evidence, with appropriate cautions about assuming that 'God-fearer' was either a uniform or a rhetorically neutral designation, in Cohen, *Beginnings*, 171–4 and Lieu, *Neither Jew nor Greek*, 31–68.
81 Note the correspondence between Paul's itinerary and Philo's list of places where Jews lived throughout the Mediterranean (*Flacc.* 281–2).
82 Paul's statement of his gospel message in 1 Cor 15:3–4 twice repeats the formula 'according to the scriptures'.
83 The most important book on Paul's religion and its ultimate divergence from the pattern of 'covenantal nomism' characterising first-century Judaism remains Sanders, *Paul and Palestinian Judaism*. On Paul and the mystery religions, see Klauck, *Religious context*, 81–152; Betz, 'Mysterien Religion', *RGG*[4] 5 (2002) and 'Religionsgeschichtliche Schule', *RGG*[4] 7 (2004); on methodological problems in comparison see Smith, *Drudgery divine*.

and the power to be had in his name, Paul's proclamation sounded a new note, even within and among other circles of Jesus-followers, in its emphasis on the cosmic significance of the death and resurrection, and its universal power of salvation for those in faith.[84]

But Paul's gospel would have had no staying power if he had not put tremendous energies into the linguistic and social creation of the new community. His proclamation and its ritual enactment in baptism, meal (what he terms 'the Lord's meal' in 1 Cor 11:20), and other liturgical acts, and his creative ecclesiological groundwork fostered a self-understanding and network of converts whose ties to one another and to a larger movement were crucial factors in its success.[85] Paul established this trans-local and thereby easily trans-generational movement through exegetical work that gave these Gentiles a new past and place among the patriarchs of Israel (see 1 Cor 10:1, 'our ancestors'). He provided an intellectual substructure to the movement[86] even as in practical terms he carried the gospel around the Mediterranean world. Further, Paul deliberately drew his converts from a wide range of social and economic classes.[87] Although social stratification and status dissonance were a factor in some of the internal church conflicts, somehow the centre held, and these fledgling communities survived and grew, apparently with individual differences subsumed into the evocative ecclesiastical images which Paul provided for them, such as 'God's house', 'God's temple', 'the body of Christ', 'the bride for the bridegroom, Christ'. But contentions about the place of slaves, women and others in the household of faith, especially in relation to the norms for their place in the Graeco-Roman household generally, were already percolating, and were to erupt into more conflict in the next generations.[88]

At the same time as he was creating this alternate theological universe, however, Paul mapped this internal group-talk onto the geographical markers of the urban and provincial structure of the *imperium Romanum*, such that he could with some audacity refer to these persons, a minute percentage of the citizens

84 While Bousset's view that Paul was the founder of the Hellenistic Christ cult (*Kyrios Christos*) is a clear overstatement, Hurtado's counter-position (*Lord Jesus Christ*, 79–153) equalises 'devotion to Jesus' among all earliest Christians in such broad terms that Paul's christological innovations and the role they played in controversies (e.g. 'another Jesus' in 2 Cor 11:4) is largely ruled out.
85 E.g. 1 Cor 1:2; see ch. 7, below.
86 See e.g. Betz, 'Christianity as religion' in his *Paulinische Studien*, 206–39; Malherbe, *Paul and the popular philosophers*.
87 See Meeks, *First urban Christians* (and ch. 7, below); Theissen, *Social setting*; debate in Meggitt, *Paul, poverty and survival*; Friesen, 'Poverty in Pauline studies'.
88 See Balch and Osiek, *Families*, and discussion below.

of these major cities, simply as 'Galatians', 'Thessalonians', 'Corinthians' or 'Romans'. And he integrated this set of practices and linguistic formations into his own apparently effective administrative missionary network.

Another apparently key persuasive force was the appeal to powerful, miraculous and charismatic/spiritual phenomena (healings, exorcisms, ecstatic speech) accompanying the message Paul preached (see Gal 3:5; cf. 1 Cor 2:4). This intersects with the strength of personality, intellect and character of Paul, including his own fervency of belief, power of self-presentation and alacrity of mind, which surely played a major role in missionary success. His carefully crafted epistles, which may also have made up for some limitations of his own physical presence,[89] with their fiery rhetoric, inventive exegesis and urgent prose, continued to animate and guide the movement he had fostered even after his death.

Other Gentile missions

No other Gentile missions are even remotely as well known to us as that of Paul and his team.[90] But we can see glimpses or gaps that point to others at work or soon to emerge, preaching the gospel among non-Jews. Paul himself may give evidence of pre-Pauline missions to the Gentiles, if what had fuelled his rage to persecute some early Jesus believers was their lack of adherence to the command to circumcise or at least laxity about Torah observance.[91] But this remains obscure, since Paul is quite ambivalent about whether he learned anything from those who went before him.[92] Luke's picture of an early Gentile mission emanating from Antioch, with roots in the 'Hellenists' in Jerusalem who were scattered by the great persecution, is taken by many as historical.[93] On that depiction, Paul came on board an existing Gentile mission, as a kind of 'junior partner' to Barnabas who took that small movement and greatly expanded its vision and activities (see Acts 9:27; 15:2; cf. 15:36–41; Gal 2:1). Some of the opponents Paul faced in his churches in Asia and Achaea were apparently

---

89 Mitchell, 'New Testament envoys'.
90 Koester, *Introduction to the New Testament*, vol. II, 93–4 on the slim evidence.
91 Gal 5:11, read in light of 1:13–14 (cf. Phil 3:6), strongly suggests this conclusion (with Donaldson, *Paul and the Gentiles*, 273–307).
92 Compare 1 Cor 15:3 with Gal 1:12, 17.
93 E.g. Hengel, *Between Jesus and Paul*; Becker, *Paul*, esp. 83–112 (including speculative reconstructions from Paul's own letters); but see Hill, *Hellenists and Hebrews*, for the range of historiographical problems attending the reconstruction of the Hellenists' position from Acts 6–7.

Jewish Christian missionaries targeting Gentile converts (were Apollos and Cephas doing so?),[94] if on different terms. Whether we treat them as part of 'Gentile Christianity' depends of course on how we define the category.[95] Johannine Christians may well represent a form of Gentile mission in Asia independent of Paul's (see esp. John 7:35; 12:20–1).[96] Even if the main Gentile mission in these provinces was Pauline, we should also expect there were other missionaries (including members of the wider Pauline missionary network, perhaps,[97] but not limited to them) who worked in between the urban areas that Paul made the measure of his circuit around the Mediterranean, such that he could say when writing Romans that he 'no longer had a place in these regions' (Rom 15:22).

What about other provinces? Luke depicts an early mission that may extend to Ethiopia, though he does not tell what happened when the eunuch baptised by Philip completed the journey home to his land and queen, Candace (Acts 8:26–40). There is little early information about missions in eastern Asia Minor and Mesopotamia,[98] though later traditions associate them with the apostle Thomas.[99] The situation is similar with other provinces that were out of the Pauline 'orbit', such as Egypt, North Africa and Mauretania, and Gaul; original missionary efforts there may have been among Jews or among Gentiles, or both.[100] Once any Christian communities have been founded, however, 'mission' may be reconfigured from itinerant outreach to networking in the present context.[101] No matter the locale, the household (and perhaps by extension the neighbourhood) seems to have been a central locus for the propagation of the faith.[102]

'Early Catholicism'

This phrase is sometimes used to refer to the developments in Gentile, particularly Pauline, Christian communities in the third generation, as they are known

---

94 1 Cor 1:12 and 3:5, 22. Luke calls Apollos an Alexandrine Jew (Acts 18:24); Becker, *Paul*, 93, a Gentile Christian missionary.
95 See discussion above, pp. 103–5.
96 See pt III, ch. 10, below.
97 The Pastoral Epistles assume Paul had delegated Ephesus, Crete and other eastern areas to his trusted emissaries when he turned west.
98 Bauckham, 'What if Paul had travelled east?'
99 See pt IV, ch. 19, below.
100 See the essays in pt IV, below, for discussion of each region.
101 Stark, *Rise of Christianity*.
102 See Klauck, *Hausgemeinde*; MacDonald, *Early Christian women*; and discussion in pt III, ch. 14, below.

to us in the Pastoral Epistles, the letters of Ignatius and Polycarp, and the Acts of the Apostles. The construct 'early catholicism' is rooted in the theory of F. C. Baur that there was a complete divide in the early church between the Jewish and Gentile missions, and that later the antithesis was resolved in such a synthesis.[103] Hence, so the theory goes, it was in this period at the beginning of the second century that a kind of constellation was formed which assured its own future by creating the monarchical episcopate and other institutional forms that locked the spontaneous faith down into an ecclesiastically sanctioned and controlled religion. In its more extreme forms, this theory brings in Weberian sociological theory to maintain that the original 'charismatic' Pauline communities later gave way to rigid, institutional forms of leadership. In recent decades the dichotomy Baur sketched has been questioned as a grand theory of Christian origins, and it has been noticed that in some ways the 'Frühkatholizismus' hypothesis involves a retrojection of Protestant/Catholic polemics back on to the early church.[104] Nonetheless, the same plot-structure of decline narrative has been retained in other terms, to the effect that the earliest Christians (Jesus and his immediate followers) were in favour of social egalitarianism, but increasingly early liberalism became subject, as the church matured, to patriarchalisation and forms of institutional oppression.[105]

Yet actually much of what is termed 'catholic' about the third Pauline generation was already to some degree present or anticipated in the first. Paul's own perspective was from the start 'catholic' in the sense of 'universal', for he set his sights on the broadest possible arena of activity and put in motion structures for each *ekklēsia* to relate to the wider network of churches. However there are developments which emerge in the later period, particularly in the extent to which the unimaginable has taken place: that Paul has become recognised as *the apostle*, and hence right thinking and right behaviour are judged in relation to (some presentation of) his views. Like Paul, a figure such as Ignatius uses letters to influence local church disputes; like him Ignatius seeks to prop up local leaders of his own choosing.[106] What is new here is the emergence of the role of the *episkopos* as the authoritative voice in the community,[107] and of provisions for the selection of *episkopoi*, *presbyteroi* and

---

103 Baur, *Church history*, vol. 1, 44–98 ('The conflict' between Paulinism and Jewish Christianity), 99–152 ('The reconciliation' into 'catholic Christianity').

104 Including, in addition to the charge of clericalism, the assumption that justification by faith was true, radical Paulinism, which (unfortunately) becomes misunderstood or diluted by the catholicising compromise (e.g. Baur, *Church history*, vol. 1, 34).

105 E.g. Schüssler Fiorenza, *In memory of her*, 251–342, a carefully nuanced position; Elliott, *Liberating Paul.*

106 Schoedel, *Ignatius of Antioch.*

107 Ign. *Eph.* 4.1–6.2, etc.

diakonoi (1 Tim 3).[108] Yet the fact that Ignatius feels he must lay down mandates for subservience to the bishop, and add his backing to Onesimus at Ephesus by name, suggests that like Paul he was writing into a contested situation. While it is an overstatement to imagine that the structure of Paul's churches was simply charismatic rather than institutional,[109] we observe a significant shift in the historical placement of the relevant figures in each generation when comparing Paul's 1 Corinthians 3:10f and the later Ephesians 2:21. Whereas for Paul there is only one foundation, Jesus Christ crucified, preached by himself as apostle, for the deutero-Pauline author the foundation is one floor up from this fundament: the church is 'built up on the foundation of the apostles and prophets, with Christ Jesus as the corner stone.' Second Thessalonians demonstrates that Paul's letters have become *the* source of his authoritative traditions (2:15; cf. 3:14), a move replicated in 1 Timothy 6:20: 'guard the deposit'! And, whereas a completely egalitarian first phase in the Pauline churches seems an overstatement, it is possible to see an increasing formalism in household relations in the later years which, while it may reflect some actual attitudes in Paul's own day,[110] was not the only or even prevailing norm, according to the evidence, in which women apparently had significant leadership roles in the movement.[111] Moreover, the third Pauline generation also included less hierarchically and household-bound figures, such as those we can glimpse in the apocryphal *Acts of Paul and Thecla*.[112] Hence while the Pauline wing of the Pastorals and Ignatius was to win out, it was not the only Gentile mission in its day. But the older hypothesis is right about the role of compromise in the settlements these documents represent – an overt attempt to read the origins of the Gentile mission as universal rather than eclectic or sectarian. In so doing, the Gentile Christian movement at the dawn of the second century was self-consciously building second and third stories onto the early Pauline housechurches in key urban settings, and ably employing the same missionary tools – letters and delegated authority – for the enactment of an empire-wide movement as had their founder, Paul.

108 1 Tim 3:1–13; Young, *Theology*, 74–96; full discussion in ch. 7, below.
109 Cf. the 'pecking order' of 1 Cor 12:28f.
110 E.g. 1 Cor 7:17–24; 11:2–16; 14:33–6.
111 Balch and Osiek, *Families*, with further literature; Schüssler Fiorenza, *In memory of her*, 168–204, for discussion of important women on Paul's missionary team.
112 MacDonald, *Legend and apostle*.

6

Johannine Christianity

HAROLD W. ATTRIDGE

The literary evidence for Johannine Christianity

The complexity of the Johannine corpus renders attempts to trace the contours of Johannine Christianity difficult. Nonetheless, the sources reveal a community of early followers of Jesus who, using an abundance of biblical symbols, defined themselves rather starkly against the Jewish milieu in which they arose. These believers cultivated an intense devotion to Jesus as the definitive revelation of God's salvific will, and understood themselves to be in intimate contact with him and with one another, under the guidance of the Spirit-Paraclete. They were conscious of their relationship to other believers with whom they hoped to be in eventual union. Their piety found distinctive expression in a reflective literary corpus that explored new ways of expressing faith in Jesus. Their common life included ritual actions known to other followers of Jesus, but they insisted on the unique spiritual value of those rites. Disputes eventually divided the community. By the middle of the second century some representatives of the Johannine tradition achieved a respected role in the emerging 'great church', the interconnected web of believers throughout the Mediterranean that provided mutual support and maintained fellowship under the leadership of emerging episcopal authorities. The Johannine community of the first century bequeathed to the universal church its distinctive literary corpus and estimation of Jesus, which came to dominate the development of later Christian orthodoxy. Other representatives of Johannine Christianity, nurturing alternative strands of tradition, influenced various second-century movements, characterised by their opponents and much modern scholarship as 'Gnostic'.

Sources

The primary source for Johannine Christianity is the anonymous gospel 'according to John'.[1] Closely related in vocabulary, style and concerns are the Johannine epistles, which are certainly interrelated, even if they address discrete problems.[2] Most scholars find in them evidence of the Johannine community wrestling with problems of the interpretation of the gospel,[3] although some associate the epistles with a late phase of the gospel itself.[4]

Date and provenance of these central texts still generate controversy. The widely accepted date for a reasonably 'final' form of the gospel[5] is the late first or early second century, although other estimates have ranged widely. Nineteenth-century scholarship tended to place the gospel in the mid- or late second century.[6] The dating of P[52] (*P. Ryl.* 457), the gospel's earliest witness, to around 125 CE, provided many twentieth-century commentators a *terminus ante quem*, although the dating of the papyrus is hardly secure, and explicit citation of the gospel does not begin until Irenaeus in the last quarter of the second century. Nonetheless, allusions to the gospel in second-century works such as the *Epistles* of Ignatius of Antioch and the *Odes of Solomon*[7] persuade most commentators that the period of 90–110 constitutes a reasonable framework for the work's composition. Some critics push the date considerably earlier, before the destruction of the temple in 70 CE, thus finding in this gospel the earliest example of the genre.[8]

The location of the community that produced the gospel and whose experience is reflected in the epistles is also a matter of conjecture. Irenaeus associates the gospel written by the Beloved Disciple, John, with Ephesus.[9] Irenaeus and

---

1 The gospel itself is anonymous, although its final colophon (21:24) suggests that it was written by the 'disciple whom Jesus loved'. By the late second century church fathers attributed the text to John (Iren. *Haer.* 3.1.1; Clement of Alexandria, cited in Euseb. *HE* 6.14.7), who is soon equated with John the son of Zebedee, named as a close companion of Jesus in the Synoptic Gospels, and briefly mentioned in John 21:2. The attribution is doubtful and the function of the character of the Beloved Disciple remains debated. On attempts to identify the figure, see Charlesworth, *Beloved Disciple*. For a history of the tradition, see Culpepper, *John*. On the literary function of the Beloved Disciple, see Attridge, 'The restless quest'.

2 On the relationship among the epistles, see Brown, *Epistles of John*, 14–35.

3 See especially Brown, *Epistles of John*, 47–115.

4 See e.g. Strecker, *Johannine letters*.

5 Some sections are clearly later additions, particularly the 'pericope of the adulteress', John 8:1–11, although when it was added remains unclear.

6 For earlier opinions, see Brown, *Introduction*, 206–10.

7 On all the second-century evidence, including the dating of P[52], see most recently Nagel, *Rezeption*. Culpepper, *John*, 107–38, offers a brief summary of the evidence.

8 See Robinson, *Priority*; Berger, *Anfang*.

9 Iren. *Haer.* 3.1.1.

other church fathers report anecdotes of John's activity in Ephesus, competing with 'Gnostic' teachers such as Cerinthus,[10] or engaged in pastoral activity.[11] While some scholars continue to think of Ephesus as a probable venue, at least for the gospel's final form,[12] others have proposed options on the Mediterranean littoral or in the Syrian hinterland.[13] Affinities between the gospel and other religious literature support such efforts. Alexandria was the home of the first-century Jewish philosopher Philo, whose complex speculation on the *logos* is often seen as a background to the Johannine prologue.[14] Alexandria was also a centre both for the speculative Christianity labelled 'Gnostic', often proposed as a background to the gospel,[15] and also for circles that generated the *Corpus Hermeticum*, a body of Graeco-Roman religious literature with affinities to the gospel's symbolic world.[16] Alternatively, the Dead Sea scrolls parallel the gospel's 'dualism' and its use of scripture,[17] prompting speculation about the gospel's Palestinian roots.[18] Further east, the *Epistles* of Ignatius and the *Odes of Solomon*, probably of second-century Syrian provenance, offer intriguing similarities to the gospel's imagery and spirituality.[19]

Other texts occasionally enter discussions of the Johannine community. Although explicitly attributed to a visionary named John, the book of Revelation is not part of the relevant literary corpus. Despite some common motifs, its language, literary style and theology clearly distinguish Revelation from the gospel and epistles.[20]

---

10 *Haer.* 3.3.4, cited by Euseb. *HE* 3.28.6. On these legends, and the importance of Irenaeus, see Culpepper, *John*, 123–28.
11 Clem. Al. *q.d.s.* 42, cited by Euseb. *HE* 3.32.5–19, reports the activity of John the Apostle and a 'lost sheep' from the region of Ephesus.
12 Most recently, see van Tilborg, *Reading John*.
13 See Brown, *Introduction*, 19–206.
14 See e.g. Borgen, *Logos*. Tobin, 'Prologue'; Boyarin, 'Gospel of the Memra'.
15 The best known proponent is Bultmann, *Gospel of John*. See also Schottroff, *Der glaubende und die feindliche Welt*. The category 'Gnostic' has come under critical scrutiny. Williams, *Rethinking 'Gnosticism'*, highlights dangers in broad generalisations but agrees that there were second-century Christian groups sharing a family resemblance, which he labels 'demiurgic creationists'. King, *What is Gnosticism?*, traces the category's polemical and scholarly uses. For primary sources, see Foerster, *Gnosis*, and Layton, *Scriptures*.
16 Noted especially by Dodd, *Interpretation*. For an English translation, see Copenhaver, *Hermetica*.
17 A connection has long been championed by James H. Charlesworth. See Charlesworth, 'Dead sea scrolls', 'Critical comparison' and *Jesus and the Dead Sea scrolls*. It is endorsed by Ashton, *Understanding*, 232–7. Others remain sceptical. See Bauckham, 'Qumran'. On the hermeneutical parallels, see Clark-Soles, *Scripture*.
18 Jews sharing the sectarian stance of the scrolls may, however, have also been in the diaspora. See Brown, *Introduction*, 199–206.
19 Lattke, *Oden*, provides a comprehensive treatment of scholarship on the *Odes*.
20 On possible relationships, see e.g. Taeger, *Johannesapokalypse*.

Two second-century texts obliquely continue the Johannine literary tradition. The *Apocryphon of John* is the most important witness to a major strand of second-century Christianity. Four copies, all surviving in Coptic translations, attest two recensions of the work,[21] which was known also to Irenaeus.[22] The slightly later *Acts of John*,[23] pious fiction typical of the period, records legends featuring the apostle. Both works witness some second-century 'Johannine' Christians with 'Gnostic' characteristics, but caution is necessary in retrojecting their evidence to the first century as background to the gospel.

The complex heart of the corpus, the gospel, defies attempts to situate the Christianity that it represents. Several surface features of the text signal the difficulties. The genre, a narrative of the life, death and resurrection of Jesus, parallels other late first-century quasi-biographical gospels.[24] A patchwork of similarities to and differences from other known gospels, particularly the Synoptics, has produced continuous debate about their relationship to John. Most recent scholars are sceptical of direct dependence,[25] although some argue that assorted pericopes, particularly the passion narrative, indicate dependence on the Synoptics.[26] A few voices alternatively argue for the dependence of one or more of the Synoptics on John.[27] The possibility of Johannine intertextual allusions has recently become even more complicated because of the possible relationship between the gospel and non-narrative Jesus traditions, particularly the *Gospel of Thomas*.[28]

To decide the relationship of John to other gospels is not simply to determine its sources and, hence, its possible historical value. Understanding the loose relationship with the Synoptics and perhaps Thomas reveals the text's

---

21 Three come from the Nag Hammadi collection of Coptic texts, discovered in 1945. The fourth survives in a Coptic codex in Berlin. For a synoptic edition, see Waldstein and Wisse, *Apocryphon*.

22 *Haer.* 1.29. For translation and discussion, see Layton, *Scriptures*, 163–9.

23 For a translation, see Schneemelcher, *NTApoc*, vol. II, 152–212. Junod and Kaestli, *Acta*, provide a new critical text and French translation. On the relationship to Johannine tradition, see Koester, *Introduction*, vol. II, 202–4.

24 The most readily comparable texts are the Synoptic Gospels, but the fourth gospel probably emerged at a time when other narratives about Jesus, now extant in fragmentary form, competed for attention. On gospels in general, see Koester, *Ancient Christian gospels*. For the texts, see Schneemelcher, *NTApoc*, vol. I.

25 For a history of the debate, see Smith, *John among the gospels*, and for recent work, Schnelle, 'Johannes'; and Denaux, *John*.

26 Lang, *Johannes*. Dunderberg, *Johannes*, finds evidence of the Synoptics in a redactional layer of John 1–9.

27 Matson, *Dialogue*.

28 For possible connections between John and Thomas, see n. 76 below.

rhetoric, which engages in a sustained reflection on the 'conventional wisdom' of various proclamations about Jesus. The writers responsible for the gospel no doubt knew of the stuff of which the Synoptics and other gospels were made, and may have even known one or more in its final form, but freely adapted both oral traditions and literary productions.[29]

The text obviously delights in symbolism. Almost everything seems to point to something else. The miracles of Jesus are 'signs', but how and what they signify is not immediately apparent. Jesus' discourses are replete with evocative terms, often pointing to himself, but introducing scriptural and general cultural themes.[30] The complex narrative collapses temporal horizons, inscribing the life of the community into the story of Jesus.[31]

The use of irony introduces further intricacies. Although hardly unknown in the other gospels,[32] the trope pervades this text.[33] Sometimes irony is a transparent dramatic device in which a character's ignorance or misunderstanding reinforces the reader's beliefs.[34] Irony obviously pervades the pivotal event of the gospel, the 'hour' of Jesus' 'glory', strangely manifest in the ignominy of crucifixion (e.g. John 12:23–33). Yet there may be even deeper irony, playing with readers' expectations in order to provoke reflection.[35] Both pervasive symbolism and irony hint that the gospel does not contain straightforward references to actual belief and practice.

Further complicating the use of the gospel as a source for historical reconstruction are numerous aporias. Features of the plot challenge its unity, such as temporal and spatial sequences that make little sense,[36] or an apparent closure in the action that subsequent developments ignore.[37] At the conceptual level, affirmations about the relationship of Jesus and his Father,[38] about

---

29 On generic ambiguity, see Attridge, 'Genre bending'.

30 See Koester, *Symbolism*.

31 This is emphasised by Martyn, *Gospel*, and his *History and theology*.

32 More than a hint of irony is evident e.g. in the centurion's declaration in Mark 15:39.

33 For recent treatments, see Duke, *Irony*, and O'Day, *Revelation*.

34 Thus Nicodemus misunderstands being born 'from above/again' in ch. 3, and the Samaritan woman (ch. 4) fails to perceive the nature of the 'living water' that Jesus offers.

35 See e.g. the play on the knowledge of Jesus' origins at 7:27. The crowds claim to know where Jesus is from (Galilee?) but insist that the origins of the Messiah will be unknown, thereby revealing their ignorance of his heavenly origin. The text may also call into question a reader's presupposition that Jesus comes from Bethlehem.

36 E.g. the apparent movement from Galilee (ch. 4), to Jerusalem (ch. 5), to Galilee (ch. 6) and back (ch. 7) is, at the very least, abrupt and unmotivated.

37 John 14:31 would make an excellent transition to 18:1. The apparent closure at 14:31 is often taken as grounds for seeing chs. 15–17 as a redactional addition.

38 John 10:30: 'The Father and I are one', and 14:28: 'The Father is greater than I'.

judgement,[39] or about eschatological salvation are often contradictory or difficult to reconcile.[40] Such difficulties have inspired attempts to trace the gospel's sources and redactional history. One widely accepted theory posits the gospel's development from a primitive collection of miracle stories, a 'signs source',[41] through a process of homiletic elaboration of sayings of Jesus, assembled by an evangelist's guiding literary hand, supplemented by other editors or redactors.

Redactional theories in turn ground construals of the history of the community behind the text. Such theories postulate that Johannine believers began as a distinctive Jesus movement that gradually conformed to the Christianity of the second century.[42] While it seems highly likely that the gospel did develop over time and therefore shows signs of rewriting and expansion,[43] the construal of redactional activity as an attempt to domesticate a 'maverick'[44] narrative remains unsatisfactory. A fundamental problem is that the supposed redactors did such a miserable job of making corrections, having left so many tensive elements in the text. It is equally plausible, and indeed even more compelling, to read such elements as a deliberate literary strategy. Too ready an appeal to redactional corrections to explain disjunctions may obscure both the functions of the literary work itself and the character of the community standing behind it.

A possible history of Johannine Christianity

The overall contours of a history of Johannine Christianity could be sketched as follows. The community began in Israel, probably in Judaea,[45] in the immediate

---

39 Does Jesus, qua 'Son of Man', not judge (John 2:17) or does he (5:22, 27)?

40 Is resurrection a future (John 5:28–9) or present (John 11:25) reality?

41 The most enduring theory about the sources and redaction of the gospel is the hypothesis of a 'signs source'. See Fortna, *Gospel of signs*, and *Fourth gospel and its predecessor*. A brief version of Fortna's results is available in Miller, *Complete gospels*, 175–95. For an alternative, see van Wahlde, *Earliest version*. For a critical review of the history of research, see van Belle, *Signs source*.

42 Brown, *Community*, popularised a version of this developmental theory. For other theories, see Bull, *Gemeinde*.

43 Coming after the colophon of 20:30–1, ch. 21 clearly seems to be an appendix, although some scholars have argued for its integral relationship with what precedes. See Minear, 'Original function'.

44 For such a notion of the gospel, see Kysar, *John, the maverick gospel*. For Bultmann, the final hand was an 'ecclesiastical redactor', who brought into line with emerging orthodoxy elements such as the realised eschatology of the gospel.

45 The initial resurrection appearances (John 20) take place in Jerusalem, where the disciples receive their commission to a ministry of forgiveness (John 20:22). Hence, as in Luke, Jerusalem is the initial focus of the post-resurrection community. The Judaean roots may

aftermath of Jesus' death and resurrection, perhaps under the leadership of a disciple of Jesus who inspired the text's Beloved Disciple. This egalitarian fellowship remembered[46] what Jesus said and did and engaged in scriptural interpretation[47] to make sense of their experience. The community interpreted the mission of their rabbi or teacher[48] with the resources of their Jewish tradition, understanding him to be one sent from God,[49] a prophet like Moses,[50] the Messiah,[51] the Son of Man,[52] Son of God,[53] an embodiment of God's word.[54] Beyond traditional titulature, the gospel appropriated symbols from Jerusalem's cultic tradition and applied them to Jesus as the new temple,[55] the source of 'living water'[56] and 'light',[57] whose life reflected the biblical liturgical cycle.[58] This Judaean Johannine community probably expanded with converts from Samaria, who introduced distinctive messianic expectations focused on a Mosaic prophet.[59] In the face of external

be even stronger. Although Jesus is said by Philip to be 'the son of Joseph, from Nazareth' (John 1:45), there is a suggestion that Judaea is also his own 'homeland'. The reference to 'his own' who did not receive him (John 1:11) is particularly true of 'the Judaeans', from whom, paradoxically, also comes salvation (John 4:22). The ignorance of the Judaeans in 7:27 may also extend to their unawareness of a Judaean origin (Bethlehem?) for Jesus.

46 'Remembering' seems to be a technical term for this community. See John 2:17, 22; 12:16.

47 On Johannine use of scripture, see Daly-Denton, *David*. On the precise form of John's biblical text, see Menken, *Old Testament quotations*.

48 For this title, see John 1:38, with both Hebrew (*rabbi*) and Greek (*didaskalos*); 3:2, 10; 11:28; 13:13–14; 20:16, again using Hebrew (*rabbouni*) and Greek (*didaskalos*) forms.

49 This is the most common way of thinking about Jesus in the gospel. Cf. 4:34; 5:23–4, 30, 37; 6:38–9; 6:44; 7:16, 28, 33; 8:16, 18, 26, 29; 9:4; 12:44–5, 49; 13:16, 20; 14:24, 26; 15:21, 26; 16:5, 7; 20:21.

50 Cf. 1:45; 4:19; 6:14; 7:40; 9:17. For background, see esp. Meeks, *Prophet-king*.

51 Cf. 1:41, where the title is handily translated as *Christos*, as at 4:25, on the lips of the Samaritan woman.

52 Cf. 1:51; 3:13–14; 5:27; 6:27, 53, 62; 8:28; 9:35 ('of God' is a variant); 12:23, 34; 13:31. The gospel's treatment of this title merits more attention. See below.

53 Cf. 1:18 (on the textual crux, see Ehrman, *The Orthodox corruption*, 78–82), 1:34, 49 (= king of Israel); 3:16–18, 35–6; 5:19–26; 6:40; 8:35–6; 10:36; 11:4, 27 (= *Christos*); 14:13; 17:1; 19:7; 20:31 (= Christ).

54 John 1:1, 14. The Christology of the prologue, with its obvious echoes of the figure of divine wisdom (Prov 8; Sir 24; Wis 7), heavily influenced the appropriation of the gospel through the centuries, but it is not the end of the gospel's christological story.

55 Cf. 2:14–16.

56 Cf. John 4:14; 7:37–9.

57 Cf. John 1:9; 8:12. Both the last reference and the water image of ch. 7 appear within the feast of Tabernacles (John 7:2), which prominently featured both symbols.

58 The cycle, based on Exod 23:14–17; Lev 23:3–44; Num 9:9–39, is partially reflected in the sequence sabbath (John 5:9); Passover (6:4); Succoth or Booths (7:2); Channukah (10:22). The sabbath is obviously a weekly festival, but is mentioned first in the pentateuchal festival calendars.

59 A Samaritan mission is attested in Acts 8, but as a post-resurrection event. John 4 suggests that Samaritans became disciples during Jesus' lifetime. That claim may be part of the historical 'palimpsest' of the gospel highlighted by Martyn.

opposition from Jewish circles, members of the community insisted ever more stridently on the heavenly source and destiny of Jesus and his intimate relationship with God.[60] In pressing these claims against considerable opposition, they took on characteristics of a 'sect', with well-defined social boundaries.[61] Their claims eventually led to their 'expulsion from the synagogue', a trauma mentioned three times in the gospel.[62] Some scholars have connected that expulsion with the *birkat hamminim*, a 'blessing', or praise of God, in fact, an imprecation against heretics. This benediction was reportedly added to the *Amidah* or Eighteen Benedictions in the last decade of the first century by rabbis at Jamnia (Yavneh). Although a bitter separation from its Jewish matrix marked the history of Johannine believers, it cannot be correlated with the introduction of the *birkat hamminim*, which is not to be dated before the third century.[63] Tensions between traditional Jews and the new followers of Jesus are widely attested in early Christian sources.[64] While the animosity attested in the fourth gospel is particularly intense, it was not unique.

Now somewhat distinct from their former Jewish environment, whether in Judaea or the diaspora,[65] these believers faced new challenges, also inscribed in the Johannine literary corpus. Doctrinal disputes, apparent in 1 John, developed over the implications of the group's characteristic christological confession. The precise roots and shape of the rejected Christology(ies) are open to debate. The opponents mentioned in 1 John may have resisted the close association of Father and Son on which the gospel insists. They may also have questioned the connection between the divine *logos* and the apparent fleshliness

---

60 On the social function of christological claims, see Meeks, 'Man'.

61 See Rebell, *Gemeinde*; Neyrey, *Ideology*. The characterisation of the Johannine community as a sect is central to the review of Johannine scholarship by Ashton, *Understanding*.

62 John 9:22; 12:42; 16:2. Whether these texts refer to a single event or a lengthy process is unclear.

63 For criticism of the hypothesis of the *birkat hamminim* as a first-century rabbinic development, see van der Horst, 'Birkat'; see also ch. 4, above, and pt III, ch. 10, below. For a more extensive critique of the historicity of 'Yavneh', see Boyarin, 'Justin Martyr'.

64 Matt 23 reveals difficulties with contemporary synagogues and predicts persecution (Matt 23:34). Paul's problems with Jewish co-religionists are apparent from his letters (1 Thess 2:14–16; Phil 3:2–11; 2 Cor 11:24; Gal 5:11), and from the dramatised narrative of Acts (13:45, 50; 14:2–5; 17:5, 13; 20:19; 21:27–36). Rivalry with a synagogue and 'Jew' as a contested self-identification are evident in Rev 3:9. These sources, however, do not mention expulsion from the synagogue.

65 A perennial problem is the identity of the opponents of Jesus, *hoi Ioudaioi*, who often seem to be specifically related to the Judaean environment of Jesus' ministry, but who may symbolise opposition to Johannine Christians in new environments. See Meeks, 'Am I a Jew?'; Ashton, 'Identity'; van Wahlde, 'Johannine "Jews"'.

of Jesus. Such a 'docetic' position may have involved theories about the relationship between the heavenly/divine and the earthly/human in Christ, or it may have denigrated the physical Jesus, on philosophical[66] or perhaps even paraenetic grounds.[67] The writer of the epistle insists, in any case, on the close connection between Father and Son (1 John 2:22–3), and maintains that Jesus really did come 'in the flesh' (1 John 4:1–3; cf. 2 John 7). Other doctrinal struggles surface in the epistle's insistence on the reality of sin and atonement (1 John 1:8–2:2; 4:10) and on the concomitant need to assume moral responsibility.[68] However 1 John relates to the gospel, its positions strongly resemble the explicit stance of many prominent second-century Christians. On crucial doctrinal issues, the position of the epistles is, in broad outline, compatible with the emergent 'Great Church'.

A second point of conflict in the Johannine community's development concerns its organisational form.[69] The gospels overtly are silent on the organisation of the communities that read them. Some texts hint at an egalitarian ideology, e.g. Matthew's rejection of honorific titles (Matt 23:9), Mark's idealisation of service (Mark 10:45), or Acts' idyllic picture of primitive 'communism' (Acts 2:44; 4:32). The situation in early communities was certainly more complex, and Paul's letters attest emerging social organisation.[70] The gospels, too, occasionally hint at the ecclesial world for which they were written, rather than the ideal fellowship that they describe. Matthew 16:18–19 famously portrays Peter as a figure of authority, perhaps rivalling the still respected scribes and Pharisees (Matt 23:3). The portrait hints at an incipient monarchical episcopacy, first evident in Ignatius of Antioch. Otherwise, governance rested in the hands of presbyteral councils, implied in Acts 20:17–38, and evident in the Pastoral Epistles (1 Tim 3:1–12) and in *1 Clement* 42.4–5, from late first-century Rome.

The fourth gospel offers little explicit information about institutional structures. It portrays the followers of Jesus as a flock (John 10) and a vine (John 15), both of which suggest special intimacy. The sheep hear and recognize their

---

66 Divine impassibility was a widespread philosophical assumption. On Middle Platonic theology, see Dillon, *Platonists*, 128, 155, 280–5.
67 Cf. the denial of the significance of suffering in Wis 2:21–3:3, based on belief in the soul's incorruptibility. 'Docetic' Christologies emerged in early second-century Christianity. On the important evidence of Ignatius of Antioch, see Schoedel, *Ignatius*, 19–29.
68 Cf. 1 John 2:3–6; 3:15–17; 4:11–12.
69 See ch. 7, below.
70 See e.g. 1 Cor 12:28 for various functional roles; 16:19 for the 'house church' of Prisca and Aquila.

shepherd's voice;[71] the vine's branches grow directly from the stalk that is Jesus (John 15:2, 5–6). The pastoral imagery further suggests the existence of other sheep (John 11:41) who should belong to the one flock. Neither metaphor, however, has any room for an intermediary structure between Jesus and his 'sheep'. If a real Beloved Disciple or his successors played a governing role, that role finds no echo in the main body of the text. The disciple's death, implied by the dialogue between Jesus and Peter at 21:21–3, may have led to community reflection on its relationship to other sources of authority.

What appears instead of simple charter myths are disciples standing in symbolic opposition. Most prominently, the Beloved Disciple contrasts with Peter.[72] At the Last Supper, he reclines in the bosom of Jesus (John 13:23),[73] and mediates Peter's access to Jesus (13:24). At the cross, the Beloved Disciple stands by Jesus and becomes his adopted brother (John 19:26), after Peter had betrayed and abandoned Jesus (John 18:17, 25, 27). Peter and the Beloved Disciple run together to the tomb on Easter morning, but the Beloved Disciple arrives first (John 20:4) and 'believes' upon seeing the folded grave cloths (John 20:8). The disciple's precedence may have ecclesiological implications, if, by the time of the gospel's composition, Peter had become associated with hierarchical structures.

If an ecclesiological subtext underlies the Beloved Disciple's portrait, other aspects of his persona may have special significance. His new status as guardian of Jesus' mother may contrast with James, the Lord's brother (Gal 1:19; Mark 6:3), whose leadership in the church of Jerusalem is attested by Paul and Acts,[74] or with the claims of Thomas, 'the twin', understood to be the sibling of Jesus in early Syrian traditions.[75] Unlike the Beloved Disciple, Thomas believes only after seeing and being invited to touch the resurrected Jesus (John 20:28).[76] Whether they are historical individuals or ideal types, the contrasts

---

71 John 10:3, 27, a motif dramatically displayed in the raising of Lazarus (11:43) and the recognition of Jesus by Mary Magdalene (20:16).

72 Quast, *Peter*, usefully reviews the evidence.

73 As the 'only begotten' had been at the Father's bosom (John 1:18).

74 Gal 2:6; Acts 15:13–21; cf. Mark 6:3. On the role of James, see most recently Chilton and Evans, *James*.

75 On this point, see Schenke, 'Function'. On Didymus Judas Thomas, see the *Gospel of Thomas* 1, 13; and the *Acts of Thomas*.

76 Several scholars have recently detected a critical stance in the fourth gospel towards 'Thomasine' Christianity. Riley, *Resurrection*, contrasts the emphasis on the physical reality of the resurrection in John with the absence of any explicit affirmation of the resurrection in the *Gospel of Thomas*. De Conick, *Seek*, finds a quest for ascent mysticism in *Gos. Thom.*, but a denial of its possibility in John, which makes Jesus the locus of revelation. Pagels, *Beyond belief*, finds a contrast between the implicit authoritarianism of

between the Beloved Disciple and other disciples suggest a critique of contemporary Christian groups, symbolised by various apostolic figures. All the disciples, nonetheless, are indeed apostles, 'sent' into the world as was Jesus (John 20:21).

The epistles provide tantalising data on disputes about the leadership of Johannine Christians, in the figure of Diotrophes, criticised in 3 John as one who 'loves first place' (*philōproteuōn*) and who 'does not receive us' (3 John 9). Diotrophes probably represents the new style of leadership, like Ignatius of Antioch, that emerged in the early second century. The 'elder' who penned 3 John, and perhaps the two other Johannine epistles as well,[77] may have represented an older form of leadership, closer to the charismatic itinerants of the first apostolic generation. The rivalry between 'the elder' and Diotrophes would then resemble the development evident in the *Didache*, the first book of church order, compiled probably in Greek-speaking Syria during the late first through early second century.[78] *Didache* 12.1–5 recognises but restricts the authority of itinerant prophets, while *Didache* 15.1–2 entrusts the future to locally elected bishops and deacons.[79]

While the portraits of the disciples in the fourth gospel score points about titular leaders and by implication their followers, the image of Peter in the last chapter takes on special significance. Rehabilitated from his triple denial of Jesus by a triple protestation of love (John 21:15–17), he is finally commissioned to 'feed the sheep' (John 21:17). This chapter acknowledges that, however much the apostle Peter and perhaps other ecclesiastical leaders were inferior to the Beloved Disciple, their authoritative position should be respected.

John 21 then suggests that Johannine believers were becoming reconciled with the wider church of the second century, which, by the time of Irenaeus, would be marked by its interconnected hierarchy, incipient canon and creedal confession.[80] The epistles also attest a schism within the community, in their reference to 'antichrists', who 'have gone out from us' (1 John 2:18–19). Perhaps those people maintained the theological positions criticised in the epistle, a docetically tinged Christology, or a denial of the reality of sin. Their legacy

---

John, where everything depends on Jesus, and *Gos. Thom.*, where wisdom may be found in every human heart. Dunderberg, 'John and Thomas', 361–80, offers a sceptical critique. For a test case of a specific sayings tradition, see Attridge, '"Seeking" and "asking"'.

77 On the issue of authorship, see Brown, *Epistles of John*, 14–35.
78 See Niederwimmer, *Didache*.
79 More distantly related is the turmoil at Corinth attested in *1 Clement*. At issue seems to have been the displacement of an older generation of leaders by a new, more youthful cadre. See *1 Clem.* 44.
80 On the development of self-defined 'orthodoxy' see pt III, ch. 13, below.

may be felt in such second-century texts as the *Apocryphon of John* and the *Acts of John*.

Distinctive features of Johannine Christianity

Johannine literature suggests that the 'community of the Beloved Disciple' had its own development within the larger Christian orbit, a development that, by the second century, led some of its number to a closer association with the type of Christianity, heavily influenced by Paul, emerging in urban centres from Antioch through Ephesus to Rome. The written record nonetheless maintains distinctive features in theology and practice, particularly in three areas, Christology, eschatology and ethics. In each area the distinctive Johannine position intensifies elements present in other forms of Christianity. In the final analysis the gospel's most distinctive features are the literary techniques through which it makes its claims.

Christology

At the heart of the gospel stands a very 'high' view of Jesus, God's creative Word in human flesh, as the prologue (John 1:1–18) proclaims.[81] This association of Jesus with God's word is certainly related to the sapiential categories exploited by other early believers for explaining the significance of Jesus.[82] Similarly, the claim that Jesus is the incarnation of a principle or agent sent from God is present in other early celebrations of Christ.[83] Distinctive of the fourth gospel is the way in which the two poles of the affirmation are maintained without explicit resolution. Jesus and the Father are one (John 10:30); yet the Father is greater than Jesus (John 14:28). Jesus is sovereign over wind and wave (John 6:19) and has preternatural knowledge (1:48, 16:30), but is reduced to tears at a friend's tomb (John 11:35).

To reduce these tensive elements to indices of documentary development ignores their conceptual role. The gospel's antinomies repeatedly reaffirm both claims of the prologue: Jesus is God's Word, and he is flesh and blood. Ultimately, his glorious divinity is most apparent when he is most visibly human, at his death.

The text's approach to claims about the significance of Jesus is evident in the series of appellations of Jesus as 'Son of Man'. Several passages evoke sayings of

---

81 For recent work, see Menken, 'Christology'.
82 Matt 11:19; 1 Cor 1:24; Heb 1:3.
83 Such celebrations often appear in material identified as hymnic: Phil 2:6–11; Col 1:15–20; Heb 1:1–3; but also in confessional formulas, e.g. 1 Cor 8:6.

the Synoptic tradition, but often with a new twist. Some (John 1:51, 5:27, 6:62) parallel elements of the 'eschatological' Son of Man sayings, the predictions of the 'coming' in heavenly glory surrounded by angels to act as judge.[84] Other verses[85] recall the passion predictions that form the backbone of Mark but are paralleled in the other gospels.[86] Others (John 6:27, 53, 9:35) portray the Son of Man in the present, offering sustenance and soliciting belief.

In all of these cases, the echoes of familiar traditions are made strange. At John 1:51, the Son of Man is not *surrounded by* angels, but, through an evocation of Jacob's ladder, he becomes a vehicle for their ascent and descent. At John 3:13–14, another biblical intertext, the healing serpent from Numbers 22 reinterprets the suffering Son of Man. At John 8:28, the 'lifting up' of the Son of Man reveals his true identity, and, at John 12:32, he promises to draw all to himself. The manipulation of Son of Man sayings through the earlier chapters anticipates the final saying at John 13:31, which boldly combines the 'glory' associated with the 'eschatological' sayings, with the event of the 'hour' when the Son of Man is 'lifted up'.

The handling of the Son of Man sayings betrays a deliberate appropriation of traditions about Jesus, holding assertions about glory and suffering in an ironic tension that invites the reader or hearer of the gospel to contemplate the significance of the cross.[87] A reflective literary hand has reshaped traditional material in order to reinforce a central Christian tenet.[88] Although the gospel has certainly been read as naively docetic,[89] the handling of such traditional christological sayings, like much else in the text, strongly emphasised the incarnate Christ as the focal point of Christian thought.[90]

Eschatology

What obtains for Christology also applies to the gospel's eschatology.[91] It is striking that the gospel lacks scenes of eschatological judgement or apocalyptic

---

84 Cf. Mark 13:26–7 and parr.; Matt 25:31–46. In general on the Son of Man in John, see Moloney, *The Johannine Son of Man*.

85 John 3:13–14; 8:28; 12:23–34; 13:31.

86 Mark 8:31; 9:31; 10:33. Among the arguments for some acquaintance with the Synoptic Gospels is the structural similarity, to Mark in particular, created by the prominence of three passion predictions utilising the motif of the Son of Man.

87 The insistence on seeing the cross with the intense eyes of faith has led to the long tradition of viewing the gospel as a 'mystical' text. See Countryman, *Mystical way*; Kangaraj, '*Mysticism*'.

88 Like Paul, the evangelist could well affirm that he knows only Christ and him crucified (1 Cor 1:23).

89 An assessment famously defended by Käsemann, *Testament*.

90 For elaboration of this point, see Schnelle, *Antidocetic Christology*.

91 In general see Frey, *Eschatologie*.

catastrophe, like those prominent on the lips of Jesus in the Synoptics and paralleled in Paul.[92] Some passages, moreover, use eschatological categories, particularly 'judgement'[93] and 'resurrection',[94] to describe not future events but the present confrontation between the individual and Christ. Yet some passages do mention a judgement and resurrection to come 'on the last day'.[95] The antinomies in the perspectives on eschatology have stimulated debate about the character of the Christianity that the gospel represents. In this material in particular, some scholars have found evidence of the hand of a corrective redactor, imposing orthodoxy on a more radical original source.[96]

Before embracing such mechanical redactional hypotheses, however, it is important to remember the reinterpretive strategy apparent in the gospel's Christology. A similar tactic is likely to be at work in the eschatological passages, where the gospel did not, in fact, break new ground. Other early Christian teachers had also used eschatological categories to suggest that hoped-for realities were part of the believers' present experience, particularly in worship. Such claims appear prominently in passages on baptism, which, in Pauline Christianity, actualises Christ's death and resurrection in the life of the believer.[97] The ritual also makes the new life of the spirit a present reality,[98] even if believers long for eschatological consummation.[99] One of the dangers that Paul himself confronted was a tendency to take the trope too literally and thereby ignore both the future hope and the contemporary ethical demand that he thought essential to life 'in Christ'.[100]

The fourth gospel's handling of eschatological expectations parallels Paul's, with a balance between present reality and future hope. Yet, in contrast to Paul, the gospel emphasises the side of the realisation of 'eternal life' in the

---

92 Cf. Matt 24–25; Mark 13; Luke 21; 1 Thess 4:13–18; 1 Cor 7:29–31; 15.

93 John 2:17–21; 8:15. Yet the Father has given judgement to the Son, according to John 5:22, 27. For a general exploration of the theme, see Blank, *Krisis*.

94 Cf. John 5:24–5; 11:25–6.

95 Cf. John 5:28–9; 6:39–40, 44, 54; 11:24; 12:48.

96 See e.g. Haenchen, *John 1*, 259–60.

97 Rom 6:1–11 uses the parallel between baptism and death/resurrection with subtlety and restraint. The future hope (v 8) and ethical reading of 'new life' (v 11) are clear. Colossians 2:12–13 emphasises more directly the participation in Christ's new life; nonetheless, future hope remains (Col 3:1–4). For deutero-Pauline applications of eschatological language to present experience, cf. 2 Tim 2:18; 2 Thess 2:2.

98 Famously celebrated at Gal 2:19–20; Phil 3:7–11; Rom 8:9–11.

99 Cf. Rom 8:18–30.

100 See e.g. the emphasis in Phil 3:12–16 on the 'not yet' element of Christian life, following close on the affirmation of being 'in Christ'. Similar concerns may underlie Paul's criticism of Corinthian self-confidence (1 Cor 4:8–9).

believer's 'abiding' relationship with God, which grounds any hope of a more conventionally conceived 'eternal life'.

The dialogue between Jesus and Martha of Bethany sharply focuses the gospel's eschatological tension. After Jesus proclaims to Martha that her brother would rise, she responds with a conventional Jewish hope[101] that her brother would rise on the last day (John 11:23–4). Without denying Martha's hopes, Jesus points to himself as resurrection, and by implication, life lived with him as eternal. Absent the life of faith, hope in a future resurrection is, the gospel suggests, vain. Similarly, at the core of the Last Supper discourses (14:1–4), Jesus, discussing the 'way' of his departure, promises to return and take his disciples with him to a heavenly 'abode' (John 14:2), the Johannine equivalent of the Pauline 'rapture' (1 Thess 4:17). The subsequent dialogues suggest that the intimacy envisioned for the post-return 'future' is already present. To those who keep Jesus' word, Jesus and the Father will come and make their 'abode' (John 14:23). Like branches on the vine, his disciples will abide in him, if they keep his commandments.[102] This sequence of eschatological moments parallels that of John 11. A traditional hope is strongly affirmed, but by implication made contingent upon the anticipatory realisation of that hope in the life of the believer. Traditional eschatology has not been eliminated but refocused on its present preconditions.[103] The figure of the Paraclete, the 'spirit of truth' (John 14:17), plays a central role in this refocusing. Present through baptismal rebirth (John 3:5), this 'Holy Spirit' (John 14:26) abides with the disciples (John 14:17), teaching them (John 14:26) and defending them against a hostile world (John 16:8–11).[104]

When seen from the perspective of the play on eschatological categories in chapters 11 and 15, the antinomies in the theme of judgement attain clearer resolution. The climactic saying on the subject at John 12:47–8 combines the tensive affirmations that the Son does and does not judge. Unlike the Son of Man seated in eschatological glory, Jesus, the Son, has not come to judge but to save (John 12:48), yet the word that he has spoken (or will speak: John 13:31)

---

101 The hope, classically expressed at Dan 12:1–3, was not universally shared, as Mark 12:18 and parr. and Acts 23:6–8 indicate. For the diversity of Jewish beliefs, see Nickelsburg, *Resurrection*.

102 John 15:5–10. The mutual indwelling of God and the believer who abides by God's command is a theme echoed in 1 John 2:24; 4:12, 16; 5:3.

103 Such focus on the initial encounter with the revealing Word and the life that flows from it may have appealed to second-century 'Gnostic' Christians. But, like the fourth gospel, they did not dispense with future eschatology. See Attridge, 'Gnosticism'.

104 On the Paraclete's role, see Brown, 'Paraclete' and Smalley, '"Paraclete"'.

provides a basis for judgement 'on the last day'. The gospel allows for an eschatological future, but it is firmly grounded in the present confrontation between the Word, both in the flesh and in the book, and those summoned to hear it.[105]

Ethics and religious practice

The followers of Jesus depicted in the Johannine literature display few of the practices that characterised their lives. Unlike the Sermon on the Mount (Matt 5–7), the fourth gospel says nothing about an ethic of non-violence, of loving enemies, turning the other cheek, renouncing divorce, walking the extra mile.

Ethics for the fourth gospel can be reduced to the single command to love one another, emphatically proclaimed at the Last Supper (John 13:31), illustrated with a proverbial saying (John 15:13) and echoed in the epistles.[106] The gospel spends little time on practical consequences, although both it and the epistles insist on the importance of forgiveness of sins.[107] Yet the love that disciples are to embody focuses on the community of fellow disciples. Such love is not deemed incompatible with harsh words against enemies (John 8:44), which perhaps mirror the hatred of an inimical 'world'.[108]

Neither the evangelist nor the writer of 1 John elaborates a detailed ethic; both focus instead on fundamental motivations for ethical behaviour. The Last Supper discourses indicate that the foundation is not simply a divine command issued by God's legate, but, in Jesus' death for his friends, it is also an embodied example of the 'greatest love' (John 15:14). This grounding of ethics in turn constitutes a soteriology: the cross reveals something that attracts (John 12:32) and heals (John 3:14–15), which, as the final discourses make clear, is love in action. In making 'the love command' central to Christian proclamation, John is hardly unique.[109] By connecting that command so closely to the cross, the evangelist innovatively fused a theoretical foundation of ethics and a doctrine of revelation.

Unconcerned about ethical details, neither does the fourth gospel worry about religious practices, such as fasting, which troubled other Christians[110] and, according to *Didache* 8.2–3, marked community boundaries. Perhaps

---

105 1 John 4:17 maintains the same structure of eschatological hope. Living the life of love provides bold confidence (*parrhēsia*) on the 'day of judgement'.
106 1 John 2:7 refers to the now 'old command', particularly celebrated in 4:7–5:4.
107 Cf. John 20:23; 1 John 1:9; 2:1.
108 John 15:18–29; 17:14. The fact that the gospel preaches love but uses harsh invective offends its most severe critics, such as Casey, *Is John's gospel true?*.
109 Cf. Matt 5:43–4; 22:35–40; Mark 12:28–34; Luke 10:25–8; Gal 5:14; Rom 13:8–10.
110 On the diverse fasting practices of early Christians, see ch. 7, below.

Johannine Christians rejected the biblical practice of fasting as did other early followers of Jesus, but the text is silent. In contrast to Matthew 7:7–13 and Luke 11:2–4, the gospel offers little explicit instruction about prayer. The final prayer of Jesus (17:1–26), faintly echoing the Lord's Prayer,[111] is not proposed for imitation. Jesus endorses petitionary prayer (John 14:13–14; 16:26), but without specifying its form. The epistles provide examples of confessional forms (1 John 4:7–10), but not prescriptions.

The text suggests that Johannine Christians baptised and conducted a sacred meal, two hallmarks of Christian communities. The gospel offers conflicting testimony on whether Jesus himself baptised,[112] but that seems irrelevant to the insistence that one must be 'born from above' by 'water and spirit' (John 3:5). The dialogue with Nicodemus offers a specifically Johannine interpretation of the action, precisely in the terminology of 'birth again/from above'. Neither a cleansing from sin,[113] nor an eschatological seal,[114] nor participation in the death of Christ,[115] baptism is, using language of Hellenistic religion, a 'rebirth'.[116] While other baptismal theologies are not in evidence, there is an intricate literary development of baptismal symbols. The 'water' through which rebirth occurs is echoed in the water from Jacob's well in John 4, where the traditional sapiential equation of water and teaching is apparent. That traditional equation receives a new twist in the note that teaching will bubble up as a fountain within each believer (John 7:38). New associations appear through the connection of the believer's 'water' with what flows from Jesus' pierced side (John 19:34).[117] Baptismal 'water' is thus ultimately connected with the believer's apprehension of the cross.[118] 1 John 2:26–7 also mentions a 'chrism' that teaches, perhaps alluding to another baptismal symbol.

That Johannine Christians celebrated a sacred meal is clear, although how they did so is not. Whatever their practice, we should not expect a standard formula in the late first or early second century.[119] Two passages are relevant

---

111 The prayers share the addressee (Father), and the motives of coming, glory/hallowing and giving.
112 The discrepancy between John 3:22 (Jesus baptised) and 4:2 (only disciples baptised) may be redactional.
113 Cf. Mark 1:4; Luke 3:3; Acts 2:38.
114 Cf. Rev 7:3; 9:4.
115 Cf. Rom 6:1–4; Col 2:12–13.
116 Cf. Corpus Hermeticum 13.
117 Some interpreters find baptismal allusions elsewhere in the gospel, but most are hardly clear. For examples, see Moloney, 'Sacraments?'; Morgan-Wynne, 'References'.
118 1 John 5:7 echoes the connection of blood and water.
119 Bradshaw, Worship, argues against positing a primitive normative form of eucharistic action, and McGowan, Ascetic eucharists, discusses the wide variety of eucharistic practices in the first two centuries.

to their practice. Chapter 13 recounts a simple final meal, with no symbolism attached to bread or wine, as in the Synoptic and Pauline accounts.[120] Instead, Jesus washes the disciples' feet and requires that they do likewise (John 13:3–17). On the other hand, Jesus' lengthy discourse on the bread of life concludes (John 6:51–8) by affirming the importance of eating Jesus' flesh and drinking his blood. This passage clearly alludes to the kind of eucharist celebrated in Pauline and Synoptic communities.

One interpretation of this evidence sees the Johannine community celebrating its own sacred meal, without 'words of institution'[121] or any reference to the symbolism of bread/body, wine/blood. A redactor, concerned to fill a gap, expanded the 'bread of life' discourse of chapter 6 to include such elements. Although some have argued for the integrity of John 6,[122] most scholars accept the theory of literary stratification and its implications for the development of Johannine eucharistic practice.

The gospel's overall literary strategy should, however, signal caution. The gospel regularly recontextualises elements of early Christian teaching and practice. One might suspect a similar strategy at work in the eucharistic materials. As a redactional move, situating the reference to sacramental eating in chapter 6 is hardly an effective device to harmonise the gospel with some newly orthodox practice. Instead, the 'eucharistic' passages of chapters 6 and 13 could be designed to work together. One must 'eat flesh' and 'drink blood' to have a part with Jesus (John 6:53); one must also know and understand his act of loving service (John 13:17). If 'eating' and 'drinking' function as traditional sapiential metaphors, then the actions contemplated in chapter 6 must be correlated with the interpretation of the actions suggested by 13.

The 'sacramental' language of chapter 6 certainly alludes to a ritual practice used by the Johannine community at some point in its development. It might have come late to the life of the community or, more likely, it describes an accepted practice the understanding of which the evangelist wanted to deepen.

Conclusion

Johannine Christianity constitutes an alternative to other forms of Christianity in the late first or early second century. It does so in part because its community

---

120 Mark 14:22–5; Matt 26:26–9; Luke 22:15–20; 1 Cor 11:23–5.
121 The 'eucharist' of *Did.* 9–10 similarly lacks the words of institution.
122 See Borgen, *Bread*, and his 'John 6'; as well as Anderson, *Christology*.

history, its oral and written traditions, and its practices may differ from those of the 'other sheep' with which it became increasingly in contact. But most of all it is distinct from its competitors because its probing analysis of traditional forms and affirmations resulted in a creative attempt to comprehend and, thus, to recontextualise the experience of Jesus and what it means to follow him.

Figure 3. Fish and loaves, Catacomb of San Callisto (Rome) (photo: Estelle Brettman, The International Catacomb Society)

7

Social and ecclesial life of the earliest Christians

WAYNE A. MEEKS

The movement that began with Jesus of Nazareth and would eventually become the Christian church in its manifold varieties developed with astonishing rapidity and exhibited diverse forms from its earliest years. Most of those early developments remain invisible to us, and scholarly attempts to plot their outline must be viewed with scepticism, but roughly we may say, with a modern sociologist, that the movement began as a Jewish sect and was soon transformed into a Graeco-Roman cult.[1] The evolution was not unilinear. Some experiments, probably more than we can know, failed; others were suppressed by rival groups. We can piece together only fragmentary pictures from several aspects of that process – the social forms of association from the Galilean beginnings to the post-Easter community in Jerusalem and the house congregations in the cities of the Roman empire, the social location of typical converts, forms of worship and ritual and other dimensions of an emerging Christian subculture.

Community organisation

Perhaps the most profound innovation that the followers of Jesus introduced into the ancient Mediterranean world was a new form of religious community. There is much truth in the assertion by Adolf von Harnack, in his classic study of 'the mission and expansion of Christianity', that by the year 300 CE it was 'this church itself . . . through its mere existence' that had replaced the activity of 'missionaries' in apostolic times, and that it was able to do so by indigenising its radical and revolutionary claims into forms that seemed 'familiar, wished-for, and natural'.[2] We can gain some sense of both early Christianity's 'naturalness' in its environment and its novelties only by comparing it with contemporary

---

1 Stark and Bainbridge, *Future of religion*, 113.
2 Harnack, *Mission und Ausbreitung*, 526–7, my trans.

social phenomena. We must keep in mind, however, that we are comparing, on both sides, reconstructions formed from scarce and sometimes random evidence.

Jesus and his followers

Several different models can be used to fill out the sparse and often contradictory picture provided by the earliest traditions about Jesus and his adherents. Some features suggest a movement we might call, somewhat anachronistically, political, that is, defined primarily by its response to the situation produced by Roman hegemony.[3] Other elements in the tradition suggest the quite different picture of a circle of disciples with a teacher,[4] while others seem to describe the clients and publicists of an exorcist and miracle worker.[5] Still other parts of the tradition seem to depict Jesus in the specifically Jewish and biblical colours of a prophet,[6] so that his followers look like an eschatological renewal movement. These different models need not be mutually exclusive.

Keeping in mind that all the stories of Jesus we have in our sources have been transformed by the posthumous reinterpretation that had to take place if the movement was going to continue after his death, the crucifixion itself is the one firm starting place for historical investigation of the group that formed around Jesus.[7] This form of execution immediately shows us how Jesus and his followers appeared to one key set of observers – the Roman governor and his advisers. The first-century Jewish historian Flavius Josephus describes several movements whose leaders met similar fates at the hands of the Roman authorities, from the time when Judaea was organised as a subprovince under Syria in 6 CE to the eve of the revolt in 66. Josephus writes as a former commander of one group of the Jewish rebel force and as a survivor who had become a client of the Flavian house; he is not an objective observer. In Roman eyes what was important about all the movements Josephus describes was that they were dangerous to the Roman peace in an area perilously close to the eastern frontier. Josephus' accounts probably magnify the anti-Roman aspects of the story by describing the disturbances with the categories and the animus

---

3 Note the importance of the title 'king of the Jews' in the trial and crucifixion narratives in all the gospels. Revolutionary elements are also clearly implied in the stories of Jesus' solemn entry into Jerusalem, his attack on practices in the temple, and his prediction of the temple's destruction and replacement.

4 The portrayal of Jesus as teacher dominates especially the gospel of Matthew.

5 Cf. for example, the sequence of stories in Mark 1:14–3:30.

6 E.g. John 6:14; Acts 3:22–6; Mark 14:65; the many prophetic judgement oracles among the sayings attributed to Jesus, such as Matt. 11:20–4; 21:22–46; Luke 6:24–6; Matt. 10:34–6.

7 See especially Dahl, 'Crucified Messiah'.

bred by the later disaster. His interest in distancing all of these movements from the native aristocracy of Judaea, in which he included himself, may also distort his descriptions. He calls several of the leaders 'bandits' (*lēistai*, e.g. *AJ* 18.7; 20.121, 160, 163, 167, 172, 185, 186), the term he also prefers for the instigators of the revolt under the governor Florus (e.g. *BJ* 2.434). The same word is used in the gospels to describe the two men crucified with Jesus (Mark 15:27; Matt 27:38, 44) and, in the fourth gospel, Barabbas (John 18:40; note also John 10:8). Others Josephus calls *goētai*, 'soothsayers', 'charlatans', though he admits they called themselves *prophētai*, 'prophets' (*BJ* 1.148–54; *AJ* 20.160, 167–72, 188). Other leaders, he reports, had royal pretensions (*BJ* 2.57, 60, 444; *AJ* 17.272, 273, 278–85).

There are several recurring elements in Josephus' narratives of failed rebellions that should warn us against a facile separation of 'political' from 'religious' factors. First, the dramatic images that attracted followers and interpreted their aims echo the sacral traditions of Israel's past: conquest of the Holy Land would come from the wilderness (*AJ* 20.167); a dry path would open through the Jordan on command (*AJ* 20.97); tabernacle implements hidden by Moses on the sacred mountain would be recovered (*AJ* 18.85–7); the city's walls would collapse on command (*AJ* 20.170). Second, the uprisings were thus eschatological: corresponding to the saving events of the past there would come in the immediate future a direct, final intervention by God to transform the social order. Third, the movements were popular, led by figures whose authority was traditional and charismatic, not institutional.

All three features are found in early traditions about Jesus and his followers. They are also characteristics of the community described in the sectarian documents discovered last century in Wadi Qumran in Judaea. In both cases, despite the obvious differences between them, we have to do with something like what modern anthropologists have called a 'renewal' or 'nativist' movement. In a traditional society that has experienced recent social and cultural change, usually by superimposition of a foreign power, a charismatic leader gathers followers for some transformative programme, cast in imagery drawn from the society's traditional defining symbols but imaginatively reformulated for the present crisis.[8]

In the early church's remembered lore about Jesus and his disciples, there are a number of elements that accord well with the 'renewal movement' model. The fact that a group of *twelve* is singled out – even though the tradition

[8] The literature on 'renewal', 'revitalisation', 'nativistic' and 'millenarian' movements is vast. One of the early classics is Wallace, 'Revitalization movements'. Two other examples: Worsley, *Trumpet*; Burridge, *New heaven*.

shows some variation in the specific names – clearly alludes to the eponymous sons of Jacob and the tribes of ancient Israel, thus suggesting some kind of repristinisation of Israel's identity. Accounts of Jesus' 'call' of disciples, sayings attributed to him that emphasise disruption of occupational and family life and adoption of a mendicant, itinerant existence correspond to the negative phase so often seen in nativistic movements, breaking with settled norms and patterns to make room for ideal patterns of culture reimagined from the past. Such itinerancy characterises the groups described by Josephus, often bringing them to resemble 'social bandits',[9] and the withdrawal of the Qumran group to the desert of Judaea is a parallel phenomenon. The elements of the Christian tradition that focus on Jesus' relationship with Jerusalem and the temple – the prophecy of the temple's destruction, the 'cleansing' of the temple, and the 'triumphal entry' – also fit this pattern.

The other two major organisational patterns – that of a teacher of wisdom with disciples and that of an exorcist-magician having adherents – seem equally deeply rooted in the traditions about Jesus. These two could easily be subsumed under the images of eschatological prophet and renewal movement, for both 'signs' and teaching, including the free appropriation of 'wisdom' forms of speech, were features of the classic depiction of the prophet in Israel. Not only the prophets of the eighth through the sixth centuries BCE, whose oracles had been collected and preserved as scripture, but also Moses and Elijah were paradigmatic.

Corresponding to the locations of Jesus' own activity as depicted in the gospels, there seem to have been two centres of activity for his early followers. One was in the villages of (mostly) rural Judaea, Galilee and Samaria, the other in Jerusalem.[10] It is in instructions by Jesus to his delegates or 'apostles' that we have our only primary source of information about the way the new sect may have established itself in the village culture of Palestine. There we see itinerant prophets who detach themselves from those ties of place and of family which, especially in a rural setting, ordinarily determine a person's identity: 'Foxes have holes, and birds of the air have nests; but the Son of Man has nowhere to lay his head' (Matt 8:20; Luke 9:58). 'If anyone comes to me and does not hate his own father and mother and wife and children and brothers and sisters, yes, and even his own life, he cannot be my disciple' (Luke 14:16; cf. Matt 10:37). On the other hand, they are made dependent for their subsistence upon the villagers to whom they are sent to proclaim their message of the reign of God (see Mark 6:8–11 and parallels).

9 Horsley and Hanson, *Bandits*.
10 See pt I, ch. 1, above.

Naturally this picture had been idealised to some extent by the time these traditions were incorporated into the written gospels. Nevertheless, it is clear that wandering, mendicant prophets or apostles played a considerable role in the spread of the Jesus sect in Jewish and Samaritan villages. Their mission was possible because they and the villagers shared a common culture which included not only the theological beliefs, the scriptures and the traditions within which Jesus' career was interpreted by his disciples, but also the socially familiar role that the disciples themselves acted out, that of the prophet. It is not so clear from our sources what kind of organised group, if any, may have emerged in the villages on those occasions when the prophets' message was accepted. Presumably there, as in the cities, adherents to the new Messiah would gather in homes for prayers, exhortations and celebration of the ritual meal, and leadership was apparently largely in the hands of the itinerants or their local deputies. In several early Christian documents (most clearly in Matthew and the *Didache*) there is evidence of conflicts between local and itinerant leaders.

Jerusalem

In the Acts of the Apostles and the earlier letters of Paul, we see a group centred in Jerusalem that seems much more stable and structured than the rural movement just described. Leadership was still relatively informal, with an indeterminate number of 'apostles' (Gal 1:17, 19; limitation of the title to the twelve is a later schematisation; cf. 1 Cor 15:4–7). Acts speaks also of 'elders' (Acts 15:6, 22), recalling local Jewish organisations.[11] Certain individuals, however, exercised special powers – pre-eminently Peter (Cephas) (Gal 1:18; 2:9; Acts 1:13, 15; 2:14, 37; chs. 3–5; 10; 15:17), often associated with Zebedee's sons, James and John (Mark 5:37; 9:2; 13:3; 14:33; perhaps these three are the 'pillars' Paul refers to in Gal 2:9) and James 'the brother of the Lord' (Gal 1:19; 2:12; Acts 12:17; 15:13; 21:18; cf. *Gos. Thom.* 12). James' rise to power in the movement contrasts with the traditions of earlier hostility towards Jesus from his immediate family (Mark 3:31–5 and parallels; John 7:3–5). Acts depicts a tightly organised sect, practising community of possessions (2:44–5; 4:32–7;

---

11 *Presbyteroi* ('elders'): *CII* 378, 581, 590, 595, 597, 663, 692; in Lifschitz's addenda to the 1975 edition, 650c, 650d, 653d, 731f; Noy, *Jewish inscriptions*, vol. 1: 59, 62, 71, 75, 148, 149, 157, 163, 181; *gerousia* and *gerousiarchēs*: *CII* 9, 95, 106, 119, 147, 189, 301, 353, 355, 368, 405, 408, 425, 504, 511, 600, cf. Frey's comments, pp. lxxxvf; Mazar, Schwabe and Lifshitz, *Beth She'arim*, 141 (vol. ii, 127–8); Noy, *Jewish inscriptions*, vol. 1: 18, 23, 76, 87, 163; vol. ii: 86, 96, 130, 189, 238, 321, 351, 354, 389, 487, 521, 554, 555. Cf. 1 Macc 7:33; 11.23; 12:35; 13:36; 14:20, 18; 2 Macc 11:27; 13:13; 14:37; 3 Macc 1:8; 6:1; Judith 6:16; 7:23; 8:10; 10:6; 13:12. *Gerousia* at Alexandria: Philo, *Flacc.* 74; Josephus, *BJ* 7.412; in Jerusalem: Josephus, *AJ* 12.138.

5:1–11), in some ways like a philosophical school, yet publicly exhibiting Jewish piety, especially in the temple, and in many ways resembling the Pharisees. Major parts of this picture are probably the results of idealisation and the special apologetic and theological aims of the writer of Acts. Actually we can be certain of very little about the forms that the first Christian communities in Jerusalem took. Yet they must have been of crucial importance for the next, decisive phase of Christian development, the move to cities outside the land of Israel.

The cities and colonies

A laconic sentence in Acts provides our only substantial clue to the beginning of the urban, inclusive mission that set the pattern for Christianity's expansion:

> Now those who were scattered because of the persecution that arose over Stephen travelled as far as Phoenicia, Cyprus and Antioch, speaking the Word to none except Jews. But there were some of them, Cypriots and Cyrenaeans, who on coming to Antioch spoke to the Greeks also. (Acts 11:19–20)

Stephen's circle is identified with a wing of the Jerusalem Christian group called *Hellēnistai* (Acts 6:1), that is, converts from the Greek-speaking Jews of Jerusalem, many of whom had probably been reared in diaspora cities and later resettled in Judaea (cf. 6:9).[12] If this statement is historically reliable, it was these Greek-speaking, Christian Jews who began the self-conscious mission to Gentiles, and the great metropolis, Antioch on the Orontes, was the starting-point. It was in that city that the former Pharisee Paul of Tarsus, after his conversion, served his apprenticeship as a Christian missionary – his earlier venture into the Nabataean kingdom ('Arabia', Gal 1:17) had apparently not been successful (cf, 2 Cor 11:32–3, and note that Arabia is not included in the 'circle' Paul outlines in Rom 15:19). According to Acts, it was in Antioch, too, that the followers of Messiah Jesus were first called *Christianoi* (Acts 11:26), most likely by outsiders who now recognised them as a sect distinguishable from the main Jewish community.

We know of a number of other cities into which Christianity was introduced within a decade or so of Jesus' execution, including Damascus and Rome, and we may guess from later evidence that Christian groups were established early in the cities of Egypt and North Africa. Unfortunately, however, we have

---

12 In nineteenth- and early twentieth-century scholarship, the 'Hellenists' were often assumed to be an organised party in opposition to the 'Jewish Christians,' and the conflict between them was taken to be the major force driving the evolution of early Christianity toward the 'synthesis' of 'early catholicism.' For a convincing refutation of this view, see Hill, *Hellenists and Hebrews*.

little or no reliable information about the beginning of any of those churches. It is only the mission of Paul and his wide-flung network of associates for which we have abundant primary evidence, thanks to the survival of letters, written by both Paul and his disciples, and to the central role accorded to Paul by the author of Acts. These sources reveal an intense effort over three or four decades, which planted Christian groups in cities on the trade routes of central and western Asia Minor, Macedonia and Greece. It is not unreasonable to assume that Christians in other places used strategies and developed social forms similar to those of the Pauline circle, but there may have been many local peculiarities of which we have no knowledge.

The key to the urban Christian strategy was the private household. Not only do we hear several times in Acts of the conversion of some person 'with all his [or her] household' (16:15, 31–4; 18:8; cf. 10:1; 11:14; John 4:53), but Paul also recalls baptising households (1 Cor 1:16; cf. 16:15–16), and in his letters he several times expressly mentions 'the assembly (*ekklēsia*) at N's house' (1 Cor 16:19; Rom 16:5; Phlm 1; Col 4:15). However, the 'basic cell'[13] of the Christian movement in the cities was not simply the household gathered for prayer. Some groups formed in households headed by non-Christians, like the four named in Romans 16:10, 11, 14, 15, not to mention the *familia Caesaris* (Phil 4:22). Conversely, not every member of a household always became a Christian when its head did, as the case of the slave Onesimus shows (Phlm 8–21). It was not unusual for a householder of some wealth to become the patron of one of the clubs or guilds that flourished so abundantly in the early Roman empire. Sometimes cultic associations with such patronage incorporated much of the household, as in the famous Dionysiac association founded by Pompeia Agrippinilla in Tusculum (early second century CE).[14] In other instances, the patron had no direct connection with the group he assisted, save for the honours that the clients returned for the favours rendered; for example, a number of synagogue inscriptions record benefactions by pagans (cf. Luke 7:5). The formation of the Christian 'assemblies' thus followed a familiar pattern.[15]

In a number of ways, however, the Christian groups of the first century were quite different both from typical cults in the Roman world and from other kinds of voluntary associations, such as craft guilds, which they otherwise resembled. Although the Christians had developed their own special rituals,

---

13 The phrase is from Gülzow, 'Die sozialen Gegebenheiten', 198.
14 *IGUR* 160; Vogliano, 'La grande iscrizione', 215–31; McLean, 'The Agrippinilla inscription'.
15 Meeks, *First urban Christians*, ch. 3; Klauck, *Hausgemeinde und Hauskirche*; White, *Social origins*. Patrons of Jewish communities: Lifshitz, *Donateurs et fondateurs*.

these were not conspicuous to outsiders. Christians had no shrines, temples, cult statues or sacrifices; they staged no public festivals, musical performances or pilgrimages. As far as we know, they set up no identifiable inscriptions. On the other hand, initiation into their cult had social consequences that were more far-reaching than initiation into the cults of familiar gods. It entailed incorporation into a tightly knit community, a resocialisation that demanded (and in many cases actually received) an allegiance replacing bonds of natural kinship, and a submission to one God and one Lord excluding participation in any other cult. Moreover, this artificial family undertook to resocialise its members by a continual process of moral instruction and admonition; hardly any aspect of life was excluded from the purview of mutual concern, if we are to believe the writings of the movement's leaders. The church thus combined features of household, cult, club and philosophical school, without being altogether like any of them.

The Christian cult groups were unusual in another respect as well. While the household assembly was Christianity's toehold in the life of the Graeco-Roman cities, each of these cells of a dozen or so persons was made constantly aware of being part of a much wider movement. The concept of a single people of the one God was a self-image that the sect had inherited from Judaism. This notion was broadened, reinforced and given practical form in two ways. Mythically, the messianic ideology of the Christians drew upon the great stories of creation and human origins in the book of Genesis – as was the beginning, so must be the end. The earliest reports of baptismal rituals are thus filled with allusions to *paradise* and *fall*: in Christ the initiate puts on again the image of God lost by Adam; in him the primeval unity of Jew and Greek, slave and free, male and female is restored (cf. Gal 3:27f.; 1 Cor 12:13; Col 3:5–15). In this mythic complex is probably to be found much of the ideological basis for the vigour of the mission to Gentiles. In turn, the practical requirements of that mission themselves reinforced the ideology of unity. The *pax Romana* and Roman road building, together with the earlier spread of the Greek language in cities of the eastern half of the empire under Alexander and his successors, had made possible an unprecedented ease of travel and communication. The Christian apostles exploited this facility, and their need for support for their travel and for continuing contact with and supervision of churches already founded led them to develop an extraordinary network of 'fellow workers', delegates and messengers. The apostolic letter, real and pseudonymous, became one of the two most important genres of Christian literature. Ironically, the ideology of unity led often to schism, for, if two factions could not convince each other of their respective versions of the single truth, they were obliged to separate.

Thus the history of schisms and the very concept of 'heresy' that emerged in the second century are ironic testimonies to the ideal of unity and the practical drive to enforce it. That drive would eventually produce, by the time of Constantine, an empire-wide complex of institutions which in some ways mirrored the empire's own provincial bureaucracy.

The invention of church 'offices'

One of the most important and distinctive developments in the organisation of the ancient church is the establishment of what came to be called 'the monarchical episcopate', that is, governance of Christian groups in each city by a single bishop (Greek *episkopos*, 'overseer'), superior to other orders of clergy called 'elders' (*presbyteroi*) and 'deacons' (*diakonoi*). As the movement spread, beginning in the second century, back into the countryside, the urban bishops presided, in principle, also over the Christians in the towns and villages dependent upon their city – the region known as the *chōra* in Greek. Yet this development, so significant for the future shape of the church, is exceedingly difficult to trace in detail, and its history remains controversial – partly because it is hard for modern historians to escape from the tendentious reading of the sources during centuries of polemics between Protestant and Catholic interpreters in the west, partly because the sources are themselves obscure. Here we can only touch upon a few of the issues.

The propensity of the Christian movement to create both local and translocal institutions did not ensure early uniformity of structure, but the contrary. From the references to organisation in the New Testament and other early documents, we get the impression of considerable variety and experimentation, and also of frequent conflict not only between different figures and groups, but also between different *modes* of authority. For example, people whose authority came from their social position, like the householders and patrons of household communities, could clash with charismatics, like local or visiting prophets (e.g. 1 Cor 12–14; 3 John). Local leaders could clash with itinerants, and different travelling 'apostles' might teach quite different beliefs and forms of behavior (e.g. *Did.* 11–13; 15).

Although inscriptions from the numerous voluntary associations with which the early Christian groups are often compared show an exuberance of nomenclature for offices – most often imitating such municipal offices as *prytanis* ('president'), treasurer, secretary, *decuriones* ('city councilmen'), *quin-quennales* ('[five-year] magistrates') and the like – there is no comparable evidence from the earliest Christian groups. In Philippi (Macedonia), we do hear of *episkopoi* and *diakonoi*, addressed as apparently distinct local functionaries in Paul's letter to that church (Phil 1:1, to be dated in the 60s) but there is no hint of their responsibilities.[16]

It is in the letters of Ignatius of Antioch, written in the time of Trajan, that the three orders of clergy are first clearly distinguished. Ignatius uses these letters and his visits to churches along his route to Rome – and indeed his carefully dramatised progress toward martyrdom[17] – to campaign for a central and unifying role for the bishop. Yet in the Pastoral Letters (1, 2 Tim, Tit), which most scholars date near the time of Ignatius or somewhat later, and whose fictive locale overlaps with the areas addressed by Ignatius, bishops and presbyters are not yet clearly distinguished (1 Tim 3:1–7; 5:17–22). From these and other sources it is evident that establishment of the single bishop did not happen in all places at once, nor did it come about without resistance.

Modern church historians usually interpret the resistance to the episcopate as an instance of the conflict between 'charismatic' and 'institutional' modes of authority. The classic depiction of such a conflict is found in the 'Teaching of the twelve apostles', an early manual of church practice commonly known from the first word of its title in Greek as the *Didache*. The *Didache* undertakes to regulate the reception in local congregations of itinerant 'apostles' and 'prophets' (ch. 11–13). Then, in language much like that found in the Pastoral Letters, *Didache* 15:1–2 prescribes the appointment of 'bishops and deacons', with the explanation, 'for they also provide for you the service of the prophets and teachers'. The appointed officers are to have equal 'honour' with the itinerants. Certainly there were conflicts between such 'official' authorities and the more unregulated modes of power, exercised by persons whose claim to be heard depended upon the perception by their hearers that they were bearers in special ways of the divine Spirit, quite apart from any formal mechanisms for selecting them. It was this conflict, as understood by late nineteenth-century church historians, upon which Max Weber based his well-known sociological typology of the modes of dominance.[18]

However, there was no single line of evolution from 'charismatic' to 'everyday' or 'routinised' structures of authority. Both institutionalisation and

---

16 Hatch, *Organization*, 36–51, thought *episkopos* and *diakonos* were terms probably borrowed from the titulature of voluntary associations, but the terms are quite rare in club inscriptions, and, where they do appear, seem to have denoted rather minor functions. For the internal organisation of the associations, see, for Latin examples, Waltzing, *Corporations professionnelles*, vol. II, 334–515; Greek counterparts, Poland, *Geschichte*, 327–423.
17 On the 'theatricality' of Ignatius's journey and his letters, see Schoedel, *Ignatius*, 11f and passim.
18 Weber, *Theory of social and economic organization*, 324–92.

conflicts over authority began in the earliest days of the Christian movement, as we have seen, and 'charismatic' figures challenged the emerging episcopal structure in a variety of ways throughout the period of our interest and long afterward. The most obvious examples are the Montanist movement of the late second century and the prerogatives accorded to 'confessors' during persecutions, reaching a climax in the Decian persecution (mid-third century).[19] Moreover, the line of conflict was not always drawn between bishop and charismatic, for the principle of election of the bishop by acclamation of the congregations meant that a person with strong popular support might be elevated to the office.[20] Popular support, to be sure, might be won by other graces than charisma. From the beginning of urban Christianity, patrons were important for the establishment and sheltering of congregations, and a patron had to have some economic and social position in order to provide the needed services. It was natural that in time the bishop would come to serve in lieu of as well as alongside lay patrons. In the third-century church we see instances of elevation to the bishopric of people who had been prepared by wealth and status to act as patrons and who, as bishops, did make use of wealth and connections to exert control over their churches, in ways quite familiar in ordinary Roman society.[21]

One of the main reasons for the development of centralised authorities was the necessity for controlling deviant behaviour and belief. Deviance was peculiarly threatening, not only because of the comparative weakness of the groups, but also because of the universal claims which the movement made for itself. In the early decades of the Christian movement, only informal and ad hoc means were available for coping with disagreements. Individual deviants were subject to persuasion and censure by other individuals, including 'prophets', 'apostles' and other leaders in a meeting of the household assembly. The strongest sanction was shunning by the other Christians, especially by banning from the common meals, or expulsion altogether from the community (1 Cor 5:1–13; Matt 18:15–18; 2 Thess 3:14–15). To be sure, physical harm by magical means was also threatened (1 Cor 11:30; Acts 5:1–11; Rev 2:22–3; cf. 1 Cor 5:5), but Christian use of force on a regular basis to suppress deviance had to wait for the post-Constantinian alliance with state power.

---

19 See pt iv., ch. 21 and pt vi, ch. 28, below.
20 Did. 15; 1 Clem. 44; Cypr. Ep. 55.8; cf. Frend, Rise of Christianity, 403; Chadwick, Early church, 50, 165.
21 Cyprian is a prime example. See Bobertz, 'Patronage networks', and 'Development of episcopal order'.

Disagreement among leaders was even more threatening to the group's stability than deviance by ordinary members – successful handling of the latter could in fact strengthen coherence – but means for dealing with it were more difficult to achieve. Essentially there were available only persuasion and influence, exercised mostly through the familiar means of Graeco-Roman rhetoric within the structures of *amicitia* ('friendship', i.e. reciprocity among social equals) and *clientela* (reciprocity between social superiors and their dependents). Classic instances of rhetorical persuasion and invective aimed at winning allegiance to one set of leaders rather than another are Paul's letter to the Galatians and 2 Corinthians 10–13. Consultation among disagreeing leaders was sometimes successful (Gal 2:1–10; Acts 15), sometimes not (Gal 2:11–13; Rev 2:21).

Unresolved differences usually led to separation between disagreeing leaders and their followers. Sometimes the separation was amicable, functional and by formal 'contract', as in the Jerusalem meeting (Gal 2:9). More often, the result was a splintering of the Christian movement, a 'schism' (1 John 2:19). Because the earliest urban congregations, as we have seen, were small associations meeting in private houses, such division could be effected by refusal to admit to the house representatives of other groups, the itinerant 'prophets' and 'apostles' who were the principal agents of the church's translocal development (2, 3 John).

Social position

In the late second century a philosopher named Celsus wrote a long, well-informed pamphlet against Christianity. Among his principal criticisms was that the movement appealed only to the uneducated, to 'slaves, women and little children', and to workers in despised trades (Origen, *C. Cels.* 3.44). This was a common complaint against the new cult by pagan writers, and Christian apologists frequently undertook to refute it.[22] Yet, at the beginning of the century, Pliny the Younger had noted with alarm that people 'of every rank' (*omnis ordinis*) were in danger of being denounced as Christians, an assessment proudly echoed a century later in North Africa by Tertullian (*Apol.* 37.4). Christianity's location within the structure of ancient society was in fact complex and variable.

---

22 For example, Min. Fel. *Oct.* 36.3–7; Justin, 2 *Apol.* 10.8; Tat. *Orat.* 32; Tert. *Apol.* 37.4.

The social level of the early Christians

The followers of Jesus have often been called 'peasants', but that is a very imprecise use of the term, which in its most direct and simplest sense denotes 'free men and women whose chief activity lay in the working of the land with their own hands'.[23] The gospel traditions depict Jesus himself as a *tektōn* or the son of one (Mark 6:3; Matt 13.55), thus of a family of independent carpenters or builders. Among his disciples are sons of fishing families with slaves and hired workers; one is a 'tax collector' (Mark 1:16–20; 2:14). Support for the itinerant band is provided by women who evidently have some means, including the wife of a commissioner of the tetrarch (Luke 8:2–3). In the cities, as we have seen, the patronage of householders, some of whom had wealth and even civic status, like Gaius and Erastus of Corinth, was indispensable. There were slaveholders as well as slaves among the faithful.

The range of social status in the early Christian groups thus seems very nearly to replicate that of the society at large, omitting the two extremes – the Roman aristocracy and the agricultural and mining slaves and the landless peasants. If there is anything peculiar about the social complexion of the Christians, it is precisely the mixing of these varying levels in such intimate communities, though efforts were made in many cases, as we have seen, to maintain a sense of hierarchy within the groups. There is some evidence, moreover, that a mixing of status indicators characterised many of the individuals who were attracted to Christianity – especially those who became its leaders. In the Pauline mission, which is the only circle of the movement for which we have substantial evidence, those individuals prominent enough to be identified either in the letters or in the Acts are typically persons of inconsistent status. That is, they rank high in some indicators of status, such as wealth or prestige within the sect, but low in others, such as servile origins, mercantile sources of their wealth or the fact that they are women.[24] More general statements in the early Christian letters and other paraenetic literature give us the impression that a great many of the converts were free traders or artisans, some of whom were reasonably well off, but many of whom could identify with 'the poor' – not merely the working poor, Greek *penētes*, but the destitute *ptōchoi* – whose cause is often upheld in early Christian aphorisms and admonitions, as it had been in Jewish wisdom literature. The epistle of James, for example, castigates Christians who would be tempted to honour a visitor who wore a splendid

---

23 MacMullen, 'Peasants', 253.
24 Meeks, *First urban Christians*, ch. 2.

toga and the gold ring of nobility while despising a *ptōchos* who entered the assembly:

> Did not God choose those who are *ptōchoi* in the world but rich in faith and heirs of the kingdom . . .? Is it not the rich who oppress you and who haul you into court? (James 2:1–7)

Care for the poor by Christians who were better off was an obligation, already familiar in Jewish communities, that was frequently urged by Christian writers. 'Remember the poor' was the one requirement laid on Gentile Christian communities by the Jerusalem apostles, as Paul reported the event (Gal 2:9), and he laboured valiantly to make good on his promise to collect money from the churches he had founded for 'the poor among the saints at Jerusalem' (1 Cor 16:1–4; 2 Cor 8–9; Rom 15:25–8), though he saw in this evidently not merely charity but also an expression of equity (*isotēs*) among the churches, particularly solidarity between the Gentile Christians and the mother church of Jerusalem. Acts draws on the classical tradition of friendship as well as the Deuteronomic picture of Israel in the wilderness to depict an ideal community of goods under the apostles in Jerusalem (Acts 4:32–5). The *Didache*, dating in its final form from the mid-second century, retained the ideal: 'Do not turn away the needy, but share everything with your brother, and do not say that it is your own' (4:8), but reveals in another place also a certain practical scepticism: 'Let your alms sweat in your hands until you know to whom you are giving' (1:6). Around 175 CE, Dionysius, bishop of Corinth, praised the Roman church as a benefactor of Christians 'in every city', helping the poor and even furnishing aid to the brothers condemned to the mines (Eusebius, *HE* 4.23.10). The satire of Lucian on the sometime Christian Peregrinus Proteus attests to the care which Christians were accustomed to take for brothers in trouble (*De mort. Peregr.* 12–13). It is reported that in Rome itself, at the middle of the third century, the orthodox clergy were assisting 1,500 needy persons (Cornelius according to Eusebius, *HE* 6.43.11).

Some evidence for the social level of at least the leaders of the Christian movement may be inferred from the style of their surviving writings. It varies widely. In the New Testament, it ranges from the barbarous grammar of the Apocalypse and the crude but not artless parataxis of Mark to the carefully composed periodic preface to Luke-Acts and the more polished rhetoric of the epistle to Hebrews and 1 Peter. Paul shows a mastery of the language, some acquaintance with rhetorical and philosophical *topoi* and a strong natural sense of rhetorical effect. However, there is no trace in Paul's letters of the atticising high style that was coming into vogue in the schools, and it remains doubtful whether he had received formal education at the tertiary level.[25] With some cogency the style of early Christian literature has been compared with that of 'professional' handbooks – medical, pharmacological and the like – with the 'diatribe' of philosophical schools and with such popular literature as the Greek romances.[26] By the late second and early third centuries, a number of Christians with advanced education and sophisticated style were writing: Origen and Clement of Alexandria, Athenagoras of Athens and the Latin writers Minucius Felix and Tertullian. It is clear that there was a drift upward in the social scale as Christianity became older and more established.[27]

Even in the first century, as noted above, a few persons of higher status were attracted to Christianity. Erastus of Corinth, named in Romans 16:23 as 'city treasurer', is probably the same person who, a few years later, paved the court of the theatre in return for being elected aedile of the colony.[28] The author of the two-volume work received into the canon as the gospel of Luke and the Acts of the Apostles dedicated it to his patron, whom he addressed as *kratistos*, 'most excellent', equivalent to the Latin *egregius*, Theophilus. Theophilus was apparently a Christian or a catechumen (Luke 1:1–4). This author was careful to portray Christianity as attracting the favourable attention of people in high station – persons of 'first rank', especially women, in both Thessalonica and Beroea (Acts 17:4, 12); the governor of Cyprus, the senator Sergius Paulus (13:12); Dionysius 'the Areopagite' of Athens (17:34); Asiarchs in Ephesus (19:31); and of course Paul himself, depicted as a Roman citizen by birth despite being both a provincial and a Jew (16:37–6; 22:25–9; 25:10–12). Though we may suspect that the author has exaggerated, it is unlikely that all these reports are fabricated.

Worship and ritual

The early Christian groups, as we have seen, resembled the other kinds of voluntary associations that were so common in the cities of the Roman empire – burial societies, craft and professional clubs, philosophical schools, cultic associations and unions of immigrants – especially those that met, as the Christians did, in private households. As we have noted, in the early decades

25 See pt III, ch. 8, below.
26 See e.g. Rydbeck, *Fachprosa*; Alexander, *Preface to Luke's gospel*; Aune, *New Testament in its literary environment*; Aune, *Greco-Roman literature*; Malherbe, *Paul and the popular philosophers*.
27 Cf. Eck, 'Eindringen', and pt III, ch. 14, below.
28 Inscription 232 in Kent, *Inscriptions 1926–1950*, 99f and plate 21; Meeks, *First urban Christians*, 58f; Murphy-O'Connor, *St Paul's Corinth*, 37.

the new movement had none of the trappings of public religion – shrines or temples, cult statues, sacrifices, professional priesthood, processions and festivals. Yet most of the clubs with which first-century observers might have compared the Christian group practised a number of rituals that we would call 'religious', usually explicitly invoking various deities. So, too, from the earliest moment for which there is any clear evidence, the devotees of Messiah Jesus developed ritual practices of their own, which served both to shape and reinforce the movement's varied but specific forms of life and belief and to help distinguish it from other groups and to separate its defining occasions from the routines of everyday life. Two of those practices are attested so widely and so early that we may say without exaggeration that they are constitutive of the movement: an initiatory ceremony centring on a water bath, called in Greek 'dipping' (*baptismos*), and a common meal first called the 'dominical meal' (*kyriakon deipnon*, usually translated 'the Lord's Supper'), later, from a prayer that came to be one of its central set-pieces, 'the thanksgiving' (*eucharistia*). Even though both rituals are often mentioned, we do not have full descriptions of the entire practice of either until the fourth century. Moreover, there are good reasons to think that practice varied widely from place to place and from one circle of Christianity to another. Consequently only a fragmentary picture of these two fundamental ritual practices can be drawn for the first two centuries.

Baptism: ritual of initiation

The central action of baptism was a bathing or washing, as the name suggests. So Justin, in the middle of the second century, could call the ritual as a whole 'the bath' (*loutron*, 1 *Apol.* 1.61.4, 12; 62.1). In one of the earliest references to the rite, a century earlier Paul could say, 'You were washed' (1 Cor 6:11; cf. Eph 5:26; Heb 10:22). Just how and where the washing was done, our earliest sources do not tell us. The fact that it could be equated metaphorically with burial (Rom 6:4; Col 2:12) suggests complete immersion in water. That would make it analogous to Jewish ritual baths. Immersion is the norm in a fourth-century compilation of various traditions reconstructed by modern scholars and until recently identified with the lost 'Apostolic tradition' attributed to Hippolytus of Rome.[29] The *Didache*, representing practice perhaps as early as the beginning of the second century, probably in Syria, also assumes immersion to be normal, but it allows that if sufficient water for immersion is not at hand, water may be

---

29 This identification has now been convincingly refuted by Bradshaw, 'Redating'; Bradshaw, Johnson, and Phillips, *Apostolic tradition*.

poured three times over the head (7:3). The latter must have been a frequent arrangement, for it corresponds with most early artistic depictions of baptism, in Roman catacombs and on sarcophagi of the third century and later. The earliest identifiable Christian meeting house known to us, at Dura Europos on the Euphrates, dating to the early third century, contained a baptismal basin too shallow for immersion.[30] Obviously local practice varied, and practicality will often have trumped whatever desire leaders may have felt to make action mime metaphor.

'Washing' in a ritual context implies a metaphorical complex dominated by the contrast between 'pure' and 'impure'. Very often in ancient religion, among both Jews and Greeks and Romans, that contrast set a boundary around a sacred *space*, with washings required for entrance; would-be initiates into mystery cults would also in the days before it undergo preparatory rites involving water.[31] For the early Christians, however, baptism was not a preparation for initiation; it *was* the initiation. Its primary function was not to draw boundaries between places and times, but to draw a *social* boundary – between the group and the 'world'. By making the cleansing rite alone bear the whole function of initiation, and by making initiation the decisive point of entry into an exclusive community, the Christian groups created something new. The bath for them marked a permanent threshold between the 'clean' group and the 'dirty' world, and 'clean' was equated, as so often in Jewish tradition, with 'holy'. Those who have been baptised are now to exhibit their 'holiness' in their behaviour, 'not . . . like the Gentiles who do not know God', 'for God did not call us to impurity but in holiness' (1 Thess 4:5–7; cf. 1 Cor 6:11; 12:2; Gal 4:8; 1 Peter 2:12; 4:3). Almost certainly Jewish practice, the *tᵉbilah*, was the ultimate model for the Christian initiatory bath, but at a twofold remove – transformed first through the eschatological rite of John the Baptist, who thus dramatised the need of all Israel to be purified in order to be ready for the impending reign of God, and, second, through association with the story of Jesus.[32]

In ritual systems, neither 'purity' nor 'holiness' necessarily has anything to do with moral evaluations, but it is very common for purity and holiness to represent moral correctness, or for moral soundness to be a necessary prerequisite for ritual purity. John's baptism was clearly understood by his contemporaries as fusing the ritual and the moral. The earliest accounts of John describe his action as 'a baptism of repentance for forgiveness of sins' (Mark 1:4; Luke 3:3; Acts 13:24; 19:4; cf. Matt 3:2, 11 and Josephus, *AJ* 18.116f.).

30 See pt VI, ch. 32, below, and Fig. 6.
31 Mylonas, *Eleusis*, 194 and fig. 70; Kerényi, *Eleusis*, fig. 14; Apul. *Met.* 11.23.
32 On the antecedents of Christian baptism, see esp. Dahl, 'Origin of baptism'.

Christian baptism, too, is often connected with repentance and forgiveness, implying that radical change of life called 'conversion' in some philosophical circles (Luke 24:47; Acts 22:16; 26:20; *Ep. Barn.* 11:1; Justin, *1 Apol.* 61; *Acts Thom.* 132).[33] Members of the new Christian group, however, were careful, at least according to the book of Acts, to distinguish baptism 'in the name of the Lord Jesus' from the baptism of John (Acts 19:5). The formula, 'in the name of (the Lord) Jesus (Christ)' was used very early and very widely (1 Cor 1:13; Acts 2:38; 8:16; 10:48; *Did.* 9:5). Soon it was expanded into the threefold formula, 'in the name of the Father and of the Son and of the Holy Spirit' (Matt 28:19; *Did.* 7:1; Justin, *1 Apol.* 61.3; *Acts Thom.* 49; 121; 132; 157; *Acts Pet.* [according to the *Actus Vercellenses* manuscript] 5; cf. already 1 Cor 6:11).

Although three of the four canonical gospels recount Jesus' own baptism by John, it is not connected expressly with Christian baptism until the early second century, when Ignatius says that Jesus was baptised 'in order to purify the water by his own submission [or suffering]' (Ign. *Eph.* 18.2). Instead, it is Jesus' death that is most clearly linked early on with baptism (cf. Mark 10:38; Luke 12:50), which can be equated with dying and rising with Christ. Reminders of baptism in the epistles express the equation in the language of analogy: 'As Christ was raised from the dead . . . so also we . . .' (Rom 6:4), in the language of participation: 'We have been baptised into his death' (Rom 6:3), and by verbs compounded in *syn-*, 'with' (Rom 6:4, 8; Col 2:12–13; Eph 2:5–6). A variation of this theme describes the state of the convert prior to baptism as itself death; baptism is a death of death, the beginning of life (Col 2:13; Eph 2:1,5). From the notion of dying and rising with Christ in baptism, it was but a short step to think of the baptised person as 'reborn' (John 3:3–5; Titus 3:5; 1 Peter 1:3; Justin, *1 Apol.* 61.3; Herm. *Sim.* 9.16.4; *Acts Thom.* 132). Accordingly, representations of baptism in early Christian art usually depict the initiate as a child. In some circles, best attested in the Pauline letters, clothing removed before baptism symbolised death with Christ as taking off 'the old human (*anthrōpos*)', 'the body of flesh' and the vices associated with it. The removal of the old body could be called 'the circumcision of Christ' (Col 2:11), that is, the Christian equivalent of Jewish circumcision of proselytes. What was 'put on' was Christ himself, 'the new human', who was 'being renewed . . . according to the image of his creator' (Col 3.10).

The early Christian poem quoted by Paul in Phil 2:6–11 was probably used sometimes in baptismal contexts. It climaxes with a scene of invisible powers

---

33 On conversion in philosophical circles, the classic work is Nock, *Conversion*. See also Malherbe, *Paul and the Thessalonians*, 21–33; Meeks, *Origins*, 18–36; Cancik, 'Lucian on conversion'.

in heaven, earth and the underworld all prostrating themselves and confessing, 'The Lord is Jesus Christ.' Very likely the newly initiated Christian thus bowed and confessed. This confession would appropriately signify the change of dominion the baptised person had undergone, from the world ruled by demonic powers, the 'elements of the world', to the realm in which 'the living God' and his Son the Christ reign. From this new Lord the initiate receives certain gifts: the Spirit and adoption as God's child – to which an early response was 'Abba! Father!' (Gal 4:6; Rom 8:15). Eventually baptism was followed by anointing with oil – widely attested from the late second century on – and possibly there is a hint of such a practice, and its association with the gift of the Spirit, much earlier, in 2 Cor 1:21 (cf. 1 John 2:20). By the mid-second century, according to Justin, the newly baptised were led immediately to the eucharist (1 Apol. 65–6; cf. Plin. Ep. 10.96; Did. 7–9).

The Lord's supper

Ritualised meals were a ubiquitous part of social and religious life in antiquity. Yet, just as baptism became an initiatory ceremony that was novel in comparison with other ritual baths, 'the dominical banquet' or 'Lord's supper' (kyriakon deipnon) developed unique symbolism and practices. The meal was the focus of regular gatherings of the initiated converts in the households of their local patrons. The book of Acts speaks of 'the breaking of bread' as one of the constitutive practices of the baptised followers of Jesus (Acts 2:42, 46; 20:7; 27:35; cf. Luke 24:28–35). Their neighbours would not have been surprised, for voluntary associations of all kinds gathered on solemn occasions for banquets that were always more or less ritualised. The symposion ('drinking together') of upper-class men was so much a part of classical Greek social life that it produced a special form of literature, still very much alive in early Christian times.[34] Even the shape of the Passover Seder as we know it from rabbinic sources and in practice still today replicates the general pattern of the symposium.[35] Any Gentile reading Luke's description of Jesus' last Passover meal with his disciples (Luke 22:14–38) would have seen a typical symposium of a teacher with his male students – though the reported topics of their discussion around the table are unusual, to say the least. The clubs that were so much a part of urban life in the Greek and Roman world met on regular occasions to eat and drink, and the inscriptions they erected frequently contain detailed rules for the provision of wine and food and behaviour at

34 See Murray, 'Symposium' and 'Symposium literature'.
35 As exemplified by Josephus, BJ 6.423 and Philo Spec. 2.148.

table.[36] Eating in the presence of the gods was common, too, and every temple of any size included a dining room. Lacking a house of sufficient capacity for a banquet, a private person would often invite friends to dinner in one of these cultic establishments: 'Herais asks you to dine in the (dining) room of the Serapeion at a banquet of the Lord Sarapis tomorrow, the eleventh, from the ninth hour.'[37] The invitation might be issued in the name of the god himself: 'The god invites you to a banquet taking place in the Thoereion tomorrow from the ninth hour.'[38] A banquet 'in the name of the Lord Jesus' would not in itself seem more unusual than 'a banquet of the Lord Sarapis'.

Nor would it seem surprising that a solemn meal was held 'as a memorial' [*anamnēsis*] of a person who had died (1 Cor 11:24–5; Luke 22:19). Funeral meals and meals on specified anniversaries of the death were celebrated in both Greek and Roman cultures over several centuries, and evidence is also abundant for similar customs among the Jews, both before and after they entered the sphere of Greek and Roman culture. The burial societies that proliferated in Roman imperial times often included such memorial meals among the benefits they offered their members. Inscriptions tell us of foundations that were endowed to fund banquets and other rites 'as a memorial'.[39]

The Christian supper not only remembered Jesus in a general way; it also commemorated a very particular occasion. The earliest description we have of the meal, citing a tradition going back to Jesus himself – 'I received from the Lord (the tradition) which I handed on to you' – is that:

> The Lord Jesus, on the night on which he was betrayed, took bread and, having given thanks [*eucharistēsas*], broke it and said, 'This is my body, which is for you. Do this as a memorial [*anamnēsis*] of me.' So also the cup after dinner: 'This cup is the new covenant in my blood. Do this, as often as you drink it, as a memorial of me.' (1 Cor. 11:23–5)

It is not absolutely clear from this passage that an account of the events of Jesus' last evening with his disciples was always recited when Christians met for the memorial supper, but assuming such a recital seems the most obvious way to explain what Paul says as well as the parallel but longer narratives in the Synoptic Gospels. It was probably in oral performances at the supper meetings

---

36 E.g. the long inscription from Andania in Messenia (first century BCE; *IG* 1390 = *SIG* 2:401–11), esp. lines 95–9. See also Waltzing, *Corporations professionnelles*, 1:373, n. 5 (examples of the *ordo cenarum*); Poland, *Geschichte*, 259–65; Smith, *Symposium to eucharist*.

37 *P. Coll. Youtie* 52, trans. Horsley, *New documents*, vol. 1, 5 (modified).

38 *P. Köln* 57, trans. Horsley, *New documents*, vol. 1, 5, modified. For a general discussion of cultic dining in antiquity, see MacMullen, *Paganism*, 36–42.

39 Klauck, *Herrenmahl*, 83–6; Reicke, *Diakonie, Festfreude und Zelos*, 111–18.

of the early disciples of the crucified and risen Jesus that the stories of his farewell to the disciples, his betrayal and arrest, and his death and resurrection took shape. Variations in practice from one group to the next would also account for the differences among the several versions of the story that survive – differences that vast scholarly industry and imagination have failed to resolve in order to yield for us 'the original' form of the supper or the words said at it. Nevertheless, it is clear that the supper – unlike baptism, which only much later was connected with the story of Jesus' own baptism – was believed from the earliest days of the new movement to re-enact Jesus' own action with his disciples.

The tradition diverged on the question whether the Last Supper was a Passover Seder. The version represented by the Synoptic Gospels states unambiguously that it was (Mark 14:12–16 and parallels), but there also appeared very early the notion that Jesus himself was the Passover sacrifice (1 Cor 5:7), and the recital of the story in circles that eventually produced the gospel of John adjusted the calendar of events accordingly. The meal with the disciples in this version took place the evening before the day when the lambs were sacrificed, so that Jesus was crucified at the very time of the sacrifice (John 13:1–5; 19:14; cf. 19:36 and 1:29). The fourth gospel does not include the sayings over the bread and cup at the Last Supper, but in the midrashic dialogue on 'bread from heaven' (6:26–71) allusions to the supper, already present in earlier versions of the feeding miracle, are multiplied. The miracle of the loaves and fishes was a natural subject for eucharistic interpretation, and that probably accounts for its popularity in early Christian funerary art.[40] The eucharistic prayer in the *Didache* identifies the bread offered to the believers with 'the bread that was scattered on the mountains and, gathered, became one' (*Didache*. 9:4; cf. John 6:12–13).[41]

The wine and bread in the early years were always part of a full meal, though their sequence with respect to the meal seems to have varied from place to place and time to time. The eucharist was celebrated as a full meal still in the circles that used the *Didache*, for the final thanksgiving was to be given 'after being satisfied' (the verb is the same as in John 6:12). Eventually, however, the symbolic elements of bread and wine came to be separated from the meal. One of the reasons for the separation may be found in the report of Pliny, governor general of the province Bithynia-Pontus, to the emperor Trajan. The Christians he had interrogated, Pliny said, had been accustomed 'to reassemble to take

---

40 See pt vi, ch. 32, below.
41 For this reading see Cerfaux, 'La multiplication des pains'.

food, but ordinary and harmless food, which practice they had stopped after my edict which I issued in accord with your mandate that clubs be banned' (*Ep.* 10.96.7). In some places the meal, separate from the eucharist, continued or reappeared, but now as a charitable institution known as the *agapē*, the Greek word for 'love'. The evidence for this development is far from clear, however, and a number of the texts that are commonly taken to refer to a 'love-feast' separate from the eucharist can just as plausibly be understood to refer to the eucharist itself (Jude 12; Ign. *Smyr.* 8.2), with emphasis on care for the poor associated with it (Tert. *Apol.* 39.16).

Eating together is so fundamental to human communities that a ritualised meal lends itself to a vast array of possible significations. In the early accounts of the banquet of the Lord Jesus, there are four constellations of symbolism that are particularly important. (1) As we have seen, the meal was a 'memorial' of Jesus. It re-enacted his last meal with his disciples, but it commemorated Jesus also in a more general way, by re-presenting significant parts of his story and, indeed, dramatically making Jesus himself present in the actions bracketing the meal: 'This is my body'; 'This is my blood'. The focus, nevertheless, was on the final day of Jesus' life on earth, so that Paul could sum up the tradition he had just quoted by declaring, 'Every time you eat this bread and drink this cup, you proclaim the *death* of the Lord' (1 Cor 11:26). That focus on the sacrificial death of Jesus would characterise the eucharistic symbolism and thought of the western church, while in the east the emphasis would be more on the presence of the resurrected and ascended Lord with the faithful at the banquet.

(2) The meal was an occasion for thanksgiving, so central to its shape that beginning early in the second century it was commonly named, by synecdoche, the eucharist, 'the thanksgiving' (e.g. Ign. *Eph.* 13.1; *Phild.* 4.1; *Smyr.* 7.1; 8.1; *Didache* 9.1,5; 10.7; Justin, *1 Apol.* 66.1). The name and the prayers that suggested it were themselves recollections of Jesus' thanksgiving (*eucharistēsas*) or blessing (*eulogēsas*) over the bread (and wine) both at the Last Supper (1 Cor 11:24; Mark 14:22–3 and parallels) and in the feeding miracles (Mark 6:41; 8:6 and parallels). But now the worshippers gave thanks for the benefits they received through Jesus (cf. Justin, *1 Apol.* 65). The earliest certain example of the eucharistic prayer of thanksgiving that has come down to us is in the *Didache* (10:2–6).[42]

(3) The common meal was a gathering of the new family of the children of God. It celebrated their solidarity 'in Christ', and it helped to register the

---

42 See Grant, 'Structure of eucharistic prayers'.

boundaries between that family and the profane world. So, for example, Paul could insist that the 'cup of blessing' was a 'sharing' or 'partnership' (*koinōnia*) in the blood of Christ and the bread 'a sharing of the body of Christ' (1 Cor 10:16). Consequently, attending a banquet in a temple dining hall (an *eidōleion*, 'idol shrine', Paul says, parodying such terms as *serapeion* that we find in the invitations) is tantamount to 'sharing a table of demons' (8:10; 10:21).[43] Further, so central was the supper to the communal life of the group that exclusion from it became a severe form of discipline in cases of misconduct (1 Cor 5:1–13; Matt 18:15–17; cf. 2 Thess 3:10, 14).

(4) Finally, the Lord's banquet was an anticipation of eschatological joy. Among the sayings of Jesus at the Last Supper remembered in the earliest traditions was this: 'Amen I say to you that I shall not again drink of the fruit of the vine until that day when I drink it new in the kingdom of God' (Mark 14:25). The tradition that Paul quotes does not include this saying, but in Paul's own added comment, in eating the supper the participants 'proclaim the death of the Lord *until he comes*' (1 Cor 11:26). The liturgical cry, 'Our Lord, come!' that Paul inserts in the closing formulas of his letter (16:22) is probably also eucharistic, as it is in the *Didache* – there, too, preserved in Aramaic, *marana tha* (*Didache*. 10.6; cf. Rev 22:20).

Other ritualised actions

In addition to baptism and the supper, the documents hint of numerous smaller ritualised actions that accompanied the major rituals or took place on other occasions when the Christians met. Some of these, like the singing of hymns or chants and the recital of blessings or prayers, have their parallels in many other Graeco-Roman cults, including Judaism, while some, such as the reading and interpreting of sacred texts, are especially close to practices of the synagogue. In addition, we may infer that the Christians quickly developed their own ways of marrying and of burying and commemorating the dead, and perhaps their special ways of ritualising yet other occasions that were commonly observed in household life, but of those we have no direct evidence at all. At our distance from the early Christian meetings, we catch only glimpses, recorded accidentally in texts written for people who knew the whole at first hand. Still, those scraps of knowledge furnish at least starting-points from which we imagine some of the varied ways in which the early Christians performed their faith.

---

43 On the complexity of Paul's tightly woven rhetoric in 1 Cor 8–10, see Meeks, *In search*, 196–209.

The poetry of worship. Chanting and singing were prominent in the meetings of the early Christians, as in most religious occasions in antiquity. The gospel of Mark tells us that at the end of the Last Supper Jesus' disciples 'sang a hymn' before they departed to the Mount of Olives (Mark 14:26). In the Pauline churches, 'psalms, hymns and spiritual odes' were customary (Col 3:16–17; Eph 5:18–20). The 'psalms' would have included some from the biblical psalter, as well as new compositions in the same style (cf. 1 Cor 14:26); both practices are attested also in the texts from Qumran and were probably common in many circles of Judaism, as were 'hymns' and 'odes' – insofar as any distinction can be made.[44] It was not only Jews, of course, who chanted their praises to their gods; similar forms were often used by different ethnic groups in the Roman empire. Scholars have detected early Christian liturgical poetry or fragments thereof in many passages of the New Testament and other early literature (e.g. Phil 2:6–11; John 1:1–5, 9–14).

Prayers, too, combined the free and the formulaic.[45] Even the Lord's Prayer, which was on its way to becoming the statutory daily prayer for Christians by the end of the first century, appears in three different forms in the earliest attestations: a short version in Luke 11:1–4, a longer version with somewhat different wording in Matt 6:7–13, and a variant of the Matthean version, with a doxology added, in *Didache.* 8.2. The *Didache* further directs that the prayer be said three times a day (8:3), thus making it the Christian replacement (or supplement) for the Jewish daily prayer.[46] Several positions for prayer were in use. Standing with arms raised and palms forward, the *orans* attitude so often represented in Hellenistic funeral art to signify piety, was certainly common in Jewish and early Christian circles. Later Christian interpreters explained it as representing crucifixion.[47] Kneeling (Acts 7:60; 9:40; 20:36; 21:5; Eph 3:14; cf. Phil 2:10) and bowing or prostrating oneself (1 Cor 14:25; cf. Rev 4:10; 7:11; 11:16; 19:4, 10; 22:9) were also common, often while speaking some confessional formula – 'The Lord is Jesus!' – or doxology – 'Glory to God!'

Reading, interpreting, exhorting. For new converts, becoming acquainted with the Jewish scriptures and the ways those texts were interpreted by the followers of Messiah Jesus was evidently an essential part of resocialisation as

---

44 E.g. 11QPs^a; 1QH^a; 4QShirShab^a; 4QDibHam^a; see further the 'poetic texts' translated in García Martínez, *Dead Sea scrolls*, 303–404; among the many studies, see Kittel, *Hymns of Qumran*; Sanders, *Dead Sea Psalms scroll*.
45 See pt III, ch. 14, below.
46 Aune, 'Worship, early Christian', 980–1.
47 *Odes Sol.* 27; Tert. *Or.* 14; Min. Fel. *Oct.* 29.8.

a member.[48] It is likely that the reading and exposition of scripture – the writings [*graphai*] that the second-century church would begin to call the Old Testament – were features of the regular meetings of Christians.[49] That assumption is plausible, though early direct evidence is lacking for both the Christian groups and for their presumed models, the early synagogues (but see Luke 4:16–21; Acts 6:9; 13:14–42). 1 Tim 4:13 directs attention to 'the reading, the exhortation, the teaching', and a few years later Justin speaks of reading either 'the memoirs of the apostles' or 'the writings of the prophets' in regular meetings on Sunday, followed by 'admonition' by the leader (1 *Apol.* 67.3f.). By 'memoirs of the apostles', Justin means the gospels, which were doubtless read in some assemblies of the Christians from very early times; indeed, oral performance of the stories and sayings of Jesus may have been one of the ways in which the gospels originated. From an even earlier time we know that letters from apostles and others were read in the churches (1 Thess 5:27; Col 4:16; Rev 1:3; 22:18f). In more than one sense, then, we may say that the reading and interpretation of texts created scripture.[50]

Ecstatic phenomena. One characteristic of the early Christian assemblies was the belief that the spirit of God or of Christ was present both in the community and within individual members of it, and that the spirit manifested itself directly in certain spontaneous activities. Perhaps the most dramatic was 'speaking in tongues' (*glōssais lalein*, whence the modern designation 'glossolalia', 1 Cor 12:10, 28, 30; 13:1, 8; 14:1–40; Acts 10:46; 19:6). Although the author of Acts rationalises tongue-speaking as a kind of instant translation service (2:2–13), the situation at Corinth addressed by Paul sounds more like the trance phenomenon often observed in some modern groups, including Pentecostal Christians. Losing conscious control, the subject pours out involuntary utterances – unintelligible to all but those with the 'gift' of interpretation (1 Cor 12:10; 14:27f) – often accompanied by rapid or sudden bodily movements, profuse sweating and other uncontrolled physical signs. Yet, while glossolalia seems the epitome of a spontaneous, anti-structural phenomenon, it happens within the context of worship, set about with ritualised behaviour. That is clear from Paul's directives in 1 Corinthians, and also from observations of modern tongue-speakers. The phenomenon occurs at predictable moments in the service, usually introduced by quite specific verbal formulas and physical actions. In adepts, there are even 'trigger words' that can induce or terminate

48 Snyder, *Teachers and texts*, 216.
49 See pt I, ch. 2, above.
50 See pt III, ch. 8, below.

the trance – and Paul seems to have assumed something similar, for he orders that the numbers of speakers and the occasions of their speaking be strictly regulated (1 Cor 14:27f.).[51]

In the New Testament, glossolalia is paired with prophecy (Acts 19:6; 1 Cor 14 passim), but there are other 'gifts' [*charismata*] of the spirit that were also common in the worship of the early Christians. So Paul can say, for example, 'When you come together, each person has a psalm, has a teaching, has a revelation [*apokalypsis*], has a tongue, has an interpretation!' (1 Cor 14:26). No sharp line should be drawn between such ecstatic behaviour and 'ritual', for on the one hand ritualised words and actions framed and even stimulated or controlled the manifestations of 'spirit possession', and on the other the utterances and actions thought to be given by the Spirit lent to the ritualised occasions much of their energy and persuasiveness.

The holy kiss. We know next to nothing about the physical gestures that may have punctuated the ritual behaviour of the early Christians in their meetings. Signing oneself with the cross, for example, is not attested until the fourth century,[52] though as we have seen some interpreted the *orans* position of prayer as a memorial of the crucifixion.[53] One particularly interesting exception is the 'holy kiss', which is mentioned already in our earliest extant Christian document (1 Thess 5:26; also Rom 16:16; 1 Cor 16:20; 2 Cor 13:12; 1 Peter 5:14), and widely thereafter (e.g. Justin, *1 Apol.* 65.2; Athenagoras, *Leg.* 32.5.8; Clem. Al. *Paed.* 3.11.81–82; *M. Perp.* 21.7; Tert. *Ad ux.* 2.4.3). Recent studies have shown that, in Roman society, the kiss (a full kiss on the mouth, not the handshake of modern churches) was customary between close relatives (and lovers). By making the kiss part of their ritual vocabulary, the Christians not only signified but helped to create a counter-family, 'the children of God'.[54] Perhaps the practice also contributed to the accusation of incestuous behaviour that opponents sometimes levelled at the Christians.[55]

Emergence of a Christian subculture

Beginning as the cult of a figure executed as an enemy of the Roman order, deriving its scriptures and initial beliefs from a distinctive ethnic group among

51 On modern glossolalia, see Goodman, *Speaking in tongues*.
52 Hipp. *Trad. apost.* 41 (ed. Botte), assuming Bradshaw's redating.
53 See above, n. 57.
54 Phillips, *Ritual kiss*; Penn, 'Performing family'.
55 See e.g. the reports by Athenagoras, *Leg.* 3.1; 31f.; Justin, *Dial.* 10.1; cf. Wilken, *Christians as the Romans saw them*, 17–21.

the subject peoples of the empire, Christianity tended from the outset to present itself in opposition to 'this world'. At the same time, it showed remarkable diversity and facility in adapting to the ways and forms of the Roman world, and the 'Christian' culture that would emerge in late antiquity carried more of the genes of its 'pagan' ancestry than of the peculiarly Christian mutations. Nevertheless, there was a cultural shift which, if not precipitous, was of vast magnitude. Christianity played a significant role in the reshaping of Graeco-Roman culture, however difficult it is to define that role with any precision.[56]

An empire within the empire

From the earliest penetration of the Christian movement into the cities outside Palestine, travel by individual Christians was of fundamental importance, not only for the spread of the cult to different places, but also for the reinforcement of the Christians' understanding of themselves as a community that transcended local connections.[57] 'Hospitality' (*philoxenia*) was a virtue much praised by early Christians, especially to be sought in bishops (1 Tim 3:2; Titus 1:8; Rom 12:13; Heb 13:2; *1 Clem.* 1:2; 10:7; 11:1; 12:1, 3; 25:1; Herm. *Mand.* 8.10; Herm. *Sim.* 9.27.2); withholding hospitality was a means of social control (2, 3 John). The significance of travel and hospitality and the power of the resulting sense of the universality of the cult are vividly portrayed by one of the earliest extant Christian inscriptions, an epitaph erected toward the end of the second century in Hieropolis, Phrygia, by a certain Abercius. Abercius, perhaps the bishop of that city (cf. Euseb. *HE* 5.16.3), describes himself as 'disciple of a pure shepherd',

> who sent me to Rome to behold a kingdom and to see a queen in golden robe and golden shoes; but I saw there a people possessing a splendid seal. I also saw the Plain of Syria and all the cities – Nisibis, when I had crossed the Euphrates. Everywhere I got companions; with me in my carriage I had Paul. Everywhere Faith went before me and set out everywhere for food the Fish from the spring, all-great and pure, whom the pure virgin caught. Him she gave at all times to friends to eat; possessing an excellent wine, she gave it, mixed, with bread.[58]

Abercius' imagery would have been cryptic to a non-Christian, but we can plainly see how the experience of the traveller, finding 'everywhere . . .

---

56 On Christian adaptations and innovations in literature and rhetoric, see pt III, ch. 8, below; on Christian art and architecture, see pt VI, ch. 32.

57 Malherbe, *Social aspects*, 92–112.

58 For text and discussion, see Klauser and Strathmann, 'Aberkios'. For the recovered fragments, see Fig. 4 (next page).

Figure 4. Abercius inscription fragments, Museo Pio Cristiano, Musei Vaticani (photo: Margaret M. Mitchell)

companions' who celebrated the eucharist and knew Paul and shared Aber-cius' faith, reinforced his grand conception of a single 'people' and 'kingdom'. Nothing about the inscription is other-worldly.[59] Apart from the special Chris-tian images, Abercius employs the usual conventions of an epitaph, including warnings of fines to be paid to the *fiscus* of Rome and to the *patris* Hieropolis by anyone found violating the tomb. Here we glimpse something of the emerging paradox of the Christian empire within the Roman empire that would disturb Decius and his successors in the third century and convince Constantine of the need to ally himself with that strange new 'kingdom'.[60]

59 Compare *Ep. Diognet.* 6:1–2: 'As the soul is in the body, so Christians are in the world. The soul is distributed through all the members of the body, and Christians in every city of the world.'
60 I have adapted some portions of this essay from an earlier one, Meeks, 'Il cristianesimo'.

PART III

*

COMMUNITY TRADITIONS
AND SELF-DEFINITION

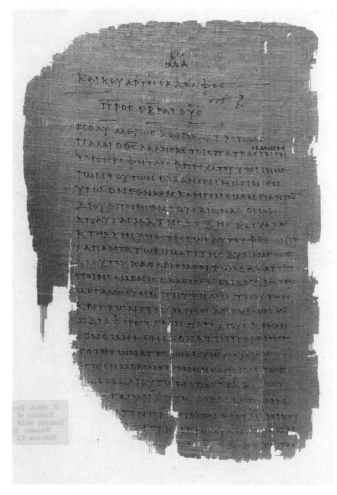

Figure 5. P⁴⁶ Chester Beatty Papyrus, fo. 21ʳ: end of Romans, incipit of Hebrews (photo: Papyrology Collection, Graduate Library, The University of Michigan)

8

The emergence of the written record

MARGARET M. MITCHELL

A battle of literatures

The oldest Christian text in Latin contains the following interrogation of a North African Christian:

> Saturninus the proconsul said, 'what are those things in your case?'
> Speratus replied, 'books and letters of Paul, a just man.'[1]

Although it is uncertain whether these 'books and letters of Paul' were produced by the defendant Speratus as evidence (and, if so, whether voluntarily or on judicial order), or brought along for the instruction and consolation of the prisoners, this encounter highlights the crucial link between Christian identity and Christian texts. In February 303, Diocletian waged a persecutorial campaign against the Christian movement by legislating three strategic actions. Tellingly, the second of these – the handing over and public burning of its texts[2] – was deemed by the emperor as crucial to the demolition of this cult as the razing of churches and civil disenfranchisement of its leaders. His diagnosis was apparently shared by his persecutorial successor, Maximinus Daia, who countered the threat of the Christian scriptures by the composition and enforced propagandisation of a counter-literature, the 'Memoirs of Pilate and the Saviour' that were to be handed on to schoolchildren for memorisation.[3] These early fourth-century bibliographic broadsides were not to prove successful (indeed, to the distress of historians no single copy remains of the 'Memoirs of Pilate and the Saviour'). Eusebius found the ultimate victory of the Christian literature in the emperor Constantine's celebratory commissioning of fifty resplendent copies of the scriptures (Old and New Testament) for distribution and use in and around the newly founded capital of his now-Christian empire.[4]

---

1 *M. Scil.* 12 (events c.180 CE).
2 Euseb. *HE* 8.2.4.
3 Euseb. *HE* 9.5.1; also 1.9.3; 9.7.1.
4 *V.C.* 3.1.5 (cf. 4.36.2–4).

This dramatic 'bibliomachy' at the end of the period covered by this volume[5] signifies an essential fact about early Christianity: it was a religious movement with texts at its very heart and soul, in its background and foreground. Its communities were characterised by a pervading, even obsessive preoccupation with and *habitus* for sacred literature. In the pre-Constantinian period, Christians succeeded in composing, collecting, distributing, interpreting and intimately incorporating a body of texts they found evocative enough to wish to live inside of.[6] But how did a movement whose founder's only recorded act of writing was a short-lived and unread finger etching on wind-swept soil,[7] within a century create, and in turn depend for its life upon, a vibrant literary culture?[8]

Earliest Christian traditions and 'scripture'

The pivotal figure in this development toward textual traditions was Paul, the earliest Christian author we know by name.[9] But Paul himself already stood within and contemporaneous to some existing Christian literary traditions. The shorthand version of the *euangelion*,[10] 'gospel message', Paul recounts in 1 Corinthians 15:3–4 (and says he has himself received) is that 'Christ died on behalf of our sins *according to the writings*', and 'he has been raised on the third day *according to the writings*'. The earliest gospel message had texts in it, texts as central to it – in this case the holy scriptures of Israel. The first followers of Jesus of Nazareth had turned to their 'scriptures', the sacred texts of Judaism in the Hebrew and Greek languages, and sought to explain the Jesus whom they had come to know by what they found there. Paul could only have confidently summarised the message that these things were 'according to the scriptures' if he were certain his audience were already familiar with the key supporting texts.[11] Because of this, and on the basis of well-attested parallels in both Jewish and Graeco-Roman literary culture, one of the earliest forms of early Christian literature was probably the 'testimonia collection'

---

5 On the 'battle of the literatures' between Homeric and Hesiodic epic and the Bible of the Christians, see Young, *Biblical exegesis*, 57.

6 'There was something about the Christian experience that drove [people] to record it in books, to express it, defend it, and explain it' (Goodspeed, *History of early Christian literature*, vi).

7 John 7:53–8:11 (fittingly, recounted in a textually uncertain passage!).

8 Later Christian authors will retroject authorial status onto Jesus (see Baarda, 'De Christi scriptis').

9 Note that Paul is the only one named by Speratus in our opening epigram.

10 See Mitchell, 'Rhetorical shorthand'.

11 E.g. Isa 53:5f; Hos 6:2; Jon 2:1.

comprised of a list of passages culled from the scriptures that Christians took to be references to Jesus – his life, actions (especially miracles), death and remarkable resurrection.[12] Hence the first element in the establishment of the Christian 'written record' was the singularly most significant decision – initially through the reflexive retention of the unquestioned literary authority of the word of God by faithful Jews, and later as a conscious step in literary appropriation by Gentiles who had previously laid no claim to these texts[13] – to carry out Christian literary activity under the umbrella of the Torah, the prophets and the writings (see e.g. Luke 24:44). Early Christian literary culture was initially, and, with only few exceptions,[14] carried out within the lexical field, plot structure, cast of characters, world-view and theological presuppositions of the scriptures of Israel, predominantly as known in the Greek translation called the Septuagint.

And it was centred on Jesus of Nazareth. In the interval between the death of Jesus (c.30 CE) and the composition of the first gospel (Mark, around 70 CE), the sayings of Jesus, like those of other holy men and philosophers, were remembered, rendered into Greek, retold, revised and recast in such common forms as *chreiai* (also termed aphorisms, pronouncement stories, and *apophthegmata*), parables, *logia* (sayings), *apokalypseis* (revelations), prophecies, macarisms and woes and *gnomai* (maxims).[15] A similar process took place with narratives about Jesus, including stories of controversy with his contemporaries (now told in the light of the early church's own contentious encounters with its neighbours) and accounts of miracle working. Gradually this process led to the collection of material, sometimes by generic type (such as parables of the kingdom,[16] cultic teachings,[17] church order instructions,[18] wisdom sayings,[19] miracle stories[20]), at other times in larger blocks of material by catchword or topical/thematic link. Elsewhere, the ordering rationale is not apparent at all, as in the *Gospel of Thomas*, a text which some scholars consider to be an early witness to Jesus' sayings largely independent of the canonical gospels, though others consider it later and derivative.[21] The reconstructed

12 See Gamble, *Books and readers*, 24–8, 65.
13 See, e.g. 1 Cor 10:1 ('our ancestors'); Gal 3–4 and Rom 4 (Abraham, 'our forefather').
14 See ch. 9, below, on Marcion.
15 Berger, 'Hellenistische Gattungen,' 1031–1432; Aune, *Westminster Dictionary*, 187–190.
16 Mark 4 and parallels.
17 See Betz, *Essays*, 1–16, 55–69; and his *Sermon on the Mount*, on Matt 6:1–18 as a 'cultic didache'.
18 Koester, *Ancient Christian gospels*, 53–4.
19 Ibid. 55–62.
20 Theissen, *Miracle stories*; Achtemeier, 'Pre-Markan miracle catenae'.
21 Koester, *Ancient Christian gospels*, 75–128, esp. 81; Aune, *Westminster dictionary*, 465–73 (with further literature).

sayings document which has generated the most intensive investigation – and dispute – is Q, 'The Synoptic sayings source,' indicated by the extensive parallelism between Matthew and Luke in places where they are clearly not relying upon their other common source, the gospel according to Mark.[22] Perhaps kept in notebooks,[23] these were 'working documents', practical texts that played a vital role in the communities where they were composed, collected, read and, as this literary process vividly demonstrates, pondered, revised and retold.[24]

The early turn to writing

Traditions about Jesus, such as that of the 'Lord's meal' (1 Cor 11:23–6; Mark 14:22–5 and parallels) existed in both oral and written form for some time.[25] But we should not presume Christians universally preferred the oral to the written, considering the former more authoritative.[26] The burgeoning of Christian literature in this same period suggests the opposite – that the written word was *highly prized* among Christ-believers, a customary and trusted medium for communicating the truths, values, roots, promises and expectations of this religious movement. Above all, the two media were not necessarily viewed as competitive, but were linked in a developing culture of composition and consumption of 'Jesus lore' that took place within the fluidity of ancient verbal culture in which 'oral' and 'written' were far less fixed than in the modern world and where reading was vocalised out loud. Full appreciation of this point requires, furthermore, that we not look for a single motivation or incitement for Christians suddenly and reluctantly to have 'switched' from oral to literary activity. This 'transition' is normally attributed to the passing on of the first generation and the fear that, with the death of the original eyewitnesses, important 'testimony' may be lost. Although this did sometimes play a role (see, for instance, John 19:35; 21:20–4), there were a host of factors that prompted early Christian literary activity:

22 See Tuckett, *Q and the history of early Christianity*; Kloppenborg Verbin, *Excavating Q*; Koester, *Ancient Christian gospels*, 128–71.
23 Stanton, 'Early reception', 59.
24 Gamble, *Books and readers*, 39, 77–8, on Christian texts as 'practical'. But this should not be set in opposition to 'aesthetic' values, which are likewise manifest in the careful literary artistry of much early Christian literature.
25 Koester, *Synoptische Überlieferung*.
26 The Papias tradition in Euseb. *HE* 3.39.3–4 has traditionally been taken this way (as recently Dunn, *Jesus remembered*, 173–254), but see the apt critiques of Alexander, 'The living voice', and Gamble, *Books and readers*, 30–1. For Paul's strategic decision to write instead of speak in person, see Mitchell, 'New Testament envoys'.

- the model of the Septuagint as 'sacred text'
- the reading and interpretation of scripture in worship in the synagogue, which served as a prototype for Christian practice[27]
- the geographical spread of missionary communities needing to stay in contact
- challenges from outsiders (Gentiles and Jews), which necessitated an organised and coherent response
- the rapidity with which internal community debates about praxis and belief arose, requiring adjudication and instigating attempts at uniformity and universality through writing and rewriting texts
- the increasing complexity of the hermeneutical tasks of self-definition and theological expression required for this religious movement delicately – and oddly – poised at the axis of Jewish and Graeco-Roman religious precedents

and, not to be neglected:

- the conspicuous literary skills of some key leaders in the first generations who made texts an effective vehicle for subsequent Christian discourse.

For all these reasons, from very early on texts became a natural and attractive medium for the religious circles developing around the name of Jesus. The emergence of the written record was neither reluctant nor hesitant, but enthusiastic.

The letters of Paul

The world in which Paul wrote to assemblies (*ekklēsiai*) he had founded in Galatia, Philippi, Thessalonica and Corinth and those ahead in territory he hoped soon to visit (Rome)[28] was quite accustomed to letters as a means of communication. A wealth of ancient Greek documentary letters written on papyrus have been preserved in Egypt which give us an insight into everyday epistolary practice in the early Roman empire.[29] We also possess the published 'literary letters' of such classical giants as Plato, Demosthenes, Isocrates, Epicurus, Cicero and Seneca, as well as later epistolary handbooks.[30] The extant letters Paul sent to early Christian churches are situated in between those two epistolary levels: they contain many of the same literary conventions as the

---

27 Gamble, *Books and readers*, 208–14.
28 See pt ii, ch. 5, above.
29 White, *Light from ancient letters*.
30 Malherbe, *Ancient epistolary theorists*.

simple everyday family and business letters (e.g. epistolary prescript, health wish, disclosure formulae, greetings, farewells), and they are real letters written to known and directly addressed readers.[31] But their epistolary bodies (i.e. the centre of the letter where its main business is accomplished) are far more elaborate, including complex and highly developed arguments which are much closer to the literary letters of the orators and philosophers (and Hellenistic Jewish authors, like the writer of the 'letter of Aristeas'), resembling a speech or a treatise more than the simple missives found among the papyri.[32] Paul's letters employ not only the epistolary *topoi* ('commonplaces' or 'clichés') of the documentary letters, but also rhetorical forms and techniques such as *hypotheseis* ('propositions'), syllogisms, *paradeigmata* ('examples for emulation'), *synkriseis* ('comparisons'), allegories and *elenchoi* ('refutations').[33] The letter was a flexible vehicle by which one could perform a range of functions: advising, instructing, admonishing, defending, excoriating, informing, consoling, administrating, requesting, explaining and warning.[34] In key instances Paul decided to write letters to address issues because they were more effective than his own voice and personal presence.[35] Remarkable products of a skilled thinker and memorable personality, the Pauline letters wrestle with the theological, ethical and pastoral meaning of the oral gospel proclamation for the subsequent history of each small group of Christians (members of local house churches) in a given city or region,[36] seen in the light of God's scriptural plan for humanity.[37]

The epistles of Paul, 'the apostle of Jesus Christ', were not written to evangelise the faith to outsiders; they presume basic knowledge of the gospel narrative, its chief characters (i.e. Jesus, God (= the God of the Jews / Israelites), the spirit, the 'rulers of this age') and essential episodes. As second- and third-order reflections on his oral 'gospel',[38] they enforce and participate in a religious world-view that Paul did much to create, and, most importantly, they script essential roles and identities for their addressees – 'the brothers and sisters', 'those who are being saved', 'the called ones', 'those who believe',[39] within the narrative of salvation so vividly sketched. This argumentative strategy allowed for an easy and natural transference of identity from the original recipients to

---

31 See Klauck, *Die antike Briefliteratur*; Aune, *Greco-Roman literature*, 158–225.
32 Closest to those among Paul's letters is Philemon.
33 Treatments in Sampley, *Paul in the Greco-Roman world*.
34 Stowers, *Letter writing*.
35 Mitchell, 'New Testament envoys'.
36 For detailed discussion, see pt II, ch. 5, above.
37 On Paul's use of scripture, see Hays, *Echoes of scripture*, and Koch, *Die Schrift*.
38 Mitchell, 'Rhetorical shorthand'.
39 E.g. 1 Cor 1:1–24.

later generations who would read and ponder these letters and find them formative of Christian identity for them, as well.[40] But Paul's letters are difficult texts, as the author of 2 Peter later lamented, even as he testifies (sometime in the early second century) that these documents have already become *graphai*, 'scripture' (3:15–16).

Pauline pseudepigrapha and the Pauline letter collection

In addition to providing fruits and nettles for this process of theological reflection, Paul's letters exemplify interpretive procedures and standards for the future. The task of Pauline interpretation that was in many ways to dominate the history of Christian thought began already in his lifetime, as he negotiated with Corinthian (e.g. 2 Cor 2:3–9; 7:11–13; 10:7–10) and other readers about the meaning and intent of his letters.[41] Because one mode of steering the meaning of those contested texts was for Paul to write a new text supplanting or building upon an earlier one,[42] after Paul's death the practice was continued by others,[43] who picked up a stylus and sent messages 'via letter[s] as though they were from him' (2 Thess 2:2). As Paul could be present from a distance across the empire, so also could he be present even after his death in letters (either his own or pseudepigraphal ones).[44] There is not complete scholarly agreement on which letters were actually written by Paul and which by these later 'Pauls', but the strongest consensus judges Ephesians, Colossians and 2 Thessalonians to be 'deutero-Paulines', and the Pastoral Epistles (1 and 2 Timothy, Titus, late first or early second century) 'trito-Paulines'. Such conclusions are based upon interlocking comparisons of historical, theological, linguistic and literary features with the presumed 'genuine' Pauline letters.[45]

For example, while Paul wrote to Christians in Thessalonica *c*.50 CE to respond to the theological crisis provoked by the delay of the *eschaton*, a later admiring reader of that letter composed a sequel using it as a literary template (replicating even oddities of its epistolary structure) to address virtually the inverse eschatological crisis: the fear that the *eschaton* had already arrived (2 Thess 2:2). This literary strategy would only work if Paul's letters were

---

40 See Dahl, 'Particularity of the Pauline epistles'.
41 Mitchell, 'Corinthian correspondence'.
42 The clearest example is 1 Cor 5:9–10, but the entire Corinthian correspondence illustrates this (Mitchell, 'Corinthian correspondence').
43 Perhaps initially members of his missionary team (Gamble, *Books and readers*, 99).
44 Betz, 'Paul's "second presence"'.
45 Koester, *Introduction*, vol. II, 241–305; Vielhauer, *Geschichte*, 58–251.

already known to be authoritative teachings (see 2 Thess 2:15; 3:14), and the readers of this new text already preconditioned to read 'as though they were Thessalonians' and hence to reap the benefit of advice (purportedly) sent to the early Macedonian Christians. This process of universalising the readership of Paul's letters was exemplified in the same period by the composition of the 'circular letter' of Ephesians, which in its earliest copies did not actually name the Ephesians in the prescript, but 'the saints and believers in Christ Jesus' in any place,[46] who would find in this imaginative compendium of statements of Paul's original letters[47] a spiritualised *enchiridion* ('handbook') of Pauline theology and ethics for their own generation.

The pseudepigraphical Pauline letters depend and draw upon the original letters and 'update' and refine them to suit later circumstances. Consequently, they presume that Paul's letters had already been collected in some form, and were in circulation as authoritative documents. We do not know exactly when this was done, or by whom, but already by the time of *1 Clement* (end of first century?) and the letters of Ignatius of Antioch (*c.*117 CE?) they are known and quoted. The earliest was probably the collection of letters to seven churches, with that number promoting a universalist audience of the epistles, a hermeneutical strategy so immediately successful that in some sense it replaced itself as more letters to churches and individuals were added, and ten-, thirteen- and fourteen-letter collections were formed.[48] Each version gave a differerent interpretive shape to the collection, by means of editorial work within individual letters (such as 2 Corinthians, which is a compilation of five individual missives),[49] the number of letters included, and the order in which they were arranged. We know of collections with Galatians, 1 and 2 Corinthians and Romans at the head.[50] It is possible that this early epistolary anthology, and the need to move around easily from letter to letter, was the reason Christians favoured the codex over the roll for their literary works.[51] That physical format was to prove equally suitable for the other characteristic genre of Christian literature,[52] which was soon packaged and disseminated in sets, also.

---

46 Marcion's text had Laodiceans in the prescript (Tert. *Marc.* 5.17; cf. Col 4:16).

47 Goodspeed, *Meaning of Ephesians*, 9, argues that 550 of the 618 short sense units of the letter have 'unmistakable parallels in Paul, in words or substance'.

48 Frede, 'Die Ordnung'; Gamble, 'Pauline corpus' and his *Books and readers*, 59–63. Trobisch, *Paul's Letter Collection*, thinks Paul began the process with his own four-letter collection.

49 Mitchell, 'Corinthian correspondence'.

50 See Fig. 5 (above) showing Romans following Hebrews in papyrus P[46] (*c.*200).

51 Gamble, 'Pauline corpus', and *Books and readers*, 49–66.

52 Skeat argued the codex was adopted for the gospels (Elliott, *Collected biblical writings of T. C. Skeat*, 73–87).

Gospel literature

Paul's letters presume,[53] but do not themselves comprise, a narrative of the life, death and resurrection of Jesus. Sometime around the conclusion to the Roman war on Judaea (66–73 CE, with the catastrophic destruction of the temple in 70 CE), an anonymous Christian with a rustic prose style and a flair for irony became the unwitting inaugurator of the gospel literature that was to become the telltale Christian literary product. From early times identified as Mark, the interpreter of Peter,[54] this writer, in penning the words of his incipit, 'the beginning of the "good news" [= "gospel"] of Jesus Christ, the Son of God' (Mark 1:1), said much more than he could ever know, for his text was to be the first in a line of early Christian 'gospels', each of which promotes a particular perspective on Jesus and his place in God's plan of salvation.

Mark

Mark's gospel is a compilation of traditions he inherited, especially miracle stories about Jesus, tales of controversy, a smaller body of Jesus' teachings, and perhaps an existing outline of the passion story. The juxtaposition of these units of tradition with his essentially Pauline conception of the 'good news' – as the death and resurrection of Jesus into which believers are baptised to gain its saving effects[55] – left Mark with several logical and theological problems. He sought to resolve these in the course of his narrative, and in so doing produced a 'diamond in the rough' of a text which for all its ruggedness is a captivating and ingenious piece of literature. The first problem is the cloaked and misunderstood identity of Jesus as the Messiah both in his lifetime and in Mark's, and the second (related to it) was the incredible incongruity of a murdered miracle worker. A compilation of the familiar and the strange (in a world that knew of other messiahs, other healers), Mark scripts an utter novelty: a verbal icon of the crucified king of Israel.

Mark's revolutionary text is 'biographic'[56] in that it follows the life of a central character (Jesus is in all but two or three scenes in the whole) in a roughly chronological order ending in his death. It opens with Isaiah the prophet (presumed to be known to the audience) whose voice interprets and

---

53 For instance, he places the Lord's Supper 'on the night on which he was betrayed' (1 Cor 11:23).
54 Papias 2.15 [= Euseb. *HE* 3.39].
55 See Marcus, 'Mark – interpreter of Paul', with bibliography on this long-standing issue of debate.
56 Terminology of Swain, 'Biography and biographic'. On the gospels as 'biographies', see Aune, *New Testament in its literary environment*, 17–76; Burridge, *What are the gospels?*

explains the action (1:2–3; 1:11; cf. Mal 3:1), so that the entire 'beginning' of Mark is situated in relation to the 'beginning' of Genesis and the anthology of biblical literature which it introduces.[57] Hence Mark's 'good news' is a new narrative that presents itself as a prophetic sequel to the scriptures of Israel[58] focused on the question, 'Who is Jesus?' (Mark 8:27). His work is also a deliberate counter-reading to those of his contemporaries associated with the powers that handed Jesus over to be crucified ('elders, chief priests, scribes' (8:31)). They contest Jesus' messianic identity (12:35–7), term it blasphemy (14:61–4) and mock his enthronement as king of Israel (15:31–2) at the very moment of his crucifixion in this upside-down drama. But the followers of Jesus[59] will triumph over those opponents (both Jesus' and theirs) when he comes in power as the Son of Man and rescues them from this world (13:27). Readers of this text (which is much more complex than it seems on the surface) are put in a privileged position whereby they can view and learn from the ignorance, not only of Jesus' cardboard cut-out evil opponents, but also his own disciples – Peter, James and John and the rest – who grapple, grope and often miss the epiphanies before their very eyes. Through the narrative scheme of the incomprehension of the disciples Mark has effected a massive theological transition from past history to 'good news' – as found in his text! – as the repository of genuine and superior religious insight. This move (together with the ritual structures in evidence in the narrative) ensures that *readers of any generation* have a mode of access to Jesus that is not only equal, but superior, to that of the historical disciples.[60]

Markan revisions

If one takes seriously this epistemological claim of Mark's gospel – that *the text* is a vehicle of divine epiphanies which were and are constantly misperceived on the level of history – then it is supremely important that the text get it right. Mark won the day on the larger point of textual mediation of divine realities, but also thereby directed attention to lacks, gaps and infelicities in his narrative that later authors sought to fill. Anonymous Christians took up that task, to revise Mark's 'beginning' composition to include more traditions about Jesus' sayings, and to revise his theological vision for their own contexts. Because Matthew and Luke made Mark's existing narrative the framework for their own, and copied much of it verbatim, these three gospels are called the

---

57 Cf. Mark 13:19; 10:6; John 1:1 will make this move definitively.
58 Differently, MacDonald, *Homeric epics*, argues that Mark wrote using the *Odyssey* as his 'hypotext'; critical assessment in Mitchell, 'Homer in the New Testament?'.
59 'Following' is Mark's technical term for being a disciple of Jesus (1:18; 2:14, 15; 6:1; 8:34; 9:38; 10:21, 28, 32, 52; 15:41).
60 The same claim Paul makes for his own apostolate (see Mitchell, 'Epiphanic evolutions').

'Synoptics' (in honour of their 'common view'). What is striking, actually, is the paradox of their strict, word-for-word fidelity to Mark's account in some places, and quite free alteration of it elsewhere. There were likely multiple motivations for the editorial activity of each evangelist and variable factors affecting the final product in each case. According to ancient rhetorical culture (the curriculum of the ancient *paideia* or educational system), a discourse should be appropriate to the subject, the speaker and the audience, the three components of the communicative act. Hence, it should not be a surprise that each gospel is in certain and various ways tailored to its expected or intended audience. Ancient traditions going back to the early second century sought to recapture the moment and place of writing of each gospel. While often legendary, these traditions, assigning Matthew to Antioch or Judaea, Luke to Achaia, Mark to Rome or Alexandria, were one way early readers grappled with the individuality and particularity of each gospel text,[61] even as the gospels were soon to become widely disseminated.[62] While we do not have to assume that each evangelist knew only a single house church or urban centre, or wrote for only a handful of friends, they do appear to address different concerns and concrete ecclesiastical contexts within the last decades of the first century.[63]

Matthew The author of Matthew's gospel appears to have lived in close proximity with non-Christian Jews and Gentile Christians sometime after the destruction of Jerusalem in 70 CE (Matt 22:7; 23:38–9). He found Mark's gospel worthy, but insufficient in its opening and closing, and too meagre in its record of the teachings of Jesus. In editing Mark to form a new version, Matthew put a new angle on Mark's enigmatic suffering Messiah by rendering him as the new Moses, both through the addition of infancy narratives which recall Moses' imperilled birth and boyhood in Egypt, and through the incorporation of blocks of traditional teaching material from Q and from his own special material in five (possibly six) long discourses of Jesus.[64] Tellingly, Matthew is the only evangelist to use the word *ekklēsia*, 'church'.[65] His Jesus is the founder of a new community of obedience to his word and command (see especially

---

61 Details in Mitchell, 'Patristic counter-evidence'.
62 All (except, significantly, Mark) well attested in the papyri from Egypt (see Metzger, *Text*, 247–56).
63 Bauckham, *Gospels for all Christians*, has rightly urged scholars not to presume that the gospel communities were isolated or completely separate. However, his proposal that all four evangelists wrote for 'any and every Christian community in the late-first-century Roman empire' (p. 1) goes too far in the other direction.
64 See the same formula in 7:28; 11:1; 13:53; 19:1; 26:1; cf. 28:19–20.
65 Matt 16:18; 18:17 (twice). Luke reserves the term for his second volume (Acts).

chapter 18), and, even beyond Moses, he is 'Emmanuel', 'God with us' from his miraculous conception, one who remains present in its midst (1:23; 28:20; 18:20; with Isa 7:14). This is just one of some dozen 'formula quotations' in Matthew, in which he solemnly emphasises that Jesus' deeds and life events are in fulfilment of 'scripture'. This sense that in the history of Jesus prophecy has been fulfilled is also applied to events since Jesus' death and its aftermath. Jesus is depicted as having foretold the destruction of Jerusalem, down to the detail of the conflagration which Titus' troops ignited (23:38; 22:7). Matthew interprets these events as divine punishment on the Jewish leaders and people for the death of Jesus (27:25) and wilful rejection of the 'gospel' message (28:11–15). When combined with the bitter invectives Matthew has Jesus deliver against the leaders of the synagogue (who were in this time period themselves seeking theological explanation for the terrible events, and finding it elsewhere),[66] Matthew's gospel became a charter document for the mission to the Gentiles, the *ethnos*, 'nation', who will bear fruit (21:43; cf. 28:19–20). Yet the parables Matthew adds to Mark's 'little Apocalypse' (Mark 13:1–37; cf. Matt 24:1–25:46), issue the unmistakable warning that the *parousia* of the Lord will only bring access to the kingdom of God for those whose deeds are in conformity with their word of confession to the Lord (see the parallelism between 7:21–7 and 25:31–46). Much is at stake, obviously, in composing a text which, like Torah itself, preserves and re-presents 'all that I commanded you' (28:20). Perhaps it is not surprising that Matthew's was the most widely read and cited gospel in the earliest church.[67]

Luke and Acts. Explicitly acknowledging his 'many' unnamed predecessors (Mark and others), this writer, probably in the early second century, argues that his new 'narrative' (*diēgēsis*) is justified by his wish to write in an orderly fashion (*kathexēs*, 1:3) the traditions, both oral and written, which he had followed 'with great precision' (*akribōs*). Luke not only claims a place for his work on the growing shelf of Christian literature, but he also, by his use of the literary form of an historiographic preface,[68] with its customary references to witnesses, prior sources and 'accuracy' and 'reliability', overtly seeks to situate his narrative about 'the things that have been fulfilled among us' among the local histories of the ancient world.[69] The shift from a well-crafted Greek

---

66 See e.g. 4 Ezra.

67 Massaux, *Influence of the gospel of Saint Matthew.*

68 See Alexander, *Preface to Luke's gospel* (who seeks to isolate technical manuals from historiographic prefaces); essays in Moessner, *Jesus and the heritage of Israel* on Luke's preface and its place in ancient historiography.

69 Sterling, *Historiography and self-definition.*

rhetorical period (Luke 1:1–4) to the conspicuously Septuagintal diction of the birth narratives (as signalled immediately in 1:5) demonstrates the dual literary standards Luke emulates, and the companions he wishes his work to have. The hybrid that results is a drama of fulfilment of divine prophetic promises in three acts, which impelled Luke to sequelise, not just Mark, but his own work, and produce a second volume (*logos*, Acts 1:1) we now know as 'The Acts of the Apostles'. In it Luke provided a foundation story for a unified Christian movement (a romantic vision which belies the primary evidence in Paul's letters) that was completely faithful to its roots in Jerusalem and Judaism (1:8f; 2:22–38; 24:44–7), yet, when spurned, turned to the Gentiles, who 'will listen to it' (Acts 28:28). Written to a patron, Theophilus, Luke-Acts is the fullest piece of early apologetics, a defence of the legitimacy of the Christian movement as a religion rooted in a 'righteous' founder, Jesus, who was no threat to Roman authority (as even the Roman governor who wrote the order for his execution averred three times),[70] and instigated a movement which has as its goal not political sedition, but universal religious salvation. The two-volume work shows the spread of the gospel from origins in Jerusalem and Jewish literary culture to Rome and a Gentile audience (1:8f; 2:22–38; Acts 28:30–1). Jesus and the movement he spawned are part of 'world history', set in relation to the Roman imperium (2:1; 3:1).

John. Scholars dispute whether John's gospel is, like Matthew and Luke, a rewrite of Mark.[71] This literary theologian trumps even the Matthean and Lukan attempts to push Mark's 'beginning' back to Jesus' ancestry to Abraham (Matt 1:1–17) or Adam (Luke 3:23–37), to the primordial, prehistorical 'beginning' *before* the creation of Genesis 1:1. His famous prologue, a poetic rendering of the career of the *logos* ('the Word'), is cleverly poised to claim for Jesus divine praises from Hellenistic Judaism and Greek philosophy. The christological question that formed the centre of Mark's narrative ('Who do people say that I am?')[72] becomes in John an inquiry about origins and destinations – 'Where is he from?' and 'Where is he going?'[73] As in Mark the reader has been clued in to the answer from the prologue, but in the act of reading s/he is given the opportunity to 'see' and 'touch' textually the divine realities which will lead to belief, and true life (John 20:30–1; 1 John 1:1–4). Like Matthew, John combines narrative material with discourse, but in his case

70 Luke 23:4, 14, 22; cf. Acts 18:15–16; 25:9–12.
71 See pt ii, ch. 6, above. I tend to think John does know Mark.
72 Mark 8:27, 29; cf. 1:24; 4:41; 6:2–3, etc.
73 John 7:27–8; 8:14; 9:29–30; 19:9, etc.

the focus is not so much ethical as christological. Jesus in John is the divine 'exegete' (1:18), who reveals God by disclosing his identity in predication (the frequent 'I am' statements) and paradox,[74] chiefly his exaltation in the very moment of crucifixion, a literal 'lifting up' from the earth (John 3:14; 8:28; 12:32–4) which is a moment of oxymoronic glorification (John 1:14; 12:16, 23, 28; 17:5). But even the divine self-exegesis of the gospel text requires update and further interpretation. The gospel of John has several endings, added over time in new editions, which allow us to glimpse the subsequent fate of the witness who stands behind the work, the 'Beloved Disciple' (see especially 21:20–5; cf. 19:35), and Peter (21:18–19), now martyred. The re-editions of the gospel are accompanied by at least one primer (perhaps written by one of the final editors?)[75] in how to read it right. First John repudiates those who have gone astray from the proper 'beginning' and not understood that 'Jesus Christ has come in the flesh' (1 John 4:2–3) in 'water and blood' (1 John 5:6; cf. John 19:34). It is not hard to see how other readers, such as the Gnostic Heracleon, could find in this gospel's portrayal of Jesus' impassivity before death[76] ample grounds for the contrary view, even as the revelation discourses in John were to be a standard literary form among the books found at Nag Hammadi.[77]

The fourfold gospel

Gnostics, and other Christians, had more gospels than these four. When Origen seeks to explain Luke's reference to 'many [who] have undertaken' to write (Luke 1:1), he names such works as 'the gospel of the Egyptians' (elsewhere, also, 'the gospel of the Hebrews'), 'the gospel of the Twelve', 'the gospel of Basilides', 'the gospel of Thomas', and 'the gospel of Matthias', among 'many others'.[78] The second century saw increasing debate about the status, authority and consistency among these various gospels. Several solutions were proposed: for a community of Christians to pick (and perhaps suitably edit)[79] one gospel that best reflects their views, to harmonise the gospels into a single composite narrative,[80] or deliberately to enshrine the diverse portraits into a

74 On paradox as characteristic of Christian discourse, see Cameron, *Christianity and the rhetoric of empire.*
75 Brown, *Gospel according to John,* vol. I, xxiv–xl.
76 Compare John 12:27 and Mark 13:32–41.
77 See *The Nag Hammadi library in English,* Robinson (ed.).
78 *Hom. Luc.* 1.4–5. See Klauck, *Apocryphal gospels,* and translated texts in *NTApoc,* vol. I.
79 See ch. 9, below, on Marcion's edition of Luke's gospel.
80 Such as Tatian's 'Diatessaron' (see pt IV, ch. 19, below).

multivolume, but definitive, collection. The champion of the latter position, which was to prove decisive, was Irenaeus of Lyons, who provided a justification for the fourfold gospel (no more, no less) as rooted in divine intention and cosmological order, just like the four winds or four pillars holding up the world.[81] This is consistent with the titles 'the gospel according to [Matthew, Mark, Luke, or John]'.[82]

A bibliographic culture

The earliest Christians did not just produce texts; they created a literary culture. Communities of readers who 'searched the scriptures' individually and in common needed tools. They found their hermeneutical tools (methods for interpretation) by naturally carrying over the standard literary-critical techniques taught in the Graeco-Roman educational system, whereby one learned to read with precision, to determine the authenticity of authorship of texts and to compile the most reliable readings and interpretations.[83] They also discovered within their texts precedents for reading their 'scriptures', including enigmatic passages like Mark 4:10–12, Galatians 4:24, 1 Corinthians 10:11, which would function increasingly as hermeneutical principles when Christian exegetes instinctively applied to their scriptures the principle of 'interpreting Homer by Homer'.[84] Every community that revolves around books – like the Jews at Qumran, or the schools of philosophers with which the early Christians had much in common[85] – makes an agreement, either tacit or overtly worked out, about what texts they read and which not.[86] This was also the case among Christians in the first three centuries. The formal fixation of the twenty-seven-book canon of the 'New Testament' lies outside this volume (Athanasius' thirty-ninth Festal Letter of 367 is usually taken as at least retrospectively a defining moment),[87] but the major corpora – Pauline letters and

---

81 Iren. *Haer.* 3.11.8, as also the four beasts of Ezek 1:18; cf. Rev 4:6–7, the source of traditional iconography of the evangelists (Burridge, *Four gospels*).

82 Hengel, *Studies in the gospel of Mark*, 64–84, argues for a first-century date for these, but this is debatable.

83 Grant, *Heresy and Criticism*; Young, *Biblical exegesis*; continued discussion in pt v, ch. 27, below.

84 Neuschäfer, *Origenes*, vol. I, 276–85. Inner-biblical interpretation is a major principle of rabbinic biblical exegesis, which also influenced Christian practice (see Kugel and Greer, *Early biblical interpretation*).

85 Especially in their focus on 'intellectual practices' (Stowers, 'Does Pauline Christianity resemble a Hellenistic philosophy?').

86 Snyder, *Teachers and texts*, esp. 94–9 ('corpus organization').

87 Metzger, *Canon*, 210–12, 312–13.

a gospel collection – were largely in place by the end of the second century, though other works remained disputed.[88]

A literary culture also requires social assets (literate persons,[89] scribes) and material tools – papyrus, parchment, ink, scriptoria, archives and libraries.[90] Significantly, Christians appear first to make a distinctive mark on material culture in the realm of books.[91] Although the codex was occasionally used for 'pocketbook editions', it was not the favoured or common format for literature in the Graeco-Roman world. Yet fully 100 per cent of papyrus gospel fragments found have been from codexes.[92] Their particular types of anthologised literature (collections of letters, of gospels) and a cast of travelling teachers apparently were some of the reasons Christians early on adopted the codex format. Whether initially so intended or not, Christian use of the codex rather than the scroll served to set them apart from both Jews and 'pagans'. Two more bibliographic peculiarities point to a unique centre of the movement: special abbreviations used for the names 'Lord', 'Jesus', 'Christ' and 'God' (called by scholars *nomina sacra*),[93] and an early use (2nd century) of a 'staurogram', a cross-shaped shorthand for the word 'cross', that may be the first piece of early Christian iconography – preserved on the pages of a papyrus codex.[94]

The genres adopted by the earliest Christian writers – letters, narrative 'gospels', histories and apocalypses – were to leave an inestimable mark on Christian identity throughout the period of this volume. Owing to Paul and his early imitators the epistolary form was to remain a favoured vehicle of Christian literary expression (twenty-one of twenty-seven New Testament documents, many of the Apostolic Fathers and subsequent figures like Dionysius of Corinth, even Constantine). Ironically, even those who may have opposed him in his lifetime, Peter and James, were later depicted as taking up Paul's weapon of choice, the epistle.[95] By incorporating Graeco-Roman rhetorical techniques into his proclamation, Paul catapulted the Christian gospel into

---

88 Euseb. *HE* 3.25; further discussion in ch. 9, below. See Barton, *Holy writings*; cf. Metzger, *Canon*, 157–62.

89 Key here is 'group literacy' (in a world in which arguably 10 per cent were literate) – if one member of the group can read, they all have access to written texts, which were customarily read aloud (valuable discussion in Gamble, *Books and readers*, 2–10).

90 Gamble, *Books and readers*.

91 Hurtado, 'Earliest evidence'.

92 Skeat in Elliott (ed.), *Collected biblical writings of T. C. Skeat*, 73–87 (esp. 79), 269–80.

93 Gamble, *Books and readers*, 74–8. The practice is attested in literary sources in *Ep. Barn.* 9.8. In Fig. 5 (above) the reader can see the abbreviation $\overline{\Theta C}$ (*th-s* for *theos*, 'God') in line 4.

94 Hurtado, 'Earliest evidence'.

95 Koester, *Introduction*, vol. II, 292–7.

the vortex of the ancient problem of rhetoric and philosophy in the quest for truth,[96] and the realm of apologetic argumentation, both of which were to constitute the enduring tasks of Christian discourse in the second century and beyond.[97] Luke's master-work of apologetic historiography was a major influence on the first church historian, Eusebius.[98] His Acts of the Apostles also spawned a cottage industry of *Acta* associated with such figures as Thomas, Peter, John, Paul, Thecla, Andrew,[99] which, echoing popular novelistic conventions,[100] were apparently widely read and avidly appreciated among Christians.[101] The narrative forms of the gospels, including sayings, miracle stories and passion narratives, were the literary template upon which martyrologies, such as *The martyrdom of Polycarp*,[102] and lives of saints, like Athanasius' *Life of Antony*, were constructed. Christians not only produced literary *Lives*, but they also lived in imitation of them, in a vital and continual interaction between text and life.[103] This extended even into death.

Apocalyptic discourses, such as are found in Paul's letters (1 Thess 4:13–5:11; 1 Cor 15), in the gospels (Mark 13 and parallels) and in a host of independent texts (*Apocalypse of Peter, Apocalypse of Paul*) remained a base-line of the Christian movement, even as they occasioned bitter controversy. The most famous of these is the Apocalypse of John, a first-century document whose authority and 'canonicity' were disputed in early centuries, but was ultimately to become the anchor leg to the New Testament (Euseb. *HE* 3.25.1–7).[104] The full anthology of 'New Testament'[105] literature that eventually became fixed ends with a bibliographic curse that now applies to the whole:

> if anyone adds to these words, God will add upon him the plagues which are written in this book; and if anyone takes away from the words of the book of this prophecy, God will remove his portion from the tree of life and from the holy city that belongs to those who have been inscribed in this book. (Rev 22:18–19).

---

96 Betz, 'Problem'; Mitchell, 'Rhetorik'.
97 See ch. 11, below.
98 Grant, *Eusebius as church historian*, 39–41.
99 Translated texts *NTApoc*, vol. 11.
100 Aune, *Westminster dictionary*, 320–3; Chance *et al.*, *Ancient fiction*.
101 Cameron, *Christianity and the rhetoric of empire*, 89–119.
102 For the deliberate parallelism, see Aune, *Westminster dictionary*, 296.
103 Cameron, *Christianity and the rhetoric of empire*, 141–54.
104 The fourth-century Codex Vaticanus may have ended with Revelation. Skeat made the case that it was one of the manuscripts Constantine commissioned (Elliott, *Collected biblical writings of T. C. Skeat*, 193–237).
105 Although a biblical phrase (Jer 31:31; 2 Cor 3:6), 'new testament' is not used of a corpus of texts until late in the second century (e.g. Iren. *Haer.* 4.28.2; Hipp. *Fr. 63 in Gen.* 2).

This scribal colophon aptly names the dynamics we have here been tracing: a literary culture of burgeoning proportions, steadfast seriousness and concern for finding its way to proper instruments of control over its productions and their meaning. The earliest Christians, who taught that the risen Jesus could not be found in tomb but in text, can readily envision a heaven without a temple (Rev 21:22), but not one without a book.

9

Marcion and the 'canon'

HARRY Y. GAMBLE

Marcion is one of the most intriguing yet elusive figures in early Christian history. It is proof of his prominence that, among the diverse forms of Christianity that flourished in the second century, his was the most frequently and forcefully attacked by anti-heretical writers, and was apparently perceived as the most dangerous.[1] Marcion has likewise interested modern scholars, not only because of the peculiarities of his teachings but also because of his possible influence on one of the most important developments in the early church, the formation of the Christian Bible.[2] In that connection, Marcion has commanded attention on two major topics: the church's appropriation of the scriptures of Judaism (which it came to call the 'Old Testament'), and the emergence of a canon of specifically Christian scriptures (a 'New Testament').

It is impossible in short space to do justice to the many difficulties that beset the study of Marcion and his influence. It has not yet become entirely clear either what Marcion taught or why he taught it. Some of his salient convictions are well known, but it remains uncertain how they arose, cohered or intersected the convictions of others. The old question whether Marcion should be regarded as a biblical theologian or as a Gnostic (or philosophical) teacher has not been answered, and cannot be answered in those terms. But, by situating Marcion within second-century Christianity and the issues that

---

1 The sources for Marcion's biography and still more for his teaching are Tert. *Marc.* and *Praescr.* (30); Iren. *Haer.* (1–3); Epiph. *Pan.* (42); Epiphanius, along with Pseudo-Tertullian, *Adversus omnes haereses*, and Filastrius, *Diversarum haereseon liber*, may preserve parts of Hippolytus' lost *Syntagma*. Justin Martyr and Theophilus of Antioch wrote treatises against Marcion, both lost, and Irenaeus states his intention to do so (*Haer.* 1.27.4). According to Eusebius, others who wrote against Marcion included Hegesippus (Euseb. *HE* 4.22), Philip of Gortyna and a certain Modestus (Euseb. *HE* 4.25). Celsus, the late second-century critic of Christianity, seems to have known only two forms of Christianity, one of which was Marcion's (Or. *C. Cels.* 2.6; 5.54; 6.57; 7.25–6).

2 The principal scholarly monographs are those of Harnack, Wilson, Knox, Blackman and Hoffmann.

preoccupied it, we can go far towards making his activity intelligible and evaluating his role.

Born in the late first or early second century, Marcion was a native of Sinope, a prosperous seaport on the Black (Euxine) Sea in the Roman province of Pontus in northern Asia Minor. Nothing certain is known of his early life. He was, by most accounts, a *nauklēros*, a shipmaster or one engaged in maritime shipping, and a well-to-do man. It is highly probable that Marcion was a Christian already in Pontus, and indeed Epiphanius (*Pan.* 42.1) represents him as the son of a Christian bishop there, but nothing certain is known of his early activity.[3] He may have been active for a time in western Asia Minor (Iren. *Haer.* 3.3.4), but he gained notoriety only when he came to Rome, sometime between 135 and 140, and became associated with the Christian community there, to which he made a munificent donation of 200,000 sesterces. Although he was initially welcomed on the presumption of his orthodoxy (Tert. *Marc.* 1.1.1), a series of disputes led to a falling out over his teaching, and in 144 he was expelled from the Roman church and his gift returned. Subsequently, Marcion proceeded with remarkable success to organise and propagate his own independent Christian community. Marcionite congregations quickly sprang up over a wide area, and, in the latter half of the second century, the Marcionite church was a formidable rival to the catholic church. Though many of its congregations were eventually absorbed into Manichaeism, it persisted with considerable strength, especially in the east, into the fifth century.[4]

Christianity according to Marcion

We are acquainted with Marcion only through the writings of his detractors, and it is uncertain how fully or accurately they have portrayed him and his teachings. There are, however, points upon which his ancient critics were widely agreed. Fundamentally, he claimed that Christianity represented a radical *novum* – a fresh and unprecedented revelation of a previously unknown God of pure goodness and perfect love. This revelation, he insisted, was discontinuous with anything that came before, and so could not have been anticipated or predicted. The emissary of this alien God was God's son, Jesus of Nazareth, who appeared suddenly in human likeness in the fifteenth year of Tiberius and proclaimed a new gospel of divine goodness to be received by faith and

3 On the pre-Roman activity: Regul, *Prologe*, 177–97.
4 Epiphanius, Adamantius, Ephraem the Syrian, Theodoret of Cyrus and Eznik of Kolb all represent Marcionism as a danger in the east in the fourth and fifth centuries.

enacted in love. According to Marcion, this gospel differed so deeply and manifestly from Judaism that the God from whom it issued could not be identified with the God of Jewish scripture, whose existence was not denied, but who had a very different character and purpose than the God proclaimed by Jesus. Thus Marcion embraced a ditheism that juxtaposed the God of Judaism and Jewish scripture on the one hand and the God of Jesus and Christianity on the other. The former he regarded as an inferior, demiurgic being who created the world and human beings, who pursued justice through a law that he had promulgated, and who recompensed persons strictly according to their merits. The latter, by contrast, was a higher God of unqualified love and mercy who, having no prior relationship with human beings, approached them entirely at his own graceful initiative and for their salvation. This conception of two Gods, one lower and one higher, one creator and one redeemer, one merely just and the other merciful and loving, stood at the heart of Marcion's thought.

A major corollary of Marcion's ditheism was a sharp disparagement of the creation. His disdain for the material order found two principal expressions. One was a thoroughgoing moral rigorism with strongly ascetic features: Marcion prescribed sexual abstinence and prohibited marriage, thinking that procreation only furthered the purposes of the creator God, and he harboured a deep repugnance towards biological processes and the nuisances of the natural world. The other was a docetic Christology, which denied the actual humanity of Jesus and, accordingly, the reality of his birth and death. In addition, Marcion taught that it was the creator God who brought about the suffering and (merely bodily) death of Jesus by crucifixion, which Marcion considered a ransom that redeemed the faithful from their thraldom to the creator. The death of Jesus was therefore held to be redemptive for those who had faith, whether living or dead. Thus Marcion regarded Jesus not as the Jewish Messiah, but as a universal saviour figure.

These convictions, though fundamental, hardly represent the full sum and substance of Marcion's teaching, for there are gaps and inconsistencies among them. But it is useful to state them before inquiring after their roots and warrants. Marcion's ancient critics routinely ranked him among Gnostic teachers, and considered his teachings, like theirs, the product of philosophical speculation run amok. Many modern scholars have continued to think of Marcion as a Gnostic.[5] Despite some resemblances – for example, ditheism, docetism and

---

5 E.g. Grant, *Gnosticism*, 120–8; Bianchi, 'Marcion'; Jonas, *Gnostic Religion*, 130–46 (noting, however, that Marcion is 'the exception to many gnostic rules' (137)); Rudolph, *Gnosis*, 313–17; and (with qualifications) Aland, 'Versuch', 423–33. But see Williams, *Rethinking 'Gnosticism'*, who questions whether 'Gnosticism' is even a meaningful category.

devaluation of the material world and the body – Marcion's teaching is in other ways distinct from Christian Gnostic systems: it lacks a cosmogonic myth, the idea of dispersed elements of the divine nature in human beings, the notion of an esoteric, redemptive *gnōsis* by which they might return to their ultimate source, the allegorical approach to Jewish scripture and the appeal to secret oral traditions.[6] But if it is not helpful to think of Marcion as a Gnostic, neither can he be easily understood merely as a 'biblical theologian' or a 'radical Paulinist' who eschewed philosophy.[7] Despite the interest he took in Jewish and Christian writings, the metaphysical elements of Marcion's teaching were not readily derivable from these texts, and it is hard to imagine that they were his starting-point or that his conception of Christianity had no other roots. Like most other educated Christians, Marcion was influenced by philosophical conceptions of his time, and his construal of Christianity was responsive to issues, ideas and trends in the philosophical theology of his day.[8] He appears to have embraced a largely philosophical conception of God, or at any rate of the high God, as an utterly transcendent and perfect being. Without discounting either the stimulus of exegetical problems posed by Jewish scripture or his commitment to the Pauline tradition, it was almost certainly from a philosophical, mainly middle Platonic, vantage point that Marcion apprehended the God of Jewish scripture as a different and inferior being.[9] He did not acquiesce, however, in the corresponding philosophical conviction that knowledge of the high God could be attained through the intellect disciplined by virtue, any more than through an esoteric *gnōsis*. Rather, for him that knowledge was mediated only by revelation in the Christian gospel and apprehended only by faith.

The peculiar character of Marcion's teaching thus seems to have arisen in an interplay between popular philosophical theology and a critical reading of texts already traditional in Christianity – above all the scriptures of Judaism and the letters of Paul. Virtually all the primary features of Marcion's teaching can be accounted for in this way, even if the logical connections and finer textures of his thought remain somewhat obscure, and perhaps were never really clear. Nevertheless, Marcion did not understand himself as a Christian

6 Aland, 'Marcion/Marcioniten', 98; Hoffmann, *Marcion*, 155–84; Norelli, 'Marcion'.
7 Famously, Harnack, *Marcion*; more recently, Hoffmann, *Marcion*. (In what follows I refer to the 2nd Geman edition, Harnack, *Marcion*, with my own translation.)
8 Gager, 'Marcion', 53–9; Woltmann, 'Hintergrund'; Aland, 'Marcion/Marcioniten', 94, 98; May, *Schöpfung*, 57–60. Marcion's portrayal of the (Jewish) creator God has much in common with the philosophical critique of the Greek myths and their representations of the gods, as noted by Dungan, 'Reactionary trends', 188–94.
9 See May, 'Marcion in contemporary views', 143–6; and esp. Drijvers, 'Marcionism in Syria', 161–9.

philosopher nor did he present his teaching in philosophical terms. He was deeply wedded to Christianity as an exclusively valid religion of salvation, and sought to sustain his teaching from fundamental resources of the Christian tradition itself, specifically from its texts.

Marcion and the scriptures of Judaism

Beyond his ditheism, what drew the strongest fire of Marcion's critics was his view of Jewish scripture. Because Christianity originated as a movement within Judaism, early Christian communities were accustomed to value the scriptures of Judaism as their own, fully convinced that the Law and the prophets pointed to Jesus as the Messiah of the God of Israel and to the church as his new covenant people. The continuity with Judaism and its scriptures felt by the earliest Jewish Christians was inevitably attenuated as Christianity acquired an increasingly Gentile constituency, and the mainly Gentile church of the second century struggled with this issue.[10] Some parts of Jewish scripture, above all the ritual law, were dismissed as inapplicable and invalid for Christians; the extent of Jewish scripture was a matter of dispute; the divergences between the Septuagint (used by Christians) and the Hebrew text were discussed; conflicts of interpretation between Christians and Jews were sharply debated; and various methods for a Christian approach to Jewish scriptures were deployed. These were lively problems among Marcion's contemporaries, and his own views become, if not less radical, then more comprehensible in this context.

Convinced of the utter incompatibility between the higher alien God of Christianity and the lower creator God of Judaism, Marcion roundly repudiated any positive Christian use of Jewish scripture. It spoke only of the creator God and his regime, and thus had nothing whatever to do with the new revelation. It was not that Marcion thought that Jewish scripture was untrue, historically inaccurate or in other ways misleading; to the contrary, he regarded it as a true revelation of the Jewish God. The problem was simply that it was *Jewish* scripture, not Christian at all, even in adumbration.[11] Hence it was irrelevant, except to demonstrate the discontinuity and, indeed, contradiction between the Jewish God and the Christian God, and between the Law and the gospel.

---

10 Still useful in this connection is Simon, *Verus Israel*.
11 Marcion allowed that Jewish scripture promises a Messiah to the Jews, but that this is not Jesus.

It was to show precisely this that Marcion composed his *Antitheses* ('Contradictions'). This work is lost, but it was available to Tertullian, who conveys a fair idea of its character.[12] Partly systematic and partly exegetical, the *Antitheses* juxtaposed passages from Jewish scripture and passages from Christian writings, together with some critical exposition, to exhibit the contrast between the creator God and the high God, between the Jewish Law and the Christian gospel, and to prove them irreconcilable (Tert. *Marc.* 1.19; 2.29; 4.6). Here Marcion relentlessly represented the creator God, not as evil but merely righteous or just, yet in a strictly retributive sense, and went on to expose him as ignorant, weak, bellicose, capricious, petty and cruel, entirely unfit to be the God of Jesus Christ and unworthy of Christian worship.

It was in fact no easy task for the early church to work out in a fully satisfactory way the relationship between the Christian revelation and the scriptures of Judaism.[13] Beyond a certain selectivity that emphasised some books and passages and neglected others, Christians relied heavily on figurative, typological and allegorical interpretations capable of deriving usefully Christian meanings from texts that, in their literal sense, were often found to be meaningless, irrelevant or even theologically intolerable. Marcion judged this studied effort to be not merely futile but counter-productive. Accordingly, he cut the Gordian knot, insisting that Christians interpret the Jewish scriptures literally and disavow hermeneutical ingenuities. This meant for Marcion that Jewish scripture could have no relevance for the church, and that Christianity could stand entirely on its own as a new revelation, unmuddled by confusions with Judaism and its scriptures.

Because of his opposition to the allegorical interpretation of Jewish scripture, Marcion's understanding of it was ironically much closer to a traditional Jewish interpretation than to any contemporary Christian one. Yet his literalistic approach to Jewish scripture had a polemical edge, for in antiquity allegorical interpretation was commonly reserved for texts believed to be particularly valuable, harbouring deep wisdom, whereas literalism was a common tool of religious argumentation, used to expose absurdities and inadequacies in the textual authorities of opponents.[14] Marcion's opponents were not, however, Jews, but Christians accustomed to appealing to Jewish scripture in support of Christian claims. Certainly Marcion sought to sharply differentiate Christians

---

12 The evidence for the nature and content of the *Antitheses* was assembled by Harnack, *Marcion*, 256*–313* (esp. 306*–312*); for his description: 89–92.
13 See the useful discussion of 'the crisis of the Old Testament canon in the second century' in Campenhausen, *Formation*, 62–102.
14 Dungan, 'Reactionary trends', 194–8.

from Jews, but there are no good reasons to assume that he was motivated by opposition to Judaism as such, let alone by anti-semitism.[15]

Marcion's rejection of the scriptures of Judaism was a radical step, but, amid the challenges posed by the Christian employment of Jewish scriptures, it had some appeal within the Gentile church. As his *Antitheses* show, Marcion nevertheless made use of Jewish scripture, yet only as a foil against which the Christian gospel might be thrown into sharper relief; otherwise, it had no relevance, let alone any authority. The positive resources of Christianity Marcion located, rather, in specifically Christian writings.

Marcion and emerging Christian scripture

Differentiating Christians and Jews as worshippers of different Gods and disavowing Christian appeals to Jewish scripture, Marcion located the authoritative basis of Christian teaching in the apostle Paul. Paul was, for him, *the* apostle – not simply the most important apostle, but the *only* apostle who had faithfully preserved the authentic Christian gospel. In various passages of his letters, Paul emphasised the startling newness of the revelation in Jesus, repeatedly drew contrasts between faith and works of the law, criticised Judaising Christians as perverters of the gospel, characterised the Mosaic dispensation as temporary, qualified the association of the Law with God and closely allied it with sin, spoke of 'the curse of the Law' (Gal 3:13) and even asserted that Christ was 'the end of the Law' (Rom 10:4). Marcion took such passages to signify a repudiation of Judaism. Furthermore, taking Paul as his theological touchstone, Marcion judged that the tradition relied upon by the church at large had been corrupted by the other apostles, who had failed either to comprehend clearly or to transmit faithfully the authentic message of Jesus. For Marcion, 'only Paul knew the truth' (Iren. *Haer*. 3.13.1), and Marcion claimed that his own teaching, because it corresponded with Paul's, was the only true Christianity.

Marcion's appeal to Paul exemplifies a widespread tendency among Christian communities in the late first and early second centuries to legitimise a particular understanding of Christianity by invoking the authority of a single apostle who was valued more highly than (and often over against) others, whereas from the mid-second century onward the predilection of Christian communities was increasingly to appeal to 'the apostles'

---

15 Cosgrove, 'Justin', suggests that Justin's *Dialogue with Trypho* is a reaction to Marcion's (and other Christians') literal approach to Jewish scripture. On Marcion and the Jews: Hoffmann, *Marcion*, 226–34; Wilson, 'Marcion and the Jews'; Bienert, 'Marcion'.

collectively.[16] Quite apart from Marcion, Paul had a singular prominence in second-century Christianity generally: he was commonly referred to as 'the Apostle', and was revered because he was the apostle to the Gentiles and the only apostle to have left a substantial literary legacy in his letters.[17] There were, to be sure, 'some things in them hard to understand, which the ignorant and unstable twist to their own destruction', as the author of 2 Peter complained (3:16), and certainly Marcion's understanding of Paul was gained at the expense of the subtleties and dialectical tensions in the apostle's teaching on topics that especially interested Marcion. Yet the boldness and complexity of Paul's thought challenged all of his second-century interpreters, and Marcion's construal of it, while unusual, could find almost as much footing in Paul's letters as competing interpretations.[18]

Claiming Paul as the sole reliable witness to Christian truth, Marcion adopted as his normative resources a set of Christian writings consisting of a gospel, usually presumed to be the gospel of Luke, and a collection of ten letters of Paul, and regarded these documents alone as the authoritative basis of genuinely Christian teaching. Believing, however, that these texts had suffered Judaising corruption in the process of their transmission, Marcion also sought to establish their original form by means of critical emendation – an effort for which he was roundly pilloried by his critics. It should not be supposed that in such editorial activity Marcion was unique, nor that it was a matter merely of conforming the texts to his own views. In fact, ancient texts of all sorts were routinely corrupted, both accidentally and intentionally, through the largely uncontrolled process of their transcription, transmission and use, so that anyone who valued a document took pains to correct it and certify its accuracy, though this was a difficult and largely conjectural endeavour.[19] Moreover, the revision of texts in accordance with theological interests was relatively common in the second century, and not only among the

16 One may think, for example, of the special esteem accorded to Peter in the gospel of Matthew (16:17–19), or to the 'Beloved Disciple' in the gospel of John, or to Paul in the deutero-Pauline letters (Eph 3:1ff, 1 Tim 1:12–16, 2 Tim 1:8–14), as well as the later appeal to Paul among the Gnostics, or to Thomas in Syrian Christianity, etc. From the dispute between Paul and Peter in Antioch (Gal 2:11–16), Marcion concluded that Peter was ignorant of the real meaning of Christianity (Tert. *Praescr.* 23; *Marc.* 4.3 and 5.3). See May, 'Streit'.

17 Rensberger, *Apostle*; Lindemann, *Paulus*.

18 On the diverse appropriations of Paul's thought in the second century: Barrett, 'Pauline controversies'; Pagels, *Gnostic Paul*; MacDonald, *Legend*; Lindemann, *Paulus*; and Dassmann, *Stachel*.

19 On the vagaries of textual transmission in antiquity and early Christianity, and the practice of emendation, Gamble, *Books and readers*, 71–2, 82–143; and, with special reference to Marcion, Grant, 'Marcion', 207–15; and *Heresy and criticism*, 59–73.

heterodox.[20] The nature and extent of Marcion's editorial work has been difficult to determine since the texts he produced have not themselves survived. Hence we shall need to attend also to the questions of how and how much Marcion may have altered the texts upon which he depended.

It is in his exclusive reliance on a gospel and the letters of Paul that many modern scholars have perceived Marcion's influence on the formation of a canon of Christian scriptures, a 'New Testament', though appraisals of this influence have been various. In his magisterial study, Adolf von Harnack asserted that Marcion was no less than 'the creator of Christian Holy Scripture'.[21] With this claim Harnack did not imagine that there were no Christian scriptures before Marcion; he supposed that the four gospels were widely known and had already been shaped into a collection, that there was already a collection of letters of Paul, and that various other Christian writings were in broad circulation and use, and he acknowledged that all of these writings possessed a measure of authority in Christian communities, though none held what he called 'an absolute dignity'.[22] Harnack meant, rather, that Marcion was the first to shape any of these writings into a fixed collection invested with 'absolute authority'.[23] Thus he maintained that Marcion was the creator of a 'canon' of Christian writings, insofar as a canon is fixed and closed, and that in this he anticipated the church at large. Harnack also claimed that Marcion's canon provided the dual form of 'gospel and apostle' upon which the canon of the catholic church was subsequently constructed, so that in both the principle of a closed canon and in its structure Marcion's scriptures were decisive for the church at large.[24] As Harnack saw it, the church both 'had to accept and did accept from Marcion everything that he had created' in the way of a canon, yet necessarily also more than that, in order to safeguard itself against Marcionite ideas.[25] In addition to emphasising Marcion's importance for the formation of the New Testament canon, Harnack also undertook to reconstruct the texts that resulted from Marcion's editorial work, and on that basis regarded a very large number of textual variants as Marcionite in origin.[26] Hence he also claimed that Marcion had a broad impact upon the textual tradition of the New Testament. Many scholars have followed Harnack in maintaining that

---

20 For the heterodox: Nestle, *Einführung*, 219–27; and more fully, Bludau, *Schriftfälschungen*; for the orthodox: Ehrman, *The orthodox corruption*.
21 *Marcion*, 151.
22 *Marcion*, 34.
23 *Marcion*, 72, 151.
24 *Marcion*, 210–213.
25 *Marcion*, 212.
26 *Marcion*, preface to the 2nd German ed. For the reconstruction itself: supp. 3 ('Das Apostolikon Marcions', 40*–176*) and supp. 4 ('Das Evangelium Marcions', 177*–255*).

Marcion's activity was the *sine qua non* of the formation of the New Testament, and that the New Testament canon arose principally or even exclusively as a reaction to him.[27] Indeed, this view was prevalent through most of the last century. Yet recent studies have eroded its foundations and drawn it ever more deeply into doubt, and modern judgements about Marcion's influence on the history of the New Testament canon must be more carefully measured.

An important general consideration is the relatively recent recognition that the New Testament canon, as a closed and fixed collection, did not come into being until the late fourth century, and indeed was not universally recognised until early in the fifth, whereas Harnack and his followers all assumed that the catholic canon had attained more or less final form by the end of the second century.[28] If, however, the church's canon was not firmly established until the fourth century, it is far more difficult to find in Marcion the stimulus to it. It is remarkable, rather, that in spite of Marcion's activity the church was *not* inclined, much less compelled, to fashion quickly a definitive canon of its own, but left the scope of Christian scripture indeterminate for quite a long time thereafter.[29] In addition, by observing a more careful distinction between 'scripture' and 'canon' – scripture being understood as religiously authoritative writings, and canon as a fixed and closed list of such documents – recent scholarship has not only been able to trace the history of the canon more clearly, but also to recognise that the church had scriptures long before it had a canon, and that various Christian writings had secured the status of scripture well before Marcion.[30] While it may be granted that Marcion

27 Many have gone further. Bauer regarded Marcion as 'the first systematic collector of the Pauline heritage', and his collection as more complete than any other (*Orthodoxy and heresy*, 221–3; cf. Hoffman, *Marcion*, 241). Knox heightened Marcion's significance by claiming that he authored the very conception of a distinctively Christian scripture, and was 'primarily responsible for the idea of the New Testament' (*Marcion*, 19–38), for prior to Marcion the church 'had no scripture except what we call the Old Testament' (24), and thus the 'sudden emergence' of the catholic New Testament, which Knox placed between 150 and 175 CE, found its entire stimulus in Marcion (*Marcion*, 77, 159, 165). Campenhausen maintained that 'the idea and the reality of a Christian Bible were the work of Marcion, and the Church which rejected his work, so far from being ahead of him in this field, from a formal point of view simply followed his example'. The idea of a normative, specifically Christian scripture 'came into existence at one stroke with Marcion and only with Marcion' (*Formation*, 147–65, esp. 148). Kinzig, 'Kaine diatheke', has urged that the designation of these scriptures as a 'New Testament' should also be traced to Marcion.

28 A key element here is the Muratorian canon list, which was commonly regarded as a late second-century and Roman document until the seminal study of A. C. Sundberg, 'Canon Muratori', whose argument for a much later dating and an eastern provenance is fully worked out by Hahneman, *Muratorian fragment*.

29 Stuhlhofer, *Gebrauch*, shows this in a particularly interesting way.

30 For the distinction between 'canon' and 'scripture', see Sundberg, 'Revised history'; and for elaborations Graham, 'Scripture'; and Barton, *Holy writings*, 9–14.

was the first to make a group of Christian texts the exclusive basis and norm of teaching, it is not clear that even his collection was definitively fixed and closed, that is, a canon in the strict sense: there are indications that Marcion's collection was enlarged by his followers.[31] And, since Marcion's emendation of the texts he considered authoritative was a work in progress, whose results were necessarily provisional, there is no reason to think that he regarded the text with which he worked as final, let alone sacrosanct. These are general grounds for denying to Marcion any original or decisive role in the history of the canon. At most he may have prompted other Christians to think more carefully about the status and use of Christian writings, or merely accelerated a process that was already well underway.[32] Yet even this probably overestimates Marcion's importance.

Marcion's significance is better gauged if he is taken merely as a witness to an early stage in what would be a protracted history of the canon. On close examination, Marcion's scriptures turn out to be very nearly what one might expect in his time and place, namely the first half of the second century on the provincial fringe of the Pauline mission field. In most respects he stands within the range of usages that are well attested in the early second century. This can be seen in connection with both his gospel and his collection of Paul's letters.

It is extremely difficult to form any clear conception of Marcion's gospel. Our knowledge of it depends almost entirely upon the testimonies of Tertullian (*Marc.* 4) and Epiphanius (*Pan.* 42). With Irenaeus, they identify it as the gospel of Luke, but all of them also indicate that Marcion had it in a much-truncated form.[33] While they concur that Marcion omitted much, Tertullian and Epiphanius frequently disagree about its content and wording, and a comparison of their comments reveals many peculiarities.[34] Tertullian's citations frequently vary, leaving doubt about what Marcion's gospel actually read; and remarkably, Tertullian frequently, and Epiphanius occasionally, fault Marcion for omitting passages that are not found in (our) Luke at all, but only in Matthew or Mark.[35]

---

31 Hahnemann, *Muratorian fragment*, 91–3.
32 See e.g. Metzger, *Canon*, 97–9; and Balas, 'Marcion revisited', 95–108.
33 Iren. *Haer.* 3.12.12, Tert. *Marc.* 4.6.2, Epiph. *Pan.* 42.11.3–6.
34 They took different approaches in characterising Marcion's text: Tertullian, aiming to refute Marcion from his own text, selectively quotes Marcion's gospel against him, without often indicating what he took to be absent or otherwise deviant by comparison with Luke; Epiphanius, alleging that Marcion 'falsifies some things and adds others out of sequence', notes that Marcion omitted the first two chapters of Luke and lists seventy-eight additional passages that he claims were altered or deleted by Marcion (*Pan.* 42.11.1–8). For the problems, see Williams, 'Marcion's gospel', 478–81.
35 See Aalders, 'Quotations'; Higgins, 'Latin text'; Williams, 'Text'; and on the general problem, Gregory, *Reception*, 175–83.

In all, there are relatively few direct quotations of Marcion's gospel made by both Tertullian and Epiphanius, and only a handful of these provide reasonable certainty about the wording of Marcion's gospel.[36]

Many of the alterations or omissions they attribute to Marcion appear to be theologically innocuous, while some passages presumably retained by Marcion seem incompatible with what we know of his theological viewpoint.[37] Further, Marcion's gospel apparently contained a fair number of non-Lucan elements. If we add to these observations the fact that Marcion himself does not appear to have known his gospel as Lucan,[38] then the most that can be claimed is that Marcion's gospel resembled our Luke more than any other gospel, discrepancies notwithstanding, but this does not mean that Marcion simply edited Luke as we know it. He may have, but he may also have used a more primitive gospel that was similar to Luke, a source for Luke, or an early version of Luke, and, of these, one that had some harmonised features.[39] Thus the nature of Marcion's gospel and extent of his editorial work upon it must remain largely obscure. While he doubtless did emend the text of the gospel he used, many of the readings attested for it that have been taken to represent his own omissions or alterations (that is, by comparison with our Luke) are also attested in 'western' textual witnesses, and such cases are better understood as early variants than as specifically Marcionite readings that have contaminated a larger tradition.

Whatever Marcion's gospel was, it is a question how he came by it and why he used that particular one. Here something depends on whether by Marcion's time a collection of four gospels had already come into being, and judgements about this vary. Our earliest and clearest evidence for the appearance of the collection of four gospels is provided by Irenaeus toward the end of the second century. His arguments in its favour (*Haer.* 3.11.8–9) suggest that it was then a relative novelty, not everywhere known or accepted. Yet it may have originated somewhat earlier, and, if so, it is just conceivable that

---

36 Williams, 'Marcion's gospel', isolates twenty-three 'explicit correlated readings' between Tertullian and Epiphanius, but considers only five of these a sound basis for the reconstruction of Marcion's text, although in a few more the variations are only minor.

37 Tertullian is often perplexed by this. See e.g. his comments in *Marc.* 4.43.7 on Marcion's gospel at Luke 24:38–9.

38 Tert. *Marc.* 4.2.3: 'Marcion attaches to his gospel no author's name.' There is no reason to think that Marcion suppressed a known title, for the association of our gospels with particular authors was only beginning in his time, and the later titles were not universally known or used in the first half of the second century.

39 Knox, *Marcion*, 77–113; Williams, 'Marcion's gospel', 481–2; Wilshire, 'Canonical Luke'; Gregory, *Reception*, 192–6. See also West, 'Primitive version', 95.

Marcion may have known it.[40] Harnack, who assumed both that Marcion's gospel was Luke and that Marcion was acquainted with an earlier collection of gospels, gave an elaborate rationale for Marcion's 'choice' of Luke, claiming that Marcion necessarily rejected the gospels of Matthew and John because of their Judaic character, and did not favour Mark because of its paucity of Jesus' teaching, but that he preferred Luke because of its Gentile Christian bias and its 'traditional and historical connection with Paul'.[41] But Harnack also acknowledged the possibility that Marcion's gospel was simply the first gospel to reach Pontus, and may for some time have been the only one known there.[42]

This last explanation is probably correct, for in the early decades of the second century it was apparently common that any given Christian community knew and used only a single gospel document. In the late second century Irenaeus (*Haer.* 3.11.7–9) faults as heterodox those who employ only one gospel, mentioning specifically the use of Matthew by the Ebionites, Luke by Marcion, Mark by docetists, John by Valentinians. But this practice must not have been exceptional, let alone heterodox, in the first half of the second century.[43] Early papyrus manuscripts of the gospels seem to have contained only single gospels, and it is first in the third century that we encounter manuscripts of multiple gospels.[44] The increasing availability to Christian communities of more than one gospel posed nettlesome problems. Various gospels were individually distinctive and at points even contradictory, so that to employ more than one required explanation of their incongruities, while multiple gospels generated doubt about the adequacy or the accuracy of any single one.[45] Such issues inhibited the use of multiple gospels, and in situations where they were available the tendency was, if not to use them only singly, then to construct harmonies. Tatian's great effort late in the second century to achieve unity,

---

40 For its origin near the middle of the second century, see now Skeat, 'Oldest manuscript'; Stanton, 'Fourfold gospel'; and Heckel, *Evangelium*. Schmid, 'Marcions Evangelium', allows that Marcion may have known it.

41 *Marcion*, 40–2.

42 *Marcion*, 42; cf. Knox, *Marcion*, 164; and Campenhausen, *Formation*, 159. The designation of a 'Luke' as a companion of Paul in the epistles (Phlm 24, Col 4:14 (cf. 2 Tim 4:11)) hardly played a role if Marcion did not know this gospel under that name.

43 Thus, among others, K. Aland and B. Aland, *Text*, 50, 67; and Parker, *Living text*, 19.

44 Checklist in K. Aland and B. Aland, *Text*, 96–101. Notably early examples include P[52] (John), P[66] (John), and P[77] (Matthew). The earliest manuscripts containing more than one Gospel are P[75] (Luke and John) and P[4+64+67] (Matthew and Luke), and the earliest to contain all four Gospels is P[45] (*c*.225). Skeat, 'Oldest manuscript' (263–8), proposes, however, that all papyri appearing to come from single-gospel codices actually come from (or presuppose) codices containing all four gospels.

45 On these issues: Cullmann, 'Plurality'; Grant, *Earliest lives*, 14–37, 52–62; Merkel, *Pluralität* and *Widersprüche*. This is already apparent from Papias (Euseb. *HE* 3.39.15–16).

consistency and completeness by weaving the texts of Matthew, Mark, Luke and John (as well as other traditions) into a single narrative, the *Diatessaron*, is only the best known of such efforts.[46]

Multiple gospels came to be known first in the large urban centres of Christianity, the natural points for the production, confluence and dissemination of Christian literature, but in provincial areas it was probably typical that at an early time only one gospel was known and used. Against this background, and lacking any evidence for his knowledge or repudiation of other gospels, Marcion's use of only one gospel can be understood as a normal and widespread practice. He may have found confirmation for this in Paul's characteristically singular use of the term 'gospel' (see esp. Gal 1:6–12), which Marcion perhaps took to refer to a written gospel rather than to the missionary proclamation, but is unlikely that this was Marcion's starting-point, or that he proceeded from this premise to locate a specifically 'Pauline' gospel. He simply used the gospel current in his native area and familiar to him from the outset.[47]

For the other and larger component of Marcion's scriptures, the letters of Paul, we are in a better position than ever before to appraise Marcion's significance. Though we hear of collections of Paul's letters prior to Marcion – multiple letters of Paul were known to the author of 2 Peter, Ignatius, Clement of Rome and Polycarp – Marcion's is the first 'edition' of the Pauline letters of which we have direct knowledge. It had ten letters of Paul in the order: Galatians, 1–2 Corinthians, Romans, 1–2 Thessalonians, Laodiceans (= our Ephesians), Colossians-Philemon, and Philippians.[48] It has often been supposed both that Marcion himself created this edition and that it reflects his particular dogmatic interests, with Galatians holding first place because of its crucial importance to his thought.[49] In addition, it is sometimes thought that Marcion deliberately excluded the Pastoral Epistles (1–2 Timothy, Titus).

It can now be recognised, however, that the edition of Paul's letters used by Marcion was not of his own making; instead, he merely took over a pre-existing collection of Paul's letters which had the same content and arrangement. Several observations sustain this conclusion. First, it can be seen that

---

46 Previously, Tatian's teacher, Justin Martyr, employed a harmony: Bellinzoni, *Sayings;* and Petersen, *Diatessaron.* The whole history of Gospel production was harmonistic: Merkel, *Pluralität.*

47 See now esp. the thorough discussion by Gregory, *Reception*, 196–210.

48 Tertullian (*Marc.* 5.21–22) considers Philemon after Philippians, but Epiphanius (*Pan.* 42.9.4, 11.8, 12) has Philemon following Colossians and preceding Philippians. For reasons given below, Epiphanius' order should be preferred.

49 Thus Harnack, *Marcion*, 35, 128; Knox, *Marcion*, 45. For Galatians' importance to Marcion, see May, 'Streit'.

with the exception of Galatians, which stands at the beginning, and Laodiceans (= Ephesians), which follows the Thessalonian letters, the letters in Marcion's edition are ordered on the principle of decreasing length, with letters to the same community (Corinthians, Thessalonians, and Colossians-Philemon) counted together as length units. This is odd, since we would expect such a principle, if adopted, to be consistently followed. Second, there is indirect but strong evidence of yet another early edition of the letters of Paul. Several early Christian sources purvey the theory that Paul wrote to exactly seven churches, and, since the number seven was taken as a symbol of totality or universality, that he therefore addressed Christendom at large.[50] This theory must have accompanied an actual edition of the Pauline letters that presented them as 'letters to seven churches'. Though this edition has not been preserved as such, its clear traces may be seen wherever the letters are arranged by decreasing length and letters to the same community are counted as a single length unit. This edition would have had the form: Corinthians (1 and 2), Romans, Ephesians, Thessalonians (1 and 2), Galatians, Philippians and Colossians-Philemon, a configuration that places the emphasis not on the number of discrete letters, but upon the number of churches to which Paul wrote.[51] The Pastoral Epistles did not belong to this edition since as personal letters they would have found no place in a collection of community letters. Such a 'seven-churches edition' has the best claim to being the most ancient edition of the *corpus Paulinum* (as distinct from earlier, smaller collections).

Marcion's edition, by virtue of counting together letters to the same community and (with the exceptions of Galatians and Laodiceans/Ephesians) arranging them by decreasing length, reveals its indebtedness to the earlier 'seven-churches edition' for which these features were fully determinative. Yet Marcion's edition is not a direct adaptation of it, nor even something original with Marcion, for the order of the letters in Marcion's *Apostolikon* is also found in the Syriac tradition and in the old Latin prologues to the Pauline letters.[52] This sequence resulted from an early effort to arrange the community letters chronologically. Galatians stood at its head because of the autobiographical materials in Galatians 1–2, and the relatively early placement of Romans was

---

50 For this theory and its witnesses: Zahn, *Geschichte*, vol. II, 73–5; Stendahl, 'Apocalypse'; and Dahl, 'Particularity of the Pauline epistles'.

51 Evidence for this edition is assembled by Frede, 'Die Ordnung', who takes it (292) to represent the earliest form of the corpus. See also Finegan, 'Original form'; and Dahl, 'Earliest prologues', esp. 253, 263. Summary and supporting considerations in Gamble, *Books and readers*, 59–62.

52 Lewis, *Catalogue*, 13–14; and Zahn, 'Neue Testament'. Evidence summarized by Frede, 'Die Ordnung', 295–7; cf. Kerschensteiner, *Paulustext*, 172–6, with hesitations. For the so-called Marcionite Prologues, Dahl, 'Earliest prologues'.

enabled by the absence of Romans 15–16 in this edition. Hence it appears that Marcion simply appropriated an existing edition of Paul's letters that was ultimately based on the seven-churches edition but had been revised to offer a chronological sequence. It is not at all likely that Marcion found this edition of Paul's letters only when he came to Rome.[53] Like his gospel, it was probably current and familiar to him in his native area.

Marcion edited his collection of Paul's letters even as he did his gospel, but the extent of this work has been much debated. Harnack himself recognised that Marcion's text of the Pauline letters was of the western type, and hence also that many readings previously taken to be Marcionite are in fact simply early western readings. Even so, Harnack regarded many other readings as tendentious alterations by Marcion.[54] The question of the text of Marcion's *Apostolikon* has now been placed on a fresh footing both by a fuller knowledge of the textual evidence and by the special studies of Clabeaux and Schmid.[55] They have demonstrated that Marcion's text was a representative form of an early (pre-140), widely current but largely uncontrolled recension of the Pauline corpus that is also reflected mainly by the Old Latin (especially the 'I' type) and the old Syriac traditions.[56] Hence many readings previously judged distinctively Marcionite can now be recognised as common variants within the pre-Marcionite Pauline textual tradition. Some of these are merely mechanical (scribal errors), some are conjectural emendations (aimed at clarification) and others are theologically tendentious. These last, however, need not or cannot be associated exclusively with Marcion since some aspects of his thought (his docetism, for example) were not unique to him. Indeed, variant readings that have any claim to be peculiarly Marcionite, and thus to have originated with Marcion, now appear to be very few, and none is certain.[57] Moreover, those that are attested only for Marcion reveal no pattern that betrays a principled, systematic and consistent editorial hand. Marcion's work of textual emendation consisted mainly and perhaps exclusively, not in revising passages to conform their wording to his teaching, but in expunging passages that he thought, however

---

53 May, 'Streit', 209.
54 *Marcion*, 44–51.
55 Clabeaux, *Lost edition*; Schmid, *Marcion*. These studies have different aims but come to similar conclusions.
56 Clabeaux, *Lost edition*, 129–48; Schmid, *Marcion*, 260–83.
57 Schmid, *Marcion*, 250–5, considers that there are some tendentious 'conjectural alterations' for which a Marcionite origin cannot be excluded, but no variant readings (as distinct from omissions) that can be confidently attributed to Marcion, though this does not mean that Marcion made no tendentious emendations; Schmid (*Marcion*, 255) thinks it likely that he did, but we can no longer tell where or how.

mistakenly, to be secondary interpolations.[58] Apart from excisions that can be traced specifically to Marcion, the texts he employed did not differ essentially from an early second-century form of the textual tradition of Paul's letters.

These findings illuminate the early textual history of the Pauline epistles, for the (pre-) Marcionite text carries the evidence back from P[46] (c.200) to the early decades of the second century. It shows that the text of Paul's letters, like that of the gospels, was in that period still fluid, susceptible both to scribal corruption and critical emendation. At the same time, it requires us to regard Marcion himself 'more as a *traditor* of a poorly controlled text than as the heavy-handed editor or fabricator of a totally new one'.[59] Thus with respect not only to the content of his scriptures but also to the text he used, Marcion presents us with nothing new, yet he serves as an interesting and important witness to an early state of affairs.

Much the same can be said about the claim that Marcion furnished the bipartite structural principle of the church's canon, consisting of gospel and apostle. The correlation as authorities of 'the Lord' (or, increasingly, 'the gospel') with 'the apostle(s)' had deep roots in earlier tradition and by no means originated with Marcion.[60] The historical succession of Jesus and the apostles gave rise to a conception of the tradition as having a dual source and form, as can be seen in many pre-Marcionite contexts (e.g. *1 Clem.* 41.7–8; with 42.1–3; Ign. *Magn.* 13.1, *Phild.* 5.1). In purely practical terms, the earliest available Christian literature consisted predominantly of gospels and 'apostolic' letters, and any appeal to documents, if those were not Jewish scriptures, was necessarily to one or the other, or both, and both had begun to acquire the status of 'scripture' well before Marcion.

With regard to the formation of Christian scriptures, then, Marcion is a figure of wonderful interest but no clear consequence: his activity had no discernible or demonstrable effect on the actual formation of the 'New Testament', whether in conception, content or chronology. He is, nevertheless, an informative witness for an early stage in the identification and use of Christian writings as scripture, for appeal to them as authoritative resources for theological exposition and argument, and for the nature of their textual traditions in his time. Although Marcion was early recognised and criticised as dangerously

---

58 Schmid, *Marcion*, 254–5. (Harnack (*Marcion*, 61) already recognised that excision was the predominant form of Marcion's editing.) Some of these omissions can be identified with confidence; others only by inference. They include: Gal 3:6–9, 14–18, 29; Rom 2:3–11; Rom 4:1–25; the larger part of Rom 9–11; and Col 1:15b–16; and all these eliminate themes that were manifestly incompatible with Marcion's theology.

59 Clabeaux, *Lost edition*, 129.

60 Bovon, 'Structure'.

heterodox, his scriptural resources, like much of his thought, are intelligible in the context of developing Gentile Christianity in the early second century. In this as in some other respects he is more aptly characterised, not as a radical innovator, but as a traditionalist and conservative.[61] Marcion is only one example of the axiom that heresy is often a matter of bad timing: he promoted in Rome near the middle of the second century a teaching and a set of scriptures that might, earlier and in more peripheral regions, have been within the range of plausible construals of Christianity, but developments in the broad stream of Christian thought and usage had already rendered them, if not obsolete, then highly objectionable to most.

The subsequent history of the formation of a New Testament

The development of distinctively Christian scriptures and the eventual formation of the New Testament canon belonged to a process that was well under way before Marcion and reached its conclusion long after his time. If, as I have argued, he had no impact upon it, there were other forces at work.

By the end of the second century the church at large held as its common scriptural resources, in addition to the scriptures of Judaism (which it steadfastly retained despite Marcion), the letters of Paul and a collection of four gospels. Paul's letters were consistently valued and used, albeit in diverse editions, from the late first or early second century onward. The collection of four gospels, however, seems to have emerged only after the middle of the second century, yet it had taken hold by the early third century everywhere except in the east, where Tatian's *Diatessaron* rivalled it until the fifth century. In addition to these gospels and Paul's letters, other documents had come into wide use, including Acts, 1 Peter and 1 John, all of which were widely acknowledged and used in the third century. Other documents that were known and used, but enjoyed no similar consensus, included 2 Peter, Jude, the *Shepherd of Hermas*, the *Epistle of Barnabas*, the *Didache, 1 Clement* and the *Apocalypse of Peter*. The Apocalypse of John (also known to English readers as the book of Revelation) was early and continuously appreciated in the west but attracted little interest in the east, whereas Hebrews was much valued in the east but virtually unknown in the west before the fourth century. There seems to have been only limited knowledge and hesitant use of 2 and 3 John and of James before the fourth century.

---

61 Barton, *Holy writings*, 42–62.

The indeterminacy in the scope of Christian scriptures that persisted throughout the third century began to be resolved in the fourth century. Eusebius's discussion (*HE* 3.25.1–7) of usages and opinions still does not move beyond three categories – the "acknowledged books" (*homologoumenoi*), which include the four gospels, the (fourteen) letters of Paul, Acts, 1 John and 1 Peter, and (provisionally) the Apocalypse of John; the 'disputed books' (*antilegomenoi*), also called 'spurious' (*nothoi*), which include James, Jude, 2 Peter, 2 and 3 John, the *Acts of Paul*, the *Shepherd of Hermas*, the *Apocalypse of Peter*, the *Didache*, the Apocalypse of John (again provisionally) and the *Gospel of the Hebrews*; and finally, 'books sponsored by heretics' as purportedly written by apostles, which are only generally referred to. For Eusebius, and presumably for the church of his time, the 'acknowledged' books still amounted to only twenty-one (or twenty-two, if the Apocalypse were counted).

The first list of Christian scriptures that corresponds precisely to the contents of the 'New Testament' as we know it is the one circulated by Athanasius, bishop of Alexandria, in his thirty-ninth Festal Letter, issued on Easter 367 and aimed at regularising usages in the Egyptian churches. While this letter presupposes persistent variations in what was read as scripture, it signals the beginning of a widespread effort to define the limits of Christian scripture and thus to fix a canon. In the latter half of the fourth century, a variety of similar lists began to appear, some in manuscripts, others as promulgations of regional synods.[62] While these lists continue to show some small variations, by the fifth century even these disappeared as the church finally arrived at a consensus supporting a New Testament canon consisting of exactly twenty-seven documents.

The forces conspiring to produce this result were many, but the most powerful among them was the actual use of Christian writings in Christian communities over a long period and over a broad area. This use consisted above all in the public reading of Christian writings, alongside Jewish scriptures, in the context of Christian worship, a practice that was both early and continuous. It was this tradition of regular liturgical reading more than anything else that prompted and directed the church's progressive recognition, and finally its definition, of the textual resources that were fundamental to its identity. That identity was still taking shape in the second century, but even by then it had become clear to most that Marcion's conception of Christian teaching, and the texts in which he sought its warrants, were far too narrow to sustain the richer heritage of Christian communities.

---

62 These lists are conveniently collected in Metzger, *Canon*, 305–15 (app. IV). For analysis, see Hahneman, *Muratorian fragment*, 132–82.

Self-definition vis-à-vis the Jewish matrix

JUDITH LIEU

To speak of early Christian self-definition is to recognise that the sense of self always implies differentiation from one or more 'others'. This and the following chapter identify those significant 'others' as the 'Jewish matrix' and the 'Graeco-Roman world'; differentiation from 'Gnostic' groups (ch. 12 below) is arguably different in kind. A significant point, then, on the path towards differentiation, although not its culmination, might be the self-understanding of the Christians as a 'third race', alongside the Greeks and the Jews; this emerges at the end of the second century, and was, perhaps, adopted from the taunts of outsiders.[1] Yet, as we shall discover, just as early Christianity necessarily remained part of the Graeco-Roman world, so in one sense it inevitably would always be positioned in relationship to a Jewish matrix. The familiar epithet, 'Judaeo-Christian tradition', while in danger of implying a common voice where none is to be heard, acknowledges a truth that is rooted in the very origins of Christianity, in the ministry of 'Jesus, the Jew'.

Our task is to plot how, within a Jewish framework, individuals and, more importantly, the groups of which they were a part, who were characterised by a commitment to the person and memory of Jesus, developed a sense of what united them over against other Jews and Jewish groups, whilst sustaining an absolute claim to what we might call their 'Jewish heritage'. This question has to be answered on the conceptual level, namely the conscious differentiation of ideas, on the linguistic or discourse level, namely the development of a rhetoric of self and 'otherness', and on the socio-cultural level, namely the formation of communities which put into practice that refusal to recognise each other as 'the same sort of thing', and, indeed, as 'the real thing'.

---

1 *Kerygma Petri* in Clem. Al. *Str.* 6.5.41; Tert. *Nat.* 1.8.1; *Scorp.*10.10; also Aristides, *Apol.* 2.1 (Greek recension); Lieu, *Image and reality*, 165–9.

In recent years this process, now a major topic for analysis and debate, has become known as 'the parting of the ways'.[2] This model starts from a recognition that Second Temple Judaism was pluralistic and lacked the organs of control that would privilege any particular interpretation of the tradition to which all looked back; out of this variety emerge two paths, eventually increasingly diverging from each other, one that will become rabbinic Judaism, particularly after the impact of the destruction of the temple in 70 CE and the loss of Jerusalem following the Bar Kochba revolt (132–5 CE), the other that will form early Christianity.

This picture represents a major shift away from an older view that saw Judaism, already in the time of Jesus, as monolithic and inherently unable to contain his message, and as subsequently consigned to sterility by the defeat of 70 CE and by the rise of a triumphant Christianity.[3] Recognition of the broad diversity of first-century 'Judaism' and of the absence of any centralised control even in the rabbinic period has invited a far more nuanced understanding of why, where and when various forms of 'Christianity' could no longer be seen as part of it. However, even within this more sensitive approach, we need to ask, 'seen by whom?'; the modern scholarly observer may be far more (or far less) tolerant of difference than were the participants at the time; a pluralistic framework may contain difference but it may also encourage a speedy sense of separation. Too often, ancient pluralism has been supposed to generate mutual toleration, a view that neither modern experience nor ancient examples, such as the community of the Dead Sea scrolls, support.

A further difficulty with the now popular model of 'the parting of the ways' is that it continues to envisage 'Judaism' and 'Christianity' as discrete and enclosed systems. Yet they have never been this, except as scholarly or political constructs. In what follows it will be difficult to avoid the terms 'Judaism' and 'Christianity' – terms actually rather rare in our sources – even though it will be argued that neither of them has a clear content, and that throughout our period both can be understood as processes. What we can ask is how specific texts, and the figures whom we hear through them, articulate a sense of who they were in antithesis to what they perceived as 'the other' of the Jews. We shall also need to ask how far the representation produced by the texts was embodied in the social practice of the groups we dimly glimpse behind them, although here any conclusions have to be far more tentative.

2 For the model and discussions of a number of the texts analysed below, see Dunn *Partings*; Dunn (ed.), *Jews and Christians*; Wilson, *Related strangers*; for a critique, Lieu, *Neither Jew nor Greek*, 11–29; Becker and Reed (eds.), *Ways that never parted*.
3 Classically expressed by Harnack, *Expansion*, vol. 1, 80–3.

Earliest witnesses

Putting the issue in these terms directs us first to Paul.[4] Paul, as a Jew, understood his own activity and his interpretation of the gospel as the proper fulfilment of 'Jewish' experience and hope (Rom 4; Gal 3). Many modern observers[5] would argue that in its own terms his interpretation was coherent, and that it was not incompatible with – or can be seen as a viable option within – the multiform 'Judaism(s)' of the first century. Yet Paul also defines those who believe in Jesus, both Jews and Gentiles, in contradistinction to those others, his 'kinsmen according to the flesh' (Rom 9:3), who do not share that faith. There is a tension here: Paul goes on to speak of Gentile believers as grafted into the olive tree of Israel, causing the language of distinction to become sharply qualified; but 'unbelieving Israel' remains 'them', not part of 'you' or 'us'. God's future eschatological purposes do encompass 'the full number of Gentiles' as well as 'all Israel' (Rom 11:17–24, 25–6);[6] but, in the present, there is an implicit antithesis in his definitions of the Jew as 'the one in secret', and of circumcision as 'of the heart in spirit not letter' (2:28–9), even though these are rooted in the scriptural tradition (Jer 4:4; 9:25–6).[7] In due course such antithetical patterns will shape the rhetoric of future Christian self-understanding.

Paul's was not the only model developing during the first century. Although constrained by the quasi-biographical gospel genre, Matthew denies any rupture with a genuine faithfulness to the ('Jewish') past, either in his presentation of the person of Jesus, whom he describes in ways recalling Moses, or in his anticipation of the *ecclēsia* (Matt 18:17). However, he does intensify the phrase he inherits from Mark, '*their* synagogues', and he predicts the persecution of the disciples there as an imminent reality and not just as an eschatological terror (Matt 10:17; contrast Mark 13:9; Luke 21:12).[8] This creates a model of opposition that prepares the ground for the positions and the accusations of hostility taken up by later writers.[9] John's gospel uses the term 'the Jews' in particular of those who do not believe, as if Jesus and his followers did not belong among them;[10] so powerfully negative is his language (for example, John 8:31–59) that many see here the roots of later Christian anti-Judaism or anti-semitism. Yet the gospel is immersed in the images and language of the

---

4 See n. 2, above, and Dunn, *Theology*, 499–532.
5 E.g. Dunn, *Partings*, 117–39.
6 Some interpreters refer 'all Israel' to the 'new Israel' of faith, cf. Gal 6:16.
7 Paul does not say (as do some translations) '*true* Jew / circumcision'.
8 See Saldarini, *Matthew's Jewish-Christian community*; Stanton, *Gospel for a new people*.
9 For the development of these charges, see Lieu, *Neither Jew nor Greek*, 135–50.
10 John 4:22 is a notable exception. On anti-Judaism in John, see pt II, ch. 6, above.

scriptures and of their interpretation in contemporary Jewish thought (for example, John 6).[11] Another pattern appears in the anonymous letter to the Hebrews, which, through meticulous exegesis of scripture, not only argues for the superiority and the finality of the Son through his sacrifice as mediator of a 'better covenant' (Heb 8:6), but also declares on the basis of Jeremiah 31:31–4 that 'in saying "new" he has rendered the first one obsolete; and what is made obsolete and is growing old will soon fade away' (Heb 8:13).[12]

With each of these examples, it is often debated whether the 'ways have parted', either because – at the conceptual level – the theological claims made could no longer be accommodated within 'Judaism', however diverse, or because – at the socio-cultural level – the communities we glimpse between and behind the lines are living in self-conscious independence of, and/or recip-rocal antagonism with, '*the* synagogue across the road'.[13] Such judgements, however, presuppose a degree of self-fulfilling definition of 'Judaism' or of 'independence from *the* synagogue', when there was no centralised authority to define the former, and often a number of synagogal communities in a city. Self-evidently, each of these writings is working within a Jewish matrix; each is also at least moving towards an exclusive claim to interpret that tradition, and so to de-legitimate other claims – at the discourse level. In social contexts where other claimants could not be avoided, a variety of consequences would have been possible, although we cannot know whether outside observers would mark differentiation more than similarity. For example, it would be possible to interpret in more than one way the praxis of the Pauline communities, which, in contrast to many other Jewish groups, did not require male circumcision, at least for Gentile members, and were ambivalent towards dietary and calendri-cal observance, and yet which, like many, still rejected any active participation in the local cult of the city (Rom 14:1–6; 1 Cor 8; 10).[14] Similarly, the apparent continued concern of the Matthaean groups for the sabbath (Matt 24:20) might also undermine clear categorisation.

A more fruitful approach might be to explore the sense of immediacy in the way that 'the other' is, implicitly if not explicitly, positioned both on the

11 The image of 'the Jews' as the offspring of the devil (John 8:44) was taken up in the long history of Christian anti-semitism. On the Jewish heritage of John 6, see Borgen, *Bread from heaven*. For the problem see Bieringer *et al.*, *Anti-Judaism and the fourth gospel*.

12 See Lindars, *Theology*; the audience and authorship of Hebrews are unknown, although it is certainly not Pauline as later supposed.

13 See nn. 2 and 8: the issue has been particularly hotly contested regarding Matthew, often with imprecise definition of 'separation', and of how, and by whom, it might be measured.

14 In each case the comparison is with 'many' other groups, since we cannot say categori-cally that Paul's was the only group to take this line.

discourse and on the socio-cultural levels, which might be very different. Most, if not all, of the Pauline communities were located in cities with an active Jewish presence; it seems probable, however, that the real opposition behind Paul's arguments in Romans and Galatians was not these 'outsiders' but an alternative position *within* the 'Jesus movement', one with more rigorous requirements for Gentile members, and hence for the character of this new 'messianic community', as defined in relationship to the Jewish polity established in scripture as well as to contemporary practice in Jerusalem, the land, and in the diaspora. There is no consensus regarding the social, temporal or geographical location of the audience of Hebrews, but many have suggested that its fears of apostasy were provoked by the specific pressures to demonstrate (or return to) loyalty to Jerusalem in the face of the first Jewish revolt (Heb 6:4–8); however, Hebrews appeals not to the traditions of the contemporary Jerusalem temple but to those of the tabernacle as described in scripture, which might rather suggest the anxieties of more intellectual circles. Matthew and John are regularly interpreted against the background not of an attractive active 'Jewish' presence but of an antagonistic one that had, perhaps, already taken steps to exclude the nascent Christians; but the contours of such a setting are blurred and too often they have been drawn by appeals to now-discredited reconstructions of the rise and influence after 70 CE of a monolithic and enclosed rabbinic Judaism.[15] By contrast, 1 Peter indicates that a group, perhaps exclusively Gentile in origin (1 Pet 1:18; 4:3–4), could be redefined in the language of the community of the Sinai covenant (2:5–10), without any hint of a challenge from other claimants to that identity. Already, then, the possible social contexts and the uses of the language of continuity or of separation are diverse, and not always easy to recover.

We cannot trace simple lines of continuity from these first-century writings into subsequent polemic and self-fashioning. There is no linear development in early Christian self-definition, and it itself never achieves a unitary form in relation to the Jewish matrix (or to anything else). Yet those that we have traced do indicate the nodal points from which future understandings of the self, and attempts to define and to deny 'the other', would grow; in time, too, they provided scriptural authority for future polemic.

Relating to a scriptural past

The difficulties of tracing a straightforward progression become evident as we move from the first into the early second century. The apparently unreflective

---

15 For such discrediting see Schwartz, *Imperialism*, 103–29; Cohen, 'Rabbi'.

claim to an unbroken continuity with the Abrahamic heritage and scriptural tradition continues: for example, *1 Clement*, with a probably Gentile readership, not only appeals to Abraham as 'our father' but also upholds as descended from Jacob, 'all the priests and levites who serve at God's altar' (*1 Clem.* 31–2);[16] however, here, as in 1 Peter, it is *scriptural* tradition that we should emphasise. The extent to which the Jewish scriptures shape the world-view of the early Christians, and provide them with a language for self-understanding within the Graeco-Roman world, appears so 'natural' in their texts that it may be too readily taken for granted by their modern interpreters.[17] It is hard to envisage how quickly or easily Gentile converts could have acquired the immersion in the Jewish scriptures necessary for them to appreciate fully some of the exegetical arguments spun from the latter (e.g. 1 Cor 10:1–5). This has led to suggestions that many such converts must have come from circles already actively interested in Judaism, a group often labelled 'God-fearers', although this may be only to push the problem of integration back a stage further.[18] On the contrary, however, much of our evidence points to Gentile converts as predominantly from a thoroughly 'pagan' background (1 Thess 1:9–10; Justin, *Dial.* 130–5).

Equally striking are those cases where there is a conscious rejection of alternative, we might say of 'Jewish', understandings of those scriptures. The *Epistle of Barnabas*, whose date is uncertain but which may belong in circumstances where political events enhanced the attraction of 'Judaism', offers an extreme example.[19] Crucial here is the anonymous author's explicit identification of the destruction of the temple not simply as divine punishment – a common theme in later writers – but as evidence that God's original intention was not a structural but a spiritual temple, now embodied in the conversion and obedience of the Gentile converts to whom he writes (*Ep. Barn.* 16). Whether or not the status of the temple is the primary motivating issue, the letter applies the same model to the scriptural provisions of sacrifice, fasting, purity, circumcision and diet: the true meaning of each is to be found in their 'spiritual' reference. The food laws inspire an allegorical exegesis of the habits of various forbidden animals as representing the vices to be avoided; Moses intended these

16 Cf. *1 Clem.* 9–12; *1 Clem.* may be dated to the last decade of the first century CE or the beginning of the second.
17 But see Young, *Biblical exegesis*.
18 In addition, the evidence for a clear profile of such circles is inadequate: see Lieu, *Neither Jew nor Greek*, 31–47. Hopkins, 'Christian number', 214–16 does conclude that the majority of Christians in this period must have been of Jewish origin.
19 For example, if it was hoped that Nerva, emperor 96–8 CE, might sanction the rebuilding of the temple; so Carleton Paget, *Epistle of Barnabas*.

'in spirit, but they took them as about food, following [their] fleshly desire' (10.10). Important to note here is, first, that such allegorical interpretation of the dietary code was already to be found in Hellenistic Judaism;[20] secondly, that the rejection of the Jews as 'carnal', and of their interpretation of scripture as literalist, in contrast to a self-definition of 'us' who interpret spiritually, was to be one of the primary fault lines in subsequent Christian exegesis, even though 'literal' and 'spiritual' could be continually redefined.[21] In practice all involved were interpreting their authoritative but often obscure texts with an eye to the present.

The *Epistle of Barnabas* is distinctive for insisting that the Law was never intended for 'literal' observance. In a telling protest probably betraying the currency of other views, he denounces those who believe that the covenant is 'theirs *and* ours'; instead, 'It is ours. They lost it completely almost as soon as Moses received it' (*Ep. Barn.* 4.6–7). The problem here was whether 'Christians', a term the *Epistle of Barnabas* does not use, had a (salvation-) historical place in God's purposes, in some sense consequent upon, and so continuous with, at least some elements within Israel's past experience, or whether rather they *alone* were the original and intended heirs of the covenantal promises. The *Epistle of Barnabas* tends towards the latter course; Justin Martyr (d. *c*.165 CE), in his *Dialogus cum Tryphone Judaeo*, comes closer to the former. Here, he drew both on prophecies of the eschatological coming of the nations and on the scriptural theme of the remnant, concluding not only that the Gentiles who believed in Jesus 'would inherit along with the patriarchs, prophets and righteous', but also that it was still possible for 'some of your people to be found Abraham's children and of the portion of Christ' (*Dial.* 26.1; 120.1–2). At the same time, he traces a parallel reverse history of Jewish ('your') disobedience from the making of the golden calf, through the fulminations of the prophets, to the present rejection of Jesus and his followers (131–5). Justin's ultimate goal is not simply to apply to the Christians the prophecies of God's eschatological people, but also to claim their right to the title 'Israel' (123–5; 135).

The conviction that Jesus Christ fulfilled the scriptural prophecies is embedded in our earliest sources (1 Cor 15:3–5; 1 Pet 1:10–12), and continues as a fundamental element in all Christian argument and self-presentation, with an ever-growing list of, often surprising, proof-texts. Justin, however, also discovers a place for Christian belief throughout the whole history of God's dealings with Israel, helped by, for example, the Greek form of the name of Joshua,

---

20 E.g. *Ep. Arist.* 142–69.
21 See Dawson, *Christian figural reading.*

'Jesus', and, more significantly, by finding the presence of Christ in the theophanies of the past, such as at Genesis 18 (*Dial.* 56–62).

Another richly articulated discovery of Christ in the scriptural record appears in Melito's *Peri pascha*: 'he is the Pascha of our salvation . . . it is he that in Abel was murdered, in Isaac bound, in Jacob exiled . . .' (*Pass.* 69).[22] On one level this is an exegetical appropriation of the scriptures; on another it means that Christians could trace back to the beginning their place as the faithful respondents to God's salvific purposes, while the one whom 'Israel' had killed was the one who had guided her through their past history, with the result that now she had forfeited all rights (83–90).[23] In each of these writers, that it was the Romans who were responsible for crucifying Jesus is increasingly forgotten in the interests of a simple oppositional pattern of salvation and rejection.[24]

A driving force in all this is the place of scripture; already here, and increasingly in subsequent writers, ways of reading the scriptures, understood largely in terms of prophecy and fulfilment, and exegeted through typology and allegory, become a primary means of Christian self-definition. Not only in texts which are at least formally directed 'against the Jews' (the *adversus Judaeos* tradition),[25] but also in numerous pastoral, doctrinal and exegetical writings, scriptural testimonies are assumed to anticipate, if positive or shaped by hope, Christ and Christians, and, if condemnatory, the Jews. Both source and goal of this is the Christian self-identification as the scripturally defined covenant people; often it leads to taking up the scriptural images, such as those of temple and priesthood, and reapplying them to the Christian community. Yet, unavoidably, such theological affirmations about their own place within God's plan demanded addressing the theological question of the place of the Jews, a demand met most frequently antithetically through the latter's characterisation by disobedience and loss. As Christianity and Judaism become conceptualised as unitary wholes, so the idea of the remnant becomes overshadowed by that of replacement, Esau supplanted by his younger brother, Jacob: 'But in Christ every blessing is found; and for this reason the latter

---

22 Usually, probably rightly, ascribed to Melito of Sardis, d. *c.*185 CE; see Hall (ed. and trans.), *Melito*.
23 Melito's Christology thus allows him to charge them with having murdered God (96).
24 The tendency to accentuate the role of the Jewish authorities in Jesus' death already appears in the New Testament gospels.
25 E.g. Cyprian (d. *c.*258 CE), *Ad Quirinum testimonia adversus Judaeos*; on the literary tradition see Schreckenberg, *Adversus-Judaeos-Texte*; Williams, *Adversus Judaeos*; on whether there were real encounters, see below.

people has snatched the blessings from the (F)ather of the former people, just as Jacob stole his blessing from Esau' (Iren. *Haer.* 4.21).

Within this framework it became imperative that Christian writers justify, to an internal as well as to an external audience, a selectivity as to which requirements of Torah were observed that was far from self-evident but that by the second century most Gentile believers took for granted.[26] While the *Epistle of Barnabas* as quoted earlier might have the sharper solution when it came to the Law – that literal observance had never been appropriate – this was one that could lead to a denial of the unity of intent, and so ultimately of identity, of the God who promulgated that Law with the Father revealed by Jesus Christ, a view later argued by Marcion.[27] Yet a response of this sort might also be unreflective, as it is in Ignatius (*c.*110 CE), who is the first to set in explicit and irreconcilable opposition 'Judaism' and 'Christianism' (*Phild.* 6.1; *Magn.* 10).[28] While he assumes the support of the prophets and even of the Law of Moses, he appears willing to jettison any argument based on the scriptures ('the archives') if it threatens his reading of 'the gospel' (*Magn.* 8.2; *Smyr.* 5.1; *Phild.* 8.2).[29] For him, Judaism is a mode of living, perhaps characterised by sabbath and circumcision, but even more by ancient myths, and its utter rejection requires no justification (*Magn.* 8.1; 9.1; *Phild.* 10.1).[30]

The retention of the scriptures as part of Christian self-understanding demanded a more sophisticated response than this. Justin's solution to the problem of the validity of the Law is that while some commandments did define 'piety and right action', and while others pointed to 'the mystery of Christ', the Law was best understood as a remedy for Israel's inveterate hardheartedness; moreover, circumcision was indeed a sign of separation for the Jews, but of separation for punishment – a conclusion supported by appeal to the fate of Jerusalem after two revolts, and, in company with most Christian authors, by ignoring the continuing vitality of Jewish life both in Palestine and in the diaspora (*Dial.* 44.2; cf. 16.2–3). This response enabled a more nuanced (or contradictory) selectivity in what Christians should obey, although ultimately at the cost of stereotyping Jewish recalcitrance and destined punishment. Indeed, perhaps already for Justin, and certainly for later polemicists, the defence against Marcion of the Christian use of the scriptures, and of their faith

---

26 But not all, see below.
27 See ch. 9, above.
28 'Christianism' is probably Ignatius' own coinage, modelled antithetically on 'Judaism', which appears first in the Maccabean literature, and infrequently thereafter.
29 On this difficult passage see Schoedel, 'Ignatius and the archives'.
30 See also Tit 1:10, 14; 3:9, which, although ascribed to Paul, many scholars date after his death.

in the one God, led smoothly into a heightened denigration of the obtuseness of the Jews who had 'failed' to perceive the true meaning of those scriptures. Hence Tertullian apparently re-used substantial parts of his earlier *Adversus Judaeos* in his *Adversus Marcionem*;[31] as probably the first Latin writer 'against the Jews', he was to have a profound influence on his successors.

Here we begin to see the multiple contexts in which the development of the discourse of separation could be worked out: in internal debate over the actual use of scripture and observance of its precepts, in the search for models of faithful and of unfaithful behaviour, in the assertion of their place in God's purposes, as well as, perhaps, in actual dealings with Jewish observers, although, as we shall see, the extent of this is debated.

Speaking to outsiders

A different context is provided by Christian apologetics to an outside world already familiar with, and sometimes contemptuous of, the Jews.[32] Most vividly, Origen has to answer the 'pagan' Celsus' charge that Christians are nothing better than apostates from their Jewish heritage – incurring the double stigma of espousing novelty against antiquity, and yet of bearing the genetic imprint of a religious tradition long derided as the antithesis of true 'classical' virtues (*Contra Celsum*).[33] Origen repeats the familiar defence that Christians are those who do not despise the Law, for it is the origin of their doctrine; rather, the Jews, through failing properly to read and obey, have reduced it to myths (2.4–5). But he also has to defend the integrity and priority of Moses, and he even brings Jews and Christians together in testifying to Abraham's holiness and efficacy for exorcism (4.21, 33, 43).

The assertion that Abraham or Moses preceded, and were the sources of, the so-called Greek wisdom was already a feature of Hellenistic Jewish apologetic for a world in which antiquity was highly prized.[34] In the second century CE, the argument was adopted by apologists like Tatian and Theophilus of Antioch for the same purpose.[35] Tatian gives a detailed and carefully documented account in order to demonstrate the antiquity of Moses and so of 'our philosophy' and 'manner of life', without ever mentioning Jesus Christ

---

31 Tränkle, *Tertulliani*, lxx–lxxiv.
32 Gager, *Origins of anti-semitism*; a more positive estimation of the standing of the Jews in the Graeco-Roman world is given by Gruen, *Diaspora*.
33 Celsus' *Alēthēs logos* ('True word') against the Christians is usually dated to *c*.177–80 CE, about seventy years before Origen's response; see Chadwick, *Contra Celsum*.
34 See ch. 11, below.
35 See Droge, *Homer or Moses?*

(*Orat.* 31–40). Here, there is no sense of antithesis with the Jewish matrix, but equally no acknowledgement of other claimants to its tradition. Justin Martyr's philosophical principles lead to a very different strategy in his *First apology*, but one that would similarly provide a venerable past for a movement liable to be dismissed as a 'novel superstition' (as by Suet. *Nero* 16); there he explicitly identifies as 'Christians' those who lived 'with the *Logos*' in the past, not only Socrates and Heraclitus, but also 'Abraham, Ananias, Azarias, Misael, Elijah and many others' (*1 Apol.* 46.3).

Tracing each of these threads has suggested that we cannot speak of 'Christian self-definition vis-à-vis the Jewish matrix' in neutral terms; 'the Jewish matrix' does not simply provide a backcloth or a rich well of resources, but was itself reconstructed or re-envisioned within and as the necessary companion of a Christian discourse of the self. This has led to vigorous debates as to whether 'the attitude of the church fathers to Jews and Judaism is synonymous with anti-Jewish polemic and with Christian anti-Judaism', and even as to whether anti-Judaism is intrinsic to all early Christian discourse and self-definition.[36] It cannot be our task here to follow further either those debates or the wider history of Christian anti-Judaism or anti-semitism, but the historical and theological challenges they lay down continue to demand reflection.

Practice versus polemic

Despite the apparent self-confidence of the authors surveyed, there was much more fluidity in practice (i.e. in the socio-cultural sphere) and in self-understanding among those who counted themselves followers of Jesus. Contrary to his theological principles, Justin is forced to acknowledge that there are those, even of Gentile birth, who do observe the Jewish Torah, and to whom he cannot deny salvation (*Dial.* 47). It may even have been the presence of similar people in the churches at Magnesia or Philadelphia that provoked Ignatius' ire against the practice of 'Judaism'. In scholarly analysis such practice is regularly labelled 'Judaising', and its extent within the early church is debated; this, however, is misleading if it is taken as implying that the boundaries were clear even when they were contravened.[37] This was far from the case. Even that doughty polemicist, Tertullian, can report without rancour that some people avoid obeisance when praying on the sabbath – a sign of its special

---

36 The first quotation comes from Hruby, *Juden und Judentum*, 6, the second position was put most forcefully by Ruether, *Faith and fratricide*; see also Taylor, *Anti-Judaism*, and for discussion, Stroumsa, 'From anti-Judaism'.

37 On this see pt II, ch. 4, above.

status – despite his preferred restriction of that practice to Sunday; for all that, he still rhetorically contrasts 'our' freedom to stretch out hands in prayer with 'Israel's' inability to do so (*Orat.* 23; cf. 14). The *Didache* urges its readers to avoid the fasts of 'the hypocrites' – perhaps referring to the Jews but equally possibly to other 'Christians' – on Mondays and Thursdays, and yet instead counsels fasting on Wednesdays and 'the day of preparation' (of the sabbath, i.e. Friday: *Did.* 8.1).[38] Some who advocated a greater continuity of practice would perhaps also tell as their story one of an unbroken continuity of divine purpose – although conceptual continuity need not imply social rapprochement with other contemporary claimants to the same 'Jewish' tradition.

Something like this appears to lie behind the second-century sources of the fourth-century Pseudo-Clementine *Recognitiones* and *Homiliae*, and perhaps also behind the *Didascalia* (possibly to be dated to the third century), both usually situated in Syria-Palestine. In the former, the religion of the apostles appears simply as that originally intended by Moses; the Gentiles have been brought in in order to complete the number originally revealed to Abraham, and so to compensate for those who did not believe.[39] Again, applying the label 'Jewish Christian' to such views may not be helpful, for it implies a high degree of uniformity as well as a clear distinction from other (Gentile) Christians, where neither are to be found.[40] None the less, such attitudes do become targeted in the anti-heretical literature that was to shape the self-understanding of the church: already Irenaeus sets a pattern by including in his list of heresies the Ebionites whom he condemns for their 'Judaic way of life' as well as for their doubts about the virgin birth (Iren. *Haer.* 1.26.2; 5.1.3). This, and the nature of the dominant development of the church and its literature, means that the eventual history of such groups and attitudes is largely lost to our view, although new approaches and the discovery of the writings of other marginalised groups is beginning to recover them and to suggest that their importance was greater than often supposed.[41]

Contacts between Jews and Christians

While internal debates, particularly about the Mosaic Law, undoubtedly stimulated reflection vis-à-vis 'the Jewish matrix', more controversial has been

---

38 See ch. 14, below.
39 See Jones, *Jewish Christian source*.
40 Jones accepts the label for his text (*Recogn.* 1.27–71) while doubting that the author would have expected circumcision, usually seen as a Jewish Christian marker, of Gentile converts (*Jewish Christian source*, 164–7).
41 See Tomson and Lambers-Petry, *Image of the Judaeo-Christians*.

whether a further impulse was provided by close encounters with Jews, individuals and communities, who merely by their existence and observance challenged a Christian self-identity, and who may also have put that challenge in active debate. Arguments that there were in fact no such encounters appeal to the general lack of interest in, or information about, actual contemporary Jewish practice in many of our writers: for them the Jews are defined, monolithically and unchangingly, by the scriptures, namely by temple, sacrifice and prophetic denunciation.[42] From this it has sometimes been concluded that 'the Jew' of their polemics is a straw figure, the rejected but ever possible alternative within, and that the *adversus Iudaeos* literature is an exercise in internal apologetic and self-affirmation. Yet certainly there were socially and religiously vibrant Jewish communities in most of the cities within which Christian groups emerged, and in many if not most cases these would have had the numerical and, perhaps, social advantage throughout our period.[43] We glimpse the ease with which some Christians could move between 'church and synagogue' when Origen and John Chrysostom denounce members of their churches for visiting the synagogue, but we have no certain way of knowing whether these are the shadows of a more substantial phenomenon.[44] Others have argued that scattered epigraphic evidence throughout and beyond our period which indicates common practices and ideas among Jews, Christians and 'pagans' demonstrates that there were many who lived in unconscious disregard of the stringent efforts of preachers and pen-pushers to maintain clear, separate boundaries. Here would be included inscriptions in Asia Minor to 'the most high God', or those displaying similar attitudes to piety or to the need for forgiveness, which have been identified either as exhibiting Jewish or Christian or 'pagan' features, or as resisting any such exclusive definition.[45]

Even more difficult to ascertain is the extent of immediate *intellectual* engagement between Jews and Christians. Justin's account of his dialogue with a Jew, Trypho, contains enough echoes of authenticity to persuade many that it is rooted in genuine encounter(s), but even it clearly betrays the controlling and constructive pen of its author.[46] Subsequent literary encounters become

---

42 E.g. Harnack, *Expansion*, vol. 1, 82.

43 See Trebilco, *Jewish communities*; and for specific examples, Lieu, *Image and reality*.

44 Or. *Sel. Lev.* 5.8; Chrys. *Adv. Jud.* 4.7.4, 7. Again, it is unhelpful to label such practice 'Judaising'. Simon, *Verus Israel* did most to re-establish the argument for the attraction of the Jewish alternative as a source of Christian anti-Jewish polemic.

45 See Mitchell, 'The cult of Theos Hypsistos'; Mitchell, *Anatolia*, vol. II, 11–51; Herz, 'Einleitung'.

46 See Lieu, *Image and reality*, 104–13.

increasingly artificial, as when Tertullian prefaces his monologue-salvo against the Jews with a dismissive reference to a debate between a Christian and a Jewish proselyte – perhaps because the Jew won (*Adv. Jud.* 1.1). Although Celsus' accusations of apostasy are placed in the mouth of a Jew, and some of the charges he lays do anticipate later Jewish anti-Christian polemic, it is still difficult to be sure whether this is much more than a clever literary device. Yet public debate was a feature of the age, and we may suppose that it continued between Jews and Christians, even if not with the triumphant conclusion often assumed by their Christian recorders.[47]

Yet the multi-faceted Origen testifies to another aspect of our equally complex problem, for he admits his debt to a 'Hebrew' for his knowledge of the language and for discussion of the relationship between the Hebrew and Greek versions of the scriptures.[48] Clement of Alexandria is familiar not only with Philo and other Hellenistic Jewish writings, but also apparently with Jewish exegesis, as is Justin. Indeed, Justin Martyr's vigorous defence suggests that he, and probably other Christians, were dependent on Jews for access to copies of the scriptures in their entirety; admitting them to be 'yours', he claims them by virtue of true understanding to be 'ours', but is still constrained to argue from the text forms they use (*Dial.* 29.2; 131.1). At some stage Christians adopted the LXX, and perhaps also the codex as the preferred material form, while Jewish communities developed alternative Greek translations and maintained the scroll format. In time Christians produced their own authoritative texts, a 'new' Testament that was to determine the lens through which the 'old' would be read but which is inconceivable without it. These moves would embody more clearly the way that the shared scriptures were becoming a focal symbol both of shared and of separate self-definition.[49]

Modelling the relationship

It is important to emphasise these contradictory thrusts of evidence for separation and for shared worlds. Earlier scholarship painted, on the one side, a Judaism that turned in on itself following the defeats of 70 CE and 135 CE, and that also expelled 'Christianity' by banning Christians from the synagogues through the 'benediction of the heretics' or *birkat hamminim*;[50] on the other

---

47 On the later tradition see Lim, *Public disputation*.
48 See de Lange, *Origen and the Jews*; it has, however, been argued that this was a Jewish Christian.
49 Horbury, *Jews and Christians*, 200–26.
50 I.e. the Twelfth of the Eighteen Benedictions which prays for the exclusion from the Book of Life of groups variously identified but including *minim* ('deviants', 'heretics'),

side, according to this view, lay a predominantly Gentile Christianity, shaped by the Hellenistic culture within which it had to articulate its faith, and troubled only by 'the Jew within', the unavoidable companion of the retention of the Jewish scriptures. We have already seen how this has been replaced by the more eirenic model of diverging paths; moreover, since it cannot be shown either that the *birkat hamminim* was targeted particularly against Christians, nor that it was known beyond the boundaries of the land of Israel, attempts to identify a single date or provocation for 'the parting' have also been abandoned. Now that rabbinic Judaism is no longer taken as the controlling norm for any reconstruction of Jewish thought throughout our period we can also recognise that Christian theology's attempts to address the Hellenistic world continued to owe much to the earlier and perhaps continuing efforts made by Jews to speak of their God in the same context.[51]

Some of the material reviewed above would take us a step further: people meeting, associating with each other, even worshipping together in ways that provoked the wrath of their more articulate and literate leaders. Christian writers' rigorous efforts to define the 'otherness' of unbelieving Jews may not betray a confident self-sufficiency so much as a fear of an ever-threatening dissolution of difference, efforts matched also by the rabbis in their own attempt to impose their world-view.[52] Here, the relationship between the world constructed by the texts, and that of popular living remains ever fraught.

Yet this new oppositional model, between text and reality, powerful elite and ordinary people, may still be too straightforward. Recent study has emphasised the intersecting worlds of Christian and Jewish exegesis: interpretations of the atoning efficacy of the 'sacrifice' of Isaac, and of the suffering and death of the martyrs, appear to have evolved through a complex pattern of implicit or explicit dialogue, of borrowing and of competition.[53] Texts like the *Testaments of the twelve patriarchs* or the *Lives of the prophets*, which were preserved by Christian scribes and readers, have often been seen as evidence for Hellenistic Judaism once they were shorn of their 'Christian' redactional layers; now many would reject both that enterprise and the utility of the separate categories employed, asking instead how these texts were read and how they would have

apostates and, at some stage in its history, *notzrim*. On this and the debate as to its relationship with the Christians, see Wilson, *Related strangers*, 179–83; Horbury, *Jews and Christians*, 67–110, 240–3; cf. pt II, chs. 4 and 6, above.

51 Particularly strongly argued by Boyarin, *Border lines*.
52 See n. 15, above.
53 See Boyarin, *Dying*; Levenson, *Death and resurrection*.

shaped their readers' self-understanding.[54] Examples such as these may lead us to recognise a shared universe of significance, one that could be shown also both to challenge and to participate in the symbolic world of Graeco-Roman antiquity.[55]

Jews and Christians share a common matrix even, or especially, when they refuse to acknowledge this.

54 See the papers in *JSJ* 32.3 (2001).
55 See Boyarin, *Border lines*; Lieu, *Christian Identity*.

11

Self-definition vis-à-vis the Graeco-Roman world

A. J. DROGE

To engage the question of Christian self-definition is to become keenly aware that it is a process of differentiations and negotiations that is never final, and that the categories of description – 'Christian', 'Jewish', 'Greek', 'Roman' – are not to be taken for granted. The communities these categories are said to designate are neither stable nor essentially known entities, but social formations continuously engaged in self-recreation.[1] With this in mind, I have endeavored to analyse a crucial moment in the second century of the formation of a 'Christian' discourse and, indeed, of the construction of 'Christianity' itself. Justin Martyr was not the first to take up the question of self-definition vis-à-vis the Graeco-Roman world, and he would certainly not be the last, but he was surely one of the most influential to do so. It was Justin more than anyone else who would set the terms in which Christianity would be represented to the wider world of antiquity, and a whole host of Christian writers would follow in his path, elaborating and expanding upon his project of self-definition. What is more, a least one 'Graeco-Roman' author of the second century appears to have taken notice of Justin's works and felt compelled to issue a response: the *Alēthēs logos* of the otherwise unknown Platonist, Celsus, represents the first systematic attack on Christianity. Taken together, Justin and Celsus signal a turning-point in the construction and contestation of Christian discourse in the second century.[2]

Atticising Moses

In his famous *Dialogue with Trypho*, Justin 'the Martyr' recounts his intellectual pilgrimage from one philosophical school to the next – Stoic, Peripatetic,

---

1 On this, see Lapin, *Religious and ethnic communities*, 1–28; and Buell, 'Rethinking the relevance', 449–76.
2 For a broader perspective on Christian 'apologetics' in the first and second centuries, see Droge, 'Apologetics, NT', vol. 1, 302–7; Grant, *Greek apologists*; and the collection of essays in Edwards *et al.* (eds.), *Apologetics in the Roman empire*.

Pythagorean and finally Platonist – at which point he tells us, 'I supposed that
I had become wise, and . . . expected to look upon God, for that is the goal
of Plato's philosophy' (*Dial.* 2.6).[3] While meditating one day by the sea, Justin
encountered an old man who 'corrected' his Platonism and then told him
of Moses and the prophets, 'more ancient than all those who are considered
philosophers [by the Greeks] . . . , who alone saw and declared the truth to
humankind' (7.1–2). Justin was converted – not to Judaism but to Christianity –
and thereafter became a teacher of the Christian 'philosophy' (8.1–2). Implied
in this highly stylised and perhaps fictional account is a new and revolutionary
recasting of the history of culture, one that not only recognises similarities
and differences between Christianity and the prevailing culture of the second
century, but also presents a theory to account for them.

In his *First apology*, addressed to the emperor Antoninus Pius, Justin declared
that 'Moses is more ancient than all Greek writers, and everything the [Greek]
poets and philosophers have said . . . they took as suggestions from the prophets,
and so were able to understand and expound them. Hence there seem to be
seeds of truth among all men' (44.8–19). In this assertion Justin was exploiting
to his own ends the recognition by the Greeks themselves of the far greater
antiquity of various 'barbarian' peoples such as the Egyptians, Phoenicians,
Babylonians and even the Jews. The idea that early Greek sages had acquired
their wisdom and learning on voyages to the 'east' could already be found in
such Greek writers as Herodotus, Hecataeus of Abdera and Diodorus of Sicily,
to mention only the most well known. Egypt, in particular, seems to have
exercised a special fascination for the Greeks. Herodotus had described the
encounter between Hecataeus of Miletus and the Egyptian priests of Thebes
as a contest between two civilisations of different antiquity. Hecataeus' sixteen
generations of ancestors simply could not compete with the Egyptian priest
who could trace his ancestry back through 345 generations (*Hist.* 2.143). In the
Timaeus Plato reported a similar encounter between the Athenian lawgiver
Solon and the Egyptian priests of Saïs. In a debate with them about archaic
history (*peri tōn archaiōn*), an amazed Solon 'discovered that neither he himself nor any other Greek knew anything at all about such matters'. Indeed,
as one Egyptian priest solemnly pointed out to him, 'Solon, there is no such
thing as an "old Greek", for you possess not a single belief that is ancient and
derived from old tradition, nor yet one science that is time-honoured' (*Ti.*
22ac). In the new international world created by Alexander and ruled over by

---

3 For the Greek text of Justin's works, I have relied on the edition of Goodspeed, *Die ältesten
Apologeten.* Translations are my own unless otherwise indicated.

his successors, including the Romans, the same point would be made again and again by 'barbarian' writers who had learned to compose history in Greek fashion: the *Babylonian history* of Berossus, the *Egyptian history* of Manetho, the *Phoenician history* of Philo of Byblos, as well as the Jewish histories of Artapanus, Eupolemus and even Flavius Josephus, all sought to present (in Greek) elaborate and sometimes quite fanciful theories about the 'barbarian' origin of Greek culture. Each of these new histories credited their own indigenous gods and heroes with being the culture-bringers responsible for the benefits of civilisation. So when Justin insisted that the Greeks had derived their wisdom from the ancient books of Moses and the prophets, he was only utilising for his own purposes an argument which in other forms was widely held.

Tertullian gave expression to this phenomenon when he wrote in his *Apology*: *Auctoritatem litteris praestat antiquitas summa* (19.1).[4] A putatively 'ancient' book carried authority as well as mystery, so much so that it was worth interpolating or even forging. Justin and his successors did their best to build their case on the ancient writings of Moses, but they exploited as well the 'ancient (pagan) prophecies' of Hystaspes and the Sibyl, apparently unaware that much of this literature had been fabricated by Jews and Christians with apologetic aims.[5] Other Christians also went to great lengths to establish the date of Moses in order to demonstrate, in the words of Tatian, Justin's student, that 'our philosophy is older than Greek culture' and that 'Moses is the originator of all barbarian wisdom' (*Orat.* 31.1). Yet, here again, it is important to bear in mind that many Greek intellectuals were making similar claims for Homer.[6]

Justin's argument for the antiquity, and hence superiority, of Christianity was, as A. D. Nock observed, 'an answer to what was at the time a most damaging criticism of Christianity – namely, that it was a new thing followed in contravention of good old customs'.[7] In particular, the 'proof from antiquity'[8] was a powerful weapon against the accusations raised by Greek intellectuals such as Celsus and Porphyry, who claimed that Christianity was a recent phenomenon and had therefore contributed nothing to the advance of culture. The intensity with which Justin and other Christian writers of the second and third centuries responded is an indicator itself of just how important the issue of 'antiquity' could be. For these Christians, as for their opponents, the assertion of 'modern' origin was equivalent to the assertion of historical insignificance.

---

4 Cf. his *Marc.* 4.5.1: 'That is truer which is prior.'
5 See Leclercq, 'Oracle', cols. 2225–6, for Jewish and Christian exploitation of the Sibyl; on the forging of 'ancient' books, see Droge, 'Lying pen', 128–34.
6 See Zeitlin, 'Visions and revisions'.
7 *Conversion*, 251.
8 See Pilhofer, *Presbyteron kreitton*.

Nothing could be both new *and* true. It was a general conviction of the age that what was 'oldest' was always best, that the 'ancients' lived nearer to the gods and the beginnings of things and therefore knew much more about them.[9] To claim, then, that Moses and the prophets were older than any of the Greek lawgivers or sages was to assert the superiority of the former and the necessary dependency of the latter. *Post hoc, ergo propter hoc* may be a logical fallacy, but it could be an effective strategy in a milieu in which so much authority was conceded to *antiquitas summa*.

Restoring philosophy

'I will present the evidence', Justin declares, 'that what we say . . . is alone true and older than all the writers who have ever lived.' This proposition, announced at *1 Apologia* 23.1 and worked out in detail in subsequent chapters, serves as the main bearing beam of Justin's argument for the superiority of his 'Christian philosophy'. To prove his case, he produced a number of 'philosophical parallels', chiefly between Moses (the putative author of the Pentateuch) and Plato. Justin claims, for example, that 'when Plato said, "The blame is his who chooses, and god is blameless" [*Rep.* 617e], he took this from the prophet Moses', who first taught that God is not the cause of evil when he said, 'Behold, before thy face are good and evil: choose the good' (*1 Apol.* 44.1, quoting Deut 30:15, 19). In other words Justin contends that Plato's teaching on fate, free will and the problem of evil was taken directly from Moses. Similarly, when Plato came to write the cosmological section of the *Timaeus* he once again relied on Moses. 'So that you may learn that Plato borrowed from our teachers . . . when he said that God made the cosmos by changing formless matter, hear the exact words of Moses, who as we said above was the first of the prophets and more ancient than all the writers among the Greeks.' There follows a quotation from Gen 1:1–3, and then Justin concludes: 'So by God's word the entire cosmos was made out of this substratum spoken of beforehand by Moses, and Plato, and those who agree with him, have learned it from [Moses]' (*1 Apol.* 59.1–5; cf. 20.4).

Perhaps the most striking proof that Plato had actually 'read' Moses occurs in the next chapter of *1 Apologia*. Here Justin claims that 'the physiological discussion concerning the son of god in the *Timaeus* of Plato, where he says, "He placed him crosswise in the universe", he [Plato] likewise took from Moses' (60.1). Justin has in mind the account of Moses' bronze snake in

---

9 On this, see Armstrong, 'Pagan and Christian traditionalism'.

Numbers 21:6–9, 'which Plato read, and clearly not understanding nor realising that it was a type of the cross, but thinking that it was a placing crosswise, said that the power next to the first god was placed crosswise in the universe' (60.5). Justin then goes on to assert that Plato also spoke of a third god:

> And as to his speaking of a third, he did this because he read, as we said above, that which was spoken by Moses, that 'the spirit of God moved over the waters' [Gen 1:2]. For [Plato] gives the second place to the *logos* which is with God, whom he said was placed crosswise in the universe; and the third place to the spirit, who was said to be borne upon the waters, saying 'And the third things around the third' (60.6–7).

This cryptic statement about 'the third' comes not from the *Timaeus*, as Justin seems to imply, but from the Pseudo-Platonic *Second epistle* 312e, a passage notoriously difficult to construe. It purports to be Plato's secret doctrine explaining 'the nature of the First': 'Related to the King of All are all things, and for his sake they exist, and of all things beautiful he is the cause. And related to the Second are the second things; and related to the Third, the third.' Whatever this obscure passage may mean, it exercised considerable fascination in later times, particularly in Pythagorean and Platonist circles. Justin is interested in this passage, however, as proof that Plato taught a triad of gods – that is to say, was in some sense a 'trinitarian' – *based on his reading of Moses*.

The point of drawing of these parallels was not to reconcile Christianity and Greek philosophy (*pace* Harnack),[10] but to demonstrate Christianity's priority and superiority to Greek philosophy. This becomes clear from a passage in the *Dialogue with Trypho*, where Justin criticises the various philosophical schools and denies that they embody the *true* and *original* philosophy.

> What philosophy really is and why it was sent down to humans have escaped the observation of most. Otherwise there would be no Platonists, Stoics, Peripatetics, Theoreticians and Pythagoreans, for philosophy is one science. I will tell you why [philosophy] has become many-headed. It happened that those who first handled it, and who were therefore esteemed illustrious individuals, were succeeded by those who made no investigation concerning truth, but . . . each thought that to be true which he learned from his teacher. Then, moreover, the latter persons handed down to their successors such things and others similar to them; and this system was called by the name of him who was styled the father of the doctrine. (*Dial.* 2.1–2)

Justin contends, in other words, that Greek philosophy as it presently exists, divided up into different schools, each contradicting the other, cannot carry out its proper function of leading people to God. Only the philosophy contained

---

10 Harnack, *Lehrbuch der Dogmengeschichte*, vol. 1.

in the books of Moses and the prophets is capable of this, as Justin makes clear through the persona of the 'old man' in the *Dialogue with Trypho*:

> There existed long before this time certain men, more ancient than all those who are considered philosophers [by the Greeks], . . . who spoke by the divine spirit, and foretold events which would take place, and are now taking place. They are called prophets . . . Their writings are still extant, and the one who has read them is very much helped in his knowledge of the beginning and end of things, and of those matters which the philosophers ought to know. (7.1–2)

It is clear from this passage that, for Justin, the true and original philosophy which 'was sent down to humans' is nothing other than that which is contained in the inspired *books* of Moses and the prophets. From this ancient source the Greek philosophers derived their doctrines, 'but they are shown not to have understood them properly because they [the philosophers and their schools] contradict one another'. Thus, Justin can claim, Christianity is 'the only safe and profitable philosophy' (*Dial.* 8.1).

Barbarian wisdom

Justin's notion of an ancient Mosaic philosophy on which the Greek philosophers depended betrays the influence of contemporary ideas about the history of philosophy. In an important study of the opening chapters of the *Dialogue with Trypho*, Niels Hyldahl argued that the source of Justin's view could be traced to the (lost) *Protrepticus* of Posidonius of Apamea.[11] According to Posidonius, philosophy was sent down to humans in primordial times, but later became corrupt when it split into various schools.

A similar perspective can also be found in the writings of Antiochus of Ascalon. Like Posidonius, Antiochus judged all philosophy after Aristotle as decadent, and urged that it was necessary to return to 'the ancients'. According to Antiochus, the true philosophy was maintained both by the early Academics and Peripatetics ('the ancients', as he called them) as late as the time of Polemo.[12] Moreover, the original unity of philosophy was not broken until Zeno, Polemo's pupil, diverged from the teachings of his predecessors and established the Stoic school.[13]

This view was modified in the second century by the Syrian Platonist Numenius of Apamea in his treatise *On the divergence of the Academics from Plato*. In

---

11 *Philosophie und Christentum*, 112–40, drawing on Diog. Laert. 7.129 and Seneca, *Ep.* 90 for a reconstruction of Posidonius' views.
12 *Apud* Cic. *Fin.* 4.3; 5.7; *Acad.* 1.34–5. For the designation 'ancients', see *Fin.* 5.14.
13 Cic. *Fin.* 4.3.

this caustic work Numenius shows himself to be an extreme *restorer* of the dogmatic teachings of the Academy, for he extends his criticism of the school well beyond Zeno. Remarkably, Numenius maintains that the genuine Platonic doctrine had been abandoned by Plato's immediate successors in the *early* academy: Speusippus, Xenocrates and Polemo (Xenocrates' 'convert'). 'They did not abide by the original tradition,' Numenius argues, 'but partly weakened it in many ways and partly distorted it.'[14] In this respect Justin's view of the history of philosophy is closer to that of Numenius than that of either Antiochus or Posidonius, for Justin laments the existence even of 'Platonists' (*Dial.* 2.1).

The belief in the original unity of philosophy led to attempts to get back to the primitive revelation or ancient theology. Among some Middle Platonists, like Atticus, there seems to have been concern only with the *Greek* antecedents of Plato: Thales, Solon, Lycurgus and so on.[15] Other Platonists, however, were prepared to admit 'barbarian' sources for Plato's wisdom. Apuleius, for example, reports that after the death of Socrates Plato visited the Pythagorean schools of Magna Graecia and then went on to Egypt, and that he also desired to visit the Indians and Persian magi.[16] Elsewhere, Apuleius relates that Pythagoras himself was instructed by the magi, and in particular by Zoroaster, as well as by the Chaldeans and Brahmans.[17]

The clearest expression of this attempt to connect Platonic philosophy with 'barbarian' sources is found in the fragmentary remains of Numenius of Apamea. In his dialogue *On the good*, Numenius claimed that the genuine philosophy of Plato could be recovered by tracing it back to Pythagoras, and from Pythagoras to the most ancient 'barbarian' peoples.

> But when one has spoken on this point, and sealed it with the testimony of Plato, it will be necessary to go back and connect it with the precepts of Pythagoras, and to appeal to the famous nations, bringing forward their rites and doctrines and institutions which are formed in agreement with Plato, all that the Brahmans, Jews, magi and Egyptians set forth.[18]

14 Fr. 24 (des Places) = Euseb. *P.E.* 14.5.1
15 In a fragment preserved by Eusebius (*P.E.* 11.2.2–4 = fr. 1 (ed. des Places)), Atticus refers to Plato 'as *one truly sent down from heaven* in order that the philosophy taught by him might be seen in its fullest proportions'. The language is strikingly similar to Justin's description of the revelation contained in the writings of Moses and the prophets (*Dial.* 2.1–2; 7.1–2).
16 *Pl.* 1.3 (ed. Thomas); cf. Cic. *Fin.* 5.87; Plut. *De Is. et Os.* 354e; Diog. Laert. 3.6; Philostr. *VA* 1.2. Clement of Alexandria (*Str.* 1.66.3) and Origen (*C. Cels.* 4.39) were familiar with this report as well.
17 *Fl.* 15 (ed. Helm); cf. Paus. 4.32.4 and the anonymous *Prolegomena philosophiae Platonicae* in *Platonis dialogi*, Hermann (ed.), vol. VI, 202.
18 Fr. 1a (ed. des Places) = Euseb. *P.E.* 9.7.1.

In other words, the distortions and corruptions with which contemporary Platonism was riddled could be compensated for through a process of triangulation among the doctrines of Plato, the precepts of Pythagoras and the rites, doctrines and institutions of the most ancient 'barbarian' peoples. The result of this process would be the recovery and reconstitution of philosophy itself.[19]

Numenius is representative of a movement that traced back Greek philosophy, and in particular Platonism and Pythagoreanism, to 'barbarian' sources. He also provides an example of the way in which 'new' ideas could be legitimated by representing them as 'ancient'. It was in this intellectual context that Justin constructed his interpretation of the history of philosophy and Christianity's place in it. Indeed, the similarities that exist between Numenius and Justin in this respect suggest that the latter may have adapted his own perspective from the former, whether directly or indirectly. It was Numenius after all who had asked, 'What is Plato but Moses speaking Attic Greek?'[20] The importance of this remark, that Plato was Moses, and not, for instance, Zoroaster, 'Atticising,' should not be underestimated, especially since Zoroaster was a popular figure among some Middle Platonists. It may be that Justin knew of Numenius' claim and that this provided the impetus for his own assertion that Plato had actually 'read' Moses. Like Numenius, Justin traced Platonic philosophy back to an ancient barbarian source, but whereas Numenius allowed that this *Ur*-philosophy derived from a variety of ancient nations and theologians, Justin claimed that the writings of Moses and the prophets were the *exclusive* source. The 'Christian philosophy' therefore was not one, or even the best, among many philosophical schools; according to Justin, it was the *only* philosophy insofar as it was the reconstitution and restoration of the original, primordial truth.

A 'pagan' response

The contemporary effectiveness of Justin's *apologia* for Christianity can best be gauged by the impassioned efforts to undermine it made by Celsus, an otherwise unknown Platonist philosopher, who, about the year 175 CE, published a polemical tract entitled the *Alēthēs logos*, by which he meant 'The true

---

19 In this same treatise Numenius singled out Moses as one of the ancient theologians and identified him with the legendary Musaeus, see fr. 9 (ed. des Places) = Euseb. *P.E.* 9.8.1–2.

20 Fr. 8 (ed. des Places) = Clem. *Str.* 1.150.4; see Stern, *Greek and Latin authors*, vol. II, 209–11 (nos. 363 a–e).

tradition' or 'The ancient norm'. In response to the perceived social, religious and political threats posed by Christianity, Celsus undertook the ambitious task of presenting a thoroughgoing refutation of the 'new' religion. In his treatise Celsus did not rely on unsubstantiated and stock charges (though there are plenty of these); rather, he sought to attack the historical foundation of Christianity in unprecedented fashion. Quoting the tag from Pindar, that 'Custom (*nomos*) is the king of all', Celsus condemned Christianity for not conforming to any of the established or recognised *nomoi*: Christians could not lay claim to any 'ancestral traditions' (*patrioi nomoi*) like those of the Egyptians, Persians or even the Jews. In fact, by rebelling against the Jews, the Christians had created a social novelty and in so doing had abandoned time-honoured customs. Christianity therefore had no historical basis for occupying a place within the Roman empire.

In its original form Celsus' treatise must have been an impressive work. Unfortunately, but not surprisingly, it is no longer extant, except for quotations made from it by Origen of Alexandria in his reply to Celsus some seventy years later. Origen's *Contra Celsum* contains so many quotations, in fact, that a substantial part of Celsus' original work can be reconstructed, though how much Origen left out – perhaps the most damaging parts – can no longer be determined. Yet even in its attenuated form the contours of Celsus' arguments can be clearly discerned.[21]

In the *Alēthēs logos* Celsus will have nothing of Justin's claim that Greek philosophy derived from Moses. To be sure, Celsus admits that there are certain superficial similarities between Greek philosophy and Christianity (e.g. that both Plato and Christ taught humility (*C. Cels.* 6.15), nonresistance to evil (7.58), and that luxury is a hindrance to virtue (6.16)). But the explanation for these 'parallels' is *not* that Plato had read Moses, as Justin claimed; on the contrary, according to Celsus, Jesus read Plato (*C. Cels.* 6.16) and Paul studied Heraclitus (6.12)!

The possibility that Celsus was responding to Justin, suggested more than a century ago by Elysée Pélagaud,[22] was argued at considerable length by Carl Andresen in his magisterial *Logos und Nomos* of 1955.[23] Andresen has convincingly shown that Celsus employed the same strategy as Justin, although

---

21 My references to Celsus indicate passages in Or. *C. Cels.*, cited usually in Chadwick's English translation, *Origen: Contra Celsum*. For the Greek text of Origen I have relied on Borret, *Origène contre Celse*.
22 *Un conservateur au second siècle*, 272–3 and 413–19.
23 *Logos und Nomos*, see esp. 345–72.

with completely opposite results. Whereas Justin claimed that the most important Greek philosophical doctrines were derived from what Moses and the prophets taught, Celsus argued that Christian beliefs and practices were nothing other than 'misunderstandings', 'counterfeits' and 'corruptions' of Greek philosophy. For example, Justin had contended that the Stoic theory of periodic cataclysms and conflagrations was a misunderstanding of what Moses had written about Noah and the flood and the fire of God's eschatological judgement.[24] To this Celsus responded that it was Moses who misunderstood the Greeks: the account of Noah's flood was a 'counterfeit' of the myth of Deucalion, and the idea of the fire of God's judgement was a 'misunderstanding of the doctrines of the Greeks and barbarians'.[25] In the manner of Justin, then, Celsus constructed a list of 'parallels' between the Bible and Greek philosophy and myth in order to demonstrate that Christianity was a 'counterfeit truth', and that the apparent similarities were at best a consequence of misunderstanding, and at worst outright corruption.[26]

Beyond individual points of intersection, it is the architecture of Celsus' argument that allows us to gain a sense of the potential cogency of Justin's project of presenting Christianity as the most ancient, and therefore only true, 'philosophy'. It is clear that Celsus will have none of it, but it is important to recognise that he does not reject the 'proof from antiquity' as *ipso facto* absurd. On the contrary, he accepts the argument as legitimate, indeed cogent, but he cleverly turns it back upon Christianity. This means that, however much they may have been at odds on specific points, they both shared a similar understanding of the history of philosophy. For Celsus, as indeed for Justin, it was evident that nothing could be both new *and* true. 'I have nothing new to say,' Celsus declared, 'but only ancient doctrines' (*C. Cels.* 4.14; cf. 2.4). Justin had asserted much the same thing in his *apologia* for Christianity. Celsus objected to Christianity not because it had borrowed from these 'ancient doctrines' but because it had 'misunderstood' them (*parakouein, C. Cels.* 3.16; 7.58), 'corrupted' them (*paraphtheirein, C. Cels.* 4.21; 7.58) and 'counterfeited' them (*paracharattein, C. Cels.* 4.41–42).[27] Moreover, according to Celsus, Christianity originated as a rebellion against Judaism, which itself was the creation of a revolutionary figure, Moses.[28] In contrast to Numenius' positive estimate of Moses as one

---

24 1 *Apol.* 60.8–9; 2 *Apol.* 7.23, identifying Noah with Deucalion.
25 *C. Cels.* 4.11, 41–2; cf. 1.19–20; 4.79.
26 Andresen has detected such an impressive number of contacts between Justin and Celsus that it seems almost certain that the latter was in fact responding to the former.
27 On this, see Andresen, *Logos und Nomos*, 146–9.
28 *C. Cels.* 2.1, 4, 6; 3.5; 5.33, 41.

of the earliest of the ancient barbarian sages, Celsus argued that it was Moses who incited the Jews to break away from their *native* Egypt,[29] and who taught them to reject the ancient theology in favour of a crude monotheism.[30] Despite its peculiarities, however, Judaism at least had the advantage of *antiquitas* on its side. About a half-century before Celsus, the Roman historian Tacitus had rendered a similar judgement: however alien the beliefs and practices of the Jews may be, they were upheld by their antiquity.[31] But not so Christianity. As far as Celsus was concerned, it had no tradition and hence no authority. Indeed, it stood at twice remove from the prevailing Graeco-Roman culture (*C. Cels.* 5.25–33).

The politics of monotheism

We have already encountered the notion of an 'ancient theology' in Nume-nius' interpretation of the history of philosophy. In the *Alēthēs logos* this idea receives its fullest expression. Whereas Justin had endeavoured to connect Christianity with this ancient theological tradition through the ancient books of Moses and the prophets, Celsus tried to drive a wedge between Christianity and this ancient tradition. 'There is an ancient doctrine (*archaios logos*),' Celsus wrote, 'which has existed from the beginning, which has always been main-tained by the wisest nations and cities and sages' (*C. Cels.* 1.14). Significantly, the list includes Greeks as well as 'barbarians': Egyptians, Assyrians, Indians, Per-sians, Odrysians, Samothracians and Eleusinians, as well as the Hyperboreans, Galactophagoi, Druids and Getae. Celsus also singles out such inspired the-ologians as Linus, Musaeus, Orpheus, Pherecydes, Zoroaster and Pythagoras, who 'understood this tradition and put down their doctrines *in books* which exist to this day' (*C. Cels.* 1.14, 16). Conspicuously absent from these lists are Moses and the Jews. Whereas Numenius had included them in his attempt to return to the origins of the tradition – from Plato to Pythagoras, and from Pythagoras to the Brahmans, Jews, magi and Egyptians – Celsus *excluded* them. In his view Moses and the Jews had misunderstood and deliberately distorted the *archaios logos* or 'ancient norm'. He writes,

> [Those] who followed Moses were deluded by clumsy deceits into thinking that there was only one god, and without any rational cause they abandoned the worship of many gods. [They] thought that there was one god called Most

---

29 *C. Cels.* 3.5; 4.31.
30 *C. Cels.* 1.21–4; 4.36; 5.41.
31 *Hist.* 5.5.1; on which see Stern, *Greek and Latin authors*, vol. II, 17–63.

High, or Adonai, or the Heavenly One, or Sabaoth . . . , and they acknowledge nothing more. But it makes no difference whether one calls the supreme God by the name used among the Greeks, or by that, for example, used among the Indians, or by that among the Egyptians (*C. Cels.* 1.23–4; cf. 5.41).

This quotation from Celsus sheds some light on what he means by an 'ancient tradition (or norm) that has existed from the beginning'. A feature of Greek philosophical theology in later antiquity was the attempt to reinterpret traditional religion in light of a form of monotheism.[32] Platonic philosophy from the time of Xenocrates held that the gods of popular religion were intermediary beings – *daimones* – negotiating between the one supreme God and the world of humankind. Similarly, the traditional deities of each *ethnos* or people were considered to be the subordinate assistants of this supreme God. In the Pseudo-Aristotelian *De mundo*, a text roughly contemporary with Justin and Celsus, this supreme deity was likened to the great king of Persia who delegated authority to generals, satraps and princes. The author writes: 'If it is beneath the dignity of Xerxes to appear himself to administer all things and to carry out his own wishes and superintend the government of his kingdom, such functions would still be less becoming for God' (398b). Celsus' contemporary, the rhetorician Maximus of Tyre, maintained that although different peoples ascribed different names to God, nevertheless, 'there is one uniform custom and doctrine (*nomos kai logos*) in all the earth, namely, that there is one God, the king and father of all, and many gods, sons of God, who rule together with him. This is believed by both Greek and barbarian alike.'[33] This is what informs Celsus' statement that 'it makes no difference whether we call Zeus the Most High, or Zen, or Adonai, or Sabaoth, or Amoun like the Egyptians, or Papaeus like the Scythians'.[34] The *De mundo* held that the supreme God controlled the universe through the *daimones*, drawing an analogy to Xerxes and the administration of the Persian empire. Celsus, a Roman imperialist, endorsed the same imperial myth, but drew the analogy home to Marcus Aurelius and the Roman empire, warning that: 'The satrap . . . or procurator of the Persian or Roman emperor . . . could do much harm if they were slighted. Would the satraps and procurators both in the air and on earth do but little harm if they were insulted?'[35]

---

32 See the discussion in Grant, *Gods and the one God*, 75–83; and the collection of essays in Athanassiadi and Frede (eds.), *Pagan monotheism*.
33 *Dialexeis* 11.5; cf. 39.5 (ed. Hobein).
34 *C. Cels.* 5.41; cf. 1.24.
35 *C. Cels.* 8.35. I owe this point to Edwards, 'Constantinian circle'.

Here it is important to note that what is at stake is not a conflict between 'Jewish (or Christian) monotheism' and 'pagan polytheism', but an attempt to distinguish between two different conceptions of monotheism – what John Dillon has called 'hard' and 'soft' monotheisms.[36]

> Soft monotheism, in the ancient Mediterranean context, is exemplified by the intellectualized version of traditional Greek religion to which most educated Greeks seem to have adhered from the fifth century BC on, according to which Zeus represents something like a supreme cosmic intellect, which can be referred to, more vaguely, as *ho theos* or *to theion*, but which is prepared to recognize also, on a lower level of reality, as it were, the full Olympic pantheon of traditional deities, and a host of little local gods as well, who can all be, if necessary, viewed as merely aspects of the supreme divinity, performing one or another specialized function.[37]

In Celsus' view, the 'hard monotheism' of the Jews represented a corruption of the true theology: 'Moses, although he heard of this doctrine, deceived his followers into thinking that there was only one God, *and no more*' (*C. Cels.* 1.21, 23–4). Yet, even though the Jews worshipped their own God as if he were the only one, at least they did so in accordance with their time-honoured native tradition. Their religion, as Celsus puts it, 'may be very peculiar, but at least it is traditional' (*C. Cels.* 5.25). The issue at stake here was not merely an arcane matter of theology, for there were potentially serious political and social consequences attached to these two types of monotheism. Celsus was a religious and social conservative who believed that the interests of a multicultural empire would best be served if the various subject peoples worshipped according to their own traditions, so long as they were willing to subscribe to a myth that all such worship was offered ultimately to the supreme God, or intellect, who oversaw the security and destiny of the empire. In such a context, 'hard monotheism' would be viewed not merely as deviant theologically; more importantly, it presented a political threat of a potentially revolutionary nature. To this extent, then, the Jews would always remain suspect in the judgement of a Celsus and those who subscribed to this imperial myth. The Jews' only salvation was their *antiquitas summa*.[38]

---

36 'Monotheism in Gnostic tradition'.
37 Dillon, 'Monotheism in Gnostic tradition', 69. Cf. e.g. Plotinus' contrast between the Greek and Christian conceptions of monotheism (*Enn.* 2.9.9).
38 Note e.g. the lengths to which Josephus went in the *Contra Apionem* to defend his *Antiquitates Judaicae* against detractors who claimed that the Jews were 'a people of recent origin' (*neōteron genos*); see Droge, 'Josephus between Greeks and barbarians', 115–42. The term *neōteron* can also bear the meaning 'strange' or 'unusual'; the plural, *ta neōtera* or *ta neōtera pragmata*, denotes 'rebellion' or 'violent revolution' (cf. the Latin *res novae*).

In comparison to Judaism, however, Christianity appeared far more dangerous, religiously *and* politically. For despite Justin's best efforts to manufacture a history for the new religion, Celsus insisted that Christianity had no native tradition to which it could legitimately appeal. 'I will ask them', Celsus writes, 'where they come from, or who is the author of their traditional laws. "Nobody!" they will say' (*C. Cels.* 5.33). Furthermore, the Christians rejected the worship of the intermediary *daimones* – the subordinate deities of the supreme cosmic God – citing the maxim of Jesus, 'No man can serve two masters.' For Celsus, this was a 'rebellious utterance of a people who have walled themselves off and broken away from the rest of humankind' (*C. Cels.* 8.2). In the face of this novel threat Celsus argues that 'soft monotheism' is the *Alēthēs logos* – 'The ancient norm' or 'The true tradition' – as he entitles his work. Following Wifstrand,[39] the title is best interpreted in connection with the *archaios logos* mentioned at *C. Cels.* 1.14 and 3.16 – a *theologia perennis* having been maintained by the most ancient nations, cities and sages, further developed and rendered precise by Plato, but later distorted by the Jews, and currently placed in jeopardy by the growing threat of Christianity.

Conclusion

Justin was no mere recorder of history; he was an inventor of it. 'Sometimes', as Bernard Lewis has written, 'the purpose of the inventors of history is not to legitimize authority but to undermine it – to assert new claims and new arguments, sometimes even a new identity, in conflict with the old order.'[40] But there is more. In staking his claim to the history of philosophy and Christianity's place in it, Justin was required to construct histories for 'paganism' and 'Judaism'. Justin was not merely spewing forth propaganda, though he was certainly not above it; in his *apologia* for Christianity, he was engaged in the construction of a Christian discourse, and, just as important, he was laying the groundwork for the very categories of 'Christianity', 'Judaism' and 'paganism'. For to claim that Moses and the prophets had inspired the Greek philosophers was to transform the heroes of Jewish tradition into 'Christian' philosophers, the scriptures into a Christian 'philosophical library' and Christianity itself into a 'philosophy'. It was also to leave open the possibility that some of the Greek philosophers themselves – Heraclitus and Socrates, for example – had actually been 'Christians' *avant la lettre*. In this project of persuasion Justin

39 'Die wahre Lehre des Kelsos'.
40 *History*, 64.

was no more recording history than he was reflecting an actually existing contemporary situation in which the borders between Christians, Jews and Greeks were clearly discernible. Rather, he was engaged in the very discursive practice that was endeavouring to bring them into existence. Both Justin *and* Celsus were labouring to produce and police the borders between Christians, Jews and Greeks – each with his own vested interest and both in the *political* context of the Roman empire – but 'their borders' were not nearly as clear as either of them would have his readers believe.

In a recent essay on the *Dialogue with Trypho*, entitled 'Justin Martyr invents Judaism', Daniel Boyarin applies Derrida's famous metaphor of Czechoslovakia and Poland to the historical situation of Jews and Christians in the second century. 'Like Czechoslovakia and Poland,' Boyarin writes, '[Jews and Christians] too resemble each other and regard each other; they are separated by a frontier that is abstract, legal, and ideal.'[41] Boyarin's application of Derrida's metaphor is revealing, but it remains incomplete unless we find a way to include the 'Greeks' as well, for Justin was inventing not only 'Christianity' and 'Judaism' in his *Dialogue with Trypho*. Let me emend the metaphor, then, by bringing it up to date: let us refer of the Czech Republic, Slovakia and Poland and apply this metaphorically to 'Christians', 'Jews' *and* 'Greeks' in the second century. To do so, is to appreciate the abstract, (il)legal, ideal, and, in a word, fabricated character of the borders Justin and Celsus were trying to draw. It is also to appreciate the high political stakes involved in their respective speech acts. Both Justin *and* Celsus were frontier guards, as it were,

> trying as best they could to police the border, and to check the passports of religious ideas and practices that wished to cross; but there were smugglers, people who respected no borders, nomads of religion [think, for example, of Numenius, a religious philosopher *sans frontières*], who kept crossing back and forth, transporting their contraband of religious goods and services.[42]

41 Boyarin, 'Justin Martyr invents Judaism', 456.
42 Boyarin, 'Justin Martyr invents Judaism', 456.

12

Self-differentiation among Christian groups: the Gnostics and their opponents

DAVID BRAKKE

When around 180 CE Bishop Irenaeus of Lyons wrote his *Detection and refutation of gnōsis falsely so-called*, known simply by the Latin title *Adversus haereses* ('Against heresies'), he hoped to bring order to a confused situation. A bewildering number of 'Christian' groups and teachers offered interested persons salvation, often in the form of *gnōsis* ('knowledge' or 'acquaintance') with God. Yet the teachings and practices of these 'Christians' displayed an astonishing diversity on such issues as the nature(s) of God and the creator of this world and the content and interpretation of scripture. Irenaeus presented his readers with a powerfully simple way to make sense of these competing claims.[1] There was, he argued, a single consistent Christian truth, deposited in a single church spread throughout the world in communities that could trace their heritage back to Christ and his original apostles. All other groups that claimed to be Christian, despite their seemingly infinite variety, in fact were manifestations of a single error, false *gnōsis*, which originated in a single teacher, Simon Magus (Acts 8:9–24). The clarity of Irenaeus' vision is so compelling that even today, after more than a century of scholarship undermining it, we moderns must exert great pains to see the Christianities of the second century in any other way.

To be sure, few scholars would now tell the story in precisely Irenaeus' terms. Most recognise that there was no single church from which Gnostic heretics deviated. Rather, Christian communities were diverse from the start, and it is probable that in some regions forms of Christianity that would later be labelled 'heresies' pre-dated those that might be identified as 'proto-orthodox'. Likewise, scholars question the assignment of numerous teachers, sects and texts to a single category of 'Gnosticism', the modern version of Irenaeus' '*gnōsis* falsely so-called', which prevents understanding of the diverse teachings of such figures as Basilides, Marcion and Valentinus.[2] The several so-called

---

1 Cf. ch. 13, below.
2 Williams, *Rethinking 'Gnosticism'*.

'Gnostic' groups did not share a single point of origin, whether Simon Magus, as Irenaeus claimed, or a pre-Christian 'Gnostic redeemer myth', as some modern scholars once thought. Perhaps the reigning non-Irenaean paradigm for understanding the second-century 'crisis of Gnosticism' resembles viewing a horse race the outcome of which one already knows. Numerous independent Christian communities, none with a fully convincing claim to exclusive authenticity as 'true Christianity', emerge from the fog of c.100 CE and jostle for position; in hindsight, we can identify the 'horse' that will emerge as the dominant orthodoxy by the end of the third century, and we watch it as it competes with and overcomes its rivals.[3]

Even this approach, although a decided improvement on Irenaeus', nonetheless retains distorting elements of the great heresiologist's vision. Self-differentiation remains a simple bilateral process between a single, albeit non-privileged, proto-orthodox self and multiple other selves who are diverse, yet equally not orthodox. This simple opposition obscures the diversity not only among proto-orthodoxy's others, but also among different representatives of the allegedly single proto-orthodox self. In several important respects, proto-orthodox teachers, such as Justin Martyr and Clement of Alexandria, were more akin to Valentinus than to Irenaeus. Christian – and, for that matter, Jewish – self-differentiation in this period was always a multilateral affair and resulted in diverse forms of Christian thought and practice. The inclusion of these varied modes of Christian piety in the single category of 'orthodoxy' was in fact the achievement of the post-Constantinian imperial church and even then was never full or complete, but always partial and contested. The student of any single Christian thinker (or group) of the second or third centuries must detect the multiple strategies by which he negotiated his relationships with a range of contemporaries – 'Jewish', 'Christian' and 'pagan' – and how these contemporaries responded to him as well.[4]

Changing approaches to 'Gnosticism' and the 'Gnostics'

Adolf von Harnack's definition of Gnosticism as 'the acute Hellenization of Christianity' may have been the culmination of the modern attempt to

---

3 Cf. Rousseau, *Pachomius*, 19.
4 E.g. on Clement of Alexandria: Buell, *Making Christians*; Dawson, *Allegorical readers*, 183–284. For differentiation from 'Judaism', an important subplot to the story told here, see ch. 10, above.

understand Gnosticism within a modified version of the Irenaean paradigm.[5] The Cambridge Platonist Henry Moore initiated this trajectory in 1669 when he coined the English word 'Gnosticism', under which he and subsequent scholars gathered nearly all the groups attacked by Irenaeus and his heresiological successors.[6] But this modern version of Gnosticism as heretical distortion of Christian orthodoxy gave way to the fresh approach of the German History of Religions school (*Religionsgeschichtliche Schule*), which dominated scholarship during most of the twentieth century and treated *Gnosis* (the German equivalent of the English 'Gnosticism') as a religion independent of Christianity. Such scholars as Wilhelm Bousset and Rudolf Bultmann traced the diverse motifs of Gnostic myths back to a single Primal Man myth that originated in India and travelled west into the Mediterranean basin through Persia; rather than an aberration from Christianity, Gnosticism was a competitor with it and, through its 'redeemer myth', a profound influence on it.[7] Although he eschewed the motif tracing of the history of religions scholars, Hans Jonas' classic *The Gnostic religion* interpreted Gnosticism as an independent world-view that expressed alienation and sought salvation in transcendence.[8] Disenchanted with the notion that one has understood a religious symbol when one has traced it to its origin, most scholars eventually turned away from the history of religions approach, which had relied on flawed dating of texts and constructed an ancient religion ('Gnosticism') with which no ancient person, even Irenaeus, would have been familiar. Still, a few scholars continue to speak of an ancient 'Gnostic religion', now often seen as originating in 'heterodox Judaism' rather than in Persia.[9]

Most contemporary scholars, however, take one of three approaches to the groups and myths that their predecessors had seen as manifestations of the religion 'Gnosticism'. Some continue to work with a category 'Gnosis' or 'Gnosticism', which they understand to be a modern typological construction designed to group together 'phenomena with related content'.[10] Movements that share certain characteristics – e.g. a distant supreme God, a lower creator God described as ignorant or evil, dualistic anthropology – are gathered under the rubric 'Gnosis', which then includes most of the persons and groups

---

5 Harnack, *Dogmengeschichte*. For the history of scholarship, see King, *What is Gnosticism?*
6 Layton, 'Prolegomena', 348–9.
7 Bousset, *Hauptprobleme*; Bultmann, 'Religionsgeschichtliche Hintergrund' and *Primitive Christianity*.
8 Jonas, *Gnostic Religion*.
9 Pearson, *Gnosticism, Judaism, and Egyptian Christianity*.
10 Markschies, *Gnosis*, 15.

that Irenaeus opposed, as well as Manichaeism.[11] Critics of the typological approach charge that it homogenises and distorts the groups gathered into its model by elevating certain of their features to 'defining characteristics', includes materials that seldom if ever evince all of the shared characteristics, and creates a reified religion, 'Gnosticism', even if its proponents understand it to be a modern category.[12] Some of these scholars propose dispensing with both the modern category 'Gnosticism' and the ancient term 'Gnostic' altogether and interpreting the texts that survive from antiquity on their own terms and without reference to these notions.[13]

A third approach agrees with the abandonment of the modern category 'Gnosticism' but notes that some ancient authors, especially Irenaeus, appear to have used the term 'Gnostic' (gnōstikos) with precision, to refer to a specific 'school of thought' or 'sect' (hairesis) that existed during the second and later centuries and adhered to a distinct myth of origins (Iren. Haer. 1.29 (–31?)).[14] Because Adam's son Seth is a prominent character in the myth, modern scholars have sometimes called the sect 'Sethian Gnostics'. This group did not include other figures and sects that modern scholars have called 'Gnostic', such as Basilides, Marcion and the Carpocratians. Valentinus and his followers adapted the myth of the Gnostics but otherwise formed a distinct Christian theological tradition. The claim to offer gnōsis, shared by the sect with many other groups in antiquity, was not distinctive of it.

Such is the approach of this essay, which will place at the beginning of its narrative the gnōstikē hairesis or 'Gnostic school of thought' and then describe the diverse strategies of self-differentiation that it used and elicited. Although this movement was probably never very large and did not reach the level of social cohesion and theological depth that the Valentinian school displayed, its mythology, approach to Jewish scriptures and modes of spirituality exerted on other forms of Christianity a profound influence that belies its size and justifies its prominent place in the Christian imagination of past and present. Christians developed diverse accounts of human salvation, practices of biblical interpretation, disciplinary procedures and modes of authority in part in response to this remarkable sect.

---

11 Most recently Markschies, Gnosis, but more famous is the definition of 'Gnosticism' proposed by a 1966 colloquium at Messina (Bianchi, Origini dello gnosticismo).
12 Williams, Rethinking 'Gnosticism', 43–50; King, What is Gnosticism?, 191–217, 225–7.
13 So Williams, Rethinking 'Gnosticism', and perhaps King, What is Gnosticism?
14 Layton, 'Prolegomena'; Logan, 'Gnosticism'; Edwards, 'Neglected texts'.

The Gnostic school of thought: self-differentiation through biblical mythology

The earliest reference to the 'Gnostic school of thought' (*gnōstikē hairesis*), whose members were known as 'Gnostics' (*gnōstikoi*), comes from Irenaeus *c*.180 CE. He reports that 'Valentinus adapted the fundamental principles of the so-called Gnostic school of thought to his own kind of system' (*Haer.* 1.11.1) and gives a summary of a myth that the Gnostics taught (*Haer.* 1.29 (–31?)), which appears also in *The secret book according to John* (*Ap. John*). They appear as a Christian group (a false one, according to Irenaeus) in whose mythology the pre-existent Christ plays a significant role. Our next sighting of these Gnostics is around the middle of the third century when they appear as rivals of the philosopher Plotinus (205–69/70): Porphyry, Plotinus' biographer, identifies the Gnostics as Christians and 'members of a school of thought' (*hairetikoi*) (*Vit. Plot.* 16). Porphyry lists a number of the Gnostics' writings, three of which – *Zostrianos* (*Zost.*), *Foreigner* (*Allogenes*), and the *Book of Zoroaster* (excerpted in *Ap. John*) – were among the texts discovered in 1945 and show dependence on the same myth recounted in *Ap. John*. In the fourth century (*c*.375), bishop Epiphanius of Salamis describes several groups that seem to share this myth, assigning to them multiple names ('Sethians', 'Archontics', as well as 'Gnostics') and social identities that range from desert monastics (Epiph. *Pan.* 40.1.1–8) to licentious, cannibalistic cults (26.3.3–17.9). These reports enable us to identify as the literary remains of the Gnostic movement a set of fourteen ancient works that share the sect's distinctive mythology.[15]

The Gnostic myth was a bold attempt to explain the origin and fate of the universe through a combination of the Jewish scriptures, Platonist mythological speculation and revelatory meditations on the structure of the human mind. Like most philosophy of the period, this cosmological speculation had a therapeutic purpose: to reconnect the human intellect with the source of its being and to ameliorate its condition of attachment to the body and its passions. The myth's ultimate God is unknowable and beyond description,

---

15 Layton, 'Prolegomena', building on Schenke, 'Das sethianische System' and 'Phenomenon and significance', as well as McGuire, 'Valentinus and the *gnōstikē hairesis*'. The fourteen works are *Ap. John*, *Zost.*, *Allogenes*, *The Book of Zoroaster* (as excerpted in *Ap. John*), *The Revelation of Adam* (*Apoc. Adam*), *The Reality of the Rulers* (*Hyp. Arch.*), *First Thought in Three Forms* (*Trim. Prot.*), *Thunder: Perfect Intellect* (*Thund.*), *The Egyptian Gospel* (*Gos. Eg.*), *The Three Tablets of Seth* (*Steles Seth*), *Marsanes*, *Melchizedek* (*Melch.*), *The Thought of Norea* (*Norea*), and the untitled treatise in the Bruce Codex. For attempts to chart the history of this literature, see Logan, *Gnostic truth*, and Turner, 'Sethian Gnosticism'.

yet its nature is to think, and this thinking resulted in a devolution of God into an 'entirety' with a complex structure of 'aeons', which are simultaneously actors, places, extents of time and modes of thought. In contrast to the spiritual entirety, this world was 'corporeal darkness' (*Zost.* 1:11–13), yet the enlightened person could experience divine stability and eternity through a process of mystical contemplation variously described as a heavenly ascent, an interior withdrawal or both. The portion of Gnostic myth most explicitly based on the Bible explained both how the human intellect found itself in this unhappy situation and how the potential for reunion with the divine persisted from the origins of time. Gnostics read the opening chapters of Genesis as a confused account of how the divine potentiality came into this world and how it survived the various attempts of the demonic forces to seize or eliminate it. The myth identified the creator of this world as a false version of divinity named Ialdabaoth, who was both the 'craftsman' (*dēmiourgos*) of Plato's *Timaeus* and the 'God' of Moses' Genesis. The final return of the lost power to the entirety and the consequent destruction of the lower universe and its rulers would follow the appearance of a saviour (the Forethought of the Entirety or the Great Seth), usually understood as present in Jesus, who would awaken Gnostics to the divine potential within them and teach them how to escape the malevolent forces of this world. Gnostic literature makes this message of awakening available to readers.

Although surviving Gnostic literature is primarily pseudepigraphic mythology, allowing little room for overt references to contemporary persons or events, it does exhibit strategies by which the Gnostics differentiated themselves from other groups. Since Gnostics differed with their competitors precisely on how to appropriate the biblical narrative in the wake of the Jesus event, most of these strategies revolved around the interpretation of the Bible. The Gnostics claimed authority for their readings primarily by appealing to sources of special divine revelation. In *Ap. John* 'the saviour' reveals the existence of the higher entirety and the true meaning of Genesis to the disciple John 'mystically' (II 32:2) in a post-ascension appearance. More typical is a revelation from a character in the biblical narrative – Adam (*Ap. Adam*), Seth (*Gos. Eg.*) or the exclusively Gnostic character Norea (*Hyp. Arch.*); after the manner of other apocalypses, the revelation is purported to have been written down and preserved secretly until the present eschatological moment. No contemporary Gnostic teacher claims his or her own interpretive authority, divine inspiration or superior education in biblical exegesis: readings are true because a divine being or divinely inspired person from the past spoke them. Despite this pseudepigraphic mode of exposition, Gnostic authors at times reveal their competition with other readers in their milieu. For example, in *Ap. John*, the saviour's statements to John that what happened 'is not as you have heard that Moses wrote' (II 22–3; cf. 13:19–21; 29:6–7) indicate the existence of a generally accepted reading that the author expects his audience to know.

Some Gnostic authors found in biblical characters or groups representatives or prototypes of contemporary persons, especially themselves,[16] and thus used the language of race and kinship to delineate themselves and other groups. The proper name of the sect was the 'Gnostic school of the thought' (*gnōstikē hairesis*), a self-promotional designation that identified it as that school of thought capable of supplying 'knowledge' (*gnōsis*). But the gnostics' terms for themselves as the ideal religious people were racial or ethnic: 'the immovable race', 'the seed of Seth', 'Those People'.[17] Such language drew both on the genealogically oriented narratives of the early chapters of Genesis and on the wider ancient practice of using ethnic or kinship language for groups that shared the same religious practices (or of seeing religious practice as part of the definition of a nation or kinship group).[18] Opponents of the Gnostics interpreted this language to mean that the Gnostics considered religious identities to be predetermined and fixed: Gnostics, as the seed of Seth, were saved 'by nature'; all other people, destined for destruction 'by nature'. But in general the use of ethnic or kinship language to speak of religious identity in antiquity did not necessarily imply such deterministic beliefs: ancient people could imagine persons moving from one 'nation' to another.[19] And in this case several Gnostic texts appear to assume that people can choose to become a Gnostic and to leave after they have joined the sect.[20] A ritual of baptism may have incorporated a person into the seed of Seth or immovable race.[21]

Responses to the Gnostic sect: heresiology, theology and authority

The Christian authors whose works provide the best evidence of self-differentiation from the Gnostic sect – Clement of Alexandria, Irenaeus, Origen and the Valentinians – inherited, adapted and supplemented a set of strategies that were developed in Rome in the early 140s by persons whose works survive much less completely than those of their successors. Marcion, Valentinus

16 Brakke, 'Seed of Seth'.
17 Layton, 'Prolegomena', 336–9.
18 Buell, 'Relevance of race', 458–66.
19 Buell, 'Relevance of race', 466–72.
20 Williams, *Rethinking 'Gnosticism'*, 189–212.
21 Sevrin, *Le dossier baptismal Séthien*.

and Justin Martyr all were active in Rome before 150 and must have known the teachings of each other and of the Gnostics. Working in the 'fractionated' environment of Roman Christianity, which lacked a single authoritative church structure able or concerned to manage diversity, each developed responses to the teachings of the Gnostic sect that not only attacked that group but also set in motion new patterns of self-differentiation that shaped Christian identities for centuries.[22]

Because none of his works survive, it cannot be proved that Marcion knew and responded to Gnostics, but such contact seems highly probable in the very small subculture of 'Christians'. Marcion's teachings offered a dramatically streamlined alternative to the Gnostic system – a Creator God who was not demonic, but merely oppressively righteous, and a Bible that excluded (rather than rewrote) the Septuagint.[23] Marcion advocated a reform that, in contrast to the Gnostics' conflicted yet engaged relationship with Jewish tradition, would more fully separate Christianity from emerging Judaism and, in response to Christian diversity in Rome, would articulate clear criteria for distinguishing true from false Christian teaching. Unable to persuade the leaders of Rome's varied Christian groups ('presbyters and teachers') to follow his programme in the summer of 144, Marcion formed his own organisation, and Marcionite churches spread throughout the Roman empire and persisted for centuries.[24]

Valentinus likewise articulated a theology that was more distinctly Christian than that of the Gnostics, but did so in part by adapting and transforming the Gnostic myth.[25] The few works that survive from this brilliant thinker suggest a less elaborate and more christocentric myth than that of the Gnostics.[26] Two fragments in particular show Valentinus in dialogue with Gnostic accounts of the creation of Adam (Clem. Al. *Str.* 2.36; 4.89–90; Layton's fragments C and D); in comparison, Valentinus emphasised the role of the Son or Word (*logos*) in depositing a share of the higher essence in Adam, and he ameliorated the antagonism between the first human being and his creators.[27] Likewise, he made more extensive use of the writings that were coming to form the canon of the New Testament: Valentinus' language, especially in his sermon *The gospel of truth*, is saturated with New Testament citations and allusions. Unlike

---

22 On 'fractionation' in second-century Roman Christianity and its effects, see Lampe, *Paul to Valentinus*, and Thomassen, 'Orthodoxy and heresy' and pt iv, ch. 22, below.

23 The classic study is Harnack, *Marcion*. Few scholars continue to call Marcion a 'Gnostic'; see ch. 9, above.

24 So Epiph. *Pan.* 42.1–2, on which see Lampe, *Paul to Valentinus*, 393, and Thomassen, 'Orthodoxy and heresy'.

25 McGuire, 'Valentinus and the *gnōstikē hairesis*', Dawson, *Allegorical readers*, 127–82.

26 Layton, *Scriptures*, 217–64. On *The gospel of truth*, see Standaert, 'L'évangile de vérité'.

27 McGuire, 'Valentinus and the *gnōstikē hairesis*', 224–30.

the Gnostics' use of pseudonymous apocalypses, Valentinus invoked his own mystical authority: according to Hippolytus of Rome, Valentinus had a visionary experience in which the Word appeared as 'a newborn babe' (Hipp. *Haer.* 6.42.2; Layton's fragment A); Valentinus himself announced, 'I have been in the place of repose' (*Gos. Truth* 43.1). His students further promoted his authority as a Christian philosopher by claiming that he had been a student of Theudas, a disciple of Paul (Clem. Al. *Str.* 7.17).[28] By all accounts, Valentinus was highly gifted, intellectually and rhetorically; his teachings, as fragmentarily as we can know them, cannot be reduced to 'Gnostic', for he drew on a range of materials, including mainstream Platonism and the emerging New Testament.[29] Still, Valentinus did, as Irenaeus claimed, 'adapt' the Gnostic myth into something more distinctively Christian and more recognisably philosophical.

Justin also presented himself as a philosopher (*Dial.* 1–3), teaching within a tradition that extended back to the appearance of God's Word in Jesus; unlike Valentinus, however, Justin did not adapt the Gnostic myth, but rejected it as a demonic invention and in the process of rejecting it invented 'heresy'.[30] Long before Justin some of the earliest Christian leaders were aware of diversity in their movement and sought to contain it, at times employing the term *hairēsis* ('sect', 'school of thought' or 'faction') (1 Cor 11:19; Gal 5:20; 2 Pet 2:1; Ign. *Eph.* 6.2). Ignatius contrasted the 'foreign plant' of *hairesis* with 'Christian food' (*Trall.* 6.1). The author of 1 Timothy attributed some false teachings to demons (1 Tim 4:1) and warned against 'what is falsely called *gnōsis*' (1 Tim 6:20) (from which Irenaeus got the title of his book). How much of this literature was known to Justin is not clear; he may have learned from these predecessors the negative sense of *hairesis* (*Dial.* 35). But while the earlier works provided some of its language and imagery, heresiology originated within a wider discourse concerning universalism and particular identity in the second-century eastern Mediterranean and within the subculture of philosophical schools in which Justin worked.[31]

When the Gnostics called themselves the *gnōstikē hairesis*, they doubtless used the term *hairesis* in its neutral philosophical sense of 'school of thought', indicating shared allegiance to a set of doctrines or to an original teacher.[32]

---

28 Basilides, an older contemporary of Valentinus, traced his academic lineage to Peter through his teacher Glaucias (Layton, 'Significance of Basilides', 146).
29 Markschies, *Valentinus*, argues that Valentinus was not a Gnostic because his teachings do not fit such typological definitions as that of the Messina colloquium. Rather, Valentinus 'prepares the way for the great systems of "gnosis"' (*Gnosis*, 89–90).
30 Le Boulluec, *La notion d'hérésie*, vol. 1, 36–91.
31 Le Boulluec, *La notion d'hérésie*; Lyman, 'Hellenism and heresy'.
32 On this usage see von Staden, 'Hairesis and heresy'.

This notion could carry with it the idea of a succession of teachers, who passed on and developed the insights of the original master(s). As we have seen, the Gnostics tended to eschew this mode of philosophical authentication, relying instead on revelations to authoritative figures of the past, but Valentinus (or at least his students), it seems, did appeal to some sort of academic succession. Justin likewise used the term *hairesis* in the sense of 'school of thought' – not in a neutral way, however, but completely negatively, and he composed a now lost work entitled *Against all the schools of thoughts that have arisen* (1 *Apol.* 26). It was by combining the philosophical concept of 'school of thought' – and its associated notions of named teachers and successions – with the Christian distrust of 'factions' as 'foreign' and even demonic that Justin put in place the essential elements of heresiology.

Justin argued that even if 'schools of thought' or, as we may now put it, 'heresies' were 'called Christians', they were in fact not so, but the creations of demons; in a degraded form of academic succession, they could be traced back through named teachers to Simon Magus (Acts 8:9–24).[33] Justin placed among the 'heretics' his contemporaries in Rome, Marcion and Valentinus (1 *Apol.* 26; cf. *Dial.* 35, 80). Justin's demonically inspired succession of heretics opposed the work of God's Word, which had sown portions of himself in pre-Christian philosophers such as Socrates, but which had appeared whole in Jesus and which true Christians now 'have' (2 *Apol.* 10, 13). Justin's 'heresy' was a demonic counterfeit both of wholly true Christianity and of its imperfectly true relative, philosophy.[34] Justin thus initiated one of the most powerful tools by which proto-orthodox Christians differentiated themselves from competing groups – heresiology, the cataloguing of 'heresies' in a perverse succession in order to demonise and trivialise them.[35] As an independent teacher, however, Justin lacked any authority to enforce his views on true and false belief on other groups in the city.

Marcion, Valentinus and Justin developed a set of responses to the Gnostic sect and/or each other that their successors borrowed and developed. These strategies ranged from outright rejection through heresiological rhetoric and withdrawal of fellowship, to adaptation and Christianisation of the Gnostic myth, to more personalised or philosophical modes of authority. Figures such as Clement of Alexandria, Ptolemy the Valentinian, Irenaeus of Lyons and Origen adapted one or more of these strategies and added ones of their own, as Christian groups multiplied and developed more complex structures.

33 King, *What is Gnosticism?*, 23–4.
34 Lyman, 'Hellenism and heresy', 218.
35 Layton, 'Significance of Basilides'.

Irenaeus took over Justin's heresiological model so successfully that Christian scribes stopped copying Justin's *Against all the schools of thought*. However, unlike Justin the independent philosopher, Irenaeus the bishop portrayed the episcopate as the holy counterpart to the demonic succession of heretics. True bishops claimed to trace their lineage back to one of the original apostles (*Haer.* 3.2–3), adopting a strategy of legitimation first deployed by figures such as Basilides and Valentinus. In response to Gnostic retellings of the Septuagint and to Marcion's rejection of it, Irenaeus promoted an embryonic biblical canon, consisting of two parts, an Old and a New Testament, with four gospels (*Haer.* 3.11; 4.9), and interpreted the Old Testament typologically to demonstrate the unity of the two parts and the single identity of their God. He argued that the Bible's overarching 'plot line' (*hypothesis*) was not the Gnostics' myth of cosmic devolution and return but the story of the single God of Israel's relationship with humanity, summarised in a 'rule of faith' (*Haer.* 1.8–10; 3.11).[36] Christ himself had delivered this rule to his apostles, who transmitted it to the bishops who followed them; thus, the rule was the same throughout the one church (*Haer.* 1.10; 3.2–4). Irenaeus faced a multitude of rival Christianities, not just the Gnostics, and emphasised the unity and consistency of the one church in contrast to the multiplicity and diversity of his opponents; his narrative of a decline from an original period of unity and truth paralleled the Gnostic myth of a fall from an original spiritual unity. Justin's heresiological model of multiple heretical teachers originating in a single source facilitated this representation.

In Irenaeus' programme, the bishop was responsible for enforcing with practical measures the truth that he received from the apostles. Differentiation from rival Christian groups was only one factor in the emergence of the monarchical episcopate, but it was an important one.[37] Bishop Victor of Rome (*c.*189–99) may serve as one example of the Irenaean paradigm in action.[38] Before Victor the diverse Christian groups in Rome usually tolerated one another and expressed their unity by sending tokens of the eucharistic elements to one another. Victor at first acted within this tradition, recognising representatives of the New Prophecy movement ('Montanism') as legitimate Christians and the Valentinian Florinus as one of his presbyters. The existence of multiple house churches hindered any simple bilateral division of 'orthodox' from

---

36 Young, *Biblical exegesis*, 19–21; Kugel and Greer, *Early biblical interpretation*, 155–76; Norris, 'Insufficiency'.
37 See ch. 14, below.
38 See Lampe, *Paul to Valentinus*, 385–96.

'others'.[39] But Irenaeus, writing from Lyons, exhorted Victor to 'expel' Florinus' writings as 'blasphemy', particularly dangerous for Christians because Florinus could claim to be 'one of you', that is, one of Victor's circle; the Christian teacher Praxeas, recently arrived from Asia Minor, likewise urged the Roman bishop to withdraw fellowship from the adherents of the New Prophecy. Victor took these actions and cut off fellowship also with another Christian teacher, Theodotus, the shoemaker.[40] Because the bishop's authority was closely tied to the eucharist over which he presided, the withdrawal of communion served him as a primary means of establishing boundaries between his own and rival Christian groups.

The immediate target of Irenaeus' heresiological work was the Valentinian school, which established itself as an attractive, more explicitly Christian alternative to the Gnostics. Valentinian teachers accepted and participated in the emerging network of episcopally led communities represented by Irenaeus and Victor, as Florinus illustrates. Adopting the character of philosophical schools, they formed study circles that existed alongside and open to other Christian groups and traced their lineage through Valentinus to Paul.[41] The Valentinian teacher Ptolemy suggested to the Christian Flora that she might be 'deemed worthy of the apostolic tradition, which even we have received by succession . . . at least if, like good rich soil that has received fertile seeds, you bear fruit' (Epiph. *Pan.* 33.7.9–10). Publishing some of the earliest known biblical commentaries and using allegorical methods, Valentinians presented their teachings as a deeper understanding of the scriptures and creeds used by most Christians. Valentinians did not refer to themselves in philosophical jargon ('Gnostics') or in genetic, racial terms ('seed of Seth'), but in Pauline language (1 Cor 2:13–16): they were those whom Paul called 'spiritual ones' (*pneumatikoi*); non-Valentinian Christians were merely 'animate' (*psychikoi*), yet worthy of their own form of salvation. The Valentinians offered a mythically based *gnōsis* akin to that of the Gnostics, but in a mode that was more explicitly Christian, and they expressed an openness to other Christians, in whom they took a pastoral interest. For Irenaeus they were wolves in sheeps' clothing (*Haer.* pref. 2), far more dangerous than the Gnostics.

In Alexandria, Clement and Origen resembled Valentinian teachers in that they offered small groups of students the opportunity to advance spiritually

---

39 Compare early third-century Carthage (Tabbernee, 'To pardon').
40 Victor and Florinus: Iren. *Frag. Syr.* 28 (in *Libros quique adversus haereses*, Harvey (ed.), vol. II, 457); Euseb. *HE* 5.15, 20. Victor and New Prophecy: Tert. *Prax.* 1. Victor and Theodotus: Euseb. *HE* 5.28.6, 9.
41 Markschies, 'Valentinian Gnosticism'.

in the study of Christian scriptures and doctrines, but each endeavoured to differentiate himself from his competitors and to stake out some relationship to the emerging network of episcopally led communities. Although Eusebius later domesticated him by making him the head of a catechetical school formally tied to the episcopate (*HE* 6.6), Clement more likely operated as a fully independent Christian teacher.[42] He challenged Gnostics and Valentinians at their own game by calling his ideal Christian 'the Gnostic, properly speaking' (*Str.* 1.13.58.2) and referring to his competitors as 'falsely named' (*Str.* 4.4.17.4). He countered the Gnostic use of genealogical and racial language to define themselves through his own use of procreative and kinship metaphors to authorise his own teachings and to delegitimate those of his rivals.[43] '*Gnōsis* itself', he argued, 'has come down by succession to a few people, transmitted by the apostles in unwritten form' (*Str.* 6.7.61.3). Echoing Ptolemy, Clement claimed that his teachers 'preserved the true tradition of the blessed doctrine in direct line from Peter, James, John and Paul, the holy apostles, child inheriting from father . . . and came with God's help to plant in us those ancestral and apostolic seeds' (*Str.* 1.1.11.3).[44] Clement pointedly did not trace his academic lineage to a single apostle, but to four, and did not name the teachers who intervened between these apostles and himself, thereby portraying himself, in contrast to his Valentinian and other competitors, as possessing not a particular strain of Christian teaching, but the fullness of apostolic teaching, transmitted in an academic succession beyond scrutiny.[45]

Clement exhibited an attitude towards episcopally supervised Christian communities that resembled that of the Valentinians in its ambivalent openness. Professing his adherence to the teachings of the wider church, Clement nonetheless offered his students a form of secret knowledge passed down not through bishops, but through his unnamed teachers (*Str.* 1.1.11–13); he made use of a range of sacred literature that belies the notion of a closed canon and very seldom referred to bishops and their communities.[46] He pointedly claimed that the person who 'has lived perfectly and gnostically' is 'really a presbyter of the church' even if 'he has not been ordained by human beings' (*Str.* 6.13.106.1–2). Clement differentiated himself on at least two fronts. On the one hand, he portrayed his 'domesticated *gnōsis*' as more faithful to original Christian doctrine than that offered by competing teachers.[47] On the other

42 Bardy, 'Aux origines de l'école d'Alexandrie'; Dawson, *Allegorical readers*, 219–22.
43 Buell, *Making Christians*.
44 Buell, *Making Christians*, 66–8, whose translation I have adapted.
45 Buell, *Making Christians*, 84–6.
46 On Clement's and Origen's semi-bounded canons, see Hanson, *Origen's doctrine*, 127–73.
47 Dawson, *Allegorical readers*, 222.

hand, he defended his philosophical speculation and advanced instruction of 'Gnostics' against 'those who are called orthodox' and who insisted on 'the bare faith alone' (*Str.* 1.9.43–5).

Origen, in contrast, clearly presented himself as a man of the church and eventually joined the clergy, but he too placed a high value on the Christian's advancement in study and discipline. After the martyrdom of his father, the brilliant young Origen made his way into the salons of wealthy and intellectually inclined Christians in Alexandria, an environment dominated by 'heretical' teachers, mainly Valentinians. Origen engaged these rivals in intellectual give-and-take, but would not worship with them (Euseb. *HE* 6.2). He worked, particularly in his *First principles*, to create a Christian 'body' (*sōma*) of thought (*Princ.* praef. 10) that could compete with those of the Gnostics and Valentinians. Like Irenaeus, Origen relied on a rule of faith – 'the teaching of the church, handed down in unbroken succession from the apostles' – to confront the 'conflicting opinions' held by professed Christians, but unlike the bishop of Lyons, he believed that the apostles deliberately left some teachings vague or unsubstantiated, so that 'lovers of wisdom,' teachers like himself and his students, would have material with which to speculate and so 'display the fruit of their ability' (*Princ.* praef. 2–3). Like the Gnostic myth, Origen's Christian story was one of a fall from an original state of spiritual unity, into a material universe marred by evil, concluding with a return of all things to God; but Origen did not assign creation to a lower God, and he placed free will at the centre of his narrative. All rational beings fell from unity with God due to their own free turning away; the bodies that they now have do not enslave them to cosmic forces but provide them with an opportunity for education in virtue.

Origen presented his views as his Valentinian rivals did – in scriptural commentaries filled with allegorical exegesis. In his *Commentary on John* Origen quoted and refuted interpretations that the Valentinian Heracleon had offered in his own similar work. Origen did not dismiss Heracleon's readings out of hand, but criticised him for proffering interpretations that did not appear substantiated by the wording of the text, for failing to consult passages from other biblical books to clarify the possible references of words and phrases in John, and for introducing doctrines that conflicted with the church's 'rule' (*Comm. Jo.* 2.100; 2.137–8; 6.109; 13.57–73; 13.98; 13.107–8).[48] Other allegorical readers he criticised for simple lack of expertise: they were 'unable to define precisely a simple ambiguity' (6.116). Elsewhere Origen condemned Jews and Christian 'heretics' who did not read the Old Testament 'according to the spiritual

---

48 See Young, *Biblical exegesis*, 130–9.

meaning but according to the bare letter' and so reached unacceptable theological conclusions (*Princ.* 4.2.2). But, in the case of allegorists such as Heracleon, the primary contrast Origen drew between himself and 'heretical' readers was his adherence to the church's rule; without such adherence, an exegete such as Heracleon simply interpreted incorrectly.

As he taught in Alexandria and especially after he moved to Caesarea Maritima and began to preach as a presbyter, Origen sought to address a variety of constituencies, ranging from ordinary churchgoers who could not read, to the educated (and not so educated) bishops who sought his theological expertise, to the aristocratic patrons who paid for his library and teams of scribes. Meanwhile, like his contemporary Victor of Rome, bishop Demetrius of Alexandria claimed increasingly broad powers to enforce doctrine and practice among Christians in his city. Negotiating his place in a changing and diverse church, Origen articulated a model of authority akin to that of Valentinus: the ideal Christian leader, whether bishop or teacher, received the gift (*charisma*) of insight into the higher meaning of scripture. Origen observed that the spiritually gifted person, the real bishop, was not always the visible bishop (*Hom. Num.* 2.1), and indeed Demetrius eventually expelled Origen from the Alexandrian church. Still, as a presbyter Origen found a place in the church of Caesarea and was able to bring into or alongside the episcopally led community a conception of charismatic authority that challenged claims based solely on office.[49]

Self-differentiation and the diversity of orthodoxy

The religious environment that the Gnostic school of thought faced in the third century differed markedly from that of the period in which it had originated. The line between 'Judaism' and 'Christianity' had become much clearer: in comparison to the Gnostics, teachers such as Justin, Valentinus, Clement and Origen made Jesus Christ more central to their theologies, and they made greater use of the Christian scriptures that would form the New Testament. The Valentinians and Origen retained elements of the Gnostic myth, but in ways that better cohered with a Christianity clearly distinct from Judaism. In response to Gnostic pseudepigraphy, genealogical rhetoric and theological claims, Christian leaders developed a repertoire of strategies of self-differentiation: (1) modes of personalised authority, expressed in claims either to visionary insight or to a succession of teachers or bishops, sometimes expressed in procreative or agricultural metaphors; (2) embryonic canons of

---

49 Trigg, 'Charismatic intellectual'.

the Bible, usually consisting of Old and New Testaments; (3) allegorical and typological methods of scriptural reading, which articulated the unity of the bipartite Bible and enabled the elaboration of speculative ideas; (4) formulation of a 'rule of faith' as a limit to such reading and speculation; (5) heresiology as a means of trivialising a range of opponents and bolstering one's own claim to single and original truth; and (6) withdrawal of communion. It is difficult to measure the success of such strategies in the pre-Constantinian era, although it is perhaps telling that Gnostic works that come from the third century (*Zost., Allogenes, Marsanes*) are in conversation less with the Septuagint and distinctively Christian themes and more with contemporary Platonist discussions, and indeed it is in the context of competition with Plotinus' circle that we hear of them *c*.250.[50]

The multilateral efforts at self-differentiation in which the gnostics and other groups played a prominent role did not produce a single 'proto-orthodox' mode of piety or spiritual formation, but a variety of such. As much as an Irenaeus and an Origen shared, the striking differences in their theological visions and conceptions of authority complicate any attempt to place them on one side of any binary picture of the 'proto-orthodox' arrayed against the Gnostics, the Valentinians and so on. If the construction of a 'Gnosticism' obscured the characters of the persons and groups assigned to it, likewise the category 'proto-orthodox' can homogenise and so distort the diversity of pre-Constantinian Christianity. Such diversity persisted into the fourth century and later, at times suppressed through anti-'heretical' measures but at times supported through, for example, the eventual embrace of monasticism. Although Irenaeus and others hoped to eliminate diversity and establish a single church with a single truth, their efforts in fact contributed to the rich multiplicity of the imperial Christian culture that emerged in late antiquity.

50 Turner and Majercik, *Gnosticism and later Platonism*; Turner, *Sethian Gnosticism*.

13

Truth and tradition: Irenaeus

DENIS MINNS

Of the several works of Irenaeus mentioned by Eusebius of Caesarea, only two survive in more than fragmentary form.[1] Both are concerned with defending the integrity of the common faith of the universal church. The longer of them, properly entitled *Detection and refutation of gnōsis falsely so-called*, is usually known simply by the Latin title *Adversus haereses* ('Against the heresies'). It survives completely only in a Latin translation, though there are significant fragments of the original Greek and also of an Armenian translation. In the first of its five books, Irenaeus offers a résumé of the teachings of Valentinus and the other heretics he opposes, and in the second a critical analysis of these. In the following three books, Irenaeus sees himself as setting forth the correct interpretation of the scriptural texts which he believes have been distorted or misunderstood in the arguments of the heretics.

The shorter work, called the *Demonstration of the apostolic preaching (Epideixis tou apostolikou kērygmatos)*, which survives only in an Armenian translation, was also intended to help the reader to 'put to shame all those who hold false opinions', as well as to 'set forth our sound and undefiled discourse in all frankness' for everyone who wanted to know it.[2] Although Irenaeus refers to *Adversus haereses* towards the end of the *Epideixis*, it has been suggested that this reference is a later addition, and that the *Epideixis* was written before *Adversus haereses*.[3] It is certainly the case that the *Epideixis* presents us with a much less sophisticated and developed theology than the larger work.

During the time Eleutherus was bishop of Rome, between approximately 174 and 189, Irenaeus was a presbyter in a Greek-speaking Christian community centred in the towns of Vienne and Lyons in Gaul.[4] Irenaeus is presumed not to have been a native of Gaul, for he mentions that when he was a boy

---

1 Euseb. *HE* 5.20.1; 26.
2 *Epid*. 1.
3 Blanchard, *Aux sources*, 113–14.
4 Euseb. *HE* 5.4.2.

he had had extensive contact with Polycarp 'in lower Asia', presumably in Smyrna, of which city Polycarp was bishop.[5] When Irenaeus went to Gaul, or how long he remained active there, is not known. Eusebius of Caesarea says that Irenaeus wrote to Victor, bishop of Rome in the last decade of the second century, remonstrating with him over his proposal to excommunicate Christian communities which differed from Victor's own practice regarding the day on which Easter was to be celebrated.[6]

Although we know so little of the details of his life, it is clear that Irenaeus identified himself as a member of a world-wide Christian community, which he calls 'the church', made up of smaller, locally based communities, which he calls 'churches', scattered throughout the Roman empire which, despite some insignificant diversity in practice, were nevertheless held together by a common, indeed unanimous, faith. It was not at all strange to Irenaeus that someone brought up in Asia Minor should find himself in a position of responsibility in a Christian community in Gaul, or that he should be sent by that community on an embassy to the bishop of Rome, or that Christian communities and individuals in quite distant parts of the Roman world should be in frequent contact with one another by letter, or should take a lively and interventionist interest in the affairs of those distant communities.

The universality of the church, its essential sameness in each of its local manifestations, is central to Irenaeus' understanding of what it is to be a Christian. It is when this sameness is challenged by local deviation in teaching that Irenaeus knows that something is amiss. It was axiomatic for him that the church, although disseminated throughout the whole world, had received its belief from the apostles and their disciples, and

> diligently guards it, as though living in a single dwelling, and believes what it believes in the same way, as though possessing one soul and one and the same heart, and proclaims, and teaches, and hands on these things with one voice, as though possessed of a single mouth. For although the languages of the world are different, the power of the tradition is one and the same. And neither the churches founded in Germany, nor those in Spain, nor those among the Celts, nor those in the east, nor those in Egypt, nor those in Libya, nor those founded in the middle regions of the world have believed different things, nor do they hand down different things. (*Haer.* 1.10.2)

When he set out to defend the authentic tradition, Irenaeus did not suppose that he had anything new to offer. He was simply restating the obvious truth

5 Euseb. *HE* 5.20.5–8.
6 Euseb. *HE* 5.24.11.

of divine revelation, against obvious distortions and manipulations of it. Nevertheless, he plainly did contribute to the reshaping of the church which he took to be an unchanging given. In wrestling with the problems posed by the heretics, he helped the church to a deeper, sharper understanding of what it was and what it believed. If heretics were succeeding in winning adherents to their perverted understanding of what Christianity was about, then there was need for a reliable measuring-stick – a canon – which would enable Christians with less confidence than Irenaeus in the obviousness of the truth to sort out what was true and what was false. Irenaeus is the most significant early witness we have to this process of orthodox self-definition in the face of what he sees as heretical distortion. We know too little of the work of his predecessors and contemporaries to be able accurately to assess the magnitude of his own contribution to the process.

Irenaeus has often been described as a founder, father, or 'first exponent of a catholic Christian orthodoxy',[7] and there is a remarkable contrast between his writings and those written only a generation or two previously by Christians whom he recognised as being within his own tradition. If we compare his writings with those of Justin Martyr and Theophilus of Antioch, for example, we can see immediately that, although he obviously stands in the same continuum with them, his theology has a newly acquired maturity: it has grown in complexity of organisation, in breadth of subject matter and in the resources it can press into service. It would be tempting to infer that Irenaeus was a brilliant and far-sighted innovator, if only it were not the case that he vigorously denies that he has done any innovating at all – innovation being, for him, precisely where the heretics he opposes have gone astray. But the very newness of the heretics' project pushes Irenaeus to a novelty of his own, though he cannot see this himself. Justin and Theophilus were apologists: their primary aim was to defend their fellow Christians from accusations brought against them by their non-Christian neighbours, and to show not only that Christianity was not an offensive, inhumane religion, but that it offered to all human beings the possibility of a genuine, God-given salvation. Irenaeus' attention was directed not outwards toward a suspicious, persecuting, non-Christian world, but inwards to fellow Christians whom he believed were poisoning the very thing that Christianity had to offer to that non-Christian world. To counter these 'heretical' fellow Christians, Irenaeus set forth what he supposed to be a straightforward account of what genuine, authentic Christianity had always been. This is, in fact, the first relatively complete picture of 'early catholicism'

7 Pyper, 'Irenaeus', 328.

that has come down to us, and some of its elements must have looked, at least in some quarters of the mainstream Christian world, quite newly minted. The Johannine and Pauline writings, for example, may have been known to Justin Martyr, as they certainly were to Theophilus of Antioch, but they had almost no impact on their respective theologies. Irenaeus is aware of the allure John and Paul have for his heretical opponents, but he insists that they are the rightful possession of mainstream Christianity, and firmly reclaims them for orthodoxy.

Irenaeus begins with the assumption that every right-thinking Christian knows what the truth of Christianity is. While he acknowledges, and is untroubled by, the existence of differences of liturgical practice in different parts of the Christian world,[8] he is convinced that the essentials of the church's self-definition will be found to be the same everywhere, in every time. Diversity of teaching can only be explained by wilful deviation from the truth handed down from the apostles, and Irenaeus believes he knows who was first responsible for this – Simon the Magician, described by Peter in the Acts of the Apostles as being 'in the gall of bitterness and the chains of wickedness' (Acts 8.23), against whom Justin Martyr had also railed.[9]

The basis of the position Irenaeus sought to defend was what he supposed was the traditional, and correct, interpretation of the revelation of God contained in what we call the Old Testament. This understanding was being assailed on the one hand by Gnostics who, if they accepted the Old Testament, interpreted it in ways radically different from the Great Church, and on the other hand by Marcionites, who dismissed it altogether, as being utterly irrelevant to the divine revelation newly made in Jesus. One of the most important elements of the self-definition of Irenaeus and of his church was a deep sense of continuity with the scriptures of the Old Testament, and with the people of God to whom that revelation had been addressed. As Irenaeus sees it, this is not a Christian usurpation. Christians are the legitimate inheritors of the promises made to Abraham. 'God is able from these stones to raise up children to Abraham', Jesus says in Matthew's gospel (Matt 3:9), and this is precisely what God has done by including Gentiles within the promises (*Haer.* 4.7.2; 8.1; 25.1). The inclusion of Gentiles was not meant to entail the exclusion of Jews, provided they accepted Jesus as the Christ.

> Abraham received the covenant of circumcision only after he was justified by faith without circumcision (cf. Rom 4:11) so that both covenants might be

---

8 *Letter to Victor* in Euseb. *HE* 5.24.12–13.
9 *Haer.* 1.27.4, cf. Justin Martyr, 1 *Apol.* 26.2–4; 56.1–4.

prefigured in him, and he might become the father of all those who follow the Word of God, and are pilgrims in this world, that is of those believers who are from the circumcised and those believers who are from the uncircumcised, just as Christ has become the cornerstone (cf. Eph 2:20), and gathers into the one faith of Abraham those from both covenants who are fit to make up the building of God. (*Haer.* 4.25.1)

In Christianity the faith of Abraham has returned to its original condition. It is faith without circumcision and without the works of the Law. This does not mean that the history and practices of Israel in the period between Abraham and Christ are to be dismissed as of no account, but they represent a temporary disposition in God's dealing with his people, adapted to the decline that accompanied their slavery in Egypt. The Decalogue encodes in writing the law which the patriarchs had written in their hearts (Haer. 4.16.3). Observance of the Decalogue remains essential to salvation, but the rest of the Mosaic Law was a yoke of slavery, needed to drag a rebellious people to obedience to God. The only difference between the obedience of slaves in the old covenant and the obedience of sons in the new is that the former had to be compelled, while the latter is freely given (*Haer.* 4.13.2).

Irenaeus did not need to define himself or his church over against Judaism, but he did need to take account of the embarrassing fact that most Jews stood apart from the movement of the gradually evolving, and divinely directed, plan of salvation. These Jews have refused to accept the interpretative key to their own scriptures which would lead them to belief in Christ, and, therefore, have been disinherited by God (*Haer.* 4.12.1; 3.21.1). Like the fleece of Gideon (Judg 6:38–40) which once was moist while all around it was dry, contemporary Judaism is now dry, while all around it is moist: that is to say, it no longer has the Holy Spirit of God, which came down upon Jesus, and was given by him to the church (*Haer.* 3.17.3).

Irenaeus' church is not defined by complete hostility or opposition to the non-Christian world. In view of the fierce persecution suffered by the Christians of Vienne and Lyons, and described by them in a letter to the churches of Asia and Phrygia,[10] he has a surprisingly relaxed attitude to the Roman empire. He acknowledges that 'it is due to them that the world is at peace, and we are able to walk on the roads without fear, and travel by sea wherever we wish' (*Haer.* 4.30.3). Like the Israelites despoiling Egypt (Exod 12:36), though with far less justification, Christians do not feel at all embarrassed at retaining the property, money, clothing and other things which they acquired before their

---

10 Euseb. *HE* 5.1.3–2.7.

conversion from the 'mammon of iniquity'. Nor after their conversion are Christians embarrassed to profit from trade with non-Christians or even to work in the imperial household (*Haer.* 4.30.1).

Irenaeus' own debt to pagan culture was heavier on the rhetorical than on the philosophical side. His prose style shows him to have had a considerable education in rhetoric, and some of his key notions, like 'hypothesis', 'economy' and 'recapitulation', have a rhetorical origin.[11] Irenaeus refers a few times to pagan poets and philosophers, but he does not show obvious signs of a deep or prolonged engagement with pagan literary or philosophical culture. Aristophanes was better at explaining the creation of things than the Valentinians, and Plato was more religious than them (*Haer.* 2.14.1; 3.25.5). But both comparisons are meant to shame Christian heretics, not to praise pagan authors. Irenaeus did, however, absorb – probably from Christian sources – the Platonist distinction between being and becoming, and deployed it to considerable effect.

Though he may thus have been reasonably comfortable in a pagan cultural environment, Irenaeus' identity was robustly Christian, and his literature was the Bible. Initially, at least, that meant the Old Testament. It was the heretics' contempt for the God revealed in the Old Testament that, more than anything else, provoked Irenaeus to counter-attack (*Haer.* 2.31.1). But since, with the exception of the Marcionites, the heretics disputed not the legitimacy but the interpretation of the Old Testament, Irenaeus had to show that his interpretation, and not that of the heretics, was the right one. At a pragmatic level, Irenaeus will argue that the scriptures should be interpreted as meaning what they say, and not as a coded way of saying something else (though he is himself no stranger to allegorical and, it might be thought, whimsical interpretation) (*Haer.* 1.9.4; 2.27.1–2). But more systematically, Irenaeus believes that the scriptures have to be interpreted against the background of what they teach, taken as a whole. Thus, it is ridiculous to suppose that the God who reveals himself in the Old Testament is a different, or a lesser, God than the one who reveals himself in Jesus. This general sense of revelation, this 'hypothesis', becomes the means of measuring the rightness or wrongness of a particular interpretation of scripture, and is therefore called, in the *Epideixis*, a canon, or rule of belief, and more frequently in *Adversus haereses*, a rule of truth.[12]

Although the Old Testament by itself, interpreted as bearing upon and looking towards the incarnation, might have satisfied Irenaeus, the argument

---

11 Grant, *Irenaeus*, 47–51.
12 *Epid.* 3; *Haer.* 1.9.4; 1.22.1; 2.27.1; 3.2.1; 3.11.1; 3.12.6; 3.15.1; 4.35.4.

of his opponents forced him to consider which Christian writings ought also to be regarded as having authoritative and binding force. Against Marcion, he is obliged to argue for a richer evangelical record; against the Gnostics, for a more restricted one. It is not possible, he argues, that there could be more or fewer gospels than the four the church actually possesses.[13]

The unity between the gospels and the Old Testament is not something that can be gauged only externally, by the application of the rule of truth. There is a dynamic unity between the Old Testament and the gospel which derives partly from the fact that it is the one Spirit which utters them and guides their interpretation when they are read conformably to the rule, and partly from the fact that the same Word of God reveals himself in both (*Haer.* 2.28.2; 3.24.1; 4.33.7). Christ is the treasure hidden in the field (Matt 13.44), that is, in the scriptures of the Old Testament (*Haer.* 4.26.1). All the appearances and utterances ascribed to God in the Old Testament have as their subject the Word who became incarnate in Jesus of Nazareth, and there is no discontinuity between what he said then and what he says in the flesh. The difference is in the manner of his communication. In the Old Testament, his utterances and appearances are prophetic of and preparatory to the permanent revelation of the Word of God in the incarnation.[14] Irenaeus is even prepared to say that in the Old Testament theophanies God was accustoming himself to humankind and accustoming humankind to himself (*Haer.* 3.17.1; 3.20.2; 4.21.3). When Jesus quotes from the Old Testament in the gospels, he is really quoting himself. It is not because he is a subordinate or second-order God that the Son is made the subject of the theophanies of the Old Testament. The incarnate Word is God made visible, and it was that God made visible that was glimpsed in the theophanies of the Old Testament. Irenaeus took quite literally the statement of Jesus in John's gospel that 'he who has seen me has seen the Father' (John 14:9). The incarnate Son is what is visible of the Father (*Haer.* 4.6.6), because he is 'the measure of the immeasurable Father' (*Haer.* 4.4.2). In the incarnation, the infinite, immeasurable and therefore incomprehensible God is measured, and therefore made comprehensible – visible, audible, touchable. But the Son 'measures' the Father only so that he can be comprehended by human beings – the incarnation does not render divinity wholly comprehensible, and so Irenaeus adds that the Father is what remains invisible of the Son. Just because he is infinite, God will never be fully comprehended by human beings, and human beings will always be able to advance in the knowledge and love of

13 *Haer.* 3.11.8.
14 *Epid.* 44–6; *Haer.* 4.5.2; 4.7.4; 4.9.1; 4.10.1.

him (*Haer.* 4.20.7). If the Son is in this way the 'steward of the Father's glory', the Holy Spirit is the means by which believers may recognise the divinity in the humanity of the Son (*Epid.* 7).

Though the Valentinians made ample use of the gospel of John (*Haer.* 3.11.7), John was a genuine disciple of the Lord (*Haer.* 3.1.1), and his gospel was actually directed against the heretical Cerinthus and the Nicolaitans (*Haer.* 3.11.1). Its teaching does not diverge from the rule of truth. Similarly, Paul had to be reclaimed for the church from those heretics who held that he alone knew the truth about the revelation made in Jesus (*Haer.* 3.13.1), or who twisted his words to deny elements of the rule of truth, such as the resurrection of the flesh. But Paul, though not the only apostle for Irenaeus, is nevertheless *the* apostle, and Irenaeus cites him more frequently than any other New Testament author, and cites all the Pauline and deutero-Pauline letters, with the exception of Philemon.[15]

Although Irenaeus relies so heavily on the writings of both testaments in defining himself as a Christian, he does not regard the scriptures as a *sine qua non* of Christian self-definition. There have been, and are, Christians who are not able to read or write, or at least not in a civilised language, yet hold fully to the true faith handed down from the apostles. What they hold is not in any way different from what is contained in the scriptures, but they have received it, by tradition, without the need for writing (*Haer.* 3.4.2).

The concept of tradition was already firmly established in Christianity before Irenaeus. It is found in Paul, for example, and in Clement of Rome.[16] But, by the time Irenaeus came to write the *Adversus haereses*, it had also been utilised by the Gnostics in order to validate those of their doctrines which were precisely *not* to be found in the scriptures. These were not to be found there because they were esoteric teachings, reserved for the elect, and handed down from the apostles to their disciples separately from the New Testament writings acknowledged by the Great Church (*Haer.* 3.2.1–2). Irenaeus insists against this that there is only one authentic tradition, and its authenticity is guaranteed by another concept often coupled with that of tradition, namely succession. This term was used of the successors to the founders of various philosophical schools, and the Gnostic Ptolemy held out to his pupil Flora the possibility that she might become worthy of the 'apostolic tradition which we too have received by succession' so that, in time, she might measure by rule against the teaching of the saviour all that he had said.[17] Clearly, if it was the case that a

15 Noormann, *Irenäus als Paulusinterpret*, 517.
16 1 Cor 11:2, 23; 15:3; 2 Thess 2:15; 3:6; 1 *Clem.* 7:2.
17 In Epiph. *Pan.* 33.7.9.

doctrine could be validated by the claim that it derived, by succession, from a secret or esoteric tradition handed down by Jesus to his disciples, then any doctrine at all could be validated in this way. In order to rescue the concept of tradition as a tool for identifying authentic doctrine, Irenaeus needed to demolish the idea that there was a secret or esoteric tradition and he did this precisely by pointing out that there was no secret about the succession in churches of apostolic foundation. If Christ handed down to his apostles any tradition, secret or otherwise, that tradition would be found in churches founded by those apostles, handed down by their successors. But we know of churches founded by the apostles of Jesus, and we know the names of the successors of those founders; therefore a doctrine can claim to be an apostolic tradition handed down by succession only if it can be shown to be identical with the doctrine taught in churches founded by the apostles. As the teachings of the heretics are manifestly not the teachings found in churches of apostolic foundation they have no claim to apostolic authenticity (*Haer.* 3.3.1–3).

Although bishops in succession from the apostles guarantee the church's claim to authentic teaching, it does not follow that hierarchical structure looms large in Irenaeus' definition of Christianity. He is sometimes credited with assigning an important, or even exclusive, role to bishops in the life of the church,[18] but, in fact, he has relatively little to say about bishops, and when he does use the term it is by no means unambiguously clear that he always thinks of a bishop as a person having sole government in a particular church. His numbering of bishops in the Roman succession list might suggest he thought that these, at least, were of such a kind, but this list may have been confected only shortly before he made use of it.[19] Irenaeus also uses other terms for church leaders, such as presbyter and leader (*proestōs*), and it is clear that he does not believe that these leaders can materially affect the content of the faith they are charged to pass on. Precisely because the faith is one and the same throughout the world, an eloquent leader will not be able to add to its content, any more than an inept one will diminish it (*Haer.* 1.10.3). If they do their work properly, they will simply hand down what had been handed down to them. The 'certain charism of truth' which presbyters receive along with episcopal succession is simply the unchanging truth handed down to them.[20]

Irenaeus held that the authentic tradition would be found in any church of apostolic foundation. But it would be both tedious and unnecessary to enumerate the succession lists of all the churches, because, if any one church

18 Cf. for example, Pagels, *Gnostic gospels*, 59–69; Brox, *Early church*, 79.
19 Cf. Lampe, *Paul to Valentinus*, 404–6.
20 *Haer.* 4.26.2; cf. Congar, *Tradition*, 28 n. 4, and 177.

of apostolic foundation preserves the authentic tradition, it will have the same doctrine as any other church of apostolic foundation. Irenaeus chose to give the succession list of the church of Rome because that church is 'very great, very ancient and known to all'. If any church of apostolic foundation will have the authentic tradition, then *a fortiori* this church will have it, because of its more excellent origin – that is, its foundation not by one, but by two apostles, and most glorious ones at that. There is no need to bother with succession lists of other churches because, by the logic of the argument, any church of apostolic foundation will have the same tradition as the Roman church (*Haer.* 3.3.2).[21]

There is no reason to doubt the sincerity of Irenaeus' confident claim that the universal church possesses, in all essential matters of faith, an identical and unchanging tradition. Nevertheless, his own writings show that he has himself drawn from orthodox Christian sources different and even contradictory theological views. Moreover, in his own theology, at least in its elaboration and its emphases, he can be seen to be redefining the orthodox tradition against the heretical opinions he opposes, if not actually fashioning it anew.

When speaking of the relationship between Father, Son and Holy Spirit, Irenaeus sometimes uses language which is suggestive of a subordinationist understanding of that relationship (e.g. *Epid.* 7; 47). But there can be no doubt that he thought of both the Son and the Spirit as being divine in the full and proper sense of the word. Irenaeus was not particularly exercised by the problem of how one God could be three persons. His interest was directed far more to the activity of Father, Son and Spirit in creation, and especially in the creation and redemption of humankind. God created the world by himself. He did not need intermediary instruments, since he had his own hands, his Word and his Wisdom, the Son and the Spirit, with which to fashion it (*Haer.* 2.10.2–4; 2.30.9). By means of his Word, he gives substantial shape to his creation; by means of the Spirit, he adorns it with beauty (*Haer.* 3.24.2; 4.20.2–4; 4.39.2; 5.1.3; 5.12.2).

Irenaeus' focus on the unity of old and new covenants, and on the unity of the God who reveals himself in both, led him to believe that there is a single divine purpose, or economy, with a single object, the creation of humankind in the image and likeness of God (*Haer.* 4. praef. 4).

The fashioning of this 'plasma' by the hands of God is not something achieved once for all in the beginning. It is a process coterminous with the economy itself. The day of Adam's creation, the sixth day of creation, is not yet over (*Haer.* 5.23.2). God *said* in the beginning, 'Let us create man in our own image and likeness,' but this will not be achieved until the resurrection of the

---

21 The best discussion of this much debated passage remains that of Abramowski, 'Irenaeus, *Adv. haer.* III.3.2'.

just (*Haer.* 5.16.2; 5.36.1–3). We have now the image of God in our flesh, because our flesh is the flesh of Adam, and it was fashioned after the pattern of the incarnate Son (*Epid.* 22; *Haer.* 5.16.2). But, at the resurrection, our incorruptible flesh, suffused, like the flesh of the risen Christ, with the Holy Spirit, will be resplendent with the Father's light (*Haer.* 4.20.2).

The Gnostics had supposed that they had discovered within themselves some spark of divinity, and that once this had been identified, nothing else mattered, certainly not the flesh. Irenaeus countered that it was precisely the flesh that did matter: it was this that God had formed from mud by his own hands; into this that he had breathed the breath of life; upon this that he would pour out his Spirit. The divine Spirit is, in fact, a constituent of a fully realised human being, but it is not there to be discovered by self-knowledge: it is bestowed by the creator God as the economy draws to its completion (*Haer.* 5.6.1).

Creation in the image and likeness of God must involve process and development, because of its inherent paradox. Human beings are creatures; God is uncreated. By the graciousness of God, it is the destiny of humankind to become 'near to the uncreated' (*Haer.* 4.11.1–2; 4.38.3–4; 4.39.2–3). To explain this, Irenaeus draws upon the Platonist distinction between being and becoming. Only God is; everything else is in a state of coming to be or passing away. Creatures cannot *be* divine, but, if it is their nature to *become*, then it is possible for them to become incrementally and infinitely more and more like God, and that is what the divine economy is all about.

Adam and Eve, though created after the pattern of Christ, were created as 'little ones', needing to grow towards their maturity (*Epid.* 12; *Haer.* 3.22.4). Being immature, they were easily misled by Satan, who used their very immaturity to crush them. Indeed, Satan encouraged them to suppose that likeness to God was something they could seize for themselves. But, just as it is the nature of God to *be*, so it is his nature to *act*, to *create*; similarly, as it is the nature of humankind to *become*, so it is its nature to be *acted upon*, to be *created*. God gives; humankind receives. Only by respecting this fundamental distinction between the nature of God and the nature of humankind will it be possible for the paradox to become real, for humankind to draw near to divinity (*Haer.* 4.11.1–2). Had God allowed Adam and Eve to achieve by themselves the immortality they hoped for, they would be immortally immature. Death, therefore, was permitted to come into the world, so that the divine economy could continue to engage with a humanity which remained pliant in the hands of God (*Haer.* 3.23.1).

Although, for polemical reasons, Irenaeus places so much emphasis on the *flesh* as the recipient of God's creative activity, he does not ignore the moral dimension of humankind's progress towards likeness to God. It was the work of the divine Spirit to lead human beings to become habitual in obedience to God, and only by retaining the moisture of the Spirit in a soft and pliable heart will they be able to be fashioned in the image and likeness of God (*Haer.* 4.39.2). The divine economy will not achieve its purpose without the obedience of faith, the acceptance of the reality of the difference between the creator and his creature, without attentiveness to the divine Word, without receptivity to divine grace.[22]

The incarnation does not represent a new departure in God's dealing with humanity: it is rather the hinge upon which the whole of the economy turns. Even in the garden in the beginning, the divine Word walked with Adam and talked with him, prefiguring the incarnation (*Epid.* 12). When expounding how Christ functions in the economy, Irenaeus introduces one of his most characteristic concepts: that of recapitulation (*anakephalaiōsis*). In its original, rhetorical context this meant a summing up of the principal points or 'heads' (*kephalaia, capita*) of an argument or discourse. The word is used in this sense by Irenaeus himself (*Haer.* 4.2.1), but it had already been pressed into theological service in the letter to the Ephesians (1:9–10), where it is said that God has 'made known to us in all wisdom and insight the mystery of his will, according to his purpose which he set forth in Christ as a plan (*oikonomia*) for the fullness of time, to recapitulate (*anakephalaiōsasthai*) all things in him, things in heaven and things on earth'.

Irenaeus understands this to mean that Christ had from all eternity a headship over things in heaven, but that in order for the economy to be fulfilled, he needed also to acquire a headship over things on earth, becoming head of the church, and drawing all things to himself (*Epid.* 6; 30; *Haer.* 3.16.6). Christ becomes the head of a redeemed humanity by recapitulating Adam in himself, which he does by being fashioned of the same flesh as Adam, and by retracing the history of Adam's disobedience and fall, but in reverse (*Haer.* 3.16.6; 3.18.7; 3.21.10; 3.23.3). Where Adam was immature and weak, Christ was fully grown and strong; where Adam was easily misled by Satan and crushed by him in death, Christ in his temptations fought back against Satan and won the prize of victory – the incorruptibility always intended for Adam's flesh (*Haer.* 3.18.2). Adam was disobedient at the tree of life, bringing death on himself and on all his flesh; Christ was obedient unto death on the cross, and rose to everlasting life. Adam's flesh already shines with divine glory in the risen Christ, but the economy of salvation has not reached its term with Christ's resurrection and

22 Aland, 'Fides und subiectio', 13–22.

ascension. At the end of the present age, the just will rise from the dead and will live in a renewed earthly Jerusalem: they will 'forget to die', and grow accustomed to immortality, in what Irenaeus calls the 'kingdom of the Son' (*Haer.* 5.35.2; 5.36.2–3). At the end of this 'thousand year reign' of the just, the unjust will rise to judgement and be cast into the lake of fire. When he has overcome his last enemy, which is death, Christ will surrender his kingdom to the Father, whose everlasting reign will then begin. What the Father's kingdom entails, we cannot say, for all that we are told is that 'no eye has seen, nor ear heard, nor the heart of man conceived, what God has prepared for those who love him' (1 Cor 2:9; *Haer.* 5.36.3). But all the just will have, according to the capacity of each, the vision of God which confers incorruptibility, and all will continue to develop in the knowledge and love of God. Even here and now, however, there is a paradise planted in this world, namely, the church (*Haer.* 5.20.2), in which the new Adam, nourished and brought into unity by the eucharist, is being fashioned in the image and likeness of God (*Haer.* 5.2.3). Christians are incorporated into this body, of which Christ is the head, by baptism and the gift of the Spirit: they become by adoption sons and daughters of God, and heirs of the promises made to Abraham. Obedience to the creative purpose of God is humanity's real glory (*Haer.* 4.14.1; 16.4), and the creative purpose of God is that humanity should receive from God the glory and power of the uncreated (*Haer.* 4.38.3–4). Human beings made full and eternally alive with the life of the Spirit are, in their turn, the glory of God (*Haer.* 4.20.7).

Irenaeus' work was widely known in the early church, and may have significantly influenced the thought of the important fourth-century theologians Marcellus of Ancyra and Athanasius of Alexandria, who, if they do not acknowledge a direct dependence on him, nevertheless seem to share some important aspects of his thought.[23] For the most part, however, it was his account of heretical opinions, rather than his own theological views, that attracted attention. His views on the relationships between the persons of the Trinity, and the relationship between humanity and divinity in Christ, were too imprecise and ambiguous to be of much use in the debates on those subjects which engulfed the church in the succeeding centuries. But that an orthodox church survived to debate these issues was in no small part due to Irenaeus' success in giving the church an understanding of itself and its doctrine which enabled it to distinguish itself from the heretics of the second century.

23 Seibt, *Theologie*, 22, 510–11; Anatolios, *Athanasius*, 23.

14

The self-defining praxis of the developing *ecclēsia*

CAROLYN OSIEK

The unknown author of the *Epistle to Diognetus*, writing probably in the late second century to an eminent patron, claimed that Christians are just like everyone else, inhabiting every land, both Greek and barbarian, living in cities, speaking the language that everyone else speaks, and wearing and eating what everyone else wears and eats. And yet, he says, they are different in subtle and often unseen ways. While they live normal lives on earth, they know that they are really here only as resident aliens, and so they can feel at home anywhere. They are in the flesh but do not live according to it. For doing good and loving everyone, they are attacked and hated, assailed as foreigners by Jews and persecuted by Greeks (*Ep. Diognet.* 3–5).

This remarkable document written in defence of Christian faith and practice reflects both the clarity and the ambiguity of Christian existence in the pre-Constantinian period as its adherents began to develop a sense of their own identity. They are both like everyone else and yet, in some significant ways, different, even to the point of being a 'third race'. The claim is put forth that being Christian did make a difference in everyday life, but not, of course, a difference that was threatening to the state or should be taken as cause for alarm by outsiders. Rather, this author and other Christian apologists like him insisted that Christians were good citizens, who were in fact not a liability but an asset to the empire. This distinct Christian identity was being forged in these important years between Jesus and Constantine through development of distinct patterns of behaviour in the areas of marriage, family and religious practice.

The author of the *Epistle to Diognetus* goes on to use the analogy of the soul in the body: what the soul is in the body, Christians are in the world, present in all of it, loving it but despised for not being fully part of it, an immortal element temporarily imprisoned in mortality. This understanding of earthly sojourn with heavenly citizenship is as old as Philippians 3:20, which asserts that we await a saviour from that heavenly state to which we belong. The 'resident alien' language of 1 Peter (1:1, 17; 2:11) reinforces this mixed identity, as does *Similitude* 1 of the Shepherd of Hermas, which exhorts hearers to remember that their own country is far away and its king may call them home at any time. If they have invested in wealth in this their alien residence, in lands, fields, buildings and businesses, they will find it perhaps too difficult suddenly to uproot. For this reason, their investments should be in works of charity towards the needy, not in earthly property and wealth. So the message that Christians are in the world but not of it was affirmed consistently from the beginning.

How did they then make use of their adoptive world's social structures? Some Christian writers claim that they rejected as immoral or sacrilegious certain customs, such as abortion, abandonment of newborns, divorce, public entertainment and participation in religious and civic rituals in honour of gods other than the true God. They also claim the creation of their own practices to help the needy. They profess a certain kind of theological (though not necessarily social) egalitarianism, to the effect that each person carried his or her own dignity before God and access to salvation directly by Christ. Yet there is no evidence that they moved to abolish any of the social structures, even within their own ranks, that contributed to social inequality. For example, the understanding of marriage and the relationship between the sexes continued to be hierarchical, and there is ample evidence that Christians continued to be slave owners, albeit perhaps with a difference. But the difference is only conjecture. As noted by a prominent historian of Roman culture, 'the means to settle the issue are not available'.[1]

Early Christian family life

The threefold division of family life into relationships of the male head of household, the *paterfamilias*,[2] with wife, children and slaves, was already popularised by Aristotle (*Pol.* 1.2.1253b passim). It continued to structure further discussions of *oikonomia*, household management, throughout the Hellenistic period and, with certain important variances, carried into the household codes of the New Testament (especially Col 3:18–4:1; Eph 5:21–6:9; 1 Pet 2:18–3:7).[3]

---

1 Garnsey, 'Sons, slaves – and Christians', 108.
2 Use of this Roman term for the male householder is widespread in today's discussions of the Roman family. In ancient texts, however, the Latin term connoted ownership of property, not family relationships. See Saller, 'Roman kinship', 7–34.
3 See Balch, 'Household codes' and 'Neopythagorean moralists'.

Marriage and celibacy

An encouragement to asceticism and celibacy began early in the Christian movement, probably prompted by two very different factors: first, adoption of a certain tendency in the Platonic world-view to see the body and the material world as obstacles to attainment of union with God; second, the historical memory of Jesus' choice to remain unmarried, probably motivated by the very different factors of apocalyptic world-view and the prophetic call. Already in 1 Corinthians 7, Paul gives advice about the question of marrying or remaining unmarried; his personal choice is clearly expressed for the latter, for eschatological reasons, though he himself may well have been married at an earlier time (1 Cor 9:5).

Two generations later, Ignatius of Antioch refers to those who remain chaste 'out of reverence for the flesh of the Lord' (Ign. *Pol.* 5.2), and in the middle of the second century, Justin tells of some in Rome, both men and women, who have remained chaste from childhood into old age (1 *Apol.* 1.15). The apocryphal acts of apostles written for popular consumption in the second and third century, especially the acts of Thomas, of John, of Peter and of Paul, teach celibacy as the authentic way of being Christian, even as the false teachers mentioned in 1 Timothy 4:3 had also forbidden marriage. Thus the pattern of celibacy chosen for religious reasons was established early. The discouragement of second marriages for church leaders was already developing in the Pastoral Epistles (1 Tim 3:2, 12; 5:9). Later, it would be extended to a general ideal, however imperfectly observed in practice.

This ambiguity about marriage must have been one characteristic, not noted by Diognetus, that also distinguished Christians. Some, always a small number, chose not to marry. Christians were not alone in this, but the practice was certainly seen as unusual. Among Jews, the best evidence suggests that the inhabitants of Qumran during its flourishing were unmarried men. Likewise, Philo tells of the Therapeutae, a group of celibate ascetic Jews in Egypt, both men and women, who lived in separate communities that came together in chorus for worship (*Contempl.* 68). In some Graeco-Roman cults, the priests and priestesses devoted to maintaining temples and offering sacrifice also did not marry.

Be that as it may, the vast majority of the population, including Christians, married and lived normal family lives. The traditional view of marriage, still prevalent in many cultures, was not of a romantic relationship between two individuals who chose each other, but a contractual relationship between two families for the enhancement of family status and property and bequeathal of that property to legitimate offspring. This did not preclude, however, loving relationships between husband and wife, sometimes developed only after the marriage. Since in Roman law and custom the agreement of the couple to live together constituted the marriage contract, the necessary ingredient was *affectio maritalis*, the intent toward each other.

Marriage customs for those living under Roman law, by the first and second centuries, was normally *sine manu*, in which case the property of husband and wife remained nominally separate, even though it might be administered jointly by the husband, so that the wife's property might be passed on to the children or, in case of divorce or childlessness of the deceased, it might revert to the wife's family rather than being absorbed into the husband's family.

The Jewish marriage contract, the *ketubah*, usually followed the same custom of specifying what property the wife brought into the marriage, so that in the case of divorce it would accompany her back into her own family. These customs regarding property were not designed for protection of the wife but rather of her paternal family's property. Nevertheless, they contributed to what is generally recognised as a new social and economic independence for women. Joined to this is evidence, again under Roman practice and to the degree that Roman influence prevailed in a given situation, of greater freedom of movement at least for women of a certain status: participation with their husbands at dinner parties, greater freedom to move about publicly and greater ease in initiating divorce.[4]

The fundamentally patriarchal structure of marriage was not abolished, however. On the contrary, it remained true that fathers were expected to be the principal decision makers in their children's marriages. Paternal authority continued theoretically and legally over adult children as long as the father was alive. But this created a tension in marriages *sine manu* in which the wife did not legally become a member of her husband's family: which male was her authority figure?

The separation of family property that was customary in Roman and Jewish marriages put a curb on the authority of husbands over wives, but by no means eliminated it. The Aristotelian world-view that only freeborn males of the right families were born to rule, while all others were born to be ruled, allied with the Platonic association of rationality and spirit with the male and sense perception and matter with the female, to produce a theoretical framework that subordinated all women, slaves and the lower classes to the

---

4 Much of this information is conveniently discussed in Winter, *Roman wives*. Cf. Corley, *Private women*; Osiek and Balch, *Families in the New Testament world*, 58–64.

interests of elite males. While an 'enlightened' Stoic philosopher like the first-century contemporary of Paul, Musonius Rufus, could argue that women have the same capacity for virtue and intelligence, and should therefore receive the same education, it was only so that they could educate their children (provided it did not compromise their chastity), while for men the same education was for participation in public affairs.[5] While Musonius Rufus and a few others like him argued that wives had just as much right to expect chaste fidelity of their husbands as husbands did of their wives, the sexual double standard was much more prevalent.

Within this world, Christians created their marriages. To the extent that household codes like those of Colossians and Ephesians were normative, Christians adapted the fundamental structures of the hierarchical household to their belief. A characteristically Christian twist, though not unknown elsewhere, is the way in which the subordinate figures of wife, children and slaves were addressed as persons in their own right, and addressed first (Col 3:18–4:1; Eph 5:22–6:9). Another is the transparency of household heads who represent God or Christ both in their reception of the submission of others and in their exercise of authority: wives are to submit to their husbands *as to the Lord*, but the husband is to love his wife *as Christ loved the church* (Eph 5:22, 25). Thus the whole familiar patriarchal structure is christologised and absorbed into Christian faith and teaching, albeit with recognition of the fundamental spiritual dignity of each member. At the same time that the authoritative position of husbands is reinforced, in the Ephesians passage, the wife is put forward as model and image of the church.

'Mixed marriages' of believers and unbelievers existed throughout the entire period covered by this volume. They are already attested in 1 Corinthians 7:12–16. These marriages witness to the relative autonomy of women to choose their own way of belief and worship, in contradiction to much of the articulated theory about the well-run marriage. When in the same chapter Paul tells widows that they are free to remarry, he expresses his desire that they marry 'in the Lord', which he would not need to say if that were taken for granted (1 Cor 7:39). Some decades later, 1 Peter 3:1 offers as a reason for the reverent submission of wives that they may thus convert unbelieving husbands.

When Tertullian writes two treatises to his wife to discourage the second marriage of the widowed, he gives a long list of troubles that the Christian wife married to a pagan husband will encounter, which constitutes one of our best descriptions not only of daily Christian practice, but also of what life in

5 Frs. 3, 4, in 'Musonius Rufus, "The Roman Socrates"', 39–49.

a mixed marriage was like. When she wants to attend Christian prayer in the early morning, he will want her to meet him at the baths. When she has a day of fast, he will throw a banquet at which he expects her attendance. When she should be performing works of charity towards the poor, he will have her deal with more urgent business for his cause. When she wants to attend all-night vigils, he will object on grounds of propriety. When she is asked to give hospitality to visiting Christians, he will refuse to accept them in his house. She will be obligated to observe family religious festivals of a faith not her own. Finally, Tertullian urges Christian women to marry Christians, even if it means an alliance below their status, something intensely disapproved of in Roman society (*Ad ux.* 2.4, 6).

Similarly, in the early third century, Hippolytus criticises his rival Callistus for allowing the marriage of higher-status women to lower-status men in order to allow more possibility for the women to find believing husbands (*Haer.* 9.12). The *Traditio apostolica* ('Apostolic tradition'), attributed to the same Hippolytus,[6] lists among Christian family customs rising in the middle of the night to pray. If, however, one has a spouse who is not a Christian, the believer should go to another room to pray so as not to awaken the non-Christian spouse (*Trad. ap.* 41). In fourth-century North Africa, the pious Christian Monica, mother of Augustine, was married to an unbeliever, evidence that the custom was still widely practised. Certainly the ideal, already expressed by Paul in 1 Corinthians 7:39, was for Christians to marry Christians; however, it seems that many did not follow that ideal.

Augustan marriage law mandated the double standard that husbands divorce their wives for adultery, but not that wives divorce their husbands. Popular treatises on marriage told wives that they should be glad if husbands expressed their debauchery elsewhere, the more to treat their wives with honour. Against widespread Jewish, Greek and Roman custom, Christians were taught the prohibition of divorce, a teaching that bore the authority of Jesus himself (1 Cor 7:10–11; Mark 10:4–12; Matt 5:31–2; 19:3–9; Luke 16:18). Special exceptions were worked out in certain situations, such as disparity of belief (1 Cor 7:12–16). The Matthean allowance of divorce in the case of *porneia* (some kind of illicit sexual activity) is disputed, but may refer to a previously exist-ing marriage that, upon entrance to a Christian Jewish community, is seen

---

6 The *Traditio apostolica* or 'Egyptian church order' is a reconstructed Greek text whose original exists only in fragments, but it is extant in several other languages and editions, and is a basis for several later church order documents. Its attribution to the Roman Hippolytus is dubious but traditional. For the history of the text, see Bradshaw *et al.*, *The apostolic tradition*, 1–17.

to be against the forbidden degrees of relationship in Levitical law. If this is not the meaning, then the passage, which already represents only the male's prerogative to initiate divorce, reinforces the patriarchal double standard and Augustan legislation by which a husband may divorce his wife for unchastity, but not the reverse (Matt 19:9).

Writing in Rome in the early second century, the Christian freedman Hermas reviews marriage regulations, reminding his listeners from a male point of view that husbands must remain faithful to their wives. But a husband who learns that his wife is adulterous must divorce her and not remarry, holding out for the possibility of reconciliation. Here Hermas follows Augustan law that requires divorce of the cuckolded husband, but departs from it and follows gospel legislation in the prohibition of remarriage (*Mand.* 4.1). Paul in 1 Corinthians 7 had been clear that in the case of incompatibility in a mixed marriage caused by disparity of belief, divorce was possible, but he had not been clear about whether remarriage was allowed upon necessary divorce. Hermas is unambiguous: it is not allowed.

Yet a few years later in the same city, the anonymous woman of Justin's story (*2 Apol.*) had followed Paul's advice to a certain extent, considering her conversion to Christianity and her husband's unacceptable ways as grounds for divorce. As a result, the husband's accusation led to the death of the wife and her catechist. Leaping ahead two centuries, to a time when Christian mores were taking over and divorce was now strongly disapproved of, Jerome's female friend Fabiola in the mid-fourth century divorced her depraved husband and remarried, yet Jerome defends her action on the basis of Matthew 19:9, arguing that for Christians, what applies to women applies equally to men, so that her first husband's licentious living justified the divorce on grounds of *porneia* (Jerome *Ep.* 77). Perhaps in these examples we have the difference between prescription and description. It seems clear that prohibition of divorce characterised Christian teaching from the first, and was something that set Christians apart from everyone else in their surroundings. Yet this does not mean that it was always and everywhere observed. This caution should guide conclusions about every characteristic of early Christian identity.

Children

In any culture, children are an investment for the future and a protection for parents in their old age, at the same time that they are the present delight of their parents. This was no less true in the environment of early Christianity. Inheritance practices and laws always cause problems in large families, yet in societies with high infant mortality, such as the ancient Mediterranean world, many children must be produced so that some will live. Even under the best of circumstances, in the wealthiest families, many children died tragically young, and Christians in the first centuries were not among those elites who could afford the best care and food.[7]

Both contraception and abortion were practised in the Graeco-Roman world, though not with much understanding or efficacy, and, as one can imagine, carried high mortality. The safer way to limit family size was the abandonment of newborns, a practice for which ancient Rome is well known.[8] At least some abandoned babies were picked up by others and raised, usually as slaves, but in what numbers we have no way of knowing. Certainly the common assumption was that these children died. Even ancient authors presumed that the majority of such abandoned children were girls. Yet Hermas identifies himself at the beginning of his work as a *threptos*, one who had been so rescued and raised in slavery. All surviving evidence indicates a preference for male rather than female slaves even for domestic service.[9]

With abortion and abandonment, we come to a distinct parting of the ways between Christians and general Graeco-Roman practice. Abortion was not without its Roman critics (e.g. Cic. *Clu.* 2.32; Ov. *Am.* 2.13–14; Juv. *Sat.* 6.592–600). Graeco-Roman writers thought the Jews unusual because they did not abandon unwanted babies (Tac. *Hist.* 5.5; Diod. Sic. 40.3). Jews themselves also claimed, like Christians after them, that this set them apart (Philo, *Spec.* 3.108–15; Josephus, *Ap.* 2.202; Pseudo-Phocylides 184–5).

Christian writers, even the very ones who want to argue that Christians are just like everyone else, stop at this point and insist that in this way Christians are entirely different. The *Didache*, a collection of teachings and procedures probably compiled at the turn of the first century in Syria, lists among forbidden practices the killing of a child that is in the womb or already born. It also forbids 'corruption of children', a sure reference to the pederasty common among elites (2.2; 5.5; parallel texts in *Ep. Barn.* 19.5; 20.2). The author of the *Epistle to Diognetus*, too, while claiming the presence of Christians everywhere doing what others do, says that they marry and have children like everyone else, but he draws the line at this difference: they do not throw their children away (5.6). Likewise, Tertullian in his characteristically aggressive rhetoric

---

7 Debate about the social status of Christians in the first generations is ongoing. Cf. pt ii, ch. 7, above. For new attempts to create a stratified model, see Meggitt, *Paul, poverty and survival*; Friesen, 'Poverty in Pauline studies', and responses: Barclay, 'Poverty in Pauline studies', and Oakes, 'Constructing poverty scales'.

8 Cf. Eyben, 'Family planning in Graeco-Roman antiquity'; on the history of abandonment, Boswell, *Kindness of strangers*, 53–179.

9 Harris, 'Roman slave trade', 119–20; Madden, 'Slavery in the Roman empire', 3–5.

accuses those who desire to see Christian blood shed of shedding blood themselves, that of their own children, either by drowning or exposure to cold, starvation or dogs. He adds that it is forbidden to Christians even to kill the child in the womb, which is a quicker kind of murder. Whether the child is born or unborn makes no difference (*Apol.* 9.6–8). An extensive chain of Christian writers argued similarly (e.g., Athenagoras, *Leg.* 35.6; Min. Fel. *Oct.* 30.2; Clem. Al. *Paed.* 2.96.1; *Apocalypse of Peter* 8 Ethiopic, 26 Akhmimic). Justin argues that some abandoned infants will die, which would make their parents murderers (1 *Apol.* 29; also Clem. Al. *Paed.* 3.3.21), and offers what is probably the most bizarre reason for forbidding the exposure of children: the child you abandoned may be raised as a slave and find her way to a brothel, where someday you may unknowingly commit incest with her (1 *Apol.* 27)!

The same household codes that directed Christian wives to submit to their husbands gave children the obligation to obey their parents. By custom mothers carried authority over their children, but not with the same social and legal pressure fathers had. The familiar stereotypes of the stern disciplinarian father and the affectionate mother existed, though we have some quite good evidence of very affectionate and intimate relationships of children with both father and mother.[10] Still, mothers might be confidants and advocates for their (especially adult) children (Matt 20.20–1),[11] but fathers were those who exercised final power.

Christian piety and practice mirrored this situation. The characteristic attribute of God as father continued as a principal way of understanding and calling upon God in the church. In this, Christians were not unique. Zeus/Jupiter was also father of gods and people. Jews, too, called on the God of Israel with paternal imagery. Yet the particular form this piety took among Christians was determined by the language ascribed to Jesus, especially the prayer in which he was said to have taught his disciples to call on God as father. Christians claimed a special relationship with their god, the one true God, under the paternal model. This filial relationship with God through Jesus was basic to their self-understanding. It put the entire Christian community in the place of children, dependent on a loving father who at the same time represented ultimate authority. In the household codes, children were admonished to obey their parents as something pleasing to the Lord. Just as wives were cast as models of the church in the Ephesian household code, so too children who obeyed their parents performed the duty of all believers towards God.

---

10 E.g. Eyben, 'Fathers and sons'; Saller, *Patriarchy, property and death.*
11 See Dixon, *Roman mother,* for examples of elite mothers arranging the political lives of their children.

Early Christian literature is strangely silent about children themselves. Other than the few admonitions to obey parents, and the brief mentions in stories about Jesus in the gospels (Mark 5:21–3, 35–43; 9:14–27; 10:13–16 and parallels), we do not learn very much. In the pages of early Christian writing, they are neither seen nor heard. We simply know they were there by implication. When one spouse belonged to the church and the other did not, did children accompany their Christian parent on the first day of the week to the Christian assembly? Paul assures the believer in this situation that both the unbelieving spouse and the children are holy because of the presence of the baptised member in the family (1 Cor 7:14). We do not know at what point infant baptism began to be practised. It is unlikely to have been this early. Yet children could not have been excluded entirely. Alternate accounts of whole households being baptised together also suggest the presence of children in Christian gatherings (1 Cor 1:16; Acts 16:15, 32–3). But the sources are largely silent about them. Perhaps this is indicative of adult attitudes.[12]

Slaves

The third human component seen as necessary in the well-ordered household was slaves, the group Aristotle regarded as most clearly born to be ruled. Domestic slavery was an institution so close to the fabric of everyday life that it was difficult to imagine life without it. For those who could afford them, slave attendants were present for every aspect of life, twenty-four hours a day, and were considered members of the household, even if in a secondary way. Alive, they could be trusted assistants and agents. Dead, they were buried in the family burial complex. Households, businesses and the imperial service were managed and maintained by slaves. Every family that possibly could owned at least one slave, who lived as one of the family if the family were of humble circumstances. Yet slaves were always viewed by the freeborn with some suspicion. They were intimate companions, and yet the strangers within. Opposing stereotypes of the slave faithful to death and the lazy potential betrayer were popular and continued to be perpetuated in Christian circles as well.[13]

---

12 In the early years of the empire, though children were sometimes beaten for discipline, an essential distinction in dignity was drawn between the child and the slave, who was much more likely to be beaten (Saller, 'Corporal punishment, authority, and obedience'). By the late fourth century, Augustine could argue for a basic equality in Christ of son and slave, which actually seems to have contributed less to cessation of slave beating than to an increase of child beating (Garnsey, 'Sons, slaves – and Christians').

13 Harrill, 'Domestic enemy'.

While by Roman law slaves could neither marry nor have legitimate children, in fact the epigraphical evidence indicates that they used marital language for their unions and considered their children to be truly theirs, with apparent approval of their owners, even though they could not make a will and pass on any acquired property to spouse or children.[14] Hence it was a kind of ambiguous existence without legal grounding that could be removed at any moment on the whim of the slaveholder. Slaves could be either in secure familial circumstances or subject to excessive cruelty, all depending on where and when they happened to be.

The practice of slavery by Christians continued without obvious change. Paul in 1 Corinthians 7:21–3 recognises slave members of the congregation, adapting the familiar Stoic theme that real slavery is subjugation to human passions, whereas true freedom does not depend on legal condition but on the human spirit. The ambiguous statement of 7:21 can be understood either that the slave should make the best of slavery, or take advantage of freedom if possible.[15] When writing to Philemon, Paul urges this host of a house church to take back his slave Onesimus, 'no longer as a slave, but as a beloved brother' (Phlm 16). It is not clear whether Paul expects Philemon to manumit Onesimus or simply to change the relationship to one that is more fraternal because Onesimus has now embraced the faith. In either case, there is no suggestion that Christians should cease to own slaves.

The household codes complete the third aspect of house management with their commands regarding the roles of slaves and slave owners. Slaves are admonished to obey their masters in everything, wholeheartedly as if to the Lord, knowing that their reward awaits them in heaven. On the other hand, masters are warned of their obligation to treat their slaves justly and evenly, with the reminder that they too have a master in heaven (Col 3:22–4:1; Eph 6:5–9). Going further, the author of 1 Timothy exhorts slaves to honour their masters and not think they can be disrespectful because both are members of the church. Rather, they should serve all the more, and not give occasion to outsiders to be critical of proper social order among Christians (1 Tim 6:1–2).[16]

Most difficult is 1 Peter, which, in its adapted household code, turns the part addressed to slaves into a long meditation on the suffering Christ as model

14 Martin, 'Slave families and slaves in families'.
15 Harrill, *Manumission of slaves*.
16 The admonition to obey one's master or mistress in everything as if to the Lord, in the context of the general expectations of the sexual availability of slaves to their owners, takes on a more ominous tone if the sexual use of one's own slaves was not always understood by Christians as a violation of the boundaries of morality. See Osiek, 'Female Slaves, *porneia*, and the limits of obedience'.

for abused slaves who must suffer without having done anything wrong (1 Pet 2:18–25). Unlike the next section addressed to wives, who by their reverent submission may win over unbelieving husbands, here there is no mention that the abuse comes from *unbelieving* slave owners. We must therefore assume that the abuse could come from either believing or unbelieving owners, a frank admission perhaps that the admonitions to slave owners as put forth in Colossians and Ephesians were not always effective.[17] The positive side of the analogy of the suffering Christ here is that another kind of christological typology is at work, as in Ephesians 5. There the reverent and submissive wife is cast as the type of the church and thus as a model for all believers. Here the abused slave is typecast as representative of Christ, a powerful image that participates in the wider mystery of the cross with its reversal of worldly expectations of honour and status.

As Christianity developed, the same kinds of exhortations continued. The *Didache*, after teaching the need to discipline sons and daughters, instructs the slave owner not to command a male or female slave in the heat of negative emotion (literally, 'in your bitterness'), lest it weaken their faith in God. The owner is reminded that God is also over him or her. The passage concludes, however, with the usual exhortation to slaves to obey their owners as a type or image of God (4.9–11). But there must eventually have been some presumption in favour of manumission, and an expectation that for those slaves who needed to buy their freedom, church funds would be allocated for this purpose. Ignatius, writing to Polycarp in the first decade of the second century, advises against this practice (Ign. *Pol.* 4.3). After first exhorting the young bishop Polycarp that he should not behave with arrogance towards slaves, he turns the advice around to ensure that slaves do not get puffed up with a sense of their own importance because they are members of the community, but serve even better as slaves of God. Ignatius adds at the end that they should not expect to be freed from the common fund 'lest they become slaves of desire' (*epithymia*) – a rather patronising excuse that adapts the Stoic adage that true slavery may begin at the moment of legal freedom, as the new freedperson becomes haughty and acquisitive and thus enslaved to one's own passions.

Throughout the literature of early Christianity, well into the fifth century, there are continued references to slavery practised by Christians. Contrary to the images we are given by the New Testament narratives of whole households

---

17 The apparent innocuousness of certain images of slavery should not blunt our awareness of its viciousness. For further discussion, see Glancy, *Slavery in early Christianity*.

converting together (Acts 10:44–8; 16:15, 31–4; 1 Cor 1:16), it seems that slaves could usually make their own decisions about faith. This was generally already true before and outside the onset of Christianity, for we know that slaves were members of private religions and other kinds of private associations. The *Apostolic tradition* attributed to Hippolytus in the early third century gives a list of occupations forbidden to those who would like to become catechumens, then specifies that a slave concubine who has been faithful to her owner/husband and raised her children well can be accepted without change. Her marital status would be considered irregular, but there was really nothing she could do about it. A slave of a Christian owner who wished to become a catechumen had to have permission and an attestation of virtue from his or her owner. In the case of a slave not of a believer, no such permission or attestation would be sought, but the slave must simply be admonished to virtues proper to slave status (*Trad. ap.* 15–16). Here it is clear that the personal initiative of each slave is the basis for seeking baptism and membership in the church. The requirement of permission from a Christian owner shows that it was not expected that their slaves would necessarily convert.

Was there anything different about the practice of slavery by Christians? The idea that real slavery is not the legal kind but enslavement to passion, which can happen in and out of legal slavery, was commonplace. The discussions of household management written throughout the Hellenistic period recognise that brutal treatment of slaves is inefficient, and encourage enlightened, though definitely authoritative, management. Encouragement will produce better results than punishment; good material treatment, including competitive incentives, will turn out better work than maltreatment.

Christian slave owners were firmly taught that abuse and uneven treatment of slaves are not to be tolerated, since slaves are their brothers and sisters in Christ, and because the slave owners themselves are slaves of God. Because something is taught, however, does not mean that it is universally observed. 1 Peter 2:18–25 does not specify that abusive owners would not be Christians, so it leaves open the possibility of mistreatment even by believers. Abusive slave owners were heartily disapproved of, but the texts sound as if slave owners were even more frightened of slaves who might adopt 'an attitude' that might compromise their authority on the basis of a common baptism. Ignatius' warning to Polycarp to avoid any kind of mutual arrogance between owner and slave may be a hint that all was not always right in these relationships. By incorporating slavery into the theological and pastoral framework of Christian life, church teaching actually reinforced the institution of slavery.

Occupations and entertainment

The *Apostolic tradition* lists occupations that are not acceptable for someone who wants to become a catechumen. They include brothel keepers, sculptors, painters (because they must deal with idolatrous images), actors (notoriously of low character), anyone involved as participant or manager in the games, priests of a pagan cult, city magistrates (presumably because they would have to offer sacrifice in the course of their duties), prostitutes, decadent persons, eunuchs, magicians and astrologers. All these must absolutely cease this occupation if they wish to become catechumens. A teacher of children should cease this work unless he has no other means of livelihood. The reason is probably because the lessons were based on the Greek and Roman classics, considered by Christians to be full of immorality and idolatry. Soldiers are a special case. They can be accepted if they are willing not to kill, even under orders, or to take the military oath that was considered an act of worship of a foreign god. These two prohibitions would in fact make it very difficult to continue as a soldier, and any catechumen or believer who is not a soldier but wishes to become one is to be rejected (*Trad. ap.* 16).[18]

Attendance at public celebrations and spectacles, along with participation in the life of baths and gymnasium, were what comprised public life for male residents of the *polis*. But Tertullian says that attendance at any of the public spectacles (theatre, races, gladiatorial events) is something that Christians do not do (*Apol.* 38.4). The reason, we would suppose, would be primarily the bloodthirsty violence, but his is different: the extent of religious ritual and meaning in them, which constitutes idolatry. Although Tertullian states that these events are forbidden to believers, the fact that he writes a whole treatise to convince Christians that they should not attend (*De spectaculis*) shows that apparently not everyone agreed to stay away from them.

Discussions like these by early Christians reveal how difficult it must have been for Christians to be full citizens. All public and many private social occasions included acts of religious worship that were off-limits for conscientious Christians. No wonder apologists, such as the author of the letter to Diognetus, wanted to stress how similar Christians were to the rest of the population, so as to remove suspicion from them. In many ways they were like everyone else, but in many ways, they were not. The differences would eventually cost some their lives.

18 The attitudes of Christians toward military service in the pre-Constantinian empire were a cause of conflict. See esp. Harnack, *Militia Christi*; Ryan, 'Rejection of military service'; Helgeland *et al., Christians and the military.*

Prayer, charity, and asceticism

Prayer, fasting, and almsgiving were already understood from their Jewish inheritance to be the fundamental acts of religious devotion for Christians.[19]

Prayer[20]

When Pliny the Younger, governor of Pontus and Bithynia in the early second century, wrote his now famous letter to Trajan inquiring what he should do with Christians he had apprehended, he reported that, from what he was able to learn, they assembled in two different kinds of meetings, once early in the morning to sing hymns to Christ as if to a god, the other later in the day for a meal, not of any sinister kind as rumour had it, but a harmless meal. Instead of binding themselves by oath to do terrible and subversive things, they instead promised to refrain from criminal actions (Plin. *Ep.* 10.96). This early morning assembly for worship in word and song sounds very much like insider reports and instructions about frequent prayer. The *Didache* teaches followers to say the Lord's Prayer three times a day (*Did.* 8.2–3). The *Apostolic tradition* teaches that the faithful should rise early, wash their hands and pray at home before going off to work, but, if it is a day when instruction is given, they should instead go to the common place.[21] We therefore assume that this instruction is given early in the morning. Later, those at home are to pray at the third, sixth and ninth hours, before going to bed and at midnight, making the sign of the cross upon their foreheads (*Trad. ap.* 35, 41–2). This continual round of daily prayer structured the lives of those who followed it.

Fasting

Fasting was also part of the discipline expected of believers. Like almsgiving, it was a custom that assumed increasing importance in post-exilic Judaism (Ezra 8:21–8; Neh 9:1; Isa 8:3–9; Joel 2:12–13; Judith 8:6). The *Didache* enjoins regular fasting on Wednesdays and Fridays (*Did.* 8.1). The Quartodeciman controversy of the second century about the correct day to celebrate Easter is presented

---

19 In the pre-exilic period, almsgiving is not singled out; the practice was part of the more general *hesed* or compassion, and hospitality. In the post-exilic period, fasting and almsgiving are given more attention and become established as inseparable works of piety (See e.g. Isa 58:3–7; Tob 4:7–11). Thanks to Toni Craven for these insights.

20 See also pt. ii, ch. 7, above.

21 The information about going immediately to work indicates that it is not the leisured class that is addressed here, but those who must labour for a livelihood. On the other hand, the directive goes on to say that, if there is no common instruction, they should read a holy book at home. So at least someone in each household is presumed to be literate.

by Eusebius as the problem of when to end the common fast in order to celebrate the Pascal feast (*HE* 5.23). Hermas, *Visions* 2.2.1; *Similitudes* 5.1, 3, depict the discipline of fasting as not only a formal practice, but also one that embraces the entirety of life. Just doing without food is not the point, but rather the full observance of God's commandments, for which fasting creates the dispositions in the person (*Sim.* 5.1.3–5; 3.7–8). Tertullian considers fasting so important that it is the subject of a treatise (*De jejunio*). The *Apostolic tradition* is a little more casual about general fasting: widows and consecrated virgins should fast often with prayer for the church. Presbyters and laity may fast as they wish. A bishop can only fast when the whole church does, since he must always be free to perform the offering of eucharist when anyone requests it (*Trad. ap.* 23). However, fasting continued to be a regular observance of ascetical practice in the church.

Almsgiving

Jewish covenantal practice required attention to the poor and needy, especially widows and their children. The first generations of Christians, being composed largely of Jews, were profoundly influenced by Jewish moral practice, which continued into the transition to Gentile Christianity. As in other aspects of community practice, Jewish emphasis on almsgiving (*eleēmosynē*) and looking to the care of the poor led to similar ways of seeing to the needy in their midst by both common collections and private patronage. While patronage and euergetism were widely practised by urban officials and other prominent citizens,[22] it is doubtful that any other religious or political entities were as thorough and regular about relief of the needy as were Jews and Christians.[23] Already Paul undertook the collection for Jerusalem with the understanding that it was for the poor there (Rom 15:25–7; 1 Cor 16:1–4; 2 Cor 8 and 9; Gal 2:10). The account of dissension between Hebrew- and Greek-speaking Christian Jews in the first years in Jerusalem reveals a custom already under way of daily food distribution, of which widows, and therefore their children as well, were the primary recipients (Acts 6:1–6). First Timothy 5 reveals elements of both communal and private patronage of widows: those who have family should be helped by them, while those who do not should be supported by the church (1 Tim 5:3–16). Help to widows and orphans was the traditional form of almsgiving (Jas 1:27; Ign. *Smyr.* 6.2; *Pol.* 4.1), while defrauding labourers was the worst offence (Jas 5:1–4). The *Didache* (15.4) links prayer and almsgiving as acts sanctioned by the gospel with community support and mutual charity.

22 For full discussion, see Hands, *Charities and social aid.*
23 Grant, *Early Christianity and society.*

One of the chief concerns of the Shepherd of Hermas[24] is neglect of community and personal responsibility to the poor by the irresponsible wealthy. The neglect is both of the common charity funds and of private patronage for poverty relief. The riches of the wealthy are a severe hindrance to them (*Vis.* 1.1.8; 3.6.5–7; *Mand.* 8.3, 10; 12.2.1; *Sim.* 8.9.1; 9.20.1–4; 9.30.4–5; 31.2) and lead them to neglect the poor (*Vis.* 3.9.3–6; *Sim.* 9.26.2). Rather, they should give with simplicity to all those in need (*Mand.* 2.4; *Sim.* 1.8–11). The second *Similitude* likens the relationship of rich and poor to a common method of viticulture in ancient central Italy, in which the small Atinian elm tree is trimmed flat on top and forced to grow horizontally so that grape vines planted at its base can be supported on its branches. The fruitless elm which supports the fruit-bearing vine is like wealthy benefactors whose intercessory prayer is not as effective as that of the poor, those who depend on them for material survival and who, because of their position, have the ear of God when they pray.

Tertullian gives quite a bit of detail about the common fund of charity collected in the church of Carthage in his day. A monthly voluntary offering from everyone goes not towards common banquets, as was customary in the burial clubs and trade guilds of the time, but to the feeding and decent burial of the poor, to the support of boys and girls without parents or property (oddly, he does not mention widows), for old domestic slaves presumably abandoned by their owners, for shipwrecked sailors, and for those in prisons or condemned to the mines, or in exile on an island for the sake of their Christian identity (*Apol.* 39.5–6). Here is a treasure of information about Christian charitable enterprises. We would like to know if those abandoned slaves and shipwrecked sailors were all Christians; probably they were. The common funds of charity were undoubtedly intended for members of the community only, and were in fact one of the attractive things about Christianity. Tertullian goes on to quote the familiar saying about Christians: 'See how they love one another' and 'See how they are ready to die for one another' (39.7).

The *Apostolic tradition* gives us a glimpse not of a common fund, but of private patronage to widows and others. Anyone who has been given a gift for a widow, sick person or someone dependent on the church must deliver it the same day; if not, the next day with something of one's own added to it, a penalty for having kept what belongs to the poor (29B (24)). Private patrons give meals for widows in their homes, which must be done in a respectable manner and concluded before evening. Alternately, one who cannot receive

---

24 Osiek, *Rich and poor in the Shepherd of Hermas*; as well as *Shepherd of Hermas: a commentary*.

widows for a meal at home may give them food and wine that they can take away to their own homes (30).

Around the same time, Clement of Alexandria urges his economically comfortable congregation to remember their responsibility toward those in need. In his treatise, *Quis dives salvetur* ('Who is the rich man who can be saved?'), on the gospel story of the rich man who seeks to follow Jesus (Mark 10:17–22; Matt 19:13–15; Luke 18:15–17), he consoles them that the call by Jesus to give away all possessions was not to be followed literally, but in the spirit: it is a call to detachment from worldly possessions in favour of mindfulness of those in need, which will take the form chiefly of personal patronage.

In these three writers, we see the two different ways in which the church organised charitable works. For Clement and the author of the *Apostolic tradition*, private patronage for the support of widows was encouraged. But Tertullian's comments reflect a tendency already in process for the role of private patrons to be gradually absorbed into the more centralised system whereby all works of charity were organised by the leaders of the assembly and distributed by them.[25] By the middle of the third century, it was reported that the Roman church was supporting over 1,500 needy widows and others in need, a sizeable number but one probably not out of proportion to other large centres of Christian life (Euseb. *HE* 6.43.11).

The practices of prayer, fasting, almsgiving and the phenomenon of martyrdom are closely interconnected. A long practice, already established in the first generations, of orientation towards the primacy of God, detachment from material possessions, and ascetic discipline prepared certain Christians for the rare times when they were called upon to exercise resistance to the point of death.[26] When the age of martyrdom ceased, the longstanding practice of asceticism was transferred to the eremitical and monastic call to the desert, which would flourish in the next few centuries. Still though, the vast majority of Christians were not involved in such extreme asceticism. But their steady daily practices of prayer, fasting and charity, learned from the parent faith of Judaism, were important factors in their self-understanding.

The ideal Christian life

A fairly clear profile of the ideal Christian life emerges from the sources: prayer many times daily, innocence of immoral conduct, stable marriage and family,

25 Bobertz, 'Role of patron'; Countryman, *The rich Christian.*
26 Tilley, 'Ascetic body and the (un)making of the martyr'.

regular fasting, constant attention to the poor and needy. Christians seem to have lived like everyone else in the midst of their neighbourhoods, except that they did not abort or expose unwanted children, they usually did not seek military service or magistracies and did not frequent temple, theatre, hippodrome or amphitheatre. The traditional hierarchical family structure, including slavery, was reinforced by theological underpinnings that nevertheless pointed the way towards respect for each baptised person as redeemed by Christ. As we have seen, these were ideals that delineated believers' lives. In the gap between ideal and reality lay their emerging sense of authentic Christian living.

PART IV

*

REGIONAL VARIETIES OF
CHRISTIANITY IN THE FIRST
THREE CENTURIES

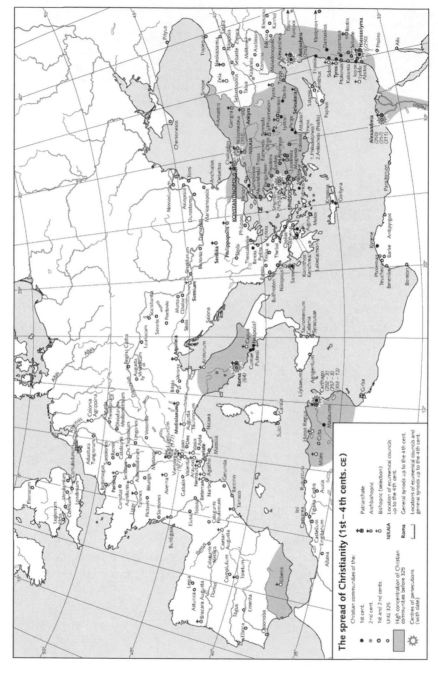

The spread of Christianity (1st–4th cents. CE)

Christian communities of the:

●	1st cent.
●●	2nd cent.
○ ○	1st and 2nd cents.
○	Until 325

High concentration of Christian communities before 325

Centres of persecutions (with date)

✝ ✝	Patriarchate
✝ ✝	Archbishopric
✝	Bishopric (selection)
NIKAIA	Location of ecumenical councils up to the 4th cent.
Roma	General synods up to the 4th cent.
⌐⌐	Locations of ecumenical councils and general synods up to the 4th cent.

Map 4. The spread of Christianity (1st–4th centuries CE)

15

From Jerusalem to the ends of the earth

MARGARET M. MITCHELL

Both the apostle Paul and the risen Jesus (according to Luke) envision a spreading of the Christian movement out from Jerusalem into the circumference of the Mediterranean world, as far as Rome, and 'to the ends of the earth' (Acts 1:8; Rom 15:19, 24). The chapters in this section will trace the progress and effects of that dispersion of Christian communities in the first three centuries – to Asia Minor, Achaea, Egypt, Syria, Mesopotamia, Gaul, North Africa and Rome. The purpose of such regional explorations is to identify the local particularities of the Christian religion as it was established in each of these places in the first three centuries, while also noting similarities and fundamental coherences and correspondences between the regional churches as they emerged. The dominant features of each region – its historical-political history in relation to the Roman empire, its local religious cults and organisations, its languages and native customs – had an undeniable impact on how the Christian mission took root and grew on that soil. But this does not mean these churches had no sense of being part of a worldwide phenomenon, supported by regular communication and interconnections, and sharing some essential beliefs and practices.[1]

In what may be the earliest extant Christian inscription (sometime before 216 CE), the famous epitaph of Abercius, bishop of Hieropolis in Phrygia Salutaris, recounts his own journeys at the end of the second century, self-consciously aligning himself with the earlier Pauline itinerary and experience – 'everywhere', he says, 'we had Paul as our companion.'[2] In his wide travels a century and a half after Paul among Christian communities from his home in Asia to Rome, to Syria, Nisibis and Mesopotamia, Abercius says he encountered

---

1 Appropriately emphasised by Markshies, *Between two worlds*; Grant, *Augustus to Constantine*, against models since Bauer that stress the great diversity among forms of Christianity and Christians. Obviously the two must be held together by the historian.
2 Lines 11–12 (I cite the text from Lüdtke and Nissen, *Die Grabschrift des Aberkios*, 36–42, along with my translations).

everywhere some constants of the Christian movement: instruction in the Lord's 'trustworthy texts' (*grammata pista*), a eucharistic celebration of common food eaten in the company of 'friends' (*philoi*), and a common 'faith' (*pistis*) leading the way (lines 12–16). He declares himself 'a disciple of a holy shepherd (*mathētēs poimenos hagnou*) who feeds flocks of sheep on mountains and plains'.[3] At the end of his epitaph, composed while he was still alive, Abercius makes a direct invocation to the passerby who might read his words, whom he invokes as 'the one who understands these things', to pray for him now that he is dead (line 19). Both the cryptic words earlier and this concluding knowing address presume a community of like-minded people who, if not known to the wider world, are recognisable to one another. Their uniting bonds are a holy shepherd and holy virgin, common texts and table, bread, wine and fish.

One significant discrepancy between Abercius and his model and spiritual companion, Paul, is that, whereas in the late 50s Paul was at great pains to visit Jerusalem one last time before heading to the west (Rom 15:23–32), Abercius passes by Jerusalem, and Judaea, without mention. He apparently was as close as 'the plains of Syria' and yet did not feel the need to veer south to see what Helena and others a century later would view as 'the Holy Land'. This oversight demonstrates a significant shift in the centre of gravity of Christian geography – real and symbolic – in the first two centuries. The focal point of Abercius' inscription is, after all, his wonder at the glories he has looked upon when visiting Rome, and seeing the church there like 'a golden-stoled, golden-sandalled queen' and 'a people who had a resplendent seal' (lines 7–9). What had happened to the church in Jerusalem in the interval?

One of the most significant facts of Christian history is the movement of the majority of Jesus' followers outside of the Galilaean and Judaean context of his ministry. Evidence of followers of Jesus in Galilee after his death may be found in the message of the young man at the tomb in Mark's gospel,[4] to the effect that the risen Jesus 'goes before them into Galilee' (16:7; cf. 14:28), and perhaps in the rural flavour of some of the sayings traditions like Q. The sources also indicate that the very earliest followers of Jesus had a centre in Jerusalem,

---

3 Lines 3–4. Earlier scholarship on the epitaph included debates over whether it was Christian, 'pagan' (Harnack, *Zur Abercius-Inschrift*), or syncretistic (Dieterich, *Die Grabschrift des Aberkios*). More recent work concludes that the density of symbols and allusions, together with the likely identification of this 'Abercius' with the anti-Montanist figure named by Eusebius as Abercius Marcellus (*HE* 5.16.2) make it much more likely that it is Christian (Wischmeyer, 'Die Aberkiosinschrift als Grabepigramm'; Merkelbach, 'Grabepigramm'; Snyder, *Ante pacem*, 247–50).

4 Mark's gospel insists that Jesus engaged in ministry in the Decapolis, which may reflect Christian communities there in his day (5:1, 20; 7:31 (confused!); 8:13, 22, etc.).

yet frustratingly little is known of the precise history of this early Palestinian church. Luke tells of early days under the leadership of James, the brother of the Lord, and Peter, with defining events, such as the martyrdoms of Stephen and James, the brother of John, and persecutions which led to a 'dispersion' of Christians, except for the apostles (Acts 8:1). Josephus and later Christian sources (Hegesippus) seem to agree on the whole about the death of James, the brother of Jesus ('the just'), at the hands of religious authorities c.61 CE, by either stoning or clubbing, according to the latter, at the site of the temple.[5] That this James, 'the brother of the Lord',[6] was a leader of the Christians in Jerusalem already in the first decades of the movement is corroborated by the earliest sources, the letters of Paul (Gal 1:19; 2:9; cf. 1 Cor 9:5). But the religious, theological and missiological position of James or of Peter is very difficult to reconstruct, because Paul's own letters are polemical rather than descriptive (see especially Gal 2:11–14), and it is hard to ascertain whether those whom Paul describes as 'some from James' in Gal 2:11 (equivalent to 'those from the circumcision' in 2:12?) were acting on his orders and authority when they prevented Peter from eating with Gentile Christians. The narrative account of the 'Jerusalem council' in Acts 15, written from a much later perspective, seeks to ally James and Peter with Paul, and with the Gentile Christian mission,[7] even as it presupposes the authority of Jerusalem as a kind of mother church. The epistle of James now in the New Testament – if 'the slave of God and the Lord Jesus' (1:1) is meant to be this 'James, the brother of the Lord' – presents him as a venerable ecclesiastical authority who writes a circular letter to believers among 'the twelve tribes in the diaspora', a perspective which also reflects a Judaean/Jerusalemite point of view.[8] But this letter, like Acts, probably reflects a Paulinisation of James from a later perspective after the Gentile, law-free mission had won out (see 1:25, championing 'the perfect law of freedom'; cf. 2:8). If this text is pseudonymous (as I think to be the case),[9]

---

5 Josephus, AJ 20.200; Hegesippus, apud Euseb. HE 2.23.
6 There has been much recent scholarly interest in James; see Chilton and Evans, The Missions of James, Peter, and Paul and James the just and Christian origins. The discovery and later discreditation of 'the James ossuary' has been an interesting, if ultimately irrelevant, part of these discussions. See the sensational claims of Shanks and Witherington, The brother of Jesus. On the debate and its exaggerated claims for significance (as well as the report of the Israeli Antiquities Authority that the ossuary in its present form has received modern 'doctoring' on the box and the inscriptions), see Mitchell, 'Does the James ossuary bring us closer to Jesus?' and 'Grave doubts about the "James ossuary"' and Painter, Just James.
7 Barrett, Freedom and obligation; Haenchen, Acts; Conzelmann, Acts; Fitzmyer, Acts of the apostles.
8 So Bauckham, James.
9 Recent champions of its authenticity include Bauckham and Johnson, The letter of James, but their arguments cannot overcome the difficulty of the comfortable Greek composition

then we must admit that we actually have no first-hand document from that early Jerusalem church of the first generation.[10] But the very fact of Paul's vigorous collection endeavour 'for the saints in Jerusalem' (1 Cor 16:1–4; 2 Cor 8 and 9; Rom 15:25–9; cf. Gal 2:9) in the 50s seems indisputable evidence that the Christian community in Jerusalem was viewed, and probably saw itself, as in some sense the matrix of the increasingly worldwide movement.[11] But this was not to last.

While we know very little of the internal development and pressures within those churches, two major socio-political events without a doubt shaped their destiny: the seige and destruction of Jerusalem by the Romans in 66–70 CE, and the crackdown against Jewish insurgency by Hadrian some sixty years later. Eusebius reports[12] that the Jerusalem Christians, warned by an oracle via a revelation (*apokalypsis*), fled from Jerusalem before its inhabitants were locked inside for the gruelling final seige so graphically depicted by Josephus in his *Bellum Judaicum*.[13] Eusebius says they were commanded to inhabit (*oikein*) Pella, a city in Perea (Transjordan, in the Roman province of Syria, and in the region of the 'Decapolis'). For him this migration (*metoikizesthai*) supports a theological argument that the destruction of Jerusalem was due to divine punishment on the Jews for having killed Jesus decades earlier.[14] He draws upon Josephus' account of the horrific sufferings in those months to accent his argument that divine vengeance was pinpointed on Jews while Christians were providentially spared.[15] Indeed, Eusebius goes so far as to say that the residency of Christians in Jerusalem earlier was what gave the city forty years of reprieve in the period between the death of Jesus and Titus' sack and seizure (*HE* 3.7.8), and he employs Josephus' own (variously directed) apologetic account to emphasise the many divine portents the Jews in Jerusalem had

---

of the letter, knowledge of Pauline tradition, and improbable provenance (for the pseud-epigraphical nature of the text, see especially Dibelius, *James*).

10 The same goes for the two epistles of Peter, both pseudepigrapha, the first of which is, like James, addressed to 'resident aliens in the diaspora' (1:1). See pt II, ch. 4 for detailed description of the sources of 'Jewish Christianity'.

11 See pt II, ch. 5, above.

12 Also references in Epiph. *Pan.* 29.7.7–8; 30.2.7, and *Mens.* 15. Koester, 'Origin and significance of the flight to Pella tradition', argues that Epiphanius was independent of Eusebius. There is also debate about whether this tradition lies behind Mark 13:14 and parallels, or was derived from it (see references in Davies and Allison, *Matthew*, vol. III, 347).

13 Euseb. *HE* 3.5.3.

14 Attridge and Hata, *Eusebius, Christianity, and Judaism*; Grant, *Eusebius as church historian*.

15 On how Josephus becomes a crucial source (ironically, towards a supercessionist, anti-Judaistic theological agenda) for patristic sources, see Schreckenberg, 'Josephus in early Christian literature'; Hardwick, *Josephus as an historical source*.

obstinately refused to heed as they raced headlong, unrepentant, to their judgement.

The second crucial event was Hadrian's suppression of the revolt of Bar Kochba in 132–5 CE, and rededication of Jerusalem as Aelia Capitolina, with Jews forbidden, not only to live there, but even to gaze upon it from a distance. When Eusebius attempts, as he does for each major location, a regular succession of Christian bishops in Jerusalem, he remarks that he had had difficulty learning details of the bishops (most of whom were short-lived) before 135, but had been able to document fifteen of them from written records. He emphasises that Hadrian's conquest of the city marked a shift in the community and leadership there, from those who were 'Hebrews in ancestry', with their 'bishops from the circumcision' (HE 4.5.3–4), to a 'church from the Gentiles', with the first bishop, Marcus, appointed (HE 4.6.4). At this point Jerusalem officially, for Eusebius, becomes, like the entire rest of the world, a part of the Gentile mission. He appears at pains to paint the history of Jewish Christianity as past and gone from that point forward.[16] Now Jerusalem is like any other city in the Mediterranean, a site of official 'pagan' worship (including the temple to Venus marking the spot where Constantine will later build a church in honour of the burial place of Jesus).

But the isolation and rededication of Jerusalem did not mean the complete eradication of either Christians or Jews from Palestine.[17] Many Jews moved to coastal cities, like Caesarea or Javneh, as also to Galilean cities, such as Sepphoris and Tiberias. Eusebius preserves an intriguing tradition of men reputed to have been the grand-nephews of Jesus (through his brother Judas) who were dragged out of Galilee and brought before the emperor Domitian (died 96 CE) on suspicion of their intent to politically enfranchise their ancestral house of David. Eusebius paints them in the hues of the martyrs of his own day by saying how, though they were rough farmers who easily persuaded Caesar of their innocuousness by showing him the roughness of their hands, their judicial ordeal (and blood connection to Jesus) led to their 'becoming leaders of the churches' (Euseb. HE 3.20.6). Eusebius' own De martyribus Palestinae ('The martyrs of Palestine'), an independent work also appended to some versions of his Historia ecclesiastica (bk VIII),[18] gives his eyewitness testimony to Christian deaths in Palestine, Phoenicia, Egypt, Syria and Asia

---

16 It may be noted here that the archaeological record is disputed as to whether there is evidence of Christians, or Jewish Christians in particular, in Palestine in the second and third centuries (see Taylor, *Christians and the holy places*).

17 Evidence collected in Mullen, *Expansion of Christianity*, 21–33.

18 The full text has been preserved in Syriac.

Minor in the early fourth century. For him, common suffering at the hands of demonically incited state authorities (in this case, the edicts under Diocletian and Maximinus Daia in 303–11 CE)[19] unifies the church of his day throughout the world, and cements their claim to be the successors of the earliest Christians whose fate they share. He tells of more than forty deaths of Palestinian Christians, including Silvanus, bishop of the churches around Gaza, and his mentor, Pamphilus, presbyter of Caesarea (*HE* 8.13.5–6). His home, Caesarea Maritima, the major Palestinian coastal city that had been for more than a century a renowned centre of Christian and Jewish life and learning, had Christian roots stretching back to the earliest days (Paul's two-year imprisonment there is told in Acts 23–6; Peter's conversion of the Roman centurion, Cornelius, in Acts 10). This splendid Hellenised coastal city, built up by Herod the Great in honour of his Roman overlords, was home to both Christians and Jews for the entire period of this volume, in which their exegetical work was mutually influenced (as invective evidences).[20] An immensely important event in its history was Origen's move to Caesarea *c.*231 from Alexandria, and his establishment there of a Christian academy, library and centre for textual production.[21]

The destruction and isolation of Jerusalem after the two revolts meant that the traditional relationship between diaspora and centre was in some sense pulled inside out, until the formation of the Christian 'Holy Land' traditions in the fourth century reversed the direction once again.[22] In the meantime, as the *Epistle to Diognetus* has it, Christians were spread throughout the empire, but, in distinction from Jews, were distinguished by neither land, language nor customs, neither special towns nor select dialect or lifestyle, living in cities both 'Gentile' and 'barbarian', in each case following local customs in dress and diet and lifestyle (*Ep. Diognet.* 5.1–5). For this anonymous author, such accession to local custom that created Christian cultural invisibility is cause for wonderment, expressed in theological paradoxes that go back to the Pauline and Johannine writings: that Christians are in the world but not of it, for they have their own commonwealth. Their sojourn is not defined by distance from Jerusalem, but from heaven: 'every alien homeland is theirs and every homeland alien' (5.5). He stresses the division between Christians

---

19 See pt VI, ch. 28, below.
20 See Hirshman, *A Rivalry of Genius*.
21 See ch. 19 and pt v, ch. 27, below. A continuous line extends for almost a century from Origen to Pamphilus to Eusebius in the stewardship of the library and academy at Caesarea.
22 Wilken, *The land called holy*; Taylor, *Christians and the holy places*; Walker, *Holy city, holy places*; see Prelude, above.

as 'soul' and the world as 'body' in order to emphasise the separation and divisibility of the two.

But he might (with a different purpose) have used the same metaphor to examine how soul and body are mutually related. For historians of ancient Christianity, this image and the concessions the author makes press the question of how these 'local customs' may have influenced the Christian movement in various places. Surely language and lifestyle, inherited and imbibed in various locales throughout the Mediterranean world, could not have been without effect on the expressions, rituals and lifestyles of these Christian communities. And each region was also conditioned by realities of Roman rule in that district (with all its permutations and constants), as well as by the conspicuous individuals and historical events that marked each in turn. No area, as we shall see, was an island unto itself, so the distinct account of each region is in part a history of interaction. But before following Paul (and Abercius, and others) in their ambit around the Mediterranean, we shall turn to the issues involved in studying the diffusion and demographics of Christianity in the early centuries. Just how many people are we talking about when we discuss the 'spread' or the 'rise' of Christianity in the pre-Constantinian period in these six regions?

16

Overview: the geographical spread
of Christianity

FRANK TROMBLEY

Methods, sources, and demographic judgements

The demographic study of earliest Christianity began with Adolf von Harnack's *Die Mission und Ausbreitung des Christentums*. Relying on the critical analysis of literary sources, Harnack saw demographically significant Christian communities wherever there was a martyrdom narrative or clear evidence for an episcopal see. This assessment was influenced by Tertullian and Origen, who both argued that Christianity was expanding rapidly in all parts of the empire, even in remote corners like Britain. Nearly a century of research since then has clarified the issue, but these studies are still in their infancy.[1] The first step is to look particularly at what evidence has become available since Harnack's pioneering work.

Three specific genres of evidence lend themselves to demographic analysis: inscriptions, papyri and archaeological artefacts. As material evidence, they permit the localisation of early Christian communities at particular sites and historical moments, as long as dates can be assigned with relative precision. Inscriptions are the most useful genre, because of their wide distribution in town and countryside, and because, as demotic documents, they give expression to the social norms and theological concepts of ordinary people. The greatest part of the epigraphy by far consists of funerary inscriptions.

Most pre-Constantinian funerary inscriptions have been discovered in Rome, in Phrygia in Asia Minor, in Roman Africa and possibly at Syracuse in Sicily.[2] Pre-fourth-century Christian inscriptions are cautious about displaying the religious affiliation of the dead and their families. Christians often used the same cemeteries as their pagan neighbours, and alluded to their beliefs in ambiguous language, but otherwise observed local burial practice. There is

---

1 Mullen, *Expansion of Christianity*.
2 *SEG* 15 (1958), nos. 580–7 (Syracuse, *c*.275–325).

a long series of Latin Christian inscriptions in the catacombs of Rome dating from the second half of the third century. The Christian stones of third-century Phrygia were often hewn in the shape of pagan funerary altars, with relief carvings of the dead and their families, with symbols of the trades they practised and with carved recesses atop the altar for sacrificial offerings to the dead. But there were also differences, as for example in the curses against breaking open the tomb that normally appeared at the end of the inscription. Departing from the conventional pagan curse, which required the tomb-breaker to pay a fine to the temple treasury and sometimes called upon subterranean divinities to punish the violator, Christian inscriptions often say simply, 'he shall be accountable to the living God.' This formula originated in the town of Eumeneia in Phrygia, where Christians outnumbered pagans, to judge from the preponderance of such inscriptions in the later third century. Christianity was not a *religio licita* ('lawful religion'). With the threat of persecution always in the air, Christian monuments displayed tact. A striking example of this is the funerary altar inscription of Abercius in the territory of Hieropolis. It is a rhetorical *tour de force* in terms of its semantic ambiguity, yet is clearly Christian. It expresses theological ideas in everyday Greek, and mentions Abercius' contacts with the Christian communities in Rome and Syria.[3] Purely Christian *nekropoleis* ('cities of the dead') also existed, providing a venue for a more vivid, and sometimes more militant, expression of the social and cultural fact of Christianity. There are, for example, the 'Christians to Christians' inscriptions of rural Phrygia. Others make use of the 'chi-rho', a ligature which was originally used as an abbreviation for the name of Christ, but which became a Christian victory symbol after 312. Where inscriptions lack Christian phrases and symbols, the burden of proof is on the epigraphist who seeks to prove that a text (and dedicatee) is Christian.

When one turns from Rome and Asia Minor, the epigraphic evidence becomes more limited. The number of datable pre-Constantinian inscriptions is very small. Christianity first identified itself with Greek language and thought at Antioch in Syria. Christian inscriptions are plentiful in its rural territory, but the series does not begin until the second quarter of the fourth century. Most cities in Roman Africa had bishops presiding over small communities, but the dated third-century epigraphic evidence is confined to a small number of towns.[4] The pre-fourth-century Christian community at Tipasa is known

---

3 See ch. 15, above, and Fig. 4.
4 Mullen, *Expansion of Christianity*, 320–6.

from the marble funerary tablet of a certain Rasinia Secunda, dating from 238.[5] It is one of the earliest known Christian inscriptions anywhere, and suggests how epigraphy and archaeology can sometimes corroborate each other. Her *praenomen* 'Rasinia' seems to be of Punic or Berber origin. There is also a small group of Christian inscriptions, one in Greek, the rest in Latin, from Clusium in Etruria that may be of late third- or early fourth-century date.[6]

Christian inscriptions can do little more than provide a *terminus ante quem* for the formation of the community in a particular locality, whether it is a large city, a rural site in its territory, or an imperial estate. The chronological origins of the local Christian community may go back decades or even centuries before the first inscription. Epigraphic evidence does much to confirm Harnack's interpretation of the pre-Nicaean literary evidence, corroborating the presence of the new religion in small towns and rural territories. But definitive conclusions are possible only by using epigraphy in combination with literary and archaeological data.

The archaeological evidence of pre-Constantinian Christianity is confined to a few localities.[7] Rome dominates the overall picture. The earliest monuments consist of the catacombs that the bishops of Rome acquired from the early third century onwards. Their artistic ornamentation gives some insight into the theological preoccupations of the Roman Christians, who made up a noticeable percentage of the population enclosed within the city by the Aurelian wall in the early 270s. The earliest surviving church building in Rome appears to be the Titulus Equitii (third century). [8] Another pre-fourth-century site is Dura Europos, a provincial town on the Euphrates frontier. The character of its community is expressed in the wall paintings of a house that was converted into a church *c*.250.[9] Its artistic themes such as the Good Shepherd have a clear resonance with the previously mentioned Abercius inscription. Late third-century Christian buildings and cemeteries have been identified in Tipasa in Numidia[10] and a cemetery at Henchir Skihra in Byzacena. The catechetical school of Alexandria must have been housed in a building ancillary to the churches (*ecclēsiae*) that Origen says were burnt down in the persecution of Decius (250–1).[11]

5 *ILCV* 3319.
6 Mullen, *Expansion of Christianity*, 190f.
7 See Snyder, *Ante pacem*.
8 Gounares, *Eisagōgē stēn palaiochristianikē archaiologia*, 57; Mullen, *Expansion of Christianity*, 200.
9 See pt VI, ch. 32, below, and Fig. 6.
10 Mullen, *Expansion of Christianity*, 325.
11 Frend, *Martyrdom and persecution*, 391.

Pre-fourth-century papyri survive exclusively from Egypt.[12] Like inscriptions, they are demotic documents. Except for a small number of second- and early third-century fragments of the Septuagint and gospels, the papyri mostly belong to the late third century and were written for family or business purposes. Personal letters contain theologically inspired observations and greetings, such as reference to 'common salvation' and 'I pray to God for your continual good health in every respect.'[13] Like inscriptions, the papyri use ambiguous phrases that can leave the religious allegiance of the writer in doubt. The papyri tell us a great deal about how ordinary Christians thought and communicated with each other, and can assist in making demographic judgements if their find spots are known from excavations, but their exact provenance is not always known.

The literary evidence remains our principal vehicle for tracing the expansion of Christianity, because it describes the behaviour of individuals and groups across a wide network of trans-Mediterranean contacts. Eusebius of Caesarea in his *Historia ecclesiastica* ('Ecclesiastical history') reports the existence of episcopal sees and correspondence networks. The papyri give proof of their scale and extent, as for example an early third-century fragment of Irenaeus of Lyons' *Adversus haereses* ('Against the heresies') that reached Oxyrhynchus in Egypt.[14] Another is a letter to a consortium of Christians in the Arsinoite nome from their agent in Rome: it mentions the help of the clerical bureaucracy in selling their grain and linen (c.264–82).[15] Eusebius' picture of the early communities is clear about the emergence of local literary traditions, and is corroborated by isolated documents, such as the canonical letter of Gregory Thaumaturgus of Neocaesarea adjudicating the affairs of the victims of a mid-third-century Sasanid Persian invasion of Asia Minor,[16] and in the letters of Cyprian of Carthage, which illustrate the social and geographical routes by which Christian ideas and personnel entered provincial life in various trans-Mediterranean destinations. Martyr narratives, theological diatribes, and other artefacts of local thought and experience followed the same routes. The bureaucratic structure of these networks, whether transmarine or terrestrial, gave local communities the institutional strength needed to disseminate ideas and attract new participants.[17]

---

12 Tibiletti, *Le lettere private*; Roberts, *Manuscript, Society and Belief*; Mullen, *Expansion of Christianity*, 271–9, 282–4; see ch. 18, below.
13 P. Oxy. 1492 (late 3rd early 4th cent.).
14 P. Oxy. 405.
15 *The Amherst papyri*, Grenfell and Hunt (eds.), I, no. 3a.
16 Gr. Thaum. *Ep. can.*
17 Leyerle, 'Communication and travel'.

Statistical estimates for Christianisation

A study by Rodney Stark estimates that the Christian population of the Roman empire was 1.9 per cent *c.*250 CE, 10.5 per cent *c.*300 CE and 56.5 per cent *c.*350 CE.[18] This framework is based on the supposition that the number of Christians increased at a rate of 40 per cent per decade between *c.*40 and 350 CE. These figures are more optimistic than traditional estimates going back to Edward Gibbon, who put the Christian population of the empire at the time of Constantine's victory at the Milvian bridge in 312 CE at somewhere near five per cent.[19] Harnack, A. H. M. Jones and R. M. Grant refused to commit themselves to precise figures.[20] Ramsay MacMullen and Keith Hopkins have suggested growth rates closer to Stark's estimate, but others have wisely viewed this with caution.[21] The fact is that no definitive estimates can be made for the Christian population of the empire as a whole before *c.*325, except perhaps for the city of Rome, which was in certain respects unique.[22] Exceptional factors include its status as the imperial residence. Its hypertrophic population growth was partly a consequence of free grain from the imperial estates being provided to the *plebs* in Caesar's name. Rome became a mecca for artisans during the building programmes initiated by Trajan, attracting skilled workers from all over the Mediterranean. This unusual combination of building activity, trade and immigration makes Rome a difficult measuring stick for the rest of the empire.

The frequency and intensity of the persecution of Christians in Rome and elsewhere are difficult to determine.[23] If known, they would only provide an index of how high a public profile the Christian communities had, but not necessarily how numerous they were. To cite one example, Cyprian's letters fail to quantify, or even hint at, the numbers of the *lapsi*, Christians who sacrificed in Rome and Carthage in accordance with the decree of Decius in 250.

Cities with Christian populations

Harnack estimated Rome's Christian population at 10,000 *c.*175 CE. This is consistent with Stark's estimate of 40,496 Christians in the whole empire *c.*150 CE,

18 Stark, *Rise of Christianity*, 7.
19 Gibbon, *Decline and fall*, vol. II, p. 69.
20 Harnack, *Mission und Ausbreitung*, 529–52; Jones, *Later Roman empire*, 96f; Grant, *Early Christianity and society*, 1–12.
21 Hopkins, 'Christian number', 198–207; MacMullen, *Christianizing the Roman empire*, 102–19; cf. Finn, 'Mission and expansion', 295f.
22 See ch. 22, below.
23 See pt VI, ch. 28, below.

but perhaps not his estimate of 217,795 c.200 CE. Late fourth-century traditions mention Christians of senatorial and equestrian rank.[24] Among them were M. Vibius Liberalis, *consul suffectus* in 166, a senator named Apollonius who confessed the *nomen Christianum* in the reign of Commodus and Valerius Victor Paternus, an equestrian (d. 297). The Roman church's bureaucracy, economic wealth and jurisdiction over the city's churches (*tituli*) were consolidated well before c.254.[25] The Christians in Rome may have numbered c.40,000 at this time, putting them in the range of 5–10 per cent of the inner city population, which has been estimated at about 700,000.[26] This may well explain the emperor Decius' quip that 'I would much rather hear that a rival emperor had risen up against me than another bishop in Rome.'[27]

It is difficult to say how accurately the Roman model reflects conditions in the provincial towns of Latin Europe. Large cities like Aquileia and Lugdunum (Lyons) had low-status expatriate populations from the Roman orient, but epigraphic evidence is scanty or non-existent, and there are few pre-fourth-century archaeological data like the possible house churches in Rome at San Giovanni e Paulo and San Clemente.[28] The Christian demography of Lugdunum is known from the letter Eusebius preserves about the martyrs there and in Vienne in 177.[29] This city, located on the upper Rhône, was a focal point for the expansion of Christianity into central Gaul. Some bishops of Gaul were executed in the Decian persecution and no successors appointed, but their communities were undoubtedly small.[30] The towns of Gaul with possible pre-Constantinian Christian buildings include Civitas Turonum (with a house church), Biturigae, Tolosa, Autessiodorum and Rotomagus.[31] In Spain, the earliest dated Christian inscription seems to come from 354, but ecclesiastical institutions are known from a letter of the churches of Leon and Merida to Cyprian in 254, from the bishops' list of the Council of Elvira (c.305–6?) and from numbers of early fourth-century Christian sarcophagi.[32] The canons of the council reveal a Christian community whose members held civic offices and married into pagan families.[33] As for Britain, there are no clear archaeological

24 *ILCV* nos. 56, 286.
25 Lampe, *Paul to Valentinus*, 142f.
26 Frend, *Martyrdom and persecution*, 245.
27 Cypr. *Ep*. 59.9.
28 White, *Architecture*, vol. II, 111–23.
29 Euseb. *HE* 5.1; Frend, *Martyrdom and persecution*, 1–30; see ch. 20, below.
30 Gregory of Tours, *Historia Francorum* 10.31. Hefele *et al.*, *Histoire des conciles*, vol. I. 1, 275–7; cf. Reynaud, *Lugdunum Christianum*; Mullen, *Expansion of Christianity*, 231.
31 Bedon, *Atlas*, 93, 122, 306, 310; cf. Mullen, *Expansion of Christianity*, 230, 236, 239, 241f.
32 *ILCV* 3932. Mullen, *Expansion of Christianity*, 253f., 256f.
33 Hefele *et al.*, *Histoire des conciles*, vol. I. 1, 215–64.

or literary data for Christians until the mid-fourth century, except the shadowy traditions about the martyrdom of St Alban, perhaps in the Decian persecution.[34]

The expansion of Christianity is hardest to trace in the smaller provincial towns of the African provinces. Some ninety bishops are said to have attended a council at Lambaesis c.240.[35] What little is known about these sees or the emergent Christian communities in towns like Altava, Satafi, Sitifi, Sufasar and Thamalla is found in a scattering of dated inscriptions. None of them gives any information about the profession or ethnicity of the persons named.[36] A third-century Christian catacomb with inscriptions existed in Hadrumetum.[37]

Literary data establish where Christian bishops and communities were before c.300. So, in quoting the memoirs of Hegesippus, Eusebius mentions bishops in Gortyna and Knossos in Crete, and Amastris on the north coast of Asia Minor.[38] Irenaeus (d. c.195) migrated through these places en route to the west. After leaving Smyrna for Rome, he went to Lugdunum and eventually become its bishop, but he continued to correspond with Rome and travelled there again.[39] Some bishops presided over small communities, but their size, composition, class structure and professional make-up cannot be determined from ecclesiastical correspondence alone.

Christianity expanded more quickly in the eastern Mediterranean coastal cities, and soon penetrated the hinterlands of Asia Minor. Literary testimony and epigraphic data document its presence in the predominantly pagan towns of Asia, Galatia, Lydia and Phrygia, and further east in Cappadocia and Pontus.[40] This culminated in the acceptance of Christianity by the semi-autonomous princes of Armenia in 314.[41] There is little evidence about Christianity in the cities of Palestine before 300; Eusebius' *De martyribus Palestinae* ('Martyrs of Palestine') indicates concentrations of Christians in Caesarea, the provincial capital, in Maiuma, the seaport of Gaza, and a scattering of persons from such places as Aelia, Diospolis, Eleutheropolis, Gadara, Jamnia and Scythopolis.[42] Egypt saw the steady growth of Christianity in towns like Oxyrhynchus. It is difficult to say how typical it was, to judge from the widely disparate numbers of papyri that have turned up from site to site. In Greece,

---

34 Thomas, *Christianity in Roman Britain*, 42–50.
35 Harnack, *Mission und Ausbreitung*, 895.
36 *ILCV* 2815, 2853 n., 3665a, 3682 n., 3956, 4038 n., 4156C.
37 Mullen, *Expansion of Christianity*, 304, 310.
38 Frend, *Rise of Christianity*, 243.
39 See pt III, ch. 13, above.
40 Mullen, *Expansion of Christianity*, 83–132.
41 Mullen, *Expansion of Christianity*, 139.
42 Taylor, *Christians and the holy places*, 56–64.

Origen speaks of a 'meek and quiet' community in Athens c.250, and one of its inscriptions from the later third century survives.[43] There also appear to be pre-Constantinian funerary inscriptions in Beroea, Corinth, Edessa, Philippi and Thessalonica.[44] The early churches in provincial Greece and the Aegean islands are known from pre-fourth-century installations and artefacts; these include a catacomb on the island of Melos, burials pre-dating the construction of the early fourth-century Sanatorium basilica in Knossos, and lamps found in burials at Philippi and Patras.[45]

Size of the Christian population and proportion to non-Christians

Christians seem to have been a tiny minority in most Mediterranean towns c.300, but there was local variation. There are only four known places where Christianity was demographically dominant c.300: at Cotiaeum and Eumeneia in Phrygia, at Orkistos, a village in the territory of pagan Nacolea, also in Phrygia, and at Maiuma, the seaport of Gaza. A smaller city, Oxyrhynchus in Egypt, already had two churches in 295; both were prominent landmarks, giving their names to streets, but the town also had at least four pagan temples.[46] A substantial number of its citizens, but perhaps not a majority, were Christian. Provincial capitals and imperial residences like Antioch, Nicomedia, Rome and Thessalonica seem to have been largely Christian only near the middle of the fourth century. Many provincial towns probably went the way of Bostra in Arabia, with a rough balance between pagans and Christians by the mid- to later fourth century.[47] In contrast, towns like Aphrodisias, Ascalon, Athens, Baalbek-Heliopolis, Carrhae-Harran, Delphi and Gaza, to name but a few, had predominantly pagan city councils until the late fourth or early fifth centuries. Estimates of the size of the Christian communities c.300 can only be made by reasoning backwards in time from later, better-documented periods, but this cannot always give satisfactory results. A. H. M. Jones' broad familiarity with the epigraphic data did not convince him of Gibbon's 5 per cent estimate, which may be a little low for some provinces to judge from the epigraphic finds from Phrygia and papyrological evidence in Egypt.[48]

---

43 Or. C. Cels. 3.30. IG 3/2 3435.
44 Mullen, Expansion of Christianity, 160–2, 164–6.
45 Laskaris, Monuments funéraires, 45f, 320, 446.
46 Trombley, Hellenic religion and Christianization, vol. II, 243f.
47 Julian, Epistulae 41.
48 Jones, Later Roman Empire, 96f; Bagnall, Egypt in late antiquity, 280f. Cf. Barnes, Constantine and Eusebius, 142.

The social class of Christians

The early Christian community of Rome drew its membership from the artisans and freedmen living in large tenement blocks (*insulae*), and from freedmen and slaves working in the imperial household, particularly in the time of Commodus, Septimius Severus and their successors. Most non-servile Christians in Rome and elsewhere were *peregrini*, expatriate citizens of the towns and their territories of the Roman orient. They enjoyed neither Roman citizenship nor Latin rights until the *Constitutio Antoniniana* of 212, the edict of emperor Caracalla that granted citizenship to most free residents of the empire. Before 212 Christians fell under the jurisdiction of the *praetor peregrinus*, who administered the large migrant population in Rome, most of them Greek-speaking easterners. The Latin-speaking Christians of late second-century Rome were African provincials. The low social status of Christians led to their victimisation in periodic persecutions designed to rid the urban centre of 'bad people' (*mali homines*) – individuals and groups who flouted the social norms, and abhorred public entertainments and religious festivals.

In the waning years of the tetrarchy,[49] there were Christians in every sector of social, economic and cultural life. Christian grammarians, rhetoricians and philosophers – like Arnobius of Sicca, Lactantius and Gregory Thaumaturgus – practised their professions at important urban centres. Men of grammatical education served as civil servants (*Caesariani*) in the offices of the imperial palaces, provincial governors and imperial estates.[50] One of them was Marcus Aurelius Prosenes (d. 217), an imperial freedman who became chamberlain of Commodus, and administrator in several departments of the emperor's private fisc. His funerary inscription mentions his reception apparently by the Christian divinity (*receptus ad deum*).[51] A Christian soldier named Aurelius Mannos is memorialised by a funerary inscription at Eumeneia in Phrygia: he was a cavalryman and horse-archer holding the special office of a *draconarius*, 'bearer of the dragon standard' in the office of Castrius Constans, who was civil governor of Phrygia and Caria shortly after 293.[52] Eusebius mentions Adauctus, a senior manager of the imperial estates in the time of Diocletian, and Dorotheus, a presbyter of the church of Antioch, who was put in charge of the imperial purple dye workshops in Tyre, a politically sensitive position. In the provinces, city councillors (*curiales*, *bouleutai*) are named in the inscriptions, particularly

---

49 See pt VI, ch. 30, below.
50 Frend, *Martyrdom and persecution*, 447.
51 *ILCV* 3332; cf. ch. 22, below.
52 *ILS* 8881.

at Eumeneia in Phrygia. Ordinary Christians practised a wide range of trades essential to the urban economy. The epigraphic and literary sources mention agricultural day-labourers, bailiffs on imperial estates, bankers, linen weavers, maritime traders, mat makers, mule keepers, rural estate owners, stonecutters and tailors, to name only some.[53]

Rural vs. urban locations

Less is known about the expansion of Christianity in the countryside, except in some parts of Asia Minor and North Africa. Agriculturists were conservative on matters of religious belief and practice, fearing violations of the 'peace of the gods'. The failure to sacrifice according to ancestral ritual was thought to alienate the chthonic and celestial gods who brought the good harvest, thereby unleashing destructive natural phenomena like drought, floods and hailstorms. Christianity first took root in the nearer territories of the towns where urban attitudes prevailed. Hermas, the narrator of the *Shepherd of Hermas*, owned a productive estate, and divided his time between Rome and his agricultural lands some hours away, where he practised viticulture and flock grazing.[54] Justin Martyr mentions rural folk attending the Christian liturgy in Rome. There is no epigraphic evidence of Christians residing in estates outside the Aurelian wall before *c.*300; they would have been a tiny percentage of the rural population in most districts outside the wall until the later fourth century.

There are pre-fourth-century examples of Christians of low social status living in the territories of provincial cities in the Roman orient. In Syria, Phoenicia and Arabia, Christianity was confined mostly to the towns; it spread slowly in the countryside because of the strong cultural roots of the varieties of Semitic religion, whether of Aramaean or Arabic origin. At Edessa, the provincial capital of Osrhoene, there were rural clergy and Christian villagers just outside the city walls at the time of the great persecution.[55] Among them was the deacon Habib from the village of Tell-She. For Palestine, Eusebius' *Onomasticon* mentions only three villages as having a mostly Christian population: Anaia, Jetheira and Kariatha.[56] His *De martyribus Palestinae* mentions the prosecution of Christians from Anaia, from a village in the territory of Caesarea, and from the village-towns of the Batanaea in Arabia.[57] The papyrus letter of the presbyter Psenoris mentions a team of Christian gravediggers at the Great Oasis,

---

53 E.g. *ILCV* 645 (Rome, 269 CE).
54 Herm. *Vis.* 1.1.2; *Vis.* 3.1.2; *Vis.* 4.1.2; *Sim.* 1.2.3; *Sim.* 1.5; 5.2.3; 6.2.1–7; 8.1.2; *Mand.* 11.8.
55 Segal, *Edessa*, 85.
56 Barnes, *Constantine and Eusebius*, 110.
57 Taylor, *Christians and the holy places*, 60f.

a settlement at al-Kharga in the western desert of Egypt, and their burial of a possible victim of the great persecution.[58] In contrast, in the territory of Antioch in Syria, no Christian inscriptions earlier than 300 have been discovered in the extensively built-up limestone massif. This applies equally to the territories of Apamea in the late Roman province of Syria II, Emesa and Damascus in Phoenice Libanensis and Bostra in Arabia.

The presence of funerary inscriptions in the countryside of Phrygia does not in itself prove the existence of Christianity in every village. Many of these belonged to urban Christians, like the city councillors of Eumeneia, who were interred in cemeteries outside the walls as a matter of imperial law and customary practice. It is difficult to estimate the number of rural Christians vis-à-vis pagans except as a small minority, perhaps 5–10 per cent. They were sufficiently rare for Origen to observe c.250 that 'some . . . have done the work of going round not only cities but *even villages and country cottages* to make others pious towards God.'[59]

Karl Holl long ago suggested that Christianity was attractive to linguistic minorities of the Mediterranean hinterlands, particularly in rural Africa, Egypt and Phrygia, where poverty alienated agricultural labourers from the landed magnates.[60] The only region where his thesis has been borne out is Africa. Onomastic study of the persons prosecuted by the proconsul of Africa at Madaura in 180 (Namphamo, Miggin, Lucitas and Sanae) indicates Punic or Berber background. In contrast, the martyrs of Scilli have common Latin names (except for Nartzalus, which is Berber or Punic). Rural poverty in Africa and Numidia found expression in a militant martyr Christianity that became dominant in the territories of the towns in the later third century.

Conclusions

The demographics of Christian expansion remain a controversial subject. Johannes Geffcken in 1920 argued lucidly that the fifty-year period between 250–300 CE saw a decisive decline in the number of votive offerings at pagan temples.[61] Similarly, W. H. C. Frend, drawing on Geffcken's analysis and much new evidence, concluded that this half-century also saw the decisive expansion of Christianity; it was this that provoked the tetrarchy into launching the great persecution.[62] The figures proposed by Hopkins, MacMullen and Stark are

58 Grenfell and Hunt (eds.), *New classical fragments*, no. 73.
59 Or. *C. Cels*. 3.9.
60 Holl, 'Das Fortleben der Volksprachen'.
61 Geffcken, *Last days of Greco-Roman paganism*, 25–34, 115–77.
62 Frend, *Martyrdom and persecution*, 440–76.

optimistic, but do not support a radical reinterpretation. Recent epigraphic discoveries have, if anything, suggested a more gradual winding down of the pagan cults than Geffcken supposed, and even continuity at some shrines until the end of the fourth century. The empty temples and dead gods are now seen more as a symptom of economic readjustment in the later third century caused by barbarian pressure on the frontiers, militarisation of the civil service and an increased demand for revenues, particularly under the tetrarchy. This was the political background to the Christians' rise to between 5 and 10 per cent of the empire's population c.300. Too little is known about the religious affiliations of those who accepted Christianity to make judgements about the deficiencies of pagan faith and ritual. What led these people to opt for Christian monotheism? The apologetics of Arnobius and Origen indicate the types of ideological persuasion, but tell little about the personal experience that drew people into the Christian catechumenate.

17

Asia Minor and Achaea

CHRISTINE TREVETT

Asia Minor and Achaea were nurseries for Christianity, as the New Testament shows. The churches there were planted, grew and changed in environs which harboured a long history, within cities (Athens and Corinth, Ephesus and Pergumum among them) in which civic pride flourished and a diversity of cultures proliferated. The context for Christians' lives was the empire[1] and, for most of them, a *polis* with its rivalries, regional grandees, associations and gathered poor.

The evidence

Asia Minor is particularly important for understanding the development and diversification of the Christians' religion. Its significant epigraphy includes *overtly* Christian inscriptions which pre-date Constantine,[2] though the Christianity they represent (catholic,[3] Montanist/New Prophet,[4] Novatianist,[5] and others) is often difficult to determine. Inscriptions help to compensate for gaps in terms of Christian writings, art and artefacts.[6] Although some may be from the late second century, there is a dearth of them through the third in areas where Christians were (e.g. Asia's western coastal region and Bithynia; cf. Plin. *Ep.* 10.96; Luc. *Alex.* 25). Of significance are (1) the openly Christian third-century epitaphs showing 'Christians' well integrated with their pagan neighbours;[7] (2) the pre-216 CE epitaph of the Phrygian Abercius (Greek:

---

1 See pt I, ch. 3, above.
2 Gibson, *The 'Christians for Christians' inscriptions*; Tabbernee, *Montanist inscriptions*.
3 Ign. *Smyr.* 8.2 has the earliest reference to 'the catholic church'; cf. M. *Polyc.* 8.1; 16.2; 19.2.
4 'Montanism' is a later designation for 'the New Prophecy'.
5 On Novatianists in Asia Minor before the fourth century see Tabbernee, *Montanist inscriptions*, 345–9. Mitchell, *Anatolia*, vol. II, 82–3, 100–2; see further pt V, ch. 26, below.
6 Snyder, *Ante pacem*; Jensen, 'Art'.
7 Tabbernee, *Montanist inscriptions*, 62–91; Gibson, *'Christians for Christians' inscriptions*; Mitchell, *Anatolia*, vol. II, 43, 57; Mitchell with Levick, *Monumenta Asiae Minoris antiqua*, vol. x (JRSM 7).

Aberkios)[8] (possibly Avircius Marcellus of Euseb. *HE* 5.16.3), telling of a common understanding of faith, hospitality and eucharist from Rome to Nisibis (cf. Iren. *Haer.* 1.10.2); and (3) the early third-century Greek and Latin inscription which seems finally to have located Tymion and the site of the New Prophets'/Montanists' Phrygian 'Jerusalem'.[9]

Many of the New Testament writings relate to Achaea and Asia Minor.[10] Overlapping them chronologically are those of the apostolic fathers to or from those regions: *1 Clement* to Corinth; Polycarp *To the Philippians*[11] and the *Martyrdom of Polycarp* (from Smyrna); Ignatius' early second-century writings (some to areas addressed in the Apocalypse (Rev. 2–3));[12] the *Fragments* of Papias, chiliast and associate of 'the Elders' (Jerome, *Vir. ill.* 18; Iren. *Haer.* 5.33.4).[13] Additionally, there remain Melito's *Peri pascha*; the *Epistula apostolorum*;[14] the *Acts of Paul and Thecla*[15] (and its embedded *3 Corinthians*); *Acts* of Andrew, Peter and John; Eusebius' fragments of Dionysius of Corinth; and anti-Montanist writers, 5 and 6 Ezra and the *Ascension of Isaiah*[16] (the provenance of some of these writings is debated).

In the 'messy' and 'confrontational' second century,[17] apologetic literature sought to justify Christians' anomalous social position,[18] with Melito, Claudius Apolinarius of Hierapolis,[19] Athenagoras of Athens and Miltiades, 'the sophist of the churches',[20] addressing Marcus Aurelius (161–80 CE) and 'secular rulers'. Aristides of Athens and the Asian (?) Quadratus (sometime *episkopos* in Athens?)[21] may have been contemporaries (Euseb. *HE* 4.3.3).

For the third and early fourth centuries there is again the evidence of Eusebius – though little is known of the once-significant figures he mentions, such

---

8 Calder, 'Epitaph', 1–4; Wischmeyer, 'Der Aberkiosinschrift als Grabepigramm'; Horsley, *New Documents*, vol II, 177–81; Frend, *Archaeology*, 95–100; Tabbernee, *Montanist inscriptions*, 53 n.13; 130; and the literature cited there. See Fig. 4, above.
9 Euseb. *HE* 5.18.2 (Apollonius). Tabbernee, 'Portals', 87–93.
10 See pt II, ch. 5, above.
11 Harrison, *Polycarp's two epistles*; Bauer, *Die Polykarpbriefe*; Hartog *Polycarp* (this last supports the unity of Poly. *Phil.*).
12 Hemer, *Letters*.
13 Lieu, *Image and reality*, 245–52. See too Körtner, *Papias von Hierapolis*; and Schoedel, 'Papias'.
14 Stewart-Sykes, 'Asian context'; Hill, '*The Epistula apostolorum*'.
15 Davis, *Thecla*.
16 Knight, *Ascension and Disciples*; Hall '*The Ascension of Isaiah*'.
17 Wagner, *After the Apostles*, 223.
18 Grant, *Greek apologists*; Young, 'Greek apologists'; Lieu, *Image and reality*, 165, 182–90; Esler, *Early Christian world*, vol. I, 577 for bibliography.
19 Euseb. *HE* 4.26.2; 4.27.1; 5.19.
20 Euseb. *HE* 5.17.5; Tert. *Val.* 5.
21 Jerome, *Vir. ill.* 19; *Ep.* 70.4. Euseb. *HE* 4.23.3; 5.17.4.

as Helenus of Tarsus, activist against the Novatianist schism and upholder of eastern practice on re-baptism of heretics (*HE* 6.46.3; 7.5.4; 7.28.1). One letter of Firmilian of Caesarea has survived, as also work from the philosopher-apologist Lactantius and accounts concerning men of the time (such as Gregory of Nyssa on Gregory Thaumaturgus).

Much early literary evidence has been lost, including most of the work of Papias,[22] Melito (Euseb. *HE* 4.26.2), Miltiades (*HE* 5.17.5; Tert. *Val.* 5) and Dionysius (*HE* 4.23). It is from opponents' writings that we learn of Cerinthus, Marcion, the New Prophets and others. There remains, nevertheless, a wide range of texts for recovering the Achaean and Asian Christian legacies.

Social and cultural characteristics

Asia Minor (from the western coast of modern Turkey to the Taurus mountain range and northwards), with its long-established Greek cities, and Achaea (Greece)[23] were linked by the common language of Greek, by proximity to the Mediterranean and its culture, and through being subject to the ubiquitous Roman administration[24] that had absorbed local leagues and made *coloniae* of the like of Corinth,[25] Achaea's capital. Over centuries Asia Minor and the regions within it had undergone many administrative and boundary-related changes.[26] Civic rivalry and civil unrest played their parts in the 'webs of power' which bound the rulers and the ruled.[27] Cities might be melting-pots of Greeks and Anatolians, Romans and Jews. Well-established Jewish communities (e.g. in Ephesus, Smyrna, Sardis, Pontus)[28] might be strongly ambivalent in response to Hellenistic culture, or actively finding means to accommodate to it.

Latin served for the imperial administration, law and the military; Greek as the first language for the majority. In pockets, other languages survived.[29]

---

22 Iren. *Haer.* 5.33.4; Euseb. *HE* 2.15.2; 3.36.2; 3.39. See too Körtner, *Papias von Hierapolis*.
23 A senatorial province from 44 CE, covering southern Greece and the Peloponnese south of Macedonia and Illyricum. Corinth, Eleusis, Epidauros, Olympia, Athens and Sparta fell within it. Aegean islands came variously under Achaean or Asian jurisdiction. See e.g. Spawforth and Mee, *Greece*; Strabo, *Geog.*, esp. bks 8–10.
24 See pt I, ch. 3, above.
25 Wiseman, 'Corinth and Rome'; Rizakis, 'Roman colonies'.
26 Magie, *Roman imperial rule*; Nörr, 'Herrschaftsstruktur'; Mitchell, *Anatolia* and 'Administration'; Jones, *Cities*; Alcock, *Early Roman empire*.
27 See too Ando, *Imperial ideology*; Huskinson (ed.), *Experiencing Rome*.
28 See Trebilco, *Jewish communities*; Conzelmann, *Gentiles, Jews, Christians*; Barclay, *Jews in the Mediterranean diaspora*; as well as pt I, ch. 2, and pt II, ch. 10, above.
29 Freeman, *Galatian language*.

Indigenous and assimilated foreign cults retained their influence. Asia Minor was long established as home to cults of Zeus, the Phrygian Men, mother goddesses (notably Cybele), divinised heroes, and monotheism as well.[30] From the site of the Mysteries at Eleusis (overrun and partially destroyed by invasion in 170 CE), through the cult of Poseidon, Ephesus' economic embrace with the cult of Artemis, and Aphrodisias' link to Aphrodite, religious symbols embedded in buildings, institutions, writings, sculpture and other artefacts were used to define, claim and retain power. The imperial cult was boosted in Domitian's time (d. 96 CE), notably in Pergamum, Smyrna and Ephesus. Christian self-definition was refined in response.[31] Gaps in the evidence and the rural and undocumented nature of much of the territory prevent a comprehensive overview of the religious and cultural interface of Christians with their surroundings.

Christianity in this context

Early Christian traditions about Ephesus[32] and Athens (Acts 17–19; cf. 1 Cor. 1:14; 15:32; 18:23; 19:1, 10) show the interface between Christians, Jews, pagans, city politics and magic.[33] The presence of diaspora Jews had been important in determining the locations for evangelism but, where confident Jewish communities existed, so might Jews, Christians, pagans and the authorities be in tension. The fourth gospel, traditionally associated with Ephesus, suggests this[34] and Luke's picture of fraught relations between evangelists, Jews, and a sometimes hostile populace in Achaea and Asia does too (e.g. Acts 13:42–51; 14:1–7; 18:5–17, 19–20).

Building on the Pauline foundation,[35] parts of urban and rural Asia Minor saw significant growth for the Christians' *superstitio* (Plin. *Ep.* 96, in 112 CE; cf. Euseb. *HE* 8.1). Epigraphy shows Christians beyond the cities, while distaste for the New Prophecy (Euseb. *HE* 5.16.7; 5.18.2) included denigration of its beginnings in a 'village' and in 'little' places in Phrygia. Most sources concern urban Christians, however.

---

30 Mitchell, *Anatolia*, vols. 1 and 11; 'The cult of Theos Hypsistos'; and Strobel, *Das heilige Land*.
31 Trummer, *Denkmäler*; Jones, 'Roman imperial cult'; Geagan, 'Roman Athens', 386–7, 398–9, 408; Brent, *Imperial cult*; Harland, 'Christ-bearers' and 'Imperial cults'.
32 On Ephesus see Koester (ed.), *Pergamon*; van Tilborg, *Reading John*; and Arnold, *Ephesians*.
33 Klauck, *Magic*; Arnold, *Ephesians*; Trevett, *Christian women*, pt 3 on Ephesus.
34 See pt 11, ch. 6, above.
35 See pt 11, ch. 5, above.

The picture was mixed. Gregory Thaumaturgus found few Christians in his native Pontus in the 240s,[36] while third-century Phrygia had Christian communities from Synnada and Iconium to the Tembris valley in the north, and not all of catholic kind. By the time of Diocletian's persecution, at least one Phrygian town was said to have been wholly Christian.[37] Many were Christian around Nicomedia in Bithynia, where Lactantius, the Cicero-loving philosopher, had been based.[38]

Public distaste for Christians was a factor throughout this period. It erupted in localised, sporadic and occasionally more systematic hostility: the Pliny-Trajan correspondence (Plin. *Ep.* 10.96.2 and 97.2); the much-debated rescript of Hadrian to Minucius Fundanus (Euseb. *HE* 4.8.5–7; 4.9; 4.26.10; Justin 1 *Apol.* 2.2);[39] the *Martyrdom of Polycarp*; Melito's reference to 'new decrees' (Euseb. *HE* 4.26.5). Christians were put to death, as Pliny indicated (cf. Ign. *Eph.* 12.2; *M. Polyc. Acts of Carpus, Papylus and Agathonike*,[40] the *M. Pion.*). They suffered in the wake of natural disasters in Cappadocia (Firmilian: Cypr. *Ep.* 75), as well as under Decius, Diocletian and Maximinus in the early fourth century.[41] Achaea was not unscathed (Euseb. *HE* 4.26.3 (and 10); 5.24.2–5; and, especially, 4.23.2). Through the martyr discourse of the *Acta*, we see clearly competing systems.[42]

Christianity and diversity

Walter Bauer (original 1934) challenged assumptions that orthodoxy must have preceded heresy,[43] but more recent analysis allows for parallel developments, takes account of dissent internal to the church about belief and practice and understands movements of internal renewal or of schism in a more nuanced way. This leads to less dogmatism about where the boundaries lay between 'insider = orthodox' and 'outsider = heretic' in a given context. It is

36 Evangelisation followed. His 'canonical letter' told of Pontus devastated by the Goths in the 250s (Gr. Nyss. *V. Gr. Thaum.* in *PG* 46.909C and 954D). Cf. Socr. *HE* 4.27; Euseb. *HE* 7.14.1; 7.28.1; Mitchell, 'Life'.
37 Euseb. *HE* 8.11.1; Lactant. *Div. inst.* 5.11. Tabbernee, *Montanist inscriptions*, 215–16.
38 Euseb. *HE* 9.6.3–8.14; 9.9a.3–6; cf. *V.C.* 11.12. Cf. too, *HE* 8.5.1–6.8.
39 Cf. the disputed rescript from the council of Asia (Euseb. *HE* 4.13).
40 Euseb. *HE* 4.15.48 (under Marcus Aurelius). See Barnes, 'Pre-Decian *Acta*' (the Latin recension links them with Decius *c*.250). For translations, see Musurillo.
41 Euseb. *HE* 8.6.6–7; 8.12.1; 8.12.6–7; 8.13.1; 9.6.3, on Cappadocia, Bithynia and Pontus. See pt VI, ch. 28, below.
42 See Perkins, *Suffering self*, e.g. 116; and pt III, ch. 14, above.
43 Bauer, *Orthodoxy and heresy*. Contrast e.g. Koester, 'ΓΝΩΜΑΙ ΔΙΑΦΟΡΟΙ'.

questionable whether we should speak of orthodoxy and heresy as categories before the council of Nicaea.[44]

The emerging catholic form of what Ignatius called *Christianism* embraced some theological, ecclesiological and regional diversity. In this period, 'insider-outsider' Christian boundaries and writings were being determined, but the lines of demarcation were not solid. The dates of some sources are disputed, and the objects of the authors' polemic are sometimes hard to establish. Thus, some credited Polycarp with authorship of the Pastoral Letters, and saw in them polemic against Marcion (cf. Iren. *Haer.* 3.3.4; Poly. *Phil.* 7.1), while the date and context for the Ignatian corpus have been variously reassessed in recent decades.[45] There is ample opportunity for mismatch when categorising groups and tendencies.

How 'Jewish' was Christianity to be?

Christians appreciative of the heritage of Judaism remained influential in the churches. Stark attributed the attacks on Marcion's anti-Jewish, ditheistic and ascetic teaching to their 'strong current ties to the Jewish world'.[46] From the outset, however (Acts, 1–2 Corinthians, Galatians, Colossians and 1 Timothy, the Revelation), Christians had disagreed about orthopraxy, involving variously circumcision, forbidden foods and sabbath, Law, angelic, apocalyptic and other speculations. Ignatius wrote of Christian 'Judaising' and 'old leaven' (Ign. *Magn.* 8–10; *Phild.* 6). Some Christians wanted at least that degree of separation from Gentiles called for in the so-called apostolic decree from Jerusalem (Acts 15:19–20; 1 Cor 8:1, 4, 10; 10:19, 28; Rev 2:14, 20), while others eschewed even those minimalist requirements. It can be hard to determine whether a writer was criticising Jews 'proper' or Christian 'Judaisers'.

There was a broad spectrum of integration and non-integration, between Christians and Christians (e.g. Ign. *Phild.* 6; *Smyr.* 5.3; 7.2), Christians and Jews, and between each and pagan society. Relations might be close, complex or fraught with tensions. Marcion's contemporary, Aquila of Sinope, converted from paganism, then was a proselyte to Judaism. His literalistic rendering of Hebrew scriptures into Greek acted as critique of the LXX version which Christians used.[47]

---

44 Williams, 'Pre-Nicene orthodoxy?' and 'Defining heresy'; McGinn, 'Internal renewal'; Frend, 'Christianity'.

45 Munier, 'La question'; Lechner, *Ignatius;* see the various works by Goulder, as well as those by Hübner.

46 Stark, *Rise of Christianity*, 64–6; also Malina, 'Social levels', 369–400.

47 K. Hyvärinen, *Aquila.*

The Quartodeciman controversy was a special case which brought into relief differences of tradition of a regional kind in Christianity.[48] This, too, related to the question of how 'Jewish' was Christianity. In the 150s, Polycarp had spoken for Asian Quartodeciman Easter practice against the alternative advocated in Rome. He and bishop Anicetus respectfully had agreed to differ, although variations in practice would have hampered ecumenical relations between Christians of different ethnic groups in Rome and elsewhere.[49] A few decades later, bishop Victor took a strong line in favour of uniformity.[50] Rome's position had many supporters, but Polycrates of Ephesus cited 'great luminaries' of the apostolic age (including John who 'lay on the Lord's breast', John 13:25), revered martyrs, Melito and his own ancestors in the episcopate (HE 5.24.2–7, cf. 5.23.1). These had kept the (arguably more 'original') Quartodeciman tradition unswervingly.[51] Undaunted, Victor excommunicated the Asian churches, a move too far for some other bishops. Irenaeus rebuked Victor for his bulldozing insensitivity (Euseb. HE 5.23.1–24.18), but, like the Arian, the Quartodeciman controversy was not quickly settled. There was not just Christian diversity but a proud distinctiveness in Asia Minor. Its catholic leaders stood their ground, despite the claims and differing practices of Rome.

Chiliasm and prophetism

Chiliasm (millenarianism) and Christian prophetism had particular associations with Asia Minor, though either might be found elsewhere. Revelation chapters 20 and 21 told of hope for a New Jerusalem / new heaven and earth, and such ideas re-emerged through Papias of Hierapolis (Iren. Haer. 5.33.3f), through Cerinthus, 'the elders', Irenaeus, and in the New Prophecy.[52] In the third century, Dionysius of Alexandria (formerly of Cappadocia) was embroiled in debates on the matter (Euseb. HE 7.24, 25) and, during fourth-century persecution, the tradition was rekindled in Methodius of Olympus (Res. 1.55.1; Symp.

---

48 Among Quartodeciman/'fourteener' Christians, the cessation of the fast and the celebration of the resurrection at Easter were reckoned in relation to the 14th of Nisan and the Jewish Passover. Commemoration of crucifixion and resurrection would not always fall on a Friday and Sunday.
49 Lampe, Paul to Valentinus; and La Piana, 'Foreign groups'.
50 La Piana, 'Roman church'.
51 See too Tabbernee, 'Trophies'; Strobel, Osterkalendar; Lohse, Passafest.
52 Euseb. HE 3.28; 7.25; Iren. Haer. 5.33.3f; Tert. Marc. 3.24 and Res. 26. Trevett, Montanism, 95–105, and the literature there.

9.5) and Lactantius (*Div. inst.* 7.21–6). Indeed, chiliastic expectation (eschewing allegorising) was another respect in which a Jewish legacy had remained strong among some Christians. Eusebius was unimpressed (*HE* 3.39.13; 7.24.1).[53]

Christian *prophetism* (attested among men and women since Paul's day, e.g. 1 Cor; Acts 21:8–11) had proved important in Asia Minor but was marginalised as institutionalisation triumphed. There had been John the Seer and others in his circle, 'Jezebel' (Rev 2:20–4),[54] Philip's daughters, Quadratus, Ammia and the New Prophet (Montanist) women and men who appealed to a 'succession' of prophesying (Euseb. *HE* 3.37.1; 5.17.4). It did not die quickly, as *The ascension of Isaiah*, *Epistula apostolorum*, *Acts of Paul and Thecla*, Cyprian, *Epistulae* 75 (on Cappadocia), and liturgical prophesying in later Montanism (Epiph. *Pan.* 49.2) indicated. The fourth-century memorial to the Christian prophetess Nanas is notable.[55] Taking into account Gnosticism, too, the incidence of female prophesying is striking. Yet, throughout this period we find that women's role in Christian ministry was contested.

Ignatius, Polycarp and Melito combined both prophet and *episkopos* roles, but tensions did emerge between one mode of authority/leadership and another. In *1 Clement* (as in the *Didache*) issues of 'class' and gender, householder rights, itinerancy and patronage contributed to such tensions.[56] The New Prophets' payment of salaries to teachers (of both sexes?) would have democratised leadership for those not well established socially (Euseb. *HE* 5.18.2 (Apollonius)) and added to the catholic side's suspicion.

The New Prophecy (later called Montanism), rising in the 160s under its leaders Priscilla, Maximilla and Montanus, differed in emphasis rather than doctrine from the catholic congregations from which it emerged, especially with regard to the exercise of authority and discipline. Its followers seceded or were driven from churches in due course,[57] under challenge to their ecstatic prophesying (Epiph. *Pan.* 48.3.4–7.8), writings[58] and rigorism. They shared in common with many Asian Christians Johannine incarnational orthodoxy, an

---

53 Nautin, *Lettres*, 143–65; *St Dionysius of Alexandria*, Feltoe (ed.).

54 Duff, *Who rides the beast?*

55 Tabbernee, *Montanist inscriptions*, 419–25; Trevett, 'Angelic visitations'; Eisen, *Women officeholders*, 63–87.

56 See Trevett, *Christian women*, pt 1; see pt iii, ch. 14, above.

57 Euseb. *HE* 5.16.9–10 (anon.); Epiph. *Pan.* 48.1.4 (his source is early and probably Asian).

58 Euseb. *HE* 6.20.3 on writings; Paulsen, 'Bedeutung'; Trevett, *Montanism*, 129–41; Denzey, 'What did the Montanists read?'; Stewart-Sykes, 'Original condemnation'.

anti-docetic[59]/Gnostic stance (this writer believes), prophetism (with appeal to New Testament and other prophets as forebears), Johannine Paraclete pneumatology, plus, perhaps, chiliasm and Quartodecimanism. If (so Hipp. *Haer.* 8.19) *some* among their followers held to Noëtus of Smyrna's monarchianism, then that too was part of the Asia Minor scene.

The New Prophecy spread rapidly to Rome, North Africa and elsewhere. More rigorist (in fasting, for example) and less forgiving of failure and lapse, its followers were not at odds with apostolic tradition nor, in principle, with episcopacy. Indeed, a hierarchy of church officials emerged, more complex than the catholic churches espoused, and including women (illustrative epigraphy survives). This Montanism retained its base in Asia Minor for centuries, albeit fragmented and diversified in theology and practice. Like Gnosticism it proved to be something against which the catholic tradition might define itself.

Diversity in theology and praxis

In the second and third centuries, developments were 'multi-directional and not easily mapped'.[60] There were many strands in the tapestry of Asian and Achaean Christian tradition, including a multiplicity of 'Paulinisms' and 'Johannisms', as various Christians appealed to ancestral teachers and community founders, just as associations and Greek cities did to theirs. The Eusebian picture was simple (*HE* 3.1.1; cf. 3.4.1), namely that the new religion had spread and diversified through various apostles' influence: Asia had had John; Achaea, Andrew; Peter for the diaspora of Asia Minor [cf. 1 Pet 1:1]; and Paul working 'from Jerusalem to Illyricum' (Acts 16:6–7; 17:10–18:1; 18:23, 19:1,10; 26:9–15; Rom 15:19). The reality was more complex.

In Achaea, as in Asia Minor, Paul was variously remembered: (a) as the admirable founding apostle by Clement in the letter to Corinth when countering schism[61] (*1 Clem.* 5.5; 47.1), and as admirable too by Ignatius (Ign. *Eph.* 12.2; *Rom.* 4.3), Polycarp (*Phil.* 3.2; 9.1), Irenaeus[62] and others; (b) as the catholic promoter of church organisation by the author of the Pastoral Epistles, as also of sound, non-ascetic, socially conservative doctrine in the face of adversaries and

---

59 Docetists (cf. Euseb. *HE* 6.12.6 (Serapion of Antioch, *c*.190s)) maintained that only seemingly was Jesus Christ a human, fleshly (rather than a spiritual) being.
60 Siker, 'Christianity in the second and third centuries', 232.
61 Trevett, *Christian women*, pt 1; Horrell, *Social ethos*; Bowe, *Church in crisis*. What the Jewish Christian Hegesippus regarded as orthodoxy lost out there after several generations (Euseb. *HE* 3.16; 4.21.2).
62 Noormann, *Irenäus als Paulusinterpret*. Paul was also mentioned in the Abercius inscription.

loss of Pauline influence in Asia (Acts 20:27–31; 1 Cor 16:9; 2 Tim 1:15; 3:1–15; 4:1–18);[63] then (c) as anti-Jewish, according to the Hellenised and marriage-denying doctrine of Marcion of Sinope,[64] in whose truncated 'canon' of scripture Paul predominated;[65] (d) as the teacher of Theodas, mentor to Valentinus,[66] according to Gnostic claims, and (e) as the promoter of non-docetic orthodoxy and of celibacy in the *Acts of Paul and Thecla* including *3 Corinthians*. Luke, Paul's associate in the New Testament, figured in the *Anti-Marcionite prologue*[67] to Luke's gospel[68] as another celibate, an Antiochene who wrote that gospel in Achaea (cf. too, Euseb. *HE* 3.4.6; Jerome, *Vir. ill.* 7), dying later in Bithynia (or Boeotia).

Encratism laid claim to Andrew, who was otherwise linked by traditions to both Achaea (Gregory of Nazianzus and Jerome, contrast Origen, so Euseb. *HE* 3.1) and Asia Minor (cf. John 1:40–4; 6:8; 12:22). In the *Acts of Andrew and Mathias in the city of cannibals*, Sinope in Pontus was the city concerned. The encratite (third-century?) *Acts of Andrew* (Euseb. *HE* 3.25.6) made of him a traveller, who moved from Pontus to Achaea and was imprisoned for teaching asceticism. One form of the text told of his crucifixion in Patras.[69]

Docetic and encratite elements, plus opposition to Simon Magus ('father' of Christian Gnosticism),[70] were combined in the *Acts of Peter* (possibly known to the author of the *Acts of Paul*). These, plus its miracle stories and the modalistic monarchianism[71] of popular Christian piety, make its thought hard to summarise.[72] Petrine influence had touched Achaea (1 Cor 1:12; 3:22; 9:5), but in Asia Minor it was 1 Peter which represented 'mainstream' Petrine tradition.

---

63 Müller, *Theologiegeschichte*; MacDonald, *Legend*; Lindemann, *Paulus*.

64 Hoffmann, *Marcion* (with caution), but also Lieu, *Image and reality*, 265–70; Schmid, *Marcion*; Hurtado, *Lord Jesus Christ*, 549–58; and items in Wilson et al. (eds.), *Anti-Judaism*, vol. II; and May et al. (eds.), *Marcion*.

65 See pt III, ch. 9, above.

66 The details of Gnostic teachers' activities in Asia Minor and Achaea are lost, but see Irenaeus (*Haer.* 1.13.5) on Marcosian influence in the family of an Asian abroad.

67 This is a modern designation. These prefaces to Mark, Luke and John vary in origin and date and were not directed against Marcion. Only the *Prologue* to Luke survives in Greek.

68 On Marcion and Luke's gospel, see pt III, ch. 9, above.

69 Prieur and Schneemelcher, 'The acts of Andrew'; MacDonald, *Acts of Andrew*; Peterson, *Andrew*.

70 Iren. *Haer.* 1.23.2–4; cf. the *Epistula apostolorum*, and [Clem.] *Recogn.* 2.1–3.49; *Hom.* 2; 3; 7; 16–19.

71 See pt v, ch. 25, below.

72 Cf. Perkins, '*Acts of Peter*'. On 'Petrine' traditions, see Berger, 'Unfehlbare Offenbarung'; and Smith, *Petrine controversies*. The *Gospel of Peter*, too, may reflect 'popular'-level Christianity and tastes. See Hurtado, *Lord Jesus Christ*, 443–7.

The legacies of more than one Asian John are hard to untangle.[73] The Johannine gospel (Iren. *Haer.* 3.1.1; Euseb. *HE* 5.20.6), with its *logos* doctrine (1:1–18) and teaching on the spirit/Paraclete (14:15–17, 25–6; 15:26–7; 16:7–15), were building bricks for the doctrine of the trinity, and valued in the east. Its prophetic (Paraclete) theology also informed the New Prophecy. Like the Johannine letters, the gospel preserved an anti-docetic christology. Jesus, the *word made flesh*, was the Christ,[74] but the text's portrayal of the descending-ascending revealer might also fuel docetism.[75] Christological conflict and docetism emerged in Asia Minor. There were accusations of aberrant teaching, schism (1 John 4.1–15; 5:1–12) and neglect of ethics and fellowship (1 John 2:4–11; 3:15–18),[76] such as troubled Ignatius (*Smyr.* 5.2; 6.2–7.2)[77] and later writers in Asia Minor.[78] Docetism was as much a general tendency as a distinct body of doctrine with associated believers.[79]

The name of Cerinthus (Euseb. *EH* 3.28.1–4),[80] adoptionist in christology, became inextricably associated with John's, though other sources either determinedly distanced John from him (Euseb. *HE* 3.28.6; Iren. *Haer.* 3.3.4) or else opposed Cerinthus while not being at odds with Johannine thought.[81] Neither John's gospel nor the Revelation (see Euseb. *HE* 7.25; 3.29.5 (Papias)) were acknowledged as authoritative without a struggle – perhaps the New Prophets' love of them alienated others – and the so-called *Alogi* (*Alogoi*, Epiph. *Pan.* 51.2–3)[82] ascribed both to Cerinthus (cf. Euseb. *HE* 7.25.1–4). In Rome, Hippolytus defended them (perhaps in a lost work *On the gospel of John and the Apocalypse*) after an attack by the catholic Caius. Caius had allegedly attributed them to

---

73 See pt II, ch. 6, above; Culpepper, *John.* On the Johns of Asia, their status and writings, cf. Iren. *Haer.* 2.22.5; 3.3.4; 3.16.5; 4.20.11; Euseb. *HE* 3.29.1; 3.31.2; 7.24.1–25.26.

74 1 John 2:18–22; 4:1–3; 5:1; 2 John 7–11. Kaestli *et al.* (eds.), *Communauté.*

75 Woll, *Johannine Christianity*; Schnelle, *Antidocetic Christology*; Strecker, 'Chiliasmus und Doketismus', 30–46.

76 See Slusser, 'Docetism'; Lieu, *Theology*; Fortna and Thatcher, *Jesus in Johannine tradition.*

77 Sumney, 'Those who "ignorantly deny"'; and Goulder, 'Ignatius' "docetists"' and 'Poor man's Christology'; Schoedel, *Ignatius of Antioch.*

78 Poly. *Phil.* 7.3; Hovhanessian, *Third Corinthians*; Schmidt, *Gespräche Jesu*; Hills, *Tradition*; Müller, 'Epistula apostolorum'; Stewart-Sykes, 'Asian context'; Hill, 'The Epistula apostolorum'.

79 Cf. Brox, 'Doketismus'; Slusser, 'Docetism'.

80 Cerinthus, Ignatius' and Polycarp's contemporary, was probably in Asia (cf. Iren. *Haer.* 3.34), rather than Egypt (Wright, 'Cerinthus').

81 *Epistula apostolorum* (1.12). Cf. Iren. *Haer.* 1.26.1; Epiph. *Pan.* 28.4.1. Stewart-Sykes, 'Asian context'; Hill, 'The Epistula apostolorum', and 'Cerinthus'.

82 Bludau, *Gegner*; Hall, 'Aloger'; Prinzivalli, 'Gaio'; Trevett, *Montanism*, 139–41. See too Iren. *Haer.* 3.11.9.

Cerinthus when in debate with the New Prophets' spokesman (Euseb. *HE* 2.25.5; 6.20.3; Dionysius, *Commentarii in Apocalypsim* 1).[83]

John's name (or Johannine tradition) was used to validate a number of different forms of belief and practice. On the one hand, there was the New Prophecy, while at the same time Johannine cosmology lent itself to Gnostic interests (see, e.g. Iren. *Haer.* 3.11.7).[84] Heracleon, Valentinus' disciple, was the first commentator on the gospel.[85] Sections 94–102 of the second-century *Acts of John* (Asian or Egyptian)[86] were transformed by Gnosticism. That work was polymorphic in its Christology, its Christ bodiless. Here was no homage to the heritage of Judaism but in these Johannine *Acts* were magic and potion-mongering and the interface of Christian power with that of the virgin goddess Artemis (cf. Acts 19; *A. Jo.* 43, cf. 37, 55).

In the developing catholic 'mainstream', apostles, those who had known them and apostolic tradition became touchstones in the face of neglect or competing versions of the truth. Thus, Irenaeus used the shadowy 'elders' to show a catholic tradition in unbroken continuity from Jesus Christ.[87]

Diversity and boundary creation

'Orthodoxy' was not the monopoly of one group throughout this period. Moreover, ideas (and their expressions in some writings) overlapped (e.g. in respect of reliance on sapiental or apocalyptic traditions) so that separating Gnostic or New Prophecy / Montanist or Marcionite teachings from a relatively ill-defined and emerging 'orthodoxy' took time.[88] What retrospectively came to be seen as aberrations (e.g. docetism or monarchianism) had been the norm for a great many Christians in time past. Challenges external, and dissent internal, prompted the church to clearer definition of its authority and doctrine. It was honed in struggle.[89]

By the 150s, Marcion's teaching of an immaterial Christ and of a good God divorced from the inferior and fickle creator demiurge had spread 'to

---

83 Dionysius bar Salibi's commentary on the Apocalypse (12th century) has preserved elements of Hippolytus' defence.
84 Naassenes and Peratai also preferred John (Hipp. *Haer.* 5.2–4 and 11–12).
85 Pagels, *Johannine gospel*.
86 Schneider, *Mystery*; Lalleman, *Acts of John*.
87 *Haer.* 2.22.5; cf. Euseb. *HE* 3.23.3. On the elders, Lieu, *Image and reality*, 241, 245–52. See, too, Körtner, *Papias von Hierapolis;* and Schoedel, 'Polycarp of Smyrna'.
88 Constantine proscribed Marcionites (Euseb. *V.C.* 3.64; cf. Cyr. H. *Catech.* 4.4). Like Montanists they were hard to eradicate completely, especially in the east.
89 Andresen, 'Siegreiche Kirche'.

every nation' (Justin, *1 Apol.* 26; *cf.*, 58; Iren. *Haer.* 3.4.3). Allegedly influenced by the Gnostic Cerdo,[90] Marcion's career in Asia Minor is unclear. In Rome, he was eventually excommunicated. That so many wrote against him points to Marcion's success.[91] He, like Valentinus and the New Prophets, had originally been in a catholic congregation. The seeds and shoots for their teachings had long existed. Gnostic ideas were part of the atmosphere, pre-dating the developed systems,[92] just as pre-existing elements in Asian Christianity, rather than paganism,[93] fuelled the (anti-Gnostic?)[94] New Prophecy.

Irenaeus counselled against extremes of judgement, e.g. with regard to prophecy[95] and Quartodeciman practice, but he countered Gnosticism (and other tendencies) at length, setting out an 'orthodox' position in *Adversus omnes haereses*. His addresses to Rome to the Asian Florinus (*On the Ogdoad* and on the *monarchia* or unity of the Godhead) would serve against the dualism of Marcion and Gnosticism alike.[96] Florinus, Irenaeus asserted, was attracted to wholly new opinions, at odds with what both of them had heard from Polycarp as the apostolic tradition.[97]

Literature was ammunition. The *Epistula apostolorum* (after epistolary beginnings) stole thunder using a format beloved of Gnostics – namely a post-resurrection revelation. But it incorporated anti-docetic christology, an orthodox theology of baptism, plus opposition to Simon Magus and Cerinthus. Alongside apologetics came Christian addresses against dissent and error within the broad spectrum of those who acknowledged Jesus, with Apollonius and the Anonymous challenging the New Prophecy, and Apolinarius and Miltiades addressing pagans, Jews and the New Prophets too (Euseb. *HE* 4.27.1; 5.16–19). Before the end of the second century, catholic leaders were gathering formally for regional discussion of major issues (Euseb. *HE* 5.16.10 (Anonymous), on the New Prophecy; *HE* 5.23.2–4, in Achaea and Pontus

90 Marcionism eschewed the kind of mythological framework beloved by gnostics.
91 See pt III, ch 9, above.
92 M. Williams, *Rethinking 'gnosticism'*.
93 Schepelern, *Der Montanismus* (Johannine rather than pagan influence). See also Strobel, *Das heilige Land der Montanisten;* Goree, 'Cultural bases'; and Elm, 'Pierced by bronze needles'.
94 Tert. *Val.* 5.1. Stewart-Sykes, 'Asian context'; McGinn, 'Internal renewal'; Froehlich, 'Montanism and gnosis'; and Denzey, 'What did the Montanists read?'.
95 Trevett, *Montanism*, 56–60.
96 Euseb. *HE* 5.20.1. Cf. too, Iren. *Haer.* 1.26 on Cerinthus. See pt III, ch. 13, above.
97 Euseb. *HE* 5.20.1 (cf. Iren. *Haer.* 1.3.4; 3.3.4); 5.20.4–8.

concerning Easter).[98] Statements of proto-'orthodox' Christian belief, a 'canon of truth' or 'rule of faith' were being formulated against alternative interpretations.[99] The first hints of this had appeared in Galatians 2:14; 6:16 (cf. Ign. *Eph.* 5.2). But these were internal matters. For their part, the governing authorities had never distinguished between catholic, New Prophet, Marcionite, or other Christians. All might have their martyrs (*M. Polyc.* 10.3; *M. Pion.* 11; cf. Or. *C. Cels.* 5.54; Euseb. *HE* 4.15.46; 5.16.21–2; 7.12).

The battle for incarnational orthodoxy merged into another for Trinitarian orthodoxy. How was Christ to be worshipped as God and Trinitarian doctrine reconciled with God's unity (*monarchia*, Tert. *Prax.* 3 and 9)? Christians of Asia Minor were prominent in the fray, and the monarchian controversy marked the beginning of a series of troubling christological and Trinitarian disputes.

In the 190s, Byzantium exported to Rome the adoptionist so-called dynamic monarchianism of Theodotus the cobbler (Hipp. *Haer.* 7.23). To Rome went the modalistic monarchianism of Noëtus of Smyrna (see Hipp. *Haer.* 9.7–12; *Noët.*; Epiph. *Pan.* 57).[100] Tertullian's 'Praxeas' (unidentified 'busybody') also had links with Asia. His modalistic monarchianism (*Prax.* 10, 27–9) had 'crucified the Father', and, in turning Rome against the New Prophecy, he had 'put to flight' the Paraclete also. In turn, Gregory Thaumaturgus challenged modalism's re-emergence in third-century Sabellianism.[101] Indeed, the anti-modalism of many Christians of the east, and their belief in Jesus Christ as the incarnation of the pre-existent and creative *logos*, was to provide fuel in the later Arian controversy.

Eastern bishops combined in support of Arius, who made Nicomedia his retreat after his excommunication. Eusebius of Nicomedia (d. *c.*342 CE), politically influential and formerly a fellow student with Arius,[102] was significant in support,[103] whereas Marcellus of Ancyra (determined upholder of the Nicaean *homoousios* language) represented one eastern camp's anti-Arian stance.[104] Once again, as in the time of the New Prophecy,[105] Christians of Ancyra were divided.

98 Synods in Synnada and Iconium (230s and 240s) considered heretics, schismatics and re-baptism (Euseb. *HE* 7.7.5). Cf. Firmilian's correspondence with Cyprian in Carthage (Cypr. *Ep.* 75).
99 Euseb. *HE* 4.23.4; cf. Iren. *Haer.* 1.9.4; Euseb. *D.E.* 3 and 6 on the rule of faith.
100 See pt v, ch. 24, below.
101 Euseb. *HE* 7.6; 7.26; Hipp. *Haer.* 9.6; Bas. *Ep.* 210.
102 Cf. Thdt. *HE* 1.5 (*PG* 82.909–12).
103 See pt vi, ch. 31, below.
104 Logan, 'Marcellus of Ancyra'; Kannengieser, 'Current theology'; Seibt, *Theologie*.
105 Euseb. *HE* 5.16.3–4; cf. Epiph. *Pan.* 51.33.

Christians with Christians

Achaea and especially Asia Minor lay as the geographical heartland between the extremes of west and east of the empire. Corinth's two ports had made it accessible to Italy and Asia alike. One of them, Cenchreae, had had a Christian presence in the 50s (Rom 16:1). Traffic and correspondence between Asia Minor and Achaea was constant.

Some Christians travelled extensively, visited, and resettled (Acts 18:1–2, 19–21; *M. Polyc.* 4; Euseb. *HE* 4.23; 5.1.17 and 49; 6.27.1; 6.32.3 (Jerome *Ep.* 33.4); 7.14.1; 7.32.5). They journeyed to debate contested matters, as when Firmilian, Helenus, Nicomas and Gregory Thaumaturgus attended synods on the Novatian schism and concerning Paul of Samosata (Euseb. *HE* 6.46.3; 7.23.1; 7.30.2–5). Origen might be found in Cappadocia or in Greece, and Firmilian in Judaea (Euseb. *HE* 6.23.4 and 32.2; 6.27). Pastoral guidance and philanthropy got around (1 *Clem.* (Euseb. *HE* 4.23.9–11; cf. 3.16; Ign. *Rom.* 3.1); Bas. *Ep.* 70; Euseb. *HE* 6.19.15–18 (lay preachers)).

Christians' texts were rhetorical implements of power, creating truth, cementing or refining relationships between individuals and churches, providing weaponry for one fray or another (Euseb. *HE* 4.23 (Dionysius)). Socrates of Corinth copied the *Martyrdom of Polycarp* in Smyrna (*M. Polyc.* 22) and it was sent to churches unnamed, apart from the one in Philomelium (Phrygia). Christians of Gaul, in correspondence and debate with Rome, Asia and Phrygia about the New Prophecy (Euseb. *HE* 5.3.4), sent to the churches an account of martyrdoms (Euseb. *HE* 5.1.2). Dionysius of Corinth wrote, sometimes by request, to inform, encourage, and provide others with ammunition against error.

What survives is the correspondence of like with like: Ignatius with Polycarp; Polycarp with a Macedonian church seething about malpractice and erroneous teaching (Poly. *Phil.*); Firmilian with Cyprian in Carthage during the controversy with Rome about the (re-)baptism of heretics (Cypr. *Ep.* 75.17; cf., Euseb. *HE* 7.5.3–5). We have no letters from Marcionites to Novatianists or Montanists to catholics. In Gaul, the Asian Irenaeus typified an empire-wide Christian vision as he mediated with Eleutherus in Rome (Euseb. *HE* 5.4.1–2) or rebuked Victor in the heat of the Quartodeciman controversy.

Within and between catholic churches (and perhaps within other kinds too), there were networks of support. Claims to a shared body of proto-orthodox belief stood alongside tensions, heightened by differences of theological and ecclesiological kinds, and by regional sensibilities. In Asia Minor and Achaea, apostles, evangelists and many unsung advocates had established and nurtured communities of Christians. But Christian belief and practice grew to be multi-faceted, so that growth towards an agreed orthodoxy was protracted. Letters and apologetic works, martyrologies and treatises, epigraphy, *Acts* and gospels are a legacy for the modern interpreter of this time, but much more has been lost.

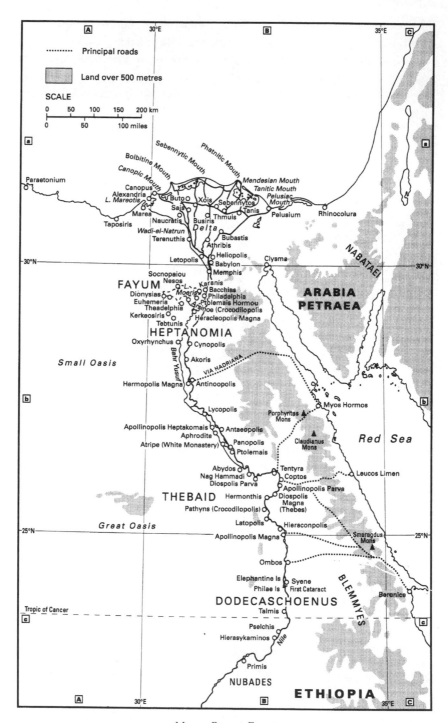

Map 5. Roman Egypt

18

Egypt

BIRGER A. PEARSON

The evidence

Evidence for Christianity in Egypt consists of non-literary and literary sources. There is virtually no archaeological evidence datable to before the fourth century, apart from a few scattered architectural fragments which are supposed to come from the earliest attested church in Alexandria, that of Theonas (bishop 282–300 CE).[1] The earliest identifiably Christian tombs date from the fourth century.[2] There are no Christian inscriptions from Egypt datable to before the fourth century.[3] The meagre iconographical evidence amounts to a couple of 'Gnostic' gems.[4] Non-literary papyri consist for the most part of what are taken to be the earliest Christian letters, and very few of these date to before the fourth century.[5]

On the other hand, the literary evidence is massive, consisting of works composed in Greek. Writings that would eventually become part of the New Testament canon were brought to Egypt very early, some probably in the first century. The earliest New Testament manuscripts, datable to the second century, consist of papyrus fragments of Matthew, Mark, John, Titus and Revelation found in Egypt.[6] Other early Christian literature introduced into Egypt and attested in second-century Greek manuscripts include the

---

1 Tkaczow, 'Archaeological sources', 432. On excavations carried out in Alexandria in the nineteenth and twentieth centuries, see Tkaczow, *Topography*; cf. Pearson, 'Alexandria'.
2 Wilfred Griggs' claims for first- and second-century Christian burials in the Fayum are 'fantasy', according to Roger Bagnall. See Griggs, 'Excavating a cemetery'; cf. Bagnall, *Egypt in late antiquity*, 279 n. 113.
3 See Lefebvre, *Recueil des inscriptions*. On later evidence see also Brown, 'Coptic and Greek inscriptions'.
4 Pearson, *Gnosticism and Christianity*, ch. 9.
5 See Naldini's edition of papyri, *Cristianesimo in Egitto*. For a good discussion of the papyrological evidence, see Judge and Pickering, 'Papyrus documentation'.
6 Roberts, *Manuscript, society and belief*, 12–13. The fragments of Mark (P^{90}) and Revelation (P^{98}) turned up since Roberts' work; see Nestle-Aland NTG^{27}, 689. P^{52}, the oldest attestation of the gospel of John, dates to the early second century.

Egerton gospel (probably from Syria), *The Shepherd of Hermas* (from Rome), *P. Oxy.* 1 (= *Gos. Thom.* 26–8, from Syria), and Irenaeus' *Adversus haereses* ('Against heresies', composed in Gaul and probably introduced into Egypt from Rome).[7]

But Egyptian Christians produced their own religious literature. Indeed, the literary output of Christians in Egypt during the second and third centuries was probably more abundant than that of any other region. Much of our evidence is fragmentary, consisting largely of quotations from patristic writers; much, too, is irretrievably lost. Our extant evidence also includes works translated into Coptic and preserved in Coptic manuscripts: twelve codices plus loose leaves from a thirteenth found near Nag Hammadi, Egypt,[8] the Berlin Gnostic codex (Papyrus Berolinensis 8502), the Askew codex (*Pistis sophia*), the Bruce codex, and fragments from another codex found at Deir el Bala'izah.

Cited in the following lists are works or authors of probable Egyptian (mostly Alexandrian) provenance:[9]

Second- and third-century apocrypha

Gospel of the Hebrews	Traditions of Matthias
Gospel of the Egyptians	Gospel of Eve
Secret Gospel of Mark	Jannes and Jambres
Gospel of the Saviour	Some Christian Sibylline oracles
Kerygma Petri ['Preaching of Peter']	Apocalypse of Elijah
Apocalypse of Peter[10]	

Apostolic fathers

Epistle of Barnabas	Epistle to Diognetus
Second Clement	

---

7 Roberts, *Manuscript, society and belief*, 13–14.

8 Cited NHC, or sometimes CG (Cairensis Gnosticus). In the Bibliography of primary sources (pp. 591–614) are listed only the Coptic–English editions of the Coptic Gnostic library project directed by James Robinson and completed in 1995. For other editions and studies see Scholer, *Nag Hammadi bibliography*. For convenient translations of the Nag Hammadi tractates, plus those of the Berlin Codex (BG), see Robinson and Meyer, *NHL*.

9 See the Bibliography of primary sources (pp. 591–614). For an extensive discussion of the literary evidence and the problems of establishing the provenance of early Christian texts see Pearson, *Gnosticism and Christianity*, 40–81. I include there discussion of works of disputed provenance, e.g. *Epistula apostolorum*, which some scholars assign to Egypt but should be assigned to Asia Minor.

10 To be distinguished from the tractate of the same title in Nag Hammadi codex VII.

Other patristic writers

Sentences of Sextus
Athenagoras
Agrippa Castor[11]
Pseudo-Justin
Clement of Alexandria

Origen
Dionysius of Alexandria
Theognostus
Pierius
Theonas[12]

Second-century Gnostic and other 'heretical' writers

Basilides and the Basilidians
Carpocrates and the Carpocratians
Valentinus

Theodotus
Heracleon
Julius Cassianus[13]

Writings preserved in Coptic Gnostic manuscripts[14]

'SETHIAN' GNOSTIC WRITINGS

Apocryphon of John (NHC II,1; III,1; IV,1; BG,2)
Hypostasis of the Archons (NHC II,4)
Gospel of the Egyptians (NHC III,2; IV,2)[15]
Three Steles of Seth (NHC VII,5)

Zostrianos (NHC VIII,1)
Melchizedek (NHC IX,1)
Thought of Norea (NHC IX,2)
Allogenes (NHC XI,3)
Trimorphic protennoia (NHC XIII,1)

---

11 His refutation of Basilides is lost, but summarized in Euseb. HE 4.7.

12 Eusebius mentions two other Alexandrian writers: Alexander, who became bishop of Jerusalem, and Anatolius, who became bishop of Laodicea (HE 6.11.3–6; 7.32.6 20). Eusebius quotes from letters of Alexander and provides an extensive quotation from Anatolius' Canons on the pascha.

13 The extensive output of another 'heretical' writer, Hieracas of Leontopolis, who wrote in both Greek and Egyptian (Coptic) according to Epiphanius (Pan. 67), is unfortunately lost.

14 Included in the bibliography of primary sources are all of the Coptic treatises; included in the following lists are only those Christian writings which are almost certainly assignable to 2nd- or 3rd-century Egypt, or those whose provenance is uncertain but which can plausibly be assigned to 2nd- or 3rd-century Egypt. Those in the latter category are Pr. Paul; Treat. res.; Tri. trac.; Interp. know.; Val. exp.; Ep. Pet. Phil.; Hypsiph.; and the Plato fragment (in a Gnostic edition). Those tractates for which a 2nd- or 3rd-century Syrian provenance is probable include Apoc. Adam (NHC V,5), Marsanes (NHC X,1), Gos. Phil. (NHC II,3), 1 Apoc. Jas. (NHC V,3), 2 Apoc. Jas. (NHC V,4), Paraph. Shem (NHC VII,1), Gos. Thom. (NHC II,2), Thom. cont. (NHC II,7), Dial. sav. (NHC III,5), Acts Pet. 12 apos. (NHC VI,1) and Act Pet. (BG,4). Probably of 4th-century Egypt are Pistis Sophia and the untitled treatise in the Bruce codex. Eugnostos (NHC III,3; V,1) probably originated in a 1st-century Alexandrian Jewish milieu. Quintessentially Egyptian (but not Christian) are the Hermetic writings: Disc. 8–9 (NHC VI,6), Pr. thanks. (NHC VI,7) and Asclepius (NHC VI,8).

15 Not to be confused with the apocryphal gospel of the same name cited above.

VALENTINIAN GNOSTIC WRITINGS

Gospel of truth (NHC i,3; xii,2) *Interpretation of knowledge* (NHC xi, 1)
Treatise on the resurrection (NHC i,4) *A Valentinian exposition* (NHC xi, 2)
Tripartite tractate (NHC i,5)

GNOSTIC WRITINGS OF UNCERTAIN AFFILIATION

Apocryphon of James (NHC i,2) *Apocalypse of Peter* (NHC vii,3)[17]
On the origin of the world (NHC ii,5; xiii,2) *Letter of Peter to Philip* (NHC viii,2)
Exegesis on the soul (NHC ii,6) *Testimony of truth* (NHC ix,3)
Sophia of Jesus Christ (NHC iii,4; BG,3) *Hypsiphrone* (NHC xi,4)
Apocalypse of Paul (NHC v,2)[16] *Gospel of Mary* (BG,1)
Thunder: perfect mind (NHC vi,2) *Books of Jeu* (Bruce codex)
Concept of our great power (NHC vi,4) Bala'izah Gnostic fragments
Second treatise of the great Seth (NHC vii,2)

NON-GNOSTIC WRITINGS

Authoritative teaching (NHC vi,3) *Sentences of Sextus* (NHC xii,1)
Teachings of Silvanus (NHC vii,4)

Alexandria ad Aegyptum

Egyptian Christianity began in Alexandria, by far the greatest of the many cities founded by Alexander the Great. Alexandria[18] was founded in 331 BCE on a site already occupied by a native village called Rhakotis (Strabo *Geog.* 17.1.6).[19] (From the third century BCE that name was used to designate the native Egyptian quarter of Alexandria, and Coptic sources use the name to designate the city as a whole.) Upon the death of Alexander in 323, Egypt came under the rule of Ptolemy, a Macedonian general and companion of Alexander. Under Ptolemy i (*Soter* = 'Saviour') the city replaced Memphis as capital of

---

16 Not to be confused with another apocryphal writing of the same name.
17 Not to be confused with the apocalypse of the same name cited above.
18 For the Ptolemaic period, see Fraser, *Ptolemaic Alexandria*. For the period from Diocletian on, see Haas, *Alexandria*. For an excellent general discussion see chapter 7 ('Alexandria, queen of the Mediterranean') in Bowman, *Egypt*; cf. also Pearson, 'Alexandria'. For the topography of Alexandria based on documentary and archaeological evidence, see Calderini, *Dizionario*, vol. i, fasc. i; and Adriani, *Repertorio d'arte*. On recent archaeological work, including underwater excavations, see Empereur, *Alexandria rediscovered*.
19 But the earliest hieroglyphic attestation of the name is an inscription dated 311 BCE, i.e. after the city's founding. See Chauveau, 'Alexandrie et Rhakotis'.

Egypt. Under Ptolemaic rule the city became the cultural, educational and commercial centre of the Hellenistic world, a position it occupied in the Roman period as well.[20]

Alexandria was a cosmopolitan city, oriented to the Mediterranean, and regarded as separate from, or 'alongside of' Egypt proper.[21] The Egyptian *chōra* ('country') consisted of the Nile valley and delta, the Fayum depression, and the desert oases (96 per cent of Egypt is desert). Greeks had penetrated into the *chōra* from the seventh century BCE on. In addition to Alexandria, there were two other Greek cities, Naukratis and Ptolemais, and a third founded by Hadrian, Antinoopolis. But Greek-speaking people were to be found in numerous Egyptian towns, and Greek cultural influence was everywhere present. Even so, Egyptian culture and religion persisted in Egypt for a long time, and manifested itself even in Alexandria under Ptolemaic sponsorship.

Jewish immigration into Egypt from Palestine had begun as early as the sixth century BCE, and Jews flowed into Alexandria in large numbers, with the result that the Alexandrian Jewish community became the most important in all of the diaspora.[22] The Jews were organised as a *politeuma* ('community', *Ep. Arist.* 310), and were encouraged by the Ptolemies and later the Roman emperors to live according to their own ancestral customs. By the first century, the Jewish population in Alexandria numbered in hundreds of thousands.

With the coming of Roman rule in 30 BCE, the favourable economic situation of the Jews in Egypt under the Ptolemies changed. A 'poll tax' (*laographia*) was imposed on native Egyptians and other non-Greek groups in 24/23 BCE. Relations with the Greek population became progressively strained, leading to a pogrom against the Jews in 38 CE. A group of Jews, led by Philo, appealed unsuccessfuly to emperor Gaius (Caligula). In 66 a riot was put down by Philo's apostate nephew, Tiberius Alexander, Roman Prefect of Egypt, with great loss of life (Josephus, *BJ* 2.487–98). A revolt of the Jews under Trajan in 115, put down in 117,[23] led to the virtual annihilation of the Jewish community (Euseb.

---

20 The topography and beautiful buildings of the city are extensively described by Strabo in book 17 of his *Geographica* (Strabo resided in the city c.24–20 BCE); cf. Fraser, *Ptolemaic Alexandria*, vol. I, 7–37; vol. II, 12–III.

21 In his oration 'to the Alexandrians' Dio Chrysostom refers hyperbolically to 'the mighty nation of Egypt' as an 'appendage' (*prosthēkē*, *Orationes* 32.36) to the magnificent city of Alexandria.

22 See pt I, ch. 2, above. The Jewish presence in Egypt in the Ptolemaic and Roman periods is fully documented in *CPJ*, which also includes inscriptions. Cf. Safrai and Stern, *Jewish people*, which concentrates on the first century; also Starobinski-Safran, 'Communauté juive'.

23 The revolt was inspired by Jewish messianism; see Hengel, 'Messianische Hoffnung'.

HE 4.2).[24] Destruction of Jewish life and property extended into the Egyptian *chōra* as well.

The development of Christianity in Egypt was impacted from the beginning by the distinctive Greek cultural and educational environment of Alexandria, and by the socio-cultural and religious life of the Jewish community in which the earliest Christians lived. As the Christian religion expanded into the *chōra*, it came under the influence of native Egyptian culture and language, resulting in the development of a distinctive Coptic ('Egyptian') Christianity which is still very much alive today.

Christian origins in Egypt

On the origins of Christianity in Egypt[25] our sources are silent until the early second century, when Alexandrian Christian literature begins to appear and doctrines of early Christian teachers begin to be reflected in texts and testimonies. The Coptic Church credits the apostle Mark with the founding of the Alexandrian church, but that tradition, attested only from the fourth century (Euseb. *HE* 2.16), is highly dubious.[26] A legend that Mark's cousin Barnabas was active in Christian mission in Alexandria, attested in the Pseudo-Clementine literature (*Hom.* 1.8.3–15.9), is also dubious.[27] There is a hint of a Christian presence in Alexandria in the New Testament in a variant reading of Acts 18:25, where it is reported that Apollos of Alexandria 'had been instructed in the word in his home country',[28] but that reading is probably secondary.

So, in discussing the origins of Christianity in Egypt, historians have been forced to extrapolate backwards from second-century sources. One still-popular view is that of Walter Bauer,[29] who accounts for the paucity of early evidence by suggesting that ecclesiastical leaders suppressed it, knowing that the earliest form of Christianity was 'heretical', specifically 'Gnostic'. This conclusion has a certain plausibility in that the earliest Christian teachers active in early second-century Alexandria of whom we have any information were the 'arch-heretics' Valentinus, Basilides and his son Isidore, and Carpocrates and his son Epiphanes. The problem with Bauer's theory, however,

---

24 See pt I, ch. 3, above.
25 Pearson, 'Earliest Christianity' and 'Christianity in Egypt'; and, more recently, Dorival, 'Les débuts'; Jakab, *Ecclesia alexandrina*, 35–61; Pearson, 'Cracking a conundrum'.
26 On the Mark legend see Pearson, 'Earliest Christianity', 137–45; also Pearson, 'Christianity in Egypt', 955–6.
27 Pearson, 'Earliest Christianity', 136–137; but see now Carleton Paget, *Epistle of Barnabas*, 36.
28 Codex Bezae (my translation), representing the 'western' text of Acts.
29 Bauer, *Orthodoxy and heresy*, 44–53.

is that it requires him to paint with 'heretical' and 'Gnostic' colours the earliest attested Alexandrian Christian literature, the *Epistle of Barnabas*, and the fragmentary apocryphal works, *Gospel of the Hebrews* and *Gospel of the Egyptians*. He also ignores other important sources such as the *Kerygma Petri*, which is obviously not a 'Gnostic' work.[30]

More plausible is the view advanced by papyrologist Colin Roberts, based on his study of the earliest Christian literary papryi, which provide no support for Bauer's view that Gnosticism was the earliest form of Christianity in Egypt. Especially important is Roberts' discussion of the *nomina sacra* (abbreviations, with superlineation, of 'sacred names' such as *Iesous, Christos, kyrios, theos* and others, fifteen in all) in early Christian manuscripts, a scribal practice which he traces back to the Jerusalem church.[31] Roberts concludes that the earliest Christianity in Egypt (i.e. in Alexandria) was Jewish. The earliest 'Christians' (if we can call them that)[32] were an integral part of the Jewish community of Alexandria.

It has recently been argued that primitive Christianity was 'annihilated' in the Jewish revolt of 115–17 'along with the entire body in which it was immersed – the Jewish community of Egypt'. On this view, the Judaeo-Christianity that came to an end in 117 was replaced by 'pagano-Christian groups' which refused to participate in the revolt.[33] While the revolt of 115–17 must have been a crucial event for Christians in Egypt, there was certainly not a complete rupture, since the existing second-century evidence points to substantial continuities between Alexandrian Judaism and post-117 Alexandrian Christianity in terms of theology, lifestyle and social organization.[34]

Social groups and Christian organisation

Following the destruction of the Jewish community in 117, much of its literary legacy survived among the Christians who treasured and preserved it, notably the Septuagint version (LXX) of the Bible (originally translated in Alexandria) and the writings of Philo and other Jewish authors. This legacy heavily impacted the literary production of Christians who now constituted a new community no longer part of the Jewish *politeuma*. A look at one of the earliest Alexandrian Christian writings, the *Kerygma Petri*, preserved in a few

---

30 Bauer, *Orthodoxy and heresy*, 47–53.
31 Roberts, *Manuscript, society and belief*, 19–21; cf. Hurtado, 'Nomina sacra'.
32 The earliest documented use of the term 'Christian' in Alexandrian Christian sources is found in fr. 2 of the *Kerygma Petri* (Clem. Al. *Str.* 6.5.41; cf. *NTApoc*, vol. ii, 39).
33 Modrzejewski, *Jews of Egypt*, 227–30.
34 Pearson, 'Cracking a conundrum', and *Gnosticism and Christianity*, 12–19, 82–99.

fragments by Clement, is instructive. Its attribution to Peter and its reference to 'the twelve' situates the text in the tradition of the apostles originally based in Jerusalem (fr. 3). It reflects a typically Alexandrian '*logos* Christology' (fr. 1) and a *credo* centred upon one God who created the world and can bring an end to it, a *credo* which can also be expressed in a typically Alexandrian 'negative theology' (fr. 2). It finds in the biblical writings prophecies of the coming, death and resurrection of Christ (fr. 4). It is the first Alexandrian writing to use the term 'Christian', defining Christians as a 'third race' (fr. 2).[35] The *Kerygma Petri* represents a variety of Christianity that lies on a trajectory leading to the 'mainline' Christianity of Clement, who quotes it approvingly.[36]

Our literary sources tell us of other varieties of Christianity which existed early on in Alexandria.[37] The *Gospel of the Hebrews* was used by Alexandrian Jewish Christians. It reflects a special allegiance to James of Jerusalem, but also the influence of Alexandrian Jewish wisdom theology. The *Gospel of the Egyptians* was in use by Greek-speaking Egyptian Christians probably resident in the Rhakotis district of Alexandria. This group was oriented to asceticism, and may have been influenced by the Jewish *Therapeutae* who, situated west of Alexandria, had a particular form of communal life, as described by Philo (*Contempl.*). Apocalyptically oriented Christianity is reflected in the *Epistle of Barnabas*, and in Alexandrian Sibylline writings in Christian dress. Apocalypticism was also probably part of the religious orientation of the simple, uneducated Christians (*simpliciores*), who left us no writings.[38]

Among the highly educated, philosophically oriented Christians would certainly have been Platonists such as are reflected in the *Authoritative teaching* (NHC VI,3)[39] and the various Gnostic groups, who also represent a kind of continuation of the different varieties of Alexandrian Judaism. The tractate *Eugnostos* (NHC III,3; V,1), for example, reflects the existence in the first century of a Jewish Gnosticism.[40] Marcionite Christianity also came to Alexandria, probably in the mid-second century;[41] Marcionites were known to Clement, who polemicises against them (e.g. *Str.* 3.3.12).

---

35 See n. 32, above.
36 The importance of the *Kerygma Petri* is underscored by Jakab, *Ecclesia alexandrina*, 56–7.
37 Van den Broek, 'Juden und Christen'.
38 Van den Broek, 'Juden und Christen', 188; Dorival, 'Les débuts', 170–1.
39 Van den Broek, 'Authentikos logos'.
40 Van den Broek, 'Jewish and Platonic speculations'; cf. van den Broek, 'Juden und Christen', 192.
41 Dorival, 'Les débuts', 171.

Christian organisation in Alexandria also exhibits a continuity with Alexandrian Judaism, especially in the form of the presbyterate. Each Christian congregation in Alexandria had its own presbyter, following the model of the synagogue.[42] To be sure, the leaders most visible to us are the early Christian teachers named in our sources. Thus, a congregation would be organised under the direction of a presbyter, but could include in its membership a prominent lay teacher. In some cases, teachers were also presbyters, as was Clement in all probability.

As for the bishops, those in the traditional list before Demetrius (189–232) going back to Mark, as given by Eusebius, seem to be nothing more than 'a mere echo and a puff of smoke'.[43] Before Demetrius, there certainly was no monarchical episcopate, such as was advocated in Asia Minor by Ignatius of Antioch. Jerome (*Ep.* 146.1) informs us of the situation in the early Alexandrian church. Before the time of the bishops Heraclas and Dionysius, the presbyters named one of themselves to serve as bishop.[44] Much later evidence is supplied by Eutychius, tenth-century Melchite patriarch of Alexandria. In his *Annals*, he speaks of twelve presbyters from whom, in case of a vacancy in the patriarchate, a new patriarch would be chosen. (His use of the term 'patriarch' for bishop is an anachronism.) Then a new presbyter would be appointed in his place in the presbytery. Eutychius also informs us that, until the time of Demetrius, he was the only bishop in Egypt; Demetrius appointed three bishops, and Heraclas, his successor, appointed an additional twenty.[45]

Demetrius played a crucial role in the development of the Egyptian Christian hierarchy. It is no wonder that he has been referred to as 'second founder of the church of Alexandria', and 'founder of the church of Egypt' for his role in the evangelisation of areas outside of Alexandria.[46] To be sure, it took some time for Demetrius to consolidate his episcopal authority. The writings of Clement and Origen attest to this evolution 'from the Christian community

---

42 Van den Broek, 'Juden und Christen', 188–91; Ritter, 'De Polycarpe à Clement', 164. On the organisation of Jewish communities in the Diaspora, see Applebaum, 'Organization'; cf. pt i, ch. 2, above. On the earliest papyrus evidence of Jewish *presbyteroi* (*P. Oxy.* 2476, 2nd century BCE), see no. 24 (by S. R. Llewelyn) in *NewDocs*, vol. ix (2002), 69–72.

43 Bauer, *Orthodoxy and heresy*, 45. The traditional list may have been constructed artificially by Julius Africanus in his (lost) *Chronographies*, one of Eusebius' sources; so Grant, *Eusebius as church historian*, 51–2. See chart, 'Roman emperors and bishops of Rome and Alexandria', pp. xxii–xxiii above.

44 See Jakab, *Ecclesia alexandrina*, 177.

45 *PG* 111.982; cf. Kemp, 'Bishops and presbyters', 137–8.

46 Telfer, 'Episcopal succession', 2.

to an institutional church',[47] and it should be added that the process begun by Demetrius was really not completed until the time of Dionysius the Great (247–64), the first 'patriarch of Egypt'.[48]

In terms of social standing, it has been argued that the earliest Christians in Alexandria were Jews of education and means, representing a 'middle class' who enjoyed a comfortable life.[49] That judgement may be a little one-sided, even though it must be admitted that the Christians depicted in Clement's *Pedagogue* were evidently people of means.[50] The pagan writer Celsus, probably writing in Alexandria in the 170s, contemptuously dismissed the Christians known to him as 'dishonourable and stupid, and only slaves, women, and little children' (Or. *C. Cels.* 3.44).[51] Athenagoras, writing around the same time as Celsus, acknowledges that some Christians were 'simple folk, artisans and old women' (*Leg.* 11.1),[52] but he also refers to some who were slave owners (*Leg.* 55).[53] Christians in Alexandria are likely to have come from all social strata.[54]

The socio-economic situation of Christians as reflected in the writings of Clement can be extended to the church itself as an institution, for by the end of the third century the Alexandrian church had become a banking institution! The evidence for this comes in a letter from an Egyptian Christian (*P. Amherst* 3a), who wrote from Rome to fellow Christians in the Arsinoite nome with instructions to make a monetary deposit in Alexandria with 'Maximus the *papas*' by giving it into the hands of the bishop's agent, Theonas.[55] Theonas later became Maximus' successor as bishop (282–300), and presided over the construction of a church building in the western part of the city.[56]

The 'Catechetical School' in Alexandria

While teachers played an important role in the Alexandrian Christian community, the earliest ones named in our sources were 'heretics' (Gnostics).[57] The first named 'orthodox' Christian teacher, Pantaenus, appears in Eusebius'

---

47 'De la communauté chrétienne à une église institutionnelle', ch. 8 in Jakab, *Ecclesia alexandrina*, 175–214.
48 Jakab, *Ecclesia alexandrina*, 215–55, esp. 252–5.
49 Jakab, *Ecclesia alexandrina*, 54–5.
50 See Jakab's discussion of the life of the 'rich Christians in Alexandria' as depicted by Clement (*Ecclesia alexandrina*, 257–92).
51 Translation by Chadwick, *Origen: contra Celsum*.
52 Crehan's translation in *Athenagoras*.
53 Barnard, *Athenagoras*, 147–9.
54 Cf. pt II, ch. 7, above.
55 Deissmann, *Light from the ancient east*, 205–13; Snyder, *Ante pacem*, 152–3.
56 Sources cited by Adriani, *Repertorio*, 217; cf. n. 1, above.
57 On the 'Catechetical School' in Alexandria, see pt v, ch. 27, below.

history in connection with events taking place during the reign of Commodus (180–92). Eusebius writes that Pantaenus, a famous teacher, was in charge of a 'school of sacred learning' (*didaskaleion tōn hierōn logōn*) which had existed in Alexandria 'from ancient custom' (*HE* 5.10.1).[58] Eusebius adds that Pantaenus was head of the school (*didaskaleion*) until his death (5.10.4) and had among his pupils Clement (5.11.1), who succeeded him in directing the school's 'instruction' (*katēchēsis*, 6.6.1). Eusebius subsequently reports that Origen was in his eighteenth year when he became head of the 'catechetical school' (*tēs katēchēseōs didaskaleion*, 6.3.3). During the persecution in 202, other teachers, including Clement, left the city. Bishop Demetrius entrusted the task of instruction (*katēchēsis*) to Origen alone (6.3.8). Afterwards, Origen shared this duty with his former pupil Heraclas (who later succeeded Demetrius as bishop), with Heraclas in charge of the more elementary instruction and Origen the more advanced (6.15). From these and other reports given by Eusebius arises the tradition of the 'Catechetical School' in Alexandria with a succession of teachers from Pantaenus on, or from unnamed predecessors as is implied by Eusebius' expression 'from ancient custom' (5.10).

A different version of the succession of Christian teachers in the *didaskaleion* at Alexandria is attributed to the fifth-century historian Philip of Side, in an abridgement of his work extant in a fourteenth-century manuscript.[59] In that account the succession of school heads begins with Athenagoras, followed by Clement, Pantaenus, Origen, Heraclas, Dionysius, Pierius, Theognostus, Serapion, Peter (bishop and martyr, d. 311), Macarius Politicus, Didymus (the Blind) and Rhodon, who is said to have moved the school from Alexandria to Side during the reign of Theodosius the Great (379–95).[60]

Diametrically opposed interpretations of the tradition concerning the 'Catechetical School' have been put forward by scholars. Some[61] argue that there was no school at all until the time of Demetrius, only independent teachers. In this view, the lay teachers in Alexandria, including Clement, could play an important role in the church, giving instruction at all levels, from prebaptismal instruction to high theology. Many of them, like Clement, were well schooled in Greek philosophy and culture; some were also biblical scholars active in a 'scriptorium' that must have existed in Alexandria by the middle of

---

58 Lake's translation in the LCL edition.
59 Pouderon, *D'Athènes à Alexandrie*, 1–70.
60 Pouderon attributes the obvious chronological errors in this account not to Philip's own work, which is lost, but to the traditors of this abridgement.
61 See esp. Bardy, 'Aux origines de l'école'; van den Broek, 'Christian "school"'; Jakab, *Ecclesia alexandrina*, 91–106.

the second century.[62] But it is only from the time of Demetrius on that one can speak of an official Christian school at Alexandria under episcopal control. Thereafter, some school heads, such as Heraclas and Dionysius, became bishops, but eventually, from the time of bishop Theophilus on (385–412), the school ceased to exist.

Other scholars,[63] while agreeing that Eusebius must be read critically, nevertheless argue that his claims should not be completely dismissed. In this view, based on a close reading of Clement, 'teaching and scholarship within the penumbra of the church was a long-established activity in Alexandria well before Origen.'[64] As for Clement, who was both a teacher and a presbyter, 'a contrast between church and school is nonexistent. His instruction moved the faithful through baptism and then toward wisdom and knowledge within the context of the church.'[65]

In fact, the full story is told neither by Eusebius nor by Clement. There were clearly other Christian teachers in Alexandria in Clement's time and there were prominent Christian teachers in Alexandria long before him of a type similar to the private teachers who represented the various philosophical traditions current in the Graeco-Roman world. Clement can be seen in a special light as one who put his instruction at the service of the Christian communities who for him constituted 'the church', in which he assumed an important leadership role. Indeed, it may be that Clement's role as a part of the Alexandrian presbytery involved a power struggle in the church that led to his departure from the city.[66] But the 'Catechetical School' of Alexandrian Christian tradition probably came into being only in the early third century as a result of the growing authority of bishop Demetrius.

Two of the school's teachers stand out in terms of their contributions to the development of Alexandrian theology, Clement and Origen. Titus Flavius Clemens, whose life is poorly documented, was probably born a pagan in Athens sometime between 140 and 150. He studied philosophy in Greece, Magna Graecia, Syria and Palestine before settling in Alexandria (*Str.* 1.11.2). The place and time of his conversion is unknown. He left Alexandria for Palestine around 202, and died there around 216. His writings reflect the strong influence of Platonism and especially of the philosophy and scriptural

62 On the Alexandrian scriptorium see Zuntz, *Text of the epistles*, 271–3.
63 See esp. Méhat, *Étude*, 62–70; van den Hoek, '"Catechetical" school'.
64 Van den Hoek, '"Catechetical" school', 76.
65 Van den Hoek, '"Catechetical" school', 71. That Clement was a presbyter is indicated in a letter by Alexander, bishop of Jerusalem, quoted by Eusebius, *HE* 6.11.6. See van den Hoek, '"Catechetical" school', 77; Nautin, *Lettres*, 114–18.
66 Nautin, *Lettres*, 18, 140.

exegesis of Philo Judaeus.[67] His major works are the *Protrepticus* ('Exhortation to the Greeks'), intended to convert pagans to Christianity, the *Paedagogus* ('Christ the educator'), a hortatory work addressed to Christians, and the *Stromata* ('Miscellanies'), intended for 'Gnostic' Christians who wish to go beyond simple faith and attain to a higher knowledge.[68] Clement takes over the term 'Gnostic' from the heretics, and distinguishes between 'true' and 'false' *gnōsis*.[69]

Origen, to whom Eusebius dedicates most of book 6 of his *Historia ecclesiastica*, was born in 185 or 186, reared as a Christian, and given a good education. Upon the martyrdom of his father Leonides in 202, he became a teacher (*didaskalos*) to support his family. Later he was given the patronage of a wealthy Christian woman, and drew many to his lectures. One of the most prolific writers of antiquity, Origen devoted all of his writings to the promotion of Christian faith, and can be regarded as the greatest scholar and theologian of the ancient church. He travelled and lectured widely, and, after a falling out with bishop Demetrius, left Alexandria for good around 234 for Caesarea, where he became even more productive. Imprisoned and tortured during the Decian persecution, he died in Tyre sometime after 251.[70]

Like Clement, Origen was a Platonist and was heavily influenced by Philo in his scriptural exegesis.[71] Most of his writings are exegetical (commentaries, homilies); his most important commentary, the one on John, was begun in Alexandria and completed in Caesarea. His impressive synopsis of the Old Testament (the *Hexapla* written in columns with the Hebrew text plus Greek translations by Aquila, Symmachus, the LXX, Theodotion and two others), of which only fragments remain, was a masterpiece of Alexandrian text-critical work.[72] His work *De principiis* ('On first principles'), composed in Alexandria, marks Origen as the church's first systematic theologian. His greatest apologetic work is his treatise *Contra Celsum* ('Against Celsus'), composed towards the end of his life in Caesarea. His Trinitarian theology and his Christology were especially influential in the subsequent development of Alexandrian theology. More controversial was his doctrine of the pre-existence (but not transmigration!) of the human soul. Much of Origen's huge output is lost,

---

67 Van den Hoek, *Clement of Alexandria*; Runia, *Philo*, 132–56.
68 Other works of Clement are listed in the bibliography of primary sources (p. 596). On lost writings see Euseb. *HE* 6.13.1–3. On Clement see Méhat, 'Clemens'.
69 Méhat, '"Vraie" et "fausse" gnose'.
70 On Origen see Williams, 'Origenes'; Nautin, *Origène*; Crouzel, *Origen*.
71 Runia, *Philo*, 157–83.
72 On this work see esp. Nautin, *Origène*, 303–361. Origen may have expanded an already existing Jewish synopsis (Nautin, *Origène*, 333–41).

some available only in Latin translations, owing to his denunciation as a heretic by emperor Justinian in 543.

Relations with Christians elsewhere

Irenaeus of Lyons[73] claimed that the church's faith, received from the apostles and their disciples, was one and the same over the entire world, in such diverse regions as Germany, Spain, Gaul, 'the east', Egypt, Libya and 'the central regions of the world' (*Haer.* 1.10.2).[74] The church inherited this claim for universal, cross-regional unity from Judaism, which, with its orientation to the temple in Jerusalem, was the only other religion in the history of Graeco-Roman religions to have this feature.

Interestingly enough, Irenaeus' work turned up in Egypt within twenty years of its composition (*P. Oxy.* 405).[75] It was certainly known to, and used by, Clement,[76] the earliest known Alexandrian writer against 'heresies'. Irenaeus' work is only one of countless writings composed outside Egypt of various genres which, from the first century on, came in a flood from such diverse regions as Palestine, Antioch, eastern Syria, Asia Minor, Greece, Rome and North Africa. And Christian authors in Egypt returned the favour. It is, first of all, through 'networks'[77] of Christians exchanging letters and literature that one can speak of relations between the church in Egypt and churches elsewhere.

The first known 'official' exchange of letters from the Alexandrian church to other churches is reported by Eusebius in connection with the controversy on the dating of Easter that arose towards the end of the second century (*HE* 5.25). He quotes from a joint encyclical letter composed by the Palestinian bishops of Jerusalem, Caesarea, Tyre and Ptolemais in support of celebrating Easter always on a Sunday, as advocated by bishop Victor of Rome, instead of on the fourteenth of the Jewish lunar month Nisan, as was the custom in Asia Minor. That letter includes the following sentence: 'And we make it plain to you that in Alexandria also they celebrate the same day as do we, for letters have been exchanged between them and us, so that we observe the holy day together and in agreement.' What is of special interest here is that no mention

---

73 See pt III, ch. 13, above.
74 For a discussion of this passage see Pearson, *Emergence*, 174–5.
75 Roberts, *Manuscript, society and belief*, 14, 23.
76 On Clement's use of Irenaeus see van den Hoek, 'How Alexandrian?', 186, 190.
77 The importance of 'network theory' in social-scientific study of early Christianity is underscored especially by Rodney Stark in his book, *Rise of Christianity*; cf. also White, *Social networks*; and Pearson, 'On Rodney Stark's foray'.

is made of the Alexandrian bishop, who at that time was Demetrius. Indeed, he had become bishop in Alexandria the same year as Victor in Rome (189). Whatever letter was sent from Alexandria to Palestine came apparently from the presbytery acting collectively, rather than the bishop, who had evidently not yet consolidated his power over the Alexandrian church.

The situation was completely different by the mid-third century, during the time of bishop Dionysius (247–64).[78] His voluminous correspondence, including 'official' letters to bishops in Rome, Antioch and elsewhere, attests to the growing importance of the Alexandrian church in the empire. By the end of the third century, the Alexandrian church was at least as influential in the east as the Roman church was in the west.

Gnosticism and Manichaeism in Egypt

In his five-volume work *Adversus haereses*, Irenaeus traces the Gnostic heresy, 'gnōsis falsely so-called', back to Simon 'Magus' of Samaria (*Haer.* 1.23.1–4; cf. Acts 8:9–24). Next in line as 'successor' to Simon is Menander, also a Samaritan (1.23.5), who became active in Antioch (cf. Justin, *1 Apol.* 26.4). Then, 'arising from these men', come Saturninus of Antioch and Basilides, who promulgated his system in Alexandria (*Haer.* 1.24.1). Eusebius, in his *Chronicon*, makes the following entry for the sixteenth year of Hadrian's reign (132): 'Basilides the heresiarch was living in Alexandria; from him derive the Gnostics.'[79] Thus, from this information one could conclude (incorrectly) that Egyptian Gnosticism began with Basilides in Alexandria.[80]

However, Irenaeus makes specific mention of a 'Gnostic' sect, whose basic myth (excerpted in *Haer.* 1.29) is not the same as the one he attributes to Basilides (*Haer.* 1.24.3–5), though it does somewhat resemble that of Saturninus (1.24.1–2). Of Basilides' contemporary in Alexandria, Valentinus, Irenaeus reports that 'Valentinus adapted the fundamental principles of the so-called "Gnostic" school of thought to his own kind of system' (*Haer.* 1.22.1).[81] As is well known, Irenaeus' excerpt of the 'Gnostic' myth (*Haer.* 1.29) corresponds

---

78 On Dionysius see esp. Bienert, *Dionysius von Alexandrien*.
79 My translation of the Latin of Jerome's version in Helm, ed., *Chronik des Hieronymus*, 201.
80 See Pearson, *Emergence*, 150–3. On Basilides, see Pearson, 'Basilides the Gnostic'. On the problem of defining 'Gnosticism' and delimiting it historically and phenomenologically, see Pearson, *Gnosticism and Christianity*, ch. 7: 'Gnosticism as a religion'. For different approaches see Williams, *Rethinking 'Gnosticism'*, and pt III, ch. 12, above. For complete bibliography on Gnosticism and the Coptic Gnostic codices, see Scholer, *Nag Hammadi bibliography*.
81 Layton's translation in Layton, *Scriptures*, 225.

to part of what we now have in the *Apocryphon of John* (NHC II,1; III,1; IV,1; BG,1). As I have argued elsewhere, that myth is not originally Christian but represents a form of Jewish Gnosticism.[82] Whether it came from Syria, or was developed in Alexandria, it was at home there before Valentinus and Basilides. *Eugnostos the blessed* (NHC III,3; V,1), a text probably known in its original Greek form to both Valentinus and Basilides, also represents an Alexandrian form of Jewish Gnosticism.

Valentinus' form of Gnosticism was thoroughly Christian, as was that of Basilides. Indeed, it has even been argued that Valentinus was not a 'Gnostic' at all.[83] However, careful reading of the fragments of Valentinus reveals that they allude to a typically Gnostic myth.[84] The same can be said of the Valentinian *Gospel of truth* (NHC I,3; XII,2), a treatise which can plausibly be assigned to Valentinus himself.[85]

The writings of Valentinus and Basilides and other Gnostic teachers in Alexandria are testimony to the strength and the extraordinary multiformity of the Gnostic 'heresy' in Egypt, and its persistence. Until the end of the second century there was among Alexandrian Christians, and later among Egyptian Christians of the *chōra*, a considerable degree of openness to a great variety of teachings. Even to speak of any sharp distinction between 'heresy' and 'orthodoxy' in early Christian Egypt is an anachronism, at least until the end of the second century in Alexandria during the episcopacy of Demetrius, and in some parts of Egypt much later.

In the third century a new form of Gnosticism made its entry into Egypt, Manichaeism, which eventually became a world religion in its own right.[86] Disciples of the prophet Mani came to Egypt from Mesopotamia as missionaries even before the prophet's death in 276. They gained a foothold early on in Upper Egypt in the area around Lycopolis, from which most of the extant Coptic Manichaean texts emanated. Missionaries, utilising well-travelled mercantile routes, would have reached the Thebaid not only via Alexandria up the Nile, but also by sea from Mesopotamia to the Red Sea coastal seaport

---

82 See e.g. Pearson, 'Pre-Valentinian Gnosticism'; *Emergence*, 122–46; and 'Jewish apocalypticism to gnosis'.
83 Markschies, *Valentinus*; also pt III, ch. 12, above.
84 For the fragments, see the bibliography of primary sources. Fragment 1 (Layton's C), for example, clearly alludes to a Gnostic anthropogony comparable to that of the *Apocryphon of John*.
85 Layton, *Scriptures*, 250–64.
86 See esp. Lieu, *Manichaeism*. For bibliography on Manichaeism, see Mikkelson, *Bibliographia Manichaica*. The standard inclusion of Manichaeism in the larger phenomenon of Gnosticism by historians of religions has recently been challenged by Jason BeDuhn, *Manichaean body*.

Berenice and overland to Hypsele, near Lycopolis. And now we have important evidence of Manichaeism's spread from Lycopolis to the Dakhleh oasis,
especially at ancient Kellis (modern Ismant el-Kharab), where archaeological excavations have turned up remains of a Manichaean community of the
early fourth century. Documentary and literary texts found there provide
new evidence of Manichaean life and religion in Egypt, complementing what
we already knew from the sensational discoveries at Medinet Madi in the
1930s.[87]

Following on the heels of this missionary enterprise, it did not take long for
anti-Manichaean literature, both pagan and Christian, to turn up in Egypt. The
earliest of these texts, one by the Platonist philosopher Alexander of Lycopolis
and the other (probably) by Theonas, bishop of Alexandria (d. 300), date already
from the late third century.[88] But there is also evidence of positive Manichaean
influences on Egyptian Christians, especially in the monasteries,[89] and on
other Gnostics of various stripes, resulting in a kind of symbiosis between
groups of Manichaeans and other Gnostics.[90]

Christian expansion into the *chōra*

Eusebius opens the sixth book of his *Historia ecclesiastica* with the following
statement (6.1.):

> Now when Severus also was stirring up persecution against the churches,
> in every place splendid martyrdoms of the champions of piety were accom-
> plished, but with especial frequency at Alexandria. Thither, as to some great
> arena, were escorted from Egypt and the whole Thebais God's champions,
> who, through their most steadfast endurance in divers tortures and modes of
> death, were wreathed with the crowns laid up with God.[91]

This is the first mention in Eusebius' *Historia* of the existence of Christians outside of Alexandria. 'Egypt' presumably refers to the Egyptian delta,
and the 'Thebaid' covers a large portion of the Nile valley, from Hermopo-
lis up (south) to Syene. One can be excused for casting a sceptical eye on

---

87 Two volumes of texts from ancient Kellis have been published thus far: Gardner, *Kellis
literary Texts*; and Gardner *et al.*, *Coptic documentary texts*.
88 For Alexander's treatise see esp. van der Horst and Mansfeld, *Alexandrian Platonist*.
Theonas' epistle is partially preserved in *P. Ryl.* 469. See Roberts, *Catalogue*, vol. III, 38–39;
van Haelst, *Catalogue*, no. 700 (p. 253).
89 Stroumsa, 'Manichaean challenge'.
90 This symbiosis is reflected in some of the Nag Hammadi tractates. See esp. Camplani,
'Trasmissione di testi gnostici'.
91 Oulton's translation in the LCL edition.

Eusebius' claims, not only respecting the role of Severus in the persecution[92] and its extent ('countless numbers [murioi] were being wreathed with the crowns of martyrdom', 6.2.3), but also the areas in Egypt whence these martyrs came. Nevertheless, it is certainly not the case that Christianity in Egypt in 190 (at the time of the paschal controversy) was 'confined to the city and its environs'.[93] Harnack, in his great work on Christianity's expansion,[94] cites for the second century only journeys into the chōra supposedly made by the heretics Basilides and Valentinus according to Epiphanius (Pan. 24.2.2, 3, 4; Pan. 31.7.1), but Epiphanius' testimony is highly dubious. As we have noted, Irenaeus contended that the church in Egypt confessed the universal creed, but he probably had no knowledge of the situation outside Alexandria.

For more reliable evidence of Christianity in Egypt outside Alexandria in the second century we must turn to the papyri preserved by Egypt's desert sands, dated on the basis of palaeography.[95] Van Haelst's Catalogue provides the following evidence: from the Fayum come fragments of the Old Testament (nos. 174, 224, and possibly 52 and 304),[96] possibly one from the New Testament (462),[97] one from the Shepherd of Hermas (657), and one from the Naassene Psalm (1066). Three fragments from an Old Testament codex come from Qarara (Hippōnōn polis, no. 33). Possibly from Panopolis or nearby come fragments from the New Testament (John, 426) and the Old Testament (Psalms, 118). Antinoopolis is represented by two Old Testament fragments (179). Of uncertain provenance are the Egerton gospel fragments (586), and a fragment of the Sibylline oracles (581). Oxyrhynchus is well represented, with fragments from the Old Testament (13, 40), the New Testament (372),[98] the Gospel of Thomas (593), a fragment from an unknown gospel (592), a fragment from Irenaeus' Adversus haereses (671), several from writings of Philo of Alexandria (696) and a magical fragment (1076). Colin Roberts has suggested that a

---

92 There seems to be no basis for the view that the emperor initiated the persecution that broke out soon after he left Alexandria in 201. See Birley, Septimius Severus, 209. The persecution was most likely a local affair, in which the prefect, Laetus, was probably involved (HE 6.2.2).
93 Telfer, 'Episcopal succession', 2.
94 Mission und Ausbreitung, vol. II, 708.
95 Cf. above, pp. 331–2; also pt III, ch. 8, above.
96 Nos. 52 and 304 are part of the Chester Beatty collection, for which alternative provenances have been suggested: Aphroditopolis or elsewhere in Upper Egypt. See van Haelst's discussion, Catalogue, 30.
97 P. Ryl. 457, which could have come from Oxyrhynchus (Catalogue, 30).
98 P. Oxy. 1683, a fragment from a codex containing (at least) the gospel of Matthew. To this should now be added P. Oxy. 3523, from a codex containing the gospel of John, on which see Llewelyn's discussion in NewDocs, vol. VII, 242–8.

Christian scriptorium existed in Oxyrhynchus by the end of the second century or beginning of the third.[99]

One caveat is in order in discussing the papyri: a certain time lag must be assumed between the composition or copying of a text on papyrus and its deposit in the place where the papyrus was found. Also, a fragment found in the *chōra* could have been copied elsewhere, most likely Alexandria. Even so, we can assume from papyrological evidence that Christianity penetrated Upper Egypt and the Fayum during the second century. It was probably present in the delta as well, though one cannot expect to find papyri from that area.

The evidence from the third century, both literary and papyrological, is much richer.[100] The most important literary evidence consists of the voluminous correspondence of bishop Dionysius partially preserved in quotations by Eusebius and others. Several of these are encyclical letters addressed to Egyptian bishops, including some establishing the date of Easter and its preceding fast.[101] It is probable that, during the course of the third century, all of the nomes of Egypt came to have their own bishops, ostensibly under the authority of the Alexandrian bishop.[102]

It is also during the third century that the Coptic language was developed, first of all for the purpose of translating the Christian scriptures into the native tongue of the Egyptians.[103] To be sure, the Coptic language itself, which appropriated Greek words and phrases into its vocabulary and syntax, is evidence of a bilingual environment. It is probably the case that Christianity spread less rapidly in rural areas, where the use of Greek was less prevalent, than in urban centres such as the nome capitals and other towns in the *chōra*.[104] But Roger Bagnall is probably right in his estimate that Christians were in the majority in Egypt by the time of the death of Constantine in 337.[105] Nevertheless, one should not speak too hastily of a Christian 'triumph', for, as David Frankfurter has shown,[106] basic patterns of Egyptian religion survived in Christian dress.

99 Roberts, *Manuscript, society and belief*, 24.
100 For the papyrological evidence, in addition to van Haelst's *Catalogue* and Naldini's collection of Christian letters (*Il cristianesimo in Egitto*), see Judge and Pickering, 'Papyrus documentation'.
101 Dionysius was the first Alexandrian bishop, so far as we know, to send out annual letters establishing the date of Easter. See Bienert, *Dionysius von Alexandrien*, 138–77.
102 Harnack, *Mission und Ausbreitung*, vol. II, 712.
103 For a convenient survey see Emmel, 'Coptic language'.
104 So Llewelyn, in *NewDocs*, vol. IV, 212.
105 Bagnall, *Egypt in late antiquity*, 281. Bagnall observes that the situation in the third century is 'unquantifiable' (ibid.), but allows that Christians were numerous.
106 Frankfurter, *Religion in Roman Egypt*.

Origins of Egyptian monasticism

Monasticism as an institution has played a greater role in the history of Egyptian Christianity than in that of any other regional church.[107] The origins of monasticism are usually associated with the fourth-century saints Antony, 'father' of the anchorite variety of monasticism, and Pachomius, 'father' of the coenobitic. Recent research has shown, however, that the origins of monasticism in Egypt are considerably earlier, and are associated with the development of a third variety of monasticism, apotactic. A papyrus document from Karanis, dated 324 CE, studied by E. A. Judge, provides evidence for this kind of monasticism, and is also the earliest attestation of the use of the term *monachos* for 'monk'.[108] In that document a man called Isidorus appeals to the local *praepositus* for justice in the case of an attack on him by two people named Pamonis and Harpalus. He reports that he would have died had it not been for the help given by 'the deacon Antoninus and the monk Isaac'.[109] The 'monk' in this case is not a desert ascetic, nor a member of a monastic community, but lives in the village and participates in civil and church affairs. His situation is illuminated by a denunciation by Jerome (*Ep.* 22.34) of a third class of monks in Egypt, in addition to the *coenobium* and the anchorites, called *remnuoth* (obviously a Coptic word meaning 'solitary'). They are monks ('solitaries') living in small household communities, who in Jerome's view exercise too much independence of clerical authority. Isaac is one of these 'solitaries' and belongs to a class of ascetics referred to in other sources as *apotaktikoi/ai* ('renouncers'; cf. Luke 14:33).[110] When Isidorus refers in his petition to a 'deacon' and a 'monk' he is referring to categories of local church members already well established by that time. Gilles Dorival has ventured to suggest that one or more groups of such ascetics could already have existed in second-century Alexandria.[111] Indeed, the use of the term *monachos* to refer to such 'solitaries' probably goes back to the second century. That Greek term occurs in the Coptic text of the *Gospel of Thomas* (sayings 16, 49 and 75) and may refer to a distinct class of Christian ascetics such as could already have existed in second-century Alexandria.

---

107 For more extensive discussion see Pearson, *Gnosticism and Christianity*, 37–40.
108 Judge, 'Earliest use of monachos'.
109 Judge, 'Earliest use of monachos', 73.
110 Judge, 'Earliest use of monachos', 79. On this class of ascetics see Goehring, *Ascetics*, 53–72.
111 Dorival, 'Les débuts', 174.

19

Syria and Mesopotamia

SUSAN ASHBROOK HARVEY

The New Testament book of Acts claims that 'in Antioch the disciples were for the first time called Christians' (Acts 11:26). Paul's letter to the Galatians and further statements from Acts present Antioch as the base from which the first Christians launched their missions out into the larger Mediterranean world. These texts depict Antioch as the place where the tensions of identity associated with Gentile and Jewish converts were first confronted and subsequently argued with the earliest believers still located in Jerusalem. Both Peter and Paul travelled to and from Antioch as they carried out their respective missions, and by virtue of their shared associations with the city granted it singular status for Christians thereafter.[1]

The familiar trajectory of Christian history traces the movement of the gospel from Jerusalem, through Antioch, westward to Rome. But Antioch was also the gateway east. Indeed, if the Abercius inscription from Hieropolis in Phrygia is Christian, it appears to attest to active Christian communities by the late second century as far east as the city of Nisibis on the Roman–Persian border. This chapter will attempt to trace the emergence of Christianity in the region broadly known as Syria: stretching from the coastal ports outside Antioch east to Palmyra and Persia, and from Mesopotamia in the north down to Palestine. While some of our most important early Christian writings survive from this region, material evidence is scarce. We have neither the abundance of inscriptions that survived in Asia Minor, nor the wealth of documentary and literary evidence found in Egypt. What shards of evidence we do have point to a larger cultural milieu in which Semitic, Hellenistic, Roman and Persian traditions and religions interacted with vigour and sophistication.[2]

---

1 Esp. Gal 2: 1–21; Acts 11: 19–30; 13: 1–3; 14: 21–8; 15: 1–41; 18: 22–3.
2 See above all Millar, *Roman near east*.

The regional context

Although a far older history exists for Syria and Mesopotamia, the region in early Christian times was strongly shaped in Graeco-Roman terms. Its major cities from Antioch or Laodicea to Edessa, Nisibis or Palmyra were almost invariably Hellenistic foundations. Damascus was an exception, but by Roman times the traces of its older past were barely visible. Hellenic civic structures and cultural expressions characterised urban life, and inscriptions were often bilingual in Greek and whatever Semitic dialect was dominant in the area. In the first century, Roman expansion made its presence felt primarily through military presence and significant construction of roads. During the second century, however, Roman rule became a stronger, more integrated aspect of the region. Antioch increasingly functioned as the eastern base for the emperors; with the tetrarchy at the turn of the fourth century, it became the imperial capital of the eastern provinces. Latin words were transmitted through Greek into Semitic languages, and bilingual inscriptions consistently appear in the public and domestic monuments of cities, as well as in documentary archives. In Dura Europos, a trilingual inscription of the third century survives in Latin, Greek and Palmyrene. In cities like Edessa or Palmyra, epigraphic evidence regularly shows Greek and Semitic deities mutually identified with one another – a situation literarily captured in Lucian of Samosata's treatise on the cult of the Syrian goddess at Hierapolis (Mabbug). Ironically, this type of evidence is almost all we know about the indigenous religions during this period: the names of deities, and some material evidence surviving in cult centres or temples. Apart from Lucian's Hellenised account, we know essentially nothing about rituals, myths or devotional practices. At the same time, we have both material and literary evidence to demonstrate, albeit piecemeal, the strength of contemporary Jewish communities throughout the region. Josephus implies (*BJ* 7.44) that the Jewish revolt of 66–73 CE in Palestine provoked anti-Jewish sentiment in Antioch, a situation recurring in the fourth century under Christian leadership.

In the course of the late first and second centuries, the Semitic dialect of Aramaic known as Syriac, prominent in the territory of Edessa ('Urhay' in Syriac), took hold as a primary Christian language of the Syrian region. Virtually every Christian Syriac text prior to the fourth century survives in both Syriac and Greek, and scholars sometimes disagree as to which was the original language. This situation underscores the larger cultural context in which Christianity developed in Syria and Mesopotamia: it was a multilingual region, thriving on international trade and the strategic importance of the

Roman–Persian frontiers, where the exchange of ideas as well as goods was a basic aspect of life. The religious situation is vividly seen in the archaeological remains of the city of Dura Europos on the middle Euphrates river, destroyed in 256 CE during Sassanian Persian incursions. Temples of Greek, Roman, Parthian and Palmyrene deities have been excavated, as well as three small religious buildings formed out of converted private homes in the western part of the city: a Mithraeum, a Jewish synagogue and the earliest surviving Christian church (see Fig. 6, below). The latter two contain brilliant, and extensive, frescoes of biblical narratives. When the Persian army relocated Christian captives into Persian territory during these same battles, there were already established Christian communities to receive them.[3]

Early communities, early literature

Antioch itself served as a kind of anchor connecting Syria to the larger Roman empire; certainly, it played that role administratively for successive Roman emperors. Because of the prominence given to Antioch in the New Testament, because of its relative proximity to Jerusalem, and because of the strength of its Jewish community, scholars have taken Antioch as a primary centre for Christianity's earliest development. Scholars have argued for Antioch as the provenance in which the gospel of Matthew was produced between the years 80 and 90 CE. The most ecclesiastically oriented of the canonical gospels, Matthew gives considerable attention to the problems of church organisation and structure. For similar reasons, many have argued that the *Didache*, perhaps the earliest Christian rule book, produced late in the first century, also came from Antioch or its surrounds. With the letters of Ignatius, bishop of Antioch, written early in the second century (probably between 107 and 117) while he was en route to his martyrdom in the city of Rome, a more concrete sense of Antioch as a centre of apostolic, ecclesiastical authority appears.

Ignatius was the earliest proponent of a tripartite ecclesiastical hierarchy.[4] But Ignatius' letters argued further for particular theological themes that would soon become characteristic of Antiochene Christianity. Against docetic or Gnostic ideas that Christ was a divine saviour whose humanity and death had been illusory, and against the Judaising view of Jesus as a pious man perhaps divinely inspired like the prophets of old, Ignatius insisted on Jesus Christ as truly Son and Word of God (Ign. *Eph.* 7; *Magn.* 8–10). Certain that such a

---

3 Brock, 'Christians in the Sasanid empire'.
4 See pt II, ch. 7, above.

view did not compromise monotheism, Ignatius proclaimed the full integrity of Christ's humanity as well as his divine sonship in terms that laid the foundations for later normative doctrine (*Trall.* 9–10). Travelling across Asia Minor through what he perceived as a bewildering array of Christian communities, practices and teachings, Ignatius argued for uniformity in structure, worship and belief.

Despite its significance as an administrative centre for Roman authorities and as an apparent locus of Christian authority, Antioch flickers in and out of view in these first Christian centuries. After Ignatius, the next significant bishop of the city was Theophilus, a convert from paganism, of whose writings two works mentioned by Eusebius (*HE* 4.24) seem to be lost and one, *Ad Autolycum* ('To Autolycus'), survives. Written around 180, the work is a loosely structured apologetic attack on pagan traditions and defence for Christianity, focused especially on notions of creation, history and moral activity. Strongly influenced by Jewish exegetical patterns as well as Stoic thought, Theophilus yet gives little if any indication of relations between Jews and Christians in the city.

Contemporaneously, but further east, Jewish scholars may well have contributed to the formation of the Syriac Bible. Most of the Peshitta Old Testament was translated between the late first and early third century CE, perhaps with the help of Jewish translators. The oldest version of the Syriac New Testament, and most commonly used well into the fifth century, was the *Diatessaron*. These biblical versions would mark emergent Syrian Christianity in particular ways. Portions of the Peshitta Old Testament show close links to Jewish exegetical traditions of the same period, an intersection that continues to flavour Syrian biblical interpretation in late antiquity. In turn, the *Diatessaron* ascribed to Justin Martyr's pupil Tatian around the year 180 (and, some would claim, produced in Antioch), may have originally been composed in either Greek or Syriac. The Syriac version has some features distinct from the Greek, and proved profoundly influential on the development of piety as well as theological motifs throughout the region of Syria and Mesopotamia.

The *Diatessaron* is often characterised by scholars as 'encratite' or strongly ascetical in flavour, but such a view distorts what we are able to reconstruct of the text. Ephrem Syrus' *Commentary on the Diatessaron*, written in the later fourth century, does not indicate an extremist view incompatible with what becomes mainstream in the post-Nicene era.[5] Rather, the desire to establish certain typological readings linking Old and New Testament passages seems

---

5 *Ephrem's commentary on the Diatessaron*, McCarthy (trans.)

to lie behind some Syriac word choices, strengthening the eschatological or soteriological force of a given text.[6] For example, John the Baptist's 'vegetarian' diet of milk and honey in the wilderness owes more to images of paradise and redemption than to any sense that the eating of meat (flesh) might in some way be sinful.[7] The importance of such a perspective will become apparent shortly.

Syria preserved the earliest known collection of Christian hymns, the *Odes of Solomon*: forty-two short hymns, surviving nearly complete in Syriac. One hymn survives also in Greek, and five in Coptic.[8] Much about this collection remains a mystery. Proposals on dating range from the late first to the late third century, but the second century seems most likely. The debate over the original language remains unresolved, with Greek, Syriac, Hebrew and Aramaic all having been proposed. While most scholars prefer Syriac, the problem remains that the poetic form of the *Odes* is unlike any other form of Syriac verse we know.[9]

Highly elusive in imagery yet hauntingly beautiful, the *Odes* show strong Johannine themes as well as parallels with the Hodayot literature from Qumran. Baptismal imagery abounds; so, too, motifs of salvific knowledge, Christ as heavenly redeemer, the descent to Sheol, the heavenly ascent of the visionary odist, and the persecution of the faithful. Laced through the sometimes puzzling images are references also to features that mark the more familiar fourth-century literature of what becomes 'normative' Syrian Christianity. For example, in Ode 19, the divine Son of God the Father is born of a virgin mother through the agency of the Holy Spirit – arguably the earliest non-biblical testimony to Mary as virgin mother, and with devotional titles that would characterise western Mariology of a significantly later period. This early appreciation of Mary's significance may lend weight to the possibility that the *Protevangelium of James*, the legendary account of Mary's own birth and upbringing, also a mid-second-century text, may have originated in Syria.[10]

As a group, the *Odes* are notable for their fully active and vividly portrayed Trinity of Father, Son and Holy Spirit, at a time when the Spirit is often missing or downplayed in other Christian writings. Powerful feminine imagery is used occasionally in these hymns for Father and Son, but especially for the Holy Spirit, a frequent characteristic of Syriac writings prior to the fifth century

---

6 Brock, 'What's in a word?'; Murray, *Symbols*, 228–36, 324–9.
7 Brock, 'The Baptist's diet'.
8 *Odes of Solomon*, Charlesworth (ed. and trans.)
9 *Odes of Solomon*, Charlesworth (ed. and trans.); Drijvers, *East of Antioch*.
10 See O. Cullmann's introduction to the *Protevangelium* in *NTApoc*, vol. I, 421–5; in favour of Syrian provenance, see Smid, *Protevangelium*.

(*ruha*, the Syriac term for 'spirit', is grammatically a feminine noun, although convention led to a change in usage around the year 400 CE).[11]

Especially prominent in these *Odes* are images of healing and bodily wholeness, of belief as a state that brings about health. The body is depicted as an essential agent of devotion to the divine, sanctified and hence made whole by its participation in activities of worship. This imagery of healing and bodily health or wholeness is one of the most pervasive and enduring themes of Syrian Christianity, appearing throughout its regions and across its various doctrinal forms.[12]

The *Chronicle of Edessa* records a flood in Edessa in the year 201 that destroyed 'the temple of the church of the Christians', indicating a community large enough to have had a building of notable importance to the city at the time.[13] Contemporaneously, the career of the great Christian philosopher and teacher Bardaisan (154–222/3 CE) flourished in the city. An aristocrat of eclectic learning – interested in astrology, philosophy, ethnography, history and apparently a fine composer of hymns – Bardaisan enjoyed the favour of the court of king Abgar VIII of Edessa. Though Eusebius (*HE* 4.30) reports that Bardaisan's prolific Syriac writings were translated quickly into Greek by his students and remained in circulation, all that survives is a dialogue on fate, in fact composed by Bardaisan's pupil Philip, known to us as the *Book of the laws of countries*.[14] Eusebius himself attests the excellence of the work, which presents an elegant argument for human free will in the literary form of a philosophical dialogue.

Bardaisan's 'school' continued for some centuries after his death as a contested Christian community in the Edessan area.[15] Eusebius (*HE* 4.30) claims that Bardaisan had been for a time an adherent of Valentinianism, and that, although he later condemned those teachings, the charge of heresy remained. Ephrem was especially contemptuous of Bardaisan's cosmology, but it appears that developments within the later 'school' may have taken Bardaisan's views to greater speculative extremes than he himself intended.

Bardaisan taught a system of thought deeply conversant with a stunning range of traditions.[16] Jewish, Iranian, Chaldaean, Christian and especially Stoic concepts strongly influenced his cosmology, which appears to have been highly original in its formulation. A primary target of Bardaisan's was the teacher Marcion (*c*.140), whose views had spread widely in the eastern territories and

---

11 Harvey, 'Feminine imagery for the divine'.
12 Murray, *Symbols*, 199–203.
13 *Chronicon Edessenum*, sec. 1.
14 *Book of the laws of countries*, Drijvers (ed. and trans.)
15 Most notably in Ephrem's *Prose refutations of Mani, Marcion, and Bardaisan*.
16 Drijvers, *Bardaisan*.

remained popular for some centuries. Ephrem, who moved to Edessa in 363, claims the Marcionites were the largest Christian group in Edessa in his time. Against Marcion, Bardaisan argued for one God, a benevolent creator in whose image humanity was made. His view of God encompassed a trinity of Father, Son and Mother of Life (a counterpart to the Holy Spirit similar to the presentation in the *Odes of Solomon*, as well as the *Acts of Thomas*, below), stressing a soteriology of redemptive knowledge made known by Christ. Scholars have noted strong similarities between the cosmologies of Bardaisan and Tatian.

Emerging themes

By the mid-third century, another highly influential Syrian work was circulating widely in Christian communities. The legendary *Acts of Thomas*, originally composed in Syriac but quickly translated into Greek, is an account purporting to tell the adventures of the apostle 'Judas Thomas' as he carried the gospel message east of Antioch, converting communities and kingdoms in Mesopotamia and India.[17] In common with other apocryphal acts of apostles, the *Acts of Thomas* shares literary motifs familiar from the Hellenistic novels. At the same time, the work includes religious and theological materials of great beauty and depth: prayers, hymns, invocations, sacramental celebrations and homilies attend the episodes. At least two of the hymns, the 'Wedding hymn' (chs. 6–7) and the 'Hymn of the pearl' (chs. 108–13), as well as the narrative of Thomas' martyrdom, also circulated independently. Both Greek and Syriac versions show signs of repeated editing, to adjust the story and its adornments to changing doctrinal positions.

In the *Acts of Thomas*, three features of conversion stand out. First, as Thomas teaches it, conversion to the gospel of Jesus Christ requires commitment to an ascetic, specifically celibate, life. Second, conversion, as Thomas effects it, is most often a response to healing from severe illness or demon possession. Jesus is frequently referred to as the Good Physician, and Thomas' prayers and invocations often call for the 'healing of soul and body'. Third, Thomas' work includes extensive ministry to the poor and suffering. The narrative presents these features as creating extreme disruption and social chaos. Hence these *Acts* are strongly based in the narrative motifs and structures of the canonical New Testament, as well as other versions of apocryphal Acts. The continuity is striking because these *Acts* vividly anticipate classic forms of Syrian asceticism that come to characterise the region when ascetic and monastic

---

17 *Acts of Thomas*, NTApoc, vol. ii.

movements develop in the late fourth and fifth centuries.[18] The ascetic monk or nun as wandering beggar is a common depiction of the later period, as is the image of the ascetic in constant interaction with domestic and civic communities. In fact, there seems to have been general stress on the values of simplicity or voluntary poverty, celibacy or continence in marriage, and responsibility for the poor or suffering in the community at large. By the third century, these became the particular obligations of men and women, known as the Sons and Daughters of the Covenant, who took vows of poverty, chastity and service to their bishop. An office distinctive to Syrian Christianity, the Members of the Covenant are found at the heart of civic church life well into the tenth century and later. Their work was not replaced by the rise of monasticism. The emphasis on these basic ideals allowed women as well as men to conduct visible and active forms of ministry.[19] The prominent roles of women characters in the *Acts of Thomas* offer some attestation, albeit idealised, for a historical counterpart in the broader social realm.

The *Acts of Thomas* further engage a number of themes central to other early Syrian texts. Healing, bodily health and bodily wholeness are especially important. More than a narrative motif in which 'physical' signifies 'spiritual' healing, as if metaphorically, these works indicate that for emergent Syrian Christianity the human body was an essential component of the human person as a religious entity. 'Healing of soul' was not opposed to 'healing of body'; rather, these were understood to be mutually inclusive actions. Here is the frame in which Thomas preached celibacy as requisite for salvation. These texts assume a cosmology in which mortality is not a natural human condition. The redeemed body promised and imaged by the resurrected Christ was a body healed of its mortality – healed of any illness or suffering, and healed, too, of the necessity of procreation.

The celibacy Thomas preaches is inextricable from the healing miracles he performs, and also from the ministry to the poor that he provides. These are significations meant to depict a redeemed life to come, when salvation will be brought to fullness in the final resurrected order: the sick will be well, the hungry fed, the blind will see and the lame walk, the sad will rejoice – and mortality, too, will be healed and restored to immortal incorruptibility. The *Acts of Thomas*, like the *Diatessaron*, present physical, bodily acts as markers of the salvation to come. The believer can and should anticipate that salvation by seeking to live, now, in that state. Celibacy could be the mark of what

---

18 Caner, *Wandering, begging monks*; Griffith, 'Asceticism'.
19 Ashbrook Harvey, 'Women's service'.

redemption will be, a rejection of the fallen order rather than of the physical body or physical world as evil. Such a sensibility is compatible with Bardaisan's insistence on the goodness of creation, on humanity in God's image, and on human choice as essential to salvation – the choice to live according to the divine will or according to the fallen order. Such a perspective will also underlie, again, much of the asceticism that characterises late antique Syrian Christianity.

Similarly, the sacramental emphasis of the *Acts of Thomas* resonates deeply with the *Odes of Solomon*, and earlier, the *Didache* and Ignatius' letters. The invocations, prayers, hymns and ritual actions of sealing by oil, baptism by immersion and shared eucharist of bread, or bread and water, or bread and 'cup', tie the *Acts* intricately into the ritual life of a larger worshipping community. Strongly Trinitarian, the ritual practices described are joined to narratives and imagery of healing. Hence, the ascetic elements of these *Acts* cannot be separated from this larger ecclesiastical and Trinitarian context.

Rival traditions

There is much in these earliest texts that anticipates coherently and emphatically the normative Christian themes that would prevail by the late fourth and early fifth centuries. At the same time, it is important to see the malleability of these themes. The same images and practices could be used within different religious and cosmological systems to uphold contrasting world-views. I have already noted the presence of Marcionite communities, strong enough to incite Bardaisan to attack at the turn of the third century, and Ephrem to fury in the 360s. Eusebius' note that Bardaisan may have supported the Valentinians at one point is not our only evidence for Valentinian popularity in Syria. Scholars have argued that the Valentinian *Gospel of Philip* may well be of Syrian origin, since a number of its passages rely on Syriac etymologies.[20] While these passages do not make a Syrian provenance essential, the text seems to have circulated broadly throughout the east. Its strong emphases on sacraments, Trinitarian depictions of God and bridal imagery all give the *Gospel of Philip* a sensibility consonant with other early Syrian literature. In the fourth century, the emperor Julian was outraged over a violent attack by Arians upon the Valentinians of Edessa.[21] Their presence was clearly not a passing one.

Scholars have sometimes argued that other works associated with the apostle Thomas – above all the *Gospel of Thomas* and the *Book of Thomas the*

20 Layton, *Scriptures*, 325–53.
21 Julian, *Epistulae* 40.

contender – originated in Syria.[22] This claim has been made in part because of the importance of the Thomas figure for Syrian Christianity. Thomas was associated with the foundations of Christianity in Mesopotamia and India apart from the *Acts* themselves. Eusebius knew an independent tradition linking Thomas to the conversion of Edessa before he evangelised Parthian Persia (*HE* 1.3; 2.1; 3.1). Edessa proudly held the relic of Thomas' bones – attested both by Ephrem and by the western pilgrim Egeria, who saw them on her visit to the city in April 384.

Thus Syrian Christianity was multi-faceted, and similar themes were refracted in contrasting ways through communities of diverse orientations. Our evidence does not help to order this fragmented picture, since prior to the fourth century it is hard to locate any of the texts. Bardaisan was an individual teacher, not an ecclesiastical official. The *Didache*, the *Odes*, the *Acts of Thomas* and other gospels are texts we cannot identify within specific groups in specific places. The exception to this situation is also the case that makes the point most dramatically: for Syria, the emergence of Manichaeism sharply demonstrates the possibilities of shared imagery with divergent functions.

The prophet Mani was born in Persian Mesopotamia in 216, son of a father who had joined the Jewish Christian baptismal sect of the Elkesaites. As a boy he began to receive revelations from his 'divine twin', leading to bitter disputes with the members and elders of his sect. In 240, at age 24, Mani received his call to heavenly discipleship and began his career as religious founder. Sending out missionaries and himself travelling to India, Mani preached a religion with himself as the final, true prophet. The Persian court under Shapor I (242–73) apparently held him in high favour. But Shapor's successors saw matters differently. Mani died a martyr following imprisonment in 276.

Mani's religious teaching drew into its complex cosmology many of the religious systems already present in the east: Judaism, Christianity, Buddhism, Zoroastrianism and Gnostic teachings. His devotees understood him to be the divine Paraclete promised by Christ in the gospel of John, thereby bringing God's revelation to its final completion. At the same time, Mani taught extensively from his own revelations, producing a huge corpus in Syriac of theological, liturgical and homiletic works. This literature, with Mani's apostles, travelled throughout the trade routes east and west, from the Silk Route to Europe, soon translated into Greek, Latin and Coptic, or, to the east, into Turkish and Chinese.[23]

22 Layton, *Scriptures*, 359–409.
23 Lieu, *Manichaeism*.

Fundamental to Mani's system was a notion of cosmic battle between good and evil, light and dark, present throughout the cosmos in 'particles'. Matter was not intrinsically evil, but it could be a prison in which light particles were trapped. The Manichaean mission was to free the light particles to return to their heavenly home. Within the elaborate mythological scheme Mani constructed, the human body had been created by demonic powers of the lower realm, a poor parody of the heavenly prototype of Adam/Eve, the androgynous humanity of divine origin. Because their spirits were of heavenly origin, humanity could liberate divine light particles from within, turning the body into a vehicle for salvation. Ritual practices as complex as this mythological scheme allowed Manichaeans to construct their daily lives so as to participate continuously in the process of transforming material reality from a realm dominated by dark particles into one not only liberating light particles, but further, serving as a harbinger or storehouse for gathering in divine forces of light.[24]

The central Manichaean ritual was that of a daily cultic meal and the elaborate practices necessary to arrange it. Two classes of adherents enabled such a ritual structure to operate: the Elect, or Adepts, whose sole task was the liberation of light particles; and the Hearers (Auditors) whose devotion was enacted through service to the Elect. As the Elect sought to live a life most suitable to liberating, or gathering in, the divine light, they had to have as little engagement in the fallen world as possible. This life of perfection was known as the Rest. Its practical expression was a life of celibacy and extreme renunciation, passed in wandering beggary. In turn, the Hearers undertook the necessarily ambiguous tasks of working in the world to obtain, prepare and distribute the food needed by the Elect. The Hearers made possible what the Elect did, and the Elect made possible the Hearers' future salvation.

Manichaean ritual life, however, was built on more than mythological narratives. It was also built on a scientific world-view that understood change to be possible: matter could be altered from prison to liberating vehicle. This was true of the cosmos; it was true of the body. The emphasis on ritual practices and especially on food was above all a focus on attaining health. Once again one finds repeated imagery of Christ as the Good Physician, healer of the wounded, who heals the collective body of the faithful even as he heals the individual bodies of the sick.

This medical imagery dominates the large corpus of Manichaean hymns that survive in Coptic, translated from Syriac originals of the third and early fourth

24 BeDuhn, *Manichaean body.*

centuries, known as the *Manichaean psalm book*.[25] Even devoid of their liturgical settings and music, these hymns are arresting in their powerful rhythms and beautiful images. Poignant prayers for healing are interlaced with lush evocations of a heavenly existence imaged in vivid sensory terms. Biblical images frame and present Mani's teachings. Additionally, borrowings from the *Acts of Thomas* are particularly striking. Indeed, the *Acts of Thomas* belong to a corpus of five apocryphal acts incorporated into the Manichaean canon. The description in the Manichaean *Psalms* of the Elect as wandering beggars is closely modelled on that of Thomas in the *Acts*. Once again, it was a clear prototype for subsequent Syrian ascetic traditions.

Thriving over vast geographical and cultural territories, Manichaeism can hardly be seen as a monolithic religion. Diversity in teachings and orientation characterise its history. Yet its popularity in Syria for some centuries cannot be lightly dismissed. Its basic themes and images draw deeply from those favoured across the varieties of earliest Syrian Christianity, reminding us that these same images could work effectively across a full spectrum of responses to bodily existence in a physical world: from renunciation as evil, to celebration as redemptive and redeemed. Just as a fundamental dualism underlay its system, so, too, did an embodied notion of healing pervade its presentation of salvation.

Achieved order, shared memory

Shortly before Mani's death, Antioch again flared into view with the notorious episcopacy of Paul of Samosata, bishop of Antioch from 260 until a special synod convened in 268 deposed him. Although subsequent generations granted him a notoriety reserved for a select few in the annals of the church, the historical evidence is difficult to reconstruct. As reported by Eusebius (*HE* 7.27–30), the bishops were scandalised as much and possibly more by Paul's behaviour than by his teachings. Their charges were cast in terms of standard invective: they opposed his allegedly dramatic preaching style, irregular liturgical practices, questionable relations with women and apparent interference with civic and provincial affairs. Nonetheless, their measures to discipline him were quite unusual. The Council of Antioch in 268 produced a synodal letter, preserved by Eusebius (*HE* 7.30), addressed nominally to the bishops Dionysius of Rome and Maximus of Alexandria and further 'to the entire catholic church throughout the world'. If local or provincial synods had become increasingly common over the course of the third century, the claim

---

25 *Manichaean psalm-book*, Allberry (ed.); Säve-Söderbergh, *Studies*.

to ecumenical authority was unprecedented. As such, it became a benchmark for later conciliar actions.

The synodal letter against Paul is the only contemporary account we have of Paul's situation, and it says little about his theology except that he taught a 'low' Christology: that Jesus Christ had been a mere man, and thus was not 'from above'. A number of later sources expand on this charge, but their accuracy is dubious, clouded as they are with the technical vocabulary and agendas of later theological disputes. Here one is given the impression that Paul distinguished between Word and Son, but it may be that Paul and his accusers were approaching Christology from different paradigms of how the human and divine elements of Jesus Christ were united in one person.[26]

In a flurry of further scandal, Paul refused to give up his church until the emperor Aurelian was drawn into the dispute and had him exiled. Despite the vindictive charges of later writers, there is no evidence that Paul was given any kind of special protection by queen Zenobia. Indeed, the so-called 'revolt' of Palmyra shortly after the emperor Aurelian's death in 272 is an event about which we know little, and which lends itself to various interpretations. But there is no basis for the idea of a separate 'Palmyrene' position which Paul might have represented, or which might have galvanised local populations against Roman rule. The immediate instability of the imperial throne appears to have been the salient issue.

Two developments of the fourth century bear upon the evidence here considered for the first three centuries. First is the appearance, essentially new, of martyrdom as a possibility for Christians of Syria and Mesopotamia. Apart from occasional (admittedly dramatic) incidents in Antioch,[27] and despite the account of the apostle's martyrdom in the *Acts of Thomas*, Christians in this region had little if any direct experience with persecution until the fourth century. The semi-autonomous political states of the Syriac-speaking territories under Roman domination lasted until well into the third century, a situation perhaps preventing the legal problems and fears that led to sporadic Roman persecutions of Christians elsewhere. In Persian territory, several martyrdoms occurred in the 270s – including the execution of Mani, but also of the Christian woman Candida. These seem to have happened only because of conversions within the royal family, offending the larger Zoroastrian frame of government.[28] But in the early fourth century, several Christians in the territory of

---

26 Behr, *Way to Nicaea*, 207–35.
27 Euseb. *HE* 6. 29, 34, 39 (Babylas). For Antioch's martyrs in the great persecution instigated by Diocletian, see further 8.12–13.
28 Brock, 'A martyr at the Sasanid court'.

Edessa were martyred during the final great persecution begun by Diocletian. The *Acts of the Edessan martyrs*, Shmona, Guria and the deacon Habib, though written later, present historically sound accounts of the events, which were notably less extreme than similar occurrences to the west.[29]

In 342, apparently in response to the changing religious loyalties of the Roman government, the Persians began to undertake sustained, widespread persecutions of Christians in their territories, accusing them of loyalty to the Christian Roman emperors.[30] In the early fifth century, the noble families of Edessa sought to re-establish their Christian past in terms more flattering to their self-image. Included in the effort was a second set of flagrantly anachronistic Edessan martyr texts, presenting the stories of Sharbil, Babai and Barsamya, members of the Edessan aristocracy, allegedly martyred in the year 105.[31] Thus, the body of Syriac martyr literature is relatively late in comparison with Greek and Latin works from the west. In this situation, the pervasive emphasis on ascetic practices and on the significance of bodily condition, characterising Syrian Christianity of all stripes from its very beginnings, cannot have been moulded by a culture of martyrdom and persecution.[32]

Secondly, by the turn of the fourth century, foundation legends begin to appear which, like the *Acts of Thomas*, purport to give accounts of apostolic missions establishing Christianity throughout greater Syria. Most famous was the legendary correspondence between Jesus and king Abgar Ukkama ('the Black') of Edessa.[33] The story is best known in the version of Eusebius (*HE* 1.13), in which the apostle Thaddaeus, one of the seventy, is sent by Thomas to convert the kingdom of Edessa. Eusebius claims to have translated this correspondence directly from Syriac into Greek (*HE* 1.13.6–10).[34]

An elaborated version of the legend appeared early in the fifth century in Syriac, known as the *Teaching of Addai*.[35] Here the correspondence is embedded in a detailed narrative in which the apostle Addai (identified with Eusebius' Thaddaeus) converts Abgar, his family and all the nobility of the region, establishing an ordered and well-governed church as Edessa becomes the first Christian 'state'.[36] By the sixth century, a further legend building from this found its

---

29 *Euphemia and the Goth with the Acts of martyrdom of the confessors of Edessa*, Burkitt (ed. and trans.); for redating, see Doran, 'Martyrdom of Habbib'.
30 Brock, 'Christians in the Sasanid empire'.
31 *Acts of Sharbil, Babai and Barsamya*, Cureton. (ed. and trans.)
32 Harvey, 'Edessan martyrs'; Griffith, 'Asceticism'.
33 *The Abgar legend*, NTApoc, vol. 1, 492–7 (introduction), 497–9 (translation).
34 Brock, 'Eusebius and Syriac Christianity'; Peppermüller, 'Griechische Papyrusfragmente'.
35 *Teaching of Addai*, Phillips (ed.), Howard (trans.)
36 Griffith, 'The *Doctrina Addai* as a paradigm'.

literary form as the *Acts of Mar Mari*. These purport to recount Addai's commission of the apostle Mari to convert Mesopotamia ('Babylon'),[37] a mission conducted through successes among royal families and aristocrats, and conversions invariably provoked by healing miracles. Unlike the *Acts of Thomas* but like the account of Addai, the *Acts of Mari* have no interest in martyrdom, and give no hint of any kind of social disruption or chaos due to the introduction of Christianity.

How do these later conversion narratives bear upon our early evidence? There is certainly no connection through historical events. The Abgar legend became greatly loved throughout the Christian world, but no trace of its story nor its events can be found earlier than Eusebius' account. However, certain threads of thematic continuity tie the later legends of Addai and Mari to the early Syrian texts. One is interest in royal favour – a theme shared with the *Acts of Thomas*, and a situation known to Bardaisan and Mani. Another is the crucial role of travel along the trade routes, again a feature of the *Acts of Thomas*, of Mani's missions, and a necessary background for Bardaisan's ethnographic interests. Most important, however, is the constant stress on healing: on Jesus as the Good Physician, on belief as a state that yields bodily health, and on the high valuation thus given to the body and its condition in the context of Christian devotion.

37 *Actes de Mar Mari*, Jullien and Jullien (eds. and trans.); *The Acts of Mar Mari the Apostle*, A. Harrak (ed. and trans.), Writings from the Greco-Roman World II (Atlanta: Society of Biblical Literature, 2005).

20

Gaul

JOHN BEHR

The evidence

Almost all we know about Christianity in Gaul during the first two or three centuries CE is connected with the Christian communities in Vienne and Lyons in the latter decades of the second century. The episcopal lists and martyrologies do not provide any reliable evidence for this period. No archaeological evidence of the Christians themselves survives to provide a tangible sense of how they constructed their own physical world. With the possible exception of one inscription, epigraphy yields nothing that can be securely dated to the pre-Constantinian era. And even the couple of references to Christianity in Gaul made by contemporary writers abroad are difficult to evaluate properly. Nevertheless, the precious excerpts, some rather lengthy, of letters written by Christians in Gaul, which Eusebius preserves, and the writings of Irenaeus of Lyons, arguably the most important Christian figure of the second century, offer a vivid picture of the remarkable vitality and diversity of these communities.

Social and cultural influences

The areas of Gaul in which Christianity appears in the second century CE are marked by the confluence of several forces and peoples. The background of the Celts, or the Gauls as the Romans called them and as they became known, lies in the so-called Hallstatt culture (named after a site near Salzburg, Austria). By 750 BCE, some had migrated to the area of Provence, beginning what is known as the La Tène culture (named after a site near Lake Neuchâtel, Switzerland), which lasted until the beginning of the Christian era, when the dominance of the Roman empire overshadowed all such distinctions. About the same time, between 734 and 580 BCE, the Mediterranean coastal regions of Gaul were colonised by Ionian Greeks from Phocaea (70 km north-west of ancient Smyrna), in search of metals and other raw materials.[1] Marseilles (Massalia) was founded around 600 BCE at the mouth of the Rhône to conduct trade with the settlements further up river. A number of other Greek colonies were established soon after along the Riviera. These settlements were clearly centres of trade and commerce during the following centuries: there is evidence of coins minted at Massalia and of trading with the Gauls, in whose graves have been found Greek, Etruscan and Massalian items, including smaller luxurious pieces made in gold, silver and amber. Gauls, from varying backgrounds, had spread out through much of Europe, even getting as far south as Rome, where in 386 BCE they sacked and burnt the city before being driven out, and as far east as Asia Minor, where some settled permanently (the 'Galatians').

The final influence on the region is, of course, that of Rome. After the defeat of Hannibal in 202 BCE, with whom the Gauls had joined forces, and other attacks by the Gauls themselves, the Romans gradually expanded throughout the Mediterranean. By 121 BCE, they had conquered the Gauls on the lower Rhône. A few years later, the first Roman colony was established at Narbonne (Narbo Martius), and the surrounding area (modern Provence) was renamed Narbonensis. In the decades that followed, the vast districts of Gaul beyond this area, from the Atlantic to the Rhine and stretching as far north as modern Holland, were gradually brought under the influence of Roman civilisation. There were no cities as such, but rather the landscape was dotted with *oppida* ('hill forts'), though there did develop some rudimentary form of government, with each *civitas*, or local polity, consisting of several *oppida*, being governed by a local, elected, chief magistrate. Some of these *civitates* began to mint their own coins, based on Greek and Roman models, so increasing the possibility for trade with Rome, and integrating Gaul into the Roman economic system. Other aspects of Greek and Roman culture also began to flourish: Julius Caesar reports that the Druids (the religious leaders of Gaul, who, along with the *equites* ('knights'), were distinguished from the commoners) even knew the Greek alphabet (*B. Gall.* 6.14). The Gauls had various deities, whom Caesar tried to identify with the Roman gods, the most important of which were the equivalent of Mercury, the Roman god of commerce (*B. Gall.* 6.12), and the mother goddesses depicted, usually in threes, in various reliefs. The Gauls were also known to practice rites of rebirth, and were even reported to have performed human sacrifices (*B. Gall.* 6.16).

---

1 On this period of Gaul, see Hodge, *Ancient Greek France*.

The most important event for the identity of Gaul during our period, and for subsequent European history, was the Gallic wars, the eight successive campaigns against Gaul and Britain lead by Julius Caesar between 58 and 50 BCE. His *Commentaries on the Gallic wars* opens by noting that Gaul is divided into three parts: that inhabited by the Belgae, north and west of the Marne and Seine rivers; that of the Aquitani, dwelling between the Garonne river and the Pyrenees; and the largest area, the remaining part, in which the Gauls lived. It is in the aftermath of these wars that the cities that will principally concern us, Vienne (Vienna) and Lyons (Lugdunum), were established as colonies for the veterans of the Gallic wars.[2] During the Gallic wars, Vienne, the former capital of the Allobroges tribe, was established as a colony, serving as a supply depot and a camp for hostages. After Caesar's assassination (44 BCE), the Allobroges, who had remained loyal to the Romans during Vercingetorix' assault on the town in 52 BCE, drove the Roman veterans out of Vienne. These soldiers, in turn, were the original settlers of the nearby town of Lyons, beginning the long-standing rivalry between the two cities. In the following year, 43 BCE, Mark Antony was sent to install another colony of veterans in Vienne, and Lucius Munatius Plancus, a general of the wars, was sent to be the governer of Lyons, establishing it as a proper colony. Despite the relative age of Vienne, Lyons unquestionably became the more important of the two cities. It is situated on the hill of Fourvière (the *forum vetus*, or 'old forum'), at the confluence of the Rhône and Saône rivers, and lay at the intersection of major trade roads. It soon became the capital of the Three Gauls, while the third division of Gaul was in turn named Lugdunensis, and an annual festival of the Three Gauls was instituted there.[3] The town was the birthplace of the future emperors Claudius (10 BCE–54 CE) and Caracalla (188–217 CE), and is mentioned by a number of Roman writers, from Livy (59 BCE–17 CE) to Ammianus Marcellinus (330–400 CE). There is a good deal of archeological evidence from Lyons indicating the assimilation of Gallic and Roman religion, such as an altar base with reliefs of the Mother Goddess, Mercury, Sucellus and Fortuna. There is also evidence for the worship of deities from the east, such as the altar, dating to 160 CE, from the shrine of Cybele, the Great Mother of the Phrygian gods. Remains of the two Roman theatres of Lyons can still be seen today on the Fourvière, the larger of which (built around 17–15 BCE) could seat 10,000 spectators, and to the north, across the Saône, lay the amphitheatre and circus, built at the beginning of the first century CE.

2 For descriptions and images of these cities and their archaeological remains, see Quentin, 'Sites and museums in Roman Gaul 1'.
3 For this festival, see Fishwick, 'Federal cult of the Three Gauls'.

The Christian community

As the shores of the Mediterranean and the valley of the Rhône had long since been home to Greeks from the east, especially Asia, who remained in contact with their fellow countrymen back home, it is not surprising that the earliest witness we have of the Christian communities in Gaul indicates such diversity. This is the 'Letter of the churches of Vienne and Lyons' to their brethren in Asia and Phrygia, written shortly after the persecutions in these two cities. The date of this pogrom and thus the letter depends upon Eusebius, who is not, however, totally consistent. His *Chronicon* would place the persecutions during the seventh year of Marcus Aurelius' reign (166–7), while his later *Historia ecclesiastica*, in which the letter is preserved, places the events a decade later, in his seventeenth year (177), the date that is generally accepted.[4] The letter seems to indicate that the founders of the two churches were among the martyrs (cf. *HE* 5.1.13), suggesting that Christianity was established in this region only in the mid-second century. That Christianity had made its way up the Rhône valley probably implies that there was already a Christian community in Marseilles, at the mouth of the Rhône, although the earliest evidence for this comes from the crypt of St Victor, which can possibly be dated as early as the mid-third century.

That the title of the letter places the church of Vienne before that of Lyons is striking, given the pre-eminence of Lyons. The leader of the community in Lyons was Pothinus, who was imprisoned during the persecution and subsequently martyred. He was already over ninety years old (*HE* 5.1.29), and so presumably was one of the original founding fathers of the church in Lyons. Around this time, Irenaeus was sent on a mission to Rome, which will be discussed below, taking with him a letter for Eleutherus, the 'bishop of the Romans' (174–89 CE), which describes Irenaeus as a 'presbyter', a word which was used interchangeably with 'bishop' during the course of the second century.[5] The fact that the letter mentions Vienne before Lyons, together with its particular style and theological tenor, makes it probable that the letter was written by Irenaeus as the leader of the community in Vienne, assuming a general oversight of Lyons while its leader was imprisoned.[6] When Irenaeus

---

4 Cf. Grant, 'Eusebius and the martyrs of Gaul'. The text of the letter can be found in Euseb. *HE* 5.1–3.

5 Euseb. *HE* 5.3.4–4.2. Irenaeus describes Polycarp as being a 'presbyter' (letter preserved in *HE* 5.20.7) and refers to Victor's predecessors as 'presbyters' (*HE* 5.24.14). The indistinct employment of the vocabulary of ecclesial office is also shown by the description, in the 'Letter of the churches of Vienne and Lyons', of Pothinus having been entrusted with 'the ministry of episcopacy in Lyons' (*tēn diakonian tēs episkopēs, HE* 5.1.29).

6 Cf. Nautin, *Lettres*, 54–61, 93–5; Doutreleau, 'Irénée de Lyon', 1928–9.

returned from Rome, after the death of Pothinus, he became bishop of Lyons, which is how he is traditionally known. Irenaeus was from the east, and the name 'Pothinus' probably indicates a similar eastern background. Irenaeus describes how, in his early youth, he had known Polycarp, the bishop of the church in Smyrna. This connection with Polycarp was important for Irenaeus: he emphasises that Polycarp had been appointed bishop of Smyrna by the apostles themselves and spoke often about his discussion with John and others who had seen the Lord.[7] Irenaeus thus brought with him to Gaul a living connection with the age of the apostles themselves. Polycarp was martyred sometime in the late 150s, after returning from a visit to Rome. It is tempting to picture both Pothinus and Irenaeus as having accompanied Polycarp to Rome, and then having moved on to Gaul, perhaps with Christians from Rome itself. Other epistolary evidence, considered below, demonstrates that links with Rome were important to the Christians in Gaul.

The letter indicates that a number of others in the Christian community of Vienne and Lyons were also immigrants from the east. It specifically mentions that Attalus, a Roman citizen, was a native of Pergamum (*HE* 5.1.17), and that Alexander, a physician, was a Phrygian who had spent many years in various parts of Gaul (*HE* 5.1.49). Alcibiades, who, as we will see later, was connected with the Montanist movement, was also from Phrygia (*HE* 5.3.2–4). The same may be true of Vettius Epagathus, who though young and 'distinguished' or 'noble' (*episēmos*), acted as the advocate for the Christians, 'having the Advocate in himself, the Spirit, more abundantly than Zacharias'.[8] The other names recorded by the letter offer evidence that these Christian communities were diverse in composition: Sanctus, the deacon of Vienne, replied to his interrogators in Latin (*HE* 5.1.20); Blandina was a slave girl, whose nameless mistress was also martyred (*HE* 5.1.17), and who also encouraged a fifteen-year-old boy called Ponticus (*HE* 5.1.53); along with Attalus, several others appear to have been Roman citizens (*HE* 5.1.47); Maturus was a 'recent convert' (*HE* 5.1.17), as perhaps was also Biblis, who initially denied her faith before 'recovering herself' and being martyred (*HE* 5.1.25–6). Finally the letter records that a number of the Christians had pagan servants, who were also seized and interrogated (*HE* 5.1.14). Thus, despite the severity of the persecution, the letter specifically mentions only eleven Christians from the two communities, ten by name and the anonymous mistress of Blandina. It is probable, however,

---

7 Cf. Iren. *Haer.* 3.3.4; and his 'Letter to Flora', cited in *HE* 5.20.4–8.

8 *HE* 5.1.9–10. The mention here of Zacharias is an allusion to the priestly father of John the Baptist (Luke 1:6), though it is also given as the (baptismal?) name of Vettius in the martyrologies. Cf. Nautin, *Lettres*, 50.

that the actual number of martyrs was larger. The later martyrologies record forty-nine names of those who perished, though some of the names seem to refer to the same person.[9] The number of Christians in both communities was certainly larger, though, again, as Eusebius mentions that the letter contained a list of the names of those who survived (*HE* 5.5.3), the overall number could not have been too extensive. The Christian communities in the cities of Vienne and Lyons were not, therefore, too large to be counted, but they were big enough to survive such a pogrom, and, as we have seen, while predominantly of eastern background, as were their leaders, they were made up of a wide cross-section of society.

Personalities and events

Of the figures mentioned in the letter, we know nothing else. However, more is known of Irenaeus, its probable author.[10] Although he had come from the east, and preferred Greek, the language in which he wrote, as he was living, he says, among the 'Celts', he had become 'accustomed for the most part to use a barbarous dialect', thus excusing, in a typically rhetorical flourish, the lack of beauty or persuasiveness of style in his own writings.[11] Irenaeus' main literary monument is his five books entitled *Detection and refutation of gnosis falsely so-called*, usually known simply by the Latin title *Adversus haereses* ('Against the heresies'). Book 3 of this work mentions Eleutherus as the current bishop of Rome (*Haer.* 3.3.3), and so it can be dated to the period between 174 and 189. The only other extant work of Irenaeus, rediscovered at the beginning of the twentieth century in an Armenian manuscript, is his *Epideixis tou apostolikou kērygmatos* ('Demonstration of the apostolic preaching'), a short summary work presenting the apostolic preaching by citing passages from the scriptures (the Law, the Psalms and the prophets). Although chapter 98 of the *Epideixis* refers the reader to the *Adversus haereses*, it is probable, given the more primitive use of the apostolic writings in the *Epideixis* and a particularity in the Armenian text at this point, that the final chapters are a later addition and that the *Epideixis* is in fact the earlier work.[12] Jerome (*c*.342–420) is the first to refer to Irenaeus as 'bishop of Lyons and martyr' (*In Esaiam* 17), though it is possible that this is a later scribal error, for Jerome does not refer to him as a martyr elsewhere.

---

9 Cf. Quentin, 'La liste des martyrs de Lyon'; Nautin, *Lettres*, 49–50.
10 See pt III, ch. 13, above.
11 *Haer.* 1.Pref.3. Cf. *Haer.* 1.10.2; 3.4.1.
12 Cf. Irenaeus, *On the Apostolic Preaching*, Behr (trans.), 3, 16 and 118 n. 229.

The first full report of his martyrdom is by Gregory of Tours (*c.*540–94, *Historia Francorum* 1.27).

Having looked at the composition of the Christian communities in Gaul, as reflected in the letter, we can turn to the events described therein. Although doubts have been raised concerning the authenticity of the letter and its account, it is generally accepted as being fairly reliable. Nevertheless, the description of the events is already shaped by theological reflection on the significance of the martyrs' suffering, drawing upon martyrological *topoi*,[13] and certainly reflecting, as we will see, Irenaeus' own theological vision. The pogrom seems to have broken out in Lyons and then spread out to Vienne, drawing in their deacon Sanctus. No particular cause is recorded, other than hostility resulting from popular prejudice against the largely immigrant Christians.[14] After suffering at the hands of the local population, the Christians were interrogated in public by the local magistrates in the forum, and then imprisoned until the arrival of the governor. The governor, as Pliny had done in Bithynia earlier (cf. *Ep.* 10.96, *c.*112 CE), wrote to the emperor for his ruling. Marcus Aurelius, like Trajan previously (cf. Plin. *Ep.* 10.97), decided that all those who recanted should be set free, but otherwise they should be condemned to the wild beasts or, if a Roman citizen, beheaded (cf. *HE* 5.1.43, 47). A number of Christians were then put to death in various ways, described in grisly detail. Finally the bodies of those who had been strangled in the prisons were thrown to the dogs, while the bodies of the other martyrs were burnt and thrown into the Rhône, perhaps following the practice of throwing into the river the losers of the oratorical contests held in honour of the Three Gauls.[15]

With its gruesome narration of the sufferings of the martyrs, the letter is concerned to present a clear theological vision, in which we can see many similarities with the theology developed by Irenaeus in his *Epideixis* and *Adversus haereses*. The most striking figure is that of Blandina, who is in many ways the heroine of the whole account (more lines are devoted to her than to any other figure, and she is named, while her mistress remains nameless), personifying the theology of martyrdom articulated by Irenaeus on the basis of Christ's words to Paul: 'My strength is made perfect in weakness.'[16] Blandina is specifically described as so 'weak in body' that the others were fearful

---

13 Thus, the letter mentions that the confessors 'heroically endured all that the people *en masse* heaped on them: abuse, blows, dragging, despoiling, stoning, imprisonment and all that an enraged mob is wont to inflict on their most hated enemies' (*HE* 5.1.7).

14 Cf. Musurillo, *Acts of the Christian martyrs*, xx–xxii.

15 *HE* 5.1.57–63. The background for this practice might in turn have been a parody of the burial rites of Celtic origin. Cf. Fishwick, 'Federal cult of the Three Gauls', 35.

16 2 Cor 12:9; cf. Iren. *Haer.* 5.2–10; Behr, *Asceticism*, 76–9.

lest she not be able to make the good confession; yet she 'was filled with such power that even those who were taking turns to torture her in every way from dawn until dusk were weary and beaten. They themselves admitted that they were beaten . . . astonished at her endurance, as her entire body was mangled and broken' (*HE* 5.1.18). Not only is she, in her weakness, filled with divine power by her confession, but she becomes fully identified with the one whose body was broken on Golgotha: when hung on a stake in the arena, 'she seemed to hang there in the form of a cross, and by her fervent prayer she aroused intense enthusiasm in those who were undergoing their ordeal, for in their torment with their physical eyes they saw in the person of their sister him who was crucified for them, that he might convince all who believe in him that all who suffer for Christ's sake will have eternal fellowship in the living God' (*HE* 5.1.41). For Irenaeus it was the martyr, no longer living by the flesh, but by the spirit, who is the truly living human being, 'the glory of God'.[17] Similarly characteristic is the description of the martyrs' deaths as their 'new birth' (*HE* 5.1.63), and the use of the term 'virgin' to refer to the church: when the ten 'stillborn' who had recanted then returned to their confession, 'the virgin mother had much joy in recovering alive those whom she had cast forth as stillborn' (*HE* 5.1.11, 45).[18] It is also noteworthy, and struck Eusebius as such, since he records this passage separately from the main narrative, that those who had survived their encounter with the wild beasts refused to be known as 'martyrs', reserving this for those alone who have endured until the end, in imitation of 'the true and faithful martyr' and 'firstborn from the dead', Christ himself.[19] Although Irenaeus had probably learnt from Justin in Rome, the theology he develops, and which is presented in this letter, comes from further east.[20] It is represented by Ignatius of Antioch, whose words on his way to his own martyrdom, 'I am the wheat of Christ, and am ground by the teeth of the wild beasts, that I may be found to be the pure bread of God', are cited by Irenaeus as coming from 'one of ours'.[21] This allusion to the eucharist is developed by Irenaeus, who sees a parallel between

---

17 Cf. *Haer.* 4.20.7; 5.9.2.

18 For Irenaeus' comments on the church as the virgin mother in whom Christians receive a new birth through martyrdom, see *Haer.* 4.33.4, 9.

19 *HE* 5.2.2–4; cf. Rev 3:14, 1:5; Col 1:18.

20 Other teachings which Irenaeus inherited from the east include the infancy of the newly created Adam, previously found only in Theophilus of Antioch (*Autol.* 2.25) and the abundant fruitfulness of the earth in the millennial kingdom of the Lord, a tradition which he received from 'the elders who saw John, the disciple of the Lord, and related that they had heard from him how the Lord used to teach in regard to these times', things which are also testified by Papias (*Haer.* 5.33.3 4).

21 *Haer.* 5.28.4; the quotation comes from Ign. *Rom.* 4.

the eucharistic offering and human death and resurrection, the fulfilment of what is prefigured in baptism: by receiving the eucharist, as the wheat and vine receive growth from the spirit, Christians are prepared, as they make the fruits into bread and wine, for their own resurrection wrought by the word, at which point, just as the bread and wine receive the word, becoming the body and blood of Christ, the eucharist, so also will their bodies receive immorality and incorruptibility from the Father.[22] Just as Christians prepare bread for the eucharist, the celebration of Christ's own death and resurrection, so also the sufferings of the martyrs prepare them for God, who celebrates their death as their new birth and entry into his own glory. The theological seeds that Irenaeus brought with him from Asia clearly flourished into a profound legacy for Christianity in Gaul.

Christian others

Beside the communities depicted for us in the letter, there were a number of others in the area who claimed to possess a higher 'knowledge' (*gnōsis*). Irenaeus describes and analyses a bewildering variety of purveyors of 'knowledge falsely so-called' in the first two books of his *Adversus haereses*.[23] But for Irenaeus this was not merely an arcane academic exercise. Some of these claimants to 'knowledge' he only knew by report, but others he claims to have encountered personally. He had read some of the 'Commentaries' of Ptolemaeus, a disciple of Valentinus, and had become acquainted with their teachings through personal contact (*Haer.* 1.Pref.2; cf. 1.8.2–5 for Ptolemaeus' commentary on the prologue to John's gospel). Irenaeus also claims to have received the testimony of women who were duped into the mystery of the 'union' with other Valentinian teachers, but later repented and confessed (*Haer.* 1.6.3). However, closer to home, Irenaeus' greatest struggle was with a certain Marcus, perhaps a disciple of Valentinus.[24] According to Irenaeus, Marcus had deceived many people, especially women (though that is, of course, a *topos*) 'in our own regions around the Rhône' (*Haer.* 1.13.7; the section 1.13.1–21.5 is devoted to Marcus). Marcus was also from Asia, where, according to Irenaeus, he defiled

---

22 *Haer.* 5.2.3. Cf. Behr, *Asceticism*, 67–78.

23 It is worth noting that Irenaeus does not describe all his opponents as 'Gnostics'; indeed, he does not call Valentinus, Basilides and their followers 'Gnostic', but reserves this term for a particular (and particularly obscure) sect who seem to hold views similar to those in the *Apocryphon of John*, in *Haer.* 1.29. See pt III, ch. 12, above.

24 Such is the implication of the present order of *Haer.* 1; though Tripp ('Original sequence of Irenaeus "Adversus haereses" 1') suggests, on the basis of the account of *Haer.* 1 given in *Haer.* 2.Pref.1, that the present order of *Haer.* 1 should be rearranged, which would then make Marcus independent of Valentinus.

in mind and body the wife of a certain deacon 'from among our own people in Asia' (*Haer.* 1.13.5). Irenaeus also records the words of 'the divinely inspired elder and preacher of the truth' against Marcus, referring probably to Pothinus (*Haer.* 1.15.6; 13.3), so that the struggle with Marcus was one which Irenaeus inherited from his predecessor. Marcus seems to have indulged in number and letter mysticism to a quite extraordinary degree (*Haer.* 1.14–17), and to have used numerous apocryphal writings (*Haer.* 1.20.1). Irenaeus mentions two particular rites of Marcus. In the first, he 'gives thanks over the cup mixed with wine and draws out at great length the prayer of invocation', making the cup appear to be purple or red, through some kind of trickery, so that it appears that 'grace from above has dropped her own blood into the cup', and then, handing the cups over to the women, he has them 'giving thanks over them in his presence' (*Haer.* 1.13.2). When the women partake of his 'grace', according to Irenaeus, they are enabled to prophesy as he himself does (*Haer.* 1.13.3). The other ritual described by Irenaeus is the 'spiritual marriage', involving a 'bridal chamber' in which they 'complete the mystic teaching with invocations of those who are being initiated' (*Haer.* 1.21.3). This rite also seems to have involved the anointing of the heads of those being initiated with a mixture of oil and water (*Haer.* 1.21.4). Irenaeus clearly wants his readers to believe that what goes on in this 'bridal chamber' is nothing other than ritualised debauchery, just as Christians were themselves accused of Thyestean feasts and Oedipal intercourse.[25] Irenaeus' accounts, rather than his interpretations and accusations, clearly indicate that these rituals were the rites of eucharist, the mixed cup over which thanks is given, and baptism, the invocation of those being initiated and their investiture with the wedding garment. However, more important for Irenaeus than the actual practices of his opponents (the historical accuracy of which can no longer be determined), is their own self-understanding, which is invariably expressed in mythological terms (as demonstrated not only in Irenaeus' accounts but also in the Nag Hammadi material). The ever more complex and bizarre mythologies elaborated by his opponents to explain themselves and their situation are taken by Irenaeus to imply an anti-cosmic moral dimension.[26] The same interrelationship is evident in Irenaeus' theology, although in his case the human being is placed firmly within the economy of God as unfolded in scripture, which entails an

---

25 See pt vi, ch. 28, below.
26 Cf. Williams, *Rethinking 'Gnosticism'*, 118, which argues that the 'Gnostics' had a much higher estimation of the body than previously thought; yet, even he speaks of a '*mythological* devaluation of the human body', in what the Gnostics *said* about their bodies rather than what they did.

asceticism understood as living the life of God as exemplified in the crucified and risen Christ.[27]

Relations with Christians elsewhere

Whilst suffering at the hands of the locals, the Christians in Gaul were intimately involved in the affairs of Christians in Rome and further east. The letter of the martyrs of Gaul was written in response to the problems which had arisen in Asia and Phrygia as a result of the 'New Prophecy' led by Montanus and usually known by his name. Several aspects of the letter indicate that the martyrs were aligned with the prophets, for instance, the description of Vettius Epagathus (*HE* 5.1.9–10) and perhaps also Alexander the Phrygian (*HE* 5.1.49–51). More explicitly, an extract from the letter, taken out of its original context by Eusebius, describes how Alcibiades led a very austere life, partaking of nothing but bread and water, but that it was revealed to Attalus, after his first contest in the amphitheatre, that Alcibiades was 'not doing well in refusing the creatures of God' and in fact was 'a stumbling block' to others, whereupon Alcibiades learnt his lesson and they 'partook of everything, giving thanks to God, for they were not deprived of the grace of God, but the Holy Spirit was their advocate' (*HE* 5.3.2–3). This emphasis on the guidance of the Spirit echoes the language of the Montanists, but is deployed to correct their excessive rigour, and significantly bases itself upon the authority of the martyrs rather than a claim to charismatic authority. This extract is placed by Eusebius just before an account of how, in addition to their letter to their brethren in Asia and Phrygia, the confessors of Gaul had also written to Eleutherus, 'the bishop of the Romans' (174–89 CE), concerning the strife which had arisen in Rome on account of the Montanists (*HE* 5.3.4–4.3). Only a short passage of the letter to Eleutherus is preserved, which seems to imply a gentle criticism of the way in which he exercised his office, contrasting it with Irenaeus, who had brought him the letter: 'if we thought that office could confer righteousness upon anyone, we should first of all have commended him as a presbyter of the church, which is his position' (*HE* 5.4.2). It seems that this embassy of peace found a positive response from Eleutherus, though this was not the end of the problem for Rome or for Asian Christianity.[28]

The further involvement of the Christians in Gaul with affairs in Rome indicates that Eleutherus and his successor, Victor (189–98 CE), were leaders of a particular community within the factionalised federation of distinct

---

27 Cf. Behr, *Asceticism*, 18–21, 25–127.
28 Cf. Trevett, *Montanism*, 56–9.

communities in Rome.[29] At some point, Irenaeus was in contact with Florinus, whom he had previously met in Polycarp's house in Asia, when he was a 'man of rank in the royal hall', but who was now a presbyter in Rome. Florinus, however, had become attracted by Valentinian teaching, and so Irenaeus wrote to him, warning him about 'the teachings which not even the heretics outside the church ever dared to proclaim'.[30] Eventually Irenaeus wrote to Victor, warning him of Florinus' teaching, which had now taken a written form that was available to him in Lyons: 'inasmuch as the books of these men may possibly have escaped your observation, but have come to our notice, I call your attention to them, that for the sake of your reputation you may expel these writings from among you ... they constitute a stumbling block to many, who simply and unreservedly receive, as coming from a presbyter, the blasphemy which they utter against God.'[31] Victor complied with Irenaeus' zeal for orthodoxy, and Florinus was obliged to lay aside his office (HE 5.15). Irenaeus intervened with Victor on one further occasion, this time concerning the conflicts that had arisen about the Quartodeciman practice of Asian Christians, that is, their celebration of Christ's Pascha on the fourteenth of Nisan. According to Eusebius, as a result of the strife Victor had 'cut off from the common unity all the communities of Asia (tēs Asias ... tas paroikias)' (HE 5.24.9). This almost certainly refers to Asian Christians in Rome, and probably to Asian Christians within Victor's own community, rather than Christians in Asia,[32] for, following the precipitous action of Victor, Irenaeus, in the name of the Christians of Gaul, reminded him that his own predecessors had tolerated a plurality of practices, so that those who 'observed' were at peace with those who did not 'observe'.[33] Most importantly, Irenaeus pointed out that when Polycarp visited Rome during the time of Anicetus, a predecessor of Victor, neither could persuade the other of their own practice, and yet Anicetus had conceded to Polycarp the celebration of the eucharist, preserving the peace (HE 5.24.16–17). As Irenaeus comments, 'the distinction in the fast emphasises

---

29 For this, see Lampe, *Paul to Valentinus*.
30 *HE* 5.20.4–5. Eusebius mentions one letter to Florinus, entitled 'On the sole sovereignty' or 'That God is not the author of evil', and mentions that he wrote another work for Florinus, entitled 'On the Ogdoad' (*HE* 5.20.1).
31 Iren. *Frag. Syr.* 28 (in *Libros quique adversus haereses*, Harvey (ed.), vol. II, 457).
32 Cf. Petersen, 'Eusebius and the paschal controversy'.
33 *HE* 5.24.14. What is being 'observed' (or not) has been a matter of great scholarly controversy, for the verb has no object. Cf. Stewart-Sykes, *Lamb's high feast*, 205. Also debated is whether Victor's community had *any* annual celebration of Pascha, for it is noteworthy that, while Eusebius records two letters from the supporters of the Quartodecimans, he does not provide any comparable evidence for an alternative practice; the (subsequent?) celebration of Pascha on the following Sunday would seem to be a compromise position.

the harmony of our faith' (*HE* 5.24.13). Once again, the Christians from Gaul had intervened in events in Rome regarding affairs which concerned their fellow Christians from Asia, indicating that they were aware and involved in the life of the church at large.

Other evidence

By the time that Cyprian (d. 254) wrote (*Ep.* 68) to Stephen in Rome, Faustinus was now the bishop in Lyons, and there was also a community in Arles, led by the bishop Marcianus, who had associated himself with Novatian. We hear nothing more of Christianity in Gaul until the beginning of the 4th century, when Gallic bishops are mentioned in the lists of the synods in Rome (313 CE), and then in Arles itself (314 CE). There is, however, one final piece of evidence from Christianity in Gaul – the inscription in Greek from the cemetery of Saint Pierre l'Estrier in Autun, which can possibly be dated to the early 3rd century:

> *Ichthuos ouraniou theion genos ētori semnōi*
> *Chrēse, labōn pēgēn ambroton en broteois*
> *Thespasiōn hydatōn. tēn sēn, phile, thalpeo psychēn*
> *Hydasin aenaois ploutodotou sophiēs.*
> *Sōtēros hagiōn meliēdea lambane brōsin,*
> *Esthie pinaōn ichthun echōn palamais.*
> *Ichthui chortaz ara, lilaiō, despota sōter.*
> *Eu heudoi mētēr, se litazome, phōs to thanantōn.*
> *Aschandie pater, tōmōi kecharismene thumōi,*
> *Sun mētri glukerēi kai adelpheioisin emoisin,*
> *Ichthuos eirēnēi seo mnēseo Pektoriouo.*

> Divine race of the heavenly Fish, with a noble heart
> draw, receiving, amongst mortals, the immortal spring
> of oracular water. Friend, warm your soul
> in the eternal waters of bounteous wisdom
> Receive the food, sweet as honey, of the Saviour of the saints;
> Eat with zest, holding the Fish in your hands.
> That I may be filled with the Fish, I ardently desire, Master and Saviour.
> That my mother may be in blessed calm, I beseech, Light of the dead.
> Ascandios, my father, so dear to my heart,
> with my sweet mother and brothers,
> in the peace of the Fish, remember your Pectorius.[34]

---

34 The text reproduced here is that transcribed in Cabrol and Leclercq (eds.), *DACL*, vol. 1, pt 2, 3196, where it is followed by a plate of the inscription. The translation is based on that given in van der Meer and Mohrmann, *Atlas of the early Christian world*, 42, where a plate of the inscription is also given.

All the central elements of the faith of Christians in Gaul are brought together in this beautiful inscription of Pectorius: baptism, eucharist (received in the hands), eternal life, prayers for the departed and request for their prayers in turn. The image of Christ as the 'Fish', emphasised by the fact that the first five lines of this inscription form an acrostic spelling out 'Fish', is based both upon the symbolism of the baptismal waters and the play made upon the Greek word for 'fish' (the letters of which, *i-ch-th-u-s*, are taken as signifying 'Jesus Christ, God's Son, Saviour'), and once again links the Christians of Gaul to Rome, where the image is found in the art of the catacombs, and Asia and Phrygia, where it occurs in the epitaph of Abercius Marcellus.[35] It is this international character that is most characteristic of Christianity in Gaul during the first two and a half centuries.

35 A translation of this epitaph can be found in Stevenson and Frend, *New Eusebius*, 110–11. See Fig. 4, above, for an image of the extant fragments.

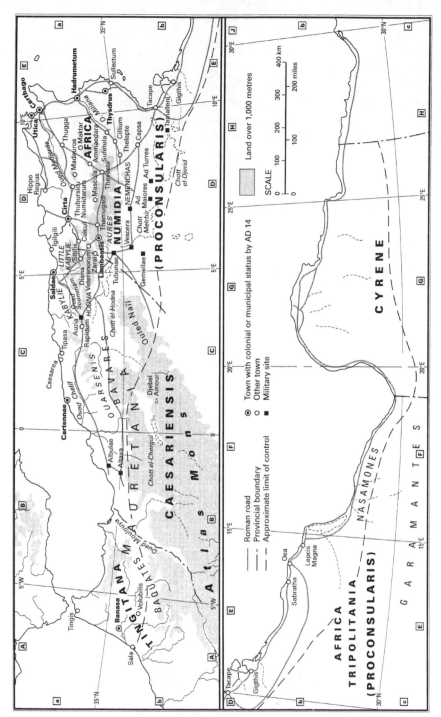

Map 6. Roman Africa

21

North Africa

MAUREEN A. TILLEY

'Africa' here refers to the land north of the Sahara, excluding Egypt and Ethiopia, but including modern-day Morocco, Algeria, Tunisia and western Libya. In this vast expanse of land, Christianity grew and provided the larger church with a bounteous crop of theological reflection. The roots of contemporary ecclesiology and sacramental theology, as well as traditions of biblical interpretation, were nourished here.

The evidence

Literary evidence for Christianity in North Africa in the first three centuries comes from Tertullian (*c.*160–*c.*225 CE), Minucius Felix (second/third century), Cyprian (d. 258), Commodian (fl. mid-third century), Pseudo-Cyprian (post-258), and various homilies and stories of martyrdom.[1] It illustrates the beliefs of the Christian communities, their structures and practices.

There are many archaeological sites in Africa, but none provides direct testimony of Christianity's early years. Not even Carthage boasts pre-fourth-century evidence. The principal obstacle to investigations into the earliest years is the fact that the churches were repeatedly rebuilt, especially during the post-Vandal conquest.

The earliest literary references to buildings used for Christian worship are all from the fourth century. The *Gesta apud Zenophilum* (320) mentions 'the house in which Christians gathered' in 303 CE. The *Martyrium Saturnini* (304 CE or shortly thereafter) mentions gathering in a lector's home during the Diocletianic persecution after the bishop's defection. An inscription at Altava (309 CE) tells of a *basilica dominica* ('dominical hall'), a shrine commemorating a martyr.[2] Gallienus' edict restoring previously confiscated churches (Euseb.

---

1 Arnobius (fl. *c.*275–*c.*311) and Lactantius (*c.*250–*c.*325) were African, too, but their surviving writings fall outside our period.
2 Février, 'Africa–Archaeology', 16.

HE 7.13) finds no echo of application in Africa. This does not mean that buildings set aside specifically as churches did not exist before 300 CE, but that there is no evidence of them.

Catacombs testify to early Christianity in Africa. The oldest, those at Hadrumetum, date from mid-third century.[3] By then the city already had a bishop. Despite the title *Bon pasteur*, there is no indication that Christians established the catacomb or that their burials constituted the majority there. There is no link to the church as an institution; epigraphy, however, attests Christian presence. Other catacombs, such as Salakta (Sullectum), Kerkenna and Gabes in Tunisia, Khenchela and Cherbet-bou-Adoufen in Algeria, and Sabratha, Sirte and Gebel Tarhuna in Libya, are not reliably dated. Only Sabratha and Khenchela, ancient Mascula, appear to have had Christian communities before 300 CE, but little is known, other than the names of their bishops.

Political, cultural, and social influences

Even before the introduction of Christianity, many different peoples contributed to African culture.[4] Pre-Punic coastal inhabitants, called Libyans by the Greek historians, leave traces in inscriptions dated as late as the second century CE and in the languages of the Tuareg.[5] Archaeology attests trade between Libyans and both Egypt and Greece. Transhumant Numidians of the highlands (called Berbers since the eighth century) figure in the Punic foundation legend of Dido and their language persists in a developed form to the present.

Phoenicians trading luxury goods[6] established small settlements about 1100 BCE and founded Carthage c.814 BCE. It became the centre of a Libyco-Punic culture.[7] Trade, agriculture, and glass and metal crafts were its economic supports.[8] Carthage was an oligarchy of wealthy and meritorious elders, but the populace retained a voice which grew stronger over the years.[9]

Trade with Greece persisted, but, over time, the expanding Phoenician trade network dominated the western Mediterranean, engulfing Greek colonies.

3 Leynaud, *Les catacombes africaines*, 11–15.
4 The political geography of Africa is not always clearly defined. In what follows I rely on Shaw, 'Formation of Africa Proconsularis'; and Adkins and Adkins, *Handbook*, 111–14.
5 Ghaki, 'Le Libyque', 204–6.
6 Lancel, *Carthage*, 5.
7 Lancel, *Carthage*, 262.
8 Fantar, 'Punic civilization', 105–6.
9 Arist. *Pol.* 2.11; Polyb. *Hist.* 6.51.

Eventually this led to conflict with Rome. At the end of the Punic wars (264–146 BCE), Rome took control of the city of Carthage, administering it and its dependencies (north-east Tunisia) as a praetorian province which supplied grain to Rome. In 67 BCE, the Romans added Cyrene to their African territories. In 46 BCE, they annexed Juba I's Mauretania, combining their Africa Vetus with this new territory of Africa Nova into a single proconsular province. Initially, civil war and concern for the protection of Rome's grain supply promoted the consolidation of the two territories. But in 42, the western part was divided into two imperial provinces, Mauretania Caesariensis and Mauretania Tingitana. In 25 BCE, the eastern part, Caesariensis, was given to Juba II to rule. Juba, reared in Rome, brought its culture to his ancestral land.[10] The western sector, Tingitana, supported one of the heaviest concentrations of Roman troops in the empire. Although few Roman cities were established there, many recruits from the area followed their fathers into the military.[11] At the turn of the second century CE the Severans, Africans themselves, came to power. With their knowledge of the local contexts, they split Numidia from Africa Proconsularis. Under Diocletian, Proconsularis and Cyrene were divided into three provinces, Africa, Byzacena and Tripolitana, and Numidia broken into three, Numidia Cirtensis, Sitifensis and Militiana. Tingitana was attached to Hispania.

All these redistributions supported Romanisation and made administration of the ill-defined frontiers more stable as Maures, Baquates, Gaetuli and other tribes pushed northwards.[12]

Specifically Punic and Graeco-Roman traces such as language and trade goods waned as one moved inland. Romanisation was strongest in coastal areas and in areas where the military was garrisoned early and intensely, e.g. around Cirta and Lambaesis. Not all cities adopted Roman mores, even forms of government. Colonies and cities which petitioned for civic status had Roman forms of government, but many larger cities, especially in Tripolitania, retained Punic forms of governance with assemblies, senates and *suffetes* assisted by *seniores*.[13] The persistence of collegial Punic forms of government depended on the convenience of Roman authorities and the degree of local elite resistance to assimilation. Where cooperation or cooptation benefited Africans, e.g. in Mauretania Caesariensis, Roman cities existed. Where it did not, e.g. in Leptis (Lepcis), dual foundations of Punic cities and Roman colonies grew up side by side.

---

10 MacMullen, *Romanization*, 43–5.
11 Shaw, 'Autonomy and tribute', 68–70.
12 On the constant renegotiation of frontier politics, see Shaw, 'Autonomy and tribute'.
13 MacMullen, *Romanization*, 35–6.

African social organisation was primarily tribal until the arrival of the Phoenicians, whose culture centred on cities. Romans diminished residual rural tribal influence by distributing large tracts of land to political supporters and by settling veterans around cities, where children assumed their fathers' civic status and strengthened Roman culture and tax revenues.[14] Juba II accelerated Romanisation by importing architectural styles, coinage, laws and religion.[15] Some Romanisation of names occurred, but, like the adoption of Roman civic forms, the balance of Punic and Roman names varied according to its utility for families' upward mobility. Punic names were often theophoric and stressed ties to pre-Roman culture. Adopted Roman names honoured Roman patrons. In general, Africans used Romanisation when it was to their own advantage, e.g. participating in Roman priesthoods and changing names, and clung to their roots when they could, e.g. in neo-Punic grave inscriptions.

African religions

Little is known of the pre-Punic traditions. Massive rock tombs attest burial of the dead with few grave goods. Scholars often hypothesise from later Saharan customs to Libyan religion, such as the veneration of meteorites and leaving cloth scraps at holy sites.[16] Phoenicians brought their Levantine heritage from Tyre, including devotion to their civic patron, Melqart. Libyco-Punic contact brought Tanit and Ba'al Hammon, minor Tyrian divinities, to prominence.[17] Theophoric names were common even in the Christian period, albeit Latinised. Tracing the religious history of Punic Carthage is complicated by Greek authors using the names of Greek divinities to describe Punic gods and by the tendency of historians of religion to fill in gaps with Phoenician or modern Maghreb traditions.

Egyptian and Greek trade influenced the religious iconography. Greek images of the divine, especially Demeter, were imported after 396 BCE, when Hamilcar raided her temple in Syracuse.[18] Isis came from Egypt and later Cybele from Asia Minor via Rome. Greek law, language and architecture

---

14 MacMullen, *Romanization*, 31; *Theodosian Code* 1.12.4.
15 Macmullen, *Romanization*, 43–5.
16 Picard, *Les religions de l'Afrique antique*, 5.
17 Picard, *Les religions de l'Afrique antique*, 26–27, 56–61.
18 Picard, *Les religions de l'Afrique antique*, 86.

perdured in Cyrenaica as the heritage of Ptolemaic rule (322–96 BCE).[19] Grave goods are not buried within the tomb but there are tables (mensae) for the living who visited and feasted the dead.[20]

Punic religion survived in cities, often assimilated to Roman cults, and, in rural areas, in less assimilated forms.[21] While large Romanised cities had Capitoline temples dedicated to Jupiter, Juno and Minerva, statues of Ba'al Hammon were still carved well into the Christian era. Tanit, the reigning goddess, was assimilated to Juno; Melqart to Hercules; and Frugifer, an agricultural deity, to Pluto, but it was grave Saturn, not Jupiter, who was chosen as the face of Ba'al. His cult was immensely popular across class lines.[22]

Sacrifice was integral to Punic religion. Sacrifices were offered by the chief priest of a collegial body.[23] Cultic remnants suggest that some sacrifices were to chthonic deities and/or the dead as libations were poured into the ground and food left at tombs.[24] Ba'al Hammon presided over graveyards and human sacrifice. During periods of stress, such as from famine and war, offerings were first-born children, but archaeological remains indicate occasional substitution of stillborns, sick older children and small animals.[25] How late and widespread human sacrifice continued is unknown, but Roman legislation and Tertullian spoke as if it extended into the first century CE.[26] After immolation, ashes were buried in urns. Otherwise the dead were buried in stone coffins or beneath rocks and clay tiles with few grave goods.

As in Rome, priesthoods held for a year – often by members of the same family – served as steps along the cursus honorum. Holding these posts was an important way of identifying with Rome. The priesthood of the imperial cult was the epitome of this practice, the summit of an African's career.[27] It was introduced, probably under Vespasian, in order to provide religious underpinning for Romanisation.[28] Thus, it represented both Roman religion and political hegemony.

19 MacKendrick, North African stones speak, 121–5.
20 Ennabli, Carthage retrouvée, 53.
21 On religion in Africa, see Rives, Religion and authority, ch. 1.
22 Rives, Religion and authority, 142–6.
23 Sznycer, 'La religion punique', 112.
24 Picard, Les religions de l'Afrique antique, 33.
25 E.g. the 200 children sacrificed in the fourth century BCE, when Agathocles of Syracuse and his troops ravaged Carthage. See Diod. Sic. 10.20; Sznycer, 'La religion punique', 114–16.
26 Tert. Apol. 9; cf. Picard, Les religions de l'Afrique antique, 103.
27 Raven, Rome in Africa, 149.
28 Ferguson, Religions of the Roman empire, 95; Taylor, Divinity of the Roman emperor, 212.

Regional particularities of early African Christianity

The Semitic roots of Punic religion raise the question of the origins of Christianity in this region. Unfortunately, they are unknown. Africans never claimed a founding apostle like other churches, such as Alexandria's Mark or India's Thomas. There was great respect for Christians at Rome, but no tradition of a foundation from that city.[29] In fact, Christian practice suggests alternate roots. Most scholars connect Christianity to Jewish communities in and around Carthage.[30] Evidence includes Hebraisms in their Latin Bible, Tertullian's familiarity with oral traditions later enshrined in the Talmud and Mishnah, and the burial of both Jews and Christian Jews in the Gamart cemetery.[31] African Christianity also exhibits some of the hallmarks of the 'Jewish Christianity' of the first centuries,[32] e.g. the apostolic decree of Acts 15:19–20 treated as normative as late as Tertullian (*Apol.* 9.13) and Minucius Felix (*Oct.* 30.6), Tertullian's knowledge that Jews knew Christians as Nazarenes, a heretical sect (*Marc.* 4.8), the angel-Christology of pseudo-Cyprian's *De centesima* (*PL*, supp. I, cols. 53–67), and the Christian observance of some Jewish festivals as late as 436 (fourth Council of Carthage, canon 89). Finally, local churches were governed by a board of elders, the *seniores laici* ('lay elders'), similar to Jewish congregations (or possibly the Punic *suffetes*). While the aggregate evidence is not conclusive, the burden of proof nonetheless is on those who would offer alternative explanations, such as a resort to a general Semitic or Punic culture.

The oldest African writing mentioning Christians, *Martyrum Scillitanorum acta* from c.180, was composed in Latin, probably because it was based on a court record. But the first language of African Christians was Greek, testimony perhaps of Christian roots among Greek-speaking, possibly Jewish diaspora, traders. The first versions of some of Tertullian's treatises were in Greek,[33] and it was the liturgical language for Perpetua (*M. Perp.* 12.2).

Whatever their origins, early Christians had a Latin Bible. The Pauline letters were available in Latin by 180 (*M. Scil.* 12) and the remainder of scripture by c.250. There is no single complete Bible extant, only short sections in various writings. Translations often differed significantly from Jerome's Vulgate (August. *Doctr.*

---

29 See the arguments against the historicity of pro-Roman texts in Lejay, 'Les origines de l'église d'Afrique', 41–7.
30 On African Jews and their relations with Christians, see Setzer, 'Jews, Christians and Judaizers', 185–200.
31 Setzer, 'Jews, Christians and Judaizers', 193–5.
32 See pt II, ch. 4, above.
33 Labriolle, *History and literature of Christianity*, 41.

chr. 2.15). They included verses unknown elsewhere but important in Africa, such as John 5:3b–4. Even within Africa, various texts circulated as late as Augustine (*Retract.* 1.7).

There is no canon list from North Africa before the *Breviarium Hipponense* (397 CE), but one may surmise the working canon from the books employed by Africans. They used all of the biblical books except James, 2 Peter and 2 and 3 John. Early non-canonical works were known in Africa, such as the *Shepherd of Hermas, Acts of Paul* and perhaps *Acts of Pilate*.[34] Stories of the martyrs were read liturgically, and a fourth-century council took pains to differentiate them from canonical texts (Council of Carthage, §5).

In tune with the political culture, collegiality was a hallmark of church governance and a gauge of the spread of Christianity. Evidence may be found in the diffusion of episcopal sees and interaction at councils.[35] The first known council was *c.*220 under the bishop Agrippinus. No list of signatories with sees survives. Not until Augustine's *De unico baptismo* 13.22 (*c.*410) were the bishops of Agrippinus' council numbered at seventy. Whether this was exact or approximate (August. *Cresc.* 3.3.3 in 405), it provides a baseline against which to measure the numbers of bishops reported later. Cyprian (*Ep.* 59.10.1) claimed that by 236/240 he could assemble ninety bishops to condemn the heresy of a Numidian bishop. Again no lists survive, but by then there were bishops scattered throughout Proconsularis and Numidia. Such a number grants some credence to a figure of seventy gathered under Agrippinus. Even in 256 between major persecutions, eighty-seven bishops gathered at Carthage, representing an area from Leptis in Tripolitania in the east to Thuburbo in the west, but concentrated primarily within 220 kilometres of Carthage.

The African tradition was one of strong reliance on bishops who gathered frequently to discuss issues of mutual concern but who were not forced to apply the consensus of the gathering in their own diocese. Even small hamlets had bishops. In the larger cities, bishops had deacons to assist them. Priests were found primarily in metropolitan areas like Carthage, where they presided over urban districts.

The intransigence of African Christianity manifests itself from the very beginning through martyrdom and apology.[36] Christians in Africa were

---

34 Labriolle, *History and literature of Christianity*, 58–9; *NTApoc*, vol. II, 214–15 (on *Acts of Paul*) and vol. I, 501–4.

35 For the numbers and diffusion of bishops, see Maier, *L'épiscopat de l'Afrique.*

36 For a treatment of this period, both in Africa and elsewhere, see Clarke, 'Christians and the Roman State'.

persecuted intermittently from 180 until 305. In assessing the strength and effects of persecution, one must recognise that not all Christians in every area of the empire were persecuted at the same time in the same way. Even imperial edicts designed to promote empire-wide uniformity depended upon local enforcement which may have been sporadic or non-existent in one place while sustained and severe elsewhere. The ambient ideal of human sacrifice, whether in war or at the altar, supported the Christian notion of the acceptability of offering one's life in fidelity, but it should be noted that no motifs of human sacrifice directly colour martyrdom narratives.[37]

The earliest martyr story, *Martyrum Scillitanorum acta*, demonstrates intransigent refusal to offer divine honours to the emperor, even in the face of death. The proconsul tried to treat his prisoners leniently, offering them opportunities to recant. They only became more steadfast in claiming the name 'Christian'. Speratus, their spokesman, made common apologetic moves (§§ 2–8). He defended Christianity as rational, worshipping God alone as the supreme ruler of the cosmos. Christians were model citizens abiding by laws and honouring the emperor. They drew the line, though, at idolatrous acts of swearing by the genius of the emperor, for it would have given the lie to their belief in God as the only divinity. In both intransigence and apologetic, Speratus provided a model for other martyr stories.

A generation later, Septimius Severus made conversion to Christianity illegal. From that period come two stories of unyielding, principled refusal to commit idolatry. The first is from Tertullian's *De corona*. A soldier was executed for refusal to wear a laurel wreath, an emblem of victory. Tertullian construed this crown as a symbol of the idolatry endemic in military life. While the juridical verdict may be interpreted more as a punishment for violation of military discipline than for adherence to the name 'Christian', there is some indication that the soldier's conduct embarrassed even some believers. However, the *Martyrium Perpetuae et Felicitatis* (203) portrays persecution specifically for adherence to Christianity. The diaries of Perpetua and her co-martyr Saturus manifest a refusal to sacrifice or even to wear priestly robes as theatrical costumes (*M. Perp.* 18.4–6). They depict a charismatic Christianity in which prophecy was respected and revelations in dreams trumped the authority of the clergy. The conflict between charismatic and ordained authority would be one of the major stress points for the African church in the 250s where it again emerged directly from the context of persecution. Likewise

---

37 The one exception may be *M. Perp.* 18.4 where Christians were forced to wear the garb of Ceres' priestesses whereby executed criminals were dedicated to the goddess. See Picard, *Les religions de l'Afrique antique*, 134.

the *Martyrium Perpetuae* would provide the model for recording the imprison-ment and execution of later martyrs like the *Martyrium Mariani et Iacobi* and the *Martyrium Montani et Lucii* in the 250s. All would follow the example of the Scillitans in their arguments with family and authorities.[38] The harder their opponents pushed the more intransigent they became.

Between Severus and Decius, there are occasional references to martyrdoms in Africa (Tert. *Scap.*, passim; Cypr. *Ep.* 39.3.1), but there was no sustained persecution comparable to what would come under Decius. While it may have been intense elsewhere or exaggerated by Eusebius, there is no evidence for widespread terror in Africa until the 250s. Edicts issued under Decius and Valerian provided the most serious threats in this era. Shortly after Decius' accession, around January 250, he ordered everyone to sacrifice. A call to religious uniformity in times of distress was not uncommon. It was a way to rally the population to ensure the *pax deorum* ('peace of the gods'). The years between 235 and 284 needed some help towards political stability. There had been eighteen emperors and many more pretenders. Turmoil on the frontiers marked the period. So the appeal for sacrifice was understandable. What was unusual, however, was the universality of the requirement and the tenacity with which it was enforced. Cyprian's writings (*Ep.* 15.4 and *Laps.* 9.25) reveal that not only heads of families but all members participated in imperial worship, pouring a libation and tasting sacrificial food (*Laps.* 25).

Those who sacrificed were given certificates of compliance (*libelli*), some of which have survived. Some tried to acquire them through proxies or bribery (Cypr. *Ep.* 21.2.1–3.2; 55.13–14), or went into voluntary exile, like Cyprian, rather than face punishment. When various pressures toward conformity failed, Christians were executed.

According to Cyprian's *De lapsis*, many Christians, including clergy, sacri-ficed. Some bishops even led their congregations in apostasy (Cypr. *Ep.* 55, 65, 67 and 69). Christians debated whether it was the act or merely consent to it that was crucial. The general consensus rested on the literalist under-standing that the physical act itself separated those who fell, the *lapsi*, from those who stood firm, the *stantes*. Many of the *lapsi*, including some clergy, sought readmission to the church. Cyprian held that it was the bishop's prerog-ative to judge case by case the degree of guilt of those returning and to apply an appropriate penalty. But until the persecution ended, Cyprian could not return to Carthage. He governed the city through correspondence with his clergy.

---

38 *M. Perp.* 3.5, 15.1–6, 18.4–6; *M. Mar.* 8.1, 4.10; *M. Mont.* 19.1–4, *inter alia*.

In his absence, individual Christians panicked. They sought readmission to the church by whatever means they could. Some pressured 'laxist' clergy; others took a path that would cause the community long-term problems. They went to *confessores*, Christians imprisoned for their refusal to sacrifice, and sought their intercession. Confessors held a peculiar place within the church. While many were not ordained, their authority was unquestioned, even by Cyprian. They had professed their allegiance to Christ and had been willing to suffer. By their imprisonment and torture, often to the brink of death, they acquired a status as close to that of a martyr as one can attain without dying. Some confessors issued repentant *lapsi* letters of reconciliation (*libelli pacis*) reincorporating them into the church. Some wrote letters on behalf of penitents to be used after their own death. Others issued blanket letters of forgiveness without specifying the names of the persons to whom they applied.

Under these circumstances, Cyprian was forced to navigate between the confessors' authority and his own articulated position on the *lapsi*. For a few years after the death of Decius in 251, Cyprian spent time setting the house of the Carthaginian church in order. Confessors were brought into the ranks of the clergy, without ordination, on the grounds that their suffering was enough to grant them the right to the deaconate and presbyterate, though not episcopacy. Repentant *lapsi* were reconciled on the bishop's terms, often with communion only *in articulo mortis* ('at the time of their death').

By 253, the interval of peace had evaporated, and under Valerian (r. 253–9) a new persecution began. As the noose tightened on the church, Cyprian began to admit more of the *lapsi* to communion. He felt that they needed spiritual strength from the sacrament and Christian fellowship to endure the next round of testing from God. In 256 Valerian issued an edict requiring higher-ranking clergy to sacrifice on behalf of the emperor, proscribing Christian assemblies, confiscating property and forbidding Christians to have their own cemeteries (*M. Cypr.* 1.7). Some clergy were sentenced to the imperial mines (Cypr. *Ep.* 76–9). During the summer of 256, the higher clergy became subject to the death penalty; upper-class men lost their status and property and, if they persisted in the faith, were also executed. Upper-class women were exiled and their property seized (Cypr. *Ep.* 80). Imperial officials had less interest in pursuing members of the lower classes since the confiscation of small properties would not be worth the effort. And, having little status in the community, they would not be significant exemplars of imperial wrath. Cyprian's elite status and position put him at risk. He was arrested at his suburban villa, brought into Carthage, tried and executed in 258.

On Valerian's death, Gallienus revoked the edict of 256. While Christianity did not become a *religio licita* ('lawful religion'), its adherents were free to assemble and could regain possession of places of worship and cemeteries. Nearly four decades of relative peace ensued. Then, in the 290s, the military began to execute soldiers, such as Maximilian of Theveste and Marcellus of Tingis, for refusal to serve after conversion. These martyrs became heroes venerated by the community. They gave Christians examples of how to resist the state in the persecutions that would come in the early 300s under Diocletian. More importantly, they reinforced Christian identity as requiring resistance to state authority. Reverence for martyrs and debates over this strict construction of Christian identity would be at the heart of the Donatist–Catholic controversies of the late fourth and early fifth centuries.

The cult of the martyrs

Parallel to other areas, the African church produced its own literature of preparation and praise for martyrdom. But Africans looked to the end of the world for vindication. As civil authorities judged martyrs on earth, martyrs would sternly judge them from heaven (*M. Perp.* 18; Tert. *Mart.* 2.4; *Apol.* 24; cf. 2 Macc 7:9–19, 35). The authority of martyrs and confessors trumped even ecclesiastical authority (*M. Perp.* 13.1; for confessors, see above).

The honouring of local martyrs on the model of biblical persons executed for fidelity to God (e.g. the Maccabees and Stephen) began in Tertullian's era. Veneration of relics in Africa commenced with Cyprian. Christians threw handkerchiefs on the ground near his execution to catch drops of his blood. Burial *ad sanctos*, i.e. close to the tomb of a martyr, is attested from 295 (*Acta Maximiliani* 3.4).

The cult of martyrs was celebrated with customs similar to widespread Roman practices for honouring deceased family members. On the anniversary of death, one's birthday into the heavenly kingdom (cf. *M. Polyc.* 18), Christians gathered at the cemetery to sing and feast, often indecorously, and to pour libations to the dead through tubes into tombs.[39] Tertullian (*Spect.* 13) and Cyprian (*Ep.* 68.6.2) condemned these celebrations as not properly Christian, but apparently met with little success since Augustine was combatting the practice of these *laetitiae* over a century and a half later (*inter alia, De civ. D.* 8.27).

There is no accurate count of the persons martyred in Africa. The impact does not seem to have been due to the sheer number but to the terror inflicted

---

39 Duval, *Recherches archéologiques à Haïdra*, vol. II, 191.

on Christians and the reaction by church leadership in demarcating Christians from the larger world. Once persecution ceased, Christians would be challenged to reformulate their attitude towards the state and to reconfigure their own self-identity.

Christians in society

In the face of that world, Christians strove to rationalise their fidelity. Apologetic literature served both to address their neighbours and to reinforce their own commitment. Along with martyrdom, it manifested their refusal to acknowledge any god but their own. Authors like Tertullian, Minucius Felix and Commodian wrote to convince their sceptical contemporaries of the value of Christianity and the absurdity of traditional cults and mystery religions. For them Christian self-identity and practice included monotheism, of course, and, as in nearly all apologetic literature, the assertion that Christians were more moral in their personal and social lives than those who were not believers (Tert. *Apol.* 3–4, 10, 30; Min. Fel. *Oct.* 30–1).

Christians claimed to be plain-living and morally upright. Their lack of ease with the ambient culture played out in paradoxical ways. Tertullian's expressed disdain for philosophy and dialectic (*Spect.* 18, *An.* 3) and Arnobius' rejection of rhetoric (*Adv. nat.* 1.59) are summed up in Tertullian's famous aphorism, 'What is there in common between Athens and Jerusalem, between academe and church, between heretics and Christians?' (*Praescr.* 7), yet even this is expressed in the best classical style. While Tertullian, writing to Christians, rejected Christian military service (*Cor.* 1), he noted that pagans should not fear Christians because they shared their civic and cultural lives, *including military service* (*Apol.* 37.4). As Minucius Felix explained, rhetoric, competently used and philosophically supported, might be useful in evangelisation (*Oct.* 39). Apologists like Minucius Felix (*Oct.* 30.3) and Tertullian (*Apol.* 9.2) especially excoriated human sacrifice. Accusing one's enemies of cannibalism was a common *topos* in the apologetic of most ancient societies. Indeed, Christians were accused of it (Tert. *Apol.* 23; Fronto in Min. Fel. *Oct.* 9). However, since Africans really had offered child sacrifice within recent memory,[40] the accusations were more cutting.[41]

Victor I provides perhaps one final example of African intransigence and collegiality. He reputedly came from Tripolitania to Rome, where he became

---

40 See the bibliography in *The Octavius of Minucius Felix*, Clarke (trans. and ed.) 334 at n. 496.
41 Benko, *Pagan Rome*, 54–78.

bishop (r. *c*.189–99). Victor was the first bishop of Rome who threatened to excommunicate Christians outside his own diocese. He was scandalised by different communities celebrating Easter on different days. But collegiality overruled his rigour. While he threatened excommunication, he never actually broke communion with anyone.

Issues of contention

Christians were largely united in their attacks on Roman traditional and mystery religions, but the church was not a monolith. Distance between cities, the small number of Christians and the existence of bishops in each small town contributed to a variety of local practices. This was expected and respected but, when the differences became too large, various movements within the African church divided Christians among themselves. Issues producing division included creation, revelation and the church.

Was creation the production of a good God or was matter itself evil? This was the basic question some gnostics asked. Against Hermogenes, Tertullian asserted God as creator and creation as good (*Herm.* 15–18). Against Marcion, he taught that the creator God of the Old Testament and the Father of Jesus were one and the same (*Marc.* 2, 4 and 5).

Was revelation complete or ongoing? Most Christians in Africa believed that God still provided revelations through dreams and visions. The editor of the *Martyrium Perpetuae* thought so, casting the present as the final days when all would prophesy. Tertullian believed that nearly everything people knew of God came through dreams, but cautioned that such revelations needed to be evaluated by the community (*An.* 9). He and his circle placed great stock in revelations given to contemporary Phrygian prophets whose rigorist movement called itself 'the New Prophecy'. It featured an imminent *eschaton* ('end of the world'), and embraced martyrdom and women as leaders. The movement appealed to many Africans. Later in life, Tertullian regarded those who did not adhere to it as so lax as to flirt with heresy, but ever collegial Africans on both sides never formed separate churches as the Montanists (as they were later called) did elsewhere, and there is no evidence of African bishops taking disciplinary measures against Montanist sympathisers.[42]

As a confessor, Perpetua felt entitled to ask God questions in prayer and to receive the answers in visions. Some had to do with martyrdom and healing. Her colleague Saturus' visions showed the superiority of confessors to clergy.

42 See ch. 17, above.

The former, closer to God, could mediate disputes among the latter (*M. Perp.* 13). A generation later Cyprian still respected dreams as revelatory.[43]

Was the church the home of saints or the refuge of sinners? The church was envisioned not simply as a gathering of baptised Christians but it was hypostatised. Tertullian was the first to use the epithet 'mother church' (*Mart.* 1), and Cyprian felt so strongly that he said, 'one cannot have God as Father who does not have the church as mother' (*Unit. eccl.* 6). Both proclaimed the unity of the church in practical ways. This dedication to unity sanctioned firm boundaries and Tertullian's rejection of any interpretation of scripture by heretics: the Bible was not theirs to interpret. The church's purity kept him from admitting that repentant adulterers might be reconciled to the Church (*Pud.* 2–3). This concept of unity also made it possible for the council which met under Agrippinus of Carthage to reject the baptism of heretics, and kept Cyprian's council in 256 from recognising the validity of baptism performed by clergy who had lapsed and later attempted to return to the Church (*Ep.* 67). For him, the church was Noah's ark. To those already baptised and tending toward separatist groups he thundered, 'Outside the church there is no salvation' (*Ep.* 73.21).[44]

Yet collegiality overruled rigour. As sympathetic as Tertullian was to the Montanists, he did not separate from the church in Africa. As strongly as any Africans defended re-baptism, they did not break communion with Romans who did not re-baptise.

Relations with Christians elsewhere

While North Africa shared a coast with Egypt, its relationship with Rome leaves more traces. The most significant interactions between the two communities focused on three issues. All betray African collegiality and devotion to unity.

The first issue was whether the church could reconcile those who had sinned after baptism. Tertullian represented the African tradition which objected that the church could not effect novelty. It was beyond its competence. Callistus, bishop of Rome *c.*217–*c.*222, argued for a more lenient policy, forcing a split at Rome between his supporters and those of Hippolytus (*c.*170–*c.*236). Despite the vehement objections of Tertullian's *De pudicitia*, Rome and Carthage never broke communion. African collegiality prevented it.

The second and third issues likewise split the community at Rome. After the Decian persecution, Cornelius (d. 253) became bishop of Rome. His

---

43 *Ep.* 4.1, 11.5, 39.1, 57.5 and 66.10, and Pontianus Diaconus, *Vita Cypriani*, 12.
44 For a thorough discussion of boundary maintenance see Burns, *Cyprian the bishop*.

reconciliation of *lapsi* irked rigourist Novatianists who impugned the validity of Cornelius' election. Later, the question was the reception of those baptised by heretics.[45] The Africans and the Roman rigorists supported re-baptism. Stephen, bishop of Rome (r. 254–7), and Cyprian engaged in a protracted debate over the issue (Cypr. *Ep.* 67–75). Even at the height of the controversy, when Cyprian enlisted overseas supporters like Firmilian of Caesarea and Stephen refused to receive his delegates, neither threatened a complete rupture.

Other features of African Christianity

Christianity in Africa tended to be literalistic and legalistic. Doctrines were articulated as a result of solving practical problems, either *in se* or as they impacted church unity. Significant areas which the Africans addressed were ecclesiology, the Trinity, the nature of the soul, biblical interpretation and roles for women.

Controversies with the gnostics were the catalyst for Tertullian's Trinitarian thought. His 'one nature, three persons' became the orthodox formula (*Pud.* 2). His explanatory metaphors used physical analogies that tended toward a subordinationist Christology (e.g. king, son, messenger; sun, light, warmth etc. in *Prax.* 8). Tertullian's contributions were spiritualised by Augustine in 419 (*Trin.*). In considering the Trinity and the soul, Tertullian tended towards a literalist interpretation of scripture and a conception of reality as material, even God, demons and the soul. Building on Irenaeus' work, Tertullian battled gnostic allegorical interpretation that created a new cosmology from the names of biblical characters. Scripture was not to be allegorised as heretics do (*Scorp.* 11.4), to create a new story that contradicted doctrine received by apostolic succession. He and Cyprian, like most Africans before Augustine, tended towards typology rather than allegory, i.e. to seeing biblical stories and figures as an overlay on current events and contemporary heroes and villains. Using typology, Cyprian's *Testimonia* solidified the links between the Old and New Testaments against the teaching of gnostics, Marcionites and Jews.

Attitudes towards and roles for women were not substantially different from those elsewhere, except by reference to the general characteristics of African Christianity. Respect for the Holy Spirit active in the church extended to inspired women, prophets whose visions were respected (Tert. *An.* 9; *M. Perp.* 1.4–5 and 4.1). Tertullian alone opposed leadership roles for women, perhaps because of his association of women's leadership with gnostic

---

45 See further pt v, ch. 26, below.

theology. Not only was he at odds with African trends but also with members of the New Prophecy outside Africa.

Aside from women as leaders, African writers supported the general mores of their society with Christian rationalisations. Tertullian took for granted the Roman valorisation of the *univira* ('a women married only once') and condemned remarriage (*Mon.* 15 and *Ad ux.* Book 2). Both he and Cyprian prescribed behaviour for women which was stricter than Carthaginian society generally, e.g. forbidding make-up, jewellery and styled hair (*Cult. fem.* and *Virg.*, and *Hab. virg.*, respectively). It should be noted, however, that while the standards of conduct for women were stricter, so too was the behaviour demanded of men in this rigorist church, especially with regard to sexual mores (e.g. Tert. *Exh. cast.* and *Mon.*).

On the whole, whether in theology or in ethics, African Christianity tended towards literal and strict interpretations of scripture and morality. It defined itself against the culture through martyrdom and apologetic. It defined itself internally by being dedicated to unity and collegiality. When the Roman emperor accepted Christianity as a licit religion, Christians who had staked their identity on opposition to the state were forced to rethink that identity. Those who accepted imperial largesse and support rationalised their acceptance by finding a positive, or at least neutral, position for the emperor in the divine plan, as did Augustine. Those who could not, saw themselves as the final remnant of the true church. In North Africa, these would be the Donatists. True heirs of African Christianity, they maintained literal and strict interpretations of scripture and a culture of martyrdom. They fostered unity and collegiality among those who continued to oppose the Roman state. All others were outsiders.[46]

46 See pt VI, ch. 28, below.

22

Rome

MARKUS VINZENT

All roads lead to Rome. The perspective adopted here is that Rome absorbed many cross-currents from around the early Christian world, and, far from itself generating or disseminating a specific theology, the Roman church was fragmented and subject to repeated internal upheavals in the first three centuries. Time and again, this church found itself affected by controversies imported by immigrants from around the empire. This seems, generally speaking, a truer characterisation than Walter Bauer's much discussed thesis that originally heretical forms of Christianity elsewhere were brought into line by Rome seeking to impose its authority on other Christian communities.[1]

The evidence

Evidence for the ancient city of Rome itself, its history and society, is far too extensive to detail here.[2] Christians had little impact on the city's life or monumental architecture prior to the major building programme undertaken by Constantine.[3]

For Christianity in Rome there are literary sources, both Christian and non-Christian, and material evidence of various types.

Literary sources include:

Letters sent to Rome: by the apostle Paul (included in the New Testament canon); also by (Pseudo-?) Ignatius, Irenaeus, Cyprian, Dionysius of Alexandria and others;

Works produced in Rome: Mark's gospel (possibly), *1 Clement*, the *Shepherd of Hermas*, and the works of Justin, Tatian, Hippolytus, Novatian; letters from

---

1 Bauer, *Orthodoxy and heresy*; Altendorf, 'Zum Stichwort'; Robinson, *The Bauer thesis*.
2 See pt I, ch. 3, above; Steinby, *Lexicon topographicum urbis Romae*; Claridge *et al.*, *Rome: an archaeological guide*; Alföldy, *Social history of Rome*.
3 See pt VI, ch. 30, below.

bishops Cornelius and Dionysius, preserved in Eusebius or Athanasius; also works by those later regarded as heretics, including possibly Valentinus, *The Gospel of truth*,[4] Ptolemy's *Letter to Flora*, and fragments of Marcion's *Antitheses* (preserved in Tertullian's refutation);

Christian sources mentioning Rome, such as the book of Acts, 2 Timothy, and 1 Peter in the New Testament; and the works of Irenaeus, Tertullian and Eusebius;

Non-Christian authors who make incidental, but vitally important references to Christians at Rome, e.g. Suetonius' apparent confirmation of Claudius' edict against the Jews (cf. Acts 18:3), with the puzzling statement that they made 'disturbances in the name of Chrestus' ['Christ'?] (Suet. *Claud.* 25.4), and the accounts of persecution of Christians by Nero as scapegoats for a terrible fire (Tac. *Ann.* 15.44, mentioning the death of Jesus under Pontius Pilate) or for purveying 'a new and wicked superstition' (Suet. *Nero* 16.2);[5]

Martyrologies, especially the *Martyrium Justini et septem sodalium* ('Martyrdom of Justin and his seven companions');[6]

Ecclesiastical succession lists, found in Irenaeus (*Haer.* 3.2–3), the catacomb of Callistus, and the later *Liber pontificalis;*

Liturgical texts, such as (Pseudo-)Hippolytus, *Traditio apostolica* ('Apostolic Tradition') (probably).[7]

Material remains,[8] which are not always easy to date and raise all kinds of interpretative questions, include:

Archaeological finds, including catacombs and church foundations; much is uncertainly traced back to the pre-Constantinian period,[9] but it may be presumed that, though 'pagan' in origin, the cemetery below the Vatican and some of the catacombs, notably what lies under San Sebastiano and those of Domitilla, Callistus and Priscilla, have some claim to be sites of interest for the time before the peace of the church;[10]

---

4 See ch. 18, above. This work, found among the Nag Hammadi discoveries, may have been produced in Egypt, and may not be the work of Valentinus.

5 See pt VI, ch. 28, below (including discussion of Dio Cassius, *Epitome* 67.14, and the possibility that Flavius Clemens and his wife, Domitilla, persecuted under Domitian, were Christians).

6 Musurillo, xvii–xx; 42–61. Additional martyrologies, such as those of Paul and Peter, Ignatius and others, are late.

7 The attribution is still contested, but its Roman origin likely; see Stewart-Sykes, *Hippolytus*.

8 See pt VI, ch. 32, below.

9 For an attempt to differentiate pre-Constantinian material see Snyder, *Ante pacem.*

10 Hertling and Kirschbaum, *Roman catacombs*; Stevenson, *Catacombs*; and Mancinelli, *Catacombs and basilicas* as well as *Catacombs of Rome.*

Inscriptions and graffiti, mostly funerary and found in catacombs or on sarcophagi;

Tomb paintings (see Figs. 3 and 7 for examples; also the Capella Graeca in the
Priscilla catacomb is especially important), and mosaics (Fig. 9);

Sarcophagi (such as that of Marcus Aurelius Prosenes (217 CE)[11] and the Via
Salaria sarcophagus (late third century))[12] which appear to be Christian,
while also reflecting conventional 'pagan' artistic imagery.

Rome the capital and Christianity within its ambit

When Christianity arrived on the scene, Rome had already extended its power
around the Mediterranean world, and had begun its transformation into a
monarchical empire.[13] The city had become a magnet and a melting pot.
Here was the arena in which native elites played politics, and the urban poor
demanded bread and circuses, as traders and travelling philosophers arrived
to seek their fortunes. Rome, the capital of the empire, provided the forum
where people could make an impression, teach and develop ideas. The city was
a complex world,[14] rather a universe within a multi-verse of cultures, religions,
ethnic groups and languages.

Rome was a natural goal. The book of Acts describes how the Christian
faith spread from Jerusalem to the limits of the world (Acts 1:8), and ends with
Rome, as do the letters of (Pseudo-?) Ignatius. Unlike Asia Minor or Egypt,
Rome hardly produced its own Christian authors. Many early Christians of
the first century – especially the leading representatives – were immigrants, as
also most prominent theologians of the second and third centuries,[15] some of
whom stayed in Rome, or even suffered martyrdom in the city, while others
only spent time there as visitors. It is interesting that Christians, despite being
resident in the Latin-speaking capital, predominantly retained Greek as their
language until well into the third century.[16] This confirms the dominance
of immigrants in the congregational groups. Even in the third and fourth
centuries, Rome remained a place of debate, and a burial and pilgrim centre

---

11 Identified as Christian because of the smaller inscription on the back (*Prosenes receptus ad
deum*, 'Prosenes received to God'), alongside cupids, dolphins and griffins (Lampe, *Paul
to Valentinus*, 330–4).

12 See Fig. 10 (Good Shepherd relief) and discussion in pt VI, ch. 32, below.

13 See pt I, ch. 3, above.

14 Plin. *Ep.* 3.9.

15 Lampe, *Paul to Valentinus*, 157–8.

16 This is attested by inscriptions and graffiti, although some are in Latin or a mixture of
languages. In literary terms, the Hippolytan writings (before 230) are in Greek; Novatian's
De Trinitate (c.250) in Latin.

in elaborate catacombs, rather than a birthplace of theology. No wonder that, in a city of so much influx, rivalry between individuals, schools and career aspirants was frequent.

When did followers of Jesus, Jewish and non-Jewish alike, arrive for the first time in the city? This is far from clear. When Paul wrote his letter – the earliest evidence we have – Christians must already have been there.[17] Another riddle is linked to the complexity of the city, namely the question about the uniformity, or rather diversity, of the Christian cells.[18] If Judaism, out of which Christianity was born, was as diverse in Rome as in Jerusalem, with numerous synagogues representing a broad variety of languages, cultures and Jewish traditions, then they provided the basis for diverse beginnings of Christianity in Rome as well.[19] This assumption is supported by Paul's letter and the description provided in Acts (28:15–30).

This variety does not necessarily imply that there was no inner coherence linking people of different languages, social backgrounds, as well as families and groups of quite different origin. Whereas scholars of the nineteenth century thought of institutions providing the link (e.g. hierarchy, creeds, doctrinal statements, sacraments), those of the twentieth century pointed to a common Christian ethic, pneumatic power, missionary success or social environment. Recent scholarship, however, has highlighted the tensions and struggles that arose from disputes (Gal 2; Acts 13–15, 18), and, if Peter Lampe's thesis is right, that applies to Rome too. The data from archaeology, epigraphy, ancient historical records, the writings of early Christians and church history support him in suggesting that

> Christianity in Rome flourished in several of the poorest and most densely populated districts . . . [It] indicates social 'fractionation' between many small cells that lacked central coordination . . . The largest proportion of Christians were Greek-speaking immigrants of low socio-economic status, though higher-class leaders, including some upper-class women, were active in smaller numbers.[20]

Even in the third century, at least until Hippolytus, who compares Christians to a 'school group' (*Haer.* 9.12), social 'fractionation' seems to have prevailed.[21] Yet, the different groups certainly thought of themselves as cells of one

---

17 See pt II, ch. 5, above.
18 Lampe, *Paul to Valentinus*, versus Scholten, 'Gibt es Quellen'.
19 Lampe, *Paul to Valentinus*.
20 Jewett, in Lampe, *Paul to Valentinus*, xiii.
21 Brent, *Hippolytus*.

church.[22] Christian sources point both to the unity of the church throughout the empire, and to the continuous tradition from the apostles through the named succession of bishops in Rome.[23] From early on, they claimed that the Christian movement was important and had an impact on the political scene. The bare support for this in non-Christian sources, however, makes us ask whether the Christian sources reflect more than wishful thinking or apologetic, missionary aims.

The city of Rome began to decline in the third century as the empire faced economic and military challenges. The persecution by Decius (250–1) probably issued from a sense that the gods who had made Rome great had to be placated if that greatness were to be maintained.[24] In the *constitutio Antoniniana* (212 CE) Roman citizenship had been granted to all within the empire, while Rome itself lost hundreds of thousands of inhabitants, 'probably attributable to the outbreaks of plague', and was immensely reduced in power during the reigns of twenty-two emperors within fifty years (235–85 CE).[25] Rome never again became the powerful centre of the empire that bore its name. When Constantine, after his usurpation in west and east, created a 'new Rome' in the fourth century, it was situated nearer to the Greek-, Syrian-, Persian- and Coptic-speaking east. The history of Christianity in Rome is in some ways the counter-history of a city in decline that rose in symbolism and ideology the more it became politically and religiously insignificant. This idealisation was willingly accepted and fostered by the Christians of Rome, who, after the empire broke into west and east in 342/3 CE, established Rome as central to the church. It was not before Gregory the Great in the sixth century that papal power surfaced in a city that for centuries had ceased to be the capital.[26]

A church of migrants

The first Roman Christians we meet in the sources are Aquila and Priscilla, who had to leave Rome because of Claudius' expulsion of the Jews (Acts 18:2). According to the Roman historian, Suetonius,[27] this was provoked by 'Chrestus'; so it is widely assumed that preaching about Christ was causing disturbances in the synagogues. Acts (18:2–3, 26) associates Aquila and Priscilla with Paul's mission, as is confirmed by greetings from them in his Corinthian correspondence (1 Cor 16:19), and also by their inclusion among the many

22 Lampe, *Paul to Valentinus*, 397–8.
23 Iren. *Haer.* 3.3.1–3.
24 See pt VI, ch. 28, below.
25 Noy, *Foreigners*, 16.
26 Markus, *Gregory the Great*.
27 *Claud.* 25.4.

individuals Paul greets in Romans 16. Presumably, they had returned to Rome after the death of Claudius in the autumn of 54, along with others – it is noticeable how many individuals Paul apparently knows in the capital, despite as yet never having been there. His letter numbers not less than twenty-eight people known to him in Rome,[28] mostly women and immigrants who belonged to the lower social classes and were either of slave origin or, when freeborn, without great wealth, reputation or prestige.[29] Some were craftsmen and traders; Paul, Aquila and Priscilla were leather workers. Migration to and from Rome is a feature of church life from the beginning.

Tradition suggests that both Peter and Paul came to Rome and suffered martyrdom under Nero.[30] *1 Clement* 5, written in Rome in the 90s, alludes to the many struggles and ultimate passage to glory of both Peter and Paul. Eusebius[31] reports that Paul was beheaded in Rome and Peter crucified, and already refers to the attachment of their names to cemeteries there – indeed, he quotes from a Roman churchman named Gaius (*c*.200): 'I can point out the monuments of the victorious apostles. If you will go as far as the Vatican or the Ostian Way, you will find the monuments of those who founded this church.' The site of the Vatican was an out-of-town cemetery, as archaeological investigations have shown. Tradition places the tomb of Peter under the altar of St Peter's.[32] One of the earliest catacombs (under the church of San Sebastiano) also gives evidence of the veneration of Peter and Paul, possibly because their relics were transferred there during persecution. Graffiti[33] suggest that pilgrimage to martyrs' tombs was already under way in the third century.

First Clement presupposes that the churches of Corinth and Rome had contact and common interests, and that hospitality was offered to travelling Christians. During the second century the arrival of various Christians in the capital confirms that this network of contacts spread around the empire.[34] (Pseudo-?) Ignatius wrote to the Roman Christians expecting to suffer martyrdom when

---

28 Some scholars (e.g. Manson, 'St Paul's letter') have – in my view unsuccessfully – questioned Rom 16, suggesting it was the close of a version of the epistle sent to Ephesus.
29 A possible exception are Christians who were part of the imperial household, mentioned in Phil 4:22 – presumably they came from Rome; see Mullen, *Expansion of Christianity*, 198.
30 Gessel, 'Das Tropaion der Petersmemorie'; see 1 Pet 5:13; if this reference 'is taken to mean Rome, then 1 Peter 1:1 & 5:12–13 preserves the tradition that Peter, Sil[v]a[nu]s, and Mark had come to Rome also . . . 1 *Clement*, 5.1–7 supports the tradition of Peter and Paul as apostles in Rome', Mullen, *Expansion of Christianity*, 198.
31 *HE* 2.25.
32 Conclusions drawn from the archaeology are highly controversial; see Snyder, *Ante pacem*.
33 Snyder, *Ante pacem*, 251–8.
34 See chs. 17 and 18, and pt III, chs. 11 and 12, above.

he arrived there under imperial escort. Justin Martyr arrived from Samaria and established a Christian philosophical school. Valentinus apparently came from Alexandria and did likewise. Only after some time did conflict with Justin's school disrupt toleration of the Valentinians,[35] while Justin's pupil, Tatian, had meanwhile returned to his place of origin, Syria, where he was himself associated with heresy.

Marcion[36] had been born in Pontus, at the commercial city and military centre of Sinope, had travelled throughout Asia and, around 140 CE, like Justin, settled in Rome. There, he generously donated the immense sum of 200,000 sesterces to the Christian community, money, however, which he was given back when a few years later he left the community again. Marcion established his own church, which spread out from Rome and survived for several centuries. The story of Marcion may be the first to illustrate what must have become a typical pattern: initially welcomed as a fellow Christian, only to find oneself creating one's own community when one's teaching was found unacceptable by others. The same kind of thing would happen to Montanists from Asia[37] and to Theodotus from Byzantium, while at the turn of the century, Epigonus, who brought to Rome the ideas of Noëtus of Smyrna, got a hearing from successive bishops[38] and attracted followers who kept the controversy going in Rome for some time into the third century. Some groups in the capital were reluctant to accept others on grounds of doctrine or practice.

So the influx and outgoings of Christian commercial people, soldiers, civil servants, tourists, teachers, students, emigrants and immigrants created rows in Rome, and also between Roman Christians and those of other cities of the empire. In the mid-second century, debate arose about the date of the Easter celebration and the breaking of the fast beforehand.[39] The issue concerned the question whether Christians should relate their Easter-dating to the Jewish calendar. Do they celebrate *Pesach* and commemorate the death of Jesus, as did the Quartodecimans who ended their fasting on the fourteenth of Nisan, or do they fast until the Sunday following the fourteenth of Nisan to celebrate Jesus' resurrection and victory over death and emphasise the distance between Christianity and Judaism? Divergence of practice and theology was certainly present in Rome itself, as Asian congregations in the capital followed the custom of their 'home' church, which was different from that of most Roman assemblies.

---

35 Lampe, *Paul to Valentinus*, 387–91.
36 See pt III, ch. 9, above.
37 See ch. 17, above.
38 See pt V, ch. 25, below.
39 See ch. 17, above.

Earlier discussions had occurred between Anicetus of Rome (bishop 155–66 CE, influenced by Marcion?) and Polycarp of Smyrna, but only after a further generation in a changed political situation did those tensions lead to a rupture within the church.[40] Victor I, just after his election as bishop (c.189 CE), assembled a synod of bishops and wrote to Polycrates of Ephesus to underline the apostolic practice of breaking the fast on Easter Sunday. Possibly he was responding to inner-Asian tensions[41] and wrote in reaction to Polycrates; nevertheless, he insisted on the Roman fasting practice in a letter that went out to all communities in Asia and those that stood in solidarity with them, threatening with excommunication those who continued to follow the Quartodeciman practice. The result was a number of letters and synods. The Asian bishops remained unconvinced by Rome, whereas the Palestinian bishops of Jerusalem, Caesarea, Tyre and Ptolemais wrote in support of Roman practice. The supportive letter by Demetrius, Victor's colleague of Alexandria, who had become bishop around the same time as he himself, apparently stemmed from the presbytery acting collectively, because they did not yet have a powerful monarchical bishop. For Rome too, the authority of the bishop may not yet have been fully developed. Irenaeus wrote[42] urging Victor to recognise long-standing diversity of practice as his predecessors had done, implying that such variety had long existed and been tolerated in Rome itself as a result of immigration. It seems likely that the whole controversy arose because of Victor's ambition to bring all the Roman congregations into uniformity under his leadership, but it had a much wider impact simply because immigrants in Rome were networking closely with the churches from which they originated.

The organisation of the Roman church

Clement wrote to Corinth on behalf of the church in Rome as a whole, but probably there was no unitary congregation; rather, he was the secretary for a group consisting of the leaders of many scattered house churches. A variety of different Christian communities is attested by Hermas, who constantly pleads for unity. The mid-second-century material suggests a number of small communities, based in households, only loosely held together, often led by immigrants. 'Schools', too, such as that of Justin, would have been house-based. This situation continued for a long period of time, with different congregations acknowledging one another by passing around a portion of the

40 Euseb. *HE* 5.23–5.
41 Vinzent, 'Viktor I', 95.
42 Euseb. *HE* 5.24.

communion bread, but actually remaining fairly independent.[43] The 'fraction-alised' house churches were scattered around various districts,[44] each with its own leadership, while the secretary or president of the overarching forum of presbyters and teachers was spokesperson for the Roman congregations collectively in relation to churches elsewhere in the empire, and perhaps also the co-ordinator of relief for the poor. The terms *presbyteros* and *episkopos* seem not to have been clearly differentiated at first, and there was a long process before a 'monarchical bishop' gained supervisory authority over all the communities.[45]

Exactly when this happened is a matter of considerable debate. Lampe[46] argued that it was the actions of Victor in the Quartodeciman controversy that effected this, noting also that the lists of bishops guaranteeing apostolic tradition seem to have been constructed in the same period.[47] Victor, however, was not entirely successful and, according to Brent,[48] Hippolytus and his supposed schism, which belong to a somewhat later period, may best be interpreted in the light of continued struggles between different congregations or 'schools' prior to the effective establishment of a monarchical episcopal authority.

Eusebius had in his library the works of a bishop called Hippolytus, but he did not know what his see was; neither did Jerome some years later. Their lists of works, now mostly lost, included one entitled *Refutatio omnium haeresium* ('The refutation of all heresies'). In 1842, a substantial amount of a work with that title was discovered in a manuscript from Mount Athos. Nineteenth-century scholarship concluded this was Hippolytus' work. Coupled with other discoveries, this contributed to the creation of a portrait of a scholarly 'anti-pope', critical of Callistus (a fact misunderstood or suppressed by Eusebius), destined to die as a martyr with Callistus' successor, Pontianus. In the mid-twentieth century, the theory that the various works by then attributed to him actually came from two different people began to disturb this picture.[49] All along a key piece of evidence had been a statue with a plinth naming works more or less corresponding with Eusebius' list. Bringing together a more critical understanding of the statue[50] and the picture of the 'fractionalised'

---

43 Lampe, *Paul to Valentinus*; Brent, *Hippolytus*; Stewart-Sykes, *Hippolytus*, introduction.
44 Lampe, *Paul to Valentinus*, maps 1 and 2, for the seven ecclesiastical districts arranged within the fourteen Augustan administrative districts.
45 See pt v, ch. 23, below.
46 Lampe, *Paul to Valentinus*, 397–408.
47 On Irenaeus' list, see pt iii, ch. 13, above.
48 Brent, *Hippolytus*.
49 Nautin and Simonetti led the discussion; for details see now Brent, *Hippolytus*.
50 Brent, *Hippolytus*, develops the earlier work of Guarducci on the statue.

Roman church proposed by Lampe, Brent[51] has painstakingly argued for a comprehensive solution. The statue is not of Hippolytus, but of a female figure with a metaphorical meaning such as 'wisdom' (recently identified – because of her bare breast and the relationship of names – as Hippolyte, the queen of the Amazons who had a son named Hippolytus);[52] the list is of works coming from a 'school', the name of Hippolytus having become attached to writings produced by his community over some decades. Hippolytus himself, who suffered martyrdom with bishop Pontianus in 235 CE, was responsible for reconciliation with the bishop, his community having been in dispute with his predecessors, Zephyrinus and Callistus. On such a theory the disputes over 'monarchianism'[53] reflect the same 'fractionalisation' as earlier evidence, and do not imply a schism.

Indeed the disputed succession after the death of bishop Fabian in the Decian persecution, when Novatian[54] opposed Cornelius, is the first case of one 'monarchical' bishop contesting the position of another. Prior to that, what we find are groups resisting attempts by the 'president' to impose his authority. This was tried by Anicetus (c.155–66 CE), Soter (c.166–75 CE), Eleutherus (c.175–89 CE), and Victor (c.189–99 CE),[55] and was one factor in the resistance of Hippolytus' group to Callistus, whom they accused of forming his own 'school'. That many of the various Christian groups in Rome were set up as 'schools' is another important feature of the period up to the time of the Decian persecution.

Christian philosophical schools in Rome

Philosophical schools were a major factor in Roman Christianity, despite the lack of any traditional basis. Philosophy is only mentioned once in the New Testament (Col 2:8) as 'hollow speculations',[56] and pagans initially dismissed Christian claims to be lovers of wisdom by calling their religion a superstition (Plin. *Ep.* 10.96.8; Suet. *Claud.* 25.3; *Nero* 16.2; Tac. *Ann.* 15.44). Nevertheless, Christians took on the mantle of philosophers. Justin in Rome in the mid-second century equates 'getting to know the Christian God' with 'understanding philosophical truth' (*Dial.* 8.1f; cf. 4.1) and represents the Old Testament

---

51 Brent, *Hippolytus*; see also Cerrato, *Hippolytus between east and west*.
52 Vinzent, 'Hippolyt von Rom'.
53 See pt v, ch. 25, below, and Hübner and Vinzent, *Der Paradox Eine*.
54 See pt v, ch. 23, below.
55 Lampe, *Paul to Valentinus*, 397.
56 Bardy, '"Philosophie"'.

prophets as philosophers (*Dial.* 7.1ff.; *2 Apol.* 2.10.8).[57] For him 'Christianity even is the crown . . . of philosophy' (*Dial.* 2.13), because 'Christianity elicits . . . piety, and justice' (*Dial.* 110.3; cf. Seneca, *Ep.* 90.3), 'as does philosophy' (*Dial.* 8.2; cf. Seneca, *Ep.* 6.1; 90.28). 'It is "certain and profitable", as is philosophy' (*Dial.* 8.1; cf. Luc. *Men.* 4). Justin's 'younger Roman contemporary (Galen) . . . was the first among the pagans to compare Christians and philosophers. He conceded that Christianity, on the basis of its high ethical standards, was a "philosophical" school.'[58] Similarly, the pagan Roman Cynic, Crescens, entered into oral discussion with Justin when this Christian philosopher instigated a dispute with him on the philosopher's way of life (see *Dial.* 2.3.[8].1ff; 11.2; Tatian, *Orat.* 19; *M. Just.* 2.3).

Once Christianity had made its way into the Roman nobility via women who had acquaintance with ethics and knowledge (*gnōsis*), we find philosophical teachers meeting their demands. Conversely, 'the work of the Christian philosophers . . . made Christianity more socially acceptable, so that . . . the higher social strata increasingly were represented in Christianity.'[59] Until that time, the modern distinction between Gnostics and orthodox Christians does not make sense and is anachronistic, because it blurs the origins of Christian philosophy.[60] The Stoic and Middle Platonic interpretation of the Jewish Torah in terms of ethics and metaphysics was an inheritance from early Christianity's Hellenistic Jewish roots, in Alexandria as well as in Rome.[61] Rome had become an attractive place for foreign philosophical teachers, non-Christian as well as Christian, for during the empire philosophical teaching was state supported, chairs had been created and financed and the social standing of philosophers raised.[62] The younger Pliny calls Rome a 'centre for liberal studies'.[63] 'Caesar granted the citizenship to . . . professors of liberal arts resident in Rome, thus inducing them to remain and tempting others to follow suit.'[64] In addition, there was the demand of the nobility to be introduced to exotic wisdom by learned foreigners, and there were the academic facilities scholars were longing for – libraries, colleges and fellow scholars to engage with in discussions. Immigrant philosophers were usually self-employed at Rome – 'the early acquisition of influential pupils or patrons at Rome would help a new

57 Lampe, *Paul to Valentinus*, 272–3.
58 Lampe, *Paul to Valentinus*, 273.
59 Lampe, *Paul to Valentinus*, 284.
60 This is my main argument against theories like those of W. Bauer.
61 See pt I, ch. 2, above.
62 Vinzent, '"Oxbridge"'.
63 Noy, *Foreigners*, 94.
64 Suet. *Jul.* 42; see Noy, *Foreigners*, 47.

arrival to become established.'[65] The friends and foes they met were teachers and pupils of rival schools – hence the often aggressive rivalry which also existed between schools amongst Christians.

Crucial steps in the shaping of inner-Christian scholarly discourse, together with the development of the categories of 'heresy' and 'orthodoxy', were taken by Justin's school. Justin, together with his pupil, Tatian, and Tatian's pupil, Rhodon, engaged in critique of pagan and Jewish teachers and philosophers, as well as of fellow Christians. Tatian describes his long journey to Rome and to his master, Justin. Born in the Syrian east (*Orat.* 42.1), he first was initiated into several pagan mysteries, passed through a Greek course of studies (*Orat.* 42.1), taught as a pagan rhetorician (*Orat.* 35.1), encountered 'many' arts and sciences and looked into the curricula of pagan scholars, particularly of grammarians and stylists, before he joined Justin's classroom. Although Christianity was not of Greek origin, he presented his newly embraced eastern religion as *paideia* and *philosophia* in the 'deeper', Middle Platonic sense of religious wisdom (*Orat.* 12.5; 31.1; 32.1; 33.2; 35.1f), even 'superior in dignity to Greek education because of the greater age of its authorities'.[66] According to Tatian, it seems that 'some Christians were held in high regard because of their Greek education before they converted to Christianity'[67] and he presents himself – in Cynic terms – as a herald of truth (*Orat.* 17.1) with an 'orientalist' slant, a barbaric philosopher who combines exotic wisdom with Greek philosophical insights. Less elaborate, and leaning philosophically more towards Stoicism, his teacher Justin had not only criticised pagan philosophers and written a lengthy dialogue with the Jew Trypho, but also challenged his philosophically influenced, but less or even anti-philosophically oriented, wealthy fellow Christian, Marcion.

For a few years, it appears, Marcion had written, worked and taught in the midst of the community before criticism had started, perhaps initiated by Justin. Marcion left in July 144 to found his own quickly expanding community, and, according to Justin, his school movement had already in the 150s gained a foothold in all the provinces. For the first time in Christian literature, with Justin as its author, a treatise was written denying fellow Christian teachers their status as Christians (*1 Apol.* 1.26). This work is lost, but from the list of teachers and schools that Justin gives in his *Apology* we can infer the names of the Christian teachers that Justin regarded as wrongly called 'Christians'. Acknowledging the diversity of teaching and lifestyle, he names teachers who are rightly persecuted by the state because of their atheist thinking or their

---

65 Noy, *Foreigners*, 95.
66 Lampe, *Paul to Valentinus*, 289.
67 Lampe, *Paul to Valentinus*, 288.

wicked deeds (*1 Apol.* 1.7; 26), amongst whom he lists Marcion and his disciples (*1 Apol.* 1.26; 58). A few years later, in his *Dialogus cum Tryphone Judaeo* ('Dialogue with Trypho the Jew'), Justin developed a genealogy of school opinions or heresies that he linked with original masterminds whom he counts as 'false prophets' (Matt 7:15) and 'false apostles' (Matt 24:11). Now Marcion heads the list, followed by other famous fellow Christian teachers of Rome (*Dial.* 35). Like Justin, the pupil of his pupil Tatian, Rhodon, continues the battle against the Marcionites and especially engages with Apelles, Marcion's best-known follower.

What was the fierce battle all about? The absence of any direct debate about monotheism or Trinity in first- or second-century literature,[68] even in discussions with Jews, shows that the heated controversy between teachers and schools in Rome did not target 'theology' in the strict sense of this word, but salvation and conduct of life. Justin could speak of the *logos* as a second God, created by the will of the superior creator God whom he revealed to other creatures, in just the same way as, already a century before, Philo of Alexandria had written in Middle Platonic terms of various forms under which God, the creator, made himself known, especially through his creative and redemptive powers, namely, his *logos* and wisdom. This revelation and the right knowledge linked with it, along with the true wisdom gained in reading the (Jewish) scriptures and practising God's laws, were the basis for human salvation. It was endangered when knowledge was cut off from the divine source, from God's word in the scriptures. The importance of God's word was recognised by all Christian schools at Rome, even by Marcion: despite his denial of the value of the traditional writings that came from the Jews, he claimed, as did Justin, that reading scripture (by which he meant the letters of Paul and his version of Luke's gospel)[69] enabled the discovery of Jesus, which meant knowing God and gaining the knowledge that brought salvation and redemption.

At least since the third century BCE, Greek and Roman philosophers had emphasised a monistic view of the world. The Middle Platonists especially taught a supreme, transcendent first principle, the unknown God, who is beyond reach and above all matter and creation.[70] Although below him various gods exist as assistant creator(s), like the world soul, or demons, the further away they are from the one God, the less divine they are, becoming in the end counter-gods. Like the Stoics, the Middle Platonists, however, believed in just one overarching providence, directing the world. How then could this

---

68 See pt v, ch. 25, below.
69 See pt III, ch. 9, above.
70 See pt III, ch. 11, above.

absolute God of providence create a world where light and dark meet, where good and evil are so intrinsically linked? According to Tertullian (*Marc.* I.2), the question of the origin of evil provoked Christian philosophy: from where does evil come? If it is only God who can save creation from evil and who saved it through Jesus Christ, how could Christ, being God and everlasting and free from limits and death, die on a cross?

Marcion, like Valentinus, Ptolemaeus, Callistus, Hippolytus and other Roman teachers, tried his best in various ways. Marcion developed Christianity as a counter-concept to Judaism: appealing to Paul's experience of the risen Christ and his ascent into the third heaven, where he gained the new and, until then, hidden divine revelation.[71] He set Paul's new divine insight against the blindness of the old people of God, the Jews, including the so-called apostles: Paul's message of the new, unknown God versus the righteous creator god of the Jews; the new creation in the risen Christ versus the old creation of death; the New Testament of the Christians (ten Pauline letters together with the 'original' version of the gospel of Luke) versus the Old Testament of the Jews; the church versus the synagogue; the body versus spirit; and so on. Valentinus and Ptolemaeus seem to have been as inventive and creative as Marcion. Many of the theological and technical terms which were much discussed in later times appear first in their writings – basic concepts such as God's person (*prosōpon*), the divine substance (*hypostasis, ousia*), Christ's being in the same divine substance as God himself (*homoousios*). In contrast to Marcion, they pursued Jewish and Hellenistic Middle Platonic philosophy, differentiating between the one, unknown and transcendent God of the Old Testament and his creative and redeeming powers and words, associating one of them with the incarnated Christ.

Roman Christians obviously lived with a fair amount of divergence of beliefs as long as those teachers were not branded 'heretics'[72] in the wake of Justin, Irenaeus, Tertullian and others, who tried to combine Jewish Middle Platonism and monarchianism, and campaigned against more systematic thinkers. Since, however, all the more systematic thinkers, like Marcion and the Marcionites, Valentinus and the Valentinians, Ptolemaeus, Carpocratians, Theodotians, Montanists, Cerdo, Epigonos, Sabellius, Hippolytus and Novatian, and even Roman Jewish Christians with Torah observance, became 'heretics', almost all the writings of the first generation of Roman theologians – except a few fragments – are lost, and their teachings can hardly, if at all, be reconstructed

71 Vinzent, 'Der Schluß'.
72 Thomassen, 'Orthodoxy and heresy'.

from the extant originals and the reports of their theological enemies. But the fact of the debates remains itself an essential datum of Roman Christianity, though we know more, and can therefore get a clearer picture of, the philosophy of those 'who were struggling to establish a normative Christianity', 'to recompose a *world*, a trustworthy social and ritual environment' against, as they saw it, the differentiations and the splits brought by the heretics.[73]

When debate did turn to questions about monotheism and Christology the same inter-school rivalry seems to be reflected in the tension between Callistus and 'Hippolytus'.[74] One survived as the author of a respected corpus of writings, the other as the official bishop in the line that hindsight established.

From 'fractionalisation' to schism

In the tradition of Hippolytus stood Novatian (d. *c.*258 CE), who, despite his eventual schism, may be regarded as one of the few known theologians of the third century at Rome,[75] as his extant treatise, *De Trinitate* ('On the Trinity'), demonstrates. Time and theological concerns, however, had drastically changed. Overshadowed by the persecution of the emperor Decius, with numerous martyrs (amongst them bishop Fabian) and countless apostates, the discussion arose about how to treat those who had offered incense or sacrifice to the gods. Throughout the persecution, Novatian held a rigorous position towards those who had apostatised (Cypr. *Ep.* 30, 31, 36), but was vehemently opposed by a strong, less rigorous party in the Roman community. The same tensions disturbed the church in North Africa, and there were frequent interactions between Rome and Carthage. At Novatian's election as bishop of Rome, an equal part of the community voted for Cornelius. The church remained divided (Euseb. *HE* 6.43), the Novatians with their theology spreading from Rome to the rest of the empire. What was the theological drive behind the schism? Novatian held that only God could reconcile – it was not in the power of the church. Although similarly rigorous, Cyprian of Carthage had accepted Cornelius' election, and argued that reconciliation (as well as any other sacrament, such as baptism) was indeed of God's grace but could only be performed within the one, united church.

Providing an example of the importance of the oneness of God's church, Cyprian handed to Cornelius' successor at Rome, Stephen, a tool which the Roman bishop would turn in his favour – the most prominent scriptural text in

---

73 Williams, 'Defining heresy', 327.
74 See pt v, ch. 25, below.
75 Wallraff, *Der Kirchenhistoriker Sokrates.*

Roman church history. Cyprian quoted Matthew 16:18f, in *De unitate ecclesiae* 4, to affirm the importance of the one church that was built on Peter, the rock. Stephen in return insisted that he was the one occupying the seat of Peter at Rome. He, therefore, claimed the power to decide in these matters of reconciliation and baptism, using the joker of his opponent and laying an important scriptural foundation for the later development of papal authority.

PART V

*

THE SHAPING OF CHRISTIAN THEOLOGY

Figure 6. Reconstruction of Christian baptistery, Dura Europos (photo: Yale University Art Gallery, Dura-Europos Collection)

23

Institutions in the pre-Constantinian
ecclēsia

STUART GEORGE HALL

By the time of Constantine the church was a sufficiently robust organisation for the emperor to engage it as a partner in unifying the empire. Systems of authority, patterns of belief and control of funds and property had turned the early household communities into an interlinked, empire-wide organisation that increasingly mirrored the structure of the empire itself. It is a telling fact that when Julian the Apostate tried to put the clock back in the 360s, he 'determined to introduce into the pagan temples the order and discipline of Christianity':[1] various degrees of ministry were instituted, teachers and readers were appointed to give instruction in pagan doctrines, hours of prayer were established, and monasteries founded for those who wanted to live in philosophical retirement; pagan priests were told to provide hospitality for travellers, to distribute corn and wine to the poor and to live holy lives, avoiding taverns and the theatre, or be deprived of office. Julian saw the discipline and benevolence of the 'atheists' as attractions dangerous to traditional religion, whereas Constantine had recognised their usefulness.

The characteristics of the early house-based communities were described in part II, chapter 7, above. There, the discussion attempted to view the phenomenon of the early church in its social and historical setting, noting how it combined features of household, cult, club and philosophical school, without being altogether like any of them. Throughout this volume the diversity of Christian groups has been observed: there was a range of possible futures. Yet, fractured and diverse as it was, Christianity began to acquire not only a coherent profile in the Mediterranean world, but also distinctive patterns of authority.[2] This may be attributed to the sense of being a single 'household of God', despite meeting in many households – unity was a desirable end in itself. So leadership was dedicated to the preservation of social harmony,

1 Soz. *HE* 5.16.
2 Lane Fox, *Pagans and Christians*; Rousseau, *Early Christian centuries*.

resolving disputes and directing liturgical life. Thus 'unity, achieved on other grounds and by other means, created a climate within which orthodoxy could assert itself'.[3] So here we consider the institutional context for the crucial debates which forged orthodoxy. Through reference to key texts, an account is offered of the process whereby there emerged the clerical orders, including the monarchical episcopate; the liturgies and credal formulations of which the clergy were the cultic leaders; together with the discipline they exercised in the community, and their conciliar authority.

Ministry

The earliest known handbook for those responsible for running early churches is the *Didache* or 'Teaching of the twelve apostles'. Compiled about 100 CE using earlier material, some probably Jewish, it contributes to or is embodied in later church manuals like the *Apostolic constitutions*. It first sets out the moral teachings which all candidates for baptism should learn, then gives directions for baptism, fasting, prayer and the eucharist, regulations for the ministers of the church and the conduct of Sunday worship, and a warning about the impending judgement of God. Its early date is verified by its divergence from later practice in many respects.

In *Didache* 11 the church leaders are teachers, apostles and prophets. The teachers are plainly those who need the manual: a new teacher is to be judged by his conformity to its contents (11.1–2). The apostles are not the twelve of the New Testament, nor the original witnesses of the resurrection (cf. 1 Cor 9:1), but travelling messengers, who receive hospitality in places they visit (11.1–6). The prophets are given most attention, whether because they play the dominant role, or cause the most trouble.[4] They are not said to travel, though like other craftsmen they may arrive and settle (13.1; cf. 12.1–5). True prophets speak in the spirit and are to be obeyed. False prophets are identified chiefly by immorality or greed (11.7–12). Prophets perhaps command the eucharistic meal to be held (11.9), and lead prayers freely at it, not being bound by the fixed forms prescribed for other officiants (9–10, especially 10.7).

The offices of apostle, prophet and teacher figure at the head of a list of appointments in 1 Corinthians (12:28), a letter in which prophecy is prominent

---

3 Rousseau, *Early Christian centuries*, 88.
4 For misleading prophecies, see Matt 7:14–16; 1 John 4:1–3. For the problems of prophets, Lucian's satire, *De morte Peregrini*; cf. the 'orthodox' reaction to the Montanists (pt IV, ch. 17, above).

among spiritual gifts (see especially 1 Cor 14). A similar ordering may lie behind passages in Matthew's gospel (Matt 23:34; 28:19–20), a document which has other affinities to the *Didache*. Such an ordering is at variance with the structure soon to emerge as universal in the churches, that of bishops, presbyters and deacons. 'Bishop' (*episkopos*) means literally 'overseer', 'superintendent' or 'inspector'. 'Presbyter', from which the English 'priest' derives, means 'elder', and was widespread in the ancient world where senior males had important political and religious roles. 'Deacon' (*diakonos*) means 'minister' or 'servant', and can refer to a menial slave or a senior official. Some hold that the classic arrangement in the church, of a bishop with his deacon supported by presbyters, is a direct borrowing from the Jewish synagogue, which was managed by a body of presbyters, one of whom presided as 'chief of synagogue' (*archisynagōgos*), and served by an officer (*hypēretēs*).[5]

The development was not, however, straightforward. The general consensus among scholars has been that, at the turn of the first and second centuries, local congregations were led by bishops and presbyters whose offices were overlapping or indistinguishable,[6] while prophets, possibly itinerant, also continued to function; this, however, smoothes out the evidence, which seems to reflect diverse developments in different areas. Already in Philippians 1:1 a ministry was ascribed to 'bishops and deacons', a formula for which Clement of Rome found biblical foundation in the Greek version of Isaiah 60:17: 'I will set up their bishops in righteousness and their deacons in faith' (*1 Clem.* 42.5). The same formula of 'bishops and deacons' is reflected in 1 Timothy 3:1–13, and appears near the end of the *Didache*:

> Elect for yourselves therefore bishops and deacons worthy of the Lord, gentle men, without avarice, true and proven; for they too minister to you the ministry of the prophets and teachers. Do not therefore despise them, for they are your honoured ones along with the prophets and teachers.[7]

This is probably a later addition to a many-layered book. The passage in full brings the earlier prescriptions of the *Didache* into line with a more formal arrangement, in which more regular officers are needed to supplement or do duty for the prophets and teachers.

Ignatius generally supposes that there is one bishop in each church, a vital figure both institutionally and symbolically:

---

5 Recently argued by Burtchaell, *From synagogue to church*.
6 For a different view, see Young, 'On *episkopos* and *presbyteros*'.
7 *Did.* 15.1–2.

All of you, go with the bishop, as Jesus Christ with the Father, and go with the presbyterium as the apostles; reverence the deacons as the appointment of God. Let none do any thing pertaining to the church without the bishop. Let that thanksgiving (*eucharistia*) be reckoned sound which is under the bishop or whoever he commit it to. Wherever the bishop is, there let the people be, just as, where Jesus Christ is, there is the universal (*katholikē*) church. It is not right without the bishop either to baptise or to conduct a charity-meal (*agapē*), but whatever he approves, that is pleasing to God, so that all you do may be secure and sound.[8]

These motifs recur with variations, each church being urged to rally round the one bishop. The context is almost certainly a looser tradition, in which each household of the faithful managed itself, and there might be several in a city. Ignatius' insistence on the importance of the bishop may be an innovation provoked by the difficulties faced in the churches, whether these involved the continuing of Jewish practices like sabbath observance, or the erroneous teaching that the flesh of Christ was apparent rather than concrete ('docetism'). House churches, without a system of control, without fixed creeds, doctrines or even clearly defined canonical scriptures, took many forms, and the religious ideas could vary immensely. The practice of appointing a single bishop in each congregation who could be recognised by other bishops and be the final local adjudicator would contribute to the development.[9]

The bishop figures in every letter of Ignatius except one, that to the Romans. Probably there was no single 'monarchical' bishop in Rome before the middle of the second century,[10] and likely later.[11] Clement of Rome, somewhat earlier, had known no such system; nor is it to be found in an influential document usually dated about 140, *The Shepherd of Hermas* of Rome. Hermas describes a set of visions in which instructions are revealed about the nature of the church, and how it is to conduct itself. Copies of his account were to be given to Clement, who is responsible for 'the outside towns', and to a female teacher, Grapte, who 'will instruct the widows and orphans': 'But you will read it in this city with the elders who preside over the church.'[12] References to apostles,

---

8 Ign. *Smyr.* 8; cf. *Trall.* 3.1.
9 Bauer, *Orthodoxy and heresy*, pioneered this analysis, though he misjudged the situation at Rome, which was probably more seriously divided than other centres; see La Piana, 'The Roman church'; Lampe, *Paul to Valentinus*; and pt IV, ch. 22, above.
10 Markschies, *Between two worlds*, 189–92.
11 According to Brent, *Hippolytus*, the progress towards monepiscopacy begins in Rome in 189 and is not complete till 235.
12 Herm. *Vis.* 2.4.3.

prophets, and teachers appear, but also to bishops (in the plural), who look like heads of houses, and are probably the same as 'presbyters'.[13]

Irenaeus,[14] writing in the 180s, combines the idea of apostolic succession, which he found in Clement, with that of the unique role of the bishop (whom he stills often calls 'presbyter'). In the face of persecution, Irenaeus calls the variegated Christians to order. Heretics have forsaken the original truth delivered to the apostles. Irenaeus rejects their claims to present secret teachings of Jesus not written in the apostolic gospels with the argument that the apostles entrusted the whole truth to those to whom they entrusted the churches, that is, to the bishops. The succession of bishops in the churches that the apostles founded is therefore a guarantee that they possess the original gospel, and that other doctrines are man-made deviations.[15] The unanimity of the churches throughout the world attests, he says, the security of the true apostolic tradition. He illustrates this by giving the succession list for bishops of Rome, fictitious in its earlier entries, and recounting his own personal links with Polycarp of Smyrna.[16]

Irenaeus' ideas, though they may not have corresponded with the reality of Christian origins, offered a tidy solution to the problem of identifying true tradition in the face of diversity of faith and practice. They were adopted enthusiastically by Tertullian in Africa, about 200 CE.[17] With them goes an increase in the power of bishops in the face of other sources of authority: the prophet, the teacher and the charismatic martyr and confessor would increasingly fall under episcopal control. This process reaches its climax in Cyprian, who, in the face of widespread lapse during persecution, and the divisions in the churches over the outcome, argued that the universal episcopate was the sole authority by which individuals and groups could be judged.[18] In his lifetime his episcopal authority was not guaranteed against the confessors and the presbyters who supported them, but the outcome cemented the monarchical bishop's authority in each locality, as well as their concerted authority in council.

Cyprian's concept derived partly from his background in civil government: the church was empire-wide, and its structures resembled those of the empire, governed from the top down. Parallels between church government and city

13 E.g. Herm. *Vis.* 3.5.1; Herm. *Sim.* 9.27.2.
14 See further pt III, ch. 10, above.
15 Iren. *Haer.* 3.3.1–3.
16 Iren. *Haer.* 3.3.4.
17 Notably in *Praescr.*
18 See ch. 26, below.

councils have often been noted.[19] The distinction between the *ordo clericus* (clergy) and the *ordo laicus* (laity) parallels that between the *plebs* (ordinary citizens) and the curial class, propertied men who had the responsibility of ruling and equipping the city's public affairs. Roman social orders (senatorial, equestrian, curial, etc.) seem reflected in the different orders within the church (bishops, presbyters, deacons, widows, virgins, subdeacons, lectors). The church took on the identity of the 'third race' (neither Jew nor Greek/Roman), and could be regarded as a state within a state.[20] Yet the lifelong 'monarchy' of the bishop was quite different from the annual magistracies and priesthoods of Roman convention.[21] The authority of the bishop was enhanced, both by Irenaeus' conception of a universal system of unanimous bishops established by the church's founders, and by their crucial function of applying biblical words to current exigencies – especially in arbitration and maintenance of order and discipline within and between church communities.

Scripture also provided a cultic 'typology', reinforcing the growing power of the bishops and other orders of ministry. Christians were originally distinct from biblical Judaism and from the pagan world around them in that they had no sacrificial cult.[22] The sacrifices of the Old Testament were interpreted in terms of personal dedication,[23] especially in the case of Jesus.[24] Widows as recipients of the church's offering are 'an altar of God'.[25] Perhaps in the same charitable sense, the *Didache* depicts the prophets as the community's 'high priests'.[26] But *1 Clement* draws a comparison between the divine appointment of the Aaronic priesthood through Moses, and the divinely ordered church under its bishop/presbyters.[27] Maybe a similar hieratic view of the bishop is present in Ignatius' picture of the church gathered round its bishop, his unity representing God's own. Close to that tradition is *Martyrium Polycarpi* ('The martyrdom of Polycarp'), which portrays bishop Polycarp offering a priestly ministry of intercession as he goes to his martyrdom.[28] In the reconstructed *Traditio apostolica* ('Apostolic tradition') attributed to Hippolytus (early third century), the prayer over a new bishop includes the words:

19 For summary and references see Torjesen, 'Social and historical setting', 188–9; an earlier statement will be found in Cochrane, *Christianity and Classical culture*, 219–20.
20 Classically Harnack, *Expansion of Christianity*, vol. I, pp. 240–78.
21 Lane Fox, *Pagans and Christians*, 545; see full discussion on 493–517.
22 So *Ep. Diognet.* 1–6; cf. Young, *Use of sacrificial ideas*.
23 Rom 12:1–2; 1 Pet 2:4–5.
24 Heb, esp. 9:11–14; 10:1–16.
25 Poly. *Phil.* 4.23.
26 *Did.* 13.3.
27 *1 Clem.* 40–4.
28 *M. Polyc.* 5.5–6.1; cf. 14.

Father, you know the heart; grant that your servant, whom you have chosen for oversight [*episcopatum*], should shepherd your flock and should serve before you as high priest without blame, serving by night and day, ceaselessly propitiating your countenance and offering the gifts of your holy church. And let him have the power of high priesthood, to forgive sins according to your command, to assign duties according to your command, to loose every tie according to the power which you gave to the apostles.[29]

This assimilates the episcopal ministry to that of the Old Testament, where the ordering of the sanctuary for prayer and sacrifice, and the government of the religious life of the people, were in the hands of a divinely instituted priestly caste, the sons of Aaron.

Soon after, Cyprian regularly calls a bishop *sacerdos* ('priest'), and a deacon *levita* ('levite'). The rebellions of Korah, Dathan and Abiram against the lawful priesthood of Aaron and their dreadful fate[30] recur continually in Cyprian's polemic against dissidents. High on his list of episcopal duties is the offering of the sacrifice, which means the eucharist of bread and wine, and binding and loosing the sins of the people. This hieratic function of the bishop and his sacrifice also presents an alternative regime to the religious foundation of the Roman empire, as Augustus had established it at the beginning of the Christian era.[31]

By the end of Cyprian's episcopate, therefore, the role of the bishops in the church appears manifold. They constitute both government and priesthood for the Christian people. Their unanimity, secured by mutual ordination, recognition and consultation, joins them throughout time and space with the church's apostolic origins, constituting a parallel body to the Roman empire itself. Bishops determine who belongs and who does not. They are the guardians and exponents of the truth once delivered to the saints. They offer the only forms of public worship acceptable to the only God. They are the living instruments of the world's salvation.

Worship and creeds

The church in every place was God's 'sanctuary'.[32] It had no temples other than the people, individually and corporately. The purity of their life was their sacrifice, in contrast to the temples and rituals of pagans and Jews. They

---

29 *Trad. ap.* 3.3–5; Stewart-Sykes (ed. and trans.), 61.
30 Num 16.
31 Full detail in Brent, *Imperial cult*.
32 Hipp. *Trad. ap.* 3.3, quoted above.

constituted the immortal soul dispersed in the body of the corrupt and dying world.[33] To become one of this people, the convert needed a decisive break with the world around. Originally, this was a symbolic washing,[34] traceable to the washings by John the Baptist 'for the forgiveness of sins', taken up by Jesus and his followers; but the resurrection of Jesus introduces a new dimension, that of the Holy Spirit.[35] The gift of the spirit is a matter of change of heart, moral reformation, the conforming of the mind to God.

The *Didache* begins with a description of the two ways, of light and darkness, good and evil, and then directs that this teaching be given to those who are to be baptised.[36] This is one version of a 'two ways' document, apparently originating in pre-Christian Judaism, which reappears in various forms throughout the patristic period, and even as late as the Carolingian empire.[37] Radical conversion to the love of God and neighbour is required, rather than theological instruction, though baptism, which is to be conducted preferably in cold, running water, was 'in the name of the Father and the Son and the Holy Spirit.'[38] This agrees with the direction given in Matthew 28:19–20, and with the other early practice.[39]

A full prescription for the ceremony appears in 'Hippolytus'.[40] Those seeking baptism are first registered as catechumens, provided they are not in the wrong trade or profession (such as idol makers, gladiators, prostitutes). They attend biblical instruction, normally for three years. Their conduct in this time is reviewed, and, if acceptable, they proceed to a course of exorcisms, they 'hear the gospel' (their earlier study having been apparently the Old Testament), and come for final vigil and prayers on a Sunday, probably Easter, morning. Water is blessed with prayer; the candidates undress and are anointed with cleansing oil, 'oil of exorcism', whereat each is required to say, 'I renounce you Satan, and all your service, and all your works.' Thus pagan religion and all the aspects of society which depend upon it are set aside. The candidate then stands in the water, and is three times dipped (or affused) by the presbyter, who interrogates him. The candidate assents to belief, with the first dipping, in God the Father Almighty, with the second, in Christ Jesus the Son of God, whose birth, passion, resurrection and future judgement are recited, and, with the

33 *Ep. Diognet.* 1–6.
34 See further pt II, ch. 7, above.
35 Mark 1:4; John 4:1–2; cf. Mark 1:8; Acts 2:38; 19:1–6.
36 *Did.* 1–7.
37 Elaborately discussed in van de Sandt and Flusser, *Didache*, 55–190.
38 *Did.* 7.
39 Cf. Justin, 1 *Apol.* 61; Hipp. *Trad. ap.* 21; Tert. *Prax.* 26.9.
40 Hipp. *Trad. ap.* 17–21; Tert. *Bapt.* gives ceremonial information largely in agreement with *Trad. ap.*

third, in 'the Holy Spirit and the holy church and the resurrection of the flesh'. After this triple baptism, the candidate is anointed again, but now with the 'oil of thanksgiving', a perfume, apparently once at the font, and once again by the bishop, with laying on of hands in the presence of the congregation. Then the newly baptised for the first time is allowed to join in the prayers and the eucharist, and receives symbolic milk, honey and water to drink, as well as the eucharistic bread and wine. By Cyprian's time special functions were attributed to parts of the rite. The anointing and laying on of hands by the bishop, for instance, was regarded as imparting the Holy Spirit, while the water gave remission of sins.[41]

This practice partly imitated what happened in the public baths, where a preliminary oiling and scraping to remove dirt was followed by bathing, and bathing concluded with the application of perfume and clean clothes. This custom prevailed in the western church, whereas in the east another practice was widespread, involving a single anointing followed by the washing or washings and a eucharistic meal.[42] The baptised were bound to a pure life, free from greed and sexual licence, as well as the many pagan religious practices with which daily life was infused. But they had other sacred duties. Already prescribed in the *Didache* are meetings for instruction (4.1–2), prayer (8.2–3), fasting (8.1; cf. 7.4), the thanksgiving with cup and bread (9–10), regular giving (4.5–8; 13; cf. 1.5) and the confession of sins (14).

Participation in the eucharist[43] would become the characteristic 'mystery' reserved only for the baptised. Already the *Didache* calls the meal *eucharistia*, 'thanksgiving', and each of the two prescribed prayers begins 'We thank you, Father . . .'. Before eating, thanks are offered over the cup for 'the holy vine of David' made known through Jesus, and over the broken bread for 'life and knowledge made known through Jesus', with a prayer for the gathering of the church in God's kingdom. The unbaptised are forbidden to participate. After eating, thanks are offered to God for making his name known through Jesus, and for food, both physical and spiritual. A different prayer is added for the preserving and gathering of the church at the end of the world. Because these prayers lack reference to the death of Christ or the Last Supper or the bestowing of the spirit to transform the gifts, scholars have usually held that this meal was not the (Catholic) Mass, the (Protestant) Lord's supper or the (Orthodox) Liturgy, but a fellowship meal or *agapē* additional to it. However,

---

41 Hence Cyprian's misunderstanding of Stephen in *Ep.* 74.5 etc. Cyprian's view is probably implied by Hipp. *Trad. ap.* 21.21; see Stewart-Sykes (ed. and trans.) 112–3.
42 E.g. *Acts Thom.* 132–3; 157.
43 See also pt II, ch. 7, above.

it is better to hold that this is about the one community meal of the *Didache*.[44] Early Christian ritual meals varied in their meaning, function and content: food other than bread was widely offered, and wine was by no means universal.[45]

The prayers and rituals associated with the formal meals of congregations are poorly attested for the early period – it is a mistake to read the contents of the great liturgical texts of the fourth century back. This has often been attempted, at the cost of ignoring the evidence for primitive variety.[46] Many scholars have tried to find a single basis for Christian eucharistic prayers in contemporary Jewish models.[47] This is called in question by recent critical research by Jewish scholars, which tends to show the same difficulties in identifying early rabbinic material as apply to Christian documents.[48] Nevertheless, turning the corporate meal into a sacrificial commemoration of the passion of Christ and the night when he was arrested is as ancient as Paul,[49] and it led to the deliberate modelling of eucharistic practice on scripture. By 250, what the Lord did was regarded as the appointment of a sacramental ceremony, and his actions were taken as the norm.[50] We find sacrificial metaphors in the *Didache* and *1 Clement*:[51] in the *Didache*, the purity of the sacrifice is achieved by mutual reconciliation and forgiveness of sins, in *1 Clement*, by the correct behaviour of the presbyters supervising the offering and of the people making it. Ignatius of Antioch appeals for total unity

> in one faith and in Jesus Christ, who was according to flesh of David's family, the Son of Man and Son of God, so that you should obey the bishop and the presbytery with undivided purpose, breaking one bread, which is the drug of immortality, an antidote so as not to die, but to live in Jesus Christ for ever.[52]

Here, Ignatius' allusion to the immortality drug should not be pressed to make eucharistic doctrine: such a drug figures in the story of Isis and the resurrection of Horus, and here it is not so much the eucharistic bread, as the obedience of gathering in one assembly under one bishop, that makes the bread-breaking medicinal. Ignatius similarly uses the metaphor of poisonous

---

44 So recently van de Sandt and Flusser, *Didache*, 301–4; by contrast, Niederwimmer, *The Didache*, 139–43.
45 See comprehensively McGowan, *Ascetic eucharists*. Stewart-Sykes (ed. and trans.) 130–2 shows how the Hippolytean meal in *Trad. ap.* 23–6 should be regarded as eucharistic.
46 See Bradshaw, *Search*.
47 So recently Mazza, *Origins*, and van de Sandt and Flusser, *Didache*.
48 Bradshaw, *Search*, 1–29.
49 1 Cor 11.17–34; cf. 10.14–22.
50 Cypr. *Ep.* 63; that orthodox African bishops are rebuked for using only water in the cup is important.
51 *Did.* 14; *1 Clem.* 40–1 and 44.4.
52 Ign. *Eph.* 20.2.

herbs for heresy, and that of a consecrated altar for the bishop and the apostolic ordinances.[53]

The early church had no official creedal formula before the Council of Nicaea in 325, and even then there is little evidence for the Nicene Creed displacing local forms of baptismal confession.[54] However, short summaries of the faith occurred in various contexts from the time when the New Testament was written.[55] Later, often against heretics, Irenaeus would rehearse summaries of 'the faith', 'the proclamation', 'the rule of truth', with no consistent wording though in substantially similar terms. Such malleable summaries are found also in Tertullian, Hippolytus and Origen during the decades following Irenaeus, and are generally referred to in modern scholarship as 'the rule of faith'.[56] It always involves confession of God as Father and creator, of Jesus and his life on earth, and usually something about the Holy Spirit, the church and the coming judgement. Some such summary appears to have been deployed by the presbyters (bishops?) who tried Noëtus for heresy late in the second century.[57] If so, that is a primitive occurrence of the 'conciliar creed' often met the next centuries as a way of settling doctrinal disputes.

Creeds as such emerged in the context of preparation for baptism, and gradually became incorporated into the liturgies. Their threefold shape is owing to the three questions (noted earlier) associated with the three washings. Prior to baptism, it became customary for the candidate to confess the faith by reciting the creed received during instruction. The eucharistic prayer became another occasion for summarising the faith of the church. The ancient practice of the eastern churches, as it comes down to us in later documents such as *The Liturgy of St James* and *The Apostolic Constitutions*,[58] celebrates the history of God's dealings with his people from the creation, through the patriarchs and prophets, to the coming of Christ and his saving death and exaltation. So creeds and summaries of the faith were not primarily deployed as tests of orthodoxy – they had their natural locus in doxology and confession of the faith in worship. This bears out the view that church leaders were concerned with the liturgical and moral life of the congregation as much as orthodoxy, if not more.

---

53 Ign. *Trall.* 6–7. For the interpretation of Ign. *Eph.* 20.2, see Schoedel, *Ignatius of Antioch*, 95–9; Wehr, *Arznei der Unsterblichkeit*, 106–11.
54 See further pt VI, ch. 31, below.
55 Classic presentation in Dodd, *Apostolic preaching*; see also Kelly, *Early Christian Creeds*, 6–29.
56 Kelly, *Early Christian Creeds*, 68–99.
57 Hipp. *Noët.* 1.7; see below.
58 *Prex eucharistica*, Hänggi and Pahl (eds.), 82–95, 244–61.

Discipline

Disputes and defections plagued the church from the start. Paul's letters already reveal disputes about male circumcision (especially Galatians), about incest, the use of flesh sacrificially slaughtered in pagan ceremonies, marriage and celibacy and belief in the bodily resurrection (all in 1 Corinthians). Such faults and disagreements soon revealed the need for a system for dealing with individuals who erred, and a procedure for settling disputes.

New Testament texts contain disciplinary decisions; inevitably these influence later practice. The man who married his mother-in-law was pronounced guilty by the apostle Paul; his sentence was to be expelled from the community.[59] Indeed, all evil-doers were to be excluded from table fellowship,[60] a restriction which might have serious implications in a community which constituted a kind of family, and provided all sorts of financial and social support for its members. By the time Matthew was written, judgement needed two or three witnesses, private expostulation and a public hearing by 'the assembly' (ecclesia) before expulsion; the decision of the assembled believers, upheld by God, should be mercifully applied.[61]

Some early texts have been taken to imply that in the earliest period serious sins after baptism were regarded as irremediable.[62] But it is clear that, while preserving the baptismal 'seal' unbroken was regarded as important,[63] repentance and forgiveness were always seen as available to those who sought it.[64] Clement of Rome, for instance, not only calls his readers to repent, but appeals to those who had removed their lawful presbyters to submit: they will be received by other churches; they should be prayed for; they will be forgiven by God, restored, small but honourable, to the flock of Christ.[65] Hermas receives in his visions extensive instructions about the building up of the church, its constant renewal and final destiny, through encouraging and facilitating the repentance of its erring members.[66] Hermas envisages a renewal of the church before the last day, and an opportunity for the sinful and lapsed members to accept discipline and be restored. His work was widely read and regarded as authoritative, as evidence from Rome, Alexandria, Carthage

---

59 1 Cor 5:1–6.
60 1 Cor 5:9–13.
61 Matt 18:15–22.
62 Notably Heb 6:5–8; 12:14–17; see Harnack, History of Dogma, vol. I, 171–3.
63 2 Clem. 6–7.
64 So Benrath, 'Buße', 452–3.
65 1 Clem. 54–7.
66 So especially Schneider, 'Propter sanctam ecclesiam'.

and Lyons before the end of the second century confirms.[67] Wherever *Hermas* was read, the view prevailed that the new life imparted at baptism could be renewed by formal repentance, an act which involved public confession, a period of exclusion and staged reintroduction to the prayers and communion of the baptised. Tertullian describes vividly what is involved in *exomologēsis*, 'confession': the penitent lives on a sparse diet, wears mourning clothes, including sackcloth and ashes, while groaning, weeping and prostrating before the clergy, and inviting the prayers of the faithful.[68] Details varied, however, from time to time and place to place.[69]

Occasionally there were protests against laxity towards the fallen. Montanism, which is better described as 'the New Prophecy',[70] was just such a rigorous movement. It is clear from Tertullian that Montanists stood for tighter discipline in various directions: veiling little girls, frequent fasts, not moving away from persecution, for instance. Such things were stipulated by utterances of the Spirit, 'the Paraclete', who removed some concession made in the time of the apostles to human weaknesses.[71] Trevett is probably correct to conclude that the disciplinary and eschatological views usually attributed to the New Prophecy were also held and propagated by others, and that the reason they were repudiated is the claim to speak with authority, inspired by the Paraclete, without due regard to the established and increasing authority of the formal ministry of the church.[72]

Though always morally rigorous, Tertullian notoriously shifted position on the question of post-baptismal sin. In his early days, he states in *De paenitentia* that the opportunity to repent again is needed because the devil attacks especially the holy. The argument is enforced with biblical examples. No sin, however grave, is apparently excluded. There are two 'planks of salvation', baptism and one further repentance with *exomologēsis*.[73] Later, expressly under the influence of the New Prophecy, he attacks a leading bishop[74] who has declared he will remit the sins of adultery and fornication after due penance.[75] It is one of the three mortal sins – idolatry, fornication and murder – forbidden

---

67 Staats, 'Hermas', 106–7.
68 Tert. *Paen.* 9; cf. Or. *C. Cels.* 3.51.
69 Brightman, 'Terms of communion', 365–77.
70 Trevett, *Montanism*, esp. 159–62; see also pt IV, ch. 17, above.
71 E.g. Tert. *Mon.* 2–3. For Tertullian's relation to Montanism, see Rankin, *Tertullian and the church*, 41–51; on repentance, Butterweck, 'Tertullian', 100–1.
72 Trevett, *Montanism*, 114–20 and elsewhere.
73 See e.g. Tert. *Paen.* 7–8; 12.9.
74 Of Carthage rather than Rome; see Hall 'Calixtus I', 562; *Letters of St Cyprian of Carthage*, Clarke (trans.), vol. III, 194–5 (Clarke's note on Cypr. *Ep.* 55.20–1).
75 Tert. *Pud.*, esp. 1.6–9.

by the apostolic decree of Acts 15.28–9 in its moralised western version, and irremissible.[76] *The Shepherd of Hermas*, whose recommendations tallied with what had been written in *De paenitentia*, is explicitly repudiated.[77]

This question apparently agitated the African church considerably, but the reconciliation of sexual sinners had become settled practice there by Cyprian's day.[78] The great quarrel now was about idolatry. The persecution under the emperor Decius, beginning in 249, led to massive defections, as Christians complied with the requirement to offer pagan sacrifice. Many then sought to return to the church, some obtaining the support of confessors and martyrs in their application.[79] The response of the clergy varied: some readmitted fallen members with little fuss; others excluded them totally. The chief records we have are from the west, where it is apparent from the correspondence of Cyprian that he himself, beginning from a fairly rigorous position, modified it in consultation with other bishops. Cyprian was as much concerned to establish episcopal authority – that of the one bishop in his own community and that of the episcopate corporately – as with resisting hasty readmissions to the church. In the first instance, it was resolved by the Council of Carthage in 251 that, after proper inquiry, those who had not sacrificed, but had only obtained a certificate, should be readmitted, and that those who were steadily penitent after actual sacrifice should be given communion if they were ill and on the point of death.[80] These arrangements were later agreed with Rome, as was the concession of general amnesty to the steadily penitent in the face of the new threat of persecution.[81] Arrangements for reconciling those who had sacrificed varied considerably,[82] but were generally stringent.

Councils

The disciplinary and baptismal controversies brought to the fore the judicial function of councils. Hamilton Hess has reviewed the beginnings and development of the council or synod as an instrument of government in the church.

76 *Pud.* 12.1–6.
77 *Pud.* 10.12.
78 Cypr. *Ep.* 55.21–22.
79 The events are outlined in ch. 26, below.
80 Cypr. *Ep.* 55.17.3, with Clarke's extended note and references to other passages, *Letters of St Cyprian*, vol. III, 191–3.
81 Cypr. *Ep.* 57, from a council dated summer 253 by Clarke, *Letters of St Cyprian*, vol. III, pp. 212–16.
82 Brightman, 'Terms of communion', 369–71, collects information on the length of time required.

Later, under the Christian emperors, it becomes a regular consultative, judicial and legislative assembly, in which bishops function like local or imperial senators. In the earliest period, it was very different. There are stories of ecclesial assemblies in Acts, the first being primarily of apostles, though a congregation of others, including Jesus' family and some women, is mentioned (1:15–26), the second consisting of a group of named prophets and teachers (13:1–3) and the third involving a formal deputation from Antioch presenting its case to the 'apostles and presbyters' in Jerusalem (15:1–35). In this latter case, a formal letter (later anachronistically dubbed 'the apostolic decree') is despatched to Antioch, and read to an assembly of the faithful there. While every one of these is a largely idealised reconstruction by Luke of events past, they give a valuable insight into the sort of process he would expect to happen in the church of his day, perhaps the last decade of the first century. Hess finds the consultations of the first two centuries largely local and congregational, only becoming inter-church councils in the third century.[83] Even this may be too sharp a distinction. If the faith began in great cities like Rome with a set of discrete house churches, among whom a single bishop ultimately emerged as superior, wide consultations must have taken place before Clement wrote on behalf of the church of Rome to that at Corinth, or when Hermas presented his weighty volume of prophecies to the presbyters and teachers at Rome. According to an unnamed writer quoted at length by Eusebius, the New Prophecy in Phrygia precipitated councils:

> When the faithful throughout Asia had met frequently and at many places in Asia for this purpose, and on examination of the new-fangled teachings had pronounced them profane and rejected the heresy, these persons were thus expelled from the church and shut off from its communion.[84]

It is not clear whether these are inter-church meetings, or simply consultations within a local congregation.

Even a local assembly, however, could benefit from the presence of a visiting expert or scholar. The same author begins his treatise by describing a local dispute at the important town of Ancyra in Galatia, how he refuted the New Prophecy, and was asked by the local presbyters to leave a written memorandum: in fact he wrote it afterwards.[85] We find similar consultation of an expert in the surviving stenographic record of Origen's doctrinal debate with the

---

83 Hess, *Early development*, 4–20.
84 Euseb. *HE* 5.16.10.
85 Euseb. *HE* 5.16.4–5.

bishop Heraclides and the bishops who suspected him.[86] His examination of Beryllus of Bostra may have been comparable, and another debate in Arabia is alleged by Eusebius to have involved a large gathering (*synodos*).[87] In all three cases, Origen appears to have talked round the opposition into agreement. Dionysius, bishop of Alexandria 247/8–264/5, was similarly successful in a three-day conference with the presbyters (bishops?) of the nome of Arsinoe, where schism had arisen over the authority and meaning of the Revelation of John.[88]

These consultations all fit the formula emphasised by Hess, that the object was consensus. Sometimes persuasion did not work. Noëtus[89] was first warned by 'the blessed presbyters' about his christological views, but, when he persisted and gathered followers, they condemned him and expelled him from the church; whereat he 'formed a school' (*didaskaleion*), in other words set up a separate church.[90] We cannot tell whether Noëtus was a bishop, though he was deposed from 'holy clerical office';[91] and, although it is likely that the 'blessed elders' are bishops of distinct churches and not the officials of a single congregation, we cannot be sure.[92]

In the case of the dispute between bishop Victor of Rome and the Quartodecimans, probably soon after 190, it is now certain that Eusebius read the dossier of letters anachronistically.[93] An attempt was made by a leading bishop to impose uniformity of paschal observance on other congregations in Rome, and correspondence with foreign bishops, in Ephesus, Lyons, Corinth, Palestine and elsewhere ensued. In Eusebius' narrative (aided perhaps by adjustments to the texts he quotes), 'synods and meetings together of bishops were held, and all with one consent set out an ecclesiastical ruling (*dogma*) that the mystery of the Lord's rising from the dead should never be celebrated on any but the Lord's day, and that on that day alone we should observe the conclusion of the paschal fasts.'[94] It is likely that the letters Eusebius saw were the fruit of discussion with local colleagues, not just personal episcopal exchanges: unless the text has been tampered with, Polycrates of Ephesus says as much.[95] But

---

86 Or. *Dial.*
87 Euseb. *HE* 6.33; 6.37.
88 Euseb. *HE* 7.24.6–9.
89 See further ch. 25, below.
90 Hipp. *Noët.* 1.3–8.
91 Hipp. *Noët.* 1.3.
92 Hess, *Early development*, 11–12.
93 Euseb. *HE* 5.23–5; Hess, *Early development*, 8–10; Brent, *Hippolytus*, 412–27, presents the argument fully, if controversially in some details.
94 Euseb. *HE* 5.23.2.
95 Euseb. *HE* 5.24.8.

the idea of systematic regional gatherings producing a decree for the universal church belongs in the fourth century, not the second.

Solid evidence for councils and their procedures begins with the fall-out of the Decian persecution, 249–51 CE. But those records themselves furnish some evidence of gatherings, a generation or more earlier, to deal with the validity of heretical baptisms, at Iconium in Phrygia, involving bishops from neighbouring provinces, as well as of the bishops of Africa and Numidia led by Agrippinus of Carthage.[96] It is usually assumed that a similar council at Carthage authorised the readmission of penitent adulterers.[97] When Cyprian returns to Carthage in 251 after his retreat, he is faced with the schism of leading clergy and deals with it by gathering a council of supportive bishops, sitting with presbyters and deacons, which agreed to rulings on the lapsed as well as on the dissident clergy.[98] A similar council in Rome was attended by sixty bishops and a greater number of presbyters and deacons.[99] After that, we have councils on record in Carthage annually till 256. By 257, renewed persecution and the execution of Cyprian apparently broke the pattern. Similar conciliar activity over the reconciliation of the lapsed and the subsequent schisms are less well recorded, but probably comparable.[100] There is evidence that annual gatherings were already being held, especially to deal with penitentiary matters,[101] something which canon 5 of Nicaea would formally prescribe in 325.

Some of these data indicate that councils were not solely episcopal. In fact, not only the various clergy, but laymen, contributed: 'bishops, presbyters, deacons, confessors and steadfast laymen' are expected to formulate a judgement.[102] When the synod acted as a court, the lay people presumably played the same role as the people did in attendance at secular courts, influencing the magistrates by their reaction to the proceedings. This grew from the fact that councils were originally local gatherings of the members of a local church, which in a city might be dispersed in several congregations. Suburban and other visiting clergy would be added to this gathering. There was thus no formal membership or voting power, though plainly those further away would need due notice and summons. This did not matter too much, since the

---

96 Euseb. *HE* 7.7.6; Cypr. *Ep.* 71.4.1; 75.7.4. On the uncertain dates and circumstances, see Clarke's notes, *Letters of St Cyprian*, vol. IV, 196–9.
97 Cypr. *Ep.* 55.20.2–21.2, with Clarke's notes.
98 Cypr. *Ep.* 51.15.1; see also ch. 26, below.
99 Euseb. *HE* 6.43.2.
100 See Clarke, *Letters of St Cyprian*, vol. II, 11–13.
101 Firmilian in Cypr. *Ep.* 75.4.3.
102 Cypr. *Ep.* 43.7.2; further examples in Hess, *Early development*, 22–4.

procedure did not involve majority voting, but aimed at consensus.[103] They were meeting to resolve a matter of conduct or of doctrine.

Hess (following Sieben) identifies three procedural styles, of which two apply to the period before Constantine,[104] the discursive and the parliamentary. The discursive were like Origen's debate with Heraclides, when questions and interpretations were offered, and conclusions reached which all accepted; it had strong educational aspects, and the involvement of the laity was significant. Synods for electing bishops probably took such a form, when both popular acclaim and visiting bishops were essential to the proceedings.[105] The parliamentary process was modelled on the Roman senate, or more significantly on the local provincial and municipal bodies, and perhaps *collegia* or guilds. We have one clear description of such a process in the *Sententiae* LXXXVII *episcoporum*,[106] edited from a stenographic record of a council held at Carthage on 1 September 256. Letters necessary to explain the issue under discussion were read; then Cyprian, as presiding bishop, outlined his view and asked for opinions. After the other eighty-six had expressed their assent, Cyprian gave his view to round off the unanimous decision. A number of Cyprian's letters announce the findings of such gatherings on a variety of topics. Sometimes it is a joint letter: Cyprian *Epistula* 57 has the names of forty-three bishops addressing their conclusion to Cornelius. In *Epistula* 71, Cyprian reports what 'a large number' of bishops had decided when summoned to meet in council; neither names nor number are given, though it is almost certainly the assembly of seventy-one bishops in the spring of 256.[107] From such origins the full transcripts and synodical *statuta* of later centuries would develop, and become a major source of canon law.

All the evidence presented so far, however, involves local, or at best provincial, synods. The one case prior to Nicaea that came nearer to involving bishops 'ecumenically' (that is, 'worldwide') is the council at Antioch which deposed Paul of Samosata. According to Eusebius, bishops assembled from surrounding provinces, and addressed their synodical letter to the bishop of Alexandria and 'all our fellow ministers throughout the world, bishops, presbyters and deacons'. The fact that the final expulsion of Paul from the church at Antioch

---

103 See esp. Hess, *Early development*, 29–33.
104 Hess, *Early development*, 24–34; Sieben, *Konzilsidee*, 466–92; Sieben's third model is the *kaiserliche Kognitionsprocess*.
105 Cyprianic evidence comprehensively summarised by Bernard, 'Cyprianic doctrine', 230–2; cf. Euseb. *HE* 6.11.1–2; 6.29.3–4.
106 *Sancti Cypriani episcopi opera*, CCSL 3E, Diercks (ed.).
107 Clarke, *Letters of St Cyprian*, vol. III, 211–12.

involved the emperor and the bishop of Rome also anticipates later develop-ments.[108]

Thus we begin to discern how it was that the internal structures of the church gave it an empire-wide focus, which, coupled with its interest in unity, made it a ready tool for Constantine in his bid to unite his dominions under one God.[109]

108 See further ch. 25, below.
109 See further pt VI, chs. 30 and 31, below.

24

Monotheism and creation

GERHARD MAY

Jewish heritage and emergent Christianity

A distinctive outcome of Christian theological reflection in the first few centuries was the doctrine of *creatio ex nihilo*. But the notion that God created the world 'out of nothing' was not simply inherited from an already well-developed Jewish or philosophical position; it was only clearly defined as monotheism[1] was defended against Gnosticism and set in debate with philosophy.

Monotheism and creation in Judaism and in Greek philosophy

The early Christians shared the monotheism of the Jews. During a long period of theological reflection, Israel had worked out the conception of one unique and universal God who, in his absolute freedom and power, had created the world and all things living in it. God's motive for creation was his goodness; his providence kept the world in being until his coming to pronounce final judgement upon it. A fully developed doctrine of monotheism is usually ascribed to Deutero-Isaiah in the sixth century BCE: the pagan gods do not really exist, and their idols are worthless.[2] In the third century BCE, a new process took its beginning: the encounter between Judaism and Greek culture. In the debates which arose about the true God, the teaching of the Bible proved to be an asset for the Jews. There also was a strong tendency toward monotheism in Greek thought, winning more and more ground under Roman rule. Apart from philosophical speculation about first principles, it was a common assumption that the gods of paganism were nothing but single aspects or powers of the one supreme God.[3] Neither Jewish nor pagan monotheism were absolutely pure: they could exist alongside belief in angels, demons or inferior gods. But the fundamental idea of monotheism was clear.

---

1 The term 'monotheism' was introduced by English thinkers in the seventeenth and eighteenth centuries.
2 Isa 40:12ff, 21–8; 43:10ff; 44:8, 23ff; 45:5f, 22.
3 See pt III, ch. 11, above.

Despite strong anti-Jewish prejudices in Greek and Roman society, the discussion about a philosophical understanding of God and his creation was profitable for both sides. Jewish missionaries won sympathisers and even made converts among the pagans all over the Mediterranean world. A fine example of the appreciation of the language of Genesis can be found in Pseudo-Longinus, an unidentified Greek author of the first century CE: Moses, he says, shows his adequate understanding of the power of God by making him bring forth light and earth merely by his word.[4] A whole historical tradition is known to us describing the Jews as a nation of philosophers.[5] However, more books were written by Jews about the agreement between Judaism and Greek philosophy than vice versa. The explanation is easy: it was more important for the Jews to be accepted as a 'philosophical' nation, while there existed no such necessity for the Greeks. Jewish teachers experienced what was virtually unavoidable in their situation: they adapted their own ideas to those of their opponents and so unconsciously changed their own views, producing tensions over the question how far Hellenisation might be pushed. Its high point is found in the work of Philo of Alexandria (of whom more later).

A hypothetical observer in the first centuries before and after Christ might have had the impression that Jewish and pagan doctrines of God were converging. The most influential philosophical school in the first two centuries after Christ was Stoicism. The Stoics were not only a group of specialised scholars, but, with their teaching and their literary work, they dominated their followers' world-view, particularly in the field of ethics. Their austerity in life appealed to seriously minded intellectuals. Although the Stoics fostered materialism, they could give a theistic turn to their language about God.[6] By the end of the second century, however, Platonism was dominant, and confrontation with this philosophy was most important for the moulding of the Jewish/Christian doctrine of creation. The period of Middle Platonism (50 BCE–250 CE) saw a definite turn towards theology.[7] God, the demiurge of the *Timaeus*, the favourite dialogue for Middle Platonism, was equated with the supreme God. From the cosmogony of the *Timaeus*, the characteristic 'three principles' doctrine was derived. Three principles of equal standing, God, ideas and matter, constitute the world. The eternity of matter, out of which the world is made, was generally accepted, but at the same time the question is debated whether the ordered cosmos had its origin in time. Cicero and Philo of Alexandria testify

---

4 *De sublimitate* 9.9; cf. Gen 1:3.
5 For full documentation, see Hengel, *Judaism and Hellenism*, vol. 2, 255-61.
6 Cleanthes, *Hymn to Zeus* [*SVF* I, p. 118, lines 24ff].
7 Dillon, *Middle Platonists*.

that in their own days the *Timaeus* was understood literally by many and that it was accepted that the world had been created at a specific moment in time. Plutarch likewise held this view, and still in the second century, when the doctrine of the eternity of the world had become practically general among the Platonists, Atticus came forward with the notion of the creation of the world in time. These views, taken from the *Timaeus*, represented the cosmology of Plato as it could be understood in the early empire. The assumption of more than one supreme principle of the universe, however, was unsatisfactory, even contradictory. Plotinus found the solution for this problem. He constructed a hierarchy of being, with the 'One', the unique and absolute ground of all being, on the top, followed in descending order by intellect (*nous*), soul (*psychē*) and matter (*hylē*). The last, which is most distant from the One, is neither being in the full sense nor absolutely non-being. It lacks all positive qualities and is identified with evil.

It was quite possible for philosophers to speak in exalted terms of God as the maker and ruler of the world. There was, however, an important qualification to be respected: divine power needed a material substrate for creative action. The heavenly creator is imagined as a craftsman who gives form to his chaotic material, taking his models from the ideas (so the majority of Platonists). Even if the world had a beginning in time (the minority opinion among the Platonists), primordial matter remained the eternal substrate of the world. The assumption that God could bring forth whatever he wished solely by his will and his power without any help from outside seemed absurd to educated people. God had to conform with the laws of nature.[8] Furthermore there was a strong sense that 'nothing comes out of nothing', and so anything without a material substrate would be a sham or or a phantom.[9]

Creation 'out of nothing'

We turn now to the core of our subject – the meaning and the use of the doctrine of 'creation out of nothing' in Hellenistic Judaism and emergent Christianity. The earliest piece of evidence in Hellenistic-Jewish literature seems to be 2 Maccabees 7:28, in which a Jewish mother under the Seleucid king Antiochus IV Epiphanes (175–164 BCE) implores her seven sons to remain steadfast under terrible torture when pressed heavily by the king to eat pork and so to betray their faith. God demonstrated his universal power by creating the world and the human race out of nothing (*ouk ex ontōn* – strictly, 'not out of

8 Dihle, *Theory of will.*
9 Ehrhardt, *The beginning.*

existing things'),[10] and in 'the time of mercy' he will raise the righteous from death.

It is difficult to interpret the formula *ouk ex ontōn* precisely. If one isolates it from its context, it could be a colloquial phrase, used without reflecting about absolute non-being, but meaning 'simply nothing'; or it could be a more pointed formula used within philosophical debate about being and non-being. Looking at the context it seems clear that, in our text, the meaning is absolute 'non-being'. Only God's omnipotence can raise the martyr from death. But there is no indication of an elaborate theory of being and non-being in the background. If the formula of 2 Maccabees 7:28 were directed against the idea of eternal matter, this should be said clearly in the context.

The German scholar G. Schmuttermayer[11] quotes a parallel text which sheds more light on the meaning of 'out of nothing'. Xenophon, the Athenian writer and pupil of Socrates (*c*.426–*c*.350 BCE), asks[12] from which persons children receive most benefits, and he gives himself the answer: from their parents, because these bring forth their children *ek men ouk ontōn*. Nobody will understand Xenophon's remark as a statement on 'non-being' in an ontological sense. 'Out of nothing' here and elsewhere means the beginning of something new, without a visible cause, as it occurs continually in the lower world.

There is a much debated linguistic variation in the Greek expressions translated 'out of nothing' – singular or plural is found, and the two Greek negatives *ou(k)* and *mē* are interchanged, apparently without distinction. For these reasons it is not always easy to know exactly what is meant. It appears also that, even when the philosophical meaning is intended, creation 'out of nothing' could involve a material substrate, since 'something' which did not exist before now comes into being.[13] The evidence is too varied and contradictory in the period before Plotinus to obtain safe results.

Philo

Philo was probably from one of the noble families of Jewish Alexandria and had received an extensive philosophical training. Although for modern scholars he is one of the earliest representatives of Middle Platonism, few contemporary Christians had a full grasp of Philo's sophisticated thinking. It is only in the latter

---

10 The word order *ouk ex ontōn* in no way changes the more common formula *ex ouk ontōn*: BDR §433.3; 2. *Makkabäerbuch*, Habicht (ed.).
11 'Vom Gott unter Göttern zum einzigen Gott'.
12 *Mem.* 2.2.3.
13 Young, 'Creatio ex nihilo'.

half of the second century that the great Alexandrian theologians Clement and Origen show familiarity with Philo's writings.

Philo's ideas of creation are rather vague. He tries to combine biblical and philosophical views of creation, but is not always successful. In his commentary on Genesis 1–3, he contrasts two opposite principles of the universe, one active, one passive. Together they form the world. The visible cosmos is temporal. The hypothesis of an eternal world, or of innumerable worlds, would exclude belief in God's providence.[14] The distinction between an active and a passive principle is probably borrowed from Stoicism.[15] But nothing is said about primeval matter. Philo is reticent on this question. In his final summary, he emphasizes five points: 1. God does exist; 2. God is unique; 3. the world is created; 4. the world is unique: God consumed all existing matter for making the world, so an infinite number of worlds is excluded; and 5. God's providence looks after the welfare of his work.[16] These aspects might well be taken as a compromise between Jewish and Greek teaching. The omnipotence of God is rigorously stressed. On the other hand, the question of eternal matter is merely touched upon and left open. The passage depends on *Timaeus* 32C–33A.[17]

In his work *De specialibus legibus* ('On special laws'), Philo tries to convince his readers of the truth of monotheism.[18] The existence of one supreme God can be shown from the perfection of nature. Our human understanding of the essence of God is never complete. It is an endless process of growing knowledge. God reveals to us as much as we can grasp of it.

Further exploration of Philo's work would not change the general impression. He emphasises the goodness, power and freedom of God, in accordance with scripture, and from time to time speaks of God creating 'out of nothing'. However, he does not draw ontological conclusions from it. Rather, he shows restraint as far as Greek cosmology is concerned. He is well acquainted with Stoic and Platonic thought about the universe, but he does not present a full view of his own ideas. He knows the controversies about the eternity of the world, about the ideas and primeval matter, but he does not take a definite position. There is a tendency towards overcoming the conception of eternal formless matter, but not more. Either Philo did not see that the concept of

---

14 Philo, *Opif.* 7–12.
15 Diog. Laert. 7.134.
16 Philo, *Opif.* 170f.
17 See also the fragment of Philo, *Prov.* 2.50f, quoted by Euseb. *P.E.* 3.21.1–4: Eusebius reads it as a proof-text for the creation of matter; cf. Schroeder and des Places in their edition of *P.E.* 7 (pp. 104–7).
18 *Spec.* 1.13–65.

eternal matter contradicted his own doctrine of divine omnipotence, or he did not want to criticise openly an important Greek idea.

The early church and the rise of heresy

Belief in the one God, maker of heaven and earth, was a precondition of the Christian message. In this respect the tradition did not change. There are reminiscences of the 'creation-out-of-nothing' formula in the New Testament (Rom 4:17; Heb 11:3), but they do not say more than the Jewish parallels. Missionary speeches elaborating the goodness and power of God assume overwhelming evidence (1 Cor 8:4–6; Acts 14:15–17; 17:23–30). But it is to the second century that we must look for more explicit attention to the questions, not least in reaction to groups generally known as Gnostics,[19] whose principal concern may have been the origin of evil,[20] but whose instinct that the whole material world is tainted with evil meant they were involved in cosmological speculations. On the whole, Gnosticism did not reach a markedly deeper understanding of the meaning of creation, but maybe its most important contribution was the widening of the educational horizon of Christian teachers. They proposed at least a few ideas which lead towards a clear conception of creation out of nothing.

Approaching 'creation out of nothing'

Marcion

Marcion, a shipowner from Pontus, came to Rome around 140 CE.[21] He concluded that Judaising Christians had falsified and misinterpreted the Christian message. Like the Gnostics, he adopted the idea of two gods, one the transcendent God, who is goodness by nature and the father of Jesus Christ, the other, the demiurge of the Jewish scriptures, the God of creation, law and punishment. He is not evil, but relentless. Marcion refused any spiritualisation of the Jewish Bible, and so its God shows all the shortcomings, self-contradictions and cruelties which a literal exposition would disclose; these scriptures he rejected, together with Christian books contaminated with such views.

In contrast to the Gnostic myth, the good God has no original connection whatever with the demiurge and his creation. Out of boundless grace and mercy, he offers salvation to the human race, sending his son to the realm of

---

19 See pt III, ch. 12, above.
20 Tert. *Praescr.* 7.5; *Marc.* I.2.2; Epiph. *Pan.* 24.6.1; Euseb. *HE* 5.27; see also Ptolemaeus, *Flor.* 7.8f.
21 See pt III, ch. 9, above.

the demiurge to preach the gospel. Nobody had known anything about the 'alien' God before; and he demanded nothing else but faith in Christ. Marcion's conception, that the good God saves the creatures of the demiurge without any previous connection, can be taken, as by Harnack,[22] as the purest possible form of grace. But the price for this gift is high: it means that the supreme God is excluded totally from creation. He is literally an 'alien' in the world of the demiurge. The problem of divine omnipotence and unity cannot be solved on Marcion's assumptions.

In his first book against Marcion, Tertullian mainly deals with the Marcionite doctrine of God. One chapter is devoted to creation.[23] From this text, full of ironical polemic, we learn that according to Marcion the demiurge made the world out of primordial matter.[24] Moreover, Tertullian discusses the possibility of another creation of the supreme God: if he was a creator, after all, he had to bring forth his own heavenly world either from eternal matter or from nothing. It seems that Marcion might be referring to the classical opposition between making the world out of nothing or shaping it from matter. This would mean that he had a clear concept of creation out of nothing. However, what Tertullian reports are his own conclusions put into the mouth of Marcion. Tertullian, writing after 200, does have a clear idea of creation out of nothing, but this cannot be presupposed for Marcion, fifty years earlier.[25] A last remark of Tertullian seems credible: Marcion imputes evil to matter.[26] From these lines of Tertullian there emerges a triad of supreme God, demiurge and matter. Similar conceptions of the constitutive principles of being can be found in Neo-Pythagoreanism, Platonism and Gnosticism.

Harnack drew the attention of his readers to one of Marcion's famous 'antitheses', showing the difference between the two gods: Elisha, the creator's prophet, needs 'matter' – water – for the healing of the leper Naaman, and this seven times (2 Kgs 5:14); Christ healed a leper by his mere word (Luke 5:12–15).[27] That Marcion deliberately used cosmological language when he described the different creative powers of his gods is possible. Perhaps Marcion envisioned two basic types of creation, each belonging to one of the two gods. The supreme God created the invisible heavenly world alone by his omnipotent

---

22 Harnack, *Marcion*, 121–43
23 Tert. *Marc.* 1.15.
24 *Marc.* 1.15.4.
25 Tert. *Herm.* 2 and throughout: the language on creation resembles that of *Marc.*
26 *Marc.* 1.15.5.
27 *Marc.* 4.9.7; cf. 4.35.4.

word, which means 'out of nothing',[28] while the demiurge depended on a material substrate for his own work as a creator. It is a likely hypothesis that Marcion, trying to distinguish the dignity of the two gods, found the idea of forming the world out of given material decisively inferior to that of creation out of nothing and a contradiction to divine omnipotence. The insight that creation out of nothing is the distinctively Christian way of understanding God's omnipotence, contrary to the doctrine of the formation of matter, marks a new precision in the Christian doctrine of God. During the second half of the second century, the majority of Christian theologians will accept it. Marcion may have been one of the first Christian teachers to discuss the problem of God's absolute power in terms of creation out of nothing, while dismissing the shaping of eternal matter as an inadequate model. Unfortunately the meagre evidence does not allow certainty about Marcion's ideas.

Basilides

The variety of Gnostic mythology and speculation extended to the language of creation. The Gnostic Basilides who lived under Hadrian (emperor 117–38) moved from Antioch to Alexandria, and there became a renowned Christian teacher.[29] The teachings ascribed to him by Irenaeus[30] and Hippolytus[31] seem hardly compatible. We pass over the more conventional report of Irenaeus and turn immediately to the Basilidian myth in Hippolytus' version. The source copied by Hippolytus is a difficult text: it shows corruptions and contradictions. Probably it comes from later Basilidian tradition rather than Basilides himself.[32]

In Hippolytus we find an extreme *theologia negativa*. The beginning quotes the myth of Protagoras in Plato's dialogue: 'There was once a time when there was absolutely nothing.'[33] God, who is himself 'non-being', creates the cosmos by his will and his word out of nothing.[34] Creation is a simultaneous act of God: he produces a 'cosmic seed' which contains the whole created world which will develop in the course of time according to the divine plan. In the context of rather bizarre ideas about 'non-being', we find that Basilides

28 *Marc.* 4.9.7: the formula 'out of nothing' does not occur, but 'by his word alone' has the same implication.
29 Löhr, *Basilides*; see pt IV, ch. 18, above.
30 Iren. *Haer.* 1.24.9–7.
31 Hipp. *Haer.* 7.20–7.
32 For the sake of convenience, the text is quoted here under the name of Basilides.
33 Hipp. *Haer.* 7.20.2, citing Pl. *Prt.* 320c.
34 Hipp. *Haer.* 7.21.4; cf. 22.16.

produces a theory of creation out of nothing, the idea for which we perhaps already found in Marcion. Basilides was the first to use the formula 'out of nothing' in a specific sense. He rejected two possible misunderstandings: there is no emanation out of the 'non-being' God, because there is no substantial outflow from God. Neither does God create the world out of pre-existent matter. As an image for emanation, Basilides mentions a spider producing its cobweb. Against creation out of matter, Basilides argues: God would not differ from a human craftsman, if his creating action was nothing but the shaping of pre-existing stuff. This latter difference was to become a standard argument against all attempts to understand God as a mere demiurge.[35]

From the text which is reproduced in Hippolytus, we may deduce that Basilides (or his pupils), starting from the theology of non-being, had formed in their mind an idea of creation out of nothing which was more precise than the conventional usage. On the other hand, the extravagance of Basilidian thought would explain why it did not, apparently, find followers. Still, Basilides shows that the formula 'creation out of nothing' could be useful for the discussion of God's creative power. One need not be surprised to find the earliest examples of a more pointed use of creation out of nothing in Gnostic literature. The Gnostics had an evident interest in proving the absoluteness of their supreme God. Creation out of nothing for them means that the true God has the power to call into being whatever he wills, breaking all limitations of Greek thought.

The school of Valentinus

Valentinus, a prominent Christian Gnostic teacher, was active in Rome around the middle of the second century, and later perhaps in Cyprus.[36] Of his literary work, only a few fragments have survived. Much richer is our evidence about the Valentinian school. From these texts, we can ascertain the good education and systematic way of thinking of those theologians.[37]

The Valentinian myth, of which several versions exist, begins with a creative act of the supreme God and first aeon, *Bythos* ('depth'). He brings forth the heavenly world (*plērōma*) constituted by thirty aeons. The last and youngest aeon, *Sophia* ('wisdom'), wants to emancipate herself from God. She tries to emanate an aeon of her own, but fails: she only produces a miscarriage, the 'second *Sophia*'. The processes of bringing forth something new in Valentinian doctrine are either described as emanation or as the formation of given material. The Valentinians were convinced that matter was generated in time.

---

35 *Haer.* 7.22.2f.
36 Epiph. *Pan.* 31.7.2; see pt III, ch. 12, above.
37 Markschies, *Valentinus.*

It was not created by a sovereign divine act, but came into being as a byproduct of the fall of *Sophia*. The passions of the 'second *Sophia*' could not simply be destroyed. They had to be transformed by the heavenly saviour, by the 'first *Sophia*' and by the demiurge in a series of successive acts of formation into cosmic substances. The foetus born by *Sophia* in another version of the myth is called formless because there was no male partner to form it with his semen. The author draws on the Aristotelian theory of sexual reproduction.[38] But formation (*morphōsis*) can also mean the Gnostic instruction.

There is only one text in which creation out of nothing appears. In the Coptic *Tripartite tractate*,[39] we read an exuberant description of God's omnipotence: 'nor is there a primordial form, which he uses as a model as he works; nor is there any difficulty which accompanies him in what he does; nor is there any material which is at his disposal, from which he creates what he creates; nor any substance within him from which he begets what he begets.'[40] Here the familiar arguments for creation out of nothing appear: God is neither in need of a model for his work nor of material stuff, nor is there an emanation from his substance. This text probably is not older than the third century. At this time creation out of nothing was no longer an object of debate, but a recognised expression for the boundless power of God.

Plato, Genesis and matter

Justin Martyr

Between 130 and 160, Gnostic teachers could regard themselves as the leading intellectuals of Christianity. During the same period, however, a growing number of theologians belonging to the 'great church' took the offensive against heresy. Connecting philosophical training with biblical insight, they became equal opponents to heretical teaching. The person who represents this gradual change was Justin Martyr.[41] Originating from Samaria, he was a Christian teacher in Rome. Justin wrote on many subjects. He addressed pagans, Jews and heretics, and he tried to win his readers for the Christian faith by means of philosophical arguments, for he was convinced that Christianity was the one true philosophy which had existed before it was split up in different schools.

---

38 Iren. *Haer.* 1.4.1.
39 NHC I, 5.
40 *Tripartite tractate* 53, lines 27–35 (trans. H. W. Attridge and D. Mueller, *NHL*, 61).
41 See pt I, ch. 3 and pt III, ch. 11, above.

Justin lays strong emphasis on the doctrine of creation. His language about God shows unmistakable echoes of Plato. Repeatedly we are reminded of the famous predicates of God from the *Timaeus*: 'Creator and father of this universe'.[42] Justin points out that the Christians and Platonists agree in saying that God, in the beginning, 'created and ordered everything' through his *logos*.[43] This is a conventional formula in the age of Justin. But he can also say: 'God in his goodness created everything from formless matter.'[44] Here Justin clearly follows Platonic teaching. As far as we know, Justin was the first Christian theologian to set out in parallel the Christian story of Genesis and the creation myth in the *Timaeus*. According to Justin, Plato took over the doctrine that God made the cosmos out of unoriginate matter from the opening verses of Genesis.[45] Justin understood Genesis 1:2 as a statement about chaotic pre-existent matter. There is no evidence to support the idea that Justin imagined that matter was created by God before he ordered it. Justin, like other educated Christians of his age, presupposed eternal matter as the stuff of creation. Obviously at this point Justin did not perceive any difference between Christian and Platonist teaching.

There is, however, another important contrast between Justin and Platonism as he understands it. Creation is good; the demons have brought evil into the world. The notion that matter could impose a limit on God's good activity, or that evil could find its basis in matter, is found nowhere in Justin's work. The idea of God working on matter like an artisan on his material simply serves for Justin as a model of the creation process. Beyond this explanatory role, the doctrine of uncreated matter plays no part in Justin's thinking.

Athenagoras of Athens

A little later than Justin, in the seventies of the second century, Athenagoras of Athens wrote his apology: *Legatio pro Christianis* ('Embassy for the Christians'). His book is more sophisticated than Justin's apologies. When he is dealing with philosophy, he is prepared to go much further with a pagan opponent than Justin would have done. The divine *logos* is at the same time the mediator of creation and contains in himself the totality of 'the ideas', the paradigms of creation. Athenagoras obviously understands the creation of the world as a mere shaping of eternal matter, comparing the process of creation with the moulding of clay by the potter. The existence of matter is presupposed, and

42 *Tim.* 28c; literally quoted in 2 *Apol.* 10.6.
43 2 *Apol.* 6.3; cf. 1 *Apol.* 20.4; *Dial.* 11.1.
44 1 *Apol.* 10.2; cf. 1 *Apol.* 67.7
45 1 *Apol.* 59.1–5.

nowhere is its origin discussed. The Platonic scheme of world formation is in no way criticised. For Athenagoras it possesses absolute validity.[46]

The attitude of Athenagoras towards matter and evil deserves special attention. Athenagoras asserts that the devil[47] and the fallen angels have an affinity with matter. Originally they were created to administer parts of the universe, while God himself took over providence for the whole world. Created as free beings, a number of angels turned away from God and became demons. These attack human beings and try to draw them to material things. Here the connection between matter and evil is obvious. However, matter is not thoroughly evil, neither is it the only ground for moral corruption. One may resist the power of evil by making use of the freedom which God has given to his creatures in the beginning.[48]

Tatian

Despite later questions about Tatian's orthodoxy, in his *Oratio ad Graecos* ('Oration to the Greeks', c.165) he defends the truth of the Christian faith in terms of Middle Platonism, and at the same time he bitterly criticises Greek culture.[49] Tatian distinguishes two stages of creation: first, God the Father himself brings forth matter, which is not without beginning like God, nor of equal power with him. Second, after the creation of matter directly through the Father, the *logos* shapes it into the ordered cosmos. Tatian describes the creation of matter using an expression which elsewhere appears as the Valentinian term for 'emanation';[50] perhaps anti-Valentinian polemic is hidden behind this language. Tatian does not speak about creation out of nothing; yet, he is the first Christian teacher to state expressly that matter, the stuff of creation, has a beginning and an end. His words foreshadow the future doctrine that God first created matter and then shaped the universe out of it.

Hermogenes of Antioch

The most ardent champion of uncreated matter was Hermogenes, a Christian painter with theological interests, who seems to have lived in the last decades of the second century, first in Antioch and later in Carthage. We can infer these biographical data from the fact that both Theophilus of Antioch and Tertullian wrote against him. Neither the works of Hermogenes nor the treatise of

---

46 *Leg.* 10.2f.
47 'Archōn ("ruler") of matter': *Leg.* 25.1.
48 *Leg.* 24.6.
49 Hunt, *Christianity in the second century.*
50 *Proballesthai: Orat.* 5.3; 12.1.

Theophilus have been preserved. Tertullian's *Adversus Hermogenem* is our most important source. Hermogenes was not so much interested in the origin of the universe; his primary concern is the origin of evil. While the Gnostics explained the existence of evil in the cosmos by the imperfection of the demiurge, Hermogenes maintains firmly the unity of God and puts evil down to matter.[51] He does not propose a Gnostic but a Platonic solution of the problem. For this reason in modern discussion Hermogenes should not be called a Gnostic, but a Christian Platonist.

Christian theology had by this time become aware of the dangers of dualism. When Hermogenes put forward his ideas, polemic against him started almost immediately. Hermogenes realised the weakness of his argument. He emphasised that matter and God do not share an equal ontological rank. God is Lord over matter. As he is eternally Lord, there must be something for him to be Lord of from eternity. God is incomparable with any other being. His very use of matter for creation is just the proof of his unique power.[52]

Hermogenes finds the biblical proof for his theory in Genesis 1:2: in the sentence 'But the earth was without form and void', 'earth' means matter, the imperfect tense 'was' means eternal duration, and by 'without form and void' the unordered chaotic state of matter is described. In Genesis 1:1 'beginning' also refers to matter, and Genesis 1:2b mentions the four elements.[53]

Matter itself is neither good nor evil, although Hermogenes derives evil from it. If matter were essentially evil, it could not have served God for his creation. Through formation matter has changed for the better, but traces of the original chaotic state have remained in every created being. This explains the presence of evil in the world. Contemporaries called Hermogenes a Platonist. According to modern research, they were right. J. H. Waszink[54] has shown in a careful analysis that most of Hermogenes' thought and terminology have parallels in Middle Platonism. In his exegesis of Genesis 1, Hermogenes follows traditions which go back to Hellenistic Judaism. Parallels are to be found in Philo, Justin, Theophilus of Antioch and Origen.

The heresy of Hermogenes was his bold synthesis of biblical doctrine with Platonism. It went too far beyond the limits which ecclesiastical theology had set. But Hermogenes was not an outsider, as his opponents wished to suggest. Christian intellectuals in the second and third century held on to the opinion that formless matter was a necessary substrate of creation. Clement of

---

51 Greschat, *Apelles und Hermogenes*, 137ff.
52 Tert. *Herm.* 7.1.
53 Tert. *Herm.* 30.1.
54 See his edition of Tertullian's *Adversus Hermogenem*.

Alexandria remained vague, as Philo had been.[55] Tertullian mentions *infirmiores* ('weaker brethren') who could not believe in creation out of nothing, preferring to assume a material substrate like the philosophers;[56] and he counts Hermogenes among other 'heretics with regard to matter',[57] refusing to take them too seriously.

The achievement of the 'Great Church'

Theophilus of Antioch

During the second half of the second century the 'Great Church' began to resist the propaganda of Marcionites and Gnostics more and more rigorously. A dividing line was drawn between heretics and ecclesiastical Christians, some of whom reflected on their own faith and tradition in order to oppose the Gnostic challenge with a better-reasoned view of Christian doctrine. The most important Christian theologians of the time before and around 200 were Theophilus, bishop of Antioch, and Irenaeus, bishop of Lyons (died *c.*200).

Theophilus of Antioch was an influential writer. He was the author of books against Marcion and Hermogenes. They were much read by contemporaries, but are lost to us. Only one work has survived, an apology of Christianity in three books, *Ad Autolycum*. However, what Theophilus says about creation, particularly creation out of nothing, seems to have a carefully thought out doctrine as its basis. Perhaps Theophilus used an older draft or statement as a model. In book I, dealing with God the Father, Theophilus declares: 'God made everything out of what did not exist' (*ex ouk ontōn*).[58]

In his second book,[59] Theophilus gives a critical outline of philosophical teaching about creation. He mainly deals with Plato, using doxographical material. Plato and his school acknowledge that God is ingenerate, 'father and maker of everything'.[60] They assume that God and matter are both ingenerate, and that matter was coeval with God. But if both, God and matter, are ingenerate, then God is not the maker of the universe, and his unique sovereignty (*monarchia*) is not demonstrated. Furthermore, as God is immutable because he is unoriginate, then matter, if it was unoriginate itself, was immutable and

---

55 For Plato calling matter *mē on*, see Clem. Al. *Str.* 5.14.89.3–7; cf. 5.14.92.3.
56 Tert. *Res.* 11.6; cf. *Marc.* 2.5.3.
57 *Herm.* 25.2.
58 *Autol.* 1.4. One need not find here a quotation of 2 Macc 7:28, as Grant suggests in his edition (*Ad Autolycum*, 7), but rather a parallel.
59 *Autol.* 2.4; the following summary partly follows the translation of Grant, *Ad Autolycum*, 22–99.
60 Pl. *Ti.* 28c.

equal with God. It would not be a great thing, if God made the world out of pre-existent matter. 'Even a human artisan, when he obtains material from someone, makes whatever he wishes out of it. But the power of God is revealed by his making whatever he wishes out of the non-existent (*ex ouk ontōn*).' God's unique power of creating out of nothing has its parallel in his unique ability to give life and motion to human beings. God 'made whatever he wished in whatever way he wished'.

In this anti-Platonic passage, Theophilus assembles the basic arguments for creation out of nothing. If matter were unoriginate like God, it would be another God. And if God had made the world out of pre-existent matter, there would be no difference between him and a human craftsman. The model of shaping matter is transcended by God's inexpressible power. This is the meaning of creation out of nothing. The Greek idea that there are natural limits to God's activity does not apply to the God of the Bible. Up to the time of Hermogenes, the central difficulty in the debate about creation was the eternity of matter. From Theophilus onwards the will of God is emphasised as the ground of creation. Creation out of nothing, originally a vague description of God's omnipotence as creator, becomes with Theophilus and Irenaeus a precise statement about the incomparable power of God.[61]

The main part of book 2 of *Ad Autolycum* is an exposition of Genesis 1–11.[62] This lengthy commentary presents Judaeo-Christian theology, as R. M. Grant has often pointed out. The first statement is: the prophets first taught us unanimously that God made everything out of non-being.[63] The biblical foundation for creation out of nothing is, as could be expected, Genesis 1:1–2. Theophilus follows the order of the days of creation, as the Hexaemeron literature since the second century does.[64] Concerning theological opponents, Theophilus is not very outspoken. The polemic against Platonic teaching about God and the world could be aimed at Hermogenes and his Christian Platonism. There are, however, few parallels between the language and thought of Hermogenes, as read in Tertullian, and that of Theophilus. Nevertheless, it is highly probable that for some time in Antioch a battle was fought about the legitimacy of Christian Platonism between Theophilus and Hermogenes. We would like to know more about Theophilus and his writings, but even what we have leaves no doubt that by fostering the idea of creation out of nothing he played an important role in its success.

61 Dihle, *Theory of will.*
62 *Autol.* 2.10–31.
63 *Autol.* 2.10.
64 van Winden, 'Hexaemeron'.

Irenaeus of Lyons

Irenaeus, a Greek from Asia Minor, became bishop of Lyons (c.180) and died about 200.[65] He and his followers were not only uncompromising defenders of the apostolic tradition; they also constructed their own synthesis of biblical teaching, following God's action from creation to the incarnation of Christ, and further to the preaching of the gospel, the foundation of the church, the resurrection of the dead and the second coming of Christ. The purpose of the deeds of God in history is to liberate humankind which is suffering under the rule of sin and to lead it to the true God. His dispositions in history, his covenants with the believers, the announcement of Christ in prophecy – all this is part of the great process of divine education for salvation.

Irenaeus was not especially interested in cosmology. But the controversy with Marcionites and Gnostics made it unavoidable for him to present an outline of ecclesiastical ideas about God and his universe. Irenaeus had received some basic philosophical education, on which he could draw when he discussed monotheism and the problems of creation. He noticed the influence of philosophy on heresy, and his arguments were directed against both. They did not differ much from the teaching of contemporary apologists. God is perfect and the source of all good.[66] God embraces everything and grants existence to all things.[67] As the Unoriginate he stands over against every originate being.[68]

God created the world through the free decision of his will.[69] This statement is directed against Gnostic ideas like the Valentinian doctrine that the demiurge was unconsciously the tool of the saviour and of *Sophia*, or that creation was the work of angels.[70] But Irenaeus goes beyond that: the freedom and will of God are in no way limited or insufficient. Neither does God's power depend on the degree to which matter can be formed. His omnipotence is absolute. Seen from a pagan viewpoint the supreme God may appear no less powerful than the God of the Bible; but in the sphere of the natural order the God of the Greeks can only will the best possible, and his will finds its limits in matter. According to the Christian view, God's freedom and will are unconditioned and boundless. One utterance of Irenaeus sounds even bolder: God 'took from himself the stuff, the pattern and the form for the things he created'.[71]

65 See pt III, ch. 13, above.
66 *Haer.* 4.11.2; cf. 1.12.2.
67 *Haer.* 4.20.6.
68 *Haer.* 2.25.3; 5.5.2.
69 *Haer.* 3.8.3; cf. 4.20.1; 2.1.1.
70 *Haer.* 2.1.1; 2.30.9.
71 *Haer.* 4.20.1; 2.30.9.

This and similar sentences need careful interpretation. It seems that Irenaeus meant to say that God took from himself the material of the created things, their ideal paradigm and their form in the cosmos. But he certainly did not wish to suggest that matter pre-existed in God before creation. We must neither take the Irenaean sentence literally nor overestimate its ontological depth. Irenaeus means to say that God depends on neither matter nor ideas from outside, but himself produces whatever he needs for creation. There is yet another of Irenaeus' ideas to be considered: he can state that 'the will of God is the substance of all things'.[72] This saying must not be understood in terms of ontology either. It simply means that the will of God is by itself its realised object. In his creative activity he is not bound to any outside conditions.

To the Valentinian speculations about the origin of matter, Irenaeus answered with the doctrine of creation out of nothing. He repeats his idea that God had used his will and his power as matter for his work.[73] This statement means that God created matter himself.[74] There is a sharp difference between divine and human creation: human beings cannot create out of nothing, but are bound to use the material given them; the superiority of God over humankind is shown by the fact that he also produces the very stuff of his creation.[75] This had been in essence the argumentation of Theophilus of Antioch. Irenaeus followed him also in deriving Gnostic cosmology from philosophy. Irenaeus names as his sources Anaxagoras, Empedocles and Plato.[76]

Irenaeus concentrates on the most important issues of the debate about creation. He reduces the complicated myth of the Valentinians to a simple structure resembling the Platonic doctrine of three principles of being. This could easily be contested. Against his opponents he argues for the absolute power and freedom of God. In pointed sentences Irenaeus expresses his central ideas: God took matter out of himself and his will is potentially its object. For Irenaeus creation out of nothing is no longer a hypothesis, but it is part of ecclesiastical teaching. Irenaeus finds it in the earlier tradition of the church: *The Shepherd of Hermas*, around 140, was for him the best witness.[77] This interpretation of *Hermas* is a projection – he still holds on to the indefinite Jewish understanding. Irenaeus, however, reads him in the light of his own new understanding.

---

72 *Haer.* 2.90.9; 4.20.1.
73 *Haer.* 2.10.2.
74 *Haer.* 2.10.3.
75 *Haer.* 2.10.4.
76 *Haer.* 2.14.4.
77 Herm. *Mand.* 1.1; see Iren. *Haer.* 4.20.2.

Conclusion

Monotheism was a fundamental article of faith from the beginning of the church. God was defined as omnipotent, as the ruler of the universe, leading the human race on the way to salvation. The Gnostics, however, despised matter as being the source of evil. They devalued the creator God of the Bible, and assumed an absolutely good God in utmost transcendence. The juxtaposition of two gods, however, was against all the tendencies of the time, and would ultimately be marginalised.

'Creation out of nothing' was originally a Hellenistic-Jewish formula expressing the power of the creator God. It was used in a rather imprecise manner. The debate about God's creative work led to two opposing alternatives: 'shaping of pre-existing matter' or 'creation out of nothing'. Despite the difficulties felt in the Greek philosophical tradition, the latter view won. It became the classic Christian formula for expressing the absolute freedom and boundless power of God.

25

Monotheism and Christology

FRANCES M. YOUNG

> If these people worshipped no other god but one, perhaps they would have a
> valid argument against the others. But in fact they worship to an extravagant
> degree this man who appeared recently, and yet think it is not inconsistent
> with monotheism if they also worship his servant.
>
> (Celsus, quoted by Origen)[1]

This theological problem lay at the heart of early Christianity, but explicit
argument about how to deal with it conceptually is not found until the third
century with the 'monarchian' controversies. A model of development has usually been used to trace a process whereby Christian doctrine was formulated.
Here, however, a more dialectical approach is adopted. Doctrinal discourse
was created by argument and counter-argument; conceptual models were
produced in the fires of controversy. To put it another way, for orthodoxy to
be discovered the counter-proposals of heresy were vital. It is in this sense
that the third century is crucial for responding to Celsus' question. As an outsider, he perhaps perceived earlier and more clearly than believers what the
distinctive mark of Christianity was, and how logically absurd it was.

In the writings of the first and second centuries, different portraits and
different expectations are associated with Jesus, many exploring the idea that
in some sense he is the pre-existent agent of the one true God (famously John
1:1–18; cf. 1 Cor 8:6; Phil 2:5–10). Furthermore, the immediate response to
Jesus was one of reverence and awe, and a rhetoric of worship is traceable in
hymnody and confession already in the New Testament.[2] However, believers
seem not to have recognised this as a radical challenge to monotheism. Rather,
in the second century it permitted a highly paradoxical discourse: the invisible
is seen; the impassible suffers; the immortal dies.[3] To attack idolatry and

---

1 C. Cels. 8.12 (trans. Chadwick, Origen: contra Celsum, 460, adjusted for capitalisation).
2 See 'Prelude', above; Hurtado, Lord Jesus Christ.
3 E.g. Mel. Fr. 13 (Hall (ed.), Melito of Sardis: On Pascha and Fragments, p. 80); such antitheses
   are shown to be widespread by Hübner and Vinzent, Der paradox Eine.

defend the one God, creator of all that is, was a key element in the second-century defence of Christianity mounted by the apologists, not least to deflect the charge of atheism, a charge based on their non-compliance with socio-religious conventions across the empire. Christians could not be involved in religious rites that honoured so-called gods who were either non-existent or mere 'daemons' (that is, supernatural beings who misled humans into providing sacrifices for them); but they did worship the one true God, and that God alone, just like the Jews, expecting to face God's ultimate judgement, and recognising that life had to be lived under divine scrutiny. From a Jewish point of view, their coupling of Jesus Christ with God in worship was blasphemy, as is already hinted at in the reports of debates with Jews in John's gospel (John 6:41–59; 8:21–59), and from a philosophical point of view, it was simply contradictory. How could they have it both ways? The apologists undoubtedly imagined they could, as they borrowed and developed an explanatory model in the notion of the *logos*,[4] but their solution was challenged in the third century. The debate would continue into the fifth century and beyond, and out of it would be forged the characteristic doctrines of Christianity: the Trinitarian concept of God and the christological claim that two natures, human and divine, were present in the one Christ.

The second century

To a surprising extent, the second century was preoccupied with other issues. The account of Eusebius, the first church historian (*HE*, bks 4 and 5), is concerned with authors who wrote apologies, with the Bar Kochba revolt and the total destruction of Jerusalem, with notorious Gnostics and famous martyrs, miracles such as the occasion when the 'thundering legion' prayed for rain and the resulting thunderstorm both quenched their thirst and routed the enemy, with the writings of Melito of Sardis, Dionysius of Corinth, Theophilus of Antioch, Irenaeus, and others, with the prophecies of Montanus and the Quartodeciman controversy. Maybe his perspective is truer than the selectivity of those scholars who seek to trace the development of Christology!

Yet theological struggles concerning cosmological issues, which were certainly at stake in the second century,[5] also impinged on the question who Jesus really was. At a remarkably early date we find opposition to the 'docetic' notion that the Christ was a supernatural being who was never fully enfleshed.[6] The

---

4 See pt iv, ch. 22, above.
5 See ch. 24, above.
6 See 'Prelude', above.

heresiologists associate such views with the lineage of those following what they dubbed 'gnosis falsely so-called' using a scriptural tag (1 Tim 6:20). If Christ revealed the true Father, who so transcended the material universe that creation was alien to the divine and produced by a lesser, fallen demiurge, then of course the Christ could not really be born, or suffer and die. Gnostic texts tend to attribute revelatory teachings to the risen Christ, their gospels often not being accounts of the life and teaching of one who existed as a human, historical person.

The stimulus for Marcion's teachings may not have been cosmological, but his contrast between the loving father of Jesus Christ and the judgemental God of the Jewish scriptures had the same effect. The material creation was devalued, and the messenger of salvation came from the superior spiritual world. So the immediate pressures of the second century concerned the defence of the material creation as ultimately the work of the one true God who said it was good. Genesis was a key text in the debates. When Irenaeus[7] composed his great work *Adversus haereses* ('Against the heresies'), he focused on the way Genesis was to be read, and on the saving effect of Christ's 'recapitulation' of Adam's path of temptation so as to reverse his 'fall' by being victorious. The over-arching story of fall and redemption was highlighted to counter appeals to pre-cosmic catastrophes and enable a positive estimate of the created order. The demiurge of Genesis was to be identified as the one true God.

So it is in the context of cosmological debate that the *logos* theology of Justin, Theophilus and other apologists is to be assessed, as also the move towards the doctrine of 'creation out of nothing'.[8] It was essential to make plausible the divine origin, yet created being, of matter, when in the culture in general, matter tended to be denigrated and regarded as unworthy of the divine, or else the divine was regarded as itself material. For matter was often contrasted with spirit, change and 'becoming' with changeless 'being'. Yet this broadly Platonic perspective was offset by the Stoic tendency to see everything as ultimately divine, to regard spirit or fire as the fundamental element from which the created order was distilled and to which it would return. The divine element, itself refined matter and immanent in all things, was the *logos* – that is, order and rationality. The macrocosm was reflected in the microcosm – human nature. To live in harmony with nature was the Stoic aim, the mind directing the body, the *logos* pervading everything. Justin has often been charged with eclecticism, but the second-century apologists, by integrating ideas of

---

7 See pt III, ch. 13, above.
8 See ch. 24, above.

transcendence and immanence from the prevailing philosophies with the legacy from Judaism, actually achieved a remarkably coherent response to the cosmological questions at issue. The way had, of course, been pioneered to some extent by Hellenised Jews before them: the Wisdom of Solomon described God's wisdom as immanent using language reminiscent of the Stoic *logos*, and Philo, the Jewish philosopher, had already explored the concept of *logos* as a complex intermediary between the multiplicity of creation and the unity of God. The apologists were doubtless aware of the prologue to the gospel of John (John 1:1–18), which provided a precedent for their use of *logos* language, even if the originator of that text was far from envisaging what it might lead to conceptually. That John's gospel was apparently a favourite text with Gnostics (the Gnostic Heracleon apparently wrote the first commentary on this gospel) may have enhanced its appropriateness: a non-Gnostic reading was required.

Whatever the amalgam of influences and ideas that contributed to their thinking, the *logos* theologians *incidentally* produced the first christological teaching which could *potentially* deliver a conceptual model capable of explanatory power – *incidentally*, I suggest, because not primarily in response to christological questions as such, but rather to the prevailing cosmological debates; and *potentially*, because sufficiently vague that interpreters with later concepts in their minds can reach opposing conclusions as to exactly what was envisaged.[9] Effectively they treated the *logos*, Stoic-like, as the immanent aspect of the divine in the material created order, whilst also affirming that the ultimate Father and source of all was the one, true, transcendent God. They noted that God created 'by his Word' (Ps 33:6) and read Genesis in the light of Proverbs 8. Thus the *logos* became the instrument through which the transcendent God created, with whom God conferred when he said, 'Let us make humanity in our own image', and through whose presence that image is constituted in human beings. The *logos* was present in Socrates, as well as the Hebrew prophets. But the culmination of God's providential plan, foretold by the Holy Spirit in the scriptures, was the full embodiment of that *logos* in Jesus Christ, restoring to humanity the image of God marred by Adam's disobedience. Thus for the apologists Christ was both human and also God's own offspring, the visible form of the invisible God, God's chosen instrument through whom creation, revelation and redemption were effected, and whose very being derived from the one, true God.

9 E.g. Theophilus' view is interpreted as 'monarchian' by Wallace-Hadrill, *Christian Antioch* and Hübner and Vinzent, *Der paradox Eine*; as 'subordinationist' by Kelly, *Early Christian doctrines*.

Justin's *Dialogus cum Tryphone Judaeo* ('Dialogue with Trypho, the Jew') 61–2 is an instructive indicator of the way this concept was forged out of the conflation of many scriptural passages. Here Proverbs 8:21–36 is quoted in full, as a way of justifying the claim that before all creatures God begat a beginning, and this is named in scripture, now the glory of the Lord, now the Son, now wisdom, now an angel, then God, and then Lord and *logos*. This is confirmed by appeal to Genesis, 'Let us make man in *our* own image', and 'Behold Adam has become as *one of us*.' The deduction is made that there were clearly two involved in the act of creation, and it was the one Solomon calls Wisdom, begotten as a beginning before all creatures, that God thus addressed. Athenagoras[10] and Theophilus[11] likewise identify personified wisdom with the Son of God who is God's *logos*. Scripture was, of course, read with the spectacles of contemporary philosophy and against cosmological speculations (of the Gnostics and Marcion) that so easily undermined the continuity between the prophetic texts received from the Jews and emerging Christian teachings. It provided a way of accounting for the veneration of Jesus within the fundamentally monotheistic outlook which had always characterised Christianity,[12] but its principal purpose was to hang on to the lines anchoring Christian belief in the created order and in the material realities of a genuinely historical life.

Maybe it was this clever but ditheistic concept (Justin at one point even uses the language of 'second god')[13] that provoked Celsus' objection[14] and turned him into the first person we can identify who effectively put his finger on the core theological problem for Christianity. If the pagan, Celsus, had difficulty with it, so would some who saw themselves as believers within the Christian tradition. It was bound to be contested. By hindsight identified as the 'orthodox' tradition, developed by Irenaeus, Tertullian, Clement and Origen, *logos* theology nevertheless had to be defended against rival appeals to scripture and tradition. The so-called monarchian controversies explicitly raised the issues.

The monarchian controversies

Our evidence for tracing the course of the monarchian controversies is confused, not least because the names of leading figures, such as Sabellius and Paul

10 *Leg.* 10.
11 *Autol.* 2.10.
12 Hurtado, *Lord Jesus Christ*.
13 *1 Apol.* 13.3.
14 See pt iv, ch. 11, above, where Droge argues that Celsus was responding to Justin.

of Samosata, were used as labels to condemn rivals in later controversies. Eusebius hardly presents the issues clearly and is vague about events in Rome, which became the epicentre of the debates. A clearer version has largely emerged from the rediscovery in the nineteenth century of the *Refutatio omnium haeresium* ('Refutation of all heresies') attributed to Hippolytus.[15] Important also is a work *Contra Noëtum* ('Against Noëtus'), with the same attribution, and the treatise written by Tertullian, *Adversus Praxean* ('Against Praxeas').

Eusebius[16] focuses on the heretical view, which he attributes to Artemon, that the saviour was merely human, seeing this as revived in his own day by Paul of Samosata. He quotes an unnamed writer who sought to refute this falsehood. From these extracts we may deduce that, when Victor was bishop of Rome (193–202), a certain Theodotus the shoemaker was excommunicated for holding such a view, and under Zephyrinus, Victor's successor, certain disciples of his, including a second Theodotus, a banker, were active in recruiting supporters. They apparently claimed that their teaching was what all earlier generations, including the apostles themselves, had taught, and it had been perverted in their own day. Their opponents contested this by reference to the very different picture in scripture, to the books of Justin, Clement, Irenaeus, Melito and others, which 'proclaim Christ as God and man', and to the liturgical compositions which 'sing of Christ as the Word of God and address him as God'. Another extract accuses these heretics of utilising syllogisms and working with corrupt texts of scripture. Clearly deductive argument was at work. There is no reason to connect this third-century movement with the so-called Ebionites.[17]

It is often assumed that what Eusebius describes was one aspect of a double-sided movement of reaction against *logos* theology, a movement concerned to protect the 'monarchy' of God.[18] Modern accounts have designated the followers of Theodotus as 'dynamic monarchians': Jesus was a 'mere man' *empowered* by God. Alongside this proposal was another, often designated 'modalist monarchianism': this resolved the problems by speaking of the one God appearing in different 'modes', now as Father, now as Son, now as Holy

---

15 For discussion of Hippolytus, see pt IV, ch. 22, and Young *et al.* (eds.), *Cambridge history of early Christian literature*, 142–51.

16 *HE* 5.28.

17 See 'Prelude' and pt II, ch. 4, above, for brief explanations.

18 Novatian, *Trin.* 30, couples together those who say Jesus Christ is the Father himself and those who turn him into a man only, indicating that they notice it is written that there is only one God. So some conclude that Christ is a man, while others argue: if there is one God, and Christ is God, then the Father is Christ; otherwise two gods are introduced contrary to the scripture. Against this, see Hübner and Vinzent, *Der paradoxe Eine*, who trace modalist views back to Melito of Sardis, regarding them as an Asian tradition, evident already in Ignatius, which opposed Gnosticism, especially its divine plurality and docetism.

Spirit. Eusebius gives us no clue about this second approach, but the *Refutatio omnium haeresium* makes clear that the latter was the more serious controversy in the Rome of Zephyrinus and Callistus. It was to oppose this teaching that Tertullian wrote his treatise *Adversus Praxean*, and later it would be indelibly associated with the name of Sabellius, 'Sabellian' becoming a label in the fourth-century Trinitarian debates with which to smear the 'Nicene' party.[19]

Two apparently different 'monarchianisms' would appear to have been addressing the same problem, appealing to some of the same scriptural texts;[20] but, as argument about the person of Christ emerged as a key issue in the third century, these two could be associated together. This is evident in Eusebius' report[21] that Beryllus of Bostra 'tried to bring in ideas alien to the faith, actually asserting that our saviour and Lord did not pre-exist in his own form of being before he made his home among men, and had no divinity of his own but only the Father's dwelling in him'. Origen was sent to straighten out his ideas, we are told, and he did this successfully. The significant point is the association of the two ideas: the saviour was a human being in whom the one God dwelt. This perhaps anticipates the teaching of Paul of Samosata, and already associates a 'modalist' view of God with a 'dynamic' view of the essentially human saviour. Some of Tertullian's arguments in his work against Praxeas also hint at a similar association of ideas.[22] Perhaps the modern distinction, while conceptually helpful, obscures the close association of the two positions.

Be that as it may, Rome under Zephyrinus and Callistus is recognised as the fulcrum of controversies which were also going on elsewhere: the evidence points to Smyrna in Asia, Antioch in Syria, Alexandria in Egypt, Libya and also North Africa. Tertullian suggests that Praxeas (according to him, the first 'modalist' teacher) imported the heresy to Rome from Asia in the time of Victor, Zephyrinus' predecessor. The fullest evidence, however, is provided by the *Refutatio omnium haeresium*.[23] Whoever he was,[24] the author of this work clearly lived through the monarchian controversies in or near Rome, and provides us with a much fuller picture than we have been able to glean from Eusebius.

Noëtus of Smyrna is the prime target of this text. At Rome his ideas were disseminated by someone called Epigonus, and Cleomenes became his disciple.

19 See pt VI, ch. 31, below.
20 Hipp. *Noët.* 3.1
21 *HE* 6.33.
22 *Prax.* 27.
23 *Haer.* bk 9.
24 See pt IV, ch. 22, above; the author of the *Refutatio* will be designated 'Hippolytus', hereafter.

Zephyrinus, the bishop, is described as accepting bribes for conniving at the activities of Cleomenes and then himself being seduced by these opinions. Callistus is closely associated with this move and, as Zephyrinus' successor, accused of continuing to collude with those who are deeply opposed by the author of this work. According to 'Hippolytus', no one is ignorant of the fact that Noëtus claims that the Son and the Father are the same. When the Father was pleased to undergo generation, having been begotten, he himself became his own Son. In this way, Noëtus intended to establish God's monarchy – Father and Son are one and the same substance, not one individual produced by another. To understand the full force of this, it is important to recognise the ambiguity of the word *archē* in Greek – it means both 'sovereignty' and 'beginning', and in philosophy was the long-standing term used to express the 'first principle' or 'source' of all reality. This double thrust indicates the comprehensive way in which it linked notions of monotheism and creation: the one source and ruler of all is the one true God, beside whom there is no other.

'Hippolytus' accuses both Zephyrinus and Callistus of being two-faced, of alleging agreement alternately with both sides of the controversy. Zephyrinus is reported to have said: 'I know that there is one God, Jesus Christ; and except for him I do not know any other that is begotten and amenable to suffering.' On another occasion, however, he affirmed: 'The Father did not die, but the Son', though he called 'Hippolytus' and his associates 'worshippers of two gods'. Sabellius is now associated with these views, and Callistus blamed for this, while the story of Callistus' suffering for the gospel is twisted against him. No credit is given for the fact that, after the death of Zephyrinus, Callistus excommunicated Sabellius – he is still charged with favouring Sabellianism and being an impostor. Like his predecessor, Callistus regards those who support 'Hippolytus' as ditheists. Callistus is presented as teaching that the *logos* himself is Son and himself Father, being one indivisible spirit; the Father is not one person and the Son another, but they are one and the same, all things transcendent and immanent, being full of the divine spirit. The spirit which became incarnate in the Virgin's womb was not different from the Father. Appeal is made to scripture, specifically John 14:11 ('Do you believe that I am in the Father and the Father in me?'). Yet Callistus wanted to avoid saying that the Father suffered, claiming that the Father suffered along with the Son. So 'Hippolytus' mocks his inconsistencies, even suggesting that he is betrayed into the error of Sabellius one minute and that of Theodotus the next. It seems that Callistus was trying to walk a tightrope, recognising the difficulties with *logos* theology and drawn to the monarchianism that seemed at first sight more adequately to represent scripture.

For all this argument about the relationship between Jesus Christ and God the Father, the issues disturbing the Roman church were clearly wide-ranging. 'Hippolytus' turns to criticism of Callistus' lax views on clerical marriage, and refusal to exercise the discipline needed to maintain the purity of the church. Over it all hang suspicions about the administration of church funds and the management of the cemetery (probably the catacomb of Callistus), together with issues arising from persecution, not to mention the offering of hospitality to Christians from abroad who arrive with suspicious books, such as the volume containing the revelations granted to Elchasai. Amongst many other doctrines disliked by 'Hippolytus', this work asserted that Christ was born in the same way as any other human being, had other births in the past, and would have more in the future. The discussion of Elchasai, however, draws 'Hippolytus' away from Callistus to discuss Jewish sects. Now the point of mentioning all this is not simply for completeness. Rather it is to emphasise the fact that it is all too easy to abstract the christological arguments from the general maelstrom of personal rivalries, ethical uncertainties and speculative views of all sorts that were around at the time. Indeed the principal objection to Callistus that 'Hippolytus' had could well have been his attempt to consolidate the 'fractionated' Roman church under a single monepiscopate undergirded by a 'monarchian' theology.[25] Be that as it may, Celsus' question clearly did exercise the church at Rome in the first part of the third century, and there was more sympathy for monarchian views of one sort and another than later historians were comfortable to recount – hence, no doubt, the inadequacies of Eusebius' account.

This may also be the right background for considering the question whom Tertullian was challenging in his work *Adversus Praxean*. There is absolutely no other evidence for a person named Praxeas, and the word could well be a pseudonym – it means 'busy-body'. According to Tertullian, he is referring to the first person to bring this 'wrong-headedness' from Asia to Rome. At first sight this might mean the person 'Hippolytus' calls Epigonus, the disciple of Noëtus of Smyrna. According to Tertullian, however, 'Praxeas' is also puffed up with boasting of his status as a confessor. Given the tales 'Hippolytus' tells of Callistus' exploitation of his imprisonment, it is hard not to wonder whether the nickname may not be a cover for criticism of the future bishop of Rome – Tertullian probably wrote about 213, some six years before Callistus succeeded Zephyrinus.

25 Brent, *Hippolytus*, and *Imperial cult*; see pt IV, ch. 22, above.

The sympathy of three successive bishops for monarchian views explains the seriousness with which both Tertullian and Hippolytus tackle the arguments. For alongside Tertullian's treatise must also be considered the work *Contra Noëtum* that is described in the manuscript as a homily by Hippolytus, archbishop of Rome and martyr.[26] The two works together bear witness to the nature of the arguments, and especially to the key proof-texts from scripture to which appeal was made. Both seem to be earlier than the account from the *Refutatio omnium haeresium* already reviewed, and it has been suggested that Hippolytus was indebted to Tertullian's work.

In these two works, then, we meet the theological arguments used by the opponents of the monarchians to refute their position. Several things are noticeable: (1) recourse to tradition, or the rule of faith, against what is treated as a novelty, a strange doctrine taught by strangers;[27] (2) the centrality of scripture – for both sides, indeed – with exegesis and counter-exegesis, and appeals to proof-texts from both Old and New Testaments; (3) the exposition of *logos* theology as a means of holding together God's oneness and the requirement to acknowledge the 'economy'.

Tertullian's[28] use of the word 'dispensation' (that is, *dispensatio* as the Latin equivalent the Greek *oikonomia*) may perhaps help to capture the meaning: it concerns God's providential 'arrangements', which dispose unity into trinity, creating a plurality without division. He draws attention to the one empire, and the fact that the emperor may share the sovereignty with his son as agent without that sovereignty being divided, even noting that provincial governors do not detract from the single monarchy. So God's monarchy is not divided by the fact that his agents are the Son and the Holy Spirit, and the angels are his ministers. Later[29] he develops the notion that God was alone, yet not alone since he always had his 'reason' within, and this became 'discourse' when God spoke and so created. Thus there was the Word, the Son, a person, another beside God, yet never separated from God, and of the same 'substance', as the shoot is 'son of the root', the river 'son of the spring', the beam 'son of the

---

26 Butterworth, in his edition of *Contra Noetum*, provides a useful discussion of the critical arguments about this work, contesting the notion that it belonged to the missing *Syntagma*, an anti-heretical compendium from an earlier date than the *Refutatio*, and arguing that it is a homily in the 'diatribe' style. It is now widely accepted that the author is not the same as the author of the *Refutatio*: this author will be distinguished from the other by dropping the quotation marks, but, if Brent is right, this work too comes from someone in Hippolytus' school rather than Hippolytus himself.

27 Hipp. *Noët*. 1.1; Tert. *Prax*. 3; see ch. 23, above, for the rule of faith.

28 *Prax*. 2–3.

29 *Prax*. 5–8.

sun'. The Trinity does not challenge the monarchy: the Son is not other than the Father by diversity but by distribution, not by division but by distinction, and there is the third, the Holy Spirit making up this relationship. This is the vital 'economy' which must be affirmed alongside the oneness of God.

Within this discussion, scripture is frequently called in as a witness: 1 Corinthians 15:27–28 speaks of the Son reigning until God has put all his enemies under his feet, and then being subjected himself so that God may be all in all – clearly there are two sharing the monarchy. Proverbs 8:22ff and Genesis 1 are woven into the Stoic-like description of God's internal conversation and the agency of creation. The latter part of Tertullian's treatise will work through the gospel of John to demonstrate the 'dispensation' whereby there are two, yet 'I and the Father are one' (John 10:30). But what is clear – even clearer in Hippolytus' *Contra Noëtum* – is the need to answer the monarchians' appeal to scripture texts, most of them from what Christians were already calling the 'Old Testament'. 'You shall have no other gods but me' (Exod 20:3); 'I am the first and the last, and besides me there is no other' (Isa 44:6); these and other such affirmations lay at the heart of their argument. Baruch 3:35–7 seems to have been a particularly important testimony: 'This is our God. No other will be compared to him. He found out the whole way of knowledge and gave it to Jacob his son and to Israel who is his beloved. Afterwards he was seen on earth and conversed with men.' From this, Hippolytus notes,[30] Noëtus deduced that the God who is the one alone was subsequently seen and talked with human beings, and so he felt himself bound to 'submit to suffering' the single God that exists. Romans 9:5, which seems to describe Christ as God over all, clinches the argument.

Hippolytus, like Tertullian, accepts that there is only one God revealed in scripture, but is not prepared to scrap the 'economy'. The argument is advanced that the texts must be put in context, that other indications in each passage point to Christ Jesus, and other texts are called in to confirm this reading.[31] Both writers are deeply troubled by the notion that the transcendent God comes into being, suffers and dies – this 'patri-passianism' is blasphemy! Tertullian charges Praxeas not only with importing modalism to Rome but also preventing the acceptance of the Montanists. His rhetoric expresses his horror that Praxeas managed two pieces of the devil's business, driving out prophecy and introducing heresy: 'he put to flight the Paraclete and crucified the Father.'[32] It is the 'economy' that allows the invisible and impassible God to

30 *Noët.* 2.5.
31 *Noët.* 4.1–7.7.
32 *Prax.* 1.

become visible and passible in his Son. The gospel of John is used extensively by both authors to demonstrate this 'economy'.

Hippolytus concludes with a telling peroration about the Word who is at the Father's side and whom the Father sent for the salvation of humanity. The Word is the one proclaimed through the Law and prophets, the one who became the 'new man' from the Virgin and the Holy Spirit, not disowning what was human about himself – hungry, exhausted, weary, thirsty, troubled when at prayer, sleeping on a pillow, sweating in agony and wanting release from suffering, betrayed, flogged, mocked, bowing his head and breathing his last. He took upon himself our infirmities, as Isaiah had said. But he was raised from the dead and is himself the resurrection and the life. He was carolled by angels and gazed on by shepherds, received God's witness, 'This is my beloved Son,' changed water into wine, reproved the sea, raised Lazarus, forgave sins. This is God who became man on our behalf – he to whom the Father subjected all things. To him be glory and power as well as to the Father and the Holy Spirit in the holy church, both now and always and from age to age. Amen.

Clearly the arguments were about articulating the implications of scripture and the liturgical confession of the church.

Origen

Contemporary with these controversies in Rome were the early years of the great scholar and thinker of the Alexandrian church, Origen. He apparently made a journey to Rome in the time of Zephyrinus,[33] and so he may have been aware of the controversies raging around at the time. Be that as it may, he developed a complex form of *logos* theology, which probably owed something to his predecessor in Alexandria, the Jewish philosopher Philo, and which, for good or ill, left a legacy for subsequent theologians of the east.

The interpretation of Origen's ideas is fraught with difficulties for a number of reasons. (1) The majority of his works have not been preserved in the original Greek: the later Origenist controversies[34] of the fourth and fifth centuries ensured, in the first place, the translation of a good deal into Latin, though somewhat adulterated by the need to defend his orthodoxy, and in the second, the destruction of his books. (2) The bulk of what he produced was scripture commentaries, where his philosophical ideas are scattered around

---

33 Euseb. *HE* 6.14.
34 Clark, *Origenist controversy*.

rather unsystematically; while his one systematic work, *De principiis* ('On first principles'), survives only in Latin and is not always consistent with views found expressed elsewhere. (3) Hostile reports of his teaching almost certainly distort what he was getting at and the context of his statements. More sympathetic assessments by modern scholars[35] point to the opening of *De principiis* which shows that he was as interested as Irenaeus and Tertullian in upholding the 'rule of faith', while exploring, as an intellectual, things it did not cover. Indeed, it looks as though he tried out various different ideas hypothetically rather than teaching them as dogma – ideas which later were rejected, such as the transmigration of souls, or the ultimate salvation of the devil. As orthodoxy sharpened up, his ideas were bound to come under fire.

So how did Origen think conceptually about the issues of monotheism and Christology? His concerns were not immediately shaped by the monarchians. Rather, Origen had Valentinus, Basilides and Marcion in his sights. Ironically he would later be accused of suggesting like his opponents that the Son was an 'emanation' of the Father, but his underlying conception was a world away from their hierarchy of many pairs of 'aeons'. For Origen there was one mediator, who in himself constituted 'a multitude of goods'. Although not spelt out in so many words, his conception reflects the pattern developed in Middle Platonism: the ultimate transcendent One, who is simple, indivisible, incorporeal and beyond understanding, gives rise to the multiplicity of things through the One–Many or Indefinite Dyad; in other words, a complex unity is the necessary ontological link between the ultimate One and the many existent things which somehow derive from it. This is the role of the many-named Son of the Father.

Scripture seemed to feed this conceptuality. The opening book of Origen's *Commentarii in evangelium Joannis* ('Commentary on John') explores all the various *epinoiai* or titles given to Christ, whether drawn from the Old or New Testament: Wisdom, Word, Life, Truth, Son of God, Righteousness, Saviour, Propitiation, Light of the World, First-born of the Dead, the Good Shepherd, Physician, Healer, Redemption, Resurrection and Life, Way, Truth, Door, Messiah, Christ, Lord, King, Vine, Bread of Life, the Living One, Alpha and Omega – First and Last, Beginning and End, Lion of Judah, Jacob / Israel, Rod, Flower, Stone, a Chosen Shaft, Sword, Servant of God, Lamb, Light of the Gentiles, Lamb of God, Paraclete, Power of God, Sanctification, High Priest. The one *logos* constitutes a plurality, many of these roles being 'relative' – for the sake of our sanctification.

35 E.g. Daniélou, *Origen*; Trigg, *Origen*; Crouzel, *Origen*.

The 'wisdom of God' is a mediating being, a distinct *hypostasis*,[36] yet begotten of God; and the Son of God must be eternal like the Father, for God cannot change – so if he is Father, he must always have had his Son. In Origen's thought the same must apply to creatures – if God is creator, he must be eternally creator. His concern here is not the material creation, which is the divine response to the 'fall' – a school to win back the souls that had failed to sustain their contemplation of God and turned aside, the incarnation being the culmination of this gracious providence. Quite apart from consideration of the material universe, Origen held that the mediating link between the one God and creatures, that is, the many pre-existent 'rational souls' (*logikoi*), is the eternal Son, who is both 'of God' and the '*archē*' ('beginning' or 'first principle') of all creation. He is the life that gives life, the Word or reason which imparts rationality, the wisdom that makes wise. He is both 'the image of the invisible God' and 'the first-born of all creation' (Col 1:15). Whether he really suggested, as implied by *De principiis* 1.2.6, that the Son has the same nature and substance as the Father is a moot point: he seems to have objected strongly to ideas that God was divisible and preferred not to use substance (*ousia*) language because of its material implications. Furthermore, while the mediator's connection to each side is crucial, the distinction between the one God and the mediator is fundamental to his system. The language he used to express the various aspects of this position provides precedents for many different positions in later controversies.[37]

Towards the end of his life Origen wrote a long refutation of Celsus' *Alēthēs logos* ('True word') – it is because he quotes Celsus in order to answer him that we have what Celsus said.[38] Here Origen speaks of offering prayers to God 'through him who is, as it were, midway between uncreated nature and that of all created things'.[39] The Son of God is 'a second God'.[40] In reply to the charge from Celsus that stands at the head of this chapter, Origen[41] refers him to the saying, 'I and the Father are one'; then he immediately safeguards himself from any suspicion of 'going over to the view of those who deny that there are two existences (*hypostaseis*), Father and Son'. He grants that some among the multitude of believers take a divergent view from his own, supposing in their rashness that the saviour is the greatest and supreme God. Monarchianism, then, he now repudiates, quoting against them, 'The Father is greater than

36 Or. *Princ.* 1.2.
37 For discussion see Williams, *Arius*.
38 See pt III, ch. 11, above.
39 *C. Cels.* 3.34 (trans. Chadwick, *Origen, Contra Celsum*, as below).
40 *C. Cels.* 5.39; 6.61; 7.57.
41 *C. Cels.* 8.12.

I'. He insists that 'we worship the Father of the truth and the Son who is the truth; they are two distinct existences, but one in mental unity, in agreement, and in identity of will. Thus he who has seen the Son, who is an effulgence of the glory and express image of the person of God, has seen God in him who is God's image' (alluding to John 14:9; Heb 1:3; Col 1:15; 2 Cor 4:4). Whether this would convince Celsus is a moot point.

The *logos* is God's self-expression, through whom we receive knowledge of God. In many ways, therefore, Origen belongs to the trajectory from Justin and the apologists, through Tertullian and Hippolytus, to later refinements of the *logos* theology tradition. In other ways the overall framework of his thought gave it a distinctive twist, which was not fully appreciated as the debates continued. Many in the east picked up his insistence on a distinct *hypostasis* and shared his tendency to think in terms of an ontological hierarchy, while suspicious of all forms of modalist monarchianism. The Arian controversy would bring to a head many of the unresolved consequences.

A generation later

The monarchian controversies took place between the late 190s and about 220. Some forty years later, there are signs of continuing anxiety about the issues. One is found in the correspondence between Dionysius of Alexandria and Dionysius of Rome. The fact that this is preserved by Athanasius,[42] writing about a century later to clarify the issues at stake in the Arian controversy, is a mark of its future significance. Another is found in the trial and deposition of Paul of Samosata.

The correspondence between the two Dionysii presupposes that complaints have been made to the bishop of Rome about the teachings of the bishop of Alexandria. The Roman Dionysius writes against those who divide and cut to pieces that most sacred teaching of the church, the divine monarchy, making it three powers, separate substances (*hypostaseis*) and indeed three godheads. He acknowledges that reaction against Sabellius' opinions is justifiable: 'for he blasphemously says that the Son is the Father, and the Father the Son'. Yet this should not lead to preaching three gods, dividing the sacred Monad into three substances foreign to one another. The divine Word is united with the God of the universe, as is the Holy Spirit. The divine triad must be gathered up into one, who is the Almighty, the God of the universe. The Son must not be regarded as a 'work', one who came into being like other creatures. Rather

---

42 Ath. *Dion.*; Ath. *Decr.*

he is in the Father as Word, wisdom and power. He was begotten of God, not made. Both the divine Triad and the holy preaching of the monarchy are to be preserved. Dionysius of Alexandria defended himself, admitting he had used some unfortunate analogies, and asserting that he later dwelt on truer examples. He compared human generation, the transmission of the parents' own nature, yet the parents are different from the children. He spoke of a plant issuing from a seed or root – different from its source yet absolutely of the same nature. The river and its spring are similar. Thus both try to steer the middle way, with the spectre of Sabellianism a common enemy. Both agree that, even though not scriptural, the term *homoousios* ('of one substance') is an acceptable word for what they are trying to articulate.

Homoousios would become the divisive term fought over throughout the fourth century. It was convenient to Athanasius that he could quote precedents for accepting it, especially since there are hints in the third-century evidence that the term was at issue when Paul of Samosata was deposed. Determining what happened at the Council of Antioch is one of the great challenges of historiography.

We begin with Eusebius' account.[43] Paul became bishop of Antioch around the same time as Dionysius became bishop of Rome. He is introduced as holding 'low, degraded opinions about Christ, in defiance of the church's teaching, regarding him as in his nature just an ordinary man'. Bishops gathered twice, possibly three times. They came from Asia, Syria and Palestine, though Dionysius of Alexandria in Egypt was too old and ill to attend. This was clearly more than a local synod. From the final meeting (268 CE) a letter was sent to all the provinces of the empire, though addressed to the bishops of Rome and Alexandria where Dionysius' successor was by now installed. Eusebius claims to reproduce this letter, though in fact he offers just selections, which cover a multiplicity of charges about lifestyle without divulging what the 'spurious and bastard doctrines' were that he promulgated. Paul was clearly a powerful public figure, and this is turned into accusations of seeking worldly honours and courting popularity, along with misappropriating church funds, blackmail and taking 'spiritual brides'. The one hint as to his doctrines appears when the subject is his liturgical innovations and preaching style: his followers say that 'their blasphemous teacher is an angel come down from heaven' whereas he will not admit that the Son of God came from heaven, but claims that Jesus Christ is 'from below'. After his excommunication, we are told, Paul refused to hand over the church building to his appointed substitute. Appeal is made

43 *HE* 7.27–30.

to the emperor Aurelian, who decided that the building belonged to those who would receive a letter from the bishops of Italy and Rome. Eusebius is scathing about the fact that Paul was thrown out by the secular authority, but in these events we can discern precedents for the ecumenical councils of Eusebius' own day, as well as the involvement of the emperor in the church's affairs.[44]

In later sources, Greek and Syriac, Paul's teaching is consistently associated with the formula 'Christ was only a man.'[45] Yet extant fragments from the dispute[46] show that this is an over-simplification. Ranged against Paul were the followers of Origen. Dionysius of Alexandria undoubtedly stood in the same tradition. Against this, Paul insisted that Father and Son are numerically identical. God is a solitary monad, whose Word remains within the divine self until it is uttered. Indeed, he would not accept that the Word, even when uttered, became a distinct *hypostasis* or person, and possibly used the term *homoousios* to convey this, though the sources are not entirely clear on this.[47] According to Epiphanius' report of Paul's teaching,[48] the Son of God is not a subsistent entity, but is in God himself, as indeed Sabellius, Noëtus and others taught as well – though Paul's doctrine is different from theirs, he adds. For while the Father and the Son are one God, the human being below is a distinct person; Jesus was a human being, and the Word from above inspired him. One fragment runs as follows: 'The *logos* was greater than Christ; for Christ became great through wisdom. The *logos* is from above; Jesus Christ is a man from here. Mary . . . bore a man like us, but greater in all respects since he was from the Holy Spirit.' It would appear, then, that Jesus was a man inspired by the wisdom or *logos* of God; and the *logos* of God is none other than the one God, the solitary Monad. So Paul probably evidenced some characteristics of both monarchian doctrines.[49]

Thus controversy drove the impulse to move from the rhetoric of devotion and confession to that of definition and doctrine. This tendency to try to shape a theological discourse of precision made the church a different kind of social organisation from most religious associations of the ancient world. Cultic practices did not normally carry 'teachings', the denial of which meant exclusion.

44 See pt VI, ch. 30, below.
45 Wallace-Hadrill, *Christian Antioch*; pp. 71f have a useful collection of quotations.
46 De Riedmatten, *Les actes*, collected the fragments.
47 The sources differ as to the use of *homoousios*: Hilary, *Epistula de synodis* 81 is probably to be preferred over Ath. *Syn.* 45. So Lampe in Cunliffe-Jones and Drewery, *History of Christian doctrine*, 88.
48 Epiph. *Pan.* 65.1.6; 7.1.
49 So Bardy, *Paul de Samosate* and De Riedmatten, *Les actes*, against Loofs, 'Paul von Samosata'.

Characterised by 'doctrine', the church was much more like a philosophical school, and different schools held various opinions (*haereses*) about the way things are. The church, however, was impelled towards unity, so that 'ironically' deviant teachings had to be excluded, and debates continually demanded decisions about what conformed to the true tradition and what did not. It was this dialectical process of determining the truth through argument which gives the impression that doctrine 'developed'. Yet a better perspective would be that of a community formulating an agreed discourse into which new converts and new generations were educated. This way of viewing the matter makes it far from surprising that early Christianity spawned philosophical schools,[50] and eventually developed a *paideia* of its own to rival that of the Graeco-Roman schools.[51]

50 E.g. in Rome; see pt IV, ch. 22, above.
51 See ch. 27, below.

26

Ecclesiology forged in the wake
of persecution

STUART GEORGE HALL

The Decian persecution and its immediate effects

The persecutions under the emperor Decius (249–51 CE) divided the churches and had lasting consequences for the way the church was perceived and organised. Before 250 CE, Christians had been persecuted from time to time. The severity and extent varied greatly, and the legal basis remains uncertain. Although there were occasional imperial rescripts or other enactments, local popular feeling and the personal attitude of local officials (always susceptible to bribes) usually determined events.[1] When the Emperor Decius had defeated his predecessor Philip (244–9 CE) in September 249, he decreed that all citizens should offer sacrifice to the gods.[2] It was not a specifically anti-Christian decree: only the worship of the gods, not renunciation, was the subject of the *libellus*, or certificate of sacrifice, which every citizen had to obtain from the examining tribunal.[3] Notable bishops fell victim: Fabian of Rome on 20/21 January 250, Babylas of Antioch soon after, and Alexander of Jerusalem died in the Caesarea prison.[4] Euctemon of Smyrna was probably not the only bishop who sacrificed, and persuaded others to do the same.[5] Dionysius of Alexandria and Cyprian of Carthage went into hiding, and tried to restore the situation, as hundreds, perhaps thousands, of Christians across the empire defected or dissimulated: both these bishops describe the rush to get certificates by making the required public offerings.[6] Decius had decreed the most systematic attempt ever made to enforce religious conformity, and, as far as the Christian

---

1 Bähnk, *Von der Notwendigkeit des Leidens*, 53–6, and generally Frend, *Martyrdom and persecution*, and pt VI, ch. 28, below.
2 The actual edict does not survive. Sage, *Cyprian*, 178–81, refutes the notion, adopted by Frend, *Martyrdom and persecution*, 406–7, that there were two phases or edicts.
3 Convenient examples in English translation in Stevenson and Frend, *New Eusebius*, 214–15, based on texts in Knipfing, 'libelli', 363ff.
4 Euseb. *HE* 6.39.1–4.
5 M. Pion. 15, 17 (Musurillo, 157, 161).
6 Cypr. *Laps.* 8–9 (see Bévenot, *St Cyprian*, 12–15); Dionysius in Euseb. *HE* 6.41.10–12.

population was concerned, had considerable success. Persecution petered out when barbarian incursions distracted the emperor, and he perished on the northern frontier in June 251.

The church in Rome could not appoint a bishop for fourteen months. The problem of mass apostasy was, however, pressing, and the remaining clergy in Rome and Carthage were obliged to make decisions. Multitudes who had been brought up as Christians had lapsed, and found themselves excluded from the benefits of church membership. Excommunication was a grave matter. While it carried with it the threat of spiritual damnation, its physical and social consequences were more immediate and pressing than would be the case in modern western Christianity. The local church was a household, a *familia*, which made mutual provision for the sick, the widowed, the orphaned and the elderly, and for the decent disposal of the dead. The lapsed therefore sought ways to get themselves restored. Surviving clergy themselves might be compromised. Cyprian from his hiding place had first to justify his flight: the Roman clergy sent a document without a named addressee to Carthage explicitly criticising faithless shepherds who forsake the sheep.[7] Cyprian, whose writings and correspondence are our chief source of information, replied by praising their martyred bishop Fabian and questioning the authenticity of the text he received. He would however consistently defend the right of Christians to flee from persecution, even regarding it as a form of confession; in this he differed from Tertullian, who had condemned flight as apostasy.[8]

Three further letters from Rome were penned on behalf of the clergy by Novatian.[9] An important figure, he was a Roman cleric who wrote fluent Latin, and had theological gifts that were acknowledged even by his opponents.[10] From his considerable output the few surviving works include *De Trinitate* ('On the Trinity'), unrivalled in surviving Roman theology of the period. Given the multitude of disputes over the persons of the Godhead which divided the church in Rome in the time of Callistus I and Hippolytus,[11] Novatian may have been responsible for the absence of such doctrinal controversy from the later conflicts.[12] He was a presbyter under bishop Fabian, and came to the fore in the vacancy caused when Fabian fell an early victim to the persecution

7 Cypr. *Ep.* 8.1, citing John 10:11–12.
8 Cypr. *Ep.* 59.6; Bähnk, *Von der Notwendigkeit des Leidens*, 296.
9 Cypr. *Ep.* 30, 31, 36.
10 See the complimentary epithets for Novatian in Cornelius *apud* Euseb. *HE* 6.43.7 and Cypr. *Ep.* 55.24.
11 Kelly, *Early Christian Doctrines*, 109–26; Hall, *Doctrine and practice*, 75–80.
12 See pt IV, ch. 22, and ch. 25, above.

instituted by the emperor Decius in 250. All Novatian's letters support Cyprian's stand against the ready reinstatement of lapsed Christians. Those who had fraudulently or by bribery obtained certificates of sacrifice were as guilty as those who actually sacrificed; the wave of requests for reinstatement based on the recommendation of confessors was to be rejected.

Sinners and confessors

When it came to the restoration of a penitent sinner, practice varied. The repentance of the baptised is clearly envisaged in some early documents.[13] The curing of sinful members by repentance is systematically urged upon the churches in the figurative revelation to Hermas in the mid-second century.[14] Where restoration was permitted, it involved penitential behaviour such as fasting, almsgiving and attendance for prayer among the catechumens for a matter of years before final restoration. The young Tertullian argued in *De paenitentia* ('Repentance') for one opportunity to repent after baptism, exactly the position of Hermas. Later, approving the severity of the New Prophecy (so-called 'Montanism'), he repudiated Hermas and argued in *De pudicitia* ('On modesty') that the church had no authority to remit post-baptismal sins, except hypothetically by the decision of a body of prophets. After the Decian calamity, churchmen were faced with the need to find a policy which would match the situation. One way forward related to the standing of confessors and martyrs. These terms (*confessor* = *homologētēs*; *martyr* = *martys*) were both applied to those who attested their faith by suffering and were often used interchangeably. A stricter definition, now conventional, had already begun to arise, whereby a martyr had died in bearing witness to the faith, whereas a confessor had suffered trial, torture or imprisonment, but had survived, or was so far surviving. In the Decian persecution few executions took place: death occurred as the result of torture, or very commonly of imprisonment.[15] Prisoners were deprived of food and drink, perhaps in order to persuade them to yield. Public confession brought such esteem among the faithful that not only were martyrs commemorated annually, but confessors were specially honoured: they enjoyed the same privileges as presbyters, and could be appointed deacon or

---

13 Matt 18:15–17; Rev 2:5 etc.; 1 *Clem.* 57–8.
14 E.g. Herm. *Vis.* 2.2 (6.1–8); 4.2 (23.5; 30.2); thorough presentation of evidence in Schneider, '*Propter sanctam ecclesiam suam*'.
15 Sage, *Cyprian*, 186–9.

presbyter without an ordination rite.[16] Such veneration is related to certain biblical texts, where the gift of the Holy Spirit is promised to those who bear witness to Christ before judges (Matt 17:17–20), or the martyrs will themselves share in Christ's reign and judgement (Rev 20:4). It was held that a confessor had the spiritual authority to remit sins, or at least to commend a penitent to the clergy for forgiveness. This happened conspicuously in the prison at Lyons in 177.[17] Tertullian repudiated this practice, arguing that a martyr atoned for his own sins alone.[18]

In Cyprian's church the confessors played a key role. In hiding in 250, and especially on his return to Carthage in the early spring of 251, he found that men who had spent some time in the prison were recommending not only serious penitents, but relatives and friends, and were issuing certificates of reconciliation to those who petitioned them.[19] Cyprian took care to praise such confessors, even while criticising their actions. His initial judgement was to urge caution: none should be rashly or immediately restored to communion. This was a view shared and supported by the Roman clergy with whom he corresponded,[20] and by a group of confessors there, to whom he had written encouragingly in their imprisonment as he did to those in Africa.[21] Cyprian would sum up his arguments in a weighty tract, De lapsis ('On the lapsed'), in which the gravity of defying the divine law is argued, and the dangers of defiance picturesquely described. Worldliness and attachment to property had caused many to fall, says Cyprian, as had the threat of torture. Now without any expiation of the crime those who had sacrificed try to take Christ's body and blood, and the clergy who connive are sacrilegious. Even martyrs and confessors cannot grant what is against God's law. Those who got certificates without actually sacrificing are guilty before God. To the heartily penitent, he holds out hope at the end: God 'can grant mercy; he can revoke his own sentence; the one who repents, does good and prays, he can in clemency forgive; he can take into consideration what martyrs have asked and clergy have done for such people'.[22] This tract was apparently presented at a council when Cyprian returned to Carthage and faced the five presbyters, and two

---

16 Hipp. Trad. ap. 10.
17 Euseb. HE 5.1.11–13, 32–5, 45–6; Hall, 'Women', 12–13.
18 Bähnk, Von der Notwendigkeit des Leidens, 213–20.
19 See Cypr. Ep. 23, on the figure Lucian who wrote in the name of a fellow confessor, Paulus, now dead (as reported to Rome in Ep. 27.1).
20 Cypr. Ep. 30 (penned by Novatian for the Roman clergy).
21 Cypr. Ep. 15; 28.
22 Cypr. Laps. 35.

others (Novatus[23] and Felicissimus), who had taken over the church in his absence, and who were responsible for the mass reconciliation of the lapsed, to which Cyprian was opposed.[24]

Ecclesiology and episcopacy

Already the outlines of Cyprian's ecclesiology were apparent: whatever authority or privilege God might grant to confessors, the fundamental structure of the church rested in the duly appointed bishops, in whom final authority was vested, and whose voice as priests God would hear.

> Our Lord, whose instructions we ought to dread and observe, setting forth the honour of the bishop and the organisation (ratio) of his church, speaks in the gospel and says to Peter: 'I say to you that you are Peter, and upon this rock I will build my church, and the gates of the underworld will not conquer it, and to you I shall give the keys of the kingdom of heaven, and things which you bind on earth shall be bound also in heaven, and whatever you set free on earth shall be set free also in heaven.' [Matt 16:18–19] Thence through the changes of times and successions the ordination of bishops and the organisation of the church have come down, so that the church is established upon the bishops, and every act of the church is directed by those same superiors (praepositos).[25]

Such was the office of bishop as Cyprian saw it. There was a network of congregations throughout the empire which corresponded in organisation to the empire itself. Each bishop was responsible for his local church and its members, for their conduct and their welfare, physical as well as spiritual. He was answerable to his superior in the metropolis, and the metropolitan bishop usually to the greater see nearby, not only for himself, but for those in his charge. The bishops of the greater sees were in communication with each other. It was already the practice that, to make a new bishop, three bishops were needed, normally with the authority, if not the actual presence, of the metropolitan.[26] An efficient metropolitan needed to keep an accurate written record of ordinations and correspondence, of synods and of judgements. The bishops thus constituted an empire-wide bureaucracy in parallel with that of the empire itself. In an imperial centre like Rome, Alexandria or Syrian Antioch,

23 Not to be confused with Novatian.
24 Cypr. *Ep.* 41–3; for Novatus, see Cyprian's hostile portrait *Ep.* 52.2.
25 Cypr. *Ep.* 33.1 (my translation).
26 So Novatian got three bishops to ordain him (Cornelius *apud* Euseb. *HE* 6.43.8–9).

the church or churches were presided over by a bishop of great influence, who not only governed in the city, but supervised neighbouring areas. This hierarchy had not always been there, though the seeds of it are as early as the territorial role attributed to Titus in the New Testament (Tit 1:5). Divine authority had been claimed for duly appointed bishops by Clement of Rome,[27] then in the Ignatian letters for a single bishop in each church.[28] Irenaeus saw the succession of bishops or 'elders' of the apostolic sees, particularly Rome, as guarantors of the genuine tradition of doctrine as against heretical deviation.[29] This thought was enthusiastically reasserted in North Africa by Tertullian,[30] and became central to the thinking of Cyprian. His most elaborate statement occurs in the book *De catholicae ecclesiae unitate* ('On the unity of the catholic church'), produced in 251, and prompted first by the schism in his native Carthage, but applied to a graver one in Rome.

The challenge of Novatian

We know little about the choice in Rome of Cornelius to succeed the martyr Fabian in the spring of 251. Cyprian says he did not rise suddenly, but had been 'promoted through all the ecclesiastical offices'.[31] Lifelong clergy like Cornelius probably resented the brilliant Novatian, who had emerged as leader during the emergency. Cornelius favoured compromise when it came to reinstating the lapsed, be they clergy or laity, and he needed defending against allegations of laxity.[32] For whatever reason, soon after Cornelius' ordination Novatian rose as champion of the gospel and was ordained by three Italian bishops, with the support of a body of Roman clergy, four or five confessors, and Novatus, who had arrived from Carthage. Cornelius and Novatian both notified other leading bishops. Dionysius of Alexandria supported Cornelius, and pleaded with Novatian to recant.[33] Fabius of Antioch apparently supported Novatian, and received remonstrations from Cornelius and Dionysius; he died soon after.[34] Cyprian sent an investigative team to Rome, an act of hesitation which required some diplomatic explanations to Cornelius.[35] It was embarrassing for

27 1 *Clem.* 40–4.
28 E.g. Ign. *Eph.* 2–6, 20; *Smyr.* 8.
29 Iren. *Haer.* 3.3–4.2.
30 *Praescr.* 20–2.
31 Cypr. *Ep.* 55.8.
32 Cypr. *Ep.* 55.11–12; note passim *communicare sacrificatis*.
33 Euseb. *HE* 6.45.
34 Euseb. *HE* 6.41.1; 43–4; 46.3–4.
35 Cypr. *Ep.* 44–5.

the champion of discipline to align himself with the laxer party at Rome and against the more rigorous Novatian. But the law of the church must prevail, he says: once Cornelius was duly appointed by bishops, most of the clergy and the voice of the laity, there was no vacancy, and Novatian was outside the church and not a bishop.[36]

Councils in Rome and Carthage met in the summer of 251 to resolve the outstanding issues. No formal records have survived, but the foremost topic was the discipline of the lapsed. In an important letter to a bishop tempted by Novatianism, Cyprian explains their conclusions. Christians are not like the Stoic philosophers, who regard all sins as equal and the good man as impeccable. The lapsed who desire remission are not so much dead as half alive, as the recommendations of martyrs and confessors indicate.[37]

> But since there is in them that which with subsequent repentance (*paeniten-tia*) might be restored to faith, and strength growing from repentance might be armed for valour . . . therefore it was determined . . . that, after indi-vidual examination, those who had received certificates (*libellatici*) should be meanwhile admitted; that those who had sacrificed should be helped at their end, for 'there is no confession in the underworld' [Ps 6.5], nor can any be urged to repentance, if the reward of repentance is taken away. If conflict [i.e. persecution] should come again, he will be found strengthened by us for the battle; but if before battle disease grows fierce, he departs with the solace of peace and communion.[38]

The final judgement of hearts and minds remains only God's, he adds. Cyprian later makes it clear that the deathbed reconciliation applies only to those who were already penitent, and have shown genuine remorse.[39] These decisions of the episcopal council in Carthage were approved by Cornelius in Rome, who had himself gathered a large council with similar results.[40] Records of both councils were sent to Dionysius of Alexandria, and in the east a widely supported episcopal council came to similar decisions, and rejected Novatianism, appointing one of their own mind to fill the place of the deceased Fabius of Antioch.[41] There would be a further development, when persecution again threatened, and an African council decreed the reception of all penitents back into the fold, so as to be prepared for impending martyrdom.[42]

36 Cypr. *Ep.* 55.8.
37 Cypr. *Ep.* 55 (*ad Antonianum*), 16.
38 Cypr. *Ep.* 55.17.
39 Cypr. *Ep.* 55.23.
40 Cypr. *Ep.* 55.6.
41 Euseb. *HE* 6.43.3.
42 Cypr. *Ep.* 57.

The outcome of all this was not so much to introduce new and more worldly standards (apostates and serious sinners had on occasion been reconciled in the past), as to strengthen the position of the bishops both individually and corporately. The role of the bishop as arbiter of membership, admission and exclusion in the local church was asserted, against the alternative of charismatically gifted confessors and martyrs: he was Peter, to whom the Lord had given the keys of the kingdom. But the standing of bishops gathered in council to resolve new issues corporately was also enhanced. This brings us to another issue.

De unitate ecclesiae

In the summer of 251, Cyprian had to deal not only with resolving the problem of the lapsed, but with the divisions in the churches which it had caused. His own church had been taken over by dissident presbyters, who found a leader in the deacon Felicissimus and went on in 252 to make one of themselves, Fortunatus, a bishop. At the same time one Maximus, who had led Novatian's delegation to North Africa, was also ordained bishop by his party, and seems to have had some support across the African provinces.[43] Support for Novatian continued, if diminished, in Rome and other provinces, and his high-principled church would last for some centuries. These divisions called forth Cyprian's important tract, *De catholicae ecclesiae unitate*, probably first presented at the council in 251. It does not specify the adversaries criticised, but constitutes a general criticism of schism, of division from what he perceived as the one true church. He begins by characterising schism and heresy as diabolic deceit: the devil dresses as an angel of light to deceive true believers (2 Cor 11:14). Schism is Antichrist. Once more he begins with the Petrine text of Matt 16:18–19.[44] Cyprian had used the same text in *Epistula* 33 to establish the bishop's unique authority. Here his exposition has come down to us in two versions, reflecting a complicated history. Both appear to be written by Cyprian, and both interpret St Peter's position as symbolic of the unity of the church.[45] One, the 'primacy text', emphasises that there can be no faith outside the unity of Peter and no church other than the one founded upon his throne: only those acknowledged by the bishop belong. It focuses totally upon Peter, directed by Christ to feed his sheep (John 21:17). Other apostles have equal power, but Christ

43 Cypr. *Ep.* 59.9.
44 Cypr. *Unit. eccl.* 4.
45 Important treatment in Bévenot, *Cyprian, de lapsis* (OECT), x–xvii, 60–7.

set up one throne (*cathedra*) and by his authority appointed one source and principle of unity. The others were indeed what Peter was, but a primacy (*primatus*) is given to Peter and one church and one throne are shown.

This has nothing to do with claims to Roman primacy (as was later to be alleged). It is directed against those in the Carthaginian church who tried to act independently of Cyprian their bishop, and against others like them. The longer 'received text' is concerned with the solidarity of the bishops, foreshadowed in the fact that Jesus commissioned one man, Peter, first (Matt 16:18–19), and later all the apostles (John 20:21–3). 'The other apostles were indeed what Peter was, endowed in equal measure with honour and power; but the beginning proceeds from oneness (*unitate*) so that the church of Christ may be shown as one.' Cyprian emphasises that it is the special duty of bishops to preserve the unity of the church by their brotherhood, to prevent any falsehood. This longer version is probably a revision designed for presentation at a council of bishops, such as that held in the summer of 252, when the local dissidents set up their rival bishop of Carthage, and the agents of Novatian were actually promoting an alternative episcopate in Africa.[46]

At chapter 5 the text of *De unitate* becomes unanimous again with the vision of the episcopate as a unity and the church spreading from its single centre over all the earth. Various scriptural arguments follow, emphasising the predicted evil of false prophets in the church,[47] denying that sectaries meet in Christ's name,[48] claiming that even martyr-death in schism is worthless, since such victims are out of charity,[49] and expressing no surprise if even confessors are deceived into sin.[50] Cyprian ends with a rousing call to unity, charity and vigilance so as not to be overcome by the devil's wiles.[51]

Schism in the church thus led Cyprian to articulate an ecclesiology promoting a concrete notion of the unity of the church, bonded in time and space by the spiritual authority of bishops duly appointed in succession from the apostles and in unanimity with each other. Individual believers might err and sin gravely, but in the bishop they had one who was judge and pastor, his judgements warranted by the unanimity of the worldwide episcopate. The bishops were the priests of divine appointment, for whom the exclusive rights

46 Bévenot dates it later, during the baptismal controversy.
47 Cypr. *Unit. eccl.* 10–11.
48 Cypr. *Unit. eccl.* 12.
49 Cypr. *Unit. eccl.* 14.
50 Cypr. *Unit. eccl.* 20–1.
51 Cypr. *Unit. eccl.* 25–7.

and duties of the Aaronic priesthood of the Old Testament were the model and rule. An act of idolatry or of schism made the priest ritually unclean, unable to perform any spiritual acts. Spiritual acts included especially the offering of the eucharist (now freely spoken of as a sacrifice) and baptism; but it included other things such as ordination and (of course) remission of sins. This concept would soon be severely tested.

Baptism and unity

By 256 both Cornelius and his successor had died, and a new bishop, Stephen, governed the church of Rome. He took positions at variance with those of Cyprian, positions which we know only from Cyprian's own letter collection. First, there was the question of allowing suspect or erring bishops to continue in office. Cyprian had already made clear his view that a bishop who committed idolatry or schism ceased to be a priest.[52] The second dispute between Cyprian and Stephen concerned whether those baptised in heresy and schism, including Novatianism, are to be treated as already baptised, or subjected to the church's baptism.[53]

Cyprian's first approach to Stephen is tactful and respectful.[54] He enclosed copies of earlier letters, and argues his usual position, that only the one church can baptise; since Novatian is outside the church, he cannot be reckoned a bishop.[55] Cyprian himself raises the matter of the baptismal creed, which for him included the phrase, 'forgiveness of sins and eternal life through the holy church'. This is a fraud when said by Novatianists, since they have not the church.[56] The heretics do not possess the Holy Spirit, and so cannot bestow him in baptism.[57] But he also notes that the matter 'seriously affects both priestly authority and the unity of the catholic church, as well as the dignity deriving from its institution by divine appointment'.[58] This is undoubtedly true, since the unanimity of the bishops is crucial to Cyprian's ecclesiology,

---

52 Significant cases include that of Trofimus (Cypr. *Ep.* 55.2.1 and 11.1–3, with Clarke's notes (*Letters*, vol. III, 35–40 and 167–84)); the Spanish bishops, Basilides and Martial (*Ep.* 67.6.1–13); and Marcian of Arles, who supported Novatian (*Ep.* 68; Novatian's own part in this is unknown (see *Ep.* 55)).

53 Cypr. *Ep.* 69.1.1.

54 Cypr. *Ep.* 72.

55 Cypr. *Ep.* 69.3.

56 Cypr. *Ep.* 69.7.

57 Cypr. *Ep.* 69.11. In *Ep.* 71 he rejects the claim that acceptance of heretics without rebaptism is an ancient custom.

58 Cypr. *Ep.* 72.1.1.

and the impending difference with Stephen affronts it. With it, he broaches the new topic, which shews that Novatianists were partly in mind: presbyters and deacons who have left the church for heresy, having rebelled against Christ, can on repentance be received back and pardoned, but only as laymen, not as clergy.[59] Stephen was perhaps more flexible. The argument advances further in Cyprian's letter to bishop Jubaianus.[60] Jubaianus had pointed out the coincidence between Novatian's baptismal practice and Cyprian's. Cyprian can shrug this off: Novatian apes the church, but what he does is irrelevant.[61] This information that Novatian held the same view as Cyprian is, however, important, as we shall see, for understanding Stephen's attitude. Cyprian continues by affirming that his policy is traditional, having been settled for Africa in the time of bishop Agrippinus, probably early in the third century.[62] Cyprian also has to deal with a document, forwarded by Jubaianus, which argued that, whoever might have conducted a baptism, the candidate received forgiveness of sins on the strength of his faith, and that even Marcionites did not need baptism, having been baptised in the name of Jesus Christ.[63] This discussion makes it plain that it is not only Novatianist baptism which is under debate, but also, perhaps chiefly, that of heretics generally. As usual, Cyprian regards baptism by any but a lawful bishop as a rebellion against the divinely appointed priesthood, using the example of the rebels against Aaron: Korah, Dathan and Abiram.[64] Perhaps revealingly, he acknowledges strong tradition on the other side, but claims that reason, and 'better' revelation by the Holy Spirit, support him.[65]

After writing this long and careful argument, Cyprian received a bombshell from Stephen, which is not in the dossier preserved. We know it from Cyprian's response to a bishop Pompeius, who had asked to know what Stephen had written.[66] The contents are dismissed as 'arrogant, irrelevant, self-contradictory, incompetent and imprudent', and only the conclusion is quoted: 'Therefore,

---

59 Cypr. *Ep.* 72.2.
60 Cypr. *Ep.* 73.
61 Cypr. *Ep.* 73.2.
62 Cypr. *Ep.* 73.3 (also an earlier allusion in *Ep.* 70.1.2 (important note in Clarke, *Letters*, vol. IV, 196–9)). For similar rulings in eastern councils, apparently in response to Montanism, see Dionysius in Euseb. *HE* 7.5.3–6; 7.7.5 (who, though supporting Stephen, pleaded for respect for these earlier rulings); Firmilian in Cypr. *Ep.* 77.3–4.
63 Cypr. *Ep.* 73.4.1; cf. 73.16–17. Clarke, *Letters*, vol. IV, 226 rejects the view that the document was the anonymous tract *De rebaptismate*, though its arguments are similar.
64 Cypr. *Ep.* 73.8, appealing to Num 16.
65 Cypr. *Ep.* 73.13; the fate of past heretics reconciled without baptism is considered at 73.23.
66 Cypr. *Ep.* 74. More details of Stephen's letter may be deduced from Firmilian's commentary in Cypr. *Ep.* 75.

if any come to you from any heresy whatsoever, let there be no innovation beyond what is traditional, that a hand be laid on them for penance, since the heretics themselves for their part do not mutually baptise those who come to them, but simply share communion.'[67] Cyprian repudiates the label 'innovator', and denies that Stephen's tradition is evangelical or apostolic. Most of his arguments are predictable, and clearly angry. But, unless he is responding to other things in Stephen's letter, he partly mistakes what Stephen writes. He argues as if Stephen lays on hands to impart the Holy Spirit, which is Cyprian's own interpretation of the rite of episcopal handlaying.[68] Stephen's words, however, are *in paenitentiam*. In other words, he would treat the converted heretic as a penitent being reconciled. His action has precedent in the actions of his predecessor Callistus before 220, who increased his congregation by accepting those coming in from other Christian groups, according to his critic Hippolytus.[69] Stephen's appeal to heretical practice is astonishing, and he is taunted with it by Cyprian.[70] But it makes sense in the Roman context, since the original multiplicity of house churches there,[71] where many differences of doctrine and practice could easily arise, meant that unity could only be achieved if the principle of 'one baptism' was adhered to in Stephen's sense. Stephen appears to have acted high-handedly towards the African churches, and towards those of Asia Minor who took the same line. He had gone so far as even to deny Cyprian's representatives bed and board in Rome, and he excommunicated the oriental bishops.[72] Such actions were incompatible with the principles, so dear to Cyprian, of the unity of the church based upon a unanimous episcopate. We have fragmentary information about Cyprian's unsuccessful attempt to negotiate in Rome, and a council was held in Carthage in 256, whose conclusions survive as *Sententiae episcoporum* ('The sentences of the bishops'). The bishops agree with Cyprian, but there were absentees who presumably dissented.[73] The most important decision, which applied both to Rome and to African dissidents, was Cyprian's declaration that none set himself up as 'bishop of bishops', but allowed each bishop to decide, and to answer

---

67 Cypr. *Ep.* 74.1. On the problems of translation, see Clarke, *Letters*, vol. IV, 237–8. My version takes *proprie* as 'for their part'.
68 Cypr. *Ep.* 74.5; that this is Cyprian's regular view is apparent from *Ep.* 69.11.3.
69 Hipp. *Haer.* 12.200–21.
70 Cypr. *Ep.* 74.4.
71 See pt IV, ch. 22, above.
72 Firmilian's sarcastic acount in Cypr. *Ep.* 75.25, and Dionysius of Alexandria in Euseb. *HE* 7.5.4; Clarke, *Letters*, vol. IV, 243.
73 Sage, *Cyprian*, 324–7.

to God, for himself. This was a position which Cyprian had suggested earlier.[74] Events overtook the dispute: when Stephen died in 257 and Cyprian was himself arrested and finally martyred in 258, Stephen's successors took steps to mend relations with other churches, aided by the mediation of Dionysius of Alexandria.[75] The debate died down, but would erupt ferociously as a prime controversy between Donatists and catholics in the fourth century. The issues were settled by conciliar decisions at Arles in 314 and Nicaea in 325, whereby those baptised in the name of the Father, the Son and the Holy Spirit were reckoned baptised (which of course included Novatianists), and those whose baptisms were not doctrinally orthodox (like the Samosatenes) were to be baptised.

Novatianism was not itself the prime subject of the baptismal dispute. It may, however, have played a key role. For Stephen, Novatian was a senior figure, a formidable theologian with a devout following. His decision not to acknowledge impure baptisms could undermine Stephen's own position, raising the spectre that faults of his predecessors or of those they allowed (like the Spanish bishops)[76] made their sacramental acts invalid. It is possible, though there is no direct evidence, that this was what led Stephen to reaffirm the old Roman tradition of acknowledging all baptisms, as a function of the faith of the individual and not of the administering priest. If so, he would have seen the stance of Cyprian and his eastern supporters as a gross betrayal, and that could account for his ire.

As to the doctrine of the church itself, this final controversy of Cyprian's short career repeated the lesson of the lapsed: the hard line is not the way to identify the truth of God as revealed in Jesus Christ. Sixty-five years before, Irenaeus had been obliged to modify his doctrine of the inspired unity of bishops in the apostolic tradition, when Rome differed from Asia over Easter.[77] Now Cyprian can only maintain that the bishops are a single body by allowing differences of baptismal discipline, as he had allowed flexibility towards the lapsed. Stephen adopted a more generous, charitable and evangelical policy, but did it with disastrous rigour. As to Novatian, his own schism and his denial of other baptisms were doubtless pursued in good faith, in response to calamity and disorder. He tried to find a faultless church, but could only produce one which essentially lacked the charity which is the church's bond and soul.

---

74 [Cyprian] CSEL iii/i 435–6; Cypr. *Ep.* 69.17.
75 Euseb. *HE* 7.2–9.
76 See n. 52 above.
77 Euseb. *HE* 5.24.11–18.

These diverse positions, which were variously replicated in the east, but are less well documented, each left its mark, positive or negative, on the later catholic church. The issues would emerge again in Donatism and Augustine, and in various guises have reappeared in the church since. The imperial church embodied Cyprian's presupposition of a single worldwide church reflecting the shape of the empire, but with Stephen's more generous and practical view of baptismal membership.

Figure 7. Christ as Philosopher, Catacomb of Domitilla (Rome) (photo: Estelle Brettman, The International Catacomb Society)

27

Towards a Christian *paideia*

FRANCES M. YOUNG

Teaching and Learning in Early Christianity

Probably in the year 245 CE, someone named Theodore delivered an oration celebrating the character and work of the great Christian scholar, Origen.[1] This panegyric has traditionally been attributed to Gregory Thaumaturgus,[2] the founder of the church in Pontus (north-east Turkey). Whoever the author was, he was clearly a student of this renowned teacher during the years that Origen spent in Caesarea. The speech is of great importance in revealing to us the kind of curriculum Origen offered. By the mid-third century, then, we have clear evidence that a Christian teacher like Origen could offer a complete philosophical education, which paralleled that which was offered in schools all over the Graeco-Roman world. Christianity was developing its own *paideia* ('education', 'training'), or at least appropriating and adapting that of the Graeco-Roman world.

Teaching and learning were characteristic of Christianity from the beginning. The term used in the gospels for the followers of Jesus is 'disciples' (*mathētai*), that is 'pupils', and Jesus himself is addressed both as 'rabbi' and 'teacher'. In second-century texts such as the *Apostolic fathers* and the Apologists, Jesus is presented as *the* teacher, with the teaching that fulfils and surpasses all others. This teaching focused on ethics, but its warrant lay in the revelation of the will of the one creator God who oversees everything, even seeing into the heart, so that not just actions but motives were laid bare.[3] Christian Gnosticism reflects this 'teaching' emphasis in its claim to have received true *knowledge* from revelations imparted by the Christ.[4] It is hardly surprising, then, that correct teaching (*dogma* in Greek, *doctrina* in Latin) became a

---

1 See pt IV, ch. 18, and ch. 25, above.
2 For discussion of the authorship, see Trigg, *Origen*, 167. Trigg follows Nautin against Crouzel in the SC edition.
3 E.g. 1 Tim 5:21, 6:13; 2 Tim 2:15; 1 *Clem.* 21.3–9, 28.4, etc.; Ign. *Eph.* 15.3; Justin 1 *Apol.* 12.
4 See pt III, ch. 12, above.

characteristic concern of early Christianity, and this made the church more like a philosophical school than a religious organisation – for it was not beliefs, doctrines or even ethics that characterised ancient religion, but traditional ritual practices performed in temples, shrines or households. Christianisation would eventually transform notions of what a religion is by emphasising creeds and correct doctrine as conditions for practising its cult.

It is plausible to suggest that some early Christian communities were modelled largely on the Jewish synagogue,[5] an organisation that had both religious and 'school'-like properties. For, while it is true that, away from Jerusalem, the synagogue was a 'prayer-house' (*proseuchē*), which to some extent replaced the temple, yet, at the heart of these Jewish communal organisations, particularly in the diaspora, was a process of learning about Jewish literature and traditions, a cultural education to match the schools of the surrounding Greek culture. As the Greeks had their law, their history, their poetry, so did the Jews. Greek schools engaged in education through the reading of ancient classical texts, from the stage of learning grammar, through education in rhetoric, to the study of philosophy – for, rightly interpreted, the whole of philosophy was to be found in ancient revered texts, like the epics of Homer. The Law and the prophets provided Jews with comparable ancient texts, and an even greater incentive to study them in that they were the Word of their God, teaching the way of life required of them to fulfil their covenant with the God who had chosen them to be his own people. Jews developed scholarly methods of literary criticism analogous to those of the Graeco-Roman grammarians;[6] and the works of Philo are evidence that at any rate some Jews also found in their scriptures the kind of intellectual and philosophical systems their Greek contemporaries found in classical texts. In the diaspora especially, reading and interpreting these texts came to constitute the heart of Jewish religious activity, rather than offering sacrifices in the faraway Jerusalem temple. So too in the Christian assembly.[7]

Teachers, as well as prophets, have a prominent role in texts coming from the earliest churches, and a teaching function is assumed for bishops; Polycarp is called 'the teacher of Asia'.[8] But perhaps the most intriguing feature of early Christianity is the prominence of people who appear to set themselves up as 'freelance' teachers, and the concern, already evident in the New

---

5 Burtchaell, *From synagogue to church*. See also pt I, ch. 2 and pt II, ch. 7, above.
6 Daube, 'Rabbinic methods of interpretation and Hellenistic rhetoric'; Lieberman, *Hellenism in Jewish Palestine*.
7 Gamble, *Books and readers*.
8 *M. Polyc.* 12.2.

Testament epistles[9] and the *Didache*, to distinguish those who teach according to the right traditions and those who do not. In the mid-second century we have the examples of Valentinus, Marcion and Justin, all of whom arrived in Rome from places further east, all of whom were apparently accepted within the Roman church, but two of whom were later excluded when the majority sensed that their teaching was aberrant.[10] Justin, however, was accepted, apparently operated as a teacher of the 'barbarian philosophy', wearing the conventional philosopher's dress and taking in pupils such as Tatian. Such a teacher substituted Moses and the biblical writings for the usual classics,[11] and developed his ideas through exegesis of texts. The presence of 'schools' among the house churches of Rome can be paralleled in Alexandria, where Valentinus and Basilides taught, as well as Pantaenus and Clement, in the years before the most famous of all, Origen.

Clearly the relationship between such semi-independent philosophical teachers and the emerging hierarchy of the church was not always straightforward. Origen found that relations with his bishop became uncomfortable, so occasioning his move from Alexandria to Caesarea. It has been suggested[12] that Arius, whose dispute with his bishop divided the church at the end of the period of this volume,[13] was behaving as if he could be an independent teacher in this older tradition at a time when social and political developments precluded it – he is described in the sources not only as a presbyter but as a scripture teacher. In the post-Constantinian period, the great teachers of the church would be the bishops – people like Basil of Caesarea, Gregory of Nazianzus, John Chrysostom, Ambrose and Augustine – while general education would become 'secularised' and remain in the hands of the rhetoricians who taught from the pagan classics.[14] In this earlier period, however, we can trace two parallel developments. On the one hand, the church, like the synagogue, had itself a strong resemblance to a school, its gatherings focusing on the reading and interpretation of texts; on the other hand, semi-independent Christian teachers were developing a Christian educational curriculum based on an alternative set of classical texts, namely the Bible.

---

9 E.g. 1 Cor 12:28; 1 Tim 3:2.
10 See pt IV, ch. 22, above.
11 Droge, *Homer or Moses?*; Young, *Biblical Exegesis*.
12 Williams, *Arius*.
13 See pt VI, ch. 31, below.
14 Fourth-century bishops had received a classical (pagan) education, and Gregory of Nazianzus defended his right to it against the edict of Julian the Apostate. This bespeaks a different attitude from the second–third centuries, where substitution of the Bible for the classics is evident; see Droge, *Homer or Moses?*

It is this latter development which chiefly concerns us in this chapter, and the principal evidence lies in the work and writings of Origen. The school of Hippolytus in Rome may have been somewhat similar, but the evidence is problematic.[15]

Origen's curriculum, according to his pupil

Theodore came to Origen after having received the standard education with the *grammatikos* and the *rhētōr*.[16] In fact, he was on his way to study Latin and Roman law in Beirut when he came across Origen – an encounter he attributed to providence – and was persuaded to study with him as well. All this underlines the fact that what Origen gave this pupil was the equivalent of tertiary (university) education, following the pattern of the established *enkyklios paideia*.[17]

Origen's love of philosophy, together with his conviction that philosophy was the foundation of true piety towards God, was what persuaded Theodore to stay in Caesarea and give up his homeland and friends, as well as his intended career. He was taken into Origen's household as a pupil, and offered friendship, a spark of love being kindled in his soul – his speech develops the 'type' of David and Jonathan, though he confesses he did not yet know of this scriptural example. He was captivated by Origen. Apart from the occasional feature, such as this reference to a biblical type, the whole discourse runs according to the cultural frames (*topoi*) of Hellenistic rhetoric. Origen's skill as a teacher is likened to the work of a gardener, taking in hand an uncultivated plot, or a wild plant that needed nurturing and pruning. Thus he took time to penetrate his students' existing knowledge – when he found potential, he cleared the ground around so as to irrigate and develop the initial growth; when he found thorns and wild growth, he cut it out. He was Socratic in his ruthless questioning and argumentation. He tamed them, like a trainer tames unbroken horses. But once the soil was softened he began to plant the seeds of truth. He taught them to search within themselves, and to be critical of sophistry.

This would seem to be a description of the teaching of logic and dialectics. So beneath all the rhetoric and moralising, we can uncover the curriculum. It

---

15 See pt IV, ch. 22, and chs. 23 and 25, above.
16 The following account is drawn from the panegyric attributed to Gregory Thaumaturgus.
17 For the classic study of ancient education, see Marrou, *History of education in antiquity*; more recently Kaster, *Guardians of language*.

went on to natural philosophy – the study of physics, geometry and astronomy, the ancient sciences about the world. Thus Origen moved his pupils beyond mere amazement and wonder at creation to a rational awareness of its order and 'economy'.[18] Then he went on to ethics, which he imparted not only by words but also by example.

The four cardinal virtues of the Greek philosophical tradition provide the core elements of his ethical teaching, but they are given their own slant by Origen's fundamental outlook: prudence – interpreted as the capacity to judge between good and evil; temperance – the ability to select what is good; justice – the capacity to give every aspect of the moral life its due; and courage – the strength of character to carry out the other virtues. Indeed, Origen urged his pupils to study the philosophy of the Greeks, but interpreted it through his Christian lifestyle. He was one who desired to 'imitate the perfect pattern' – the encomiast therefore refuses to call Origen himself the perfect pattern, despite presenting him as exemplary, and so one can detect, not just his avowed refusal to go beyond the truth, but a sense that he knew, though he never explicitly says so, that Origen's life was patterned on Christ. The highest word of wisdom was 'Know yourself' – the classic maxim of the Socratic tradition, for the soul then beholds itself as in a mirror, and reflects the divine mind in itself. Again and again one senses, as here, the confluence of the Greek philosophical tradition and notions that derive from the biblical tradition. Theodore confesses – still reflecting standard *topoi* – that Origen never succeeded in instilling all the virtues into his pupil, because of his dull nature, but his teacher did make him a lover of virtue, and Origen did get him to understand that piety is what undergirds the ethical life, which is only achieved through divine grace. The ultimate object is to become like God, so as to draw near to the divine and abide within it.

Theology, then, was the climax of all these studies. Origen thought it important that his pupils should study what was written by the philosophers and by the ancient poets, excluding only the work of the atheists who deny both God and providence (doubtless a reference to the Epicureans). He clearly tackled with them the well-rehearsed criticism that philosophers came up with so many different theories, each school having its own set of dogmas, each philosopher sure he is right and unwilling to listen to the opinions of others. Theodore describes such thinkers as caught in quagmire or labyrinth from which they cannot escape. To secure his pupils against such a fate, Origen did

18 The Greek word *oikonomia* literally means 'household management', but is used in theological writing to refer to God's providential management of the universe, the divine saving purposes effected through the incarnation, and even the divine self-disposition into Trinity (see ch. 25, above).

not introduce them to a single school of philosophy. He set before them what was useful and true from all the various philosophies. Thus he made a virtue of eclecticism. Origen's students were to attach themselves not to any human teacher, but devote themselves to God and to the prophets.

So the highest study of all was the interpretation of the scriptures, and it was for this that all the study of philosophy was a preparation. The prophets often wrote words that are dark and enigmatical, especially to those who have wandered far from God. Theodore suggests that Origen was a skilled and discerning listener to God, who was able to elucidate what was obscure, because the Divine Spirit had made him his friend, and given him the gift of investigating and explaining the divine oracles. To interpret scripture required inspiration. That Theodore had learned something about the scriptures from Origen is then demonstrated as he takes his leave, comparing his departure to Adam leaving paradise, to the prodigal going off to a far country and the deportation of the Jews to Babylon.

It would appear that the philosophical education Origen gave Theodore differed little from that he had received himself from the Platonist, Ammonius Saccas. The conventional three disciplines of dialectic (or logic), physics and ethics provided the basic structure. The classical *paideia* provided this Christian teacher with his curriculum. Yet the goal, for Origen, was to provide foundations for theology and biblical study.

The question of Origen's 'school'

Theodore's description of his studies with Origen does not sit well with Eusebius' suggestion that Origen succeeded Clement, who succeeded Pantaenus, as head of the so-called Catechetical School in Alexandria.[19] Of course Theodore's account refers to Origen's teaching activities, not in Alexandria, but towards the end of his life in Caesarea. Yet even so, there seems to be a disjunction between this programme of 'tertiary' education and the practice of initial Christian education prior to baptism traditionally associated with the term 'catechesis'. In the one case, Origen would seem to have been a 'freelance' philosophical teacher, taking pupils into his household, even though at this stage he had also been ordained presbyter and gave homilies in an ecclesiastical setting. In the other case, he would seem to have been some kind of official appointee, in a succession of teachers, providing, at least until he lost

---

19 *HE* 6.6. The nature of this succession was questioned by G. Bardy, 'Aux origines de l'école d'Alexandrie' and 'Pour l'histoire de l'école d'Alexandrie'.

the favour of his bishop, elementary instruction in the Christian faith. Can we resolve these tensions, and come to some kind of consistent picture of Origen's teaching activity?

It is important to disabuse ourselves of the inevitable assumptions drawn from analogies with schools as we experience them in modern societies: schools were not institutions. Greek cities did provide salaries for some teachers to offer public education, but the majority of teachers operated on a freelance basis, gathering groups of students whose size depended on the teacher's popularity. Their classes might be held in the gymnasium or other public locale, or at their own house or some other private place. Depending upon their social status, pupils would either drop out at some stage, or move from the elementary teacher to the *grammatikos* and then to the *rhētōr*, as and when they were ready to do so. They might then proceed to some philosopher. When one philosophical teacher followed another as his successor, the word 'school' might be used for this continuous succession – the best-known case being the Academy which stemmed from Plato and lasted several centuries. The word 'school' could have a variety of possible connotations.

Eusebius may be using multiple sources to construct his account of Origen's life and teaching activities – it is in any case a rather episodic narration, broken up by the insertion of other material, on account of Eusebius' attempts to order his material chronologically rather than topically. Several different descriptions are apposite to our enquiry. (1) After his father's martyrdom, a rich woman became Origen's patron so that he could pursue his studies, and he rapidly reached the stage where he could earn well as a *grammatikos*.[20] (2) During the persecution, all the Christian catechists had left Alexandria. Various pagans approached Origen for instruction in the Word of God. So at the age of seventeen the bishop, Demetrius, appointed him head of the catechetical school. He came under increasing pressure as soldiers were posted around the house where he was living, because of the large numbers who came to him for elementary instruction in the faith, and he had to keep moving from house to house.[21] (3) Responsibility for catechesis was entrusted by Demetrius to Origen alone, and he soon saw pupils coming to him in increasing numbers. He decided that this responsibility was not compatible with being a *grammatikos*, so he sold his library in order to gain some financial independence, and devoted himself to study of the scriptures. (4) After a trip to Rome, Origen decided that his catechetical work was too distracting from his

---

20 *HE* 6.2.
21 *HE* 6.3.

study of theology and his scholarly work on the scriptures.[22] So he divided up his pupils and entrusted the introductory lessons to Heraclas, one of his most promising students, while concentrating on the higher education of more advanced pupils. Eusebius speaks of the many educated people who came to Origen's school, where, after preparatory studies including geometry and arithmetic, he instructed them in Greek philosophy, discussing the different systems of the philosophers, and giving many a general grounding which would stand them in good stead for study of the scriptures.[23] This begins to sound more like the account given by Theodore of his curriculum in Caesarea.

What then was this 'catechetical school'? The notion of something like the Academy, of which there was a series of well-known heads, both prior and subsequent to Origen's tenure, is probably imposed on the material by hindsight, though it may represent Eusebius' attempt to identify the lineage of orthodox teachers in a context where heterodox teachers also practised. The accounts suggest something rather simpler: that the bishop asked Origen to undertake the necessary catechesis of converts in an emergency; and that in response to demand, Origen combined duties for which he was patronised by the bishop with the development of a more advanced programme undertaken as a freelance teacher. In other words, Origen engaged in different levels of teaching activity concurrently.

Interestingly enough, this suggestion coheres well with recent reassessment[24] of the distinction, which Origen apparently makes in his writings, between different levels of Christian believer, classifying people according to their capacity to read scripture literally, morally or spiritually. It seems that, so far from categorising persons, Origen means to suggest that the three levels of meaning relate to three stages in an educational process. He knew it was possible to move from one level to another, and that none of the levels of meaning was exclusive of the others. It is clear from his homilies that Origen was aware of differing levels of understanding in his audience, and in response to Celsus' jibes, Origen is pleased to admit that Christianity could educate even slaves and women to be good, unlike philosophy, with its elitist character.[25] Maybe these attitudes were the fruit of his experience of teaching at a wide range of levels concurrently during the years in Alexandria. His teaching activities in Caesarea, as priest, homilist and philosophical teacher, would appear to have been similarly diverse.

22 *HE* 6.15.
23 *HE* 6.18.
24 Torjesen, '"Body", "Soul", and "Spirit"'. See further below, p. 498.
25 *C. Cels.* 3.49ff.

Reading the scriptures

Most of Origen's literary activity went into the production of commentaries on scripture. He had a patron, Ambrosius, who helped to finance this work.[26] A huge amount is lost, though some has survived in translation or excerpted in compendia of various kinds. Origen also discusses the pitfalls and methods of interpreting scripture in his work, *De principiis* ('On first principles'). For a long time the latter was taken as a basic account of his approach. More recent study, however, has sought to examine his actual practice of biblical interpretation in the extant commentaries and homilies.[27] What is clear is that scripture lay at the heart of his philosophy, and its reading was the goal of his educational programme. Inevitably his mind was as shaped by Platonic assumptions as modern scholarship has been by evolutionary ones. So his exegetical interests often produce comments which now seem far from the point – indeed, the classic study of Origen's biblical work in English tends to suggest that, since he had no historical sense, he had no hope of understanding the texts.[28] Yet Origen simply approached the task of interpretation in recognisably the same ways as many of his contemporaries.

Texts lay at the heart of the normal educational processes of antiquity. So most interpretation went on in the classroom, and we have no record of this oral activity. We can, however, discern something of what went on from various rhetorical handbooks and other surviving material. Because of its full discussion of the various stages of education, Quintilian's *Institutio oratoria* ('Training in oratory'), a Latin work dating from the late first century CE, enables us to observe the various exegetical moves commonly made, which are also found in Origen's commentaries.[29]

Texts in the ancient world were handwritten on parchment or papyrus. The first thing the teacher had to do was to see that the various copies being used in the class actually had the same wording. In other words, textual criticism was unavoidable, and it had long been practised in Alexandria. It is quite clear that Origen understood the necessity of discussing what the correct wording of a text was where there was an inconsistency or doubt. One example will prove the point: Matthew 19:19 in some copies had the added words, 'You shall love your neighbour as yourself.' Origen thought it had been added, and that the addition is confirmed by the absence of these words in Mark and

---

26 Euseb. *HE* 6.18.
27 See particularly Neuschäfer, *Origenes als Philologe*, and Young, *Biblical exegesis*.
28 Hanson, *Allegory and event*.
29 The following exposition re-presents that found in Young, *Biblical exegesis*.

Luke. He suggests that it would irreverent to make such a suggestion if it were not for the fact that there is much diversity in our copies, whether by the carelessness of certain scribes, or by some culpable rashness in the correction of the text, or by some people making arbitrary additions or omissions in their corrections.[30]

Origen was also well aware that a translated text could never quite represent the exact wording of the original. Eusebius tells us[31] how he produced the *Hexapla* – a massive work in which he placed the Hebrew, a Hebrew transliteration and four or more Greek versions side by side for comparison. The questions how much Hebrew Origen actually knew[32] and how much he consulted Jewish scholars are vexed. He does claim in a number of places[33] to have heard Jews interpreting scripture, or himself enquired of Jews about particular passages. The complete *Hexapla* was probably never copied, and the original has long since been lost. It is an indication, however, of how seriously Origen took the scholarly endeavour to ensure that every jot and tittle of the text was just right.

In ancient texts there was no word division or punctuation, so reading involved analysis of the text to see how the words fitted together and where the phrases ended. All reading in the ancient world was aloud, and had to be prepared, by studying the grammar and construction of the sentences. Then understanding required attention to vocabulary and etymology, since ancient texts often used archaic words. Commentators would build up concordances so as to discern the Homeric meaning of words;[34] Origen did the same to establish biblical meanings, listing cross-references to elucidate the text before him. Besides this, figures of speech had to be noted – simile and metaphor, onomatopeia, irony and so on. If the linguistic 'turn' (*tropē*) was not identified, the wrong meaning would emerge – after all, irony is saying the opposite of what you mean with a particular tone of voice, so failing to identify that in a text would be to misread it entirely. Origen expends considerable effort in identifying such linguistic features. He recognises that you cannot take a metaphor literally without completely misreading the text. There are times when taking a text 'according to the letter' is impossible. Origen simply adopts here the standard methodology of the schools of grammar and rhetoric, applying it to

30 Or. *Comm. Matt.* 15.14.
31 *HE* 6.16.
32 Euseb. *HE* 6.16 claims he knew the language, but it seems from his writings that his knowledge was slight; de Lange, *Origen and the Jews*.
33 E.g. *Comm. Jo.* 6.83; *Hom. in Ezech.* 4.8; *C. Cels.* 1.45, 55; de Lange, *Origen and the Jews* for full discussion of his debt to Jewish scholars.
34 Lamberton, *Homer the theologian*.

the scriptures. But as he does so, metaphor becomes an indicator that the text has a deeper meaning. Indeed, figures of speech and *aporiai* – puzzles that are not easily resolvable – become jumping-off points for allegory. Origen suggests that such 'stumbling blocks' were deliberately put into the text by the Holy Spirit so as to stimulate the reader into seeking the spiritual meaning (*Princ.* 4.3.1). God cannot have eyes and ears or walk in the Garden of Eden – for God is the transcendent 'other', invisible and incorporeal. Similarly God cannot be angry, since the divine is impassible; yet God accommodates the divine self to our need, appearing to be angry so as to stimulate us to greater righteousness. Study of the letter of the text at times precludes literal reading. From study of the wording, Origen could generate symbolic readings, as if the text were a kind of code. Etymology helps to crack this code, and becomes a tool of philosophical reading.

The other aspect of Origen's commentaries can also be paralleled in the practices of the schools. Explanatory comment was necessary to help understand allusions in the text, in the case of classical texts, things like the gods and heroes, the mythical stories, and many other features. Quintilian warns against overdoing it, showing off one's erudition, which suggests it was common practice to do just that. Sometimes it would be allusion to natural phenomena or historical events, or geographical, astronomical, or musical information, that would need explanation – indeed, texts could easily provide the programme for a huge curriculum, and conversely the curriculum was widely regarded as providing the basis for reading texts – as we saw earlier in Origen's case. Origen's capacity to disregard any warning against overdoing is evidenced by his disquisition on the pearl,[35] provoked by the parable in Matthew 13:45 about a merchant who, on finding a pearl of exceptional value, sold all he had to purchase it. We are told all about pearls – the best places for finding them, how they are formed, indeed, everything a learned person like Origen might know about them. Investigation into such features of the text was called *historia*, and sometimes involved a focus on what we might call the 'facts' behind the text. Faced with the gospel story of the crowds wondering where Jesus got his wisdom, given his lowly origins as a carpenter's son, Origen alerts his readers to the fact that the crowd was ignorant of the virgin birth – hence the puzzlement, and to confirm this explanatory 'fact' he adds the tradition from apocryphal sources that the brothers of Jesus were sons of Joseph by a former wife.[36]

---

35 *Comm. Matt.* 10.7–10.
36 *Comm. Matt.* 10.17.

Narratives not only required informative expansion, however. In the schools, pupils were taught to assess the probability of stories,[37] to find ways of proving or disproving them, the point being that this kind of criticism would be vital when they came to act as lawyers in court. Origen had his own skills here: he treats as 'myth' Celsus' version of the birth of Jesus, whereby Mary had a child by a soldier called Panthera, and so was turned out by Joseph to whom she was betrothed.[38] In his gospel commentaries he does not hesitate to note discrepancies in different versions of particular stories. One example is the story of the so-called cleansing of the temple.[39] Quite apart from minor differences, there is a huge discrepancy in the matter of timing: according to John's gospel this incident came at the very beginning of Jesus' career; according to the other gospels it immediately preceded his arrest and condemnation. Origen 'conceives it to be impossible for those who admit nothing more than the history in their interpretation to show that these discrepant statements are in harmony with one another'.[40] He demonstrates the implausibility of the Johannine timing, and then goes on to discuss the deeper meaning of that narrative. Turning to the Matthaean version, he again draws attention to features which are implausible as they stand, looking for the deeper intent of each evangelist. Just as in the case of his grammatical and lexical analysis, so here, puzzles and problems are a pointer to the fact that the 'material' level of the text is not sufficient of itself for one seeking to discover the true meaning. The *aporiai* stimulate the sensitive reader to go beyond the letter to the spirit. Scripture is full of 'enigmas' or 'parables'.

It was accepted by rhetoricians that orators might speak falsehood for the benefit of the hearer. Origen believes that God does something similar, accommodating himself to the human level. Frequently he speaks of God acting as a father dealing with an infant son, or as a doctor dealing with a patient: 'the whole of divine scripture is full of such medicines', he suggests.[41] In this way he made the obscure and difficult 'barbarian' books, written in awkward translationese, acceptable to educated enquirers. Its crude language and anthropomorphisms were explained. The important thing was to grow in understanding so as to move beyond the 'letter' of the text, to discover its moral and spiritual level. No wonder Theodore saw the interpretation of scripture as the object of Origen's curriculum.

37 For further discussion see Grant, *Earliest lives*.
38 *C. Cels.* 1.32–7.
39 *Comm. Jo.* 10.119–22.
40 *Comm. Jo.* 10.130.
41 *Hom. Jer.* 20.3.

This sense that the whole aim of *paideia* is to be able to read and interpret scripture is reflected also in the work known as *De principiis*. This appears to be his earliest surviving work, yet it presents us with an overview of Origen's thinking at a time when he was developing his teaching activities in Alexandria. It may have been written as a defence of his exegetical procedures.[42] It is a kind of 'systematic theology', but its genre is now understood as akin to philosophical handbooks used in ancient schools, dealing with the 'first principles' both of the universe and of logic. Because Origen's views became highly controversial at a later date, only fragments survive in the original Greek, but the whole work is extant in Rufinus' fourth-century Latin translation. Unfortunately, it is evident that Rufinus' version is somewhat apologetic in character and not entirely reliable. Nevertheless, the work remains an important summary of Origen's theological and exegetical principles.

The work begins with the affirmation that the words and teaching of Christ are not confined to what he said when on earth. Moses and the prophets were inspired by Christ. But the interpretation of these scriptures has caused many conflicting opinions, so it is important to begin with the accepted 'rule of faith', the doctrines inherited from the apostles. Origen is clear, however, that anyone with a philosophical bent will need to enquire beyond this basic core of doctrine. His initial enquiry concerns the nature of God, and immediately it is clear how scriptural texts inform his argument that God is incorporeal. As the work proceeds, he deals with a range of topics in order: Christ, the Holy Spirit, rational creatures, angels, the material creation, the incarnation, the soul, free will, the devil, the consummation and so on. Book 4 then tackles the question of scripture, beginning with a discussion of its divine inspiration and the prophetic meaning of Moses and the prophets, and then indicating that it is all too easy not to read the scriptures aright.

So with polemical intent, doubtless informed by his own experience of debates with Jews and others, Origen introduces the problems of literal reading. Jews cannot see the prophecies fulfilled in Christ because the wolf did not literally feed with the lamb nor the leopard lie down with the kid, nor the calf and bull and lion feed together, led by a little child.[43] Heretics dwell on texts about the wrath of God and say the creator God of the Jewish scriptures is imperfect, and so cannot be the perfect God revealed by the Saviour. Even the simple-minded in the church attribute to God things they would not believe of even the most savage and unjust human beings. The reason, Origen asserts,

---

42 Trigg, *Origen*, 91.
43 Isa 11:6–7 in *Princ.* 4.2.1.

is that the Bible is interpreted according to the bare letter rather than being understood in its spiritual sense.

Origen has a series of Pauline texts which constantly justify his discernment of a spiritual or christological reading.[44] They are repeatedly found in his writings, and include Romans 7:14; 1 Corinthians 2:2, 10, 12–13, 16; 1 Corinthians 9:9–10; 1 Corinthians 10:4 and 11; 2 Corinthians 3:6, 15–17; and Galatians 4:24. In addition we find in the *De principiis* reference to Hebrews 8:5, an epistle which Origen here appears to accept as coming from the apostle despite his acknowledgement elsewhere that no one apart from God knows who wrote this letter.[45] On the basis of such indicators, the Bible is to be regarded as full of mysteries – some simply incomprehensible, others 'types' of what is to come. Prophecies are full of riddles and dark sayings. It is hardly surprising that thousands make mistakes in their interpretation. Origen finds the key in Proverbs 22:20–1, which he understood to be an instruction to set forth words of truth in a threefold way.[46] The simple are to be edified by the flesh of scripture, that is, the obvious interpretation; the person who has made progress is to be edified by scripture's soul; and the one who is perfect will be edified by the spiritual law, which has 'a shadow of the good things to come'. According to the apostle, he will 'speak wisdom among the perfect; yet a wisdom not of this world, nor of the rulers of this world, which are coming to nothing; but we speak God's wisdom in a mystery, even the wisdom hidden, which God foreordained before the worlds for our glory' (1 Cor 2:6–7). As a person consists of body, soul and spirit, so does scripture. However, it is difficult to apply this threefold theory, as spelt out in the *De principiis*, to his actual exegetical practice. In most of his commentaries and other exegetical writings, Origen actually operates with multiple possible meanings that fall into two categories: 'according to the letter' and 'according to the spirit'. *Prima facie* those scripture passages which he exploited to justify his approach also suggest a twofold meaning.

In his theoretical discussion, Origen hastens on to show that some passages have 'no bodily sense at all', and the reader must immediately search for the soul or spirit of the passage. Origen is worried that, if the meaning were transparent, the reader would never realise what lay beyond it. So, he suggests, the Word of God has arranged for certain stumbling blocks, as it were, and hindrances and impossibilities to be inserted in the midst of the law and the history, in order that we may not be completely drawn away by the sheer attractiveness of the

---

44 Heine, 'Gregory of Nyssa's apology for allegory'.
45 Quoted in Euseb. *HE* 6.25.
46 *Princ.* 4.2.4.

language, and so either reject the true doctrines absolutely, on the grounds that we learn from the scriptures nothing worthy of God, or else, by never moving away from the letter, fail to learn anything of the more divine element.[47]

Origen asserts that occasionally the Spirit wove fiction into the historical narratives, not just of the pre-Christian writings, but even of the gospels, so that sequences should follow the mystical events to which they point rather than earthly factuality. His illustrations begin[48] with the narrative of creation, continue with the story of Jesus' temptation by the devil, and focus particularly on the Mosaic Law, some gospel teachings, and the Exodus. Nevertheless, it is quite clear that Origen believed that most of the Bible had a perfectly satisfactory meaning to edify the simple-minded according to the letter.[49] He takes a pride in the fact that, whereas philosophy could only make the elite good, Christianity was capable of bettering every human being.

Origen's approach to the scriptures is indebted to contemporary philosophical approaches to texts, as well as to the philological traditions already mentioned. Plato had attacked the poets for the immorality of their tales, and in his ideal state wanted to outlaw their educational use (*Res.* 10. 595Af.). But tradition prevailed, and people like Plutarch had developed ways of justifying the 'moral' use of literature in education.[50] The stories could be exemplary, or they could be warnings. Teachers should always attempt to draw out the 'moral' of the story. By Origen's time, the influence of Stoic philosophy meant that philosophical teachers would, generally speaking, regard literature as allegorical, and that what Homer was really talking about were moral or philosophical truths.[51] The exegete should tease out these hidden meanings as a way of teaching philosophy. Clement of Alexandria was entirely at one with Plutarch in thinking that all religious truth comes in symbols and riddles – for the divine is beyond human language and comprehension.[52] The interesting thing about Origen is the degree to which he proves the point from the scriptures themselves. Later he would be condemned, at least in part, for his cavalier treatment of scripture – his propensity, through the means of allegory, to spiritualise away key elements of the over-arching Christian story, like the creation and paradise, the resurrection of the body and the kingdom of God.[53]

---

47 *Princ.* 4.2.9.
48 The illustrations form the bulk of *Princ.* 4.3.
49 *Princ.* 4.2.6.
50 Plut. *Lib. ed.* (*Moralia* 1a–14c) and *Adol. poet. aud.* (*Moralia* 14d–37b).
51 Lamberton, *Homer the theologian*.
52 Plut. *Superst.* (*Moralia* 164e–171f); *De Is. et Os.* (*Moralia* 351c–384c) and *Def. orac.* (*Moralia* 409e–438d). Cf. Clem. Al. *Str.* 5.4f.
53 Young, 'Fourth century reaction against allegory'.

Yet the legacy of his critique of anthropomorphic language, his recognition of the difficulties of speaking about the spiritual mysteries or knowing the reality of God, and his emphasis on God's accommodation of the divine self to our level would bear fruit in the theology of the Cappadocians and the eastern Orthodox tradition.

The contribution of Origen was to stimulate the development of a genuine intellectual tradition within Christianity. This bore many resemblances to the intellectual traditions and educational systems of the ancient world. Books were at the heart of it, ancient books that passed down the wisdom of long ago,[54] but needed interpretation. The cycle of studies began with the reading of texts to acquire basic skills, but also culminated in sophisticated re-readings of traditional texts to find philosophical truth. Origen substituted the Bible for the literary canon of the Greek classical tradition. Scripture became the crown of his Christian *paideia*. The study of scripture became the source of all truth, and the justification of a lifelong process of spiritual exploration. It lay at the heart of an integrated intellectual spirituality, which took the soul on a journey beyond the simple framework of agreed creedal dogma. It is hardly surprising that Origen's legacy was deeply influential in succeeding centuries. Yet his free spirit of inquiry[55] became increasingly problematic, and many of his ideas were perceived to be unsatisfactory, as new controversies led to the articulation of doctrinal formulae adverse to the reception of his theological hermeneutics.

54 Hatch, *Influence of Greek ideas*. More recently, Young, 'Books and their "aura"'.
55 See ch. 25, above; Crouzel, *Origen*.

PART VI

*

'ALIENS' BECOME CITIZENS:
TOWARDS IMPERIAL
PATRONAGE

Figure 8. Temple of Trajan at Pergamum (photo: Marion Kosem)

28

Persecutions: genesis and legacy

W. H. C. FREND

In the 250 years that separate the Neronian persecution in 64 CE from the conversion of Constantine to Christianity, c.312, Christianity was an illegal and suspect religion whose members were subject to arrest, condemnation and, in many cases, death. In the second century, acts of persecution would be carried out on the authority of provincial governors, but, in the third century, the emperors themselves began to become involved until under Valerian (253–60) edicts were promulgated through the senate that were aimed at suppressing the worship of the church and inflicting damage on its adherents. For their part, the Christians expected alienation from surrounding provincial society and subjection to persecution. Not all, however, were, like the deacon Euplus in Catania in 304, volunteer martyrs,[1] but the tradition of righteous suffering, inherited from Judaism, was strong and was reinforced by the recorded example of Jesus himself, as well as the great prophets of Israel.[2] Unfortunately for future history, the legacy of persecution, now aimed against heretics and non-believers, was not to die with the grant of toleration to the church.

The first encounter between the Christians and the Roman authorities was both fortuitous and disastrous. Up to the point at which Luke ends the Acts of the Apostles in 62 CE, relations with the provincial authorities had been tolerable.[3] On arrival in Rome, Paul and his followers were still considered to be authentic, if suspect and unpopular, members of the Jewish community (cf. Acts 28:22). This relationship appeared unlikely to change in the next two years. On 19 July 64, however, a massive fire broke out in Rome.[4] Fanned by the high

---

1 *Acta Eupli* i (= no. 25 in Musurillo, 210–11).
2 See e.g. Heb 11:37.
3 It is possible that Suet. *Claud.* 25.4, recording the expulsion of the Jews from Rome in 49 CE because of 'disturbances at the instigation of Chrestus', may refer to action against the Christians. Aquila and Priscilla moved from Rome as a result of this edict (Acts 18:2). For tolerance of the Claudian age, however, see Acts 18:12–17 (Gallio at Corinth).
4 See Stevenson and Frend, *New Eusebius*, 2–3, for a translation and notes on Tacitus' account of the fire and its consequences for the Christians (Tac. *Ann.* 15.44.2–8).

wind, the conflagration destroyed three entire quarters of the city. Thousands were made homeless. The reaction was similar to that experienced when Rome confronted the Bacchanal conspiracy in 186 BCE, recorded in detail by Livy.[5] The guardian gods of the city had been violated. Expiation must be severe. But suspicion fell on Nero himself, well known for his grandiose schemes which it was believed included the replanning of Rome on a scale he considered fitting for an imperial city. Then, to quote Tacitus (writing, however, fifty years after the event, in 115), 'Nero fastened the guilt and inflicted the most exquisite tortures on a class hated for their abominations called Christians.'[6] As with Livy's account of the suppression of the Bacchanals, 'an immense number' were arrested, and those 'who confessed' (to being Christians?) were condemned and put to death, probably in Nero's amphitheatre near what is now the Vatican. Some were crucified, others done to death in a crude parody of the fate of Actaeon, torn to pieces by dogs, or, in the case of the women, impersonating the Dirce, fastened to the horns of bulls, or the Danaids, exposed in the arena to attacks by wild beasts.[7] This purge was to appease the gods by the extreme method of human sacrifice.

The public pitied the victims and did not exonerate Nero. 'It was not as it seemed for the public good but to glut one man's cruelty that they were being destroyed.'[8] Tacitus' contemporary, Suetonius, does not mention Christians in connection with the fire, but a list of miscellaneous acts of Nero, not necessarily unreliable, states that 'punishment was inflicted on the Christians, a class of men given to a new (i.e. novel or revolutionary) and wicked superstition.' The word used, maleficus, has the connotation of 'magic' or 'black magic'.[9] Henceforth, therefore, the Christians were associated with arson and revolutionary aims pursued through the agency of black magic. They were 'hostile to society' and had no right to exist.[10] The events of 64 and actions taken in response to them, summed up by Tertullian in 197 in the words institutum neronianum, were to be long remembered.[11]

Such was the genesis of the persecutions. Curiously, the disaster of 64 was not followed by similar actions elsewhere, especially in the provinces of Asia

---

5 Livy 39.8.
6 Ann. 15.44.3.
7 The reference to Danaids and Dirce is given in 1 Clem. 6.2. See also Coleman, 'Fatal charades', 44–7; cf. 65.
8 Tac. Ann. 15.44.8.
9 Suet. Nero 16.2. He blames Nero for starting the fire (38.2). For Jesus himself, regarded as a magician in the second century, see Celsus as cited by Or. C. Cels. 1.6.
10 Odium generis humani (Tac. Ann. 15.44.6), a charge also levelled against the Jews (see Tac. Hist. 5.5.1).
11 Tert. Nat. 1.7.9 (cf. Apol. 5.3). The institutum was not a law, but what was customary.

Minor where the Christians were strongest. For the next thirty years we gather that they did 'suffer for the name' (1 Pet 4:12–16) and, by the end of the century, intense popular ill feeling in the province of Asia was manifesting itself towards them, which resulted in persecution and martyrdom (Rev 6:9), but there was no further documented state intervention against Christians until near the end of the reign of Domitian (81–96 CE).

This emperor was a not unsuccessful soldier and administrator, but was cursed by a deeply suspicious nature that saw philosophers and, towards the end of his reign, members of the aristocracy as his enemies. 'Master and god'[12] were the titles by which he expected to be known. On the other hand, like Vespasian (69–79 CE) before him, he had a vision of the unity of the empire chacterised by urbanisation and romanisation, and consolidated, especially in the eastern provinces, through the cult of Roma and the emperor.[13] While Tacitus describes how temples and fora were being built in the towns of Britain,[14] in the provinces of Asia, statues and temples in honour of the emperor were characteristic of Ephesus, Laodicea, Smyrna and Pergamum, where the Council of Asia (*koinon tēs Asias*) met and games in the emperor's honour were celebrated.[15]

In these circumstances, religious non-conformity would not be tolerated. Jews might be accepted on payment of two *denarii* a year to the treasury (the *fiscus iudaicus*), but not their imitators. Dio Cassius relates how, in 95 CE, the emperor's cousin, Flavius Clemens, and his wife, the emperor's niece, Flavia Domitilla, were charged with 'atheism' (being *atheotai*). Clemens was executed; his wife exiled to the island of Pandataria. Other aristocrats were accused of 'falling away into Jewish customs', and the penalty was either execution or confiscation of property.[16] The consul, Acilius Glabrio, was charged in addition with 'having revolutionary aims' (*molitor rerum novarum*).[17] While nothing should be deduced from the fact that the catacomb of Domitilla was in Christian possession by the third century,[18] 'atheism' was the term applied to Christianity at Smyrna in 156 (see below). The aristocrats punished by Domitian had appeared to reject the Roman gods; as they were not Jews, they put themselves outside the protection of the law. Tertullian regarded

---

12 Suet. *Dom.* 13.2.
13 See pt I, ch. 3, above.
14 Tac. *Agr.* 21; cf. Suet. *Tit.* 4.
15 See Charlesworth, 'Flavian dynasty', 39–40 and footnotes.
16 Dio Cassius 67.14.2; Suet. *Dom.* 15. For an account of the incident, see Streeter, 'Rise of Christianity', 254–5.
17 Suet. *Dom.* 10.
18 Lampe, *Paul to Valentinus*, 206.

Domitian as a persecutor of Christians after Nero,[19] but whether this incident amounted to persecution is a matter for debate.

Domitian was murdered in September 96. An echo of these events may perhaps be found in the coinage of his successor, Nerva (96–8 CE), proclaiming *fisci judaici calumnia sublata* ('abuse of the *fiscus judaicus* abolished'), issued in 96. Tertullian claims that the exiles were recalled.[20] Christianity does not figure again among Classical writers until Pliny's report to the emperor Trajan (98–117 CE) from Bithynia-Pontus, probably in 111.

Pliny (C. Plinius Caecilius Secundus) was born into a family of local aristocrats of the town of Comon (Como) in North Italy.[21] Connected with the Flavian administration through an uncle, Pliny was well placed to attempt a senatorial career. He was lucky with his friends, advancing to the rank of *quaestor*, which automatically admitted him to the senate. He survived Domitian's reign and was consul in 100, Trajan's third year of reign. He was trusted by that emperor and, when, in *c*.108, the affairs of Bithynia-Pontus reached crisis point, largely through corrupt government, he was appointed *legatus Augusti* with full powers to restore the finances and administration in the province. The exact dating of his term is uncertain. He may have been in the province as early as 109 and remained there until 111, rather than the more usual dating of 112–13. He appears to have died not long afterwards, before 114 when Trajan assumed the title of *Optimus*.[22]

Pliny's mandate had nothing to do with Christianity. It included the regulation of the finances of five Bithynian cities, curtailing the misuse of the imperial post, a check to massive overruns in building expenses, and the regulation, or more usually, the suspension of unlicensed *collegia* ('guilds' or 'clubs') as possible centres of crime and sedition. These Pliny banned.[23] It was not until the second year of his tour of the province, at some point between Amisus and Amastris at the eastern end of Pontus, that he appears to have encountered Christians.[24] These were brought before him *tanquam Christiani*, 'as Christians'. Profession of Christianity was illegal, and the penalty for its profession was death. Hence, despite his assertion in his letter to the emperor

19 Tert. *Apol.* 5.13–14.
20 ibid.
21 Pliny's family history and official career are given in Sherwin-White, *Letters of Pliny*, 69–82.
22 Sherwin-White, *Letters of Pliny*, 81–2.
23 Pliny to Trajan, *Ep.* 10.33 and Trajan's uncompromising reply (relating to a *collegium* of firemen at Nicomedia which Pliny had commended, *Ep.* 10.34); see Sherwin-White, *Letters of Pliny*, 606–10.
24 Pliny to Trajan, *Ep.* 10.96. Translated with notes in Stevenson and Frend, *New Eusebius*, 18–20. On the spread of Christianity in Asia Minor, see pt. IV, ch. 17, above.

that he had never previously taken part in investigation of Christians, and that he did not know the nature of the crime usually attributed to them, Pliny had had no hesitation in ordering the execution of those who persisted in affirming their Christianity in the face of a thrice repeated question.[25] And he felt no doubt, since in any case their 'obstinacy and unbending perversity deserved to be punished'. This, as Sherwin-White maintained, was now an additional ground for condemning Christians to death,[26] as the Scillitan confessors were to discover when brought before the proconsul Saturninus at Carthage in July 180. In the case of Roman citizens, Pliny sent them off to Rome for trial and punishment.

Then, there was a complication. An anonymous pamphlet listed individuals whom it denounced as Christian. Pliny, an honest administrator, began to investigate further. Those who denied ever having been Christians, he released once they had recited a prayer to the gods, 'made supplication with wine and incense', and, finally, 'cursed Christ' – a striking illustration of the maleficent nature of the Christian faith as understood even in the upper echelons of Roman society. Of the remainder, some said that they had ceased to be Christians three or more and some as many as twenty years before. They explained part of the liturgy,[27] probably the recitation of the Ten Commandments and the eating of a communal *agapē* after the eucharist, and emphasised that this consisted of ordinary food, an indication that Christians were suspected of consuming vile concoctions for the purpose of black magic or, even, of engaging in cannibalism. After taking further evidence from two maidservants (deaconesses?), Pliny concluded that Christianity was *nihil aliud . . . quam superstitionem pravam et immodicam* ('nothing more . . . than a perverse and extravagant superstition'), and, now that the temples were being frequented once more, 'a place for repentance should be granted'.[28]

Trajan agreed. His replies to Pliny's letters were almost invariably terse and to the point. He commended his legate's actions and instructed that, while 'nothing can be laid down as a general ruling involving something like a set procedure', Christians were 'not to be sought out', that is, not to be treated as common malefactors, sacrilegious or brigands. But theirs was still not a legal religion, and, if accused and convicted, they were to be punished. Every

25 Sherwin-White, *Letters of Pliny*, 693–700. See also, de Ste Croix, 'Why were the early Christians persecuted?'
26 Sherwin-White, *Letters of Pliny*, 599.
27 Sherwin-White, *Letters of Pliny*, 700–9. For a still useful discussion of the Christian liturgy at this time, see Lietzmann, *Messe und Herrenmahl*, 257–60.
28 I.e. Pliny understood Christianity as simply a noxious foreign cult. See Wilken, *Christians as the Romans saw them*, 21–5.

chance, however, should be given them to recant, and, if so, they could be pardoned. Anonymous accusations were to be rejected as 'a very bad example and unworthy of our time'.[29]

This was a decisive moment in the relations between the Christians and the Roman authorities. The text of this correspondence was known widely throughout the second century. This rescript (i.e. a letter containing official instructions) was applied by the provincial governor to Christians arrested at Lyons in 177,[30] and was quoted and mocked by Tertullian some twenty years later.[31] Confused and contradictory though it might seem to be, Trajan's response provided the Roman authorities with guidance on how to deal with an increasingly intractable problem.

Ten years later, there were evidently riots against the Christians in some of the cities in the provinces of Asia. In c.125, the emperor Hadrian (117–38 CE) sent a rescript to the proconsul, Caius Minucius Fundanus,[32] referring to a report sent to him by the proconsul's predecessor, Serenius Granianus, probably asking for instructions in the face of popular outbreaks against the Christians. Hadrian would allow regular charges to be brought against them, but the rescript reiterated his predecessor's indignation against anonymous and vexatious denunciations. Prosecutions of Christians would, therefore, be more difficult, though Justin Martyr was hardly justified in regarding the rescript as securing them from persecution.[33] Its significance lies also in the fact that the provincials were being roused against the Christians. The feeling was growing that the monotheism and morality they were preaching were incompatible with the way of life accepted readily by the vast majority of their contemporaries. The emperor, the great provincial deities and their myriad satellite divinities look after the common welfare. Middle Platonism and Stoicism provided religious philosophies superior to that purveyed by Moses, or by the Hebrew prophets, who extolled the virtues of a Jew crucified in Palestine as a rebel in the reign of Tiberius.[34] It would take another century before Christians were able to turn the table on their opponents.

A lengthy interval of comparative peace ended in the 150s. The grim warnings by the prophet Hermas (c. 130) concerning 'strife, imprisonment, great

---

29 Pliny, *Ep.* 10.97; Sherwin-White, *Letters of Pliny*, 710–12. Trajan insists merely that Christians should 'worship our gods'. 'Cursing Christ' was evidently not required.
30 Euseb. *HE* 5.1.
31 Tert. *Apol.* 2.6–9.
32 Text in Stevenson and Frend, *New Eusebius*, no. 18, pp. 21–2.
33 1 *Apol.* 68.6–10.
34 On the various philosophies open to an educated provincial, especially in the east, see Hunt, *Christianity in the second century*, 74–98; Dodds, *Pagan and Christian in the age of anxiety*, chs. 2–3.

afflictions, crucifixions, wild beasts for the sake of the Name' had not materialised.[35] At Smyrna, however, on 22 February 156, bishop Polycarp was brought before the proconsul on a wave of popular anger and accused of 'atheism'. Having refused all pleas from that official to 'consider his age', 'swear by the genius of Caesar', and 'denounce the atheists', Polycarp was condemned to be burnt alive.[36]

By now provincial antagonism was being formalised into a series of deadly accusations. Our earliest source is Fronto, a North African, possibly from Cirta in Numidia, but who had made his career as a lawyer in Rome, where he had prospered and been appointed tutor to the future emperor Marcus Aurelius (161–80 CE). Hence, his speech, which was perhaps delivered to the senate, must date to c.150–5. Part of it is preserved by Minucius Felix, in the *Octavius*, though that work was compiled some eighty years later. Fronto accused the Christians of 'sacred rites more foul than any sacrilege'. At what one presumes was an *agapē* ('gathering at a banquet'), 'there were drunken orgies, there was incest and some horrid rituals involving a tethered dog'.[37] Twenty years later, similar charges were being spread around in the east, c.176, when Athenagoras, making a plea for toleration of Christians, wrote his *Legatio pro Christianis* to the emperors Marcus Aurelius and Commodus. The more gruesome charge of cannibalism was added to the list (*Leg.* 35) that included the hated accusation of 'atheism'.[38] At Lyons in 177, the same charges were made by the mob that hounded and harassed the Christians before hauling them before the governor.[39] The latter acted in the spirit of Trajan's ruling, by consulting the emperor. Marcus Aurelius pronounced the decision that those who recanted be freed, but the obdurate condemned to the beasts. Roman citizens were to be beheaded.[40] The letter recounting these events describes them as eliciting the delight of the populace, with pity confined to retorts that their lives had been needlessly thrown away.[41] The Christians themselves,

35 Herm. *Vis.* 3.2.1; cf. Herm. *Sim.* 8.3.7. For Hermas' strongly anti-Roman views, see Frend, *Martyrdom and persecution*, 193–5.

36 According to *Mart. Polyc.*, a long letter sent by the church of Smyrna to the church at Philomelium in Phrygia recounting Polycarp's martyrdom (large portions of which are quoted by Euseb. *HE* 4.15). It is significant that Polycarp had remained unmolested as the 'father' of the Christians from the time of Ignatius of Antioch's martyrdom c.107, until his own arrest.

37 Min. Fel. *Oct.* 8.9. As with Pliny's examination of the Christians, suspicion in Fronto's mind fastened on the *agapē* and rumours connected with it.

38 Athenagoras argued that, if Christians were atheists, so too was Plato, and he stressed the loyalty of Christians to the empire and its rulers (*Leg.* 6.2).

39 Euseb. *HE* 5.1.14; see pt IV, ch. 20, above.

40 Euseb. *HE* 5.1.47.

41 Euseb. *HE* 5.1.66. 'Where is their god, and what good to them was their worship, which they preferred beyond their lives?'

however, were described as triumphant, for they went to their deaths 'readily and with joy'.[42]

A final episode in the second century provides a striking illustration of the growing conflict. Previously, it was the Christians who stressed the divide, but now the Roman authorities themselves were becoming conscious of the irreconcilable gulf that separated the two systems of belief, cultic practice and ethics. On 17 July 180, a group of North Africans from the town of Scilli, probably near Carthage, were brought before the proconsul Saturninus.[43] He opened the proceedings by saying to them, 'You may merit the indulgence of our lord the emperor, if you return to a right frame of mind,' that is, recant and be freed, along the lines of Trajan's ruling. Speratus, the spokesman for the Scillitans, replied uncompromisingly that they gave thanks when ill treated 'because we hold our own emperor in honour'. Saturninus reminded him that 'We also are a religious people', swearing by the genius of the emperor, and urged Speratus and his followers to do the same. It was of no use. Speratus proclaimed, 'I do not recognise the empire of this world. Rather, I serve that God whom no man has seen . . .' The *obstinatio* was complete, and, after having confessed to being a Christian and refusing time to reconsider, the Scillitans were condemned to death. 'Thanks be to God' was the reaction. 'Today we are martyrs in heaven.' North African Christianity would continue to be 'the church of the martyrs', guided to that end by the Holy Spirit.[44] The same spirit was being shown by Christian confessors from one province to another, who believed that in martyrdom they would finally be with their Lord, and share with him the Day of Judgement at the expense of their pagan enemies.[45]

During the last half of the second century, instinctive popular anger against the Christians generated the violent, sporadic persecutions recorded by Eusebius.[46] The Jews are now less prominent, though at this time the Platonist critic Celsus still regarded the Christians as apostates from Judaism.[47] He also criticised them for their refusal to take on the responsibilities of public or military service and their apparent wish for a martyr's death. Yet all the time, Christianity was gaining strength and also a measure of respect.[48] The third century would see a contest over whether the immortal gods or the Christian God would watch over the destinies of the empire.

---

42 Euseb. *HE* 5.1.63; cf. 5.1.55.
43 Text and translation in Musurillo, 86–9.
44 See pt IV, ch. 21, above.
45 Cf. Tert. *Spect.*, ch. 30. See Frend, *Martyrdom and persecution*, 368–9.
46 Euseb. *HE* 5.1.
47 Or. *C. Cels.* 2.4; cf. also 4.18.
48 See, for instance, Wilken, *Christians as the Romans saw them*, 68–93.

The third century

Through most of the third century, popular hostility continued to be one of the principal factors in rousing persecution against the Christians, but the emperors and their officials now became more active. Previously, they appear to have been, except perhaps in the case of the Scillitans, the passive recipients of demands from the people for the destruction of the Christians. Now, they began to take the initiative.

The first indication that things were changing comes in the years 202–6. There seems no reason to doubt the authenticity of the end of a rescript of Septimius Severus (193–211 CE), preserved by Spartian, his alleged biographer, forbidding conversion either to Judaism or Christianity and dated to 202 CE.[49] This was to be the last time that the two religions were bracketed in joint infamy. The Christians were probably the main sufferers. Though nothing seems to have befallen the Christian leaders in either Rome, Carthage or Alexandria, new Christians were punished, and ugly scenes occurred there and in Corinth.[50] At Alexandria, Leonides, Origen's father, was a victim.[51] The converts Perpetua and Felicitas and their companions were executed in Carthage in March 203. The detailed account of their martyrdom shows the damage which conversion to Christianity could inflict on one of the leading families in Carthage and once more the 'unbending perversity' of the Christians, rejecting with contempt pleas from Perpetua's father and from the procurator to recant. They were fanatics, threatening eternal punishment on the procurator while being marched round the amphitheatre at Carthage, enduring the sadistic pleasure of the spectators at their deaths.[52]

There was no sympathy for Christianity or Christians. Tertullian (c.197) writes of the 'instinctive fury' of the populace of Carthage as a prime cause of persecution.[53] Christians were blamed for every natural disaster. In a well-remembered sentence, he summed up the attitude of the people. 'If the Tiber reaches the walls, if the Nile does not rise to the fields, if the sky does not move or the earth does, if there is famine, if there is plague, the cry is at once, "The Christians to the lion." All of them to one lion!'[54] To the charge of illegality

---

49 *Sept. Sever.* 17.1.
50 For Alexandria, see Euseb. *HE* 6.3.3 'under Aquila' (early in 202). For Corinth, the fate of a 'noble Christian lady who blasphemed both the times and the emperors and spoke ill of the idols' is recorded by Pall. *H. Laus.* 65. See also Frend, *Martyrdom and persecution*, 321–4 (cf. Barnes, 'Legislation').
51 Euseb. *HE* 6.2.12, probably in 202, 'when he (Origen) was not quite seventeen'.
52 *M. Perp.* 18.
53 *Apol.* 37.2.
54 *Apol.* 41.1.

was being added that of outspoken opposition to 'the Roman gods' and to the Roman state. At the turn of the third century, the Christians were being perceived as prime internal enemies of the empire and of the values for which it stood.

Other factors, however, were turning in the new religion's favour. In the first half of the third century, Christianity could no longer be identified with 'the lower orders fomenting discontent'. Origen replying to Celsus *c.*248 describes how an increasing number of educated individuals were becoming Christians: 'When on account of the multitude of people coming to the faith even rich men and persons in positions of honour, and ladies of high refinement and birth, favourably regard adherents of the faith, one might venture to say that some become leaders of the Christian teaching for the sake of a little prestige.'[55] This was happening alike in east and west, Alexandria as well as North Africa.

This change in social composition was accompanied by greater self-confidence. In the west, Tertullian's *Apologeticus* and other writings speak for themselves. *Fiunt non nascuntur Christiani* ('Christians are made, not born')[56] was probably the truth. In Alexandria, Clement's *Protrepticus* (*c.*190) is the first open attempt to convert educated Greek-speaking citizens to Christianity. Defence of the faith was no longer based solely on scriptural proof-texts showing that Jesus was Messiah, but on demonstrations that Christianity was the true philosophy. This was a significant change in Christian apologetics from the second to the third century, corresponding largely to a change in the composition of the membership of the church.[57]

A time of quasi-toleration lasted from the final years of Septimius Severus to the death of Alexander Severus in March 235 at the hands of rebellious soldiers. It was a period of Christian advance. Tertullian, though writing some years earlier, boasts 'We are but yesterday, and we have filled everything you have – cities, tenements, forts, towns, exchanges, yes! and camps, tribes, palace, senate, forum.'[58] This was gross exaggeration, but the house church at Dura Europos, and the first Roman catacombs, as well as the careers of Prosenes, an imperial chamberlain,[59] and Julius Africanus, onetime officer in Septimius Severus' army and earliest known Christian chronographer and friend of Alexander Severus, bear witness to the growing strength and visibility of the church.[60]

---

55 *C. Cels.* 3.9.
56 *Apol.* 18.4.
57 See pt III, ch. II, and pt v, ch. 27, above.
58 *Nat.* 1.14, written *c.*197 CE; compare a similar statement written in 212 CE, Tert. *Scap.* 2.
59 On Prosenes, see McKechnie, 'Grave inscriptions'.
60 For Julius Africanus, see Euseb. *HE* 3.2 and 6.31; Simonetti, 'Julius Africanus'.

These signs of prosperity were abruptly challenged by Alexander Severus' supplanter, Maximin (235–8 CE), a rough Thracian soldier who evidently had no time for unlawful religions. For the first time an emperor takes the initiative against the Christians by aiming at their leaders.[61] Origen's friend, Ambrosius, was among those who believed themselves threatened. The threat, however, passed quickly. Maximin was murdered in 238, and another eleven years of peace and progress followed.[62] In Rome, new catacombs were created, and the church there was developing into a vast charitable organisation, with 'up to 1,500 widows and poor persons' receiving support from its coffers.[63]

But storms were gathering. In 248 there was a massive pogrom of Christians in Alexandria,[64] and Origen shows that in the east Christians were being blamed for the instability of the times.[65] Once again the wheel turned. On the Danube frontier, the empire was threatened by attacks from a powerful confederation of Germanic tribes, the Goths. The emperor Philip (244–9 CE) proved an incompetent soldier. In September 249, his army was defeated at Verona by one of his generals, and he lost his life. The victor, Decius (249–51 CE), was determined to restore both the empire's frontiers and the traditional values of Rome. He assumed the name 'Trajan' in honour of that illustrious emperor, and, to make the point, issued a series of coins commemorating the *consecratio* of many of his predecessors. It was probably in the same spirit that the new emperor issued a decree in the first months of his reign ordering all the inhabitants to sacrifice to the gods, taste the sacrificial meat and swear that they had sacrificed.[66] The annual sacrifice on the Capitol on 3 January 250 provided a weighty example which the cities of the empire must follow. J. B. Rives has ably pointed out that the aim of the decree was positive. 'It was in some way the religious analogue to Caracalla's citizen decree: while the latter replaced the mishmash of local citizenships with a universal and homogeneous citizenship, the former summarised the huge range of local cults in a single religious act that signalled membership in the Roman Empire.'[67] Decius' decree was not aimed, therefore, specifically against the Christians, but as prime non-conformists they were especially subject to sanctions, for they were not prepared even to 'recognise' the Roman gods. This *obstinatio* accounts for the acute divisions that resulted within individual Christian communities.

61 Euseb. *HE* 6.28.
62 Euseb. *HE* 6.36.
63 Euseb. *HE* 6.43.11.
64 Euseb. *HE* 6.1–7.
65 *C. Cels.* 3.15.
66 See Rives, 'Decree of Decius', 135.
67 Rives, 'Decree of Decius', 153.

Members were forced to choose between obedience to the emperor and obedience to the church, and the recent increase in the number of Christians, many of whom were nominal, made the dilemma worse.

Prominent individuals, such as Fabian, bishop of Rome, and Babylas, bishop of Antioch, were arrested, tried and executed almost at once.[68] Cyprian of Carthage was publicly proscribed and had left the city by March.[69] On 12 March,[70] the presbyter Pionius was executed at Smyrna. Proceedings, however, dragged on. In Egypt, the sacrifice test appears not to have been applied until the middle of the year. Forty-four certificates of sacrifice (libelli) have survived, dating from 12 June to 14 July, the elaborate formulae used attesting to the solemnity of the occasion.[71]

Available evidence suggests that the emperor's policy met with immediate success. The church was still very largely urban, and its leaders would be well known. They lost control of the situation. At Carthage there was mass apostasy. The crowd of would-be sacrificers was so great that the priests begged them to return the next day.[72] At Smyrna, Polycarp's see, bishop Euctemon readily sacrificed, and encouraged others to do so.[73] According to the dramatic account of events in the Martyrium Pionii, the pagan population, despite nearly two centuries of Christian mission, was clearly on top, alternately mocking the presbyter Pionius and his few companions and beseeching him not to throw away his life so foolishly. Although their urging was in vain, it was evident that the church had suffered a mighty blow, and, had the persecution been followed up, its recovery would have been slow and difficult.

As it was, fortune favoured the Christians. Decius and his son were killed in battle against the Goths in June 251. There were two more years of stress under the short-lived emperor Gallus (251–3 CE),[74] enough for the mob to shout 'Cyprian to the lion'[75] and for pope Cornelius to die in exile at Centumcellae in 253. In the same summer, however, the situation was partly stabilised by the removal of Gallus and the accession of Decius' friend, Valerian (253–60 CE).

68 Cypr. Ep. 55.9 (Fabian); Euseb. HE 6.39.4 (Babylas).
69 Cypr. Ep. 66.4.1. Rives, 'Decree of Decius', 141.
70 M. Pion. 23.
71 See Knipfing, 'Libelli of the Decian persecution', 363ff. A full list is given by Selinger, Mid-third century persecutions, 137–55.
72 Cypr. Laps. 8.
73 M. Pion. 15. See Lane Fox, Pagans and Christians, 460–92, for a brilliant sketch of the events leading to Pionius' martyrdom.
74 See Frend, Martyrdom and persecution, 411–12. For an account of the confused events of the year 253, see Alföldi, 'Age of Decius', 168–9.
75 Cypr. Ep. 59.8. On the number of Christian martyrs under Decius, see Frend, Martyrdom and persecution, 413.

The new emperor had the reputation of being at first 'exceptionally friendly' towards the Christians.[76] The evidence shows that the great Christian centres of Rome, Carthage and Alexandria recovered quickly. At Carthage, bishop Cyprian returned to his city early in 251. He dealt rapidly with the problems raised by the multitude of lapsed Christians who wanted to return to the church, and asserted his episcopal authority against the claims of the confessors that, as 'friends of Christ', they, and not the bishop, had the right to forgive sins.[77] However, Cyprian's victory was short-lived.[78]

The persecution that resulted in his execution differed from that of Decius. Decius had made no attempt to confiscate the goods of the church. Now, this was to be a prime aim. According to Eusebius,[79] quoting a letter from bishop Dionysius to a fellow bishop, Herammon, the trouble started in Egypt with jealousy between 'the synagogue of Egyptian magicians' and Christians. The magicians were accused by the latter of performing horrible rites involving infanticide (just as the Christians had been accused earlier in the century). Unfortunately for the Christians, the 'ruler of the synagogue' was Macrianus, a former, yet still powerful, official who had been in charge of the imperial finances. He harboured hopes of gaining the empire for himself, and apparently (there is a lengthy gap in the text here) persuaded Valerian that the Christians posed a danger to the empire at a time when the empire itself was being threatened by Persian invaders.

The aim of the persecution was to destroy the church, financially and socially, by confiscating its not inconsiderable property and by preventing the leadership from functioning. The first aim was understandable as within a few years the coin in common use, the *antoninanus*, would suffer a catastrophic devaluation. In addition, Christian services were forbidden, and Christian places of worship confiscated. There was good reason for these new tactics. In the previous thirty years, the social composition of the church in Rome had been changing. No longer 'the dregs of the population', but *matronae* ('wives of the aristocracy or near-aristocracy') and the influential *Caesariani* ('imperial freedmen'), were among its numbers. Moreover, catacombs, often the burial places of retainers of the leading houses in Rome, were passing into Christian hands, those of Calepodius and Domitilla being prime examples. The authorities were faced with a formidable task.

---

76 Dionysius of Alexandria, quoted by Euseb. *HE* 7.10.3.
77 Cypr. *Ep.* 23 (the statement of the confessor Lucian to Cyprian). In the previous century, the confessors of Lyons had assumed without question the right of 'binding and loosing' (Euseb. *HE* 5.2.5).
78 See pt v, ch. 26, above.
79 *HE* 7.10.4.

The two edicts aimed at destroying the power of the church and emphasising its illegality were promulgated by the emperor and senate in July 257 and August 258. The first usually involved exile, or condemnation to the mines,[80] the second, death. The authorities had no doubt now that Christianity was a religion openly hostile to the state. On 14 September 258, Cyprian, having been sent into comfortable exile at Curubis as a result of the first edict,[81] was brought before the proconsul of Africa, the ailing Galerius Maximus. It was charged that he had 'lived long an irreligious life and drawn together a number of men bound by an unlawful association, and professed (himself) an open enemy of the gods and the religion of Rome'.[82] Cyprian refused to 'conform to the Roman rites' and was executed the same day. The grounds for persecution could not be clearer. What the first martyrs in North Africa, the Scillitans, had confessed in July 180 and what Tertullian had proclaimed was so: Christianity could not be reconciled with the religion of the Roman gods. Were they or Christ to be the guardian of the empire?

In Alexandria, where Dionysius, bishop through two persecutions, was an eyewitness, we find the same conflict but without equally tragic results. His account of his interrogation by the deputy prefect, Aemilian, is preserved by Eusebius.[83] After first forbidding the holding of Christian services, Aemilian conducted a reasonably civilised discussion with Dionysius and his priestly companions. But when Dionysius refused to worship 'the gods that preserve the empire and forget those gods that are contrary to nature', he was sent into exile to Cephro, an oasis in Libya. Characteristically, he built a large church there that became a centre of worship for Egyptian Christians. In Rome, pope Sixtus II and four of his deacons met their deaths on 6 August 258 in cimiterio, probably the catacomb of Callistus.

The persecution, perhaps more severe in the west than in the east,[84] was cut short by Valerian's capture and death at the hands of the Persians in a battle near the city of Edessa in June 260. His son, Gallienus, now sole ruler (260–8 CE), hastened 'by decrees (dia programmatōn)' to end the persecution.[85] One of these, addressed to the bishops in Egypt, has survived, restoring 'the places of worship to them' (i.e. to the Christian bishops) and ordering that 'none

---

80 See Cypr. *Ep.* 76–9; and Davies, 'Condemnation'.
81 *Acta proconsularia* of St Cyprian 1 (CSEL 3.3, pp. x–xiv); English translation in Stevenson and Frend, *New Eusebius*, no. 222, pp. 247–9.
82 *Acta proconsularia* 3–4 (CSEL 3.3, pp. xii–xiii).
83 *HE* 7.11.3–11.
84 Frend, *Martyrdom and persecution*, 427–8.
85 Euseb. *HE* 7.13.1.

should molest them'.[86] In Rome, the Christians had not waited. As soon as the news of Valerian's capture had arrived, a new bishop, Dionysius (260–9 CE), was elected.[87]

The vigour and self-assurance of this response were not confined to Rome. For the next forty-three years the church enjoyed peace. There were occasional, isolated persecutions, but 'churches everywhere were at peace'.[88] Though the historian lacks the close-knit documentation provided, for instance, by Cyprian's letters, literary and material evidence combine to show that this was a period of Christian advance through the empire, to a level that would frustrate Diocletian's hopes of destroying Christianity through the Great Persecution of 303–12.

In Rome itself, the catacombs tell the story. At the catacomb 'Aux deux lauriers', by 300 CE there were 11,000 burials over a two-kilometre area on the site, the majority of whom had been laid to rest in the previous fifty years.[89] Other catacombs, such as those of Maximus, Pamphilius and Thrason, were newly constructed. That of Novatian (died c.258 CE) has yielded inscriptions dating from 266 and 270.[90] In this period, pope Dionysius made regulations for the cemeteries under his jurisdiction, and it would seem that by the end of the century every *titulus* (parish) had its own cemetery.

Other sites, not least in Asia Minor, also provide evidence for the growth of Christianity. At Nicomedia, Diocletian's capital, an imposing church stood in full view of the imperial palace by 300. When Maximin entered the city in 311, he found that 'nearly all the inhabitants were Christians'.[91] In Phrygia, cities such as Orcistus and Eumeneia were strongly Christian, and one unnamed town in the province was the scene of a massacre involving the entire population during the Great Persecution.[92] Elsewhere, the city of Cirta in Numidia provides an example of the popular change of attitude towards the Christians. Whereas in 259 the confessors Marianus and Jacobus were hounded before the magistrates,[93] fifty years later, Victor the fuller was prepared to offer 20 *folles* to become a presbyter.[94]

---

86 Euseb. *H.E.* 7.13.
87 Before 20 July 260. See Marichal, 'Date des graffiti', 119.
88 Euseb. *H.E.* 7.15.
89 Guyon, *Cimitière*, 101.
90 See Stevenson, *Catacombs*, 33–4; for the 'vast development of catacombs', see 250–300.
91 Euseb. *HE* 9.9.5.
92 Euseb. *HE* 8.11.
93 M. *Mar.* 1, 2 and 5, 'blind madness of the pagans', and 'the blind and bloodthirsty prefect caused persecution'. The anti-pagan emphasis of this *passio* is exceptional.
94 Optatus, *De schismate Donatistarum* (see Optatus, *Against the Donatists*, Edwards (ed. and trans.), appendix, p. 194 (top)).

All over the empire, including the Celtic lands of north-west Europe, Christianity had advanced. But the real problem facing any would-be persecutor was its progress into the countryside. For reasons that are by no means clear, in the provinces bordering the Mediterranean from the south, the traditional deities that had watched over the respective populations for millennia lost favour and support. In Numidia, hitherto devoted to the worship of Saturn (Baal Hammon), the last dated inscriptions in his honour are from 272.[95] In Cyrenaica, Apollo has no dedicatory inscription after 287.[96] In Egypt, the last known inscription in hieroglyphs dates from 250,[97] and from 270 onwards the Copts were moving towards an alternative form of religion in monasticism. By 300, persecution of the Christians could no longer count on the completely willing support of public opinion, either in town or countryside.

By this time, Christianity had emerged as the final obstacle to Diocletian's (284–305 CE) policy of unifying the empire under the aegis of the Latin language, the Roman gods and, in particular, Jupiter and Hercules as the guides of a uniform administration. In 286, imperial power was divided into a dyarchy, Diocletian taking Maximian as his colleague responsible for the west. Then in 293 each emperor appointed a deputy or Caesar, Galerius in the east and Constantius in the west. In Diocletian himself, however, resided the wisdom of the gods, the *providentia* associated with Jupiter, while Maximian was associated with Hercules, who represented heroic energy combined with willing obedience. The establishment of the tetrarchy was followed by other measures promoting unification and uniformity. Traditional city mints, including that of Alexandria, were scrapped, and in 295–6 a single uniform currency was struck featuring on the reverse of its most common unit, the *follis*, a dedication 'to the genius of the Roman people' (*genio populi Romani*).[98] Provincial administration was also reorganised,[99] and in 301 the Edict of Prices attempted to impose a uniform system of valuation for a vast range of goods throughout the empire.[100]

---

95 From Novar (Sillegue), *CIL* 8.20435. See Frend, *Donatist church*, 83–4. A later dedication, dated November 323, has been found on a temple site near Beja in western Tunisia, but the *tria nomina* of the dedicant (Marcus Gargilius Zabo) suggests that by the early fourth century the cult had become aristocratic rather than popular, although there seems also to have been a priestly hierarchy. See Beschaouch, 'Une stèle consacrée à Saturne', 258–9.

96 Roques, *Synésios de Cyrene*, 318.

97 Geffcken, *Der Ausgang des griechisch-römischen Heidentums*, 25.

98 See Mattingly, 'Quattuor principes,' 337–8, for discussion of Diocletian's coinage reform.

99 See Ensslin, 'Development of paganism'.

100 Lactant. *Mort.* 7.6–7. Fragments of the inscription have been found on more than 40 sites in the east but, so far, none in the west. On its relatively limited purpose, see Barnes, *Constantine and Eusebius*, 11.

Uniformity was the rule. As in the reign of Decius, the Christians were seen as the great non-conformists.

There had been ample warnings of the conflict to come. The decade 290–300 had witnessed a vigorous propaganda war against the Christians represented by Porphyry of Tyre's fifteen books *Against the Christians (Kata Christianōn)*.[101] The genesis of the Great Persecution, however, lay in a trivial incident in Antioch in 298. Christians were blamed for the absence of entrails in animals sacrificed to the gods in honour of the successful conclusion of the Persian war, and the emperor ordered them removed from the army and civil services.[102] Thereafter, Eusebius records, 'little by little persecution against us began.'[103] The attitude of the emperors had already been foreshadowed in their decree against the Manichaeans, directed to the proconsul of Africa.[104] The gods had made Rome great. Innovation might bring divine wrath upon the empire. *Disciplina* must be observed in all aspects of life. Manichaean books would be seized and adherents of the sect burnt alive. The example was there when the time came to act against the Christians.

That moment arrived late in 302. There was still an immense belief in the authority of oracles, when Diocletian and Galerius visited the oracle of Apollo at Didyma near Miletus. But they found its utterances confused and demoralised by the influence of Christianity.[105] So their minds were made up. They would strike to remove the Christian challenge to the gods. The day set was 23 February, the feast of Terminalia. It would mark the end of the rival religion.

Eusebius could find no logical reason for the persecution.[106] On 23 February 303, Diocletian issued an edict requiring that Christians hand over their scriptures on pain of imprisonment, their churches be destroyed, and they be banned from pleading in the courts. Upper class Christians (the *honestiores*) were to lose their social status; the *Caesariani* (imperial freedmen), as under Valerian, reduced to slavery; and Christian slaves barred from being manumitted. But, according to Lactantius, who was at Nicomedia at the time, Diocletian opposed the shedding of blood.[107] No martyrs were to be made,

---

101 See Frend, 'Prelude'.
102 Lactant. *Mort.* 10; cf. *Div. inst.* 4.27.
103 *Chron.*, at the year 301.
104 English translation of Diocletian's decree against the Manichaeans (dated *c.*297 or by others to 31 March 302), in Stevenson and Frend, *New Eusebius*, no. 236, pp. 267–8.
105 Lactant. *Div. inst.* 11; Euseb. *V.C.* 2.50.
106 Euseb. *HE* 8.1.1–6, points instead to the church's great prosperity and apparent enjoyment of imperial favour.
107 *Mort.* 10; see Moreau's commentary (SC), vol. ii, 264.

and there was no order yet for a general sacrifice.[108] That was reserved for the spring of the following year with the fourth edict of persecution, which was the work of Diocletian's Caesar, Galerius.

In the meantime, a second and third edict had been promulgated, the second ordering the imprisonment of clergy, the third, coinciding with the celebration of the twentieth anniversary of Diocletian's reign (his *vicennalia*) in Rome in the summer of 303, releasing those who were prepared to sacrifice. Force was used to break the will of the reluctant.[109] At first, matters seemed to be going well for the authorities. As Eusebius points out,[110] the initial measures were aimed at bishops (and clergy) only. In North Africa, we hear of bishops either apostatising, such as Repostus of Abitina, prevaricating, like Paul of Cirta, or handing over heretical (Manichaean?) or spurious works, as did the primate, Mensurius of Carthage. In some towns such as Apthungi, in Byzacena, the bishops and local leaders of the city council were on friendly terms. In the spring of 304, however, the fourth edict, which demanded a general sacrifice by all, changed this and brought about what proved to be the final battle between the old and the new.

North Africa and Egypt, followed by Palestine, saw the most savage of the persecutions. In North Africa, lay Christians were willing to defy the authorities and court martyrdom. The most celebrated of these was Crispina, an upper class woman from Thagora in western Tunisia who was brought before the proconsul Annius Anulinus at Theveste. Despite every argument by the latter, not discourteously expressed, Crispina held firm to her faith, refused to sacrifice to the gods, and was beheaded with five supporters on 22 December 304.[111] Her resting place became a centre of pilgrimage throughout the fourth century. In Carthage, forty-eight Christians caught celebrating the liturgy at Abitina after the apostasy of their bishop were imprisoned and had to contend with the hostility of the Carthaginian clergy as well as that of the authorities. In a step of the utmost significance for the future of the church in North Africa, these prisoners held a council in February 304, at which they decreed that none of those who collaborated with the authorities would have peace with the holy martyrs and participate in the joys of paradise with

---

108 *Mort.* 11; cf. Moreau's commentary (SC), vol. II, 273. For death-dealing reprisals after a fire in the imperial palace allegedly started by Galerius, see *Mort.* 14.
109 Lactant. *Div. inst.* 5.9 and 11 (an eyewitness account of what he saw in Bithynia).
110 *Mart. Pal.* 3.1.
111 *M. Crisp.* The contrast between the relative patience of the administrators and the obstinate fervour of the confessors is highlighted in the martyrologies of this period.

them.[112] The schism in the church of North Africa between the catholics, who were prepared not to provoke the authorities, and their opponents, for whom martyrdom was the highest Christian good, may be said to have started at this point.[113]

In Palestine, there were forty-seven executions recorded by Eusebius in his *Martyrs of Palestine*, most for provoking the authorities. The majority of recalcitrant Christians, however, were sent to work in the mines of Egypt. It was there that the worst horrors of the persecution, witnessed by Eusebius in 311 in Upper Egypt, took place. After describing a number of horrific tortures meted out to Christians in the Thebaid, Eusebius continues: 'And we ourselves beheld, when we were at these places, many all at once in a single day, some of whom suffered decapitation, others the punishment of fire; so that the murderous axe was dulled, and worn out, and was broken in pieces while the executioners grew utterly weary and took it in turns to succeed one another.' Yet the volunteers for martyrdom never ceased and received 'the final sentence with gladness'.[114]

Maximin was an energetic ruler. He ordered the reform of the pagan cults in the cities of the east on hierarchical lines. He had anti-Christian propaganda such as the 'Memoirs of Pilate and the Saviour' circulated and, when he took over the provinces of Asia Minor on Galerius' death (5 May 311), he encouraged provincial and city councils to petition him to have the 'atheists' removed from their boundaries. An inscription from Colbasa in Lycia and Pamphylia records the emperor's congratulations to the city for 'having been freed from blind and wandering ways to have returned to a right and goodly frame of mind'.[115]

But at this point pagan morale was crumbling. Too many people were asking themselves why Christians hated the gods to the extent of giving their lives rather than worship them.[116] Persecution in the west had ended upon the abdication of Diocletian and Maximian on 1 May 305. The palinode of Galerius, issued on 30 April 311, admitted the ill success of the measures designed to bring the Christians back to the religion of Rome, and now allowed 'that Christians may exist again'.[117] This sealed the fate of the gods as no longer the sole protectors of the empire. Constantine took his cue from what he had seen. His

---

112 M. *Saturn*. 18 (*PL* 8, col. 701 B).
113 See pt IV, ch. 21, above.
114 *HE* 8.9.4–5.
115 See Mitchell, 'Maximinus'. The text of the Aricanda inscription (*CIL* 3.12132) is given in translation in Stevenson and Frend, *New Eusebius*, no. 247, p. 281.
116 Lactant. *Div. inst*. 5.23.
117 Lactant. *Mort*. 34; translation in Stevenson and Frend, *New Eusebius*, no. 246, pp. 280–1.

victory over the western usurper, Maxentius, at the Milvian bridge outside Rome on 28 October 312, brought an end to the Great Persecution, finally achieved by his meeting with his colleague Licinius at Milan in February 313. Within a decade of Diocletian's first edict, Christianity had become the favoured religion of the empire.

What was the legacy of the persecutions? Diocletian's great effort to bring the Christians at least to acknowledge the immortal gods had failed, but the results were not to be altogether favourable to the Christians. In the two territories where the persecution had claimed the most lives, Egypt and North Africa, divisions between those who had co-operated with the authorities and those who courted a martyr's death were as deep as those that separated the collaborators and the Resistance at the end of the Second World War. In Egypt only the martyrdom of Peter, bishop of Alexandria, on 25 November 311, prevented the schism, initiated by Melitius, bishop of Lycopolis, from gaining the support of the majority of Egyptian Christians. As it was, Melitius and his hardline supporters continued to embarrass bishop Alexander and Athanasius to the middle of the century and exerted an influence on the development of the Arian controversy for a generation after the Council of Nicaea (325 CE).[118]

Events in North Africa took a more serious turn. We do not know the fate of the Abitinians, though their martyrdom may be presumed. There was also another memory, that of the archdeacon Caecilian forcibly preventing food from reaching them in prison. When in 311 bishop Mensurius died, Caecilian was elected bishop of Carthage in his place. There was an immediate hostile reaction. Indicative of the increased strength of the church in Numidia, at some time after the death of Cyprian, the Numidian bishops had acquired the right of assisting at the consecration of a new bishop of Carthage. This time they arrived too late. Frustrated, the primate, Secundus of Tigisis, who had arrived with seventy bishops (a formal number inherited from the number of the Jewish Sanhedrin), joined the Carthaginian opposition. He accused Caecilian of being consecrated by a *traditor* bishop (i.e. one who had surrendered the scriptures), probably Mensurius' deputy, Felix of Abthungi in Byzacena. He now assembled a council that promptly deposed Caecilian. Schism had broken out. This was the situation that greeted Constantine on his entry into Rome on 29 October 312. Rashly, the emperor decided that Caecilian was true bishop of Carthage and threatened to punish his opponents. The state had intervened to crush dissenters. By the summer of 313, the latter had found an able leader in Donatus, bishop of a community on the edge of the Numidian steppes

---

118 See ch. 31, below.

at Casae Nigrae. Despite successive condemnations by bishop Miltiades of Rome, the Council of Arles in August 314, and finally by the emperor himself in November 316, the church of Donatus survived, claiming to be the church of the martyrs. It was so to dominate Christian North Africa throughout the fourth century.[119]

The Donatist church was the prime legacy of the Great Persecution in the west, maintaining so long as it lasted the tradition of martyrdom, the exclusive nature of the church, and the belief in the complete separation of church and state. The last would remain a feature of western theology through the European Middle Ages.

In the remainder of the church, in both east and west, the virtues associated with martyrdom became identified with monasticism. The monks took over much of the role of the martyr. Persecution left its own mark on the history of the church. But its legacy was not religious liberty, as one might have expected. Defence of the age-old established religion of guardian deities watching over the Roman empire and the peoples of the provinces gave way to the guardianship of a single God, whose demands were ever more exacting. This God desired complete and unreserved commitment to divine doctrines. Those who dissented felt the power of God's wrath exercised in his name by the state. One form of persecution gave way to another, a legacy which has lasted until our own day.

119 Euseb. *HE* 7.30.19. For the origins of the Donatist schism, see Frend, *Donatist church*, ch. 1.

29

Church and state up to *c*.300 CE

ADOLF MARTIN RITTER

The problem

The world in which the Christian church assembled was, without doubt, already politically structured. One is scarcely permitted, however, to draw the conclusion that the relation between 'church and state' was regarded, from the beginning, as a particularly important problem. As a matter of fact, this wording appropriately characterises a central problem of *modern* times, in the same way as 'state' is a *modern* concept, arising in the Italian Renaissance. Even with reference to the Middle Ages it can be applied only to a point. The famous 'investiture struggles' were, of course, exactly *not* conflicts between 'church and state'; to transfer this scheme to early Christian times would definitely involve the danger of introducing a great many anachronisms which tend to obstruct our understanding of the real challenges of those days.

The New Testament takes the existence of political authorities for granted and proposes instructions as to the appropriate Christian attitude towards Jewish and Roman rulers. Christian apocalyptic uses, beyond that, a categorical contrast between the people of God and the 'world' power inimical to God. Within the one tradition, spanning from Matthew 22:15–22 (the section on the payment of tribute to Caesar) to Romans 13:1–8, we certainly meet the 'state' or, better, the Roman empire, but not the church. Again, in the persecuted servants of God we can find, it is true, the church, but her counterpart is not really the state as a political ordering power, nor is it the Roman empire, but precisely the 'world' inimical to God. This difference already hinders us from forming a simple contrast between one tradition as positive and another as critical with respect to the 'state' (or the political circumstances, respectively), although there is no doubt that Romans 13 and Revelation 13 reflect on the Roman empire from completely different points of view. The history of interpretation of these two texts until the time of Constantine I[1] reveals that the ancient church

---

1 Cf. Strobel, 'Schriftverständnis'.

never played one text off against the other and obviously never detected any contrast, let alone contradiction, between them. This confirms our point that the early church reflected on her relation with the 'state', if at all, in her own way, not in ours. Or, to give it a positive formulation: the first four centuries CE are the period during which the problem of the relation between 'church and state' has simply been *detected*, as a result of a long historical development.

Presuppositions of early Christian 'political' thinking

According to a strong and influential research tradition,[2] there were mainly three concepts that were the basis for early Christian thinking as to 'church and state'. All three, it is said, can be traced back to current Hellenistic Jewish attitudes towards the Roman empire. As their main representatives, on the one hand, rank the Jewish philosopher Philo of Alexandria (*c*.25 BCE–40 CE),[3] a great admirer of the Roman empire, especially of the emperor Augustus (as unifier of the human race and bringer of peace after a long period of civil wars), and, on the other, the apostle Paul, and his younger Jewish contemporary, Rabbi Hananiah. Paul and Hananiah shared the opinion that the empire is a God-given institution, destined to protect and discipline humanity; otherwise 'everybody would swallow his neighbour alive'.[4] But there was also, according to this interpretive tradition, already in pre-Christian Judaism a third attitude. This attitude was much more revolutionary and hostile, or at least more critical, vis-à-vis the civil power than the aforementioned two. It is that of apocalyptic, as found e.g. in the book of Daniel,[5] in the Jewish passages of the Sibyllines,[6] and in the apocalypses of Ezra[7] and of Baruch.[8] Although to some extent overlapping, by and large, we are assured:

> the categories stand, and it is interesting that the first, most favourable view of the empire should predominate almost immediately among the Christians in the Greek east . . . while Paulinist and eschatological (others would prefer to say apocalyptic) attitudes prevailed in Rome and the west.[9]

2 Cf. e.g. Harnack, *Mission und Ausbreitung*, esp. 272–81; Frend 'Church and state', esp. 42f.
3 Cf. e.g. Philo, *Legat.* 8–10, 13, 147, 309–11, with Euseb. *L.C.* 5.1–5.
4 *Pirqe avot* 3.2.
5 Cf. Dan 2 (the vision of the four empires), Dan 6 (the story of Daniel in the lion's den), or Dan 3 (the three holy children defying Nebuchadnezar in the fiery furnace).
6 Cf. e.g. *Orac. Sib.* 3.350–61.
7 *4 Ezra* 5: 3.
8 *Apocalypse of Baruch* (also known as *3 Baruch*) 40: 1–2.
9 See Frend, 'Church and state', 43.

That this analysis – notwithstanding its indisputable element of truth (*particula veri*) – runs, nevertheless, the risk of oversimplifying things a bit,[10] we shall see in the next paragraphs. For the moment, we should recall another important presupposition of early Christian 'political' thinking: the Christians' attitude(s) towards the surrounding 'world'. Of course, we cannot treat this problem exhaustively, either, but we must again be content with tracing the most essential shifts.

We start with the apostle Paul. In his first letter to the Corinthians (1 Cor 7:29–31), he writes that the time we live in (*ho kairos*) will not last long (literally: it 'is pressed together'). It is therefore advisable for all those who meanwhile 'use the world' not to count on 'using it to the full, because this world in its specific frame is vanishing'. Only a few decades later (*c*.96 CE), in the so-called first letter of Clement of Rome to the Corinthians (*1 Clem.*), we meet a remarkably different climate. The 'world' (*kosmos*) is now presented as persevering in peace and harmony (ch. 20), under the rule (*dioikēsis*) of the divine Word (*logos*) which permeates the universe; it appropriately serves as an ethical paradigm for Christians.

A next marked stage of development is documented by the correspondence of bishop Ignatius of Antioch. In his letter to the Ephesians (before 115 CE?), the author describes Christ's epiphany as a cosmic crisis (ch. 19): 'Now began what God had prepared. The whole created universe henceforth started to move in all its parts [cf. Rom 8:19–22], because [God] worked for the destruction of death' (19:3).

At the turning-point from the second to the third century CE, the unknown author of the *Epistle to Diognetus*, presumably a cultivated Alexandrian Christian, already dares to depict the Christian church as a political society disseminated throughout other political societies, saying:

> what the soul is in the body (i.e. the centre from which all its motions start, the vital as well as the spiritual and intellectual), that the Christians are in the world. The soul is disseminated throughout all members of the body, and Christians throughout the cities of the world. The soul dwells *in* the body, but is not *of* the body, and Christians dwell *in* the world, but are not *of* the world. (*Ep. Diognet.* 6:1–3; cf. 5:9; John 15:19; 17:11, 14, 16)

This represents a breathtaking development, no doubt, or at least a remarkable progress of thought, from the Pauline conviction that 'this world in its

---

10 A glance at the New Testament should already alert us to the fact that this is a real danger (cf. Theissen, *Gospel writing*; his *Gospels in context*; as well as his 'Political dimension of Jesus' activities'; see also Popkes in his review article, 'Zum Thema "Anti-imperiale Deutung"').

specific frame is *vanishing* to 'a synthesis of the Clementine, so to speak still naive, yes (*sc.* vis-à-vis the world) and the Ignatian surmounted no', for the time being, and thereafter to an 'intra-mundane existential dialectics'![11] Small wonder that a renowned German patristics scholar twenty-five years ago found all this 'so striking, that it is hard to dispense with *Hegelian* categories',[12] if you wish to interpret and understand this phenomenon appropriately.

The 'Romans' as the 'Christians' saw them

The Christian attitudes towards the Roman empire[13] during the first three centuries CE seem to have generally followed what the bipartite Christian Bible (Old and New Testament) recommended.[14] The *eschatological* orientation of early Christianity could only with great difficulties, if at all, be harmonised with those interpretations of the established Roman empire which placed, together with Rome's own persistence (*Roma aeterna*), the continuance of the world in the foreground. But, by referring to prophecies like Daniel 2: 31–45; 7: 7 and Revelation 13: 11f, it *was* possible to see in the Roman empire the last political structure in the course of history, which will be replaced by God's own reign (*basileia tou theou*) at the end of the days.[15]

Following 2 Thessalonians 2:7, it was also possible, certainly, to attribute to the Roman empire a *protracting* function, 'a postponement of the end' (*mora finis*),[16] because it stops or, better, delays the eschatological appearance of that 'lawless man whom the Lord Jesus will exterminate with his mouth's breath . . . Satan' (2 Thess 2: 8f), by maintaining peace, order and justice on earth or at least by trying to do so (cf. Rom 13: 3, 4; 1 Pet 2:13–17; 1 Tim 2:1f).

All this must include a realisation that there were not only rivalries or conflicts, but also common interests and goals between 'Romans' and 'Christians', which the latter, as a rule, increasingly emphasised as their expectation for a near return of their Lord weakened (cf. Matt 25:1–46; Rev 3:11; 22: 7, 12, 20 etc.). This was especially true of the early Christian apologists, who struggled for toleration by a suspicious and antagonistic pagan society. Some of their main positions we should now briefly introduce.

---

11 Wickert, 'Christus kommt zur Welt', 474.
12 Wickert, 'Christus Kommt zur Welt', 474 (italics added).
13 Cf. Gärtner, 'Imperium Romanum', esp. 1168–78.
14 See pp. 524–6, above.
15 Cf. e.g. Iren. *Haer.* 5.26.1; 5.30.3. As Gärtner, 'Imperium Romanum', 1169, correctly states, this Jewish Christian theory is a reversal of the pagan concept of *translatio imperii* (see pt 1, ch. 3, above).
16 Tert. *Apol.* 39.2; cf. also 32.1; *Scap.* 2.6; August. *De civ. D.* 20.23.

Early Christian apologists

The first Greek-speaking Christian apologist whose work we know beyond chance fragments[17] – and probably the most important, at least of the second century CE – is Justin, 'philosopher and martyr'.[18] He was born in Samaria (Flavia Neapolis, modern Nablus), and died around 165 CE in Rome, where he (with interruptions) had lived for quite a time. He describes the Christians as 'truly pious and philosophers', like the imperial addressees of his *apologia*.[19] And, by exploiting traditional themes of Platonic philosophy, from the beginning of his treatise forward Justin likewise introduces himself as a philosopher and hence congenial to the situation in which he writes.[20] But, what is more interesting for us is the fact that he likes to emphasise the Christians' loyalty vis-à-vis the emperor and his agents, as well as their persistent prayers for the benefit of the polity, even in times of persecution (whether by Roman authorities or with their silent toleration). For instance, he contends:

> Much more than all other people we are your[21] helpers and allies in the struggle for peace, convinced that it is alike impossible for the evil doer, the avaricious, the perfidious as well as the virtuous man to escape the notice of God; but everybody will face eternal punishment or salvation, according to the quality of his deeds . . . Taxes and tolls we are, more than others, willing to offer to the officials you have installed; because our Lord himself has taught us that . . . [cf. Matt 22:15–22 and parallels]. Therefore we adore (*proskynoumen*), it is true, God alone, but in all other respects we willingly obey you,[22] recognising you as emperors and rulers of men and praying (to God) that you may be, all the time, together with the imperial power, in the possession of prudence and discernment (*sōphrōn logismos*).[23]

17 As is the case e.g. with Quadratus, who, as far as we know, was the first to submit an *apologia* on behalf of the Christians to the emperor (in this case to Hadrian, 117–38 CE). Eusebius has preserved a few lines of it (*HE* 4.3.2–3), but they do not bear specifically on our subject.

18 This honorary title, which, as far as we know, Tertullian (*Val.* 5.1) was the first to bestow on him, was to be Justin's enduring epithet.

19 Cf. *1 Apol.* 1. 2.

20 This is in striking contrast to his own pupil, the Syrian Tatian, and to Theophilus of Antioch, his contemporary. Both also wrote apologies for their Christian faith which have likewise completely survived, but such treatises are more attacks against 'worldly wisdom' than apologies for Christianity, destined to convert cultivated Greeks to the 'barbarian' philosophy of the Christians (Tatian). In his biting critique of Greek philosophy, Theophilus is the first Christian author who spoke about 'the Hellenic theft from the sacred writings' of Jews and Christians (*Autol.* 3.1.14; 3.2.37). See also ch. 11.

21 Justin's addressees in his first *apologia* are the emperor Antoninus Pius (138–61) and his adoptive son L. Verus.

22 Cf. Thphl. Ant. *Autol.* 1.11.1 ('In a word, I prefer to pay honour to the emperor not by worshipping him (*proskynōn autōi*), but by praying for him').

23 Justin, *1 Apol.* 12. Such a presumption was not mere audacity, but a fair expectation, if one took seriously the pretensions of the Roman emperors of the second and the first half of

Referring to the often-discussed 'synchronisms' between the history of the Roman empire and salvation history in Luke 1:5; 2:1; 3:1, and in deliberate conformity with the Roman propaganda and the general feeling, especially of the higher classes, another, younger Christian apologist, Melito of Sardis in Asia Minor, pens his apology (*c*.172).[24] He depicts the time since Augustus (27 BCE–14 CE) as a period of brilliance and glory, explaining this by the fact that the Roman empire, enlarged and pacified under the 'magnificent government' of Augustus, and the Christian church are 'foster-sisters' (*syntrophoi*) born at (nearly) the same time and breast-fed by the same nurse. That means that the contemporaneity of Augustus and Jesus Christ is not at all fortuitous, but providential! As the unification and pacification of the Mediterranean world (*pax Augusta*) created, in concordance with the divine will, a favourable precondition for the Christian propaganda (*pax Christi*), so it is, in Melito's eyes, owing to the support Roman authorities granted to the Christians

> that the might of the Romans increased to great and splendid proportions. You[25] are now his [Augustus'] desired successor, and such you will continue to be, together with your son,[26] provided that you protect that philosophy[27] which began with Augustus and was reared along with the empire. Your prede cessors [*sc.* since Augustus and including him] have respected [this philosophy], in addition to the other religions . . . Among all [the emperors] only Nero and Domitian,[28] seduced by some malevolent persons, made an exception and tried to bring our doctrine into discredit.[29]

Melito subsequently[30] refers to a series of prior imperial interventions and encyclical letters regarding Christians, especially those of Hadrian (117–38 CE)[31]

---

the third century (see pt 1, ch. 3, above). Athenagoras, another contemporary of Tatian and Theophilus, specifies the content of the Christian intercessions for the emperors and the common welfare. Lawfulness and worldwide extension of the Roman rule are, accordingly, his main concerns (Athenagoras, *Leg.* 37.2).

24 Fragmentarily preserved in Euseb. *HE* 4.26.4–11; because addressed solely to the emperor Marcus Aurelius (161–80 CE), it appears to date from the short period of his autocracy (171/172 CE).

25 Cf. the previous note.

26 Commodus (reigning 180–92 CE).

27 Cf. Malingrey, *Philosophia*, esp. 185f, as to the reasons why early Christians could designate their own doctrine and austere lifestyle a 'philosophy' and self-confidently oppose it to the 'pagan'.

28 With the names of Nero (51–68 CE) and Domitian (81–96 CE) are usually associated – rightly or wrongly – the first persecutions of Christians in the Roman empire (see ch. 28, above). Both were regarded also by cultivated pagans as detestable, because they were enemies of the Roman senate.

29 Euseb. *HE* 4.26.7.9.

30 Euseb. *HE* 4.26.7.10.

31 Preserved by Eusebius (*HE* 4.9.1–3); cf. the commentary of Klein in Gyot and Klein, *Das frühe Christentum*, 325f.

and Antoninus Pius.[32] But nearly nothing has survived,[33] and what was preserved gives the impression of having been forged or at least interpolated by
Christians. Nevertheless, with his thesis – that the contemporaneity of Augustus and Jesus was providential – Melito was to find many adherents, among
eastern as well as western theologians.[34]

Millenarianists and anti-millenarianists

There persisted, however, strong apocalyptic traditions, including the expectation of an eschatological renewal of heaven *and earth* (cf. Rev 21:1–5, with Isa
31:9–32:1; 54:11–14; 65:18–22) and a millenarian rule of the 'just', i.e. of 'those
who had not worshipped the beast and its image'. They will finally 'reign with
Christ' on earth (Rev 20: 4, 6, 7), after Satan (the Antichrist) will have appeared,
and all nations, subordinated to him, have been destroyed.

An important and influential witness of these traditions is Irenaeus, who was
born in Asia Minor (before 150 CE), but served for many decades (until his death,
c.200 CE) as a presbyter and bishop in southern Gaul (Lyons, Lugdunum).[35]
His major work is a sharp polemic against nearly all kinds of Gnostic heresy
(written between about 174–89 CE) which many regarded – and some still
regard – as pleading for ideas that were 'nihilistic' as far as their attitude
towards the 'world' and its political structures is concerned.[36] But that is not
Irenaeus' main point, except as it is a part of his critique of those who prefer
to allegorise the millenarian ('chiliastic') hope instead of interpreting it as
an earthly reality or perspective.[37] The 'inhabited earth' (*oikoumenē gē, orbis
terrarum*) is only interesting for him as the arena in which the Christian teaching
gains ground;[38] the Roman empire only as a force guaranteeing peace.[39] Like
Paul he is convinced that 'the world in its specific frame is vanishing'; not so

---

32 Also preserved by Eusebius (*HE* 4.13.1–7); cf. Harnack, *Das Edikt des Antoninus Pius*;
Freudenberger, 'Christenreskript'; and Klein's commentary in Gyot and Klein, *Das frühe
Christentum*, 430.
33 The same is true of book 7 of the famous Roman jurist Ulpian's *De officio proconsulis*.
The Christian Lactantius (see below) claimed to know that this book contained several
imperial constitutions referring to the Christians (Lactant. *Div. inst.* 5.11.18).
34 See e.g. Iren. *Haer.* 4.30.3; Or. *C. Cels.* 2.30; Ambrose *Exp. Ps. 118* 45.21; Klein, 'Das Bild
des Augustus'.
35 See pt III, ch. 13, above.
36 Cf. in particular the classic work of Jonas, *Gnostic religion*, esp. 320–40 ('Epilogue: Gnosticism, nihilism and existentialism').
37 Iren. *Haer.* 5.35.36.
38 *Haer.* 1.10.1; 2.9.1.
39 *Haer.* 4.30.3

God (together with his servants).[40] The Roman empire is the last before the end will come.[41]

Hippolytus was perhaps also born in Asia Minor (before 170 CE) and for a long time served as a presbyter in Rome, before dying in exile in Sardinia under Maximinus Thrax (235 CE). He follows in Irenaeus' footsteps, e.g. in his commentary on Daniel (*Commentarium in Danielem*), the first known Christian commentary on this biblical book, and in his 'Demonstration on Christ and Antichrist' (*Demonstratio de Christo et antichristo*). In both works, Hippolytus intensifies the apocalyptic point of view by admitting that 'Rome' *is* indeed the restraining power of 2 Thessalonians 2: 6, 7 (*mora finis*),[42] but it is also the precurser of the Satanic regime which will finally be destroyed by Jesus Christ.[43] The expansion of the Roman empire was for him only possible because it tried, under Satanic inspiration (cf. 2 Thess 2:9), to imitate the Christian church.[44] Hence, Hippolytus does not deny the coincidence between the 'Augustan principate' and Christ's coming, but he draws from it conclusions quite opposite to those of Melito.

The great North African Tertullian (c.160–220 CE), in all probability the first Latin Christian author, in any case 'a master of rhetorical style and intellectual debate',[45] also shares Irenaeus' and Hippolytus' ardent expectation of the near end of this world, especially in those texts aimed at the edification of his fellow Christians,[46] although no one, he assures, is yearning after the eschatological *horrors*; all are willing, instead, to pray *in a body* 'for the emperors and so for the whole world and the stability and power of the Roman empire' (*pro imperatoribus et ita universo orbe et omni statu imperii rebusque Romanis*).[47] A 'master of the apologetic genre',[48] Tertullian nevertheless takes a path that is distinctive as compared to other early Christian apologists (such as Justin). Instead of pointing out a *maximum* of common ground between 'Romans' and 'Christians', he starts from the beginning of his apologetic masterpiece, the *Apologeticus* (written c.197 CE), with a counter-attack denying that the Roman *res publica* has any significance for Christians, because the one 'state' *they* know,

---

40 *Haer.* 3.1.
41 *Haer.* 5.26.1; cf. 30.3.
42 Hipp. *Dan.* 4.21.3; cf. also 12: 2.
43 *Dan.* 4.12.4f; *Antichr.* 49.28.
44 *Dan.* 4.9.2f.
45 O'Donovan and O'Donovan, *Irenaeus to Grotius*, 23.
46 Cf. Tert. *Cult. fem.* 2.9.8; esp. Tert. *Or.* 5.1–4.
47 Cf. *Apol.* 30.1–33.1; *Scap.* 2.6.
48 O'Donovan and O'Donovan, *Irenaeus to Grotius*, 23f.

of which *they* all are citizens, is the universe (*mundus*).[49] The Romans' rule over the world is *not* the result of (or a reward for) their scrupulous veneration of the traditional gods, as Cicero and many others believed,[50] but it was accomplished by wanton destruction of cities, assassination of citizens and priests and sacking of sacred, as well as profane, buildings. How could anyone imagine that the captured gods would grant an 'empire without end' (*imperium sine fine*) to their *enemies* of all people?[51]

More than once we gain the impression that in the heat of the moment Tertullian has tangled himself up in contradictions. Taking up what was likely the apocryphal 'letter of Pontius Pilate to Claudius'[52] (a forgery dating from the end of the second century CE), Tertullian infers from its very detailed reports of Jesus' miracles and documentation of his resurrection that its author, Pilate, must have become a Christian. This leads to further remarks about how far Roman and Christian might mix:

> Whatever happened with Christ, Pilate – himself already a Christian as far as his conviction is concerned – wrote all that to the emperor at that time, Tiberius.[53] But the emperors, too, would have believed in Christ, if either emperors were not necessary for conducting the affairs of this world, or Christians could also be emperors (*si aut Caesares non essent necessarii saeculo, aut si et Christiani potuissent esse Caesares*)![54]

An astonishing statement, no doubt; astonishing as well as astonishingly contradictory, as it seems to be! Never before in Christian sources have we met such a far-reaching acceptance of the Roman order (without which 'the world' couldn't manage), an acceptance which is obviously untouched even by criticisms of the persecutions Christians had to endure from time to time and for which only some individuals seem to be made responsible. Like the Middle Platonist Celsus (flourishing about 150 CE),[55] although surely not for the same reasons, Tertullian is evidently convinced that one can only be *either* emperor *or* Christian. Neither here nor elsewhere are we told *why* he sees here no other alternative. The only plausible explanation may well be the intimate interweaving of civil society and its institutions, especially of the emperor's office

---

49 Tert. *Apol.* 38.3; cf. 17.1 and Philostr. *VA* 7.14, 19 (!).
50 Cic. *N.D.* 2.8.72; *Har. resp.* 9.19.
51 Tert. *Apol.* 25.12–17.
52 Contained in the *Acts of Peter and Paul* (*Acta Petri et Pauli*), 40–2.
53 Tiberius was emperor at the time of the procuratorship of Pilate, not Claudius (as the pseudepigraphical letter wrongly has it).
54 *Apol.* 21.24.
55 In his anti-Christian polemic (*alēthēs logos*, preserved in Or. *C. Cels.* 8. 68). See pt III, ch. 11, above.

(*as* 'supreme pontiff' (*pontifex maximus*) of the official cult), with *idolatry*. This interweaving seems to be 'so much the fundamental reality for the pre-Nicene church, that it swallowed up all other reasons'.[56]

A dozen chapters later in the same great apology Tertullian can, none the less, exclaim:

> But, why say more about the religious awe and loyalty of the Christians towards the emperor? We simply *must* respect him, because it is *our* God who has elected him [cf. Rom 13:1f, 4]. So it is apt if I say: Caesar is more ours than yours [because he is] installed by *our* God (*Noster est magis Caesar, a nostro deo constitutus*).[57]

Tertullian's younger, eastern contemporary Origen (*c*.185–253 CE), one of the major thinkers in pre-Constantinian times, if not the most learned Greek theologian within antiquity, is a sharp critic of all millenarian ideas. He was convinced that

> the end of the world will come as soon as everybody will have received the punishment which his sins merited; God alone knows the time . . . [cf. Matt 24:36, and parallels]. We believe, at any rate, that God's loving-kindness by his Christ will lead the whole creation to one and only end in which also the enemies will be subjected [cf. Ps 109:1 [110:1]; 1 Cor 15:25].[58]

Those 'who will have nothing to do with intellectual effort, pupils of the mere letter' (*litterae solius discipuli*), who interpret the 'future promises' of the Bible 'carnally' and not 'spiritually' (cf. Rom 8:9; 1 Cor 2:6–16 etc.), Origen can only treat with pity.[59] As far as his attitude towards the Roman empire is concerned, Origen, like Melito, combines political and salvation history, seeing in the contemporaneity of Augustus and Christ a providential act. This must be so, because

> how could this (Christian) doctrine, which preaches peace and does not even allow retaliation against one's enemies, have held its own, unless the circumstances on earth had everywhere been changed and a milder spirit predominated at the advent of Jesus?[60]

---

56 O'Donovan and O'Donovan, *Irenaeus to Grotius*, 24.
57 *Apol.* 33.1.
58 Or. *Princ.* 1.6.1; cf. also Origen's *Comm. Matt.* on 24:9–14 (preserved in Latin). The first passage is a clear expression of Origen's expectation of a 'restitution of all things' (*apokatastasis pantōn*).
59 *Princ.* 2.11.2; cf. 2.3.2–4; *Or.* 25.1.2.
60 *C. Cels.* 2.30.

And even more than that, Origen can, it seems, imagine that there will be, one day, a *Christian imperium Romanum*! The pagan philosopher Celsus, entertaining for argument's sake the outlandish possibility that Romans could be persuaded to neglect the honours paid to their traditional gods and the old customs and, proving themselves 'losers', worship the 'most high' god of Jews and Christians, regarded the sure consequences of such a religious reorientation to be political catastrophe.[61] Origen, on the other hand, boldly replies:

> if, according to Celsus' hypothesis, all the Romans were convinced (by the Christian preaching) and prayed (to the true God), they would overcome their enemies or would not even have any reason for fighting, because God's power would protect them, he, who promised to preserve five entire cities for the sake of fifty righteous men (Gen 18:24–6) . . . If it is, however, his will that we should again wrestle (suffer) and fight for our religion, let our antagonists (competitors) come forward. We shall say to them: 'I have strength for anything by our Lord Jesus Christ who gives me power' (Phil 4: 13).[62]

Meanwhile, Origen maintains, Christians will continue to be loyal to the pagan authorities, 'help the emperor' with all their power, 'and co-operate with him in what is right', just as Celsus demanded, but exclusively with their own means and weapons – by rendering *divine* help to the emperors or, if one may say so, 'by taking up even the whole armour of God' (cf. Eph 6:11). In doing it this way, they merely claim one of the privileges that the Roman authorities were prepared to concede to their pagan 'priests', namely, immunity from military service.[63] Why this reserve about Christian military service? Is it the impossibility of shedding blood, even in the service of those authorities whom God had empowered to bear the sword (Rom 13)? Origen does not tell us. But we may surmise that it is once again the indissoluble association with idolatry that in Origen's eyes excludes military office for Christians, rather than pacifism as a matter of principle.[64]

---

61 *C. Cels.* 8.69. Celsus points out that, 'instead of being masters of the whole world, the former [i.e. the Jews] have been left not even a clod, not even a fireplace', after Jerusalem was captured and destroyed (70 CE) and the emperor Hadrian proscribed the Jews from living there (as a consequence of Bar Kochba's rebellion, 132–5/6 CE). Further, in the case of the Christians, 'if anyone does still wander about in secret [undetected], he will be [sometime] sought out and condemned to death.'

62 *C. Cels.* 8.70.

63 *C. Cels.* 8.73; for the general immunity of pagan priests from military service, cf. Plut. *Cam.* 41; Wissowa, *Religion und Kultus*, 499.

64 The same is true for Tertullian's treatise 'The military crown' (*De corona militis*), written just before his breach with his fellow Christians over the New Prophecy (Montanism).

The 'Constantinian turn' and its literary reflex

Only five to seven decades after Origen's death (254 CE), the African layman Lactantius (*c*.250–325 CE) and the Palestinian bishop Eusebius (*c*.264/5–339/40 CE) would witness the 'revolution' which Origen would not have completely excluded, although he could hardly have counted on it. The 'christianisation' of the Roman empire (or, better, its beginning) is normally associated with the name of emperor Constantine (reigning 305/6–337 CE) and therefore called the 'Constantinian turn' or 'revolution' respectively, although this 'turn' was in reality a process of a longer duration.[65] To describe this process is not our task in this chapter.[66] We confine ourselves to asking how these two Christian eyewitnesses, both skilled authors, one from the western and one from the eastern part of the Roman empire, experienced the fundamental reorientation of the religious policy of the Roman empire and reflected on it in their writings.

Lactantius was engaged between 290 and 300 CE by Diocletian as a teacher of Latin rhetoric at his court in Nicomedia and, later on (314/15), by Constantine as a tutor of his son Crispus in Treves, where he possibly had also some influence on the emperor's politics and legislation. Lactantius was an exponent of a millenarian orientation of Christian eschatology, in the footsteps of Irenaeus, Hippolytus and Tertullian (also Cyprian), as can be seen unambiguously in the last book (bk 7) of his *Divinae institutiones* ('Divine institutions'), his major theological writing, and the last five chapters of its abridged version (or *Epitome*).

What does Lactantius' millenarianism mean for his attitude towards the Roman empire? If one compares his various exhortations, delivered over an extended period of time, for Christians to intercede for the Roman authorities, a remarkable change can be observed. According to a passage in the first 'edition' of the *Divinae institutiones*, written before the 'Constantinian turn' (exactly between 304 and 311 CE), Christians have to intercede (pray) for the 'Romans' in order that the horrors preceding the millenarian rule be delayed (the Roman empire as *mora finis*).[67] But in his work *De morte persecutorum* ('On the deaths of the persecutors'), written between 313 and 316 CE – after such momentous events as the publication of emperor Galerius' edict of toleration (311), Constantine's defeat of the 'tyrant' Maxentius (28 October 312), Licinius' victory over the great enemy of the Christians, Maximinus Daia (30 April 313), and, last of all, the agreement made by Constantine and Licinius at Milan

---

65 Grant, *Augustus to Constantine*.
66 See ch. 30, below.
67 *Div. inst.* 7.25.8.

(February 313), which the latter promulgated four months later on behalf of the eastern part of the Roman empire (13 June 313) – Christian intercessions for the benefit of the 'Romans' are now to be primarily aimed at the 'lasting tranquillity of the flourishing church' (*florescentis ecclesiae perpetuam quietem*).[68] Still later, in the addresses to the emperor in the second 'edition' of the *Divinae institutiones* (*c*.324 CE), 'Christian' intercessions are now strikingly similar to the former 'pagan' prayers for the emperor, following the old Roman (as well as Hellenistic) conviction that true cult (piety) is the necessary precondition of 'public welfare' (*salus publica*) and that peace is its fruits.[69] No doubt – and small wonder! – that Lactantius welcomes Constantine's rise and final autocracy, seeing in it the fulfilment of many prayers of faithful Christians.[70]

Eusebius of Caesarea, one of the leading figures in the east when Constantine's reign begins there (324 CE), fully agrees with Lactantius in this respect. Like Melito, he is convinced that there is a special affinity between *monarchy* and *monotheism* (*one* emperor – *one* God),[71] especially, but not only, when a 'friend' and imitator 'of God' (*tōi theōi philos*), like Constantine is in possession of the throne.[72] Eusebius can describe the present time of the Roman empire, like Lactantius, with formulae traditionally used for the *eschatological* reign of peace. The properly eschatological expectations, including also a critique of the actual present circumstances, recede into the background in view of the Christian *pax Romana* realised by the Roman empire. Thus Eusebius becomes an exponent of the so-called 'political theology'.[73]

Conclusion

It would be tempting to follow the previous section with another correspondingly entitled, 'The Christians as the Romans saw them'.[74] But that would inevitably involve us in a debate over the motives and background of the persecutions of Christians in pre-Constantinian times, and whether Roman authorities initiated these persecutions or tolerated popular anti-Christian

---

68 *Mort.* 52: 4f.; cf. 1 Tim 2:2b (*ut quietam et tranquillam vitam agamus in omni pietate et castitate*).
69 *Div. inst.* 7.27.17; cf. Plin. *Pan.* 1.94.1.
70 *Mort.* 1.1ff.
71 Euseb. *D.E.* 3.7; cf. 6 and Cic. *Rep.* 1.56/60.
72 *L.C.* 5.1–5, with many reminiscences of the Hellenistic idea of kingship (cf. Plut. *Princ. inerud.*; Delatte, *Les traités*).
73 Gärtner, 'Imperium Romanum', 1178, with references mainly to Peterson, *Der Monotheismus*, 71–82; Winkelmann, *Euseb von Kaisareia*, 136–59.
74 So the title of the fascinating book by Wilken.

riots and dirty tricks. So it must be left undone here.[75] Yet there is much to the view that, despite all the resistance, contradiction and even hatred against Christians within the Roman society, rather than the *cause* of the triumph of Christianity, the 'Constantinian turn' 'was an astute *response* to rapid Christian growth that had already made them a major political force'.[76]

Our study has focused on the development of early Christian thinking on the political order. Eastern and western theologians contributed to this development in a comparable way. We have found interesting nuances and different accentuations, but no signs of a *fundamental difference* between east and west as to the basic understanding of 'church and state' or 'religion and politics' in the period up to Constantine.[77]

---

75 See ch. 28, above. For a (short, but fairly exhaustive) list of motives for anti-Christian hatred, collected from pagan as well as Christian sources, cf. Gottlieb, *Christentum und Kirche*, 93–102.

76 Stark, *Rise of Christianity*, 2.

77 Cf. my paper on 'Augustine and Photius on religion and politics', to be published in the proceedings of the Fourteenth International Conference on Patristic Studies (Oxford, 18–23 August 2003), with a critique of the theory of Berkhof, *Kirche und Kaiser*, and Rahner, *Church and state*, adopted also by Frend, 'Church and state', esp. 38f, 47–9, among others.

30

Constantine and the 'peace of the church'

AVERIL CAMERON

The reign of Constantine (306–37 CE) was momentous for Christianity. Before it, and indeed during Constantine's first years, Christians continued to suffer persecution; after it, all but one emperor followed Constantine's example in supporting Christianity. Christianity did not become the official religion of the empire under Constantine, as is often mistakenly claimed, but imperial hostility had turned into enthusiastic support, backed with money and patronage. However, some of Constantine's actions opened up splits between the Christians themselves. The term the 'peace of the church', used by Christians to denote the ending of persecution,[1] is something of a misnomer in light of the violent quarrels which followed during the rest of the fourth century and after. Nevertheless, Constantine's patronage of the church set it on an altogether different path and made it in a real sense a public institution with a legal presence and official recognition.

Sources

The successive literary works by Eusebius, bishop of Caesarea (d. *c*.349 CE), breathe the amazement, and at first almost the disbelief, of a Christian who had visited mutilated clergy in Egypt during the Diocletianic persecution, and then found all his expectations suddenly reversed. Eusebius's *Historia ecclesiastica* ('History of the church'), perhaps begun even before the outbreak of persecution in 303 CE and written over a long period of years, had to be revised more than once as events succeeded each other in startling sequence. After Constantine's victory at the battle of the Milvian Bridge in 312 CE, Eusebius was still occupied with his lengthy refutation of pagan ideas,[2] but later he revised his *Historia ecclesiastica* and composed a *De vita Constantini* ('Life of Constantine'),

---

1 E.g. Lactant. *Mort.* 52.4; the same usage is found earlier in Cyprian.
2 In the two apologetic works known as the *Praeparatio evangelica* ('Preparation for the gospel') and *Demonstratio evangelica* ('Demonstration of the gospel').

designed to explain and extol the rise of this Christian ruler. He also delivered speeches for the emperor's thirtieth anniversary and on the dedication of his church in Jerusalem, setting out a new philosophy of Christian government.[3] Anyone who reads Eusebius can sense the sheer excitement felt by men like him at this unexpected and, from their point of view, clearly divinely inspired reversal. In his *De vita Constantini*, which describes the death of the emperor, they might also feel his anxiety lest this precedent for Christian rulership should now find itself in jeopardy without a successor.

Eusebius is our most important source for Constantine as a Christian emperor, but his view is highly partisan, as was that of Lactantius, whom Constantine chose as tutor for his son Crispus, and whose work *De morte persecutorum* ('On the deaths of the persecutors') demonises and gloats over the persecuting emperors. In total contrast, the pagan historian Zosimus, reflecting earlier pagan accounts, presents a secular and highly critical picture of Constantine.[4] Several surviving Latin panegyrics, most of them anonymous, provide favourable but tendentious versions of events.[5] The fourth-century *Origo Constantini imperatoris* ('The lineage of the emperor Constantine') and fourth-century epitomators (Aurelius Victor, Eutropius) provide valuable and often more neutral information,[6] and the literary sources must be supplemented by the evidence of coins, inscriptions and legal texts. Modern scholars have dealt with this wealth of contradictory and often difficult information in accordance with their own preconceptions, sometimes by attacking the reliability of sources not to their taste.[7] Still today, arriving at a fair appreciation of Constantine requires extreme caution and not a little good judgement; by no means all specialists would agree with the interpretation advanced in this chapter.

Historical setting

Constantine was born at Naissus (modern Nish), perhaps in 272 or 273 CE, the son of Constantius Chlorus by his first wife or perhaps concubine Minervina.[8] Constantius was at first Caesar (junior emperor) and then Augustus (senior

---

3 Drake, 'Lambs into Lions'.
4 Zosimus; *Historia nova* ('New history'), 2.8–39.
5 See Nixon and Rodgers, *In praise of later Roman emperors*; L'Huillier, *L'empire des mots*; Rees, *Layers of loyalty*.
6 See however Fowden, 'Last days of Constantine'.
7 This has been the case especially with Eusebius's *De vita Constantini*, but see Baynes, *Constantine the Great*; Cameron and Hall, *Life*, 4–9.
8 For the problems concerning Constantine's family and early years see Callu, 'Naissance'.

emperor) in the west (293 and 305 CE) under the Diocletianic system of power sharing known as the tetrarchy. Constantine's background and education were Latin rather than Greek (thus his effort to speak in Greek at the Council of Nicaea in 325 CE was much appreciated by the Greek-speaking bishops who were in the majority). According to some sources he had been held in his youth as a hostage away from his father at the court of Diocletian in Nicomedia.[9] When the Diocletianic or 'Great' persecution began in 303 CE, Constantius seems to have been lukewarm about taking action: Eusebius later tried to depict him as a virtual Christian.[10] This was in contrast with his eastern colleagues, especially Galerius, and later Maximin, who continued to persecute Christians after Diocletian's retirement from power in 305.[11] It seems clear that there was division of opinion in the high levels of government about the policy, and that the treatment of Christians could be used as a means of political leverage. Nevertheless, the experience of persecution was real, especially in the east and in North Africa; when it was called off, serious issues of ecclesiology emerged between rigorists and those who believed in the forgiveness and inclusion of the lapsed within the church as a whole.[12] This was the scenario in which Constantine rose to power.

The fate of the tetrarchy

The years 305–12 CE saw the breakdown of the tetrarchic system established by Diocletian under the pressure of individual ambition, of which Constantine was by no means innocent. The idea had been that there would be two emperors (Augusti) in east and west, and two Caesars who would eventually succeed them, thus providing a smooth succession and avoiding the civil strife and competition that marked the third century. It worked well enough until Diocletian and his co-emperor Maximian both retired from power in 305; thereafter stability was lost. Constantine found himself excluded from the succession and, according to some, managed a dramatic 'escape'[13] from Diocletian's successor Galerius in Nicomedia.[14] When Constantius died in York in 306, Constantine was proclaimed emperor there by his father's troops on 25 July. He knew that it was critical to establish his position and quickly left Britain for Gaul, where,

---

9 *Origo Constantini imperatoris* 2; Lactant. *Mort.* 18.10 presents him as favoured by Diocletian.
10 Euseb. *V.C.* 1.13–18; cf. Lactant. *Mort.* 8.7.
11 See ch. 28, above.
12 See pt IV, ch. 21, and pt V, ch. 26, above.
13 Lactant. *Mort.* 24; Euseb. *V.C.* 1.20; contrast Aurel. Vict., *Caes.* 40.2; Zos. *Hist.* 2.8.2. According to *Origo Constantini imperatoris* 2, he was sent for by Constantius.
14 Lactant. *Mort.* 19.1–4.

despite the disapproval of Galerius, he soon obtained the title of Augustus from the senior emperor, Maximian, who had re-emerged from retirement. This politically useful endorsement was sealed by a dynastic marriage between Constantine and Maximian's daughter Fausta (307).[15] At this stage it is clear that Constantine was willing to use the title Herculius, which was part of the apparatus of tetrarchic imperial cult.[16] Nevertheless, there were others jostling for power, including Maxentius (the son of Maximian), Maximin Daia, Galerius and Licinius.[17] This is a confused period of intermittent warfare and alliances, for which we have no complete narrative history, and which can be reconstructed only with difficulty, with the help of numismatic and legal evidence.[18]

Constantine was as ruthless as any in his pursuit of personal ambition, and sought divine help where he found it expedient. Probably implausibly, Lactantius claims that Constantine supported Christians from as early as 306.[19] A Latin panegyric written in Gaul in 310 depicts him as having had a vision of Apollo, and dedications to the Unconquered Sun (Sol Invictus) featured on his coins until as late as the early 320s.[20] After 307 Maximian's fortunes were chequered; he was forced to retire a second time in 308, but even then re-emerged; he committed suicide after Constantine defeated him in 310.[21] But his son Maxentius held Rome, and Constantine's next priority was to march through Italy on Rome and to defeat him. His advance south through Italy, including his siege of Verona, and his victorious entry into Rome are depicted in the sculptures on the Arch of Constantine (315 CE) which still stands beside the Colosseum in Rome.[22] To save Constantine's reputation, the Christian sources paint Maxentius as a tyrant and a usurper; they do the same with Licinius, who was for the moment a necessary ally but was clearly destined to be a further target. Constantine's actions in the months following his victory

15 Pan. Lat. 7 (307); on these events see Rees, Layers of loyalty, 153–84.
16 Pan. Lat. 7 (307) 2.5, 8.2; for the title see Nixon and Rodgers, In praise of later Roman emperors, 44–51; Kolb, Diocletian, 63–6.
17 For the evidence see Barnes, New empire, especially ch. 4.
18 See Barnes, New empire, with Barnes, Constantine and Eusebius, 28–43; Kolb, Diocletian; Sutherland and Carson, Roman imperial coinage, vol. VI, introduction; Cameron, 'Reign of Constantine, 306–37'.
19 Lactant. Mort. 24.9.
20 For the vision: Pan. Lat. 6 (310). 21.4–22.1, on which see Nixon and Rodgers, In praise of later Roman emperors, 249–50; Rodgers, 'Constantine's pagan vision'; van Dam, 'The many conversions of the emperor Constantine', 135; coins: Bruun in Sutherland et al., Roman imperial coinage, vol. VII. Modern scholars have often argued for Constantine's continuing devotion to the cult of Sol Invictus.
21 Pan. Lat. 6 (310) 14.3–6; 20.1–4; Lactant. Mort. 29.7–8; both accounts are highly tendentious.
22 Elsner, Imperial Rome, 16–22, 187–9.

over Maxentius at the battle of the Milvian Bridge late in 312 demonstrate his support for Christians, but it is important to note that even now he was still constrained by political realities and was not solely responsible for the change in religious policy. Not only had Galerius, emperor in the east, already called off persecution in 311;[23] the so-called Edict of Milan of 313 which proclaimed toleration was in fact the policy of Licinius, emperor in the east. As he had done with Maximian in 307, Constantine hastened to make an alliance with his powerful rival, cementing it by marrying his half-sister Constantia to Licinius.[24] The latter had been initially presented in Eusebius's *Historia ecclesiastica* as a pro-Christian emperor like Constantine; it was only later and following their hostilities in 316 and 324 that Eusebius rewrote his story so as to make Licinius into a tyrant and persecutor.[25] It is important to remember that Constantine's victory gave him power only in the west; it was not until Licinius had been defeated in 324 that Constantine became sole emperor. The Christian accounts of Constantine's rise to power are deeply tendentious; if there was a tetrarchic 'system', it had been destroyed by Constantine himself.

Instinctu divinitatis

Constantine is remembered for his alleged vision of a cross in the sky immediately before he went into battle against Maxentius. This version depends on the later and highly embellished story in Eusebius's *De vita Constantini*, which he claims came from the emperor himself.[26] Accounts nearer in time to the event also attribute his victory to divine assistance, though with some confusion as to the form this aid actually took. While in Lactantius' version Constantine is told in a dream to mark his soldiers' shields, apparently with a chi-rho sign,[27] a contemporary panegyrist offers a pagan account.[28] On the Arch of Constantine of 315, the emperor is said to have delivered the city from the grip of a tyrant 'by divine inspiration' (*instinctu divinitatis*), a phrase which carefully leaves the identity of the divinity unspecified. None of these accounts

---

23 Lactant. *Mort.* 34, where Galerius is depicted as motivated by remorse.
24 Lactant. *Mort.* 45.1, 48; Euseb. *HE* 10.5.2–14; in fact the resulting 'edict' was a letter sent out by Licinius. The marriage had been offered before the battle against Maxentius: Lactant. *Mort.* 43.2.
25 Euseb. *HE* 10.8.7–9.5; *V.C.* 1.49–59, 2.1–5; on Licinius see Corcoran, 'Hidden from history'; Barnes, 'Editions of Eusebius' *Ecclesiastical history*'.
26 Euseb. *V.C.* 1.28–32; Constantine is here credited with both a vision and a dream of Christ (29.1); for discussion see Cameron and Hall, *Life*, 204–213; Weiss, 'Vision of Constantine'.
27 Lactant. *Mort.* 44.5.
28 *Pan. Lat.*12 (313), e.g. 25.1 (Constantius rejoices from heaven); 4 (321) 14.1–4 (divine troops sent to Constantine's aid).

tells this as a conversion experience, although Eusebius claims that Constantine now had to inquire from clergy what the sign meant, and even which divinity his father had honoured.[29]

Maxentius and his army were driven into the river Tiber and drowned with their horses and armour, enabling an apt comparison with the chariots of Pharaoh.[30] But the test of Constantine's religious conviction came only in the actions which followed. These included the meeting with Licinius in Milan and announcement of toleration, but Constantine had already decided to favour Christians by offering the same immunity from civic requirements that pagan priests enjoyed, a well-meaning act which immediately gave rise to trouble. In an empire in which Christians were a small minority,[31] a full identification of the emperor with Christianity emerged only slowly, but from now on Constantine never deviated from this decision to support the church, even if it took time before even the emperor himself came to see its full implications. In 315 he celebrated the tenth anniversary of his accession in Rome without the usual sacrifices.[32] Soon after becoming sole emperor in 324 he issued edicts regulating religious affairs: God, he said, had directed his own rise to power and given him victory, and the persecutors had met deserved ends; Christians who had suffered were to be reinstated and receive back confiscated property; even the imperial treasury was to be compelled to make restitution where it was due. Moreover, while no one was to be coerced, polytheists should recognise the error of their ways and cease to put their trust in oracles.[33] As late as the 330s he allowed the erection of a temple for the imperial cult in Umbria, but only in a sanitised form.[34] Yet the weight of tradition bore hard on him, and there were few unambiguous symbols of Christianity on his coins.[35] Equally, the inauguration ceremonies for Constantinople in 324 and 330 seem to have incorporated elements of ancient Roman tradition, even though Eusebius claims that the new city named after the emperor was Christian through and through.[36] The reality was more complex than Eusebius acknowledges: Constantine's 'New Rome' developed on the site of an older and non-Christian city, and it seems to have been planned as much as a seat of imperial power as a Christian capital. Yet later the emperor prepared a mausoleum for himself

---

29 Euseb. V.C. 1.27.2–3, 32.1–3.
30 Euseb. HE 9.8.5–8.
31 Several recent estimates put the Christian population at 10 per cent of the total, but this may well be too high; see pt IV, ch. 16, above.
32 Euseb. V.C. 1.48.
33 Euseb. V.C. 2.23–43, 47–60.
34 Hispellum: CIL 11.5265 = ILS 705 (333–5 CE).
35 Bruun, 'Christian signs on the coins of Constantine'.
36 Euseb. V.C. 3.48; cf. Zos. Hist. 2.31, who claims that Constantine built new temples there.

at Constantinople in which he would be surrounded by sarcophagi representing the twelve apostles and referred to himself as 'the bishop of those outside'.[37]

Legislation can be a poor indicator of a ruler's personal beliefs, but here too there are relatively few obviously Christian elements in the surviving laws of Constantine.[38] For example, his surviving enactments on marriage and celibacy, which Eusebius claims as inspired by Constantine's zeal to reward ascetics, can be seen to have been part of a much longer piece of legislation with less clearly Christian import.[39] Forbidding crucifixion and branding on the face, as the image of the divine, might be felt to be clear enough indicators of Christian motivation, but Constantine's law establishing the observance of Sunday ('the day of the sun') makes no reference to Christian practice.[40] Judging his real allegiance was no easier for contemporaries than for modern historians; for some pagan critics, whose opinions are reflected by Zosimus, Constantine was a dangerous innovator who disturbed the ancient traditions of Rome, but other non-Christian sources present him in far more religiously neutral terms.[41] Nevertheless, certain steps which Constantine took were to prove vitally important in the history of Christianity.

Steps towards Christian enfranchisement

One such step was his crucial decision to grant clergy immunities, which in North Africa exposed the fact that the legitimacy of Caecilian the bishop of Carthage had been challenged by rigorists. The dismay with which Constantine greeted the news that Christians themselves were seriously at odds is evident in his own letters to officials and to the North African bishops.[42] He was put on the spot when the followers of Caecilian's rival, Donatus, directed an appeal to him as emperor, but he did not hesitate in accepting his obligation to act, calling meetings of bishops, first in Rome and then at Arles in 314.[43]

---

37 Mausoleum: Euseb. V.C. 4.60; some may have been shocked by such boldness: Mango, 'Constantine's mausoleum'; *episkopos tōn ektos*: Euseb. V.C. 4.24; Barnes, *Constantine and Eusebius*, 270.

38 Euseb. V.C. 4.17–21 presents a partial view; see Cameron and Hall, *Life*, for discussion.

39 Euseb. V.C. 4.26.2–5; Evans Grubbs, *Law and family in late antiquity*, esp. 128–30.

40 Barnes, *Constantine and Eusebius*, 51.

41 Fowden, 'Last days of Constantine'; Zos. *Hist.* 2.29–39; Ammianus Marcellinus's section on Constantine has not survived, but there are enough hints to allow us to see that he was not enamoured of Constantine. For a more neutral view, see the *Origo Constantini imperatoris*, a fourth-century Latin account which later received some Christian revision.

42 Mainly preserved in Optatus, Appendix. See Barnes, *New empire*, 238–47 for chronology.

43 Millar, *Emperor in the Roman world*, 584–91.

Thus he initiated a momentous precedent for Christian rulers of intervening in church disputes. Nor did he hesitate to denounce and legislate against what he saw as 'sects' – Novatians, Valentinians, Marcionites and Cataphrygians – banning their meetings, confiscating their buildings, and seeking out their books for destruction.[44] This was later followed by more book burning, including the writings of the pagan Porphyry and some Arian material.[45] Those, like the Donatists in North Africa, who refused to conform to council decisions attracted attempts to enforce them by force, and those who still dissented at Nicaea were exiled. In the following years Constantine changed his position and brought back the exiles but banished others, including Athanasius (336). In a letter of 321, in which he admitted to the catholics of North Africa whose church had been seized by Donatists that he could not help them, he appealed to them to await the medicine of God;[46] earlier, however, he had threatened to come to North Africa and sort out the dispute himself but was prevented only by military preoccupations connected with his rivalry with Licinius.[47]

In one of the most momentous precedents of his reign, during Constantine's twentieth anniversary celebrations in 325, some 250 bishops[48] assembled at Nicaea in the emperor's presence and at his order to settle difficult issues of contention across the empire about the date of Easter, episcopal succession and Christology.[49] Constantine made a point of deferring to the bishops. He did not preside himself and only took his seat when they did,[50] but it was the emperor who had summoned the council, and the sanctions that followed for the small number of dissenters including Arius were also imposed by him. Afterwards he entertained the bishops at a splendid banquet in the palace. Eusebius was bowled over by such imperial generosity and by the amazing prospect of an emperor who would support the church; in his highly admiring account of the council, his own theological ambivalence has been temporarily set aside.[51]

It was natural that Constantine looked to bishops as a key part of the organisation of Christianity. He had already ordered governors to provide for their travel to the Council of Arles at state expense, and he gave bishops an

---

44 Euseb. *V.C.* 3.63–5; Hall, 'Sects under Constantine'.
45 Socr. *HE* 1.9.30–1.
46 Optatus, Appendix 10.
47 Optatus, Appendix 5.
48 The numbers given range from *c.*250 (Eusebius) to more than 300; later the number of 318 (cf. Gen 14:14) became canonical.
49 See ch. 31, below.
50 Euseb. *V.C.* 3.10.5.
51 See Cameron and Hall, *Life*, for commentary on Euseb. *V.C.* 3.10–14.

important privilege by granting them judicial power.[52] These were critical steps for the future. Successful bishops came to hold great influence in their cities and elsewhere, including by the end of the century such powerful figures as Ambrose of Milan and John Chrysostom, as well as ascetic leaders like Basil of Caesarea. Now that churches could legally own property, they also soon started to have access to considerable wealth. It has recently been argued that the bishops on their part did their best to manipulate the emperor and pushed him further in some directions than he would otherwise have gone.[53] Doubtless some tried: the years after Nicaea, for example, were a time of episcopal competition and anxiety, when Constantine found himself inevitably drawn into ecclesiastical politics.[54] But the favour shown by him to bishops in general proved to be critical in the further process of Christianisation and the growth of the church as an institution at a time when as yet no parish system existed.

One of the most influential steps that Constantine took, in relation to the future visibility and spread of Christianity, was his church building. Before this period, though there were some substantial churches (e.g. in Diocletian's own capital of Nicomedia), there was nothing to compare with the grand basilicas of the post-Constantinian period. Most that are extant, such as the rotunda of St George in Thessalonica,[55] or the church at Dura Europos in eastern Syria, were buildings erected originally for other purposes but later converted into church use.[56] Constantine set a different example, by inaugurating elaborate church buildings in and around Rome, in Antioch, and above all in and around Jerusalem. These included the octagonal 'Golden Church' of Constantine on the island of Antioch, no longer surviving but depicted on a fifth-century mosaic, which was begun in 327 as a replacement for the church at Nicomedia burnt at the outbreak of the Diocletianic persecution.[57] Church building in Rome concentrated on sites already associated with early Christian worship, on the edges of the city itself, but Constantine was able to build the Lateran basilica on land which was formerly the camp of the *equites singulares* in the centre, and the church of Santa Croce in Gerusalemme stands on the site of the Sessorian palace traditionally associated with Helena;[58] St Peter's, on

52 For the *episcopalis audientia* and the enhanced position of bishops after Constantine see Brown, *Power and persuasion*, esp. 96–103.
53 So Drake, *Constantine and the bishops*.
54 See Barnes, 'Emperors and bishops'.
55 This probably dates from the time of Galerius, whose palace and triumphal arch are nearby (see Lowden, *Early Christian and Byzantine art*, 13–16).
56 See ch. 32, below.
57 Euseb. *L.C.* 9.15; *V.C.* 3.50; Downey, *History of Antioch*, 342–9; Kondoleon, *Antioch*, 115.
58 See Prelude, above.

the Vatican hill and built over an existing cemetery, is associated with the venerable site of the tomb of St Peter.[59] The dates of these churches are not easy to determine, despite the large amount of apparently circumstantial information in the later *Liber pontificalis*, but the intention and the impact are clear enough.[60] The same policy was even more apparent in the Holy Land towards the end of the reign. Here Constantine founded a basilica dedicated in 335 on the supposed site of the resurrection and of Golgotha, the hill of the crucifixion, and another church at Mamre, where Abraham was visited by the three angels; and his mother Helena is credited with the churches of the Nativity at Bethlehem and the Ascension on the Mount of Olives.[61] Eusebius makes great claims for Constantine's building programme (though he does not know about the churches in Rome and writes only vaguely about Constantinople).[62]

Recent scholarship suggests that Hagia Sophia in Constantinople, the Golden Church at Antioch, and St Peter's in Rome owe more to his sons and successors Constans and Constantius II than to Constantine himself, and the rotunda at the site of the tomb of Christ in Jerusalem, like the church of the Holy Apostles attached to Constantine's mausoleum in Constantinople, was also built later.[63] Nevertheless it was Constantine who took the important step of devoting imperial and public funds to church building. He also endowed his churches with wealth and lands to provide revenue for their clergy and upkeep. In a sense he was simply following the example set by his pagan predecessors, for whom building programmes had been an important aspect of imperial patronage. Nevertheless his activities set a pattern for others, and by the end of the fourth century every self-respecting city, however small, had at least one church, and in many cases a lavishly appointed set of buildings with substantial endowments. Christians felt confident when they saw and worshipped in such buildings, and the richer ones were encouraged to become ecclesiastical patrons themselves. By his church building programme in Palestine, Constantine had also inaugurated the transformation of the Roman colony of Aelia Capitolina, as Jerusalem became in the time of Hadrian after the Bar Kochba revolt, into what would become during late antiquity a largely Christian holy

59 Barnes, *Constantine and Eusebius*, 49; Krautheimer, *Rome*, 3–31. For Rome see also Curran, *Pagan city*.
60 For St Peter's see Bowersock, 'Peter and Constantine', esp. 217, 'very probably after Constantine'.
61 Euseb. *L.C.* 9.16–17; *V.C.* 3.25–40, 51–3, 41–3. See Walker, *Holy city, holy places*; Biddle, *The tomb of Christ*; and Prelude, above, on the legends of Helena and the true cross and the Holy Sepulchre.
62 Euseb. *V.C.* 3.48.
63 For the Holy Apostles see Euseb. *V.C.* 4.58–60, with Mango, 'Constantine's mausoleum'.

city; thus, he set in train the practical realisation of a Christian Holy Land, ushering in the practice of pilgrimage which would become one of the most characteristic features of the late antique and medieval world.[64]

Constantine's Christianity

Constantine's own religious belief has always been and no doubt will remain a matter for speculation. It is certainly hard to be sure of what happened in 312, and the contemporary sources variously project their own interpretations onto the emperor. For Eusebius in particular, Constantine's faith was beyond doubt, and there is no denying that he may have exaggerated in his enthusiasm. However, Constantine has left what seems to be testimony of his own. The letters relating to the Donatist affair in North Africa preserved by the catholic bishop Optatus display a strong sense of religious duty and a determination to establish 'right belief' in the empire. The authenticity of the edicts quoted by Eusebius in the *De vita Constantini* has been challenged in the past, but these are now generally accepted, especially since the text of one of the most important of the Constantinian documents in the *Vita* was identified on an early papyrus.[65] Here again Constantine's language is strong; he comes across as a man convinced that persecution of Christians has been punished by God and with a mission to persuade polytheists of the error of their ways. He is equally forceful in the language he uses in his denunciation of Christian sects. Eusebius tells us that the emperor regularly preached to his court, much to their surprise, and that his sermons took the form of an attack on polytheistic error, a call to Christ and an exhortation to repentance.[66] It was a matter of note for Eusebius that Constantine used his own words, not those of speechwriters.[67] The emperor also composed a remarkable speech, which still survives, and which is known today as *Oratio ad sanctorum coetum* ('Oration to the saints'). It was written in Latin and translated into Greek, and takes the form of an apology for Christianity, justifying its truth with reference to Sibylline prophecy and to a Christian interpretation of the child prophesied in Vergil's fourth *Eclogue*.[68] He was also credited with the successful *homoousios* formula agreed at Nicaea, and indeed the *Oratio ad sanctorum coetum* belies the frequent suggestion that he

---

64 Wilken, *The land called holy*, 83–100; Hunt, *Holy Land pilgrimage*.
65 Jones and Skeat, 'Notes on the genuineness of the Constantinian documents'.
66 Euseb. *V.C.* 4.29.
67 Euseb. *V.C.* 4.29.1.
68 The date when the *Oratio* was delivered and its place of delivery are a matter of debate: for the place as Rome and the date as 315, see Edwards, *Constantine and Christendom*, xxiii–xxix; cf. Prelude, above.

was a kind of untutored rough soldier.[69] According to Eusebius, Constantine continued writing speeches to the very end, discoursing before his death on the immortality of the soul and on divine punishment.[70]

Scholars have often wondered why Constantine was baptised only when death was approaching,[71] and have taken this as a sign that his Christianity was even then uncertain or lukewarm. However, infant baptism was not yet the norm and, since Constantine accepted that once baptised his worldly life as emperor would have to change,[72] he had a strong reason for delaying it. When he fell ill, he was on his way to make war on the Persians, in what was at least in part presented as a mission to help the Christians ill-treated by Shapur.[73] It is hard to justify in conventionally Christian terms Constantine's hand in the deaths of his eldest son, Crispus and his wife Fausta in 326, and the Christian sources have quite naturally written out both the events and the suggestion in the work of pagan historians of remorse or expiation on Constantine's part.[74] However, zeal for the church did not absolve him from the harsh realities of power.

In practical terms, it was Constantine who ended the persecution of Christians – at least by their non-religionists. But did he in so doing contribute to the history of religious toleration?[75] One text in which toleration is promoted is Lactantius' *Divinae institutiones* ('Divine institutes'), of which a second edition was dedicated to Constantine, who knew Lactantius and his work, and even drew on it in his *Oratio ad sanctorum coetum*.[76] However the *Institutiones* took shape during the years of Constantine's rise to power and before persecution of Christians had been called off; thus, Lactantius wrote as a Christian apologist in time of persecution, answering pagan arguments against Christianity and arguing for religious toleration for all. After 313, and certainly after 324, the situation had changed dramatically, and new problems presented themselves, not least the handling of dissident Christian groups. If we accept the evidence

---

69 Based on *Origo Constantini imperatoris* 2.
70 Euseb. *V.C.* 4.55.1–2.
71 Euseb. *V.C.* 4. 61–63.
72 Euseb. *V.C.* 4.62.3.
73 *Origo Constantini imperatoris* 35; Eusebius does not connect his illness and death near Nicomedia with the campaign. See Barnes, 'Constantine and the Christians of Persia', and Fowden, 'Last days of Constantine'.
74 See in contrast Zos. *Hist.* 2.29.2–3.
75 See Stanton and Stroumsa, *Tolerance and intolerance*; Drake, 'Lambs into Lions'; also Digeser, 'Lactantius' and her *Making of a Christian empire*.
76 Barnes, *Constantine and Eusebius*, 74; Digeser, *Making of a Christian empire*, ch. 5, esp. 133–8, who argues that Lactantius was reading his work to Constantine's court at Trier before 313; similarly Drake, *Constantine and the bishops*, 207; for the *Institutiones* see Lactantius, *Divine institutes*, Bowen and Garnsey (eds. and trans.).

of Eusebius,[77] Constantine did not restrain his anger at Christian division or his strong conviction that polytheism represented the darkest kind of error. The letter to Arius and Alexander (332/3) denounces Arius as 'the mouthpiece of Satan'.[78] Constantine was, however, a pragmatist. The fact that he did not take stronger measures against pagans[79] does not prove that he had a policy of toleration; rather, it is indicative of the simple fact that non-Christians comprised the vast majority of the population. Even when sole emperor neither Constantine nor his successors could seriously ignore that fact, and no emperor tried to make polytheism itself illegal until Theodosius I at the end of the fourth century. This suggests that their agendas were more concerned with the internal issues affecting Christians; above all, Constantine was determined to try to unify the Christian church throughout the empire. A tension between Christian innovation and traditional religion can be seen again in Eusebius' account of Constantine's funeral. The ceremony was Christian, and Constantine was interred in his mausoleum in Constantinople, whereas previous Roman emperors had been cremated and received apotheosis; yet, like his predecessors, Constantine too was recognised as 'divine' (divus).[80] This seems to reflect the uncertainty and the diversity of views held at the time of his death, not the emperor's own policy of toleration.

The Constantinian legacy

When Constantine died, it cannot have been obvious, at least to sceptics, that the new direction in which he had taken the empire would be continued under his successors. Indeed, in their emphasis on the continued posthumous guidance of Constantine over his three surviving sons, the preface and conclusion to Eusebius' De vita Constantini betray a distinct anxiety for the future. After the death of Crispus in 326, no formal measures had been taken about the succession until 335, when Constantine attempted to set up a division of the empire between his other three sons and two from the family of Constantine's half-brothers.[81] His optimism let him down. In the months after his death in May 337, his three sons turned on their rivals and then began to fight among themselves, in a bloody epilogue to Constantine's reign. Nevertheless,

---

77 Despite some probable exaggerations: for example, whether Constantine forbade pagan sacrifice (Euseb. V.C. 2.45) is debated, and while Eusebius makes extravagant claims for the destruction of temples (L.C. 8), he cites only three specific examples (V.C. 3.55–8).
78 Barnes, Constantine and Eusebius, 233.
79 Perhaps indeed Eusebius' high claims about this in L.C. 7–9 are to be read as apologetic.
80 Euseb. V.C. 4.65–73.
81 Euseb. V.C. 4.51–2.

Constantius II, the sole survivor, did not waver in his own Arian Christianity, and his reign was marked by as much imperial intervention – or attempted intervention – in the affairs of the church as his father's had been.[82] Nor was toleration any more a hallmark of his policies than it had been of Constantine's. Certainly Christians no longer had to fear persecution by the state, so long as they were of the right theological persuasion. But inordinate attention was now paid to doctrinal and other differences within the church itself. Moreover the allegiance of the reigning emperor to this or that variety of Christianity became a critical factor for the rest of the century. It could and often did result in the exile and condemnation of individual bishops. Constantine had not succeeded in settling these differences and doctrinal, especially christological, issues dominated imperial and church politics for several centuries.

What then had changed, and what had Constantine achieved? He did not make Christianity the official religion of the Roman state, as many continue to assume, nor did he declare polytheism illegal. Indeed the majority of the population remained non-Christian at least into the fifth century. But would the transformation of Christianity into a world religion have happened without Constantine? Or would some other Christian emperor have come along soon enough? These are natural questions, but they are not the sorts of question that historians can easily answer. For the enthusiastic Eusebius, Constantine was quite simply God's vice-gerent on earth, and earth the microcosm of heaven,[83] an optimistic view which Augustine's *City of God* was to modify in the light of tragic experience but which remained the basis for a political theory accepted for centuries by eastern Christians in the Byzantine empire. In founding or rather re-founding and renaming Byzantium as Constantinople, Constantine was not to know that the city would become the capital of the eastern and Orthodox empire known to us as Byzantium, or that this empire would bequeath Orthodoxy to Europe. Nor did he establish himself as head of the church. But his actions did bring the Christian church and the Roman state together in a completely new way, and in this his reign was fundamental for subsequent history.

82 Barnes, *Athanasius and Constantius*.
83 See Euseb. *L.C.* for the expression of this view.

31

The first Council of Nicaea

MARK EDWARDS

The first Council of Nicaea was summoned in 325 CE by Constantine, within seven months of the victory that installed him as sole ruler of the empire. It was held, according to Socrates (*HE* 1.8), because the Christian sovereign hated discord and had, therefore, set himself three tasks: to resolve the Melitian schism in Alexandria, to establish a date for Easter, and to bring the church to a common mind in the wake of the controversy ignited by Arius, an Alexandrian presbyter. These issues will be explained below, but we may begin by noting that the council itself was a sign that Christianity had assumed a new mode of government, as well as a new position in the empire. Hitherto, no dispute had been debated in full synod by representatives of all provinces. Doctrine had seldom divided the bishops, and each had therefore imposed the orthodoxy of his forebears on his own clergy; synods convened to chastise a truculent churchman seldom required the notice, let alone the personal attendance, of bishops from outside his province. It was because the questions pending were so momentous, because Christendom was now too large to act as a body even in matters which touched it as a body, and, above all, because the monarchy of Constantine could not tolerate a fragmented church, that this became the first 'oecumenical council', to use the expression of an illustrious participant, Eusebius of Caesarea.

Eusebius, the archivist of church affairs for the three preceding centuries, is also the chief historian of his own epoch. It is from his elliptical narrative in the *De vita Constantini* that we learn most about the prelude to the council and the imperial correspondence that succeeded it; most versions of the creed that it framed against Arius are based upon the letter that he addressed to Caesarea in vindication of his own signature. For the rest, we depend on retrospective allusions, on the stitching together of papyrus fragments, on the partisan testimony of Athanasius (who, if present at all, as deacon to

Alexander of Alexandria,[1] would not have been a participant in debate) and on the ecclesiastical historians, some four of whom – Rufinus, Socrates, Sozomen and Theodoret – offer credible increments to our knowledge, while two of the most loquacious, Philostorgius and Gelasius of Cyzicus, may have done little more than embellish or parody what they read elsewhere. The later the historian, the more apt he is to follow Athanasius in assuming that the defence or definition of a contested orthodoxy was the main object of the council. Yet the creed itself – the vague yet polemical *Symbolum Nicaenum* which will furnish the centrepiece of the present chapter – is an expression not so much of unanimity as of a common desire for unity. Those bishops (the great majority) who came nursing other quarrels may have seen in it nothing more than a placebo for a new, abstruse and local controversy, which, like any other controversy, would be forgotten once it had been resolved.

The protagonists

Constantine himself, though an apologist, was never a dogmatic theologian. He could tolerate a modest idiosyncrasy in doctrine far more readily than conspicuous disparity in practice. In 314 he had used the Council of Arles[2] to subject the west to the Roman calendar, which required that Easter always fall on the Sunday after the new moon which succeeded the vernal equinox. In Asia Minor, however, many churches held to the 'Quartodeciman' reckoning, according to which the remembrance of the Passion was to coincide with the day of preparation for the Passover (14 Nisan), whenever that Jewish festival chanced to fall. To the first Christian emperor, a Judaising anomaly was peculiarly unpalatable, and Constantine's instructions to the bishops after the Nicene council[3] give the immediate force of law to the Roman date. It is not the creed but the paschal computation that was remembered in the canons attached to the Council of Antioch in 341,[4] and even today the date of the chief Christian holiday continues to rotate according to principles laid down in 325.

Eusebius of Caesarea, the biographer and encomiast of Constantine, seems none the less to disapprove of the Council of Nicaea altogether when he

---

1 His attendance is recorded first by Gregory of Nazianzus (*Or.* 21); in a list preserved by Gelasius of Cyzicus, he is the only cleric of a lower order to sign the creed (*HE* 2.38.2). In his tract *De decretis Nicaenae synodi*, Athanasius speaks of the delegates in the third person.

2 Jonkers, *Acta*, 23–4.

3 Euseb. *V.C.* 3.17–19, with 3.5.1–2; see Eusebius, *Life of Constantine*, Cameron and Hall (eds. and trans.), 268–71.

4 Often assigned now to the earlier council which deposed Eustathius.

imputes the beginnings of it to malevolence or *phthonos*.[5] He was certainly not inimical to public shows of harmony. Eusebius records with satisfaction the unanimity of the bishops who approved the Roman date for Easter in the late second century (*HE* 5.24), and he counts the suppression of synods among the impieties of Licinius, the pagan precursor of Constantine in the east (*V.C.* 1.51.1). If Eusebius thus admits that there were matters which required a synod after 321, he could hardly think it a fault in Constantine, the first Christian emperor, to convene one in 325, within a few months of assuming the eastern throne. Unity of doctrine was, however, not so clearly a matter for an episcopal gathering as was conformity in worship. Eusebius does not tell us in his *Historia ecclesiastica* – though it was subsequently accepted by all parties as a fact – that the Council of Antioch in 268 had denounced the application of the adjective *homoousios* ('consubstantial') to the persons of the Trinity; and in his *Demonstratio evangelica*, written before the Nicene council, he discourages the pursuit of any question to which the answer is not revealed in the sacred texts. To judge from the events that followed the council, the prescription of Eusebius – uniformity of practice within the latitude of opinion permitted by the scriptures – commanded wide support among the prelates of the east.

Theological inquiry in Alexandria was, however, more tenacious – which is not to say more philosophical, let alone more Platonic. This was the seedbed of the controversy which became – at least in retrospect – the main business of the council. During the previous hundred years, the catechists and clergy of the city had taken every opportunity to castigate the Libyan Sabellius for his teaching that the Father and the Son are a single entity (*prosōpon*). The view of the majority in Egypt, and throughout the eastern empire, was that the Father, Son and Spirit are three *hypostases*, or self-identical beings, who coexist as a triad, but without compromising the unity of God. This was the opinion of Arius,[6] an Alexandrian presbyter, who proclaimed the distinctness of the three hypostases with such vehemence that his bishop, Alexander, rightly suspected him of denying that the second and third participated in a common Godhead. Arius in turn accused Alexander of an inclination to Sabellianism. When Alexander demanded a recantation of his tenet that the Son was 'out of nothing' (*ex ouk ontōn*),[7] he refused, and an Egyptian synod was convened against him. As was their wont, the bishops of this province cast their votes en bloc with

---

5 Euseb. *V.C.* 3.4; cf. 2.61 and his comment on the origins of the council at Tyre (4.41). Athanasius bears the stigma of anonymity throughout Euseb. *V.C.*

6 On his theology see Williams, *Arius*, 95–116. Dates are much contested, but the letters of Alexander and Arius were probably composed between 318 and 323.

7 See Arius' letter to Eusebius of Nicomedia (Epiph. *Pan.* 69.7; Thdt. *HE* 1.5). Stead, 'Word', surmises that Arius rested his theology on Prov 8:22.

the patriarch – all except two Libyans, Theonas and Secundus, who were particularly wary of any statement which might seem to lend support to their fellow countryman, the errant Sabellius.[8] Far from submitting, Arius sought the protection of Eusebius, the astute and powerful bishop of Nicomedia in Bithynia, and by some accounts a courtier of Licinius, who resided there as monarch of the east.

Three considerations may have induced Eusebius of Nicomedia to take up the cause of Arius. First, as he was reminded at the end of Arius' letter, both were pupils of the eminent scholar Lucian of Antioch, to whom Constantine's new capital, Constantinople, was later dedicated. Next, there may have been rivalry between Nicomedia and Alexandria, for while the former was an imperial seat, the latter remained the wealthiest city of the Greek world and claimed the apostle Mark as the founder of its church. Finally, Eusebius may have thought in good faith that his suppliant had been wrongly condemned, for, while he does not appear to have held that the Son was 'out of nothing', one of his letters denies that the Son proceeds from the being or *ousia* of the Father.[9] Whether or not this statement was intended to contradict the ancient principle that the Son is 'from the *hypostasis* of the Father',[10] it certainly excludes the term *homoousios*, which, however the second half of it is rendered, must imply that the *ousia* (being, substance, entity or essence) of the Son and the Father is one.

Arius also shunned this term: in a letter to Alexander[11] he explains that to conceive of the Son as a *homoousion meros* ('consubstantial part') of the Father would be to follow the Manichaeans by introducing passibility and division into the Godhead. Even after the Council of Nicaea, opponents of the *homoousion* declared that it could only connote the homogeneity between two lengths of the same material, or else the result the result of kneading two materials into a stuff of uniform texture.[12] Arius concedes that one could also preserve the unity of nature between the Father and the Son by 'dividing the monad', like Sabellius, by making the Son a physical projection from the Father, like Valentinus, or by likening him to a fire lit from a fire, like Hieracas. But all these would be blasphemies: the First Commandment requires that all divinity be invested in the Father, and consequently the Son must be a *ktisma* or creation,

8 Cf. Soz. *HE* 2.18.
9 Letter to Paulinus of Tyre at Thdt. *HE* 1.6.
10 Cf. Tertullian, *ex substantia patris* at *Prax.* 7.14, which, like the phrase translated by the same Latin terms in Or. *Comm. Heb.* (Pamph. *Ap. Or.*, in *PG*, vol. xvii, 581–2), seems to paraphrase the dictum at Heb 1:3 that the Son is the impression (*charaktēr*) of the Father's *hypostasis* (Latin *substantia*). The Council of Antioch in 325 invoked the same text; see Stevenson and Frend, *New Eusebius*, 336.
11 Ath. *Decr.* 1.16; Soz. *HE* 1.15.
12 See Hanson, *Search for the Christian doctrine*, 190–202; Williams, *Arius*, 218–22.

albeit the first and 'not as one of the creatures'. Perfectly, unchangeably and timelessly, the Son retains the likeness of the Father – but only by virtue of the Father's will.

Alexander retorted that, if the Son is unchangeable only by the Father's will, he is changeable by nature. For evidence that the Son is derived uniquely from the Father, he proceeds in his encyclical,[13] we need look no further than the title *logos* in the gospel of John; for this means speech, and what is speech, as Psalm 44 reminds us, but an effusion of the heart? Arius in fact made sparing use of this appellation before Nicaea, but in a subsequent confession of faith he employed it in a position which suggests that he took *logos* to signify not the speech of God but the rational principle of governance in creation. Origen held a similar view, denouncing those who had reasoned from the same psalm that Christ was merely an epiphenomenon or function of the Father (*Comm. Jo.* 1.24); and there were no doubt many contemporaries of Arius who feared that Alexander's words, in the manner of his Egyptian predecessor, Valentinus, subjected the Father himself to change. Yet Origen had his detractors also, chiefly bishop Marcellus of Ancyra (modern Ankara), who accused him of inferring, from a dubious equation of Christ with the Wisdom of Proverbs 8, that the second *hypostasis* is a creature and therefore no part of the Godhead. The principal exponent of this fallacy in his own time, for Marcellus, was Eusebius of Caesarea, who, as a keen admirer of Origen, had gone so far as to say that the Son and the Father were not only two *hypostases* but two *ousiai*.[14] In response, Marcellus denied (according to Eusebius) that God was a triad before the incarnation. In terms that would once again have savoured of Valentinianism to some contemporaries, he spoke of the nativity as the evolution of uttered speech (*logos prophorikos*) from the latent reason (*logos endiathetos*), which eternally inhabits the mind of God.

Both Eusebius and Marcellus in fact had exposed themselves to censures that had already been passed on Origen;[15] each had appropriated half the vocabulary of bishop Dionysius of Alexandria, who, but for age and infirmity, would have presided over the deposition of Paul of Samosata in the third century.[16] Their quarrel became more strident after the council, and was to prove fatal to the tenure of Marcellus; up to 325, however, it seems to have embroiled no other

---

13 This letter, *henos sōmatos* ('of one body'), is preserved by Socr. *HE* 1.6, and ascribed to Athanasius by Stead, 'Athanasius' earliest written work'. Alexander's letter to Alexander of Byzantium concedes that the Father, as father, is prior to his Word, though not in rank or nature (Thdt. *HE* 1.3, citing John 14:28).

14 Defended by Euseb. *Marcell.* 1.4.45.

15 For Origen's supposed Valentinianism, see *PG*, vol. xvii, 582.

16 See n. 37; Ath. *Dion.* 14–25.

parties except for the shadowy Narcissus of Neronias and one Theodotus of Laodicea.[17] The controversy in Alexandria may have been fanned by the presence of a faction which acknowledged a rival claimant to the bishopric. It seems that one Melitius of Lycopolis had appointed himself lieutenant to the imprisoned bishop Peter in Alexandria during the years of persecution.[18] When Peter died without resuming office, his place was taken by Achillas, but Melitius refused to give up the right of ordination. On the death of Achillas, Melitius and his cohort turned their rancour on his successor Alexander. We have no reason to think that the Melitians made common cause with Arius at the outset,[19] but such concerted insubordination could not fail to impair the authority of the patriarch. That a bishop should not inquire into the opinions of his presbyters, but that, if he did, the presbyter should submit to his superior, was the advice of Constantine in a letter quoted with approbation by Eusebius (V.C. 2.64–72); but how was any truce possible, when one had a see to rule and the other a conscience to defend?

In matters of this kind, Constantine desired nothing so much as 'peace' (Socr. HE 1.10). This is not to say that he failed to comprehend the debate, for his Oratio ad sanctorum coetum, if authentic, must have been delivered at the latest within a few years of the council.[20] Adopting terms that would have been old-fashioned had they not been used concurrently by Marcellus, he speaks of Christ as the logos prophorikos issuing from the logos endiathetos. He assumes the Son's inferiority to the Father, but this tenet, though it came to be regarded as an accommodation to the views of Arius, was at that time a harmless platitude, designed to forestall the inference that the Father was not the cause of the Son, and hence that there were not so much two hypostases as two independent gods.[21] Whatever his own convictions, he handed over the theological question to a preliminary hearing at Antioch early in 325.[22] In a fragment of a Syriac record, the president's name is given as Eusebius, yet we learn from other sources that Eusebius of Caesarea was condemned here for his

---

17 See Eusebius, Life of Constantine, Cameron and Hall (eds. and trans.), 262, with notes below on the Council of Antioch in 325.

18 The evidence, as appraised by Barnes, Constantine and Eusebius, 202–3, suggests that Peter had delegated authority to Melitius in the Thebaid, but had not approved his role in Alexandria.

19 Williams, 'Arius and the Melitian schism'. A coalition before the Nicene council is alleged by Socr. HE 1.6 and by Soz. HE 1.15.2. Athanasius, however, says nothing of it, while Epiph. Pan. 68.4 reports that Melitius was an early critic of Arius.

20 For bibliography and discussion, see Edwards, Constantine and Christendom.

21 See Edwards, 'The Arian heresy'.

22 For what follows see Stevenson and Frend, New Eusebius, 334–7; Chadwick, 'Ossius'. Lane Fox, Pagans and Christians, 643–4, suggests that Const. Or. s.c. was delivered on this occasion.

assertion of two *ousiai* in the Godhead, and Narcissus for his bolder but more consistent assertion of three. Eusebius of Nicomedia would not have taken offence at either statement; scholars have therefore proposed the emendation of 'Eusebius' to 'Ossius', a change of only one letter in the Syriac. In that case the inquisitor was Ossius (or Hosius) of Cordova, an aging statesman of the Latin church whom Constantine had retained as his confessor. His judgement, like the emperor's *Oratio ad sanctorum coetum*, reveals a solicitude for the unity of the Godhead which was characteristic of the Latin west.

It was known by now that a plenary session would be unavoidable, but the Syriac record anticipates a 'great council' not at Nicaea, but at Ancyra.[23] If, as has been suggested, the notoriety of its bishop made Ancyra an unsuitable location, it is difficult to account for the substitution of Nicaea, whose bishop, Theognis, in contrast to Marcellus and the majority of the participants, was deposed in the wake of the council. If the object is to be inferred from the outcome, it seems more probable that Constantine resolved on a change of venue because he was now assured of the innocence of Marcellus, while Nicaea was appointed as a tribunal for Theognis (just as Antioch was for Paul in 268 and Sirmium for Marcellus' friend Photinus in 351).

Enactments of the council

Constantine's letter summoning the bishops to Nicaea commends its climate and its accessibility to western travellers;[24] Eusebius, who coined the expression 'oecumenical council' for this occasion, adds that the name connoted 'victory' (*nikē*). He states that the number of bishops who attended it exceeded 250, with an 'incalculable' retinue of presbyters and deacons.[25] His estimate is confirmed by extant lists of those who signed the creed, though later historians raised it to 300, and it was soon fixed by tradition at 318, one for every member of Abraham's household.[26] This figure is attained in an Arabic list, but the total in Greek and Latin versions never rises above 220.[27] Twenty came from Egypt and Libya, another fifty from Palestine and Syria, over a hundred from Asia Minor. We read of only six from provinces ruled by Constantine before 324: Ossius of Cordova, Caecilian of Carthage, Protogenes of Sardica, Marcus from Calabria, Domnus from Pannonia and Nicasius from Gaul. Silvester the bishop

23 Logan, 'Marcellus', 440, suggests that Constantine moved the council to Nicaea to make his own attendance possible.
24 Stevenson and Frend, *New Eusebius*, 338.
25 See Euseb. *V.C.* 3.6.1 and 3.8, with Chadwick, 'Origin'.
26 See Eustathius and Liberius at Socr. *HE* 4.12.
27 Figures from Gelzer, Hilgenfeld and Cuntz, *Patrum Nicaenorum nomina*.

of Rome was represented by two legates, in accordance with a precedent set at Arles in 314.[28]

The debates which preceded the signing of the creed wore on from early June[29] to late July; the common sentiment of the church historians is conveyed in Socrates' anecdote that on the eve of the council idle disputants traded subtleties in public, until a simple old man reminded them that faith, not eloquence, is the key to heaven.[30] Rufinus says that the Emperor, showered with letters from litigious bishops, burnt them on his arrival without having read them (Ruf. *HE* 1.2). Eusebius dwells on the august mien of Constantine, his eirenic counsels, the shrewdness of his kindly interventions. These he made in Greek, though at the outset, having been welcomed by the 'bishop in the first row',[31] he replied in Latin (Euseb. *V.C.* 3.10–11). This oration has not survived, although the words ascribed to Constantine by Rufinus – 'you are not to be judged of men, you are as gods to us' – are characteristic of him, and not such as a theologian would have coined.[32]

An encyclical issued after the council shows that Alexander gained the better part of a compromise in the Melitian controversy. Melitian ordinations were upheld, but on condition that Alexander be acknowledged as the bishop of Alexandria, and that no further ordinations be performed without his consent (Socr. *HE* 1.9). Canon 6 confirmed the supremacy of the metropolitan in his province;[33] another, which could be taken as a reflection on Eusebius of Nicomedia, forbade the translation of bishops from see to see, and was widely flouted after the council, as before.[34] The *philanthrōpia* ('humanity') of the ruling on those who had lapsed under persecution would have been more gratifying to Eusebius, whose intimacy with Licinius had exposed him to suspicion and reproach.[35] Penance, after a period of exclusion, was to be the price of return for those who had sacrificed, the heaviest burden falling on

---

28 See, Opt. Appendix 4. Ossius and the legates (or Silvester) come first in all lists.

29 Though Socr. *HE* 1.13 states that it opened on 20 May.

30 Socr. *HE* 1.8. In a different encounter (Ruf. *HE* 1.3, much expanded in Gel. *HE*, bk 2), an old man armed with nothing but the scriptures converts an Arian philosopher. On the sentiment of the historians see Lim, *Public disputation*, 217–29.

31 Identified as Eusebius of Nicomedia by the chapter heading, by Theodoret as Eustathius of Antioch (Thdt. *HE* 1.7), and by Sozomen as the historian himself (Soz. *HE* 1.19).

32 Ruf. *HE* 1.2; cf. Opt. *Donat.* 1.23.4. On the speech attributed to Constantine by Gel. *HE* 2.7.1–41 see Ehrhardt, 'Constantinian documents'.

33 Especially in Egypt; canon 7 gives Jerusalem second rank in Palestine after Caesarea. For the text see Jonkers, *Acta*, 38–47.

34 On canon 15 see Socr. *HE* 7.38, with Bright, *Notes*, 47–51. Alexander had made it a charge against Eusebius of Nicomedia that he migrated there from Berytus / Beirut (Socr. *HE* 1.6).

35 Constantine calls him a creature of Licinius, according to Thdt. *HE* 1.19.

those who apostatised under Licinius, when there was no threat to their lives (canons 11 and 12).

Clergy of the Novatianist or 'puritan' sect,[36] who refused to hold communion with lapsed ministers or with those who had contracted a second marriage, could be reconciled to the catholic church by the laying on of hands. Their orders would remain valid, though a bishop of the Novatianists would become a presbyter under a catholic bishop (canon 8). The followers of Paul of Samosata,[37] on the other hand, were mere heretics who could not be readmitted until they received a new baptism in the threefold name (canon 18). Although this canon intimates by its silence that the baptisms of Novatianists were valid, this is not expressly stated. We owe to Socrates the information that the council licensed the marriage of lower clergy (Socr. *HE* 1.11); he also tells us that the Novatianists, having declined the summons of Constantine, were so far from being appeased by the decisions of the council that they subsequently took up the Asiatic date for Easter although they had hitherto observed the Roman calendar.[38] There is nothing to corroborate the tradition that the bishops removed another source of discord by proclaiming a canon of scripture. But since there is no evidence, apart from Constantine's letter, of a regulation on the date of Easter, it seems probable that more work was transacted at Nicaea than our records now disclose.

The creed

As to the composition of the creed, we possess conflicting testimonies. Basil of Caesarea in Cappadocia (the Turkish hinterland) ascribes it to his own countryman Hermogenes (*Ep.* 81). Eusebius the historian, in a letter to the church of Palestinian Caesarea, asserts that, at the beginning of the council, he recited their local creed, which was then adopted by the council except that Constantine required the addition of the term *homoousios*.[39] In the creed that he recited, there was in fact a great deal more that found no place in the Nicene version, and there is also more than one clause in the creed which was not anticipated in the Caesarean formula. Yet the story may be true in part, his own account of the episode in which, Theodoret tells us, the confession of one Eusebius was read out and condemned.[40] Theodoret fails to say which

---

36 Including Donatists? See Epiph. *Pan.* 59.13.
37 See Euseb. *HE* 7.30.11 on his denial of Christ's divinity.
38 Socr. *HE* 1.10 on the abstention of Acesius; 4.28 on the Phrygian calendar.
39 Appendix to Ath. *Decr.*
40 Thdt. *HE* 1.8.1; see Stead, "Eusebius".

Eusebius suffered this misadventure, whether it was he or another person who read the document, and whether the rehearsal was intended as a proof or as a test of his orthodoxy. At any rate, Theodoret cannot (if he is right) be describing the formal deposition of either Eusebius, for both retained their sees throughout the council. Notwithstanding the presence – and, as some maintain, the presidency[41] – of Ossius, the sentence passed at Antioch on Eusebius of Caesarea had plainly been revoked.

Text and translation

Whatever the provenance of the 'Nicene symbol', our earliest text of it is quoted in the letter of this Eusebius, which is appended to the treatise of his opponent Athanasius, *De decretis Nicaenae synodi*. In the following translation, I have italicised those phrases which are lacking in previous creeds: [42]

> We believe in one God, Father almighty, maker of all things seen and unseen;
> And in one Lord Jesus Christ, the Son of God, *begotten from the Father*
> *monogenēs*,[43] that is, *from the substance of the Father*,
> God from God, light from light, *true God from true God*,
> *begotten not made* (poiētheis), homoousios *with the Father*,
> through whom all came to be, both things in the heavens and those on earth
> the one who on account of us humans and our salvation
> came down and took flesh, becoming man,
> suffering and rising again on the third day and going up [*or* back] to the heavens,
> and who is coming again to judge living and dead;

> And in the Holy Spirit.

> *But those who say 'there was when he was not',*
> *and 'before being begotten he was not',*
> *and 'he came to be from what was not',*
> *or assert that the Son of God is from another* hypostasis *or* ousia*,*
> *or created* (ktistos)[44] *or alterable or changeable:*
> *These the church catholic anathematises.*

41 Barnes, 'Emperors and bishops', 57, marshalls Ath. *Apol. sec.* 5.2 and *H. Ar.* 42.3 against those who opine that the emperor presided.
42 Greek text of Creed and anathemas follows Jonkers, *Acta*, 38–9. Eusebius' letter is also cited by Socr. *HE* 1.8; for the Eustathian version see Socr. *HE*. 4.12; for Alexandrian and Cappadocian variants, Cyril of Alexandria, *Third Letter to Nestorius* 3 and Bas. *Ep.* 125. Hilary of Poitiers, *Adversus Valentem et Ursacium* ('Against Valens and Ursacius') 1.9.1 transcribes an early Latin rendering. See n. 49 and Dossetti, *Simbolo di Nicea*.
43 Eustathius appears to omit this term.
44 See n. 49.

Commentary on the creed

Monogenēs may signify either 'unique' or 'only begotten'.[45] It was not perverse of Arius to take it in the former sense, for even after Nicaea *unicus* rather than *unigenitus* was the common reading of the Apostles' Creed in Latin writers. The council, however, enforced the meaning 'only begotten', adding a gloss that foreshadows and partly elucidates the word *homoousios* in a later clause. It appears that the older phrase 'from the *hypostasis* of the Father' was now deemed insufficient to exclude the 'Arian' tenet that the Son was a product of the Father's will. Origen, while asserting this, had granted a common *physis* or 'nature' to the two *hypostases*,[46] but neither he nor other Greeks had chosen to characterise the Godhead as a single *ousia*. When used in contradistinction to *hypostasis*, the noun *ousia* denotes the stuff or substrate of a concrete individual; here it perhaps implies that the first *hypostasis* is not merely the cause but the source or ground of the second, propagating his attributes by an act which, while it cannot but transcend mundane analogies, resembles a corporeal emanation.

If we believe Philostorgius, it was Alexander and Ossius who conspired to introduce the word *homoousios* (Philost. *HE* 1.7). Athanasius contends that the word was Alexander's only means of forcing an open rupture, as the Arians were able to put their own construction on every other article. Though not defined, the term seems to be paraphrased obliquely by the juxtaposition of 'God from God' as well as by the gloss on *monogenēs*. Nevertheless, Eusebius of Caesarea, in a letter addressed to his congregation within a few weeks of the council, could assert that the *homoousion* merely predicates divine attributes of the Son without determining anything as to his mode of origin. This letter, our only comment on the creed by one of its signatories, is quoted by Athanasius to prove that Eusebius subscribed to it, not to convict him of deceit. Thus it appears that, while the Alexandrians knew their own meaning, they were forced to concede some latitude of interpretation in order to win the suffrage of the majority.

'God from God' is traditional, but 'light from light' rehabilitates a metaphor from Justin and Hieracas, which was impugned in Arius' letter to Alexander. 'True God from true God' vindicates the eternal deity of Christ the Son against the teaching that he became divine through adoption or by fiat. The council assumed, against Arius, that the 'one true God' who is certainly the Father at

---

45 See Skarsaune, 'Neglected detail'. Logan, 'Marcellus', 441–6, argues that Marcellus was a prime mover in the drafting of the Creed.

46 *Or. Comm. Jo.* 2.10; see also n. 10.

John 17:3 is the Son at 1 John 5:20. For all that, the creed affirms not the equality of the persons and an identity of nature – or, as Eusebius held, community of attributes. The procession of the Son was asserted only to prove his likeness to the Father, and nothing was said to countermand the western view that this procession entailed subordination within the triune monarchy. Monarchy and the one substance (*una substantia*) are concomitants, if not synonyms, in Tertullian, and we have already seen that, according to Eusebius, it was Constantine, the Latin-speaking emperor, who enjoined the addition of the *homoousion*. This story is the more likely to be true because Eusebius credits Constantine with the argument that Christ is the *logos prophorikos* who issues from the *logos endiathetos*[47] – a doctrine wholly consonant with Tertullian and the sovereign's own *Oratio ad sanctorum coetum*, but not with the idiom of Eusebius elsewhere. Moreover it is clear that both before and after the council there were many Greeks who regarded the *homoousion* as a treacherous neologism: who but Constantine could have induced them to accept it with such unanimity in 325?

The assertion 'before he was begotten, he was not' was made by Arius in his letter to Alexander, against the notion of a latent or anhypostatic existence of the *logos* in the Father before he became (or acquired) a distinct *hypostasis*. The Alexandrian signatories concurred with him (and thus disowned the teaching of Marcellus) by rejecting this ingenerate phase, but they presupposed a doctrine of eternal generation which was expressly denied by Arius and discreetly overlooked in the polemics of Eusebius against Marcellus after the council. Arius postulated not an eternal but a timeless generation, and it is consequently improbable that he ever wrote 'there was when the Son was not'. Unless, then, the third anathema is a caricature of his thought, it will have been aimed at a different target. On the other hand, there is no doubt that it was Arius who said that the Son was 'out of nothing'. For him this phrase secured the impassibility of the Godhead while distinguishing the Son from all the beings created through him out of matter; for many at the council, it served only to estrange Christ from his Father, making nonsense of his titles and his cult. In the fourth anathema, on those who derive the Son 'from another *hypostasis* or *ousia*', a distinction may be intended between the Father as cause and the Father as source; on the other hand, terms of similar import are often coupled in legal documents to ensure that an offender cannot escape by giving his crime a different name.[48]

---

47 Ath. *Decr.* 33.16; cf. Const. *Or. s.c.* 9.
48 Bindley, *Oecumenical documents*, 51, considers the words synonymous; Hanson, *Search for the Christian doctrine*, 167, suspects deliberate ambiguity.

The anathema on the words changeable (*treptos*) and alterable (*alloiōtos*) was most probably inspired by Alexander's charge that, if the Arian Christ is unchangeable only by the Father's will, he is changeable by nature. Athanasius states (or surmises) that the life of Christ on earth was seen by Arius as a probation of the Son, the attributes of divinity being conferred on him as the prize of merit – not, however, posthumously, as Philippians 2:9–12 suggests, but proleptically, as the Father foresaw his victory in the hour of his generation (Ath. *Apol. sec.* 1.5–6). Eusebius, however, turns the anathema against those – and here he can only mean Marcellus – who assert that the Godhead undergoes some change in the propagation of the Son. The prohibition of the term 'created' (*ktistos*) he does not explain at all, and, in his writings against Marcellus after the council, he continues to urge that creation and generation are synonymous in the Bible. There are a number of witnesses, including bishop Cyril of Alexandria, successor and disciple of Athanasius, who quote the Nicene Creed without the anathema on *ktistos*.[49] Some suspect Athanasius of a poor memory, if not of wilful fraud.[50]

In any case, the creed was drafted cleverly enough to win the assent of the great majority (including Eusebius), while the recusants – Theonas, Secundus and Arius – were excommunicated. Theognis of Nicaea and Eusebius of Nicomedia were deposed, although the subsequent restitution of Eusebius, and the letter by which he procured it (Socr. *HE* 1.14), suffice to prove that he withheld his signature only from the anathemas. So far as we know, the creed was not intended for the laity; we do not hear that it was ever recited at baptism or inserted (like the creed of 381) into regular services of the church.

The aftermath

Few delegates can have been entirely satisfied with their work at the Nicene council. It had promulgated a formula which was neither strict nor latitudinarian – not strict, since (as Eusebius showed) its sense was often equivocal, yet not latitudinarian, as it had canonised a term which, being new, unbiblical and uninterpreted, could hardly fail to irritate the conscience. The last twelve years of Constantine's reign saw a change in the tide of affairs that is often

---

49 Cyril, *Third Letter to Nestorius* 3. Cf. Theodoret, citing Eusebius, *HE* 1.12; Hilary of Poitiers, *Adversus Valentem et Ursacium* 1.9; Bas. *Ep.* 125; Eustathius at Socr. *HE* 4.12. *Ktistos* appears in the latter's transcript of the Eusebian letter (*HE* 1.8), as well as in Ath. *Ep. Jov.* 3 and in his appendix to *Decr.*, which is the first citation of Eusebius' letter.

50 On Whiston's view see Wiles, 'Textual variant'. 'Made' (*poiētheis*), which does not imply perfection and nearness to God, was indisputably condemned.

described, after Athanasius, as an 'Arian reaction'.[51] Perhaps the first prominent casualty, condemned in his native city, was Eustathius of Antioch; yet, although he was a harsh critic of both Arius and Origen, the charge against him was not heresy but traducing the Emperor's mother.[52] Marcellus of Ancyra was condemned as a Sabellian, something worse than an Arian in the eyes of many easterners.[53] Eusebius of Nicomedia, on the other hand, was not only restored to his see but underwent a new translation in 338 to the see of Constantinople (Thdt. *HE* 1.19). Constantine himself was reconciled, at least temporarily, to Arius by the submission of a creed which did not contain the words 'true God' or *homoousios* (Socr. *HE* 1.26). The Alexandrian church, however, refused to comply with the emperor's demand that he be admitted to communion, and Constantine appears to have reverted at some time to a more hostile view of Arius. The knot that human wiles could not untie was cut in 335, when Arius died painfully in the privy – an event which Athanasius ascribed to the mercy of the Triune God.[54]

There was no concerted denunciation of the Nicene faith and no explicit championship of Arian tenets; yet those who had opposed the opponents of Arius were in the ascendant outside Alexandria. Even there the new bishop Athanasius was under siege from the time when he succeeded Alexander on his death in 328. It is true that he was reproached not with errors in doctrine but with tyranny in government, not by Arians but by the followers of Melitius;[55] he, however, professed to believe that his trials were orchestrated by an Arian conclave under the direction of Eusebius of Nicomedia, with the connivance of Eusebius of Caesarea.[56] He was charged with murder, riot, fornication, breaking a chalice, arresting the grain supply from Alexandria; even when the gravest accusations had been refuted at Tyre (he tells us), he was found guilty of the sacrilege.[57] He appealed to Constantine, who at first reinforced

51 See Ath. *H. Ar.* 1; Elliott, 'Constantine and the Arian reaction'.
52 Ath. *H. Ar.* 4–5. This occurred late in 328, according to Burgess, 'Date of the deposition'. For Eustathius' denunciation of Eusebius of Caesarea see Socr. *HE* 1.23.
53 This event follows hard on the plot against Eustathius in Ath. H. *Ar.* 6; yet, Socr. *HE* 1.35–6 implies a date of 335, while 336 is proposed by Barnes, 'Emperors and bishops', 64. Barnes observes that Schwartz ('Eusebios von Caesarea') suggested 328 and Bardy ('La réaction Eusébienne') 330.
54 See Ath. *Ep.* 54 (to Serapion on the death of Arius). The tergiversations of Constantine continue to baffle historians: for one account see Barnes, *Constantine and Eusebius*, 229–34.
55 A papyrus containing part of their indictment has been discovered: Arnold, *Early episcopal career*, 187–9. For a less sympathetic account of Athanasius' career than that of Arnold, see Barnes, *Athanasius and Constantius*.
56 Euseb. *V.C.* 4.41–8 makes Athanasius (without naming him) the cause of his own misfortunes.
57 See Ath. *H. Ar.* 71–89, with Ruf. *HE* 1.17 and Soz. *HE* 1.25.12–19. In 335, a council in Jerusalem rescinded the sentence on Arius.

his deposition by exile; a brief restoration followed, but Constantius II, the heir of Constantine, confirmed the decision of Tyre in 339. Ejected from his diocese, Athanasius joined Marcellus as a petitioner to Julius of Rome.

Relations between Alexandria and Rome were always cordial, and Julius was quickly convinced of the plot against Athanasius. Marcellus was absolved on the recitation of a creed resembling the so-called Apostles' Creed of the Latin church.[58] In 341, the Greek bishops met at Antioch, where, denying that they were Arians, they drafted a creedal statement that repeated most of the articles from Nicaea, not excepting (in one statement) an anathema on the word *ktistos*.[59] Yet the word *homoousios* did not appear in any of them, and their insistence that the Son is the Father's image seemed to militate against the doctrine of a common nature.[60] The policy of the easterners from 341 to 360 was to steer between the (imaginary) heretics who posited two unbegotten entities (*duo innata*) and those (not so imaginary) who reduced the Godhead to a single person or *prosōpon*. Both errors could have been substantiated by an aberrant reading of the word *homoousios*. Meanwhile in 343, an attempt to bring east and west together at Serdica foundered; the easterners held their own council, while the westerners took occasion to confirm the prerogatives of the Roman see.[61] They issued a creed asserting 'one *hypostasis*' in the Godhead – an injudicious rendering of *substantia*, which ripened into heresy if *hypostasis* was assumed to bear its usual sense in Greek.[62]

The Council of Antioch, known for the next two decades as the 'great council', had ratified the condemnation of Arius while purging the creed of clauses which, in the eyes of many easterners, were more of a snare than a prop to orthodoxy. The western council of Serdica, while asserting Christ's divinity in its own fashion, had accorded to Rome a position which enabled her to pose henceforth as the champion and interpreter of Nicaea. Oecumenical force was given to the canons of western Serdica by annexing them to those of 325. It cannot be said, however, that the council and its creed became prescriptive for the whole of Christendom until 381, when, after forty years of schism and vacillation, Theodosius I convened the Second Oecumenical Council at Constantinople. The Nicene Creed was ratified, though it was still considered

---

58 Kinzig and Vinzent, 'Recent research'.
59 Ath. *Decr.* 23. See 22–5 for other formularies, with Kelly, *Early Christian creeds*, 265–74, and Jonkers, *Acta*, 57–61. The so-called 'second creed', which contains the anathema on *ktistos*, is the one that is clearly a statement of the whole council.
60 Cf. Euseb. *Marcell.* 1.4.40 and 2.4.30–2.
61 For text and translation of the canons, see Hess, *Early development of canon law*, 212–55.
62 Ath. *Tom.* 5; Hess, *Early development of canon law*, 105–6. Liberius (Socr. *HE* 4.12) cites only this term of the Nicene anathema.

expedient to omit the gloss on *monogenēs*, to dispense with the anathemas, to add that the Holy Spirit proceeds from the Father, and to append the clauses on baptism, the church and resurrection which had figured in older creeds. In the west the Apostles' Creed held sway as the rule of faith, though it was common enough for the papacy to resist any innovation from the east on the ground that no increment to the doctrine of Nicaea was necessary. For all that, when the west adopted the amplified creed of 381, it enlarged it again to accommodate the purely western tenet that the Spirit proceeds *a patre filioque*, 'from the Father *and the Son*'. It seems to have been the catholics of Visigothic Spain in the late sixth century who made this interpolation as a defence of the Son's divinity against Arian innuendo. Two centuries later the Franks made it an instrument of policy, in their rivalry with Byzantium, to impose this tenet on Rome and hence on the whole of western Christendom.[63] The so-called *filioque* took its place at the head of a swelling list of grievances which were freely exacerbated by both sides until in 1054 the Old Rome excommunicated the New. The divisions between the churches since that date have been too deep to admit of any reunion by a form of words.

63 Kelly, *Early Christian creeds*, 357–68.

32

Towards a Christian material culture

ROBIN M. JENSEN

Christians, idols and the invisible God

In his address at the Athenian Areopagus, the apostle Paul (according to Luke) points out similarities as well as differences between the worship of the locals and the God he proclaims. Distressed to find the city filled with idols, he remarks that Athenians must be extremely religious people, since, among all those objects of worship, he noted an altar dedicated to 'an unknown god'. This find leads him to distinguish the Christian God from other gods, specifically in terms of their material accoutrements:

> The God who made the world and everything in it, he who is Lord of heaven and earth, does not live in shrines made by human hands, nor is he served by human hands . . . Since we are his offspring, we ought not to think that the deity is like gold, or silver, or stone, an image formed by the art and imagination of mortals. (Acts 17: 22–9, NRSV)

If Paul's pronouncement actually had guided subsequent Christian practice, this religion indeed would have appeared to be a 'strange new teaching' – radically different from other religions in terms of constructing shrines to house or images to portray its deity. Graeco-Roman polytheism was visually oriented. Temples and statues were central to most of the 'foreign' religions practiced by diverse ethnic groups in the empire, while religious pluralism and experimentation were characteristic of the era. Paul's Athenian contacts are described as eager to hear and tell about 'something new', and Paul's proclamation of a deity beyond visual representation and inhabiting all of space *was* something new. But besides worshipping their own invisible and omnipresent God, Christians stubbornly refused to respect their neighbour's gods and boycotted the civic and imperial cult. They were not pluralistic in their attitude towards religion, and either denied that other gods existed, or claimed that they were demonic inventions. Such antisocial and unpatriotic behaviour led to Christians being characterised as atheists and often charged with criminal impiety or sacrilege.[1]

The late second-century apologist Marcus Minucius Felix portrays such Christian effrontery in a (probably fictional) dialogue between the pagan Caecilius and the Christian Octavius. Caecilius claims that Christians despise temples, spit on the gods' images, sneer at pagan rites, treat priests with contempt and scorn the purple robes of public office.[2] Octavius proves him right by characterising polytheism as gullible, naive, and simple minded – the creation of long-dead mortals who elevated ordinary human beings to divine status, and then crafted worthless statues of them on which birds might nest, or spiders hang webs. He goes on, ridiculing pagan rituals, making fun of their priests, and flatly stating that only the superstitious or deranged would participate in such a religion. He contrastingly describes his Christian God as 'too bright for sight', ungraspable, immeasurable and an unnameable boundless infinity.[3] Other early Christian writers shared these views, including Minucius Felix's African contemporary, Tertullian, who condemns most of Roman culture as essentially idolatrous, including attending the games or theatre, wearing fashionable clothing, drawing up contracts, or teaching literature. Above all, Tertullian regards making images of foolish 'nonentities', who neither see, smell, hear nor feel but yet are deemed gods, as an utterly depraved activity. By contrast, he describes the Christian God as invisible, indescribable and inconceivable, and yet manifest in everything and known in every historical event. Moreover, this God will curse and condemn anyone who would either make or worship an idol.[4]

There were, however, certain groups within the surrounding culture who might have shared Octavius' view of the pagan gods or their images, or thought Tertullian's condemnation justified. Paul had been arguing in the synagogue with devout Jews and addressed his speech on the Areopagus to Epicurean and Stoic philosophers. In contrast to traditional Roman polytheists, such groups may have been well disposed to the proclamation of a transcendent, singular and invisible god, who had neither image nor shrine. The Stoics, for example, opposed the making of divine images, following the teachings of their founder Zeno, who was known for his opposition to temples and statues.[5] And Christian apologists often noted that Christian teaching was

---

1 Justin, 1 *Apol.* 6; 13; 25; Tert. *Apol.* 10; Athenagoras, *Leg.* 4; M. *Polyc.* 9; Arnobius, *Adv. nat.* 1.29; 3.28; 5.30.
2 Min. Fel. *Oct.* 8.4.
3 Min. Fel. *Oct.* 18–24.
4 Tert. *Idol.* passim.
5 For example, see Cic. *N.D.* 1.36.101–2; cited in Balch, 'Areopagus speech', 59–79.

consistent with teachings of earlier, pre-Christian philosophers and poets, although they insisted that on all points Christian teaching was fully complete and true.[6] Similarly, some Christian writers pointed to Jewish repudiation of images and the prohibition against idolatry in the Ten Commandments (Exod 20:4; Deut 5:8) to defend Christian rejection of divine images and even visual art in general. The third-century Egyptian writer, Origen, for instance, praised Jews for expelling both painters and image makers from their state, and condemning the art that drags the eyes of the soul away from God to the earth.[7]

Christian enculturation

Based on such assertions, a modern reader might assume that early Christians, behaving like pious Jews, scrupulously avoided the trappings of the polytheistic culture that surrounded them, especially its visual art and architecture. However, a visit to the excavations below St Peter's basilica in Rome offers a contradiction – an ancient Christian tomb with an overhead mosaic portraying Christ in the guise of the sun god driving a chariot drawn by four white horses. The radiate halo around Christ's head extends golden beams and his tunic and cloak fly in the breeze. In his left hand he holds the orb of the world, a symbol of his dominion. His right hand (mostly missing) must have either held the reins, or perhaps made a gesture of greeting or blessing. Incongruously, however, the space over which his chariot flies is neither a cloudless sky nor a starry heaven, but a lush grapevine (fig. 9).

In this place visitors encounter the vestiges of a much earlier time, when Christians were not yet securely dominant or powerful, and the signs of their existence reflected their tenuous and ambiguous relationships with their non-Christian neighbours. Excavations below St Peter's basilica undertaken in the mid-twentieth century under Pope Pius XII confirmed that the high altar of the original St Peter's was actually set over an ancient shrine of the saint himself. As significant as this discovery was, the simultaneous exploration of a network of pagan and Christian tombs also revealed much about the relationships of Christian and non-Christian Romans in the first three centuries. St Peter's basilica was first built by Constantine in the 320s, to mark and enclose the site where pilgrims came to visit and venerate Peter's grave, situated in the ancient cemetery on the Vatican hill. In order to build this great pilgrimage

---

6 Min. Fel. *Oct.* 18–19; Justin, *1 Apol.* 20; Clem. Al. *Protr.* 6.
7 Or. *C. Cels.* 4.31; cf. Clem. Al. *Protr.* 4.

Figure 9. Christ/Apollo mosaic, Vatican Necropolis (photo: Estelle Brettman, The International Catacomb Society)

church, the emperor had to level the surrounding necropolis, and fill in a great number of surrounding tombs, most of them pagan, but a few also belonging to families who at some point included Christian converts among their members. The Julius family mausoleum, which features the mosaic described above, was built in the early third century and adorned with Christian motifs some decades later. The inclusion of the figures of Jonah, the Good Shepherd and a fisherman allows observers to identify the resplendent figure in the chariot as a representation of Christ.

Based on this iconographic programme, a viewer may deduce that the mausoleum was decorated in order to convey a Christian hope in the resurrection. The adaptation of an image of Sol riding through a Dionysian grapevine to this end, however, might provoke questions about the supposed Christian convictions of those buried within or whether they were confused about the identity of their god. Yet, rather than point to this image as an example of religious syncretism, one might instead argue that it demonstrates that Roman Christians chose to express their faith using an already-established and familiar symbolic vocabulary. Thus, what we see is neither religious confusion nor ambivalence, but the adaptation of a familiar type, giving it a new, Christian significance. The identity of the character in the chariot, therefore, is beside the point. To ask whether this is Christ, Apollo or some hybrid character is to misunderstand the function of artistic expression in general. This probably is less a portrait of a god than the representation of an idea – the deity's transcendence of darkness and death. In this context, the reference is to the work of Christ in terms of the traditional symbolism of Sol or Apollo, which is both supported and elaborated by the rest of the iconographic programme of the tomb.

Such use of a familiar image or metaphor to convey a new meaning also occurs in literature. For example, when Clement of Alexandria urges pagans to convert (c.190–200 CE), he summons the figure of Helios as a metaphor for the resurrected and cosmic Christ: 'Hail, Light! . . . That light is eternal life, and whatever shares in it, lives. But night pays homage to light, receding through fear, ceding place to the day of the Lord. Everything has become a sleepless light and the setting has been transformed into rising.' Clement earlier had cited Ephesians 5:14, and seems to describe the sun god: 'Awake, sleeper, rise from the dead and Christ will shine upon you. The sun of the resurrection, the one born before the dawn, whose beams give light, will give you life.'[8] In both places, vivid poetic language boldly borrows the imagery of a radiant Sol, riding over the heavens from dawn to dusk, in order to symbolise the transcendent power and beauty of the Christian god. Clement spoke to his audience in language that would have meaning for them.

The motif of the vine and the grape harvest which appears in traditional Roman decorative art also appears in early Christian literature. The lusciously ornamental and loaded vines being harvested by small children (*putti*) or winged cherubs simply could be attractive symbols of prosperity and abundance or they could be references to the cult of Bacchus/Dionysos, the god of the vine who triumphed over death and whose cult offered devotees some

---

8 Clem. Al. *Protr.* 11 and 9, my trans.

kind of blessed afterlife. At the same time, the image of the vine and harvest can be a Christian symbol, since Jesus spoke of himself as the true vine (John 15:1–5) and his blood was symbolized in the cup of fermented grape juice in the sacrament of the Eucharist. Thus, the grape harvest could refer either to pagan or Christian religious aspirations (or both). For example, one Christian writer described such a scene in order to express the mystical union with and divine presence of Christ in the eucharist:

> The spiritual vine is the savior, the shoots and branches are his saints, the bunches of grapes are his martyrs, the trees which are joined with the vine reveal the passion, the vintagers are the angels, the baskets full of grapes are the apostles, the winepress is the church and the wine is the power of the Holy Spirit.[9]

These and other visual and literary applications of familiar symbols demonstrate that, though their original signification was maintained, they were simultaneously being charged with new meaning. Christians expressed their faith through widely recognisable forms that were generally understood within their cultural environment but that also had particular meaning for them – a practical and natural way to explain and spread their religion. The images chosen were complex enough to carry multiple meanings, and flexible enough to cross both religious and secular boundaries. Thus, to view such 'borrowings' as evidence of syncretism, religious confusion, crypto-paganism or religious ambivalence misunderstands the power and malleability of images. Once the new religion was well understood and truly entrenched in its environment, new visual images emerged to express its central teachings, values and community identity.

The emergence of these new forms gradually drove out the older ones, a pattern which coincided with the church's transition from persecuted minority to powerful, imperially supported majority. These shifts took time, but they are clearly discernible, and move from initial adaptation of traditional Graeco-Roman motifs, to invention of new Christian imagery during the period of church growth in the third century. Eventually a second phase of merging Christian and Roman identity in the early Byzantine era produced a highly evolved iconography that reflected that consolidation and the ascendant position of Christianity over its earlier competitors.

Such an application, however, of traditional forms for a new religious purpose raises the question of how different Christians were, culturally, from their

---

9 Hipp. *Ben. Is. Iac.* 25, my trans.

non-Christian neighbours, and how their distinct beliefs and practices were manifested across time and space, or diverged according to social status or economic security. Christianity's interaction with and adaptation of the culture in which it emerged must be viewed in the context of particular circumstances or communities. Varying according to the time or place of our examination, we see that Christians suffered sporadic episodes of persecution, alternating with periods of relative peace. Each of these greatly affected the process of enculturation, until at last Christianity moved from the edges of Roman culture to its centre. Thus, although the evolution of an identifiable Christian material culture was far from steady or consistent, it did finally arrive.

The emergence of Christian visual culture

Most historians agree that few extant examples of recognisably Christian art and architecture can be identified and dated prior to the beginning of the third century. Although older scholarship sometimes argued that this 'late arrival' of Christian art was due to Christians' original resistance to visual art or specially constructed worship spaces, more recent studies have pointed to the difficulty of distinguishing pagan artefacts from Christian ones or secular domestic architecture from house churches, noting the gradual transition from adaptation to innovation discussed above.[10] Scholars no longer insist that early Christians were uniformly opposed to figurative art or church buildings, and thus had none. Instead, the absence of artefacts from the first two centuries may be explained partly as a problem of identification. The absence may also be explained by the vicissitudes of survival. Many of the earliest datable artefacts and iconography probably endured because they were made for subterranean burials or were covered by later structures, while a great many others perished through urban renewal, the ravages of war or weather, and even iconoclastic attacks at various points in history.

What has survived has a limited provenance and milieu. The great majority of Christian artefacts come from a funerary context, especially from the Roman catacombs. Notable exceptions include terracotta lamps, finger rings, glasses or tableware that were moulded, etched or stamped with Christian motifs, dated as early as the late second or early third century. Clement of Alexandria even provides a list of appropriate motifs for signet rings, including a dove, fish, ship or anchor, but he bans images of swords, drinking cups or portraits

---

10 Breckenridge, 'Reception of art', 361–9; Grigg, 'Aniconic worship', 428–9; Murray, 'Art and the early church', 304–45.

of lovers.[11] And although many of these objects were found in tombs, their evident mass production and widespread dissemination may suggest that they were in daily use.

At the other end of the spectrum from funerary art or modest personal artefacts is the mid-third-century Christian house church discovered at Dura Europos in eastern Syria, which contains an extensively decorated room used for baptism (see fig. 6, above, p. 414). Other evidence of pre-Constantinian church building outside of Rome exists. A fifth-century octagonal church building at Capernaum was built over an existing domestic structure, believed to have been an early house church located in St Peter's house. A double church building at Aquileia incorporates an oratory that might be dated to the reign of bishop Theodore (308–19). Documents mentioning the existence of Christian church structures, books and furnishings in various parts of the Roman empire offer further evidence of growing Christian communities in the mid- to late third century, that had a relative degree of security, wealth and permanence, and had moved from modest gatherings in homes to larger crowds in imposing edifices. For example, Porphyry complains: 'But the Christians, imitating the construction of temples, erect great buildings in which they meet to pray, though there is nothing to prevent them from doing this in their own homes.'[12]

Nevertheless, the most extensive collection of early and identifiably Christian artefacts are the paintings in the Roman catacombs, and of those the oldest are in the Catacomb of Callistus on the ancient Via Appia, an early Christian necropolis dated to the first decade of the third century. Other early Christian Roman catacombs include those of Sebastian, Domitilla and Priscilla, all providing material evidence of early Christian culture. These catacombs contained small family burial chambers (*cubicula*) with paintings on their walls and ceilings, often divided into fields and registers by lines and decorative frames. In addition to these, however, are examples of carved plaques used to cover the horizontal graves (*loculi*) cut into the gallery walls, a few rare mosaics and a considerable number of carved stone sarcophagi. In addition to wall paintings and relief carvings are a small but significant group of sculptures in the round. All of these objects have been identified as belonging to a Christian milieu, either by their content or by their placement within a larger programme of Christian imagery. Not all of the iconography, however, is uniquely Christian in its themes and its style, and in technique it closely parallels the

---

11 Clem. Al. *Paed.* 11; cf. Tert. *Pud.* 7.1–4; 10f (on shepherd cups).
12 Porph. *Christ.* frag. 76, trans. White, *Social origins of Christian architecture*, vol. 11, 104; cf. Euseb. *HE* 8.1–2.

type of painting in neighbouring pagan tombs as well as more general interior decoration.[13]

The art of the Roman catacombs was clearly made for private family tombs, rather than public spaces, and so is not necessarily representative of what the 'official' church may have permitted or even commissioned for the decoration of its congregational meeting spaces. Since the only surviving church wall paintings from this period come from the baptistery of the Dura Europos house church, conclusions are tenuous at best. Nevertheless, it seems unlikely that Dura was unique, and the frescoes in the Roman catacombs indicate that church officials probably permitted and even encouraged figurative painting, at least in a funerary venue. Such approval is demonstrated by the fact that the Catacomb of Callistus bears the name of its supposed first supervisor, who eventually became bishop of Rome (217–22 CE), and the fact that the catacomb itself contains the tombs of several subsequent third-century popes.

Within a short time, the graves of the community's heroes, bishops and martyrs became pilgrimage destinations, and thus warranted particular markers or structures to identify the saint's shrine. The above-mentioned shrine of St Peter on the Vatican is an example. According to tradition, from the beginning of the third century, Peter's grave was indicated by a small columned architectural structure with an opening to give visitors access to the tomb itself. Martyrs' graves in other cemeteries were similarly marked, and in time covered with larger structures to offer shelter and seating space to pilgrims who often celebrated a memorial meal at the shrine. These memorial meals represented the continuance of a traditional pagan practice of funerary banquets at the graves of deceased family members, and so burial sites were equipped with benches and small tables (*mensae*) that allowed the pouring of libations or placement of food offerings for the dead. During the fourth century, these structures were enlarged and eventually transformed into pilgrimage churches with eucharistic tables placed over the saint's grave, thus continuing the ancient practice of dining with the honoured dead.

Early Christian iconography in cultural context and transition

The oldest datable motifs painted on the walls, or inscribed on funeral plaques of these underground tombs, usually are decorative or religiously ambiguous

---

13 On the catacombs and their iconography, see Snyder, *Ante pacem*; Nicolai et al., *Christian catacombs of Rome*; Finney, *Invisible God*; Mancinelli, *Catacombs of Rome*; Stevenson, *Catacombs*; Hertling and Kirschbaum, *Roman catacombs*.

images drawn from traditional Roman decorative art such as flowers, fruit, birds, grapevines and garlands, as well as certain figures that might be imbued with particular Christian meanings such as the fish or fisher, dove, boat, anchor and shepherd. While many of the latter would be indistinguishable from their pagan counterparts if detached and hung on a museum wall, their placement within a larger artistic programme, along with the addition of inscribed epitaphs, helps to identify them as Christian and as relaying a particular Christian message. The fish in the Catacomb of Callistus, for example, is shown with a basket of bread and a vial of wine, probably indicating the sacrament of the eucharist (see fig. 3, above p. 144).

As noted above, many of these were standard motifs found in Roman religious and secular iconography. For example, the image of the shepherd, which references the many uses of the metaphor in Christian and Jewish scripture (e.g. John 10:11: 'I am the Good Shepherd'), may have been adapted from a Roman representation of Hermes carrying a ram. Hermes, the god who carried messages from the gods to humans and served as a guide to souls in the underworld (*psychopompos*), was appropriately portrayed in funereal settings. His Christian version is often hard to distinguish from the non-Christian, especially when the provenance of the object is unknown, as is often true of small shepherd figurines. Similarly, the figure of Orpheus was adapted to convey the nature of Christ's work. Orpheus, the tamer of wild beasts and the rescuer of the dead (Eurydice), was transformed into Christ the tamer of human passions and saviour from death.[14]

The representation of Christ the teacher with his students, as in the Catacomb of Domitilla (see fig. 7, above, p. 484), has a well-known parallel in the representation of a philosopher such as Socrates. Other motifs, common to both Christian and pagan burial iconography, include the representation of a funeral banquet (five or seven persons seated at semicircular table), a seated male reading a scroll, and a veiled female praying figure (*orant*), her hands stretched out and up. Both of these expressed traditional Roman virtues of wisdom and piety, and may have been meant to represent the deceased's habits or character. However, to a Christian patron or viewer, the *orant* also could represent the Christian soul awaiting resurrection, while the teacher or seated reader could allude to Christian teaching as true philosophy.[15]

The well-known Via Salaria sarcophagus provides an example of the difficulty in distinguishing between a Christian object and a pagan one in the early

14 Murray, *Rebirth and afterlife*, 37–63.
15 See pt v, ch. 27, above.

Figure 10. Christ as Good Shepherd, Via Salaria sarcophagus, Museo Pio Cristiano, Musei Vaticani (photo: Robin M. Jensen)

period. Dated to the late third century and usually identified as an example of early Christian relief sculpture, this large marble coffin bears an imposing ram's head on each end and a central frieze of images that have religious, but not obviously Christian, signification. In the centre a shepherd figure stands with a ram over his shoulders. To his left a man sits reading a scroll, and to his right is a seated woman holding a rolled scroll. Both the man and woman have companions, one of them in the posture of prayer. Such religiously ambiguous iconography might have come from artisans' workshops, with a limited catalogue of motifs, which were patronised by pagan and Christian clients.

By the mid-third century, however, many of these more universal images were joined by narrative scenes from the Christian Old and New Testaments. Some stories are far more common than others. Initially figures from the Old Testament outnumbered scenes from the New Testament in both wall painting and relief carving. Among these are representations of Adam and Eve, Abraham and Isaac, Noah, Moses, Daniel, the three youths in the fiery furnace and Jonah, who was the most popular of all. Although some of these scenes seem to have no clear pre-Christian prototypes and so to have been invented *de novo*, others are clearly influenced by particular pagan models. Daniel, for example, is almost always portrayed nude, like such classical heroes as Hercules or Meleager. In illustrations from the gospel stories of Jesus working such wonders as changing water to wine, he holds a wand, the widely recognised attribute of a magician.[16]

The iconography of Jonah offers another example of a borrowed and adapted classical prototype. Jonah reclining nude under the gourd vine strikes a pose identical to that of the mythical Endymion on pagan sarcophagi. Endymion was cursed – or blessed (depending on your point of view) – with both eternal youth and everlasting sleep, and visited each night by Selene, the moon goddess who bore him fifty daughters. Instead of an allusion to his disobedience or humiliation, when Jonah is portrayed in the same posture, he symbolises the hope of eternal and blissful repose (fig. 11, below, p. 580). However, since the story also calls to mind the 'sign of Jonah' as a figure of Christ's death and resurrection (Matt 12:39–40), his iconography may have a soteriological significance. Additionally, Jonah's nudity, watery plunge and re-emergence from the belly of a sea creature may allude to the Christian ritual of baptism, thus adding a sacramental dimension to the symbolism.

In addition to holding a wand, when Jesus appears in scenes of healing or wonderworking, he normally appears as a beautiful and beardless youth.

---

16 Mathews, *Clash of gods*, 54–91.

Figure 11. Jonah/Endymion sarcophagus relief, Museo Pio Cristiano, Musei Vaticani
(photo: Robin M. Jensen)

His face and body type in these images look remarkably like those of Apollo
or one of the other Graeco-Roman saviour gods (e.g. Dionysos, Hermes or
Orpheus). These physical features do not necessarily suggest that Jesus was
identified (or confused) with these other gods, but that he (truly) possessed
certain attributes associated with them. In early, rare representations of Jesus
with a beard, he appears in the guise of a philosopher teacher, imparting the
true wisdom to his disciples.[17] In other places where Jesus appears as a teacher,
however, he may appear as beardless (fig. 7, above, p. 484).

A different bearded type emerges only in the late fourth century in which
Jesus' face resembles the traditional representations of such regal, senior pagan
gods as Jupiter and Neptune. These images emphasised Christ's transcendent
glory and role as judge and lawgiver rather than his earthly miracles or role as
saviour god (fig. 2, above, p. 86).[18] Artistic representations of Christ's passion
or resurrection were similarly unknown prior to the mid- to late fourth century. In addition, iconography portraying Jesus' baptism by John, as well as

17 Zanker, *Mask of Socrates*, 297–327; Mathews, *Clash of gods*, 109–11.
18 Mathews, *Clash of gods*, 108–9; Jensen, *Understanding early Christian art*, 119–20.

the adoration of the magi, appeared markedly earlier than other scenes from Jesus' earthly life, including such images more common in later Christian art as the Last Supper or the transfiguration. And with the arrival of scenes of the passion and the enthroned Christ came other new iconographic types now usually identified with imagery of the Christian emperor, such as an empty cross surmounted by the chi-rho within a wreath (fig. 13, below, p. 587). In conjunction with this transformation in iconography was the gradual disappearance of the earliest motifs, including the shepherd and Jonah.

The new iconography of the trial, passion, triumph and enthronement of Christ excluded any representation of the actual crucifixion – a striking contrast with the extensive discussion of Christ's passion in Christian literature of this period. In fact, with few exceptions, images of the crucifixion cannot be dated earlier than the early fifth century, and they are extremely rare until the sixth or even the seventh. Different theories have been offered to explain this apparent exclusion: that early Christians de-emphasised the death of Jesus, that the scene was too shocking to be portrayed, or that the central mystery of the faith should be hidden from the uninitiated.[19] None of these theories by itself adequately explains the absence of crucifixion imagery, however, especially considering the existence of depictions of other scenes from the passion story, which neither underplayed nor disguised the means of Jesus' death. Furthermore, images of violent or sacrificial death were well known in the pagan world, and might have provided possible models.[20] Whatever the reason for its early absence, the eventual appearance of crucifixion imagery coincides with the rising popularity of pilgrimages to the Holy Land in the fourth century and beyond, and the dissemination of relics of the cross.[21]

Enculturation of architecture: from house church to basilica

Although Paul asserted that the Christian God has no human-made shrine, early Christians nevertheless needed space where they might meet for communal prayer and meals. At first it appears that they continued to spend time together in the temple as well as gathering in homes to eat and perhaps to pray and study (cf. Acts 2:46, 5:42 and 20:7–9). In this sense they were like another

---

19 Grabar, *Christian iconography*, 132; Milburn, *Early Christian art*, 109; van der Meer, *Early Christian art*, 120–2; Jensen, *Understanding early Christian art*, 133–7.
20 Balch, 'Suffering of Isis/Io', 25–42.
21 Jensen, *Understanding early Christian art*, 150–1.

Jewish group, the Pharisees.[22] These activities required no special architecture. A member of the group who owned a home hosted the gathering in the public rooms of the house, either the reception room or dining room or both (cf. Rom 16:5; 1 Cor 16:19; Col 4:15; and Philem 2).[23] As the community grew, the house could be renovated or even built over to accommodate a larger gathering or a more formal meeting. The church built into Peter's house at Capernaum is such a place. In the beginning, however, Paul and other apostles also taught in the synagogue and, when that became more and more difficult, they found other accommodating spaces, such as a local lecture hall (cf. Acts 9:20, 13:5, 14–43; 19:8–9). Examination of the churches of San Clemente or Santi Giovanni e Paolo in Rome indicates that other functional and available structures may have been used and renovated, such as rooms in apartment blocks (*insulae*), former shops or warehouses.[24] While these spaces lacked distinguishing characteristics that would identify them as Christian gathering spaces, they were not hiding places. By the end of the third century, some may even have been impressive in size and design, and well known to the Roman authorities who were able to seize or destroy them.[25]

Synagogues, like those mentioned in the New Testament, were places where members of the community would gather for communal scripture reading and study (probably not prayer). Synagogues seem to have emerged in the diaspora, as an alternative to the temple, but after the temple's destruction (70 CE) they began to be central to Jewish religious and social life. Yet, even second-century synagogues were probably still rather modest and, like early Christian spaces, often started as renovated houses. Thus, the development of synagogue architecture parallels Christian church building rather than serving as a model for it.[26] By the middle of the third century, however, synagogues could be found throughout the Roman empire, and some of them were relatively large and imposing. The synagogue at Dura Europos, converted from a domestic structure in the mid-third century, had a main hall that was approximately 14 × 9 metres in size, elaborately decorated with wall paintings and furnished with a Torah shrine on its western wall. Its counterpart, the Christian house church (fig. 6, above, p. 144), was comparable in size, and probably was decorated by the same artisans.[27]

---

22 White, *Social origins of Christian architecture*, vol. 1, 103.
23 Osiek and Balch, *Families in the New Testament world*, 193–212; Snyder, *Ante pacem*, 128–36.
24 Krautheimer, *Early Christian and Byzantine architecture*, 28–30.
25 M. *Saturn.* 2; Euseb. *HE* 8.2.
26 Rutgers, 'Diaspora synagogues', 92–5. See also pt 1, ch. 2, above; Levine, *Ancient synagogues revealed*.
27 Jensen, 'Dura Europos synagogue',184–7.

While the gradual development of a specific Christian architecture parallels the development of distinctively Christian iconographic motifs, one reason for the relatively slower emergence of the former is undoubtedly a lack of economic or social resources. Construction or renovation of buildings requires more financial means than the manufacture of small art objects, and additionally it requires both land and a great deal of skilled labour of various kinds. The establishment of a church building, not to mention its renovation, also presumes a degree of public acceptance, even if the buildings were privately owned and maintained.

At the same time (and contrary to their borrowings from the motifs of pagan iconography), early Christians seem intentionally to have avoided using worship spaces that looked like typical pagan temples or shrines. And when they began to build new structures, they deliberately adopted a particular design that came out of the surrounding secular, instead of religious, culture. Apart from wanting to distinguish their worship from that of the traditional gods (and the idolatry they associated with it), Christians would have found typical temple architecture impractical for their kind of assembly and their developing liturgical ceremonies. Roman temples were essentially designed for public rites that mainly took place out of doors. Such temples tended to be located in main city squares, and their rituals included public processions and open-air sacrifices. Although such buildings were a main feature of the urban landscape, they were not meant to house large gatherings. The inner sanctum (*cella*) of pagan temples was not a place for communal worship, but a small room that housed a cult statue. By contrast, early Christian communities consisted of voluntary and initiated members who met in regular assemblies and whose rituals needed to be out of the public view.

Based on these needs alone, however, Christian meeting spaces might have been like those used by other voluntary associations, including the clubs, burial societies (*collegia*) and mystery cults popular in late antiquity. Like early Christians, these groups held exclusive gatherings where members shared a meal and performed a variety of rituals. Their activities were secret and thus required interior, private spaces. The devotees of the god Mithras were such a group. Gathered in small groups, they met in small, windowless chambers that featured benches along their long walls that served as dining couches. Like Christians and Jews, their meeting places (*mithraea*) often were renovated homes. The *mithraeum* in Dura Europos was first built into a single room and eventually expanded to the whole house.[28]

---

28 White, *Social origins of Christian architecture*, I, 47–59; Snyder, *Ante pacem*, 140–52.

Figure 12. Santa Sabina, exterior view (Rome) (photo: Mark L. Brack)

By the mid-third century, however, Christian communities would have found such a space too small and restrictive. Rather than gathering in small, local and exclusive groups, Christians tended to have one larger community within an urban area, under the guidance of a bishop who was supported by a staff of other church office holders including elders (presbyters) and deacons. The provision of material and economic support for groups of widows and orphans demanded storage rooms for food and clothing. The ceremonies of the liturgy involved special furniture, books and ritual implements that had to be kept secure when they weren't in use. Screens, stairs or raised platforms provided separate spaces for clergy and laity. Finally, as the ritual of Christian baptism changed from an outdoor event in a natural setting to an indoor and secret rite, it required a special room equipped with a font deep enough for immersion.[29] The Christian house church at Dura Europos provides an excellent example of an early baptismal room with a large water tank at one end (fig. 6, above, p. 414).

The Constantinian era brought about the most marked stage in the evolution from renovated, existing spaces to newly built church buildings. Shortly after he signed the Edict of Milan (313 CE), Constantine launched a major church building programme in Rome and the Holy Land. The architectural plan for

29 See Davies, *Architectural setting of baptism* and Jensen, *Living water*.

these first churches was based on the design of the basilica, originally a civic or secular building that provided impressive interior space for the housing of grand ceremonies. The first of the churches Constantine built in Rome was the Lateran basilica constructed on land owned by his wife. A palace on the site became the residence of the bishop of Rome, and the newly built church featured a five-aisled nave, 76 meters in length, with a large apse at its far (west) end. The sanctuary that was encompassed by the apse included the throne of the bishop and semicircular benches to either side for his presbyters. The opulent interior decoration of the building included silver statues, a golden altar and glittering mosaics, in addition to two interior rows of green marble columns with imposing capitals.[30] Such a building symbolised the beginning of Christianity's transition from a minority community adapting what it had available and expressing itself in familiar terms, to a powerful, wealthy and dominant segment of the population, now able to determine the forms and styles by which it expressed its own cultural identity. The imposing scale and potential grandeur of the basilica design well suited the gradually more elaborate liturgy, even as it reflected the changed social and political status of the church and became a definitive and monumental symbol of the church's new self-understanding and cultural integration. Although the Lateran basilica today no longer has its original appearance, the fifth-century church of Santa Sabina in Rome has been both preserved and restored so that it still shows this traditional basilica form (fig. 12, above, p. 584). Eusebius of Caesarea, who lived through the transition from the time of persecution to the 'peace of the church',[31] sums up this dramatic transition, writing that an 'unspeakable gladness' came over those who saw, in the place of desolation and destruction, newly built 'temples rising from their foundations to an immense height and far more splendid than the ones that had been destroyed'.[32]

30 *Liber pontificalis* 1.181.
31 See ch. 30, above.
32 Euseb. *HE* 10.2.

Conclusion: retrospect and prospect

While Eusebius of Caesarea could account for subsequent events by issuing new editions with updated endings to his *Historia ecclesiastica*, we must bring this first volume to a definitive close. Like Eusebius, we take Constantine as our line in the sand, but, with the gift of historical perspective, we know that there is a long and convoluted story of Christianity reaching beyond him. We can happily leave it to the next eight volumes to sketch and analyse that once unimaginable history – in Europe, Latin America, Africa, China, in the medieval west, the Byzantine east, in Renaissance and reformation, modernity and even post-modernity – that is yet to come. But where does this volume leave us in the project of rendering an adequate historiographic account of the Christian religion? Is it possible to trace in the acorn the lineaments of the oak tree, with its main trunk and many branches? In telling their history, Christian churches through the ages have either claimed organic continuity with 'Christian origins' or sought a radical return to origins they feel have been betrayed. Yet all along, both creativity and a process of adaptation to varieties of cultural experience have vied with conservative instincts, such that one might well ask: can ancient Christianity really be regarded as the true foundation for subsequent history?

To the extent that, by the end of our period, a roughly coherent shape has emerged from a rather amorphous range of initial possibilities, it is perhaps possible to respond in the affirmative. The essays in this volume have documented how, in various locations over the first three centuries, Christians set in place the structures and forms of discourse that transformed the early missionary groups into a religious movement that spread throughout the Mediterranean basin and beyond it, one capable of transmission from one generation to the next. They developed texts, rituals, lifestyles, institutions, laws, forms of education and socialisation, and various modes of historical self-understanding which were to mark the movement from there forward. Devotion to the figure of Jesus, seen in diverse ways, was central to all versions of the early cult, despite diversity in language, theology and specifics of ritual

Figure 13. Christogram on fourth-century sarcophagus, Museo Pio Cristiano, Musei Vaticani (photo: Robin M. Jensen)

practice. The symbols of life, death, resurrection, divine gift and sacred story provided dynamic, permanent sources for ongoing critical, mystical and theological reflection. The Christian 'gospel' by the time of Constantine, even if it were by no means the universal religion of the empire, had put in place elements of a cultural system that would transform, even as it assimilated, the cultural resources of the Graeco-Roman world.[1] That very sense of unity, however, was achieved and protected through the eventual exclusion of groups

1 Markus, *The End of Ancient Christianity*.

587

such as the Gnostics and Manichaeans, a process that would be reinforced by the powerful alliance of church and empire which would increasingly define orthodoxy.

What ancient Christianity surely bequeathed to all its descendants was a set of tensions or problematics that would preoccupy each generation of followers of Jesus for the next millennia.

Unity and diversity. The earliest period demonstrates that, while there is a cohering point in Jesus of Nazareth (variously understood!), Christians were continually from the earliest period testing the limits of diversity and conformity, inclusion and exclusion. Older models that regarded the earliest period as an inexorable evolution towards a recognised 'orthodoxy' have given way to an increasing attention to the range of persons who thought of themselves as 'Christian', while articulating that faith and acting it out in ritual and ethics in quite different fashions. These different groups did not just go their own way, but were mostly mutually engaged, debating and disputing. Earliest Christianity produced such eloquent calls for unity as Paul's 1 Corinthians[2] and Cyprian's *De unitate ecclesiae* ('The unity of the church') while also defying that harmonious vision in practice time and again. What are the acceptable conditions of this unity? What are the limits on diversity? These questions were and would never be far from view.

Definition and indeterminacy. From the very beginning Christians engaged in tasks of interpretation – who was this Jesus, and how did he relate to the promises of the God of Israel? Forms of religious knowledge – received 'wisdom' known in ancient sacred texts and contemporary revelations of divine mysteries as 'new' experience – competed with one another. The injunction to 'Test the spirits' (1 John 4:1) calls for an intersection of these two modes of knowing and talking about God, and sums up the tensive task of Christianity as a communal (not merely individual) religion: to adjudicate between various proposals about religious truth, not all of which can be right, but not all of which are subject to clear verification or invalidation. As Averil Cameron has cogently observed, from early on the die was cast that 'Christianity was to be a matter of articulation and interpretation.'[3] Yet the characteristic form of Christian religious poetics was the paradox that sought to hold in tension such poles as God's transcendence and immanence, the assurance of past

---

2 Or the later Paulinist's Ephesians.
3 Cameron, *Christianity and the rhetoric of empire*, 13–14.

redemption and need for future hope, and even the adequacy and inadequacy of religious language itself to express truth.

Church and world. Early Christian discourse as we have come to know it is both worldly and other-worldly. The apostle Paul said 'the form of this world is passing away' even as he founded churches and spoke of 'laying a foundation' (1 Cor 7:31; 3:10–11). While some think it was Constantine who 'sold out' and transformed a counter-cultural church into an enfranchised political establishment,[4] the relationship between Christians and the social order was from the start much more complex and mutually influencing. It was to remain so, with some figures fleeing the city for the desert,[5] and others finding in the city the proper home for Christian life and vocation. The tension between living in this world and hoping for the next is reincarnated by Christians in each age, always impacted by the current political situation and events, and triggered by key figures, like the Montanists, who rekindle apocalyptic fervour for their times when it seems to have faded. This view is unfailingly greeted by a mixed response: some applaud them as the true faithful, others as extremist heretics.

Beginnings and endings, old and new. The earliest Christians sought to defend their faith as simultaneously very ancient, rooted in the prophets of Israel, and a novelty of cosmic divine revelation in recent times. Christian self-identity, rooted as it was in scriptures appropriated from the Jews, was then and always thereafter would be defined in relation to Jews and Judaism; though the parameters have continually changed, tragically the ancient mode of apologetic invective has been continually re-enacted in quite different historical epochs. The project of self-definition, in antiquity and beyond, has always involved the construction of beginnings, and a claim of unique or special fidelity to them. In that sense the present volume stands in a malleable relationship to the ones which follow. The complex analytical framework we have sought to provide here is an aggregate scholarly reconstruction of ancient events and developments. But, in the history of Christianity, this narrative has been written – in texts and in lives – in Christian communities in every time and place. Ancient Christianity provides the raw materials – Peter and Paul, Jerusalem and Rome, Alexandria and Antioch, martyrs and monks, bishops and prophets – that will be reconfigured and recast in the mosaic self-portraits of each generation to come in manifold ways.

---

4 Crossan, *Jesus: a revolutionary biography*, 201: 'Is it time now, or is it already too late, to conduct, religiously and theologically, ethically and morally, some basic cost accounting with Constantine?'
5 Brown, *Body and society*.

Bibliographies

General bibliography of sources cited

Primary sources

The following is a list of sources, texts and editions referred to by authors in this volume, not an exhaustive bibliography. For a more complete catalogue, readers should consult F. Young, L. Ayres and A. Louth (eds.), *Cambridge history of early Christian literature* (Cambridge: Cambridge University Press, 2004), and S. Döpp and W. Geerlings (eds.), *Dictionary of early Christian literature*, M. O'Connell (trans.) (New York: Crossroad, 2000).

See List of Abbreviations, pp. xxxvii–xliv, for acronyms of series and periodicals.

A. Non-literary sources: inscriptions and papyri

The Amherst papyri, 2 vols., B. P. Grenfell and A. S. Hunt (eds.) (London: Oxford University Press, 1977, original 1900–1).

Betz, H. D. (ed.). *The Greek magical papyri in translation*, 2nd ed. (Chicago: University of Chicago Press, 1992).

Corpus inscriptionum Iudaicarum, 2 vols., J. Frey (ed.), Sussidi allo Studio delle Antichità Cristiane (Vatican City: Pontificio istituto di archeologia cristiana, 1936–52).

Corpus papyrorum Judaicarum, 3 vols., V. Tcherikover and A. Fuks (eds.) (Cambridge: Harvard University Press, 1957–64).

Gardner, I. (ed.). *Kellis literary texts*, MDOP 4 (1996).

Gardner, I. *et al.* (eds.). *Coptic documentary texts from Kellis*, MDOP 9 (1999).

Gibson, E. *The 'Christians for Christians' inscriptions of Phrygia: Greek texts, translation and commentary*, HTS 32 (1978).

Grenfell, B. P., and A. S. Hunt (eds.). *New classical fragments and other Greek and Latin papyri*, Greek papyri ser. 2 (Oxford: Clarendon Press, 1897).

Heine, R. E., *The Montanist oracles and testimonia*, PatrMS 14 (1989).

Horbury, W. and D. Noy (eds.). *Jewish inscriptions of Graeco-Roman Egypt* (Cambridge: Cambridge University Press, 1992).

Inscriptiones Graecae, 14 vols. (Berlin: De Gruyter, 1913–).

Inscriptiones Graecae urbis Romae, L. Moretti (ed.). Studi pubblicati dall' Istituto Italiano per la storia antica 17 (Rome, 1968–).

Inscriptiones Latinae Christianae veteres, 3 vols., E. Diehl, J. Moreau, and H. I. Marrou (eds.), 4th ed. (Berlin: Weidmann, 1925–85).

Inscriptiones Latinae selectae, 3 vols., H. Dessau (ed.), 3rd ed. (Berlin: Weidmann, 1962).

Kent, J. H. *Inscriptions 1926–1950*, Corinth: Results of excavations conducted by the American School of Classical Studies at Athens 8/3 (Princeton: Princeton University Press, 1966).

Kölner papyri, B. Kramer, R. Hübner and M. Gronewald (eds.), 10 vols., Abhandlungen der Rheinisch-Westfälischen Akademie der Wissenschaften, Sonderreihe papyrologica Coloniensia 7 (Opladen: Westdeutscher Verlag, 1976–).

Labriolle, P. de. *Les sources de l'histoire du Montanisme: textes grecs, latins, syriaques*, Collectanea Friburgensia 24 (Paris: Leroux, 1913).

Lefebvre, G. *Recueil des inscriptions grecques-chrétiennes d'Egypte* (Cairo: IFAO, 1907).

Mazar, B., M. Schwabe and B. Lifshitz (eds.). *Beth She'arim*, 3 vols. (New Brunswick, NJ: Rutgers University Press, 1973–4).

Monumenta Asiae Minoris antiqua, 10 vols., Publications of the American Society for Archaeological Research in Asia Minor [JRSM] (London: Longmans, Green, 1928–93).

Naldini, M. *Il cristianesimo in Egitto: lettere private nei papiri dei secoli II–IV* (Florence: Le Monnier, 1968).

Noy, D. *Jewish inscriptions of Western Europe*, vol. I: *Italy (excluding the city of Rome), Spain and Gaul* (Cambridge: Cambridge University Press, 1993).

—. *Jewish inscriptions of Western Europe*, vol. II: *The city of Rome* (Cambridge: Cambridge University Press, 1995).

The Old Syriac inscriptions of Edessa and Osrhoene: texts, translations, and commentary, H. J. W. Drijvers and J. F. Healey (eds. and trans.) (Leiden: Brill, 1999).

Orientis Graeci inscriptiones selectae, 2 vols., W. Dittenberger (ed.) (Leipzig, 1903–5; repr. Hildesheim: Olms, 1970).

The Oxyrhynchus papyri, 67 vols., B. P. Grenfell and A. S. Hunt (eds.) (London: Egypt Exploration Fund, 1916–2001).

Roberts, C. H. (ed.). *Catalogue of the Greek and Latin papyri in the John Rylands Library*, vol. III: *Theological and literary texts (nos. 457–551)* (Manchester: Manchester University Press, 1938).

Sylloge inscriptionum Graecarum, 4 vols., W. Dittenberger (ed.), 3rd ed. (repr., Hildesheim: Olms, 1960).

Tabbernee, W. *Montanist inscriptions and testimonia: epigraphic sources illustrating the history of Montanism*, PatrMS 16 (1997).

B. *Literary Sources* (Christian and Non-Christian)

Abgar legend [ET: *NTApoc*, vol. I].

Act of Peter [BG, 4; ET: *NHL*].
NHS II, D. Parrott (ed.) (1979), 473–93.

Acta Joannis [ET: *NTA poc*, vol. II].

Acta Maximiliani [Musurillo, 244–9].

Acta proconsularia, in *S. Thasci Caecili Cypriani opera omnia*, G. Hartel (ed.), CSEL 3.3 (1868–71).

Les Actes de Mar Mari, 2 vols. C. Jullien and F. Jullien (eds. and trans.), CSCO 602–3, Scriptores Syri 234–5 (2003).

The Acts of Mar Mari the Apostle, A. Harrak (ed. and trans.), Writings from the Greco-Roman World (Atlanta: Society of Biblical Literature, 2005).

Acts of Andrew [ET: *NTApoc*, vol. II].

  Text: *Acta Andreae*, J.-M. Prieur (ed.), CCSA 5–6 (1989).

Acts of Andrew and Matthias in the city of cannibals [ET: James (ed.), *Apocryphal New Testament*].

  Text: *Acta apostolorum apocrypha*, R. A. Lipsius, M. Bonnet and H. Kraft (eds.) (Leipzig: Hinrichs, 1891), vol. I.

  Text and Trans.: *The Acts of Andrew and The Acts of Andrew and Matthias in the city of cannibals*, D. R. MacDonald (ed. and trans.) (Atlanta: Scholars Press, 1990).

Acts of Paul [ET: *NTApoc*, vol. II].

  Text: *Acta apostolorum apocrypha*, R. A. Lipsius, M. Bonnet and H. Kraft (eds.) (Leipzig: Hinrichs, 1891), vol. I.

Acts of Paul and Thecla [ET: *NTApoc*, vol. II].

  Text: *Acta apostolorum apocrypha*, R. A. Lipsius, M. Bonnet and H. Kraft (eds.) (Leipzig: Hinrichs, 1891), vol. I.

Acts of Peter [ET: *NTApoc*, vol. II].

  Text and French trans.: *Les Actes de Pierre: introduction, textes, traduction et commentaire*, L. Vouaux, Documents pour servir à l'étude des origines chrétiennes (Paris: Letouzey et Ané, 1922).

Acts of Peter and Paul [ET: *ANF* 8].

  Text: *Acta apostolorum apocrypha*, R. A. Lipsius, M. Bonnet and H. Kraft (eds.) (Leipzig: Hinrichs, 1891), vol. I.

Acts of Peter and the twelve apostles [NHC VI, 1; ET: *NHL*].

  NHS 11, D. Parrott (ed.) (1979), 197–229.

Acts of Pilate [ET: *NTApoc*, vol. I].

Acts of Sharbil, Babai and Barsamya [ET: *ANF* 8].

  Text and ET: *Ancient Syriac documents relative to the earliest establishment of Christianity in Edessa and the neighbouring countries*, W. Cureton (ed. and trans.) (Amsterdam: Oriental Press, 1967, original 1864).

Acts of Thomas [ET: *NTApoc*, vol. II].

  Text: *La version Copte de la prédication et du martyre de Thomas*, P.-H. Poirier (ed.), with E. Lucchesi, Subsidia hagiographica 67 (Brussels: Société des Bollandistes, 1984).

  Text and ET: *The Acts of Thomas: introduction, text, and commentary*, 2nd rev. ed., A. F. J. Klijn (ed.), NovTSup 108 (2003).

Albinus. *Epitome*, in *Albinos: Épitomé*, P. Louis (ed.) (Paris: Les Belles Lettres, 1945).

Alexander of Lycopolis. *Alexandri Lycopolitani contra Manichaei opiniones disputatio*, A. Brinkmann (ed.), Teubner (1895).

  ET: *An Alexandrian Platonist against dualism: Alexander of Lycopolis' treatise 'Critique of the doctrines of Manichaeus'*, P. W. van der Horst and J. Mansfield (eds.) (Leiden: Brill, 1974), 48–97.

Allogenes [NHC XI, 3; ET: *NHL*].

  NHS 28, C. W. Hedrick (ed.) (1990), 173–267.

Ambrose of Milan [ET: *NPNF*[2] 10].

—. *De fide*. Text: *Sancti Ambrosii opera* VIII, O. Faller (ed.), CSEL 78 (1962),

—. *De obitu Theodosii*. Text: *Sancti Ambrosii opera* VII, O. Faller (ed.), CSEL 73 (1955).

  ET: *Sancti Ambrosii Oratio de obitu Theodosii*, M. D. Mannix (ed. and trans.), Catholic University of America patristic studies 9 (Washington, DC: Catholic University of America, 1925).

—. *Explanatio psalmorum XII*. Text: M. Petschenig (ed.), CSEL 64² (1999).

Apocalypse of Adam [NHC v, 5; ET: *OTP*, vol. I; *NHL*].
   NHS 11, D. Parrott (ed.) (1979), 151–95.

Apocalypse of Baruch [ET: *OTP*, vol. I, *APOT*, vol. I].
   Text and French trans.: *Apocalypse de Baruch*, P. Bogaert (ed. and trans.), *SC* 144 (1969).

Apocalypse of Elijah [ET: *OTP*, vol. I].
   Text: G. Steindorff, *Die Apokalypse des Elias: eine unbekannte Apokalypse und Bruchstücke der Sophonias-Apokalypse*, TU 17 (1899).
   ET: D. Frankfurter, *Elijah in Upper Egypt: the Apocalypse of Elijah and early Egyptian Christianity*, SAC 7 (1993), 299–328.

(First) Apocalypse of James [NHC v, 3; ET: *NHL*].
   NHS 11, D. Parrott (ed.) (1979), 65–103.

(Second) Apocalypse of James [NHC v, 4; ET: *NHL*].
   NHS 11, D. Parrott (ed.) (1979), 105–49.

Apocalypse of Paul [NHC v, 2; ET: *NHL, NTApoc*, vol. II].
   NHS 11, D. Parrott (ed.) (1979), 47–63.

Apocalypse of Peter [NHC VII, 3; ET: *NHL, NTApoc*, vol. II].
   NHMS 30, B. A. Pearson (ed.) (1996), 201–47.

Apocryphal New Testament [See Elliott, *The Apocryphal New Testament*; James, *The Apocryphal New Testament*].

Apocryphon of James [NHC I, 2; ET: *NHL*].
   NHS 22–3, H. W. Attridge (ed.) (1985), 13–53.

Apocryphon of John [NHC II, 1; III, 1; IV, 1; BG, 2; ET: *NHL*].
   NHMS 33, M. Waldstein and F. Wisse (eds. and trans.) (1995).

Apostolic constitutions [ET: *ANF* 7].
   Text and French trans. *Les constitutions apostoliques*, 3 vols., M. Metzger (ed. and trans.), SC 320, 329, 336 (1985–7).

Apostolic fathers. Text and German trans.: *Die apostolischen Väter*, F. X. Funk, K. Bihlmeyer, M. Whittaker, A. Lindemann and H. Paulsen (eds. and trans.) (Tübingen: Mohr Siebeck, 1992).
   Text and ET: *The Apostolic fathers*, LCL, 2 vols., B. D. Ehrman (ed. and trans.) (2003).
   Text and ET: *The Apostolic fathers*, LCL, 2 vols., K. Lake (ed. and trans.) (1912–13).
   Text and ET: *The Apostolic fathers*, 5 vols., J. B. Lightfoot (ed. and trans.) (London: Macmillan, 1885–90).
   Text and ET: *The Apostolic fathers: Greek texts and English translations of their writings*, 2nd ed., J. B. Lightfoot and J. R. Harmer (eds. and trans.), M. W. Holmes (ed. and rev.) (Grand Rapids, MI: Baker, 1992).
   Text and French trans.: *La doctrine des douze apôtres (Didachè)*, W. Rordorf and A. Tuilier (eds. and trans.), SC 248 (1978).
   Text and ET: *The Didache: text, translation, analysis, and commentary*, A. Milavec (ed. and trans.) (Collegeville, MN: Liturgical Press, 2003).
   Text and French trans.: *Lettres: Ignace d'Antioche, Polycarpe de Smyrne, martyre de Polycarpe*, P. T. Camelot (ed. and trans.), SC 10² (1998).
   Text and French trans.: *Lettres: martyre de Polycarpe*, 2nd ed., P. Th. Camelot (ed. and trans.), SC 10 (1951).
   Text: *Der Hirt des Hermas*, M. Whittaker (ed.), GCS 48 (1967).

Apuleius. Text: *Apulei Platonici Madaurensis opera quae supersunt*, 3 vols., R. Helm, P. Thomas and C. Moreschini (eds.), Teubner (1908–13, 1991–2001).

Aristeas, Letter of. Text and French trans.: *Lettre d'Aristée à Philocrate*, A. Pelletier (ed. and trans.), SC 89 (1962).

    Text and ET: *An introduction to the Old Testament in Greek*, H. B. Swete (ed.) (Cambridge: Cambridge University Press, 1902), 499–574.

Aristides of Athens. *Apologia.* Text: Goodspeed, *Die ältesten Apologeten*.

    ET: *The apology of Aristides on behalf of the Christians: from a Syriac ms. preserved on Mount Sinai*, J. R. Harris and J. Armitage Robinson (eds. and trans.), 2nd ed., Texts and studies: contributions to biblical and patristic literature 1.1 (Cambridge: Cambridge University Press, 1891).

Aristotle. *Politica.* Text and ET: LCL, H. Rackham (ed. and trans.) (1932).

[Aristotle]. *De mundo.* Text: *Aristotelis qui fertur libellus de mundo*, W. L. Lorimer (ed.) (Paris: Les Belles Lettres, 1933), 47–103.

Arnobius. Text: *Adversus nationes libri VII*, A. Reifferscheid (ed.), CSEL 4 (1875).

    ET: Arnobius, *The case against the pagans*, 2 vols., G. E. McCracken (trans.), ACW 7–8 (1949).

Ascension of Isaiah [ET: *NTApoc*, vol. II].

    Text: *Ascensio Isaiae*, 2 vols., P. Bettiolo, A. G. Kossova, C. Leonardi, E. Norelli and L. Perrone (eds.), CCSA 7–8 (1995).

    ET: J. Knight, *The ascension of Isaiah*, Guides to apocrypha and pseudepigrapha (Sheffield: Sheffield Academic Press, 1995).

Asclepius 21–29 [NHC VI, 8; ET: *NHL*].

    NHS 11, D. Parrott (ed.) (1979), 395–451.

Athanasius of Alexandria [ET: *NPNF*² 4].

    Text: *Athanasius Werke*, vol. II, pt 1, vol. III, pt 1, H. G. Opitz (ed.) (Berlin: De Gruyter, 1934–41).

Athenagoras. *Legatio sive supplicatio pro Christianis.* Text: *Legatio pro Christianis*, M. Marcovich (ed.), PTS 31 (1990).

    Text and ET: in *Athenagoras: Legatio and De resurrectione*, W. R. Schoedel (ed. and trans.), OECT (1972).

    Text and French trans.: *Supplique au sujet des chrétiens*, G. Bardy (ed. and trans.), SC 3 (1943).

    ET: *Early Christian fathers*, C. C. Richardson, E. R. Fairweather, E. R. Hardy and M. H. Shepherd (eds. and trans.), LCC 1 (1970).

    ET: *Athenagoras: Embassy for the Christians; the resurrection of the dead*, J. H. Crehan (trans.), ACW 23 (1956).

Augustine. *Contra Cresconium Donatistam = Asconium Grammaticum parties Donati: Sancti Aureli Augustini Scripta contra donatistas*, M. Petschenig (ed.), CSEL 52 (1909).

—. *De civitate Dei.* Text: *Sancti Aurelii Augustini episcopi De civitate Dei, libri XXII*, B. Dombart and A. Kalb (eds.), 5th ed., Teubner (1981).

    Text and ET: *Augustine: City of God*, LCL, 7 vols., W. M. Green, P. Levine, G. E. McCracken, E. M. Sanford and D. S. Wiesen (eds. and trans.) (1957–72).

—. *De doctrina Christiana.* Text: J. Martin (ed.), CCSL 32 (1962).

    Text and ET: R. P. H. Green (ed. and trans.), OECT (1995).

—. *De trinitate.* Text: *De trinitate libri XV*, 2 vols., W. J. Mountain (ed.), CCSL 50–50A (1968).

ET: *The Trinity*, S. McKenna (trans.), FC 45 (1963).

ET: *The Trinity*, E. Hill (trans.), John E. Rotelle (ed.), in *The works of Saint Augustine*, pt 1, vol. v (Brooklyn, NY: New City Press, 1991).

—. *Retractationes*. Text: *Sancti Aurelii Augustini Retractationum libri II*, P. Knoll (ed.), CSEL 36 (1902).

Text: *Sancti Aurelii Augustini Retractationum libri II*, A. Mutzenbecher (ed.), CCSL 57 (1984).

ET: *The retractations*, M. I. Bogan (trans.), FC 60 (1968).

Aurelius Victor. *Liber de Caesaribus*. Text: F. Pichlmayr and R. Gruendel (eds.), Teubner (1970).

ET: *Liber de Caesaribus*, H. W. Bird (trans.), TTH 17 (1994).

Authoritative teaching [NHC VI, 3; ET: *NHL*].

NHS 11, D. Parrott (ed.) (1979), 257–89.

Bala'izah Gnostic fragments [ET: *NTApoc*, vol. 1].

P. E. Kahle, Jr., *Bala'izah: Coptic texts from Deir el-Bala'izah in Upper Egypt*, 2 vols. (London: Oxford University Press, 1954), vol. I, 473–7.

Barnabas, Epistle of [See *Apostolic fathers*].

Basil of Caesarea, *Epistulae*. Text and French trans: *Lettres*, 3 vols., Y. Courtonne (ed.) (Paris: Les Belles Lettres, 1957–61).

ET: *Letters*, A. C. Way (trans.), FC 13, 28 (1951–5).

—. *Homiliae*. Text: *PG* 85.

ET: *Exegetic homilies*, A. C. Way (trans.), FC 46 (1963).

Basilides. Text: *Quellen zur Geschichte der christlichen Gnosis*, W. Völker (ed.), Sammlung Ausgewählter Kirchen- und Dogmengeschichtlicher Quellenschriften, n.s. 5 (Tübingen: Mohr Siebeck, 1932), 38–44.

ET: Foerster, *Gnosis*, vol. I, 59–83.

ET: *The Gnostic scriptures*, B. Layton (ed.) (Garden City, NY: Doubleday, 1987), 427–44.

The book of the laws of countries: dialogue on the fate of Bardaisan of Edessa, H. J. W. Drijvers (ed. and trans.) (Assen: van Gorcum, 1965).

Book of Thomas the Contender [NHC II, 7; ET: *NHL*].

NHS 20–1, B. Layton (ed.) (1989), vol. II, 173–205.

Books of Jeu [ET: *NTApoc*, vol. 1]

NHS 13, C. Schmidt (ed.) (1978), 1–211.

Julius Caesar. Text: *Commentarii rerum gestarum*, vol. I: *Bellum Gallicum*, W. Hering (ed.), Teubner (1987).

Text and ET: *The Gallic war*, LCL, H. J. Edwards (ed. and trans.) (1917).

Carpocrates. ET: Foerster, *Gnosis*, vol. I, 36–40.

Testimonia: M. Smith, *Clement of Alexandria and a secret gospel of Mark* (Cambridge, MA: Harvard University Press, 1973), 295–350.

Chronicon Edessenum. Text: *Chronica minora*, 6 vols., I. Guidi, E. W. Brooks, J. B. Chabot (eds.), CSCO 1–6.; Scriptores Syri, ser. 3, pt 4 (1955), vol. I.1, pp. 1–13 (Syriac), and vol. II.2, pp. 1–11 (Latin trans.).

Chrysostom, John [ET: *NPNF*¹ 9–14].

—. *Adversus Judaeos*. Text: *PG* 48.

ET: *John Chrysostom, Discourses against Judaizing Christians*, P. W. Harkins (trans.), FC 68 (1979).

—. *Homiliae in Johannem.* Text: *PG* 59.
　ET: *Commentary on Saint John the apostle and evangelist*, 2 vols., T. A. Goggin (trans.), FC
　31, 43 (1957–60).
Cicero. Text: M. *Tulli Ciceronis scripta quae manserunt omnia*, 28 vols., C. F. Müller, W. Friedrich
　et al. (eds.), Teubner (1914–).
　Texts and ET: LCL, 28 vols., H. M. Hubbell, H. Rackham, E. W. Sutton *et al.* (eds. and
　trans.) (1913–2002).
Cleanthes. *Hymn to Zeus.* Text: *SVF*, vol. I.
　ET: C. J. de Vogel. *Greek philosophy: a collection of texts, selected and supplied with some notes
　and explanations*, 4th ed. (Leiden: Brill, 1973), no. 943, vol. III, 82–3.
1 *Clement* [See *Apostolic fathers*].
2 *Clement* [See *Apostolic fathers*].
[Clement] [See *Clementina*].
Clement of Alexandria [ET: *ANF* 2].
—. *Paedagogus.* Text: *Clemens Alexandrinus*, vol. I: *Protrepticus und Paedagogus.* O. Stählin, and
　U. Treu (eds.), GCS 12, 2nd ed. (1974).
　Text and French trans.: *Clément d'Alexandrie: le Pédagogue*, 3 vols., M. Harl, H.-I. Marrou,
　C. Matray and C. Mondésert (eds. and trans.), SC 70, 108, 158 (1960–70).
　ET: *Clement of Alexandria (Exhortation to the Greeks, Rich man's salvation, To the newly
　baptized)*, LCL, G. W. Butterworth (ed. and trans.) (1919).
　ET: *Clement of Alexandria: Christ the educator*, S. P. Wood (trans.), FC 23 (1954).
　ET: *Alexandrian Christianity: selected translations of Clement and Origen with introductions
　and notes*, J. E. L. Oulton and H. Chadwick (eds. and trans.), LCC 2, Ichthus edition
　(1977).
—. *Protrepticus.* Text: *Clementis Alexandrini Protrepticus*, M. Marcovich (ed.), VCSup 34 (1995).
　Text: *Protrepticus und Paedagogus*, O. Stählin and U. Treu (eds.), 3rd ed., GCS 1 (1972).
　Text and French trans.: *Le protreptrique*, C. Mondésert and André Plassart (eds. and trans.),
　3rd ed. rev., SC 2 (1976).
—. *Stromateis.* Text: O. Stählin, L. Früchtel, and U. Treu (eds.), GCS 52, 2nd ed. (1985) (bks 1–6);
　O. Stählin and L. Früchtel (eds.), GCS 17, 2nd ed. (1970) (bks 7–8).
　ET: *Clement of Alexandria, Stromateis, books one to three*, J. Ferguson (trans.), FC 85 (1991).
—. *Excerpta ex Theodoto.* Text and ET: R. P. Casey, *The Excerpta ex Theodoto of Clement of
　Alexandria*, SD 1 (1934).
—. *Letter to Theodore.* Text and ET: M. Smith, *Clement of Alexandria and a secret gospel of Mark*
　(Cambridge, MA: Harvard University Press, 1973), 445–53.
Clementina.
—. *Ascents of James.* ET: Robert E. van Voorst, *The ascents of James: history and theology of a
　Jewish-Christian community*, SBLDS 112 (1989).
—. *Epistula Petri ad Jacobum* [ET: *NTApoc*, vol. II].
—. *Homilies* [ET: *ANF* 8].
　Text: *Die Pseudoklementinen*, vol. I: *Homilien*, B. Rehm, J. Irmscher and G. Strecker (eds.),
　GCS (unnumbered), 3rd ed. corrected (1992).
—. *Kerygma Petrou* [ET: *NTApoc*, vol. II].
—. *Recognitions* [ET: *ANF* 8].
　Text: *Die Pseudoklementinen*, vol. II: *Rekognitionem*, B. Rehm and F. Paschke (eds.), GCS
　51 (1965).

The Cologne Mani codex: 'Concerning the origin of his body', R. Cameron and A. J. Dewey (eds. and trans.), SBLTT 15 (1979).

Commodian. *Carmina*. Text: J. Martin (ed.), CCSL 128 (1960).

Concept of our great power [NHC vi, 4; ET: *NHL*].

NHS 11, D. Parrott (ed.) (1979), 291–323.

Concilium Carthaginense quartum habitum ab episcopis numero ducentis quatuorum, era ccc-cxxxvi. Text: *Concilia Africae A. 345–A. 525*, C. Munier (ed.), CCSL 149 (1974).

Constantine. *Oratio ad sanctorum coetum*. Text: *Eusebius, Werke*, vol. i, I. A. Heikel (ed.), GCS 7 (1902).

ET: *Constantine and Christendom: the Oration to the saints, the Greek and Latin accounts of the discovery of the cross, the edict of Constantine to Pope Silvester*, M. J. Edwards (trans.), TTH 39 (2003).

Cyprian of Carthage [ET: *ANF* 5].

Text: *Sancti Cypriani episcopi opera*, 6 vols., G. F. Diercks, G. W. Clarke *et al.* (eds.), CCSL 3, 3A–E (1972–).

—. *Epistulae*. ET: *The letters of St Cyprian of Carthage*, 4 vols., G. W. Clarke (trans.), ACW 43–4, 46–7 (1984–9).

—. *De lapsis and De ecclesiae catholicae unitate*, M. Bévenot (ed. and trans.), OECT (1971).

ET: *St Cyprian, 'The lapsed' and 'The unity of the catholic church'*, M. Bévenot (trans.), ACW 25 (1957).

—. *Sententiae episcoporum numero lxxxvii de haereticis baptizandis*. Text: G. F. Diercks (ed.), CCSL 3E (2004).

Cyril of Alexandria.

Text: *Opera*, 7 vols., P. E. Pusey (ed.) (Oxford: Clarendon Press, 1868–77).

Text: E. Schwartz, *Acta conciliorum oecumenicorum: iussu atque mandato societatis scientiarum argentoratensis* (Berlin: De Gruyter, 1914), 1.1.1, pp. 33–42.

Text and trans.: *Cyril of Alexandria: select letters*, I. R. Wickham (ed. and trans.), OECT (1983).

ET: J. I. McEnerny (trans.), FC 76, 77 (1987).

Cyril of Jerusalem [ET: *NPNF²* 7].

Text: *Cyrilli Hierosolymorum archiepiscopi opera quae supersunt omnia*, 2 vols., W. C. Reischl and J. Rupp (eds.) (Munich: Lentner, 1848–60; repr. Hildesheim: Olms, 1967).

ET: *The works of Saint Cyril of Jerusalem*, 2 vols., L. P. McCauley and A. A. Stephenson (trans.), FC 61, 64 (1969–70).

—. *Catechesis Mystagogicae* Text and French trans.: *Catéchèses mystagogicae*. A. Piédagnel and P. Paris (eds. and trans.), SC 126 (1966).

—. 'Epistula ad Constantium imperatorem', in E. Bihain, 'L'épître de Cyrille de Jérusalem à Constance sur la vision de la croix', *Byzantion* 43 (1973), 286–91.

Dead Sea scrolls. *Qumran Cave i*, D. Bartholémy and J. T. Milik (eds.), DJD 1 (1955).

Text and ET: *The Dead Sea scrolls study edition*, 2 vols., F. García Martínez and E. J. C. Tigchelaar (eds.) (Leiden: Brill, 2000).

[Demetrius]. *On style*, D. C. Innes (trans.), in *Aristotle*, vol. xxiii, LCL (1995).

Dialogue of the savior [NHC iii, 5; ET: *NHL, NTApoc*, vol. i].

NHS 26, S. Emmel (ed.) (1984), 37–95.

Didache [See *Apostolic fathers*].

Didascalia Apostolorum.
> Syriac text and ET: *The Didascalia apostolorum in Syriac*, A. Vööbus (ed. and trans.), CSCO, 401–2, 407–8, Scriptores Syri, vols. 175–6, 179–80 (Louvain: Secrétariat du Corpus SCO, 1979).
>
> Latin text: *Didascalia et Constitutiones apostolorum*, 2 vols., F. X. Funk (ed.) (Turin: Bottega d'Erasmo, 1962).
>
> Latin text: *Didascaliae apostolorum; Canonum ecclesiasticorum; Traditionis apostolicae versiones Latinae*, E. Tidner (ed.), TU 75 (5th ser., vol. xix) (Berlin: Akademie-Verlag, 1963).
>
> ET: *Didascalia apostolorum: the Syriac version translated and accompanied by the Verona Latin fragments, with an introduction and notes*, R. H. Connolly (trans.) (Oxford: Clarendon Press, 1929, repr. 1969).

Dio Cassius. Text and ET: *Dio Cassius: Roman History*, LCL, 9 vols., E. Cary (ed. and trans.) (1914–27).

Dio Chrysostom. Text and ET: *Dio Chrysostom*, LCL, 5 vols., J. W. Cohoon and H. L. Crosby (eds. and trans.) (1932–51).

Diodorus Siculus. Text and ET: *Diodorus Siculus*, LCL, 12 vols., C. H. Oldfather, C. L. Sherman, C. Bradford Welles, R. M. Geer and F. R. Walton (eds. and trans.) (1933–67).

Diogenes Laertius. Text: *Diogenis Laertii vitae philosophorum*, 3 vols., M. Marcovich (ed.), Teubner (1999).
> Text and German trans.: Diogenes Laertius, *Leben und Meinungen berühmter Philosophen*, 2 vols., O. Apelt and K. Reich (eds. and trans.), Philosophische Bibliothek 53–4 (Hamburg: Meiner, 1998).
>
> Text and ET: *Diogenes Laertes, Lives of eminent philosophers*, LCL, 2 vols., R. D. Hicks (ed. and trans.) (1925).

Diognetus, Epistle to [See *Apostolic fathers*].

Dionysius of Alexandria. Text: *The letters and other remains of Dionysius of Alexandria*, C. L. Feltoe (ed.), Cambridge patristic texts (Cambridge: Cambridge University Press, 1904).
> ET: *St Dionysius of Alexandria: letters and treatises*, C. L. Feltoe (trans.), TCL ser. 1 (1918).

Dionysius bar Salibi, *Commentari in Apocalypsim.*
> Latin and Syriac texts: *In Apocalypsim, Actus et Epistulas catholicas*, Jaroslav Sedlácek (ed.), 2 vols. in 1, CSCO 53, 60; Scriptores Syri ser. 2, vol. ci (Paris: Typographeus Reipublicae, 1909–10).

Dioscurides Pedianus. Text: *De materia medica libri quinque*, 3 vols., M. Wellmann (ed.), (Berlin: Weidmann, 1906–14).

Discourse on the eighth and ninth [NHC vi, 6; ET: *NHL*].
> NHS 11, D. Parrott (ed.) (1979), 341–73.

Egerton gospel [*Egerton papyrus 2*; ET: *NTApoc*, vol. 1].
> Text and ET: H. I. Bell and T. C. Skeat, *Fragments of an unknown gospel and other early Christian papyri* (London: British Museum, 1935).

Elliott, J. K. (ed.). *The Apocryphal New Testament: a collection of apocryphal Christian literature in an English translation* (Oxford: Oxford University Press, 1993).

Ephrem. *Saint Ephrem's commentary on Tatian's Diatessaron: an English translation of Chester Beatty Syriac MS 709*, C. McCarthy (trans.), JSS Sup 2 (1993).

—. *Hymns against heresy* in *Des heiligen Ephraem des Syrers Hymnen contra haereses*, 2 vols., E. Beck (ed. and trans.), CSCO 169–70, Scriptores Syri 76–7 (1957).

—. *St Ephraim's prose refutations of Mani, Marcion, and Bardaisan*, 2 vols., C. W. Mitchell, A. A. Bevan and F. C. Burkitt (eds. and trans.) (London: Williams and Norgate, 1912).

Epictetus. Text and ET: *Epictetus*, LCL, 2 vols., W. A. Oldfather (ed. and trans.) (1925–8).

Epiphanius. *Panarion (Adversus haereses)*. Text: *Epiphanius i–iii*, K. Holl and J. Dummer (eds.), 2nd ed., GCS 25, 31, 37 (1980–5).

Text and ET: *The Panarion of Epiphanius of Salamis*, 2 vols., F. Williams (trans.), NHS 35–6 (1987–94).

Epistula apostolorum [ET: *NTApoc*, vol. i; Elliott, *Apocryphal New Testament*].

Text: *Gespräche Jesu mit seinen Jüngern nach der Auferstehung*, C. Schmidt (ed.), I. Wajnberg (trans.), TU 43 (1913).

Text and French trans.: *L'Épître des apôtres, accompagnée du Testament de notre Seigneur et notre saveur Jésus-Christ*, J. N. Pérès (ed. and trans.), Apocryphes 5 (Turnhout: Brepols, 1994).

Eugnostos the Blessed [NHC ii, 6; ET: *NHL*].

Euphemia and the Goth with the Acts of martyrdom of the confessors of Edessa, Shmona, Guria, and Habib, F. C. Burkitt (ed. and trans.), Text and Translation Society Publications (London: Williams and Norgate, 1913).

NHS 27, D. Parrott (ed.) (1991).

Eusebius [ET: *NPNF²* 1].

Texts: *Eusebius Werke*, 9 vols., I. A. Heikel, E. Schwartz, E. Klostermann *et al.* (eds. and trans.), GCS 7, 9, 11, 14, 20, 23–4, 34, 43, 47, n.s. 6.1 (1902–75).

—. *Demonstratio evangelica*. Text: *Eusebius Werke*, vol. vi: *Die Demonstratio evangelica*, I. A. Heikel (ed.), GCS 23 (1913).

ET: *Eusebius, The proof of the gospel*, 2 vols., W. J. Ferrar (trans.), TCL ser. 1 (1920).

Text and Italian trans.: *Dimostrazione evangelica*, P. Carrara (ed. and trans.), Letture cristiane del primo millennio 29 (Milan: Paoline, 2000).

—. *De ecclesiastica theologia* and *Contra Marcellum*. Text: *Eusebius Werke*, vol. iv: *Gegen Marcell; Über die kirchlichen Theologie*, E. Klostermann (ed.), G. C. Hansen (rev.), GCS 14 (1972).

—. *Historia ecclesiastica*. Text and French trans.: *Histoire ecclésiastique*, rev. and corr. ed., E. Schwartz (ed.), G. Bardy (trans.), SC 31, 41, 55, 73 (2001–).

Text and ET: *Eusebius: The ecclesiastical history*, LCL, 2 vols., K. Lake, J. E. L. Oulton and H. J. Lawlor (trans.) (1926–32).

ET: *Eusebius, bishop of Caesarea: the Ecclesiastical history and the Martyrs of Palestine*, H. J. Lawlor and J. E. L. Oulton (trans.) (London: SPCK, 1927).

ET: *Ecclesiastical history*, R. J. Deferrari (trans.), FC 19, 29 (1953–6).

ET: *The history of the church from Christ to Constantine*, G. A. Williamson (trans.) and Andrew Louth (rev.) (London: Penguin, 1989).

—. *Laus Constantini*. Text: I. A. Heikel (ed.), GCS 7 (1902).

—. *Praeparatio evangelica*. Text and French trans.: *Eusebius: la Préparation évangélique, livre* vii, G. Schroeder and E. des Places (eds. and trans.), SC 215 (1975).

Text and ET: *Eusebius, Praeparatio evangelica*, 5 vols., E. H. Gifford (ed.) (Oxford: Clarendon Press, 1903).

—. *De vita Constantini*. Text: *Eusebius Werke*, vol. i, F. Winkelmann (ed.), GCS 1 (1975, rev. 1992).

ET: *Eusebius, Life of Constantine: introduction, translation, and commentary*, Averil Cameron and S. G. Hall (eds. and trans.) (Oxford: Clarendon Press, 1999).

Eutropius. *Breviarium ab urbe condita*. Text: F. Ruehl (ed.), Teubner (1975).

ET: *The Breviarum ab urbe condita of Eutropius*, H. W. Bird (trans.), TTH 14 (1993).

Eutychius. *Annales*. Text: *PG* 111.

Exegesis on the soul [NHC 11, 6; ET: *NHL*].

    NHS 20–1, B. Layton (ed.) (1989), 11. 136–69.

4 Ezra [ET: *OTP*, vol. 1, *APOT*, vol. 11].

    Text: *Die Esra-Apokalypse (IV. Esra)*, A. F. J. Klijn (ed.), GCS (un-numbered) (1992).

    Text: *Die Esra-Apokalypse (IV. Esra)*, 2 vols., B. Violet (ed.), GCS 18, 32 (1910–24).

Filastrius. *Sancti Filastrii episcopi Brixiensis Diversarum hereseon liber*, F. Marx (ed.), CSEL 38 (Vienna: F. Tempsky, 1898).

—. *Filastrii episcopi Brixiensis Diversarum hereseon liber*, F. Heylen (ed.), CCSL 9 (Turnhout: Brepols, 1957).

Foerster, W. *Gnosis: a selection of Gnostic texts*, 2 vols.; R. McL. Wilson, (trans.) (Oxford: Clarendon Press, 1972–4).

Gelasius of Cyzicus. *Historia ecclesiastica*. Text: *Anonyme Kirchengeschichte (Gelasius Cyzicenus)*, G. C. Hansen (ed.), GCS n.s. 9 (2002).

Gesta apud Zenophilum.

    Text: *S. Optati Milevitani libri VII*, K. Ziwsa (ed.), CSEL 26 (1893), 185–97.

Goodspeed, E. J. *Die ältesten Apologeten: Texte mit kurzen Einleitungen* (Göttingen: Vandenhoeck & Ruprecht, 1914).

The gospel of the Egyptians [NHC 11, 2; IV, 2; ET: *NHL*].

    NHS 4, A. Böhlig and F. Wisse (eds. and trans.) (1975).

The gospel of Eve [ET: *NTApoc*, vol. 1].

The gospel of the Hebrews [ET: *NTApoc*, vol. 1].

The gospel of Mary [BG,1; ET: *NTApoc*, vol. 1, *NHL*].

    NHS 11, D. Parrott (ed.) (1979), 453–71.

The gospel of Peter [ET: *NTApoc*, vol. 1].

    Text and French trans.: *Evangile de Pierre*, M. G. Mara (ed. and trans.), SC 201 (1973).

The gospel of Philip [NHC 11, 3; ET: *NTApoc*, vol. 1, *NHL*].

    NHS 20–1, B. Layton (ed.) (1989), 1.131–217.

The gospel of the Saviour.

    Text and ET: *Gospel of the Savior: a new ancient gospel*, C. W. Hedrick and P. Mirecki (eds. and trans.) (Santa Rosa, CA: Polebridge, 1999).

The gospel of Thomas [ET: *NTApoc*, vol. 1, *NHL*].

    NHS 20–1, B. Layton (ed.) (1989), 1.38–128.

    ET: *The critical edition of Q*, J. M. Robinson, P. Hoffman and J. S. Kloppenborg (eds.) (Minneapolis: Fortress, 2000).

The gospel of truth [NHC 1, 3; XII, 2; ET: *NHL*].

    NHS 22–3, H. W. Attridge (ed.) (1985), 1.55–117.

The gospel of the twelve [ET: *NTApoc*, vol. 1].

Gregory of Nazianzus. *Orations* [ET in *NPNF*[2] 7].

    Text and French trans.: *Discours*, J. Bernardi, J. Mossay, P. Gallay and C. Moreschini (eds. and trans.), SC 247, 250, 270, 284, 309, 318, 358, 384, 405 (1978–).

Gregory of Nyssa. *De vita Gregorii Thaumaturgi.* Text: *Gregorii Nysseni opera*, vol. x, pt ii, bk i: *Sermones*, G. Heil, J. P Cavarnos, O. Lendle (eds.) (Leiden: Brill, 1990).

Gregory Thaumaturgus. *Epistula canonica.* Text: *PG* 10.

ET: 'Canonical letter', in P. J. Heather and J. Matthews, *The Goths in the fourth century*, TTH 11 (1991).

—. *In Originem oratio panegyrica.*

Text and French trans.: *Remerciement à Origène, suivi de la lettre d'Origène à Grégoire*, H. Crouzel (ed. and trans.), SC 148 (1969).

ET: *St Gregory Thaumaturgus: Life and Works*, M. Slusser (trans.), FC 98 (1998).

Gregory of Tours. *Historia Francorum.*

Text and German trans.: Gregory of Tours, *Zehn Bücher Geschichten*, 2 vols., W. Giesebrechts and R. Buchner (eds. and trans.), 4th ed., Ausgewählte Quellen zur deutschen Geschichte des Mittelalters 2–3 (Darmstadt: Wissenschaftliche Buchgesellschaft, 1970).

Text and French trans.: Gregory of Tours, *Histoire des Francs*, 2 vols., R. Latouche (ed. and trans.), Classiques de l'histoire de France au moyen age 27–28 (Paris: Les Belles Lettres, 1963–5).

Text and Italian trans.: *Storia dei Franchi: i dieci libri delle storie*, 2 vols., M. Oldoni (ed. and trans.), Nuovo medioevo 55 (Naples: Liguori, 2001).

ET: Gregory of Tours, *The history of the Franks*, L. Thorpe (trans.), Penguin classics (Baltimore: Penguin, 1974).

Hänggi, A. and I. Pahl. *Prex eucharistica: textus e variis liturgiis antiquioribus selecti*, Spicilegium Friburgense 12 (Fribourg: Éditions Universitaires, 1968).

Heracleon. *Fragmenta.* Text: A. E. Brooke, *The fragments of Heracleon* (Cambridge: Cambridge University Press 1891).

ET: Foerster, *Gnosis*, vol. i, 162–83.

Hermas, Shepherd of (*Visions, Mandates and Similitudes*) [See *Apostolic fathers*].

Hermetica. Text: *The Greek Corpus Hermeticum and the Latin Asclepius in a new English translation, with notes and introduction*, B. P. Copenhaver (ed. and trans.) (Cambridge: Cambridge University Press, 1992).

Hilary of Poitiers [ET: *NPNF²* 10].

—. *Adversus Valentem et Ursacium.* Text: *S. Hilarii episcopi Pictaviensis opera*, vol. iv, A. Feder (ed.), CSEL 65 (1916).

ET: *Hilary of Poitiers: conflicts of conscience and law in the fourth-century church*, L. R. Wickham (ed. and trans.), TTH 25 (1997).

—. *Epistula de synodis.* Text: A. Feder (ed.), CSEL 65 (1916).

Hippolytus [ET: *ANF* 5].

Texts: *Hippolytus Werke*, GCS 1, 26, 36, 46, G. N. Bonwetsch, H. Achelis, P. Wendland and A. Bauer (eds.) (1897–).

—. *Commentarii in Danielem.* Text and French trans.: *Commentaire sur Daniel*, G. Bardy and M. Lefèvre (eds. and trans.), SC 14 (1947).

—. *contra Noëtum.* Text: *Contro Noeto*, M. Simonetti (ed.), Biblioteca Patristica 35 (Bologna: EDB, 2000).

ET: *Contra Noëtum*, R. Butterworth (ed. and trans.), Heythrop monographs 2 (London: Heythrop College, 1977).

—. *Refutatio omnium haeresium.* Text: M. Marcovich (ed.), PTS 25 (1986).

ET: *Philosophoumena, or, The refutation of all heresies*, F. Legge (trans.), TCL ser. I (1921).

[Hippolytus?]. *Traditio apostolica*. Text and French trans.: *Hippolyte de Rome: la Tradition apostolique d'après les anciennes versions*, 2nd ed., B. Botte (ed. and trans.), SC 11 bis; (1968).

ET: *The treatise on the 'Apostolic tradition'*, G. Dix (ed. and trans.), H. Chadwick (ed.), 2nd ed., (London: SPCK, 1968).

ET: *The Apostolic tradition: translation and commentary*, P. F. Bradshaw, M. E. Johnson and L. E. Phillips (eds. and trans.), Hermeneia (Minneapolis: Fortress, 2002).

ET: *On the apostolic tradition*, A. Stewart-Sykes (ed. and trans.) (Crestwood, NY: St Vladimir's Seminary Press, 2001).

Historia Augusta. Text and ET: *Scriptores historiae Augustae*, LCL, 3 vols., D. Magie (trans.), 1924–32.

Holladay, C. R. *Fragments from Hellenistic Jewish authors*, vol. I: *Historians*, vol. II: *Poets*, vol. III *Aristobulus*, vol. IV, *Orphica* (Missoula, MT: Scholars Press, 1983–96).

Hypostasis of the Archons [NHC II, 4; ET: *NHL*].

NHS 20–1, B. Layton (ed.) (1989), 1.220–59.

Hypsiphrone [NHC XI, 4; ET: *NHL*].

NHS 28, C. W. Hedrick (ed.) (1990), 269–79.

Ignatius of Antioch. *Epistulae* [See *Apostolic fathers*].

Interpretation of Knowledge [NHC XI, 1; ET: *NHL*].

NHS 28, C. W. Hedrick (ed.) (1990), 21–88.

Irenaeus [ET: *ANF* 1].

—. *Adversus haereses*. Text and French trans.: *Irénée de Lyon, Contre les hérésies*, A. Rousseau and L. Doutreleau (eds. and trans.), SC 100, 152–3, 210–11, 263–4, 293–4 (1969–82).

Text and Latin trans.: *Libros quinque adversus haereses*, 2 vols., W. W. Harvey (ed.) (Cambridge: Typis Academicus, 1857).

Armenian text: *Irenäus, Gegen die Häretiker*, K. Ter-Mekerttschian and E. Ter-Minassiantz (eds.), TU 35.2 (1910).

Partial ET: *Irenaeus of Lyons: Against heresies*, R. M. Grant (trans.), Early church fathers (London: Routledge, 1997).

ET: *Five books of St. Irenaeus, bishop of Lyons, Against heresies*, J. Keble (trans.) (Oxford: J. Parker, 1872).

ET: *St Irenaeus of Lyons Against the heresies*, D. J. Unger (trans.), J. J. Dillon (rev.), ACW 55 (1992).

—. *Epideixis tou apostolikou kērygmatos*. Text and French trans.: *Irénée de Lyon: Demonstration de la prédication apostolique*, A. Rousseau (ed. and trans.), SC 406 (1995).

Armenian text and German trans.: *Des heiligen Irenäus Schrift zum Erweise der apostolischen Verkündigung*, K. Ter-Mekerttschian und E. Ter-Minassiantz (eds. and trans.), TU 31.1 (1907).

Armenian text and English and French trans.: *Epideixis tou apostolikou kērygmatos* = *The proof of the apostolic preaching, with seven fragments*, K. Mekerttschian, S. G. Wilson, Max, Prince of Saxony, J. Barthoulot and J. Tixeront (eds. and trans.), PO 12.5 (1919; repr. 1989).

ET: *Irenaeus' Demonstration of the apostolic preaching: a theological commentary and translation*, I. M. MacKenzie (trans.) (Aldershot, Hants: Ashgate, 2002).

ET: *On the apostolic preaching*, J. Behr (trans.) (Crestwood, NY: St Vladimir's Seminary Press, 1997).

ET: *Proof of the apostolic preaching*, J. P. Smith (trans.), ACW 16 (1952).

ET: *The demonstration of the apostolic preaching*, J. A. Robinson (trans.), TCL ser. 4 (1920).

—. *Fragmenta*. Text and German trans.: *Fragmente vornicänischer Kirchenväter aus den Sacra Parallela*, K. Holl (ed. and trans.), TU 20.2 (1899).

Text and German trans.: *Armenische Irenaeusfragmente*, H. Jordan (ed. and trans.), TU 36.3 (1913).

James, M. R. (ed. and trans.). *The Apocryphal New Testament* (Oxford: Clarendon Press, 1955).

Jannes and Jambres [ET: *OTP*, vol. II].

Jerome [Text in PL 22–30; PLS, vol. II, 18–328; ET: *NPNF*² 6].

—. *Chronicon*. Text: *Chronik des Hieronymus*, R. Helm (ed.), GCS 47.

—. *Commentariorum in Amos* [ET: *NPNF*² 6].

S. *Hieronymi presbyteri opera*, pt I: *Opera exegetica*, vol. VI, *Commentarii in prophetas minores*, M. Adriaen and D. Vallarsi (eds.), CCSL 76 (1969).

—. *Commentariorum in Epistulam ad Galatas* [ET: *NPNF*² 6].

Text: PL 26.307–438.

—. *Commentariorum in Ezechielem* [ET: *NPNF*² 6].

Text: S. *Hieronymi presbyteri opera*, pt I: *Opera exegetica*, vol. IV, *Commentarii in Hiezechielem libri* XIV, F. Glorie (ed.), CCSL 75 (1964).

—. *Commentariorum in Habacuc* [ET: *NPNF*² 6]

Text: S. *Hieronymi presbyteri opera*, pt I: *Opera exegetica*, vol. VI, *Commentarii in prophetas minores*, M. Adriaen and D. Vallarsi (eds.), CCSL 76A (1970).

—. *Commentariorum in Isaiam* [ET: *NPNF*² 6]

Text: S. *Hieronymi presbyteri opera*, pt I: *Opera exegetica*, vol. II, *Commentariorum in Esaiam libri I–XI*, M. Adriaen (ed.), CCSL 73 (1963).

Text: S. *Hieronymi presbyteri opera*, pt I: *Opera exegetica*, vol. IIA, *Commentariorum in Esaiam libri XII–XVIII in Esaia parvula adbreviatio*, M. Adriaen (ed.), CCSL 73A (1963).

—. *Commentariorum in Jeremiam* [ET: *NPNF*² 6].

Text: S. *Hieronymi presbyteri opera*, pt I: *Opera exegetica*, vol. III, *In Hieremiam libri VI*, S. Reiter (ed.), CCSL 74 (1960).

Sancti Eusebii Hieronymi in Hieremiam prophetam libri VI, S. Reiter (ed.). CSEL 59 (1913).

—. *Commentariorum in Matthaeum* [ET: *NPNF*² 6].

Text: S. *Hieronymi presbyteri opera*, pt I: *Opera exegetica*, vol. VII, *Commentarii in Mattheum libri IV*, D. Hurst and M. Adriaen (eds.), CCSL 77 (1969).

—. *De viris illustribus* [ET: *NPNF*² 3].

Text: *Hieronymus liber De viris inlustribus: Gennadius liber De viris inlustribus*. E. C. Richardson (ed.), TU 14.1a (1896).

Text: *Hieronymi De viris inlustribus liber: accedit Gennadii Catalogus virorum inlustrium*, G. Herding (ed.), Teubner (1924).

—. *Epistulae*. Text: *Hieronymus, Epistulae*, 3 vols., I. Hilberg (ed.), CSEL 54–6, 2nd ed. (1996).

ET: *The Letters of Saint Jerome*, C. C. Mierow and T. C. Lawler (eds. and trans.), ACW 33 (1963).

—. *Onomasticon*. Text in Eusebius, *Werke*, vol. III, pt 1, *Das Onomastikon der biblischen Ortsnamen*, E. Klostermann (ed.), GCS 11.1 (1904).

Josephus. Texts: *Opera*, 7 vols., B. Niese (ed.) (Berlin: Weidmann, 1955).

Text and ET: *Josephus*, LCL, 10 vols., H. St. J. Thackeray, R. Marcus, A. Wikgren and L. H. Feldman (eds. and trans.) (1926–65).

—. *De bello Iudaico*. Text: *Der jüdische Krieg*, 3 vols., O. Michel and O. Bauernfeind (eds. and trans.) (Munich: Kösel, 1959–69).

—. *Vita*. ET: *Flavius Josephus: translation and commentary*, S. Mason (ed.) (Leiden: Brill, 2000).

Julian. Text and ET: *Julian*, LCL, 3 vols., W. C. Wright (ed. and trans.) (1913–23).

Justin [ET: *ANF* 1].

Text: Goodspeed, *Die ältesten Apologeten*.

—. *1–2 Apologia*. Text: *Iustini Martyris apologiae pro Christianis*, M. Marcovich (ed.), PTS 38 (1994).

ET: *The first and second Apologies: translated with introduction and notes*, L. W. Barnard (ed. and trans.), ACW 56 (1997).

ET: *Saint Justin Martyr: the first Apology, the second Apology, Dialogue with Trypho, Exhortation to the Greeks, Discourse to the Greeks, The monarchy or the rule of God*, T. B. Falls (trans.), FC 6 (1977).

ET: *Early Christian fathers*, C. C. Richardson, E. R. Fairweather, E. R. Hardy and M. H. Shepherd (eds. and trans.), LCC 1 (1970).

—. *Dialogus cum Tryphone*. Text: M. Marcovich (ed.), PTS 47 (1997).

ET: *Dialogue with Trypho*, T. B. Falls (trans), T. P. Halton and M. Slusser (eds.), FC 3 (2003).

[Justin]. Text: *Pseudo-Justinus: Cohortatio ad Graecos, De monarchia, Oratio ad Graecos*, M. Marcovich (ed.), PTS 32 (1990).

Juvenal. Text and ET: *Juvenal and Persius*, LCL, G. G. Ramsay (ed. and trans.) (1918).

Kerygma Petri [ET: *NTApoc*, vol. II].

Text and French trans.: *Kerygma Petri: textus et commentarius*, M. Cambe (ed. and trans.), CCSA 15 (2003).

Kerygmata Petrou [ET: *NTApoc*, vol. II].

Lactantius [ET: *ANF* 7].

Text: *L. Caeli Firmiani Lactanti opera omnia*, S. Brandt and G. Laubmann (eds.), CSEL 19 (1890).

—. *Divinae institutiones*. Text and French trans.: *Lactantius, Institutions divines*, P. Monat (ed. and trans.), SC 204–5, 326, 337, 377 (1986–7).

ET: *Lactantius: Divine institutes*, A. Bowen and P. Garnsey (trans.), TTH 40 (2003).

ET: *Lactantius: The divine institutes, books 1–7*, M. F. Macdonald (trans.), FC 49 (1964).

—. *De morte persecutorum*. Text and ET: *De mortibus persecutorum*, J. L. Creed (ed. and trans.), OECT (1984).

Text: *De mortibus persecutorum*, S. Brandt and G. Laubmann (eds.), CSEL 27.2 (1897).

Text and French trans.: *De la mort des persecuteurs*, 2 vols., J. Moreau (ed. and trans.), SC 39 (1954).

—. *Minor works*, M. F. Macdonald (trans.), FC 54 (1965).

Layton, B. (ed.). *The gnostic scriptures* (Garden City, NY: Doubleday, 1987).

Liber pontificalis. Text: *Le Liber pontificalis: texte, introduction et commentaire*, 3 vols., L. Duchesne and C. Vogel (eds.), Bibliothèque des écoles françaises d'Athènes et de Rome, 2nd ser. (Paris: E. de Boccard, 1981, original 1955–7).

ET: *The book of pontiffs: the ancient biographies of the first ninety Roman bishops to* AD *715*, R. Davis (trans.), TTH Latin ser. 5 (1989).

Livy. Text and ET: *Livy*, LCL, 14 vols., B. O. Foster, F. G. Moore, E. T. Sage and A. C. Schlesinger (eds. and trans.) (1919–59).

[Longinus]. *De sublimitate*. Text and ET: *The Poetics*, Aristotle, LCL, D. A. Russell (ed. and trans.) (1995).

Lucian. Text: *Luciani opera*, M. D. Macleod (ed.), OCT (1974–87).

Text: *Luciani Samosatensis opera*, K. Iacobitz (ed.), Teubner (1913–21).

Text and ET: *Lucian*, LCL, 8 vols., A. M. Harmon, K. Kilburn and M. D. Maleod (eds. and trans.) (1913–67).

—. *De dea Syria*. Text and ET: *On the Syrian goddess*, J. L. Lightfoot (ed. and trans.) (Oxford: Oxford University Press, 2003).

Lucretius. *De rerum natura*. Text and ET: *Lucretius*, LCL, W. H. D. Rouse (ed. and trans.), M. F. Smith (rev.) (1992).

2 Maccabees. Text: *2. Makkabäerbuch*, C. Habicht (ed.), Jüdische Schriften aus hellenistisch-römischer Zeit, vol. I, Historische und legendarische Schriften, pt 3 (Gütersloh: Mohn, 1976).

A Manichaean psalm-book, pt II. *Text*, C. R. C. Allberry (ed.), Manichaean manuscripts in the Chester Beatty collection 2 (Stuttgart: Kohlhammer, 1938).

Marcus Aurelius. Text and ET: *Marcus Aurelius*, LCL, C. R. Haines (ed. and trans.) (1916).

Marsanes [NHC x; ET: *NHL*].

NHS 15, B. A. Pearson (ed.) (1981), 119–347.

Martyrium Crispinae [Text and ET: Musurillo].

Martyrium Cypriani [Text and ET: Musurillo].

Martyrium Justini et septem sodalium [Text and ET: Musurillo].

Martyrium Mariani et Iacobi [Text and ET: Musurillo].

Martyrium Montani et Lucii [Text and ET: Musurillo].

Martyrium Perpetuae et Felicitatis [Text and ET: Musurillo].

Martyrium Pionii [Text and ET: Musurillo].

Martyrium Polycarpi [See *Apostolic fathers*; Text and ET: Musurillo].

Martyrium Saturnini et Dativi et aliorum [Text: *PL* 8].

Text and Italian trans.: *Note agiografiche*, vol. VIII, P. Franchi de' Cavalieri (ed. and trans.), Studi e testi 65 (Rome: Tipografia Vaticana, 1935), 47–71.

Martyrum Scillitanorum acta [Text and ET: Musurillo].

Maximus of Tyre. Text: *Maximi Tyrii philosophumena*, H. Hobein (ed.), Teubner (1910).

Text: *Dissertationes*, M. B. Trapp (ed.) Teubner (1994).

Text with commentary: *Maximus Tyrius Philosophumena: Dialexeis*, G. L. Koniaris (ed.), Texte und Kommentare 17 (Berlin: W. de Gruyter, 1995).

ET: *The philosophical orations*, M. B. Trapp (trans.) (New York: Oxford University Press, 1997).

Melchizedek [NHC IX, I; ET: *NHL*].

NHS 15, B. A. Pearson (ed.) (1981), 19–85.

Melito of Sardis. *Peri pascha*. Text and ET: *Melito of Sardis: On Pascha and Fragments: texts and translations*, S. G. Hall (ed. and trans.), OECT (1979).

Text and French trans.: *Meliton de Sardes: Sur la pâque et fragments*, O. Perler (ed. and trans.), SC 123 (1966).

Methodius of Olympus. Text: *Methodius*, G. Nathanael Bonwetsch (ed.), GCS 27 (1917).
    ET: *The Writings of Methodius*, A. Roberts (trans.), Ante Nicene Christian library 14 (Edinburgh: T & T Clark, 1880).
——. *Symposium.* Text and French trans.: *Le banquet*, H. Musurillo (ed. and trans.), SC 95 (1963).
    ET: *The symposium: a treatise on chastity*, H. Musurillo (trans.), ACW 27 (1958).
Minucius Felix. *Octavius.* Text: *M. Minuci Felicis Octavius*, B. Kytzler (ed.), Teubner (1982).
    Text and ET: LCL, T. R. Glover and G. H. Rendall (eds. and trans.) (with Tertullian, *Apology, de spectaculis*) (1931).
    ET: *The Octavius of Minucius Felix*, G. Clarke (trans. and ed.), ACW 39 (1974).
    German trans.: *Octavius*, H. von Geisau (ed.), 3rd ed. (Münster: Aschendorff, 1955).
Mishnah. Text: *Shishah Sidre Mishnah*, C. Albeck (ed.) (Jerusalem: Mosad Byalik, 1975).
    ET: *The Mishnah*, H. Danby (trans.) (Oxford: Oxford University Press, 1933).
    ET: *The Mishnah: a new translation*, J. Neusner (ed. and trans.) (New Haven: Yale University Press, 1988).
Musonius Rufus. Text: *C. Musonii Rufi reliquiae*, O. Hense (ed.), Teubner (1905, repr. 1990).
    Text and ET: 'Musonius Rufus, "The Roman Socrates"', C. E Lutz (ed. and trans.), *Yale classical studies* 10 (1947), 3–147.
Musurillo, H. (ed. and trans.). *Acts of the Christian martyrs*, OECT (1972).
The Nag Hammadi library in English, James M. Robinson (ed.), 4th ed. (San Francisco: Harper & Row, 1988).
Nautin, P. (ed.). *Lettres et écrivains chrétiens des IIe et IIIe siècles* (Paris: Editions du Cerf, 1961).
New Testament Apocrypha, 2 vols., W. Schneemelcher and R. McL. Wilson (eds.), rev. ed. (Louisville, Ky: Westminster John Knox, 1991–2).
Novatian ET: *ANF* 5.
——. *De Trinitate liber.* Text: *Novatiani opera quae supersunt*, G. F. Diercks (ed.), CCSL 4 (1972).
    Text: *Novatiani Romanae urbis presbyteri De Trinitate liber: Novatian's treatise on the Trinity*, W. Y. Faussett (ed.), Cambridge patristic texts (Cambridge: Cambridge University Press, 1909).
    ET: *The treatise of Novatian on the Trinity*, H. Moore (ed. and trans.), TCL, ser. 2 (1919).
    ET: *Novatian, The Trinity, The spectacles, Jewish foods, In praise of purity, Letters*, R. J. DeSimone (ed. and trans.), FC 67 (1974).
Numenius. *Fragmenta.* Text and French trans.: *Numénius: fragments*, E. des Places (ed. and trans.) (Paris: Les Belles Lettres, 1973).
Odes of Solomon [ET: *OTP*, vol. II].
    Text and ET: *The odes of Solomon: the Syriac texts*, J. H. Charlesworth (ed. and trans.), SBLTT 13 (1978).
    Text and German trans.: *Oden Salomos: Text, Übersetzung, Kommentar*, M. Lattke (ed. and trans.), NTOA 41 (1999).
On the origin of the world [NHC II, 5; XIII, 2; ET: *NHL*].
    NHS 20–1, B. Layton (ed.) (1989), 2.12–134.
Optatus of Milevis. Text: *S. Optati Milevitani libri VII*, K. Ziwsa (ed.), CSEL 26 (1893).
    Text and French trans.: *Optatus de Milève, Traité contre les Donatistes*, 2 vols., J. Labrousse (ed. and trans.), SC 412–413 (1996–7).

Text and French trans.: *Le dossier du Donatisme*, 2 vols., J.-L. Maier (ed. and trans.), TU 134–5 (1987–9).

ET: *Optatus, Against the Donatists*, M. Edwards (ed. and trans.), TTH 27 (1997).

—. Appendices to *Against the Donatists*. Text: *S. Optati Milevitani libri VII*, C. Ziwsa (ed.), CSEL 26 (1893).

Text: *Le dossier du Donatisme*, vol. I, J.-L. Maier (ed.), TU 134 (1987).

Origen [ET: *ANF* 4, 10].

Text: *Origenes Werke*, 12 vols., P. Koetschau, E. Klostermann, E. Preuschen and W. A. Baehrens (eds.), GCS 2–3, 6, 10, 22, 29–30, 33, 35, 38, 40, 41 (1899–1955).

—. *Commentarii in evangelium Joannis*. Text and French trans.: *Commentaire sur Saint Jean*, C. Blanc (ed. and trans.), SC 120², 157, 222, 290, 385 (1966–92).

ET: *Commentary on the gospel according to John*, 2 vols., R. E. Heine (trans.), FC 80, 89 (1989–93).

—. *In Matthaeum commentariorum series*. German trans.: *Der Kommentar zum Evangelium nach Mattäus*, 3 vols., Herman J. Vogt (ed. and trans.), Bibliothek der griechischen Literatur, Abteilung Patristik 18, 30, 38 (Stuttgart: A. Hiersemann, 1983–93).

—. *Contra Celsum*. Text and French trans.: *Contre Celse: introduction, texte critique, traduction et notes*, M. Borret (ed. and trans.), SC 132, 136, 147, 150, 227 (1967–76).

ET: *Contra Celsum*, H. Chadwick (trans.) (Cambridge: Cambridge University Press, 1980).

—. *Dialogus cum Heraclide*. Text: *Entretien d'Origène avec Héraclide et les évêques, ses collègues, sur le Père, le Fils et l'âme*, Jacques Scherer (ed.), Publications, textes et documents, Société Fouad I de Papyrologie (Cairo: Imprimerie de l'Institut Français d'Archéologie Orientale, 1949).

Text and ET: *Alexandrian Christianity: Selected translations of Clement and Origen with introductions and notes*, J. E. L. Oulton and H. Chadwick (eds. and trans.), LCC 2 (1977), pp. 430–55.

—. *Hexapla*. Text: *Origenis Hexaplorum quae supersunt*, 2 vols., F. Field (ed.) (repr. Hildesheim: Olms, 1964).

—. *Homiliae in Numeros*. Text and French trans.: *Homélies sur les Nombres*, A. Méhat (ed. and trans.), SC 29 (1951).

—. *De oratione*. ET: *Origen: Prayer, Exhortation to martyrdom*, J. J. O'Meara (trans.), ACW 19 (1954).

—. *De principiis*. Text and French trans.: *Traité des principes*, H. Crouzel and M. Simonetti (eds. and trans.), SC 252, 268 (1978, 1980).

ET: *On first principles*, G. W. Butterworth (trans.) (London: SPCK, 1936).

—. *Selecta in Leviticum (fragmenta e catenis)*, PG 12, cols. 397–404.

—. *Selections from the commentaries and homilies of Origen*, R B. Tollinton (ed. and trans.), TCL, ser. I (1929).

Collected, partial English translations of Origen's works:

—. *Origen*, R. A. Greer (ed. and trans.) (New York: Paulist, 1979).

—. *Origen*, J. W. Trigg (ed. and trans.), Early church fathers (London: Routledge, 1998).

—. J. E. L. Oulton and H. Chadwick (eds. and trans.), *Alexandrian Christianity: selected translations of Clement and Origen with introductions and notes*, LCC 2 (1977).

Origo Constantini imperatoris. Text and German trans.: *Origo Constantini, Anonymus Valesianus,* I. König (ed. and trans.), Trierer Historische Forschungen 11 (Trier: Trierer Historische Forschungen, 1987).

ET: *From Constantine to Julian: pagan and Christian views, a source history,* S. N. C. Lieu and D. Montserrat (eds.) (London: Routledge, 1996).

Orosius. *Historiae adversum paganos* [Text: *PL* 31].

Text: *Historiarum adversum paganos libri* VII, W. Zangemeister (ed.), Teubner (1889).

Ovid. *Heroides: Amores.* Text and ET: *Ovid: The art of love and other poems,* LCL, G. Showerman (ed. and trans.), G. P. Goold (rev.), 2nd ed. (1977).

Palladius. *Historia Lausiaca.* Text: *The Lausiac history of Palladius: a critical discussion together with notes on early Egyptian monachism,* 2 vols., E. C. Butler (ed.), Texts and studies: contributions to Biblical and patristic literature 6.1–2 (Cambridge: Cambridge University Press, 1898–1904).

ET: *The Lausiac history of Palladius,* W. K. L. Clarke (ed. and trans.), TCL, ser. 1 (1918).

ET: *Palladius: the Lausiac history,* R. T. Meyer (trans.), ACW 34 (1965).

Pamphilus, *Apologia pro Origine.* Text: *Pamphile et Eusèbe de Césarée, Apologie pour Origène: suivi de Rufin d'Aquilée, Sur la falsification des livres d'Origène,* R. Amacker and E. Junod (eds. and trans.), SC 464 (2002).

Panegyrici latini. Text: *XII panegyrici Latini,* E. Baehrens and W. A. Baehrens (eds.), Teubner (1911).

Text: *XII panegyrici Latini,* R. A. B. Mynors (ed.), OCT (1964).

ET: *In praise of later Roman emperors: the Panegyrici Latini: introduction, translation, and historical commentary, with the Latin text of R. A. B. Mynors,* C. E. V. Nixon and B. S. Rodgers (eds. and trans.), TCH 21 (1994).

Papias. *Fragments.* See *Apostolic fathers.*

Paraphrase of Shem [NHC VII, 1; ET: *NHL*].

NHMS 30, B. A. Pearson (ed.) (1996), 15–127.

Peter to James, epistle of [ET: *ANF* 8].

Peter to Philip, letter of [NHC VIII, 2; ET: *NHL*].

NHMS 31, J. Sieber (ed.), NHMS 31 (1991), 227–51.

Petronius. *Satyricon.* Text and ET: *Petronius,* LCL, M. Heseltine (ed. and trans.), E. H. Warmington (rev., 1969).

Philo. Text: *Philonis Alexandrini opera quae supersunt,* 7 vols., L. Cohn and P. Wendland (eds.) (Berlin: De Gruyter, 1930–62).

Text and ET: *Philo,* LCL, 10 vols., F. H. Colson, G. H. Whitaker and F. H. Colson (trans.) (1929–62).

—. *Philonis Alexandrini Legatio ad Gaium,* E. M. Smallwood (ed. and trans.) (Leiden: Brill, 1961).

Philodemus. *On piety,* pt 1: *Critical text with commentary,* D. Obbink (ed.) (Oxford: Clarendon Press, 1996).

Philostorgius. *Historia ecclesiastica.* Text: *Philostorgius, Kirchengeschichte: mit dem Leben des Lucian von Antiochien und den Fragmenten eines arianischen Historiographen,* J. Bidez (ed.), F. Winkelmann (rev.), 2nd ed., GCS 21 (1972).

ET: *The Ecclesiastical history of Sozomen and the Ecclesiastical history of Philostorgius, as epitomised by Photius, patriarch of Constantinople,* E. Walford (trans.), Bohn ecclesiastical library (London: H. G. Bohn, 1855).

Philostratus. Text and ET: *Philostratus, The Life of Apollonius of Tyana*, LCL, 2 vols., F. C. Conybeare (ed. and trans.) (1912), C. P. Jones (rev.) (2005). *Philostratus and Eunapius: Lives of the Sophists*, LCL, W. C. Wright (ed. and trans.) (1921).

Pirqe avot. Text and ET: *Sayings of the Jewish fathers*, C. Taylor (ed. and trans.), Library of Jewish classics (New York: Ktav, 1969).

Pistis Sophia [ET: *NHL, NTApoc*, vol. I].

NHS 9, C. Schmidt (ed.), V. MacDermot (trans.) (1978).

Plato. Text: *Platonis dialogi secundum Thrasylli tetralogias dispositi*, 6 vols., K. F. Hermann and E. M. Wohlrab (eds.) Teubner (1915–27).

Text: *Opera*, J. Burnet (ed.) (Oxford: Clarendon Press, 1900, repr. 1967).

Text and ET: *Plato*, LCL, 12 vols., H. N. Fowler, W. R. M. Lamb, P. Shorey, and R.G. Bury (eds. and trans.) (1914–27).

—. *Republic* 588A–589B [NHC VI, 5; ET: *NHL*].

NHS 11, D. Parrott (ed.) (1979), 325–39.

Pliny the Elder. *Historiae naturalis*. Text and ET: *Pliny: Natural History*, LCL, 10 vols., H. Rackham, W. H. S. Jones, A. C. Andrews and D. E. Eichholz (eds. and trans.) (1938–63).

Pliny the Younger. *Epistulae*. Text: *epistularum libri novem, epistularum ad Traianum liber*, M. Schuster and R. Hanslik (eds.), Teubner (1958).

Text and ET: *Letters and Panegyricus*, LCL, 2 vols., B. Radice (ed. and trans.) (1969).

Plotinus. Text and ET: *Plotinus*, LCL, 7 vols., A. H. Armstrong, P. Henry and H.-R. Schwyzer (eds. and trans.) (1966–88).

Plutarch. *Moralia*. Text and ET: LCL, 17 vols., F. C. Babbitt, W. C. Helmbold, P. H. De Lacy *et al.* (eds. and trans.) (1927–69).

—. *Parallel Lives*. Text and ET: LCL, 11 vols., B. Perrin (ed. and trans.) (1914–26).

—. *De Iside et Osiride*. Text and ET: J. Gwyn Griffiths (ed. and trans.) (Cardiff: University of Wales Press, 1970).

Polybius. *Historiae*. Text and ET: *Polybius*, LCL, 6 vols., W. R. Paton (ed. and trans.) (1922–7).

Pontianus Diaconus. *Vita Caecilii Cypriani*. Text: *Cypriani opera omnia*, W. Hartel (ed.), CSEL 3.3 (1871).

Pontius Pilate, letter to Claudius [ET: James, *Apocryphal New Testament*].

Porphyry. Text: *Porphyrii Philosophi fragmenta*, A. Smith and D. Wasserstein (eds.), Teubner (1993).

—. *De antro nympharum*. Text: *Porphyry: The cave of the nymphs in the Odyssey*, Seminar classics 609, Arethusa monographs (Buffalo: Department of Classics, State University of New York, 1969).

—. *Contra Christianos*. Text: *Porphyrius 'Gegen die Christen', 15 Bücher Zeugnisse, Fragmente und Referate*, A. von Harnack (ed.), Abhandlungen der preussischen Akademie der Wissenschaften, Philosoph.-hist. Kl. 1 (Berlin: Reimer, 1916).

Text: *Neue fragmente des Werks des Porphyrius gegen die Christen: die Pseudo-Polycarpiana und die Schrift des Rhetors Pacatus gegen Porphyrius*, A. von Harnack (ed.) (Berlin: Verlag der Akademie der Wissenschafter, 1921).

—.*Vita Plotini*. Greek text: *Plotini opera*, P. Henry and H.-R. Schwyzer (eds.) (Leiden: Brill, 1951), vol. I, 1–41.

Text and ET: *Plotinus*, LCL, vol. I, A. H. Armstrong (ed. and trans.) (1966).

Prayer of the apostle Paul [NHC I, 1; ET: *NHL*].

NHS 22–3, H. W. Attridge (ed.) (1985), 5–11.

Prayer of thanksgiving [NHC vi, 7; ET: *NHL*].
   NHS 11, D. Parrott (ed.) (1979), 375–87.
Prex eucharistica: textus e variis liturgiis antiquioribus selecti, A. Härggi and I. Pahl (eds.),
   Specilegium Friburgense 12 (Fribourg: Editions Universitaires, 1968).
Protevangelium of James [ET: *NTApoc*, vol. i].
Pseudo-Phocylides. Text and ET: *The Sentences of Pseudo-Phocylides: with introduction and
   commentary*, P. W. van der Horst (ed. and trans.), Studia in Veteris Testamenti pseude-
   pigrapha 4 (Leiden: Brill, 1978).
Ptolemaeus. *Epistula ad Floram*. Text: *Brief an die Flora*, A. von Harnack (ed.), 2nd ed., Kleine
   Texte für theologische Vorlesungen und Ubungen 9 (Bonn: A. Marcus und E. Weber,
   1912).
   Text and French trans.: *Lettre à Flora: analyse, texte critique, traduction, commentaire et index
   grec*, G. Quispel (ed. and trans.), 2nd ed., SC 24 bis (1966).
Quintilian. *Institutio oratoria*. Text and ET: *Quintilian: The Orator's Education*, LCL, 5 vols.,
   D. A. Russell (ed. and trans.). (2001).
Reardon, B. P. (ed.). *Collected ancient Greek novels* (Berkeley: University of California Press,
   1989).
Res gestae divi Augusti, E. Weber (ed. and trans.), 3rd ed., Tusculum-Bücherei (Munich:
   Heimeran Verlag, 1975).
Robinson, J. M. (ed.). *The Coptic Gnostic library: a complete edition of the Nag Hammadi codices*,
   5 vols. (Leiden: Brill, 2000).
Robinson, J. M. and R. Smith (eds.). *The Nag Hammadi library in English*, 4th ed., rev. (Leiden:
   Brill, 1996).
Rufinus. *Historia ecclesiastica*. Text: *Kirchengeschichte*, T. Mommsen (ed.), appendix to *Euse-
   bius, Werke*, vol. ii. 2: *Kirchengeschichte* ii, E. Schwartz (ed.), GCS 9.1 (1908).
Second treatise of the great Seth [NHC vii, 2; ET: *NHL*].
   NHMS 30, B. A. Pearson (ed.), (1996), 129–99.
Secret gospel of Mark. Text and ET: M. Smith, *Clement of Alexandria and a secret gospel of Mark*
   (Cambridge, MA: Harvard University Press, 1973), 445–53.
Seneca. Text and ET: *Seneca*, LCL, 10 vols., F. J. Miller, R. M. Gummere, J. W. Basore and T.
   H. Corcoran (eds. and trans.) (1917–72).
Sentences of Sextus [NHC xii, 1; ET: *NHL*].
   NHS 28, C. W. Hedrick (ed.) (1990), 295–327.
   ET: *The Sentences of Sextus: a contribution to the history of early Christian ethics*, H. Chadwick
   (trans.), TS 5 (1959).
Sententiae episcoporum numero lxxxvii *de haereticis baptizandis*. Text: *Cypriani opera omnia*,
   3 vols., W. Hartel (ed.), CSEL 3.1 (1871).
Sherk, R. K. *Roman documents from the Greek east:* Senatus consulta *and* Epistulae *to the age
   of Augustus* (Baltimore: Johns Hopkins University Press, 1969).
—. *The Roman empire: Augustus to Hadrian*, Translated documents of Greece and Rome 6
   (Cambridge: Cambridge University Press, 1988).
Sibylline oracles [ET: *OTP*, vol. i and *NTApoc*, vol. ii].
   Text: *Die Oracula Sibyllina*, J. Geffcken (ed.), GCS 8 (1902).
   Text and German trans.: *Sibyllinische Weissagungen: Griechisch–Deutsch*, J.-D. Gauger (ed.
   and trans) (Düsseldorf: Artemis & Winkler, 1998).

Text and French trans.: *La troisième Sibylle*, V. Nikiprowetzky (ed. and trans.), Études juives 9 (Paris: École Practique des Hautes Études, 1970).

Socrates Scholasticus. *Historia ecclesiastica* [ET: *NPNF*² 2].

Text: *Kirchengeschichte*, G. C. Hansen and M. Sirinjan (eds.), GCS n.s. 1 (1995).

Text and French trans.: *Socrate de Constantinople: Histoire ecclésiastique, livre I*, G. C. Hansen (ed.), P. Périchon and P. Maraval (eds. and trans.), SC 477 (2004).

Sophia of Jesus Christ [NHC III, 4; BG, 3; ET: *NHL, NTApoc*, vol. 1].

NHS 27, D. Parrott (ed.) (1991).

Sozomen. *Historia ecclesiastica*. [ET: *NPNF*² 2].

Text: *Sozomenus, Kirchengeschichte*, J. Bidez (ed.), GCS n.s. 4 (1995).

Text: *Sozomenus, Kirchengeschichte*, G. C. Hansen (ed.), GCS 50 (1960).

Spartian. *Vita Septimii Severi*. Text and ET: *Scriptores historiae augustae*, LCL, vol. 1, D. Magie (ed. and trans.) (1921).

Strabo. Text and ET: *The geography of Strabo*, LCL, 8 vols., H. L. Jones (ed. and trans.) (1917–32).

Suetonius. *De vita Caesarum*. Text: *C. Suetoni Tranquilli opera*, vol. 1: *De vita Caesarum, libri VIII*, M. Ihm (ed.), Teubner (1958, repr. 1978).

Text and ET: *Suetonius*, LCL, 2 vols., J. C. Rolfe (trans.), rev. ed. (1997–8).

Tacitus. Text: *Cornelii Taciti libri qui supersunt*, S. Borzsák and K. Wellesley (eds.), Teubner (1986–).

Text: *Cornelii Taciti annalium ab excessu divi Augusti libri*, C. D. Fisher (ed.), OCT (1946).

Text: *Cornelii Taciti historiarum libri*, C. D. Fisher (ed.), OCT (1962).

Text and ET: *Tacitus*, LCL, 5 vols., M. Hutton, W. Peterson, R. M. Ogilvie *et al.* (trans. and rev.) (1970, 1985).

Tatian [ET: *ANF* 2].

—. *Oratio ad Graecos*. Text: *Tatiani Oratio ad Graecos*, M. Marcovich (ed.), PTS 43 (1995).

Text: Goodspeed, *Die ältesten Apologeten*.

Text and ET: *Oratio ad Graecos and Fragments*, M. Whittaker (ed. and trans.), OECT (1982).

The Teaching of Addai, G. Phillips (ed.), G. Howard (trans.), SBLTT 16 (1981).

Teachings of Silvanus [NHC VII, 4; ET: *NHL*].

NHMS 30, B. A. Pearson (ed.) (1996), 249–369.

Tertullian [ET: *ANF* 3–4].

Text: *Tertulliani opera quae supersunt omnia*, 3 vols., F. Oehler (ed.) (Leipzig: T. O. Weigel, 1851–4).

Text: *Quinti Septimi Florentis Tertulliani opera*, 2 vols., E. Dekkers, J. G. P. Borleffs, R. Willems *et al.* (eds.), CCSL 1–2 (1954).

—. *Adversus Hermogenem*. Text: *Adversus Hermogenem liber quem ad fidem codicum recensuit*, J. H. Waszink (ed.), Stromata patristica et mediaevalia 5 (Antwerp: Spectrum, 1956).

Text and French trans.: *Contre Hermogène*, F. Chapot (ed. and trans.), SC 439 (1999).

ET: *The treatise against Hermogenes*, J. H. Waszink (trans.), ACW 24 (1956).

—. *Adversus Marcionem*. Text and French trans.: *Contre Marcion*, R. Braun and C. Moreschini (eds.), SC 365, 368, 399, 456, 483 (1990–2001).

Text and ET: *Adversus Marcionem*, 2 vols., E. Evans (ed. and trans.), OECT (1972).

—. *De idololatria*. Text and ET: *Quinti Septimi Florentis Tertulliani De idololatria*, P. G. van der Nat (ed.) and P. H. van Huizen (trans.) (Leiden: Saint Lucas Society, 1960).

Text and ET: *De idololatria,* J. H. Waszink, J. C. M. van Winden and P. G. van der Nat (eds. and trans.), VCSup 1 (1987).

—. *Adversus Praxean.* Text and ET: *Tertullian's treatise against Praxeas,* E. Evans (ed. and trans.) (London: SPCK, 1948).

—. *Ad uxorem.* Text and French trans.: *A son épouse,* C. Munier (ed. and trans.), SC 273 (1980).

ET: *Treatises on marriage and remarriage: To his wife, an exhortation to chastity, monogamy,* W. P. Le Saint (trans.), ACW 13 (1951).

—. *Apologeticus.* Text: H. Hoppe and E. Kroymann (eds.), CSEL 69–70 (1939–42, repr. 1964).

Text and ET: *Apology, De spectaculis.* LCL, T. R. Glover and G. H. Rendall (eds. and trans.) (1931).

Text and French trans.: *Apologétique: texte établi et traduit,* J.-P. Waltzing and A. Severyns (eds. and trans.), Collection des universités de France (Paris: Les Belles Lettres, 1929).

Text and German trans.: *Apologeticum: Verteidigung des Christentums,* C. Becker (ed. and trans.) (Munich: Kösel, 1952).

Text and German trans.: *Tertullians Apologeticum: Werden und Leistung,* C. Becker (ed. and trans.) (Munich: Kösel, 1954).

—. *De baptismo.* Text: A. Reifferscheid and G. Wissowa (eds.), CSEL 20 (1890).

Text and French trans.: *Traité du baptême,* F. Refoulé (ed. and trans.), SC 35 (1952).

Text and ET: *Tertullian's homily on baptism,* E. Evans (ed. and trans.) (London: SPCK, 1964).

—. *De praescriptione haereticorum.* Text and French trans.: *Traité de la prescription contre les hérétiques: introduction, texte critique, et notes,* F. Refoulé and P. de Labriolle (eds. and trans.), SC 46 (1957).

Testimony of truth [NHC IX, 3; ET: *NHL*].

NHS 15, B. A. Pearson (ed.) (1981), 101–203.

Theodoret of Cyr [ET: *NPNF²* 3].

—. *Historia ecclesiastica.* Text: L. Parmentier (ed.), 3rd ed., GCS n.s. 5 (1998).

Theodosiani libri XVI cum constitutionibus Sirmondianis et leges novellae ad Theodosianum pertinentes; consilio et auctoritate Academiae litterarum regiae borussicae, 2 vols., T. Mommsen, P. M. Meyer and J. Sirmond (eds.) (Berlin: Weidmann, 1905).

ET: *The Theodosian code and novels, and the Sirmondian constitutions,* C. Pharr, T. S. Davidson and M. Brown Pharr (trans.), Corpus of Roman law 1 (Princeton: Princeton University Press, 1952).

Theodotus. Text and French trans.: *Extraits de Théodote,* F. Sagnard (ed. and trans.), SC 23 (1970).

Text and ET: *The Excerpta ex Theodoto of Clement of Alexandria,* R. P. Casey (ed. and trans.), SD 1 (1934).

Theognostus. ET: L. B. Radford, *Three teachers of Alexandria: Theognostus, Pierius, and Peter* (Cambridge: Cambridge University Press, 1908), 1–47.

Theonas. *Against the Manichaeans.* Text: *Catalogue of the Greek and Latin papyri in the John Rylands Library,* C. H. Roberts (ed.) (Manchester: Manchester University Press, 1938), vol. III, 38–9.

Theophilus of Antioch. *Ad Autolycum.* Text and ET: *Ad Autolycum,* R. M. Grant (ed. and trans.) (Oxford: Clarendon Press, 1970).

Text: Goodspeed, *Die ältesten Apologeten.*

Thought of Norea [NHC ix, 2; ET: *NHL*].
  NHS 15, B. A. Pearson (ed.) (1981), 87–99.
Three steles of Seth [NHC vii, 5; ET: *NHL*].
  NHMS 30, B. A. Pearson (ed.) (1996), 371–421.
Thunder: perfect mind [NHC vi, 2; ET: *NHL*].
  NHS 11, D. Parrott (ed.) (1979), 231–55.
Traditions of Matthias [ET: *NTApoc*, vol. ii].
Treatise on the resurrection [NHC i, 4; ET: *NHL*].
  NHS 22–3, H. W. Attridge (ed.) (1985), 1.123–57.
Trimorphic protennoia [NHC xiii, 1; ET: *NHL*].
  NHS 28, C. W. Hedrick (ed.) (1990), 173–267.
Tripartite tractate [NHC i, 5; ET: *NHL*].
  NHS 22–3, H. W. Attridge (ed.) (1985), 1.159–337.
Unidentified fragments from Nag Hammadi [NHC xii, 3; ET: *NHL*].
  NHS 28, C. W. Hedrick (ed.) (1990), 349–55.
Untitled tractate in the Bruce codex.
  NHS 13, C. Schmidt (ed.), V. MacDermot (trans.) (1978), 214–317.
A Valentinian exposition [NHC xi, 2; ET: *NHL*].
  NHS 28, C. W. Hedrick (ed.) (1990), 89–172.
Valentinus. *Fragmenta.* Text: *Quellen zur Geschichte der christlichen Gnosis*, W. Völker (ed.),
  Sammlung Ausgewählter Kirchen- und Dogmengeschichtlicher Quellenschriften,
  n.s. 5 (Tübingen: Mohr Siebeck, 1932), 57–60.
  Text and German trans.: *Valentinus Gnosticus? Untersuchungen zur valentinianischen
  Gnosis mit einem Kommentar zu den Fragmenten Valentinus*, C. Markschies, WUNT 65
  (1992).
  ET: Foerster, *Gnosis*, vol. i, 59–74, 121–61.
Vergil. Text and ET: *Virgil*, LCL, 2 vols., H. R. Fairclough (ed. and trans.), G. P. Goold (rev.)
  (1999).
Xenophon. *Memorabilia.* Text and ET: *Xenophon*, vol. iv: *Memorabilia and Oeconomicus,
  Symposium and Apologia*, LCL, E. C. Marchant and O. J. Todd (eds. and trans.)
  (1923).
Zosimus [ET: *ANF* 10].
  Text and French trans.: *Zosime, Histoire nouvelle*, 3 vols., F. Paschoud (ed. and trans.),
  Collection des universités de France (Paris: Les Belles Lettres, 1971–89).
  ET: *Zosimus*, R. T. Ridley (trans.), Byzantina Australiensia 2 (Canberra: Australian Asso-
  ciation for Byzantine Studies, 1982).
Zostrianos [NHC viii, 1; ET: *NHL*].
  NHMS 31, J. Sieber (ed.) (1991), 7–225.

Secondary sources

The following is a listing of secondary sources referred to by authors in several
chapters of this volume. For studies specific to individual essays, the reader is referred to the
'Specialized Bibliographies by Chapter', found below.

Adkins, L. and R. A. Adkins. *Handbook to life in ancient Rome* (New York: Facts on File, 1994).
Aland, B. 'Marcion–Marcionites–Marcionism', *EECh* (1992), vol. i, 523–4.

Aland, K. and B. Aland. *The text of the New Testament* (Grand Rapids, MI: Eerdmans, 1987).

Alexander, L. *The preface to Luke's gospel: literary convention and social context in Luke 1.1–4 and Acts 1.1*, SNTSMS 78 (1993).

Alföldy, G. *The social history of Rome*, D. Braund and F. Pollock (trans.) (Baltimore: Johns Hopkins University Press, 1988).

Andresen, C. '"Siegreiche Kirche" im Aufstieg des Christentums. Untersuchungen zu Eusebius von Caesarea und Dionysius von Alexandrien', *ANRW* II.23.1 (1979), 387–459.

Applebaum, S. 'The organization of the Jewish communities in the diaspora', in *The Jewish people in the first century: historical geography, political history, social, cultural and religious life and institutions*, 2 vols., S. Safrai and M. Stern (eds.), CRINT I.1–2 (1974–6), vol. I, 464–503.

Attridge, H. W. and G. Hata (eds.). *Eusebius, Christianity, and Judaism*, StPB 42 (1992).

Aune, D. E. (ed.). *Greco-Roman literature and the New Testament: selected forms and genres*, SBLSBS (1988).

—. 'Magic in early Christianity', *ANRW* II.23.2 (1980), 1507–57.

—. *The New Testament in its literary environment*, LEC (1987).

—. *Prophecy in early Christianity and the ancient Mediterranean world* (Grand Rapids, MI: Eerdmans, 1983).

—. *The Westminster dictionary of New Testament and early Christian literature and rhetoric* (Louisville, KY: Westminster John Knox, 2003).

Bagnall, R. A. *Egypt in late antiquity* (Princeton: Princeton University Press, 1993).

Balch, D. L. and C. Osiek (eds.). *Early Christian families in context: an interdisciplinary dialogue* (Grand Rapids, MI: Eerdmans, 2003).

Barclay, J. M. G. *Jews in the Mediterranean diaspora from Alexander to Trajan (323 BCE–117 CE)* (Edinburgh: T&T Clark, 1996).

Bardy, G. 'Aux origines de l'école d'Alexandrie', *RSR* 27 (1937), 65–90.

Barnard, L. W. *Athenagoras: a study in second century Christian apologetic*, ThH 18 (1972).

Barnes, T. D. *Athanasius and Constantius: theology and politics in the Constantinian empire* (Cambridge, MA: Harvard University Press, 1993).

—. *Constantine and Eusebius* (Cambridge, MA : Harvard University Press, 1981).

—. *Early Christianity and the Roman empire* (London: Variorum Reprints, 1984).

—. 'Emperors and bishops 324–44: some problems', *AJAH* 3 (1978), 53–75.

—. 'Pre-Decian *Acta martyrum*', *JTS* 19 (1968), 509–31.

Barrett, C. K. *Essays on Paul* (London: SPCK, 1982).

—. 'Pauline controversies in the post-Pauline period', *NTS* 20 (1974), 229–45.

Bartlett, J. R. (ed.). *Jews in the Hellenistic and Roman cities* (London: Routledge, 2002).

Barton, J. *Holy writings, sacred text: the canon in early Christianity* (Louisville, KY: Westminster John Knox, 1998).

Bauckham, R. *Jude and the relatives of Jesus in the early church* (Edinburgh: T&T Clark, 1990).

—. 'Papias and Polycrates on the origin of the fourth gospel', *JTS* 44 (1993), 24–69.

Bauer, W. *Orthodoxy and heresy in earliest Christianity*, ET of 2nd German ed. (1964), W. Bauer, R. A. Kraft and G. Krodel (eds. and trans.) (London: SCM Press, 1972).

BeDuhn, J. *The Manichaean body in discipline and ritual* (Baltimore: Johns Hopkins University Press, 2000).

Behr, J. *Asceticism and anthropology in Irenaeus and Clement*, OECS (2000).

Benko, S. 'Pagan criticism of Christianity during the first two centuries A.D.', *ANRW* II.23.2 (1980), 1055–1118.

—. *Pagan Rome and the early Christians* (Bloomington: Indian University Press, 1984).

Biddle, M. *The tomb of Christ* (Stroud, Glos.: Sutton, 1999).

Bienert, W. *Dionysius von Alexandrien: zur Frage des Origenismus im dritten Jahrhundert*, PTS 21 (1978).

Bieringer, R., D. Pollefeyt and F. Vandecasteele-Vanneuville (eds.). *Anti-Judaism in the fourth gospel* (Louisville, KY: Westminster John Knox, 2001).

—. *Anti-Judaism and the fourth gospel: papers of the Leuven colloquium, 2000* (Assen: Van Gorcum, 2001).

Birley, A. R. *Septimius Severus: the African emperor* (London: Eyre & Spottiswoode, 1971).

Bisbee, G. A. *Pre-Decian acts of martyrs and commentarii* (Philadelphia: Fortress, 1988).

Bludau, A. *Die ersten Gegner der Johannes Schriften*, BibS(F) 22. 1–2 (1925).

Borgen, P. (ed.). *Early Christianity and Hellenistic Judaism* (Edinburgh: T&T Clark, 1996).

Boyarin, D. 'Justin Martyr invents Judaism', *CH* 70 (2001), 427–61.

Bradshaw, P. F. *Early Christian worship: a basic introduction to ideas and practice* (London: SPCK, 1996).

—. 'Redating the Apostolic tradition: some preliminary steps', in *Rule of prayer, rule of faith: essays in honor of Aidan Kavanagh, OSB*, J. Baldovin and N. Mitchell (eds.) (Collegeville, MN: Liturgical Press, 1996), 3–17.

Bradshaw, P. F., M. E. Johnson and L. E. Phillips. *The apostolic tradition: a commentary*, Hermeneia (Minneapolis: Fortress, 2002).

Brent, A. *Hippolytus and the Roman church in the third century: communities in tension before the emergence of a monarch-bishop*, VCSup 31 (1995).

—. *The imperial cult and the development of church order: concepts and image of authority in paganism and early Christianity before the age of Cyprian*, VCSup 45 (1999).

Brown, P. *The body and society: men, women, and sexual renunciation in early Christianity*, Lectures on the history of religions, n.s. 13 (New York: Columbia University Press, 1988).

Brown, R. E. *The community of the beloved disciple* (Paramus, NJ: Paulist/Newman, 1979).

Brown, R. E. and J. P. Meier. *Antioch and Rome: New Testament cradles of Catholic christianity* (New York: Paulist, 1983).

Brox, N. 'Doketismus – eine Problemanzeige', *ZKG* 95 (1984), 301–14.

Buell, D. K. 'Rethinking the relevance of race for early Christian self-definition', *HTR* 94 (2001), 449–476.

Bousset, W. *Kyrios Christos: a history of the belief in Christ from the beginnings of Christianity to Irenaeus*, J. E. Steely (trans.) (Nashville, TN: Abingdon Press, 1970).

Bultmann, R. K. *The gospel of John: a commentary*, G. R. Beasley-Murray (trans.) (Oxford: Blackwell, 1971).

—. *History of the synoptic tradition*, J. Marsh (trans.) (Oxford: Blackwell, 1963).

—. *Jesus and the word*, L. Pettibone Smith and E. Huntress Lantero (trans.) (New York: Scribners, 1934).

—. *Primitive Christianity in its contemporary setting*, R. H. Fuller (trans.) (Philadelphia: Fortress, 1980).

—. *Theology of the New Testament*, 2 vols., K. Grobel (trans.) (London: SCM Press, 1952–5).

Burridge, R. A. *Four gospels, one Jesus? A symbolic reading* (London: SPCK, 1994).

Burkert, W. *Ancient mystery cults* (Cambridge, MA: Harvard University Press, 1987).

Burtchaell, J. T. *From synagogue to church: public services and offices in the earliest Christian communities* (Cambridge: Cambridge University Press, 1992).

Buschmann, G. *Das Martyrium des Polycarp*, KAV 6 (1998).

Calder, W. M. 'The epitaph of Avircius Marcellus', *JRS* 29 (1939), 1–4.

Cameron, Averil. *Christianity and the rhetoric of empire: the development of Christian discourse*, Sather Classical lectures 55 (Berkeley: University of California Press, 1991).

Cameron, Averil and S. G. Hall. *Eusebius: Life of Constantine* (Oxford: Clarendon Press, 1999).

Carleton Paget, J. *The Epistle of Barnabas: outlook and background*, WUNT 2/64 (1994).

Chadwick, H. *Early Christian thought and the classical tradition* (New York: Oxford University Press, 1966).

—. *The early Church*, PHC 1 (1967).

— (trans. and ed.). *Origen: contra Celsum* (Oxford: Oxford University Press, 1953).

Charlesworth, M. P. 'The Flavian dynasty', *CAH¹*, vol. 11 (1936), 1–45.

Chilton, B. and C. A. Evans. *James the just and Christian origins*, NovTSup 98 (1999).

Cohen, S. J. D. *The beginnings of Jewishness: boundaries, varieties, uncertainties* (Berkeley: University of California Press, 1999).

Crossan, J. D. *Jesus: a revolutionary biography* (San Francisco: HarperSanFrancisco, 1994).

Crouzel, H. *Origen*, A. S. Worrall (trans.) (San Francisco: Harper & Row, 1989).

Cullmann, O. 'The plurality of the gospels as a theological problem in the ancient church', in O. Cullmann, *The early Church*, A. J. B. Higgins and S. Godman (trans.) (Philadelphia: Westminster, 1956), 39–54.

Culpepper, R. A. *John the son of Zebedee: the life of a legend* (Columbia: University of South Carolina Press, 1994).

Dahl, N. A. 'The particularity of the Pauline epistles as a problem in the ancient church', in *Neotestamentica et Patristica: eine Freundesgabe, Herrn Professor Dr. Oscar Cullmann, zu seinem 60. Geburtstag überreicht*, NovTSup 6 (1962), 261–71; repr. in N. A. Dahl, *Studies in Ephesians: introductory questions, text- and edition-critical issues, interpretation of texts and themes*, D. Hellholm, V. Blomkvist and T. Fornberg (eds.), WUNT 131 (2000), 165–78.

Davies, W. D. and D. C. Allison, Jr. *A critical and exegetical commentary on the gospel according to Matthew*, 3 vols., ICC (1988–97).

Dehandschutter, B. 'The *Martyrium Polycarpi*: a century of research', *ANRW* 11.27.1 (1993), 485–522.

Deissmann, A. *Light from the ancient east: the New Testament illustrated by recently discovered texts of the Graeco-Roman world*, L. R. M. Strachan (trans.) (London: Hodder & Stoughton, 1910).

Dillon, J. M. *The Middle Platonists, 80 B.C. to A.D. 220*, rev. ed. (Ithaca, NY: Cornell University Press, 1996).

Donfried, K. P. *The Romans debate: revised and expanded version* (Peabody, MA: Hendrickson, 1991).

Drijvers, J. W. *Helena Augusta: the mother of Constantine the Great and the legend of her finding of the true cross* (Leiden: Brill, 1992).

Droge, A. J. *Homer or Moses? Early Christian interpretations of the history of culture*, HUT 26 (1989).

Dunn, J. D. G. *Jesus remembered*, Christianity in the making 1 (Grand Rapids, MI: Eerdmans, 2003).

Eck, W. 'Das Eindringen des Christentums in den Senatorenstand bis zu Konstantin dem Grossen', *Chiron* 1 (1971), 381–406.

Edwards, M. J. *Constantine and Christendom: the Oration to the saints, the Greek and Latin accounts of the discovery of the cross, the Edict of Constantine to Pope Silvester*, TTH 39 (2003).

Ehrman, B. *The orthodox corruption of scripture: the effect of early christological controversies on the text of the New Testament* (New York: Oxford University Press, 1993).

Elliott, J. K. (ed.). *The Apocryphal New Testament: a collection of apocryphal Christian literature in an English translation* (Oxford: Oxford University Press, 1993).

Elsner, J. *Art and the Roman viewer: the transformation of art from the pagan world to Christianity* (Cambridge: Cambridge University Press, 1995).

—. *Imperial Rome and Christian triumph: the art of the Roman empire* AD 100–450, Oxford history of art (Oxford: Oxford University Press, 1998).

Esler, P. F. (ed.). *The early Christian world*, 2 vols. (Routledge: London, 2000).

Fine, S. *Jews, Christians and polytheists in the ancient synagogue: cultural interaction during the Greco-Roman period* (London: Routledge, 1999).

Fitzgerald, J. T. (ed.). *Greco-Roman perspectives on friendship*, SBLRBS 34 (1997).

Frede, H.–J. 'Die Ordnung der Paulusbriefe und der Platz des Kolosserbriefes im Corpus Paulinum', *VL* 24 (1969), 290–303.

Fredriksen, P. *From Jesus to Christ: the origins of the New Testament images of Jesus* (New Haven: Yale University Press, 1988).

Frend, W. H. C. *The archaeology of early Christianity: a history* (Minneapolis: Fortress, 1996).

—. 'Christianity in the second century: orthodoxy and diversity', *JEH* 48 (1997), 302–13.

—. *Martyrdom and persecution in the early church* (Oxford: Blackwell, 1965).

—. *The rise of Christianity* (Philadelphia: Fortress, 1984).

Friesen, S. J. *Imperial cults and the Apocalypse of John: reading Revelation in the ruins* (Oxford: Oxford University Press, 2001).

—. 'Poverty in Pauline studies: beyond the so-called New Consensus', *JSNT* 26 (2004), 323-61.

—. *Twice Neokoros: Ephesus, Asia and the cult of the Flavian imperial family*, Religions in the Graeco-Roman world 116 (Leiden: Brill, 1993).

Gamble, H. Y. *Books and readers in the early church: a history of early Christian texts* (New Haven: Yale University Press, 1995).

García Martínez, F. and E. J. C. Tigchelaar. *The Dead Sea scrolls study edition*, 2 vols. (Leiden: Brill, 1997–8).

Geffcken, J. *The last days of Greco-Roman paganism*, S. MacCormack (trans.), Europe in the Middle Ages 8 (New York: North Holland, 1978; ET of *Der Ausgang des griechisch-römischen Heidentums*, Religionswissenschaftliche Bibliothek 6 (Heidelberg: C. Winter, 1929).

Grant, R. M. *Augustus to Constantine: the rise and triumph of Christianity in the Roman world*, rev. ed. (Louisville, KY: Westminster John Knox, 2004).

—. *Jesus after the gospels: the Christ of the second century* (Louisville, KY: Westminster John Knox, 1990).

—. *The earliest lives of Jesus* (New York: Harper & Row, 1961).

—. *Early Christianity and society* (New York: Harper & Row, 1977).

—. *Eusebius as church historian* (Oxford: Clarendon Press, 1980).

—. *Gnosticism and early Christianity*, 2nd ed. (New York: Harper, 1966).

—. *Gods and the one God*, LEC 1 (1986).

—. *Greek apologists of the second century* (Philadelphia: Westminster, 1988).

—. *Heresy and criticism: the search for authenticity in early Christian literature* (Louisville, KY: Westminster John Knox, 1993).

—. *The letter and the spirit* (London: SPCK, 1957).

—. *Irenaeus of Lyons*, Early church fathers (London: Routledge, 1997).

Gruen, E. *Diaspora: Jews amidst Greeks and Romans* (Cambridge, MA: Harvard University Press, 2002).

Hall, S. G. *Doctrine and practice in the early church* (London: SPCK, 1991).

—. 'Women among the early martyrs', in *Martyrs and martyrologies: papers read at the 1992 summer meeting and the 1993 winter meeting of the Ecclesiastical History Society*, D. Wood (ed.), SCH 30 (1993), 1–21.

Harland, P. A. *Associations, synagogues and congregations: claiming a place in an ancient Mediterranean society* (Minneapolis: Fortress, 2003).

Harnack, A. von. *Lehrbuch der Dogmengeschichte*, 3 vols. (Tübingen: Mohr Siebeck 1990; repr. of 4th ed., 1909); ET: *The history of dogma*, 7 vols. in 4, trans. from the 3rd German ed., N. Buchanan (trans.) (Gloucester, MA: Peter Smith, 1976).

—. *Marcion: das Evangelium vom fremden Gott, ein Monographie zur Geschichte der Grundlegung der katholischen Kirche* (Leipzig: Hinrichs, 1921; 2nd ed. corr. and expanded 1924, repr. Darmstadt: Wissenschaftliche Buchgesellschaft, 1960, 1985); ET: *Marcion: the gospel of the alien God*, J. Steeley and L. Bierma (trans.) (Durham, N.C.: Labyrinth Press, 1990).

—. *Die Mission und Ausbreitung des Christentums in den ersten drei Jahrhunderten*, 2 vols., 4th ed. (Leipzig: Hinrichs, 1924); ET: *The mission and expansion of Christianity in the first three Centuries*, 2 vols., 2nd ed., J. Moffatt (trans.) (London: Williams and Norgate, 1908).

Harrill, J. A. The manumission of slaves in early Christianity, HUT 32 (1995).

Hayes, C. E. *Gentile impurities and Jewish identities: intermarriage and conversion from the Bible to the Talmud* (New York: Oxford University Press, 2002).

Helleman, W. E. (ed.) *Hellenization revisited: shaping a Christian response within the Greco-Roman world* (Lanham, MD: University Press of America, 1994).

Hengel, M. *The four gospels and the one gospel of Jesus Christ* (London: SCM Press, 2000).

—. *Judaism and Hellenism: studies in their encounter in Palestine during the early Hellenistic period*, 2 vols., J. Bowden (trans.) (London: SCM Press, 1974).

—. 'Messianische Hoffnung und politischer "Radikalismus" in der "jüdisch-hellenistischen Diaspora"', in *Apocalypticism in the Mediterranean world and the Near East: proceedings of the international colloquium on apocalypticism, Uppsala, August 12–17, 1979*, D. Hellholm (ed.) (Tübingen: Mohr Siebeck, 1983), 655–86.

Hertling, L. and E. Kirschbaum. *The Roman catacombs and their martyrs*, M. J. Costelloe (trans.) (Milwaukee, WI: Bruce, 1956).

Hill, C. C. *Hellenists and Hebrews: reappraising division within the earliest church* (Minneapolis: Augsburg Fortress, 1992).

Hoffmann, R. J. 'How then know this troublous teacher? Further reflections on Marcion and his church', *SecCent* 6 (1987–8), 173–91.

—. *Marcion, On the restitution of Christianity: an essay on the development of radical Paulinist theology in the second century*, AAR Academy series 46 (1984).

Hopkins, K. 'Christian number and its implications', *JECS* 6 (1998), 185–226.

Horsley, G. H. R. and S. R. Llewelyn (eds.). *New documents illustrating early Christianity*, 9 vols. (North Ryde, NSW: Ancient History Documentary Research Centre, Macquarie University, 1981–2005).

Horsley, R. A. and J. S. Hanson. *Bandits, prophets, and messiahs: popular movements in the time of Jesus* (Minneapolis, MN: Winston, 1985).

Hübner, R. M. 'Thesen zur Echtheit und Datierung der sieben Briefe des Ignatius von Antiochien', *ZAC/JAC* 1 (1997), 44–72.

Hübner, R. M. and M. Vinzent. *Der Paradox Eine: antignostischer Monarchianismus im zweiten Jahrhundert*, VCSup 50 (1999).

Hunt, E. D. *Holy Land pilgrimage in the later Roman empire*, AD 312–460 (Oxford: Oxford University Press, 1982).

Hunt, E. J. *Christianity in the second century: the case of Tatian* (London: Routledge, 2003).

Hurtado, L. W. 'The earliest evidence of an emerging Christian material and visual culture: the codex, the *nomina sacra* and the staurogram' in *Text and artifact in the religions of Mediterranean antiquity: essays in honour of Peter Richardson*, S. G. Wilson and M. Desjardins (eds.) (Waterloo, Ont.: Wilfrid Laurier University Press, 2000), 271–88.

—. *Lord Jesus Christ: devotion to Jesus in earliest Christianity* (Grand Rapids, MI: Eerdmans, 2003).

—. 'The origin of the *nomina sacra*: a proposal', *JBL* 117 (1998), 655–73.

Huskinson, J. (ed.). *Experiencing Rome: culture, identity and power in the Roman empire* (London: Routledge, 2000).

Jensen, R. M. 'Art', in *The early Christian world*, 2 vols., P. F. Esler (ed.) (London: Routledge, 2000), vol. II, 747–72.

Johnson, L. T. *The Letter of James: a new translation with introduction and commentary*, AB 37A (1995).

Jonas, H. *The Gnostic religion: the message of the alien god and the beginnings of Christianity*, 3rd ed. (Boston: Beacon Press, 2001).

Jones, A. H. M. *The cities of the eastern Roman provinces*, 2nd ed. (Oxford: Clarendon Press, 1971).

Jones, D. L., 'Christianity and the Roman imperial cult', *ANRW* II.23.2 (1980), 1023–54.

Käsemann, E. *The testament of Jesus: a study of the gospel of John in the light of chapter 17*, G. Krodel (trans.), New Testament library (London: SCM Press, 1968).

Kelly, J. N. D. *Early Christian creeds*, 3rd ed. (London: Longman, 1972).

—. *Early Christian doctrines*, 5th rev. ed. (London: A. & C. Black, 1985).

King, K. L. *What is Gnosticism?* (Cambridge, MA: Belknap Press of Harvard University, 2003).

Klauck, H.-J. *Hausgemeinde und Hauskirche im frühen Christentum*, SBS 103 (1981).
—. *Magic and paganism in early Christianity* (Edinburgh: T&T Clark, 2000).
—. *The religious context of early Christianity: a guide to Graeco-Roman religions*, B. McNeil (trans.), Studies of the New Testament and its world (Edinburgh: T&T Clark, 2000).
Koester, H. *Ancient Christian gospels: their history and development* (Philadelphia: Trinity Press International, 1990).
—. *Introduction to the New Testament*, vol. I: *History, culture and religion of the Hellenistic age*; vol. II: *History and literature of early Christianity*, 2nd ed. (Berlin: De Gruyter, 1995–2000).
—. 'The origin and significance of the Flight to Pella tradition', *CBQ* 51 (1989), 90–106.
Kugel, J. L., and R. A. Greer. *Early biblical interpretation*, LEC 3 (1986).
Labriolle, P. de. *La réaction païenne: étude sur la polémique antichrétienne du Ier au VIe siècle* (Paris: L'Artisan du Livre, 1934).
Lampe, P. *From Paul to Valentinus: Christians at Rome in the first two centuries*, M. Steinhauser (trans.) (Minneapolis: Fortress, 2003).
Lane Fox, R. *Pagans and Christians in the Mediterranean world from the second century to the conversion of Constantine* (New York: Knopf, 1987).
Lange, N. de. *Origen and the Jews: studies in Jewish-Christian relations in third-century Palestine* (Cambridge: Cambridge University Press, 1976).
Lattke, M. *Die Oden Salomos in ihrer Bedeutung für Neues Testament und Gnosis*, 4 vols. in 5 (Göttingen: Vandenhoeck & Ruprecht, 1979–98).
Layton, B. *The Gnostic scriptures* (Garden City, NY: Doubleday, 1987).
Leon, H. J. and C. Osiek. *The Jews of ancient Rome*, updated ed. (Peabody, MA: Hendrickson, 1995).
Levinskaya, I. A. *The book of Acts in its diaspora setting*, The book of Acts in its first century setting 5 (Grand Rapids, MI: Eerdmans, 1996).
Lieu, J. M. *Image and reality: the Jews in the world of the Christians in the second century* (Edinburgh: T&T Clark, 1996).
—. '"Impregnable ramparts and walls of iron": boundary and identity in early "Judaism" and "Christianity"', *NTS* 48 (2002), 297–313.
—. *Neither Jew nor Greek?: constructing early Christianity*, Studies of the New Testament and its world (London: T&T Clark, 2002).
—. *The Theology of the Johannine epistles* (Cambridge: Cambridge University Press, 1991).
Lieu, J. M., J. A. North and T. Rajak (eds.). *The Jews among pagans and Christians in the Roman empire* (London: Routledge, 1992).
Lieu, S. N. C. *Manichaeism in the later Roman empire and medieval China*, 2nd ed., WUNT 63 (1992).
Lindars, B., R. B. Edwards and J. M. Court (eds.). *The Johannine literature* (Sheffield: Sheffield Academic Press, 2000).
Logan, A. H. B. 'Marcellus of Ancyra and the councils of A.D. 325: Antioch, Ancyra and Nicaea', *JTS* 43 (1992), 428–46.
Long, A. A. *Hellenistic philosophy: Stoics, Epicureans, Sceptics*, 2nd ed. (Berkeley: University of California Press, 1986).
Lowden, J. *Early Christian and Byzantine art* (London: Phaidon, 1997).
MacDonald, D. R. *The legend and the apostle: the battle for Paul in story and canon* (Philadelphia: Westminster, 1983).

MacMullen, R. *Christianizing the Roman empire (A.D. 100–400)* (New Haven: Yale University Press, 1984).

——. *Paganism in the Roman empire* (New Haven: Yale University Press, 1981).

Malherbe, A. J. *Paul and the popular philosophers* (Minneapolis: Fortress, 1989).

——. *Paul and the Thessalonians: the philosophic tradition of pastoral care* (Philadelphia: Fortress, 1987).

——. *Social aspects of early Christianity*, 2nd ed. (Philadelphia: Fortress, 1983).

Mancinelli, F. *Catacombs and basilicas: the early Christians in Rome*, C. Wasserman (trans.) (Florence: Scala, 1981).

——. *The catacombs of Rome and the origins of Christianity*, C. Wasserman (trans.) (Florence: Scala, 1981).

Marcus, J. 'Mark – interpreter of Paul', *NTS* 46 (2000), 473–87.

Markschies, C. *Between two worlds: structures of earliest Christianity*, J. Bowden (trans.) (London: SCM Press, 1999).

——. *Valentinus Gnosticus? Untersuchungen zur valentinianischen Gnosis mit einem Kommentar zu den Fragmenten Valentins*, WUNT 65 (1992).

Markus, R. A. *The end of ancient Christianity* (Cambridge: Cambridge University Press, 1990).

May, G. *'Creatio ex nihilo': the doctrine of 'creation out of nothing' in early Christian thought*, A. S. Worrall (trans.) (Edinburgh: T&T Clark, 1994).

Mazza, E. *The origins of the eucharistic prayer* (Collegeville, MN: Liturgical Press, 1995).

McGowan, A. B. *Ascetic eucharists*, OECS (1999).

Meeks, W. A. *The first urban Christians: the social world of the apostle Paul* (New Haven: Yale University Press, 1983).

Méhat, A. 'Clemens von Alexandrien', *TRE* 8 (1981), 101–13.

——. *Étude sur les 'Stromates' de Clément d'Alexandrie*, Patristica Sorbonensia 7 (Paris: Éditions du Seuil, 1966).

——. '"Vraie" et "fausse" gnose d'après Clément d'Alexandrie', in *The rediscovery of Gnosticism: proceedings of the international conference on Gnosticism at Yale, March 1978*, vol. 1: *The school of Valentinus*, B. Layton (ed.), SHR 41 (1980), 426–33.

Metzger, B. M. *The canon of the New Testament: its origin, development and significance* (Oxford: Oxford University Press, 1987).

——. *A textual commentary on the Greek New Testament* (New York: United Bible Societies, 1971).

Mikkelsen, G. B. *Bibliographia Manichaica: a comprehensive bibliography of Manichaeism through 1996*, Corpus fontium manichaeorum, Subsidia 1 (Turnhout: Brepols, 1997).

Millar, F. *The Roman near east, 31 BC–AD 337* (Cambridge, MA: Harvard University Press, 1993).

Mitchell, M. M. 'The Corinthian correspondence and the birth of Pauline hermeneutics', in *Paul and the Corinthians: studies on a community in conflict: essays in honour of Margaret E. Thrall*, T. J. Burke and J. K. Elliott (eds.), NovTSup 109 (2003), 17–53.

——. 'Epiphanic evolutions in earliest Christianity', *Illinois Classical studies* 29 (2004), 183–204.

——. 'New Testament envoys in the context of Greco-Roman diplomatic and epistolary conventions: the example of Timothy and Titus', *JBL* 111 (1992), 641–62.

——. *Paul and the rhetoric of reconciliation: an exegetical investigation of the language and composition of 1 Corinthians*, HUT 28 (1991; Louisville, KY: Westminster John Knox, 1992).

—. 'Rhetorical shorthand in Pauline argumentation: the functions of "the gospel" in the Corinthian correspondence', in *Gospel in Paul*, L. A. Jervis and P. Richardson (eds.) (Sheffield: Sheffield Academic Press, 1994), 63–88.

Mitchell, S. *Anatolia; land, men and gods in Asia Minor*, 2 vols. (Oxford: Clarendon Press, 1993).

—. 'The cult of Theos Hypsistos between pagans, Jews and Christians', in *Pagan monotheism in late antiquity*, P. Athanassiadi and M. Frede (eds.) (Oxford: Clarendon Press, 1999), 81–148.

Modrzejewski, J. M. *The Jews of Egypt: from Rameses II to emperor Hadrian*, R. Cornman (trans.) (Philadelphia/Jerusalem: Jewish Publication Society, 1995).

Mullen, R. L. *The expansion of Christianity: a gazetteer of its first three centuries*, VCSup 69 (2004).

Murphy-O'Connor, J. *Paul: a critical life* (Oxford: Clarendon Press, 1996).

—. *St. Paul's Corinth: texts and archaeology*, GNS 6 (1983).

Musurillo, H. (ed. and trans.). *Acts of the Christian martyrs: introduction, texts, and translations*, OECT (1972).

Nautin, P. (ed.). *Lettres et écrivains chrétiens des IIe et IIIe siècles* (Paris: Éditions du Cerf, 1961).

—. *Origène: sa vie et son oeuvre* (Paris: Beauchesne, 1977).

Neuschäfer, B. *Origenes als Philologe*, 2 vols., Schweizerische Beiträge zur Altertumswissenschaft 18. 1–2 (Basel: Reinhardt, 1987).

Niederwimmer, K. *The Didache: a commentary*, Hermeneia (Minneapolis: Fortress, 1998).

Nock, A. D. *Conversion: the old and the new in religion from Alexander the Great to Augustine of Hippo* (Baltimore: Johns Hopkins University Press, 1998, original 1933).

Noormann, R. *Irenäus als Paulusinterpret: zur Rezeption und Wirkung der paulinischen und deuteropaulinischen Briefe im Werk des Irenäus von Lyon*, WUNT 2.66 (1994).

Pagels, E. H. *The Gnostic Paul: Gnostic exegesis of the Pauline letters* (Philadelphia: Fortress, 1975).

Osiek, C. *Shepherd of Hermas: a commentary*, Hermeneia (Minneapolis: Fortress, 1999).

Osiek, C. and D. L. Balch. *Families in the New Testament world: households and house churches* (Louisville, KY: Westminster John Knox, 1997).

Pearson, B. A. 'From Jewish apocalypticism to gnosis', in *The Nag Hammadi texts in the history of religions: proceedings of the international conference at the Royal Academy of Sciences and Letters in Copenhagen, September 19–24, 1995, on the occasion of the 50th anniversary of the Nag Hammadi discovery*, S. Giversen, T. Petersen and J. P. Sørensen (eds.), Historisk-filosofiske skrifter 26 (Copenhagen: The Royal Danish Academy of Sciences and Letters, 2002), 146–63.

—. *Gnosticism and Christianity in Roman and Coptic Egypt* (London: T&T Clark, 2004).

—. *Gnosticism, Judaism, and Egyptian Christianity* (Minneapolis: Fortress, 1990).

Porter, S. E. *Handbook of classical rhetoric in the Hellenistic period, 330 B.C.–A.D. 400* (Leiden: Brill, 1997).

Poschmann, B. *Paenitentia secunda: die kirchliche Buße im ältesten Christentum bis Cyprian und Origenes: eine dogmengeschichtliche Untersuchung*, Theophaneia 1 (Bonn: Hanstein, 1940).

Pouderon, B. *D'Athènes à Alexandrie: études sur Athénagore et les origines de la philosophie chrétienne*, Bibliothèque copte de Nag Hammadi, Études 4 (Louvain: Peeters, 1997).

Price, S. R. F. *Rituals and power: the Roman imperial cult in Asia Minor* (Cambridge: Cambridge University Press, 1984).

Radford, L. B. *Three teachers of Alexandria: Theognostus, Pierius, and Peter: a study in the early history of Origenism and anti-Origenism* (Cambridge: Cambridge University Press, 1908).

Rawson, B. (ed.). *The family in ancient Rome: new perspectives* (Ithaca, NY: Cornell University Press, 1986).

Reed, J. L. *Archaeology and the Galilean Jesus* (Harrisburg, PA: Trinity Press International, 2000).

Roberts, C. H. *Manuscript, society and belief in early Christian Egypt* (London and New York: Oxford University Press, 1979).

Rosenmeyer, P. A. *Ancient epistolary fictions: the letter in Greek literature* (Cambridge: Cambridge University Press, 2001).

Rudolph, K. *Gnosis: the nature and history of Gnosticism*, R. McL. Wilson (ed.) (San Francisco: Harper & Row, 1987).

Runia, D. *Philo in early Christian literature: a survey*, CRINT III.3 (1993).

Safrai, S. and M. Stern (eds.). *The Jewish people in the first century: historical geography, political history, social, cultural and religious life and institutions*, 2 vols., CRINT 1.1–2 (1974–6).

Sage, M. M. *Cyprian*, Patristic monograph series 1 (Cambridge, MA: The Philadelphia Patristic Foundation Ltd., 1975).

Saldarini, A. J. *Matthew's Christian-Jewish Community* (Chicago: University of Chicago Press, 1994).

Sanders, E. P. *Jesus and Judaism* (Philadelphia: Fortress, 1985).

—. (ed.). *Jewish and Christian self-definition*, vol. 1: *The shaping of Christianity in the second and third centuries* (London: SCM Press, 1980).).

—. *Jewish law from Jesus to the Mishnah: five studies* (London: SCM Press, 1990).

—. *Judaism: practice and belief 63 BCE–66 CE* (London: SCM Press, 1992).

Sanders, J. A. *The Dead Sea Psalms scroll* (Ithaca, NY: Cornell University Press, 1967).

Schmid, U. *Marcion und sein Apostolos: Rekonstruktion und historische Einordnung der marcionitischen Paulusbriefausgabe*, ANTF 25 (1995).

Schneider, A. *'Propter sanctam ecclesiam suam': die Kirche als Geschöpf, Frau und Bau im Bußunterricht des Pastor Hermae*, SEAug 67 (1999).

Schnelle, U. *Antidocetic christology in the gospel of John*, L. M. Maloney (trans.) (Minneapolis: Fortress, 1992); ET of *Antidoketische Christologie im Johannesevangelium*, FRLANT 144 (1987).

Schoedel, W. R. *Ignatius of Antioch: a commentary on the letters of Ignatius of Antioch*, Hermeneia (Philadelphia: Fortress, 1985).

Schürer, E. *The history of the Jewish people in the age of Jesus Christ (175 B.C.– A.D. 135)*, 3 vols., E. Schürer, G. Vermes, F. Millar *et al.* (revs. and eds.) (Edinburgh: T&T Clark, 1973–87).

Schwartz, D. R. *Agrippa I: the last king of Judaea*, TSAJ 23 (1990).

Schwartz, S. *Imperialism and Jewish Society 200 B.C.E. to 640 C.E.* (Princeton: Princeton University Press, 2001).

Schweitzer, A. *The quest of the historical Jesus*, 1st complete ed., J. Bowden (ed.), W. Montgomery, J. R. Coates, S. Cupitt and J. Bowden (trans.) (Minneapolis: Fortress, 2001).

Simon, M. *Verus Israel: a study of the relations between Christians and Jews in the Roman empire (AD 135–425)*, H. McKeating (trans.), Littman library of Jewish civilization (Oxford: Oxford University Press, 1986).

Smallwood, E. M. *Philonis Alexandrini Legatio ad Gaium*, 2nd ed. (Leiden: Brill, 1970).

Snyder, G. F. *Ante pacem: archaeological evidence of church life before Constantine*, 2nd ed. (Macon, GA: Mercer University Press, 2003).

Snyder, H. G. *Teachers and texts in the ancient world: philosophers, Jews and Christians*, Religion in the first Christian centuries (London: Routledge, 2000).

Stanton, G. N. *A gospel for a new people: studies in Matthew* (Edinburgh: T&T Clark, 1992).

Stanton, G. N. and G. G. Stroumsa (eds.). *Tolerance and intolerance in early Judaism and Christianity* (Cambridge: Cambridge University Press, 1998).

Stark, R. *The rise of Christianity: a sociologist reconsiders history* (Princeton: Princeton University Press, 1996).

Stark, R. and W. S. Bainbridge. *The future of religion: secularization, revival, and cult formation* (Berkeley: University of California Press, 1985).

Sterling, G. E. *Historiography and self-definition: Josephos, Luke-Acts, and apologetic historiography*, NovTSup 64 (1992).

Stern, M. *Greek and Latin authors on Jews and Judaism*, 3 vols. (Jerusalem: Israel Academy of Sciences and Humanities, 1976–84).

Stevenson, J. *The catacombs: rediscovered monuments of early Christianity* (London: Thames and Hudson, 1978).

Stevenson, J. and W. H. C. Frend. *A new Eusebius: documents illustrating the history of the church to AD 337* (London: SPCK, 1987).

Stewart-Sykes, A. *The lamb's high feast: Melito, Peri pascha and the Quartodeciman paschal liturgy at Sardis*, VCSup 42 (1998).

Strecker, G. *The Johannine letters: a commentary on 1, 2 and 3 John*, L. M. Maloney (trans.), Hermeneia (Minneapolis: Fortress, 1996).

Taylor, J. E. *Christians and the holy places: the myth of Jewish-Christian origins* (Oxford: Clarendon, 1993).

Theissen, G. *The Gospels in context: social and political history in the synoptic tradition* (Edinburgh: T&T Clark, 1992).

Thomassen, E. 'Orthodoxy and heresy in second-century Rome', HTR 97 (2004), 241–256.

Trebilco, P. R. *Jewish communities in Asia Minor*, SNTSMS 69 (1991).

Trevett, C. *Montanism: gender, authority and the New Prophecy* (Cambridge: Cambridge: University Press, 1996).

van Tilborg, S. *Reading John in Ephesus*, NovTSup 83 (1996).

Vielhauer, P. *Geschichte der urchristlichen Literatur: Einleitung in das Neue Testament, die Apokryphen und die Apostolischen Väter* (Berlin: De Gruyter, 1975).

Walker, P. W. L. *Holy city, holy places: Christian attitudes to Jerusalem and the Holy Land in the fourth century*, OECS (1990).

Weiss, J. *Earliest Christianity: A history of the period A.D. 30–150*, 2 vols., F. C. Grant (ed. and trans.) (New York: Harper, 1937).

White, L. M. (ed.). *Social networks in the early Christian environment: issues and methods for social history*, Semeia 56 (1992).

—. *The social origins of Christian architecture*, 2 vols., HTS 42 (1996–7).

Wilken, R. L. *The Christians as the Romans saw them*, 2nd ed. (New Haven: Yale University Press, 2003).

—. *The land called holy: Palestine in Christian history and thought* (New Haven: Yale University Press, 1992).

Williams, M. A. *Rethinking 'Gnosticism': an argument for dismantling a dubious category* (Princeton: Princeton University Press, 1996).

Williams, R. *Arius: heresy and tradition*, 2nd ed. (London: SCM Press, 2001).

—. 'Defining heresy', in *The origins of Christendom in the west*, A. Kreider (ed.) (Edinburgh: T&T Clark, 2001), 313–35.

— 'Does it make sense to speak of pre-Nicene orthodoxy?', in *The making of orthodoxy: essays in honour of Henry Chadwick*, R. Williams (ed.) (Cambridge: Cambridge University Press 1989), 1–23.

—. 'Origenes/Origenismus', *TRE* 25 (1995), 397–420.

Wilson, S. G. *Related strangers: Jews and Christians 70–170 CE* (Minneapolis: Fortress, 1995).

Wischmeyer, W. K. 'Die Aberkiosinschrift als Grabepigramm', *JAC* 23 (1980), 22–47.

Young, F. M. *Biblical exegesis and the formation of Christian culture* (Cambridge: Cambridge University Press, 1997).

Young, F. M., L. Ayres and A. Louth. *The Cambridge history of early Christian literature* (Cambridge: Cambridge University Press, 2004).

Zanker, P. *The mask of Socrates: the image of the intellectual in antiquity*, A. Shapiro (trans.), Sather Classical lectures 59 (Berkeley: University of California Press, 1995).

Zuntz, G. *The text of the epistles: a disquisition upon the Corpus Paulinum* (London: British Academy, 1953).

Specialised bibliographies by chapter

Prelude: Jesus Christ, foundation of Christianity

Frances M. Young

Allison, D. C. *Jesus of Nazareth: millenarian prophet* (Minneapolis: Fortress, 1998).

Bauckham, R. *The climax of prophecy* (Edinburgh: T&T Clark, 1993).

Bockmuehl, M. N. A. (ed.). *The Cambridge companion to Jesus* (Cambridge: Cambridge University Press, 2001).

Chilton, B. *Rabbi Jesus: an intimate biography* (New York: Doubleday, 2000).

Crossan, J. D. *The historical Jesus: the life of a Mediterranean Jewish peasant* (San Francisco: HarperSanFrancisco, 1991).

Crossan, J. D. and J. L. Reed. *Excavating Jesus: beneath the stones, behind the text* (San Francisco: HarperSanFrancisco, 2001).

Davies, S. L. *Jesus the healer: possession, trance, and the origins of Christianity* (New York: Continuum, 1995).

Dodd, C. H. *Parables of the Kingdom* (London: Nisbet, 1935).

Downing, F. G. *Christ and the Cynics* (Sheffield: Sheffield Academic Press, 1988).

Drake, H. A. 'Eusebius on the true cross', *JEH* 36 (1985), 1–22.

Ehrman, B. D. *Jesus: apocalyptic prophet of the new millennium* (Oxford: Oxford University Press, 1999).

Funk, R. W. and the Jesus Seminar (eds.). *The acts of Jesus: the search for the authentic deeds of Jesus* (San Francisco: HarperSanFrancisco, 1998).

Funk, R. W., R. W. Hoover, and the Jesus Seminar (eds.). *The five gospels: the search for the authentic words of Jesus* (New York: Macmillan, 1993).

Gelston, A. *The Eucharistic prayer of Addai and Mari* (Oxford: Clarendon Press, 1992).

Gibson, S. and J. E. Taylor. *Beneath the Church of the Holy Sepulchre, Jerusalem: the archaeology and early history of traditional Golgotha*, Palestine Exploration Fund monograph series maior 1 (London: Palestine Exploration Fund, 1994).

Hick, J. (ed). *The myth of God incarnate* (London: SCM Press, 1977).

Hooker, M. D. *Jesus and the servant: the influence of the servant concept of deutero-Isaiah in the New Testament* (London: SPCK, 1959).

Horsley, R. A. *Jesus and the spiral of violence: popular Jewish resistance in Roman Palestine* (San Francisco: Harper & Row, 1987).

Kiley, M. C. *et al.* (eds). *Prayer from Alexander to Constantine: a critical anthology* (London: Routledge, 1997).

Klausner, J. *Jesus of Nazareth*, H. Danby (trans.) (London: George Allen and Unwin, 1925).

Lincoln, A. T. *Paradise now and not yet*, SNTSMS 43 (1981).

Lindars, B. *The gospel of John*, New Century Bible (London: Oliphants, 1972).

Maccoby, H. *Jesus the Pharisee* (London: SCM Press, 2003).

Meier, J. P. *A marginal Jew: re-thinking the historical Jesus*, 3 vols. (New York: Doubleday, 1991–2001).

Neill, S. C. and N. T. Wright. *The interpretation of the New Testament, 1861–1986* (Oxford: Oxford University Press, 1988).

Paulus, H. E. G. *Das Leben Jesu als Grundlage einer reinen Geschichte des Urchristentums* (Heidelberg: C. F. Winter, 1828).

Powell, M. A. *The Jesus debate: modern historians investigate the life of Christ* (Oxford: Lion, 1998).

Reimarus: fragments, C. H. Talbert (ed.), R. S. Fraser (trans.) (London: SCM Press, 1971).

Rowland, C. *The open heaven: a study of apocalyptic in Judaism and early Christianity* (London: SPCK, 1982).

Sanders, E. P. *The historical figure of Jesus* (London: Penguin Books, 1993).

Smith, M. *Jesus the magician* (New York: Harper & Row, 1978).

Strauss, D. F. *The life of Jesus critically examined*, reprint, P. C. Hodgson (ed.), trans. from the 4th German ed. by George Eliot (Ramsey, NJ: Sigler, 1994).

Taylor, J. E. 'Golgotha: a reconsideration of the evidence for the sites of Jesus' crucifixion and burial', *NTS* 44 (1998), 180–203.

Theissen, G. and D. Winter. *The quest for the plausible Jesus: the question of criteria*, M. E. Boring (trans.) (Louisville, KY: Westminster John Knox, 2002).

Thiede, C. P. and M. d'Ancona. *The quest of the true cross* (London: Wiedenfeld and Nicolson, 2000).

Vermes, G. *Jesus the Jew* (London: Collins, 1973).

—. *The religion of Jesus the Jew* (London: SCM Press, 1993).

Webb, M. *The churches and catacombs of early Christian Rome: a comprehensive guide* (Brighton: Sussex Academic Press, 2001).

Witherington, B., III. *Jesus the sage: the pilgrimage of wisdom* (Minneapolis: Fortress, 1994).

—. *Jesus the seer: the progress of prophecy* (Peabody, MA: Hendrickson, 1999).

Wrede, W. *The messianic secret*, J. C. G. Greig (trans.), Library of theological translations (Cambridge: J. Clarke, 1971).

Wright, N. T. *Jesus and the victory of God* (London: SPCK, 1996).

Young, F. M. 'Temple, cult and law in early Christianity: a study in the relations between Jews and Christians in the early centuries', *NTS* 19 (1973), 325–38.

1. Galilee and Judaea in the first century

Seán Freyne

Arav, R. and R. A. Freund. *Bethsaida, I and II: 'A city by the north shore of the sea of Galilee'* (Kirksville, MO: Thomas Jefferson State University Press, 1995, 1999).

Barag, D. 'Tyrian currency in Galilee', *INJ* 6/7 (1982/3), 7–13.

Ben-David, A. *Jerusalem und Tyros: ein Beitrag zur palästinensischen Münz- und Wirtschaftsgeschichte (126 a. C.–57 p. C)* (Basel: Kyklos, 1969).

Betz, H. D. 'Jesus and the Cynics: survey and analysis of a hypothesis', *JR* 74 (1994), 453–75.

Chancey, M. A. *The myth of a Gentile Galilee*, SNTSMS 118 (2002).

Crossan, J. D. *The birth of Christianity* (San Francisco: HarperSanFrancisco, 1998).

Edwards, D. R. and C. T. McCollough (eds.). *Archaeology and the Galilee: texts and contexts in the Greco-Roman and Byzantine periods*, South Florida studies in the history of Judaism 143 (Atlanta: Scholars Press, 1997).

Fiensy, D. A. *The social history of Palestine in the Herodian period* (Lewiston, ME: Mellen, 1991).

Frankel, R. 'Galilee, prehellenistic', *ABD* vol. II, 879–94.

—. 'Har Mispe Yamim, 1988/89', *Excavations and surveys in Israel* 9 (1989), 100–102.

—. 'Some oil-presses from western Galilee', *BASOR* 286 (1992), 39–71.

Frankel, R. and R. Ventura. 'The Mispe Yamim bronzes', *BASOR* 311 (1998), 49–59.

Freyne, S. 'Archaeology and the historical Jesus', in S. Freyne, *Galilee and Gospel: collected essays*, WUNT 125 (2000), 160–182.

—. 'Behind the names: Galileans, Samaritans, *Ioudaioi*', in S. Freyne, *Galilee and gospel: collected essays*, WUNT 125 (2000), 114–31.

—. 'Galilean questions to Crossan's Mediterranean Jesus', in S. Freyne, *Galilee and gospel: collected essays*, WUNT 125 (2000), 208–29.

—. *Galilee from Alexander the Great to Hadrian: a study of Second Temple Judaism* (Wilmington, DE: Michael Glazier and Notre Dame, IN: Notre Dame University Press, 1980; repr. Edinburgh: T&T Clark, 1998).

—. *Galilee, Jesus and the gospels: literary approaches and historical investigations* (Philadelphia: Fortress, 1988).

—. 'The geography of restoration: Galilee–Jerusalem relations in early Jewish and Christian experience', *NTS* 47 (2001), 289–311.

—. 'The geography, politics and economics of Galilee and the quest for the historical Jesus', in *Studying the historical Jesus: evaluations of the current state of research*, B. Chilton and C. A. Evans (eds.) (Leiden: Brill, 1994), 75–121.

—. 'Herodian economics in Galilee: searching for a suitable model', in S. Freyne, *Galilee and gospel: collected essays*, WUNT 125 (2000), 86–113.

—. 'Jesus and the urban culture of Galilee', in S. Freyne, *Galilee and gospel: collected essays*, WUNT 125 (2000), 183–207.

—. 'Urban–rural relations in first-century Galilee: some suggestions from the literary sources', in S. Freyne, *Galilee and gospel: collected essays*, WUNT 125 (2000), 45–58.

Goodman, M. *The ruling class of Judaea: the origins of the Jewish revolt against Rome A.D. 66–70* (Cambridge: Cambridge University Press, 1993).

Hanson, K. C. 'The Galilean fishing economy and the Jesus tradition', *BTB* 27 (1997), 99–111.

Hanson, R. S. *Tyrian influence in the upper Galilee* (Cambridge, MA: American School of Oriental Research , 1980).

Herrenbrück, F. *Jesus und die Zöllner*, WUNT 2.41 (1990).

—. 'Zum Vorwurf der Kollaboration des Zöllners mit Rom', *ZNW* 78 (1987), 186–99.

Hoehner, H. W. *Herod Antipas*, SNTSMS 17 (1972).

Horsley, R. A. *Archaeology, history and society in Galilee: the social context of Jesus and the rabbis* (Valley Forge, PA: Trinity Press International, 1996).

—. *Galilee: history, politics, people* (Valley Forge, PA: Trinity Press International, 1995).

—. *Sociology and the Jesus movement* (New York: Crossroads, 1989).

Jeremias, J. *Jerusalem in the time of Jesus* (London: SCM Press, 1969).

Kraabel, A. T. 'New evidence of the Samaritan diaspora has been found in Delos', *BA* 47 (1984), 44–6.

Lenski, G. E. *Power and privilege: a theory of social stratification* (New York: McGraw-Hill, 1966).

Levine, L. I. (ed.). *The Galilee in late antiquity* (New York: The Jewish Theological Seminary of America, 1992).

Mendels, D. *The rise and fall of Jewish nationalism: Jewish and Christian ethnicity in ancient Palestine* (New York: Doubleday, 1992).

Meyers, E. M. (ed.). 'Galilean regionalism as a factor in historical reconstruction', *BASOR* 221 (1976), 95–101.

—. (ed). *Galilee through the centuries: confluence of cultures* (Winona Lake, IN: Eisenbrauns, 1999).

—. (ed.). *The Oxford encyclopedia of archaeology in the near east*, 5 vols. (New York: Oxford University Press, 1997).

Meyers, E. M., E. Netzer and C. L. Meyers. *Sepphoris* (Winona Lake, IN: Eisenbrauns, 1992).

—. 'Sepphoris, the ornament of all Galilee', *BA* 49 (1986), 4–19.

Meyers, E. M., J. F. Strange and D. E. Groh. 'The Meiron excavation project: archaeological survey in Galilee and Golan, 1976', *BASOR* 230 (1978), 1–24.

Nagy, R. M. (ed.). *Sepphoris in Galilee: cross currents of culture* (Raleigh: North Carolina Museum of Modern Art; Winona Lake, IN: Eisenbrauns, 1996).

Netzer, E. 'Herod's building projects: state necessity or personal need?', in *Jerusalem cathedra* 1, L. I. Levine (ed.) (Jerusalem: Izhak Ben-Zvi Institute, 1981), 48–67.

Netzer, E. and Z. Weiss. *Zippori* (Jerusalem: Israel Exploration Society, 1994).

Nun, M. *Ancient anchorages and harbours around the sea of Galilee* (Kibbutz Ein Gev: Kinnereth Sailing Co., 1988).

Oakman, D. E. *Jesus and the economic questions of his day* (Lewiston, NY: Mellen, 1986).

Oakman, D. E. and K. C. Hanson. *Palestine in the time of Jesus: social structures and social conflicts* (Minneapolis: Fortress, 1998).

Overman, J. A. 'Recent advances in the archaeology of the Galilee in the Roman period', *Current research in Biblical studies* 1 (1993), 35–57.

Raynor, J. T. and Y. Meshorer. *The coins of ancient Meiron* (Winona Lake, IN: Eisenbrauns, 1988).

Richardson, P. *Herod, king of the Jews and friend of the Romans* (Columbia: University of South Carolina Press, 1996).

Safrai, Z. *The economy of Roman Palestine* (London: Routledge, 1994).

Stemberger, G. *Jews and Christians in the holy land: Palestine in the fourth century*, R. Tuschling (trans.) (Edinburgh: T&T Clark, 2000).

Stern, E. (ed.). *The new encyclopedia of archaeological excavations in the Holy Land*, 4 vols. (Jerusalem: Jerusalem Exploration Society & Carta; New York: Simon & Schuster, 1993).

Stern, M. 'Aspects of Jewish society: the priesthood and other classes', in *The Jewish people in the first century: historical geography, political history, social, cultural and religious life and institutions*, 2 vols., S. Safrai and M. Stern (eds.), CRINT I. I–II (1974–6), vol. II, 561–630.

Strange, J. 'Some implications of archaeology for New Testament studies', in *What has archaeology to do with faith?*, J. H. Charlesworth and W. P. Weaver (eds.) (Philadelphia: Trinity Press International, 1992), 23–59.

Strange, J. F., D. E. Groh and T. R. W. Longstaff. 'Excavations at Sepphoris: the location and identification of Shikhin: Part I', *IEJ* 44 (1994), 216–27.

—. 'Excavations at Sepphoris: the location and identification of Shikhin: Part II', *IEJ* 45 (1995), 171–87.

Syon, D. 'The coins from Gamala: an interim report', *INJ* 12 (1992/3), 34–55.

Tcherikover, V. 'Palestine under the Ptolemies: a contribution to the study of the Zenon papyri', *Mizraim* 4–5 (1937), 9–90.

Theissen, G. *Social reality and the early Christians: theology, ethics and the world of the New Testament*, M. Kohl (trans.) (Edinburgh: T&T Clark, 1993).

—. *Sociology of early Palestinian Christianity* (Philadelphia: Fortress, 1978).

2. The Jewish Diaspora

Tessa Rajak

Abusch, R. 'Negotiating difference: genital mutilation in Roman slave law and the history of the Bar Kokhba revolt', in *The Bar Kokhba war reconsidered: new perspectives on the second Jewish revolt against Rome*, P. Schäfer (ed.), TSAJ 100 (2003), 71–91.

Applebaum, S. *Jews and Greeks in ancient Cyrene*, SJLA 28 (1979).

Barclay, J. M. G. (ed.). *Negotiating diaspora: Jewish strategies in the Roman empire* (New York: T&T Clark, 2004).

Bar-Kochva, B. *Pseudo-Hecataeus 'On the Jews': legitimizing the Jewish diaspora* (Berkeley: University of California Press, 1996).

Bickerman, E. J. *The Jews in the Greek age* (Cambridge, MA: Harvard University Press, 1988).

Brooten, B. J. *Women leaders in the ancient synagogue*, BJS 36 (1982).

Chaniotis, A. 'The Jews of Aphrodisias: new evidence and old problems', *SCI* 21 (2002), 209–42.

Cohen, S. J. D. 'Epigraphical rabbis', *JQR* 72 (1981/2), 1–17.

Cohen, S. J. D. and S. E. Frerichs (eds.). *Diasporas in antiquity*, BJS 288 (1993).

Collins, J. J. *Between Athens and Jerusalem: Jewish identity in the Hellenistic diaspora*, 2nd ed. (Grand Rapids, MI: Eerdmans, 2000).

Collins, J. J. and G. E. Sterling (eds.). *Hellenism in the land of Israel* (Notre Dame, IN: University of Notre Dame Press, 2001).

Doran, R. 'The Jewish Hellenistic historians before Josephus', *ANRW* II.20.1 (1987), 246–97.

Feldman, L. H. *Jew and Gentile in the ancient world: attitudes and interactions from Alexander to Justinian* (Princeton: Princeton University Press, 1993).

Gafni, I. M. *Land, center and diaspora: Jewish constructs in late antiquity*, JSPSup 21 (1997).

Gibson, E. L. *The Jewish manumission inscriptions of the Bosporus kingdom*, TSAJ 75 (1999).

Goodenough, E. R. *Jewish symbols in the Greco-Roman period*, 13 vols. (New York: Pantheon, 1953–68).

Goodman, M. (ed.). *Jews in a Graeco-Roman World* (Oxford: Clarendon Press, 1998).

—. 'Jewish proselytizing in the first century', in *The Jews among pagans and Christians in the Roman empire*, J. M. Lieu, J. A. North and T. Rajak (eds.) (London: Routledge, 1992), 53–78.

—. *Mission and conversion: proselytizing in the religious history of the Roman empire* (Oxford: Clarendon Press, 1994).

—. 'Trajan and the origins of the Bar Kokhba war', in *The Bar Kokhba war reconsidered: new perspectives on the second Jewish revolt against Rome*, P. Schäfer (ed.), TSAJ 100 (2003), 23–29.

Grabbe, L. L. *Judaism from Cyrus to Hadrian*, 2 vols. (Minneapolis: Fortress, 1992).

Gruen, E. S. *Heritage and Hellenism: the reinvention of Jewish tradition* (Berkeley: University of California Press, 1998).

Hachlili, R. *Ancient Jewish art and archaeology in the diaspora*, HO 7.1 (1998).

Honigman, S. 'The Jewish *politeuma* at Heracleopolis', *SCI* 21 (2002), 251–66.

—. *The Septuagint and Homeric scholarship in Alexandria: a study in the narrative of the Letter of Aristeas* (London: Routledge, 2003).

Isaac, B. H. *The invention of racism in Classical antiquity* (Princeton: Princeton University Press, 2004).

—. 'Roman religious policy and the Bar Kokhba war', in *The Bar Kokhba war reconsidered: new perspectives on the second Jewish revolt against Rome*, P. Schäfer (ed.), TSAJ 100 (2003), 36–54.

Jones, S. and S. Pearce (eds.) *Jewish local patriotism and self-identification in the Graeco-Roman period*, JSPSup 31 (1998).

Kasher, A. *The Jews in Hellenistic and Roman Egypt: the struggle for equal rights*, rev. ed., TSAJ 7 (1985).

Kraemer, R. S. 'Typical and atypical family dynamics: the cases of Babatha and Berenice', in *Early Christian families in context: an interdisciplinary dialogue*, D. L. Balch and C. Osiek (eds.) (Grand Rapids, MI: Eerdmans, 2003), 130–56.

Levine, L. I. *The ancient synagogue: the first thousand years* (New Haven: Yale University Press, 2000).

Lewis, N., Y. Yadin and J. C. Greenfield. (eds.). *The documents from the Bar Kochba period in the Cave of Letters*, JDS 2 (1989).

Lieu, J. 'The race of the God-fearers', *JTS* 46 (1995), 483–501.

Linder, A. (ed). *The Jews in Roman imperial legislation* (Detroit: Wayne State University Press, 1987).

Olsson, B. and M. Zetterholm (eds.). *The ancient synagogue: from its origins until 200 CE* (Stockholm: Almqvist and Wiksell, 2003).

Oppenheimer, A. 'The ban on circumcision as a cause of the revolt: a reconsideration', in *The Bar Kokhba war reconsidered: new perspectives on the second Jewish revolt against Rome*, P. Schäfer (ed.), TSAJ 100 (2003), 55–69.

Overman, J. A. and R. S. MacLennan (eds.). *Diaspora Jews and Judaism: essays in honor of, and in dialogue with, A. Thomas Kraabel* (Atlanta: Scholars Press, 1992).

Pucci Ben Zeev, M. *Jewish rights in the Roman world: the Greek and Roman documents quoted by Josephus Flavius*, TSAJ 74 (1998).

Rajak, T. 'The ancient synagogue' (review article), *SPhilo* 15 (2003), 100–8.

—. 'Inscription and context: reading the Jewish catacombs of Rome', in *Studies in early Jewish epigraphy*, J. W. van Henten and P. W. van der Horst (eds.), AGJU 21 (1994), 226–41.

—. *The Jewish dialogue with Greece and Rome: studies in cultural and social interaction*, AGJU 48 (2001).

—. 'Josephus in the diaspora', in *Flavius Josephus in Flavian Rome*, J. C. Edmondson, S. Mason, and J. B. Rives (eds.) (Oxford: Oxford University Press, 2005), 79–97.

—. 'Synagogue and community in the Graeco-Roman diaspora', in *The Jews in the Hellenistic and Roman cities*, J. R. Bartlett (ed.) (London: Routledge, 2002), 22–38.

Reynolds, J. M. and R. Tannenbaum. *Jews and God-fearers at Aphrodisias: Greek inscriptions with commentary*, Proceedings of the Cambridge Philological Society 12 (Cambridge: Cambridge Philological Society, 1987).

Runesson, A. *The origins of the synagogue: a socio-historical study* (Stockholm: Almqvist and Wiksell, 2001).

Rutgers, L. V. *The hidden heritage of diaspora Judaism* (Louvain: Peeters, 1998).

—. *The Jews in late ancient Rome: evidence of cultural interaction in the Roman diaspora*, RGRW 126 (1995).

Schäfer, P. (ed.) *The Bar Kokhba war reconsidered: new perspectives on the second Jewish revolt against Rome*, TSAJ 100 (2003).

—. *Judeophobia: attitudes towards the Jews in the ancient world* (Cambridge, MA: Harvard University Press, 1997).

Schwartz, D. R. 'From the Maccabees to Masada: on diasporan historiography of the Second Temple period', in *Jüdische Geschichte in hellenistisch-römischer Zeit*, A. Oppenheimer (ed.) (Munich: Oldenbourg, 1999), 29–40.

Smallwood, E. M. *The Jews under Roman rule: from Pompey to Diocletian*, SJLA 20 (1976).

Tcherikover, V. *Hellenistic civilization and the Jews*, S. Applebaum (trans.) (Philadelphia: Jewish Publication Society of America, 1961).

van der Horst, P. W. *Ancient Jewish epitaphs: an introductory survey of a millennium of Jewish funerary epigraphy (300 BCE–700 CE)*, CBET 2 (1991).

van Henten, J. W., and P. W. van der Horst (eds.). *Studies in early Jewish epigraphy*, AGJU 21 (1994).

Williams, M. *The Jews among the Greeks and Romans: a diasporan sourcebook* (London: Duckworth, 1998).

—. 'The structure of the Jewish community in Rome', in *Jews in a Graeco-Roman world*, M. Goodman (ed.) (Oxford: Clarendon Press, 1998), 215–28.

3. The Roman empire

Hans-Josef Klauck

Albrecht, M. von. *A history of Roman literature from Livius Andronicus to Boethius: with special regard to its influence on world literature*, 2 vols., G. L. Schmeling and M. von Albrecht (revs.), Mnemos.Sup. 165 (1997).

Alföldy, G. 'Pontius Pilatus und das Tiberieum von Caesarea Maritima', *SCI* 18 (1999), 85–108.

Alvarez Cineira, D. *Die Religionspolitik des Kaisers Claudius und die paulinische Mission*, HBS 19 (1999).

Baltrusch, E. *Die Juden und das römische Reich: Geschichte einer konfliktreichen Beziehung* (Darmstadt: Wissenschaftliche Buchgesellschaft, 2002).

Beard, M., J. A. North and S. R. F. Price. *Religions of Rome*, 2 vols. (Cambridge: Cambridge University Press, 1998).

Boardman, J. (ed.). *The Oxford history of classical art* (Oxford: Oxford University Press, 1993).

Boyle, A. J. 'Introduction: reading Flavian Rome', in *Flavian Rome: culture, image, text*, A. J. Boyle and W. J. Dominik (eds.) (Leiden: Brill, 2003), 1–67.

Boyle, A. J. and W. J. Dominik, (eds.). *Flavian Rome: culture, image, text* (Leiden: Brill, 2003).

Bradley, K. R. *Slavery and society at Rome*, Key themes in ancient history (Cambridge: Cambridge University Press, 1994).

Braund, D. *Rome and the friendly king: the character of the client kingship* (London: Helm, 1984).

Cambell, J. B. *The Roman army, 31 BC–AD 337: a sourcebook* (London: Routledge, 1994).

The Cambridge ancient history, vol. x. *The Augustan empire, 43 BC–AD 69*, A. K. Bowman, E. Champlin and A. Lintott (eds.), 2nd ed. (Cambridge: Cambridge University Press, 1996).

The Cambridge ancient history, vol. xi: *The high empire, AD 70–192*, A. K. Bowman, P. Garnsey and D. Rathbone (eds.), 2nd ed. (Cambridge: Cambridge University Press, 2000).

Casson, L. *Travel in the ancient world* (repr., Baltimore: Johns Hopkins University Press, 1994, original 1974).

Clauss, M. *Kaiser und Gott: Herrscherkult im römischen Reich* (Stuttgart: Teubner, 1999).

Coarelli, F. *The column of Trajan*, C. Rockwell (trans.) (Rome: Editore Colombo and German Archaeological Institute, 2000).

Colish, M. L. *The Stoic tradition from antiquity to the early middle ages*, vol. i: *Stoicism in Classical Latin Literature*, 2nd ed. (Leiden: Brill, 1990).

Colledge, M. A. R. 'Art and architecture', *CAH²*, vol. xi (2000), 966–83.

Danker, F. W. *Benefactor: epigraphic studies of a Graeco-Roman and New Testament semantic field* (St. Louis, MO: Clayton, 1982).

Dihle, A. *Greek and Latin literature of the Roman empire: from Augustus to Justinian*, M. Malzahn (trans.) (London: Routledge, 1994).

Freudenberger, R. *Das Verhalten der römischen Behörden gegen die Christen im 2. Jahrhundert dargestellt am Brief des Plinius an Trajan und den Reskripten Trajans und Hadrians*, MBPF 52 (1967).

Gager, J. G. (ed.). *Curse tablets and binding spells from the ancient world* (New York: Oxford University Press, 1992).

Garnsey, P. and R. P. Saller. *The Roman empire: economy, society and culture* (London: Duckworth, 1987).

Glad, C. E. *Paul and Philodemus: adaptability in Epicurean and early Christian psychagogy*, NovTSup 81 (1995).

Goodman, M. *The Roman world, 44 BC–AD 180* (London: Routledge, 1997).

Gradel, I. *Emperor worship and Roman religion*, Oxford classical monographs (Oxford: Clarendon Press, 2002).

Graf, F. *Magic in the ancient world*, RA 10 (1997).

Harrill, J. A. 'Slavery', in *Dictionary of New Testament background*, C. A. Evans and S. E. Porter (eds.) (Downers Grove, IL: InterVarsity, 2000), 1124–7.

Harris, W. V. *Ancient literacy* (Cambridge, MA: Harvard University Press, 1989).

Heichelheim, F. M. 'Bevölkerungswesen', in *Der kleine Pauly* 1 (1964), 879–80.

Labahn, M. and J. Zangenberg (eds.). *Zwischen den Reichen: Neues Testament und römische Herrschaft*, TANZ 36 (2002).

Laffi, U. 'Le iscrizioni relative all'introduzione nel 9 a.C. del nuovo calendario della provincia d'Asia', *SCO* 16 (1967), 5–98.

Lémonon, J.-P. *Pilate et le gouvernement de la Judée: textes et monuments*, EBib (1981).

Morford, M. P. O. *The Roman philosophers: from the time of Cato the Censor to the death of Marcus Aurelius* (London: Routledge, 2002).

Newlands, C. E. 'The emperor's *saturnalia*: Statius, *Silvae* 1.6', in *Flavian Rome: culture, image, text*, A. J. Boyle and W. J. Dominik (eds.) (Leiden: Brill, 2003), 499–522.

Novak, R. M. *Christianity and the Roman empire: background texts* (Harrisburg, PA: Trinity Press International, 2001).

Pollitt, J. J. 'Rome: the republic and early empire', in *The Oxford History of Classical Art*, J. Boardman (ed.) (Oxford: Oxford University Press, 1993), 217–95.

Radt, W. *Pergamon: Geschichte und Bauten einer antiken Metropole* (Darmstadt: Wissenschaftliche Buchgesellschaft, 1999).

Reale, G. *A history of ancient philosophy*, vol. IV: *The schools of the imperial age*, J. R. Catan (ed. and trans.) (Albany: State University of New York Press, 1990).

Riepl, W. *Das Nachrichtenwesen des Altertums, mit besonderer Rücksicht auf die Römer* (repr. Hildesheim: Olms, 1972, original 1913).

Roth, J. P. *The logistics of the Roman army at war (264 BC–AD 235)*, CSCT 23 (1999).

Saller, R. P. *Personal patronage under the early empire* (Cambridge: Cambridge University Press, 1982).

Schubert, C. *Studien zum Nerobild in der lateinischen Dichtung der Antike*, Beiträge zur Altertumskunde 116 (Leipzig: Teubner, 1998).

Shelton, J.-A. *As the Romans did: a sourcebook in Roman social history*, 2nd ed. (Oxford: Oxford University Press, 1998).

Sherk, Robert K. *Roman documents from the Greek east*: senatus consulta *and* epistulae *to the age of Augustus* (Baltimore: Johns Hopkins University Press, 1969).

Strobel, K. *Untersuchungen zu den Dakerkriegen Trajans: Studien zur Geschichte des mittleren und unteren Donauraumes in der Hohen Kaiserzeit*, Antiquitas, ser. 1, Abhandlungen zur alten Geschichte, vol. 33 (1984).

Swain, S. *Hellenism and empire: language, classicism, and power in the Greek world, AD 50–250* (Oxford: Clarendon Press, 1996).

Torelli, M. 'Roman art, 43 BC to AD 69', *CAH²*, vol. X (1996), 930–58.

Urner, C. 'Kaiser Domitian im Urteil antiker literarischer Quellen und moderner Forschung' (Diss. phil., University of Augsburg, 1993).

van Nijf, O. M. *The civic world of professional associations in the Roman east*, DMAHA 17 (1997).

Veyne, P. *Le pain et le cirque: sociologie historique d'un pluralisme politique*, L'univers historique (Paris: Du Seuil, 1976); ET *Bread and circuses: historical sociology and political pluralism*; abridged version, O. Murray (ed.), B. Pearce (trans.) (London: Penguin, 1990).

Wengst, K. *Pax romana and the peace of Jesus Christ*, J. Bowden (trans.) (London: SCM Press, 1987).

Woolf, G. 'Romanisierung', *Der neue Pauly* 10 (2001), 122–7.

Zanker, P. *The power of images in the age of Augustus*, A. Shapiro (trans.), Jerome lectures 16 (Ann Arbor: University of Michigan Press, 1989).

4. Jewish Christianity

Joel Marcus

Achtemeier, P. J. *1 Peter: a commentary on First Peter*, Hermeneia (Minneapolis: Fortress, 1996).

Alexander, P. S. '"The parting of the ways" from the perspective of rabbinic Judaism', in *Jews and Christians: the parting of the ways, AD 70 to 135*, The second Durham–Tübingen research symposium on earliest Christianity and Judaism (Durham, September 1989), J. D. G. Dunn (ed.), WUNT 66 (1992), 1–25.

Allison, D.C. 'The fiction of James and its *Sitz im Leben*', *RB* 108 (2001), 529–70.

Bagatti, B. *The church from the circumcision: history and archaeology of the Judaeo-Christians*, Publications of the Studium Biblicum Franciscanum, Smaller Series no. 2 (Jerusalem: Franciscan Printing Press, 1971).

Bauckham, R. 'The parting of the ways: what happened and why', *ST* 47 (1993), 135–51.

Baur, F. C. 'Die Christuspartei in der korinthischen Gemeinde, der Gegensatz der petrinischen und paulinischen Christenthums in der ältesten Kirche, der Apostel Petrus in Rom', *Tübinger Zeitschrift für Theologie* 4 (1831), 61–206.

Berger, K. *Die Gesetzesauslegung Jesu: ihr historischer Hintergrund im Judentum und im Alten Testament*, pt 1: *Markus und Parallelen*, WMANT 40 (1972).

Bernheim, P.-A. *James, brother of Jesus*, J. Bowden (trans.) (London: SCM Press, 1997).

Borg, M. *Conflict, holiness and politics in the teaching of Jesus* (New York: Mellen, 1984).

Brock, S. 'Jewish traditions in Syriac sources', *JJS* 30 (1979), 212–32.

Brown, R. E. *The churches the apostles left behind* (New York: Paulist, 1984).

—. 'Not Jewish Christianity and Gentile Christianity, but types of Jewish/Gentile Christianity', *CBQ* 45 (1983), 74–9.

Carleton Paget, J. 'The definition of "Jewish Christian/Jewish Christianity" in the history of research', in *A history of Jewish believers in Christ from antiquity to the present*, vol. 1, R. Hvalnik and O. Skarsaune (eds.) (Peabody, MA: Hendrickson, 2006).

—. 'Jewish Christianity', in *The Cambridge history of Judaism*, vol. III: *The early Roman period*, W. Horbury, W. D. Davies and J. Sturdy (eds.) (Cambridge: Cambridge University Press, 1999), 731–75.

Casey, M. *From Jewish prophet to Gentile God: the origins and development of New Testament Christology* (Cambridge: James Clarke & Co., 1991).

Daniélou, J. *The theology of Jewish Christianity*, J. A. Baker (trans.), Development of Christian doctrine before the Council of Nicaea 1 (London: Darton, Longman & Todd, 1964).

de Boer, M. C. *Johannine perspectives on the death of Jesus*, Contributions to biblical exegesis and theology 17 (Kampen: Kok Pharos, 1996).

—. 'The Nazoreans: living at the boundary of Judaism and Christianity', in *Tolerance and intolerance in early Judaism and Christianity*, G. N. Stanton and G. G. Stroumsa (eds.) (Cambridge: Cambridge University Press, 1998), 239–62.

Draper, J. A. 'Torah and troublesome apostles in the *Didache* community', in J. A. Draper (ed.), *The* Didache *in modern research*, AGJU 37 (1996), 340–63.

Dunn, J. D. G. 'The Colossian philosophy: a confident Jewish apologia', *Bib* 76 (1995), 153–81.

—. 'Jesus and ritual purity: a study of the tradition-history of Mark 7.15', in J. D. G. Dunn, *Jesus, Paul and the Law: studies in Mark and Galatians* (Louisville, KY: Westminster John Knox Press, 1990), 37–60.

—. *Jesus, Paul and the Law: studies in Mark and Galatians* (Louisville, KY: Westminster John Knox Press, 1990).

Fee, G. D. *The first epistle to the Corinthians*, NICNT (1987).

Ford, J. M. 'Was Montanism a Jewish-Christian heresy?', *JEH* 17 (1966), 145–58.

Frankfurter, D. 'Jews or not? Reconstructing the "other" in Rev 2:9 and 3:9', *HTR* 94 (2001), 403–25.

Georgi, D. *The opponents of Paul in Second Corinthians* (Philadelphia: Fortress, 1986).

Herford, B. A. *Christianity in Talmud and Midrash* (Clifton, NJ: Reference Book Publishers, 1966 (orig. 1903)).

Jervell, J. *Luke and the people of God: a new look at Luke-Acts* (Minneapolis: Augsburg, 1972).

—. *The theology of the Acts of the Apostles* (Cambridge: Cambridge University Press, 1996).

Jones, F. S. 'The Pseudo-Clementines: a history of research', *SecCent* 2 (1982), 1–33, 63–96.

Käsemann, E. 'Epheserbrief', *RGG*³ 2 (1958), 517–20.

Kimelman, R. '*Birkat ha-minim* and the lack of evidence for an anti-Christian Jewish prayer in late antiquity', in *Jewish and Christian self-definition*, vol. II: *Aspects of Judaism in the Graeco-Roman period*, E. P. Sanders, A. I. Baumgarten and A. Mendelson (eds.) (Philadelphia: Fortress, 1981), 226–44.

Klijn, A. F. J. *Jewish-Christian gospel tradition*, VCSup 17 (1992).

Kruse, H. 'Die 'dialektische Negation' als semitisches Idiom', *VT* 4 (1954), 385–400.

Lane, W. L. *Hebrews*, 2 vols., WBC 47AB (1991).

Laws, S. *A Commentary on the epistle of James*, HNTC (1980).

Loader, W. R. G. *Jesus' attitude towards the Law: a study of the gospels*, WUNT 2/97 (1997).

Luedemann, G. *Opposition to Paul in Jewish Christianity*, E. M. Boring (trans.) (Minneapolis: Fortress, 1989).

Malina, B. J. 'Jewish Christianity or Christian Judaism: toward a hypothetical definition', *JSJ* 7 (1976), 46–57.

Marcus, J. 'Authority to forgive sins upon the earth: the Shema in the gospel of Mark', in *The gospels and the scriptures of Israel*, C. A. Evans and W. Stegner (eds.), JSNTSup 104; SSEJC 3 (1994), 196–211.

—. 'The circumcision and the uncircumcision in Rome', *NTS* 35 (1989), 67–81.

—. 'James', in *The books of the Bible*, 2 vols., B. W. Anderson (ed.) (New York: Charles Scribner's Sons, 1989), vol. 1, 339–43.

—. 'The Jewish war and the *Sitz im Leben* of Mark', *JBL* 111 (1992), 441–462.

—. *Mark 1–8: a new translation with introduction and commentary*, AB 27 (2000).

Marjanen, A. '*Thomas* and Jewish religious practices', in *Thomas at the crossroads: essays on the* Gospel of Thomas, R. Uro (ed.) (Edinburgh: T&T Clark, 1998), 163–82.

Martyn, J. L. *The gospel of John in Christian history: essays for interpreters*, Theological Inquiries (New York: Paulist, 1978).

—. *History and theology in the fourth gospel*, 2nd ed. (Nashville: Abingdon, 1979).

Meier, J. P. *Law and history in Matthew's gospel: a redactional study of Mt. 5:17–48*, AnBib 71 (1976).

Overman, J. A. *Matthew's gospel and formative Judaism: the social world of the Matthean community* (Minneapolis: Fortress, 1990).

Painter, J. *Just James: the brother of Jesus in history and tradition*, Studies on personalities of the New Testament (Columbia: University of South Carolina Press, 1997).

Pancaro, S. *The Law in the fourth gospel*, NovTSup 42 (1975).

Petersen, W. L. 'The Diatessaron of Tatian', in *The text of the New Testament in contemporary research*, B. D. Ehrman and M. W. Holmes (eds.) (Grand Rapids, MI: Eerdmans, 1995), 77–96.

Pritz, R. A. *Nazarene Jewish Christianity from the end of the New Testament period until its disappearance in the fourth century*, StPB 37 (1988).

Riches, J. K. *Jesus and the transformation of Judaism* (London: Darton, Longman & Todd, 1980).

Riegel, S. X. 'Jewish Christianity: definitions and terminology', *NTS* 29 (1978), 410–15.

Rouwhorst, G. 'Jewish liturgical traditions in early Syriac Christianity', *VC* 51 (1997), 72–93.

Sanders, E. P. 'Jewish association with Gentiles and Galatians 2:11–14', in *The conversation continues: studies in Paul and John in honor of J. Louis Martyn*, B. R. Gaventa (ed.) (Nashville: Abingdon, 1990), 170–88.

Schiffman, L. H. 'At the crossroads: Tannaitic perspectives on the Jewish-Christian schism', in *Jewish and Christian self-definition*, vol. II: *Aspects of Judaism in the Greco-Roman period*, E. P. Sanders, A. I. Baumgarten and A. Mendelson (eds.) (Philadelphia: Fortress, 1981), 115–56.

Segal, A. F. *Two powers in heaven: early rabbinic reports about Christianity and gnosticism*, SJLA 25 (1977).

Shepherd, M. H. 'The gospel of John', in *The interpreter's one-volume commentary on the Bible*, C. M. Laymon (ed.) (Nashville: Abingdon, 1971), 707–28.

Sim, D.C. *The gospel of Matthew and Christian Judaism: the history and social setting of the Matthean community*, Studies of the New Testament and its world (Edinburgh: T&T Clark, 1998).

Simon, M. 'Réflexions sur le Judéo-Christianisme', in *Christianity, Judaism and other Greco-Roman cults: studies for Morton Smith at sixty*, 4 vols., J. Neusner (ed.), SJLA 12 (1975), vol. 3, 53–76.

Smith, D. M. 'The contribution of J. Louis Martyn to the understanding of the gospel of John', in *The conversation continues: studies in Paul and John in honor of J. Louis Martyn*, R. T. Fortna and B. R. Gaventa (eds.) (Nashville: Abingdon, 1990), 275–94.

Strecker, G. 'On the problem of Jewish Christianity', appendix 1 in *Orthodoxy and heresy in earliest Christianity*, W. Bauer (ed.) (Philadelphia: Fortress, 1972), 241–85.

ter Haar Romeny, R. B. 'Hypotheses on the development of Judaism and Christianity in Syria in the period after 70 CE', in *Matthew and the Didache: two documents from the same Jewish-Christian milieu?*, H. van de Sandt (ed.) (Assen: Van Gorcum; Minneapolis: Fortress, 2004), 1–21.

Visotzky, B. L. 'Prolegomenon to the study of Jewish Christianities in rabbinic literature', in B. L. Visotzky, *Fathers of the world: essays in rabbinic and patristic literatures*, WUNT 80 (1995), 129–49.

Westerholm, S. *Jesus and scribal authority*, ConBNT 10 (Lund: Gleerup, 1978).

Whittaker, M. *Jews and Christians: Graeco-Roman views*, Cambridge commentaries on writings of the Jewish and Christian world 200 BC to AD 200, vol. 6 (Cambridge: Cambridge University Press, 1984).

Wolthuis, T. 'Jude and Jewish traditions', *CTJ* 22 (1987), 21–45.

Wright, N. T. *The epistles of Paul to the Colossians and to Philemon: an introduction and commentary*, TNTC (1986).

Wyschogrod, M. 'Letter to a friend', *Modern theology* 11 (1995), 165–71.

5. Gentile Christianity

Margaret M. Mitchell

Bauckham, R. 'What if Paul had travelled east rather than west?' *BibInt* 8 (2000), 171–84.

Baur, F. C. *The church history of the first three centuries*, vol. 1, 3rd ed., A. Menzies (trans.) (London: Williams and Norgate, 1878).

—. *Paul, the apostle of Jesus Christ: his life and work, his epistles and his doctrine: a contribution to a critical history of primitive Christianity*, 2 vols., 2nd ed., A. Menzies and E. Zeller (eds. and trans.) (London: Williams and Norgate, 1875–6).

Becker, J. *Paul, apostle to the Gentiles*, O. C. Dean, Jr. (trans.) (Louisville, KY: Westminster John Knox, 1993).

Betz, H. D. *2 Corinthians 8 and 9*, Hermeneia (Philadelphia: Fortress, 1985).

—. *Antike und Christentum, Gesammelte Aufsätze*, vol. IV (Tübingen: Mohr Siebeck, 1998).

—. *Galatians*, Hermeneia (Philadelphia: Fortress, 1979).

—. 'The gospel and the wisdom of the barbarians', *Biblica* (forthcoming).

—. 'Mysterienreligion, II: Christlicher Kult und Mysterien. I. Urchristentum und Alte Kirche', *RGG*⁴ (2002), cols. 1640–2.

—. *Paulinische Studien, Gesammelte Aufsätze*, vol. III (Tübingen: Mohr Siebeck, 1994).

—. 'Religionsgeschichtliche Schule', *RGG*⁴ (2004), cols. 323–6.

Buell, D. K. and C. J. Hodge. 'The politics of interpretation: the rhetoric of race and ethnicity in Paul', *JBL* 123 (2004), 235–51.

Donaldson, T. L. *Paul and the Gentiles: remapping the apostle's convictional world* (Minneapolis: Fortress, 1997).

Dunn, J. D. G. *The Cambridge companion to St Paul* (Cambridge: Cambridge University Press, 2003).

Elliott, N. *Liberating Paul: The justice of God and the politics of the apostle* (Maryknoll, NY: Orbis, 1994).

Engberg-Pedersen, T. (ed.). *Paul beyond the Judaism/Hellenism divide* (Louisville, KY: Westminster John Knox, 2001).

—. (ed.). *Paul in his Hellenistic context* (Minneapolis: Fortress, 1995).

Fitzmyer, J. A. *Romans*, AB 33 (1993).

Fredriksen, P. 'Judaism, the circumcision of Gentiles, and apocalyptic hope, another look at Galatians 1 and 2', in *The Galatians debate*, M. D. Nanos (ed.) (Peabody, MA: Hendrickson, 2002), 235–60.

Gager, J. G. *Reinventing Paul* (Oxford: Oxford University Press, 2000).

Georgi, D. *The Opponents of Paul in 2 Corinthians* (Philadelphia: Fortress, 1986).

—. *Remembering the poor: the history of Paul's collection for Jerusalem* (Nashville: Abingdon, 1992).

Grant, R. M. *Paul in the Roman world: the conflict at Corinth* (Louisville, KY: Westminster John Knox, 2001).

Güttgemanns, E. *Der leidende Apostel und sein Herr: Studien zur paulinischen Christologie*, FRLANT 90 (1966).

Haenchen, E. *The Acts of the Apostles: a commentary*, B. Noble and G. Shinn (trans.) (Philadelphia: Westminster, 1971).

Hall, R. G. 'Circumcision', *ABD* vol. I, 1025–31.

Hays, R. B. *The faith of Jesus Christ: the narrative substructure of Gal 3:1–4:11*, rev. ed., The biblical resource series (Grand Rapids, MI: Eerdmans, 2001).

Hengel, M. *Between Jesus and Paul* (London: SCM Press, 1983).

Horsley, R. A. (ed.). *Paul and empire: religion and power in Roman imperial society* (Harrisburg, PA: Trinity Press International, 1997).

Johnson, L. T. 'Luke-Acts, book of', *ABD* vol. IV, 403–20.

Klein, G. 'Paul's purpose in writing the epistle to the Romans', in *The Romans debate*, K. P. Donfried (ed.), rev. ed. (Peabody, MA: Hendrickson 1991), 29–43.

Knox, J. *Chapters in a life of Paul*, rev. ed., D. R. A. Hare (ed.) (Macon, GA: Mercer University Press, 1987).

Lightfoot, J. B. *St Paul's epistle to the Galatians* (Peabody, MA: Hendrickson, 1993 (orig. 1865)).

—. *St Paul's epistles to the Colossians and Philemon* (Peabody, MA: Hendrickson, 1993 (orig. 1875)).

MacDonald, M. Y. *Early Christian women and pagan opinion: the power of the hysterical woman* (Cambridge: Cambridge University Press, 1996).

Martyn, J. L. *Galatians*, AB 33A (1997).

Meggitt, J. J. *Paul, poverty and survival* (Edinburgh: T&T Clark, 1998).

Mitchell, M. M. '1 and 2 Thessalonians', in *The Cambridge companion to St Paul*, J. D. G. Dunn (ed.) (Cambridge: Cambridge University Press, 2003), 51–63.

—. 'Paul's letters to Corinth: the interpretive intertwining of literary and historical reconstruction', in *Urban religion in Roman Corinth*, D. N. Schowalter and S. J. Friesen (eds.), HTS 53 (2005), 307–38.

Moessner, D. P. (ed.). *Jesus and the heritage of Israel: Luke's narrative claim upon Israel's legacy* (Harrisburg, PA: Trinity Press International, 1999).

Mount, C. N. *Pauline Christianity: Luke-Acts and the legacy of Paul*, NovTSup 104 (2002).

Munck, J. *Paul and the salvation of mankind*, F. Clarke (trans.) (London: SCM Press, 1959).

Ollrog, W.-H. *Paulus und seine Mitarbeiter: Untersuchungen zu Theorie und Praxis der paulinischen Mission*, WMANT 50 (1979).

Räisänen, H. *Jesus, Paul and Torah: collected essays*, D. E. Orton (trans), JSNTSup 43 (1992).

—. *Paul and the law* (Philadelphia: Fortress, 1983).

Riesner, R. *Paul's early period: chronology, mission strategy, theology*, D. Stott (trans.) (Grand Rapids, MI: Eerdmans, 1998).

Roetzel, C. J. *Paul: a Jew on the margins* (Louisville, KY: Westminster John Knox, 2003).

Sampley, J. P. *Pauline partnership in Christ: Christian community and commitment in light of Roman law* (Philadelphia: Fortress, 1980).

—. (ed.). *Paul in the Greco-Roman world: a handbook* (Harrisburg, PA: Trinity Press International, 2003).

Sanders, E. P. *Paul* (Oxford: Oxford University Press, 1991).

—. *Paul and Palestinian Judaism: a comparison of patterns of religion* (Philadelphia: Fortress, 1977).

—. *Paul, the Law and the Jewish people* (Philadelphia: Fortress, 1983).

Schüssler Fiorenza, E. *In memory of her: a feminist theological reconstruction of Christian origins*, 10th anniversary ed. (New York: Crossroad, 1994).

Scott, J. M. *Paul and the nations: the Old Testament and Jewish background of Paul's mission to the nations with special reference to the destination of Galatians*, WUNT 84 (1995).

Segal, A. F. *Paul the convert: the apostolate and apostasy of Saul the Pharisee* (New Haven: Yale University Press, 1990).

Smith, J. Z. *Drudgery divine: on the comparison of early Christianities and the religions of late antiquity* (Chicago: University of Chicago Press, 1990).

Stendahl, K. *Paul among Jews and Gentiles and other essays* (Philadelphia: Fortress, 1976).

Theissen, G. *The social setting of Pauline Christianity: essays on Corinth*, J. H. Schütz (ed. and trans.) (Philadelphia: Fortress, 1982).

Vollenweider, S. 'Paulus', *RGG*[4] 6 (2003), 1035–66.

Young, F. M. *The theology of the Pastoral Letters* (Cambridge: Cambridge University Press, 1994).

Young, F. M. and D. F. Ford. *Meaning and truth in 2 Corinthians* (London: SPCK, 1987).

Ziesler, J. A. *Pauline Christianity*, rev. ed. (Oxford: Oxford University Press, 1990).

6. Johannine Christianity

Harold W. Attridge

Anderson, P. N. *The Christology of the fourth gospel: its unity and disunity in the light of John 6*, WUNT 2/78 (1996).

Ashton, J. 'The identity and function of the *Ioudaioi* in the fourth gospel', *NovT* 27 (1985), 40–75.

— . *Understanding the fourth gospel* (Oxford: Clarendon, 1991).

Attridge, H. W. 'Genre bending in the fourth gospel', *JBL* 121 (2002), 3–21.

—. 'Gnosticism and apocalypticism: Valentinian and Sethian apocalyptic traditions', *JECS* 8 (2000), 173–211.

—. 'The restless quest for the Beloved Disciple', in *Early Christian voices in texts, traditions, and symbols: essays in honor of François Bovon*, D. H. Warren, A. Graham Brock and D. W. Pao (eds.), BIS 66 (2003), 71–80.

—. '"Seeking" and "asking" in Q, Thomas and John', in *From quest to Q: Festschrift James M. Robinson*, Jon Ma. Asgeirsson, K. de Troyer and M. W. Meyer (eds.), BETL 146 (2000), 295–302.

Bauckham, R. 'Qumran and the fourth gospel: is there a connection?' in *The scrolls and the scriptures: Qumran fifty years after*, S. E. Porter and C. A. Evans (eds.), JSPSup 26, Roehampton Institute London papers 3 (1997), 267–79.

Berger, K. *Im Anfang war Johannes: Datierung und Theologie des vierten Evangeliums*, 2nd ed. (Gütersloh: Gütersloher Verlagshaus, 2003).

Blank, J. *Krisis: Untersuchungen zur johanneischen Christologie und Eschatologie* (Freiburg im Breisgau: Lambertus, 1964).

Borgen, P. *Bread from heaven: an exegetical study of the concept of manna in the gospel of John and the writings of Philo*, NovTSup 10 (1965).

—. 'John 6: tradition, interpretation and composition', in *Critical readings of John 6*, R. A. Culpepper (ed.), BIS 22 (1997), 95–114, repr. in P. Borgen, *Early Christianity and Hellenistic Judaism* (Edinburgh: T&T Clark, 1996), 205–29.

—. *Logos was the true light, and other essays on the gospel of John* (Trondheim: Tapir, 1983).

Boyarin, D. 'The gospel of the Memra: Jewish binitarianism and the prologue to John', *HTR* 94 (2001), 243–84.

Brown, R. E. *The epistles of John*, AB 30 (1982).

—. *An introduction to the gospel of John*, F. J. Moloney (ed.) (New York: Doubleday, 2003).

—. 'The Paraclete in the fourth gospel', *NTS* 13 (1967), 113–32.

Bull, K.-M. *Gemeinde zwischen Integration und Abgrenzung: ein Beitrag zur Frage nach dem Ort der johanneischen Gemeinde(n) in der Geschichte des Urchristentums*, BBET 24 (1992).

Casey, M. *Is John's gospel true?* (London: Routledge, 1996).

Charlesworth, J. H. *The Beloved Disciple: whose witness validates the gospel of John?* (Valley Forge, PA: Trinity Press International, 1995).

—. 'A critical comparison of the dualism in 1QS 3:13–4:26 and the "dualism" contained in the gospel of John', in *John and the Dead Sea scrolls*, J. H. Charlesworth (ed.) (New York: Crossroad, 1990 (orig. *John and Qumran* (London: Chapman, 1972)), 76–106.

—. 'The Dead Sea scrolls and the gospel according to John', in *Exploring the gospel of John: in honor of D. Moody Smith*, R. A. Culpepper and C. C. Black (eds.) (Louisville, KY: Westminster John Knox, 1996), 289–300.

—. *Jesus and the Dead Sea scrolls: the controversy resolved* (New York: Doubleday, 1992).

Clark-Soles, J. *Scripture cannot be broken: the social function of the use of scripture in the fourth gospel* (Boston: Brill, 2003).

Countryman, L. W. *The mystical way in the fourth gospel: crossing over into God* (Philadelphia: Fortress, 1987).

Culpepper, R. A. (ed.). *Critical Readings of John 6*, BIS 22 (1997).

Daly-Denton, M. *David in the fourth gospel: the Johannine reception of the Psalms*, AGJU 47 (2000).

De Conick, A. D. *Seek to see him: ascent and vision mysticism in the gospel of Thomas*, VCSup 33 (1996).

Denaux, A. (ed.). *John and the Synoptics*, BETL 101 (1992).

Dodd, C. H. *The interpretation of the fourth gospel* (Cambridge: Cambridge University Press, 1953, 1968).

Duke, P. D. *Irony in the fourth gospel* (Atlanta: John Knox, 1985).

Dunderberg, I. *Johannes und die Synoptiker: Studien zu Joh 1–9*, Annales academiae scientiarum fennicae, Dissertationes humanarum litterarum 69 (Helsinki: Suomalainen Tiedeakatemia, 1994).

—. 'John and Thomas in conflict?' in *The Nag Hammadi library after fifty years: proceedings of the 1995 Society of Biblical Literature commemoration*, J. D. Turner and A. M. McGuire (eds.), NHMS 44 (1997), 361–80.

Fortna, R. T. *The fourth gospel and its predecessor: from narrative source to present gospel*, Studies in the New Testament and its world (Edinburgh: T&T Clark, 1989).

—. *The gospel of signs: a reconstruction of the narrative source underlying the fourth gospel*, SNTSMS 11 (1970).

Frey, J. *Die johanneische Eschatologie*, vol. I: *Ihre Probleme im Spiegel der Forschung seit Reimarus*; vol. II: *Das johanneische Zeitverständnis*; vol. III: *Die eschatologische Verkündigung in den johanneischen Texten*, WUNT 96, 110, 117 (1997, 1998, 2000).

Haenchen, E. *John 1: a commentary on the gospel of John chapters 1–6*, R. W. Funk (trans.), Hermeneia (Philadelphia: Fortress, 1984).

Junod, E. and J.-D. Kaestli. *Acta Iohannis*, 2 vols., CCSA 1–2 (1983).

Kangaraj, J. J. *'Mysticism' in the gospel of John: an inquiry into its background*, JSNTSup 158 (1998).

Koester, C. R. *Symbolism in the fourth gospel: meaning, mystery, community*, 2nd ed. (Minneapolis: Fortress, 2003).

Kysar, R. *John, the maverick gospel* (Atlanta: John Knox, 1976).

Lang, M. *Johannes und die Synoptiker: eine redaktionsgeschichtliche Analyse von Joh 18–20 vor dem markinischen und lukanischen Hintergrund*, FRLANT 182 (1999).

Martyn, J. L. *The gospel of John in Christian history: essays for interpreters* (New York: Paulist, 1978).

—. *History and theology in the fourth gospel*, rev. ed. (Nashville: Abingdon, 1979).

Matson, M. A. *In dialogue with another gospel? The influence of the fourth gospel on the passion narrative of the gospel of Luke*, SBLDS 178 (2001).

Meeks, W. 'Am I a Jew? Johannine Christianity and Judaism', in *Christianity, Judaism and other Greco-Roman cults: studies for Morton Smith at 60*, 4 vols., J. Neusner (ed.) (Leiden: Brill, 1975), vol. I, 163–86.

—. 'The man from heaven in Johannine sectarianism', *JBL* 91 (1972), 44–72, repr. in *Interpretations of the fourth gospel*, J. Ashton (ed.) (London: SPCK, 1986), 141–73.

—. *The Prophet-king: Moses traditions and the Johannine Christology*, NovTSup 14 (1967).

Menken, M. F. F. 'The Christology of the fourth gospel: a survey of recent research', in *From Jesus to John: essays on Jesus and New Testament Christology in honour of Marinus de Jonge*, M. de Boer (ed.), JSNTSup 84 (1993), 292–320.

—. *Old Testament quotations in the fourth gospel: studies in textual form*, CBET 15 (1996).

Miller, R. J. (ed.). *The complete gospels: annotated scholars version* (Sonoma, CA: Polebridge, 1994).

Minear, P. 'The original functions of John 21', *JBL* 102 (1983), 85–98.

Moloney, F. J. *The Johannine Son of Man*, 2nd ed., BSRel 14 (1978).

—. 'When is John talking about sacraments?' *ABR* 30 (1982), 10–33.

Morgan-Wynne, J. E. 'References to baptism in the fourth gospel', in *Baptism, the New Testament and the church*, S. E. Porter and A. R. Cross (eds.), JSNTSup 171 (1999), 116–35.

Nagel, T. *Die Rezeption des Johannesevangeliums im 2. Jahrhundert: Studien zur vorirenäischen Aneignung und Auslegung des vierten Evangeliums in christlicher und christlich-gnostischer Literatur*, AzBiG 2 (2000).

Neyrey, J. H. *An ideology of revolt: John's Christology in social-science perspective* (Philadelphia: Fortress, 1988).

Nickelsburg, G. W. E. *Resurrection, immortality and eternal life in intertestamental Judaism*, HTS 26 (1972).

O'Day, G. R. *Revelation in the fourth gospel: narrative mode and theological claim* (Philadelphia: Fortress, 1986).

Pagels, E. H. *Beyond belief: the secret gospel of Thomas* (New York: Random House, 2003).

Quast, K. *Peter and the Beloved Disciple: figures for a community in crisis*, JSNTSup 32 (1989).

Rebell, W. *Gemeinde als Gegenwelt: zur soziologischen und didaktischen Funktion des Johannese-vangeliums* (New York: P. Lang, 1987).

Riley, G. J. *Resurrection reconsidered* (Minneapolis: Fortress, 1995).

Robinson, J. A. T. *The priority of John*, J. F. Coakley (ed.) (London: SCM Press, 1985).

Schenke, H.-M. 'The function and background of the Beloved Disciple in the gospel of John', in *Nag Hammadi, Gnosticism and early Christianity*, C. W. Hedrick and R. Hodgson, Jr. (eds.) (Peabody, MA: Hendrickson, 1986), 111–25.

Schnelle, U. 'Johannes und die Synoptiker', in *The four gospels 1992: Festschrift Frans Neirynck*, 3 vols., F. van Segbroeck (ed.), BETL 100/1–3 (1992), vol. III, 1799–1814.

Schottroff, L. *Der glaubende und die feindliche Welt: Beobachtungen zum gnostischen Dualismus und seiner Bedeutung für Paulus und das Johannesevangelium*, WMANT 37 (1970).

Smalley, S. S. '"The Paraclete": pneumatology in the Johannine gospel and Apocalypse', in *Exploring the gospel of John: in honor of D. Moody Smith*, R. A. Culpepper and C. C. Black (eds.) (Louisville, KY: Westminster John Knox, 1996), 289–300.

Smith, D. M. *John among the gospels: the relationship in twentieth-century research* (Minneapolis: Fortress, 1992).

Taeger, J.-W. *Johannesapokalypse und johanneischer Kreis: Versuch einer traditionsgeschichtlichen Ortsbestimmung am Paradigma der Lebenswasser-Thematik*, BZNW 51 (1989).

Tobin, T. 'The prologue of John and Hellenistic Jewish speculation', *CBQ* 52 (1990), 252–69.

van Belle, G. *The signs source in the fourth gospel: historical survey and critical evaluation of the Semeia hypothesis*, BETL 116 (1994).

van der Horst, P. 'The birkat ha-minim in recent research', *ExpT* 105 (1994), 363–8.

van Wahlde, U. C. *The earliest version of John's Gospel: recovering the gospel of signs* (Wilmington, DE: Glazier, 1989).

—. 'The Johannine "Jews": a critical survey', *NTS* 28 (1981/2), 33–60.

7. Social and ecclesial life of the earliest Christians

Wayne A. Meeks

Aune, D. E. 'Worship, early Christian', *ABD* vol. VI, 973–89.

Bobertz, C. A. 'The development of episcopal order', in *Eusebius, Christianity and Judaism*, H. W. Attridge and G. Hata (eds.), StPB 42 (1992), 183–211.

—. 'Patronage networks and the study of ancient Christianity', in *StPatr* 24 (1993), 20–7.

Burridge, K. *New heaven, new earth: a study of millenarian activities*, The pavilion series: social anthropology (New York: Schocken, 1969).

Cancik, H. 'Lucian on conversion: remarks on Lucian's dialogue *Nigrinos*', in *Ancient and modern perspectives on the Bible and culture: essays in honor of Hans Dieter Betz*, A. Yarbro Collins (ed.) (Atlanta, GA: Scholars Press, 1998), 26–48.

Cerfaux, L. 'La multiplication des pains dans la liturgie de la Didachè: Did 9:4', *Bib* 40 (1959), 943–948.

Dahl, N. A. 'The crucified Messiah', in *Jesus the Christ: the historical origins of christological doctrine*, D. H. Juel (ed.) (Minneapolis: Fortress, 1991), 27–47.

—. 'The origin of baptism', in *Interpretationes ad Vetus Testamentum pertinentes Sigmundo Mowinckel septuagenario missae*, N. A. Dahl and A. S. Kapelrud (eds.) (Oslo: Land og kirke, 1955), 36–52.

Goodman, F. D. *Speaking in tongues: a cross-cultural study of glossolalia* (Chicago: University of Chicago Press, 1972).

Grant, R. M. 'The structure of eucharistic prayers', in *Antiquity and humanity: essays on ancient religion and philosophy presented to Hans Dieter Betz on his 70th birthday*, A. Yarbro Collins and M. M. Mitchell (eds.) (Tübingen: Mohr Siebeck, 2001), 321–32.

Gülzow, H. 'Die sozialen Gegebenheiten der altchristlichen Mission', in *Kirchengeschichte als Missionsgeschichte*, 2 vols., H. Frohnes and U. W. Knorr (eds.) (Munich: Chr. Kaiser, 1974), vol. I, 189–226.

Hatch, E. *The organization of the early Christian churches*, 4th ed. (London: Longmans, Green, 1892).

Kerényi, C. *Eleusis: Archetypal image of mother and daughter*, R. Manheim (trans.) (New York: Schocken, 1977).

Kittel, B. *The hymns of Qumran*, SBLDS (1981).

Klauck, H.-J. *Herrenmahl und hellenistischer Kult: eine religionsgeschichtliche Untersuchung zum ersten Korintherbrief*, NTAbh (1982).

Klauser, Th. and H. Strathmann. 'Aberkios', *RAC* I (1950), cols. 12–17.

Lifshitz, B. *Donateurs et fondateurs dans les synagogues juives: répertoire des dédicaces grecques relatives à la construction et à la réfection des synagogues*, Cahiers de la revue biblique 7 (Paris: J. Gabalda, 1967).

MacMullen, R. 'Peasants, during the principate', *ANRW* II.1 (1974), 253–261.

McLean, B. H. 'The Agrippinilla inscription: religious associations and early church formation,' in *Origins and methods: towards a new understanding of Judaism and Christianity: essays in honour of John C. Hurd*, B. H. McLean (ed.), JSNTSup 86 (1993), 239–70.

Meeks, W. A. 'Il cristianesimo,' in *Storia di Roma*, 4 vols., A. Momigliano and A. Schiavone (eds.) (Turin: Einaudi, 1992), vol. II.3, 283–319.

—. *The origins of Christian morality: the first two centuries* (New Haven: Yale University Press, 1993).

—. *In search of the early Christians: selected essays*, A. R. Hilton and H. G. Snyder (eds.) (New Haven: Yale University Press, 2002).

Murray, O. 'Symposium', *OCD*³ (1996), 1461.

—. 'Symposium literature', *OCD*³ (1996), 1461.

Mylonas, G. E. *Eleusis and the Eleusinian mysteries* (Princeton: Princeton University Press, 1961).

Neusner, J. *The idea of purity in ancient Judaism: the Haskell lectures, 1972–73*, SJLA 1 (1973).

Penn, M. 'Performing family: ritual kissing and the construction of early Christian kinship', *JECS* 10 (2002), 151–74.

Phillips, L. E. *The ritual kiss in early Christian worship* (Cambridge: Grove Books, 1996).

Poland, F. *Geschichte des griechischen Vereinswesens*, Preisschriften 38 (Leipzig: Teubner, 1909).

Reicke, B. I. *Diakonie, Festfreude und Zelos, in Verbindung mit der altchristlichen Agapenfeier* (Uppsala: Lundequistska bokhandeln, 1951).

Rydbeck, L. *Fachprosa, vermeintliche Volkssprache und Neues Testament: zur Beurteilung der sprachlichen Niveauunterschiede im nachklassischen Griechischen*, Studia Graeca Upsaliensia (Uppsala: Uppsala Universitetet, 1967).

Smith, D. E. *From symposium to eucharist: the banquet in the early Christian world* (Minneapolis: Fortress, 2003).

Vogliano, A. 'La grande iscrizione Bacchia del Metropolitan Museum: I', *AJA* 2nd series, 37 (1933), 215–31.

Wallace, A. F. C. 'Revitalization movements', *AmAnthr* 58 (1956), 264–81.

Waltzing, J.-P. *Étude historique sur les corporations professionnelles chez les romains depuis les origines jusqu'à la chute de l'empire d'occident*, Mémoires couronnés et autres mémoires publiés par l'Académie Royale (Brussels: Hayez, 1895–1900).

Weber, M. *The theory of social and economic organization*, A. M. Henderson and T. Parsons (eds. and trans.) (New York: Free Press, 1957).

Worsley, P. *The trumpet shall sound: a study of 'cargo' cults in Melanesia*, 2nd ed. (London: MacGibbon & Kee, 1968).

8. The Emergence of the Written Record

Margaret M. Mitchell

Achtemeier, P. J. 'The origin and function of the pre-Markan miracle catenae', *JBL* 91 (1972), 198–221.

Alexander, L. 'The living voice: skepticism towards the written word in early Christian and in Graeco-Roman texts', in *The Bible in three dimensions*, D. J. A. Clines, S. E. Fowl and S. E. Porter (eds.), JSOTSup 87 (1990), 221–47.

Baarda, T. *'De Christi scriptis'*: Jesus as author in early Christian literature', SNTS presidential address, 1 August 2001.

Bauckham, R. (ed.). *The gospels for all Christians: rethinking the gospel audiences* (Grand Rapids, MI: Eerdmans, 1998), 9–48.

Berger, K. 'Hellenistische Gattungen im Neuen Testament', *ANRW* II.25.2 (1984), 1031–1432.

Betz, H. D. *Essays on the Sermon on the Mount*, L. L. Welborn (trans.) (Philadelphia: Fortress, 1985).

—. 'Paul's "second presence" in Colossians', in *Texts and contexts: biblical texts in their textual and situational contexts. Essays in honor of Lars Hartmann*, T. Fornberg and D. Hellholm (eds.) (Oslo: Scandinavian University Press, 1995), 507–18.

—. 'The problem of rhetoric and theology according to the apostle Paul', in *L'Apôtre Paul: personnalité, style et conception du ministère*, A. Vanhoye (ed.), BETL 73 (1986), 16–48.

—. *The Sermon on the Mount: a commentary on the Sermon on the Mount, including the Sermon on the Plain (Matthew 5:3–7:27 and Luke 6:20–49)*, A. Yarboro Collins (ed.), Hermeneia (Minneapolis: Fortress, 1995).

Brown, R. E. *The gospel according to John*, 2 vols., AB 29–29A (Garden City, NY: Doubleday, 1966–70).

Burridge, R. A. *What are the gospels? A comparison with Graeco-Roman biography*, 2nd ed. (Grand Rapids, MI: Eerdmans, 2004).

Chance, J. B., R. F. Hock and J. Perkins (eds.). *Ancient fiction and early Christian narrative*, SBLSymS 6 (1998).

Elliott, J. K. (ed.). *The collected biblical writings of T. C. Skeat*, NovTSup 113 (2004).

Gamble, H. Y. 'The Pauline corpus and the early Christian book', in *Paul and the legacies of Paul*, W. S. Babcock (ed.) (Dallas: Southern Methodist University Press, 1990), 265–80.

Goodspeed, E. J. *A History of early Christian literature*, rev. ed., R. M. Grant (ed.) (Chicago: University of Chicago Press, 1966 (original 1942)).

—. *The meaning of Ephesians* (Chicago: University of Chicago Press, 1933).

Hays, R. B. *Echoes of scripture in the letters of Paul* (New Haven: Yale University Press, 1989).

Hengel, M. *Studies in the gospel of Mark*, J. Bowden (trans.) (Philadelphia: Fortress, 1985).

Klauck, H.-J. *Die antike Briefliteratur und das Neue Testament: ein Lehr- und Arbeitsbuch*, Uni-Taschenbücher 2022 (Paderborn: Schöningh, 1998).

—. *Apocryphal gospels: an introduction*, B. McNeil (trans.) (London: T&T Clark, 2003).

Kloppenborg, J. S. *The formation of Q: trajectories in ancient wisdom collections* (Philadelphia: Fortress, 1987).

—. *Q parallels: synopsis, critical notes, and concordance* (Sonoma, CA: Polebridge Press, 1988).

Kloppenborg Verbin, J. S. *Excavating Q: the history and setting of the sayings gospel* (Minneapolis: Fortress, 2000).

Koch, D.- A. *Die Schrift als Zeuge des Evangeliums: Unterschungen zur Verwendung und zum Verständnis der Schrift bei Paulus*, BHT 69 (1986).

Koester, H. *Synoptische Überlieferung bei den apostolischen Vätern*, TU 65, ser. 5, vol. x (1957).

MacDonald, D. R. *The Homeric epics and the gospel of Mark* (New Haven: Yale University Press, 2000).

Malherbe, A. J. *Ancient epistolary theorists*, Sources for biblical study 19 (Atlanta: Society of Biblical Literature, 1988).

Massaux, É. *The influence of the gospel of Saint Matthew on Christian literature before Saint Irenaeus*, N. J. Belval and S. Hecht (trans.), A. J. Bellinzoni (ed.), New gospel studies 5/1–3 (Macon, GA: Mercer, 1990–3; first French ed. 1950).

Metzger, B. M. *The text of the New Testament: its transmission, corruption and restoration*, 3rd enlarged ed. (New York: Oxford University Press, 1992).

Mitchell, M. M. 'Epiphanic Evolutions in Earliest Christianity', *Illinois Classical Studies* 29 (2004), 183–204.

—. 'Homer in the New Testament?' *JR* 83 (2003), 244–60.

—. 'Patristic counter-evidence to the claim that "The gospels were written for all Christians"', *NTS* 51 (2005), 36–79.

—. 'Rhetorik, I. Antike, 3. Christlich', *RGG*[4](2005), vol. 7.

Moessner, D. P. *Jesus and the heritage of Israel; Luke's narrative claim on Israel's legacy*, Luke the interpreter of Israel 1 (Harrisburg, PA: Trinity Press International, 1999).

Robinson, J. M., P. Hoffmann and J. S. Kloppenborg (eds.). *The critical edition of Q* (Minneapolis, MN: Fortress, 2000).

Sampley, J. P. (ed.). *Paul in the Greco-Roman world: a handbook* (Harrisburg, PA Trinity Press International, 2003).

Stanton, G. 'The early reception of Matthew's gospel: new evidence from papyri?' in *The Gospel of Matthew in current study: studies in memory of William G. Thompson, S. J.*, D. E. Aune (ed.) (Grand Rapids, MI: Eerdmans, 2001), 42–61.

Stowers, S. K. 'Does Pauline Christianity resemble a Hellenistic philosophy?' in *Paul beyond the Judaism/Hellenism divide*, T. Engberg-Pedersen (ed.) (Louisville, KY: Westminster John Knox, 2001), 81–102.

—. *Letter writing in Greco-Roman antiquity*, LEC 5 (1986).

Swain, S. 'Biography and biographic in the literature of the Roman empire', in *Portraits: biographical representation in the Greek and Latin literature of the Roman empire*, M. J. Edwards and S. Swain (eds.) (Oxford: Clarendon Press, 1997), 1–37.

Theissen, G. *The miracle stories of the early Christian tradition*, F. McDonagh (trans.) (Philadelphia: Fortress, 1983).

Trobisch, D. *Paul's letter collection: tracing the origins* (Minneapolis: Fortress, 1994).

Tuckett, C. M. *Q and the history of early Christianity: studies on Q* (Edinburgh: T&T Clark, 1996).

White, John L. *Light from ancient letters* (Philadelphia: Fortress, 1986).

9. Marcion and the 'Canon'

Harry Y. Gamble

Aalders, G. J. D. 'Tertullian's quotations from St Luke', *Mnemosyne* 5 (1937), 241–82.

Aland, B. 'Marcion: Versuch einer neuen Interpretation', *ZTK* 70 (1973), 420–47.

—. 'Marcion/Marcioniten', *TRE* 22 (1992), 89–101.

Balas, D. L. 'Marcion revisited: a "post-Harnack" perspective', in *Texts and testaments*, W. E. March (ed.) (San Antonio, TX: Trinity University Press, 1980), 95–108.

Barton, J. 'Marcion revisited', in *The canon debate*, L. M. McDonald and J. A. Sanders (eds.) (Peabody, MA: Hendrickson, 2002), 241–354.

Bellinzoni, A. J. *The sayings of Jesus in the writings of Justin Martyr*, NovTSup 17 (1967).

Bianchi, U. 'Marcion, théologien biblique ou docteur gnostique?' *VC* 21 (1967), 141–9.

Bienert, W. 'Marcion und der Antijudaismus', in *Marcion und seine kirchengeschichtliche Wirkung*, G. May and K. Greschat (eds.), TU 150 (2002), 191–205.

Blackman, E. C. *Marcion and his influence* (London: SPCK, 1948).

Bludau, A. *Die Schriftfälschungen der Häretiker: ein Beitrag zur Textkritik der Bibel*, NTAbh 11 (1925).

Bovon, F. 'The canonical structure of gospel and apostle', in *The canon debate*, L. M. McDonald and J. A. Sanders (eds.) (Peabody, MA: Hendrickson, 2002), 516–27.

Campenhausen, H. von. *The formation of the Christian Bible*, J. A. Baker (trans.) (Philadephia: Fortress, 1972).

Clabeaux, J. J. *A lost edition of the letters of Paul: a reassessment of the text of the Pauline corpus attested by Marcion*, CBQMS 21 (1989).

Cosgrove, C. H. 'Justin Martyr and the emerging Christian canon: observations on the purpose and destination of the Dialogue with Trypho', *VC* 36 (1982), 209–32.

Dahl, N. A. 'The origin of the earliest prologues to the Pauline letters', *Semeia* 12 (1978), 233–77.

Dassmann, E. *Der Stachel im Fleisch: Paulus in der frühchristlichen Literatur bis Irenäus* (Munster: Aschendorff, 1979).

Drijvers, H. J. W. 'Marcionism in Syria: principles, problems, polemics', *SecCent* 6 (1987–8), 153–72.

Dungan, D. L. 'Reactionary trends in the gospel producing activity of the early Church: Marcion, Tatian, Mark', in *L'évangile selon Marc: tradition et rédaction*, M. Sabbe (ed.), BETL 34 (1974), 179–201.

Finegan, J. 'The original form of the Pauline collection', *HTR* 49 (1956), 85–104.

Gager, J. G. 'Marcion and philosophy', *VC* 26 (1972), 53–9.

Graham, W. A. 'Scripture', *ER*, vol. XIII, 133–45.

Grant, R. M. 'Marcion and the critical method', in *From Jesus to Paul: studies in honor of Francis Wright Beare*, P. Richardson and J. C. Hurd (eds.) (Toronto: Wilfrid Laurier University Press, 1984), 207–15.

Gregory, A. *The reception of Luke and Acts in the period before Irenaeus: looking for Luke in the second century*, WUNT 2/169 (2003).

Hahneman, G. M. *The Muratorian fragment and the development of the canon*, OTM (1992).

Heckel, T. K. *Vom Evangelium des Markus zum viergestaltigen Evangelium*, WUNT 120 (1999).

Higgins, A. J. B. 'The Latin text of Luke in Marcion and Tertullian', *VC* 2 (1951), 1–42.

Kerschensteiner, J. *Der altsyrische Paulustext*, CCSO 315 (1970).

Kinzig, W. 'Kaine diatheke: the title of the New Testament in the second and third centuries', *JTS* 45 (1994), 519–44.

Knox, J. *Marcion and the New Testament: an essay in the early history of the canon* (Chicago: University of Chicago Press, 1942).

Lewis, A. S. *Catalogue of the Syriac MSS in the convent of St Catharine on Mt Sinai*, Studia Sinaitica 1 (London: Clay, 1894).

Lindemann, A. *Paulus im ältesten Christentum: das Bild des Apostels und die Rezeption der paulinischen Theologie in der frühchristlichen Literatur bis Marcion*, BHT 58 (1979).

May, G. 'Marcion in contemporary views: results and open questions', *SecCent* 6 (1987–8), 129–51.

—. *Schöpfung aus dem Nichts: die Entstehung der Lehre von der creatio ex nihilo*, AKG 48 (1978); ET: *Creatio ex nihilo: the doctrine of 'creation out of nothing' in early Christian thought*, A. S. Worrall (trans.) (Edinburgh: T&T Clark, 2004, 1994).

—. 'Der Streit zwischen Petrus und Paulus in Antiochien bei Markion', in *Von Wittenberg nach Memphis: Festschrift für R. Schwarz*, W. Homolka and O. Ziegelmeier (eds.) (Göttingen: Vandenhoeck & Ruprecht, 1989), 204–11.

May, G., and K. Greschat (eds.). *Marcion und seine kirchengeschichtliche Wirkung*, TU 150 (2002).

McDonald, L. M. and J. A. Sanders (eds.) *The canon debate* (Peabody, MA: Hendrickson, 2002).

Merkel, H. *Die Pluralität der Evangelien als theologisches und exegetisches Problem in der Alten Kirche* (Berne: Lang, 1978).

—. *Die Widersprüche zwischen den Evangelien: ihre polemische und apologetische Behandlung in der alten Kirche bis zu Augustin*, WUNT 13 (1971).

Nestle, E. *Einführung in das griechische Neue Testament*, 3rd ed. (Göttingen: Vandenhoeck & Ruprecht, 1909).

Norelli, E. 'Marcion: ein christlicher Philosoph oder ein Christ gegen die Philosophie?', in *Marcion und seine kirchengeschichtliche Wirkung*, G. May and K. Greschat (eds.), TU 150 (2002), 113–30.

Parker, D. *The living text of the gospels* (Cambridge: Cambridge University Press, 1997).

Petersen, W. L. *Tatian's Diatessaron: its creation, dissemination, significance and history in scholarship*, VCSup 25 (1994).

Regul, J. *Die antimarcionitischen Evangelienprologe*, Aus der Geschichte der lateinischen Bibel 6 (Freiburg: Herder, 1969).

Rensberger, D. 'As the apostle teaches: the development of the use of Paul's letters in second century Christianity' (Ph.D. dissertation, Yale University, 1981).

Schmid, U. 'Marcions Evangelium und die neutestamentlichen Evangelien: Ruckfragen zur Geschichte und Kanonisierung der Evangelienüberlieferung', in *Marcion und seine kirchengeschichtliche Wirkung*, G. May and K. Greschat (eds.), TU 150 (2002), 67–78.

Skeat, T. C. 'The oldest manuscript of the four gospels', NTS 43 (1997), 1–34, repr. in *The collected biblical writings of T. C. Skeat*, J. K. Elliott (ed.), NovTSup 113 (2004), 158–92.

Stanton, G. N. 'The fourfold gospel', NTS 43 (1997), 317–46.

Stendahl, K. 'The Apocalypse of John and the epistles of Paul in the Muratorian fragment', in *Current issues in New Testament interpretation*, W. Klassen and G. S. Snyder (eds.) (New York: Harper & Row, 1962), 239–45.

Stuhlhofer, F. *Der Gebrauch der Bibel von Jesus bis Euseb: eine statistische Untersuchung zur Kanongeschichte* (Wuppertal: Brockhaus, 1988).

Sundberg, A. C. 'Canon Muratori: a fourth century list', HTR 66 (1973), 1–41.

—. 'Toward a revised history of the New Testament canon', StEv 4; TU 102 (1968), 452–61.

West, H. P. 'A primitive version of Luke in the composition of Matthew', NTS 14 (1967), 75–95.

Williams, D. S. 'On Tertullian's text of Luke', SecCent 8 (1991), 193–9.

—. 'Reconsidering Marcion's gospel', JBL 108 (1989), 477–96.

Wilshire, L. E. 'Was canonical Luke written in the second century? A continuing discussion', NTS 20 (1974), 246–53.

Wilson, R. S. *Marcion: a study of a second century heretic* (London: Clarke, 1932).

Wilson, S. G. 'Marcion and the Jews', in *Anti-Judaism in early Christianity*, 2 vols., S. G. Wilson (ed.) (Waterloo: Wilfrid Laurier University Press, 1986), vol. II, 45–58.

Woltmann, J. 'Der geschichtliche Hintergrund der Lehre Markions vom "Fremden Gott"', in *Wegzeichen: Festgabe zum 60. Geburtstag von Prof. Dr. Hermengild M. Biedermann*, E. C. Suttner and C. Patock (eds.) (Würzburg: Augustinus, 1971), 15–42.

Zahn, Th. *Geschichte des neutestamentliche Kanons*, 2 vols. (Erlangen: Deichert, 1888–92).

—. 'Das Neue Testament Theodors von Mopsuestia und der ursprüngliche Kanon der Syrer', *NKZ* 11 (1900), 788–806.

10. Self-Definition vis-à-vis the Jewish Matrix

Judith Lieu

Becker, A. H. and A. Y. Reed (eds.). *The ways that never parted: Jews and Christians in late antiquity and the early middle ages*, TSAJ 95 (2003).

Borgen, P. *Bread from heaven: an exegetical study of the conception of manna in the gospel of John and the writings of Philo*, NovTSup 10 (1965).

Boyarin, D. *Border lines: the partition of Judaeo-Christianity*, Divinations (Philadelphia: University of Pennsylvania Press, 2004).

—. *Dying for God: martyrdom and the making of Christianity and Judaism* (Stanford: Stanford University Press, 1999).

Cohen. S. 'The rabbi in second-century Jewish society', in *The Cambridge history of Judaism*, vol. III: *The early Roman period*, W. Horbury, W. D. Davies and J. Sturdy (eds.) (Cambridge: Cambridge University Press, 1999), 922–90.

Dawson, J. D. *Christian figural reading and the fashioning of identity* (Berkeley: University of California Press, 2002).

Dunn, J. D. G. (ed.). *Jews and Christians: the parting of the ways AD 70 to 135*, WUNT 66 (1992).

—. *The partings of the ways between Christianity and Judaism and their significance for the character of Christianity* (London: SCM Press, 1991).

—. *The theology of Paul the apostle* (Grand Rapids, MI: Eerdmans, 1998).

Gager, J. G. *The origins of anti-semitism: attitudes towards Judaism in pagan and Christian antiquity* (Oxford: Oxford University Press, 1985).

Herz, P. 'Einleitung', in *Ethnische und religiöse Minderheiten in Kleinasien: von der hellenistischen Antike bis in das byzantische Mittelalter*, P. Herz and J. Kobes (eds.) (Wiesbaden: Harrassowitz, 1998), xiii–xx.

Horbury, W. *Jews and Christians in contact and controversy* (Edinburgh: T&T Clark, 1998).

Hruby, K. *Juden und Judentum bei den Kirchenvätern* (Zurich: Theologischer Verlag, 1971).

Jones, F. S. *An ancient Jewish Christian source on the history of Christianity: Pseudo-Clementine recognitions 1.27–71* (Atlanta: Scholars Press, 1995).

Krauss, S. *The Jewish-Christian controversy from the earliest times to 1789*, vol. 1: *History*, W. Horbury (ed. and rev.), TSAJ 56 (1995).

Levenson, J. D. *The death and resurrection of the beloved son: the transformation of child sacrifice in Judaism and Christianity* (New Haven: Yale University Press, 1993).

Lieu, J. M. *Christian identity in the Jewish and Graeco-Roman world* (Oxford: Oxford University Press, 2004).

Lim, R. *Public disputation, power, and social order in late antiquity*, TCH 23 (1995).

Lindars, B. *The theology of the letter to the Hebrews* (Cambridge: Cambridge University Press, 1991).

Ruether, R. *Faith and fratricide: the theological roots of anti-semitism* (New York: Seabury, 1974).

Schoedel, W. R. 'Ignatius and the archives', *HTR* 71 (1978), 97–106.

Schreckenberg, H. *Die christlichen Adversus-Judaeos-Texte und ihr literarisches und historisches Umfeld (1.–11. Jh.)*, 2nd ed., Europäische Hochschulschriften, ser. 23, Theology, vol. CLXXII (Frankfurt am Main: Lang, 1990).

Stroumsa, G. 'From anti-Judaism to antisemitism in early Christianity?', in *Contra Iudaeos: ancient and medieval polemics between Christians and Jews*, O. Limor and G. Stroumsa (eds.) (Tübingen: Mohr Siebeck, 1996), 1–26.

Taylor, M. *Anti-Judaism and early Christian identity: a critique of the scholarly consensus*, StPB 46 (1995).

Tomson, P. J. and D. Lambers-Petry. *The image of the Judaeo-Christians in ancient Jewish and Christian literature*, WUNT 158 (2003).

Tränkle, H. *Q. S. F. Tertulliani adversus Iudaeos* (Wiesbaden: Steiner, 1964).

Williams, A. L. *Adversus Judaeos: a bird's-eye view of Christian apologiae until the Renaissance* (Cambridge: Cambridge University Press, 1935).

11. Self-definition vis-à-vis the Graeco-Roman world

A. J. Droge

Andresen, C. *Logos und Nomos: die Polemik des Kelsos wider das Christentum*, AKG 30 (1955).

Armstrong, A. H. 'Pagan and Christian traditionalism in the first three centuries', in *Studia patristica XV: papers presented to the seventh international conference on patristic studies held in Oxford, 1975*, E. A. Livingstone (ed.), TU 128 (1984), 414–31.

Athanassiadi, P. and M. Frede (eds.). *Pagan monotheism in late antiquity* (Oxford: Clarendon Press, 1999).

Bader, R. *Der Alethes logos des Kelsos*, TBA 33 (1940).

Barnard, L. W. *Justin Martyr: his life and thought* (Cambridge: Cambridge University Press, 1967).

Borret, M. *Origène contre Celse*, 5 vols., SC 132, 136, 147, 150, 227 (1967–76).

Des Places, E. 'Platonisme moyen et apologétique chrétienne au IIᵉ siècle ap. J.-C.: Numénius, Atticus, Justin', in *Studia patristica XV: papers presented to the seventh international conference on patristic studies held in Oxford, 1975*, E. A. Livingstone (ed.), TU 128 (1984), 432–41.

Dillon, J. 'Monotheism in gnostic tradition', in *Pagan monotheism in late antiquity*, P. Athanassiadi and M. Frede (eds.) (Oxford: Clarendon Press, 1999), 69–79.

Droge, A. J. 'Apologetics, NT', *ABD* vol. I, 302–7.

—. 'Josephus between Greeks and barbarians', in *Josephus' Contra Apionem: studies in its character and context*, L. H. Feldman and J. R. Levison (eds.), AGJU 34 (1996), 115–42.

—. '"The lying pen of the scribes": of holy books and pious frauds', *Method & theory in the study of religion* 15 (2003), 117–47.

Edwards, M. J. 'The Constantinian circle and the *Oration to the saints*', in *Apologetics in the Roman empire: Pagans, Jews and Christians*, M. J. Edwards, M. Goodman, S. R. F. Price and C. Rowland (eds.) (Oxford: Oxford University Press, 1999), 251–75.

Edwards, M. J., M. Goodman, S. R. F. Price and C. Rowland (eds.), *Apologetics in the Roman empire: Pagans, Jews and Christians* (Oxford: Oxford University Press, 1999).

Gager, J. G. *Moses in Greco-Roman paganism*, SBLMS 16 (1972).

Geffcken, J. *Zwei griechische Apologeten*, Sammlung wissenschaftlicher Kommentare zu griechischen und römischen Schriftstellern (Leipzig: Teubner, 1907).

Goldhill, S. (ed.), *Being Greek under Rome: cultural identity, the second sophistic and the development of empire* (Cambridge: Cambridge University Press, 2001).

Goodenough, E. R. *The theology of Justin Martyr* (Jena: Frommann (Biedermann), 1923).

Hoffmann, R. J. *Celsus on the true doctrine: a discourse against the Christians* (New York: Oxford University Press, 1987).

Holte, R. 'Logos spermatikos: Christianity and ancient philosophy according to St Justin's Apologies', *ST* 12 (1958), 109–68.

Hyldahl, N. *Philosophie und Christentum: eine Interpretation der Einleitung zum Dialog Justins*, ATD 9 (1966).

Lapin, H. (ed.), *Religious and ethnic communities in later Roman Palestine* (Bethesda: University Press of Maryland, 1998).

Leclerq, H. 'Oracle', *DACL* 12 (1935–6), cols. 2225–6.

Lewis, B. *History: remembered, recovered, invented* (Princeton: Princeton University Press, 1975).

Momigliano, A. *Alien wisdom: the limits of Hellenization* (Cambridge: Cambridge University Press, 1975).

Murray, O. 'Hecataeus of Abdera and Pharaonic kingship', *JEA* 56 (1970), 141–71.

Osborn, E. F. *Justin Martyr*, BHT 47 (1973).

Pélagaud, E. *Un conservateur au second siècle: étude sur Celse et la première escarmouche entre la philosophie antique et le christianisme naissant* (Lyon: Georg, 1878).

Pépin, J. 'Le "challenge" Homère-Moïse aux premiers siècles chrétiens', *RSR* 29 (1955), 105–22.

Peterson, E. *Der Monotheismus als politisches Problem* (Leipzig: Hegner, 1935).

Pilhofer, P. *Presbyteron kreitton: der Altersbeweis der jüdischen und christlichen Apologeten und seine Vorgeschichte*, WUNT 2/39 (1990).

Waszink, J. H. 'Some observations on the appreciation of "The philosophy of the barbarians" in early Christian literature', in *Mélanges offerts à Mlle Christine Mohrmann*, L. J. Engels et al. (eds.) (Utrecht: Spectrum, 1963), 41–56.

Whittaker, J. 'Moses Atticizing', *Phoenix* 21 (1967), 196–201.

Wifstrand, A. 'Die wahre Lehre des Kelsos', *Bulletin de la Société Royale des Lettres de Lund 1941–42* 5 (1942), 391–431.

Zeitlin, Froma I. 'Visions and revisions of Homer', in *Being Greek under Rome: cultural identity, the second sophistic and the development of empire*, S. Goldhill (ed.) (Cambridge: Cambridge University Press, 2001), 196–266.

12. Self-differentiation among Christian groups: the gnostics and their opponents

David Brakke

Bianchi, U. (ed.). *Le origini dello gnosticismo: colloquio di Messina, 13–18 Aprile 1966*, SHR 12 (1970).

Bousset, W. *Hauptprobleme der Gnosis*, FRLANT 10 (1907, repr. 1973).

Brakke, D. 'The seed of Seth at the flood: biblical interpretation and gnostic theological reflection', in *Reading in Christian communities: essays on interpretation in the early church*, C. A. Bobertz and D. Brakke (eds.), CJA 14 (2002), 41–62.

Buell, D. K. *Making Christians: Clement of Alexandria and the rhetoric of legitimacy* (Princeton: Princeton University Press, 1999).

Bultmann, R. K. 'Der religionsgeschichtliche Hintergrund des Prologs zum Johannes Evangelium', in *Eucharisterion: Studien zur Religion und Literatur des Alten und Neuen Testaments*, 2 vols., H. Schmidt (ed.), FRLANT n.s. 19 (1923), vol. II, 3–26.

Dawson, D. *Allegorical readers and cultural revision in ancient Alexandria* (Berkeley: University of California Press, 1992).

Edwards, M. J. 'Neglected texts in the study of Gnosticism', *JTS* n.s. 41 (1990), 26–50.

Hanson, R. P. C. *Origen's doctrine of tradition* (London: SPCK, 1954).

King, K. L. *Revelation of the unknowable God*, California Classical library (Santa Rosa, CA: Polebridge, 1995).

Layton, B. 'Prolegomena to the study of ancient Gnosticism', in *The social world of the first Christians: essays in honor of Wayne A. Meeks*, L. M. White and O. L. Yarbrough (eds.) (Minneapolis: Fortress, 1995), 334–50.

—. 'The significance of Basilides in ancient Christian thought', *Representations* 28 (1989), 135–51.

Le Boulluec, A. *La notion d'hérésie dans la littérature grecque, IIe–IIIe siècles*, 2 vols. (Paris: Études Augustiniennes, 1985).

Logan, A. B. *Gnostic truth and Christian heresy* (Edinburgh: T&T Clark, 1996).

—. 'Gnosticism', in *The early Christian world*, 2 vols., P. F. Esler (ed.) (London: Routledge, 2000), vol. II, 907–28.

Lyman, R. 'Hellenism and heresy', *JECS* 11 (2003), 209–22.

Markschies, C. *Gnosis: an introduction*, J. Bowden (trans.) (London: T&T Clark, 2003).

—. 'Valentinian Gnosticism: toward the anatomy of a school', in *The Nag Hammadi Library after fifty years: proceedings of the 1995 Society of Biblical Literature commemoration*, J. D. Turner and A. M. McGuire (eds.), NHMS 44 (1997), 401–38.

McGuire, A. M. 'Valentinus and the *gnōstikē hairesis*: an investigation of Valentinus's position in the history of Gnosticism' (Ph.D. dissertation, Yale University, 1983).

Norris, R. A. 'The insufficiency of scripture: *Adversus haereses* 2 and the role of scripture in Irenaeus's anti-gnostic polemic', in *Reading in Christian communities: essays on interpretation in the early church*, C. A. Bobertz and D. Brakke (eds.), CJA 14 (2002), 63–79.

Rousseau, P. *Pachomius: the making of a community in fourth-century Egypt*, TCH 6 (1985).

Schenke, H.-M. 'The phenomenon and significance of gnostic Sethianism', in *The rediscovery of Gnosticism: proceedings of the international conference on Gnosticism at Yale, New Haven, Connecticut, March 28–31, 1978*, 2 vols., B. Layton (ed.), SHR 41 (1980–1), vol. II, 588–616.

—. 'Das sethianische System nach Nag-Hammadi Handschriften', in *Studia Coptica*, P. Nagel (ed.), Berliner byzantinistischer Arbeiten 45 (Berlin: Akademie Verlag, 1974), 165–73.

Sevrin, J.-M. *Le dossier baptismal séthien: études sur la sacramentaire gnostique* (Quebec: Presses de l'Université Laval, 1986).

Standaert, B. 'L'évangile de vérité: critique et lecture', *NTS* 22 (1976), 243–75.

Tabbernee, W. 'To pardon or not to pardon? North African Montanism and the forgiveness of sins', *StPatr* 36 (2001), 375–86.

Trigg, J. W. 'The charismatic intellectual: Origen's understanding of religious leadership', *CH* 50 (1981), 5–19.

Turner, J. D. 'Sethian Gnosticism: a literary history', in *Nag Hammadi, Gnosticism, and early Christianity*, C. W. Hedrick and R. Hodgson (eds.) (Peabody, MA: Hendrickson, 1986), 55–86.

—. *Sethian Gnosticism and the Platonic tradition*, Bibliothèque copte de Nag Hammadi, section études 6 (Quebec: Presses de l'Université Laval, 2001).

Turner, J. D. and R. Majercik (eds.). *Gnosticism and later Platonism: themes, figures, and texts*, SBLSymS 12 (2000).

von Staden, H. 'Hairesis and heresy: the case of the *haireseis iatrikai*', in *Self-definition in the Graeco-Roman world*, B. F. Meyer and E. P. Sanders (eds.) (Philadelphia: Fortress, 1982), 76–100.

13. Truth and tradition: Irenaeus

Denis Minns

Abramowski, L. 'Irenaeus, *Adv. haer.* III.3.2: ecclesia romana and omnis ecclesia; and ibid. 3.3: Anacletus of Rome', *JTS* 28 (1977), 101–4.

Aland, B. 'Fides und subiectio: zur Anthropologie des Irenäus', in *Kerygma und Logos: beiträge zu den geistesgeschichtlichen Beziehungen zwischen Antike und Christentum. Festschrift für Carl Andresen zum 70. Geburtstag*, A. M. Ritter (ed.) (Göttingen: Vandenhoeck & Ruprecht, 1979), 9–28.

Anatolios, K. *Athanasius: the coherence of his thought.* (London: Routledge, 1998).

Andia, Y. de. *Homo vivens: incorruptibilité et divinisation de l'homme selon Irénée de Lyon* (Paris: Études Augustiniennes, 1986).

Bacq, P. *De l'ancienne à la nouvelle Alliance selon s. Irénée: unité du livre IV de l'Adversus haereses* (Paris: Lethielleux, 1978).

Bengsch, A. *Heilsgeschichte und Heilswissen: eine Untersuchung zur Struktur und Entfaltung des theologischen Denkens im Werk 'Adversus haereses' des hl. Irenäus von Lyon*, Erfurter theologische Studien 3 (Leipzig: St Benno-Verlag, 1957).

Benoît, A. *Saint Irénée: introduction à l'étude de sa théologie*, Études d'histoire et de philosophie religieuses 52 (Paris: Presses Universitaires de France, 1960).

Berthouzoz, R. *Liberté et grâce suivant la théologie d'Irénée de Lyon: le débat avec la gnose aux origines de la théologie chrétienne*, Études d'éthique chrétienne 8 (Fribourg: Universitaires; Paris: Éditions du Cerf, 1980).

Blanchard, Y.-M. *Aux sources du canon: le témoignage d'Irénée*, Cogitatio fidei 175 (Paris: Éditions du Cerf, 1993).

Brox, N. *A history of the early church*, J. Bowden (trans.) (London: SCM Press, 1994).

—. *Offenbarung, Gnosis und gnostischer Mythos bei Irenäus von Lyon: zur Charakteristik der System*, Salzburger patristische Studien 1 (Salzburg: Pustet, 1966).

Congar, Y. M.-J. *Tradition and traditions: an historical and a theological essay*, M. Naseby and T. Rainborough (trans.) (London: Burns and Oates, 1966).

Donovan, M. A. *One right reading? A guide to Irenaeus* (Collegeville, MN: Liturgical Press, 1977).

Fantino, J. *La théologie d'Irénée: lecture des écritures en réponse à l'exégèse gnostique, une approche trinitaire* (Paris: Éditions du Cerf, 1994).

Jaschke, H.-J. *Der Heilige Geist im Bekenntnis der Kirche: eine Studie zur Pneumatologie des Irenäus von Lyon im Ausgang vom altchristlichen Glaubensbekenntnis*, MBT 40 (1976).

Joppich, G. *Salus carnis: eine Untersuchung in der Theologie des hl. Irenäus von Lyon*, Münsterschwarzacher Studien 1 (Münsterschwarzach: Vier-Türme-Verlag, 1965).

MacKenzie, I. M. *Irenaeus' Demonstration of the apostolic preaching: a theological commentary and translation* (Aldershot, Hants: Ashgate, 2002).

Minns, D. *Irenaeus*, Outstanding Christian thinkers (London: Geoffrey Chapman, 1994).

Orbe, A. *Antropología de san Ireneo*, BAC, seccion IV: Teológia y canones 286 (1969).

—. *Espiritualidad de san Ireneo*, Analecta gregoriana 256, series Facultatis theologiae, sectio A, no. 33 (Rome: Editrice Pontificia Università Gregoriana, 1989).

—. *Parábolas evangélicas en san Ireneo*, 2 vols., BAC 331–2 (1972).

—. *Teología de san Ireneo: comentario al libro v del 'Adversus haereses'*, 3 vols., BAC, Maior 25, 29, 33 (1985–8).

—. *Teología de san Ireneo IV: traducción y comentario del libro IV del 'Adverus haereses'*, BAC, Maior 53 (1996).

Osborn, E. F. *Irenaeus of Lyons* (Cambridge: Cambridge University Press, 2001).

Pagels, E. H. *The gnostic gospels* (New York: Random House, 1979).

Pyper, H. S. 'Irenaeus', in *The Oxford companion to Christian thought*, A. Hastings, A. Mason and H. S. Pyper (eds.) (Oxford: Oxford University Press, 2000), 328–9.

Seibt, K. *Die Theologie des Markell von Ankyra*, AKG 59 (1994).

Sesboüé, B. *Tout récapituler dans le Christ: christologie et sotériologie d'Irénée*, Collection 'Jésus et Jésus-Christ' 80 (Paris: Desclée, 2000).

Tremblay, R. *La manifestation et la vision de Dieu selon saint Irénée de Lyon*, MBT 41 (Münster: Aschendorff, 1978).

Wingren, G. *Man and the incarnation: a study in the biblical theology of Irenaeus*, R. Mackenzie (trans.) (Edinburgh: Oliver & Boyd, 1959).

14. The self-defining praxis of the developing *ecclēsia*

Carolyn Osiek

Balch, D. L. 'Household codes', in *Greco-Roman literature and the New Testament*, D. E. Aune (ed.), SBLSBS 21 (1988), 25–50.

—. 'Neopythagorean moralists and the New Testament household codes' in *ANRW* II 26.1 (1992), 380–411.

Barclay, J. M. 'Poverty in Pauline studies: a response to Steven Friesen', *JSNT* 26 (2004), 363–6.

Bobertz, C. A. 'The role of patron in the *cena dominica* of Hippolytus' *Apostolic tradition*', *JTS* 44 (1993), 170–84.

Boswell, J. *The kindness of strangers: the abandonment of children in western Europe from late antiquity to the Renaissance* (New York: Pantheon, 1988).

Corley, K. E. *Private women, public meals: social conflict in the synoptic tradition* (Peabody, MA: Hendrickson, 1993).

Countryman, L. W. *The rich Christian in the church of the early empire: contradictions and accommodations* (New York: Mellen, 1980).

Dixon, S. *The Roman mother* (Norman: University of Oklahoma Press, 1988).

Eyben, E. 'Family planning in Graeco-Roman antiquity', *Ancient society* 11 / 12 (1980–1), 5–82.

—. 'Fathers and sons', in *Marriage, divorce, and children in ancient Rome*, B. Rawson (ed.) (Canberra: Humanities Research Centre; Oxford: Clarendon Press, 1991), 114–43.

Garnsey, P. 'Sons, slaves – and Christians', in *The Roman family in Italy: status, sentiment, space*, B. Rawson and P. R. C. Weaver (eds.) (Canberra: Humanities Research Centre; Oxford: Clarendon Press, 1999), 101–21.

Glancy, J. A. *Slavery in early Christianity* (Oxford: Oxford University Press, 2002).

Hands, A. R. *Charities and social aid in Greece and Rome* (Ithaca, NY: Cornell University Press, 1968).

Harnack, A. von. *Militia Christi: the Christian religion and the military in the first three centuries*, D. M. Gracie (trans.) (Philadelphia: Fortress, 1981).

Harrill, J. A. 'The domestic enemy: a moral polarity of household slaves in early Christian apologies and martyrdoms', in *Early Christian families in context: an interdisciplinary dialogue*, D. L. Balch and C. Osiek (eds.) (Grand Rapids, MI: Eerdmans, 2003), 231–54.

Harris, W. V. 'Towards a study of the Roman slave trade,' *Memoirs of the American Academy in Rome* 36 (1980), 117–40.

Helgeland, J., R. J. Daly and J. P. Burns. *Christians and the military: the early experience* (Philadelphia: Fortress, 1985).

Madden, J. 'Slavery in the Roman empire: numbers and origins', *Classics Ireland* 3 (1996), 3–5.

Martin, D. B. 'Slave families and slaves in families', in *Early Christian families in context: an interdisciplinary dialogue*, D. L. Balch and C. Osiek (eds.) (Grand Rapids, MI: Eerdmans, 2003), 207–230.

Meggitt, J. *Paul, poverty and survival* (Edinburgh: T&T Clark, 1998).

Oakes, P. 'Constructing poverty scales for Graeco-Roman society: a response to Steven Friesen's "Poverty in Pauline studies"', *JSNT* 26 (2004), 367–71.

Osiek, C. *Rich and poor in the Shepherd of Hermas*, CBQMS 15 (1983).

—. 'Female slaves, *Porneia*, and the limits of obedience', in *Early Christian families in context: an interdisciplinary dialogue*, D. L. Balch and C. Osiek (eds.) (Grand Rapids, MI: Eerdmans, 2003), 255–74.

Ryan, E. 'The rejection of military service by the early Christians', *TS* 12 (1952), 1–32.

Saller, R. P. 'Corporal punishment, authority, and obedience in the Roman household', in *Marriage, divorce, and children in ancient Rome*, B. Rawson (ed.) (Canberra: Humanities Research Centre; Oxford: Clarendon Press, 1991), 144–65.

—. *Patriarchy, property, and death in the Roman family*, Cambridge studies in population, economy, and society in past time 25 (Cambridge: Cambridge University Press, 1994).

—. 'Roman kinship: structure and sentiment', in *The Roman family in Italy: status, sentiment, space*, B. Rawson and P. R. C. Weaver (eds.) (Canberra: Humanities Research Centre; Oxford: Clarendon Press, 1999), 7–34.

Tilley, M. 'The ascetic body and the (un)making of the world of the martyr', *JAAR* 59 (1991), 467–79.

Winter, B. W. *Roman wives, Roman widows: the appearance of new women and the Pauline communities* (Grand Rapids, MI: Eerdmans, 2003).

15. From Jerusalem to the ends of the earth

Margaret M. Mitchell

Barrett, C. K. *Freedom and obligation: a study of the epistle to the Galatians* (Philadelphia: Westminster, 1985).

Bauckham, R. *James: wisdom of James, disciple of Jesus the sage* (London: Routledge, 1999).

Chilton, B. and C. A. Evans. *The missions of James, Peter, and Paul*, NovTSup 115 (2005).

Conzelmann, H. *Acts of the Apostles*, Hermeneia (Philadelphia: Fortress, 1987).

Dibelius, M. *James*, rev. by H. Greeven, M. A. Williams (trans.), Hermeneia (Philadelphia: Fortress, 1976).

Dieterich, A. *Die Grabschrift des Aberkios* (Leipzig: Teubner, 1896).

Fitzmyer, J. A. *The acts of the apostles*, AB 31 (New York: Doubleday, 1998).

Haenchen, E. *The acts of the apostles*, B. Noble *et al.* (trans.) (Philadelphia: Westminster, 1971).

Hardwick, M. E. *Josephus as an historical source in patristic literature through Eusebius*, BJS 128 (1989).

Harnack, A. von. *Zur Abercius-Inschrift*, TU 12/4b (1895).

Hirshman, M. *A rivalry of genius: Jewish and Christian biblical interpretation in late antiquity*, B. Stein (trans.) (Albany: State University of New York Press, 1996).

Lüdtke, W. and T. Nissen. *Die Grabschrift des Aberkios: ihre Überlieferung und ihr Text*, Teubner (1910).

Merkelbach, R. 'Grabepigramm und Vita des Bischofs Aberkios von Hierapolis', *Epigraphica Anatolia* 28 (1997), 125–39.

Mitchell, M. M. 'Does the James ossuary bring us closer to Jesus?', *Sightings*, January 2003.

—. 'Grave doubts about the "James ossuary"' *Sightings*, June 2003.

Painter, J. *Just James: the brother of Jesus in history and tradition*, 2nd ed. (Columbia: University of South Carolina Press, 2004).

Schreckenberg, H. 'Josephus in early Christian literature and medieval Christian art', in *Jewish historiography and iconography in early and medieval Christianity*, H. Schreckenberg and K. Schubert (eds.), CRINT III/2 (1992), 7–138.

Shanks, H. and B. Witherington, III. *The brother of Jesus: the dramatic story and meaning of the first archaeological link to Jesus and his family* (San Francisco: HarperSanFrancisco, 2003).

16. Overview: the geographical spread of Christianity

Frank Trombley

Bedon, R. *Atlas des villes, bourgs, villages de France au passé romain* (Paris: Picard, 2001).

Finn, T. M. 'Mission and expansion', in *The early Christian world*, 2 vols., P. F. Esler (ed.) (London: Routledge, 2000), vol. 1, 295–315.

Gibbon, E. *The history of the decline and fall of the Roman empire*, 7 vols., J. B. Bury (ed.) (New York: AMS Press 1974, repr. of the 1909–14 ed.).

Gounares, G. G. *Eisagōgē stēn palaiochristianikē archaiologia*, vol. 1: *Architektonikē*, 2nd ed. (Thessalonike: University Studio Press, 2000).

Hefele, K. J. von (ed.). *A history of the councils of the church, from the original documents*, 5 vols. (New York: AMS Press, 1972; ET of *Histoire des conciles d'après les documents originaux*, 21 vols. (Hildesheim: Olms, 1973, orig. 1907)).

Holl, K. 'Das Fortleben der Volksprachen in Kleinasien in nachchristlicher Zeit', *Hermes* 43 (1908), 240–54.

Jones, A. H. M. *The later Roman empire, 284–602: a social, economic and administrative survey*, 2 vols. (Baltimore: Johns Hopkins University Press, 1986, orig. 1964).

Laskaris, N. G. *Monuments funéraires paléochrétiens (et byzantins) de la Grèce* (Athens: Les Éditions Historiques Stéfanos D. Basilopoulos, 2000).

Leyerle, B. 'Communication and travel', in *The early Christian world*, 2 vols., P. F. Esler (ed.) (London: Routledge, 2000), vol. 1, 452–74.

Reynaud, J.-F. *Lugdunum Christianum: Lyon du ivᵉ au viiiᵉ s.: topographie, nécropoles et édifices religieux*, Documents d'archéologie française 69 (Paris: Éditions de la maison des sciences de l'homme, 1998).

Segal, J. B. *Edessa, the 'blessed city'* (Oxford: Clarendon Press, 1970).

Thomas, C. *Christianity in Roman Britain to AD 500* (Berkeley: University of California Press, 1981).

Tibiletti, G. *Le lettere private nei papiri greci del iii e iv secolo d. C.: tra paganesimo e cristianesimo* (Milan: Vita e Pensiero, 1979).

Trombley, F. R. *Hellenic religion and Christianization, c.370–529*, 2 vols., Religions in the Graeco-Roman world 115, 1–2 (Leiden: Brill, 1993–4).

17. Asia Minor and Achaea

Christine Trevett

Alcock, S. E. (ed.). *The early Roman empire in the east* (Oxford: Oxbow Books, 1997).

—. *Graecia capta: the landscapes of Roman Greece* (Cambridge: Cambridge University Press, 1993).

Ando, C. *Imperial ideology and provincial loyalty in the Roman empire* (Berkeley: University of California Press, 2000).

Arnold, C. E. *The Colossian syncretism: the interface between Christianity and folk belief at Colossae*, WUNT 2/77 (1995).

—. *Ephesians, power and magic: the concept of power in Ephesians in light of its historical setting*, SNTSMS 63 (1989).

Bauer, J. B. *Die Polykarpbriefe*, KAV 5 (1995).

Bergren, T. A. *Sixth Ezra: the text and recensions* (Oxford: Oxford University Press, 1998).

Berger, K. 'Unfehlbare Offenbarung: Petrus in der gnostischen und apokalyptischen Offenbarungsliteratur', in *Kontinuität und Einheit: für Franz Mussner*, P.-G. Müller and W. Stenger (eds.) (Freiburg: Herder, 1981), 261–326.

Bienert, W. A. 'The picture of the apostle in early Christian tradition', *NTApoc*, vol. ii, 5–27.

Boatwright, M. T. *Hadrian and the cities of the Roman empire* (Princeton: Princeton University Press, 2000).

Bowe, B. E. *A church in crisis: ecclesiology and paraenesis in Clement of Rome*, HDR 23 (1988).

Bremmer, J. N. (ed.). *The apocryphal acts of Paul and Thecla* (Kampen: Kok Pharos, 1996).

Brent, A. 'Luke-Acts and the imperial cult in Asia Minor', *JTS* 48 (1997), 411–38.

Brown, C. T. *The gospel and Ignatius of Antioch* (New York: Lang, 2000).

Cadoux, C. J. *Ancient Smyrna: a history of the city from the earliest times to 224 A.D.* (Oxford: Blackwell, 1938).

Chow, J. K. *Patronage and power: a study of social networks in Corinth*, JSNTSup 75 (1992).

Conzelmann, H. *Gentiles, Jews, Christians: polemics and apologetics in the Greco-Roman era*, M. E. Boring (trans.) (Minneapolis: Fortress, 1992).

Davis, S. J. *The cult of Saint Thecla: a tradition of women's piety in late antiquity*, OECS (2001).

Denzey, N. 'What did the Montanists read?', *HTR* 94 (2001), 427–48.

Desjardins, M. 'Bauer and beyond: on recent scholarly discussions of *hairesis* in the early Christian era', *SecCent* 8 (1991), 65–82.

Dignas, B. *Economy and the sacred in Hellenistic and Roman Asia Minor* (Oxford: Clarendon Press, 2002).

Drijvers, J. W. and J. W. Watt (eds.). *Portraits of spiritual authority: religious power in early Christianity, Byzantium and the Christian orient*, RGRW 137 (1999).

Duensing, H. and A. de Santos Otero. 'The fifth and sixth books of Esra', *NTApoc*, vol. II, 641–652.

Duff, P. B. *Who rides the beast? Prophetic rivalry and the rhetoric of crisis in the churches of the apocalypse* (Oxford: Oxford University Press, 2001).

Edwards, D. R. *Religion and power: pagans, Jews, and Christians in the Greek east* (Oxford: Oxford University Press, 1996).

Eisen, U. E. *Women officeholders in early Christianity: epigraphal and literary studies*, L. M. Maloney (trans.) (Collegeville, MN: Liturgical Press, 2000).

Elm, S. '"Pierced by bronze needles": anti-Montanist charges of ritual stigmatization in their fourth-century context', *JECS* 4 (1996), 409–40.

Esler, P. F. *Galatians* (London: Routledge, 1998).

—. 'The Mediterranean context of early Christianity', in *The early Christian world*, 2 vols., P. F. Esler (ed.) (London: Routledge, 2000), vol. I, 3–25.

Ficker, G. 'Widerlegung eines Montanisten', *ZKG* 26 (1905), 447–63.

Fortna, R. T. and T. Thatcher. *Jesus in Johannine tradition* (Louisville, KY: Westminster John Knox 2001).

Freeman, P. *The Galatian language: a comprehensive survey of the language of the ancient Celts in Greco-Roman Asia Minor* (Lewiston, NY: Mellen, 2001).

Froehlich, K. 'Montanism and gnosis', *OrChrAn* 195 (1973), 91–111.

Geagan, D. J. 'Roman Athens: some aspects of life and culture, I. 86 B.C.–A.D. 267', *ANRW* II. 7.1 (1980), 371–437.

Gebhard, E. R. *The Isthmian games and the sanctuary of Poseidon in the early empire*, JRASup 8 (1993).

Gibson, E. L. 'Jewish antagonism or Christian polemic: the case of the *Martyrdom of Pionius*', *JECS* 9 (2001), 339–58.

Gill, D. W. J. and C. H. Gempf (eds.). *The book of Acts in its first century setting*, II: *The book of Acts in its Graeco-Roman setting* (Grand Rapids, MI: Eerdmans, 1994).

Goree, B. W. 'The cultural bases of Montanism' (Ph.D. dissertation, Baylor University, 1980).

Goulder, M. D. 'Ignatius' "docetists"', *VC* 53 (1999), 16–30.

—. 'A poor man's Christology', *NTS* 45 (1999), 332–48.

—. *A tale of two missions* (London: SCM Press, 1994).

Griffin, M. 'The Flavians', *CAH²*, vol. XI (2000), 1–83.

Hall, J. M. *Hellenicity: between ethnicity and culture* (Chicago: University of Chicago Press, 2002).

Hall, R. G. 'The *Ascension of Isaiah*: community situation, date and place in early Christianity', *JBL* 109 (1990), 289–306.

Hall, S. G. 'Aloger', *TRE* 2 (1978), 290–5.

—. 'The origins of Easter', *StPatr* 15.1 (1984), 554–67.

Harland, P. A. 'Christ-bearers and fellow-initiates: local cultural life and Christian identity in Ignatius's letters', *JECS* 11 (2003), 481–99.

—. 'Imperial cults within local cultural life: associations in Roman Asia', *Historia* 17 (2003), 85–107.

Harris, B. F. 'Bithynia: Roman sovereignty and the survival of Hellenism', *ANRW* II.7.2 (1980), 857–901.

Harrison, P. N. *Polycarp's two epistles to the Philippians* (Cambridge: Cambridge University Press, 1936).

Hartog, P. *Polycarp and the New Testament: the occasion, rhetoric, theme and unity of the epistle to the Philippians and its allusions to New Testament literature*, WUNT 2/134 (2002).

Hemer, C. J. *The letters to the seven churches of Asia in their local setting*, JSNTSup 11 (1986).

Hill, C. E. 'Cerinthus, Gnostic or chiliast: a new answer to an old question', *JECS* 8 (2000), 135–72.

—. 'The *Epistula apostolorum*: an Asian tract from the time of Polycarp', *JECS* 7 (1999), 1–53.

Hills, J. V. *Tradition and composition in the Epistula apostolorum*, HDR 24 (1990).

Horbury, W. *Jews and Christians in contact and controversy* (Edinburgh: T&T Clark, 1998).

Hovhanessian, V. *Third Corinthians: reclaiming Paul for Christian orthodoxy* (New York: Lang, 2000).

Horrell, D. G. 'Early Jewish Christianity', in *The early Christian world*, 2 vols., P. F. Esler (ed.) (London: Routledge, 2000), vol. I, 136–67.

—. *The social ethos of the Corinthian correspondence: interests and ideology from 1 Corinthians to 1 Clement* (Edinburgh: T&T Clark, 1996).

Horsley, G. H. R. 'The inscriptions of Ephesos and the New Testament', *NovT* 34 (1992), 105–68.

Hübner, R. M. 'Die antignostische Glaubensregel des Noët von Smyrna (Hippolyt *Refutatio* IX,10,9–12 und X,27,1–2) bei Ignatius, Irenaeus und Tertullian', *MTZ* 40 (1989), 279–311.

Hyvärinen, K. *Die Übersetzung von Aquila*, ConBOT 10 (1977).

Kaestli, J.-D., J.-M. Poffet and J. Zumstein (eds.). *La communauté johannique et son histoire: la trajectoire de l'évangile de Jean aux deux premiers siècles* (Geneva: Labor et Fides, 1990).

Kannengiesser, C. 'Arius and the Arians', *ThSt* 44 (1983), 456–75.

Knight, J. *The Ascension of Isaiah*, Guides to apocrypha and pseudepigrapha (Sheffield: Sheffield Academic Press, 1995).

—. *Disciples of the beloved one: the Christology, social setting and theological context of the 'Ascension of Isaiah'*, JSPSup 18 (1996).

Koester, H. 'ΓΝΩΜΑΙ ΔΙΑΦΟΡΟΙ: the origin and nature of diversification in the history of early Christianity', *HTR* 58 (1965), 280–318; repr. in H. Koester and J. M. Robinson (eds.), *Trajectories through early Christianity* (Philadelphia: Fortress, 1971), 114–43.

—. (ed.). *Ephesos, metropolis of Asia: an interdisciplinary approach to its archaeology, religion and culture* (Valley Forge, PA: Trinity Press International, 1995).

—. (ed.). *Pergamon: citadel of the gods* (Harrisburg, PA: Trinity Press International, 1998).

Körtner, U. H. J. *Papias von Hierapolis: ein Beitrag zur Geschichte des frühen Christentums*, FRLANT 133 (1983).

La Piana, G.. 'Foreign groups in Rome during the first centuries of the empire', *HTR* 20 (1927), 183–403.

—. 'The Roman church at the end of the second century', *HTR* 18 (1925), 201–77.

Lalleman, P. J. *The acts of John: a two-stage initiation into Johannine gnosticism*, Studies in the apocryphal acts of the apostles 4 (Leuven: Peeters, 1999).

Lechner, T. *Ignatius adversus Valentinianos? Chronologische und theologiegeschichtliche Studien zu den Briefen des Ignatius von Antiochien*, VCSup 47 (1999).

Levick, B., S. Mitchell, J. Potter and M. Waelkens (eds.). *Monumenta Asiae Minoris antiqua*, vol. x: *Monuments from the upper Tembris valley, Cotiaeum, Cadi, Synaus, Ancyra and Tiberiopolis recorded by C. W. M. Cox, A. Cameron and J. Cullen*, JRSM 7 (London: Society for the Promotion of Roman Studies, 1993).

Lindemann, A. *Paulus, Apostel und Lehrer der Kirche: Studien zu Paulus und zum frühen Paulusverständnis* (Tübingen: Mohr Siebeck, 1999).

Lohse, B. *Das Passafest der Quartodecimaner*, BFCT 2/54 (1953).

MacDonald, M. Y. *Early Christian women and pagan opinion: the power of the hysterical woman* (Cambridge: Cambridge University Press, 1996).

Macro, A.D. 'The cities of Asia Minor under the Roman imperium', *ANRW* II.7.2 (1980), 658–97.

Magie, D. *Roman rule in Asia Minor, to the end of the third century after Christ*, 2 vols. (Princeton: Princeton University Press, 1950).

Malina. B. J. 'Social levels, morals and daily life', in *The early Christian world*, 2 vols., P. F. Esler (ed.) (London: Routledge, 2000), vol. I, 369–400.

May, G., K. Greschat and M. Meiser (eds.). *Marcion und seine Kirchengeschichte*, TU 150 (2002).

McGinn, S. E. 'Internal renewal and dissent in the early Christian world' in *The early Christian world*, 2 vols., P. F. Esler (ed.) (London: Routledge, 2000), vol. II, 893–906.

Mitchell, S. 'The administration of Roman Asia from 133 BC–AD 250' in *Lokale Autonomie und römische Ordnungsmacht in den kaiserzeitlichen Provinzen vom 1. bis 3. Jahrhundert*, W. Ech (ed.), Schriften des historischen Kollegs Kolloquien, 42 (Munich: Oldenbourg, 1999), 17–46.

—. 'Ethnicity, acculturation and empire in Roman and late Roman Asia Minor', in *Ethnicity and culture in late antiquity*, S. Mitchell and G. Greatrex (eds.) (London: Duckworth, 2000), 117–51.

—. 'The life and *Lives* of Gregory Thaumaturgus', in *Portraits of spiritual authority: religious power in early Christianity, Byzantium and the Christian orient*, J. W. Drijvers and J. W. Watt (eds.), RGRW 137 (1999), 99–138.

—. 'The *Life* of St Theodotus of Ancyra', *AnSt* 32 (1982), 93–113.

Mueller, J. 'Anti-Judaism in the New Testament Apocrypha: a preliminary survey', in *Anti-Semitism and early Christianity*, C. A. Evans and D. A. Hagner (eds.) (Minneapolis: Fortress, 1993), 253–68.

Müller, C. D. G. 'Apocalypse of Peter', *NTApoc*, vol. II, 620–38.

—. 'Ascension of Isaiah', *NTApoc*, vol. II, 603–20.

—. 'Epistula apostolorum', *NTApoc*, vol. I, 249–84.

Müller, U. B. *Zur frühchristlichen Theologiegeschichte: Judenchristentum und Paulinismus in Kleinasien an der Wende vom ersten zum zweiten Jahrhundert nach Christ* (Gütersloh: Mohn, 1976).

Munier, C. 'Où en est la question d'Ignace d'Antioche? Bilan d'un siècle de recherches 1870–1988', *ANRW* II.27.1 (1993), 359–484.

Nörr, D. 'Zur Herrschaftsstruktur des römischen Reiches: Die Städte des Ostens und das Imperium', *ANRW* II.7.1 (1979), 3–20.

Orbe, A. 'Marcionitica', *Augustinianum* 31 (1991), 195–244.

Pagels, E. H. *The Johannine gospel in gnostic exegesis: Heracleon's commentary on John*, SBLMS 17 (1973).

Paulsen, H. 'Die Bedeutung des Montanismus für die Herausbildung des Kanons', *VC* 32 (1978), 19–52.

Pekáry, T. 'Kleinasien unter römischer Herrschaft', *ANRW* II.7.2 (1980), 595–657.

Perkins, J. 'The social world of the *Acts of Peter*', in *The search for the ancient novel*, J. Tatum (ed.) (Baltimore: Johns Hopkins University Press, 1994), 296–307.

—. *The suffering self: pain and narrative representation in the early Christian era* (London: Routledge, 1995).

Peterson, P. M. *Andrew, brother of Simon Peter: his history and legends*, NovTSup 1 (1958).

Prieur, J.-M. and W. Schneemelcher. 'The acts of Andrew', *NTApoc*, vol. II, 101–51.

Prigent, P. 'L'hérésie asiate et l'église confessante: de l'apocalypse à Ignace', *VC* 31 (1977), 1–22.

Prinzivalli, E. 'Gaio e gli Alogi', *Studi storico-religiosi* 5 (1981), 53–68.

Rapske, B. *The book of Acts and Paul in Roman custody*, The book of Acts in its first century setting 3 (Grand Rapids, MI: Eerdmans, 1994).

Rizakis, A.D. 'Roman colonies in the province of Achaia', in *The early Roman empire in the east*, S. E. Alcock (ed.) (Oxford: Oxbow Books, 1997), 15–36.

Robbins, V. K. *The tapestry of early Christian discourse: rhetoric, society and ideology* (London: Routledge, 1996).

Robbins, V. K., P. Borgen and D. B. Gowler (eds.). *Recruitment, conquest and conflict: strategies in Judaism, early Christianity and the Greco-Roman world*, Emory studies in early Christianity 6 (Atlanta: Scholars Press, 1998).

Schepelern, W. *Der Montanismus und die phrygischen Kulte: eine religionsgeschichtliche Untersuchung* (Tübingen: Mohr Siebeck, 1929).

Schmidt, C., P. Lacau and I. Wajnberg (eds. and trans.). *Gespräche Jesu mit seinen Jüngern nach der Auferstehung; ein katholisch-apostolisches Sendschreiben des 2. Jahrhunderts nach einem koptischen Papyrus des Institut de la mission archéol. française au Caire*, TU 43 (1919).

Schneider, P. G. 'The acts of John: the gnostic transformation of a Christian community', in *Hellenization revisited: shaping a Christian response within the Greco-Roman world*, W. E. Helleman (ed.) (Lanham, MD: University Press of America, 1994), 241–70.

—. *The mystery of the acts of John: an interpretation of the hymn and the dance in light of the acts' theology* (San Francisco: Mellen Research University Press, 1991).

Schoedel, W. R. 'Papias', *ANRW* II.27.1 (1993), 235–70.

—. 'Polycarp of Smyrna and Ignatius of Antioch', *ANRW* II.27.1 (1993), 272–358.

Scholer, D. M. (ed). *Gnosticism in the early Church* (New York: Garland, 1993).

Seibt, K. *Die Theologie des Markell von Ankyra*, AKG 59 (1994).

Siker, J. S. 'Christianity in the second and third centuries', in *The early Christian world*, 2 vols., P. F. Esler (ed.) (London: Routledge, 2000), vol. I, 231–57.

Slusser, M. 'Docetism: a historical definition', *SecCent* 1 (1981), 163–72.

Smith, T. V. *Petrine controversies in early Christianity: attitudes towards Peter in Christian writings of the first two centuries*, WUNT 2/15 (1985).

Spawforth, A. and P. Cartledge. *Hellenistic and Roman Sparta: a tale of two cities*, rev. ed. (London: Routledge, 2001).

Spawforth, A. and C. Mee. *Greece*, Oxford archaeological guides (Oxford: Oxford University Press, 2001).

Stewart-Sykes, A. 'The Asian context of the New Prophecy and of *Epistula apostolorum*,' *VC* 51 (1997), 416–38.

—. 'The original condemnation of Asian Montanism', *JEH* 50 (1999), 1–22.

Strecker, G. 'Chiliasmus und Doketismus in der johanneischen Schule', *KD* 38 (1992), 30–46.

Strobel, A. *Das heilige Land der Montanisten: eine religionsgeographische Untersuchung*, RVV 37 (1980).

—. *Ursprung und Geschichte des frühchristlichen Osterkalendars*, TU 121 (1977).

Sumney, J. L. 'Those who "ignorantly deny him": the opponents of Ignatius of Antioch', *JECS* 1 (1993), 345–65.

Syme, R. *Anatolica: studies in Strabo*, A. R. Birley (ed.) (Oxford: Clarendon Press, 1995).

Tabbernee, W. '"Our trophies are better than your trophies": the appeal to tombs and reliquaries in Montanist-orthodox relations', *StPatr* 31 (1997), 206–17.

—. 'Portals of the Montanist new Jerusalem: the discovery of Pepouza and Tymion', *JECS* 11 (2003), 87–93.

Tiessen, T. L. 'Gnosticism as heresy: the response of Irenaeus', in *Hellenization revisited: shaping a Christian response within the Greco-Roman world*, W. E. Helleman (ed) (Lanham, MD: University Press of America, 1994), 339–360.

Trevett, C. '"Angelic visitations and speech she had": Nanas of Kotiaeion', in *Prayer and spirituality in the early Church*, P. Allen, W. Meyer and L. Cross (eds.) (Everton Park, QLD: Centre for Early Christian Studies, Catholic University of Australia, 1999), vol. II, 259–77.

—. *Christian women and the time of the apostolic fathers (pre 160 C.E.): Corinth, Rome and Asia Minor* (Cardiff: University of Wales Press, 2005).

—. 'Spiritual authority and the "heretical" woman: Firmilian's word to the church in Carthage', in *Portraits of spiritual authority: religious power in early Christianity, Byzantium and the Christian orient*, J. W. Drijvers and J. W. Watt (eds.), RGRW 137 (1999), 45–62.

Trummer, R. *Die Denkmäler des Kaiserkults in der römischen Provinz Achaia*, University of Graz dissertation series 52 (Graz: Technische Universität Graz, 1980).

von Campenhausen, H. *Ecclesiastical authority and spiritual power in the church of the first three centuries*, J. A. Baker (trans.) (London: A. & C. Black, 1969).

Wagner, W. H. *After the apostles: Christianity in the second century* (Minneapolis: Fortress, 1994).

Walzer, R. *Galen on Jews and Christians* (London: Oxford University Press, 1949).

Weidmann, F. W. *Polycarp and John: the Harris fragments and their challenge to the literary tradition*, CJA 12 (1999).

Wilson, S. G. (ed.). *Anti-Judaism in early Christianity*, vol. II: *Separation and polemic*, Studies in Christianity and Judaism 2 (Waterloo: Wilfrid Laurier University Press, 1986).

Winter, B. W. *After Paul left Corinth: the influence of secular ethics and social change* (Grand Rapids, MI: Eerdmans, 2001).

Winter, B. W. and Clarke, A. D. (eds.). *The book of Acts in its ancient literary setting*, The book of Acts in its first century setting 1 (Grand Rapids, MI: Eerdmans, 1993).

Wiseman, J. 'Corinth and Rome I: 228 B.C.–A.D. 267', *ANRW* II.7.1 (1979), 438–548.

Wisse, F. 'The use of early Christian literature as evidence for inner diversity and conflict', in *Nag Hammadi, gnosticism and early Christianity*, C. W. Hedrick and R. Hodgson, Jr. (eds.) (Peabody, MA: Hendricksen, 1986), 177–90; repr. in *Gnosticism in the early church*, D. M. Scholer (ed.) (New York: Garland, 1993), 365–78.

Woll, D. B. *Johannine Christianity in conflict*, SBLDS 60 (1981).

Wright, B. G., III. 'Cerinthus *apud* Hippolytus: an inquiry into the traditions about Cerinthus' provenance', *SecCent* 4 (1984), 103–15.

Young, F. M. 'Greek apologists of the second century', in *Apologetics in the Roman empire: pagans, Jews, and Christians*, M. J. Edwards, M. Goodman, S. R. F. Price and C. Rowland (eds.) (Oxford: Oxford University Press, 1999), 81–104.

18. Egypt

Birger A. Pearson

Adriani, A. (ed.). *Repertorio d'arte dell'Egitto greco-romano*, ser. C, vols. I (text) and II (tables) (Palermo: Fondazione 'Ignazio Mormino' del Banco di Sicilia, 1966).

Alexandrie: une mégapole cosmopolite: Actes du 9ème colloque de la Villa Kérylos à Beaulieu-sur-Mer les 2 & 3 octobre 1998 (Paris: Academie des Inscriptions et Belles-Lettres, 1999).

Alexandrina: hellénisme, judaïsme et christianisme à Alexandrie. Mélanges offerts au P. Claude Mondésert (Paris: Éditions du Cerf, 1987).

Bardy, G. 'Aux origines de l'école d'Alexandrie', *RSR* 27 (1937), 65–90.

Bowman, Alan K. *Egypt after the Pharaohs, 332 BC–AD 642* (Berkeley: University of California Press, 1986).

Brown, S. Kent. 'Coptic and Greek inscriptions from Christian Egypt: a brief review', in *The roots of Egyptian Christianity*, B. A. Pearson and J. E. Goehring (eds.) (Minneapolis: Fortress, 1992), 26–41.

Calderini, A. *Dizionario dei nomi geografici dell'Egitto greco-romane*, vol. I, fasc. I: *Alexandreia* (Milan: Cisalpino-Golardica, 1935).

Camplani, A. 'Sulla trasmissione di testi gnostici in copto', in *L'Egitto cristiano: aspetti e problemi in età tardo-antica*, A. Camplani (ed.), SEAug 56 (1997), 121–75.

Chauveau, M. 'Alexandrie et Rhakotis: le point de vue des Égyptiens', in *Alexandrie: une mégapole cosmopolite: Actes du 9ème colloque de la Villa Kérylos à Beaulieu-sur-Mer les 2 & 3 octobre 1998* (Paris: Academie des Inscriptions et Belles-Lettres, 1999), 1–10.

Dorival, G. 'Les débuts du christianisme à Alexandrie', in *Alexandrie: Une mégapole cosmopolite: Actes du 9ème colloque de la Villa Kérylos à Beaulieu-sur-Mer les 2 & 3 octobre 1998* (Paris: Academie des Inscriptions et Belles-Lettres, 1999), 157–74.

Emmel, S. 'Coptic language', *ABD* vol. IV, 180–8.

Empereur, J.-Y. *Alexandria rediscovered*, M. Maehler (trans.) (New York: Braziller, 1998).

Frankfurter, D. *Religion in Roman Egypt: assimilation and resistance* (Princeton: Princeton University Press, 1998).

Fraser, P. M. *Ptolemaic Alexandria*, 3 vols. (Oxford: Clarendon, 1972).

Godlewski, W. (ed.), *Coptic studies: acts of the third international congress of Coptic studies, Warsaw, 20–25 August 1984* (Warsaw: PWN- Éditions Scientifiques de Pologne, 1990).

Goehring, J. E. *Ascetics, society, and the desert: studies in early Egyptian monasticism* (Harrisburg, PA: Trinity Press International, 1999).

Griggs, C. W. 'Excavating a Christian cemetery near Seila in the Fayum region of Egypt', in *Coptic studies: acts of the third international congress of Coptic studies, Warsaw, 20–25 August 1984*, W. Godlewski (ed.) (Warsaw: PWN- Éditions Scientifiques de Pologne, 1990), 145–50.

Haas, C. *Alexandria in late antiquity: topography and social conflict* (Baltimore: Johns Hopkins University Press, 1997).

Jakab, A. *Ecclesia alexandrina: evolution sociale et institutionnelle du christianisme alexandrin (IIᵉ et IIIᵉ siècles)* (Bern: Lang, 2001).

Judge, E. A. 'The earliest use of monachos for "Monk" (*P. Coll. Youtie* 77) and the origins of monasticism', *JAC* 20 (1977), 72–89.

Judge, E. A. and S. R. Pickering. 'Papyrus documentation of church and community in Egypt to the mid-fourth century', *JAC* 20 (1977), 47–71.

Kemp, E. W. 'Bishops and presbyters at Alexandria', *JEH* 6 (1955), 125–42.

Meinardus, O. *Christian Egypt, ancient and modern*, 2nd ed. (Cairo: American University in Cairo Press, 1977).

Pearson, B. A. 'Alexandria', in E. M. Meyers (ed.), *The Oxford encyclopedia of archaeology in the Near East*, 5 vols. (Oxford: Oxford University Press, 1997), vol. I, 65–9.

—. 'Basilides the gnostic', in *A companion to second-century Christian 'heretics'*, A. Marjanen and P. Luomanen (eds.), VCSup 76 (2005).

—. 'Christianity in Egypt', *ABD* vol. I, 954–60.

—. 'Cracking a conundrum: Christian origins in Egypt', *ST* 57 (2003), 61–75.

—. 'Earliest Christianity in Egypt: some observations', in *The roots of Egyptian Christianity*, B. A. Pearson and J. E. Goehring (eds.) (Minneapolis: Fortress, 1990), 132–59.

—. *The emergence of the Christian religion: essays on early Christianity* (Harrisburg, PA: Trinity Press International, 1997).

—. *Gnosticism and Christianity in Roman and Coptic Egypt* (London: T&T Clark International, 2004).

—. 'On Rodney Stark's foray into early Christian history', *Religion* 19 (1999), 171–6.

—. 'Pre-Valentinian gnosticism in Alexandria', in *The future of early Christianity: essays in honor of Helmut Koester*, B. A. Pearson (ed.) (Minneapolis: Fortress, 1990), 455–66.

Pearson, B. A. and J. Goehring (eds.). *The roots of Egyptian Christianity* (Minneapolis: Fortress, 1990).

Ritter, A. M. 'De Polycarpe à Clement: aux origines d'Alexandrie chrétienne', in *Alexandrina: hellénisme, judaisme et christianisme à Alexandrie. Mélanges offerts au P. Claude Mondésert* (Paris: Éditions du Cerf, 1987), 151–72.

Roberts, C. H. (ed.), *Catalogue of the Greek and Latin papyri in the John Rylands library*, 3 vols. (Manchester: Manchester University Press, 1938).

Scholer, D. 'Bibliographia gnostica: supplementum II/1', *NovT* 40 (1998), 73–100.

—. *Nag Hammadi bibliography 1948–1969*, NHS 1 (1971).

—. *Nag Hammadi Bibliography 1970–94*, NHMS 32 (1997).

Starobinsky-Safran, E. 'La communauté juive d'Alexandrie à l'époque de Philon', in *Alexandrina: hellénisme, judaïsme et christianisme à Alexandrie. Mélanges offerts au P. Claude Mondésert* (Paris: Éditions du Cerf, 1987), 45–75.

Stroumsa, G. G. 'The Manichaean challenge to Egyptian Christianity', in *The roots of Egyptian Christianity*, B. A. Pearson and J. E. Goehring (eds.) (Minneapolis: Fortress, 1990), 307–19.

Telfer, W. 'Episcopal succession in Egypt', *JEH* 3 (1952), 1–13.

Tkaczow, B. 'Archaeological sources for the earliest churches in Alexandria', in *Coptic studies: acts of the third international congress of Coptic studies, Warsaw, 20–25 August 1984*, W. Godlewski (ed.) (Warsaw: PWN- Éditions Scientifiques de Pologne, 1990), 431–5.

—. *Topography of ancient Alexandria (an archeological map)*, Travaux du Centre d'Archéologie mediterranéenne de l'Academie polonaise des Sciences 32 (Warsaw: PWN- Éditions Scientifiques de Pologne, 1993).

van den Broek, R. 'The *Authentikos logos*: a new document of Christian Platonism', in R. van den Broek, *Studies in gnosticism and Alexandrian Christianity*, NHMS 39 (1996), 206–34.

—. 'The Christian "school" of Alexandria in the second and third centuries', in R. van den Broek, *Studies in gnosticism and Alexandrian Christianity*, NHMS 39 (1996), 197–205.

—. 'Jewish and Platonic speculations in early Alexandrian theology: Eugnostos, Philo, Valentinus, Origen', in R. van den Broek, *Studies in gnosticism and Alexandrian Christianity*, NHMS 39 (1996), 117–30.

—. 'Juden und Christen in Alexandrien im 1. und 3. Jahrhundert', in R. van den Broek, *Studies in gnosticism and Alexandrian Christianity*, NHMS 39 (1996), 181–96.

—. *Studies in gnosticism and Alexandrian Christianity*, NHMS 39 (1996).

van den Hoek, A. 'The "Catechetical" school of early Christian Alexandria and its Philonic heritage', *HTR* 90 (1997), 59–87.

—. *Clement of Alexandria and his use of Philo in the* Stromateis: *an early Christian reshaping of a Jewish model*, VCSup 3 (1988).

—. 'How Alexandrian was Clement of Alexandria? Reflections on Clement and his Alexandrian background', *HeyJ* 31 (1990), 179–94.

van der Horst, P. W. and J. Mansfeld. *An Alexandrian Platonist against dualism: Alexander of Lycopolis' treatise 'Critique of the doctrines of Manichaeus'* (Leiden: Brill, 1974).

van Haelst, J. *Catalogue des papyrus littéraires juifs et chrétiens* (Paris: Sorbonne, 1976).

19. Syria and Mesopotamia

Susan Ashbrook Harvey

Aune, D. E. *The cultic setting of realized eschatology in early Christianity, NovTSup* 28 (1972).

BeDuhn, J. *The Manichaean body in discipline and ritual* (Baltimore: Johns Hopkins University Press, 2000).

Behr, J. *The way to Nicaea: The formation of Christian theology*, vol 1 (Crestwood, NY: St Vladimir's Seminary Press, 2001).

Brock, S. P. 'The Baptist's diet in Syriac sources', *OrChr* 54 (1970), 113–24.

—. 'Christians in the Sasanid empire: a case of divided loyalties', in S. P. Brock, *Syriac perspectives on late antiquity* (London: Variorum Reprints, 1984), ch. 6.

—. 'Eusebius and Syriac Christianity', in *Eusebius, Christianity and Judaism*, H. W. Attridge and G. Hata (eds.), StPB 42 (1992), 212–34.

—. 'Greek and Syriac in late antique Syria', in *Literacy and power in the ancient world*, A. K. Bowman and G. Woolf (eds.) (Cambridge: Cambridge University Press, 1994), 149–60.

—. 'A martyr at the Sasanid court under Vahran II: Candida', *AnBoll* 96 (1978), 167–81.

—. 'What's in a word? An intriguing choice in the Syriac *Diatessaron*', in *Understanding, studying and reading: New Testament essays in honour of John Ashton*, C. Rowland and C. H. T. Fletcher-Louis (eds.), JSNTSup 153 (1998), 180–7.

Caner, D. *Wandering, begging monks: spiritual authority and the promotion of monasticism in late antiquity*, TCH 33 (1998).

Doran, R. 'The martyrdom of Habbib the deacon', in *Religions of late antiquity in practice*, R. Valantasis (ed.) (Princeton: Princeton University Press, 2000), 413–23.

Drijvers, H. J. W. *Bardaisan of Edessa* (Assen: Van Gorcum, 1966).

—. *Cults and beliefs at Edessa*, EPRO 82 (1980).

—. *East of Antioch: studies in early Syriac Christianity* (London: Variorum, Reprints, 1984).

Griffith, S. H. 'Asceticism in the church of Syria: the hermeneutics of early Syrian monasticism', in *Asceticism*, V. L. Wimbush and R. Valantasis (eds.) (New York: Oxford University Press, 1995), 220–45.

—. 'The *Doctrina Addai* as a paradigm of Christian thought in Edessa in the fifth century', *Hugoye: Journal of Syriac Studies* 6.2 (July 2003).

Harvey, S. A. 'The Edessan martyrs and ascetic tradition', in *Symposium Syriacum V, 1988: Katholieke Universiteit, Leuven, 29–31 août 1988*, R. Lavenant (ed.), OrChrAn 236 (1990), 95–206.

—. 'Feminine imagery for the divine: the Holy Spirit, the *Odes of Solomon* and early Syriac tradition', *SVTQ* 37 (1993), 111–39.

—. 'Women's service in ancient Syriac Christianity', in *Mutter, Nonne, Diakonin: Frauenbilder im Recht der Ostkirchen*, Kanon 16 (2001), 226–41.

Jefford, C. N. (ed.). *The Didache in context: essays on its text, history and transmission*, NovTSup 77 (1995).

Meeks, W. A. and R. L. Wilken. *Jews and Christians in Antioch in the first four centuries of the Common Era*, SBLSBS 13 (1978).

Murray, R. *Symbols of church and kingdom: a study in early Syriac tradition* (Cambridge: Cambridge University Press, 1975; rev. ed. Piscataway, NJ: Gorgias, 2004).

Peppermüller, R. 'Griechische Papyrusfragmente der Doctrina Addai', *VC* 25 (1971), 289–301.

Ross, S. K. *Roman Edessa: politics and culture on the eastern fringes of the Roman empire, 114–242 CE* (New York: Routledge, 2001).

Säve-Söderbergh, T. *Studies in the Coptic Manichaean psalm-book: prosody and Mandaean parallels* (Uppsala: Almqvist and Wiksells, 1949).

Slee, M. *The church in Antioch in the first century CE: communion and conflict*, JSNTSup 244 (2003).

Smid, H. R. *Protevangelium Jacobi: a commentary*, G. E. van Baaren-Pape (trans.) (Assen: Van Gorcum, 1965).

Zetterholm, M. *The formation of Christianity in Antioch: a social-scientific approach to the separation between Judaism and Christianity* (London: Routledge, 2003).

20. Gaul

John Behr

Doutreleau, L. 'Irénée de Lyon (saint). I. Vie. II. Oeuvres', in *Dictionnaire de spiritualité ascétique et mystique, doctrine et histoire*, M. Viller, C. Baumgartner and A. Rayez (eds.), 17 vols. (Paris: Beauchesne, 1932–7), fasc. L–LX, pp. 1923–38.

Fishwick, D. 'The federal cult of the three Gauls', in *Les martyrs de Lyon (177)*, J. Rougé and R. Turcan (eds.), Colloques internationaux du Centre National de la Recherche Scientifique 575 (Paris: CNRS, 1978), 33–45.

Grant, R. M. 'Eusebius and the martyrs of Gaul', in *Les martyrs de Lyon (177)*, J. Rougé and R. Turcan (eds.), Colloques internationaux du Centre National de la Recherche Scientifique 575 (Paris: CNRS, 1978), 129–36.

Griffe, É. *La Gaule chrétienne a l'époque romaine*, vol. I, *Des origines chrétiennes à la fin du IVᵉ siècle* (Paris: Picard, 1947).

Hodge, A. T. *Ancient Greek France* (Philadelphia: University of Pennsylvania Press, 1999).

Petersen, W. L. 'Eusebius and the paschal controversy', in *Eusebius, Christianity and Judaism*, H. W. Attridge and G. Hata (eds.), StPB 42 (1992), 311–25.

Quentin, H. 'La liste des martyrs de Lyon de l'an 177', in *AnBoll* 39 (1921), 113–38.

—. 'Sites and museums in Roman Gaul I', in *Athena review: journal of archaeology, history, and exploration* 1.4 (1998) (www.athenapub.com).

Thompson, J. W. 'The alleged persecution of the Christians at Lyons in 177', *AJT* 16 (1912), 359–84.

Tripp, D. H. 'The original sequence of Irenaeus "Adversus haereses" I: a suggestion', *SecCent* 8 (1991), 157–62.

van der Meer, F. and C. Mohrmann. *Atlas of the early Christian world*, M. F. Hedlund and H. H. Rowley (eds. and trans.) (London: Nelson, 1958).

21. North Africa

Maureen A. Tilley

Baudrillart, A., A. Vogy and U. Rouzines (eds.). *Dictionnaire d'histoire et de géographie ecclésiastiques*, 27 vols. (Paris: Letouzey et Ane, 1912–).

Burns, J. P., Jr. *Cyprian the bishop* (London: Routledge, 2002).

—. 'Christians and the Roman state: 193–324', <http://people.vanderbilt.edu/~james.p.burns/chroma/>.

Clarke, G. W. 'Christianity in Roman Africa', <http://people.vanderbilt.edu/~james.p.burns/chroma/>.

Duval, N. and F. Prévot (eds.). *Recherches archéologiques à Haïdra*, vol. II: *La basilique I dite de Melléus ou de Saint-Cyprien*, Collection de l'École française de Rome 18 (Rome: École française de Rome, 1981).

Ennabli, A. *Carthage retrouvée* (Paris: Herscher, 1995).

Fantar, M. 'Punic civilization', in *Carthage: a mosaic of ancient Tunisia*, A. Ben Abed Ben Khader and D. Soren (eds.) (London: W. W. Norton, 1987), 88–109.

Ferguson, J. *The religions of the Roman empire* (Ithaca: Cornell University Press, 1970).

Février, P.-A. 'Africa–Archaeology', *s.v.* 'Africa IV', *EECh* (1992).

Frend, W. H. C. 'Jews and Christians in third century Carthage', in *Paganisme, Christianisme: influences et affrontements dans le monde antique. Mélanges offerts à Marcel Simon* (Paris: Boccard, 1978), 185–94.

Ghaki, M. 'Le Libyque', in *Carthage: l'histoire, sa trace et son echo: [exposition] les musées de la ville de Paris, Musée du Petit Palais, 9 mars–2 juillet 1995* (Paris: Association Française d'Action Artistique, 1995), 204–9.

Labriolle, P. C. de. *History and literature of Christianity from Tertullian to Boethius*, H. Wilson (trans.) (London: Kegan Paul, Trench, Trubner, 1924).

Lancel, S. *Carthage: a history*, A. Nevill (trans.) (Oxford: Blackwell, 1995).

—. 'Carthage et les échanges culturelles en Mediterranée', in *Carthage: l'histoire, sa trace et son écho: [exposition] les musées de la ville de Paris, Musée du Petit Palais, 9 mars–2 juillet 1995* (Paris: Association française d'action artistique, 1995), 24–48.

Lejay, M. 'Les origines de l'église d'Afrique et l'église romaine', in *Mélanges Godefroid Kurth*, vol. II: *Mémoires littéraires, philologiques et archéologiques*, J. P. Waltzing, K. Hanquiet and J. Closon (eds.) (Paris: Les Belles Lettres, 1908), 41–7.

Leynaud, A.-F. *Les catacombes africaines: Sousse-Hadrumète*, 2nd ed. (Algiers: Jules Cabonel, 1922).

MacKendrick, P. L. *The North African stones speak* (Chapel Hill: University of North Carolina Press, 1980).

MacMullen, R. *Romanization in the time of Augustus* (New Haven: Yale University Press, 2000).

Maier, J.-L. *L'épiscopat de l'Afrique romaine, vandale et byzantine* (Rome: Institut Suisse de Rome, 1973).

Picard, G.-C. *Les religions de l'Afrique antique* (Paris: Plon, 1954).

Raven, S. *Rome in Africa*, 3rd ed. (London: Routledge, 1993).

Rives, J. B. *Religion and authority in Roman Carthage from Augustus to Constantine* (Oxford: Clarendon Press, 1995).

Saxer, V. *Morts, martyrs, reliques en Afrique chrétienne aux premiers siècles: les témoignages de Tertullien, Cyprien et Augustin à la lumière de l'archéologie africaine* (Paris: Beauchesne, 1980).

—. *Vie liturgique et quotidienne à Carthage vers le milieu du IIIe siècle* (Vatican City: Pontificio Istituto di Archeologia Cristiana, 1969).

Setzer, C. 'Jews, Christians and Judaizers in North Africa', in *Putting body and soul together: essays in honor of Robin Scroggs*, V. Wiles, A. R. Brown and G. F. Snyder (eds.) (Valley Forge, PA: Trinity Press International, 1997), 185–200.

Shaw, B. 'Autonomy and tribute: mountain and plain in Mauretania Tingitana', in *Désert et montagne au Maghreb: hommage à Jean Dresch: ouvrage publié avec le concours du Centre National des Lettres*, Revue de l'Occident mussulman et de la Méditerranée 41–2 (Aix en Provence: Edisud, 1987), 66–89.

—. 'The formation of Africa Proconsularis', *Hermes* 105 (1977), 369–80.

Soren, D. 'Introduction', in *Carthage: a mosaic of ancient Tunisia*, A. Ben Abed Ben Khader and D. Soren (eds.) (London: W. W. Norton, 1987), 14–37.

Sznyccr, M. 'La religion punique à Carthage', in *Carthage: l'histoire, sa trace et son echo: [exposition] les musées de la ville de Paris, Musée du Petit Palais, 9 mars–2 juillet 1995* (Paris: Association française d'action artistique, 1995), 100–16.

Taylor, L. R. *The divinity of the Roman emperor* (Middletown, CT: American Philological Association, 1931).

Tilley, M. A. 'The ascetic body and the (un)making of the world of the martyr', *JAAR* 59 (1991), 467–80.

—. 'The passion of Perpetua and Felicity', in *Searching the scriptures*, vol. II: *A feminist commentary*, E. Schüssler Fiorenza (ed.) (New York: Crossroad, 1994), 829–58.

Trevett, C. 'Montanism', in *The early Christian world*, 2 vols., P. F. Esler (ed.) (London: Routledge, 2000), vol. II, 929–51.

van Oort, J. 'Jewish elements in the origin of North African Christianity', in *Ancient Christianity in the Caucasus*, T. Mgaloblishvili (ed.), Caucasus world: Iberica Caucasica I (Richmond, Surrey: Curzon, 1998), 97–105, 218–221.

22. Rome

Markus Vinzent

Altendorf, H.-D. 'Zum Stichwort: Rechtgläubigkeit und Ketzerei im ältesten Christentum', *ZKG* 80 (1969), 61–74.

Andresen, C. and A. M. Ritter. *Handbuch der Dogmen- und Theologiegeschichte*, vol. 1: *Die Lehr-entwicklung im Rahmen der Katholizität*, 2nd ed. (Göttingen: Vandenhoeck & Ruprecht, 1999).

Bardy, G. '"Philosophie" et "philosophe" dans le vocabulaire chrétien des premiers siècles', *Revue d'ascétique et de mystique* 25 (1949), 97–108.

Cerrato, J. A. *Hippolytus between east and west: the commentaries and the provenance of the corpus*, OTM (2002).

Claridge, A., J. Toms and T. Cubberley. *Rome: an Oxford archaeological guide to Rome*, Oxford archaeological guides (Oxford: Oxford University Press, 1998).

Gessel, W. M. 'Das Tropaion der Petersmemorie: eine Quellenrelecture', in '. . . *zur Zeit oder Unzeit': Studien zur spätantiken Theologie-, Geistes- und Kunstgeschichte und ihrer Nachwirkung: Hans Georg Thümmel zu Ehren*, A. M. Ritter, W. Wischmeyer and W. Kinzig (eds.), Texts and studies in the history of theology 9 (Mandelbachtal and Cambridge: Edition Cicero, 2004), 135–41.

Gwatkin, H. M. *Early church history to A.D. 313*, 2 vols. (London: Macmillan 1909).

Hübner, R. M. 'Die Anfänge von Diakonat, Presbyterat und Episkopat in der frühen Kirche', in *Das Priestertum in der Einen Kirche: Diakonat, Presbyterat und Episkopat*, A. Rauch and P. Imhof (eds.), Koinonia 4 (Aschaffenburg: Kaffke-Verlag, 1986), 45–89.

Jeffers, J. S. *Conflict at Rome: social order and hierarchy in early Christianity* (Minneapolis: Fortress, 1991).

Lüdemann, G. *Heretics: the other side of early Christianity*, J. Bowden (trans.) (London: SCM Press, 1996).

—. 'Zur Geschichte des ältesten Christentums in Rom', *ZNW* 70 (1979), 86–114.

Manson, T. W. 'St Paul's letter to the Romans – and others', in *The Romans debate: revised and expanded version*, K. P. Donfried (ed.) (Peabody, MA: Hendrickson, 1991), 3–15.

Markus, R. A. *Gregory the Great and his world* (Cambridge: Cambridge University Press, 1997).

Noy, D. *Foreigners at Rome: citizens and strangers* (London: Duckworth, 2000).

Robinson, T. A. *The Bauer thesis examined: the geography of heresy in the early Christian church*, Studies in the Bible and early Christianity 11 (Lewiston, NY: Mellen, 1988).

Scholten, C. 'Gibt es Quellen zur Sozialgeschichte der Valentinianer Roms?', *ZNW* 79 (1988), 245–61.

Speigl, J. 'Der Ökumenische Patriarch: zur Entstehung und kanonischen Bestätigung einer frühkirchlichen Institution im Spannungsfeld mit der Kirche von Rom', in '. . . *zur Zeit oder Unzeit': Studien zur spätantiken Theologie-, Geistes- und Kunstgeschichte und ihrer Nachwirkung: Hans Georg Thümmel zu Ehren*, A. M. Ritter, W. Wischmeyer and W. Kinzig (eds.), Texts and studies in the history of theology 9 (Mandelbachtal and Cambridge: Edition Cicero, 2004), 53–75.

Steinby, E. M. (ed.). *Lexicon topographicum urbis Romae*, 6 vols. (Oxford: Oxford University Press, 1995–2000).

Stewart-Sykes, A. (ed. and trans.). *Hippolytus: On the apostolic tradition* (Crestwood, NY: St Vladimir's Seminary Press, 2001).

Vinzent, M. 'Die Entstehung des römischen Glaubensbekenntnisses', in *Tauffragen und Bekenntnis: Studien zur sogenannten 'Traditio apostolica', zu den 'Interrogationes de fide'* und zum 'Römischen Glaubensbekenntnis', W. Kinzig, C. Markschies, and M. Vinzent (eds.), AKG 74 (1999), 185–410.

—. 'Die frühchristlichen Lehrer, Gnostiker und Philosophen, und die Ziele ihres Unterrichts', *Das Altertum* 41 (1996), 177–87.

—. 'Hippolyt von Rom und seine Statue', in '. . . *zur Zeit oder Unzeit': Studien zur spätantiken Theologie-, Geistes- und Kunstgeschichte und ihrer Nachwirkung: Hans Georg Thümmel zu Ehren*, A. M. Ritter, W. Wischmeyer and W. Kinzig (eds.), Texts and studies in the history of theology 9 (Mandelbachtal and Cambridge: Edition Cicero, 2004), 125–34.

—. '"Oxbridge" in der ausgehenden Spätantike, oder ein Vergleich der Schulen von Athen und Alexandrien', *ZAC/JAC* 4 (2000), 49–82.

—. 'Der Schluß des Lukasevangeliums bei Marcion', in *Marcion und seine kirchengeschichtliche Wirkung*, G. May and K. Greschat (eds.), TU 150 (2002), 79–94.

—. 'Viktor I, Bischof von Rom', *TRE* 35 (2003), 93–97.

Vinzent, M. and W. Kinzig. 'Recent research on the origin of the Creed', *JTS* n.s. 50 (1999), 534–59.

Wallraff, M. *Der Kirchenhistoriker Sokrates: Untersuchungen zu Geschichtsdarstellung, Methode und Person*, FKDG 68 (1997).

Wander, B. *Gottesfürchtige und Sympathisanten: Studien zum heidnischen Umfeld von Diasporasynagogen*, WUNT 104 (1998).

—. *Trennungsprozesse zwischen frühem Christentum und Judentum im 1. Jahrhundert n. Chr. Datierbare Abfolgen zwischen der Hinrichtung Jesu und der Zerstörung des Jerusalemer Tempels*, TANZ 16 (1994, 2nd rev. ed. 1997).

23. Institutional structures in the pre-Constantinian *ecclēsia*

Stuart George Hall

Bähnk, W. *Von der Notwendigkeit des Leidens: die Theologie des Martyriums bei Tertullian*, FKDG 78 (2001).

Benrath, G. A. 'Buße v', *TRE* 6 (1981), 452–73.

Bernard, J. H. 'The Cyprianic doctrine of the ministry', in *Essays on the early history of the church and the ministry*, 2nd ed., H. B. Swete (ed.) (London: Macmillan, 1921), 215–62.

Bradshaw, P. *Daily prayer in the early church: a study of the origin and early development of the divine office*, Alcuin Club Collections 63 (London: Alcuin Club/SPCK, 1981).

—. *The search for the origins of Christian worship: sources and methods for the study of early liturgy*, 2nd ed (New York: Oxford University Press, 2002).

Brightman, F. E. 'Terms of communion, and the ministration of the sacraments, in early times', in *Essays on the early history of the church and the ministry*, 2nd ed., H. B. Swete (ed.) (London: Macmillan, 1921), 313–408.

Bulley, C. J. *The priesthood of some believers: developments from the general to the special priesthood in the Christian literature of the first three centuries*, Paternoster biblical and theological monographs (Waynesboro, GA: Paternoster Press, 2000).

Butterweck, C. 'Tertullian', *TRE* 33 (2002), 93–107.

Cochrane, C. N. *Christianity and Classical culture* (Oxford: Oxford University Press, 1940).

Dodd, C. H. *The apostolic preaching and its developments* (London: Hodder and Stoughton, 1936).

Goldhahn-Müller, I. *Die Grenze der Gemeinde: Studien zur Problem der zweiten Buße im Neuen Testament unter Berücksichtigung der Entwicklung im 2. Jh. bis Tertullian*, GTA 39 (1989).

Hall, S. G. 'Calixtus I', *TRE* 7 (1981), 559–63.

Hess, H. *The early development of canon law and the council of Serdica*, OECS (2002.).

La Piana, G. 'The Roman church at the end of the second century', *HTR* 18 (1925), 201–77.

Lindemann, A. 'Antwort auf die "Thesen zur Echtheit und Datierung der sieben Briefe des Ignatius von Antiochien"', *ZAC/JAC* 1 (1997), 185–94.

Neumann, J. 'Bischof I', *TRE* 6 (1980), 653–82.

Neymeyr, U. *Die christlichen Lehrer im zweiten Jahrhundert: ihre Lehrtätigkeit, ihr Selbstverständnis, und ihre Geschichte*, VCSup 4 (1989).

Rankin, D. *Tertullian and the church* (Cambridge: Cambridge University Press 1995).

Rousseau, P. *The early Christian centuries* (London: Longman, 2002).

Sieben, H. J. *Die Konzilsidee der alten Kirche*, Konziliengeschichte, Reihe B, Untersuchungen (Paderborn: Schöningh, 1979).

Staats, R. 'Hermas', *TRE* 16 (1986), 100–8.

Swete, H. B. (ed.). *Essays on the early history of the church and the ministry*, 2nd ed. (London: Macmillan, 1921).

Torjesen, K. J. 'Social and historical setting: Christianity as culture critique', in *The Cambridge history of early Christian literature*, F. M. Young, L. Ayres and A. Louth (eds.) (Cambridge: Cambridge University Press, 2004), 181–99.

van de Sandt, H. W. M. and D. Flusser. *The Didache: its Jewish sources and its place in early Judaism and Christianity*, CRINT III/5 (2002).

Wehr, L. *Arznei der Unsterblichkeit: die Eucharistie bei Ignatius von Antiochien und im Johannesevangelium*, NTAbh n.s. 18 (1987).

Young, F. M. 'On *episkopos* and *presbyteros*', *JTS* n.s. 45 (1994), 142–8.

—. *The use of sacrificial ideas in Greek Christian writers from the New Testament to John Chrysostom*, Patristic monograph series 5 (Cambridge, MA: The Philadelphia Patristic Foundation Ltd 1979).

24. Monotheism and creation

Gerhard May

Armstrong, A. H. (ed). *The Cambridge history of later Greek and early medieval philosophy* (Cambridge: Cambridge University Press, 1967).

Dihle, A. *The theory of will in classical antiquity*, Sather classical lectures 48 (Berkeley: University of California Press, 1982).

Ehrhardt, A. *The beginning: a study in the Greek philosophical approach to the concept of creation from Anaximander to St John* (Manchester: Manchester University Press, 1968).

Grant, R. M. *The early Christian doctrine of God* (Charlottesville: University of Virginia Press, 1966).

Greschat, K. *Apelles und Hermogenes: zwei theologische Lehrer des zweiten Jahrhunderts*, VCSup 48 (2000).

Levenson, J. D. *Creation and the persistence of evil* (San Francisco: Harper & Row, 1988).

Löhr, W. A. *Basilides und seine Schule: eine Studie zur Theologie- und Kirchengeschichte des zweiten Jahrhunderts*, WUNT 83 (1996).

Meijering, E. P. *God being history* (Amsterdam: North Holland, 1975).

Norris, R. A. *God and world in early Christian theology* (New York: Seabury, 1965).

Schmuttermayer, G. 'Vom Gott unter Göttern zum einzigen Gott', in *Freude an der Weisung des Herrn: Beiträge zur Theologie der Psalmen: Festgabe zum 70. Geburtstag von Heinrich Gross*, E. Haag and F.-L. Hossfeld (eds.), SBB 13 (1986), 349–74.

Sorabji, R. *Time, creation and the continuum* (London: Duckworth, 1983).

van Winden, J. C. M. 'Hexaemeron', *RAC* 14 (1988), 1250–69.

Young, F. M. '"Creatio ex nihilo": a context for the emergence of the Christian doctrine of creation', *SJT* 44 (1991), 139–51.

25. Monotheism and Christology

Frances M. Young

Bardy, G. *Paul de Samosate* (Bruges: Imprimerie Sainte-Catherine, 1923).

Clark, E. A. *The Origenist controversy: the cultural construction of an early Christian debate* (Princeton: Princeton University Press, 1992).

Cunliffe-Jones, H. and B. Drewery (eds.). *A history of Christian doctrine* (Edinburgh: T&T Clark, 1978).

Daniélou, J. *Origen*, W. Mitchell (trans.) (New York: Sheed & Ward, 1955).

De Riedmatten, H. *Les actes du procès de Paul de Samosate: étude sur la christologie du IIIe au IVe siècle* (Fribourg en Suisse: Editions St Paul, 1952).

Grillmeier, A. *Christ in Christian tradition*, vol. 1: *From the apostolic age to Chalcedon (451)*, 2nd rev. ed., J. Bowden (trans.) (London: Mowbray, 1975).

Loofs, F. *Paulus von Samosata*, TU 44/5 (1924).

Millar, F. 'Paul of Samosata, Zenobia and Aurelian: the church, local culture and political allegiance in third century Syria', *JRS* 61 (1971), 1–17.

Trigg, J. W. *Origen: the Bible and philosophy in the third century church* (London: SCM Press, 1983).

Wallace-Hadrill, D. S. *Christian Antioch: a study of early Christian thought in the east* (Cambridge: Cambridge University Press, 1982).

26. Ecclesiology forged in the wake of persecution

Stuart George Hall

Alexander, J. S. 'Novatian/Novatianer', *TRE* 24 (1994), 678–82.

Bähnk, W. *Von der Notwendigkeit des Leidens: die Theologie des Martyriums bei Tertullian*, FKDG 78 (2001).

Benrath, G. A. 'Buße v', *TRE* 6 (1981), 452–73.

Bévenot, M. 'Cyprian von Karthago', *TRE* 8 (1981), 246–54.

— *(trans.)*. St Cyprian, 'The lapsed' and 'The unity of the catholic church', ACW 25 (1957).

Burns, J. P. *Cyprian the bishop* (London: Routledge, 2002).

Gülzow, H. *Cyprian und Novatian: der Briefwechsel zwischen d. Gemeinden in Rom u. Karthago z. Zeit d. Verfolgung d. Kaisers Decius*, BHT 48 (1975).

Hinchliff, P. B. *Cyprian of Carthage and the unity of the Christian church* (London: Geoffrey Chapman, 1974).

Knipfing, J. R. 'The *libelli* of the Decian persecution', *HTR* 16 (1923), 345–90.

May, G. 'Kirche III', *TRE* 18 (1989), 218–27.

Neumann, J. 'Bischof I', *TRE* 6 (1980), 653–82.

Sebastian, J. J. ". . . *baptisma unum in sancta ecclesia* . . .": *a theological appraisal of the baptismal controversy in the work and writings of Cyprian of Carthage* (Delhi: ISPCK, 1997).

27. Towards a Christian *paideia*

Frances M. Young

Bardy, G. 'Pour l'histoire de l'école d'Alexandrie', *Vivre et penser* 2 (1942), 80–109.

Daube, D. 'Rabbinic methods of interpretation and Hellenistic rhetoric', *HUCA* 22 (1949), 239–64.

Hanson, R. P. C. *Allegory and event: a study of the sources and significance of Origen's interpretation of scripture* (Louisville, KY: Westminster John Knox, 2002, orig. 1959).

Hatch, E. *The influence of Greek ideas on Christianity* (New York: Harper, 1957 (orig. 1890)).

Heine, R. E. 'Gregory of Nyssa's apology for allegory', *VC* 38 (1984), 360–70.

Kaster, R. A. *Guardians of language: the grammarian and society in late antiquity*, TCH 11 (1988).

Lamberton, R. *Homer the theologian*, TCH 9 (1986).

Lieberman, S. *Hellenism in Jewish Palestine* (New York: Jewish Theological Seminary of America, 1950).

Marrou, H.-I. *A history of education in antiquity*, G. Lamb (trans.) (New York: Sheed and Ward, 1956; ET of *L'histoire de l'éducation dans l'antiquité*, 2nd ed. (Paris: Éditions du Seuil, 1948)).

Torjesen, K. J. '"Body", "soul" and "spirit" in Origen's theory of exegesis', *AThR* 67 (1985), 17–30.

—. *Hermeneutical procedure and theological structure in Origen's exegesis*, PTS 28 (1985).

Trigg, J. W. *Origen: the Bible and philosophy in the third-century church* (Atlanta: John Knox, 1983).

Young, F. M. 'Books and their "aura": the functions of written texts in Judaism, paganism and Christianity during the first centuries CE', in *Religious identity and the problem of historical foundation*, J. Frishman, W. Otten and G. Rouwhorst (eds.), Jewish and Christian perspectives series 8 (Leiden: Brill, 2004), 535–52.

—. 'The fourth century reaction against allegory', *StPatr* 30 (1997), 120–5.

28. Persecutions: genesis and legacy

W. H. C. Frend

Alföldi, A. 'Introduction: the age of Decius, Gallus and Aemilianus', *CAH¹*, vol. XII, 165–9.

Barnes, T. D. 'Legislation against the Christians', *JRS* 58 (1968), 32–50.

Baynes, N. H. 'The Great Persecution', *CAH¹*, vol. xii, 646–77.

Beschaouch, A. 'Une stèle consacrée à Saturne le 8 novembre 323', *Bulletin archéologique* 4 (1968), 253–68.

Bowersock, G. W. *Martyrdom and Rome* (Cambridge: Cambridge University Press, 1995).

Clarke, G. W. 'Some observations on the persecution of Decius', *Antichthon* 3 (1969), 63–76.

Coleman, K. M. 'Fatal charades: Roman executions staged as mythological enactments', *JRS* 80 (1990), 44–73.

Davies, J. G. 'Condemnation to the mines: a neglected chapter in the history of the persecutions', *University of Birmingham historical journal* 6 (1958), 99–107.

de Ste Croix, G. E. M. 'Why were the early Christians persecuted?' *Past and present* 26 (1963), 6–38.

Dodds, E. R. *Pagan and Christian in an age of anxiety* (Cambridge: Cambridge University Press, 1965).

Dörries, H. *Constantine and religious liberty* (New Haven: Yale University Press, 1960).

Ensslin, W. 'The development of paganism in the Roman empire', *CAH¹*, vol. xii, 409–49.

Francis, J. A. *Subversive virtue: asceticism and authority in the second-century pagan world* (University Park: Pennsylvania State University Press, 1995).

Frend, W. H. C. *The Donatist church: a movement of protest in Roman North Africa* (Oxford: Clarendon Press, 2000, orig. 1952).

—. 'The failure of the persecutions in the Roman empire', *Past and Present* 16 (1959), 10–30.

—. 'Prelude to the Great Persecution: the propaganda war', *JEH* 38 (1987), 1–18.

Grégoire, H. *Les persécutions dans l'empire Romain*, 2nd rev. ed., Académie Royale des Sciences, des Lettres et des Beaux-arts de Belgique, Classe des lettres et des sciences morales et politiques, Mémoires, 2nd ser., vol. lvi, fasc. 5 (Brussels: Palais des Académies, 1964).

Guyon, J. *Le cimetière aux deux Lauriers: recherches sur les catacombes romaines*, Roma sotterranea cristiana 7 (Rome: École Française de Rome, 1987).

Hardy, E. G. *Christianity and the Roman government* (London: Allen & Unwin, 1925).

Knipfing, J. R. 'The libelli of the Decian persecution', *HTR* 16 (1923), 345–90.

Last, H. 'The study of the "persecutions"', *JRS* 27 (1937), 80–92.

Lietzmann, H. *Messe und Herrenmahl: eine Studie zur Geschichte der Liturgie*, AKG 8 (1926).

Marichal, R. 'La date des graffiti de la basilique de Saint-Sebastien à Rome', *Nouv. Clio* 5 (1953), 119–20.

Mattingly, H. '*Quattuor principes mundi*', *CAH¹*, vol. xii, 331–9.

McKechnie, P. 'Christian grave inscriptions from the *familia Caesaris*', *JEH* 50 (1999), 427–41.

Mitchell, S. 'Maximinus and the Christians in A.D. 312: a new Latin inscription', *JRS* 78 (1988), 105–24.

Molthagen, J. *Der römische Staat und die Christen im zweiten und dritten Jahrhundert*, Hypomnemata: Untersuchungen zur Antike und zu ihrem Nachleben 28 (Göttingen: Vandenhoeck & Ruprecht, 1970).

Momigliano, A. (ed.). *The conflict between paganism and Christianity in the fourth century* (Oxford: Oxford University Press, 1970).

Perler, O. 'Das vierte Makkabaerbuch, Ignatius von Antiochien und die ältesten Martyrerberichte', *Rivista di archaeologia cristiana* 25 (1949), 47–72.

Rives, J. B. 'The decree of Decius and the religion of the empire', *JRS* 89 (1999), 135–54.

Roques, D. *Synésios de Cyrène et la Cyrénaïque du bas empire* (Paris: Éditions du Centre national de la recherche scientifique, 1988).

Selinger, R. *The mid-third century persecutions of Decius and Valerian* (New York: Lang, 2002).

Sherwin-White, A. N. 'The early persecutions and Roman law again', *JTS* n.s. 3 (1952), 199–213.

Simonetti, M. 'Julius Africanus', *EECh*, vol. I, 460.

Sordi, M. *Il cristianesimo e Roma*, Storia di Roma 19 (Bologna: Cappelli, 1965).

Speigl, J. *Der römische Staat und die Christen: Staat und Kirche von Domitian bis Commodus* (Amsterdam: Hakkert, 1970).

Streeter, B. H. 'The rise of Christianity', *CAH*[1], vol. XI, 253–93.

Turcan, R. 'Le culte impérial au IIIe siècle', *ANRW* II.16.2 (1978), 996–1084.

Wlosok, A. *Rom und die Christen: zur Auseinandersetzung zwischen Christentum und römischem Staat* (Stuttgart: Klett, 1970).

29. Church and state up to *c*.300 CE

Adolf Martin Ritter

Barnes, T. D. 'Pagan perceptions of Christianity', in *Early Christianity: origins and evolution to AD 600: in honour of W. H. C. Frend*, I. Hazlett (ed.) (London: SPCK, 1991), 231–43.

Berkhof, H. *Kirche und Kaiser: eine Untersuchung der Entstehung der byzantinischen und der theokratischen Staatsauffassung im vierten Jahrhundert* (Zollikon – Zurich: Evangelischer Verlag, 1947).

Chadwick, H. *The church in ancient society: from Galilee to Gregory the Great* (Oxford: Oxford University Press, 2001).

Delatte, L. *Les traités de la royauté d'Ecphante, Diotogène et Sthénidas*, Bibliothèque de la faculté de philosophie et lettres de l'Université de Liége, fasc. XCVII (Paris: Droz, 1942).

Frend, W. H. C. 'Church and state – perspective and problems in the patristic era', E. A. Livingstone (ed.), *StPatr* 17.1 (1982), 38–54.

Freudenberger, R. 'Christenreskript: ein umstrittenes Reskript des Antoninus Pius', *ZKG* 78 (1967), 1–14.

—. 'Die Überlieferung vom Martyrium des römischen Christen Apollonius', *ZNW* 60 (1969), 111–30.

—. *Das Verhalten der römischen Behörden gegen die Christen im 2. Jh., dargestellt am Brief des Plinius an Trajan und den Reskripten Trajans und Hadrians*, MBPF 52 (1967).

Gärtner, H.-A. 'Imperium Romanum', *RAC* 17 (1996), 1142–98.

Gottlieb, G. *Christentum und Kirche in den ersten drei Jahrhunderten* (Heidelberg: C. Winter, 1991).

Gross, K. 'Augustus. B (Christentum u. Augustus)', *RAC* I (1950), 999–1004.

Guyot, P. and Klein, R. *Das frühe Christentum bis zum Ende der Verfolgungen: eine Dokumentation*, 2 vols., Texte zur Forschung 60 (Darmstadt: Wissenschaftliche Buchgesellschaft, 1997).

Harnack, A. von. *Das Edikt des Antoninus Pius*, TU 13/4a (1898).

Hazlett, I. (ed.). *Early Christianity: origins and evolution to AD 600: in honour of W. H. C. Frend* (London: SPCK, 1991),

King, N. 'Church-State relations', in *Early Christianity: origins and evolution to AD 600: in honour of W. H. C. Frend*, I. Hazlett (ed.) (London: SPCK, 1991), 244–55.

Klein, R. 'Das Bild des Augustus in der frühchristlichen Literatur', in *Rom und das himmlische Jerusalem: die frühen Christen zwischen Anpassung und Ablehnung*, R. von Haehling and P. Mikat (eds.) (Darmstadt: Wissenschaftliche Buchgesellschaft, 2000), 205–36.

Kretschmar, G. 'Der Weg zur Reichskirche', *VF* 13 (1968), 3–44.

Malingrey, A. M. *Philosophia: étude d'un groupe de mots dans la littérature grecque des présocratiques au 4ᵉᵐᵉ siècle après J.-C.* (Paris: Klincksieck, 1961).

O'Donovan, O. and J. Lockwood O'Donovan. *From Irenaeus to Grotius: a sourcebook in Christian political thought, 100–1625* (Grand Rapid, MI: Eerdmans, 1999).

Peterson, E. 'Der Monotheismus als politisches Problem: ein Beitrag zur Geschichte der politischen Theologie im Imperium Romanum' (Leipzig: Hegner, 1935), repr. in E. Peterson, *Theologische Traktate* (Munich: Beck, 1951), 45–147.

Popkes, W. 'Zum Thema "Anti-imperiale Deutung neutestamentlicher Schriften"', *ThLZ* 127 (2002), 850–62.

Rahner, H. *Church and state in early Christianity*, L. D. Davis (trans.) (San Francisco: Ignatius Press, 1992; ET of *Kirche und Staat im frühen Christentum: Dokumente aus acht Jahrhunderten und ihre Deutung* (Munich: Kösel, 1961)).

Ritter, A. M. *'Kirche und Staat' im Denken des frühen Christentums: Texte und Kommentare zum Thema Religion und Politik in der Antike*, Traditio Christiana 13 (Bern: Lang, 2005).

Schneemelcher, W. 'Kirche und Staat im Neuen Testament', in *Kirche und Staat: Festschrift H. Kunst*, K Aland and W. Schneemelcher (eds.) (Berlin: De Gruyter, 1967), 1–18.

Strobel, F. A. 'Schriftverständnis und Obrigkeitsdenken in der ältesten Kirche (Eine auslegungs- und problemgeschichtliche Studie zum Verhältnis von Kirche und Staat, vor allem bis zur Zeit Konstantins des Großen)' (Ph.D. dissertation, University of Erlangen, 1956); cf. the abstract in *ThLZ* 82 (1957), 69–71.

—. 'Zum Verständnis von Rm 13', *ZNW* 47 (1956), 67–93.

Theissen, G. *Gospel writing and church politics: a socio-rhetorical approach*, Chuen King lecture series 3 (Hong Kong: Theology Division, Chung Chi College, CUHK, 2001).

—. 'The political dimension of Jesus' activities'. in *The social setting of Jesus and the Gospels*, W. Stegemann, B. J. Malina and G. Theissen (eds.) (Minneapolis, MN: Fortress, 2002), 225–50.

Wickert, U. 'Christus kommt zur Welt: zur Wechselbeziehung von Christologie, Kosmologie und Eschatologie in der Alten Kirche', in *Kerygma und Logos: Beiträge zu den geistesgeschichtlichen Beziehungen zwischen Antike und Christentum: Festschrift für Carl Andresen*, A. M. Ritter (ed.) (Göttingen: Vandenhoeck & Ruprecht 1979), 461–81.

Winkelmann, F. *Euseb von Kaisareia: der Vater der Kirchengeschichte* (Berlin: Verlags-Anstalt Union, 1991).
Wissowa, G. *Religion und Kultus der Römer*, 2nd ed. (Munich: Beck, 1971).

30. Constantine and the 'peace of the church'

Averil Cameron

Barnes, T. D. 'Constantine and the Christians of Persia', *JRS* 75 (1985), 126–36.
—. 'The editions of Eusebius' *Ecclesiastical history*', *GRBS* 21 (1980), 191–201.
—. *The new empire of Diocletian and Constantine* (Cambridge, MA: Harvard University Press, 1982).
Baynes, N. H. *Constantine the Great and the Christian church*, British Academy, annual Raleigh lecture 1930 (New York: Haskell House, 1975, 1930).
Borgehammar, S. *How the Holy Cross was found: from event to medieval legend* (Stockholm: Almqvist & Wiksell, 1991).
Bowersock, G. W. 'Peter and Constantine', in *'Humana sapit': études d'antiquité tardive offertes à Lellia Cracco Ruggini*, J.-M. Carrié and R. Lizzi Testa (eds.), Bibliothèque de l'antiquité tardive 3 (Turnhout: Brepols, 2003), 209–17.
Brown, P. *Power and persuasion in late antiquity: towards a Christian empire* (Madison: University of Wisconsin Press, 1992).
Bruun, P. 'The Christian signs on the coins of Constantine', *Arctos* n.s. 3 (1962), 5–35.
—. 'The disappearance of Sol from the coins of Constantine', *Arctos* n.s. 2 (1958), 15–37.
Callu, J.-P. 'Naissance de la dynastie constantinienne: le tournant de 314–316', in *'Humana sapit': études d'antiquité tardive offertes à Lellia Cracco Ruggini*, J.-M. Carrié and R. Lizzi Testa (eds.), Bibliothèque de l'antiquité tardive 3 (Turnhout: Brepols, 2003), 111–20.
Cameron, Averil. 'The reign of Constantine, 306–337', *CAH²*, vol. xii (2005), 90–109.
Corcoran, S. 'Hidden from history: the legislation of Licinius', in *The Theodosian Code*, J. Harries and I. Wood (eds.) (London: Routledge, 1993), 97–119.
Curran, J. *Pagan city and Christian capital: Rome in the fourth century* (Oxford: Clarendon Press, 2000).
Digeser, E. D. 'Lactantius, Porphyry and the debate over religious toleration', *JRS* 88 (1998), 129–46.
—. *The making of a Christian empire: Lactantius and Rome* (Ithaca, NY: Cornell University Press, 2000).
Downey, G. *A history of Antioch in Syria from Seleucus to the Arab conquest* (Princeton: Princeton University Press, 1961).
Drake, H. A. *Constantine and the bishops: the politics of intolerance* (Baltimore: Johns Hopkins University Press, 2000).
—. *In praise of Constantine* (Berkeley: University of California Press, 1976).
—. 'Lambs into lions: explaining early Christian intolerance', *Past and present* 153 (1996), 3–36.
Evans Grubbs, J. *Law and family in late antiquity: the emperor Constantine's marriage legislation* (Oxford: Oxford University Press, 1995).
Fowden, G. 'The last days of Constantine: oppositional versions and their influence', *JRS* 84 (1994), 146–70.

Hall, S. G. 'The sects under Constantine', in *Voluntary religion: papers read at the 1985 summer meeting and the 1986 winter meeting of the Ecclesiastical History Society*, W. J. Sheils and D. Wood (eds.), Studies in church history 23 (Oxford: Blackwell, 1986), 1–13.

Harries, J. and I. N. Wood (eds.). *The Theodosian Code* (London: Routledge, 1993).

Jones, A. H. M. and T. C. Skeat. 'Notes on the genuineness of the Constantinian documents in Eusebius' *Life of Constantine*', *JEH* 5 (1954), 196–200.

Kolb, F. *Diocletian und die Erste Tetrarchie: Improvisation oder Experiment in der Organisation monarchischer Herrschaft?* Untersuchungen zur antiken Literatur und Geschichte 27 (Berlin: De Gruyter, 1987).

Kondoleon, C. (ed.). *Antioch: the lost ancient city* (Princeton: Princeton University Press, 2000).

Kraft, H. (ed.). *Konstantin der grosse*, Wege der Forschung 31 (Darmstadt: Wissenschaftliche Buchgesellschaft, 1974).

Krautheimer, R. *Rome: profile of a city, 312–1308* (Princeton: Princeton University Press, 1980).

Leeb, R. *Konstantin und Christus: die Verchristlichung der imperialen Repräsentation unter Konstantin dem grossen als Spiegel seiner Kirchenpolitik und seines Selbstverständnisses als christlicher Kaiser*, AKG 58 (1992).

L'Huillier, M.-C. *L'empire des mots: orateurs gaulois et empereurs romains 3ᵉ et 4ᵉ siècles*, Centre de recherches d'histoire ancienne 114 (Paris: Les Belles Lettres, 1992).

Lieu, S. N. C. and D. Montserrat. *Constantine: history, historiography and legend* (London: Routledge, 1998).

—. *From Constantine to Julian: a source history* (London: Routledge, 1996).

Magdalino, P. (ed.). *New Constantines: the rhythm of imperial renewal in Byzantium, 4th–13th centuries*, Papers from the twenty-sixth spring symposium of Byzantine studies, St Andrews, March 1992 (Aldershot: Variorum, 1994).

Mango, C. 'Constantine's mausoleum and the translation of relics', *BZ* 83 (1990), 51–61.

Millar, F. *The emperor in the Roman world* (London: Duckworth, 1977).

Nixon, C. E. V. and B. S. Rodgers (eds. and trans.). *In praise of later Roman emperors: the Panegyrici Latini: introduction, translation, and historical commentary, with the Latin text of R. A. B. Mynors*, TCH 21 (1994).

Pietri, C. *Roma Christiana: recherches sur l'église de Rome, son organisation, sa politique, son idéologie de Miltiade à Sixte III (311–440)*, Bibliothèque des écoles françaises d'Athènes et de Rome 224 (Paris: L'École Française de Rome, 1976).

Rees, R. *Layers of loyalty in Latin panegyric, AD 289–307* (Oxford: Oxford University Press, 2002).

Rodgers, B. S. 'Constantine's pagan vision', *Byzantion* 50 (1980), 259–78.

Sutherland, C. H. V. and R. A. G. Carson. *The Roman imperial coinage*, vol. VI: *From Diocletian's reform (A.D. 294) to the death of Maximinus (A.D. 313)* (London: Spink, 1967).

Sutherland, C. H. V., R. A. G. Carson and P. Bruun. *The Roman imperial coinage*, vol. VII: *Constantine and Licinius, A.D. 313–337* (London: Spink, 1966).

van Dam, R. 'The many conversions of the emperor Constantine', in *Conversion in late antiquity and the early Middle Ages: seeing and believing*, K. Mills and A. Grafton (eds.) (Rochester, NY: University of Rochester Press, 2003), 127–51.

Wallraff, M. 'Constantine's devotion to the sun after 324', *StPatr* 34 (2001), 256–69.

Weiss, P. 'The vision of Constantine', *JRA* 16 (2003), 237–59.

31. The first Council of Nicaea

Mark Edwards

Arnold, D. W. H. *The early episcopal career of Athanasius*, CJA 6 (1991).

Bardy, G. 'La réaction Eusébienne et le schisme de Sardique', ch. 2 of J.-R. Palanque, G. Bardy and P. de Labriolle, *Histoire de l'Eglise depuis les origines jusqu'à nos jours*, vol. III: *De la paix constantinienne à la mort de Théodose*, A. Fliche and V. Martin (eds.) (Paris: Bloud & Gay, 1936), 97–130.

Bindley, T. H. *The oecumenical documents of the faith: the Creed of Nicaea, three epistles of Cyril, the Tome of Leo, the Chalcedonian definition* (London: Methuen & Co., 1899).

Bright, W. *Notes on the canons of the first four general councils* (Oxford: Clarendon Press, 1882).

Burgess, R. W. 'The date of the deposition of Eustathius of Antioch', *JTS* 51 (2000), 150–60.

Campenhausen, H. von. 'Das Bekenntnis Eusebs von Caesarea', *ZNW* 67 (1976), 123–39.

Chadwick, H. 'The origin of the title "Oecumenical council"', *JTS* 23 (1972), 132–5.

—. 'Ossius of Cordova and the presidency of the Council of Antioch, 325', *JTS* n.s. 9 (1958), 292–304.

Dossetti, G. L. *Il Simbolo di Nicea e di Constantinopoli: edizione critica, ricerca condotta col contributo del Consiglio nazionale delle ricerche*, Testi e ricerche di scienze religiose 2 (Rome: Herder, 1967).

Edwards, M. J. 'The Arian heresy and the oration to the saints', *VC* 49 (1995), 379–87.

Ehrhardt, C. T. H. R. 'Constantinian documents in Gelasius of Cyzicus', *JAC* 23 (1980), 48–57.

Elliott, T. G. 'Constantine and the Arian reaction after Nicaea', *JEH* 43 (1992), 169–94.

Gelzer, H., H. Hilgenfeld and O. Cuntz (eds). *Patrum Nicaenorum nomina Latine, Graece, Coptice, Syriace, Arabice, Armeniace* (Stuttgart: Teubner, 1995, orig. 1898).

Hanson, R. P. C. *The search for the Christian doctrine of God* (Edinburgh: T&T Clark, 1988).

Hess, H. *The early development of canon law and the Council of Serdica*, OECS 1 (2002).

Jonkers, E. *Acta et symbola conciliorum quae quarto saeculo habita sunt*, Textus minores in usum academicum 19 (Leiden: Brill, 1954).

Kinzig, W. and M. Vinzent. 'Recent research on the origin of the Creed', *JTS* 50 (1999), 534–59.

Lim, R. *Public disputation, power and social order in late antiquity*, TCH 23 (1995).

Schwartz, E. 'Eusebios von Caesarea', PW 6 (1907), cols. 1370–1439.

—. 'Zur Geschichte des Athanasius VIII', *Nachrichten von der königlichen Gesellschaft der Wissenschaften zur Göttingen. Philologisch-historische Klasse aus dem Jahre 1911* (Berlin: Weidmann, 1911), 367–426); repr. as ch. 8 of E. Schwartz, *Zur Geschichte des Athanasius, Gesammelte Schriften*, vol. III (Berlin: De Gruyter, 1959), 188–264.

Skarsaune, O. 'A neglected detail in the creed of Nicaea (325)', *VC* 41 (1987), 34–54.

Stead, G. C. 'Athanasius' earliest written work', *JTS* 39 (1988), 76–91.

—. '"Eusebius" and the Council of Nicaea', *JTS* 24 (1973), 85–100.

—. 'The word "from nothing"', *JTS* 49 (1998), 671–84.

Wiles, M. F. 'A textual variant in the creed of the Council of Nicaea', *StPatr* 26 (1993), 428–33.

Williams, R. D. 'Arius and the Melitian schism', *JTS* 37 (1986), 35–52.

32. Towards a Christian material culture

Robin M. Jensen

Balch, D. L. 'The Areopagus speech: an appeal to the Stoic historian Posidonius against later Stoics and the Epicureans', in *Greeks, Romans, and Christians: essays in honor of Abraham J. Malherbe*, D. L. Balch, E. Ferguson and W. A Meeks (eds.) (Minneapolis: Fortress, 1990), 52–79.

—. 'The suffering of Isis/Io and Paul's portrait of Christ crucified (Gal. 3.1): frescoes in Pompeian and Roman houses and in the temple of Isis in Pompeii', *JR* 83 (2003), 24–55.

Breckenridge, J. D. 'The reception of art into the early church', *Atti del IX congresso internazionale di archeologia cristiana* 9.1 (1978), 361–9.

Davies, J. G. *The architectural setting of baptism* (London: Barrie and Rockliff, 1962).

Elsner, J. (ed.). *Art and text in Roman culture* (Cambridge: Cambridge University Press, 1996).

Fine, S. (ed.). *Sacred realm: the emergence of the synagogue in the ancient world* (New York: Oxford University Press, 1996).

Finney, P. C. (ed.). *Art, archaeology and architecture of early Christianity*, E. Ferguson (ed.), Studies in Early Christianity 18 (New York: Garland, 1993).

—. *The invisible God: the earliest Christians on art* (New York: Oxford University Press, 1994).

Grabar, A. *The beginnings of Christian art, 200–395*, S. Gilbert and J. Emmons (trans.) (London: Thames and Hudson, 1967).

—. *Christian iconography: a study of its origins*, T. Grabar (trans.) (Princeton: Princeton University Press, 1968).

Grigg, R. 'Aniconic worship and the apologetic tradition', *CH* 45 (1976), 428–33.

Jensen, R. M. 'The Dura Europos synagogue, early Christian art, and religious life in Dura Europos', in *Jews, Christians, and polytheists in the ancient synagogue*, S. Fine (ed.) (London: Routledge, 1999), 174–89.

—. *Face to face: portraits of the divine in early Christianity* (Minneapolis: Fortress, 2005).

—. *Living water: the images, symbols, and settings of early Christian baptism* (Leiden: Brill, forthcoming).

—. *Understanding early Christian art* (London: Routledge, 2000).

Krautheimer, R. *Early Christian and Byzantine architecture*, 4th ed. (Harmondsworth: Penguin, 1986).

Levine, L. I. *Ancient synagogues revealed* (Jerusalem: Israel Exploration Society, 1982).

Mathews, T. F. *The clash of gods: a reinterpretation of early Christian art*, rev. ed. (Princeton: Princeton University Press, 1999).

Milburn, R. L. P. *Early Christian art and architecture* (Berkeley: University of California Press, 1988).

Murray, Sr Charles. 'Art and the early church', *JTS* n.s. 28 (1977), 303–45.

—. *Rebirth and afterlife: a study of the transmutation of some pagan imagery in early Christian funerary art* (Oxford: BAR, 1981).

Nicolai, V. F., F. Bisconti and D. Mazzoleni. *The Christian catacombs of Rome: history, decoration, inscriptions* (Regensburg: Schnell & Steiner, 1999).

Rutgers, L. V. 'Diaspora synagogues: synagogue archaeology in the Greco-Roman world', in *Sacred realm: the emergence of the synagogue in the ancient world*, S. Fine (ed.) (New York: Oxford University Press, 1996), 67–95.

van der Meer, F. *Early Christian art*, P. Brown and F. Brown (trans.) (Chicago: University of Chicago Press, 1967).

Index

The index lists subjects and persons – ancient and modern – treated in the text, not including the notes or Bibliographies.

DATE DUE